HARTRAMPF'S
Vocabulary-Builder

HARTRAMPF'S
Vocabulary-Builder

REVISED AND ENLARGED EDITION

By

GUSTAVUS A. HARTRAMPF

With Special Introduction and
Vocabulary Tests by

ROSS McLAURY TAYLOR, Ph.D.

Grosset & Dunlap · *Publishers*

NEW YORK

Printed and Bound in the U. S. A.
By Kingsport Press, Inc., Kingsport, Tenn.

HOW THIS VOCABULARY-BUILDER
WILL WORK FOR YOU

THE FAMOUS English dictionary-maker, Dr. Samuel Johnson, was once taken to task by a user of his great book for the omission of several words which she deemed important. "I am really very much surprised, Doctor Johnson," she said. "Whatever made you omit those important words?" "Ignorance, Madam, sheer ignorance," was the reply of the learned doctor.

Nowadays, with our tremendously improved facilities for self-education, this disarming reply would not suffice. We have at our disposal thousands upon thousands of reference tools which even the leading scholars of Dr. Johnson's day lacked. And one of the simplest and most effective ways for you to *guarantee* that you will have the right word at your fingertips at the right time is to make a daily practice of using Hartrampf's VOCABULARY-BUILDER.

You will find the method of using this book simplicity itself. Let us assume that you are a motion-picture critic faced with the need for describing the newest and brightest performance of Hollywood's leading comedienne. You toy with such adjectives as *gay, laughable, entertaining* and *clever,* but all of them lack freshness and vigor. None of them has the punch that the actress' own performance had.

So you turn to Hartrampf's VOCABULARY-BUILDER and look in the index at the back of the book where you will find the following entry:

entertain 99A, 48A, 114, 113

Turn to section 99A, which can easily be found from the numbers at the top of every page, and there you will find dozens upon dozens of verbs, adjectives and nouns conveying every conceivable shade of meaning of the words *entertain, entertaining,* and *entertainment.* Here, to describe your comedienne's performance, you will find *blithe, engaging, vivacious, droll, gladsome, joyous* and many others. The picture itself may have *elated, beguiled,* or *captivated* you. And the sum total of your reaction to the film was a mood of *enchantment, fascination,* or even *enthrallment.*

And all this, mind you, from looking in only *one* place, There is no need to search through hundreds of pages of a dictionary or similar reference book. Here in one place are all the synonyms and associative words you are ever likely to need. Should you find even these dozens of choices insufficient, you may wish to look up the other sections referred to in the index under *entertain* — sections 48A, 114, and 113. In almost every instance, however, you will find more variations than you can possibly use in the very first section you turn to.

In brief, the best and simplest way to use Hartrampf's VOCABULARY-BUILDER is this:

1. Find in the index at the back of the book the word for which you want a substitute.
2. Note the section number following the word.
3. Turn back to this section in the front part of the book. There you will find the right word to express your thought.

Here, then, is your new VOCABULARY-BUILDER. Use it daily and you will find, almost before you know it, that you have gained real mastery over words.

VOCABULARY: YOUR KEY TO SUCCESS

By ROSS McLAURY TAYLOR, Ph.D.

Professor of English, University of Wichita
Author of *Brazos, The Saddle and the Plow*, etc.

IF YOU HAVE EVER FELT the paralyzing and strangling helplessness of hunting for the right word when you need it the most, then you know the real value of a rich vocabulary. There is no man on earth so alone as the one who is addressing a group of associates and, at the moment of putting across an "idea" which may make the future for him, finds himself struggling hopelessly for the right word to convey that idea. He is alone then; there is no one who can help him, no matter how much we may wish to. He is alone with a mind that is struggling valiantly to broadcast the right word conveying the right idea.

Unless the right word is immediately available, the idea may as well have died at the very moment of conception. Remember there is more truth than poetry to the old jingle " . . . for want of a horseshoe nail a kingdom was lost." It is equally true that for the lack of a single word one's whole future may be lost.

WHY ARE WORDS IMPORTANT?

What is a word that it should be so important? There are many definitions for a word: a word may be a *noun,* the name of something; a word may be a *verb,* an action word or one that implies action; a word may be an *adjective,* a word that qualifies or colors or limits a noun; and so on. Each definition leaves the word itself lifeless. One is, in effect, standing outside looking at the word. What goes on inside of the word? We must know how a word functions, why more and more words add to our ability to think, and why an increase in our thinking adds to our mental growth. Then we can understand why an enriched vocabulary often is an index to our prospects for future success.

HOW DO WORD-MEANINGS CHANGE?

As we know, each word stands for something and that something is more often than not shaded in the light of one's own experience. The word *cold,* for instance, to a Southerner who enjoys a temperate climate even in the dead of winter, does not mean the same thing that it does to a native of northern Minnesota. To a Grand Banks fisherman the word does not mean the same thing that it does to the Minnesotean. Nor does it mean the same thing to the high altitude flyer who has suffered a lack of oxygen as well as cold. Each one of us colors the word in our own way.

Think also of such words as *pain, hunger, thirst, fear, anger, hate*—these words are basic to our very existence. If a word is mentioned in our hearing or if we read it, we immediately associate some familiar experience with the word. But, if we increase the range of the words and steadily lift our thinking above the level of these basic items of human experience, what happens? We find that it is not so easy to associate some personal experience with each word — the word becomes less a specific thing and becomes more an intangible something we cannot grasp so easily. It requires not one but several words to explain. And we find this to be increasingly true the farther we move away from our basic vocabulary.

A WORD IS THE SYMBOL OF AN IDEA

The more we explore this truth in words, then, the more we realize that each word stands for some one idea, whether it be simple or complex. We can then say that *a word is the symbol of an idea*. When we use words we are expressing ideas.

Two qualities mark mankind. One quality is his physical attitude, his physical presence. The other quality is his intellect — shown by his ability to think, and to organize his thinking, and especially by his ability to express and to exchange ideas with others. The first of these qualities is obvious at first glance. One looks at a man, one sees him, one appraises his appearance and passes a first judgment. But the second quality, that of intellect, is not at first discernible, for it becomes apparent only after you know a man and exchange ideas with him. If this second quality does not exist, then it is apparent to all of us that here is only the shell of a man, a hollow figure.

IDEAS AND THEIR EXPRESSION MAKE THE MAN

It follows that the more we advance and the more we become civilized — the more interested we are in our ability to think and to express thoughts. This ability is almost wholly dependent upon vocabulary or store of words. The open door, the key to that interior person we want all of our world to know is the vehicle by which we express our ideas — words.

As children our thoughts were relatively simple. We were hungry or cold or warm or thirsty or tired, and with a few rather well chosen simple words we could convey the idea to our elders and get results. As we grew up, our ideas became more complicated. We wanted not just cold water, but water with ice in it, or iced water with sirup and coloring in it. In each instance, as our ideas became more complicated, we needed a greater range of vocabulary to put across the idea of what we desired. And now we find our adult life increasingly complicated by our need for more words and better words to grasp the complicated world situation or a tangled business problem. Despite a highly mechanized and scientific age, our ideas are still conveyed by words.

IS A MINIMUM VOCABULARY ENOUGH?

Many of us are downright lazy. Most of us, conceivably, should find it more convenient to use a minimum vocabulary. Certainly it would not require so much mental activity. If it were possible for us to accomplish all we wish in life with the basic minimum vocabulary of eight hundred words, we should scarcely have needed to go beyond the original vocal gymnastics of the caveman.

Miss Helen Keller, born deaf, dumb, and blind, is a splendid example of the constant striving of the human mind to reach beyond the boundaries imposed by a limited vocabulary. The blind person expends every effort in learning Braille so he can read. He learns to use the stylus and prepared paper to keep his own notes.

He even learns the touch system on the typewriter and develops other senses to compensate for the loss of sight. The person born dumb first learns to express himself by sign language, then progresses beyond that slow and inefficient method and starts to write notes or to use the typewriter so that he can more quickly and fully express broadening ideas. In each instance, it is an endless cycle — the more words, the more ideas; the more ideas, the more words with which to express the ideas; and so on *ad infinitum*. To be sure, this process is typical only of a person who is *determined* to push beyond all boundaries, physical and intellectual, a determination which is characteristic of all who are sincerely interested in this volume, *Hartrampf's Vocabulary-Builder*.

WHAT THE VOCABULARY-BUILDER IS

This volume is a truly splendid collection of related vocabularies so arranged that the user can place his finger immediately upon the category of words that he needs for use or for study. To make these collections even more readily accessible for use and study, the collections of words have been divided vertically into groups. These are the major divisions for all words of *verbs, adjectives,* and *nouns,* the inverse order to the one by which we learned our words as children, but the correct order in which we must learn our words as adults to improve and enrich our vocabularies.

Thus we have first our lists of "power" words, the words that give our vocabulary its strength, its capacity to be tough when toughmindedness is needed, to be gentle when the velvet glove is needed. Secondly, we have our lists of adjectives, those words that limit nouns or qualify or add to nouns, the words that add color and emotional depth to our statement or argument or plea. And thirdly we have our lists of nouns, nouns which are synonymous with each other and nouns which, though associated in meaning, also enable us to go far afield from an original idea and to follow new paths of thought.

HOW IT CAN WORK FOR YOU

It is this study of *new* or *associative* verbs, adjectives and nouns which enables us to avoid the bad habits of a limited vocabulary. Using trite or hackneyed expressions is one of the bad habits picked up as a child. We hear a word; we like it. We use the word or the phrase over again and again in order to learn it. But the next thing we know it has become a trite part of our vocabulary. The word or the phrase sounded good. We liked it. So, after we learned it, we used it over and over the way a parrot would. In the course of time, the word ceased to have the original value it may have possessed but, because it once had a charm for us, we keep on using it. So remember that triteness of word usage can and does occur on every level of diction from the most literary English to that level we call the vulgar — particularly so in slang.

We need to watch for triteness, for the hackneyed word or phrase, the cliché, as it is known. Triteness and the cliché are prime indicators of the limited vocabulary, of the mind that refuses to grow.

A dictionary often is thought of as a vocabulary builder. Actually, it is a tool, an indispensable tool, of the person who needs to know an exact word and its meanings. For vocabulary building it relies on the inherent interest of the person using it and on his talent and skill in calculating associative words. But, to go beyond the limitations of the dictionary, a person determined to build a stronger, more forceful vocabulary must use a volume designed for that purpose, *Hartrampf's Vocabulary-Builder.*

The dictionary contains a word's background, its level of usage, and sometimes an account of its origin, but seldom does it go beyond that stage. It may, and often does, list a synonym. But the dictionary does not and cannot give you the *families* of words nor can it divide vertically those categories of words into verbs, adjectives, and nouns for convenience and interest in study.

It is in the wealth of synonyms and synonymous usages contained in this volume that you will find most assistance in ridding yourself of the habit of using the cliché. Remember that cliché means stereotyped, stiff, trite, worn-out and over-used. It is the one error, where words and vocabulary are concerned, that we must learn to avoid at all costs. If not corrected, triteness can and will eventually dull your mind, limit its capacity, and narrow its ability to grasp or express new thought and ideas.

Here are several practice sentences, each containing a typical cliché or over-worked word in *italic* type. After the first sentence you will see how the use of the *Hartrampf Vocabulary-Builder* helps you improve the sentence.

"He was *busy as a bee.*" Now look up *busy* in the back half of your book. On page 421 you will find:

    busy 144B, 39, 11A

Now check the first reference (144B) in the front half of your book and you will find an entry labelled:

    ADJECTIVES **Busy,** Etc.

Here you have twenty synonyms for the trite "busy as a bee." How much fresher your sentence will sound when you rephrase it, for example:

    "He was bustling and industrious."

Now go ahead and test your new *Vocabulary-Builder* on some more dull and tired words and phrases, such as:

    "He was *proud possessor* of a new automobile."

    "Thanks a lot. I had a *grand* time.

    "Isn't the baby *cute?*"

    "He drove at *breakneck* speed."

In every case, you will find that *Hartrampf's Vocabulary-Builder* can help you find the right, fresh, meaningful word that you are looking for. And, if you do not find what you want under the *first* number in the index, look up the other numbers where you will find even a greater number of synonyms or associated words.

VOCABULARY BUILDING DAY BY DAY

You should remember, also, that a good, well-rounded vocabulary comes only as a result of practice. It is a very wise practice for every one interested in improving his vocabulary to carry a small pocket notebook to write down every good, unusual word or phrase he encounters in his daily conversation and reading or in his radio listening. It is during such daily activity that one is most likely to hear an exceptional phrase or an unusual word that strikes home and creates an idea that may in the course of time pay real dividends.

It is equally wise for you to make it a daily habit to refer to the *Vocabulary-Builder* — not just any time during the day, but at the *same* time each day, so it becomes an unbreakable habit. Perhaps you will want to find an improvement on a poor selection of word or phrase or to strengthen your grasp on a good word or phrase by learning its family of related verbs, adjectives, and nouns. It is only when you make a constant, *daily* habit of using the *Vocabulary-Builder* that you can surely expect to make the word or phrase a permanent possession and give it a depth and perspective that will enhance it all the more for your own use.

Remember that you think *all of the time.* Thinking isn't a mental exercise that you indulge in only early in the morning or late at night. Your daily existence depends completely upon your constant use of your mental faculties. Keep the *Vocabulary-Builder* close at hand, literally at your finger tips where it is readily accessible for use and *use it!* It is only by deliberate intention on your part that your vocabulary can be built and strengthened and polished.

HOW VOCABULARY AFFECTS YOUR CAREER

Did you know that an individual's vocabulary does not increase beyond the end of a college career unless *a conscious effort* is made to add to it? Mr. Johnson O'Connor, one of the most outstanding testers of business men in this country, has reported that tests of the vocabularies of one hundred successful business executives, when compared with the results of similar tests given one hundred college graduates, showed a remarkable difference in that only 9 per cent of the college graduates made a score as high as the *average* of the major executives.

In other words, there is a close relationship between the person's determination to succeed and the range of his vocabulary. Likewise we can say that a good and rich vocabulary goes hand in hand with success no matter what you wish to do in life. We cannot assume that these executives were especially equipped with vocabularies to begin with, nor that they were initially hired because of their vocabulary. We can say that, in carrying out their determination to succeed, they realized that a good, rich vocabulary was essential for success. Therefore, a *conscious effort* to increase and enhance their vocabularies materially helped these individuals to succeed in their chosen fields.

An increase in your vocabulary unlocks, once and for all time, doors that have previously been locked. It not only makes for material success, but for happiness, a new capacity to enjoy pleasures you may not even have been aware of. It cannot be done for you; you must do it yourself. *And you can do it!*

With the key to thousands of heretofore unknown words and phrases placed in your hand, with a daily routine built up and maintained, you and you alone set the pace and decide the results you wish to obtain. You can acquire greater understanding of the thoughts and the ideas of others. You can increase the degree of success you wish to obtain by expressing your own ideas more clearly. And you can take a long step towards your goal by building your power over words.

VOCABULARY TESTS

ON THE RIGHT of each word in *italics* are four words or phrases, lettered **a, b, c,** or **d.** Check or underline the one you think is closest in meaning to the italicized word. When you have finished all twenty questions, turn to page xvii, where you will find the correct answers.

You will find that the tests become harder as you proceed from number I to VIII. We recommend that you score yourself on these tests and keep an accurate record. After a month of using Hartrampf's VOCABULARY-BUILDER according to the instructions in Professor Taylor's article, take these tests for a second time. You will be surprised at the improvement in your score!

TEST I

1. *Stoic:* **a.** ancient; **b.** indifferent to pleasure or pain; **c.** stubborn; **d.** philosophical.
2. *Torpid:* **a.** tubelike; **b.** swift; **c.** inert; **d.** violent.
3. *Mitigate:* **a.** aggravate; **b.** make less severe; **c.** move to a new abode; **d.** bless.
4. *Recluse:* **a.** enclosure; **b.** consort; **c.** pilgrim; **d.** hermit.
5. *Stolid:* **a.** worthwhile; **b.** muddy; **c.** dull; **d.** vivacious.
6. *Lucid:* **a.** long; **b.** muddy; **c.** loose; **d.** clear.
7. *Parlous:* **a.** risky; **b.** debatable; **c.** peaceful; **d.** indifferent.
8. *Empiric:* **a.** a charlatan; **b.** a ruler; **c.** employee; **d.** head of an empire.
9. *Culpable:* **a.** not capable; **b.** deserving blame; **c.** unified; **d.** evasive.
10. *Nuance:* **a.** type of cloud, **b.** innovation; **c.** shade of difference; **d.** friendship.
11. *Pugnacious:* **a.** peaceful; **b.** disposed to fight; **c.** distasteful; **d.** inclined to dishonesty.
12. *Puerile:* **a.** childish; **b.** liquid; **c.** non-pure; **d.** aged.
13. *Penury:* **a.** servitude; **b.** avarice; **c.** destitution; **d.** dishonesty.
14. *Mulct:* **a.** acquire dishonestly; **b.** cover with mulch; **c.** to milk; **d.** to confuse.
15. *Ignominious:* **a.** stingy; **b.** very ignorant; **c.** humiliating; **d.** loud.
16. *Maudlin:* **a.** messy; **b.** disorderly; **c.** joyful; **d.** sentimental.
17. *Perfidious:* **a.** untrustworthy; **b.** faithless; **c.** perfect; **d.** ruthless.
18. *Virago:* **a.** North American bird; **b.** vitality; **c.** a shrew; **d.** slander.
19. *Paranoia:* **a.** a soporific; **b.** persecution complex; **c.** fear of height; **d.** desire for leadership.
20. *Erudite:* **a.** hidden; **b.** stupid; **c.** friendly; **d.** learned.

TEST II

1. *Ephemeral:* **a.** effeminate; **b.** lasting; **c.** interesting; **d.** short-lived.
2. *Persiflage:* **a.** light raillery; **b.** disguise; **c.** anger; **d.** thermal measurement.
3. *Desultory:* **a.** dreary; **b.** designing; **c.** aimless; **d.** lonely.
4. *Profligate:* **a.** set fire to; **b.** recklessly extravagant; **c.** humdrum; **d.** hateful..
5. *Blatant:* **a.** dark; **b.** bland; **c.** obnoxious; **d.** noisy.
6. *Foment:* **a.** to extinguish; **b.** to smoothe out; **c.** to nurse to life; **d.** to make bubble-like
7. *Soporific:* **a.** dreamy; **b.** sleep inducing; **c.** of exceptional swiftness; **d.** viscous.
8. *Collate:* **a.** compare; **b.** lather; **c.** cloth; **d.** add.
9. *Uxorious:* **a.** slavishly devoted; **b.** urgent; **c.** usurping; **d.** laborious.
10. *Pariah:* **a.** father; **b.** an outcast; **c.** an ancient; **d.** a foreigner.
11. *Banal:* **a.** vivid; **b.** imaginative; **c.** fraternal; **d.** commonplace.
12. *Chicanery:* **a.** poultry; **b.** admiration; **c.** petty trickery; **d.** stubborn pride.

13. *Diffident:* **a.** unusual; **b.** unconfident; **c.** various; **d.** routine.
14. *Quixotic:* **a.** swift; **b.** insane; **c.** practical; **d.** romantically idealistic.
15. *Potable:* **a.** drinkable; **b.** transportable; **c.** elementary; **d.** poisonous.
16. *Mundane:* **a.** pecuniary; **b.** worldly; **c.** municipal; **d.** weekly.
17. *Necropolis:* **a.** a large city; **b.** cemetery; **c.** lovers' land; **d.** site of a guillotine.
18. *Didactic:* **a.** poetic; **b.** entertaining; **c.** instructive; **d.** pertaining to diets.
19. *Truculent:* **a.** portable; **b.** amiable; **c.** stiffly formal; **d.** fiercely resentful.
20. *Opulent:* **a.** wealthy; **b.** industrious; **c.** overweight; **d.** impoverished.

TEST III

1. *Filial:* **a.** transparent; **b.** equine; **c.** pertaining to son or daughter; **d.** fatherly or parental.
2. *Adamant:* **a.** yielding; **b.** stubborn; **c.** sparkling; **d.** primitive.
3. *Augury:* **a.** an omen; **b.** a bird cage; **c.** a drilling tool; **d.** a miracle.
4. *Onus:* **a.** musical composition; **b.** debt; **c.** high praise; **d.** burden or duty.
5. *Mien:* **a.** Chinese food; **b.** external appearance; **c.** method; **d.** possession.
6. *Taciturn:* **a.** talkative; **b.** grasping; **c.** habitually silent; **d.** generous.
7. *Amity:* **a.** hatred; **b.** cotton material; **c.** honesty; **d.** friendship.
8. *Harbinger:* **a.** a forerunner; **b.** a sailor; **c.** a witch; **d.** a kind of gun.
9. *Jocose:* **a.** melancholy; **b.** sportively humorous; **c.** recalcitrant or unmanageable; **d.** impertinent.
10. *Spurious:* **a.** counterfeit; **b.** thorny; **c.** genuine; **d.** porous.
11. *Savant:* **a.** a doctor of medicine; **b.** a forerunner of trouble; **c.** a scholar; **d.** a student.
12. *Placable:* **a.** difficult to please; **b.** stationary; **c.** movable; **d.** able to be appeased.
13. *Demise:* **a.** a kind of underwear; **b.** death; **c.** birth; **d.** a halfway place.
14. *Mentor:* **a.** a faithful counselor; **b.** an orator; **c.** a liar; **d.** a beggar.
15. *Mendacity:* **a.** cure; **b.** poverty; **c.** deceit; **d.** capacity.
16. *Indigenous:* **a.** earthy; **b.** inedible; **c.** foreign; **d.** native.
17. *Natal:* **a.** pertaining to birth; **b.** fatal; **c.** pertaining to nature; **d.** mortal.
18. *Rapacious:* **a.** abstemious; **b.** ecstatic; **c.** greedy; **d.** rapid.
19. *Nascent:* **a.** declining; **b.** beginning to grow; **c.** stubborn; **d.** non-odorous.
20. *Optative:* **a.** visual; **b.** wealthy; **c.** bearing a grudge; **d.** expressing a desire.

TEST IV

1. *Incorrigible:* **a.** incorruptible; **b.** unhealthy; **c.** impertinent; **d.** unmanageable.
2. *Complicity:* **a.** complexion; **b.** partnership; **c.** an international agreement; **d.** a law suit.
3. *Unctuous:* **a.** harsh; **b.** soothing; **c.** suave; **d.** belonging to an uncle.
4. *Ebullient:* **a.** hateful; **b.** fearful; **c.** viscous; **d.** bubbling.
5. *Carnage:* **a.** kind of decoration; **b.** slaughter; **c.** two wheeled cart or buggy; **d.** a festival.
6. *Diatribe:* **a.** dual debate; **b.** musical form; **c.** savage group; **d.** abuse.
7. *Chauvinism:* **a.** exaggerated patriotism; **b.** religiousness; **c.** provincial mindedness; **d.** oriental philosophy.
8. *Chimerical:* **a.** commonplace; **b.** dishonest; **c.** fantastic; **d.** routine.
9. *Vacillation:* **a.** bubbling; **b.** process of distillation; **c.** whirling or spinning; **d.** irresolution.
10. *Lethargic:* **a.** dull or morbidly drowsy; **b.** alert; **c.** vivacious; **d.** overwhelming.
11. *Umbra:* **a.** spiteful dictation; **b.** braggadocia; **c.** shrewdness; **d.** shade.
12. *Sedulous:* **a.** routine; **b.** deep rooted; **c.** untiring or diligent; **d.** restful.
13. *Contretemps:* **a.** embarrassing occurrence; **b.** international combine; **c.** sequence of events; **d.** turn of the seasons.
14. *Siccate:* **a.** to compel secrecy; **b.** to dry; **c.** to reduce to powder; **d.** to make fun of.
15. *Predaceous:* **a.** anything that follows another; **b.** living by preying on other animals: **c.** parasitic; **d.** following in order.
16. *Attenuate:* **a.** to lift up; **b.** to strengthen; **c.** to dilute or to thin; **d.** to give strength to.
17. *Laconic:* **a.** tired; **b.** verbose; **c.** terse; **d.** loudly angry.
18. *Phlegmatic:* **a.** painful; **b.** composed, calm; **c.** highly colored; **d.** out of the ordinary.
19. *Invidious:* **a.** exciting ill will; **b.** secretive; **c.** complimentary; **d.** abusive.
20. *Eclectic:* **a.** choosing or selecting from various sources; **b.** foreign to one's nature; **c.** liking sports or physical activity; **d.** reclusive.

xiii

TEST V

1. *Anachronous:* **a.** up to the minute; **b.** remote from the present; **c.** true to tradition; **d.** belonging to another time.
2. *Plagiarize:* **a.** to borrow momentarily; **b.** to steal and pass off as one's own; **c.** to write anything under the name of another; **d.** to reduce a play in length.
3. *Jingoism:* **a.** use of vulgar language; **b.** insular mindedness; **c.** practice of being belligerent in international relations; **d.** use of arbitration in settling disputes.
4. *Satiate:* **a.** to tire out; **b.** to feed to the limit; **c.** to dampen one's spirits; **d.** to arouse one's emotions.
5. *Ideology:* **a.** ideal government; **b.** tendency toward extreme nationalism; **c.** visionary theorizing or thinking; **d.** worship of ancient standards.
6. *Saturnine:* **a.** majestic in proportion; **b.** light hearted; **c.** retiring or shy; **d.** grave or gloomy; dull.
7. *Acrimonious:* **a.** sanctimonious; **b.** caustic or bitter; **c.** hypocritical; **d.** debatable.
8. *Cursory:* **a.** vulgar or profane treatment; **b.** routine or orderly; **c.** thorough-going and complete; **d.** superficially performed.
9. *Irascible:* **a.** prone to anger; **b.** prone to excitement; **c.** quiet dispositioned; **d.** steady and unexcitable.
10. *Abstemious:* **a.** miserly in habit; **b.** prone to excess; **c.** moderate or temperate in appetites; **d.** reclusive or fearful.
11. *Interstice:* **a.** period of quiet between two nations; **b.** period of mourning; **c.** changes in the moon's phases; **d.** space between two things.
12. *Entrepreneur:* **a.** a political appointee; **b.** one who assumes responsibility and management in business; **c.** one with revolutionary ideas; **d.** employee of a business firm.
13. *Axiomatic:* **a.** contrary to nature's laws; **b.** self-evidently true; **c.** outside the normal; **d.** almost, but not quite, true.
14. *Malefaction:* **a.** a practical joke; **b.** an organized group of men; **c.** an evil deed; **d.** a political party.
15. *Petulant:* **a.** peevish or cross; **b.** small in stature; **c.** angry or hateful; **d.** happy dispositioned.
16. *Clandestine:* **a.** conducted in groups; **b.** off color; **c.** unorganized activity; **d.** secret or furtive.
17. *Frangible:* **a.** emanating out of France; **b.** brittle or breakable; **c.** stern or tough in quality; **d.** light in touch.
18. *Parapet:* **a.** low wall at edge of platform; **b.** stand for lecturer's notes; **c.** fence; **d.** a governmental boundary.
19. *Sequester:* **a.** to cover up; **b.** to waste away; **c.** to expand disproportionately; **d.** to set apart or separate.
20. *Contiguous:* **a.** continuing from one to another; **b.** equalling something else; **c.** adjacent or near to another; **d.** two objects equally distant from a third.

TEST VI

1. *Accolade:* **a.** an award or decoration; **b.** a verdict handed down by courts; **c.** decision rendered by international court; **d.** a special dispensation.
2. *Redolent:* **a.** harsh in scent; **b.** fragrant; **c.** overflowing; **d.** repetitious in nature.
3. *Anomalous:* **a.** similar to another; **b.** routine and regular; **c.** diminutive; **d.** out of the ordinary.
4. *Hebdomadal:* **a.** occurring at intervals of seven days; **b.** varying at long intervals; **c.** any idolatrous worship; **d.** a seasonal variation.
5. *Insensate:* **a.** undeveloped; **b.** small in size; **c.** high sensory reaction; **d.** without sensation.
6. *Calumny:* **a.** catastrophic action; **b.** false accusation; **c.** just accusation before a court; **d.** a settling of guilt.
7. *Porcine:* **a.** characteristically hoggish in appearance; **b.** round bodied and smooth; **c.** high handedness; **d.** lacking energy.
8. *Tautology:* **a.** to pull something taut or tight; **b.** a kind of philosophy; **c.** terseness in diction; **d.** needless repetition of meaning in other words.

9. *Vestige:* **a.** power of office given to officials; **b.** a trace of something no longer existent; **c.** early sign of sprouting seeds; **d.** evidence of destruction.
10. *Effulgent:* **a.** filling to overflowing; **b.** feeding until corpulent; **c.** pouring out a stream of radiant light; **d.** retiring in nature.
11. *Euphony:* **a.** repetitious sound; **b.** musical variation; **c.** characteristic of organization; **d.** sweet sound.
12. *Prescience:* **a.** preliminary investigation; **b.** a phase of science; **c.** crystal; **d.** foresight or knowledge of the future.
13. *Postulate:* **a.** protest; **b.** reply to a statement; **c.** a musical phrase; **d.** proposition taken for granted.
14. *Gourmand:* **a.** an habitual drunkard; **b.** one who delights in fine foods; **c.** a coffee taster; **d.** a government examiner.
15. *Cacophony:* **a.** discord or harsh sound; **b.** section of a symphony orchestra; **c.** a type of symphonic music; **d.** type of music played on string instruments only.
16. *Alliteration:* **a.** any group of illiterate people; **b.** period of vernal equinox; **c.** prelude used in music; **d.** repetition of same sounds in verse.
17. *Curmudgeon:* **a.** one who is grasping; **b.** a kind of walking stick; **c.** a type of overcoat; **d.** a public spirited citizen.
18. *Impasse:* **a.** low-lying mountain pass; **b.** an awkward moment; **c.** predicament without an escape; **d.** a disagreement.
19. *Narcissism:* **a.** love of flowers; **b.** love of one's self; **c.** general physical condition; **d.** a kind of dance.
20. *Succinct:* **a.** compressed or brief; **b.** sugary or sweet; **c.** loud; **d.** in organized fashion.

TEST VII

1. *Lucubration:* **a.** system of oiling machinery; **b.** process of thinking; **c.** laborious study; **d.** process of cultivating land.
2. *Enucleate:* **a.** to tie things together; **b.** to raze a structure; **c.** to peel out of a shell or to explain; **d.** to break something.
3. *Verisimilar:* **a.** resembling something; **b.** related mathematically; **c.** contrary to reality; **d.** having appearance of reality or truth.
4. *Depurate:* **a.** to appoint a deputy; **b.** to free of impurities; **c.** to delegate authority; **d.** to incorporate a group.
5. *Lustrate:* **a.** to make pure by offerings; **b.** to point out something; **c.** to show by illustration; **d.** to pay homage.
6. *Cozenage:* **a.** study of family relations; **b.** a type of humorous play; **c.** organized play; **d.** art or practice of fraud.
7. *Comprador:* **a.** high administrative official; **b.** an Oriental potentate; **c.** native agent hired to supervise native employees; **d.** one who deals in foreign trade.
8. *Ominous:* **a.** thunderous or noisy; **b.** foreboding; **c.** vacillating action; **d.** definitely true.
9. *Hegemony:* **a.** leadership in government; **b.** marriage between reigning families; **c.** line of succession; **d.** organization of political adherents.
10. *Flatulent:* **a.** explosive; **b.** without order or plan; **c.** thin or flat; **d.** pretentious.
11. *Pother:* **a.** to confuse; **b.** to be contrary; **c.** to plan; **d.** to organize.
12. *Fecund:* **a.** sourish; **b.** hateful; **c.** miserly; **d.** prolific.
13. *Apostasize:* **a.** to proclaim; **b.** to request; **c.** to renounce; **d.** to petition.
14. *Cortege:* **a.** a parade; **b.** a jury for a high court; **c.** a train of assistants; **d.** an audience.
15. *Eleemosynary:* **a.** electing by popular vote; **b.** receiving alms or favors; **c.** sanguine in disposition; **d.** apathetic in attitude.
16. *Pertinacious:* **a.** loosely held; **b.** tending to give up; **c.** proceeding on a straight line; **d.** unyielding.
17. *Tumid:* **a.** swollen; **b.** dampish; **c.** gigantic; **d.** thin.
18. *Obfuscate:* **a.** to examine closely; **b.** to consider; **c.** to bewilder or to perplex; **d.** to weigh fully.
19. *Adventitious:* **a.** dangerous; **b.** casual; **c.** routine; **d.** grasping.
20. *Celibate:* **a.** one who lives loosely; **b.** married many times; **c.** a public figure; **d.** unmarried person.

TEST VIII

1. *Insouciant:* **a.** vitally interested; **b.** indifferent; **c.** curious; **d.** quiescent.
2. *Ratiocination:* **a.** avoiding an issue; **b.** random thinking; **c.** reasoning exactly; **d.** process of adding up.
3. *Veridical:* **a.** untruthful; **b.** greenish; **c.** vertical or upright; **d.** truthful or accurate.
4. *Metonymy:* **a.** regular and repeated sounds; **b.** a kind of suicide; **c.** a musical composition; **d.** use of one word for another.
5. *Cognate:* **a.** allied by origin; **b.** deriving from known facts; **c.** generally understood; **d.** factually stating.
6. *Cognomen:* **a.** an unknown man; **b.** a surname; **c.** one's given name; **d.** a writer's pen name.
7. *Hiatus:* **a.** a drunken revel; **b.** an opening; **c.** a mistake; **d.** an awkward moment.
8. *Rodomontade:* **a.** a deliberate statement; **b.** a salacious remark; **c.** idle gossip; **d.** vain boasting.
9. *Apocryphal:* **a.** of highest veracity; **b.** unquestioned; **c.** spurious; **d.** dogmatic.
10. *Assiduous:* **a.** foolish; **b.** persistent or devoted; **c.** malicious; **d.** regular.
11. *Collusion:* **a.** a chance running together of two or more vehicles; **b.** a contractual agreement; **c.** a secret agreement for wrongful purposes; **d.** an improper advance.
12. *Xenophobia:* **a.** hatred of foreigners; **b.** the nature of madness; **c.** passion; **d.** liking for things that are ancient.
13. *Hedonistic:* **a.** practical minded; **b.** pleasure loving; **c.** empiricist; **d.** introvertive.
14. *Viviparous:* **a.** violent tempered; **b.** sagacious; **c.** dull witted; **d.** producing living young.
15. *Ascetic:* **a.** sourish; **b.** reclusive; **c.** hateful; **d.** determined.
16. *Misogynist:* **a.** a religious cultist; **b.** a miser; **c.** a rabble rouser; **d.** a woman hater.
17. *Iconoclast:* **a.** an introvert; **b.** one who is lonely; **c.** a breaker of traditions; **d.** a beggar.
18. *Autonomy:* **a.** quality of being generous; **b.** pertaining to political units within a state or union; **c.** one who is selfish; **d.** a self-governing state.
19. *Multifarious:* **a.** single-mindedness; **b.** planned for evil purposes; **c.** concentrating on one of many; **d.** having great diversity.
20. *Lubricity:* **a.** coyness; **b.** slipperiness; **c.** strength; **d.** suaveness.

ANSWERS TO VOCABULARY TESTS I-VIII

I	II	III	IV
1. b.	1. d.	1. c.	1. d.
2. c.	2. a.	2. b.	2. b.
3. b.	3. c.	3. a.	3. c.
4. d.	4. b.	4. d.	4. d.
5. c.	5. d.	5. b.	5. b.
6. d.	6. c.	6. c.	6. d.
7. a.	7. b.	7. d.	7. a.
8. a.	8. a.	8. a.	8. c.
9. b.	9. a.	9. b.	9. d.
10. c.	10. b.	10. a.	10. a.
11. b.	11. d.	11. c.	11. d.
12. a.	12. c.	12. d.	12. c.
13. c.	13. b.	13. b.	13. a.
14. a.	14. d.	14. a.	14. b.
15. c.	15. a.	15. c.	15. b.
16. d.	16. b.	16. d.	16. c.
17. b.	17. b.	17. a.	17. c.
18. c.	18 .c.	18. c.	18. b.
19. b.	19. d.	19. b.	19. a.
20. d.	20. a,	20. d.	20. a.

V	VI	VII	VIII
1. d.	1. a.	1. c.	1. b.
2. b.	2. b.	2. c.	2. c.
3. c.	3. d.	3. d.	3. d.
4. b.	4. a.	4. b.	4. d.
5. c.	5. d.	5. a.	5. a.
6. d.	6. b.	6. d.	6. b.
7. b.	7. a.	7. c.	7. b.
8. d.	8. d.	8. b.	8. d.
9. a.	9. b.	9. a.	9. c.
10. c.	10. c.	10. d.	10. b.
11. d.	11. d.	11. a.	11. c.
12. b.	12. d.	12. d.	12. a.
13. b.	13. d.	13. c.	13. b.
14. c.	14. b.	14. c.	14. d.
15. a.	15. a.	15. b.	15. b.
16. d.	16. d.	16. d.	16. d.
17. b.	17. a.	17. a.	17. c.
18. a.	18. c.	18. c.	18. d.
19. d.	19. b.	19. b.	19. d.
20. c.	20. a.	20. d.	20. b.

WORD GAMES

NOTE: These word games are designed to help you check your familiarity with all aspects of our language. Follow the instructions at the beginning of each game and, when you have finished, check your answers against those on page xxi.

I. What is the adjective that ends in *ous* and

1. Beginning with *g*, means "living in flocks; liking company?"
2. Beginning with *p*, "insecure?"
3. Beginning with *l*, means "talkative?"
4. Beginning with *f*, means "humorous; witty?"
5. Beginning with *v*, means "greedy?"
6. Beginning with *c*, means "intemperate in drinking?"
7. Beginning with *l*, means "lustful?"
8. Beginning with *p*, means "mentally advanced?"
9. Beginning with *o*, means "excessively submissive?"
10. Beginning with *s*, means "resonant?"
11. Beginning with *u*, means "omnipresent?"
12. Beginning with *v*, means "substituted?"
13. Beginning with *s*, means "arrogant?"
14. Beginning with *l*, means "ridiculously funny?"
15. Beginning with *f*, means "foolish?"

II. What is the adjective ending in *ine* that means "like" or "pertaining to" the following animal:

1. dog	9. mouse
2. cat	10. sheep
3. horse	11. wolf
4. cow	12. fox
5. lion	13. bear
6. hare	14. swallow
7. fish	15. goat
8. pig	

III. Find the words in the following list that are misspelled and then correct them.

1. jejune	9. surreptitious
2. canteloupe	10. homey
3. lacey	11. belligerancy
4. develope	12. inane
5. ecstacy	13. sporatic
6. nickle	14. bouyancy
7. elliptical	15. innuendo
8. annoint	

IV. Match the correct definitions to the following numbered verbs. Place the letter of the definition after the word it defines:

1. abrogate ....a. to strive to equal another
2. inhume ....b. to blot out, to erase
3. abridge ....c. to spread in all directions
4. retaliate ....d. to make shorter, condense

xviii

5. ridicule ....e. to use another's words or ideas
6. plagiarize ....f. to annul by an authoritative act
7. scintillate ....g. to sparkle with wit or humor
8. procrastinate ....h. to make hallow or sacred
9. expunge ....i. to be attached, to cling
10. adhere ....j. to return like for like
11. supplicate ....k. to bury in the earth
12. emulate ....l. to implore humbly
13. sanctify ....m. to shame by slander
14. diffuse ....n. to put off until a future time
15. traduce ....o. to laugh at mockingly

V. Which of these often-confused words should fill the blanks in the following sentences:

1. affect-effect. Lectures had no .... upon him.
2. principal-principle. John was the .... character in the novel.
3. stationary-stationery. The letter was written on her new ....
4. ascetic-aesthetic. The picture pleases her .... sense.
5. mantel-mantle. The clock sat on the ....
6. complement-compliment. The two departments .... each other.
7. allusion-illusion. No .... was made to the weather.
8. eminent-imminent. The rain storm was ....
9. explicit-implicit. The child's trust was ....
10. except-accept. They took everyone .... Charles.
11. ingenious-ingenuous. Her smile was ....
12. dual-duel. They fought the .... with swords.

VI. Answer yes or no, whether the definition fits the word.

Word	Yes or No	Definition
1. succumb	....	1. shake violently
2. stipend	....	2. clasp
3. wanton	....	3. untamed
4. recondite	....	4 profound
5. lucid	....	5 free
6. torpid	....	6. numb
7. hiatus	....	7. flower
8. procrastinate	....	8. be punctual
9. onus	....	9. duty
10. ague	....	10. chill
11. canard	....	11. coward
12. neophyte	....	12. corpse
13. carnage	....	13. mass movement
14. mulct	....	14. cheat
15. flagrant	....	15. burning

VII. Substitute one word with the required number of letters for the italicized expressions in the following sentences.

1. Many people are troubled with *inability to sleep.* ....
(8 letters)

2. The cave was *a series of winding passages.* ....
(9 letters)

3. The world sought a *universal remedy or medicine.* ....
(7 letters)

4. That ritual has not taken place for a *space of 1000 years.* ....
(10 letters)

5. They vacationed at a *mineral springs resort.* ....
(3 letters)

6. It took her a long time to become *adapted to the climate.* ....
(10 letters)

7. Many of the old folk tales are *of unknown authorship.* ....
(9 letters)
8. The criminal was arrested on the charge of *maliciously setting fire* to a house.

....
(5 letters)
9. Lace curtains are *easily set afire.* ....
(11 letters)
10. Some people are *able to use either hand with equal ease.* ....
(12 letters)

VIII. Use the following foreign words and phrases to fill the blanks in the sentences below.

faux pas	denouement
laissez faire	coterie
bourgeois	esprit de corps
savoir faire	coup d'etat
a la carte	ersatz

1. The French Revolution was a ....
2. Unless you prefer table d'hote, you probably order ....
3. Noninterference, especially in economics, is termed ....
4. A congenial social group is called a ....
5. A man with the "know-how" has ....
6. In a play or novel the outcome could be called a ....
7. The common spirit of the group, its enthusiasm and devotion, is called ....
8. A person of the middle class in society could be called a ....
9. Your embarrassing social blunder could be called a ....
10. A substitute of inferior quality is called ....

IX. Determine whether the two words of each line are *similar* or *opposite.* Indicate your answer by encircling one of the two initials.

1. altruistic	s	o	selfish
2. refractory	s	o	recalcitrant
3. perfidy	s	o	loyalty
4. verbose	s	o	talkative
5. senile	s	o	young
6. adamant	s	o	stubborn
7. sanguinary	s	o	bloody
8. dilate	s	o	contract
9. obesity	s	o	corpulence
10. malaise	s	o	feeling-of-fitness
11. onerous	s	o	buoyant
12. placate	s	o	irritate
13. subvert	s	o	overthrow
14. desultory	s	o	methodical
15. orthodox	s	o	radical

ANSWERS TO WORD GAMES I-IX

I.

1. gregarious
2. precarious
3. loquacious
4. facetious
5. voracious
6. crapulous
7. libidinous
   or lascivious
8. precocious
9. obsequious
10. sonorous
11. ubiquitous
12. vicarious
13. supercilious
14. ludicrous
15. fatuous

II.

1. canine
2. feline
3. equine
4. bovine
5. leonine
6. leporine
7. piscine
8. porcine
9. murine
10. ovine
11. lupine
12. vulpine
13. ursine
14. hirundine
15. hircine

III.

1. ok
2. cantaloupe
3. lacy
4. develop
5. ecstasy
6. nickel
7. ok
8. anoint
9. ok
10. ok
11. belligerency
12. ok
13. sporadic
14. buoyancy
15. ok

IV.

1. f.
2. k.
3. d
4. j
5. o
6. e
7. g
8. n
9. b
10. i
11. l
12. a
13. h
14. c
15. m.

V.

1. effect
2. principal
3. stationery
4. aesthetic
5. mantel
6. complement
7. allusion
8. imminent
9. implicit
10. except
11. ingenuous
12. duel

VI.

1. no
2. no
3. yes
4. yes
5. no
6. yes
7. no
8. no
9. yes
10. yes
11. no
12. no
13. no
14. yes
15. no

VII.

1. insomnia
2. labyrinth
3. panacea
4. millennium
5. spa
6. acclimated
7. anonymous
8. arson
9. inflammable
10. ambidextrous

VIII.

1. coup d'Etat
2. a la carte
3. laissez faire
4. coterie
5. savoir faire
6. denouement
7. esprit de corps
8. bourgeois
9. faux pas
10. ersatz

IX.

1. o
2. s
3. o
4. s
5. o
6. ?
7. s
8. o
9. s
10. o
11. o
12. o
13. s
14. o
15. o

CAUSE—CAUSATION   see—

     vs. Impotence—Exhaustion 128A
     vs. Effect—Consequence 144C

ASSOCIATIVE

1

VERBS

Cause

cause, effect
conduce, cause
effect, cause
exert, effect
influence, effect
occasion, cause

Predispose

destine, predispose
determine, dispose
dispose, fix
fix, predispose
predestinate, predispose
predetermine, predispose
predispose, prepare

Prepare

buckle, prepare
prepare, dispose
prime, prepare
project, prepare

Prevail

overbear, prevail
pervade, prevail
predominate, prevail
prevail, predominate
sway, predominate

ADJECTIVES

Causing

active, causative
causative, effective
conducive, causative
conductive, effective
determinant, causative
effective, conductive

Predisposing

influential, effective
important, momentous
momentous, weighty

ADJECTIVES (Continued)

motive, causing motion
weighty, effective

Preparative

designing, causative
preparative, conductive
preparatory, preparative

Prevalent

indefeasible, invincible
invincible, absolute
inviolable, invincible
omnipotent, inviolable
prevalent, prevailing
rife, prevalent

Actual

absolute, inviolable
actual, real
material, real
real, absolute
realistic, actual

Spiritual

spiritual, supernal
supernal, supernatural
supernatural, Godly

NOUNS

Causation

causation, cause of effect
cause, causation
determinant, cause
exertion, determinant
first-cause, fundamental
influence, cause
occasion, cause
reason, cause

Prevalence

absolutism, supreme cause
almightiness, omnipotence
domination, prevalence
might, prevalence
omnipotence, absolutism

NOUNS (Continued)

predominance, prevalence
prevalence, domination

Base

base, principle
foundation, base
fundamental, foundation
ground, cause
principle, source
root, basis

Origin

birthplace, nativity
cradle, origin
creation, nature
mother, source
nativity, cradle
nature, great cause
origin, first cause
source, cause
spring, source

Virtue

faculty, virtue
virtue, inherent cause
vis, virtue

Impulse

breath, life
dint, force
energy, power
exertion, force
fermentation, vital cause
force, active cause
impulse, sudden force
leaven, active cause
life, vital force
power, motive cause
vitality, vital principle

CREATOR

Creator, God, Great Cause
God, Creator
Omnipotence, God

CAUSE—PROMOTION

Word-groups that represent causes or stimuli in promoting effects

CHANGE—START

Word-groups that imply CHANGE in circumstance or quality

TENDENCY—INCLINATION   see—   ASSOCIATIVE

vs. Stability—Inertia 11B

Effort—Endeavor 41C
Desire—Expectation 39
Soul—Life—Inherence 137C

2

VERBS

Tend
conduce, tend
dispose, incline
impend, incline
incline, tend
lean, tend
prepare, dispose
propend, incline
tend, lean
trend, tend
  Intend
aim, intend
decide, determine
design, intend
determine, resolve
intend, resolve
mean, intend
purpose, resolve
resolve, intend
will, resolve
  Endeavor
attempt, try
endeavor, attempt
try, endeavor
  Gravitate
drift, tend steadily
gravitate, drift
stream, drift

ADJECTIVES

Tending
bent, disposed
biased, inclined
disposed, inclined
inclined, tending
intentional, disposed
intentioned, intentional
minded, inclined
prepense, inclined
prone, tending
tending, inclined
voluntary, intentional
willing, inclined
  Intent
determined, resolute
firm, determined
intent, purposeful
purposeful, intentional
resolute, determined
  Intense
ardent, fervid
fervid, resolute
intense, ardent
  Gravitational
gravitational, drifting
momentous, weighty
weighty, momentous
  Ready
alert, ready
imminent, impending

ADJECTIVES (Continued)

impendent, impending
impending, ready
poised, ready
prepared, ready
ready, disposed
  Possible
apt, likely
latent, potential
likely, disposed
pending, inclined
potential, ready
possible, potential
potent, potential
probable, likely
virtual, potential
  Innate
autodynamic, spontaneous
automatic, autodynamic
automatous, spontaneous
conative, instinctive
constitutional, inherent
immanent, constitutional
impulsive, instinctive
inherent, innate
innate, naturally inclined
instinctive, innate
intrinsic, inherent
live, conative
native, inherent
natural, constitutional
pithy, constitutional
reflex, instinctive
spiritual, inherent
spontaneous, instinctive
staminal, constitutional

NOUNS

Tendency
bent, inclination
inclination, tendency
proclivity, inclination
proneness, propensity
propensity, tendency
predisposition, propensity
tendency, inclination
tenor, tendency
trend, tendency
  Intention
aim, purpose
attempt, aim
effort, attempt
intent, purpose
intention, intent
predetermination, design
purport, design
purpose, intention
  Intensity
ardor, intensity
(B). ardour
fervency, fervor

NOUNS (Continued)

fervor, ardor
intensity, fervency
  Gravitation
current, tendency
destiny, spiritual trend
drift, trend
gravitation, drift
gravity, tendency
impetus, momentum
momentum, impetus
predestination, destiny
  Readiness
alacrity, readiness
imminence, potential evil
potency, readiness
preparation, preparedness
preparedness, readiness
readiness, preparedness
  Possibility
aptitude, tendency
latency, potentiality
likelihood, disposition
possibility, potentiality
potential, possibility
potentiality, propensity
probability, potentiality
  Natural Bent
automatism, conation
conation, spontaneity
constitution, temperament
disposition, temper
elan, ardor
excitability, spontaneity
faculty, disposition
immanency, inherence
impulse, instinct
inbeing, inherence
inherence, constitution
instinct, conation
nature, natural tendency
spontaneity, automatism
talent, faculty
temper, constitution
temperament, nature
vein, disposition
verve, artistic excitability
virtue, disposition
  Predilection
animus, animated bent
bias, propensity
humor, tendency
(B). humour
mood, temperament
obsession, bias
penchant, inclination
predilection, inclination
prejudice, bias
stomach, inclination
(Continued on page 5)

vs. Stability—Inertia 11B

Start 4
Rhythmic Change 3B
Reactive Change 3C

3A

VERBS

Change

alter, change
change, modify
conjugate, modify
convert, change
evolve, transform
ferment, alter character
inflect, modulate
leaven, ferment
melt, transform
metamorphose, transform
modify, alter
modulate, change
mutate, change
render, modify
temper, modify
transfigure, alter
transform, transfigure
transmute, alter
transubstantiate, convert
turn, change

Displace

alienate, replace
displace, remove
proselytize, convert
replace, supersede
substitute, exchange
supersede, supplant
supplant, replace
transpose, substitute
transplant, replant

Vary

alternate, change about
diversify, vary
variate, change
vary, modify

Move

budge, move
move, shift
shift, move

Exchange

commute, exchange
exchange, swap
interchange, exchange
reciprocate, interchange
swap, exchange

Reverse

invert, reverse
reverse, change about
revert, reverse

Reform

reform, change anew
regenerate, reform
revolutionize, reform

ADJECTIVES

Changing

actinic, chemical

ADJECTIVES (Continued)

allotropic, actinic
alterant, noting change
alterative, transformatory
changeable, versatile
chemical, actinic
metabolic, transformatory
metamorphic, alterative
protean, assuming change
transformatory, alterative
transitive, changing
versatile, changeable

Interchangeable

commutative, converse
converse, interchangeable
interchangeable, converse
mutual, reciprocal
reciprocal, mutual
transitional, commutative

Reversionary

atavic, reversionary
reverse, interchangeable
reversible, changing back
reversionary, atavic
revulsive, changing

NOUNS

Change

accidence, inflection
actinism, chemical change
alchemy, transformation
allomorphism, actinism
allotropy, chemical change
alteration, change
change, mutation
changeability, change
chemistry, transformation
conjugation, modification
conversion, mutation
currency, continual change
declension, inflection
diversion, change
evolution, advancing change
fomentation, mutation
inflection, variation
metabolism, change of character
metamorphism, change in rock
metamorphosis, change in forms
modification, alteration
modulation, variation
mutation, change
transfiguration, change
transformation, mutation

NOUNS (Continued)

transubstantiation, spiritual conversion
transmutation, transformation

Displacement

alienation, diversion
displacement, substitution
metathesis, substitution
metempsychosis, transmigration
proselytism, conversion
substitution, exchange
supersedure, replacement
transmigration, change to another body
transposition, substitution
transplantation, replanting

Variation

alternation, exchange
diversification, variation
diversion, alteration
variation, change

Transition

metabasis, transition
move, change
movement, move
transition, metamorphosis
transitiveness, transition

Exchange

communion, exchange
commutability, exchange
commutation, exchange
exchange, reciprocation
interchange, exchange
intercourse, interchange
metagenesis, alternation of generations
mutuality, reciprocity
osmosis, reciprocal change
permutation, exchange
reciprocation, interchange
reciprocity, reciprocation
shift, change
vicissitude, interchange

Reversion

atavism, reversion
catabolism, change to simple forms
devolution, reversion
fermentation, decomposing change
leaven, fermentation
reversion, atavism

Crisis

climacteric, change in life
conjuncture, crisis
crisis, decisive change
emergency, sudden change
(Continued on page 7)

4

START— COMMENCEMENT		ASSOCIATIVE
COMMENCEMENT	Birthplace 141D	Musical Beginnings 68C
see—	Excite—Rouse 8	Time Preceding 148A
vs. Stop, Cessation....12	Change 3A	Cause 1
	Opening—Foreword 73	

4

VERBS

Begin
begin, commence
buckle, prepare
commence, start
prepare, start
resume, begin anew
start, begin

Arise
arise, originate
become, begin
dawn, begin
originate, begin
spring, start

Enter
broach, open
enter, begin
launch, act
lead, open
open, begin
pioneer, open

Act
act, begin
bestir, start
stir, act

ADJECTIVES

Initial
accessional, commencing
first, original
initial, beginning
initiative, introductory
initiatory, introductory
introductory, initiatory
original, initial
preliminary, introductory
preparatory, preliminary
primary, first

Inceptive
elemental, rudimental
elementary, incipient

ADJECTIVES (Continued)
embryonic, inchoate
inceptive, beginning
inchoate, elementary
inchoative, incipient
incipient, initial
nascent, incipient
rudimental, embryonic

Spontaneous
automatic, self-acting
automatous, spontaneous
autodynamic, spontaneous
conative, instinctive
instinctive, spontaneous
spontaneous, self-beginning

Basic
basic, initial
cardinal, fundamental
fundamental, basic
radical, fundamental

NOUNS

Beginning
accession, commencement,
  as in disease
alpha, beginning
beginning, commencement
commencement, start
initiative, first step
initiation, introduction
introduction, preparation
origin, beginning
preparation, commence-
  ment
start, beginning

Inception
birth, beginning
dawn, beginning
dawning, dawn
genesis, beginning
inception, beginning
inchoation, inception
incipience, inception
rise, origin

NOUNS (Continued)

Action
act, start
action, beginning
actuation, a starting
impulse, sudden act
step, action

Spontaneity
ideomotion, muscular act
  arising unconsciously
spontaneity, original im-
  pulse

Base
base, beginning
foundation, origin
fundament, foundation
fundamental, base
first, beginning

Entrance
door, entrance
entrance, start
opening, entrance
threshold, entrance

Source
cradle, source
fountain, origin
fountain-head, source
source, beginning
spring, source

Rudiment
element, rudiment
embryo, incipient life
germ, embryo
rudiment, germ

Beginner
beginner, initiator
leader, beginner
pioneer, leader
starter, beginner

BEING
Janus, god of beginning
  and ending

3A (Continued)
NOUNS (Continued)
juncture, change
MEDIUMS
alterative, changing me-
  dium
changer, converter
chemical, alterative

MEDIUMS (Continued)
commutator, alternating
  transmitter
converter, transformer
modulator, converter
transformer, transmuter
transmuter, converter

PERSONS
alchemist, one who trans-
  mutes metals, etc.
chameleon, color-changing
  reptile
chemist, transformationist

3C (Continued)
NOUNS (Continued)
frivolity, caprice
instability, changeability
inconsistency, instability
lubricity, frivolity
slipperiness, instability
volatility, changeableness

NOUNS (Continued)
Frailness
flimsiness, flaccidity
fragileness, frailness
fragility, flimsiness
frailness, fragility

MEDIUMS
elastic, a rubber
recoil, spring
rubber, an elastic material
spring, recoil

Encouragement 7	Remedy 136B
Improvement 6	Luck, Good Fortune 134D
Stimulation 8	Appointment 139A
Subservient 46B	Exaltation 139B

5A

VERBS

Aid
aid, help
assist, help
attend, assist
help, assist
succor, aid
(B). succour

Contribute
abet, aid
accommodate, aid
collaborate, assist
conduce, contribute
contribute, aid
coöperate, collaborate
favor, accommodate
serve, accommodate
subserve, support
subsidize, aid financially

Grease
grease, oil
lubricate, facilitate
oil, lubricate
soap, make slippery

Alleviate
alleviate, lighten
disburden, lighten
ease, facilitate
facilitate, lighten
lighten, facilitate
obviate, facilitate
pave, facilitate
relieve, aid
simplify, facilitate

Support
bolster, support
prop, stay
stay, support
support, succor
uphold, support

ADJECTIVES

Helpful
assistant, helpful
assistful, helpful
beneficial, helpful
buoyant, helpful
helpful, beneficial
serviceable, useful
useful, helpful

Auxiliary
accessory, aiding
accommodating, assistful
ancillary, auxiliary
auxiliary, accessory
coefficient, coöperative
collusive, aiding
contributory, aiding
coöperative, collaborative

ADJECTIVES (Continued)
collaborative, contributive
serviceable, helpful
subsidiary, aiding

Greased, Etc.
frictionless, facile
greased, lubricated
greasy, facilitated
lubricated, facilitated
oily, lubricated
slick, facile
slippery, slick
soapy, greasy
smooth, frictionless
unctuous, greasy

Convenient
convenient, advantageous
easy, facile
facile, not difficult
handy, convenient
light, handy
simple, easy

Advantageous
advantageous, favorable
applicable, practical
auspicious, favorable
expedient, advantageous
feasible, practicable
favorable, expedient
institutional, serviceable
instrumental, helpful
Machiavellian, noting un-
  scrupulous expediency
practicable, serviceable
practical, useful
propitious, favorable
relevant, propitious
reliable, trustworthy
trustworthy, reliable

NOUNS

Help
aid, assistance
alleviation, succor
assistance, help
benefice, aid
beneficence, benefice
favor, kindness
help, assistance
kindness, aid
relief, aid
sake, benefit
service, help
succor, help
(B). succour
support, aid

Auxiliary
accommodation, favor

NOUNS (Continued)
collaboration, coöperation
collusion, connivance
coöperation, mutual aid
connivance, collusion
contribution, aid
fomentation, an abetting
subsidy, financial aid

Convenience
convenience, facility
facility, easiness
facilitation, convenience
simplification, facilitation

Advantage
advantage, convenience
agency, instrumentality
expediency, convenience
expedient, advantage
feasibility, practicability
instrumentality, aid
Machiavellianism, unscru-
  ulous expediency
pertinency, expediency
practicability, feasibility
relevancy, pertinency
snap, easy advantage
serviceableness, benefice
utility, serviceableness

Accessory
accessory, auxiliary
adjunct, auxiliary
agent, auxiliary
apparatus, contrivance
appliance, medium
appurtenance, adjunct
auxiliary, an aid
coefficient, auxiliary
contrivance, device
device, medium
equipment, outfit
expedient, device
implement, tool
instrument, medium
invention, device
medium, an aid
outfit, equipment
stop-gap, expedient
tool, implement

Means
agent, auxiliary
factor, agent
function, medium
means, agency

INSTITUTIONS
agency, agent's office
bureau, office

(Continued on page 10)

AID—HELP—MEDIUMS (Continued)

5B NOUNS (Specific Mediums)	5C NOUNS (Substance)	5C (Continued) NOUNS (Substance)
cue, billiard rod	brick	stuff
canvas, a sail	clay	substance
gavel, mallet	commodity	sand
hammer, driving tool	cotton	stick
handle, heft	dirt	stone
heft, handle	earth	staple
helve, ax-handle	flax	stock
hilt, handle	fibrin	soil
implement, tool	gluten	wares
knob, round handle	ground	wood
loom, oar-handle	glass	wool
mallet, hammer	goods	Etc., Etc.
oar, long boat-paddle	import	
sail, canvas sheet	iron	The vocabulary SUB-
scull, short oar	land	STANCE is seldom referred
sledge, hammer	merchandise	to by the desiderator where-
spanker, sail	moveables	fore the thousands of terms
tool, any implement	mercury	belonging in this vocabu-
trigger, hammer-release	material	lary are omitted.
utensil, implement	matter	
wheel, rotating device	mud	
yoke, frame for carrying	marble	
water	mire	
Etc., Etc.		

5D

NOUNS (Elements)—The progressive numbers indicate the number of electrons said to constitute the atoms in the respective elements.

1 Hydrogen	24 Chromium	47 Silver	70 Ytterbium
2 Helium	25 Manganese	48 Cadmium	71 Lutecium
3 Lithium	26 Iron	49 Indium	72 Hafnium
4 Beryllium	27 Cobalt	50 Tin	73 Tantalum
5 Boron	28 Nickel	51 Antimony	74 Tungsten
6 Carbon	29 Copper	52 Tellurium	75 Rhenium
7 Nitrogen	30 Zinc	53 Iodine	76 Osmium
8 Oxygen	31 Gallium	54 Xenon	77 Iridium
9 Fluorine	32 Germanium	55 Caesium	78 Platinum
10 Neon	33 Arsenic	56 Barium	79 Gold
11 Sodium	34 Selenium	57 Lanthanum	80 Mercury
12 Magnesium	35 Bromine	58 Cerium	81 Thallium
13 Aluminum	36 Krypton	59 Praseodymium	82 Lead
14 Silicon	37 Rubidium	60 Neodymium	83 Bismuth
15 Phosphorus	38 Strontium	61 Illinium	84 Polonium
16 Sulphur	39 Yttrium	62 Samarium	85 ....?*
17 Chlorin	40 Zirconium	63 Europium	86 Niton
18 Argon	41 Niobium	64 Gadolinium	87 ....?*
19 Potassium	42 Molybdenum	65 Terbium	88 Radium
20 Calcium	43 Masurium	66 Dysprosium	89 Actinium
21 Scandium	44 Ruthenium	67 Holmium	90 Thorium
22 Titanium	45 Rhodium	68 Erbium	91 Uranium X
23 Vanadium	46 Palladium	69 Thulium	92 Uranium

*These are elements not yet found and named.
According to current theory, elements more complex than No. 92 might exist under extraordinary or unknown conditions.

IMPROVEMENT—		ASSOCIATIVE	
BETTERMENT see—	Increase 10	Aid—Help 5A	
vs. Injury 130G	Teaching 81	Stimulation 8	
vs. Negligence 126B	Manufacture 144B	Nurture 48	
vs. Reduction 14	Cure—Remedy 136B	Invention 144A	

6

VERBS

Improve, Etc.

ameliorate, improve
benefit, improve
better, benefit
favor, patronize
foster, nurture
further, promote
improve, make better
meliorate, improve
patronize, foster
progress, improve
promote, advance
support, further

Prepare

capacitate, qualify
fit, qualify
practice, rehearse
prepare, qualify
qualify, capacitate
rehearse, prepare

Advance

advance, promote
elaborate, improve
enhance, heighten
enrich, improve
heighten, elaborate
intensify, elaborate
refine, heighten
forward, improve

Develop

cultivate, improve by labor
develop, elaborate
exploit, develop
grow, progress

VERBS (Continued)

protagonist, advocate
hammer, develop
nurture, develop
ply, improve
propagate, grow

ADJECTIVES

Miscellaneous

accultural, cultural
conductive, promotive
cultural, promotive
developmental, promotive
elaborate, highly improved
intensive, elaborate
preparative, promotive
preparatory, preparative
progressive, promotive
promotive, developmental

NOUNS

Improvement

amelioration, improvement
benefit, improvement
benefice, patronage
betterment, benefit
emendation, improvement
improvement, promotion
melioration, improvement
progression, improvement
patronage, support
promotion, advancement
support, furtherance
reformation, improvement

Preparation

practice, rehearsal
preparation, intensification

NOUNS (Continued)

qualification, preparation
rehearsal, preparation

Advancement

acculture, culture
advancement, improvement
culture, refinement
elaboration, improvement
enhancement, enrichment
enrichment, refinement
furtherance, improvement
intensification, exploitation
refinement, improvement

Development

cultivation, improvement
development, improvement
evolution, development
exploitation, improvement
growth, progress
maturation, growth
nurture, development
propaganda, propagation
propagation, cultivation
tillage, cultivation

MEDIUMS

cultivator, one who, or that
  which, cultivates
reformatory, place for improvement

PERSONS

advocate, supporter
benefactor, patron
patron, supporter
leader, promoter
promoter, developer

5A (Continued)

INSTITUTIONS (Cont'd)

institution, agency
office, service branch
portfolio, office

PERSONS

accessary, assistant
accessory, accomplice

PERSONS (Continued)

accomplice, an aid
advocate, supporter
agent, factor
ally, confederate
assistant, helper
auxiliary, assistant
collaborator, mutual aid

PERSONS (Continued)

confederate, accomplice
factor, agent
functionary, one who functions in an office
helper, assistant
henchman, assistant

Page 10

ENCOURAGEMENT see—
   vs. Difficulty 13

ASSOCIATIVE

Stimulation 8	Pleasing 99A
Consolation 136A	Objective 149H

7

VERBS	VERBS (Continued)	ADJECTIVES (Continued)
Encourage	**Inspire**	**inspirational,** buoyant
abet, encourage	**breathe,** inspire	**Promethean,** life-giving
boost, encourage	**buoy,** inspirit	**promising,** encouraging
embolden, encourage	**elate,** inspirit	**reassuring,** heartening
encourage, inspire	**enthuse,** inspirit	**sympathetic,** condolatory
fortify, encourage	**inspire,** uplift	**NOUNS**
hearten, cheer	**inspirit,** inspire	**assurance,** encouragement
nerve, hearten	**uplift,** hearten	**buoyancy,** support
Assure		**comfort,** assurance
assure, hearten	**ADJECTIVES**	**encouragement,** reas-
cheer, encourage	**buoyant,** encouraging	surance
condole, hearten	**cheering,** buoyant	**illumination,** inspiration
comfort, inspirit	**condolatory,** sympathetic	**inspiration,** encouragement
promise, encourage	**encouraging,** heartening	**promise,** encouragement
reassure, hearten	**heartening,** inspiriting	**reassurance,** encourage-
sympathize, condole	**inspiriting,** inspiring	ment
		support, reassurance

8

STIMULATION—URGING   see—

   vs. Discouragement 13
   vs. Oppression 130B

ASSOCIATIVE

Encouragement 7	
Consolation 136A	
Influence 135B	
Pleasing 99A	

8

VERBS	VERBS (Continued)	VERBS (Continued)
Stimulate	**stir,** incite	**concern,** interest
energize, vitalize	**startle,** excite	**engage,** absorb
engender, excite	**sway,** captivate	**engross,** engage
inspirit, vivify	**thrill,** exhilarate	**grip,** engage
instil, engender	**wake,** rouse	**interest,** awaken
invigorate, energize	**work,** excite	**Charm**
magnetize, electrify	**waken,** animate	**bewitch,** captivate
stimulate, animate	**Incite**	**captivate,** charm
vitalize, animate	**agitate,** excite	**charm,** fascinate
vivify, vitalize	**bestir,** foment	**enchant,** bewitch
warm, stimulate	**foment,** excite	**fascinate,** bewitch
Stir	**impel,** incite	**infatuate,** captivate
actuate, animate	**incense,** fire	**Compel**
affect, stir	**incite,** instigate	**compel,** force
animate, vivify	**inflame,** fire	**drive,** urge
arouse, excite	**instigate,** provoke	**enforce,** oblige
awake, arouse	**precipitate,** impel	**force,** enforce, oblige
awaken, wake	**prompt,** incite	**goad,** spur
elate, excite	**provoke,** incense	**make,** oblige
electrify, energize	**whet,** incite	**necessitate,** compel
elevate, animate	**Impassion**	**oblige,** necessitate
enkindle, fire	**heat,** excite	**spur,** exhort, goad
enliven, exhilarate	**holden,** sensualize	**whip,** exhort
excite, rouse	**(B). hoyden**	**Insist**
exhilarate, animate	**impassion,** excite	**egg,** urge
fire, enkindle	**sensualize,** impassion	**exhort,** urge
influence, actuate	**Refresh**	**hie,** urge
kindle, inflame	**reanimate,** revivify	**importune,** urge
light, kindle	**refresh,** reanimate	**insist,** press
move, rouse	**reinvigorate,** refresh	**obtrude,** urge
quicken, excite	**rejuvenate,** reanimate	**press,** urge
raise, rouse	**revive,** reanimate	**urge,** insist
rouse, animate	**revivify,** revive	(Continued on page 12)
start, actuate	**Interest**	
	absorb, engage	

ADJECTIVES

Stimulative
incentive, stimulative
inspirational, incentive
stimulant, stimulating
stimulating, stimulative
stimulative, quickening
vivifying, animative

Stirring
affecting, animative
animate, motive
animative, stirring
emotive, animative
exciting, stirring
fiery, spirited
motive, animative
quickening, exciting
ripping, exciting
rousing, stirring
sensational, rousing
spectacular, rousing
spirited, fiery
startling, excitatory
stirring, exciting
thrilling, exciting
touching, affecting

Provocative
agitative, instigating
incendiary, inflammatory
incitative, exhortatory
inflammatory, inciting
provocative, rousing

Interesting
engaging, engrossing
engrossing, interesting
gripping, engrossing
interesting, affecting

Charming
bewitching, enchanting
captivating, fascinating
charming, bewitching
enchanting, charming

ADJECTIVES (Continued)
fascinating, impassioning
magnetic, captivating

Compelling
compelling, compulsive
compulsive, obligatory
compulsory, compulsive
obligatory, compelling

Insistent
exhortative, inciting
exhortatory, inciting
hortative, inciting
importunate, urgent
insistent, urgent
persistent, urgent
pressing, persistent
urgent, pressing

NOUNS

Stimulation
excitation, stimulation
excitement, excitation
incentive, stimulation
inducement, motive
influence, excitation
inspiration, excitation
interest, stimulus
stimulation, excitation
stimulus, excitation

Excitation
actuation, impulsion
animation, stimulus
excitation, stimulus
impulse, excitation
impulsion, excitation
motive, incentive
revival, reanimation

Provocation
agitation, excitation
fomentation, excitation
incitement, provocation
incitation, instigation

NOUNS (Continued)
instigation, incitement
provocation, excitation
provocative, incitement

Charm
beguilement, captivation
bewitchment, enchantment
charm, bewitchment
enchantment, charm
fascination, bewitchment

Compulsion
compulsion, sway
enforcement, compulsion

Insistence
egging, urgency
exhortation, urgency
importunity, urgency
insistence, importunity
jog, incentive
spur, incentive
stress, urgency
urgency, spur

PERSONS
agitator, excitant
instigator, agitator
revivalist, revivifier

MEDIUMS
excitant, stimulant
stimulator, excitant
stimulant, stimulator

Goad
goad, excitant
rowel, goad of a spur
whip, excitant

Starter
hair-trigger, easy trigger
starter, excitant
trigger, starter

NOUNS (Continued)

Impetuosity
impetuosity, precipitation
precipitancy, haste

NOUNS (Continued)
precipitation, dash
salience, a leaping
vehemence, impetuosity

PERSONS
clipper, speedster
scorcher, fast driver

9

HASTE—HURRY—RUN—JUMP   see—   ASSOCIATIVE

vs. Slowness—Negligence ....126B   {
Leave—Escape 15
Short Time 148D
Vibrant 3B
}

9

VERBS

Hasten
accelerate, hasten
bestir, hurry
dispatch, expedite
expedite, hasten
haste, hasten
hasten, hurry
hie, hasten
hurry, hasten
press, hurry
quicken, hurry

Speed
bolt, dash
boom, go with a rush
dart, dash
dash, rush
flit, dart
fly, run
race, speed
run, speed
rush, hurry
scoot, run
scurry, scoot
scuttle, run
scud, scuttle
scorch, sky-hoot
shoot, dart
sky-hoot, speed
skirr, scurry
skim, skate, scoot
skate, skim
slide, scoot
speed, rush
spin, scorch
sweep, whisk
tear, dash
whisk, scud, scorch
snap, dash

Spring
bounce, spring
bound, spring
hop, skip
hurtle, bound
hump, leap
jump, leap
leap, jump
ramp, spring
skip, bound
spring, leap
vault, bound

Gallop, Etc.
canter, gallop
career, speed
gallop, career
jog, trot
scamper, speed
sprint, race
trot, jog

VERBS (Continued)

Prance, Etc.
capriole, prance
cavort, prance
prance, capriole

Bustle
brisk, hurry (brisk up)
bustle, hurry
hustle, bustle
rustle, hustle
stir, bustle

ADJECTIVES

Hasty
brisk, quick
expeditious, speedy
fleeting, quick
hasty, hurried
hurried, swift
immediate, instant
instant, prompt
prompt, quick
quick, rapid
sudden, quick

Speedy
fast, speedy
fleet, swift
flying, swift
rapid, fast
sky-hooting, speeding
speedy, fleet
swift, fast

Bustling
active, lively
agile, quick
alive, sprightly
animated, lively
bustling, hurried
chipper, lively
dynamic, active
flitting, fleet
frisky, sprightly
lissom, nimble
lively, quick
mercurial, volatile
nimble, chipper
perky, lively
snap, brisk
spry, swift
sprightly, brisk
spirited, lively
stirring, bustling
vivacious, lively
volant, nimble
volatile, spry

Impetuous
fugacious, fleeting
headlong, hasty
impulsive, hasty
impetuous, impulsive

ADJECTIVES (Continued)
precipitant, hasty
precipitate, headlong
precipitous, impetuous
salient, leaping
saltant, salient

NOUNS

Haste
acceleration, hurry
celerity, rapidity
despatch, celerity
dispatch, despatch
expedition, despatch
haste, hurry
hurry, expedition
promptness, quickness
promptitude, quickness
quickness, hurry

Speed
dash, speed
fleetness, swiftness
rapidity, despatch
race, career
run, spurt
rush, haste
snap, dash
speed, swiftness
spurt, dash
swiftness, speed
velocity, speed

Spring
bound
hop
jump
leap
ramp
skip
spring
vault

Gallop, Etc.
career, a run at full speed
dog-trot, gentle trot
gallop, career
jog, trot

Bustle
activity, animation
agility, nimbleness
alacrity, briskness
animation, liveliness
briskness, liveliness
bustle, hurry
flurry, hurry
friskiness, agility
liveliness, animation
scamper, haste
scurry, scamper
spirit, liveliness

(Continued on page 12)

INCREASE—
   ENLARGEMENT see—
   vs. Decrease 14

ASSOCIATIVE

Give 43A
Improvement 6
Stimulation 8

Continuation 11A
Many—Large........147I, 147J
Remedy 136B

10

VERBS

Increase

add, increase
augment, increase
complement, supplement
conduce, contribute
contribute, add
entail, augment
increase, augment
multiply, increase
redouble, increase much
supervene, contribute
supplement, augment

Enhance

accent, accentuate
accentuate, emphasize
aggrandize, augment
aggravate, intensify
amplify, enlarge
appreciate, enhance
emphasize, accentuate
enhance, increase
exaggerate, overdo
heighten, intensify
intensify, augment
magnify, amplify
stimulate, intensify
strengthen, intensify

Enlarge

broaden, enlarge
deepen, as in depth
dilate, distend
distend, expand
enlarge, augment
expand, enlarge
extend, enlarge
inflate, enlarge
protract, extend
puff, swell
stretch, extend
swell, grow distended
widen, enlarge

Introduce

imbrue, instil
implant, inoculate
infuse, introduce
ingraft, implant
inoculate, ingraft
instil, infuse
introduce, complement

Grow

accrete, grow
accrue, accrete
batten, fatten
bloom, wax
blossom, bloom
develop, grow
fatten, accrete fat
flourish, thrive

VERBS (Continued)

grow, develop
progress, develop
thrive, grow
wax, grow

Cultivate

cultivate, develop
foster, rear
nurture, rear
propagate, multiply
raise, rear
rear, nurture
till, cultivate

ADJECTIVES

Additional

accessional, additional
accessory, extra
additional, supplemental
augmentative, increasing
complemental, supple-
  mental
extra, additional
further, additional
supplemental, additional
supplementary, supple-
  mental

Ampliative

accentual, emphatic
ampliative, supplemental
emphatic, accentual
enhancing, increasing
intensive, ampliative

Growing

accrescent, growing
accretive, accrescent
accultural, accumulative
accumulative, cumulative
adolescent, growing
autumnal, growing
blooming, maturing
crescent, growing
cumulative, accretive
embryonic, developing
gradatory, advancing
growing, accretive
roseate, blooming
nascent, embryonic

ADVERBS

also, likewise
besides, too
further, besides
furthermore, moreover
likewise, moreover
moreover, besides
still, yet
yet, further
too, also

NOUNS

Addition

addition, increase
augmentation, increase
complement, supplement
contribution, augmentation
entailment, augmentation
raise, increase
supervention, an adding
supplement, addition

Enhancement

accent, stress
accentuation, accent
aggrandizement, augmenta-
  tion
amplification, augmentation
emphasis, accent
enhancement, increase
intensification, increase
intensity, intensification
magnification, amplification
stimulation, intensification
stress, accent

Enlargement

distension, extension
enlargement, increase
expansion, extension
extension, enlargement
inflation, expansion

Introduction

impregnation, propagation
infusion, instillation
inoculation, impregnation
instillation, infusion
introduction, infusion

Growth

accession, advance
accretion, growth
accrual, accretion
adolescence, growth
advance, progress
development, growth
enhancement, advance
gradation, advancement
growth, development
increase, enlargement
increment, increase
progression, growth
progress, progression
progressiveness, growth
rise, increase

Cultivation

cultivation, propagation
propagation, multiplication
tillage, cultivation

11

STABILITY—CONTINUATION

11A

CONTINUATION—PERPETUATION
ASSOCIATIVE

see— { Stability 11B
vs. Decrease—Lessen ....14 { Long Time 148C

11A

VERBS

Continue
continue, last
dwell, continue
endure, persist
last, endure
outlast, endure
persevere, persist
persist, endure
remain, stay
wear, last

Preserve
can, preserve
embalm, preserve
pickle, preserve
preserve, make lasting
souse, preserve

Perpetuate
commemorate, preserve
immortalize, perpetuate
perpetuate, cause to endure

Stay
abide, remain
await, abide
bide, wait
exist, live
live, subsist
stand, endure
stay, continue
subsist, live
wait, stay

Sustain
buoy, sustain
conserve, preserve
extend, prolong
foster, support
hold, maintain
keep, hold
maintain, hold, keep
prolong, protract
protract, prolong
rescue, save
save, preserve
support, sustain
survive, outlive
sustain, maintain
wage, do continually

State of Being
am, to be
are, exist
be, exist
is, exist

ADJECTIVES

Eternal
boundless, limitless
deathless, everlasting
endless, unceasing
eternal, perpetual
everlasting, eternal
immortal, deathless

ADJECTIVES (Continued)
imperishable, permanent
infinite, interminable
interminable, endless
limitless, endless
perpetual, ceaseless
undying, deathless

Conservatory
commemorative, preserving
conservatory, preserving
preserving, conserving
preservative, preserving

Durable
abiding, lasting
durable, lasting
enduring, constant
extant, enduring
firm, steadfast
fixed, permanent
lasting, permanent
monumental, enduring
permanent, enduring
steady, steadfast
stable, firm

Sustained
ceaseless, incessant
chronic, recurring
constant, steadfast
continual, endless
incessant, unceasing
invariable, constant
long, enduring
perennial, perpetual
protracted, sustained
sustained, continual
unabating, incessant
unbroken, continuous
unceasing, ceaseless
undiminished, enduring
unending, ceaseless
unfailing, steadfast
uninterrupted, unremitting
unimpeded, continuing
unmitigated, unabating

Persistent
assiduous, steadfast
busy, industrious
determined, persistent
diligent, assiduous
engaged, busy
indefatigable, unremitting
industrious, diligent
occupied, engaged
persevering, steadfast
persistent, constant
relentless, uninterrupted
resolute, steadfast
resolved, firm
sedulous, persevering
steadfast, constant
sisyphean, unceasing

ADJECTIVES (Continued)
tireless, indefatigable
unflagging, indefatigable
unfaltering, continual
unremitting, persevering
unrestrained, constant
untiring, tireless
unwearied, unflagging
unwavering, steadfast

ADVERBS
always
ay
(B). aye
ever
evermore
forever

NOUNS

Eternity
eternity, perpetuity
immortality, eternal life
infinity, boundlessness
infinitude, infinity

Perpetuation
conservation, preservation
commemoration, preservation
perpetuation, immortalization
preservation, conservation

Durability
durability, lastingness
permanence, durability
permanency, continuance
perpetuity, permanence
stability, firmness

Constancy
constancy, firmness
continuation, continuance
continuity, continuation
continuance, steadiness
durance, duration
duration, continuation
maintenance, support
salvation, a saving
support, maintenance
survival, continuance
survivorship, a living on
sustenance, support
sustentation, maintenance
prolongation, sustentation
protraction, continuance

Persistence
assiduity, steadfastness
diligence, assiduity
endurance, perseverance
firmness, sedulity
indefatigability, assiduity
industry, diligence
perseverance, sedulity

(Continued on page 17)

STABILITY—REST see—

11B

VERBS

Stabilize
crystallize, fix
establish, found
fix, stabilize
found, establish
ground, establish
institute, found
ratify, validate
settle, fix
stabilize, settle
validate, establish
Rest
be, exist
exist, prevail
lie, rest
lodge, perch
obtain, prevail
perch, sit
prevail, be current
recline, rest
remain, stay
repose, rest
rest, stay
roost, lodge
sit, rest
stand, stay
stay, remain
set, stabilize
Silence
calm, still
hush, quiet
quiet, silence
silence, hush
still, quiet

ADJECTIVES

Stable
changeless, fixed
established, fixed
fixed, fast
founded, established
settled, established
stable, firm
static, fixed
traditional, unchanged
Stationary
fast, firm
firm, fixed
immovable, fast
stationary, fixed
staid, steady
steadfast, steady

ADJECTIVES (Continued)

steady, stable
unshaken, firm
unwavering, steady
Silent
mute, silent
noiseless, silent
quiet, still
silent, still
soundless, silent
taciturn, silent
Unbending
inflexible, unbending
rigid, inflexible
stiff, rigid
unbending, stiff
unyielding, unbending
Inactive
disinclined, inactive
immobile, motionless
inactive, inert
indifferent, unmoved
indisposed, disinclined
inert, inactive
motionless, inactive
passive, inactive
sedentary, sitting
statuesque, immobile
still, inert
stockstill, motionless
unchanged, inert
unconcerned, indifferent
Unrelenting
inexorable, unyielding
positive, settled
rigorous, uncompromising
stern, steadfast
stony, inflexible
uncompromising, firm
unrelenting, stony
wilful, inexorable
Permanent
durable, stable
inconvertible, unalterable
indefectible, steadfast
indestructible, permanent
insoluble, fixed
permanent, durable
Ineffaceable
indelible, ineffaceable
ineffaceable, unalterable

ADJECTIVES (Continued)

mordant, fixed in color
unfading, mordant
Unalterable
absolute, fixed
immutable, unchangeable
inalienable, unalterable
irrevocable, unalterable
invariable, immutable
inviolable, unalterable
unalterable, immutable
unchangeable, immutable

NOUNS

Stability
fixedness, stability
fixity, permanence
immobility, immovableness
immutability, permanence
inalienability, unchange-
   ableness
inexorability, inflexibility
inflexibility, immutability
indelibility, fixedness
indestructibility, perma-
   nence
permanence, durability
rigidity, stiffness
stability, firmness
Silence
hush, quiet
muteness, silence
quiescence, quiet
quiet, silence
silence, stillness
stillness, hush
taciturnity, silence
Inaction
disinclination, indifference
inaction, inertness
indifference, passivity
indisposition, disinclination
inertia, inaction
passivity, inactivity
quietus, rest
rest, inaction
sedentariness, a sitting
standstill, inaction
Foundation
base
foundation
ground

11A (Continued)

NOUNS (Continued)
persistence, firmness
sedulity, perseverance
steadiness, stability

PERSONS
commemorator, conservator
conservator, preserver
immortal, one who survives
   in name, fame, etc.

PERSONS (Continued)
savior, one who saves
(B). saviour
survivor, one who survives

MEDIUMS
elixir, a supposed preservative of life
pickle, preservative

MEDIUMS (Continued)
preservative, that which
   preserves
souse, a preservative

SYMBOL
scarab, symbol of immor-
   tality

12

REDUCTION—HINDRANCE

STOP—PREVENT see— vs. Start— Commence 4

{ Stability—Rest ....11B Ban—Prohibition 35
{ Close—Ending ....74 Conquest 50

VERBS

Stop

cease, desist
desist, stop
discontinue, stop
halt, stop
lie, rest
pause, halt
repose, rest
rest, pause
set, sit
sit, set
stop, cease
stay, stop
stand, stay
surcease, stop

Conclude

accomplish, conclude
close, finish
complete, conclude
conclude, consummate
consummate, finish
culminate, consummate
dispatch, finish
end, terminate
fill, consummate
finish, consummate
terminate, complete

Expire

die, finish
expire, perish
perish, die

Suppress

abate, suppress
allay, quiet
arrest, stay
check, stop
discontinue, stop
end, stop
estop, arrest
halt, arrest
quell, end
silence, stop
stay, stop
stanch, stop
stint, stop
stop, halt
suppress, stop
suspend, stop
whoa, (interj) stop

Interrupt

adjourn, postpone
defer, postpone
delay, deter
deter, hinder
detain, restrain
hinder, detain
impede, hinder
interfere, interrupt
intermit, interrupt
interpose, interrupt

VERBS (Continued)

interrupt, interfere
postpone, suspend
preclude, hinder
prevent, preclude
prorogue, postpone
reprieve, postpone
respite, postpone
restrain, hinder
retard, detain
scotch, check

ADJECTIVES

Conclusive

conclusive, final
final, conclusive
last, final
ultimate, final
utmost, last

Decisive

abrupt, decisive
decisive, conclusive
terminal, final

Interruptive

detentive, hindering
impeditive, detentive
preventive, hindering

Concluded

accomplished, done
complete, finished
concluded, ended
done, accomplished
ended, finished
finished, ended
grown, ripe
mature, grown
ripe, mature

NOUNS

Stop

abeyance, discontinuance
cessation, stop
halt, stop
pause, stop
repose, rest
rest, pause
stop, cessation
stoppage, halt

Conclusion

accomplishment, finish
climax, close
close, finish
completion, finish
conclusion, completion
consummation, completion
culmination, consummation
end, close
ending, end
expiration, termination
expiry, death
finale, end

NOUNS (Continued)

finality, conclusion
finis, end
finish, end
fulfilment, close
omega, the end, the last
termination, end

Death

death, final end

Interruption

adjournment, postponement
closure, stoppage, end
deferment, postponement
delay, suspension
detention, restraint
halt, stop
hindrance, restraint
intermission, interruption
interruption, hindrance
interregnum, suspension
postponement, suspension
preclusion, prevention
prevention, hindrance
restraint, prevention
retardation, interruption
stop, detention
stoppage, prevention
suspension, halt

Stay

armistice, truce
respite, truce
stay, a detent
truce, suspension

Suppression

abatement, suppression
quietus, a suppressing
suppression, prevention

Stopper

detent, a stop
stopgap, detent
stopper, stopgap

Goal

aim, end, goal
butt, end
bourn, goal
destination, goal
end, object
extremity, end
goal, aim
issue, end
mark, target
motive, aim
Mecca, goal
object, end
point, issue
purpose, motive
sake, purpose
target, point
terminus, end

(Continued on page 21)

13

VERBS

Trouble
burden, embarrass
embarrass, trouble
engulf, overwhelm
irk, trouble
strand, embarrass
task, burden
trouble, obtrude
weigh, burden

Puzzle
baffle, confound
bamboozle, mystify
bewilder, perplex
confound, confuse
confuse, mystify
distract, bewilder
dumbfound, bewilder
mystify, perplex
nonplus, bewilder
obfuscate, perplex
perplex, puzzle
pose, puzzle
puzzle, perplex
stump, dumbfound

Hide
conceal, hide
hide, conceal
obscure, hide

Complicate
complicate, involve
entangle, complicate
implicate, entangle
involve, entangle
tangle, entangle

Aggravate
aggravate, trouble
annoy, aggravate
bother, trouble
depress, dispirit
discourage, dishearten
dishearten, dispirit
dismay, discourage
dispirit, discourage
disturb, bother
harass, worry
importune, harass
intrude, bother
meddle, bother
obtrude, trouble
penalize, burden
tamper, meddle
tax, burden
worry, bother

Impede
clog, impede
cumber, burden
encumber, impede
hinder, interfere
hobble, embarrass

VERBS (Continued)
hamper, impede
impede, hinder
interfere, obtrude

Toil
drudge, work hard
labor, travail
plod, weary
toil, labor
travail, toil
trudge, plod
weary, toil hard

Inconvenience
handicap, burden
incommode, inconvenience
inconvenience, involve
weight, handicap

Strain
exert, stretch
force, exert might
push, shove
shove, exert force
strain, exert
stretch, strain
tax, strain

ADJECTIVES

Difficult
arduous, difficult
difficult, arduous
embarrassing, aggravating
hard, difficult
irksome, troublesome
tedious, wearisome
ticklish, difficult
tough, arduous
toughish, difficult
trying, difficult

Puzzling
abstruse, incomprehensible
bewildering, baffling
confounding, confusing
confusing, disconcerting
cryptic, hidden
deep, abstruse, complex
discomposing, confusing
disconcerting, dumbfounding
distracting, confusing
dumbfounding, perplexing
enigmatic, puzzling
finedrawn, abstruse
finespun, finedrawn
illegible, baffling
mysterious, perplexing
nonplussing, discouraging
obfuscating, perplexing
obscure, deep
perplexing, puzzling

ADJECTIVES (Continued)
profound, abstruse
puzzling, deep
recondite, profound
uncanny, mysterious
unfathomable, baffling

Hidden
hidden, secret
secret, cryptic

Baffling
baffling, Serbonian
Gordian, nonplussing
impossible, Gordian
incomprehensible, baffling
inconceivable, baffling
incredible, inconceivable
incredulous, unbelievable
indefinable, nondescript
inexpressible, unutterable
insuperable, baffling
insurmountable, baffling
nondescript, perplexing
unbelievable, baffling
unimaginable, baffling

Complex
complex, intricate
complicate, complex
complicated, complicate
entangled, knotted
intricate, difficult
knotty, difficult
manifold, complex
trackless, perplexing

Aggravating
aggravating, troublesome
annoying, embarrassing
bothersome, troublesome
discouraging, Serbonian
disheartening, Serbonian
dispiriting, discouraging
distressing, annoying
meddlesome, bothersome
objectionable, bothersome
obtrusive, bothersome
officious, bothersome
troublesome, embarrassing
vexatious, troublesome

Impeditive
boggy, impeditive
impeditive, embarrassing
Serbonian, marshy, difficult

Dangerous
critical, perilous
dangerous, perilous
grave, serious
hazardous, dangerous
perilous, hazardous
risky, perilous
serious, dangerous
(Continued on page 21)

ADJECTIVES (Continued)

Toilsome
laborious, toilsome
tiresome, toilsome
toilsome, difficult
wearisome, tiresome

Burdensome
burdensome, irksome
cumbersome, burdensome
cumbrous, unwieldy
heavy, burdensome
onerous, burdensome
unwieldy, cumbersome

Inconvenient
inconvenient, bothersome
inexpedient, inconvenient
unfavorable, embarrassing
unpropitious, unfavorable

Strenuous
severe, hard
strenuous, laborious

NOUNS

Difficulty
crush, jam
difficulty, embarrassment
embarrassment, dilemma
emergency, dilemma
jam, squeeze
lurch, difficulty
pickle, embarrassment
pinch, difficulty
rub, difficulty
scrape, difficulty
squeeze, difficulty
strait, difficulty
trial, difficulty
trouble, bother

Dilemma
dilemma, difficulty
hole, dilemma, (colo.)
impossibility, nonplus
nonplus, difficulty
perplexity, dilemma
plight, predicament
predicament, plight
Serbonian Bog, plight
stew, perplexity

Concealment
cache, hiding place
concealment, crypt, etc.
crypt, secret place
obscurity, concealment

NOUNS (Continued)

Mystery
enigma, puzzle
charade, enigma
conundrum, riddle
mystery, puzzle
poser, conundrum
puzzle, entanglement
rebus, puzzle
riddle, puzzle
secret, closed fact
trick, puzzle

Complexity
complication, intricacy
complexity, complication
entanglement, difficulty
imbroglio, difficulty
intricacy, difficulty
knot, difficulty
tangle, difficulty

Maze
bewilderment, jungle
bog, quagmire
jungle, tangled forest
labyrinth, maze
maze, labyrinth
morass, quagmire
marsh, morass
quagmire, marsh
quicksand, bog
swamp, bog
tangle, wilderness
wilderness, jungle

Aggravation
aggravation, bother
annoyance, vexation
bother, annoyance
botheration, bother
damper, discouragement
discouragement, nonplus
incubus, difficulty
intrusion, bother
kill-joy, discouragement
nuisance, annoyance
obtrusion, onus
penalty, handicap
vexation, bother

Impediment
encumbrance, impediment
hindrance, difficulty
impediment, hindrance
impedimenta, encumbrance
interference, bother

NOUNS (Continued)
snag, impediment
tax, burden

Danger
danger, hazard
hazard, difficulty
pitfall, danger

Toil
drudgery, work
labor, work
toil, labor
work, toil
travail, hard labor

Burden
burden, load
load, difficulty
onus, burden
weight, onus.

Inconvenience
disadvantage, difficulty
drawback, disadvantage
handicap, difficulty
inconvenience, difficulty
unfavorableness, rub

Strain
effort, exertion
exertion, stress
strain, tension
stress, strain
tension, stress

Responsibility
care, responsibility
charge, responsibility
duty, task
fate, lot
job, task
lot, duty
obligation, duty
responsibility, lot
task, burden
work, task

Handicap
hurdle, interference
handicap, a difficulty
interference, a handicap

PERSONS
Gordius, King who tied a
 difficult knot
meddler, intruder
intruder, meddler

NOUNS (Continued)

Incentive
allurement
attraction
beguilement
call
challenge

NOUNS (Continued)
enticement
glamour
invitation
incentive
inducement
interest

NOUNS (Continued)
lure

BEING
Janus, god of beginnings
 and endings

DECREASE—		ASSOCIATIVE	
REDUCTION see—	Stop—Prevention 12	Decay 128C
vs. Increase—	Slowness—Negligence 126B	Brevity 58
Enlargement 10	Lowness—Abasement 129B	Solidify 146B

14

VERBS

Decrease
abate, lessen
attenuate, lessen
bate, lower
decrease, lessen
dim, lower
diminish, lessen
dwarf, reduce
lessen, diminish
lighten, lessen
lower, reduce
minimize, reduce
modify, moderate
reduce, lessen
subdue, lower
stunt, dwarf
thin, attenuate

Moderate
alleviate, mitigate
assuage, alleviate
extenuate, lessen
mitigate, palliate
moderate, lessen
palliate, extenuate
tone, mitigate

Deduct
deduct, subtract
discount, deduct
dock, deduct
subduct, subtract
subtract, deduct

Curtail
abridge, shorten
contract, condense
curtail, reduce
epitomize, abridge
prune, trim
retrench, curtail
shorten, curtail
trim, clip

Detract
bear, depreciate
cheapen, lessen
degrade, lower
depress, cheapen
depreciate, lessen
derogate, detract
detract, depreciate
disrate, degrade
impoverish, beggar

Shrink
desiccate, dry
dry, wither
parch, shrivel
shrink, shrivel
shrivel, shrink
wither, shrivel
wrinkle, shrivel

VERBS (Continued)

Condense
compress, condense
condense, contract
crystallize, harden
fossilize, petrify
harden, crystallize
indurate, harden
petrify, harden

Dwindle
decline, lapse
degenerate, retrograde
deteriorate, lapse
drop, fall
dwindle, lapse
ebb, fail
evanesce, dwindle
fade, fail
fail, grow less
fall, wane
lapse, dwindle
lose, waste
relax, abate
retrograde, degenerate
subside, fall
vanish, evanesce
wane, dwindle
wear, deteriorate

Waste
boil, simmer
effervesce, evaporate
evaporate, waste
simmer, boil down
waste, dwindle

ADJECTIVES

Alleviative
alleviative, mitigative
assuaging, mitigative
demulcent, lenitive
emollient, lenitive
extenuatory, mitigative
lenitive, palliative
mitigative, alleviative
palliative, mitigative
sedative, alleviating

Deductive
deductive, subtractive
subtractive, deductive

Detractive
degrading, derogatory
depreciating, derogatory
derogatory, lowering

Dwindling
decrescent, failing
dwindling, decrescent
evanescent, dwindling
failing, dwindling
gradient, falling
obsolescent, failing

ADJECTIVES (Continued)

vanishing, evanescent
waning, dwindling
Wasting
effervescent, evaporating
hectic, wasting
wasting, failing

NOUNS

Decrease
decrease, diminution
decrement, decrease
reduction, diminution
temperance, moderation
Moderation
alleviation, mitigation
assuagement, alleviation
extenuation, palliation
mitigation, alleviation
moderation, reduction
palliation, extenuation
Deduction
deduction, subtraction
discount, deduction
stoppage, deduction
subtraction, deduction
Curtailment
contraction, condensation
curtailment, reduction
recision, retrenchment
retrenchment, curtailment
Detraction
degradation, depreciation
depreciation, derogation
derogation, detraction
detraction, depreciation
Decline
abatement, drop
abeyance, abatement
autumn, decline
decline, wane
declension, diminution
decrescence, decline
degeneration, a lapsing
descension, decline
depression, decline
diminution, decrease
drop, slump
evanescence, decrescence
fall, decline
obsolescence, decline
shrinkage, decline
slump, fall
wane, decline
Waste
effervescence, waste
evaporation, waste
loss, waste
waste, loss

MEDIUMS
lenitive, that which allays

PASSAGE—TRANSPORTATION

CARRIERS—PASSENGERS

PASSAGEWAYS—OPENINGS

LEAVE—WITHDRAWAL　　see—　　**ASSOCIATIVE**

15

VERBS

Leave
bundle, depart
depart, leave
go, depart
leave, depart
pack, depart
part, leave
quit, leave
sequester, withdraw
withdraw, leave

Depart
abscond, depart
decamp, desert
elope, abscond
escape, levant
levant, escape
scape, escape
vamose, decamp

Desert
abandon, desert
apostatize, abandon
backslide, apostatize
crab, back out
crawfish, withdraw
desert, abandon
fail, forsake
forsake, desert

Debark
debark, leave
deplane, debark
detrain, leave
disembark, leave

Vanish
disappear, escape
elapse, glide away
evanesce, vanish
fade, vanish
lapse, disappear
vanish, disappear

Withdraw
abdicate, secede
evacuate, abandon
relinquish, quit
resign, abdicate
secede, withdraw
vacate, depart

Flee
bolt, run
flee, run
flunk, skedaddle
fly, flee
run, flee
skedaddle, flee
stampede, flee in panic

Issue
debouch, sally
disembogue, issue

VERBS (Continued)
emerge, leave
emigrate, migrate
exit, leave
issue, leave
migrate, emigrate
sally, issue forth

Return
ebb, recede
recede, retreat
retire, withdraw
retreat, withdraw
retrocede, recede
return, ebb

Avoid
avoid, evade
dodge, evade
duck, dodge
elude, evade
evade, elude
shun, escape
skulk, sequester

ADJECTIVES

Miscellaneous
apostate, apostatical
apostatical, abandoning
centrifugal, leaving center
efferent, leaving
elusive, escaping
elusory, evasive
emigrant, leaving one's country
evanescent, vanishing
evasive, elusive
fleeting, fleeing
fugacious, fugitive
fugitive, fleeing
migratory, emigrant
parting, leaving
seditious, noting tumultuous withdrawal
vanishing, disappearing

NOUNS

Leave
departure, withdrawal
farewell, departure
going, a leaving
goodby, farewell
leave, departure
parting, departure
sequestration, retirement

Desertion
abandonment, withdrawal
apostasy, abandonment
backsliding, withdrawal
defection, desertion

NOUNS (Continued)
dereliction, abandonment
desertion, abandonment

Debarkation
debarkation, departure
disembarkation, debarkation

Disappearance
disappearance, escape
evanescence, lapse
lapse, disappearance

Withdrawal
abdication, evacuation
evacuation, retirement
recession, withdrawal
relinquishment, abandonment
resignation, withdrawal
retiracy, withdrawal
secession, withdrawal
sedition, abdication
withdrawal, retirement

Flight
elopement, flight
escape, flight
flight, departure
flush, flight (of birds)
French leave, escape
stampede, disordered flight

Issue
efference, a leaving
egress, departure
emersion, act of emerging
emergence, exit
emigration, migration
exit, departure
exodus, departure
issue, departure
migration, emigration
sally, sudden egress

Return
ebb, reflux
reflux, return
regression, a going
retirement, withdrawal
retreat, retirement
retrogression, regression
return, depart

Avoidance
avoidance, escape
evasion, escape
tergiversation, evasion

PERSONS
abdicator, a relinquisher
anchoret, hermit

(Continued on page 26)

FLOW—DISCHARGE   see—   ASSOCIATIVE

vs. Acquirement—Absorption 49A

16
VERBS
Exude
bleed, flow blood
distill, trickle
drip, fall in drops
effuse, pour
extravasate, force out, as blood
exude, emanate
exomose, exude
filter, trickle
gutter, drip
leak, issue accidentally
ooze, issue
percolate, filter
perspire, sweat
shed, pour
sweat, perspire
transude, issue
trickle, flow

Plunge
drop, fall, as rain
fall, plunge
plunge, fall

Swirl
eddy, swirl
swirl, whirl
whirl, eddy

Overflow
billow, surge
deluge, inundate
flood, inundate
inundate, overflow
overflow, flow over
regurgitate, flow back
surge, billow
submerge, inundate
swash, flood
well, flow

Flow
circulate, to move, as blood
drift, flow
flow, stream
glide, flow
meander, circulate
rill, flow
ripple, rill
run, flow
stream, flow

Rain, Snow, Etc.
drizzle, rain
hail, sleet
mizzle, drizzle
rain, fall in drops
sleet, hail
snow, to fall in flakes

Drain
drain, empty
empty, discharge
exhaust, drain

VERBS (Continued)
Expectorate
expectorate, spit
hawk, heave mucus
spit, expectorate

Defecate
defecate, excrete
evacuate, excrete
excrete, discharge excretion
stale, urinate
stool, excrete
urinate, emit urine

Ventilate
fume, reek
reek, emit vapor
ventilate, emit bad air

Emit Air
blow, puff
breathe, expel air
exhale, breathe
huff, puff
pant, blow
puff, blow
respire, breathe
sigh, respire
whiff, puff

Cough, Vomit, Etc.
belch, eject wind
cough, erupt from the throat
disembogue, discharge
disgorge, heave
drivel, slaver
drool, drivel
eructate, belch
hiccup, hiccough
hiccough, discharge by hiccups
heave, vomit
puke, vomit
retch, heave
sneeze, erupt from the nose
spew, vomit
slaver, drool
snivel, run at the nose
vomit, puke

Erupt—Discharge
decant, pour
discharge, emit
emanate, issue
emit, discharge
erupt, discharge
gush, spout
issue, emanate
jet, spout
pour, decant
proceed, issue
spout, jet

VERBS (Continued)
spurt, spout
squirt, spout
Evaporate
effervesce, bubble forth
evaporate, effervesce
steam, evaporate

ADJECTIVES
Discharging
see VERBS, adding ing to form adjectives, as:—
belching
blowing
coughing
etc., etc.

Flowing, Falling
see VERBS, adding ing to form adjectives, as:—
billowing
bleeding
etc., etc.
circulatory, meandering
confluent, flowing together
decurrent, flowing
flowing, streaming
lachrymal, tearful
rippling, rilling
tearful, flowing tears

NOUNS
Exudation
bleeding, blood-flow
desudation, perspiration
drip, regular dripping
effusion, a shedding forth
endosmose, slow osmose
exosmose, fast osmose
extravasation, a forcing out blood
exudation, emanation
filtration, percolation
leak, accidental flow
leakage, leak
ooze, a slow issue
osmose, mutual passage
percolation, filtration
perspiration, sweat
sudation, perspiration
sweat, perspiration
transudation, perspiration

Plunge
dive, plunge
drop, fall
fall, drop
plunge, fall

Vortex
circulation, flow
eddy, vortex
(Continued on page 26)

NOUNS (Continued)

gulf, whirlpool
maelstrom, whirlpool
vortex, whirlpool
whirlpool, maelstrom

Overflow

billow, a surge
breaker, a breaking wave
effluent, overflowing stream
ground-swell, a rolling sea
inundation, flood
overflow, inundation
surge, a swell
swell, a sea
sea, billow
suffusion, inundation
tide, a rising and falling of the sea
wave, billow

Stream

bottom, river
branch, rivulet
brook, branch
brooklet, brook
burn, rivulet
cove, creek
current, flow
drift, flow
flow, a streaming
gill, brook
jet, stream
river, a stream
rill, rivulet
rivulet, brook
runnel, brook
reach, a stream
stream, a flowing body
trickle, rivulet

Tributary

confluence, tributary
tributary, a joining stream

Wild Stream

cascade, cataract
cataclysm, flood

NOUNS (Continued)

cataract, waterfall
debacle, cataclysm
Niagara, waterfall
race, a swift stream
rapids, a race
torrent, cascade

Rain, Snow, Etc.

cloud-burst, downpour
deluge, downpour
downpour, a hard rain
dribble, drizzle
drizzle, fine rain
hail, sleet
mizzle, drizzle
rain, falling drops
snow, a snowfall
snowfall, falling snow
sleet, hail
shower, rain
serein, fine rain

A Contrary Flow

reflux, a flowing back
regurgitation, reflux
undercurrent, underflow
undertow, contrary underflow

Expectoration

expectoration, a spitting
spitting, expectoration

Defecation

defecation, evacuation
excretion, evacuation
evacuation, excretion
stool, evacuation

Exhalation

breath, respiration
exhalation, breath
respiration, a breathing

Cough, Vomit, Etc.

belch, eructation
catarrh, abnormal mucus action
cough, violent exhalation

NOUNS (Continued)

eructation, a belch
heave, a vomiting
hiccough, a contracted eruption, hiccup
rheum, flux, as from nose and eyes
salivation, abnormal action of saliva
sneeze, violent eruption from nose and mouth
snivel, a running from the nose
vomiting, a spewing

Miscellaneous

acne, pustular eruption
brash, rash or eruption
course, menses
drainage, an emptying
hemorrhage, a bleeding
incontinence, involuntary discharge
menses, menstruation
menstruation, menses
rash, brash

Eruption, Discharge

affusion, a pouring
discharge, ejection
douche, effusion
effluence, emanation
efflux, emanation
emanation, a flowing out
emission, emanation
eruption, outbreak
flux, flow
fluxion, flux
gush, a gushing
influx, a flowing in
issue, emanation
outbreak, eruption

Ebullition

ebullition, effervescence
effervescence, ebullition

PERSONS (Continued)

apostate, deserter
ascetic, hermit
deserter, renegade
emigrant, migrator
fugitive, runaway

PERSONS (Continued)

hermit, recluse
migrator, emigrant
recluse, anchoret
refugee, one who flees
renegade, deserter

PERSONS (Continued)

runagate, renegade
runaway, fugitive
seceder, abdicator
skulk, sneak
sneak, skulk

PERSONS (Continued)

airman, aeronaut
aviator, aeronaut
balloonist, aeronaut
birdman, aviator
bluejacket, sailor
boatman, traveler by boat
canoeist, boatman

PERSONS (Continued)

circumnavigator, navigator
flier, aviator
marine, soldier-seaman
mariner, navigator
navigator, seaman
seaman, navigator
sailor, seaman

PERSONS (Continued)

salt, tar
swimmer, one who swims
skipper, seaman
tar, sailor
yachtsman, yacht navigator

RISING—VAULTING　　see—　　**ASSOCIATIVE**

vs. Descent—Fall 22	Elevation—Height 149F
vs. Low—Below 149G	Exaltation 139B
	Excellence—Distinction 140B

17

VERBS

Rise

ascend, mount
aspire, ascend
arise, ascend
billow, surge
emerge, issue
fly, soar
issue, arise
rear, arise
rise, ascend
rocket, ascend
soar, fly
surge, billow
tower, soar

Jump

hop, vault
jump, spring
leap, vault
spring, jump

Surmount

culminate, surmount

VERBS (Continued)

escalade, scale
exalt, surmount
scale, escalade
surmount, scale
vault, surmount

Mount

clamber, climb
climb, mount
mount, ascend
ramp, climb
shin, climb
top, mount

ADJECTIVES

ascendant, ascending
ascending, rising
billowing, rising
eminent, towering
rising, soaring
rocketing, mounting

ADJECTIVES (Continued)

soaring, rocketing
surging, billowing
transcendent, surmounting
towering, soaring

NOUNS

ascent, ascension
ascension, rise
climb, a mounting
culmination, transcendency
elevation, rise
hop, a leap
jump, a spring
leap, a spring
mount, a climbing
rise, ascent
spring, a leap
skip, a hop
soar, a flying
surge, a rising
transcendency, culmination
transit, a passage over

STAGGER—SHAMBLE
(Irregular Walking)　　see—

vs. Walk—March—Step 19B

ASSOCIATIVE

Stray—Ramble 18B
Turn—Whirl—Shift 18C
Unskilfulness 126D
Walk—March—Step 19B

18A

VERBS

Stagger

flounder, stumble
halt, limp
hobble, limp, totter
limp, halt
reel, stagger
slip, totter
stagger, totter
stumble, stagger
toddle, totter
totter, stagger

Lurch

dash, pitch
fall, tumble
lurch, plunge
pitch, plunge
plunge, lurch
trip, totter
tumble, fall

Trudge

crawl, drag
creep, crawl
drag, lag
lag, plod
plod, trudge
shamble, shuffle

VERBS (Continued)

shuffle, shamble
slouch, shamble
sprawl, shamble
trudge, drag

Waddle

daddle, waddle
wabble, waddle
waddle, waggle
waggle, wabble
wobble, waddle

ADJECTIVES

awkward, clumsy
clumsy, gawky
floundering, stumbling
gangling, awkward
gawky, ungainly
graceless, ungainly
inelegant, awkward
lame, halting
lubberly, awkward
poky, sluggish
shambling, shuffling
shuffling, shambling
sluggish, clumsy
stumbling, staggering

ADJECTIVES (Continued)

tardy, poky
uncouth, ungainly
undignified, graceless
ungainly, clumsy
ungraceful, graceless
unsteady, wabbling
wabbling, wabbly
wabbly, unsteady

NOUNS

halt, a limping
hobble, a limp
limp, a halt
staggers, titubation
titubation, a wabbling
waddle, a wobbling
waggle, a waddling
wobble, a waddling

PERSONS

gawky, a hobbledehoy
hobbledehoy, looby
looby, awkward fellow
lout, looby
lubber, swab
swab, looby, sluggard, lout

STRAY—RAMBLE
(Desultory Passage)

vs. Advance—Proceed 19A

ASSOCIATIVE

Irregularity 126A
Stagger—Shamble 18A
Turn—Whirl—Shift 18C
Walk—March—Step 19B
Error—Fault—Defect 126C

18B
VERBS

Stray

drift, ramble
loaf, wander
loiter, loaf
ramble, rove
roam, ramble
rove, wander
straggle, wander
stray, straggle
tramp, wander
wander, ramble

Frisk

caper, gambol
curvet, frisk
frisk, rollick
gambol, frisk
rampage, romp
rollick, romp
romp, rollick

Meander

meander, wend
range, rove

VERBS (Continued)

saunter, stroll
stroll, wander
thread, wend
wend, meander

ADJECTIVES

adrift, discursive
astray, wandering
desultory, excursive
devious, rambling
discursive, desultory
errant, roving
erratic, wandering
excursive, rambling
rambling, excursive
roaming, wandering
roving, rambling
stray, wandering
strolling, rambling
vagrant, wandering

NOUNS

desultoriness, discursiveness

NOUNS (Continued)

discursiveness, a tramping
rampage, a romping
romp, a rollicking
saunter, a strolling
tramp, a wandering
vagrancy, idle roving

PERSONS

beach-comber, vagrant
Bohemian, rover
gipsy, Bohemian
hobo, tramp
loafer, vagrant
rambler, rover
nomad, wanderer
ranger, rover
roamer, wanderer
rover, wanderer
straggler, vagrant
stroller, rover
tramp, vagrant
vagrant, loafer
wanderer, rover

TURN—WHIRL—SHIFT

vs. Advance—Proceed 19A

ASSOCIATIVE

Dancing 99F
Circular—Curved 150C
Stray—Ramble 18B
Stagger—Shamble 18A
Walk—March—Step 19B

18C
VERBS

Turn

bend, turn
boxhaul, veer
caracole, swerve
clubhaul, turn
curve, swerve
kedge, warp
luff, turn
oscillate, swing
shift, turn
sidle, move sidewise
skid, swerve
swerve, turn
swing, turn
tend, turn
turn, wheel
veer, turn
warp, swerve
wear, turn
whiffle, veer
yaw, whiffle

VERBS (Continued)

Avoid

avoid, shy
balk, swerve
dodge, shift
shy, turn

Twist

squirm, wriggle
twist, squirm
wriggle, squirm
writhe, twist

Circle

circle, wind
compass, go around
eddy, swirl
gyrate, revolve
mill, wind
pirouette, whirl
revolve, gyrate
roll, revolve
rotate, revolve
spin, gyrate

VERBS (Continued)

swirl, whirl
twirl, whirl
wheel, rotate
whirl, gyrate

Zigzag

circulate, wind
flutter, move about quickly
meander, wend
sinuate, wind
stay, tack
tack, zigzag
wend, meander
wind, wend
zigzag, tack

Diverge

depart, deviate
detour, diverge
deviate, diverge
digress, swerve
diverge, deviate
(Continued on page 29)

VERBS (Continued)
divert, turn
shunt, divert

Miscellaneous
deflect, swerve
hinge, pivot
invert, reverse
pass, shunt
pivot, hinge
port, turn left
reverse, shift
revert, turn back
trend, have bent

ADJECTIVES

Roundabout
circuitous, roundabout
devious, diverging
indirect, devious
rambling, devious
roundabout, devious
sinuate, winding
sinuous, meandering
tortuous, zigzag
wavy, sinuous
winding, wending
zigzag, having short turns

Miscellaneous
aberrant, straying
circulatory, moving around
digressive, indirect
divergent, devious
gyratory, revolving
heliotropic, turning with
   the sun
oblique, indirect

ADJECTIVES (Continued)
reverse, shifting back
revolving, rotary
rolling, turning
rotary, revolving
saltatory, dancing
swerving, turning
Terpsichorean, saltatory
transverse, crossing
trochlear, pulley-like
trochilic, noting a rotary
   motion

NOUNS

Turn
cant, a turn
caracole, a swerving
deflection, deviation
departure, digression
deviation, digression
digression, divergence
divergence, digression
shift, a turning
shunt, a turning aside
swerve, deviation
turn, deflection
warp, a turning

A Circling
circulation, a moving
   around
gurgitation, a whirling
gyration, a revolving
revolution, rotation
rotation, a turning
swirl, an eddying

NOUNS (Continued)
whir, a quick turning
whirl, a revolving

Miscellaneous
aberration, digression
aberrance, a straying
avoidance, a dodging
detour, divergence
distortion, a twisting
heliotropism, a turning with
   the sun
pirouette, a whirling upon
   the toes
return, reversal
reversal, a turning back
reversion, a returning
tack, a zigzagging

MEDIUMS
deflector, bending medium
flexor, bending muscle
gig, a whirligig
gyroscope, top
heliotrope, a flower which
   turns with the sun
propeller, rotating device
pulley, power-wheel
revolver, that which rotates
screw, propeller
top, gyroscope
wheel, rotating device
windlass, power drum
whirligig, revolving device

19A

ADVANCE—PROCEED—TRAVEL   see—
   vs. Leave—Withdrawal—Escape 15

19A
VERBS

Advance
advance, approach
drive, travel
proceed, progress
progress, advance
push, proceed

Approach
approach, near
approximate, approach
come, draw near
near, advance

Go
circumnavigate, voyage
cruise, voyage
go, proceed
itinerate, travel
jaunt, march
journey, travel
march, jaunt

VERBS (Continued)
move, proceed
pass, traverse
traverse, progress
travel, journey
trek, travel
thread, trek
tour, travel
voyage, cruise
wander, travel

Resort
haunt, resort
migrate, resort
resort, go often
retrace, return
return, retrace
visit, resort

ADJECTIVES

Miscellaneous
advancing, approaching

ADJECTIVES (Continued)
approaching, nearing
en route, transient
expeditionary, en route
forthcoming, approaching
homing, returning
itinerant, transient
locomotive, progressive
migratory, transient
moving, locomotive
nomadic, wandering
onward, advancing
passing, transient
processional, proceeding
progressive, advancing
transient, moving
transmigratory, transient
(Continued on page 30)

NOUNS

Advancement

advance, approach
advancement, progress
approach, a nearing
approximation, approach
course, progress
procedure, advancement
progress, advancement
progressiveness, progress
progression, progress

Trip

circuit, journey
cruise, voyage
drive, excursion
excursion, trip
jaunt, excursion
journey, excursion
march, jaunt
pilgrimage, journey
sally, excursion
trek, journey by wagon
trip, journey
tour, excursion
voyage, cruise

NOUNS (Continued)

Movement

action, progress
going, progression
locomotion, progression
motion, movement
movement, action
move, action

Travel

itineracy, travels
migration, travel
nomadism, a wandering
perambulation, travel
peregrination, travel
passage, progress
transit, passage
transmigration, passage
travel, a journeying

Expedition, Etc.

caravan, company of travelers
cavalcade, procession
excursion, excursionists
excursionists, travelers
expedition, excursion

NOUNS (Continued)

parade, procession
procession, traveling body
safari, expedition

PERSONS

aviator, aerial traveler
circumnavigator, globe-trotter
commuter, passenger
excursionist, traveler
globe-trotter, traveler
itinerant, traveler
navigator, traveler by sea
nomad, wanderer
passenger, traveler
perambulator, traveler
peregrinator, traveler
pilgrim, traveler
stowaway, hidden passenger
tourist, traveler
traveler, one who travels
voyager, navigator
voyageur, boatman
wayfarer, traveler
wanderer, nomad

WALK—MARCH—STEP   see—

vs. Stagger—Stumble 18A

19B

ASSOCIATIVE

Advance—Proceed 19A
Stray—Ramble 18B
Stagger—Shamble 18A
Haste—Hurry 9

19B

VERBS

Walk

pace, step
stalk, strut
step, stride
stride, pace
strut, swagger
swagger, stride
tread, walk
walk, tread

Jaunt

amble, stroll
hike, tramp
jaunt, ramble
march, walk
perambulate, walk
promenade, stroll
ramble, stroll
stroll, amble
tramp, march
wade, walk in water

ADJECTIVES

Miscellaneous

afoot (adv.), walking
ambulatory, walking
ambulent, walking
apace (adv.), stepping fast
astir (adv.), moving
gradatory, gradient
gradient, ambulant
itinerant, peripatetic
pedal, moving by foot
pedestrian, ambulatory
peripatetic, pedestrian
plantigrade, pedal

NOUNS

Miscellaneous

amble, pace
ambulation, a walk
constitutional, stroll
gait, walk
hike, march
jaunt, stroll
march, tramp

NOUNS (Continued)

pace, step
perambulation, a walking
promenade, stroll
step, pace
stride, step
stroll, promenade
strut, a swagger
swagger, strut
somnambulism, a walking
in sleep
tramp, a march
walk, stroll

PERSONS

ambulator, walker
hiker, walker
itinerant, walker
perambulator, ambulator
peripatetic, ambulator
pedestrian, walker
somnambulist, sleeping walker
walker, pedestrian

ENTRANCE—PENETRATION   see—   ASSOCIATIVE
   vs. Leave—Withdrawal 15   { Inside—Middle 149L
                 { Confinement—Enclosure 52H

20

VERBS

Enter

enter, pass into
immigrate, enter
permeate, pervade
penetrate, pervade
pervade, permeate
reenter, enter again
return, reenter
thread, penetrate

Pierce

bore, drill
drill, bore
perforate, pierce
pierce, penetrate
puncture, pierce
tunnel, penetrate

Embark

board, enter on passage
embark, board
enplane, embark
entrain, board
launch, enter

Intrude

descend, invade
encroach, intrude
insinuate, obtrude

VERBS (Continued)

intrude, obtrude
invade, intrude
obtrude, intrude
rush, enter eagerly

ADJECTIVES

Miscellaneous

centripetal, centerward
endosmotic, noting reciprocal penetration
immigrant, entering
intrusive, obtrusive
obtrusive, insinuating
penetrating, penetrative
penetrative, piercing
piercing, penetrating

NOUNS

Miscellaneous

diffusion, reciprocal permeation
diosmose, reciprocal inflow-
 ing
endosmose, reciprocal
 penetration
encroachment, intrusion
entrance, entry

NOUNS (Continued)

entry, ingress
ingress, entry
entree, entrance
illapse, influx
immigration, entrance
influx, a flowing in
incursion, invasion
inroad, incursion
insinuation, obtrusion
intrusion, obtrusion
invasion, incursion
irruption, invasion
obtrusion, insinuation
osmose, reciprocal permeation
penetration, entrance
penetrability, penetration
penetrativeness, penetrability
perforation, puncture
permeation, penetration
permeability, permeation
pervasion, permeation

PERSONS

immigrant, in-comer

SUBMERSION—DIPPING   see—   ASSOCIATIVE
   vs. Leave—Withdrawal 15   { Descent—Fall 22
   vs. Rising—Vaulting 17   { Low—Below 149G
                  { Lowness—Abasement 129B

21

VERBS

Submerge

bog, sink
draw, sink proportionately
founder, sink
mire, bog
sink, submerge
submerge, engulf
subside, sink

Dip

dip, steep
dive, plunge
douse, souse
launch, plunge or float
pitch, dip
plunge, souse
souse, plunge

VERBS (Continued)

Engulf

deluge, overflow
engulf, inundate
flood, deluge
inundate, flood
overflow, inundate

Immerse

baptize, immerse
immerge, immerse
immerse, submerge
steep, immerse
wade, walk submerged

ADJECTIVES

foundering, sinking
plunging, diving

ADJECTIVES (Continued)

sinking, submerging
submarine, submerged

NOUNS

Miscellaneous

baptism, immersion
dip, submersion
dive, plunge
ducking, a dipping
flood, inundation
header, head-dive
immersion, baptism
inundation, a flooding
plunge, a dive
submersion, a dipping
souse, plunge

vs. Rise—Vaulting 17

Submersion—Dipping 21
Exudation—Flow 16
Low—Below 149G

22

VERBS

Descend
descend, pass down
dip, swoop
drop, fall
fall, descend
flop, fall
plunge, drop suddenly
shoot, swoop
sink, fall
slump, sink
swoop, shoot down
topple, fall
tumble, topple

Gravitate
coast, glide
drift, float
float, gravitate
flow, float
gravitate, move toward attraction
toboggan, coast

VERBS (Continued)
volplane, float down

Depend
append, hang from
depend, hang
droop, hang down
hang, suspend
nod, let the head fall or droop
sag, hang
suspend, hang
swag, sag

Settle
set, sink
settle, set
subside, settle

ADJECTIVES
Miscellaneous
deciduous, dropping off
descendent, descending
downward, descending

ADJECTIVES (Continued)
falling, dropping
fugacious, falling
sinking, settling

NOUNS
Miscellaneous
collapse, a falling together
descension, passage down
descent, descension
drop, fall
downfall, drop
ebb, a flowing back
fall, descent
gravitation, movement due to attraction
lapse, a falling by degrees
plunge, sudden drop
suspension, a hanging
subsidence, a sinking
slump, a sinking
tumble, disorderly fall

---

vs. Descent—Fall 22

Travel, Etc. 24I
Haste—Hurry 9
Advance—Proceed 19A
Rising—Vaulting 17

23

VERBS

Fly
aviate, fly by a machine
boom, go with a rush
flit, fly
fly, soar
soar, fly
swing, soar
wing, fly

Navigate
boat, navigate
circumnavigate, sail round
coast, sail
course, navigate
luff, sail close to the wind
navigate, sail
sail, coast
scud, sail
ship, navigate

Float
float, glide
flow, glide
glide, go smoothly
meander, float
skate, slide
slide, glide
slip, slide

VERBS (Continued)
swim, progress in water
volplane, glide
waft, float

ADJECTIVES
Miscellaneous
aerial, flying in the air
aeronautic, aviatory
aviatory, flying
afloat, floating
alar, winging
alary, alar
aquatic, natatorial
buoyant, afloat
flitting, flying
floating, gliding
marine, maritime
maritime, aquatic
natant, swimming
natatorial, natant
naval, natatorial
volant, flying
volatile, fleeting

MEDIUMS
natatorium, swimming-pool
oar, propeller

MEDIUMS (Continued)
paddle, oar
pinion, wing
propeller, oar
skate, ice slide
ski, foot slide
wing, pinion

NOUNS
Miscellaneous
aeronautics, aerial travel
aviation, art of flight
ballooning, balloon travel
circumnavigation, a sailing round
flight, a flying
flying, aviation
flotation, a floating
natation, art of swimming
navigation, art of sailing
swimming, natant travel
yachting, navigation with yachts

PERSONS
aeronaut, airman
aeroplanist, airman
(Continued on page 26)

TRANSPORTATION—CARTAGE   see—

vs. Laxity—Neglect 126B
vs. Rest—Stability 11B

ASSOCIATIVE

24A
VERBS

Transport
convey, carry
drive, convey
forward, convey
move, convey
remove, transfer
transport, transfer

Haul
cab, convey by cab
cart, haul
freight, haul
haul, freight
ride, convey
roll, wheel along
sled, convey by sled
truck, haul by truck
train, haul by train
trundle, roll along

To Boat
boat, carry by boat
canoe, convey by canoe
ferry, ship
raft, haul by raft
ship, convey by ship

Pull
drag, tow
draw, pull
lug, tug
pull, drag
siphon, draw by siphon
tow, drag by rope
tug, pull
warp, tow

Deliver
commit, deliver
consign, deliver
deliver, send forth
devolve, transmit
extradite, deliver
hand, pass by hand

VERBS (Continued)
pass, convey
transfer, transmit
transmit, convey

Dispatch
delegate, dispatch
dispatch, express
entrain, dispatch
export, send away
express, dispatch
mail, send by mail
post, mail
speed, dispatch

Attend
accompany, escort
attend, accompany
convoy, escort
escort, convoy

Conduct
conduct, lead
direct, guide
guide, maneuver
lead, conduct
maneuver, guide
pilot, guide
steer, guide
take, lead

To move in water
float, convey by water
paddle, row
row, move with oars

Carry
bear, carry
bring, carry, bear
carry, transport
fetch, carry

ADJECTIVES
angelic, messenger-like
conductive, conveying

ADJECTIVES (Continued)
deferent, conveying
equestrian, moving by horse
peristaltic, moving worm-like

NOUNS

Transportation
carriage, transportation
cartage, carriage
haul, cartage
haulage, cartage
lug, a pull
marine, shipping
portage, carriage
rafting, haulage by raft
removal, transference
shipping, transportation
sledding, moving by sled
transportation, conveyance

Delivery
commitment, delivery
consignment, delivery
conveyance, carriage
deliverance, transmission
delivery, transference
extradition, deliverance
remittal, transmission
transmission, conductance
transfer, transmission
transference, transfer

Conductance
conductance, transmission
conduction, transmission
conductivity, conduction
guidance, conductance
logistics, maneuver
maneuver, guidance
pilotage, guidance

LIFT—HOIST

ASSOCIATIVE

vs. Laxity—Neglect 126B
vs. Rest—Stability 11B

Transportation 24A
Impulsion 24C
Delivery 43B
Gift—Givers 43A
Change 3A

24B

VERBS

Lift

elevate, lift
heave, lift
hoist, lift
lift, raise
raise, elevate
rear, raise
uplift, raise aloft

Load

freight, load
lade, load
load, lade

VERBS (Continued)

Boost

boost, lift
purchase, hoist
upheave, heave

ADJECTIVES

add ing to verbs

NOUNS

boost, a lift
elevation, uplift
heave, a lift
leverage, lifting degree

NOUNS (Continued)

lift, uplift
upheaval, a heaving
uplift, a lifting

LIFTING MEDIUMS

derrick, hoist
elevator, a lift
escalator, moving stairway
handscrew, jack
hoist, a lift
jack, lever
lever, lifting device
windlass, a lift

24C

VERBS

Impel

bowl, roll
impel, drive
precipitate, throw
project, hurl
propel, drive forward
roll, bowl
wheel, roll

Throw

cast, throw
chuck, pitch
dart, throw
dash, hurl
discharge, fire
drop, pitch
fillip, throw
fire, shoot
fling, hurl
flirt, jerk
heave, hurl
hurl, project
hurtle, impel
jerk, fillip
pitch, throw
send, cast
shoot, hurl
sling, hurl
shy, fling
toss, chuck
throw, hurl

VERBS (Continued)

Push

boom, push
hustle, push roughly
push, shove
ram, push
shove, push
shuffle, push about
sweep, hurl
thrust, impel

Discharge

decant, pour
discharge, empty
dump, discharge
empty, pour out
pour, discharge

ADJECTIVES

Miscellaneous

abroach, pouring
dumping, discharging
hurtling, impellent
impellent, propelling
projectile, impelling
propellent, driving forth
protrusive, pushing forward
pushing, shoving
shoving, hurtling
tossing, throwing

NOUNS

Miscellaneous

cast, a hurl

NOUNS (Continued)

discharge, pulsion
drive, impulsion
hurl, act of throwing
impetus, momentum
impulse, impulsion
impulsion, an impelling
infusion, a pouring in
injection, a throwing into
jerk, a push or pull
momentum, impetus
projection, impulsion
propulsion, projection
pulsion, a driving forth
shot, a discharge
thrust, a push

IMPELLENT MEDIUMS

(See ARMS 130-I)

decanter, a pouring vessel
helm, tiller
impellent, driving medium
oar, hand propeller
paddle, canoe propeller
projector, projecting medium
propeller, driving device
rudder, guiding device
squirt, syringe
syringe, a squirt
tiller, helm
turbine, a driving wheel
warp, a towing rope

TRANSPORTATION MEDIUMS   see—   **ASSOCIATIVE**

vs. Laxity—Neglect 126B
vs. Rest—Stability 11B

Transportation 24A
Lift—Hoist 24B
Impulsion—Hurling 24C
Delivery—Distribution 43B

24D
ROTARY MEDIUMS

ball	marble	wheel
bowl	pulley	caster
hoop		

24E CARRIERS
PERSONS

PERSONS

Carrier

bearer, porter
caravaneer, caravan head
carrier, conveyancer
coolie, porter
conductor, transport head
conveyancer, carrier
hauler, carrier
porter, carrier
transferrer, conveyancer

Boatman

bargeman, barge workman
canoeist, boatman
ferryman, ferry conductor

PERSONS (Continued)

gondolier, boatman
longshoreman, stevedore
oarsman, boatman
pilot, boat conductor
raftsman, raft attendant
stevedore, wharfman
sailor, seaman
seaman, sailor
yachtsman, yacht boatman

Equestrian, Etc.

equestrian, horseman
equestrienne, horsewoman
jockey, equestrian
mahout, elephant driver
teamster, team driver

PERSONS (Continued)

Driver, Etc.

bicyclist, cyclist
chauffeur, auto driver
charioteer, chariot driver
coachman, coach driver
cyclist, bicycle rider
driver, wagoner, etc.
engineer, engine driver
expressman, express
  worker
hackman, hack driver
jehu, coachman
motorist, chauffeur
motorman, motor driver
wagoner, wagon driver
wheelman, cyclist

24F
MESSENGERS

ablegate, Pope's envoy
angel, messenger
archangel, chief angel
beadle, court messenger
button, page

courier, messenger
delegate, envoy
delegation, delegate body
envoy, messenger

messenger, courier, etc.
page, messenger
post, messenger
pursuivant, state
  messenger

24G
BEASTS OF BURDEN

ass	charger	filly	jennet	racer
barb	courser	goer	llama	reindeer
bidet	cuddy	hack	mule	roadster
broncho	donkey	hackney	mustang	roan
burro	drag	horse	nag	sheltie
camel	dromedary	jackass	ox	steed
carrier-pigeon	elephant	jade	pony	yak

24J (Continued)
SHIPS—BOATS, Etc.

skiff, canoe
umiak, Eskimo boat
wherry, rowboat

Ferry

back, ferryboat
ferry, ferryboat
ferryboat, crossing V.
pontoon, floating bridge

Galley, Etc.

foist, light galley
four, 4-oared boat
galley, oar-boat

V.—vessel

lymphad, a galley
pinnace, 6 or 8-oared boat
quadrireme, a ship with 4
  banks of oars
trireme, galley
galleass, armed galley

Pleasure Boat

funny, pleasure boat

Motor-boat

motor-boat, power-boat
motor, motor-boat

paddle, paddle-wheel
side-wheeler, paddle
steamboat, steamer
steamer, steamboat

Freight Boat

bumboat, freighter
casco, freight V.
cat, small boat
collier, coaling V.
freighter, merchantman
keel boat, freight boat

vs. Laxity—Neglect 126B

{ Delivery—Distribution 43B
Gift—Givers 43A
Change 3A

24H
CARRIERS ON LAND

Vehicle
car, vehicle
conveyance, vehicle
equipage, carriage
rig, vehicle
team, horse and V.
transport, conveyance
vehicle, a conveyance

Motor-Car
auto, automobile
automobile, motor vehicle
auto-truck, motor truck
Ford, a motor car
jitney, small fare V.
limousine, motor-car
locomotive, engine
motor-car, auto
motor-truck, power-truck
sedan, closed motor-car
taxi, taxicab
taxicab, motor-cab

Carriage, Etc.
brougham
buggy
cariole
carriage
chaise
chariot
curricle
dearborn
four-in-hand
Gladstone
landau
landaulet
phaeton
rockaway
shay
stanhope
sulky
surrey
tarantass
trap
Victoria

V.—vehicle

CARRIERS, ETC. (Cont'd.)
Litter, Etc.
bier, litter
brancard, horse litter
kago, palanquin
litter, stretcher
palanquin, a conveyance
  borne on shoulders
stretcher, litter

Sled, Etc.
cutter, sled
hurdle, frame-drag
pung, sleigh
skate, a gliding instrument
ski, snow-runner
sled, sledge
sledge, sled
sleigh, sled
toboggan, sled

Cycle
autocycle, motor-cycle
bicycle, two-wheeled V.
cycle, bicycle
motorcycle, motor-bicycle
tricycle, 3-wheeled V.
unicycle, one-wheel cycle
velocipede, a cycle

Elevator
elevator, a lift
escalator, moving stairway
hoist, elevator
lift, elevator

Wagon, Etc.
buckboard, light wagon
caravan, a van
dray, a heavy wagon
fourgon, luggage-van
freight-car, public carrier
freighter, wagon, etc.
gondola, flat freight-car
hearse, funeral V.
lorry, platform wagon
truck, heavy cart
trundle, truck

CARRIERS, ETC. (Cont'd.)
van, large wagon or car
wagon, 4-wheeled V.
wain, wagon

Tractor, Etc.
caterpillar, tractor
tank, armored car
tractor, motor V.

Coach, Tram, Etc.
bus, omnibus
cab, one-horse carriage
cabriolet, carriage
char-a-bancs, passenger V.
coach, a passenger V.
drag, coach
express, a fast conveyance
growler, cab
gyroscope car, balance V.
hack, a traveling V.
hackney, coach
local, suburban train
omnibus, bus
stage, traveling V.
tallyho, coach
train, coupled railway
  coaches
tram, tramcar
trolley, trolley car

Barrow, Etc.
barrow, wheelbarrow
limber, gun-carriage V.
perambulator, baby V.
pushcart, two-wheeled cart
tumbrel, two-wheeled cart
wheelbarrow, barrow

Cart, Etc.
cart
dogcart
gig
go-cart
hansom
jinrikisha
tandem
tilbury

24I
AIRCRAFT

Airplane, Etc.

aeroplane, flying machine
aircraft, airplane, etc.
airplane, airship
airship, balloon, etc.
albatross, a type of airplane
biplane, two-plane airship
blimp, dirigible balloon
dirigible, airship
escadrille, airplane squadron
gyroplane, a form of airplane

AIRCRAFT (Continued)

gyropter, a form of airplane
helicopter, a direct lift airplane
hydro-airplane, a water and air vessel combined
hydroplane, a boat with aerial propellers
monoplane, airplane with a single plane
ornithopter, a flying machine with wings

AIRCRAFT (Continued)

plane, airplane
seaplane, combination water and aeroplane
Zeppelin, a dirigible balloon

Balloon, Etc.

aerostat, balloon
balloon, a device for flying
kite, a captive flying device
parachute, a device for descending slowly in the air

24J
SHIPS—BOATS, Etc.

Boat

ark, large boat
bateau, light boat
boat, small watercraft
bottom, a vessel
conveyance, transport
craft, a vessel
decker, ship with decks
liner, a vessel
packet, small boat
ship, seagoing vessel
transport, troop ship, etc.
vessel, ship or boat

Sailing Vessel

bark, small sailboat
barkantine, sailing V.
bilander, two-masted V.
boyer, Flemish Sloop
brig, square-rigged V.
brigantine, sailing V.
bucentaur, a state barge
caique, sailing vessel
catboat, sailboat
clipper, sailing vessel
dhow, Arabian V.
doni, Ceylonese vessel
droger, West India boat
galleon, 3-decker, Spanish
grab, light V.
hooker, Dutch V.
hulk, unseaworthy V.
Indiaman, vessel of India
junk, Chinese V.
ketch, sailing V.
lorcha, Chinese V.
pilot-boat, pilot's boat
pink, narrow-sterned V.
polacre, Mediterranean V.
prahu, proa
proa, Malaysian V.
saic, sailing V.
sail, ship or vessel
sailer, sailing V.

V.—vessel
SHIPS, Etc. (Continued)

schooner, sailing V.
settee, sailing V.
sloop, sailing V.
snow, sailing vessel
store-ship, supply ship
tartan, Mediterranean V.
tender, auxiliary V.
tug, towing V.
whiff, outrigged boat
xebec, sailing V.

Fishing Vessel

buss, fishing vessel
coble, flat fishing V.
cob, fishing boat
dogger, Dutch fishing V.
fisherman, fishing V.
hatch-boat, fishing V.
koff, fishing V.
lugger, fishing V.
smack, fishing boat
trawler, trawling V.
whaler, whaling V.

Warship

corvette, wooden war V.
cruiser, war vessel
destroyer, torpedo boat
dreadnaught, war vessel
frigate, warship
launch, man-of-war boat
man-of-war, warship
monitor, warship
submarine, submersible V.

Raft, Float

barge, flatboat
catamaran, Indies raft
float, raft
lighter, barge
praam, flat-bottomed V.
punt, flat-bottomed boat
raft, flatboat
scow, flatboat

Trading Vessel

argosy, merchant V.
carack, merchantman

SHIPS, Etc. (Continued)

coaster, coast-trade V.
felucca, Mediterranean V.
galiot, Dutch merchantman
hoy, coasting V.
merchantman, trading V.
slaver, slave-trade V.

House Boat

dahabiyeh, house boat
house boat, dwelling boat
sampan, Chinese house boat

Fleet

armada, merchant fleet
caravel, body of vessels
fleet, vessels in company
flotilla, small fleet

Ship's Boat

cockboat, small boat
dingey, East India boat
gig, a ship's boat
jolly-boat, ship's boat
lifeboat, ship's boat
longboat, ship's boat
yawl, sloop

Racing Vessel

outrigger, racing boat
sonder-yacht, racing yacht
yacht, racing V.

Rowboat, Etc.

canoe, small boat
cockleshell, light boat
coracle, a boat of hides
dory, skiff
dugout, canoe
gondola, Venetian boat
ice boat, ice glider
ice canoe, ice boat
kayak, Eskimo boat
oomiak, umiak
pair-oar, V. for two oarsmen
shallop, rowboat
piroque, canoe
randan, rowboat
(Continued on page 35)

PASSAGEWAYS   see—   ASSOCIATIVE

25

VERBS

Penetrate
enter, penetrate
penetrate, tunnel
perforate, pierce
pierce, penetrate
punch, perforate

Bore
bore, drill
burrow, tunnel
drill, bore
tap, bore
tunnel, excavate

Open
broaden, make wider
clear, free of obstruction
dig, excavate
ditch, excavate
excavate, hollow out
groove, furrow
hollow, excavate
open, make passable
space, leave an opening
widen, broaden

ADJECTIVES

Accessible
accessible, open
ajar, open
circumnavigable, open for
  sailing around
clear, unobstructed
fordable, open for fording
gaping, ajar
hollow, open
navigable, open for ships
open, admitting passage
passable, unobstructed
spacial, open
unclosed, open

Spacious
ample, roomy
broad, open, wide
capacious, spacious
commodious, roomy
expansive, spacious
extensive, expansive
large, spacious
roomy, spacious
spacious, roomy
vast, extensive
wide, broad

Deep
abysmal, deep

ADJECTIVES (Continued)
cavernous, hollow
deep, hollow
yawning, abysmal

Perforate
alveolate, pitted deeply
cribriform, sieve-like
perforate, full of holes
pitted, full of pits
porous, having pores

Crannied, Etc.
canaliculate, grooved
crannied, having crevices
crevassed, deep-fissured
furrowed, trenched
galleried, having galleries
grooved, lined deeply
honey-combed, full of cells
interstitial, crevassed
rimose, having fissures

Vascular
arterial, having arteries
intestinal, having canals
vascular, having vessels
venal, having veins
venous, having veins

NOUNS

Accessibility
access, entry
adit, mine opening
archway, entrance
entrance, passage
entry, entrance
ingress, entrance
inlet, entrance
mouth, opening
muzzle, mouth
nozzle, mouthpiece

Opening
aperture, opening
eyelet, hole for thread
gap, opening
ingate, opening in a mold
mesh, opening in a net, etc.
opening, aperture
orifice, opening
perforation, a bored hole
rift, opening

Outlook
loophole, opening in a fortification

NOUNS (Continued)
outlook, opening
peephole, hole for peeping
porthole, opening in a
  ship's side
port, porthole
vista, opening for view

Window
bay, wall opening
bay window, projecting
  window
casement, opening
dormer, roof window
embrasure, wall-opening
oriel, bay window
window, opening

Door, Gate, Etc.
door, passageway
doorway, door
gate, passage in a wall
hatch, deck opening
hatchway, hatch
portal, entrance-way
postern, gate
scuttle, small hatchway
sluice, water gate
threshold, entrance
wicker, small door, etc.
wicket, small gate

Outlet
debouch, opening in a fortification
embouchure, opening at the
  mouth of a cannon, river,
  etc.
floodgate, water gate
leak, accidental opening
outlet, opening
ostiary, river's mouth
sally port, exit for troops
scupper, deck drain
vent, opening for air

Hole, Pit, Etc.
bore, bored opening
cavity, hollow
excavation, artificial opening or clearance
hole, deep opening
hollow, hole
pit, cavity
well, deep opening

25A
NOUNS

Area
area, extent
breadth, expanse
compass, sweep
expanse, area
extent, compass
latitude, range
range, area
room, space
reach, stretch
scope, area
sphere, range

NOUNS (Continued)
stretch, range
surface, area
sweep, extent, expanse

Space
air, spatial fluid
atmosphere, air
ether, atmosphere
emptiness, unobstructed
    space
inane, infinite space
interval, space
space, void
void, emptiness

NOUNS (Continued)
Arena, Ring, Etc.
amphitheater, vast arena
arena, field of action
Colosseum, amphitheater
course, field
field, arena
floor, area
floorage, floor space
gridiron, football field
ring, arena
rink, place for skating
stadium, course

25B
PATHS—WALKS—
ROADS

Course, Path
airline, bee line
beat, course
bee line, straight course
circuit, course
course, track
lap, a course
orbit, course
pass, passage
path, course
route, course
rut, beaten track
track, path
turf, race course
way, path

Passage
access, approach
alley, lane
approach, avenue
cut-off, short road
defile, narrow pass
drift, a mine passage
hall, hallway
hallway, passage
lane, passage
passage, patch
tunnel, underground pass

PATHS, Etc. (Continued)
Road, Highway
avenue, driveway
boulevard, thoroughfare
byway, detour
causeway, thoroughfare
corduroy road, log road
detour, circuitous way
drive, vehicular road
ghaut, mountain pass
highroad, highway
highway, public road
pavement, paved road
pike, road
road, highway
street, road
subway, underground
    course
thoroughfare, street
tracing, track
turnpike, toll road
trocha, military road

Railway
extension, railway branch
line, railway
tram, tramway
tramway, railway
railroad, tramway
railway, railroad

PATHS, Etc. (Continued)
Bridge
bateau bridge, pontoon
bridge, spanning passage
crossing, cross path
drawbridge, convertible
    bridge
gangway, narrow bridge
pontoon, bridge of boats
trestle, bridge
viaduct, bridge

Walk
aisle, passage
ambulatory, a walk
arbor, bower
banquette, sidewalk
bower, arbor
esplanade, shore drive
flagstone, paved course
mall, shaded walk
path, walk
pergola, covered walk
promenade, esplanade
sidewalk, foot walk
walk, path

Quay, Etc.
dock, wharf
pier, wharf
quay, wharf
wharf, pier

25C
STAIRWAY—STEP
escalator, moving stairway
ladder, an ascending frame
newel, winding stair

perron, outside stair
stair, steps
staircase, stairway

stairway, stair
steps, stairway
stile, steps over a fence

25D
ARTIFICIAL AREAS
arcade, arched gallery
bridge deck, partial deck
corridor, gallery
court, yard-like space
deck, ship's floor
gallery, corridor

lobby, vestibule
peristyle, open court
parquet, space back of or-
    chestra
piazza, porch
plaza, open square

porch, portico
portico, covered walk
proscenium, front stage
vestibule, porch
veranda, portico
yard, space by a house

PASSAGEWAYS
vs. Obstruction 36

See—(ASSOCIATIVE 25)

25E
ORGANIC PASSAGES

alimentary canal, excreta duct
adenoid, throat gland
anus, excremental orifice
artery, blood vessel
basilic, arm vein
bowel, gut
breast, milk organ
canal, duct, channel, etc.
capillary, blood vessel
duct, canal
entrails, intestines

gland, a bodily organ
glandule, small gland
gullet, throat
gut, intestinal canal
intestine, bowel
muscle, a fibrous medium for conducting energy
nerve, fibrous duct
nipple, teat of breast
nostril, nose opening
organ, functional medium

orifice, small opening
pap, nipple
rectum, anus
sinew, a fibrous conductor
swallow, gullet
teat, nipple
throat, gullet
tendon, the fibrous medium connecting muscles
vein, duct
weasand, windpipe, throat

25F
ARTIFICIAL CONDUCT-
ING MEDIUMS

Canal, Etc.
canal, waterway, duct
channel, watercourse
flume, water channel
watercourse, canal
Drain, Etc.
culvert, sewer
ditch, trench
drain, canal
drainage, drain
gutter, drain
sewer, drain
sink, drain
Vent, Etc.
chimney, vent
chute, inclined trough
flue, chimney

(Continued)
smokestack, chimney
shaft, cut
upcast, ventilating shaft
vent, flue
Pipe, Tap, Conduit
aqueduct, water conduit
cannula, tube
conductor, conduit
conduit, canal or pipe
cylinder, tube
faucet, pipe valve
funnel, conical tube
hooka, pipe
hose, flexible tube
hydrant, water valve
nozzle, mouthpiece
pipe, tube

(Continued)
siphon, conveying tube
tap, release pipe
tube, cylinder
wire, electrical conductor

Trench, Ditch
cut, trench
dike, ditch
grip, trench
groove, shallow channel
moat, ditch
sap, trench
trench, narrow excavation
Gutter, Etc.
kennel, gutter
strip, trough
trough, chute

25G
LAND BODIES OR
AREAS

Tract, Region
acreage, area in acres
area, tract
continent, geographical area
country, territory
ground, land
land, territory
latitude, range, scope
province, region
range, territory
region, territory
scope, latitude
territory, area
tract, plot

Valley, Dale
dale, glen
dell, small valley
glen, narrow valley
lea, meadow
lowland, level country
mead, meadow (Poet.)

(Continued)
meadow, lowland
vale, valley
valley, lowland
wadi, deep valley
wady, wadi
Swamp, Marsh
bog, morass
everglade, Florida swamp
fen, marsh land
marsh, swamp land
morass, fen
quagmire, marsh
slough, bog
swamp, marsh
Field, Plain
delta, alluvial land
field, open country
flat, plain
heath, moorland
llano, grassy plain
moorland, moor
moor, wasteland
pampas, prairie

(Continued)
plain, level country
prairie, plain
plateau, elevated flat land
savannah, extensive meadow
steppe, plains of Russia
tundra, Siberian plain
veld, open country
Shore
beach, strand
coast, area by the sea
littoral, area by a shore
shore, coast
strand, shore
Island
eyot, small island
holm, river island
isle, island
island, land surrounded by water
islet, island
key, island
(Continued on page 41)

PASSAGEWAYS
vs. Obstruction 36

25G LAND BODIES OR AREAS (Continued)

Forest, Desert

desert, barren tract
frontier, bordering land
forest, wilderness
wilderness, barren region
wood, forest

Common, Etc.

common, public ground
park, common
parade, review ground

Lawn, Clearing

clearing, open space
glade, clearing
greensward, lawn
green, grass plot
lawn, green
link, golf course
plat, plot
plot, plat of land
sod, turf

sward, sod
terrace, raised level
turf, green

Promontory

cape, headland
headland, promontory
isthmus, a neck of land
peninsula, land almost surrounded by water
promontory, cape

25H

cave, natural cavity
cavern, cave
cavity, hollow

HOLLOW-FISSURE, ETC.

Hollow, Gulf

abyss, gulf
bowl, hollow
chasm, deep opening
crater, cup-shaped cavity
gap, cleft, hiatus
gulf, abyss
hiatus, gap, chasm
hole, hollow
hollow, cavity, etc.

(Continued)

lacuna, pit, hiatus
pit, hole
vault, cavern

Cleft, Gorge

breach, opening, gap
caldera, caldron-like cavity
canon, gorge
canyon, gorge
chap, crack
chink, crack
cleft, crevasse
clough, gorge
crack, fissure, chink
cranny, fissure, crevice

(Continued)

crevasse, deep fissure
crevice, small fissure
dingle, hollow between
 hills
ditch, gully
gash, gap
gorge, canyon
grotto, cavern
gulch, canyon
gully, ravine
interstice, crevasse
ravine, gorge
recess, cavity
slit, cleft

25I

WATER BODIES

(See FLOW 16)

Stream, River

branch, rivulet
broad, overflow of a river
bourn, rivulet
brook, rivulet
brooklet, brook
confluence, tributary
course, stream
cove, brook
creek, cove
estuary, tidal river en-
 trance
fleet, creek
floss, small stream
gill, brook
inlet, creek
mesh, shallow river
reach, stream
rill, rivulet
river, stream

(Continued)

rivulet, brook
runlet, rivulet
runnel, brook
stream, river
streamlet, rivulet
tributary, connecting
 water

Lake, Etc.

bay, a shore lake
bayou, stream
bight, small bay
firth, arm of the sea
frith, firth
harbor, haven for ships
lagoon, shallow lake
lake, water surrounded by
 land
loch, bay
lough, lake
pond, lake
pool, pond
tarn, mountain lake

(Continued)

Ocean, Etc.

archipelago, island-dotted
 waters
deep, ocean
gulf, a sea partially surrounded by land
main, the ocean
ocean, a vast expanse of
 water
offing, depth off the shore
sea, large water body

Channel, Etc.

canal, channel
channel, flume
flume, channel
gut, strait
sound, narrow waterway
strait, a narrow water

BEING

Neptune, god of the seas
 and all inland waters

26

OPPOSITION—REPELLENCE

vs. Insufficiency 37
vs. Exhaustion 128A

Unrestraint 125C
Many—Large 147I
Lavishness 43A

26
VERBS
Miscellaneous
cloy, over-fill
exceed, excel
excel, surpass
overdo, do in excess
overflow, exceed
redound, be redundant
regurgitate, surge back
surcharge, overload
surpass, exceed

ADJECTIVES
Excessive
copious, overflowing
de trop, excessive
excessive, superabundant
extreme, excessive
exuberant, superabundant
luxuriant, superabundant
overflowing, excessive
plethoric, excessive
redundant, superabundant
superabundant, excessive
superfluous, excessive
unessential, superfluous
unnecessary, superfluous
useless, unnecessary
utmost, extreme
ultra (prefix), beyond

Adequate
abundant, copious
adequate, plenty

ADJECTIVES (Continued)
commensurate, equal
corresponding, equal
enough, adequate
equal, equivalent
equivalent, proportional
plenty, enough
proportional, equivalent
proportionate, equal
sufficient, enough
tantamount, equivalent

Extra
extra, spare
spare, superabundant
surplus, excessive
supernumerary, extra

Full
brimful, filled
congested, overcrowded
crammed, congested
filled, full
flooded, overflowing
full, replete
replete, too full
saturated, soaked
soaked, saturated

Sated
blasé, sated
flushed, surfeited
jejune, blasé
satiated, sated
sated, too full
stuffed, satiated

ADJECTIVES (Continued)
surfeited, stuffed
sodden, saturated
uninterested, jejune

NOUNS
Excess
congestion, excess
excess, overplus
extremes, excess
exuberance, abundance
luxuriance, abundance
overflow, excess
overplus, superabundance
plethora, excess, fullness
redundance, superfluity
regurgitation, a surging
repletion, plethora
superabundance, overplus
superfluity, excess

Adequacy
abundance, great plenty
adequacy, fullness
impregnation, saturation
plentitude, fullness
saturation, fullness
sufficiency, adequacy

Satiety
ennui, satiety
fill, satiety
satiety, surfeit
surfeit, satiety

---

31 (Continued)
NOUNS (Continued)
bereavement, woe
disconsolation, sadness
dolor, sorrow
(B). dolour
heartache, grief
hopelessness, despondency
infelicity, misery
loneliness, bereavement
misery, distress
pensiveness, sadness
sadness, sorrow

NOUNS (Continued)
seediness, wretchedness
tribulation, deep sorrow
woe, misery

Pain
ache, pain
pain, anguish
pang, pain
sore, pain
stitch, sharp pain
twinge, pain

PERSONS
wince, a pain
allopath, passive sufferer
dupe, victim
mourner, a bereaved person
martyr, sufferer for a
   cause
penitent, repenter
scapegoat, victim
victim, unwilling sufferer
wretch, a sufferer

OPPOSITION
ASSOCIATIVE

REBELLION see—		
	Ban—Prohibition 35	Dislike—Hatred 28
vs. Desire 39	Protestation 67A	Anger—Wrath 29
vs. Submission 46B	Disputation 66	Complaint 67B
	Contention 41D	Reproof—Satire 64
	Threat—Menace 33	Attack—Encounter 130F
	Protection 34	Disbelief—Doubt 30

27

VERBS

Oppose

differ, disagree
disagree, oppose
object, oppose
oppose, resist
resent, oppose
resist, object

Countervail

breast, stem
buck, oppose
confront, oppose
contravene, oppose
counteract, oppose
countervail, counteract
insist, persist
negative, countervail
persist, breast
resolve, persist
stem, resist
withstand, oppose

Repel

abnegate, refuse
apostatize, renounce
decline, refuse
deny, renounce
dishonor, refuse
disown, deny
rebuff, refuse
refuse, reject
reject, decline
renounce, disown
shun, decline
spurn, reject
won't, refuse

Rebel

balk, refuse
disobey, rebel
mutineer, revolt
mutiny, revolt
rebel, revolt
revolt, mutiny

Contest

aggress, militate
antagonize, aggress
contest, litigate
kick, contest
litigate, contest

ADJECTIVES

Oppositional

adverse, opposed
adversative, antithetical
antithetical, opposite
conflicting, opposite

ADJECTIVES (Continued)

contrary, adverse
counter, contrary
counteractive, negative
dissentient, oppositional
dissenting, dissentient
negative, contrary
objectionable, opposed
opposable, oppositional
oppositional, opposed
opposite, contrary
pessimistic, not optimistic
reactive, contrary
resistant, negative

Repellent

inhospitable, uninviting
repellent, repulsive
repulsive, inhospitable
uncongenial, inhospitable
uninviting, inhospitable
unwelcome, uninviting

Rebellious

factious, turbulent
incendiary, seditious
insurgent, rebellious
insurrectionary, mutinous
malcontent, rebellious
mutinous, revolutionary
rebellious, mutinous
revolutionary, rebellious
schismatic, factious
seditious, rebellious

Persistent

bent, determined
determined, resolute
fixed, immovable
insistent, persistent
persistent, obstinate
purposeful, resolute
resolute, persistent
set, obstinate
stanch, steadfast
steadfast, resolute

Pertinacious

arbitrary, self-willed
balky, stubborn
dogged, stubborn
froward, obstinate
headstrong, obdurate
morose, sullen
mulish, stubborn
obdurate, obstinate
obstinate, stubborn
pertinacious, obstinate
pigheaded, stubborn
recusant, obstinate
refractory, obstinate

ADJECTIVES (Continued)

restive, stubborn
stiff-necked, obstinate
stubborn, obstinate
sullen, stubborn
tenacious, obstinate
wayward, wilful

Serious

earnest, serious
grave, serious
serious, determined
stern, determined

Wilful

conclusive, decisive
decisive, positive
final, decisive
flinty, obdurate
hard, unyielding
immovable, implacable
impassive, unmoved
implacable, inexorable
inexorable, inflexible
inflexible, obstinate
positive, wilful
unmoved, resolute
unyielding, inexorable
wilful, headstrong

Intolerant

bigoted, intolerant
captious, resentful
contumelious, scornful
forbidding, intolerant
incompatible, irreconcilable
intolerant, bigoted
irreconcilable, intolerant
resentful, intolerant
scornful, intolerant

Unmanageable

cantankerous, perverse
contumacious, rebellious
disobedient, insubordinate
incorrigible, unruly
indocile, intractable
intractable, unmanageable
insubordinate, insurgent
obstreperous, unruly
perverse, intractable
recalcitrant, refractory
refractory, insubordinate
riotous, insurrectionary
turbulent, rebellious
uncontrollable, unruly
ungovernable, refractory
unmanageable, indocile
unruly, rebellious
untoward, perverse

(Continued on page 45)

ADJECTIVES (Continued)

Aggressive

aggressive, militant
antagonistic, aggressive
belligerent, militant
conflicting, contentious
contentious, militant
litigant, litigious
litigious, contentious
militant, belligerent
pugnacious, militant

Averse

averse, reluctant
backward, averse
inattentive, negative
loath, averse
neutral, uninterested
reluctant, unwilling
tardy, reluctant
uninterested, negative
unwilling, averse

CONJUNCTIONS

albeit, although
although, though
but, except
however, notwithstanding
neither, nor
nevertheless, yet
nor, neither
notwithstanding, although
still, nevertheless
though, however
yet, however

PREPOSITIONS

against, opposite
barring, excepting
but, except
except, barring

ADVERBS

but, only
anyhow, notwithstanding
anyway, anyhow
merely, nothing but
nay, no
nevertheless, anyway
no, nay
none, not any
notwithstanding, in spite of
not, negatively
only, merely
simply, merely

NOUNS

Opposition

antithesis, oppositeness
contrariety, opposition
contrariness, disagreement
contravention, opposition
counteraction, negation
difference, disagreement
discontent, dissatisfaction
disagreement, difference

NOUNS (Continued)

dissatisfaction, dissent
dissension, dissent
dissent, opposition
friction, opposition
inconsistency, contrariety
misunderstanding, disagreement
negation, opposition
objection, opposition
oppositeness, antithesis
opposition, contrariety
resistance, opposition
stand, resistance

Repellence

abnegation, refusal
denial, rejection
refusal, rejection
rebuff, refusal
rejection, rebuff
repellence, rebuff
resentment, opposition

Rebellion

apostasy, sedition
faction, turbulence
insubordination, revolt
insurrection, revolt
mutiny, insurrection
rebellion, insurrection
renunciation, rebellion
revolt, rebellion
revolution, rebellion
riot, rebellion
rising, insurrection
schism, faction
sedition, dissension
strike, rising
treason, sedition
turbulence, uprising
uprising, insurrection

Persistence

backbone, determination
decision, determination
determination, persistence
insistence, determination
persistence, insistence
purpose, resolution
resolution, determination

Pertinacity

contumacy, obstinacy
impenitence, obduracy
implacability, inexorability
inexorability, obduracy
inflexibility, obstinacy
obduracy, obstinacy
obdurateness, obduracy
obstinacy, stubbornness
pertinacity, obstinacy
perverseness, obstinacy
refractoriness, obstinacy
stubbornness, obstinacy

Intolerance

arbitrariness, contrariety
bigotry, intolerance

NOUNS (Continued)

incompatibility, difference
intolerance, bigotry
pessimism, opposition to optimism
stoicism, intolerance

Indocility

disobedience, indocility
incorrigibleness, insubordination
indocility, intractability
recalcitration, indocility

Aggression

aggression, militancy
belligerence, aggression
contention, militancy
litigation, contention
militancy, contention
obtrusion, pugnacity
pugnacity, militancy

Aversion

aversion, reluctance
disinclination, reluctance
indifference, disinclination
indisposition, unwillingness
neutrality, indifference
nolition, unwillingness
reluctance, unwillingness
tardiness, reluctance
unwillingness, tardiness

PERSONS (Miscellaneous)

apostate, reactionist
appellee, defendant
bigot, fanatic
contestant, litigant
defendant, litigant
demagogue, incendiary
dissenter, nonconformist
dissentient, dissenter
donkey, a stubborn person
hothead, a quick dissenter
impenitent, an unrepentant person
incendiary, revolutionist
insurgent, revolutionist
intransigeant, oppositionist
litigant, contestant
malcontent, nonconformist
militant, combative person
mule, a stubborn person
mutineer, insurgent
nonconformist, malcontent
opponent, contestant
oppositionist, nonconformist
pessimist, one opposed to optimism
reactionist, oppositionist
rebel, insurgent
recusant, nonconformist
renegade, rebel
revolutionist, insurgent
sorehead, malcontent
traitor, rebel

DISLIKE—HATRED— SPITE see—	ASSOCIATIVE	
	Opposition 27	Punishment 130N
vs. Liking—	Anger—Wrath 29	Destruction 130-O
Esteem 38	Disputation 66	Insult 65
vs. Love—	Blame 65	Ridicule 64
Affection 39A	Threat 33	Crime 130A
vs. Desire—Hope ..39	Attack 130F	Fear 32
	Infliction 130G	Flight—Escape 15
	Cruelty 130M	Banishment 35A

28

VERBS

Disdain

abhor, hate
abominate, loathe
begrudge, have hostile
  want
despise, hate
detest, loathe
disdain, detest
dislike, detest
envy, begrudge
hate, detest
loathe, abhor
resent, bridle
revolt, have disgust
scorn, disdain
stomach, resent
spurn, disdain

Shun

avoid, evade
dodge, avoid
evade, shun
shun, abhor

Snub

bristle, frown
bridle, bristle
disregard, ignore
frown, scowl
glower, scowl
ignore, snub
rise, be hostile
scowl, frown
snub, have contempt

ADJECTIVES

Disdainful

abhorrent, hateful
abominable, antipathetic
contemptuous, disdainful
disdainful, supercilious
hateful, adverse
scornful, disdainful

Arrogant

aloof, haughty
arrogant, disdainful
cavalier, supercilious
chesty, haughty
haughty, arrogant
highflown, haughty
lofty, proud
overbearing, arrogant
proud, arrogant
snobbish, aloof
supercilious, disdainful

ADJECTIVES (Continued)

toplofty, arrogant
uppish, arrogant

Cold-blooded

chill, haughty
cold, indifferent
cold-blooded, frigid
cool, cold
frigid, haughty
frosty, frigid
icy, cold

Spiteful

bloodthirsty, vengeful
caustic, spiteful
feudal, vindictive
jealous, revengeful
retaliative, vindictive
revengeful, feudal
sanguinary, bloodthirsty
spiteful, malignant
splenetic, spiteful
splenic, rancorous
vengeful, vindictive
vindictive, revengeful

Fiendish

atrocious, diabolical
devilish, diabolical
diabolical, fiendish
fiendish, diabolical
flagitious, atrocious
hellish, diabolical
infernal, hateful
nefarious, hellish
satanic, hellish
Stygian, hellish

Malicious

baleful, malignant
bitter, caustic
evil, malicious
implacable, satanic
invidious, envious
insidious, hostile
malevolent, spiteful
malign, ill-willed
malignant, spiteful
malicious, malignant
nasty, spiteful
rancorous, spiteful
venomous, spiteful
vicious, spiteful
viperous, malignant
virulent, malignant

Averse

antipathetic, adverse

Page 46

ADJECTIVES (Continued)

averse, unfavorable
disclined, antipathetic
fastidious, squeamish
heedless, unconcerned
impatient, intolerant
inadvertent, indifferent
inappreciable, indifferent
indisposed, indifferent
inattentive, adverse
indifferent, unconcerned
nonchalant, indifferent
phlegmatic, antipathetic
stoic, indifferent to irrelevant interests
unconcerned, antipathetic

Hostile

adverse, hostile
antagonistic, hostile
bristling, hostile
hostile, inimical
inhospitable, hostile
inimical, hostile
repugnant, hostile
resentful, repugnant

Impudent

discourteous, rude
impolite, rude
impudent, rude
indignant, resentful
petulant, pert
pert, saucy
rude, uncivil
saucy, impudent
ungentlemanly, rude

Opprobrious

contumelious, supercilious
cynical, sardonic
derisive, spiteful
ironical, sardonic
Mephistophelian, cynical
opprobrious, scornful
poignant, bitter
sardonic, scornful
wry, sardonic

Sinister

envious, jealous
grim, vengeful
harsh, unkind
ill, unfriendly
misanthropic, hating man
severe, harsh
sinister, hateful
sulky, ill-willed

(Continued on page 47)

ADJECTIVES (Continued)
uncharitable, adverse
unfatherly, hostile
unfriendly, inimical
ungracious, hateful
unkind, hostile
unneighborly, unsocial
unsocial, inimical

Disgusted
disgusted, adverse
horrent, abhorrent
nauseous, having loathing
sick, disgusted
squeamish, easily disgusted

NOUNS
Disdain
abhorrence, detestation
abomination, abhorrence
contempt, scorn
cynicism, contempt
detestation, abhorrence
disdain, contempt
dislike, aversion
displeasure, dislike
fleer, contempt
hate, loathing
hatred, detestation
loathing, abomination
odium, hatred
repugnance, aversion
scorn, contempt

Arrogance
arrogance, hauteur
arrogation, presumption
crest, pride, hauteur
hauteur, arrogance
lordliness, hauteur
presumption, arrogance
pride, arrogance
stomach, haughtiness
superciliousness, disdain

Spite
despite, spite
evil-eye, malicious influence
feud, enmity
grudge, malice
revenge, vengeance
spite, hatred
spitefulness, spite
vengeance, vindictiveness
vindictiveness, revenge

NOUNS (Continued)
Malice
acrimony, bitterness
asperity, bitterness
bitterness, spite
gall, spleen
implacability, grim malignancy
malevolence, spite
malice, rancor
maliciousness, spite
malignancy, spite
malignity, spite
rancor, spleen
spleen, malice
venom, spite
virulence, malignity

Aversion
antipathy, dislike
aversion, antipathy
avoidance, a shunning
consequence, hauteur
detachment, aloofness
disinclination, aversion
impatience, petulance
indifference, disdain
indisposition, aversion
nonchalance, indifference
phlegm, dislike
sang-froid, indifference
unconcern, indifference

Hostility
animus, hostility
animosity, hatred
antagonism, hostility
enmity, ill-will
hostility, unfriendliness
indignation, angry dislike
resentment, angry scorn
strife, enmity
vendetta, active enmity

Impudence
affront, insolence
audacity, insolence
brass, impudence
cheek, impudence
disrespect, indignity
effrontery, impudence
impertinence, effrontery
impudence, audacity
indignity, insult
insult, affront

NOUNS (Continued)
insolence, indignity
pertness, impertinence
sauciness, pertness

Opprobrium
contumely, contempt
derision, scorn
irony, contempt
opprobrium, contumely
poignancy, acrimony

Unfriendliness
disaffection, ill-will
envy, malice
jealousy, revengefulness
misanthropy, hatred of mankind
misogyny, hatred of women
sulkiness, ill-will
unfriendliness, hostility

Disgust
boredom, ennui
disgust, loathing
distaste, aversion
dudgeon, sullen dislike
ennui, wearisome dislike
nausea, disgust

PERSONS
arch-enemy, chief enemy
basilisk, serpent
cynic, a scornful person
devil, fiend
enemy, hostile person
feudalist, a foeman
feudist, feudalist
fiend, a malicious person
foe, enemy
foeman, foe
iceberg, a forbidding person
misanthrope, one who hates mankind
misogynist, woman hater
serpent, a malignant person
viper, venomous person

BEING
Gnomes, Norse dwarfs who symbolize malice
serpent, evil one

NOUNS (Continued)
vehemence, rage
violence, ferocity

PERSONS
catamaran, vixen
codger, peevish old man

PERSONS (Continued)
fury, termagant
harridan, shrew
hothead, fiery person
shrew, vixen, scold
Tartar, hothead
termagant, violent woman

PERSONS (Continued)
tigress, furious woman
virago, turbulent woman
vixen, ill-tempered woman
wasp, irritable person
Xanthippe, shrew

ANGER—WRATH— FURY see—	ASSOCIATIVE	
vs. Joy—Mirth— Gladness ....71A vs. Friendliness 38	Opposition ....27 Sorrow—Grief ....31 Dislike ....28 Disputation ....66 Blame ....65 Threat 33	Attack ....130F Infliction ....130G Cruelty ....130M Punishment ....130N Crime ....130A Death—Disaster 130-O

29

VERBS

Miscellaneous

boil, rage
broil, boil
burn, fume
foam, rage
froth, foam
fume, rage
rage, be furious
rankle, broil
rave, rage
resent, be angered
storm, broil
vex, irritate

ADJECTIVES

Angry

angry, wrathful
irate, angry
mad, rabid
possessed, mad
wrathful, irate
wroth, angry

Sulky

dumpy, sulky
glum, ill-humored
grouchy, sullen
grouty, cross
grumpy, surly
ill-humored, cross
moody, glum
morose, gloomy
mumpish, sulky
sulky, grouchy
sullen, glum
surly, snarling
ugly, ill-natured

Irritable

bilious, prone to anger
bitter, poignant
cantankerous, ill-tempered
choleric, bilious
churlish, snappish
crabbed, ill-tempered
cranky, irritable
cross, fretful
cross-grained, cross
crusty, snappish
currish, crusty
doggish, currish
fitful, irritated
fractious, cross
fretful, irritable
hot, furious
impatient, peevish

ADJECTIVES (Continued)

irascible, hot-tempered
irritable, crabbed
irritated, irate
peevish, fretful
peppery, irascible
perverse, petulant
petulant, peevish
piquant, ill-natured
poignant, piquant
snarling, churlish
snappish, currish
techy, peevish
testy, irritable
touchy, peevish

Resentful

aggravated, indignant
angered, maddened
aroused, furious
displeased, aggravated
enflamed, exasperated
enraged, angry
envenomed, bitter
exasperated, fiery
excited, exasperated
fired, incensed
incensed, exasperated
indignant, incensed
inflamed, exasperated
infuriated, rageful
maddened, rankled
nettled, irritated
piqued, angered
provoked, wrathful
rankled, angered
resentful, indignant
roiled, furious
ruffled, nettled
vexed, angered

Rageful

black, rabid
ferocious, savage
fierce, furious
fiery, irascible
frantic, furious
frenzied, rageful
furious, tempestuous
passionate, angry
rabid, rageful
rageful, shrewish
savage, fierce
shrewish, vile-tempered
termagant, raging
tigrin, tigerish
tigerish, tiger-like
truculent, ferocious

NOUNS

Anger

anger, wrath
bile, ill-humor
dander, anger
ire, anger
wrath, fury

Sulkiness

dudgeon, sullen anger
grouch, bad temper
grumpiness, crossness
sulkiness, sullen anger
sullenness, sulkiness
surliness, irritability

Irritability

choler, irascibility
irritability, irascibility
petulance, peevishness
peevishness, testiness
pique, anger
piquancy, pique
testiness, peevishness

Acerbity

acerbity, severity of temper
acridity, bitterness of temper
acrimony, bitterness
austerity, severity
bitterness, passion
severity, acridity

Resentment

exception, indignation
huff, resentment
indignation, resentment
offense, anger
(B). offence
resentment, indignation
tiff, huff
touchiness, irritability

Rage

ferocity, fury
fierceness, ferocity
frenzy, fury
fury, rage
heat, rage
irascibility, truculence
passion, rage
rage, wrath
rampage, furious excitement
storming, violent anger
tantrum, fury
transport, rage
truculence, ferocity

(Continued on page 47)

DISBELIEF—DOUBT—DISTRUST see—
vs. Belief—Opinion 113
vs. Intelligence—Wisdom 117

ASSOCIATIVE
Wonder—Perplexity 112
Fear—Irresolution 32

30

VERBS
Miscellaneous
disbelieve, discredit
discredit, doubt
distrust, mistrust
doubt, distrust
mistrust, doubt
question, doubt
suspect, doubt
suspicion, mistrust

ADJECTIVES
Distrustful
diffident, distrustful
distrustful, skeptical
doubtful, having doubt
doubting, skeptical
inconceivable, incredible
incredible, distrustful
incredulous, skeptical
questionable, doubtful
skeptical, unbelievable
suspicious, mistrusting
Faithless
antichristian, heterodox
atheistic, disbelieving
faithless, not believing
heretical, contrary in faith
heterodox, antichristian

ADJECTIVES (Continued)
infidel, heretical
pagan, heretical
perfidious, faithless

NOUNS
Miscellaneous
agnosticism, disbelief in the
ultimate knowledge of the
nature of things
atheism, disbelief in God
difficulty, perplexity
diffidence, distrust
disbelief, unbelief
discredit, mistrust
distrust, discredit
doubt, distrust
heresy, disbelief in the
orthodox
hesitation, doubt
heterodoxy, heresy
incredulity, disbelief
indecision, doubt
infidelity, disbelief in God
nihilism, disbelief that anything can be known
perplexity, doubt
Pyrrhonism, exaggerated
skepticism

NOUNS (Continued)
quandary, doubt
question, doubt
scruple, hesitation
skepticism, incredulity
suspense, doubt
suspension, indecision
unbelief, disbelief

PERSONS
agnostic, a disbeliever in
the existence of mind or
knowledge
atheist, infidel
giaour, infidel
heathen, an unbeliever
heretic, infidel
infidel, one who does not
believe in divine revela-
tion
Kaffir, infidel (Mohamme-
dan)
nihilist, one who doubts
that anything, even existence, can be known
skeptic, disbeliever
zendik, unbeliever

---

32 (Continued)
NOUNS (Continued)
funk, cowardice
gliff, sudden fear
horror, terror
panic, consternation
stampede, terrified flight
start, sudden fright
terror, fright
Fear
abhorrence, fear
alarm, fright
anxiety, apprehension
apprehension, fear
fear, dread
foreboding, apprehension
horripilation, shuddering
fear
presentiment, foreboding
restiveness, uneasiness
trepidation, terror
uneasiness, apprehension
Timidity
archness, coyness

NOUNS (continued)
bashfulness, shyness
diffidence, timidity
shyness, timidity
timidity, diffidence
Caution
caution, circumspection
circumspection, caution
discretion, prudence
hesitancy, vacillation
hesitation, hesitancy
indecision, irresolution
irresolution, diffidence
prudence, caution
qualm, scrupulosity
reluctance, hesitancy
scruple, caution
scrupulosity, hesitancy
vacillation, diffidence
weariness, caution
Modesty
bashfulness, shyness

NOUNS (Continued)
delicacy, archness
humiliation, shame
modesty, delicacy
mortification, shame
shame, humiliation

PERSONS
caitiff, cowardly wretch
coward, caitiff
craven, caitiff
cur, coward
dastard, coward
groveler, caitiff
howler, coward
poltroon, dastard
recreant, cur
skulk, sneak
skulker, coward
slink, skulker
sneak, coward

---

34 (Continued)
PERSONS (Continued)
sacristan, churchwarden
scout, advance guard
sentinel, sentry
sentry, guard
shepherd, sheep guard
tutor, guardian
warden, guardian
warder, guard

BEINGS
Cerberus, guarding dog of
Hades
Neith, guardian goddess
Nephthys, protecting god-
dess of the dead
Savior, Redeemer
(B). saviour

BEINGS (Continued)
Silvanus, Roman god who
presided over fields, cattle, etc.
Vesta, guardian goddess of
home and fireside

PAIN—SORROW   see—

vs. Joy—Mirth........71A

ASSOCIATIVE

{ Weakness—Debility ....128A   Cowardice 132
    Sickness ....128B   Misfortune 127B
    Apathy—Stupor 110A

31
VERBS

Suffer
ache, suffer
agonize, endure agony
ail, suffer
suffer, bear
twinge, suffer
wince, twinge
writhe, agonize

Endure
abide, endure
bear, suffer
bide, endure
endure, suffer
quail, smart
smart, endure
sustain, endure
tolerate, endure
undergo, suffer

Have Sorrow
atone, have sorrow
brood, to sorrow
brook, to sorrow
commiserate, feel pity
despair, despond
despond, brood
expiate, atone
languish, despond
mope, brood
pine, languish
pity, commiserate
repent, regret
rue, repent
sadden, sorrow
sorrow, grieve
sympathize, commiserate
worry, brood

Struggle
chafe, bear pain
irk, weary
labor, be hard pressed
struggle, agonize
toil, irk
travail, bear child

Strangle
smother, suffocate
stifle, suffocate
strangle, suffocate
suffocate, stive

Lament
bemoan, bewail
bewail, lament
blubber, weep
cant, whine
complain, grieve
condole, lament
cry, weep
deplore, lament

VERBS (Continued)
fret, complain
grieve, lament
groan, grieve
lament, bewail
moan, lament
mourn, grieve
murmur, lament
pule, whine
regret, bewail
repine, complain
scream, bewail
sigh, grieve
snivel, cry
sob, lament
wail, lament
weep, grieve
whine, lament
whimper, deplore
yelp, lament

ADJECTIVES
Suffering
aching, suffering
agonizing, suffering
painful, suffering
sore, painful
tired, weary
uneasy, uncomfortable
weary, worn, tired

Tolerant
deplorable, grieving
discomforted, distressed
grievous, pitiable
infelicitous, unhappy
passive, suffering
pathetic, grief-stricken
patient, bearing pain
pensive, sad
piteous, sorrowful
pitiable, pathetic
pitiful, pathetic
ruthful, sad
sad, sorrowful
saddened, sad
suffering, enduring
tolerant, enduring
uncomfortable, distressed

Regretful
attrite, repentant
contrite, penitent
expiatory, atoning
penitent, repentant
penitential, penitent
regretful, remorseful
remorseful, penitent
repentant, contrite
rueful, sad
sorry, regretful

ADJECTIVES (Continued)
Sympathetic
commiserate, having pity
compassionate, commiserate
sympathetic, compassionate

Lamenting
elegiac, plaintive
howling, grief-stricken
lachrymose, tearful
lamentable, mournful
maudlin, tearful
mournful, tearful
plaintive, mournful
tearful, mournful
weeping, mournful
whimpering, crying
whining, plaintive
yelping, lamentable

Embarrassed
abashed, ashamed
ashamed, shamefaced
embarrassed, distressed
mortified, distressed
shamefaced, abashed

Harassed
aggrieved, sorrowful
annoyed, miserable
bored, annoyed
burdened, discouraged
harassed, vexed
harried, harassed

Distressed
anxious, worried
distracted, distressed
distressed, sad
frantic, distracted
hysterical, distressed
worried, anxious

Lonely
abandoned, miserable
bereaved, lonely
desolate, miserable
forlorn, lonely
lonely, lonesome
lonesome, dreary

Abused
abused, harassed
badgered, abused
basted, beaten
battered, beaten
bayoneted, wounded
beaten, flogged
beset, harassed
bitten, wounded
bothered, harassed

(Continued on page 51)

ADJECTIVES (Continued)

bumped, bruised
bruised, injured
castigated, chastened
chastened, punished
chastized, chastened
clawed, lacerated
cowhided, chastized
crippled, lame
cudgeled, clubbed
drubbed, beaten
flayed, flogged
flogged, beaten
goaded, lacerated
gored, wounded
gouged, wounded
garroted, strangled
hurt, stricken
impaired, injured
impaled, transfixed
injured, stricken
kicked, bruised
knifed, wounded
lashed, beaten
larruped, beaten (colloq.)
leathered, larruped
licked, chastized
mutilated, maimed
maimed, disabled
persecuted, plagued
pestered, harassed
plagued, pestered
racked, tortured
saddled, burdened
scourged, punished
stricken, calamitous
tortured, racked
transfixed, impaled
wounded, maimed

Dejected

blue, unhappy
broody, moody
chapfallen, dejected
crestfallen, dispirited
damp, dejected
dejected, dispirited
depressed, sad
discouraged, dispirited
dismal, dejected
dispirited, dejected
doleful, sad
dolorous, doleful
downcast, sad
drear, sorrowful
dreary, cheerless
funereal, sad
ghostly, dismal
gloomy, depressed
glum, moody
heavy, sorrowful
hypochondriac, depressed
lowspirited, dispirited
lugubrious, dismal
melancholic, depressed
melancholy, gloomy
moody, melancholic
morose, moody

ADJECTIVES (Continued)

poor, dejected
saturnine, morose
seedy, miserable
somber, cheerless
sombrous, somber
sorrowful, sad
sullen, dismal

Miserable

cheerless, unhappy
despairing, forlorn
despondent, disconsolate
disconsolate, sad
downhearted, sad
hapless, sad
heartbroken, hapless
inconsolable, hapless
mirthless, sad
miserable, wretched
tragic, sorrowful
woebegone, doleful
unhappy, hapless
woeful, sorrowful
wretched, miserable

NOUNS

Suffering

affliction, pain
agony, anguish
anguish, pain
excruciation, agony
passion, anguish
suffering, anguish
throe, agony
torment, anguish
torture, agony

Tolerance

cross, suffering
endurance, sufferance
fortitude, sufferance
hardship, endurance
martyrdom, tolerance
patience, endurance
sufferance, endurance
tolerance, sufferance
toleration, sufferance
trial, sufferance

Regret

atonement, penitence
attrition, sorrow for sin
compunction, contrition
contriteness, contrition
contrition, penitence
expiation, atonement
penance, contrition
penitence, repentance
regret, sorrow
remorse, deep regret
repentance, contrition
ruth, sorrow
shame, regret
sorrow, grief

Sympathy

commiseration, compassion
compassion, sympathy
condolence, sympathy
pathos, compassion

NOUNS (Continued)

pity, compassion
sympathy, commiseration

Struggle

cramp, pain
labor, pain
struggle, convulsive pain
strangulation, a choking
suffocation, distress
travail, labor with pain

Lamentation

cry, a lament
crying, lamentation
groan, a lament
lamentation, distress cry
moaning, a lament
outcry, bewailment
plaint, lamentation
plaintiveness, lamentation
sigh, an audible lament
sob, a smothered lament
wail, lamentation
weeping, tearful lament
whine, plaintive lament

Distress

anxiety, uneasiness
calamity, distress
desolation, deep misery
disappointment, distress
discomfort, distress
discomfiture, discomfort
displeasure, grief
dissatisfaction, displeasure
distress, anxiety
embarrassment, distress
grief, misery
grievance, displeasure
hysteria, morbid emotion
mourning, grief
oppression, discomfiture
trouble, distress
uneasiness, discomfort
unhappiness, wretchedness
vexation, distress
worry, anxiety
worriment, worry
wretchedness, unhappiness

Dejection

blue devils, despondency
dejection, melancholy
depression, dejection
despair, despondency
despondency, misery
doldrums, despondency
dumps, dejection
gloom, melancholy
heaviness, grief
horror, deep depression
hypochondria, melancholy
melancholia, despondency
melancholy, despondency
moodiness, melancholy

Misery

bale, woe
(Continued on page 43)

COWARDICE—FEAR—TIMIDITY see—   ASSOCIATIVE

     vs. Bravery—Daring 42

32

VERBS

Cower
blench, quail
blush, have shame
cower, quail
cringe, cower
crouch, cringe
flinch, recoil
funk, dread
grovel, cower
kneel, bend in fear
quail, cower
recoil, quail
shrink, blench
slink, cringe
wince, quail

Fear
apprehend, fear
dread, fear
fear, dread
worry, apprehend

Tremble
abhor, shun, shudder
quake, tremble
quiver, quake
shiver, tremble
shudder, quiver
tremble, shudder

Skulk
skulk, sneak
sneak, move slyly

Evade
avoid, evade
dodge, evade
eschew, avoid
evade, avoid
shun, avoid
shy, dodge

Hesitate
beware, be cautious
falter, hesitate
fluctuate, falter
hesitate, waver
pause, hesitate
shilly-shally, waver
scruple, hesitate
waver, hesitate

Startle
skedaddle, run terrified
start, recoil
startle, be alarmed
stampede, flee in fear

ADJECTIVES

Cowardly
caitiff, cowardly
cowardly, fearful
craven, cowardly
cringing, cowardly

ADJECTIVES (Continued)
crouching, craven
currish, cowardly
dastardly, cowardly
flinching, shrinking
groveling, dastardly
obsequious, cringing
quailing, cringing
recreant, cowardly
servile, obsequious
shirking, dodging
shrinking, cringing
wincing, shrinking

Terrified
abhorrent, horrified
aghast, terrified
alarmed, terrified
appalled, aghast
awe-struck, appalled
bewildered, distracted
distracted, frantic
frantic, alarmed
frenzied, frantic
frightened, fearful
horrified, terrified
horror-stricken, fearful
panicky, terrified
petrified, horrified
startled, frightened
terrified, startled
terror-stricken, frightened

Fearful
afraid, fearful
anxious, apprehensive
apprehensive, fearful
fearful, timorous
gun-shy, shy of a gun
nervous, timid
restive, uneasy
scared, afraid
uneasy, apprehensive

Trembling
creepy, shuddering
quivering, quaking
shaky, trembling
shuddering, quivering
trembling, tremulous
tremulous, quaking

Skulking
hangdog, sneaking
skulking, sneaking
slinking, skulking
sneaking, apprehensive

Timid
chicken-hearted, timid
diffident, timid
fainthearted, diffident
henpecked, diffident
meticulous, timid

ADJECTIVES (Continued)
skittish, timorous
timid, fearful
timorous, fearful

Cautious
advised, cautious
careful, cautious
cautious, wary
chary, cautious
circumspect, cautious
discreet, prudent
faltering, wavering
hesitating, wavering
indecisive, wavering
irresolute, wavering
prudent, cautious
reluctant, wavering
scrupulous, cautious
vacillating, wavering
wary, cautious
wavering, hesitating
weak, vacillating

Modest
abashed, ashamed
ashamed, abashed
backward, shy
bashful, shy
blushful, bashful
blushing, blushful
coy, bashful
modest, shy
shamefaced, blushing
shy, timid
sheepish, shy
skew, shy

Pusillanimous
invertebrate, spineless
nerveless, cowardly
pusillanimous, cowardly
sapless, spiritless
spineless, spiritless
spiritless, pusillanimous
white-livered, cowardly

NOUNS

Cowardice
cowardice, unworthy fear
dastardliness, cowardice
pusillanimity, cowardice
servility, obsequiousness

Terror
acrophobia, fear of elevation
awe, reverential fear
consternation, terror
dismay, terror
dread, terror
fright, alarm
(Continued on page 49)

33

VERBS

Threaten

admonish, warn
alarm, startle
bluff, intimidate
caution, admonish
daunt, intimidate
forewarn, admonish
fulminate, threaten
intimidate, frighten
menace, threaten
threaten, menace

Bully

bluster, bully
browbeat, bully
bully, terrorize
bullyrag, intimidate
cow, bully
hector, bully
huff, bully

Discourage

brandish, threaten
challenge, dare
dare, daunt
defy, dare
deter, frighten
discourage, dishearten
dishearten, deter
dispirit, dishearten
flourish, brandish
impend, threaten
lower, browbeat
scowl, lower
shoo, startle

Terrify

appall, frighten
awe, appall
dismay, terrify
faze, frighten
frighten, terrify
horrify, terrorize
petrify, scare stiff
scare, frighten
shock, dismay
terrify, frighten
terrorize, horrify

ADJECTIVES

Threatening

admonitory, cautionary
alarming, frightful
cautionary, admonitory
ill-omened, ominous
imminent, impending
impending, threatening

ADJECTIVES (Continued)

lowering, threatening
menacing, lowering
minatory, threatening
monitorial, monitory
monitory, admonitory
ominous, appalling
portentous, terrible
premonitory, admonitory
threatening, menacing

Discouraging

dangerous, threatening
defiant, challenging
deterrent, frightening
detrimental, deterrent
discouraging, deterrent
hazardous, dangerous
perilous, dangerous

Formidable

awesome, appalling
black, threatening
dismal, appalling
eerie, scary
fearful, frightful
fearsome, terrible
formidable, terrible
ghastly, weird
grave, awesome
grim, frightful
gruesome, horrible
impressive, grave
serious, solemn
solemn, awesome
somber, awesome
(B). sombre
unearthly, horrible
weird, scary

Fierce

fierce, dreadful
fiery, fierce
redoubtable, terrible
ruthless, frightful
volcanic, terrifying

Terrifying

appalling, dreadful
cyclopean, terrifying
dire, dreadful
direful, dire
dread, awful
dreadful, horrifying
frightful, fearsome
grisly, terrible
harrowing, dreadful
hideous, dreadful

ADJECTIVES (Continued)

horrible, terrible
horrid, dreadful
horrific, horrible
scary, frightful
shocking, alarming
terrible, dreadful
terrific, terrible
terrifying, frightful
thunderous, ominous
tremendous, dreadful

Wild

uncurbed, unrestrained
unrestrained, wild
untamed, wild
wild, untamed

NOUNS

Miscellaneous

alarm, warning
admonition, warning
bluff, deterrence
bluster, bluff
caution, admonition
challenge, dare
danger, impending harm
dare, danger
defiance, dare
embracery, threat
Frankenstein, self-made peril
frightfulness, horribleness
fulmination, threat
gravity, awesomeness
gruesomeness, frightfulness
hazard, danger
horribleness, gruesomeness
imminence, pending evil
impressiveness, awesomeness
incubus, nightmare
intimidation, threat
menace, threat
nightmare, dreadful dream
peril, danger
ruthlessness, frightfulness
scare, a fright
solemnity, awesomeness
terribleness, frightfulness
terror, frightfulness
terrorism, terror
threat, menace
threatening, a menace
warning, admonition
(Continued on page 55)

PROTECTION—
GUARDIANSHIP see—

vs. Negligence 126B
vs. Attack 130F
vs. Offend 130C

ASSOCIATIVE

Defense 36	Clothing 106B
Secrecy—Hiding 103A	Confinement 52H
Disguise 103B	Fence, etc. 36D
Watchfulness 119G	Dwellings 53D
Opposition 27	Settlement—Town 53F
Soldiery 36G	Threat—Menace 33

34

VERBS

Protect

cherish, protect
defend, protect
fend, guard
keep, guard
man, guard
protect, shield
shield, protect
ward, fend
watch, guard

Guard

chaperon, escort
convoy, escort
escort, convoy
guard, protect
patrol, guard
scout, patrol
shepherd, guard
tend, guard

Ensconce

canopy, cover
cover, shelter
ensconce, secure
fence, shelter
house, shelter
roof, shelter
shelter, ensconce

Insure

guarantee, warrant
immunize, safeguard
indemnify, secure
insure, secure
patronize, warrant
redeem, save
safeguard, secure
save, secure
secure, immunize
warrant, secure

ADJECTIVES

Guarding

Cerberean, guarding
guarded, protected
pastoral, protective
protective, guarding
talismanic, guarding by a
 talisman
tutelary, protective

Secure

covert, protected
ensconced, secure
immune, safe
insured, protected
safe, secure
secure, ensconced
sure, safe

NOUNS

Guardianship

auspice, patronage
chaperonage, protection
defense, protection
(B). defence
guardianship, guardship
guardship, protection
protectorate, guardianship
tuition, protection
tutelage, guardianship
tutorship, guardianship

Security

coverture, protection
guaranty, warranty
immunity, protection
indemnification, security
indemnity, insurance
insurance, warranty
palladium, security
patronage, guardianship
policy, insurance
protection, safeguard
redemption, salvation
safeguard, protection
safety, security
safe-conduct, protection
salvation, redemption
security, protection
warranty, security

Wild Shelter

basket, grove
boscage, thicket
brake, wooded swamp
bush, forest
chaparral, thicket
clump, thicket
copse, underwood
covert, thicket
forest, deep woods
grove, wooded expanse
ruck, forest
thicket, wooded shelter
tope, grove
underbrush, under-growth
under-growth, tangled
 growth
weald, forest
wold, forest
wood, wold

Shelter

ark, refuge
covert, shelter
coverture, covert
ceiling, inner roof
harbor, haven
haven, refuge

NOUNS (Continued)

home, refuge
house, shelter
port, harbor
refuge, shelter
roof, shelter
shelter, refuge

Covers

afghan, carriage robe
awning, canvas covering
blanket, covering
canopy, covering
cover, blanket
covering, blanket
coverlet, quilt
quilt, blanket
robe, cover
tilt, arched wagon cover

Apron, Etc.

apron
bib
breast-cloth

Charms

amulet, talisman
charm, amulet
fetish, protective charm
obi, charm
talisman, charm

PERSONS

Cerberus, alert guard
chaperon, escort
churchwarden, church
 guard
coastguard, coast guardian
conservator, protector
convoy, escort
custodian, guardian
duenna, chaperon
escort, guardian
gendarme, policeman
gnome, gnomide
gnomide, mine-guard
griffin, alert guard
guarantor, insurer
guardian, protector
guard, warden
patrol, guard
patron, protector
patroness, protectress
picket, sentry
police, community guard
policeman, as above
protector, guardian
redeemer, savior

(Continued on page 49)

BAN—PROHIBITION—EXCLUSION

see—

vs. Persuasion—Invitation 40A
vs. Appointment—Installation 94

ASSOCIATIVE

35

VERBS

Prohibit
bar, prohibit
ban, prohibit
blackball, debar
blacklist, boycott
forbid, prohibit
hoodoo, ban
inhibit, prohibit
outlaw, ban
pill, blackball
prohibit, forbid
proscribe, interdict
quarantine, prohibit
taboo, ban

Exclude
boycott, debar
debar, exclude
deprive, debar
eliminate, exclude
except, exclude
exclude, debar
leave, except
lockout, debar
omit, leave out
suspend, debar

Intervene
enjoin, prohibit
interfere, prevent
interdict, forbid
intervene, interfere
obviate, prevent
preclude, prevent
prevent, obviate
suppress, prevent
veto, prohibit

Disown
decline, reject

VERBS (Continued)
disown, bar
reject, decline
refuse, reject
reprobate, disown

ADJECTIVES

Miscellaneous
barring, excepting
contraband, prohibitive
exclusive, prohibitive
forbidding, prohibitive
illegal, unlawful
illegitimate, illegal
illicit, unlawful
inadmissible, prohibitive
inhibitive, prohibitive
interdictive, prohibitive
preclusive, preventive
preventive, barring
prohibitive, preclusive
proscriptive, prohibitive
unauthorized, not allowed
unconstitutional, illegal
unlawful, interdictive
unlicensed, unauthorized
unwarranted, unauthorized

NOUNS

Miscellaneous
ban, prohibition
blacklist, exclusion list
boycott, prohibition
constitution, prohibitive
measures
embargo, cargo ban
estoppel, prohibition
exception, exclusion

NOUNS (Continued)
exclusion, ban
expropriation, exclusion
from land-ownership
illegality, unlawfulness
illegitimacy, illegality
injunction, interdiction
interdiction, prohibition
interference, prevention
intervention, interference
law, constitution
lockout, ban on workmen
omission, exception
outlawry, interdiction
preclusion, prohibition
prevention, preclusion
prohibition, interdiction
proscription, interdiction
protractionism, prohibition
by the imposition of duty
quarantine, prohibition of
plague contact
refusal, rejection
rejection, refusal
taboo, ban
unlawfulness, illegality

PERSONS
exclusive, one who excludes
all but chosen fellowship
prohibitionist, a supporter
of prohibition
protectionist, one who sup-
ports protectionism
Signify other persons by
adding affix to verbs

33 (Continued)

PERSONS, Etc.
bete noire, bugbear
bluffer, bully
bogy, hobgoblin
bugaboo, bugbear
bugbear, a vain terror
bulldozer, bully
bully, bulldozer
bounder, bully
elf, mischievous spirit
Frankenstein, self-made
peril

(Continued)
goblin, a frightful creature
gorgon, terrible monster
gorgon, a hideous object
grizzle, fierce bear
hell-hound, fearful creature
hobgoblin, bugbear
hoodlum, bully
monster, fearful creature
mumbo-jumbo, bugbear
ogre, frightful monster

(Continued)
rowdy, ruffian
ruffian, bully
scarecrow, cause of terror
terrorist, one who terrifies
tough, ruffian

BEINGS
Scylla, frightful monster
who became a rock in the
sea and menaced ships
Durga, Hindu goddess in
fear-inspiring form

BANISHMENT—		ASSOCIATIVE	
REMOVAL see—	Shed—Doff 145G	Cleansing 138A	
	Prohibition 35	Purification 138B	
vs. Appointment ..94	Opposition 27	Dumping 24C	
vs. Acquirement—	Obstruction 36A	Attack 130F	
Gain 49A	Threat 33	Punishment 130N	
	Guardianship 34	Annulment 131A	
	Command 94	Destruction 130-O	

35A
VERBS

Remove
abolish, remove
banish, exile
bare, divest
deport, banish
dethrone, remove
discharge, dismiss
dismiss, discharge
dispose, dismiss
displace, dispose
divest, strip from
drum, expel
eliminate, remove
exile, banish
expel, banish
extrude, expel
evacuate, remove
maroon, abandon
obviate, remove
remove, dismiss
sack, dismiss
strip, divest
transport, banish
unburden, unload
unload, remove

Dismiss
anathematize, ban
bounce, oust
bundle, dismiss
chase, drive off
clear, remove
detach, send away
disburden, remove
disperse, dismiss
discard, cast away
dislodge, remove
dispel, disperse
drive, chase
eject, evict
excommunicate, banish
exorcise, cast out
expatriate, banish
evict, bounce
fire, discharge
jilt, discard
ostracise, extrude
oust, eject
pack, bounce
reject, throw away
relegate, dismiss
remit, send back

VERBS (Continued)
rid, clear
rouse, drive from a covert
rout, disperse
rusticate, banish students
send, dispose

Efface, Etc.
bowdlerize, expurgate
efface, obliterate
erase, efface
expurgate, bowdlerize
obliterate, efface
rub, erase
weed, remove weeds
winnow, remove chaff
wipe, efface
wring, compress water
from

Order Away
avaunt
begone
clear out
depart
dodge
duck
flee
fly
get out
go
leave
levant
move
run
skedaddle
skat
vamose

ADJECTIVES
Miscellaneous
ablative, removing what is
unnecessary
depilatory, having the quality of removing hair
dispersive, causing to vanish
ejective, noting ejection
excommunicable, noting excommunication
expulsive, expelling
expurgatory, noting expurgation

NOUNS
Miscellaneous
ablation, removal of ines-
sentials
abolition, removal
banishment, expulsion
censorship, expurgation
deportation, banishment
dethronement, removal
from a throne
discharge, dismissal
dislodgment, removal
dismissal, removal
divestiture, removal
divestment, divestiture
elimination, relegation
ejection, expulsion
ejectment, ejection
eviction, ejection
excommunication, banish-
ment from the church
exile, banishment
exorcism, the dispelling of
evil spirits
expulsion, ejection
extrusion, expulsion
ostracism, banishment
relegation, removal
removal, dismissal
riddance, removal
rustication, dismissal or
suspension from college
sack, dismissal
transportation, banishment

MEDIUMS
cowcatcher, a device for removing obstructions from
a track
depilatory, hair remover
knock-out, removing device

PERSONS
abolitionist, expurgator
bouncer, ejector
censor, expurgator
ejector, evictor
evictor, bouncer
expurgator, one who expur-
gates
jilt, one who discards a
lover

OBSTRUCTION—		ASSOCIATIVE

OBSTRUCTION—
DEFENSE   see—

vs. Openings—
Passageways ..25
vs. Persuasion—
Invitation 40A
vs. Surrender—
Submission 46B

Guardianship 34
Soldiery 36G
Opposition 27
Prohibition 35
Banishment 35A

ASSOCIATIVE

Ban 35
Disputation 66
Threat 33
Secrecy 103A
Anger—Fury 29

36
VERBS

Obstruct

bar, obstruct
block, obstruct
clog, impede
close, shut out
cross, obstruct
encumber, obstruct
obstruct, block
obviate, shut out difficulty
preclude, shut out
shut, close

Impede

estop, place a legal impediment
filibuster, obstruct with
delay
hinder, obstruct
impede, obstruct
interfere, prevent
intercept, prevent
interpose, intervene
interrupt, obstruct
intervene, interfere
intrude, interfere
meddle, interfere
prevent, obstruct
retard, obstruct
stop, stem

Uphold

crusade, exert vigorous
defense
defend, ward off
maintain, defend
preserve, defend
protect, defend
rescue, deliver
save, prevent
safeguard, fortify
shelter, shield
shield, guard
uphold, defend

Fortify

arm, fortify
bank, embank
barricade, fortify
dam, obstruct
defilade, raise a rampart
embank, fortify with a
bank
fence, obstruct with a fence
fortify, obstruct

VERBS (Continued)

garrison, fortify with
troops
impale, obstruct with a
fence
intrench, fortify with a
trench
mail, armor with mail
moat, fortify with a moat
palisade, fortify by fence
picket, palisade
rampart, build a rampart
screen, fortify by screen
stem, dam, obstruct
stockade, palisade
wall, protect with a wall

Withstand

avert, ward off
fend, ward off
foil, frustrate
forefend, fend
frustrate, thwart
guard, defend
parry, ward off
rebuff, repel
rebut, rebuff
repel, repulse
repress, press back
repulse, drive back
resist, withstand
thwart, foil
traverse, thwart
withstand, thwart

ADJECTIVES

Obstructive, Etc.

barring, obstructing
bristling, defensive
defensive, having defense
detentive, obstructing
impedimental, obstructive
obstructive, detentive
pragmatic, interfering
preventive, obstructive
protective, defensive
repellent, repelling
repulsive, repellent
repressive, repellent
retardative, obstructive
resistant, preventive
retuse, depressing

Fortified, Etc.

anti-aircraft, noting de-
fense against air-craft

ADJECTIVES (Continued)

armored, protected
castellated, fortified
embattled, having battle-
ments
gauntleted, wearing mailed
gloves
heeled, well armed
ironclad, fortified by iron
pachydermatous, having
thick-skinned protection
panoplied, completely
armored
safe, invincible
secure, safe

Invincible

baffling, redoubtable
impassable, inaccessible
impenetrable, impregnable
impermeable, impenetrable
impervious, impermeable
inaccessible, impenetrable
impregnable, invincible
incontestable, impregnable
indomitable, irrepressible
insuperable, unconquerable
insurmountable, insuper-
able
invincible, unconquerable
invulnerable, unconquer-
able
irrepressible, impregnable
irresistible, impregnable
redoubtable, indomitable
unconquerable, invincible
unsurmountable, insuper-
able

NOUNS

Miscellaneous

champerty, defense in consideration of a share
crusade, defense
defense, resistance
(B). defence
defensive, a warding off
detention, intervention
frustration, nonplus
guard, defense
impenetrability, impregnability
impermeability, impenetrability

(Continued on page 58)

36A, 36B

OBSTACLES—OBSTRUCTIONS   See—(ASSOCIATIVE 36)
    vs. Openings 25

36A

balk, obstacle
bar, obstruction
barrier, bar
cowcatcher, fender
check, obstruction
detent, a stop
door, gate
encumbrance, hindrance
estoppel, legal impediment
fender, protective bar

gate, postern
guard, a detent
hitch, obstruction
hindrance, obstruction
impediment, obstruction
interference, obstruction
interposition, interference
interruption, check
obstacle, obstruction
obstruction, impediment

postern, gate
prevention, preventive
preventive, interference
quarte, guard in fencing
retardation, hindrance
stoppage, obstruction
ward, guard
BEING
Janus, god of gates and
    doors

FORTIFICATIONS   See—(ASSOCIATIVE 36)
    vs. Vulnerability 128A

36B

abatis, barricade of trees
acropolis, citadel
barbette, breastwork
barbican, defense tower
bastile, defense tower
bastion, a projection work
barricade, defense
bartizan, battlement
battlement, parapet with
    openings
battery, cannon station
block, blockade
blockage, obstruction
blockade, defense line
blockhouse, stronghold
boon, water obstruction to
    enemy ships
breastwork, a defense
bridge-head, a bridge de-
    fense
bulwark, any defense
caponiere, covered
    lodgment
casement, shellproof
    battery
castle, fortress
citadel, fortress
contravallation, besiegers'
    works thrown around an
    enemy
cordon, defense line
defense, protective work
donjon, defense of last re-
    sort
dugout, defense trench
dun, fortified eminence

earthwork, a defense
    embankment
embankment, a defensive
    work
enceinte, the main en-
    closure of a fortress
entanglement, a barbed-
    wire obstruction
epaulement, a side protec-
    tive work
fastness, a natural strong-
    hold
footing, assured position
fortification, a defensive
    work
fort, fortified place
fortress, castle
gabionnade, a defense made
    of gabions
garrison, fortified place
glacis, a defensive slope in
    front of a fortification
keep, stronghold
laager, a defense formed of
    wagons, etc.
mantelet, movable rampart
moat, a water barrier
muniment, stronghold
orillon, a defense for
    cannon
outwork, a defense beyond
    the main fort
palisade, a fortification of
    pointed stakes
palladium, a citadel or
    safeguard

parapet, rampart
picket, fortification
portcullis, a defensive work
    for lowering in front of
    an entrance
postern, a protected pas-
    sage closed by a gate
protection, defensive work
rampart, an elevation
    around a fortified place
redan, a V-shaped fortifica-
    tion with the apex toward
    the enemy
redoubt, a work without
    flanks for strengthening
    a position
rideau, an earth curtain or
    concealment
refuge, stronghold
retrenchment, a defense in-
    side another
revetment, a retaining wall
    around the lower part of
    a rampart, etc.
safeguard, protection
sconce, small fort
shelter, refuge
stockade, a barrier of posts
stronghold, fortress
testudo, a defense made of
    shields
tete-de-pont, a defense at a
    bridge entrance
tower, bastile
trench, a defensive ditch
wall, rampart
zariba, a fortified camp

36 (Continued)

NOUNS (Continued)
impregnability, invincibility
interference, prevention
intervention, interference
invincibility, irresistibility

invulnerability, impregna-
    bility
irresistibility, invincibility
maintenance, defense
nonplus, insuperableness
preclusion, act of cutting
    off

prevention, intervention
rebuff, repulse
repellence, repulsion
repellency, repellence
repression, a putting down
repulse, a beating back
repulsion, repulse

36C
PERSONAL ARMOR   See—(ASSOCIATIVE 36)
vs. Vulnerability 128A

armature, armor
armor, body covering of defensive material
(B). armour
brassard, armor for the arm
breastplate, armor for the front of the body
buckler, ancient shield
casque, helmet

corselet, light armor
crest, helmet
cuirass, breastplate
ecu, mediæval shield
gauntlet, mailed glove
gorget, throat armor
habergeon, neck and breast mail
hauberk, armor made of steel rings

helm, helmet
helmet, head armor
mail, armor of steel netting, etc.
morion, open helmet
panoply, complete suit of armor
sallet, helmet
shield, defensive armor carried on the arm

36D
FENCE—HEDGE, ETC.
fence, barrier of rails
hedge, fence of bushes

paling, fence of pales
rail, a bar

railing, fence of rails

36E
DEFENSE MATERIALS
fascine, bundle of sticks used in fortification

gabion, a basket of earth used in defense works

munition, military stores for defense

36F
SKIN—BARK—RIND
bark, tree covering
carapace, upper shell of a tortoise
cuticle, scarf skin
derma, true skin
ectoderm, external skin
epicardium, scalp of the skull

epicarp, under-skin of a fruit
epidermis, outer skin
film, a thin skin
hide, leather-like skin
hull, fruit or nut covering
husk, outer covering
integument, tegument

rind, a skin or covering
scale, a plate-like fish covering
skin, integument
tegument, skin
testa, integument of a seed

36G
PERSONS
attorney, legal defender
defendant, one who is on the defense

busybody, meddler
defender, one who defends
marplot, one who hinders
meddler, interferer

obstructionist, one who obstructs
rebutter, one who defends with a contrary answer

36H
BANK—LEVEE—SHORE
bank, edge of a water course
beach, strand
border, brink
breakwater, a structure for breaking the force of waves
brim, edge

brink, brim
coast, shore
curb, curbstone
curbstone, a path's edge made of stone
dam, a water barrier
dike, levee
edge, brink

embankment, bank
lasher, weir
levee, embankment
margin, rim
rim, brim
shore, coast
strand, shore
weir, dam

36I
GRILL—DOOR—WINDOW
baluster, pilaster
balustrade, protecting rail
banister, baluster
door, gate
gate, door

grill, an open grating
hatch, door
pilaster, part of a wall
screen, sheltering shield
shield, screen

shutter, screen
window, transparent protection against the wind, etc.

36J
UMBRELLA
gingham, umbrella

parasol, sunshade

umbrella, rain screen

DESIRE—WANT—NEED

NEED—INSUFFICIENCY	ASSOCIATIVE	
see—	Tendency 2	Allurement 40A
	Liking 38	Search 119E
vs. Repletion—	Friendliness 38	Inquiry 41A
Overabundance ..26	Desire 39	Appeal 40B
	Love 39A	Demand 41B
	Passion 39B	Contention 41D
	Weakness 128A	Endeavor 41C

37

VERBS

Miscellaneous

desiderate, need
entail, necessitate
famish, starve
gasp, need breath
hunger, need
lack, need
miss, need
need, lack
necessitate, need
require, need
smother, suffocate
starve, hunger
stifle, suffocate
stive, stifle
strangle, suffocate
suffocate, need air
thirst, need drink

ADJECTIVES

Needful

anxious, eager
desiderative, needing
discontented, needful
dissatisfied, needful
famished, starved
hungry, needing food
insatiable, unsatisfied
intent, anxious
malcontent, needful
needful, destitute
smothering, needing breath
strangling, smothering
suffocating, strangling
starved, famished
thirsty, needing drink

Deprived

deprived, destitute
deserted, lonely
destitute, needful
impecunious, needful
indigent, needy
lonely, deserted
lonesome, yearning
necessitous, needy
needy, necessitous
poor, necessitous

Empty

empty, needful
exhausted, empty
vacant, empty
void, wanting

Inane

analgesic, anesthetic

ADJECTIVES (Continued)

blind, sightless
comatose, lethargic
deaf, deficient in hearing
dumb, wanting speech
inane, wanting, void
inanimate, inane
jejune, not vital
spiritless, inane
voiceless, dumb

Deficient

deficient, needful
inadequate, insufficient
incommensurate, needful
insufficient, deficient
lacking, wanting
missing, needful
needed, lacking
scarce, scanty
scant, insufficient
short, inadequate

Requisite

absent, lacking
incompetent, inadequate
incomplete, lacking
prerequisite, requisite
requisite, needful
unfilled, inadequate
wanting, needful

Necessary

essential, necessary
exigent, urgently needful
indispensable, necessary
necessary, essential
urgent, exigent
vital, essential

NOUNS

Need

anxiety, eagerness
discontent, need
discontentment, discontent
dissatisfaction, want
famine, hunger
hunger, need
loneliness, need of companionship
need, want
starvation, famine
strangulation, suffocation
suffocation, need of breath
thirst, need of drink
want, need

Deprivation

destitution, poverty

NOUNS (Continued)

impecuniosity, poverty
indigence, need
penury, poverty
poverty, destitution

Emptiness

chasm, a great want
emptiness, need
exhaustion, emptiness
gap, void
gulf, insatiable void
hiatus, a step wanting in a chain of proof
vacancy, emptiness
vacuity, emptiness
vacuum, void
void, emptiness

Inanity

inanition, inanity
inanity, emptiness
wanness, inanity

Deficiency

dearth, scarcity
deficiency, want
drought, dearth
scarceness, scarcity
scarcity, dearth
shortage, deficiency
shortcoming, deficiency

Requirement

absence, lack, want
deficit, deficiency
desideratum, something needed
inadequacy, wantage
incompetence, insufficiency
insufficiency, inadequacy
lack, want
needfulness, necessity
requirement, exigency
requisiteness, necessity
requisition, requirement
wantage, deficiency

Necessity

crisis, pressing need
destiny, inevitable necessity
emergency, necessity
essential, indispensability
essentiality, necessity
exigency, urgent need
indispensability, necessity
necessity, indigence
urgency, exigency

ESTEEM— FRIENDSHIP, Etc. see—	ASSOCIATIVE	
	Desire 39	Praise 63
vs. Dislike 28	Love 39A	Inquiry 41A
vs. Opposition 27	Passion 39B	Need 37
	Courtship 40	Tendency 2
	Endeavor 41C	Relish 51A
	Allurement 40A	Licentiousness 39B
	Appeal 40B	Caress 98C
	Demand 41B	Goodness 140A
	Contention 41D	Brag—Bluster 76

38

VERBS

Appreciate

admire, esteem
adore, cherish
appreciate, esteem
cherish, esteem
dote, adore
esteem, prize
glorify, worship
hallow, revere
harbor, cherish
honor, esteem
(B). honour
idolize, adore
like, esteem
love, cherish
prize, esteem
regard, esteem
respect, be deferential
revere, respect
reverence, worship
treasure, harbor
value, esteem
venerate, worship
worship, revere

Befriend

acknowledge, honor
befriend, favor
embosom, cherish
endear, embosom
favor, befriend
(B). favour
hobnob, be friendly
ingratiate, court favor
recognize, acknowledge
remember, cherish
sympathize, condole
thank, be appreciative
welcome, befriend

Pursue

employ, exercise
exercise, pursue
frequent, use often
practice, pursue
pursue, practice
use, employ

ADJECTIVES

Appreciative

appreciative, noting esteem
appreciatory, appreciative
grateful, appreciative
honorary, having esteem

ADJECTIVES (Continued)

respectful, reverential
thankful, appreciative

Friendly

amicable, friendly
close, intimate
convivial, festive
cordial, sincere
deferential, respectful
endearing, loving
friendly, amiable
genial, cordial
hearty, cordial
ingratiating, courting
    favor
intimate, close
near, intimate
neighborly, friendly
obsequious, ingratiating
salutory, cordial
sincere, cordial

Agreeable

affectionate, loving
agreeable, cordial
amateur, in devoted pursuit
amiable, affectionate
attentive, regardful
dear, loving
familiar, affable
fond, ardent
good, kind
goody, weakly devoted
gentle, agreeable
kind, friendly
lovable, loving
lovely, attentive
loving, affectionate
philharmonic, fond of
    harmony
tender, loving

Polite

affable, friendly
bland, affable
Chesterfieldian, suave
chivalrous, courteous
civil, complaisant
complacent, affable
complaisant, courteous
courteous, polite
debonair, suave
gallant, chivalrous
gracious, affable
knightly, chivalrous

ADJECTIVES (Continued)

mannerly, polite
polite, mannerly
suave, gracious
urbane, polite

Humane

benevolent, kind
charitable, benevolent
humane, benevolent
magnanimous, benevolent
philanthropic, humane
sympathetic, compassionate

Devoted

assiduous, devoted
constant, devoted
devoted, loving
dilettante, devoted to art
faithful, loyal
fast, faithful
firm, stanch
leal, true-hearted
loyal, faithful
patriotic, loyal
stanch, faithful
staunch, stanch
steadfast, loyal
true, loyal

Worshipful

devotional, religious
devout, heartfelt
idolatrous, worshipful
pious, reverential
religious, pious
reverend, reverential
reverent, respectful
reverential, worshipful
worshipful, religious

Egotistic

arrogant, proud
conceited, vain
egotistic, conceited
overweening, conceited
proud, vain
vain, conceited
vainglorious, vain

NOUNS

Appreciation

acknowledgment, gratitude
appreciation, gratitude
attention, regard
deference, regard
(Continued on page 63)

NOUNS (Continued)

esteem, respect
gratitude, appreciation
honor, esteem
(B). honour
regard, esteem
respect, regard
reverence, deep respect
service, professed respect
thanks, acknowledgment
thanksgiving, gratitude
valuation, esteem
veneration, deep regard

Friendship

benevolence, kindness
charity, benevolence
compassion, sympathy
conviviality, fellowship
favor, kindness
(B). favour
fellowship, friendship
friendliness, kindness
friendship, friendliness
goodwill, friendliness
grace, kindness
graciousness, grace
kindness, friendliness
neighborliness, friendliness
philanthropy, benevolence
reception, welcome
sympathy, compassion
sincerity, friendliness
welcome, friendliness

Admiration

admiration, adoration
adoration, love
affection, love
amiability, lovableness
amity, love
attachment, affection
eclat, admiration
endearment, affection
fancy, liking
fondness, liking
hero-worship, love for
 heroes
infatuation, foolish passion
intimacy, attachment
liking, fondness
love, adoration
philoprogenitiveness, in-
 stinctive love for off-
 spring
shine, fancy for a person

Pursuit

addiction, habit
custom, practice
dilettanteism, devotion to
 the fine arts
employment, use
habit, pursuit
Hellenism, Grecian love and
 culture of art
idealism, quest of the ideal

NOUNS (Continued)

ideality, devotion to ideals
practice, employment
profession, pursuit
pursuit, practice
use, practice
utopianism, idealism
vice, addiction

Preference

bent, disposition, bias
bias, prejudice
favoritism, preference
(B). favouritism
obsession, prejudice
partiality, prejudice
penchant, inclination
predilection, partiality
predisposition, partiality
prejudice, bias
preference, partiality
preferment, preference
propensity, preferment

Agreeableness, Etc.

affability, complaisance
amenity, gentleness
chivalry, knightliness
civility, courtesy
comity, politeness
complacence, complaisance
complaisance, politeness
cordiality, heartiness
courtesy, politeness
empressement, animated
 cordiality
gallantry, chivalry
geniality, cordiality
heartiness, cordiality
obsequiousness, complai-
 sance
politeness, courtesy
politesse, overacted politeness
suavity, pleasant manner
urbanity, politeness

Loyalty

Chauvinism, extravagant
 patriotism
fealty, loyalty
loyalty, patriotism
patriotism, loyalty
sans-culottism, loyalty to
 republicanism
sectionalism, loyalty to a
 section

Worship

cult, religious devotion
devotion, religious zeal
hyperdulla, worship given
 the Virgin Mary as the
 highest of saints
dulia, veneration given
 saints and angels
idolatry, idol worship
piety, religious devoutness

NOUNS (Continued)

religion, devotion to God
reverence, worship
sectarianism, devotion to
 sect
worship, religious reverence

Egotism

arrogance, excessive pride
complacence, self-approval
conceit, vanity
confidence, faith
crest, pride
ego, inherent affinity
egoism, self-interest
egotism, self-esteem
pride, self-esteem
rest, confidence
trust, faith
vainglory, pride
vanity, pride

PERSONS

Devotee

addict, votary
adherent, votary
amateur, devotee
devotee, one devoted
dilettante, amateur
enthusiast, votary
esthete, a votary of art
(B). aesthete
esthetician, esthete
(B). aesthetician
fan, enthusiast
fanatic, zealot
fancier, amateur
follower, adherent
habitue, votary
idealist, esthete
votary, devotee
zealot, devotee

Friend, Etc.

friend, one who is friendly
loyalist, patriot
patriot, one devoted to his
 country
philanthropist, a lover of
 mankind
sectarian, adherent to sect

Miscellaneous

bibliolater, book worshiper
bibliomaniac, one who has
 a mania for rare books
bibliopege, lover of bindings
bibliophile, lover of books
dipsomaniac, a craver for
 alcohol
Zoophile, lover of animals

Gallant

cavalier, gallant
Chesterfield, gallant
gallant, cavalier
(Continued on page 67)

DESIRE—		ASSOCIATIVE	
EXPECTATION,	Need 37	Allurement 40A
Etc. see—	Tendency 2	Appeal 40B
	Liking 38	Demand 41B
vs. Opposition 27	Friendliness 38	Contention 41D
vs. Dislike 28	Love 39A	Search 119E
vs. Neglect 126B	Passion 39B	Inquiry 41A
	Endeavor 41C	Relish 51A
	Courtship 40	Licentiousness 39B

39
VERBS

Miscellaneous

abide, await
affect, have liking
aim, have design
allure, attract
anticipate, expect
apprehend, expect
aspire, desire
attract, allure
await, expect
begrudge, envy
burn, desire ardently
care, be anxious
champ, be impatient
choose, prefer
concern, have interest
covet, desire
crave, yearn
cultivate, cherish deeply
decide, choose
desiderate, desire
desire, crave
drive, aim
enthuse, be zealous
envy, grudge
expect, anticipate
fain, wish gladly
fancy, like strongly
fidget, be anxious
flame, burn
flare, flame
gape, be in open-mouthed
  expectation
gasp, desire with eager
  expression
grudge, envy
hanker, crave
hark, listen eagerly
hope, wish
hover, linger expectantly
hunger, desire
interest, attract
itch, crave
languish, be wistful
long, desire
pant, crave
persevere, ply
pine, languish
ply, persist in want
rage, be violently eager
resolve, determine
thirst, crave
wait, expect

VERBS (Continued)

want, desire
wish, hope
wonder, gape
worry, be anxious
yearn, crave

ADJECTIVES
Desirous

aspiring, desirous
athirst, thirsty
craving, eager
desirous, wishful
eager, anxious
fain, joyously eager
hankering, craving
hungry, having hunger
lackadaisical, affectedly
  sentimental
longing, earnest
solicitous, eager
thirsty, feverish

Passionate

frantic, rageful
impatient, eager
impetuous, vehement
passionate, ardent
rabid, rageful
rageful, vehement
raging, rageful
ravenous, rageful
restless, impatient
wolfish, ravenous

Vehement

ablaze, eager
ardent, eager
fervent, earnest
fervid, eager
feverish, vehement
fiery, vehement
flaming, flaring
flaring, excitedly eager
hot, ardent
impassioned, ardent
intense, ardent
mawkish, sentimental
sentimental, impassioned
tense, eager
vehement, passionate
warm, fervid

Earnest

determined, resolved
earnest, eager
resolved, resolute
serious, earnest
sincere, serious

ADJECTIVES (Continued)
Diligent

assiduous, steadfast
busy, assiduous
constant, assiduous
diligent, assiduous
indefatigable, diligent
industrious, diligent
persevering, assiduous
persistent, persevering
pertinacious, persistent
purposeful, assiduous
pushing, enterprising
resolute, determined
sedulous, diligent
steadfast, persevering
steady, assiduous
unflagging, sedulous
unwavering, unflagging

Enterprising

adventurous, ambitious
ambitious, zealous
energetic, enterprising
enterprising, adventurous
strenuous, energetic

Enthusiastic

enthusiastic, zealous
fanatical, zealous
soulful, fervent
stanch, zealous
zealous, ardent

Maniacal

dipsomaniacal, raging for
  alcohol
homesick, nostalgic
jealous, envious
nostalgic, longing for home

Acquisitive

acquisitive, grasping
avaricious, grasping
covetous, avaricious
envious, coveting
grasping, avaricious
greedy, grasping
grudging, envious
insatiable, avaricious
miserly, covetous
niggardly, miserly
parsimonious, penurious
penurious, miserly
selfish, niggardly
sordid, avaricious
worldly, selfish

Concerned

anxious, earnest
(Continued on page 65)

39 (Continued)

ADJECTIVES (Continued)

careful, anxious
concerned, careful
interested, concerned
uneasy, anxious
worried, anxious

Expectant

agog, expectant
alert, eager
confident, expectant
curious, agog
expectant, anxious
hopeful, wishful
optimistic, hopeful
prospective, expectant
sanguine, confident
wishful, hopeful
wistful, longing

Volitional

anticipative, expectant
desiderative, desiring
optative, having desire
optional, noting choice
volitional, optional
volitive, volitional

Affinitive

affinitive, drawing
attractive, drawing
conative, reciprocally
  attractive
magnetic, attractive
suant, seeking after

NOUNS

Desire

alertness, eagerness
appetite, hunger
aspiration, desire
craving, longing
desire, aspiration
eagerness, anxiousness
hankering, a longing
hunger, ardent desire
longing, desire
thirst, eagerness
want, desire
wish, hope

Passion

impatience, eagerness
itch, teasing desire
passion, rage
penchant, strong liking
rage, passion

Vehemence

ardency, zeal
fire, ardor
fieriness, fervency
flare, ardor
heat, ardor
intensity, eagerness
vehemence, ardency
warmth, passion

Earnestness

determination, resolution
earnestness, ardor

NOUNS (Continued)

resoluteness, determination
resolution, determination
seriousness, ardor
sincerity, earnestness

Diligence

application, assiduity
assiduity, diligence
constancy, assiduity
diligence, assiduity
perseverence, assiduity
persistence, assiduity
pertinacity, resoluteness
sedulity, assiduity

Enterprise

aim, aspiration
ambition, aspiration
enterprise, ambition
motive, purpose
purpose, resolution
undertaking, enterprise
wanderlust, love for travel

Enthusiasm

ardor, ardency
(B). ardour
elan, ardor
enthusiasm, zealousness
fanaticism, wild enthusiasm
fervor, eagerness
spirit, ardor
verve, enthusiasm
zeal, ardency

Mania

bibliomania, mania for rare
  books
craze, passing infatuation
dipsomania, craving for
  drink
homesickness, nostalgia
mania, inordinate desire
nostalgia, homesickness
xenomania, mania for for-
  eign persons or things
zoophily, a love for animals

Acquisitiveness

acquisitiveness, greed
avarice, greed
avidity, eagerness
covetousness, avarice
cupidity, inordinate desire
envy, grudging
greed, selfish desire
greediness, greed
insatiability, avarice
miserliness, avarice
niggardliness, miserliness
parsimony, niggardliness
penury, miserliness
stinginess, niggardliness
worldliness, temporal want

Concern

anxiety, concern
care, anxiety
concern, care
interest, concern

NOUNS (Continued)

jealousy, suspicious anxiety
suspense, anxiety
tension, suspense
uneasiness, anxiety
worry, anxiety

Expectation

confidence, optimism
curiosity, inordinate prying
expectancy, expectation
expectation, anticipation
hope, wish
optimism, hopefulness
prospect, expectation

Volition

affection, fondness
anticipation, hope
desiderata, pl. for desideratum
desideratum, general desire
fancy, strong liking
option, rightful
partiality, particular
  liking
volition, optative choice

Affinity

affinity, attraction
alimentiveness, affinity for
  food
attraction, affinity
conation, reciprocal
  affinity
gravitation, attractive
  force
gravity, attraction
magnetism, attraction

Solicitude

sentiment, tenderness
solicitude, anxiety
tenderness, solicitousness

PERSONS

Votary

addict, devotee to a
  practice
adherent, votary
amateur, devotee
devotee, enthusiast
dilettante, amateur
enthusiast, zealot
esthete, votary of art
(B). aesthete
esthetician, esthete
fan, enthusiast
fanatic, zealot
fancier, amateur
follower, adherent
habitue, votary
idealist, esthete
proponent, adherent
votary, one devoted to a
  pursuit
zealot, adherent
(Continued on page 67)

LOVE—SEXUAL AFFECTION

LOVE—SEXUAL AFFECTION	see—	ASSOCIATIVE			
		Liking—Esteem 38	Appeal 40B		
		Desire 39	Caress 98C		
vs. Dislike—Hatred 28		Passion 39B	Allurement 40A		
vs. Anger—Wrath ..29		Courtship 40	Licentiousness 39B		

39A

VERBS

adore, love intensely
bear, cherish
burn, flame with ardor
cherish, regard as dear
foster, cherish
glow, burn with passion
love, have strong affection
spoon, make love

ADJECTIVES

affectional, affectionate
affectionate, loving
amative, full of love
amatorial, amatory
amatory, noting love
amorous, amative
assiduous, devoted
erotic, amorous
fond, affectionate
idolatrous, over-fond
lovelorn, love-sick
love-sick, lovelorn
loving, affectionate

ADJECTIVES (Continued)

moony, sentimental
sentimental, erotic
soulful, amative
spoony, making love
tender, loving
uxorious, excessively fond of one's wife

NOUNS

adherence, attachment
adoration, ardent love
affection, love
amativeness, affection
attachment, affection
bosom, love
devotion, ardent love
dotage, excessive love
eroticism, sexual love
glow, passion
heat, affection
idolatry, excessive love
love, affection
passion, intense love

PERSONS

admirer, lover
beau, suitor
cavalier, beau
Cupid, god of love
dotard, foolish admirer
flame, sweetheart
gallant, beau
inamorata, sweetheart (f)
inamorato, lover (male)
lover, inamorato
masher, inamorato
mistress, sweetheart
spark, beau
suitor, lover
swain, a rustic lover
sweetheart, lover
valentine, sweetheart

BEINGS

Cupid, god of love
Erato, muse of love
Eros, Greek Cupid
Kama, Hindu Cupid
Venus, goddess of love

39B

SEXUAL PASSION—LUST	see—	ASSOCIATIVE		
		Desire 39	Caress 98C	
vs. Dislike—Hatred 28		Love 39A	Allurement 40A	
		Courtship 40	Licentiousness 39B	

39B

VERBS

chafe, lust
covet, desire
desire, lust after
gloat, stare lustfully
lust, desire sexual pleasure
ogle, look admiringly

ADJECTIVES

carnal, lustful
concupiscent, lustful
covetous, lustful
erotic, sexually passionate
fiery, passionate
hot, passionate
impulsive, vehement
incestuous, lascivious
lascivious, lustful
lecherous, lustful
libidinous, lustful
licentious, wanton
lustful, sensuous
meretricious, lustful

ADJECTIVES (Continued)

passionate, sensual
prurient, lascivious
ruttish, libidinous
salacious, lecherous
sensual, carnal
sensuous, passionate
wanton, lustful
warm, passionate
vehement, passionate

NOUNS

affinity, sex attraction
amativeness, sexual desire
ardor, passion
(B). ardour
bosom, the passions
carnalism, lustfulness
concupiscence, lechery
concupiscibleness, lechery
covetousness, lust
cupidity, lust

NOUNS (Continued)

desire, passion
eroticism, sexual love
erotomania, morbid lust
emotion, passion
flame, passion
honeymoon, first period of marriage
incest, sexual relations between relatives
infatuation, fatuous lust
lasciviousness, lust
lechery, lust
lust, sexual passion
motion, passion
passion, intense desire
prurience, itching passion
pruriency, prurience
rut, desire of animals
salaciousness, lust
salacity, lustfulness

PERSONS (See 146D, 39C)

SEXUAL INTERCOURSE—		ASSOCIATIVE	
SENSUALITY see—	Lust 39B	Incontinence 125C	
	Love 39A	Allurement 40A	
vs. Dislike—Hatred 28	Desire 39	Caress 98C	
vs. Weakness—Debility 128A	Courtship 40	Licentiousness 39B	

39C

VERBS

debauch, indulge carnally
fornicate, have illicit sex
  relations
prostitute, debauch
ravish, fornicate against a
  woman's will
sensualize, debauch
whore, prostitute

ADJECTIVES

bawdy, unchaste
bestial, sensual
carnal, sensual
cyprian, licentious
dissolute, licentious
goatish, sensual
holden, dissolute
immodest, unchaste
immoral, dissolute
incontinent, wanton
indelicate, unchaste
lascivious, lewd
lewd, licentious
libertine, licentious
licentious, dissolute
lydian, sensuous
profligate, dissolute
ribald, profligate
sensual, lewd
sensuous, voluptuous
unchaste, wanton
unreserved, dissolute

ADJECTIVES (Continued)

unrestrained, wanton
voluptuary, licentious
wanton, licentious

NOUNS

amour, illicit love
bawdiness, lewdness
bawdy, bawdiness
carnalism, sensuality
debauchery, licentiousness
eroticism, sexual sensuality
fornication, illegal sexual
  intercourse
free-love, licentiousness
harlotry, whoredom
immorality, lewdness
idolatry, whoredom
incontinence, amour
indelicacy, lewdness
liaison, secret amour
libertinism, debauchery
lewdness, profligacy
lubricity, sensuality
profligacy, debauchery
prostitution, whoredom
ravishment, illegal sexual
  gratification
seduction, foul carnalism
sensuality, gratification of
  lust
venery, sexual indulgence
whoredom, prostitution

PERSONS

adulterer, one who violates
  the marriage bed (male)
adultress, a woman who
  violates the marriage bed
bawd, prostitute
carnalist, sensualist
courtezan, prostitute
cyprian, courtezan
debauchee, sensualist
Don Juan, libertine
fornicator, sensualist
harlot, prostitute
hussy, jade
incontinent, sensualist
jade, unchaste woman
lecher, a lewd man
libertine, debauchee
lorette, a woman of the
  demi-monde
Lothario, libertine
paramour, illicit lover
profligate, carnalist
prostitute, whore
quean, prostitute
rake, debauchee
ribald, libertine
roué, fashionable sensualist
sensualist, profligate
strumpet, prostitute
trollop, strumpet
voluptuary, sensualist
wastrel, profligate
whore, prostitute

---

38 (Continued)

PERSONS (Continued)

Egoist
egoist, egotist
egotist, a vain person
ego-maniac, egoist

PERSONS (Continued)

Worshiper
idolator, idol worshiper
idolatress, as above (fem.)
worshiper, votary

BEING

Eloes, Norse fairies who
  symbolized friendliness

---

39 (Continued)

PERSONS (Continued)

Desiderator
adventurer, one who seeks
  social distinction
aspirant, one who aspires
candidate, aspirant
desiderator, desirer

PERSONS (Continued)

optimist, one who is habitually hopeful
prospector, one engaged in
  exploring for minerals
Miser
curmudgeon, miser

PERSONS (Continued)

miser, niggard
niggard, skinflint
skinflint, miser
BEING
Mammon, god of desire for
  wealth

40

VERBS

Court
court, woo
solicit, court
sue, court
woo, court

Gallivant
coquet, flirt
flirt, coquet
gallivant, flirt
philander, gallivant

Spoon
coo, spoon
fawn, spoon
mash, enamor
spoon, court

Seduce
flatter, flirt
gallant, court
seduce, court the passions
vamp, enamor

Captivate
captivate, charm
charm, fascinate
enamor, captivate
(B). enamour
enrapture, charm
fascinate, charm
infatuate, enrapture

ADJECTIVES
bawdy, seductive

ADJECTIVES (Continued)
bewitching, charming
captivating, fascinating
charming, fascinating
coquette, coquettish
coquettish, flirtatious
epigamic, relating to animal
  methods in obtaining
  mates during the pairing
  season
fascinating, charming
fawning, wooing
flirtatious, coquettish
seductive, coquettish
siren, bewitching
wooing, courting

NOUNS

address, a lover's attention
adulation, interested praise
allurement, captivation
bewitchment, allurement
captivation, bewitchment
charm, fascination
coquetry, flirtation
courtship, wooing
fascination, bewitchment
fawning, adulation
flattery, adulation
flirtation, coquetry
flirting, flirtation

NOUNS (Continued)
gyneolatry, excessive
  homage to women
gallantry, chivalrousness
love, courtship
love-making, courtship
seduction, foul allurement
  to carnalism
seductiveness, allurement
suit, courtship
wooing, courtship

PERSONS

coquette, flirt
courtier, wooer
Delilah, Philistine vamp
flapper, flirt
flirt, coquette
fizgig, flapper
fortune-hunter, one who
  seeks fortune through
  marriage
gallant, courtier
grisette, coquette
libertine, paramour
Lothario, libertine
lover, suitor
paramour, seducer
seducer, Lothario
siren, vamp
suitor, lover
vamp, an alluring person
wooer, courtier

40B (Continued)

PERSONS
advocate, barrister
advocator, advocate
apologist, one who asks excuse
appellant, one who appeals
applicant, one who applies
attorney, advocate
barker, touter
barrister, attorney
beggar, mendicant
candidate, a solicitor for
  votes
canvasser, solicitor

PERSONS (Continued)
conjuror, one who conjures
dervish, a beggar monk
lawyer, barrister
lobbyist, one who solicits
  legislative votes
mendicant, beggar
mumper, beggar
pettifogger, a petty lawyer
plaintiff, petitioner
touter, solicitor
solicitor, canvasser
suppliant, one who suppli-
  cates

PERSONS (Continued)
supplicant, petitioner
worshiper, suppliant

EXCLAMATIONS
help, cry for succor
peccavi, prithee
prithee, corruption of I
  pray thee
S. O. S., wireless call for
  help

ADVERB
why? for what cause

TEMPTATION—
    PERSUASION see—⎧ Courtship 40
                       ⎨ Appeal 40B
    vs. Threat—Menace..33 ⎩ Promise 89

ASSOCIATIVE
Praise 63
Friendliness 38
Beauty 108

40 A

VERBS

Tempt
abduce, persuade
allure, entice
attract, allure
bait, tempt
coax, cajole
cozen, entice
crimp, decoy
decoy, allure
dissuade, persuade
draw, allure
elicit, induce
entice, beguile
inveigle, allure
lure, entice
reason, persuade
seduce, entice
tantalize, deceptively offer
tempt, allure
wile, entice

Persuade
ask, invite
call, invite
importune, solicit
invite, solicit
obtrude, importune
persuade, induce
solicit, invite
summon, invite

Offer
bid, offer
bribe, offer a bribe
challenge, invite
induce, offer
offer, tempt
proffer, tender
propose, offer
tender, offer
underbid, offer less
volunteer, offer service

Beguile
blandish, entice
beguile, allure
cajole, beguile
flatter, cajole
wheedle, cajole

Charm
bewitch, charm
captivate, charm
charm, allure
fascinate, charm

ADJECTIVES

Charming
alluring, tempting

ADJECTIVES (Continued)

attractive, inviting
bewitching, charming
charming, alluring
enchanting, charming
engaging, engrossing
engrossing, absorbing
entrancing, enchanting
fascinating, charming
glamorous, bewitching
lovely, inviting
ravishing, entrancing
seductive, enticing
siren, bewitching
vivacious, entrancing

Miscellaneous
absorbing, engrossing
affable, inviting
bland, affable
dissuasive, persuading
  against
enticing, alluring
flattering, cajoling
importunate, soliciting insistently
interesting, engaging
inviting, tempting
meretricious, artfully attractive
obtrusive, importunate
opportune, inviting
persuasive, alluring
pleasing, charming
promising, tempting
propositional, proposing
smooth, bland
suasive, persuasive
tantalizing, alluring and
  disappointing
tempting, alluring
voluntary, offering a service
wheedling, cajoling

NOUNS

Temptation
allurement, enticement
attraction, allurement
bait, tempting offer
decoy, enticement
enticement, temptation
ignis-fatuus, hollow attraction
incentive, enticement
lure, enticement
seducement, seduction
seduction, enticement

NOUNS (Continued)

seductiveness, fascination
temptation, enticement
tantalization, a disappointing offer

Persuasion
call, invitation
invitation, offer
persuasion, a coaxing
persuasiveness, persuasion
solicitation, invitation
suasion, persuasion

Offer
advance, overture
advantage, opportunity
bid, offer
bidding, offers
bribery, bribing offer
challenge, invitation
inducement, allurement
offer, invitation
offering, proffer
opportunity, promise
overture, proposal
proffer, offer
promise, inducement
proposal, offer
proposition, proposal
ultimatum, final offer

Beguilement
beguilement, allurement
blandishment, winning artifice
blarney, wheedling speech
buncombe, suasive speech
cajolery, flattery
flattery, beguilement
sugar, flattering bait

Charm
bewitchery, charm
captivation, charm
charm, allurement
fascination, bewitchment
glamour, fascination

PERSONS

crimp, one who decoys men
  into naval service
seducer, one who seduces
siren, seductress
tempter, seducer
volunteer, one who offers
  service, etc.

BEING

Tantalus, god of disap-
  pointing promisers

40B
VERBS

Appeal
adjure, appeal
apologize, ask pardon
appeal, entreat
beg, implore
beseech, beg
bless, invoke blessing
call, appeal
conjure, appeal
crave, ask humbly
entreat, beseech
impetrate, appeal
implore, entreat
induce, persuade
intercede, plead for
invoke, pray
obsecrate, implore
palaver, coax
persuade, entreat
petition, ask
plead, implore
postulate, entreat
pray, petition
sue, beg
supplicate, beseech

Solicit
apply, petition
ask, request
bespeak, ask in advance
curry, ask with flattery
evoke, call forth
exhort, incite by appeal
halloo, call
invite, ask
request, ask
solicit, entreat
tout, solicit

Bleat
bleat, plead
cant, plead whiningly
cry, lament imploringly
mump, cant
pule, mump
repine, pule
snivel, pule
whimper, pule
whine, pule

Importune
crowd, importune
dun, importune
importune, solicit unduly
ply, solicit regularly

Canvass
campaign, canvass

VERBS (Continued)
canvass, solicit
electioneer, canvass
lobby, solicit legislatures
stump, campaign

Imprecate
beshrew, call a curse upon
imprecate, beshrew

ADJECTIVES
Miscellaneous
affable, inviting
appealing, solicitous
appellate, noting appeal
appellatory, appellate
apologetic, asking pardon
beggarly, suppliant
beseeching, imploring
canting, suppliant
convocational, calling together
craven, beggarly
entreating, beseeching
impetrative, noting prayer
  for personal good
imploring, beseeching
importunate, noting urgent
  solicitation
importune, importunate
imprecatory, praying evil
  upon
incantatory, chanting
  prayer
inviting, affable
liturgic, praying in customary form
mendicant, begging
persuasive, inviting
petitionary, prayerful
plaintive, suppliant
pleading, petitionary
prayerful, beseeching
pressing, importunate
puling, plaintive
recreant, begging mercy
solicitous, persuasive
soulful, prayerful
suppliant, beseeching
supplicatory, prayerful

NOUNS
Appeal
advocacy, appeal
apology, request for pardon
appeal, entreaty
appellation, appeal
conjuration, incantation
entreaty, appeal

NOUNS (Continued)
excuse, apology
impetration, entreaty
intercession, prayer
invocation, prayer
obsecration, entreaty
outcry, clamor
persuasion, entreaty
petition, prayer
plea, supplication
supplication, entreaty

Solicitation
application, petition
blarney, wheedling
calling, invitation
invitation, request
palaver, a wheedling
recourse, plea for help
request, invitation
solicitation, application
suit, petition

Lamentation
bewailment, lamentation
cant, a whining appeal
jeremiad, lamentation
lamentation, appeal
plaint, lamentation
wail, lamentation

Importunity
dun, importunate request
importunity, solicitation
mendicancy, beggary

Canvass
campaign, political canvass
candidature, campaign
canvass, solicitation
electioneering, a canvassing
  for votes

Imprecation
imprecation, a praying evil
  upon

Prayer
angelus, a devotion
benediction, invocation
blessing, invocation
collect, a short prayer
deprecation, petition of delivery from evil
incantation, conjuration
litany, a form of prayer
liturgy, as above
paternoster, Lord's prayer
prayer, entreaty
rogation, litany
worship, devotional prayer
(Continued on page 68)

QUESTION—INQUIRY

vs. Indifference—Negligence 126B

41A, 41B
see—

ASSOCIATIVE

Appeal—Request 40B
Demand 41B
Search—Inspection 119E

41A

VERBS

ask, interrogate
bombard, fire questions
confer, consult
consult, ask advice
derogate, weaken by questioning
examine, question
heckle, ask teasingly
inquire, ask
interpellate, seek through questioning
interrogate, question
interview, question
ply, question earnestly
probe, inquire deeply
propound, put a question for solution
pry, probe
pump, question artfully
question, inquire
quiz, pry

ADJECTIVES

curious, inquisitive
derogatory, weakening tes-

ADJECTIVES (Continued)

timony by questioning
inquisitive, prying
inquisitorial, inquisitive
interrogative, questioning
interrogatory, inquiring
prying, curious

NOUNS

conference, consultation
consultation, a seeking advice
cross-examination, a re-questioning in court
cross-question, a questioning again
counsel, consultation
curiosity, inquisitiveness
derogation, a weakening of testimony by questioning
disquisition, interview
examination, inquisition
inquest, inquisition
inquiry, question
inquisition, judicial inquiry

NOUNS (Continued)

inquisitiveness, curiosity
interrogation, inquiry
interrogative, a word used in asking a question
interview, disquisition
problem, a question for solution
quest, inquiry
query, question
question, inquiry
questionary, a series of questions
questionnaire, questionary
trial, judicial examination

PERSONS

council, an assembly in consultation
inquisitor, questioner
prier, quidnunc
questioner, inquisitor
querist, questioner
quidnunc, inquisitive questioner

DEMAND—SUMMONS see—

vs. Cowardice—Fear......32

41B

ASSOCIATIVE

Question—Inquiry 41A
Courtship 40
Allurement 40A
Search—Inspection 119E

Seizure—Capture 49C
Robbery—Piracy 49G
Conquest 50

41B

VERBS

Demand

charge, demand
demand, exact
exact, demand
press, postulate
require, exact

Summon

arraign, summon
call, summon
cite, summon
challenge, call from sentry
command, summon
convoke, summon
hail, call loudly
summon, call

Claim

arrogate, demand
assume, claim
claim, demand
postulate, demand

Expostulate

expostulate, insist against

VERBS (Continued)

haggle, claim
higgle, haggle
importune, expostulate
insist, press or demand
litigate, demand by law
palter, haggle
remonstrate, expostulate
sue, litigate
urge, demand

Vociferate

clamor, demand
(B). clamour
encore, call for repetition
run, demand in concert
vociferate, clamor
wrangle, vociferate

Amerce

amerce, demand a fine
fine, charge
mulct, fine

Recall

recall, call back

VERBS (Continued)

reclaim, recall
revoke, recall

ADJECTIVES

Miscellaneous

arrogant, assuming exorbitant claims
clamorous, urgent
crying, clamoring
demagogic, expostulatory
exacting, demanding
exigent, urgent
expostulatory, urging insistently
insistent, exacting
importunate, urgent
litigant, litigious
litigious, noting demand through litigation
obstreperous, clamorous
remonstrant, expostulatory
(Continued on page 72)

ADJECTIVES (Continued)
requisite, exigent
revocable, that which calls
  or may be called back
seditious, remonstrant
urgent, insistent
vociferous, clamorous

NOUNS

Demand
demand, requisition
exaction, demand
exigency, pressing demand
pressure, demand
requirement, demand
requisition, requirement

Summon
arraignment, summons
call, summons
calling, convocation
challenge, a summons
citation, summons
command, demand
convocation, summons
hail, a call

NOUNS (Continued)
summons, authoritative
  call

Claim
arrogance, undue claim
claim, demand
postulate, a claim

Expostulation
expostulation, remonstrance
importunity, urgency
insistence, exaction
litigation, legal demand
remonstrance, expostula-
  tion
urgency, importunity

Outcry
battle cry, slogan
clamor, vociferation
(B). clamour
encore, call for repetition
hue, clamor
hue and cry, early method
  of pursuing a criminal

NOUNS (Continued)
outcry, clamor
rappel, battle call of a
  drum
run, concerted demand
slogan, a rallying cry
vociferation, clamor
war cry, summons to battle
wrangle, noisy demand

Recall
recall, revocation
revocation, a recalling

PERSONS
claimant, one who claims
demagogue, unprincipled
  politician
remonstrant, one who urges
  against
suffragette, a woman who
  demands the right to vote
wrangler, remonstrant

41C

41C
VERBS

Endeavor
aim, attempt
attempt, endeavor
endeavor, attempt
(B). endeavour
essay, endeavor
experiment, try by test
try, endeavor

Undertake
hazard, attempt
launch, venture
undertake, attempt
venture, undertake

Pursue
chase, pursue
emulate, strive to excel
hound, chase
launch, venture
prosecute, pursue
pursue, chase
seek, endeavor
stalk, pursue steadily

Struggle
clamber, seek a height
flounder, strive
gasp, try for breath
grapple, struggle
pull, struggle
retch, try at vomiting

VERBS (Continued)
scramble, endeavor con-
  fusedly
struggle, strive
toil, struggle

Strain
endeavor, strive
exert, strive
spurt, strive briefly
strain, strive
strive, endeavor
tug, pull

ADJECTIVES

Miscellaneous
assiduous, steady in pur-
  suit
conative, attempting to-
  gether
empiric, experimental
emulous, trying to excel
energetic, assiduous
experimental, trying by
  test
hazardous, trying through
  risk
intent, eager in pursuit
iterative, attempting again
intense, straining
pursuant, intent
sedulous, assiduous

ADJECTIVES (Continued)
struggling, sedulous
tentative, experimental
venturesome, empiric

NOUNS

Miscellaneous
aim, attempt
assiduity, diligence in pursuit
attempt, effort
chase, pursuit
conation, concerted effort
dead-lift, discouraging
  effort
diligence, assiduity
effort, endeavor
endeavor, attempt
essay, trial
exertion, strain
experiment, trial through
  test
gasp, effort to breathe
heft, effort
industrialism, constant
  pursuit
industry, diligent pursuit
pain, diligent effort
project, a scheme projected
  with hope of success
(Continued on page 75)

CONTENTION—
COMPETITION   see—
vs. Cowardice—Fear ..32
vs. Submission 46B

ASSOCIATIVE
Desire 39
Effort—Endeavor 41C
Search 119E
Courtship 40
Allurement 40A
Inquiry 41A

41D
VERBS

Contest
campaign, contend
compete, contest
contend, contest
contest, compete
cope, contend
pit, set in competition
plump, cast single vote
rival, contend against
vie, rival

Race, Box, Etc.
box, spar
duel, contend with arms
gamble, compete for money
joust, cope in mock combat
litigate, contend
race, run
run, contend in a race
spar, to box

Wager
bet, wager
lay, wager
stake, wager
wager, contend by betting

Encounter
antagonize, contend
  against
encounter, conflict
engage, encounter
grapple, contend

Combat
battle, fight
beleaguer, surround a force
combat, fight
conflict, battle
crusade, combat
fight, combat
militate, conflict
rencounter—rencontre,
  meet suddenly
skirmish, fight slightly
wage, contend in warfare

Pursue
angle, engage with a hook
chase, pursue
fish, angle
hunt, pursue
pursue, hunt
sniggle, fish
track, pursue footprints

Breast
buck, meet manfully
buffet, contend against
breast, buck
stem, breast
stickle, contend firmly

Scuffle
scuffle, fight

VERBS (Continued)
strive, contend
struggle, strive
tussle, struggle
wrestle, struggle

ADJECTIVES
Miscellaneous
antagonistic, militant
belligerent, antagonistic
combatant, antagonistic
combative, pugnacious
competitive, rival
conflicting, opponent
contentious, litigious
emulous, rivaling
gladitorial, litigious
litigious, contending
  legally
militant, warlike
opponent, rival
pugilistic, implying boxing
pugnacious, combative
vying, competing

NOUNS
Contest
bout, contest
campaign, political competition
competition, contest
contention, strife
contest, competition
emulation, competition
match, contest
rivalry, contest
tournament, contest

Race, Duel, Etc.
course, a race
duel, contest with arms
jiu-jitsu, Japanese system
  of wrestling
joust, mock combat
litigation, legal contest
mill, a prize-fight
prize-fight, boxing match
pugilism, fist-fighting
race, competition
regatta, rowing match
scratch race, open race
setto, boxing contest
spar, setto
tilt, contest with lances

Wager
bet, a wager
stake, a wager
sweepstake, entire stake
wager, a bet

Encounter
antagonism, contention

NOUNS (Continued)
encounter, conflict
engagement, encounter
recounter, rencontre
rencontre, hostile meeting

Combat
affray, fight
agnostics, combative
  science
altercation, contention
battle, fight
belligerence, warfare
combat, conflict
conflict, altercation
crusade, campaign
fight, conflict
militancy, warfare
skirmish, slight fight
war, warfare
warfare, conflict

Pursuit
chase, pursuit
hunt, pursuit of game
pursuit, chase

Scuffle
grapple, a close fight
scuffle, hand to hand fight
strife, contention
struggle, strife
wrestling, throwing contest

PERSONS
adversary, opponent
athlete, competitor
antagonist, foe
belligerent, combatant
candidate, political con-
  testant
competitor, opponent
contestant, competitor
dicer, gambler
emulator, competitor
foe, adversary
gambler, one who plays at
  games of chance
gladiator, deadly foe
hunter, one who pursues
  game
huntsman, hunter
litigant, legal contender
Mars, god of war
opponent, adversary
pack, dogs in concerted effort
pugilist, a boxer
racer, one who races
rival, opponent

(Continued on page 75)

BRAVERY—DARING   see—

vs. Cowardice—Fear......32

ASSOCIATIVE

Threat	33	Torture	130N
Opposition	27	Murder—Slaughter	130-O
Anger—Fury	29	Wickedness	130A
Robbery	49G	Military Force	36G
Conquest	50	Strength	137B
Brag	76	Goodness	140A
Attack	130F	Effort	41C
Cruelty	130M	Contention	41D

42

VERBS

Miscellaneous

adventure, hazard
affront, confront
brave, dare
breast, meet bravely
challenge, dare
cheek, face impudently
confront, face
dare, defy danger
defy, dare
determine, resolve
embark, venture
face, defy
hazard, venture
presume, be over-confident
resolve, be unwavering
risk, dare
sauce, be pert
venture, risk
wage, risk

ADJECTIVES

Brave

Amazonian, bold
aweless, brave
bold, brave
brave, courageous
courageous, brave
daring, bold
dauntless, fearless
defiant, daring
fearless, dauntless
intrepid, fearless

Plucky

gritty, intrepid
hardy, venturesome
manful, courageous
manly, courageous
mettlesome, daring
nervy, plucky
plucky, courageous
spunky, plucky

Heroic

chivalrous, courageous
epic, heroic
gallant, brave
heroic, courageous
high-spirited, chivalrous
lion-hearted, fearless
magnanimous, courageous
noble, valorous
splendid, heroic
valiant, heroic
valorous, intrepid

ADJECTIVES (Continued)

Doughty

bulldog, redoubtable
determined, resolute
doughty, valorous
formidable, valorous
headstrong, undaunted
indefeasible, indomitable
indomitable, resolute
invincible, indomitable
redoubtable, valiant
resolute, indomitable
strenuous, bold
tiger-like, fearless
undaunted, fearless
unfearing, fearless
unflinching, fearless

Confident

broad, bold
confident, bold
horrent, defiant
independent, confident
mannish, valorous
masculine, courageous
self-reliant, confident
stalwart, brave
stanch, valorous
stout, brave

Venturesome

adventuresome, bold
adventurous, daring
enterprising, venturesome
hazardous, venturesome
venturesome, daring

Reckless

dare-devil, reckless
desperate, reckless
forward, bold
foolhardy, reckless
hasty, reckless
headlong, reckless
heady, reckless
hotspur, dauntless
incautious, reckless
indiscreet, incautious
precipitate, reckless
precipitous, rash
rash, reckless
reckless, desperate
unwary, incautious

Audacious

audacious, bold
barefaced, impudent
brash, shameless (coloq.)
brazen, shameless

ADJECTIVES (Continued)

cheeky, impudent
immodest, shameless
impudent, bold
indelicate, immodest
pert, impudent
presumptuous, bold
saucy, impudent
shameless, bold
unabashed, shameless
unblushing, unabashed

NOUNS

Bravery

boldness, pluck
bravado, defiance
bravery, intrepidity
courage, valor
daring, bravery
defiance, daring
fearlessness, daring
intrepidity, boldness

Pluck

backbone, grit
crest, courage
grit, courage
grittiness, grit
heart, valor
mettle, courage
nerve, manliness
pluck, courage
sand, courage
spirit, courage
spunk, pluck

Heroism

chivalry, valor
gallantry, heroism
heroism, brilliant bravery
prowess, valor
valor, intrepidity
(B). valour
virtue, valor

Doughtiness

determination, resolution
doughtiness, valor
fortitude, courage
hardihood, boldness
resoluteness, fortitude
resolution, hardihood

Confidence

assurance, confidence
assuredness, confidence
confidence, boldness
face, confidence

(Continued on page 75)

NOUNS (Continued)
front, boldness
independence, confidence
manfulness, courage
manhood, heroism
manliness, bravery
morale, courage
reliance, confidence

Adventure
adventure, boldness
cartel, challenge
challenge, defiance
enterprise, boldness
exploit, a deed of heroism
hazard, daring
risk, hazard

Recklessness
desperation, recklessness
foolhardiness, daring
precipitation, daring
rashness, recklessness

NOUNS (Continued)
recklessness, foolhardiness
temerity, rash boldness

Audacity
affront, audacity
audacity, daring
cheek, impudence
effrontery, shamelessness
gall, impudence
impudence, cheek
presumption, audacity
sauciness, boldness
shamelessness, boldness

PERSONS
adventurer, knight-errant
Amazon, a fearless woman
blood, high-spirited man
brave, a blood
bravo, a daring villain
fire-eater, hotspur

PERSONS (Continued)
dare-devil, fire-eater
desperado, bravo
dreadnaught, dare-devil
gallant, hero
Hector, a blustering hero
hero, one noted for valor
heroine, same as hero
  (fem.)
hotspur, dare-devil
knight-errant, gallant
lion, dreadnaught
madcap, fire-eater
thunderbolt, dreadnaught

BEING
Ajax, Greek hero

SYMBOL
Gold Star, heroic military
  death

41C (Continued)

NOUNS (Continued)
prosecution, pursuit
pursuit, diligent effort
strain, exertion
struggle, endeavor
test, trial

NOUNS (Continued)
trial, attempt
tug, a pulling exertion
undertaking, attempt
venture, undertaking
yank, a tug

PERSONS
prosecutor
pursuer

41D (Continued)

PERSONS (Continued)
sportsman, one interested
  in sport, games, etc.
toreador, bullfighter
turfman, race follower
wrestler, a contestant

GAMES (Miscellaneous)
backgammon
badminton
baseball
basketball
chess
cricket
croquet
domino

(Continued)
football
game
golf
hockey
kotch
keno
leapfrog
lotto
ping-pong
polo
roly-poly
roulette
tennis

(Continued)
tournament
tug-of-war

CARD GAMES
bridge
casino
cribbage
euchre
hearts
nap
pinochle
poker
seven-up
solitaire
Etc., etc.

43

GIVE—TRANSFER

GIFT—GENEROSITY see—

vs. Hold—Keep 52A
vs. Desire—Envy 39

ASSOCIATIVE

Aid—Help 5A
Distribution 43B
Pay—Reward 45

Many—Much 147I
Fortune—Luck 134D
Unrestraint—Excess ..125C

43A

VERBS

Lavish

enrich, lavish
lavish, give freely
luxuriate, lavish
pour, lavish
shower, lavish

Contribute

appropriate, confer
contribute, donate
donate, contribute
subscribe, contribute

Benefit

benefit, bestow
dole, succor
favor, bestow
(B). favour
patronize, favor
share, give a part
spare, share
succor, benefit
(B). succour

Bequest, Etc.

amortize, convey
bequeath, will
convey, transfer
demise, will
devise, bequeath
dower, endow
endow, bestow
entail, leave inheritance
grant, confer
leave, will
transfer, grant
will, bequeath

Confer, Etc.

afford, yield
bestow, confer
confer, bestow
dispense, impart
give, confer
hand, present
impart, give
present, bestow
subsidize, aid financially
tip, give a tithe
yield, give

Volunteer

dedicate, set apart
devote, dedicate
offer, make sacrifice
sacrifice, offer
tender, offer
volunteer, tender

ADJECTIVES

Generous

freehanded, generous
generous, liberal

ADJECTIVES (Continued)

gracious, magnanimous
golden, rich
handsome, generous
lavish, extravagant
liberal, generous
magnanimous, unselfish
munificent, generous
open, free
princely, munificent
rich, lavish

Abounding

abounding, bounteous
bounteous, lavish
bountiful, generous
copious, lavish
profuse, lavish

Extravagant

extravagant, lavish
prodigal, extravagant
spendthrift, extravagant
wasteful, extravagant

Beneficent

altruistic, benevolent
benevolent, charitable
beneficent, benevolent
benign, generous
charitable, benevolent
eleemosynary, charitable
gratifying, unselfish
hospitable, charitable
impartial, magnanimous
noble, magnanimous
philanthropic, benevolent
sacrificial, unselfish
supererogatory, unsparing
ungrudging, generous
unselfish, ungrudging
unsparing, liberal
unstinted, unsparing

Contributive

contributive, donative
donative, contributive
tributary, contributive

Bequesting, Etc.

patrimonial, by patrimony
testamentary, bequesting
testate, given by will

Gratuitous

free, liberal
gratuitous, free
voluntary, gratuitous

NOUNS

Generosity

bounty, generosity
extravagance, lavishness
generosity, liberality
lavishment, munificence

NOUNS (Continued)

lavishness, generosity
liberality, generosity
magnanimity, altruism
munificence, generosity
prodigality, lavishness

Abundance

abundance, liberality
shower, lavish bestowal

Contribution

allocation, allowance
allowance, bestowal
appropriation, apportion-
ment
apportionment, allocation
contribution, donation
donation, appropriation
donative, gift
subscription, contribution
tribute, contribution

Beneficence

altruism, benevolence
beneficence, benefit
benignity, beneficence
benevolence, charity
hospitality, altruism
patronage, benefice
philanthropy, benevolence
supererogation, unselfish-
ness beyond duty

Benefaction, Etc.

advowson, benefice
alms, charity
benefice, endowment
benefaction, beneficence
bestowment, gift
boon, gift
charity, alms
succor, benefit
(B). succour

Bequest, Etc.

amortization, transfer
bequest, gift by will
birthright, heritage
demise, will
devise, will
dower, widow's estate
endowment, gift
entail, bequest
grant, endowment
heirloom, heritage
hereditament, heritage
heritage, birthright
inheritance, heritage
jointure, woman's settle-
ment
legacy, hereditament
testacy, will

(Continued on page 85)

DISTRIBUTION—PURVEYANCE see—

43B

VERBS

Distribute
allocate, allot
allot, distribute
allow, provide
assign, allot
attribute, assign
apportion, allot
deal, distribute
disburse, distribute
dispense, distribute
dispose, distribute
distribute, apportion
dole, deal
mete, allot
portion, allot

Minister
accommodate, supply
administer, dispense
aliment, furnish with food
dish, dispense
enable, furnish means
endue, furnish
furnish, supply
grubstake, finance
help, pass food, etc.
indue, supply
maintain, supply means
minister, supply need
provide, furnish
serve, supply
support, provide
sustain, support
victual, provide

Bestow
address, consign
afford, supply
alienate, transfer
award, assign
bestow, impart
confer, bestow
consign, deliver
convey, impart
deliver, convey
finance, supply funds
hand, pass
impart, bestow
pass, hand
present, bestow
render, bestow
transfer, hand

Complement
complement, supply a de-
ficiency
conduce, contribute
contribute, bestow

VERBS (Continued)
supplement, complement

Gratify
cater, supply
gratify, cater
pander, gratify
pimp, pander
spread, cater

Commit
commit, bestow
extradite, hand over
recommit, commit anew
remand, recommit

Supply
deposit, place with
recruit, supply anew
replenish, resupply
retrocede, rebestow
store, supply
stock, supply
supply, furnish

ADJECTIVES

Miscellaneous
agrarian, redistributing
land
alimental, supplying food
attributive, contributive
auxiliary, attributive
beneficial, beneficent
beneficent, contributive
conducible, contributive
contributive, ministrant
contributory, contributive
dispensatory, distributive
dispensable, dispensatory
distributive, dispensatory
ministrant, dispensatory
presentative, ministrant
provisional, providing
supplemental, complemen-
tary
tributary, contributive

NOUNS

Distribution
agrarianism, redistribution
of land
aliment, allowance of food
allocation, assignment
allowance, allotment
allotment, distribution
apportionment, allotment
assignment, allotment
attribution, an assigning

NOUNS (Continued)
colportage, distribution of
religious books
deal, allotment
disbursement, expenditure
dispensation, distribution
disposal, distribution
distribution, allotment
dole, sparing allotment
expenditure, disbursement
ordering, distribution
supply, dispensation

Ministration
accommodation, comple-
ment
administration, dispensa-
tion
maintenance, supply
ministration, dispensation
patronage, special support
provision, purveyance
purveyance, a furnishing
support, maintenance
sustentation, support

Bestowment
alienation, transference
bestowal, an imparting
bestowment, bestowal
consignment, delivery
delivery, bestowal
presentation, bestowal
presentment, presentation
transference, delivery

Complement
complement, supplement
contribution, accommoda-
tion
subscription, contribution
supplement, complement

Gratification
gratification, a satisfying
procuration, a providing
for immoral purposes

Commitment
commitment, consignment
extradition, a handing over
recommitment, a com-
mitting anew
remand, recommitment

PERSONS
administrator, one who dis-
penses an estate

(Continued on page 79)

44
VERBS
Sell
auction, sell on a bid
auctioneer, auction
market, sell
peddle, sell
prostitute, exchange basely
retail, vend
sell, vend
vend, sell

Bargain
bargain, trade
barter, bargain
exchange, barter
haggle, barter
hawk, carry for sale
higgle, haggle
negotiate, exchange
swap, exchange
trade, barter
traffic, trade
treat, trade
truck, barter

Transfer
amortize, sell
(B). amortise
assign, deed
convey, deed
deed, transfer
enfeoff, sell
transfer, deed

Credit
credit, sell on trust
obligate, render indebted
oblige, obligate
trust, credit

ADJECTIVES
Miscellaneous
commercial, mercenary
mercantile, commercial
mercenary, done for gain

ADJECTIVES (Continued)
meretricious, prostituting
sex
professional, occupational
or mercenary
salable, marketable
venal, mercenary
vendible, commercial
vocational, occupational
occupational, active in mercenary pursuit

NOUNS
Miscellaneous
assignation, deed of
transfer
assignment, assignation
auction, sale to the highest
bidder
barter, exchange
business, commerce
calling, business
commerce, interchange of
trade
employment, occupation
exchange, barter
harlotry, prostitution for
hire
negotiation, exchange
occupation, business
profession, occupation
professionalism, mercenary
sports
prostitution, harlotry
sale, mercenary exchange
swap, exchange
trade, commerce
trading, commerce
traffic, barter
venality, prostitution of
talents
vendue, auction
vocation, profession
wholesale, sale in quantities

TRADE PLACES
whoredom, harlotry
bazaar, store
dairy, milk depot
debouch, mart
emporium, large shop
grocery, food shop
haberdashery, men's fur-
nishing store
market, mart
mart, market
shop, store
store, mart

PERSONS
auctioneer, seller at auction
banker, financier
bargainer, trader
bibliopole, book seller
broker, a dealer
chapman, hawker
creditor, obligee
dealer, trader
duffer, hawker
fishmonger, a fish-seller
grocer, dealer in groceries
haberdasher, a dealer in
men's goods
hawker, peddler
mercenary, vendor
merchant, tradesman
obligee, creditor
peddler, hawker
professional, a mercenary
sportsman
prostitutor, mercenary
sutler, provision seller
trader, barterer
tradesman, trader
vendor, seller
vintner, wine dealer

BEING
Mercury, god of commerce

43B (Continued)
PERSONS (Continued)
administratrix, as above,
(f.)
agrarian, one who favors
the redistribution of land
colporteur, Bible distributor
commissariat, supply officer
consignor, deliverer

PERSONS (Continued)
contributor, one who con-
tributes
dealer, apportioner
fruiterer, fruit dealer
granter, grantor
grantor, transferer
pimp, one who provides
gratification to others

PERSONS (Continued)
procurer, a provider for
immoral purposes
purser, commissariat
purveyor, provider
supplier, one who supplies
sutler, an army follower
who caters to troops

45

VERBS

Pay
fulfil, pay
liquidate, settle
pay, compensate
remit, settle
settle, pay

Expend
defray, pay an expense
disburse, pay out
expend, pay out
spend, expend
squander, spend lavishly

Compensate
award, give recompense
compensate, recompense
countervail, compensate
crown, reward
recompense, pay equivalent
reciprocate, interchange
remunerate, recompense
reward, recompense

Reimburse
address, redress
atone, make reparations
disgorge, make restitution
expiate, redress
forfeit, give up
indemnify, pay for loss
propitiate, atone
rebate, refund
recoup, indemnify
redress, requite
refund, repay
reimburse, refund
render, pay or give back
repay, pay back
requite, recompense
restore, redress
return, repay
revest, return to owner
satisfy, settle
serve, requite

Aliment
aliment, provide food
pension, superannuate
superannuate, pension

Pledge
advance, pay beforehand
deposit, place a pledge
entrust, deposit
hock, secure a loan
impawn, pawn
lend, entrust
loan, lend
mortgage, give security
pawn, pledge
pledge, pawn

VERBS (Continued)
prepay, advance
retain, pay advance fee
secure, impawn

Redeem
bail, secure freedom
ransom, pay for liberation
redeem, ransom
replevy, give bail

Bribe, Etc.
bribe, lure political aid
Gerrymander, compensate
  political parties with unnatural advantages
graft, bribe
hire, bribe

Swap, Etc.
cash, exchange for money
change, give in return
exchange, swap
interchange, exchange
negotiate, exchange
swap, exchange

Retaliate
avenge, revenge
punish, retaliate
retaliate, requite
revenge, retaliate

Thank
thank, give appreciation

ADJECTIVES

Miscellaneous
beneficial, beneficent
beneficent, compensative
commensurable, retaliative
commensurate, compensa-
  tive
compensative, remunera-
  tive
condign, retributive
countervailing, offsetting
deserved, retributive
duteous, countervailing
fat, lucrative
lucrative, remunerative
merited, deserved
negotiatory, exchangeable
pensionary, paying regu-
  larly for past services
piacular, expiatory
profitable, remunerative
propitiatory, atoning
reciprocal, interchangeable
remunerable, lucrative
remunerative, lucrative
remuneratory, profitable
retaliative, retributive

ADJECTIVES (Continued)
retributive, retaliative
satisfactory, commensurate
solvent, countervailing
talismanic, employing ex-
  traordinary advantage
  paid
thankful, appreciative
tributary, paying together

NOUNS

Payment
defrayal, outlay
disbursement, outlay
expenditure, expense
expense, outlay
liquidation, settlement
outgo, payment for general
  expenses
outlay, expenditure
overhead, general cost
pay, compensation
payment, pay
remittance, payment
settlement, recompense

Compensation
compensation, recompense
recompense, compensation
remuneration, payment
reward, recompense

Reimbursement
atonement, reparation
amends, redress
damage, payment for in-
  jury
demurrage, pay for deten-
  tion of a carrier
expiation, reparation
fine, payment for wrong
forfeiture, penalty
indemnification, payment
  for loss
indemnity, indemnification
penalty, fine
propitiation, expiation
rebate, return for overpay
redress, reparation
refund, rebate
reimbursement, refund
reparation, amends
restitution, reparation
return, satisfaction
satisfaction, reparation

Salary
emolument, remuneration
salary, recompense
stipend, salary

(Continued on page 81)

NOUNS (Continued)
wage, wages
wages, pay for labor

Public Service Pay
ballastage, ballast toll
brokerage, commission
cartage, pay for hauling
commission, brokerage
dockage, pay for dock use
ferriage, pay for ferrying
freightage, hauling cost
haulage, hauling pay
pilotage, pay for piloting
porterage, pay for carriage
primage, pay for loading
and unloading vessel
salvage, pay for saving a
vessel or goods

Ecclesiastic's Pay
curacy, pay of a curate
parsonage, ecclesiastical
benefice
prebend, ecclesiastic's pay
provostry, benefit of a
provost
rectory, benefice of a
rector
vicarage, benefice of a
vicar

Gratitude
appreciation, gratitude
gratitude, thankfulness
thankfulness, appreciation

Reward
award, favor
bakshish, tip (oriental)
bay, laurel
bounty, reward
crown, reward
cup, prize
gratification, reward
gratuity, reward
guerdon, reward
laurel, crown
mead, reward
merit, just reward
perquisite, gratuity
plate, prize for racing
prize, reward
reward, prize
tip, slight reward
veil, gratuity

Aliment, Etc.
aliment, decreed allowance
alimony, decreed aliment
allowance, regular payment
dowry, consideration given
a husband when married
livelihood, living
living, return for service
maintenance, livelihood
pension, allowance paid for
past services
sinecure, remuneration

NOUNS (Continued)
without employment
superannuation, pension for
infirmity

Pledge, Etc.
advance, prepayment
bail, security for release
bailment, delivery in trust
earnest, retainer
love-gift, a pledge of love
love-token, love-gift
mortgage, security deed
pawn, pledge
pledge, security
ransom, payment for re-
lease
replevy, security for wrongfully seized goods
respondentia, advance paid
on a cargo
retainer, advance fee
security, valid assurance

Bribery, Etc.
bribe, corrupt payment
bribery, as above
graft, bribe

Retaliation
exchange, reciprocal change
desert, requital
doom, sentence, punishment
offset, reprisal
punishment, retribution
recaption, reprisal
reciprocation, act
reciprocity, as above
reprisal, retaliation
requital, retaliation
retaliation, offset
retribution, requital
revenge, retaliation
sentence, punishment
tit-for-tat, offset

Duty, Task
duty, due performance
obligation, payment of
bond due
onus, duty
task, duty
work, duty performed

Tax, Tribute
capitation, tax
custom, duty on import or
export
duty, pay as duty
impost, tribute
tax, annual tribute
toll, tax tribute
tribute, tax

Interest, Profit
bonus, the sum paid above
what is due
boot, incast

NOUNS (Continued)
dividend, payment of a
profit share
gain, repayment
incast, good measure
interest, pay for the use of
money
premium, dividend
profit, return
seigniorage, minting charge
return, repayment
repayment, pay in gain
revenue, tax
royalty, payment for right

Cost, Charge
charge, cost
cost, outlay
fee, commission
hire, pay
honorarium, honorary fee
price, charge

Miscellaneous
fare, pay for passage
feud, payment for tenancy
fief, fee
insurance, premium
premium, pay for insurance
render, rental
rent, rental
rental, pay for rent
tuition, payment for in-
struction, etc.

PERSONS
bailor, one who delivers
goods in bailment
boodler, one who gives or
accepts boodle
bursar, treasurer
compensator, liquidator
drawee, one who pays a
draft
liquidator, one who settles
his affairs
mortgagor, a mortgage
giver
purser, paymaster
teller, payer in a bank
treasurer, bursar
tributary, a person or state
paying tribute

INTERJECTIONS
gramercy, great thanks

MEDIUM OF EXCHANGE
(See QUANTITY 147B)
assets, property
cash, money
finance, funds
funds, convertible assets
money, revenue
revenue, finance

46A

PERMISSION—COMPLIANCE   see—   ASSOCIATIVE
     vs. Opposition—Refusal 27   ⎰ Submission—Subordination 46B
     vs. Ban—Prohibition 35   ⎱ Pardon—Forgiveness 47

46A
VERBS

Permit
admit, permit
allow, permit
let, permit
permit, allow

Approve
approbate, sanction
approve, sanction
assent, consent
consent, comply
countenance, allow
ratify, sanction
sanction, authorize
subscribe, consent

Authorize
affranchise, privilege to
   vote, etc.
authorize, grant authority
empower, authorize
enfranchise, privilege
license, permit
privilege, grant a benefit
warrant, authorize

Lease, Etc.
charter, privilege
charter-party, charter a
   vessel
lease, license, permit, rent
rent, lease

Concur
accede, consent
accept, acquiesce
accord, grant
acquiesce, agree
agree, consent
comply, assent
concede, accord
concur, agree
connive, permit
grant, permit
vouchsafe, grant

Indulge
gratify, acquiesce
humor, gratify
(B). humour
indulge, gratify
oblige, gratify
satisfy, gratify
temporize, humor

Tolerate
brook, tolerate
condescend, permit
defer, yield
deign, defer
quiesce, be passive
suffer, allow
take, tolerate
tolerate, permit

VERBS (Continued)
unbend, condescend
yield, suffer

Immunize
exempt, grant privilege
forego, waive
immunize, exempt
waive, forego

ADJECTIVES

Permissive
allowable, permissive
alternative, allowing choice
facultative, permissive
leisurely, optional
optional, privileged
permissible, granting permission
permissive, concessive
tacit, passive
unforbidding, tolerant
willing, agreeable

Approbative
accessional, assenting
approbative, sanctioning
approbatory, authoritative
assentient, consenting
concessionary, complaint
concessive, concessionary
consentient, assentient

Authoritative
authoritative, lawful
constitutional, legally authorized
lawful, constitutional
legal, lawful
legitimate, legal
licit, lawful
privileged, authorized
warranted, authorized

Concurrent
accordant, agreeing
agreeable, acquiescent
concordant, concurrent
concurrent, accommodating
consentaneous, mutually
   agreeing
entente, agreeable
mutual, consentaneous
reciprocal, mutual
unanimous, concurrent

Indulgent
accommodating, acquies-
   cent
accommodative, compliant
acquiescent, consentient
affable, condescending
compliable, compliant
compliant, agreeable
complaisant, agreeable
condescending, kind

ADJECTIVES (Continued)
deferential, acquiescent
gracious, deferential
gratifying, obliging
indulgent, tolerant
kind, indulgent
obliging, agreeable
satisfying, gratifying

Tolerant
patient, tolerant
sufferable, permissive
suffering, sufferable
tolerant, indulgent

Immune
exempt, privileged
immune, exempt

ADVERBS
fain, willingly
yes, aye
aye, yes
kindly, agreeably
willingly, agreeably

NOUNS

Permission
admission, permission
allowance, authority
alternative, privilege of
   choice
entree, admission
leisure, permit to use time
   as desired
opportunity, permission
option, privilege to choose
permit, authority
permission, permit

Approbation
accession, assent
approbation, consent
approval, approbation
assent, accession
assentation, consent
consent, permission
imprimatur, mark of ap-
   proval
sanction, approval

Authority
authority, permit
authorization, authority
boon, privilege
brevet, license
carte blanche, unconditional
   authority
charter, agreement
charter-party, grant to the
   use of a vessel
commonage, privilege of
   pasture on common land
concession, privilege
(Continued on page 85)

SUBMISSION—SUBORDINATION see—

vs. Opposition—Rebellion 27

ASSOCIATIVE

Permission—Compliance 46A
Flight—Abdication 15
Useful Materials 5B
Workmen 144D

46B

VERBS

Submit

acquiesce, yield
bend, submit
capitulate, surrender
cede, surrender
comply, yield
desist, yield
drop, submit
forego, yield
give, yield
heed, obey
keel, surrender
kneel, submit
knuckle, submit
mind, obey
obey, heed
quiesce, acquiesce
relax, desist
remise, surrender
resign, surrender
relinquish, desist
slacken, bend
stomach, acquiesce
submit, yield
succumb, submit
stoop, submit
surrender, yield
truckle, knuckle
yield, submit
waive, surrender

Serve—Slave

attend, serve
char, serve
drudge, slave
labor, work
render, serve
serve, wait upon
slave, toil
subserve, attend
toil, labor
work, toil

Be Subject

behoove, be subject
depend, be subject
owe, be obligated
rely, depend
toady, be servile

ADJECTIVES

Submissive

acquiescent, submissive
amenable, obedient
biddable, obedient
cessionary, surrendering

ADJECTIVES (Continued)

consentient, acquiescent
corrigible, amenable
docile, tractable
ductile, tractable
duteous, obedient
dutiful, duteous
facile, pliant
flexible, pliant
gentle, docile
henpecked, submissive
humble, submissive
implicit, unquestioning
involuntary, acquiscent
limber, pliant
manageable, docile
meek, submissive
obedient, duteous
obsequious, submissive
passive, submissive
patient, passive
plastic, yielding
pliable, flexible
pliant, yielding
pregnable, vincible
quiescent, passive
resigned, submissive
reverent, respectful
suasible, acquiescent
submissive, yielding
supple, yielding
susceptible, yielding
tractable, docile
vincible, conquerable
vulnerable, vincible

SERVING

ancillary, subservient
assistant, subservient
attendant, assistant
auxiliary, subsidiary
companion, attendant
collateral, auxiliary
liable, subject
menial, servile
servile, serving meanly
slavish, servile
subsidiary, auxiliary
tributary, subordinate
subservient, subsidiary

Enslaved—Captive

captive, imprisoned
caged, captive
cloistered, interned
confined, interned
enclosed, confined
encompassed, enclosed

ADJECTIVES (Continued)

enslaved, in bondage
entombed, confined
immured, imprisoned
impounded, immured
imprisoned, impounded
incarcerated, imprisoned
incased, confined
incastellated, confined
inescapable, captive
interned, confined
liege, bound in service
unemancipated, enslaved

Subject—Inferior

achievable, subject
answerable, liable
available, subject
beholden, indebted
commodious, useful
dependent, subordinate
due, beholden
easy, convenient
eligible, subject
expedient, convenient
handy, convenient
incidental, subordinate
indebted, beholden
inferior, subordinate
liable, subject
mercenary, available
negotiable, achievable
obliged, beholden
owing, beholden
payable, due
practicable, subject to use
proletariat, subject
responsible, answerable
secondary, subordinate
serviceable, useful
subaltern, subordinate
subject, subordinate
substitute, subordinate
usable, serviceable
useful, subject to use
utilitarian, serviceable
vicarious, subordinate

NOUNS

Submission

acquiescence, submission
amenability, tractableness
capitulation, surrender
cessation, surrender
cession, surrender

(Continued on page 84)

NOUNS (Continued)

delivery, surrender
docility, tractability
dutifulness, obedience
humble-pie, humility
humiliation, humility
humility, submissiveness
obedience, docility
passiveness, submission
patience, passiveness
pliability, submissiveness
quiescence, passiveness
relinquishment, surrender
remittal, surrender
resignation, surrender
submission, acquiescence
surrender, capitulation
susceptibility, docility
tractability, docility
vulnerability, susceptibility

Service

civil service, public service
drudgery, labor
flunkyism, obsequiousness
labor, toil
service, subservience
servility, flunkyism
subservience, a serving
sycophancy, servility
toil, work
work, service

Slavery—Bondage

bondage, slavery
drudgery, labor
harlotry, serfdom
serfage, slavery
serfdom, slavery
servitude, slavery
slavery, bondage
thralldom, bondage
vassalage, serfdom
villanage, serfdom
yoke, bondage

Subjectiveness

availability, facility
convenience, usefulness
dependence, subjection
dutifulness, indebtedness
eligibility, liability
expediency, utility
facility, ready pliancy

NOUNS (Continued)

handiness, convenience
indebtedness, obligation
liability, indebtedness
makeshift, expediency
obligation, liability
serviceableness, utility
usefulness, facility
utility, usefulness

PERSONS

Surrenderer

capitulator, surrenderer
submitter, capitulator
yielder, submitter

Slave, Etc.

bondman, slave
drudge, slave
feudatory, vassal
helot, slave
liege, vassal
man, vassal
peasant, rustic
peon, Mexican bondman
rustic, laborer
serf, slave
slave, thrall
thrall, bondman
vassal, bondman

Subject

obligor, one who is obligated
subject, one who is amenable

Retinue, Etc.

cortege, train of assistants
retinue, attendants of a personage
train, retinue

Agent—Laborer, Etc.

agent, factor
assistant, helper
attendant, one who accompanies
auxiliary, assistant
ayah, nurse, (Anglo-Ind.)
batman, attendant
boots, boot servant
butler, chief servant
caddie, golfer's assistant

PERSONS (Continued)

chamberlain, male servant
clerk, assistant
collaborator, auxiliary
domestic, servant
employee, mercenary
equerry, nobleman's aid
eunuch, harem assistant
factor, subordinate
factotum, man of all work
famulus, assistant
fellah, peasant
flunky, servant
footman, servant
garcon, waiter
groom, hostler
hand, laborer
handmaid, maid
handyman, factotum
help, servant
helper, servant
henchman, hireling
hind, peasant
hireling, servant
hostler, groom
jackal, myrmidon
janitor, building-keeper
laborer, workman
lackey, servant
maid, female servant
menial, servant
mercenary, hireling
minion, henchman
minister, servant
myrmidon, base minion
orderly, military aid
peasant, fellah
proletarian, workman
pursuivant, attendant
scrub, menial
scullion, menial
servant, domestic
slavy, maid servant
subaltern, subordinate
subordinate, aid
sycophant, henchman
toady, sycophant
valet, man's servant
waiter, servant
wench, colored slavy
woman, female attendant
workman, mercenary

NOUNS (Continued)
testament, will
will, gift by one dead

Gift
gift, present
handsel, gift
largess, present
present, gift

Nepotism
favoritism, preferment
(B). favouritism
nepotism, favoritism
preferment, elevation in rank
subsidy, pecuniary grant
subvention, subsidy

Gratuity
bakshish, tip (oriental)

43A (Continued)
NOUNS (Continued)
dole, gratuity
gratuity, gift
tip, small gratuity

Offering
oblation, offering
offering, sacrifice
sacrifice, offering

PERSONS
advowee, patron
almoner, benefactor
altruist, philanthropist
befena, fairy patron
benefactor, patron
contributor, donator
devisor, bequeather

PERSONS (Continued)
donator, giver
donor, donator
patron, benefactor
philanthropist, benefactor
prodigal, lavish person
Samaritan, benefactor
wastrel, prodigal

INSTITUTIONS
almonry, almshouse
almshouse, house of alms
hospice, Alpine shelter

SYMBOL
Key, symbol of hospitality

46A (Continued)
NOUNS (Continued)
copyright, exclusive privilege
dispensation, license
enfranchisement, privilege to vote, etc.
entente, agreement
favor, privilege
franchise, privilege
grant, privilege
lease, legal permit
license, legal permission
marque, ship's license for making reprisals
pass, permit
patent, legal grant
piscary, license to fish
pratique, an uninfected ship's license to trade
preemption, privilege to purchase before others
prerogative, peculiar privilege
privilege, franchise
suffrage, franchise
warrant, authority
warranty, authority

NOUNS (Continued)
Law
constitution, legal authority
law, legal authority

Concurrence
accord, concurrence
accordance, sanction
acquiescence, accession
agreement, concordance
bargain, agreement
compact, agreement
compliance, acquiescence
concord, agreement
concordance, concord
concordant, compact
concurrence, accord
connivance, passive consent
consensus, concordance
unanimity, concordance

Indulgence
accommodation, compliance
affability, deference
agreeability, agreement
complaisance, deference

NOUNS (Continued)
condescension, deference
deference, condescension
deferment, deference
grace, deference
gratification, grace
indulgence, gratification

Tolerance
forbearance, patience
fortitude, forbearance
impunity, toleration
patience, tolerance
sufferance, negative consent
tolerance, sufferance
toleration, tolerance

Immunity
exemption, special privilege
immunity, exemption

Freedom
freedom, privilege of liberty
furlough, leave of absence
leave, permit
liberty, special privilege
parole, leave of absence

vs. Punishment—Torture	...........130N	Esteem—Friendliness	38
vs. Retaliation—Payment	45	Praise—Approval	63
vs. Vengeance—Hatred	28	Reward—Recompense	45

47
VERBS

Forgive
absolve, forgive
condone, pardon
dispense, excuse
excuse, pardon
forbear, excuse
forgive, pardon
pardon, forgive
quit, absolve
remit, pardon
spare, forgive

Liberate
acquit, absolve
affranchise, liberate
deliver, free
discharge, release
emancipate, free
enfranchise, emancipate
free, release
liberate, free
manumit, emancipate
release, pardon
relieve, release
respite, suspend execution

Relent
desist, forbear
melt, relent
relax, relent
relent, desist

VERBS (Continued)
thaw, relent

ADJECTIVES

Miscellaneous
absolvatory, forgiving
clement, absolvatory
compassionate, merciful
forgiving, compassionate
forbearing, excusing
lenient, relenting
merciful, compassionate
pardoning, forgiving
placable, forgiving
relenting, yielding
sympathetic, compassionate
venial, pardonable

NOUNS

Forgiveness
absolution, pardon
amnesty, pardon
condonation, pardon
dispensation, remission
excuse, pardon
forgiveness, pardon
pardon, forgiveness
remission, pardon
shrift, absolution

Liberation
acquittal, acquittance

NOUNS (Continued)
acquittance, acquittal
deliverance, delivery
delivery, a setting free
discharge, liberation
emancipation, liberation
enfranchisement, emancipation
liberation, emancipation
manumission, emancipation
quittance, release
release, liberation
relief, release
respite, remission

Mercy
clemency, compassion
compassion, leniency
forbearance, excuse
leniency, clemency
mercy, clemency
placability, forbearance

PERSONS
deliverer
emancipator
liberator
pardoner
preserver
Savior
(B). Saviour

48

NURTURE—FOOD

FOOD—DRINKS, Etc.   see—   ASSOCIATIVE

vs. Impairment—Deprivation 130D
vs. Weakness—Poverty 128A

Seasoning—Taste 48P
Purveyance—Providers 43B
Gift—Generosity 43A
Help—Aid 5A

48A

VERBS

Nurture
aliment, nurture
board, lodge and feed
maintain, nurture
mother, nurture
nurse, nourish
nurture, nourish
nourish, feed
suckle, nurse
support, nurture
sustain, nurture

Entertain
banquet, feast
breakfast, give breakfast
cater, supply food
dine, give dinner
entertain, banquet
feast, entertain
lunch, give lunch
regale, feast

Feed, Etc.
dose, give a dose
feed, give food
forage, supply forage
mess, feed
pasture, furnish pasture
quench, allay thirst
slake, quench
victual, supply food

ADJECTIVES

Miscellaneous
alimental, nourishing
alimentary, nutritive
beneficent, wholesome
edible, alimental
esculent, edible
healthful, wholesome
mammalian, suckling young
mammary, mammalian
nourishing, nutritive
nutrient, nourishing
nutritious, nutrient
nutritive, nutritious
prandial, pertaining to
  meals
salutary, wholesome
wholesome, nutritious

NOUNS

Nurture
aliment, food
alimentation, maintenance
board, meals and lodging
keep, subsistence
maintenance, sustenance
nurture, food

NOUNS (Continued)
nourishment, nutriment
nutriment, food
nutrition, nutriment
subsistence, sustenance
support, maintenance
sustenance, nutriment
sustentation, support

Entertainment
banquet, sumptuous food
entertainment, spread
feast, sumptuous repast
refection, light meal
refreshment, food, etc.
repast, meal
spread, a feast
table, repast
table d'hote, meals for several persons at the same
  price

Provision
diet, food
feed, food
food, aliment
grub, food
larder, provisions
pabulum, food
prey, food of beasts
provision, foods
viands, victuals
victuals, food

Dish, Dose, Etc.
bee-bread, food for bees
breath, food of lungs
concoction, a prepared food
  or drink
cud, ruminant's food
decoction, a boiled food
dish, food
dose, prescribed quantity
esculent, a fit food
morsel, a bit of food
ration, food allowance
service, a course

Meal
breakfast, a first meal
dejeuner, breakfast
dinner, principal meal
lunch, a light repast
luncheon, lunch
meal, repast
snack, hasty repast
supper, the last meal

PERSONS
Boniface, inn-keeper
caterer, host

PERSONS (Continued)
dry-nurse, one who rears
  without the breast
feeder, caterer
host, inn-keeper
hostess, as above (female)
mammal, suckling species
mammalia, as above (plu.)
purveyor, caterer
restauranteur, caterer
victualer, caterer
wet-nurse, a suckling nurse

48B

FOOD PLACES
automat, eating place with
  automatic service
barroom, saloon
cabaret, cafe
cafe, restaurant
cafeteria, restaurant
canteen, refreshment place
caravansary, khan
dispensary, an institution
  for providing the poor
gin-mill, drinking place
gin-place, saloon
groggery, saloon
grog-shop, groggery
hostel, inn
hostelry, inn
hotel, a superior inn
inn, hostelry
khan, caravan's lodgment
manger, feeding box
rathskeller, basement cafe
refectory, eating room
restaurant, eating place
saloon, groggery
tavern, inn

48C

NUTS
black walnut
Brazil nut
butternut
chestnut
chinkapin
coconut
English walnut
filbert
hickory nut
nut
peanut
pecan
walnut
Etc.

FOOD—DRINKS, Etc.   see—   **ASSOCIATIVE**

    Seasoning—Taste 48P
  vs. Impairment—Deprivation ......130D Purveyance—Providers 43B
  vs. Weakness—Poverty ....128A Gift—Generosity 43A
    Help—Aid 5A

48D
SOUPS—STEWS—MEATS PUDDINGS—SALADS

aspic, dish of game, etc.
bacon, prepared hog meat
barbecue, roasted animal
batter, a cooked mixture
beef, flesh of cattle
bisk, a soup
bouilli, a meat soup
bouillon, clear meat soup
brace, broth
braise, braised meat
broth, soup
brose, porridge
chop-suey, stewed meat, etc.
chowder, food of fish
cole-slaw, salad
consomme, a strong soup
croquette, food in balls
curry, a stew
dal, a rice food
dumplings, cooked dough
fillet, boneless meat
fricassee, hash-like food
gippo, a soup
goulash, meat stew
grillade, grilled meat
gruel, a liquid food
gumbo, a soup
ham, smoked thigh
haricot, a stew of meat, etc.
hash, haricot
hodge-podge, pudding
hotchpotch, hodge-podge
jerk, jerked beef
kickshaw, hotchpotch
mayonnaise, salad dressing
meat, flesh
noodle, stripped dough
pap, soft food
pemmican, cakes of meat
potpourri, a mixed dish
pottage, soup
porridge, boiled oatmeal
pudding, soft food
ragout, stewed meats
salad, dish of herbs, etc.
salmagundi, chopped meats
salmi, roasted game, etc.
sandwich, meat, etc., between sliced bread
sausage, ground meat
spaghetti, cord-like food
steak, sliced meat
stew, food stewed
succotash, vegetable dish

48E
BREADS—CAKES—PIES

bannock, a bread-cake
pastry, pies, etc.
bread, baked dough
bread-fruit, a fruit eaten like bread
biscuit, cake-like bread
cake, sweetened bread
cracknel, fancy biscuit
custard, a food mixture
dough, unbaked bread
eclair, a cream cake
fritter, a small cake
flapjack, pancake
gingerbread, a cake
griddle cake, cake
hardtack, hard bread
loaf, a bread
macaroon, a cake
pancake, flapjack
pie, a baked food
pretzel, a hard bread
roll, a bread
sconce, oatmeal cake
shortcake, bread-cake
tart, an open pie
toast, browned bread
waffle, indented cake

48F
CONFECTIONS, ETC.

ambrosia, delicious fruit dish
bonbon, a confection
candy, a confection
caramel, a chocolate
chocolate, a confection
confection, any sweetmeat
confectionery, sweetmeats
cooky, a sweetmeat
dainty, a nice edible
delicacy, dainty
delicatessen, dainties
dessert, a sweet course
entree, a side dish
entremets, a side dish
hokey-pokey, an ice cream
ice cream, a refrigerant
lozenge, a sweetmeat
licorice, a confection
marmalade, a confection
rarebit, a dainty morsel
refrigerant, refreshment
sherbet, a refrigerant
sondhi, an ice cream
sundæ, as above
taffy, a candy
titbit, rarebit

48G
FRUITS—BERRIES

almond, a fruit kernel
apple, fruit
apricot, fruit
bacca, berry
banana, fruit
bergamot, lemon
berry, a small fruit
bilberry, whortleberry
blackberry, berry
blackcap, berry
catawba, a grape
cherry, fruit
crab, crab apple
cranberry, berry
currant, dried grape
date, a fruit
fig, a fruit
fruit, seeded edible
gooseberry, berry
grenandine, a plum
grape, clustered fruit
hamburg, a grape
huckleberry, berry
kaki, a plum
kumquat, a citrus fruit
lemon, an acid fruit
lime, a sour fruit
mandarin, orange
mangosteen, citrus fruit
mulberry, a berry
olive, a fruit
orange, a juicy fruit
nectarine, a peach
peach, a fruit
pear, a fruit
persimmon, a plum-like fruit
pineapple, a fruit
pippin, an apple
plum, a fruit
pomegranate, a fruit
prune, dried plum
prunella, prune
raisin, dried grape
raspberry, berry
sloe, plum
strawberry, berry
tangerine, orange

BEINGS

Ceres, goddess of fruits and cereals
Dionysus, god of fruits, etc.
Pomona, goddess of fruits

ASSOCIATIVE

FOOD—DRINKS—TOBACCO   see—

vs. Impairment—Deprivation 130D
vs. Weakness—Poverty 128A

Seasoning—Taste 48P
Purveyance—Providers 43B
Gift—Generosity 43A
Help—Aid 5A

48H

JAM, Etc.
honey
jam
jelly
molasses
preserves
syrup
treacle

48I

CURD, Etc.
cheese
cheese-
  cake
curd
flummery
gravy
junket

48J

NON-INTOXICANTS

adam's ale, water
beverage, any drink
bishop, a beverage
bumper, overflowing cup
buttermilk, a milk
cider, apple juice
cobbler, a cooling drink
cocoa, a beverage
chocolate, a beverage
coffee, a beverage
dose, draft
draft, a drink
drink, a potion
elixir, rejuvenating liquid
ginger ale, a beverage
ginger beer, a beverage
lemonade, a beverage
milk, a wholesome liquid
nectar, wine of the gods
orangeade, a beverage
potion, draft
soft-drink, a drink
soft-water, a drink
spruce, a beverage
sup, a small mouthful
water, refreshing liquid

48K

VEGETABLES, Etc.

artichoke
asparagus
beet
broccoli
cabbage
cantaloupe
carrot
cauliflower
celery
cole
colewort
cucumber
gherkin
granadilla
kale

melon
pickle
potato
pumpkin
radish
rape
rutabaga
spinach
spud
sweet-corn
sweet potato
tomato
turnip
vegetable

48L

INTOXICATING DRINKS

absinthe, French brandy
ale, a liquor
alcohol, spirituous liquor
beer, a liquor
bhang, hashish
bitters, a liquor
booze, whisky
Bordeau, a French wine
brandy, a liquor
buck-beer, a strong beer
bumper, overflowing cup
canary, a light wine
caudle, wine
cherry, a wine
chloral, a narcotic
claret, a wine
cocktail, American drink
cognac, French brandy
cup, potation
dram, drink of whisky
eye-opener, dram
fire-water, ardent spirits
gin, alcoholic drink
grog, a drink
guzzle, a whisky
hashish, an intoxicant
hermitage, French wine
highball, whisky and soda
hock, Rhine wine
intoxicant, alcohol, etc.
julep, a brandy
kava, a beverage
liquor, a beverage
Madeira, a wine
mint-julep, brandy
pony, a small drink
potation, a drink
punch, whisky
purl, an ale or gin
red-eye, new whisky
rum, spirits
sherry, a wine
sweet, a homemade wine
tent, sacramental wine
tipple, a liquor
vin ordinaire, common wine
vintage, season's wine
vodka, Russian intoxicant
wassail, a flavored liquor
whisky, spirituous liquor
white-wine, clear wine

BEING

Bacchus, god of wine

48M

MEAL—FLOUR, Etc.

barley
bran
cereal
corn
cornstarch
farina
flour
grain
grist
grit
grout
hominy
meal
oat
rice
rye
wheat

BEING

Ceres, goddess of fruits and
  cereals

48N

PROVENDER, Etc.

alfalfa
browse
clover
ensilage
fodder
forage
grass
hay
lucerne
meadow
pasture
pasturage
provender
shack
smooth

48-O

TOBACCO

cheroot
cigar
cigarette
fag
snuff
stogy
tobacco
weed

APPETIZERS—CONDIMENTS   see—{ Food—Drinks—Tobacco 48A
    vs. Unpalatableness ....48Q   { Entertainment 99A

48P
VERBS

Miscellaneous

curry, to spice
devil, make peppery
flavor, impart taste
(B). flavour
pepper, devil
peptonize, impart pepsin
relish, flavor
salt, season with salt
savor, flavor
(B). savour
season, spice
sauce, give relish
smack, have relish
spice, season
sweeten, make sweet
taste, have flavor

ADJECTIVES

Delectable

ambrosial, delicious
appetizing, toothsome
candied, sweet
cooling, refreshing
delectable, delicious
delicious, exquisite
exquisite, ambrosial
fleshy, succulent
juicy, succulent
luscious, delicious
mild, pleasant
nectareous, ambrosial
palatable, savory
pleasant, savory
refrigerant, refreshing
refreshing, delectable
rich, delectable
savory, palatable
(B). savoury
succulent, juicy
sugary, sweet
sweet, sugary
tasteful, palatable
tasty, savory
toothsome, palatable

Enjoyable

admirable, delightful
delicate, enjoyable

ADJECTIVES (Continued)

delightful, admirable
enjoyable, delightful
good, admirable

Seasoned

biting, racy
honeyed, sweet
hot, peppery
lickerish, appetizing
peppery, pepper-like
peptic, having pepsin
pungent, sharp
racy, sharp
saccharin, sugar-like
sapid, savory
saporous, giving taste
seasoned, palatable
sharp, racy
spicy, racy
stinging, sharp

Fit

fit, ripe
mature, ripe
mellow, savory
pappy, soft
ripe, fit

NOUNS

Miscellaneous

cuisine, quality of cooking
delectability, deliciousness
delicacy, delectability
dosage, flavor which distinguishes wines
flavor, particular taste
(B). flavour
gastronomy, the flavoring of foods
palatability, delectability
palatableness, savoriness
pungency, sharpness
raciness, strong flavor
relish, agreeable flavor
sapidity, flavor
sapor, excitation of flavor
savor, flavor
(B). savour
savoriness, relish

NOUNS (Continued)

(B). savouriness
smack, flavor
spiciness, pungency
succulence, juiciness
sweetness, sweet taste
tang, peculiar flavor
taste, particular flavor
toothsomeness, palatableness
wholesomeness, toothsomeness
zest, agreeable flavor

CONDIMENTS, ETC.

allspice, a spice
appetizer, condiment
basil, a mint
betel, a pepper
butter, a food substance
catchup, tomato sauce
capsicum, condiment
cayenne, a pepper
clove, a spice
condiment, a seasoning
cubeb, a pepper
curry, a spice
flavoring, condiment
(B). flavouring
garlic, a pungent bulb
horseradish, a condiment
ketchup, a sauce
lard, a cooking substance
mustard, a condiment
nutmeg, a flavoring
oil, a cooking substance
onion, edible bulb
pepper, condiment
peppermint, a flavoring
pepsin, a stimulant for digestion
pimiento, a pepper
relish, appetizer
sage, a flavoring
salt, a seasoning
sauce, a relish
seasoning, flavoring
spice, a seasoning
sugar, a sweetening
vinegar, a condiment

UNPALATABILITY

48Q

see—

ASSOCIATIVE

{ Foods—Drink—Tobacco 48A

vs. Deliciousness, etc. ....48P { Annoyance—Abomination 130C

48Q

VERBS

Miscellaneous

acetify, make sour
acidify, make sour
acidulate, render acid
disgust, cause aversion
nauseate, cause nausea
sicken, disgust

ADJECTIVES

Unpalatable

disgusting, nauseous
mawkish, sickening
nasty, nauseous
nauseous, sickening
sickening, nauseous
unsavory, disgusting
(B). unsavoury

Harsh

acid, sharp
acidic, acid
acidiferous, acidic
acidific, acidic

ADJECTIVES (Continued)

acidulent, tart
acidulous, acid-like
acrid, stinging
austere, sour
bitter, acrid
bitterish, bitter
brackish, saltish
briny, salty
caustic, burning
harsh, acrid
pungent, stinging
saltish, briny
sharp, bitter
sour, acrid
tart, acrid

Unfit

green, unfit
raw, uncooked
unfit, not good
unripe, green

Tasteless

flat, insipid

ADJECTIVES (Continued)

flavorless, flat
insipid, tasteless
spiceless, flat
stale, tasteless
tasteless, insipid
vapid, insipid

NOUNS

Miscellaneous

acid, anything sour
acidity, sourness
acridity, a burning taste
flummery, insipidity
insipidity, tastelessness
nastiness, nauseousness
nausea, that which sickens
nauseation, nausea
pungency, acridity
staleness, insipidity
unsavoriness
(B). unsavouriness, dis-
    agreeableness
vapidity, insipidity

49

TAKE—HOLD—RESIDE—RESIDENCE
ACQUIREMENT—SEIZURE—GAIN

EATING—DRINKING—INHALING

HOLD—BIND—CONFINE

CAPACITY—(HOLDING) MEDIUMS

OCCUPATION—DWELLERS

ACQUIREMENT—
    RECOVERY   see—

    vs. Waste—Dissipation 125C
    vs. Dismissal—Removal 35A

ASSOCIATIVE

Seizure	49C	Robbery	49G
Acceptance	49B	Conquest	50
Commerce	44	Hoarding	49E
Purchase	49D	Luck	134D
Theft	49F	Learning	116
Roguery	130A	Reduction	14

49A
VERBS

Acquire
achieve, gain
acquire, attain
attain, acquire
gather, select
get, procure
obtain, acquire
procure, obtain
secure, obtain
take, get possession

Appropriate
adopt, choose ownership
affiliate, adopt
anticipate, take beforehand
appropriate, take as one's own
arrogate, appropriate
assume, appropriate
borrow, obtain
import, get from without

Select
ballot, vote
choose, select
cull, choose
elect, choose
pick, select
select, choose
vote, choose by vote

Derive
betake, resort
derive, draw, receive
partake, share
participate, partake
recruit, take new supplies
repair, resort
resort, draw upon
share, partake
taste, participate

Gain
avail, profit
deserve, merit
earn, gain justly
enlist, gain over
gain, obtain
land, gain
merit, deserve
profit, gain
trump, win
win, gain

Thrive
accrete, attain growth
accrue, attain increment
become, attain a station
flourish, thrive
grow, thrive

VERBS (Continued)
prosper, accrue richly
thrive, prosper

Miscellaneous
absorb, take in
attract, draw to
drain, exhaust
draw, pull
exhaust, take completely
milk, draw milk
mine, get from a mine
pull, extract
quarry, take stone from
raise, obtain an army, tax, etc.
soak, absorb

Extract
abstract, take from
deduct, take away
dock, deduct
excerpt, select from a writing
extract, draw from
subtract, deduct
withdraw, abstract

Recover
extricate, rescue
find, gain by luck
glean, gather leavings
pinch, gain painfully
ransom, redeem
reclaim, recover
recover, regain
recoup, regain
redeem, reclaim
regain, gain again
replevy, gain by replevin
rescue, redeem
retrieve, recover
save, rescue

Tax
excise, levy a tax
impost, fix a duty
levy, impose tax
surtax, tax additionally
tax, acquire by taxation

ADJECTIVES

Acquisitive
acquisitive, acquiring
covetous, acquisitive
miserly, grasping
niggardly, miserly

Appropriative
adoptive, appropriative

ADJECTIVES (Continued)
anticipant, taking before
appropriative, adoptive
assumptive, appropriative

Selective
avocational, having recourse
choice, selective
elective, selective
eclectic, selective
optional, noting choice
occupational, occupied for gain
preferential, taking by choice
select, choosing
selective, selecting
vocational, occupational

Discriminating
discriminating, scrupulous
fastidious, meticulous
finical, fastidious
meticulous, finical
particular, fastidious
scrupulous, particular

Thriving
accretive, attaining by growth
flourishing, prosperous
gainful, gaining
growing, accretive
industrious, thrifty
profitable, gainful
prosperous, accruing richly
successful, prosperous
thrifty, thriving
thriving, prosperous

Miscellaneous
absorbent, soaking up
absorptive, absorbent
attractive, attaining by attraction
capillary, having porous attraction
sorbefacient, soaking up

Extractive
abstractional, appropriative
abstractive, abstractional
derivative, drawn from another
eductive, drawing from
extractible, pulling out
participant, sharing
subtractive, deductive

(Continued on page 95)

ADJECTIVES (Continued)
Recovering
redemptive, reclaiming
redemptory, redemptive
retrievable, recovering

NOUNS
Acquisition
achievement, acquirement
acquirement, acquisition
acquisition, attainment
acquisitiveness, acquirement
attainder, attainment by outlawing a right
attainment, acquirement
coup, sudden achievement
obtainment, acquirement

Appropriation
adoption, appropriation
affiliation, adoption
anticipation, assumption
appropriation, adoption
arrogation, assumption
assumption, arrogation
bottomry, a borrowing on security of a ship
importation, acquirement from abroad
opportunism, gaining
opportune, advantage
sabotage, workers' acquirement by reducing work

Selection
alternative, choice
ballot, vote
choice, selection
election, choice
option, rightful choice
pick, selection
predilection, preferment
preference, choice
preferment, preference
prerogative, predilection
privilege, prerogative
recourse, choice
right, privilege
selection, choice
vote, choice by vote

Gain
behoof, gain
desert, merit
earnings, gain
find, lucky gain
gain, success
income, gain
merit, desert
profit, gain
profitableness, profit
prosperity, lavish gain

NOUNS (Continued)
return, profit
revenue, income
seigniorage, minting profit
success, prosperity
trove, a find
trump, a winning medium
vails, profit
winnings, gain

Miscellaneous
absorbability, absorptivity
absorbency, absorptivity
absorptivity, absorption
absorption, an absorbing
attraction, accretion
capillarity, attraction through pores, etc.
eduction, exhaustion
exhaustion, utter appropriation
gravitation, attraction
magnetism, attraction
participation, a sharing
suction, a sucking

Extraction
abstraction, a drawing
deduction, subtraction
extraction, abstraction
subtraction, deduction

Recovery
recovery, a regaining
redemption, recovery
replevin, recovery from wrongful seizure
retrievableness, recovery
trover, legal recovery

Tax
capitation, tax
custom, duty
duty, impost
excise, tax levy
impost, tax
levy, impost
poll-tax, capitation tax
surtax, capitation tax
tax, taxation
taxation, impost
tribute, tax

Thriving
accretion, assimilation
accruement, accretion
assimilation, accretion
augmentation, accretion
growth, accretion
increment, accretion

Employment
avocation, occupation for gratification

NOUNS (Continued)
employment, occupation
livelihood, employment
occupation, vocation
procuration, occupation of white-slavery
vocation, employment

Diligence
diligence, industry
industry, employment
thrift, employment
thriftiness, thrift

MEDIUMS
catchpenny, article for catching small profits
nucleus, accretive center
protractor, instrument for extracting substances

PERSONS
appropriator, taker
beachcomber, retriever on a beach
eclectic, one who chooses from different creeds
electorate, assemblage entitled to vote or choose
electoral college, assemblage for choosing a U. S. A. President
extractor, abstractor
financier, one engaged in the acquisition of wealth
finder, one who finds
getter, acquirer
merchant, one engaged in commerce
participator, sharer
participant, participator
profiteer, one who profits on public expense
ransomer, redeemer
redeemer, one who redeems
redemptioner, redeemer
rescuer, redeemer
retriever, recoverer
Savior, redeemer
selector, one who selects
stipendiary, one who acquires by service
winner, one who acquires through contest

BEING
Hermes, god of commerce

49B

ACCEPTANCE— RECIPIENCE see—		ASSOCIATIVE	
	Acquirement 49A	Roguery 130A	
vs. Rejection—Opposition 27	Seizure 49C	Robbery 49G	
vs. Ban—Prohibition 35	Purchase 49D	Learning 116	
	Theft 49F	Hoarding 49E	

49B

VERBS

Miscellaneous

accept, take
admit, receive
benefit, derive help
catch, receive
conceive, receive into the womb
derive, receive
draw, receive
embrace, receive willingly
graft, take bribery
inherit, derive from a deceased
reap, receive
receive, accept
take, accept

ADJECTIVES

Recipient

acceptable, accepting
conceptive, noting mental or uterine reception
receivable, receptive
receptive, receiving
recipient, receiving
taking, accepting

Beneficiary

accessional, receiving or assuming in succession
abintestate, succeeding to an estate left without a will
beneficiary, receiving benefit
eleemosynary, receiving alms
heritable, implying inheritance
metronymic, deriving from one's mother or female ancestor
patrimonial, deriving from one's father or ancestor
parcenary, inheriting through co-heirship
pensionary, receiving a pension

MEDIUMS

depository, treasury
mortise, a receiving hole for a tenon
repository, receiving warehouse
treasury, a financial institution
socket, a receiving device

NOUNS

Miscellaneous

acceptability, acceptation
acceptance, recipience
acceptation, acceptance
accession, attainment through succession
admission, reception
birthright, reception by inheritance
catch, reception of something tossed
conception, reception into the mind or ovum
heritage, inheritance
inheritance, derivation from an ancestor
patrimony, inherited right
primogeniture, inheritance by right of seniority
receipt, reception
recipience, reception
reception, recipience
receptibility, reception
treasureship, the function of receiving and paying as in a treasury

PERSONS

Recipient

acceptor, receiver
receiver, recipient
recipient, one who receives
taker, acceptor

Beneficiary

advowee, receiver of a benefice
almsman, one who receives alms
annuitant, recipient of an annuity
beneficiary, one who receives a benefit
bursar, a student who receives an allowance
devisee, one who receives a bequest
donee, one who receives a donation
eleemosynary, the recipient of alms
grantee, the recipient of a grant
heir, the recipient of an inheritance

PERSONS (Plural)

heiress, as above (female)
heir apparent, one who has the right to succeed if he outlives an ancestor
heir presumptive, the one to become an heir if one nearer in succession is not born
legatee, the recipient of a legacy
parcener, a co-heir
parvenu, the recipient of new wealth
pensionary, pensioner
pensioner, the recipient of a pension
scion, heir
stipendiary, the recipient of compensation
upstart, parvenu

Miscellaneous

appointee, one who receives an appointment
assignee, recipient of an assignment
bailee, one who receives goods from a bailor
concessionaire, recipient of a concession
consignee, recipient of a consignment
depositary, recipient of goods for safekeeping
exercitor, the recipient of a ship's profits
fence, the receiver of stolen goods
grafter, the acceptor of bribes
guest, the recipient of hospitality
indorsee, an assignee
medalist, the recipient of a medal
mortgagee, the recipient of a mortgage
payee, the recipient of payment
presentee, the recipient of an ecclesiastical benefice
teller, receiving teller
treasurer, one who receives and disburses funds
trustee, depositary

Page 96

SEIZURE—CAPTURE see—

vs. Rejection—Dismissal 27
vs. Ban—Prohibition 35

ASSOCIATIVE

49C
VERBS

Seize

catch, grasp
grab, nab
nab, seize
pounce, seize suddenly
seize, take forcibly
snatch, seize suddenly
swoop, pounce

Apprehend

apprehend, seize
arrest, intercept
attach, seize
capture, intercept
clasp, hook into
clutch, grasp
collar, seize
cop, capture
engage, attach to
fasten, seize
grapple, engage
grasp, seize
grip, seize tightly
gripe, seize
hook, clasp
intercept, seize
stop, intercept
tackle, grapple
take, seize

Trap, Snare, Etc.

bag, capture
corral, capture
corner, corral
creel, catch
ensnare, trap
entrap, ensnare
gin, to trap
land, capture
lasso, catch with a rope
net, catch with a net
noose, lasso
pit, to trap
pocket, take into a pocket
sack, catch with a sack
snare, catch
trap, ensnare

Wrest, Yank, Etc.

jerk, yank
pluck, pull
pull, pluck
wrench, wrest
wrest, twist from
yank, wrest

Deprive, Confiscate

commandeer, impress

VERBS (Continued)

confiscate, seize
conscript, impress
crusade, seize under the
   banner of the cross
deprive, confiscate
disseize, deprive unlawfully
distrain, seize
draft, conscript
embrace, take close
impress, commandeer
levy, distrain
possess, seize
screw, take by oppression
sequester, seize property
   pending the establish-
   ment of a claim
shanghai, impress unjustly

ADJECTIVES

captious, seizing upon
confiscatory, possessory
grasping, prehensile
possessory, embracing
prehensible, prehensile
prehensile, having the
   faculty of grasping
tentacular, prehensile

NOUNS

Confiscation, Etc.

ablation, a taking from
angaria, forcible seizure
apprehension, seizure
appropriation, angaria
attachment, seizure
capture, seizure
confiscation, angaria
conscription, impressment
crusade, seizure, as by
   Christian power
deprivation, confiscation
disseizin, unjust seizure
distraint, levy
draft, conscription
impressment, confiscation
levy, forcible seizure
prehension, a seizing with
   the hand, etc.
seizen, forcible seizure
sequestration, seizure of
   property for the benefit
   of creditors
seizure, apprehension

PERSONS

appropriator, taker
captor, apprehender
confiscator, sequestrator
deadhead, appropriator of
   advantage without pay
irredentist, appropriator
opportunist, one who seizes
   what is opportune
press-gang, seamen em-
   powered to seize for
   service
sequestrator, one who
   sequestrates
skinflint, one who habitually bereaves his victims
taker, apprehender

MEDIUMS

Claw, Etc.

claw, prehensile extremity
clutches, claws
paw, a foot with claws
talons, claws

Trap, Snare, Etc.

bow-net, trap-like holder
bolas, roped balls for ensnaring animals
cobweb, a snare
deadfall, trap
drop, a trap
fishgig, a fishing device
fishhook, a snare
fyke, fish trap
gin, trap
lariat, lasso
lasso, an ensnaring rope
net, a corded trap
pit, trap
pitfall, trap
seine, fish net
snap, a spring catch
snare, noose, etc.
trap, a snare

Clasp, Latch, Etc.

buckle, clasp
button, a fastening disk
bolt, a door catch
catch, latch
clasp, latch
crotch, hook
hasp, clasp
hook, a catch
latch, a catch
lock, a spring catch
(Continued on page 98)

BUYING (Acquisition by Exchange) see—	ASSOCIATIVE	

BUYING (Acquisition
by Exchange) see—
vs. Selling—Venders..44

ASSOCIATIVE

Seizure 49C
Acquirement 49A
Hoarding 49E

Theft 49F
Roguery 130A
Robbery 49G

49D

VERBS

Buy, Etc.

buy, purchase
commute, exchange
engross, buy in bulk
exchange, give for another
invest, buy
purchase, buy equivalent
purvey, buy provisions
swap, exchange

Trade, Etc.

barter, haggle in trade
dicker, barter
gamble, speculate
market, buy and sell
speculate, invest with risk
trade, barter
traffic, trade

Spend

disburse, buy with funds
expend, disburse
spend, expend

Forestall

bribe, exchange corruptly
contract, negotiate
forestall, buy in advance
incur, become obligated
lease, buy a privilege .
monopolize, forestall
negotiate, exchange
preempt, forestall
rent, lease

VERBS (Continued)

Employ

employ, hire
engage, employ
farm, hire land on shares
hire, employ
occupy, employ
use, employ
utilize, use

ADJECTIVES

commutable, exchanging
expensive, sumptuary
monopolistic, preempt
preempt, buying before-
  hand
simoniacal, trafficking in
  sacred things
speculative, buying with
  risk
sumptuary, purchasing or
  expending

PERSONS

banker, dealer in finance
broker, a dealer
buyer, purchaser
commuter, one who buys
  passage, etc.
dealer, trader
investor, dealer
jobber, a dealer in mer-
  cantile commodities
merchant, dealer in mer-
  chandise

PERSONS (Continued)

monger, trafficker
monopolist, preemptor
piker, timid investor
preemptor, an acquirer
  beforehand
purchaser, buyer
trader, dealer

NOUNS

agiotage, the business of
  exchanging one kind of
  money for another
barter, trafficking
commutation, the purchase
  of passage, etc.
disbursement, expenditure
engrossment, monopoly
exchange, swap
expenditure, disbursement
expense, expenditure
investment, purchase
monopoly, preemption
negotiation, exchange
preemption, a purchasing
  before others
purchase, a buying
purveyance, the purchase
  of provisions
simony, a trafficking in
  sacred interests
speculation, risky trading
swap, an exchange
trade, purchase or sale

49C (Continued)

MEDIUMS (Continued)

padlock, a clasp lock
pintle, a bolt

Tongs, Pincers

clamp, clamp-like holder
cramp, a holding device
forceps, pliers
monkey-wrench, wrench
nippers, pincers

MEDIUMS (Continued)

pincers, nippers
pinchers, pincers
pliers, nippers
tongs, large pliers
tweezers, pincers
vise, a holding medium
wrench, a twisting device

Anchor

anchor, an engaging device

MEDIUMS (Continued)

fluke, an anchor point
grapnel, anchor
kedge, anchor

Tentacle, Etc.

finger, a prehensile digit
hand, a prehensile medium
tentacle, prehensile organ
tendril, plant tentacle

AMASSMENT   see—

    vs. Dissipation 125C

ASSOCIATIVE

Many—Much 147I	Seizure 49C
Acceptance 49B	Theft 49F
Acquirement 49A	Robbery 49G
Purchase 49D	Possession 52A

49E

VERBS

Miscellaneous

accumulate, amass
amass, hoard
assemble, accumulate
collect, accumulate
cumulate, accumulate
garner, gather
gather, accumulate
glean, collect
harvest, gather
hoard, accumulate
pluck, gather
reap, harvest
save, treasure
store, hoard
scrape, glean
treasure, hoard

ADJECTIVES

Miscellaneous

accumulative, collective
autumnal, noting the
    autumn harvest
collective, accumulative
cumulative, accumulative
mercenary, niggardly
miserly, hoarding miserlike
niggardly, miserly
saving, hoarding
venial, mercenary

NOUNS

Miscellaneous

accumulation, an amassing
amassment, accumulation
collection, accumulation
cumulation, accumulation

NOUNS (Continued)

gleaning, gathering follow-
    ing the reaping
harvesting, a reaping
hoarding, an amassing
miserliness, mean hoarding
niggardliness, miserliness
philately, the collection of
    stamps
reaping, harvesting

PERSONS

accumulator, collector
capitalist, owner of capital
cashier, money custodian
collector, gatherer
connoisseur, collector of
    arts
curioso, collector of
    curiosities
harvester, reaper
mercenary, one occupied
    with gaining money
millionaire, wealthy man
miser, one who hoards
    meanly
muckworm, miser
multimillionaire, a man
    with many millions
nabob, a very wealthy man
niggard, miser
philatelist, stamp collector
reaper, harvest gatherer
treasurer, connoisseur

THINGS AMASSED

Amassment

accumulation, mass
aggregation, collection
amassment, heap

THINGS AMASSED

(Continued)

collection, aggregation
fascicle, collection
glean, collected gleanings
harvest, a gathering in
hoard, accumulated
    commodity
increment, amassment

Mass

deposit, accumulation
heap, mass
lodgment, deposit
mass, pile
pile, heap
stock, store
store, accumulated stock

Property

assets, property
goods, assets
means, resource
possession, property
property, assets, goods
resources, money, means

Treasure

bonanza, a mine of wealth
El Dorado, vast treasure
Golconda, mine of wealth
mine, bonanza
treasure, riches

Wealth

affluence, wealth
fortune, riches
mammon, great wealth
opulence, wealth
plum, a large fortune
riches, wealth
wealth, riches

49F (Continued)

PERSONS (Continued)

grafter, embezzler of the
    public trust
misappropriator, peculator
peculator, embezzler

Usurer

body-snatcher, one who
    steals from graves
contrabandist, smuggler
ghoul, body-snatcher
plagiarist, appropriator of
    another's writings
poacher, a game-thief
smuggler, contrabandist
stowaway, passage thief
usurer, smuggler

PERSONS (Continued)

Deceiver

cat's paw, one who serves
    the knavery of another
decoy, humbugger
stool pigeon, decoy

Swindler

bam, a cheat
bilk, swindler
blackleg, a cheat
card-sharp, a cheat at
    cards
cheat, swindler
crimp, knave
crook, swindler

PERSONS (Continued)

deadbeat, crook
duffer, swindler
fake, swindler
forger, swindler
fraud, cheat
humbug, a cheat
humbugger, a humbug
jockey, a cheat
huckster, a cheat
knave, a swindler
rogue, knave
rook, swindler
sharper, swindler
swindler, a cheat

THEFT—FRAUD   ASSOCIATIVE

(Sly Acquirement)   see— Robbery ....49G   Dishonesty 130A

Seizure ....49C   Hoarding 49E

vs. Honesty—Justice ..140A   Acquirement 49A

49F

VERBS

Thieve, Spirit

abduct, steal off with
bag, steal
bone, steal
burglarize, take by theft
cadge, steal
crib, steal
filch, steal
finger, steal
kidnap, steal (a child)
lift, steal
pick, pilfer
pilfer, steal
purloin, steal
sneak, steal on advantage
spirit, kidnap, sneak
steal, take secretly
swipe, steal
thieve, steal

Misappropriate

defalcate, misappropriate
default, misappropriate
embezzle, defalcate
misappropriate, default
peculate, embezzle

Usurp

encroach, usurp stealthily
poach, steal game
smuggle, take past duty
usurp, take wrongfully

Deceive

beguile, delude
circumvent, delude
crimp, delude
deceive, beguile
delude, cheat
foist, deceive
gull, cheat
hawk, foist
hocus, deceive
plagiarize, foist the work
of another as one's own

Swindle

bam, cheat
bamboozle, humbug
bilk, cheat
bishop, bamboozle
bunco, swindle
cheat, defraud
chouse, swindle
cozen, cheat
defraud, cheat
diddle, cheat
do, swindle
dupe, cheat
ensnare, take by a ruse

VERBS (Continued)

entrap, ensnare
fake, swindle
fiddle, cheat
finesse, take by artifice
fleece, cheat
humbug, cheat
jockey, cheat
palm, cheat
rook, swindle
skin, cheat
sponge, deceive
swindle, defraud
trick, cheat
victimize, swindle

ADJECTIVES

Miscellaneous

burglarious, thievish
deceptive, meretricious
feline, treacherous
foxy, treacherous
fraudulent, swindling
furtive, stolen
ghoulish, stealing from
graves
knavish, swindling
larcenous, thievish
meretricious, deceptive
pilfering, thievish
roguish, knavish
sacrilegious, stealing from
a temple
surreptitious, deceptive
swindling, cheating
thievish, addicted to stealing
treacherous, untrustworthy
tricky, deceptive
unauthorized, treacherous
untrustworthy, knavish

NOUNS

Thievery

abduction, a kidnapping
burglary, theft
crib, petty theft
kidnapping, abduction
kleptomania, tendency to
steal
robbery, thievery
roguery, theft
sacrilege, theft from
temples
shoplifting, theft from
stores

Misappropriation

defalcation, embezzlement
embezzlement, defalcation

NOUNS (Continued)

larceny, embezzlement
malversation, dishonesty
misappropriation, larcency
peculation, embezzlement

Usurpation

encroachment, surreptitious
usurpation
piracy, plagiarism
plagiarism, misappropria-
tion of another's work
smuggling, usurpation
usurpation, smuggling

Deception

beguilement, fraud
deceit, delusion
deceitfulness, deception
deception, humbuggery
delusion, imposition
imposition, deceit

Swindling

bunco, fraud
confidence game, fraud
craft, fraud
forgery, fraud
fraud, swindling
fraudulence, fraud
humbuggery, fraud
jobbery, fraud
knavery, fraud
swindle, fraud
trickery, fraud

PERSONS

Thief

abductor, kidnaper
biblioklept, book thief
crib, thief
fingerer, thief
kidnaper, abductor
kleptomaniac, one who
insanely steals
pickpocket, thief
pilferer, thief
sacrilegist, temple thief
sneak, thief
thief, burglar

Robber

burglar, thief
cracksman, burglar
robber, burglar
yeggman, safe robber

Misappropriator

defalcator, embezzler
defaulter, embezzler
embezzler, defaulter
(Continued on page 99)

ROBBERY—PILLAGE
(Open Robbery)   see— {   (ASSOCIATIVE 49F)
vs. Honesty—Justice ....140A {

49G

VERBS

Rob, Etc.

abduct, kidnap
garrote, strangle and rob
harry, rob
holdup, rob
kidnap, take forcibly
pick, rob
raven, rob
ravish, take by force
rob, take by force

Plunder, Etc.

depredate, pillage
despoil, pillage
divest, despoil
foray, pillage
gut, plunder
invade, plunder
loot, pillage
maraud, plunder
pillage, plunder
plunder, depredate
prey, plunder
raid, pillage
ransack, plunder
rapine, pillage
ravage, despoil
rifle, pillage
sack, pillage
spoil, plunder
strip, rob
swoop, invade suddenly

Extort, Etc.

blackmail, extort
bleed, extort
deprive, appropriate
exact, bleed
extort, exact
fleece, plunder
usurp, take by force
wring, extort

Pirate

buccaneer, pillage
filibuster, buccaneer
pirate, plunder
privateer, plunder

ADJECTIVES

Miscellaneous

depredatory, predatory
extortionate, extortionary

ADJECTIVES (Continued)

extortionary, wringing
  from
lupine, wolfish
pillaging, depredatory
piratic, pirate-like
plundering, predatory
predacious, preying upon
predatory, plundering
rapacious, predatory
ravenous, plundering madly
usurious, extortionate
vulturine, rapacious

NOUNS

Loot, Plunder

boodle, public plunder
booty, spoils of plunder
blood-money, money for
  murder
goods, booty
loot, spoils
pelf, loot
pillage, spoils
plunder, booty
prey, booty
spoils, plunder
swag, booty

Miscellaneous

abduction, a kidnaping
accroachment, usurpation
badger-game, foul exaction
blackbirding, the kidnap-
  ing of negroes
blackmail, extortion by
  intimidation
brigandage, robbery
dacoity, robbery by gangs
depredation, pillage
exaction, extortion
extortion, foul seizure
foray, raid
hold-up, highway robbery
incursion, raid
inroad, raid
invasion, incursion
irruption, sudden invasion
pillage, robbery
piracy, sea raiding
raid, predatory incursion
rapacity, ravening
rape, forcible seizure
rapine, plunder

NOUNS (Continued)

raven, pillage
ravening, preying
  propensity
robbery, active plundering
spoliation, robbery, etc.
usurpation, foul seizure
usury, usurpation

PERSONS

Robber, Etc.

abductor, kidnaper
bandit, brigand
brigand, robber
bushranger, highwayman
decoit, bandit
depredator, pillager
footpad, highwayman
garroter, one who strangles
  and robs
guerrilla, depredator
harpy, plunderer
highwayman, robber
kidnaper, abductor
ladrone, robber
marauder, depredator
peeler, plunderer
picaroon, marauder
rifler, robber
robber, brigand
ruffian, robber
spoiler, depredator
thug, robber
tyrant, a usurper of power
vulture, depredator
wolf, depredator
wrecker, plunderer

Interloper

interloper, foul interceptor
land-grabber, land usurper
usurer, one who seizes
  foully

Pirate, Etc.

buccaneer, pirate
filibuster, buccaneer
freebooter, buccaneer
pirate, high-sea robber
privateer, plunderer
ranger, marauder
reefer, one who entices and
  plunders vessels
rover, pirate
viking, pirate

CONQUEST—	ASSOCIATIVE
ACHIEVEMENT see— ⎧ Government 133A	Imprisonment 52H
vs. Failure ....127B ⎨ Opposition 27	Strength—Force 137B
vs. Submission ....46B ⎩ Decree—Law 94	Superlativeness 140B

50

VERBS

Conquer

bow, subdue
conquer, subdue
crush, vanquish
disarm, subdue
dragoon, vanquish
subdue, conquer
subjugate, subdue
triumph, vanquish
vanquish, conquer

Achieve

achieve, accomplish
attain, achieve
avail, profit
carry, win
fare, succeed
gain, succeed
land, achieve
profit, gain
prosper, succeed
reach, attain
realize, profit
score, win
speed, prosper
succeed, accomplish
tally, score
trump, win
win, achieve

Conclude

accomplish, effect
cap, culminate
complete, accomplish
conclude, complete
crown, complete
culminate, crown
consummate, accomplish
finish, culminate
fulfil, conclude

Commit

commit, execute
do, commit
effect, achieve
execute, accomplish
perform, do
perpetrate, perform

Frustrate

baffle, defeat
balk, baffle
beat, defeat
bridle, subdue
cast, defeat at law
checkmate, defeat
circumvent, outwit
defeat, vanquish
foil, frustrate
frustrate, defeat

VERBS (Continued)

kibosh, defeat
outdo, defeat
outwit, frustrate
rebuff, repel
thwart, frustrate

Suppress

abate, suppress
check, curb
constrain, compel
convince, silence
curb, subdue
muzzle, subdue
quell, crush
reduce, subdue
repress, restrain
restrain, subdue
silence, subdue
smother, suppress
squelch, crush
suppress, subdue

Compel

chain, enslave
coerce, compel
compel, enforce
enforce, compel
enslave, enthrall
enthrall, enslave
force, compel
impose, compel
impress, compel
make, compel
necessitate, compel
oblige, compel
oppress, impose
press, force
subject, subjugate
subordinate, subject

Humble

disappoint, frustrate
discomfit, defeat
disconcert, frustrate
faze, discomfit
humble, subdue
tame, subdue

Prevail

dominate, prevail
domineer, dominate
overbear, overpower
overcome, vanquish
overpower, overcome
overthrow, conquer
predominate, prevail
preponderate, overpower
prevail, preponderate
subvert, overthrow
surmount, overcome
top, surmount

VERBS (Continued)

Surpass

distance, outstrip
eclipse, excel
exceed, excel
excel, surpass
outgo, distance
outstrip, distance
outwit, eclipse
pass, surpass
scrape, barely exceed
surpass, outdo
survive, outlast
transcend, excel
weather, survive

Mesmerize

bewitch, mesmerize
captivate, bewitch
charm, captivate
enchant, fascinate
enthrall, charm
fascinate, charm
hypnotize, mesmerize
infatuate, fascinate
magnetize, mesmerize
mesmerize, bewitch
witch, bewitch

ADJECTIVES

Conquering

conquering, victorious
triumphal, triumphant
triumphant, victorious
victorious, triumphant

Successful

prosperous, successful
successful, triumphant
thriving, successful

Conclusive

absolute, dominant
conclusive, decisive
convincing, conclusive
decisive, positive
fatal, fateful
fatalistic, absolute
fateful, unavoidable
inescapable, decisive
inevitable, unavoidable
positive, conclusive
unavoidable, irresistible
utter, absolute

Unconquerable

incontestable, invincible
indefeasible, indomitable
indomitable, invincible
inexorable, compelling
insuperable, invincible

(Continued on page 103)

ADJECTIVES (Continued)
invincible, unconquerable
irrepressible, invincible
irresistible, indomitable
resistless, irresistible
spartan, exceptionally
  brave
unconquerable, invincible

Compulsive
coercive, compulsory
compelling, compulsory
compulsive, coercive
compulsory, compulsive
incumbent, obligatory
obligatory, compelling
relentless, compelling

Prevalent
circumventive, outwitting
dominant, ruling
oppressive, overpowering
overpowering, dominating
predominant, prevailing
prevailing, prevalent
prevalent, predominant
ruling, dominant
subversive, dominant
superior, ruling
surpassing, superior
transcending, surpassing

NOUNS
Conquest
conquest, victory
triumph, victory
victory, conquest

Achievement
achievement, attainment
attainment, accomplish-
  ment
gain, achievement
prosperity, success
realization, achievement
speed, success
success, achievement
weal, prosperity
welfare, prosperity

Conclusion
accomplishment, deed
completion, fulfilment
conclusion, fulfilment
consummation, conclusion
culmination, consummation
finality, culmination
finish, fulfilment
fruition, fulfilment

NOUNS (Continued)
Commission
fulfilment, culmination
career, commission
commission, performance
coup, master stroke
deed, commission
execution, accomplishment
feat, performance
performance, achievement
perpetration, deed

Frustration
checkmate, defeat
defeat, conquest
frustration, defeat
kibosh, (slang) defeat
rebuff, defeat
reversal, overthrow
subjection, subjugation
subjugation, bondage
subordination, subjection
subversion, overthrow

Suppression
abatement, suppression
arrest, abatement
constraint, repression
quietus, a suppressing
reduction, subjugation
repression, constraint
restraint, enforcement
suppression, constraint

Compulsion
compulsion, enforcement
coercion, compulsion
duress, compulsion
enforcement, compulsion
imposition, compulsion
incumbency, obligation
obligation, incumbency
oppression, imposition

Prevalence
absoluteness, dominance
absolutism, absoluteness
advantage, superiority
ascendancy, domination
control, dominance
debacle, overthrow
dominance, domination
domination, control
influence, ruling force
invincibility, absoluteness
mastery, domination
overthrow, defeat
predominance, prevalence
predomination, prevalence
prevalence, superiority
superiority, invincibility

NOUNS (Continued)
sway, domination
weight, influence

Mesmerism
bewitchery, captivation
captivation, charm
charm, bewitchery
conjuration, enchantment
enchantment, captivation
fascination, charm
hypnosis, mesmerism
hypnotism, mesmerism
mesmerism, hypnotism
spell, conjuration
vampirism, bewitchery
witchcraft, conjuration

Enslavement
bondage, enslavement
enslavement, thralldom
enthrallment, bondage
serfdom, bondage
slavery, bondage
thralldom, slavery
thrall, bondage
vassalage, bondage
villenage, vassalage
yoke, bondage

Destiny
decree, eternal purpose
destiny, inevitable lot
doom, fate
fatalism, inevitability
fate, destiny
fatality, fate
foredoom, destiny
inevitability, fate
kismet, fate

PERSONS
champion, hero
conqueror, victor
hero, victor
hypnotist, mesmerist
master, victor
medalist, winner
mesmerist, hypnotist
subjugator, victor
successor, victor
suppressor, conqueror
survivor, successor
winner, successor
victor, conqueror

BEINGS
Nike, goddess of victory
Ashur, god of military
  prowess

EATING—DRINKING, Etc.   **see—**   **ASSOCIATIVE**

51A

vs. Starvation—Need 37   { Food 48A
{ Learning—Study 116

51A

VERBS

Eat
browse, graze
consume, devour
eat, chew and swallow
feed, eat
graze, eat grass
mess, eat together
munch, eat noisily
pick, eat fastidiously

Assimilate
assimilate, digest
digest, assimilate
incorporate, assimilate
stomach, assimilate

Subsist
batten, thrive
board, take meals
exist, live
fare, eat
live, subsist
subsist, take sustenance
thrive, subsist

Devour
bolt, swallow hurriedly
devour, bolt
gobble, gorge
prey, devour
raven, devour
swallow, to stomach

Glut
cram, glut
engorge, devour
glut, gormandize
gluttonize, gormandize
gorge, glut
gormandize, eat to excess
hog, gormandize
sate, surfeit
satiate, sate
stuff, gorge
surfeit, gorge

Feast, Etc.
banquet, feast
breakfast, eat on rising
carouse, feast
dine, eat dinner
feast, eat sumptuously
junket, feast
lunch, eat lightly
revel, feast
sup, take supper

Relish, Etc.
enjoy, relish
relish, eat with gusto
savor, relish
smack, savor
taste, smack

Inhale
aspire, breathe
breathe, inhale

VERBS (Continued)
gape, yawn
gasp, breathe violently
inhale, inspire
inspire, breathe
smoke, inhale smoke
respire, breathe
yawn, respire gapingly

ADJECTIVES

Assimilative
assimilative, digesting food
digestive, assimilative

Respectively Subsisting
anthropophagous, feeding on human flesh
cannibalistic, eating one's own kind
carnivorous, feeding on flesh
ghoulish, feeding on corruption
graminivorous, eating grass
granivorous, eating grain
herbivorous, eating herbs
ichthyophagous, fish-eating
idiotrophic, taking affinitive nourishment, said of living cells
insectivorous, eating insects
ogreish, devouring humans
omnivorous, eating anything
omophagic, eating raw flesh
pantophagous, omnivorous
parasitic, eating at the expense of others
phytivorous, phytophagous
phytophagous, eating plants
sarcophagous, carnivorous
xylophagous, feeding on wood

Rapacious
ferocious, rapacious
greedy, gluttonous
rapacious, greedy
ravenous, voracious
swinish, ravenous
voracious, rapacious
vulturine, rapacious

Gluttonous
crapulent, gluttonous
edacious, voracious
Gargantuan, gluttonous
gluttonous, edacious
hoggish, gluttonous
intemperate, gluttonous
piggish, hoggish

ADJECTIVES (Continued)

Festive, Etc.
Epicurean, gratifying the appetite
festive, feasting
gastronomic, Epicurean
gustatory, having relish
gustful, gustatory
gusty, gustful

Inhaling
aspiratory, breathing
breathing, respiratory
inspiratory, aspiratory
pulmonary, implying respiration
pulmonic, pertaining to the lungs, etc.
respiratory, pertaining to breathing

NOUNS

Appetence, Etc.
alimentiveness, instinct for food
appetence, appetite
appetite, relish
hunger, keenness of appetite
stomach, appetite

Assimilation
assimilation, digestion
digestion, assimilation
incorporation, assimilation

Subsistence
board, daily meals
breakfast, first meal
mess, an eating together
subsistence, living

Rapacity
avidity, rapacity
greediness, rapacity
rapacity, greediness
voracity, rapacity

Gluttony
edacity, gluttony
engorgement, rapacity
gluttony, excessive eating
satiety, surfeit
surfeit, gluttony

Festivity, Etc.
banquet, a feasting
carnival, the feast before Lent, when flesh is eaten
conviviality, festivity
feast, sumptuous eating
festivity, a feasting
fete, festivity
junket, a feasting
kermess, feast in the open
love-feast, religious feast
(Continued on page 105)

NOUNS (Continued)
lunch, light meal
luncheon, lunch
picnic, excursion feast
revelry, festivity

Relish, Etc.
delectation, enjoyment
enjoyment, relish
Epicureanism, relish for food
gastronomy, Epicureanism
gusto, relish
palate, relish
relish, gusto in eating
savor, relish
smack, savor
taste, gustful perception
tooth, relish
zest, keen relish

Respective Subsistence
cannibalism, the custom of eating one's kind
deglutition, a swallowing
geophagism, the practice of eating earth
geophagy, geophagism
hippophagy, eating of horseflesh
parasitism, a living on others
pantophagy, the eating of all kinds of food

NOUNS (Continued)
symbiosis, living made on a parasite
vegetarianism, the eating of vegetables

Inhalation
breath, respiration
inhalation, breath
inspiration, inhalation
respiration, breathing
smoke, act of smoking

PERSONS
Epicure, Etc.
epicure, one who gratifies the appetite
Epicurean, epicure
gourmet, epicure
gastronomist, epicure
lotus-eater, one who eats in order to forget
reveler, feaster

Glutton, Etc.
cormorant, glutton
glutton, excessive eater
gormand, glutton
gourmand, gormand
hog, glutton

Vulture, Etc.
carrion crow, carrion eater
cobra-de-capello, a ravenous snake

PERSONS (Continued)
vulture, one who preys on others

Respective Subsisters
anthropophagi, pl. cannibals
cannibal, one who eats the flesh of his own kind
carnivora, flesh-eating animals
eleemosynary, one who subsists on alms
ghoul, one who feeds on the dead in graves
herbivora, herb-eating animals
hippophagist, horse-flesh eater
ogre, man-eating monster
pantophagist, indiscriminate eater
parasite, one or that which exists at the expense of others
scavenger, that which eats refuse
sponge, a parasite
vampire, fabulous monster that sucks the blood of the sleeping
vegetarian, one who eats vegetables

DRINK

see— 51B
vs. Abstentation 132C

ASSOCIATIVE
{ Food—Nourishment 48A
{ Learning—Study 116

51B

VERBS
Drink, Etc.
booze, drink liquor
carouse, drink merrily
drink, imbibe
guzzle, gulp
hobnob, drink with friends
imbibe, drink
quaff, gulp
swig, drink greedily
swill, swig
tipple, booze
tope, booze

Swallow, Etc.
gobble, gulp
gulp, swallow eagerly
swallow, gulp
take, swallow

Suck, Sip, Etc.
absorb, drink
lap, lick up
lick, lap
sip, imbibe lightly
sponge, absorb
suck, imbibe

VERBS (Continued)
suckle, suck
sup, sip

ADJECTIVES
Drinking
absorbent, soaking up
absorptive, absorbent
bacchantic, drinking merrily
bacchic, bacchantic
bibulous, taking drink
crapulent, intemperate
intemperate, drinking too much
sucking, suctorial
suctorial, living by sucking

NOUNS
Drinking
carousal, noisy drinking
debauchery, riotous drinking
deglutition, swallowing process

NOUNS (Continued)
draft, act of drinking
drinking, an imbibing
gulp, a swallowing
intemperance, debauchery
nip, a small drink
orgy, carousal
potation, drinking bout
propination, a drinking before another to indicate absence of poison
sip, a light drink
suck, a drawing or drinking
sucking, a drinking
symposium, carousal
wassail, festivity

PERSONS
Drinkers
bacchanal, debauchee
bacchanate, as above (fem.)
bibber, guzzler
debauchee, guzzler
guzzler, debauchee
tippler, bibber

RESTRAINT

(Holding Back) see—

vs. Permission 46A

{
Abstentation 132C
Keep 52A
Binding—Cords, etc. 52B
}

ASSOCIATIVE

Confinement 52H
Obstruction 36A
Ban—Prohibition 35

52A

VERBS

Hold, Retain

adhere, hinder
cleave, cling
cling, hold firmly
hold, restrain
inhibit, restrain
keep, hold
repress, check
retain, hold
stick, cling
withhold, hold

Restrain, Etc.

apprehend, restrain
arrest, apprehend
coerce, constrain
constrain, restrain
reprehend, restrain
restrain, detain

Detain, Etc.

check, restrain
detain, hold back
deter, restrain
embarrass, hinder
encumber, impede
hamper, hinder
hinder, restrain
impede, restrain
interrupt, hinder
prohibit, hinder
stay, restrain
stop, hinder

Curb, Etc.

bond, limit
bridle, curb
circumscribe, restrict
collar, restrain
curb, restrain
halter, tie to a halter
limit, restrain
muzzle, hinder
restrict, limit

Fetter, Etc.

enchain, fetter
fetter, shackle
gyve, fetter the legs
hamshackle, restrain
hobble, shackle

VERBS (Continued)

iron, fetter
manacle, fetter
pinion, fetter
shackle, manacle

Tie, Hitch, Etc.

anchor, hold by anchor
hitch, tie up
leash, tie by a leash
picket, hitch
tether, tie
tie, tether

ADJECTIVES

Miscellaneous

coercible, constraining
coercive, restrictive
detentive, restrictive
deterrent, detentive
inhibitive, restraining
Malthusian, having restraining measures to prevent overpopulation
reprehensible, coercive
reprehensive, coercive
repressive, restrictive
restrictive, restraining

NOUNS

Miscellaneous

apprehension, arrest
arrest, detention
check, restraint
coercion, restraint
constraint, restriction
detainment, detention
detention, restraint
embracery, a restraining influence
hindrance, restraint
hitch, restraint by tether
hold, restraint
impeachment, a coercive accusation
interruption, hindrance
limitation, restriction
Malthusiasm, measure for restraining overpopulation

NOUNS (Continued

repression, restraint
restraint, hindrance
restriction, limitation
sabotage, hindrance of production to force increase in pay

MEDIUMS

Fetter, Etc.

anklet, a fetter
bilboes, fetters
darbies, manacles
fetter, a shackle
gyve, fetter for the legs
handcuff, fetter
irons, fetters
manacle, wrist fetters
pinion, a shackle
shackle, a fetter

Halter, Tether, Etc.

barnacle, instrument for holding horses
breeching, harness
bricole, man harness
bridle, a restraint
check, a curb
collar, a restraint
curb, a restraint
hackmore, halter
halter, a restraint
harness, stay, straps, etc.
martingale, strap for holding the head down
muzzle, a deterrent
rein, a bridle
snaffle, bridle
traces, harness, straps
tether, rope for confining
trammel, shackle for horses

Deterrent

brake, a friction device
detainer, deterrent
deterrent, preventer
fastening, deterrent
retainer, a holder
stopper, deterrent

BINDING—ADHESION see—

vs. Division—Separation 145A

ASSOCIATIVE

Unification 146A
Confinement 52H
Seizure 49C
Keep 132C

52B

VERBS

Bind, Tie, Etc.
astrict, bind closely
baste, stitch lightly
belay, make fast
bind, make fast
constrict, bind tightly
constringe, constrict
cord, tie
furl, secure, as a sail
gird, bind
girdle, gird
lace, fix with a lace
lash, secure tightly
leash, fix with a leash
pin, fix with a pin
rope, fix with a rope
secure, fasten
sew, stitch together
stitch, sew
strap, fix with a strap
swaddle, bind tightly
swathe, bandage
tie, fix with a cord
truss, bind closely

Attach, Affix, Etc.
affix, attach
append, attach
attach, fasten
concatenate, interlink
connect, join
couple, link together
fasten, make fast
fix, fasten
hinge, attach to a hinge
jam, wedge

VERBS (Continued)
join, connect
link, connect in links
skewer, fix with a meat pin
wedge, fix in place

Bolt, Latch, Etc.
bolt, fasten with a bolt
dovetail, interlock
interlock, lock together
latch, lock
lock, latch
padlock, lock with a pad-
lock

Hitch, Chain, Etc.
cable, fix with a cable
chain, fix with a chain
enchain, bind strongly
girt, moor with two cables
hitch, fix by a hitch
moor, secure or anchor

Brad, Etc.
brad, secure with a brad
clinch, rivet
nail, fix with a nail
rivet, brad
screw, fix with a screw
tack, fix with a tack

Braze, Etc.
braze, solder
solder, unite by solder
weld, fuse

Buckle, Hook, Etc.
buckle, fix with a buckle
button, fix with buttons

VERBS (Continued)
clamp, fix with a clamp
cramp, make fast
hook, fix with a hook
knot, fix with a knot

Twist, Etc.
entwine, twine around
envelop, wrap within
splice, interwind
spin, twist into thread
twine, unite closely
twist, twine
wrap, secure by wrapping

ADJECTIVES

Binding
astringent, binding
connecting, joining
constrictive, binding
constringent, binding
gordian, knotted

NOUNS

Binding
astriction, a binding
attachment, connection
binding, a making fast
concatenation, a linking
connection, fastening
connective, connection
constriction, a binding
engagement, attachment
fastening, connection
moorage, mooring place
splice, an interweaving
stitching, act of sewing

52C

NOUNS

Fiber
abb, yarn for weaving
fiber, a binding medium
fibril, a small fiber
filament, a fine thread
yarn, spun thread

Special Fibers
arrasene, wool thread
cotton, a plant fiber
fibroin, raw silk
flax, a fiber
hemp, cordage fiber
jute, rope fiber
oakum, loose hemp
silk, a fine fiber

Cord, Line, Etc.
binder, a binding medium
brail, binding rope
cord, a binding medium
funicle, a small cord
funiculus, funicle

NOUNS (Continued)
lace, a cord
leash, a thong
ligature, band or tie
line, a cord
strand, twist of a rope
strap, a binding strip
string, a small line
tab, a latchet
thong, strip of leather
thread, fine cord
twine, strong thread
twist, a cord
wire, a metallic line

Rope, Etc.
cordage, ropes
forestay, mast rope
guy, rope, chain, etc.
halyard, hoisting rope
hank, rope or coil
hawser, rope or cable
painter, a fastening rope

NOUNS (Continued)
rigging, ship's cordage
rope, twisted cord
tackle, rigging

Cable, Etc.
cable, rope or chain
chain, a linked bond
moorings, cables, etc.

Band, Etc.
band, binder
bandage, band
bandlet, small band
bond, a band
cinch, saddle girth
collar, band
cordon, a band
fillet, headband
garter, girdle
girth, saddle band
ribbon, band of silk, etc.
roller, broad bandage

(Continued on page 108)

52C (Continued)

NOUNS (Continued)
swathe, bandage
tape, a narrow band
tire, band
wrapper, binder

NOUNS (Continued)
Knot, Tie, Etc.
clinch, a sure knot
knot, a tie
tie, a flexible bond

NOUNS (Continued)
Tendon, Etc.
leader, tendon
ligament, elastic tissue
muscle, fibrous organ
tendon, organic fiber

52D

NOUNS
Pin, Tack, Etc.
belaying pin, binding pin
brad, a nail
brock, a spike
bolt, a stout pin
dowel, spike-like pin
hairpin, pin for the hair

NOUNS (Continued)
hatpin, pin for fastening hats
linchpin, a wheel pin
nail, metal spike
peg, wooden pin
pin, pointed fastener
picket, a fastening stake
pivot, shaft

NOUNS (Continued)
rivet, bolt for clinching
screw, spiral-grooved nail
skewer, pin for fixing meat
spike, a large nail
stake, wooden post, etc.
staple, looped pin
tack, broad-headed nail
treenail, peg

52E

BINDING—ADHESION—
INHERENCE
vs. Division—Separation 145A

see— { (ASSOCIATIVE 52B)

52E

VERBS (Adhere)
adhere, stick
agglutinate, glue together
braze, fuse
cement, stick with cement
cleave, stick fast
cling, cleave
coalesce, grow together
cohere, stick together
concrete, unite solidly
congeal, freeze together
conglutinate, glue
fuse, melt together
glue, adhere
paste, stick
regelate, fuse
seal, fasten with wax
solder, fuse
stick, adhere
wax, unite with wax
weld, fuse

ADJECTIVES (Adhesive)
adherent, sticking fast
adhesive, sticking
agglutinant, adhesive
coalescent, fusing
coherent, cleaving
concrete, coalescent
conglutinant, glued
conglutinative, fit to glue
conglutinous, glue-like
gelatinous, like gelatin
glairy, viscous
gluey, sticky
glutinous, sticky
mucilaginous, gluey
mucous, viscous
pertinacious, tenacious
ropy, viscous
sticky, viscous
tenacious, sticking
viscid, glutinous
viscous, glutinous

NOUNS (Adhesion)
adherence, adhesion
adhesion, a sticking
adhesiveness, adhesion
agglutination, adhesion
coalescence, a coalescing
coherence, adherence
cohesion, coherence
concretion, coalescence
congelation, a freezing
conglutination, a gluing
pertinacity, tenacity
regelation, congelation
ropiness, viscosity
stickiness, viscidity
tenacity, adhesion
viscidity, glutinousness
viscosity, viscidity

52F

ADHESIVE MEDIUMS
adhesive, glue, etc.
agglutinant, glue, etc.
birdlime, a gluey snare
cement, strong glue
concrete, a coalescent
coalescent, strong paste
daub, a mortar
dextrin, a gum
gelatin, a pasty substance
glair, a viscid substance

(Continued)
gluten, a viscid substance
glue, a viscid cement
grout, a cement
gum, a viscid substance
jelly, a semisolid paste
mortar, a cement
mucilage, an adhesive
mucus, a viscid matter

(Continued)
paste, a sticky substance
plaster, a cement
putty, a glazier's cement
soldering, metallic cement
size, a weak glue
starch, viscid paste
wafer, a paste disk
wax, a tenacious substance

52G (See 137C.)

VERBS (Inhere)
appertain, belong by nature
coalesce, inhere by growth
fix, unite
ground, root
grow, take root
implant, plant
inhere, unite inseparably
plant, root
radicate, plant firmly
root, inhere
seat, fix
set, plant
transplant, replant
unite, coalesce

ADJECTIVES (Inhering)
coalescent, inherent
constitutional, inherent
deep-rooted, radical
fast, fixed
fixed, inherent
hidebound, inseparable
infrangible, inseparable
inherent, inseparable
inseparable, vitally inherent
inveterate, deeply rooted
radical, constitutional
rooted, inherent

NOUNS (Inherence)
coalescence, inherent growth
coherence, fixedness
fixation, act of fixing
fixedness, inherence
fixity, inseparableness
inherence, inseparable coherence
inveteracy, deep-rootedness
planting, act of rooting
transplantation, a replanting

52H

CONFINEMENT see—
vs. Release—Forgiveness 47

Conquest 50
Seizure 49C
Restraint 52H
Tomb—Grave 104H

ASSOCIATIVE
Guardianship 34
Keep 132C
Grave—Coffin, etc. 53L

52H

VERBS
Confine, Etc.
besiege, surround
confine, imprison
encompass, inclose
restrict, confine
siege, besiege
surround, encompass

Imprison, Etc.
cage, shut in
cloister, confine in a convent
coop, confine
immure, confine
impound, imprison
imprison, confine
incarcerate, imprison
intern, imprison
jail, imprison
jug, jail
pen, confine in a pen
pound, confine
prison, imprison
yoke, confine

Inclose, Etc.
bottle, place in a bottle
box, place in a box
buckle, confine
close, inclose
dam, confine by a dam
incase, place in a case
inclose, shut in

Bury, Etc.
bury, entomb
entomb, place in a tomb
inhume, inter
inter, bury

ADJECTIVES
Close
airtight, hermetic

ADJECTIVES (Continued)
close, confining
confining, held within
hermetic, tight
tight, sealed

Secured
bound, confined
clamped, held
closeted, confined
confined, secured
corraled, inclosed
encaved, inclosed
entombed, interred
fastened, tied
haltered, hitched
held, secured
hitched, haltered
imprisoned, incarcerated
incarcerated, jailed
jailed, imprisoned
locked, fastened
manacled, handcuffed
pilloried, shackled
secured, fastened
shackled, confined
tied, fastened

NOUNS
Miscellaneous
bond, confinement
bondage, imprisonment
boundary, confining limit
burial, interment
captivity, thraldom
confine, confinement
confinement, imprisonment
custody, imprisonment
durance, imprisonment
duress, imprisonment
entombment, interment
imprisonment, confinement

NOUNS (Continued)
incarceration, imprisonment
interment, burial
restriction, confinement
sepulture, entombment
thraldom, bondage

MEDIUMS
Prison, Etc.
bastile, prison
bridewell, a lockup
calaboose, jail
gaol, jail
jail, prison
jug, jail
lockup, jail
penitentiary, prison
prison, confinement
reformatory, bridewell

Cell, Cage, Etc.
black-hole, dungeon
cage, cell or coop
cell, small confinement
coop, confinement
donjon, underground prison
dungeon, prison
pillory, confining frame
stocks, pillory
tomb, dungeon
vault, prison

Enclosure
aviary, bird enclosure
closure, enclosure
corral, pen for stock
crawl, pen for turtle, etc.
enclosure, inclosure
inclosure, confinement
menagerie, animal enclosure

(Continued on page 115)

CONTAIN—EMBODY

see—
vs. Need 37

Storage Houses, etc. ..53B	Satchel, Trunk, etc. 53J
Community Places 53C	Utensils, Dishes 53M
Residential Places 53D	Jar, Tub, Barrel 53N
Compartments, Rooms 53E	Baskets, etc. 53K
Town, District, etc. 53F	Organic Containers 53Q
Heavenly Abodes 53H	Bed, Chair, Cushions ..53O
Infernal Abodes 130N	Furniture, etc. 53P
Footing, Base 53G	Coffin, Tomb, etc. 104H
Embodiment 53A	Framing, Supports 53R
Eating Places 48B	Miscellaneous 53I

53A—EMBODIMENT

VERBS

appertain, belong with
bear, possess
belong, appertain
comprehend, include
comprise, comprehend
compose, constitute
concern, pertain
consist, constitute
constitute, comprise
contain, include
embody, include
embrace, include
engage, contain
engross, comprehend
have, possess
hold, contain
imply, include
include, contain
occupy, hold or keep
own, possess
pertain, belong with
prepossess, occupy beforehand
subsist, consist

ADJECTIVES

appertaining, pertinent
appurtenant, appertaining
capacious, spacious
composite, holding in combination
comprehensive, inclusive
inclusive, including
pertaining, appertaining
pertinent, belonging with
possessive, noting inclusion
possessory, possessive
proprietory, owned or held
 by a proprietor
prepossessing, possessing
 beforehand
regarding, relative
relative, pertinent
roomy, capacious
spacious, roomy
tenable, appurtenant

NOUNS

appurtenance, a belonging
 with
bearing, inclusion

NOUNS (Continued)

berth, adequate room
burden, ship's capacity
capacity, cubical contents
composition, constitution
comprehension, embodiment
comprisal, a containing
concern, inclusion of a relation
constitution, embodiment
cubical contents, capacity
embodiment, inclusion
engagement, occupation
engrossment, embodiment
inclusion, comprehension
habit, constitutional conduct
pertinence, appurtenance
possession, ownership
prepossession, possession
 beforehand
ownership, possession
right, ownership
routine, inclusive conduct
tenability, appurtenance

53B

STORAGE HOUSE, Etc.

aerodrome, hangar
archive, place for records
armory, arsenal
(B). armoury
arsenal, magazine
bank, a money vault
barn, a farm building
basin, reservoir
bay, space in a barn
building, structure
cache, concealed storage
cesspool, filth reservoir
construction, structure
cistern, reservoir
container, receptacle
depository, storehouse
depot, a repository
edifice, building

(Continued)

exchequer, a treasury
fabric, edifice
gallery, art repository
garage, auto shed
gasometer, gas reservoir
granary, grain building
hangar, aircraft shed
hold, ship's storage
hothouse, flower house
house, building
magazine, warehouse
mine, natural reservoir
receptacle, container
repertory, repository
repository, warehouse
reservoir, fluid container
rotunda, circular building
shed, a slight building

(Continued)

silo, feed container
skyscraper, a high building
stable, stock shed
stall, stable
stand, small structure
still, liquor repository
storeroom, repository
store, warehouse
storehouse, warehouse
structure, house
sub-treasury, branch
 treasury
tank, reservoir
thesaurus, storehouse
treasury, repository
vein, mineral reservoir
warehouse, storage place

53C
COMMUNITY PLACES, Etc.
Church, Temple
cathedral, church
chapel, place of worship
church, temple
kirk, church
pagoda, temple
synagogue, church
tabernacle, church
temple, church
Convent, Cloister
abbey, cloister
cloister, abbey
convent, cloister
monastery, cloister

(Continued)
priory, monastery
Asylum, Hospital
asylum, an institution
hospital, infirmary
infirmary, hospital
lazaretto, pest house
orphanage, orphan asylum
pandemonium, insane asylum
sanitarium, hospital
workhouse, poorhouse
Station, Forum, Etc.
basilica, assembly hall
casino, entertainment hall

(Continued)
depot, station
forum, resort
harbor, port
pavilion, assembling place
port, harbor
resort, forum
station, terminus
terminus, station
Barrack, Camp
armory, soldiers' hall
barrack, soldiers' lodgment
bivouac, encampment
camp, temporary lodgment
cantonment, barrack
encampment, camp

53D
DWELLINGS, Etc.
Dwelling
abode, habitation
dwelling, abode
domicil, residence
establishment, residence
habitation, abode
homestead, first home
house, abode
residence, domicil
settlement, legal abode
site, residence
sojourn, temporary abode
stay, abode
Home, Etc.
fireside, home
hearth, domicil
home, abode
ingleside, fireside
Kind of Abode
apartment, suite of rooms
box, country house
bungalow, cottage
cabin, cottage
cot, cottage
cottage, small dwelling
flat, residential division
grange, farm dwelling
hacienda, rural abode
hermitage, hermit's abode
house-boat, abode on water
igloo, snow house
kayak, seal-skin house boat
kiosk, summer house
lean-to, penthouse
lodge, gate-keeper's cottage
lodging, temporary abode
log cabin, log house
penthouse, lean-to, annex
pueblo, tribal abode
ranch, rancho
rancho, ranchers' abode
rustication, country abode
suite, set of rooms
tenement, dwelling house

(Continued)
villa, country seat
Manor, Castle, Etc.
castle, noble mansion
chateau, manor
manor, mansion
mansion, castle
messuage, mansion
palace, stately house
Specific Abode
allodium, estate
earldom, earl's estate
harem, seraglio
legation, diplomats' abode
manse, minister's residence
parsonage, parson's abode
pastorate, pastor's office
prefecture, prefect's abode
seraglio, Mohammedan abode
White House, Executive Mansion
zenana, harem (India)
Hut, Hovel
chalet, herdman's hut
cote, hut
dump, hovel
hole, hovel
hovel, a mean abode
hut, small cabin
kraal, hut
shack, hut
shanty, shack
shed, shanty
thatch, straw shack
Haven, Resort
ark, refuge
covert, shelter
haven, shelter
refuge, shelter
resort, frequented place
rest, abode
retreat, shelter
repose, abode
sanctuary, refuge
shelter, refuge

(Continued)
Haunt, Habitat
habitat, natural resort
haunt, resort
menagerie, vivarium
vivarium, habitat of animals
Stall, Cell, Etc.
cell, hovel
crib, stall
cubby-hole, snug place
stable, animal's stall
stall, animal's rest
Tent, Etc.
teepee, wigwam
tent, canvas shelter
tilt, tent
wickiup, teepee
wigwam, teepee
Brothel
brothel, low resort
dive, low resort
stew, brothel
Den, Lair
burrow, rabbit hole
cave, den
den, cave
dugout, cave, den
hibernation, winter den
kennel, lair of a fox
lair, beast's covert
Nest
aerie, eagle's nest
eyry, aerie
nest, abode of a bird
nidus, nest
rookery, group of nests
Roost, Hive, Etc.
apiary, bee house
beehive, abode of bees
dovecote, box for doves
hive, abode of bees
perch, roost
roost, abode of birds

53E
COMPARTMENT, Etc.
Room, Etc.
antechamber, a lesser room
anteroom, antechamber
cabin, room on a ship
room, compartment

Private Room
bedroom, sleeping room
boudoir, woman's room
chamber, a private room
dormitory, sleeping hall
lavatory, retiring room
refuge, chamber
sacristy, vestry
sanctuary, sanctum
sanctum, private place
sanctum sanctorum, place
  of utmost privacy
vestry, sacristy

Assembly Room
aula, great hall
divan, council chamber
drawing-room, main room
green-room, actors' room

See—(ASSOCIATIVE 53A)
(Continued)
hall, assembly room
parlor, drawing-room
salon, drawing-room
stateroom, elegant room

Court, Etc.
atrium, a court
court, enclosure
peristyle, interior court

Pantry, Etc.
crib, manger
cuisine, kitchen
kitchen, cookroom
kitchenette, small kitchen
larder, pantry
manger, feeding box
pantry, larder
scullery, kitchen room

Cell, Closet, Etc.
alcove, recess
booth, temporary stall
box, compartment
cabinet, small compartment

(Continued)
cell, small room
closet, small room
compartment, apartment
crypt, cell
press, closet and shelves
recess, alcove
stall, compartment

Loft, Etc.
attic, loft
belfry, bell tower
garret, loft
loft, garret

Cellar, Hole, Etc.
basement, cellar
cellar, underground room
cockpit, pit
cubby-hole, small space
hold, freight compartment
hole, a hollow
pit, hole
steerage, passenger deck
vault, cellar

53F
TOWN—DISTRICT
Nativity, Empire
country, native land
dominion, territory
empire, dominion
fatherland, nativity
kingdom, King's dominion
nativity, fatherland
realm, empire

District, Etc.
county, district
district, territory
diocese, bishop's see
place, territory

(Continued)
parish, district
precinct, district
province, territory
state, territory
territory, district

City, Etc.
capital, chief city
city, important town
metropolis, capital
municipality, town, city

Town, Etc.
borough, town
hans-town, associate town

(Continued)
town, large village
township, town

Village, Etc.
colony, settlement
ham, village
hamlet, village
kraal, African village
plantation, new colony
settlement, colony
village, large hamlet

Slum, Etc.
ghetto, Jewish quarter
slum, a low quarter

53G
FOOTING—BASE
Miscellaneous
abutment, support
base, support
buttress, support
earth, prime support
floor, foot support

(Continued)
footing, support
foundation, support
ground, support
pedestal, base
platform, raised stand
plinth, support
pulpit, speaker's stand

(Continued)
rostrum, platform
slab, plinth
socle, plinth
stage, platform
stand, platform
support, foundation
thill, coal-mine floor

53H
HEAVENLY ABODES
Miscellaneous
Abode of the blessed,
  heaven
Arcadia, Eden
Bowers of bliss, Arcadia
Celestial City, heavenly
  Jerusalem
City Celestial, heaven
Eden, Paradise
Elysian Fields, heaven
Elysium, Greek paradise
Empyreal, Empyrean

See—(ASSOCIATIVE 53A)
(Continued)
Empyrean, heavenly abode
Eternal Home, heaven
Future State, heaven
Garden of the Hesperides
Happy Hunting Grounds,
  Indians' heaven
Heaven, God's abode
Heavenly City, heaven
Heavenly Kingdom, heaven
Holy City, heaven
Holy Kingdom, heaven
Kingdom of God, heaven

(Continued)
Kingdom of heaven, heaven
Nirvana, Buddhists' heaven
Olympus, home of the gods
Paradise, Eden
Seventh Heaven
Third Heaven
Throne of God, heaven
Valhalla, Norse heaven
Walhalla, Valhalla
Zion, Heavenly Jerusalem
See Hell, Etc., 130N

53I
MISCELLANEOUS
bin, grain receptacle
bunker, large bin
capsule, small container
chalice, eucharist cup
commode, night-stool
drawer, loose compartment
envelope, paper container
grail, chalice

(Continued)
grate, fuel frame
hod, brick container
holster, pistol case
horn, powder case
locker, safety receptacle
manger, trough
pigeonhole, small receptacle
rack, hay container

(Continued)
scabbard, sheath
sheath, sword covering
shell, hollow case
socket, a receptacle
tabernacle, holy vessel
till, drawer
trough, box-like container

53J
POCKET—SATCHEL, Etc.
bag, wallet
boot, baggage holder
box, square case
budget, bag and contents
caddy, small box
caisson, box
case, box
chest, large box
coffer, chest
fob, small pocket
grip, valise
haversack, knapsack

(Continued)
hutch, box
imperial, baggage case
knapsack, traveling bag
pocket, small bag
pocketbook, wallet
portemonnaie, purse
portfolio, brief bag
portmanteau, traveling bag
pouch, pocket
purse, moneybag
pyx, coin box
reliquary, chest

(Continued)
reticule, handbag
safe, steel chest
satchel, book bag
scrip, satchel
trunk, traveling chest
valise, portmanteau
vinaigrette, box for aro-
  matics
wallet, pocketbook
bandbox, hatbox

53K
BASKETS
basket, flexible container
bassinet, basket
crate, wicker hamper
creel, fishing basket

(Continued)
hamper, wicker-like basket
hopper, seed basket
hoppet, hand basket
pannier, basket

(Continued)
pottle, conical basket
skip, basket

53L
COFFIN, GRAVES, Etc.
  (See 52H and 104H)
casket, coffin
catacomb, burial place
cemetery, burial ground

(Continued)
coffin, burial casket
God's Acre, cemetery
grave, place of burial
graveyard, cemetery

(Continued)
necropolis, cemetery
sarcophagus, stone coffin
sepulcher, grave

53M
UTENSILS—DISHES, Etc.
beaker, drinking vessel
brazier, charcoal pan
caldron, boiler
crucible, melting pot
cup, drinking vessel
cupule, little cup

(Continued)
cuspidor, spittoon
dipper, ladle-like vessel
dish, broad vessel
epergne, flower stand
fork, table implement
glass, tumbler

(Continued)
goblet, drinking vessel
griddle, cake pan
gridiron, cooking vessel
jardiniere, flower stand
jorum, drinking bowl
(Continued on page 114)

53M (Continued), 53N, 53-O, 53P

53M (Continued)
UTENSILS—DISHES, Etc.
kettle, boiler
ladle, deep spoon
laver, washing vessel
mortar, pounding bowl
mug, cup
noggin, mug
olla, cooking vessel
pan, shallow vessel
plate, shallow vessel

See—(ASSOCIATIVE 53A)
(Continued)
platter, fish dish
porringer, porridge dish
pot, boiler
salver, tray
saucer, vessel for cup
schooner, beer glass
scoop, ladle
shovel, scoop
skillet, cooking vessel

(Continued)
spittoon, cuspidor
spoon, table implement
tankard, drinking vessel
toby, mug
tray, flat vessel
trencher, wooden plate
trowel, mortar implement
tumbler, drinking vessel
tureen, soup dish

53N
JAR—TUB—BARREL, Etc.
amphora, wine vessel
ampulla, drinking vessel
barrel, cask
basin, water vessel
black-jack, leather vessel
bottle, liquid container
bowl, hollow vessel
bucket, water vessel
butt, 117 gallon cask
calabash, gourd-like vessel
can, tin vessel
canteen, soldier's flask
carboy, jacketed bottle
cask, barrel
caster, cruet
coal-scuttle, scuttle
container, receptacle
crock, pot
crockery, earthenware
cruet, glass vessel

(Continued)
cruse, vessel
cupel, a porous vessel
decanter, wine bottle
demijohn, carboy
earthenware, clay vessels
epergne, flower vessel
ewer, water jug
firkin, small tub
flagon, drinking vessel
flask, bottle
goglet, gurglet
gurglet, earthen vessel
hogshead, large cask
jar, pot
jardiniere, flower stand
jug, vessel for liquids
keg, small barrel
kit, large bottle
magnum, wine bottle
pail, bucket

(Continued)
phial, vial
pipkin, pot
pitcher, water vessel
pot, a vessel
pottery, earthenware
press, wine vat
puncheon, wine cask
receptacle, container
samovar, tea urn
scuttle, coal vessel
stoup, flagon
tub, cask
tun, large cask
urn, a roundish vessel
vase, flower vessel
vat, tub
vessel, utility container
vial, small bottle

53-O
BED—SOFA—CHAIR, Etc.
armchair, easy-chair
bed, place of rest
bedding, sleeping straw
bedstraw, bedding
bedtick, bedding
bench, long seat
berth, sleeping place
bolster, long pillow
box, driver's seat
bunk, berth
camp-stool, folding stool
chair, seat
couch, bed, sofa
cot, small bed
cradle, crib
crib, child's bed

(Continued)
cushion, pillow
divan, couch
faldstool, bishop's chair
hammock, swinging bed
hassock, kneeling pad
howdah, seat on elephant
litter, bedding
mattress, tick of bedding
morris chair, easy-chair
ottoman, cushioned seat
pad, cushion
pallet, bed
pillion, soft saddle
pillow, cushion
pew, church bench
rocking-chair, easy-chair

(Continued)
saddle, horseback seat
seat, a rest
sedilia, altar seats
settee, long seat
sofa, cushioned seat
squab, sofa
stool, seat
shakedown, bed
stretcher, litter
tabouret, cushioned stool
truckle-bed, trundle-bed
trundle-bed, bed on casters
woolsack, Lord Chancellor's
seat

53P
FURNITURE
(Miscellaneous)
andirons, firedogs
bookcase, book holder
buffet, sideboard
bureau, commode
cabinet, commode
canterbury, music stand

(Continued)
chiffonier, sideboard
commode, bureau
console, low table
counter, shop table
cupboard, shelved chest
davenport, writing desk
desk, table

(Continued)
dresser, cupboard
escritoire, bureau
easel, stand
firedogs, andirons
furniture, house utilities
hatrack, hat-frame
(Continued on page 115)

Page 114

53P (Continued)
FURNITURE (Continued)

hat-tree, hatrack
hob, grate shelf
mantel, shelf

(Continued)

rack, frame
shelf, a support
sideboard, buffet

(Continued)

stand, small table
wardrobe, portable closet

53Q
ORGANIC CONTAINERS

abdomen, belly
aërocyst, air bladder
belly, stomach
bladder, membranous bag
capsule, membranous sac
craw, crop
crop, craw

(Continued)

cyst, bladder
gizzard, stomach
maw, stomach
pericarp, pod
pod, seed vessel
pouch, belly
sac, pouch

(Continued)

saccule, cyst
sack, pouch
stomach, pouch
udder, glandular sac
ventricle, organic cavity
vesicle, bladder

53R
FRAMING—SUPPORTS
(See 53G)

abacus, crowning slab
architrave, chief beam
board, plank
bracket, support
beam, long support
bear, support
block, support of wood
branch, limb
branchlet, small limb
cantilever, supporting arm
cleat, supporting piece
column, round pillar
cornerstone, chief stone
flooring, floor material
frame, support

(Continued)

girder, main beam
hip, rafter
joist, floor support
leg, an under support
limb, branch
lintel, an over support
log, an undressed timber
lumber, building material
mast, sail support
masthead, top of a mast
outrigger, sail beam
panel, frame board
plank, board
pilaster, square column
pillar, column
post, erect timber

(Continued)

prop, support
rafter, roof support
scaffold, support
scaffolding, scaffold
shaft, column
shank, leg
skeleton, framework
sleeper, track support
slab, first cut from a log
stanchion, post
strut, support of timber
summer, girder
support, prop
timber, lumber
transom, crossbeam

52H (Continued)
MEDIUMS (Continued)

paddock, enclosure
pen, enclosure or prison
pound, prison or cattle pen
stockade, enclosure
sty, pen
vivarium, confinement for
  animals
warren, a crawl

MEDIUMS (Continued)

yard, enclosure

Miscellaneous

blockade, cordon of ships,
  etc., for restricting
cloister, convent
convent, house for monks
cul-de-sac, sack-like
  closure

PERSONS

custodian, guardian
guard, keeper
guardian, warden
incarcerator, jailor
jailor, prison guard
keeper, jailor
turnkey, jailor
warden, keeper
warder, keeper

54C (Continued)
RACE—NATIONALITY

(Continued)

Inca, aboriginal Peruvian
Indian, N. American Red
  man
Israelite, Jew
Jew, Israelite
Japanese, native of Japan
Martian, inhabitant of
  Mars

(Continued)

muzhik, Russian peasant
Negrito, native of the Malay Archipelago
negro, native of Africa
negroid, negro
Ottoman, Turk
Parisian, native of Paris

(Continued)

pigmy, one of a dwarfish
  race
ryot, East Indian peasant
Senegalese, French African
  negro native
Turk, native of Turkey

RESIDENCE—INMATE—INHABITANT
vs. Wandering—Rover 18B

ASSOCIATIVE

see— { Inmate—Inhabitant 54B
{ Race—Nationality 54C

54A
VERBS
abide, reside
bide, reside
camp, lodge temporarily
dwell, inhabit
encamp, camp
frequent, resort often
hibernate, to winter
inhabit, dwell
live, reside
lodge, reside
nest, dwell
nestle, lodge
occupy, inhabit
reside, dwell
rest, dwell

VERBS (Continued)
remain, abide
roost, nest
rusticate, live rurally
settle, dwell
sojourn, dwell shortly
stay, dwell
stop, sojourn
tabernacle, sojourn
winter, hibernate

ADJECTIVES
arboreal, living in trees
domiciliary, residing
habitual, residential
indigenous, native

ADJECTIVES (Continued)
monastic, in seclusion
native, indigenous
resident, domiciliary
residential, resident

NOUNS
feud, fief
fief, tenure
habitation, occupancy
inhabitation, habitation
occupancy, tenure
possession, occupancy
residence, habitation
tenancy, occupancy
tenure, tenancy

54B
INMATE—INHABITANT, Etc.
aborigine, autochthon
anchoret, fixed habitant
autochthon, aborigine
burgh, burgess
burgess, burg's citizen
burgher, burgh
citizen, city dweller
colonist, colony dweller
commoner, inhabitant
compatriot, countryman
countryman, native
cosmopolitan, world's citizen
denizen, inhabitant
dweller, resident
habitant, dweller

(Continued)
habitue, frequenter
indigene, native
inhabitant, countryman
inmate, dweller
lessee, tenant
lodger, sojourner
native, original dweller
occupant, dweller
patriot, countryman
peasant, rustic
provincial, native of a province
resident, dweller
rustic, countryman
settler, colonist
sojourner, brief dweller

(Continued)
squatter, settler
tenant, lessee
townsman, citizen
villager, village dweller

COLLECTIVE
autochthones, aborigines
aborigines, first inhabitants
clan, tribe
commonality, commoners
house, clan
household, house
menage, household
peasantry, rural dwellers
tenantry, tenants collectively
tribe, a primitive people

54C
RACE—NATIONALITY
African, African native
Africander, native of Africa born of white parents
alien, outlander
American, citizen of America
Apache, Apache Indian
Arab, Arabian native
Assyrian, Assyrian native
Aztec, Aztec native
Bedouin, nomadic Arab
Bermudian, Bermuda native
Boer, Dutch S. African

(Continued)
Briton, British native
Bushman, bush dweller
Canadian, Canadian native
Canuck, Canadian
Castilian, citizen of Castile
Caucasian, one of the white race
Celestial, Chinese native
Celt, Indo-European
Chinese, Celestial
Cockney, Londoner
Czech, inhabitant of Czecho-Slovakia
Digger, Digger Indian

(Continued)
Eskimo, Greenland native
Ethiopian, African negro
Filipino, native of the Philippine Islands
foreigner, alien
German, German native
Gipsy, one of a wandering tribe
greaser, Mexican
Hawaiian, a native of Hawaii
Hebrew, Israelite
Igorote, native of Luzon
(Continued on page 115)

SPEECH—MELODY—SOUND

SPEECH (Vocal)   see—
   vs. Apathy 110A

ASSOCIATIVE

Symbolic Speech	.............55B	Melody—Eloquence	........68A
Assertion	80	Dissonance	.......................70˙
Announcement	79	Brevity	58
Disclosure	78	Verbosity	56
Prophecy	77	Laughter	...........................71B
Narration	...........................85A	Subdued	.............................69A
Conversation	90	Moderate	..........................69C
Exclamation	91	Loud	.................................69B

55A

VERBS

Speak, Etc.
accost, address
address, speak to
articulate, speak
broach, accost
communicate, address
enunciate, utter
express, remark
observe, remark
phrase, express
remark, say
say, speak
sound, utter
speak, utter
talk, speak
tell, address
utter, remark
word, phrase

Vocalize, Etc.
aspirate, breathe speech
assibilate, hiss
breathe, whisper
hiss, sibilate
sibilate, assibilate
vocalize, utter
whisper, aspirate

Speak Variously
cant, talk affectedly
convey, communicate
coo, utter lovingly
couch, express in words
deliver, utter
drop, utter casually
exclaim, utter suddenly
extemporize, talk offhand
hurl, utter vehemently
neologize, coin new words
phone, telephone
pour, utter
pronounce, articulate
prose, speak in prose
telephone, speak by phone

ADJECTIVES
Miscellaneous
adjectival, qualificative
adverbial, qualificative
articulate, lingual
colloquial, familiar
Doric, noting dialect of the
   Dorians
dialectic, colloquial

ADJECTIVES (Continued)
exclamatory, impromptu
expressive, communicative
extemporaneous, im-
   promptu
extempore, impromptu
guttural, throaty
impromptu, offhand
idiomatic, dialectic
interjectional, exclamatory
labial, with the lips
lingual, vocal
oral, spoken
polyglot, in many tongues
significant, expressive
speaking, expressive
verbal, oral
vernacular, idiomatic
vocal, oral

UTTERANCE
assibilation, hissing speech
articulation, speech
comment, remark
communication, speech
enunciation, articulation
expression, speech
language, speech
mention, utterance
remark, comment
say, utterance
soliloquy, a talking to one's
   self
speech, articulation
talk, expression
tongue, speech
utterance, voice
vent, utterance
ventriloquism, speech from
   a deceptive source
whisper, toneless speech
word, speech
pronunciation, articulation
vocalization, speech
voice, speech

DIALECT—IDIOM, Etc.
alloquialism, manner of address
Anglicism, English idiom
argot, slang
brogue, dialect
cant, jargon
colloquialism, parlance
delivery, diction

DIALECT—IDIOM, Etc.
(Continued)
dialect, peculiar speech
diction, manner of speech
idiom, vernacular
jargon, brogue
lingo, dialect
localism, idiom
locution, idiom
parlance, diction
patois, illiterate dialect
phraseology, parlance
provincialism, patois
slang, jargon
style, diction
talk, dialect
tongue, dialect
vernacular, localism

PERSONS
articulator, distinct speaker
elocutionist, skilled speaker
linguist, one skilled in languages
speaker, elocutionist, etc.
ventriloquist, one skilled in
   throwing the voice

NATIONAL SPEECH, Etc.
(L.—Language.)
Assyrian, Assyrian L.
Chinese, Chinese L.
Danish, Danish L.
English, English L.
Esperanto, international L.
Finnish, Finnish L.
French, French L.
German, German L.
Greek, Greek L.
Ido, a universal L.
Italian, Italian L.
Japanese, Japanese L.
Latin, ancient Roman L.
Norwegian, Norwegian L.
Portuguese, Portuguese L.
Russian, Russian L.
Sanskrit, ancient Hindu L.
Scotch, Scotch L.
Spanish, Spanish L.
Swedish, Swedish L.
Turkish, Turkish L.
Volapuk, a universal L.
Etc., etc.

(Continued on page 120)

SPEECH
   (Symbolic)   see—
   vs. Apathy 110A

ASSOCIATIVE

Literary Symbols 55B	Melody—Eloquence 68A
Vocal Speech 55A	Dissonance 70
Assertion 80	Brevity 58
Announcement 79	Verbosity 56
Disclosure 78	Laughter 71B
Prophecy 77	Subduedness 69A
Narration 85A	Moderation 69C
Conversation 90	Loudness 69B
Exclamation 91	

55B

VERBS

address, subscribe
cable, communicate by cable
compose, prose, etc.
engross, write in a round hand
inscribe, address
jot, write
pen, write
print, stamp
prose, write in prose
publish, print by press
scrawl, scribble
scribble, write badly
signal, communicate by signs
stamp, print
superscribe, inscribe
telegraph, communicate by wire
wire, telegraph
write, communicate by symbols

ADJECTIVES

alphabetic, expressed with letters
cuneiform, expressed in ancient wedge-shaped letters
heptaglot, written in seven languages
phonetic, expressed in elementary sounds
phonographic, phonetic
runic, expressed in ancient characters
typographical, expressed in type
written, expressed in writing

PERSONS

amanuensis, stenographer
calligrapher, skilled penman
penman, calligrapher
stenographer, shorthand writer
typist, typewriter
typewriter, typist

NOUNS (Symbolic Speech)

calligraph, beautiful penmanship
calligraphy, calligraph
cereography, art of writing, engrossing, etc., in wax
chirography, art of writing, engrossing, etc.
cryptogram, a writing in cypher
cryptography, writing in secret characters
dactylology, communication by fingered signs
engrossment, the engrossing of documents
palimpsest, a writing upon indiscernible writing
penmanship, art of writing
phonography, shorthand
phonology, science of articulate sounds
phonotype, the printed representation of sounds with distinct type
script, style of writing
shorthand, symbolic writing
stenography, art of writing in shorthand
typography, art of printing

**SENTENCE—
PARAGRAPH—METER**

amphibrach, foot of three syllables
anapest, amphibrach
clause, sentence
column, division of writing
dactyl, a foot of three syllables, one long followed by two short
dissyllable, word of two syllables
foot, measure of poetic rhythm
hendecasyllable, a line of eleven syllables
item, newspaper paragraph
meter, a rhythmic arrangement of syllables
monosyllable, a word of one syllable

**SENTENCE—
PARAGRAPH—METER**
   (Continued)

paragraph, short passage
passage, clause
period, complete sentence
phrase, short sentence
poem, poetic composition
poetry, metric composition
proposition, complete sentence
prose, non-metric writing or speaking
sentence, series of words
syllable, single sound

NOUNS (Literary Symbols)

alphabet, letters of speech
accent, writing character
asterisk, reference mark
bracket, interpolation mark
braille, raised character for the blind
caret, insert mark
character, symbolic letter
colon, pause mark
comma, pause mark
crotchet, bracket
dagger, reference mark
dash, qualificative mark
dieresis, pronunciation mark
double-dagger, reference mark
exclamation, ejaculatory mark
figure, character
hieroglyphic, writing character
homograph, similar mark, symbol, etc.
homonym, word alike in sound but different in meaning
homophone, letter representing the same sound as another
hyphen, combining mark
ideograph, symbol representing an idea, etc.
interrogation, question mark
keynote, token
keyword, sign
   (Continued on page 120)

NOUNS (Literary Symbols)
(Continued)

labial, mark indicating utterance formed by the lips
letter, character
obelisk, double-dagger
parenthesis, insert mark
period, stop mark
phonogram, sound symbol
neologism, new word
quotation, citation mark
semicolon, pause mark
sign, symbol
symbol, letter, character
token, sign
word, symbol of speech or force

NOUNS (Continued)

runic, alphabet of early Teutons

NOUNS

(Talking and Writing Mediums)

dictaphone, phonograph
electrotype, plate for printing
font, a particular assortment of type
linotype, printing machine
megaphone, sound magnifier
phonotype, phonetic type

NOUNS (Continued)

phonoscope, an instrument for recording characters
phonograph, machine for reproducing sound
pen, ink writer
pencil, lead writer
stencil, marking pattern
stereotype, metal plate for printing
talking machine, phonograph
telescriptor, electric typewriter
typewriter, writing machine
type, letters for printing

SPEECH—SOUND (Radio-active) see— ⎰ (ASSOCIATIVE 55)
vs. Apathy ....110A ⎱

55C

55C

VERBS
radiate, send rays
telegraph, wire
telephone, talk by wire
wire, telegraph
wireless, telegraph by air

ADJECTIVES
radio-active
telegraphic
telephonic

NOUNS
marconigram
radio

NOUNS (Continued)
radio-activity
radiation
telegram
telegraphy
telepathy
wire
wireless
wireless-telegraphy
wireless-telephony

INSTRUMENTS
aerophone
electrophone
gramophone

INSTRUMENTS
(Continued)
microphone
telegraph
telegraphone
telephone
radio

PERSONS
announcer
operator
telegrapher
telephonist
Etc., etc.

55A (Continued)

PARTS OF SPEECH, Etc.
ablaut, a vowel differing from the vowel in the base word, as **do, did**
adjective, a qualificative word
adverb, a word which qualifies a verb or adjective
anagram, a significant word or phrase transposed from another of different form
antonym, a word of opposite meaning
aphthong, a letter not sounded in a word
articles, a, an, the
asyndeton, a disconnected figure of speech
conjunction, a word expressing connection

(Continued)

consonant, non-vowel sound
dental, a sound formed with the teeth
diphthong, union of vowels
etymon, the root or primitive significance of a word
guttural, throat sound
interjection, an exclamation
labial, lip sound
liquid, a consonant sound
mute, unpronounced consonant
note, sound
noun, substantive, name
paradigm, grammatical inflection of a word

(Continued)

preposition, a word placed before noun or pronoun to express relationship to some other word
pronoun, a word used in place of a noun
root, the part of a word which signifies its primitive meaning
shibboleth, a peculiar pronunciation characteristic of a race
substantive, noun
synonym, a word similar to another
verb, a word which expresses action
vocable, a vocal sound
vowel, open note or sound

56

VERBS

Palaver

diffuse, expatiate
dwell, prose
flourish, be flowery
harp, dwell
palaver, dwell
pour, diffuse
prose, diffuse
rhapsodize, be rhapsodic

Expatiate

amplify, expatiate
dilate, expatiate
enlarge, amplify
expatiate, enlarge
launch, be diffuse
paraphrase, restate

Chatter, Prattle

babble, prattle
chatter, babble
clack, chatter
gab, babble
patter, chatter
prate, palaver
prattle, babble
rattle, prattle

ADJECTIVES

Fluent

copious, effusive
diffusive, effusive
effusive, voluble
exuberant, copious
flowing, copious
fluent, flowing
glib, voluble
linguistic, fluent

ADJECTIVES (Continued)

loquacious, talkative
profuse, wordy
prolix, verbose
verbose, wordy
versatile, linguistic
voluble, fluent
wordy, verbose

Chattering

babbling, talkative
chatty, talkative
garrulous, talkative
gushing, effusive
talkative, diffusive

Commonplace

commonplace, prosaic
dull, prosaic
hackneyed, commonplace
humdrum, monotonous
monotonous, dull
prosaic, commonplace
tedious, redundant

Redundant

circumlocutory, tedious
paraphrastic, restating
pleonastic, redundant
redundant, superfluous
superfluous, pleonastic

NOUNS

Fluency

flow, fluency
fluency, copiousness
loquacity, talkativeness
prolixity, verbosity
tongue, fluency
verbiage, verbosity

NOUNS (Continued)

verbosity, loquacity
versatility, varying fluency
volubility, windiness
wordiness, loquacity

Chatter

babble, loquaciousness
chatter, talkativeness
clack, chatter
gab, loquacity
garrulity, loquacity
palaver, empty talk
patter, prattle
prattle, babble
prattle-prattle, loquacity
rigmarole, garrulity
talkativeness, loquacity
windiness, verbosity

Prose, Etc.

platitude, commonplaceness
prose, tedious discourse
prosiness, tediousness

Redundancy

circumlocution, verbosity
periphrasis, circumlocution
pleonasm, redundancy
redundancy, wordiness

Digression

desultoriness, digression
digression, discursiveness
discursiveness, digression
excursion, excursiveness
excursus, digression

PERSONS

babbler, prattler
chatterbox, babbler
Etc., etc.

57 (Continued)

NOUNS (Continued)

homophone, a letter expressing the same sound as another
hyperbole, equivocation
palindrome, that which reads backward as well as forward
proxonym, word pronounced like another but different in meaning

NOUNS (Continued)

trope, an expression used in a sense different from its usual sense

Indeterminate Terms

any, anything
anything, thing
aught, anything
thing, aught

PERSONS

diplomat, tactful person
diplomatist, diplomat
Machiavellis, tricky person
mystic, oracle
oracle, enigmatic person
punster, one who makes puns
sophist, a skilled but pernicious disputer
sphinx, mystic

vs. Definiteness 84

Falsehood 62
Foolishness 60
Uncertainty 127A
Surprising 96A
Difficulty 13

Verbosity 56
Religious Dogma 82A
Isms and Ologies 83
Hiding—Secrecy 103A

57

VERBS

Deceive

bamboozle, mystify
camouflage, dissimulate
deceive, mislead
dissimulate, make ambiguous
equivocate, quibble
foist, mislead
mislead, equivocate
quibble, equivocate

Allude

allude, intimate indirectly
insinuate, intimate
intimate, allude
rumor, report on hearsay
simulate, insinuate

Mystify

confound, perplex
confuse, confound
muddle, perplex
mystify, obscure
nonplus, perplex
obfuscate, confuse
obscure, dissimulate
perplex, puzzle
puzzle, perplex
quiz, puzzle
stump, perplex

Exaggerate

exaggerate, hyperbolize
hyperbolize, exaggerate, as "swift as the wind"
overstate, exaggerate
rhapsodize, be extravagant in speech
strain, exaggerate
stretch, strain

Complicate

complicate, involve
dogmatize, utter without proof
digress, muddle
entail, involve
entangle, involve
involve, complicate
tangle, complicate

ADJECTIVES

Ambiguous

absurd, fantastic
ambiguous, doubtful
amphibolic, equivocal
anomalous, absurd
backhanded, ambiguous
casuistic, equivocal
equivocal, ambiguous

ADJECTIVES (Continued)

homonymous, equivocal
homophonous, equivocal
incongruous, ambiguous
macaronic, incongruous
oblique, ambiguous

Deceitful

captious, quibbling
deceitful, misleading
deceptive, misleading
delusive, deceptive
evasive, quibbling
misleading, deceptive
quibbling, ambiguous
sophistical, misleading

Unauthentic

apocryphal, unauthentic
dogmatic, uncertain
exegetic, dogmatic
hearsay, rumor
inconsistent, doubtful
ptolemaic, inconsistent
unaccredited, unauthorized
unauthorized, unauthentic
unauthentic, hearsay
unorthodox, apocryphal
unreliable, unauthentic
untrustworthy, unreliable

Questionable

agitable, uncertain
conjectural, doubtful
controversial, inconclusive
debatable, inconclusive
disputable, inconclusive
doubtful, questionable
dubious, doubtful
hypothetic, uncertain
problematic, doubtful
questionable, doubtful
unconvincing, questionable

Indefinite

comparative, inconclusive
general, indefinite
inconclusive, doubtful
indefinite, indeterminate
indeterminate, undefined
uncertain, doubtful
undefined, doubtful
unexplained, strange
vague, indefinite

Odd

odd, strange
peculiar, odd
quaint, dubious
strange, unexplained

Allusive

allusive, indirect

ADJECTIVES (Continued)

flippant, equivocal
impersonal, not specific

Illusory

chimerical, fantastic
fanciful, chimerical
fantastic, incongruous
illusive, deceptive
illusory, deceptive
imaginative, illusory

Mysterious

allegoric, hidden
confusing, puzzling
elusive, mystifying
enigmatic, puzzling
hidden, mysterious
incomprehensible, mystic
inscrutable, hidden
mysterious, puzzling
mystic, mysterious
mystifying, perplexing
oracular, ambiguous
paradoxical, incredible but true
perplexing, puzzling
puzzling, ambiguous
quizzical, puzzling
recondite, hidden

Occult, Hidden

abstruse, obscure
concealed, hidden
cryptic, hidden
occult, hidden
occulted, occult
prognostic, noting an uncertain foreshadowing
shrouded, hidden

Obscure, Dark

cimmerian, intensely dark
dark, obscure
foggy, obscure
hazy, obscure
impenetrable, inscrutable
imperceptible, obscure
inconspicuous, indistinct
indistinct, undefined
indistinguishable, obscure
misty, obscure
nebulous, obscure
obscure, undefined
shadowy, deceptive

Inexplicable

indefinable, subtle
inexplicable, enigmatic
infinite, undefined
infinitive, indeterminate
unaccountable, puzzling

(Continued on page 123)

ADJECTIVES (Continued)

Finespun

artful, subtle
canny, subtle
delicate, subtle
diplomatic, strategic
downy, artful
fine, subtle
finedrawn, finespun
finespun, uncertain
glossarial, ambiguous
metaphrastic, close but inconclusive
pragmatic, philosophic
subtile, finespun
subtle, finespun
wily, artful

Incredible

extravagant, hyperbolic
fishy, incredible
hyberbolic, equivocal
inconceivable, incredible
incredible, inexplicable
preposterous, incredible
prolix, stretched
rhapsodic, ambiguous
stretched, exaggerated
unbelievable, incredible

Complex

complected, interwoven
complex, involved
complicated, complected
intricate, puzzling
involved, complected
knotty, involved
manifold, complected
paronymous, ambiguous

Excursive

circumlocutory, roundabout
circumstantial, indirect
desultory, digressive
digressive, wandering
discursive, desultory
excursive, desultory
indirect, ambiguous
periphrastic, circumlocutory

NOUNS

Ambiguity

absurdity, a puzzling significance
ambiguity, doubtful significance
anomaly, absurdity
equivocation, ambiguity
equivoque, ambiguous term
incongruity, ambiguity
inconsistency, incongruity
quiddity, trifling nicety
quirk, equivocation

Deception

artifice, equivocation
camouflage, dissimulation
casuistry, sophism

NOUNS (Continued)

chicane, sophistry
deception, artifice
diplomacy, subtle negotiations
dissimulation, duplicity
duplicity, ambiguity
finesse, artifice
lubricity, uncertainty
quibbling, equivocation
quibble, equivocation
simulation, camouflage
sophism, deceptive argument
sophistry, a subtly deceptive disputation
speciousness, verisimilitude
stratagem, artifice
subtlety, artfulness

Unreliability

apocrypha, something of doubtful authorship
dogma, seemingness
dogmatism, ambiguity
elusiveness, mystification
fame, current report
hearsay, rumor
mystification, mystery
perplexity, entanglement
prognosis, uncertain opinion of a disease
rumor, hearsay
talk, rumor
unreliability, mere talk

Indefiniteness

generality, indefiniteness
indefiniteness, vagueness
probability, uncertainty
questionability, uncertainty
rhapsody, confused sentence
uncertainty, doubtfulness
vagueness, indefiniteness
verisimilitude, probability

Illusion

apparition, phantasm
chimera, misleading imagery
delusion, phantasm
hallucination, delusion
ignisfatuus, misleading influence
illusion, phantom
mirage, phantasm
phantasm, deception
phantom, apparition

Allusion

allusion, indirect reference
flare, ambiguous expression
hint, intimation
innuendo, oblique hint
insinuation, allusion
intimation, allusion

Mystery, Etc.

charade, enacted enigma

NOUNS (Continued)

conundrum, riddle
enigma, riddle
mystery, enigma
myth, unproved tradition
paradox, a seeming contradiction—possibly true
poser, enigma
problem, perplexing question
pun, equivocation
puzzle, enigma
quiz, enigma
rebus, enigmatical phrase
riddle, enigma
tickler, something puzzling

Incredibility

fishiness, incredibleness
imperceptibility, inscrutability
incomprehensibility, inscrutability
inconceivability, incomprehensibility
incredibility, absurdity
inscrutability, infinity

Complexity

complexity, complication
complicacy, complexity
complication, problem
entanglement, complication
intricacy, complicacy
labyrinth, intricacy
maze, labyrinth
ramification, intricacy
tangle, complication
wilderness, maze

Excursiveness

circumlocution, indirect expression
desultoriness, digression
digression, equivocation
discursiveness, digression
discursion, circumlocution
excursion, digression
knot, intricacy
periphrasis, circumlocution

Obscure Terms

abscission, a broken sentence leaving one to infer its meaning
amphibolic, an ambiguous sentence or proposition
double entendre, word or phrase with two meanings—usually identical
glossary, obscure or ambiguous terms
homograph, a word spelled like another with a different meaning
homonym, a word like another in sound but with a different idea
(Continued on page 121)

58

VERBS

Miscellaneous

abbreviate, shorten
abridge, epitomize
abstract, epitomize
brief, epitomize
condense, reduce
contract, condense
curtail, abbreviate
epitomize, abridge
initial, abbreviate
mention, say briefly
recapitulate, summarize
reduce, curtail
shorten, curtail
summarize, abridge
syncopate, contract by
   omission of the middle

ADJECTIVES

Brief

brief, concise
concise, terse
laconic, brief
short, brief
succinct, concise
terse, forcibly concise

Abridged

abridged, epitomized
compendious, succinct
condensed, abridged
contracted, condensed
summary, brief

Decisive

abrupt, broken short
bluffy, brusque
brusque, abrupt
clipped, abrupt
crisp, terse
curt, abrupt
decisive, laconic
sententious, terse

ADJECTIVES (Continued)

sharp, concise

Direct

direct, pointed
emphatic, decisive
pointblank, direct
pointed, sharp
pronounced, emphatic
straightforward, direct

Energetic

energetic, sententious
forceful, pithy
powerful, decisive
strong, energetic
vigorous, energetic

Significant

gnomic, pithy
minute, pointed
pithy, terse
plain, pointed
significant, pointed
virtual, pithy

NOUNS

Abbreviation

abbreviation, contraction
apocope, deletion of the
   last syllable or letter of
   a word
contraction, abbreviation
curtailment, abbreviation
initial, abbreviation
syncopation, contraction by
   omission of the middle
systole, shortening of a
   long syllable

Brevity

brevity, conciseness
conciseness, terseness
terseness, conciseness

Abridgment

abbreviature, compendium

NOUNS (Continued)

abridgment, epitome
abstract, epitome
brief, an epitome
compendium, abridgment
condensation, abridgment
conspectus, synopsis
compend, abridgment
compression, condensation
digest, abridgment
docket, synopsis
draft, short outline
epitome, abridgment
pandect, digest of Roman
   or civil law
scenario, brief sketch
summary, compendium
synopsis, conspectus
syllabus, compendium

Energy

abruption, sudden termination
brusqueness, abruptness
energy, sententiousness
emphasis, force
force, energy
power, energy
rigor, force
(B). rigour
strength, sententiousness

Significance

gist, main point
pith, pithiness
pithiness, terseness
point, terse significance
significance, point

Notation

memorandum, note
mention, brief notice
minute, memorandum
notation, short note
note, brief outline

59

VERBS

aphorize, utter pithily
(B). aphorise

ADJECTIVES

acute, pointed
artful, cunning
astute, crafty
brainy, wise

ADJECTIVES (Continued)

bright, brilliant
brilliant, sparkling
clever, witty
cunning, crafty
crafty, artful
cute, clever
diplomatic, tactful
epigrammatic, witty

ADJECTIVES (Continued)

intelligent, clever
keen, sharp
judicious, sagacious
logical, rational
pointed, terse, pithy
rational, judicious
sagacious, judicious
(Continued on page 127)

	see—	Stupidity—Idiocy 110B	Error 126C
vs. Wit—Cleverness	59	Ambiguity 57	Dissonance 70
vs. Wisdom—Intelligence	117	Falsehood 62	Talkativeness 56

60

VERBS

Miscellaneous

babble, talk childishly
blather, talk foolishly
cackle, blather
chatter, babble
drivel, blather
drool, drivel
fiddle-faddle, talk nonsense
gabble, fiddle-faddle
gibber, be incoherent
jabber, chatter
prate, talk idly
prattle, prate
rattle, cackle
rave, talk wildly
rehash, utter tritely
smatter, blather
splutter, utter confusedly
stutter, splutter
tattle, prate
trifle, fiddle-faddle
twaddle, blather

ADJECTIVES

Senseless

foolish, silly
inane, senseless
nonsensical, senseless
senseless, unintelligible
silly, foolish
thoughtless, reasonless

Chattering

babbling, pointless
cackling, chattering
chattering, babbling
gibberish, incoherent
jabbering, incoherent

Frivolous

banal, meaningless
casual, cursory
cursory, superficial
empty, hollow
flatulent, windy
flippant, thoughtless
frivolous, frothy
frothy, senseless
glib, flippant
groundless, hollow
hollow, superficial
meaningless, empty
platitudinous, trite
pointless, stupid

ADJECTIVES (Continued)

shallow, superficial
superficial, hollow
transitory, cursory
unimportant, inconsequent
windy, flatulent
wishy-washy, empty

Incongruous

absurd, unintelligible
contrary, inconsistent
extravagant, visionary
far-fetched, illogical
illogical, irrational
inarticulate, incoherent
incoherent, absurd
inconclusive, hollow
incongruous, inconsistent
inconsequent, inconsistent
inconsistent, illogical
inept, absurd
irrational, absurd
preposterous, unreasonable
reasonless, senseless
ridiculous, absurd
sophistical, unsound
unmeaning, senseless
unreasonable, unsound
unsound, illogical

Unintelligible

confused, incoherent
desultory, irrational
discursive, desultory
rhapsodic, confused
unintelligible, senseless

Stupid

dull, inane
stupid, dull

NOUNS

Nonsense

bosh, nonsense
froth, vapid speech
fudge, nonsense
gab, idle chatter
guff, nonsense
nonsense, incongruity
punk, nonsensical talk
rot, nonsense
rubbish, nonsense
stuff, nonsense
wind, empty talk

NOUNS (Continued)

Chatter

babble, foolish talk
blather, gibberish
cackle, silly talk
chatter, gibberish
chitchat, trifling talk
diddle-daddle, nonsense
fiddle-faddle, nonsense
fiddledeedee, nonsense
gabble, incoherent talk
gibberish, gabble
rattle, empty talk
splutter, confused talk

Frivolity

balderdash, nonsense
extravaganza, rhapsody
flatulence, emptiness
flippancy, babble
folderol, nonsense
foolishness, nonsense
frivolity, folderol
frothiness, froth
inconsequence, idle chatter
jargon, incongruity
levity, inconsistency
malapropism, absurd use of
  fine words
prattle, empty talk
rabble, incoherent dis-
  course
rhapsody, rigmarole
rigmarole, foolish talk
tomfoolery, nonsense
twaddle, silly talk
windiness, flatulence

Incongruity

absurdity, nonsense
contrariety, inconsistency
desultoriness, incoherence
fallacy, unsound argument
illogicalness, inconsistency
incongruity, incoherence
inconsistency, incongruity
sophism, unsound argument
sophistry, sophism
superficiality, flatulence

PERSONS

blatherskite, a foolish
  talker
stick, inconsistent speaker

	ASSOCIATIVE	
Truisms—Maxims 61B	Wisdom, Wittiness........117	
Disclosure 78	Assertion 80	
Prophecy 77	Proof, Witness..............93	
Teaching, Education ..81	Religious Dogma............82A	
Justice, Honesty 140A	Isms and Ologies 83	

61A

VERBS

State Truth

affirm, declare true
allege, affirm
assert, affirm
aver, declare truthfully
avouch, declare true
certify, attest as true
declare, reveal
divulge, reveal
prove, reveal
vow, declare openly

Reveal

actualize, make a fact
attest, certify
confirm, verify
ratify, confirm
reveal, divulge
testify, solemnly declare true
verify, prove true
vouch, attest

Admit

acknowledge, confess
admit, acknowledge
avow, confess
confess, acknowledge
own, acknowledge

ADJECTIVES

Declarative

affirmative, ratifying
declarative, affirmative
emphatic, declarative

Actual

absolute, veritable
actual, true
factual, actual
fundamental, real
genuine, real
infallible, factual
invincible, infallible
paradoxical, apparently absurd but true
philosophic, sound
real, true
scientific, philosophic
sound, founded on reality
true, actual
valid, sound
veritable, actual
very, real

Truthful

faithful, truthful
loyal, faithful
truthful, true
veracious, truthful

ADJECTIVES (Continued)

Credible

authentic, genuine
authoritative, absolute
believable, trustworthy
careful, credible
competent, authoritative
credible, believable
gospel, veritable
orthodox, considered sound
reliable, truthful
reputable, reliable
responsible, truthful
trustworthy, truthful

Frank

artless, frank
candid, truthful
earnest, sincere
fair, honest
frank, candid
guileless, frank
honest, frank
impartial, fair
ingenuous, frank
innocent, frank
naive, artless
open, frank
serious, earnest
sincere, honest
unbiased, honest
unfeigned, truthful
unprejudiced, fair
unreserved, outspoken

Straight-spoken

outspoken, frank
straightforward, frank
straight-spoken, true
unexaggerated, veritable
unvarnished, unexaggerated
upright, outspoken

Indisputable

incontrovertible, indubitable
indisputable, indubitable
indubitable, without doubt
inviolable, undeniable
undeniable, true
unquestionable, not to be questioned

NOUNS

Declaration

affirmation, averment
allegation, affirmation
assertion, declaration
averment, affirmation

NOUNS (Continued)

declaration, assertion

Revelation

actualization, verification
attestation, certification of truth
certification, statement of truth
confirmation, verification
disclosure, verification
ratification, confirmation
revelation, disclosure
verification, confirmation

Actuality

actuality, reality
absoluteness, actuality
fact, truth
gospel, verity
infallibility, inviolability
integrity, soundness
inviolability, actuality
paradox, truth when apparently an absurdity
reality, truth
science, truth
solidity, validity
soundness, reality
truth, actuality
validity, truth
verity, reality
virtue, soundness

Truthfulness

accuracy, truth
authenticity, truth
fidelity, truthfulness
probity, truthfulness
sooth, truth
truthfulness, truth
veracity, truthfulness

Credibility

credibility, probability
probability, credibility
verisimilitude, the appearance of truth

Frankness

artlessness, frankness
candor, frankness
earnestness, sincerity
fairness, candor
frankness, candor
honesty, truthfulness
ingenuousness, frankness
naivete, artlessness
sincerity, truthfulness

(Continued on page 127)

TRUISM—MAXIM—MOTTO   see—   **ASSOCIATIVE**

61B

VERBS

aphorize, moralize
moralize, aphorize

ADJECTIVES

aphoristic, proverbial
axiomatic, evident as equal
  to a truth
epigrammatic, having the
  pith of an epigram
gnomic, proverbial
pointed, epigrammatic
proverbial, evident as a
  truth
sententious, axiomatic

NOUNS

acrostic, a motto or phrase
  formed by the perpendicular front edge of a composition
adage, proverb
aphorism, proverb
apothegm, a pithy saying
apologue, moral
axiom, truism
dictum, aphorism
epigram, pithy phrase
fable, moral
folk-lore, maxims, etc.
gnome, maxim

NOUNS (Continued)

institute, maxim
maxim, proverb
moral, an evident truth
mot, a witty saying
motto, a pithy truth
parable, allegory conveying
  a pithy truth
precept, maxim
proverb, aphorism
rule, maxim
saw, aphorism
saying, adage
slogan, mot
truism, self-evident truth
war-cry, aphorism

59 (Continued)

ADJECTIVES (Continued)

sage, wise
sapient, discerning
sensible, clever
sharp, acute
shrewd, sagacious
smart, shrewd
tactful, clever
wise, learned
subtle, clever
urbane, witty

ADJECTIVES (Continued)

versatile, witty
witty, clever

NOUNS

acuteness, sagacity
cleverness, wit
cuteness, cleverness
facetiæ, witticism
judiciousness, wisdom
rationality, judiciousness

NOUNS (Continued)

sagacity, acuteness
sally, sudden wit
sapience, sagacity
subtlety, acuteness
tact, skilful expression
wisdom, wise saying
wit, witty remark
witticism, wit

61A (Continued)

NOUNS (Continued)

Admission

acknowledgment, admis-
  sion of truth
admission, acknowledg-
  ment
confession, acknowledg-
  ment

Password

parole, the true password
  used daily in a garrison

NOUNS (Continued)

password, parole
shibboleth, a word when
  uttered correctly de-
  noted a compatriot
watchword, password

Fundamental

fundamental, truth
foundation, fundamental

NOUNS (Continued)

principle, fundamental
  truth
rudiment, first principle

INTERJECTIONS

fact, quotha
indeed, in truth
quotha, indeed
amen, adv. verily
verily, adv. amen

vs. Truth 61A	Dishonesty 130A
	Ambiguity 57
	Mystification 103A

Dark—Nebulous 97
Flattery—Praise 63
Foolishness—Nonsense 60

62

VERBS

Lie

belie, lie
equivocate, deceive
excuse, whitewash
fib, tell a white lie
forswear, swear falsely
lie, utter falsely
perjure, swear falsely
whitewash, misrepresent

Exaggerate

exaggerate, overstate
hyperbolize, exaggerate, as "swift as the wind"
(B). hyperbolise
imp, exaggerate
magnify, exaggerate
stretch, exaggerate

Deceive

beguile, deceive
deceive, chicane
delude, deceive
diddle, deceive
flam, deceive
flare, deceive boldly
foist, introduce deceptively
fudge, foist a fallacy
illude, deceive
mislead, deceive

Humbug

canard, deceive by a hoax
chicane, trick with pretense
gammon, impose a hoax
humbug, deceive
quack, pretend
trick, delude

Pervert

bias, instil deceptively
distort, misrepresent
falsify, misrepresent
misrepresent, present falsely
pervert, distort
prejudice, bias
traduce, misrepresent
vitiate, pervert

Prevaricate

prevaricate, quibble
quibble, prevaricate
tergiversate, equivocate
whiffle, prevaricate

Fabricate

dogmatize, fabricate
(B). dogmatise
fable, to fib
fabricate, fabulize
fabulize, compose fables
(B). fabulise
romance, yarn

VERBS (Continued)

yarn, fabricate

Pretend

cant, utter hypocritically
counterfeit, feign
feign, pretend
malinger, feign sickness
pretend, mislead
sham, pretend
simulate, deceive

ADJECTIVES

Lying

false, untrue
lying, false
perjured, perfidious
perverted, false
wry, false

Exaggerated

exaggerated, overwrought
extravagant, exaggerated
fantastic, exaggerated
hyperbolic, exaggerating the fact
outre, exaggerated
overwrought, exaggerated
reckless, untrustworthy

Deceptive

ambidexterous, deceitful
collusory, deceptive
crafty, deceptive
deceitful, deceptive
deceptive, quibbling
designing, deceitful
disingenuous, deceptive
double-faced, deceptive
fallacious, deceptive
illusive, deceptive
insidious, deceitful
mendacious, lying
quackish, pretentious
quibbling, deceptive
tricky, deceitful
two-faced, deceptive

Perversive

counterfeit, spurious
distorted, false
spurious, false
unreal, fictitious

Prevaricating

fishy, apparently false
hollow, false
inconsistent, wanting truth
tortuous, deceitful
ungrounded, false
unreliable, whiffling
untrue, false
untrustworthy, unreliable

ADJECTIVES (Continued)

Fabricating

dogmatic, fabricated
fabulous, fictitious
fictional, fictitious
fictitious, false
mythic, romantic
mythical, unreal
romantic, extravagant

Hypocritical

canting, hypocritical
hypocritical, shamming
mock, false
necromantic, noting pretended divination
pharisaical, hypocritical
pretentious, shamming
pseudo, prefix—false
sanctimonious, hypocritical
unctuous, deceitfully bland

Treacherous

apostate, false
disloyal, false
faithless, disloyal
perfidious, false
traitorous, false
treacherous, traitorous

NOUNS

Lying

duplicity, deceit
equivocation, prevarication
fallacy, untruth
falsehood, deceit
lying, falsehood
perjury, false swearing
untruth, falsehood

Lie

fib, falsehood
lie, a falsehood
thumper, barefaced lie
white lie, a lie in the interest of good
whopper, notorious lie

Exaggeration

exaggeration, extravagant statement
hyperbole, exaggeration
screamer, gross exaggeration

Deception

artifice, deception
deceit, falsehood
deceitfulness, deceit
deception, falsehood
falsity, deceit
flam, falsehood
guile, deceit

(Continued on page 130)

PRAISE—ACCLAIM ETC.	see—	**ASSOCIATIVE**	
		Exaltation 139B	Songs—Melody 68B
vs. Reproof 64		Reward 45	Love—Affection 39A
vs. Defamation 65		Trophy—Palm, etc. 104B	Esteem 38
		Memorials 104H	Courtship 40
		Badge—Cross, etc. 104B	Joy—Bliss 71A

63

VERBS

Praise
eulogize, extol
(B). eulogise
extol, praise highly
glorify, reflect glory upon
honor, glorify
(B). honour
laud, extol
lionize, glorify
magnify, exalt
panegyrize, praise
(B). panegyrise
praise, laud

Compliment
compliment, congratulate
congratulate, felicitate
delight, please highly
felicitate, wish joy to
gratify, delight
revere, venerate
venerate, honor
worship, venerate

Acclaim
acclaim, shout applause
applaud, acclaim
cheer, applaud
encore, recall with applause
hurrah, shout applause
toast, honor in drinking
trumpet, extol loudly

Flatter
beslaver, praise fulsomely
beslobber, beslaver
flatter, gratify with praise
honey, flatter
puff, praise fulsomely
sugar, flatter
toady, flatter obsequiously
wheedle, toady

Commemorate
celebrate, extol
commemorate, celebrate
consecrate, dedicate
dedicate, commemorate
immortalize, exalt to fame
(B). immortalise
solemnize, celebrate
(B). solemnise

Approve
advocate, recommend
approbate, approve
approve, commend
commend, praise
indorse, sanction
recommend, commend
sanction, approve

VERBS (Continued)

Greet
greet, welcome
hail, greet
salute, greet
welcome, honor

Thank
bless, praise
thank, bless

ADJECTIVES

Praising
acclamatory, laudatory
encomiastic, eulogistic
eulogistic, laudatory
laudatory, eulogistic
laureate, giving honor
panegyric, eulogistic
plauditory, giving applause

Complimentary
complimentary, praiseful
congratulatory, approbative

Flattering
adulatory, flattering
flattering, adulatory
fulsome, rich in praise
oily, flattering
smooth, flattering
suave, unctuous
unctuous, flattering

Approbative
approbative, commendatory
approbatory, approbative
commendatory, approbative
recommendatory, approving

Greeting
salutatory, wishing well

Benedictory
benedictive, benedictory
benedictory, blessing
halleluiah, praising God

Thankful
gracious, thankful
grateful, fulsome
thankful, grateful

Farewell
farewell, valedictory
good-by, farewell
valedictory, saying fare-
well

NOUNS

Praise
encomium, formal praise
eulogy, high praise

NOUNS (Continued)
homage, worship
hero-worship, laureation
honor, homage
(B). honour
laudation, praise
panegyric, eulogy
praise, laudation
tribute, praise

Compliment
admiration, worship
compliment, praise
congratulation, felicitation
felicitation, congratulation
felicity, praise
reverence, veneration
veneration, worship
worship, ardent praise

Acclamation
acclaim, shout of applause
acclamation, applause
applause, audible praise
boom, burst of applause
cheer, audible acclaim
encore, applause
furor, great enthusiasm
gush, outburst of praise
ovation, acclamation
plaudit, applause
salvo, burst of applause
toast, praise with drinking

Flattery
adulation, praise
blandishment, flattery
blarney, wheedling
flattery
fawning, servile flattery
flattery, excessive praise
flummery, flattery
logrolling, mutual praise
puff, flattery
puffing, puff
sycophancy, servile flattery
taffy, blarney (slang)
unction, flattery
wheedling, blarney

Commemoration
celebration, dedication
commemoration, celebration
dedication, commemoration
glorification, laudation
laureation, formal honor

(Continued on page 130)

NOUNS (Continued)

Approval

approbation, commendation
approbativeness, approval
approval, approbation
commendation, approval
indorsement, approval
recommendation, approval
testimonial, certificate of
   approval

Greeting

greeting, welcome
salute, greeting
salutation, salute
welcome, greeting

Benediction

benediction, blessing
benison, blessing
blessing, gift of grace
doxology, glory to God
eloge, funeral eulogy
gloria, ascription of praise

63 (Continued)
NOUNS (Continued)

halleluiah, gloria

Thankfulness

grace, gratitude
gratitude, thanks
thankfulness, gratitude

Farewell

adieu, farewell
farewell, valediction
good-by, a farewell
valedictory, oration of
   praise and farewell

PERSONS

adulator, flatterer
claque, hired applauders
claqueur, as above (sing.)
congratulator, felicitator
encomiast, laudator
eulogist, encomiast
flatterer, puffer
laudator, praiser

PERSONS (Continued)

laureate, laureate poet
lickspittle, sycophant
panegyrist, eulogizer
puffer, adulator
sycophant, servile flatterer
trumpeter, self-proclaimer
tuft-hunter, sycophant
valedictorian, one who delivers a valedictory

INTERJECTIONS

all-hail, vive!
bravo, good!
bully, bravo! (slang)
good, well done!
hosanna, praise to God!
hurrah, bravo!
viva, hurrah!
vive, long life or success!

---

62 (Continued)
NOUNS (Continued)

mendacity, falsehood

Humbuggery

bosh, humbuggery
canard, hoax
fudge, made-up story
gammon, hoax
hoax, deceptive trick
hocus, deception
humbuggery, falsehood
imposture, deception
invention, fabrication
quackery, imposture
trick, hoax
trickery, deception

Perversion

bull, distortion of facts
casuistry, sophistry
charlatanism, quackery
chicane, sophistry
distortion, perversion
falsification, fabrication
Jesuitism, subtle duplicity
Machiavellianism, unprin-
   cipled deception in politics
misrepresentation, untruth
perversion, falsification
sophism, sophistry
sophistry, specious falsity

Prevarication

excuse, subterfuge
fishiness, inverisimilitude
inveracity, untruthfulness
inverisimilitude, falsehood

NOUNS (Continued)

prevarication, pretext
quibble, falsehood
quibbling, petty deceit
subterfuge, falsehood
tergiversation, subterfuge
whiffling, prevarication

Fabrication

dogma, statement of belief
dogmatism, dogma
fable, fabrication
fabrication, fiction
fiction, invention
figment, fiction
story, fictitious narrative
tale, story
yarn, tale

Hypocrisy

cant, hypocrisy
hypocrisy, false profession
mockery, falsehood
necromancy, pretension to
   divination
pharisaism, hypocrisy
pretense, prevarication
pretension, pretense
pretext, pretense
sciolism, pretense to
   knowledge
sham, pretense
speciousness, deceptive
   fairness
veneer, pretense

Treachery

faithlessness, falsehood

NOUNS (Continued)

infidelity, faithlessness
perfidy, treachery
treachery, faithlessness
treason, treachery

PERSONS

Ananias, the liar who fell
   dead when rebuked by
   Peter
charlatan, pretender to
   knowledge
deceiver, imposter
dissembler, deceiver
fabricator, prevaricator
fabulist, fabricator of
   fables
fibber, fibster
fibster, petty liar
forger, a falsifier
hypocrite, one who pretends
   to be what he is not
imposter, montebank
liar, one who lies
Machiavellian, a cunning
   unprincipled politician
necromancer, pretender at
   divination
Pharisee, deceiver
pretender, quack
prevaricator, misrepre-
   senter
quack, charlatan
sophist, one who argues
   cleverly but fallaciously

see—

ASSOCIATIVE

64

VERBS

Reproach
admonish, reprove
blame, condemn
carp, reproach
check, reprove
lecture, reprimand
rail, reproach
reprimand, reprove
reflect, cast reproach
reprove, chide
rebuke, reprove
reproach, upbraid
reprobate, censure
upbraid, reproach
warn, admonish

Denounce
abjure, renounce
abnegate, denounce
condemn, disapprove
decry, denounce
denounce, censure
disapprove, decry
fulminate, denounce
objurgate, rebuke
renounce, denounce

Censure
animadvert, criticize
berate, scold
censure, castigate
chide, scold
criticize, censure
(B). criticise
fuss, scold
inculpate, censure
nag, censure
reprehend, censure
scold, chide sharply
slate, criticize severely
vent, utter ill feelings

Castigate
castigate, criticize severely
excoriate, chastize verbally
keelhaul, censure
lash, scourge with satire
rate, excoriate
roast, scold

Growl, Etc.
growl, admonish
snarl, admonish

Deride
deride, ridicule
fiddle-faddle, twit
gibe, taunt
gird, taunt

VERBS (Continued)
hoot, gibe
ridicule, scoff
scoff, gibe
taunt, gibe, reproach
twit, upbraid

Insult
affront, insult
huff, affront
insult, affront
sauce, insult
snub, affront

Curse
anathematize, curse
(B). anathematise
beshrew, imprecate
curse, invoke evil upon
damn, condemn
execrate, curse
imprecate, curse
inveigh, censure severely
rip, swear
swear, curse
vituperate, curse abusively

ADJECTIVES
Reproachful
admonitory, reproachful
captious, carping
carping, fault-finding
fussy, carping
invective, vituperative
reprehensive, reproachful
reproachful, censorious

Denunciatory
condemnatory, denunciatory
damnatory, condemnatory
damning, condemning
denunciatory, objurgatory
depreciating, denunciatory
objurgatory, censorious

Censorious
animadversive, censorious
censorious, denunciatory
censurable, fault-finding
critical, censorious
naggy, censorious
vituperative, censorious

Castigatory
castigatory, censorious
cutting, sarcastic
mordant, sarcastic
scathing, censorious
slashing, sarcastic

ADJECTIVES (Continued)
trenchant, scathing

Harsh
acrimonious, caustic
acrid, stinging
biting, acrimonious
bitter, sarcastic
caustic, sarcastic
grating, acrid
harsh, grating
poignant, bitter
pungent, sarcastic
severe, scathing
shrewish, scolding
snarling, surly
stinging, acrimonious
surly, snarling
tart, stinging

Sarcastic
sarcastic, cuttingly severe
sardonic, derisive
satirical, sarcastic

Derisive
derisive, ironical
ironical, satirical
scoffing, derisive

Insulting
audacious, impudent
brassy, impudent
brazen, insolent
impertinent, impudent
impudent, saucy
insolent, impertinent
insulting, insolent
lippy, impertinent
malapert, impudent
pert, saucy
saucy, impudent

NOUNS
Reproach
admonition, reproof
blame, reproach
obloquy, reproach
rebuke, reprehension
reproach, severe blame
reprobation, reproach
reproof, censure
warning, admonition

Denunciation
abjuration, renunciation
condemnation, denunciation
damnation, condemnation
denunciation, censure

(Continued on page 134)

vs. Exaltation 139B
vs. Praise—Acclaim 63

65

VERBS

Defame

asperse, slander
backbite, slander
belie, calumniate
blackguard, vilify
blaspheme, revile
calumniate, accuse falsely
defame, disgrace
desecrate, defame
libel, defame
malign, slander
profane, debase
revile, vilify
scandalize, defame
(B). scandalise
slander, calumniate
traduce, slander
vilify, defame
violate, profane

Disparage

abase, humble
belittle, depreciate
degrade, lower, debase
depress, humble
disgrace, dishonor
dishonor, defame
disparage, belittle
humble, degrade
humiliate, humble
lower, humble
mortify, humiliate
obscure, make mean
prostrate, humble
slur, disparage

Abuse

abuse, defame
brutalize, brutify
brutify, debase
corrupt, debase
debase, corrupt
deprave, debase
depreciate, disparage
derogate, detract
detract, disparage
disqualify, disrate
disrate, degrade

Stigmatize

attaint, disgrace
bespatter, asperse
blacken, defame
blemish, defame
brand, stigmatize
stigmatize, defame
(B). stigmatise

Accuse

accuse, blame
arraign, accuse

VERBS (Continued)

ascribe, impute
attribute, impute
blame, accuse
charge, accuse
complain, charge
criminate, accuse
impeach, arraign
impute, charge
incriminate, accuse
inculpate, criminate
indict, charge
lay, impute
recriminate, countercharge

Denounce

cast, condemn
condemn, blame
decry, disparage
denounce, accuse
inveigh, denounce

Curse

anathematize, curse
(B). anathematise
ban, curse
beshrew, execrate
curse, blaspheme
damn, curse
damnify, curse
execrate, curse
imprecate, curse

ADJECTIVES

Defamatory

blasphemous, vilifying
calumnious, defamatory
contumelious, abusive
defamatory, derogatory
evil, foul
foul, scurrilous
infamous, libelous
libelous, scandalous
obscene, foul
pornographic, obscene
profane, blasphemous
scandalous, defamatory
slanderous, calumnious
scurrilous, opprobrious
venomous, scurrilous
villainous, infamous
virulent, venomous

Disparaging

degrading, disparaging
disparaging, depreciatory
humiliating, mortifying
mortifying, humiliating

ADJECTIVES (Continued)

Abusive

abusive, humiliating
depreciatory, derogatory
derogatory, disparaging
discreditable, disparaging
disgraceful, degrading
ignominious, derogatory
inglorious, disparaging
opprobrious, disgraceful
outlandish, infamous
scornful, disparaging
unflattering, opprobrious

Accusatory

accusatory, accusing
ascribable, blamable
attributive, ascribing
blamable, accusatory
blameful, accusatory
invective, accusatory
recriminatory, accusatory

Denunciatory

apostatical, renunciatory
damnatory, denunciatory
demagogic, denunciatory
denunciatory, accusatory
imprecatory, cursing

NOUNS

Defamation

aspersion, slander
blackguardism, calumniation
blackguard, slander
blasphemy, profanity
billingsgate, slander
calumniation, slander
contumely, scornful abuse
defamation, aspersion
desecration, defamation
indignity, abuse
infamy, ignominy
libel, slander
obloquy, slander
profanation, blasphemy
scandal, defamation
scurrility, slander
slander, defamation
vilification, defamation
violation, profanation

Disparagement

abasement, disparagement
debasement, defamation
degradation, abasement
disparagement, defamation

(Continued on page 133)

DISPUTE—QUARREL

see—

vs. Admission—
Compliance 46A

ASSOCIATIVE

66

VERBS

Dispute
contradict, dispute
disagree, dispute
differ, disagree
dispute, debate
gainsay, contradict
impugn, gainsay

Contend
altercate, dispute
argue, debate
contend, dispute
contravene, dispute
controvert, debate
contest, dispute
debate, dispute
discuss, argue
litigate, contend
militate, contend
ratiocinate, argue

Quarrel
agitate, discuss
bicker, altercate
brawl, quarrel
fuss, quarrel
heckle, interrupt
higgle, dispute
jangle, quarrel
quarrel, dispute
squabble, quarrel
wrangle, dispute

ADJECTIVES

Disputatious
contradictory, diametrically
  opposed
discordant, wrangling
disputatious, dissentient
dissentient, controversial

ADJECTIVES (Continued)
dissonant, quarrelsome

Contentious
argumentative, disputa-
  tious
contentious, quarrelsome
controversial, controvertible
debatable, being debated
forensic, in public dispute
litigious, forensic
polemic, disputatious
polemical, polemic
ratiocinative, argumen-
  tative

Quarrelsome
cantankerous, quarrelsome
irascible, quarrelsome
quarrelsome, disputatious
querulous, dissentient
pugnacious, quarrelsome
wrangling, disputatious

NOUNS

Dispute
contentiousness, disputa-
  tion
contradiction, contraven-
  tion
controversy, disputation
diatribe, long disputation
difference, controversy
disputation, controversy
dispute, quarrel
dissidence, dispute
dissonance, disagreement

NOUNS (Continued)
disagreement, contraven-
  tion
polemics, controversy

Contention
altercation, dispute
argument, debate
argumentation, dispute
contention, debate
contest, dispute
contravention, debate
debate, argument
litigation, legal dispute
logomachy, furious argu-
  ment

Quarrel
agitation, argument
bickering, wrangling
embroilment, disputation
friction, dispute
imbroglio, fracas
strife, quarrel
wrangling, disputation

Miscellaneous
brawl, quarrel
broil, a quarrel
clash, disputation
feud, quarrel
fracas, noisy quarrel
fray, quarrel
fuss, quarrel
gale, quarrel
quarrel, dispute
row, wrangle
ruction, row
spat, quarrel
squabble, dispute
tiff, spat

---

65 (Continued)

NOUNS (Continued)

Abuse
abuse, slander
depreciation, decrial
derogation, disparagement
detraction, derogation

Stigma
blemish, stigma
brand, stigma
disgrace, humiliation
dishonor, infamy
humiliation, mortification
ignominy, defamation
slur, aspersion

NOUNS (Continued)
stigma, infamy
umbrage, foul expression

Accusation
accusation, blame
arraignment, ascription
ascription, blame
attribution, imputation
blame, accusation
charge, accusation
complaint, charge
countercharge, recrimina-
  tion
crimination, accusation

NOUNS (Continued)
impeachment, accusation
imputation, ascription
inculpation, incrimination
incrimination, accusation
indictment, charge
invective, violent accusation
objurgation, blame
philippic, invective
recrimination, accusation
reproach, disgrace

(Continued on page 134)

NOUNS (Continued)

jeremiad, sarcastic lament
objurgation, blame
renouncement, objurgation
renunciation, objurgation
thunder, denunciation
thunderbolt, denunciation

Censure

animadversion, censure
belles-lettres, facile
   criticism
censure, reproof
criticism, censure
curtain lecture, scolding
fuss, a scolding
lecture, reprimand
reprimand, reproach
reprehension, censure
scolding, sharp rebuke
wigging, scolding rebuke

Castigation

castigation, severe
   criticism
decrial, clamorous censure
diatribe, abusive criticism
dressing, reprimand
gratings, harsh abuse
stricture, censure
tirade, violent censure
vituperation, censure

Harshness

acerbity, acrimony
acridity, acrimony
acrimony, asperity
asperity, acerbity
poignancy, acrimony
spleen, acrimony

Sarcasm

cynicism, sarcasm
irony, subtle sarcasm
railing, satire
raillery, satire
sarcasm, bitter satire
satire, sarcasm

NOUNS (Continued)

Derision

catcall, reproof
derision, hostile ridicule
dudgeon, malicious jeering
gibe, a taunting
hoot, jeering, disapprobation
horse-laugh, derision
ridicule, derision
scoffing, ridicule
sneer, scoff
taunt, bitter reproach

Insult

affront, indignity
audacity, insolence
brass, impudence
cheek, reproof
effrontery, impudence
flippancy, impudence
impertinence, impudence
impudence, insolence
indignity, insult
insolence, insult
insult, effrontery
pertness, impudence
sauciness, impudence

Lampoon, Etc.

broadside, conspicuous
   newspaper attack
lampoon, abusive satire
pasquinade, lampoon
skit, brief satire
slant, sarcastic remark

Growl, Hiss, Etc.

growl, warning grumble
grumbling, growling
hiss, sibilation
sibilation, warning hiss
snarl, acrimonious growl

Curse

anathema, curse
curse, imprecation
execration, a cursing

NOUNS (Continued)

imprecation, curse
malediction, imprecation
malison, malediction
oath, curse

PERSONS

castigator, one who rebukes
   severely
critic, one who judges cap-
   tiously
criticaster, petty critic
cynic, a captious person
demagogue, one who in-
   veighs against authority
iconoclast, one who attacks
   sham, etc.
railleur, one who attacks
   jestingly
satirist, a writer of satire
scold, a scolding woman
scoffer, one who scoffs
shrew, vixen
spitfire, one who is fitfully
   acrimonious
termagant, a noisy, violent
   woman
vixen, harsh woman
Xanthippe, a scolding
   woman

INTERJECTIONS

bah, contempt
boo, contempt
faugh, disgust
fiddle-de-dee, disapproval
fiddlestick, disapproval
fie, disapproval
fugh, disapproval
hoity-toity, disapproval
lush, contempt
pish, contempt
pshaw, contempt
pugh, contempt
sirrah, fellow, sir (surly)

NOUNS (Continued)

Denunciation

condemnation, blame
damnation, imprecation
decrial, disparagement
demagogism, denunciation
denunciation, accusation
fulmination, denunciation
opprobrium, condemnation
renunciation, disparage-
   ment
scorn, opprobrium

NOUNS (Continued)

Curse

anathema, formal curse
ban, a curse
curse, imprecation
damn, a curse
execration, imprecation
expletive, curse
imprecation, malediction
malediction, curse
malison, execration
profanity, malediction

PERSONS

apostate, one who re-
   nounces his party
blackguard, reviler
demagogue, a political re-
   nouncer
denunciator, denouncer
maligner, slanderer
muckraker, an abusive
   writer or speaker
reviler, defamer

REMONSTRANCE—

DENIAL see—
vs. Compliance 46A
vs. Submission 46B

ASSOCIATIVE

Disputation 66	Demand 41B
Complaint 67B	Anger 29
Reproof 64	Hatred 28
Opposition 27	Conversation 90

67A

VERBS

Remonstrate

confute, disprove
contradict, deny
contravene, controvert
controvert, refute
decline, deny
demur, disagree
deplore, remonstrate
deprecate, protest
differ, dissent
disagree, dissent
disapprove, dissent
disprove, demur
dissent, expostulate
expostulate, remonstrate
gainsay, contradict
impugn, contradict
object, protest
oppose, object
protest, remonstrate
refuse, decline
refute, disprove
reject, refuse
remonstrate, expostulate
traverse, deny formally

Resent

antagonize, defy
(B). antagonise
challenge, defy
dare, defy
defy, dare
resent, kick

Snarl, Etc.

bellow, roar defiance
foam, rage
gnash, grit defiance
grit, gnash the teeth
growl, snarl defiance
grumble, murmur protest
kick, remonstrate
lip, resent
rage, growl, gnash
rant, protest, rave, rage
rave, rage
roar, bellow defiance
snap, defy sharply
snarl, growl defiance
storm, defy stormily
tear, rage

Repudiate

abjure, renounce
apostatize, renounce
(B). apostatise
deny, abjure
disclaim, repudiate
disavow, disclaim

VERBS (Continued)

disown, disclaim
forswear, deny
recant, deny
renounce, disclaim
repudiate, disclaim

ADJECTIVES

Remonstrant

adverse, contrary
apostate, renunciatory
contradictory, denying
contrary, contradictory
controversial, contra-
  dictory
deprecatory, disapproving
dissentient, controversial
dissenting, negative
expostulatory, dissentient
negative, oppositious
opponent, controversial
oppositious, protesting
protestant, expostulatory
refutable, disprovable
remonstrant, expostulatory
renunciatory, dissentient
tutelar, protesting

Resentful

antagonistic, negative
bellicose, contentious
belligerent, hostile
cantankerous, contentious
contentious, contradictory
defiant, antagonistic
fiery, cantankerous
grievous, sorely negative
hostile, antagonistic
indignant, resentful
inimical, hostile
militant, hostile
peppery, fiery
perverse, petulant
pettish, petulant
petulant, resentful
pugnacious, hostile
resentful, expostulatory
splenetic, peppery

Snarling, Etc.

growling, cantankerous
grumbling, growling
grumpy, hostile
mumpish, grumbling
snappish, petulant
snarling, snappish
waspish, snappish

Harsh, Etc.

austere, stern

ADJECTIVES (Continued)

grave, solemnly negative
harsh, austere
serious, solemn
severe, austere
solemn, stern
stern, severe

Repudiative

agnostic, denying God, etc.
adjuratory, renunciatory
apostatical, renunciatory
renunciatory, repudiating
repudiative, renunciatory

NOUNS

Remonstrance

confutation, denial
contradiction, denial
contravention, opposition
demurrer, objection
denial, contradiction
disagreement, dissension
disapprobation, disapproval
disapproval, dissension
discord, dissonance
dissent, contravention
dissension, difference
difference, disagreement
dissidence, disagreement
dissonance, disagreement
expostulation, protest
negation, denial
objection, remonstrance
opposition, protestation
protest, remonstrance
protestation, protest
refusal, denial
refutation, denial
rejection, refusal
remonstrance, protest
traverse, formal denial
variance, difference

Resentment

antagonism, militancy
bravado, defiance
contention, antagonism
contentiousness, petulance
challenge, protest
dare, a challenge
defiance, dare
hostility, militancy
militancy, antagonism
peevishness, dissonance
petulance, peevishness
pugnacity, contentiousness
resentment, strong protest

(Continued on page 138)

COMPLAINT see—		ASSOCIATIVE	
vs. Contentment—	⎧ Remonstrance 67A	Disputation 66
Laughter 71B	⎨ Reproof 64	Opposition 27

67B

VERBS	VERBS (Continued)	NOUNS

VERBS

Deplore

bemoan, bewail
bewail, lament
complain, murmur
deplore, complain
fret, deplore
grieve, deplore
lament, bewail
murmur, moan

Cry, Etc.

blubber, deplore
cry, bewail
groan, moan
moan, deplore
pule, deplore
scream, shriek deploringly

VERBS (Continued)

sigh, deplore
snivel, weep
sob, weep
wail, bewail
weep, deplore
whimper, weep
whine, complain
yelp, bewail

ADJECTIVES

Miscellaneous

doleful, complaining
dolesome, doleful
mournful, dolesome
plaintive, mournful
querimonious, complaining
querulous, complaining

NOUNS

Miscellaneous

complaint, deprecation
cry, bewailment
deprecation, entreating
protest
grievance, complaint
groan, doleful moan
lamentation, complaint
moan, lamentation
murmur, moan
plaint, a lament
plaintiveness, bewailment
scream, shrill cry
sob, doleful crying
whimper, sob
whine, plaint

MELODY—		ASSOCIATIVE	
ELOQUENCE see—	⎧ Song—Melody 68B	INSTRUMENTS	
vs. Dissonance 70	⎨ Persons 68H, 68I, 68J	Stringed 68D
	⎪ Symbols 68K	Percussion 68E
	⎩ Speech 55A	Pneumatic 68G

68A

VERBS	VERBS (Continued)	ADJECTIVES (Continued)

VERBS

Melodize

attune, bring in accord
harmonize, be in accord
jazz, play lively music
melodize, harmonize
(B). melodise
play, express in music
serenade, sing or play
   tenderly
symphonize, harmonize
   with a full band
(B). symphonise

Sing, Etc.

carol, warble
chant, sing
chime, harmonize
chirp, utter chirpingly
croon, sing softly
hum, croon
lilt, sing to swaying
quaver, trill
sing, chant
trill, sing quaveringly
warble, trill
yodle, warble

Fiddle, Fife, Etc.

ding, sound like a bell
drum, play on a drum
fiddle, play a violin
fife, play a fife or flute
intone, sound a note

VERBS (Continued)

pipe, whistle
ring, sound bell-like
roll, drum a long sound
sound, intone
tingle, ring
tinkle, ring softly
tune, harmonize
whistle, blow a tune

Portray Eloquently

declaim, speak rhetorically
depict, portray
flourish, be flowery
paint, depict
portray, paint verbally
recite, declaim

ADJECTIVES

Melodious

dulcet, harmonious
elegiac, sadly tuneful
enharmonic, in harmony
harmonic, concordant
harmonious, musical
incantatory, enchanting
liquid, mellifluous
lyric, in the music of a lyre
mellifluent, sweet-sounding
mellifluous, mellifluent
melodious, dulcet
musical, melodious
Orphean, melodious

ADJECTIVES (Continued)

sweet, mellifluous
symphonic, orchestral
tuneful, harmonic

*Figuratively
Melodious*

agreeable, pleasant
beautiful, delightful
delightful, pleasing
enchanting, pleasing
exquisite, delightful
pleasant, delightful
pleasing, delightful

*Distinctively
Melodious*

clarion, distinct
clear, clarion
gentle, tender
low, soft
mellow, soft
orotund, resonant
resonant, resounding
rich, harmonious
ringing, clear
silvery, clear
soft, dulcet
sonant, resonant
sonorific, sounding
sonorous, resonant
soothing, tender

(Continued on page 137)

ADJECTIVES (Continued)

tender, soft
warbling, trilling

Vocal, Orchestral, Etc.

choral, sung in choir
chromatic, in semitones
instrumental, orchestral
operatic, in musical drama
orchestral, played in
  orchestra
vocal, sonant

Concordant

assonant, sonant
concordant, consonant
consonant, harmonious
rhythmic, harmonious

Vocally Distinctive

alto, contralto
barytone, voiced between
  bass and tenor
bass, deep-sounding
contrabass, sounded an
  octave lower
contralto, alto
diatonic, regular in pitch
falsetto, higher than chest
  voice
mezzo-soprano, between
  soprano and contralto
soprano, noting the highest
  female voice
tenor, noting the highest
  male voice
treble, soprano

Eloquent, Etc.

altisonant, high-sounding
declamatory, rhetorical
elocutionary, rhetorical
eloquent, artful, persuasive
euphemistic, pleasing
euphonic, euphonious
euphonious, exquisite
exquisite, highly pleasing
fine, grand
florid, flowery
flowery, oratorical
fluent, eloquent
grand, grandiose
grandiose, grandiloquent
grandiloquent, lofty in
  expression
magniloquent, grand
oratorical, rhetorical
recitative, uttered
  musically
rhetorical, elegant in
  speech

ADJECTIVES (Continued)

Implying Diction

clear, definite
definite, distinct
grammatical, correct in
  speech
measured, rhythmic
puristic, affectedly precise
rhythmic, recitative

NOUNS

Melody

glee, minstrelsy
harmony, concordance
jazz, form of syncopation
melody, harmony
minstrelsy, music
music, melody
psalmody, psalm singing
ragtime, syncopated music
symphony, harmony
syncopation, form of jazz

Tremolo, Etc.

quaver, vibrating tone
resonance, vibrant tone
tremolo, tremulous effect
trill, a quaver
warble, sweet flow of sound

Concordance

accord, harmony
attunement, harmonization
concord, harmony
concordance, concord
consonance, harmony
rhythm, rhyme
unison, concordance

Intonation, Etc.

bravura, brilliant range
cadenza, musical flourish
cadence, a musical run
cantillation, an intoning
chord, notes in harmony
diapason, entire range
diminuendo, decrease in
  tone
dulciana, a pleasing stop
gamut, entire range
intonation, quality of tone
modulation, varying tone
roulade, musical movement

Note, Pitch

flat, depressed tone
note, tone
pitch, quality of tone
sharp, higher note
tone, quality of sound

Eloquence, Etc.

assonance, euphony

NOUNS (Continued)

Atticism, eloquence
elegance, magniloquence
eloquence, gripping
  utterance
euphony, pleasing speech
flourish, magniloquence
fluency, eloquence
grandiloquence, grand
magniloquence, grand
  speech
oratory, eloquence
refinement, elegance

Figurative Eloquence

artistry
portraiture
beauty
charm
bewitchment
enchantment
dignity
elegance
grace
stateliness
brilliance
fire
resplendence
sparkle
force
intensity
power
strength
character
importance
prestige
significance
cleverness
genius
profundity
wisdom
magnificence

Diction, Etc.

diction, elocution
elocution, pleasing speech
poetry, poetic speech
purism, precise speech
rhetoric, elegant speech
rhyme, poetry

Voice

See Adjectives

PERSONS

orator, artful speaker
speaker, orator
spellbinder, orator

SONG—AIR—MELODY

accompaniment, a subordinate rendition
air, melody
anthem, triumphal song
antiphon, hymn by alternating choirs
antiphony, responsive chanting
antistrophe, alternate singing
aria, an air
arietta, short aria
ballad, a music and dance rendition
barcarole, gondolier song
berceuse, cradle-song
bolero, music for a Spanish dance
cantata, a choral composition
canticle, a song
canto, a singing
canto fermo, plain song
canzona, a song
canzonet, short song
carillon, an air on bells
carol, song of joy
cavatina, short melody
cento, a composition with mixed pieces
chant, a song
chantey, sailors' song
charivari, mock serenade
choral, a melody
concert, musical entertainment
concertino, abridged concerto
concerto, musical composition
cotillion, dance music
descant, a varied melody
dirge, funeral hymn
ditty, a little song
divertimento, an air
divertissement, ballet

(Continued)

doxology, hymn of praise
duet, a piece for two
duetino, a short duet
elegiac, elegy
elegy, dirge
extravaganza, fantastic composition or drama
fantasia, extravaganza
fugue, a composition with parts repeated
gallopade, dance music
glee, composition for voices
gradual, response song
Gregorian, a chant
halleluiah, a rendition of praise
hymn, sacred dole
hyporcheme, Greek dance song
improvisation, improvised rendition
incantation, an enchantment
introit, an entering psalm
lay, a simple song
lilt, a song with rhythmic movement
love-ditty, a love-song
lullaby, a cradle song
lyric, rendition on a lyre
madrigal, amorous song
Magnificat, a chant
march, a composition for marching
melody, a tune
minstrelsy, production of ballads, poetry, etc.
minuet, a dance music
monody, plaintive song
musette, a soft air
music, harmonic sounds
musicale, harmonic entertainment
music-drama, splendid harmony
nocturne, lullaby

(Continued)

ode, a short song
opera, musical drama
operetta, opera
opus, musical composition
oratorio, a sacred melody
oratory, oratorio
orchestration, orchestral rendition
pæan, triumphal song
paraphrase, sacred hymn
parody, a burlesque
pastoral, a rural song
psalm, sacred ode
philter, love-song
potpourri, musical medley
recital, musical entertainment
redowa, Bohemian music or dance
refrain, a repeated strain
requiem, musical mass for a deceased
rondeau, a light air
rondelet, refrain
roundelay, ancient song or dance
saltarello, vivacious music or dance
saraband, music for a Spanish dance
serenade, a tender strain
service, a devotional piece
solo, piece rendered singly
sonata, composition for one instrument
sonatina, miniature sonata
song, poetical strain
strain, melody
symphony, an orchestration
syncopation, syncopated piece
tune, a melody
vespers, evening song
yodel, song in natural and falsetto voice

67A (Continued)
NOUNS (Continued)

Snarl, Etc.

bellow, defiant roar
gust, violent outburst
roar, defiant bellow
scream, yell of rage
snarl, defiant growl
tantrum, sudden outburst

Repudiation

abjuration, repudiation
disavowal, denial
recantation, denial
renouncement, repudiation

NOUNS (Continued)

renunciation, denial
repudiation, disavowal

PERSONS

agitator, controversialist
antagonist, opponent
complainant, remonstrant
controversialist, disputant
controvertist, disputant
disclaimer, disowner
disputant, disclaimer
dissenter, remonstrant

PERSONS (Continued)

dissentient, remonstrant
dissident, ranter, etc.
growler, remonstrant
grumbler, growler
opponent, controversialist
Polemic, controversialist
ranter, boisterous preacher
remonstrant, expostulator
repudiator, disclaimer
shrew, vixen
wasp, vixen
wrangler, disputant

68C, 68D, 68E, 68F, 68G, 68H, 68I, 68J, 68K   See—(ASSOCIATIVE 68A)

68C

INTRODUCTION—END-ING—INTERLUDE

dulciana, pleasing stop
epode, last part of an ode
exode, interlude
interlude, a playing be-tween
intermezzo, a lively playing between
overture, introduction
prelude, musical preface
recessional, a rendition as the clergy departs
reveille, an awakening by drum or bugle
ritornelle, an introductory or concluding symphony
symphony, instrumental in-troduction or ending of a vocal composition
taps, bugle command for "lights out"
tattoo, drumbeat for re-tirement

68D

STRINGED INSTRUMENTS

Æolian harp	koto
banjo	lute
bass viol	lyre
cello	mandolin
cithara	penta
cithern	piano
clavichord	pianoforte
clavier	pianola
contrabasso	psaltery
dulcimer	sackbut
fiddle	Stradivarius
gittern	ukulele
grand	viol
guitar	viola
harp	violin
harpsichord	violone
hautboy	violoncello
hept	zither
hexa	Etc., etc.
kin	

68E

PERCUSSION INSTRUMENTS

bell
castanet
chime
cymbal
drum
gong
tambourine
tom-tom
xylophone

68F

INSTRUMENTS—MISCELLANEOUS

graphophone, phonograph
instrument, music piece
phonograph, graphophone

68G

AIR INSTRUMENTS

accordion	flute
alpenhorn	harmonium
autophon	harmonica
bagpipe	horn
basshorn	jew's harp
bassoon	ophicleide
bombardon	organ
bugle	piccolo
calliope	saxhorn
clarinet	saxophone
clarion	trombone
concertina	trumpet
cornet	tuba
euphonium	whistle
fife	

68H

MUSICIANS

artiste, singer, etc.
band, orchestra
banjoist, banjo player
bassoonist, bassoon player
drummer, drum player
fiddler, violinist
fuguist, performer
flutist, flute player
harmonist, melodist
lyrist, lyre player
maestro, a master in music
melodist, music maker
minstrel, musician
musician, minstrel
orchestra, band
organist, organ player
performer, player
pianist, piano player
player, musician
soloist, solo singer
trumpeter, trumpet sounder
tuner, harmonizer
violinist, violin player
virtuoso, a skilful player
waits, nocturnal musicians

BEINGS

Euterpe, muse of music
Apollo, god of music, etc.
Orpheus, mythical musician

68I

VOCALISTS, Etc.

artiste, singer
barytone, intermediate tone
bass, bass singer
basso, bass
basso profundo, low bass
bard, singer
cantor, chief singer
choir, company of singers
chorister, choir member
chorus, choir
contralto, contralto singer
cantatrice, female singer
falsetto, falsetto singer
nightingale, sweet singer
octet, eight singers
parodist, one who parodies
prima donna, a principal female singer
psalmist, psalm singer
psalmodist, psalmist
quartet, four singers
quintet, five singers
sextet, six singers
singer, one who sings
songster, singer
soprano, highest female voice
tenor, highest male voice
troubadour, lyric poet
virtuoso, master musician
vocalist, singer
warbler, singer

68J

PERSONS (Miscellaneous)

composer, writer of music
impresario, director
improviser, composer
precentor, leader of a choir
prelector, precentor

68K

MUSICAL SYMBOLS

clef, pitch symbol
bass-clef
tenor-clef
scale, etc., etc.

FAINTNESS—LOW SOUND   see—   ASSOCIATIVE

vs. Loudness 69B

- Stability—Rest 11B
- Insensibility—Apathy 110A
- Moderate Sound 69C
- Speech 55A

69A

VERBS

Hush
hush, be subdued or silent
silence, hush
sough, blow softly
still, hush

Mutter
buzz, hum
coo, murmur softly
drone, utter monotonously
gurgle, sound purlingly
hum, drone
muffle, say in undertone
murmur, mutter
mutter, be low-voiced
purl, murmur gently

Aspirate
aspirate, breathe utterance
breathe, whisper
fizz, sound hissingly
hiss, utter a hiss
sizzle, sound hissingly
whisper, utter with breath

Patter
crackle, crepitate
crepitate, crackle lightly
palpitate, beat softly
patter, sound softly
ripple, crepitate softly
rustle, sound softly
tick, be faint-sounding
tinkle, ring softly

ADJECTIVES

Hushed
hushed, inaudible
inaudible, not heard
noiseless, inaudible
quiet, hushed
silent, inaudible
stifled, suppressed
still, inaudible
subdued, low
suppressed, muffled
soundless, inaudible

Muttering
audible, faint
bland, soft
faint, almost silent
gentle, soft
indistinct, faint
low, not loud
muffled, indistinct
soft, not harsh
sotto voce, in undertone

Aspirate
aspirate, soft
hissing, having a hiss
sibilant, hissing
susurrant, rustling gently
whispering, breathing
  utterance

Pattering
crepitating, crackling
pattering, sounding softly
tinkling, ringing softly
tintinnabular, tinkling

NOUNS

Hush
faintness, a faint sound
hush, inaudibleness
silence, a hush
stillness, silence

Mutter
drone, dull tone
hum, low sound
murmur, low utterance
mutter, low utterance
undertone, subdued tone
whirr, humming sound

Aspiration
aspirate, breath-like sound
aspiration, aspirate
lisp, indistinct utterance
sibilation, hissing sound
sough, hollow murmur
susurrus, gentle rustling
whisper, breathed utterance

Pattering
crepitation, light crackling
palpitation, inaudible
  beating
pattering, soft sounds
ripple, a murmuring
rustle, whispering sound
tapping, light sound
tinkling, soft ringing
tintinnabulation, tinkling

69B (Continued)

NOUNS (Continued)

Stridulation, Etc.
jangle, a howling
raucity, harsh noise
splutter, confused noise
sputter, splutter
stridulation, shrillness

Bellow, Etc.
bark, sharp cry
bellow, a roar
bray, donkey-like cry
howl, prolonged cry
scream, shrill cry
screech, shrill noise
shriek, scream
squawk, a squall

NOUNS (Continued)
squall, loud crying
ululation, a howling

Report, Etc.
blare, blast
blast, violent blowing
discharge, explosion
explosion, detonation
fulmination, thunder
report, explosion
roar, thundering noises
rumbling, deep sound
thunderbolt, loud report

Trumpeting, Etc.
salvo, simultaneous firing
tattoo, drum-beat

NOUNS (Continued)
volley, salvo

Clang, Ring, Etc.
clang, metallic noise
clangor, clang
(B). clangour
crack, sharp sound
knell, a bell toll
peal, loud sound
ring, peal
stroke, peal
tang, twang
toll, peal of a bell
twang, sharp sound

VOCIFERATION   see—

vs. Low Sound........69A

ASSOCIATIVE

69B

VERBS

Thunder, Etc.

crash, sound crashingly
detonate, thunder
explode, detonate
fulminate, thunder
noise, sound loud
re-echo, reverberate
resound, re-echo
reverberate, resound
roar, bellow
roll, make a deep sound
rumble, resound
shriek, scream
swell, increase in sound
thunder, fulminate

Vociferate, Etc.

clamor, be turbulent
(B). clamour
exclaim, vociferate
hallo, shout
hollo, shout
hoop, whoop
shout, yell
vociferate, utter loudly
whoop, shout
yell, shout

Bellow, Etc.

bark, make barking sound
bay, bark deeply
bawl, utter loudly
bellow, roar
bleat, utter a bleat
bray, sound donkey-like
caw, sound crow-like
cackle, utter a cackle
chirp, peep
croak, sound frog-like
crow, sound rooster-like
cry, scream
gobble, sound turkey-like
howl, sound a wail
jangle, yelp or howl
low, bellow
mew, utter a mew
moo, sound cow-like
neigh, sound a neigh
peep, chirp
pipe, utter shrilly
scream, utter shrilly
screech, sound shrilly
snore, be stertorous
shrill, shriek
squawk, squall
squall, cry loudly

VERBS (Continued)

squeak, utter shrilly
squeal, shrill
snort, sound with a snort
wail, howl

Trumpet, Etc.

blare, trumpet
drum, beat a tattoo
trumpet, blare

Clang, Ring, Etc.

bang, sound with a bang
boom, make a deep sound
clang, sound metallic-like
clank, clang
peal, vociferate
ring, peal

ADJECTIVES

Thundering, Etc.

deafening, violently loud
ear-splitting, deafening
howling, yelling
roaring, uproarious
thundering, thunder-like
thunderous, thundering
tumultuous, riotous
turbulent, noisy
uproarious, tumultuous

Vociferous

bawling, wailing
blatant, bawling
boisterous, noisy
clamorous, vociferous
clangorous, clamorous
flamboyant, boisterous
loud-mouthed, flamboyant
obstreperous, boisterous
riotous, noisy
vociferous, clamorous
windy, boisterous

Sonorous, Etc.

clarion, loud
declamatory, noisy
deep, grave in pitch
full, sonorous
high, shrill
high-toned, high-pitched
hollow, deep-toned
loud, clarion
powerful, sonorous
resonant, resounding
resounding, reverberatory
reverberant, resounding

ADJECTIVES (Continued)

reverberatory, resounding
sepulchral, hollow
sounding, resonant
sonorous, loud-sounding
stentorian, loud-voiced

Stridulous

highstrung, high-pitched
piercing, shrill
piping, shrill
shrill, loud and sharp
stertorous, snoring loudly
stridulous, shrill

NOUNS

Thunder, Etc.

bedlam, uproar
crashing, violent noise
din, deafening noise
disorder, uproar
disturbance, uproar
hubbub, uproar
hullabaloo, uproar
noise, uproar
pandemonium, uproar
racket, clattering noise
rabble, noise
riot, uproar
rumpus, uproar
shindy, uproar
spatterdash, noise
thunder, loud report
tumult, uproar
turbulence, turmoil
turmoil, noise and bustle
uproar, clamor, noise

Vociferation, Etc.

clamor, vociferation,
(B). clamour
hallo, a shout
hue, clamor
outcry, clamor
shout, outcry
whoop, a shout

Sonorousness

booming, hollow report
detoning, explosion
intonation, a sounding
resonance, reverberation
reverberation, a reechoing
sonorousness, clear sound
volume, fullness of sound

(Continued on page 140)

MODERATE SOUND

       see—
   vs. Quiet 11B

ASSOCIATIVE

69C

VERBS

Sound

accent, accentuate
accentuate, emphasize
emphasize, accentuate
(B). emphasise
intone, utter monotone
sound, make a tone, note, etc.

Vibrate

clink, sound with a ring
jingle, tinkle
quaver, utter tremulously
ring, tinkle
tink, clink
tinkle, ring
tong, sound bell-like
twang, sound in vibration
vibrate, to sound

Crepitate, Etc.

clack, sound sharply
clatter, make sharp noises
crackle, sound sharply
creak, sound gratingly
crepitate, crackle
rattle, sound sharply
snap, sound sharp

VERBS (Continued)

sputter, sound sputteringly

Squeak, Etc.

squeak, make a small noise
swish, sound whistle-like
wheeze, sound wheezingly
whiz, sound whizzingly

ADJECTIVES

Miscellaneous

accentual, having accent
bleating, sounding a bleat
crackling, crepitant
creaky, grating
crepitant, rattling
distinct, easily heard
emphatic, accentual
monotonous, even-toned
quavering, tremulous
stridulous, crackling
tremulous, quavering
vibratory, tremulous
wheezy, sounding wheezy

NOUNS

Sound

accent, accentuation

NOUNS (Continued)

accentuation, emphasis
cadence, full voice
emphasis, accent
inflection, modulation
note, sound
sound, audible note, tone, etc.
tempo, musical speed
tone, note or sound

Vibration

tinkle, tintinnabulation
tintinnabulation, tinkling
tremolo, fluttering tone
vibration, tremolo

Crepitation, Etc.

clatter, sharp sounds
creak, creaking sound
crepitation, a rattling
flip-flap, flapping sound
pit-a-pat, quick noise
thud, dull sound
thump, thud

Squeak, Etc.

sizzle, sizzling sound
squeak, small noise
swish, sharp whistling

DISSONANCE— INELEGANCE see— vs. Melody 68A	ASSOCIATIVE

70
VERBS

Croak, Etc.

belch, eructate noisily
bray, utter coarsely
cackle, caterwaul
caterwaul, sound harshly
croak, utter croakingly
gobble, sound turkey-like
grate, utter harshly
grunt, utter in grunts
stammer, stutter
stutter, stammer
scrape, sound harshly
snuffle, speak with a nasal
   dissonance
snore, sleep noisily
wheeze, breathe harshly

Mumble, Etc.

drawl, utter lazily
drone, utter boresomely
falter, stammer
lisp, utter imperfectly
mumble, sound mumblingly
mump, mutter
mutter, mumble
muffle, mutter

ADJECTIVES

Croaking, Etc.

asthmatic, wheezing
croaking, cacophonous
grunting, uttering grunts
guttural, croaking
hoarse, rough and harsh
husky, hoarse
hollow, husky
jarring, discordant
piping, cacophonous
raucous, hoarse
rough, harsh
sepulchral, hollow
snoring, raucous
stammering, stuttering

ADJECTIVES (Continued)

stuttering, stammering
stertorous, snoring
strident, harsh
stridulous, strident
throaty, guttural
wheezing, harsh

Discordant, Etc.

cacophonous, discordant
cracked, discordant
disagreeable, discordant
discordant, dissonant
dissonant, discordant
grating, harsh
harsh, discordant
inarticulate, indistinct
inharmonious, discordant
scraping, harsh
sour, cracked
tuneless, discordant

Noisy

boisterous, rude
noisy, boisterous
termagant, noisy

Shrill

piercing, shrill
screaming, shrieking
screeching, shrieking
shrieking, shrill
shrill, piercing

Mumbling, Etc.

drawling, inelegant
droning, monotonous
faltering, inarticulate
lisping, inarticulate
muffled, mumbling
mumbling, murmuring
murmuring, muttering
muttering, mumbling
monotonous, dull
singsong, monotonous

Vulgar

bawdy, foul-mouthed

ADJECTIVES (Continued)

coarse, vulgar
dirty, filthy
filthy, indecent
flat, ribald, foul
foul, obscene
indecent, obscene
inelegant, coarse
low, obscene
obscene, vulgar
pornographic, obscene
ribald, obscene
rude, vulgar
smutty, obscene
vulgar, common, rude

NOUNS

Miscellaneous

hoarseness, huskiness
huskiness, hoarseness
monotone, tiresome drone
monotony, dull speech
singsong, monotony
stammering, stuttering
stuttering, stammering

Discord, Etc.

cacophony, dissonance
croaking, raucous noise
discord, dissonance
dissonance, discord
jangle, discord
noise, dissonance
raucity, huskiness
screed, shrill sound
stridulation, shrillness
wheeze, a wheezing
yawp, uncouth outcry

Vulgarity

bawdry, obscene speech
obscenity, vulgarity
ribaldry, bawdry
smut, obscene talk
vulgarism, low expression
vulgarity, vulgarism

JOY—MIRTH—GLADNESS   see—   **ASSOCIATIVE**

vs. Sorrow—Grief 31	Laughter 71B
vs. Anger—Wrath 29	Jocularity 72
	Song—Melody 68B
	Praise 63

71A

VERBS

Miscellaneous

appreciate, enjoy
bask, enjoy
blush, flush
carouse, feast joyously
delight, rejoice
disport, play
divert, relax
enjoy, rejoice
exult, be glad
flush, be overcome
flutter, be excited
frolic, gambol
gambol, frisk joyously
glory, rejoice
jubilate, exult
junket, revel
luxuriate, live richly
marvel, wonder
play, disport
recreate, enjoy one's self
rejoice, be glad
relax, divert
relish, enjoy
revel, be merry
rollick, be jovial
snuggle, enjoy intimately
taste, enjoy
triumph, rejoice
wile, pass pleasantly
wonder, be amazed

ADJECTIVES

Jubilant

agog, eagerly excited
delighted, elated
elated, jubilant
enthusiastic, exuberant
excited, agog
exuberant, elated
exultant, jubilant
gleeful, joyous
hilarious, jubilant
intoxicated, excited
joyful, gleeful
joyous, joyful
jubilant, rejoicing
overjoyed, elated
rhapsodic, exuberant
tickled, elated
triumphant, rejoicing

Vivacious

airy, gay
amused, pleased
frisky, gay
frolicsome, merry
gamesome, merry
happy-go-lucky, rollicking

ADJECTIVES (Continued)

larking, frolicsome
lively, vivacious
perky, gay
playful, lively
rollicking, jovial
sparkling, lively
sportful, merry
sportive, merry
sprightly, vivacious
vivacious, gay

Happy

blithe, joyous
bonny, gay
boon, gay
buoyant, joyous
buxom, jolly
cavalier, gay
cheerful, glad
cheery, cheerful
felicitous, happy
gay, cheerful
genial, cheerful
glad, joyous
gladsome, gay
gustful, zestful
halcyon, happy
jolly, mirthful
jovial, merry
merry, mirthful
mirthful, joyful
primrose, gay

Ecstatic

captivated, charmed
charmed, fascinated
delirious, ecstatic
ecstatic, blissful
enrapt, rapt
enraptured, enrapt
entranced, enraptured
fascinated, enraptured
rapt, overjoyed
raptured, enrapt
thrilled, enrapt
transported, rapt

Spellbound

amazed, astonished
astonished, spellbound
astounded, thunderstruck
breathless, thunderstruck
dazzled, amazed
spellbound, astonished
thunderstruck, spellbound

Blissful

beatific, blissful
blithesome, mirthful
blissful, happy
Elysian, blissful

ADJECTIVES (Continued)

Proud

arrogant, proud
conceited, proud
egotistic, self-satisfied
overweening, self-satisfied
proud, pleased, elated
vain, proud
vainglorious, elated

Festive

bacchanal, in revelry
bacchantic, jovial
Bacchic, bacchanal
carousing, festive
convivial, jovial
festive, joyous
riotous, carousing

Contented

comfortable, contented
contented, satisfied
cozy, comfortable
luxurious, gratified
snug, comfortable
warm, comfortable

Heartened

assured, heartened
buoyed, cheered
cheered, heartened
condoled, comforted
consoled, condoled
comforted, heartened
heartened, cheered

Appreciative

appreciative, gratified
complacent, pleased
grateful, thankful
gratified, pleased
pleased, gratified
satisfied, pleased
thankful, appreciative

NOUNS

Jubilation

elan, verve
enthusiasm, exuberance
excitement, furor
exuberance, exultation
exultation, rejoicing
flurry, excitement
furor, enthusiasm
gale, gaiety
heyday, time of joy
hilarity, noisy merriment
jollification, gaiety
jollity, gaiety
joviality, joyfulness
(Continued on page 145)

NOUNS (Continued)

joy, gladness
jubilation, exultation
jubilee, jubilation
rhapsody, exuberance
rejoicing, jubilation
verve, enthusiasm

Vivacity

airiness, gaiety
alacrity, liveliness
buoyancy, joyousness
lark, frolic
liveliness, gaiety
levity, gaiety
playfulness, gaiety
readiness, cheerfulness
sportiveness, jollity
sprightliness, jollity
skylarking, a frolicking
vivacity, gayness

Happiness

cheer, gladness
cheerfulness, joy
cheeriness, gladness
gaiety, merriment
geniality, cheerfulness
gladness, joy
glee, joy
happiness, joyfulness
humor, merriment
(B). humour
merriment, mirth
mirth, gaiety
pleasantry, merriment
weal, happiness
welfare, weal

Ecstasy

afflatus, exaltation
charm, intoxication
delirium, rapture
ecstasy, transport
elation, exultation
exaltation, transport
exhilaration, exaltation
fascination, charm
inspiration, exaltation
intoxication, exhilaration
rapture, ecstasy
ravishment, transport
thrill, exquisite sensation
trance, ecstasy
transport, ecstasy
triumph, jubilation

Blissfulness

beatitude, bliss

NOUNS (Continued)

blessedness, bliss
bliss, perfect joy
blissfulness, beatitude
Elysium, bliss
felicity, blissfulness
glory, beatitude

Pride

arrogance, pride
conceit, pride
crest, egotism
egotism, conceit
presumption, egotism
pride, elation
self-importance, egotism
self-respect, pride
vanity, conceit

Festivity

carnival, revelry
carousal, revelry
conviviality, joviality
festival, joyfulness
festivity, gaiety
fete, festival
honeymoon, honey-month
   of marriage
kermess, festival
kettledrum, conviviality
orgy, revelry
revelry, jollification
Saturnalia, unrestrained
   revelry
shindy, carousal
spree, carousal
symposium, a merry-
   making
wassail, carousal

Contentment

comfort, contentment
consolation, contentment
content, complacence
contentedness, content
contentment, complacence
ease, contentment
luxury, pleasure
rest, ease
solace, contentment

Recreation

amusement, recreation
avocation, diversion
diversion, enjoyment
divertisement, enjoyment
frolic, gaiety
fun, mirth
hobby, divertisement

NOUNS (Continued)

leisure, recreation
pastime, diversion
play, leisure
recreation, diversion
relaxation, recreation
sport, merriment
vacation, recreation

Appreciation

appreciation, gladness
complacence, satisfaction
delectation, delight
delight, pleasure
enjoyment, pleasure
gratification, pleasure
gratitude, appreciation
gusto, enjoyment
indulgence, gratification
pleasure, enjoyment
relish, enjoyment
satisfaction, contentment
taste, relish
zest, enjoyment

PERSONS

addict, habitual user
amateur, devotee
bacchanal, reveler
bacchante, female
   bacchanal
devotee, votary
dilettante, amateur
egotist, a self-satisfied
   person
egoist, egotist
esthete, votary of art
(B). aesthete
epicure, one devoted to
   luxury
sportsman, one devoted to
   sports
reveler, bacchanal
vacationist, one who is on
   a vacation
votary, devotee

BEINGS

Billiken, image of good
   cheer
Euphrosyne, a grace who
   made life cheerful
Venus, goddess of laughter
Terpsichore, muse of gaiety,
   grace, dance, song, etc.

ASSOCIATIVE

vs. Grief—Moaning 31
vs. Anger—Wrath 29

Facial Emotions 98B
Joy—Mirth 71A
Jocularity 72
Song—Melody 68B
Praise 63

71B

VERBS

Miscellaneous

cachinnate, laugh loudly
chortle, chuckle
chuckle, chortle
convulse, choke in laughter
exult, be delighted
giggle, laugh foolishly
groan, rumble in laughter
ha, express gladness
kink, laugh immoderately
laugh, be in laughter
simper, smile silly-like
smile, have pleased aspect
snicker, simper
snigger, snicker
titter, snicker

ADJECTIVES

Delightful

delectable, delightful
delicious, exquisite
delightful, pleasing
effusive, rollicking
exquisite, sparkling

ADJECTIVES (Continued)

pleasing, glad
humorous, laughing

Laughing

exultant, delightful
gushing, effusive
hilarious, rollicking
laughing, risorial
risible, laughing louder
  and louder
risorial, laughing

NOUNS

Miscellaneous

cachinnation, loud laughter
chuckle, suppressed
  laughter
exultation, joyous laughter
fleer, a titter
giggle, silly laughter
guffaw, boisterous laughter
hilarity, noisy laughter
horselaugh, coarse laughter

NOUNS (Continued)

humor, laughter
(B). humour
jubilation, triumphant
  laughter
laugh, pleased expression
laughter, joyous expression
levity, humor
risibility, rising laughter
sally, wild laughter
simper, silly smile
smile, pleased expression
snicker, suppressed
  laughter
tehee, a little laughter
titter, restrained laughter

INTERJECTIONS

ha, expression of joy
hoity-toity, ha
hurrah, shout of joy

BEING

Venus, goddess of laughter,
love

72

ASSOCIATIVE

vs. Praise—Acclaim 63

Satire—Reproof 64
Defamation 65
Laughter 71B
Joy—Mirth 71A
Song—Melody 68B

72

VERBS

Jest

bandy, exchange banter
banter, make fun of
chaff, banter
illude, play tricks
jest, joke
joke, banter
jolly, banter
josh, jolly
quiz, banter

Deride

catcall, jeer
deride, ridicule
gibbet, ridicule
guy, ridicule
rail, scoff
ridicule, deride
scoff, deride
taunt, guy

VERBS (Continued)

Scoff

croak, jeer
flaunt, jeer
fleer, mock
gibe, scoff
hoot, jeer
jeer, scoff
laugh, jeer
mock, deride

Burlesque

burlesque, ridicule
caricature, make
  ridiculous
lampoon, satirize
parody, burlesque
pasquinade, satirize
rally, satirize
satirize, pasquinade
(B). satirise
squib, lampoon

ADJECTIVES

Jesting

facetious, jocular
Falstaffian, jocular
funny, humorous
humorous, droll
jesting, jocose
jocose, sportive
jocular, making jokes
jocund, jocose
sportive, jocund
waggish, jokesome
whimsical, droll

Derisory

bizarre, droll
convulsive, risible
derisive, scoffing
derisory, mocking
droll, ridiculous
ludicrous, ridiculous
(Continued on page 147)

FOREWORD—OPENING   see—   **ASSOCIATIVE**

vs. Close—Ending 74

- Salutation 98C
- Start 4
- Musical Openings 68C

73

VERBS	**ADJECTIVES** (Continued)	**NOUNS** (Continued)

VERBS

begin, open
broach, begin
commence, begin
hail, utter salute
introduce, broach
open, begin
precede, preface
preface, introduce
prefix, place before
prelude, preface
premise, introduce
prologue, preface
propound, premise

ADJECTIVES

aforementioned, preceding
aforesaid, preceding
antecedent, preceding
foregoing, former
former, preceding

ADJECTIVES (Continued)

initiatory, introductory
introductory, opening
opening, introductory
preceding, foregoing
prefatory, introductory
preliminary, introductory
prelusive, introductory
preparatory, introductory

NOUNS

alpha, beginning
antecedence, precedence
antecedent, precedent
augment, a vowel prefix
beginning, opening
caption, introduction
commencement, opening
exordium, preface
forespeech, preface
foreword, introduction

NOUNS (Continued)

greeting, introduction
hail, opening salute
hello, greeting
introduction, opening
opening, preface
preamble, introduction
precedence, antecedence
preface, introduction
prefix, a placing before
preliminary, introduction
prelude, preface
premise, preamble
proem, introduction
prologue, preface
salutation, greeting
salutatory, opening oration

PERSONS

prolocutor, presider
salutatorian, opening
  speaker

---

72 (Continued)

ADJECTIVES (Continued)

ridiculous, humorous
risible, ridiculous
scoffing, derisive

   Sarcastic

ironic, ironical
ironical, sarcastic
pungent, sarcastic
sarcastic, ironic
satiric, satirical
satirical, ridiculing
witty, satirical

   Burlesque, Etc.

burlesque, jocose
serio-comic, seriously
  jocose

NOUNS

   Jesting

badinage, raillery
banter, raillery
chaff, banter
comedy, drollery, etc.
facetiae, coarse wit
fun, drollery
high-jinks, badinage
horseplay, buffoonery
jest, pleasantry
jesting, joking
jocularity, jocosity
jocosity, sportiveness
jocundity, jocularity
joke, a jest
joking, waggery
persiflage, banter

NOUNS (Continued)

pleasantry, trick or joke
pun, witticism
sally, outburst of wit
screamer, a funny joke
shivaree, sportive reception
sport, jesting
waggery, jocularity
witticism, jocular remark

   Derision

buffoonery, drollery
derision, ridicule
drollery, buffoonery
mockery, ridicule
raillery, jocularity
ridicule, mockery
scoffing, derision
slam, pungent attack
taunt, a scoff

   Scoff

catcall, a jeering
hoot, shout of ridicule
horselaugh, derisive laugh
scoff, a jeer

   Sarcasm

antiphrasis, a quality
  reversed, as when the
  Furies were called the
  kindly ones
irony, sarcasm
sarcasm, ridicule
satire, irony
scurrility, foul
  jocularity

NOUNS (Continued)

   Burlesque, Etc.

burlesque, ludicrous
  parody
bathos, ludicrous descent
caricature, ridicule
lampoon, satire
parody, burlesque
pasquinade, satire
skit, a burlesque
squib, lampoon
travesty, burlesque

PERSONS

buffo, burlesquer
buffoon, low jester
harlequin, humorist
humorist, wag
jester, joker
joker, wag
jokesmith, professional
  wag
merry-andrew, buffoon
puck, mischievous spirit
punch, harlequin
punster, a wit
satirist, one active in
  satire
scoffer, derider
wag, wit
wit, humorist

BEING

Thalia, muse of comedy

74, 75

CLOSE—ENDING—APPENDIX   see—

ASSOCIATIVE

vs. Foreword—Opening—Prefix 73

{
Finish—Completion 50
Musical Endings 68C
Increase—Enlargement 10
}

74

VERBS

Close
close, finish
closure, end a debate
conclude, close
culminate, conclude
end, close
finish, end
perorate, conclude
terminate, close

Supplement
add, affix
affix, append
annex, join to
append, annex
attach, connect
postfix, affix
suffix, add to the end
supplement, add

ADJECTIVES

Closing
crowning, culminal
culminal, final
definitive, conclusive
farewell, closing
final, concluding
posthumous, after death
valedictory, farewell

Supplemental
additional, supplemental
supplemental, adding

ADJECTIVES (Continued)
supplementary, supple-
mental
closing, concluding
concluding, final
conclusive, closing

NOUNS

Close
climax, culmination
close, finish
conclusion, termination
culmination, conclusion
end, close
ending, end
finale, end
finality, conclusion
finis, end
finish, conclusion
omega, end
termination, conclusion
ultima, last, farthest

Outcome
consequence, sequel
denouement, outcome
outcome, sequel
sequel, succeeding result
sequence, sequel

Anticlimax
anticlimax, ludicrous close
bathos, ludicrous descent
catastrophe, climax

NOUNS (Continued)
fiasco, ludicrous finish
flunk, failure

Closure, Etc.
closure, closing of a debate
cue, the last word of preceding speech
epilogue, concluding speech
epode, last of an ode
peroration, ending oration

Retirement
peace, rest
quiet, rest
rest, retirement
retirement, rest
taps, bugle command for
"lights out"
tattoo, drum-beat for
retirement

Supplement
addendum, necessary
addition
addition, supplement
affix, something added
appendage, addition
appendix, appendage
augmentative, an added expression which amplifies
context, following part
postscript, appendix
suffix, affix
supplement, appendix

75

REPETITION—DUPLICATION   see—

ASSOCIATIVE

vs. Brevity 58

{
Enumeration 86
Verbosity 56
Custom—Habit 132D
}

75

VERBS

Repeat
imitate, do in imitation
iterate, repeat
quote, repeat
recite, repeat from memory
rehearse, repeat
reiterate, repeat again
repeat, do again

Duplicate
copy, duplicate
duplicate, reproduce
recapitulate, summarize
reduplicate, duplicate
again
reproduce, duplicate

VERBS (Continued)
summarize, repeat in
substance
(B). summarise

Harp, Etc.
din, repeat noisily
ding, din
drill, hammer
drum, repeat often
hammer, repeat often
harp, repeat often
parrot, imitate

Recur
echo, repeat sound
recur, repeat
re-echo, repeat again

ADJECTIVES

Repetitional
alliterative, repeating the
first letter as: "Apt al-
literation's artful aid"
repeated, iterative
repetitional, repeating

Duplicate
duplicate, repeated
imitative, in imitation
quotative, repeating
recapitulative, repeating
briefly

Redundant, Etc.
harping, repeating often
(Continued on page 149)

ADJECTIVES (Continued)

pleonastic, redundant
redundant, repeating
  unnecessarily
tautological, repeating in
  different words

Recurring

consecutive, successive
customary, habitual
frequent, repeated often
frequentative, frequent
habitual, in routine
incessant, continuous
periodical, recurrent
recurrent, periodical
recurring, recurrent
regular, habitual
rhythmic, regular
successional, successive
successive, recurrent
usual, habitual

ADVERBS

afresh, anew
again, repeated
anew, repeated
anon, again

NOUNS

Repetition

alliteration, see alliterative
encore, repetition
iteration, repetition
quotation, repeating
recapitulation, repetition
  in brief
recital, repetition from
  memory
recitation, recital
rehearsal, private recital
reiteration, repetition
reiterative, a word or part
  of a word reduplicated
repetition, a repeating

Duplication

ditto, a duplication
duplicate, duplication
duplication, reproduction
echo, repetition
imitation, duplication
reduplication, a duplicating
  again
replication, repetition
reproduction, repetition

NOUNS (Continued)

Redundance, Etc.

harping, regular repetition
pleonasm, unnecessary
  repetition
redundance, unnecessary
  repetition
tautology, repetition in
  different words
tautophony, repetition of
  the same sound

Recurrence

frequency, recurrence
periodicity, regular
  recurrence
practice, routine
recurrence, repetition
revolution, recurrence
rhythm, regular recurrence
rote, mechanical repetition
routine, regular practice
succession, regular
  recurrence

PERSONS

imitator
repeater
etc., etc.

76

BRAG—BLUSTER see—

vs. Modesty 132C

ASSOCIATIVE

Ostentation—Pomp 95D
Nonsense 60
Exaggeration 62
Unrestraint 125C

76

VERBS

Brag

bluster, boast
boast, vaunt
brag, boast
crack, boast
crow, boast
domineer, bluster
Hector, bluster
rant, bluster
tear, rant

Puff

blow, brag
gas, boast
gasconade, gas
puff, boast

Vaunt

plume, boast
rodomontade, brag
vaunt, brag, boast

Swagger

blazon, boast
display, brag
fanfaronade, gasconade
flaunt, bluster
mouth, utter pompously
swagger, bluster
trumpet, brag

ADJECTIVES

Braggart

blatant, bombastic
blustering, boastful
boastful, bumptious
boasting, gasconading
braggart, boastful

Puffy

frothy, bombastic
fustian, frothy
gasconading, boastful
inflated, bombastic
puffing, boasting
puffy, bombastic
tumid, turgid
turgid, bombastic

Vainglorious

arrogant, boastful
conceited, egotistic
egotistic, inordinate in self-
  praise or esteem
overweening, conceited
proud, arrogant
vain, conceited
vainglorious, boastful
vaunted, boastful

Swaggering

bombastic, ostentatious

ADJECTIVES (Continued)

bumptious, chesty
chesty, boastful
Falstaffian, boastful
grandiloquent, pompous
highfaluting, bombastic
highflown, turgid
knightly, grandiloquent
magniloquent, bombastic
ostentatious, bombastic
pedantic, ostentatious with
  learning
pretentious, ostentatious
pompous, pretentious
spread-eagle, defiantly
  bombastic
stilted, pompous
swaggering, pompous
thrasonical, boastful

NOUNS

Brag

blurb, fulsome puff
bluster, vain talk
boasting, vainglorious
  speech
brag, boastful language
(Continued on page 151)

PROPHECY   see—   **ASSOCIATIVE**

77

VERBS
Prophesy
augur, prognosticate
bode, augur
divine, foretell
predict, forecast
prophesy, foretell
soothsay, predict
vaticinate, foretell

Portend
forebode, forecast
forecast, foretell
foretell, prognosticate
omen, prognosticate
portend, forebode
presage, predict
prognosticate, foretell

Announce
announce, proclaim
annunciate, announce
harbinger, foretell
herald, proclaim
notify, foretell
proclaim, announce

ADJECTIVES
Prophetic
astrological, predictive
necromantic, predictive
oracular, prophetic
predictive, foretelling
prophetic, portentous
pythonic, prophetic
sibylline, prophetic

Portentous
admonitory, premonitory
adumbrant, shadowing
forth
monitorial, monitory
monitory, admonitory
ominous, foreboding

ADJECTIVES (Continued)
portentous, presaging
precursory, premonitory
premonitory, admonitory
prognostic, foreshadowing

Announcing
announcing, heraldic
heraldic, proclaiming

NOUNS
Prophecy
ariolation, a soothsaying
astrology, prediction
augury, prediction by signs
auspice, augury
bodement, prediction
divination, prediction
   through supernatural
   agencies
chiromancy, palmistry
forecast, a foretelling
necromancy, prophecy
oracle, prophecy
palmistry, chiromancy
prediction, prophecy
prognostication, a fore-
   telling
prognosis, prediction
prophecy, prediction
pythonism, prediction
vaticination, prophecy

Portent
alarm, warning
admonition, warning
knell, ill omen
monition, warning
omen, prognostication
presage, prediction
portent, omen
warning, notification

NOUNS (Continued)
Announcement
announcement, notification
annunciation, announce-
   ment
harbinger, announcement
notice, monition
notification, announcement
proclamation, announce-
   ment

PERSONS
astrologer, diviner
augur, predictor
banshee, fairy who foretells
   death
forecaster, predictor
forerunner, precursor
foreteller, prognosticator
herald, precursor
necromancer, one who foretells through medium of
   the dead
monitor, forewarner
monitress, as above (fem.)
oracle, prophet
precursor, prognosticator
predictor, prophet
prognosticator, foreteller
prophet, predictor
pythoness, prophetess
seer, prophet
soothsayer, precursor
vaticinator, prophet

BEINGS
Apollo, god of prophecy,
   etc.
Cassandra, a prophetess
   (Myth.)
Sibyl, a prophetess (Myth.)

DISCLOSURE	see—	ASSOCIATIVE	

78

VERBS

Disclose

bare, reveal
betray, divulge
disabuse, disclose
disclose, reveal
display, unfold
divulge, reveal
enlighten, reveal
expose, bare
gibbet, expose to ridicule
nail, expose a lie
peach, betray (colloq.)
reveal, divulge
transpire, reveal
unfold, divulge

Air

air, divulge freely
babble, blab
blab, tell thoughtlessly
blow, report
blurt, blab
bolt, blurt
bruit, expose
noise, spread by rumor
publish, divulge
report, publish
rumor, report abroad
tattle, divulge
trumpet, publish
ventilate, air

Tell

communicate, tell
extend, communicate
inform, disclose

VERBS (Continued)

tell, reveal

Confide

breathe, confide
confide, disclose
earwig, whisper covertly
whisper, confide

Confess

acknowledge, confess
admit, acknowledge
avouch, confess
avow, acknowledge
confess, own
own, admit
profess, acknowledge
unbosom, confess

ADJECTIVES

Miscellaneous

communicative, unreserved
confidential, trusting to
  another
patent, open to all
professed, acknowledged
unreserved, communicative

NOUNS

Disclosure

disclosure, revelation
exposition, disclosure
exposure, disclosure
revelation, disclosure

Airing

airing, exposure
bruit, a broadcast rumor

NOUNS (Continued)

notoriety, publicity
publicity, exposure
rumor, report
ventilation, airing

Confession

acknowledgment, confession
avowal, confession
confession, disclosure
confessional, confession
  before a priest
recognizance, acknowledgment
shrift, confession

Miscellaneous

communication, disclosure
confidence, revelation
information, exposure
intelligence, communication
stink, unpleasant exposure

PERSONS

communicant, informer
confessor, one who
  confesses
informant, informer
informer, exposer
telltale, informer
tipster, touter
tout, one who tells secrets
touter, tout
traitor, one who betrays a
  confidence

76 (Continued)

NOUNS (Continued)

Puff

buncombe, bombast
flatulence, conceit
froth, vapid eloquence
frothiness, froth
fustian, inflated speech
gas, bombast
gasconade, bluster
poppycock, boastful speech
puff, flatulence
turgescence, bombast
windiness, brag

Vainglory

arrogance, exorbitant
  claim
conceit, egotism
egoism, egotism
egotism, conceit or brag

NOUNS (Continued)

rodomontade, boasting
vainglory, rodomontade
vanity, egotism
vaunting, vaingloriousness

Swagger

bombast, high-sounding
  words
braggadocio, brag
fanfaronade, blustering
  talk
fanfare, flourish of
  trumpets
flaunt, a boast
highfaluting, bombast
knight-errantry, fanfare
magniloquence, bombast
pedantry, display of
  learning

NOUNS (Continued)

rant, empty declamation
swagger, boastfulness
Thrason, boasting

PERSONS

blusterer, braggart
boaster, braggart
braggadocio, boaster
braggart, braggadocio
ego-maniac, an extremist
  in self-esteem
egotist, self-praiser, etc.
knight-errant, one who is
  ostentatiously valorous
pedant, one who is showy
  with learning
Thraso, boaster

ANNOUNCEMENT see—

vs. Secrecy 103A

ASSOCIATIVE

79

VERBS

Announce
announce, make known
annunciate, announce
blazon, proclaim
cry, proclaim
declare, proclaim
enunciate, proclaim
harbinger, announce
herald, proclaim
neologize, blazon
proclaim, announce
promulgate, publish
pronounce, proclaim
publish, announce
resound, proclaim

Communicate
advise, apprise
apprise, inform
communicate, acquaint
inform, apprise
notify, apprise
report, make known
return, report officially
state, declare

Introduce, Etc.
acquaint, inform
intimate, make known
introduce, acquaint
impart, communicate
mention, inform briefly
prefer, present
present, introduce
refer, give reference

Warn
admonish, warn
alarm, warn
caution, admonish
warn, give notice

Broadcast
advertise, make public
broadcast, announce widely
bruit, report
noise, rumor
rumor, spread report
strike, notify by sound

Post
bulletin, state by bulletin
circularize, announce by
   circulars

VERBS (Continued)
placard, post
post, inform fully

ADJECTIVES
Miscellaneous
admonitory, monitive
alarming, admonitory
angelic, bearing message
communicative, patent
current, circulating
encyclical, announcing by
   circular letter
heraldic, introductory
introductory, heraldic
monitive, warning
monitorial, admonitory
patent, open for all
prognostic, foretelling
referential, giving reference
warning, monitive

NOUNS
Announcement
announcement, notice
ban, proclamation
declaration, proclamation
edict, proclamation
manifesto, declaration
notice, notification
notification, announcement
proclamation, announce-
   ment
prognostication, announcement
promulgation, announce-
   ment
pronunciamento, proclama-
   tion
publication, report

Communication
brief, letter
communication, message
dispatch, official announcement
epistle, missive
errand, message
letter, message
message, notification
missive, letter
note, brief
report, announcement
return, official report

NOUNS (Continued)
telegram, telegraphic
   message

Introduction, Etc.
intimation, announcement
introduction, notification
mention, brief notice
reference, mention

Warning
admonition, warning
alarm, warning
caution, notice of warning
warning, notification

Broadcast
broadcast, publicity
fame, public report
heraldry, business of
   heralds
noise, rumor, report
publicity, publication
rumor, popular report

News
intelligence, news
news, tidings of events
tidings, news
word, news

Ads, Circulars, Etc.
ad, advertisement
advertisement, notice in
   print
bull, encyclical
bulletin, official notice
cablegram, cable message
circular, printed notice
circularization, act of
   circularizing
encyclical, circular letter
placard, posted announce-
   ment
poster, advertising bill

PERSONS
advertiser, monitor
angel, God's herald
bellman, town-crier
crier, one who proclaims
forerunner, herald
harbinger, announcer
herald, proclaimer
messenger, herald
monitor, one who warns
precursor, herald
promulgator, announcer

DECLARATION   see—   **ASSOCIATIVE**

vs. Secrecy 103A

Announcement 79	Conspicuity 95E
Show—Display 95A	Proof—Citation 93
Disclosure 78	Teaching 81
Speech 55A	Explanation 84
Prophecy 77	Suggestion 87
Truth 61A	Answer 88
Truism 61B	Messenger 24F

80

VERBS

Assert
allege, assert
assert, avouch
contend, assert
declare, assert
enunciate, declare
maintain, affirm
profess, declare
relate, state
state, declare

Avow
affirm, aver
aver, declare
avouch, aver
avow, avouch
find, declare judicially
vow, declare openly

Attribute
ascribe, attribute
assign, attribute
asseverate, affirm
attribute, declare
dogmatize, aver on belief
(B). dogmatise
impute, attribute

VERBS (Continued)
predicate, affirm
refer, assign

ADJECTIVES
Miscellaneous
affirmative, assertory
assertory, declarative
attributive, declarative
declarative, affirmative
declaratory, declarative
dogmatic, positive
enunciative, declaratory
flat, positive
peremptory, positive
positive, assertory
predicative, affirmative

NOUNS
Assertion
affirmative, that which
  declares
allegation, assertion
assertion, a positive
  statement
declaration, assertion
enunciation, declaration
issue, declaration
maintenance, affirmation

NOUNS (Continued)
manifesto, declaration
peremptoriness, positive-
  ness
point, issue
positiveness, forcible
  declaration
protestation, affirmation

Avowal
affirmation, averment
averment, assertion
avowal, open declaration
finding, verdict
recognizance, avowal
verdict, assertion

Attribution
ascription, attribution
asseveration, affirmation
attribution, assertion
dictum, dogmatic assertion
dogma, asserted doctrine
predicability, that which
  may be affirmed
predication, affirmation

PERSONS
affirmant, one who declares
assertor, affirmant

81

TEACHING   see—   **ASSOCIATIVE**

vs. Secrecy 103A
vs. Neglect 126B

Scientific Teachings........83	Notification 79
Religious Doctrines........82A	Explanation 84
Truth 61A	Publications 85B
Truisms 61B	Pithiness—Brevity 58
Disclosure 78	Wittiness 59

81

VERBS

Instruct
instruct, teach
school, instruct
teach, instruct
tutor, teach

Acquaint
acquaint, familiarize
enlighten, instruct
familiarize, acquaint
(B). familiarise
impart, instruct
inform, instruct
show, teach

Inculcate
engraft, root deeply
ground, engraft

VERBS (Continued)
Helenize, imbue with
  Greek Wisdom
imbue, cause to absorb
implant, inculcate
inculcate, instil
indoctrinate, imbue with
  learning
indue, clothe mentally
infuse, instil
instil, instruct
inspire, imbue with ideas
penetrate, reach the mind

Educate
cultivate, propagate
edify, instruct
educate, teach

VERBS (Continued)
elevate, uplift
nourish, nurture
nurture, educate
propagate, disseminate
rear, educate
refine, educate

Discipline
coach, instruct
din, ding
ding, impress repeatedly
discipline, train
drill, ding, instruct
hammer, impress
train, drill
(Continued on page 154)

VERBS (Continued)

Impress

allegorize, instruct by allegory

(B). allegorise

engrave, impress deeply

impress, implant

stamp, impress

Disseminate

civilize, enlighten

(B). civilise

descant, comment freely

discourse, instruct

disseminate, diffuse knowledge

preach, teach publicly

sermonize, preach

(B). sermonise

Miscellaneous

catechize, instruct by catechism

(B). catechise

initiate, instruct in rudiments

rudiment, initiate

ADJECTIVES

Instructive

cultural, educational

disciplinary, instructive

edifying, educational

educational, instructive

enlightening, edifying

esoteric, privately doctrinal

instructional, educative

instructive, educational

Disseminating

clinical, imparting medical instruction

disseminating, exoteric

doctrinal, pertaining to that which teaches

exoteric, publicly doctrinal

suant, disseminating, as water seeks its level, suant culture spreads to man

Pedagogic

pedantic, pedagogic

pedagogic, noting the science of teaching

professorial, pertaining to professors, teaching, etc.

scholastic, pertaining to scholar or schools

tutorial, educational

Didactic

allegoric, instructing by allegory

catechetical, teaching by questions and answers

didactic, adapted to teaching

exegetic, interpretative

ADJECTIVES (Continued)

monitorial, impairing instruction

preceptory, noting instruction

Collegiate

academic, active in education

collegiate, learning or teaching in associated bodies

polytechnic, varied in arts and sciences

Introductory

initiative, introductory

initiatory, initiative

introductory, imparting rudiments

NOUNS

Instruction

instruction, tutelage

lesson, instruction

schooling, instruction

teaching, instruction

tuition, instruction

tutelage, instruction

tutorship, instructorship

Inculcation

inculcation, instruction

infusion, instillation

information, injecta

impression, inculcation

instillation, instruction

initiation, instruction in rudiments

Education

civilization, enlightenment

(B). civilisation

culture, training

edification, education

education, culture

kultur, culture

nurture, education

Discipline

coaching, instruction in athletics

discipline, training

exercise, a lesson or example

training, culture

Dissemination

baccalaureate, sermon to a graduating class

discourse, sermon

dissemination, propaganda

propaganda, the propagation of principles, etc.

propagandism, zealous propaganda

propagation, dissemination of instruction

sermon, discourse

NOUNS (Continued)

Pedagogy

allegory, instruction by analogy

didactics, art of teaching

exegesis, a descanting on text

illumination, edification

pedagogics, science of teaching

pedagogism, as above

pedagogy, pedagogics

Curriculum, Etc.

catechetics, instruction by questions and answers

curriculum, prescribed instructions

doctrine, that which is taught

lore, instruction

organon, rules for guidance

prosody, grammatical treatise

rule, concise direction

PERSONS

abecedarian, teacher of rudiments

academician, promoter of education, science, etc.

catechist, instructor

coach, instructor

disciplinarian, martinet

disseminator, instructor

dominie, schoolmaster

duenna, governess

educationist, educator

educator, teacher

esoterist, philosophic instructor

faculty, instructors collectively

falconer, trainer of falcons

governess, instructress

initiator, instructor in rudiments

instructor, teacher

luminary, instructor

martinet, disciplinarian

mentor, teacher

monitor, instructor of fellow pupils

monitress, as above (fem.)

pedagogue, pedant

pedant, schoolmaster

preceptor, teacher

professor, instructor

professorate, faculty

propagandist, one who propagates a principle or system

regent, teacher in a vicarious capacity

schoolmaster, tutor

(Continued on page 159)

RELIGIOUS DOGMA

see—

vs. Heresy 30
vs. Dishonesty 130A
vs. Hell, etc. 130N

Various Doctrines 82B
God—Spiritual Beings ..82E
Religious Teachers 82F
Religious Executives 82G
Religious Supporters 82D
Religious Institutions ..82C

ASSOCIATIVE

Scientific Teachings 83
Instruction 81
Truth 61A
Truisms 61B
Goodness—Honesty 140A
Heavenly Abodes 53H

82A

VERBS

dogmatize, form a religious belief for acceptation (B). **dogmatise**
indoctrinate, dogmatize

ADJECTIVES

Scriptural

Biblical, pertaining to Bible teachings
canonical, Biblical
deistic, Christian
doctrinal, Biblical
dogmatic, doctrinal
religious, dominical
scriptural, Biblical
theistic, pertaining to the teachings of God
theological, having the nature of God
theosophic, pertaining to nature, God, man and their relationship

Orthodox

Calvinistic, noting the teachings of Calvinism
catholic, pertaining to the whole of Christianity
Christian, dominical
dominical, pertaining to Christian teachings
Episcopal, Episcopalian
Episcopalian, pertaining to Episcopal teachings
Jewish, noting Jewish teachings, etc.
Mohammedan, pertaining to Mohammed
orthodox, pertaining to the teaching of established doctrines
pastoral, dominical
Presbyterian, holding to Presbyterianism

Unorthodox

atheistic, without belief in God

ADJECTIVES (Continued)

gnostic, noting the religious teaching that knowledge, rather than belief, is the true salvation
heretic, heterodox
heretical, heretic
heterodox, holding other than orthodox teachings
idolatrous, believing or teaching idolatry
materialistic, not spiritualistic

In Religious Office

apostolate, pertaining to the office of the Pope
diocesan, pertaining to a bishop
partriarchate, noting the office of a patriarch
prelatic, pertaining to a prelate
rectorial, pertaining to a rector

Ecclesiastical

clerical, pertaining to the clergy
ecclesiastical, noting the church and its organization
hierarchic, ecclesiastical
priestly, hieratical

RELIGIOUS CREEDS

(See 82B Dogma)

Alcoran, Koran
apocalypse, last book of the New Testament
Apostles' Creed, the shortest of the creeds
apocrypha, certain scriptural writings regarded as authentic by some and rejected by others
Bible, Old and New Testaments
breviary, formulary
canon, rules of religious conduct

RELIGIOUS CREEDS

(Continued)

canon-law, canon
canonicity, canon
commandments, decalogue
creed, doctrine
credenda, articles of faith
decalog, ten commandments
decalogue, decalog
decretal, book of edicts
doctrine, tenet of a sect
dogma, supposititious assertions
ecclesiology, doctrine of the church as an organized society
faith, doctrine
formulary, book of prayers, rituals, etc.
golden-rule, rule of life: "Whatsoever ye would that men should do to you, do ye even so to them."
Gospel, Christian Creed
institute, book of laws and principles
Koran, Mohammedan Bible
orthodoxy, commonly accepted doctrine
phylactery, parchment texts worn by Jews
polyglot, Bible in several languages
pragmatism, doctrine of practical results
religion, doctrine or faith
ritual, book of rites
ritualism, doctrine based on excessive forms of worship
scripture, sacred writings
tenet, doctrine maintained as true
testament, volume containing the New Testament
theology, doctrine of divine government
Word, Holy Scripture

82B
DOGMA

Indefinite Dogma
belief, religion
cult, a religion
doctrine, religion
dogma, suppositious assertion
faith, religion
principle, tenet
precept, dogma
religion, any theology
sect, cult, religion
tenet, dogma

Kind of Dogma
agnosticism, doctrine of revelation by contact only
angelology, treatise on the nature of angels
Anglicanism, doctrine of the Anglican Church
animism, doctrine of life arising from spiritual causes
anthropomorphism, doctrine of human heritage from divinity
Arianism, doctrine denying the divinity of Christ
astrotheology, theology founded on the stars
atheism, doctrine or denial of deism
Baalism, idolatry
Brahmanism, Hinduism
Buddhism, religion of Buddha
Calvinism, doctrine of predestination, selection, etc.
Catholicism, religion of the Roman Catholic Church
catholicity, universality
Christendom, Christianity
Christianity, doctrines founded by Christ
Christian Science, doctrine founded by Mary Baker Eddy
deism, doctrine based on a personal God
demonolatry, doctrine based on demons
demonology, treatise or doctrine based on demons
divinity, theology

DOGMA (Continued)
dualism, doctrine of good and evil in all
ecclesiology, doctrine of the Church as an organized society
fatalism, doctrine based on overruling destiny
fetishism, doctrine of fetish worship
Gnosticism, doctrine intermediate between Christianity and paganism
heliolatry, doctrine of sun-worshipers
heresy, heterodoxy
heterodoxy, doctrine which departs from accepted doctrine
heathenism, doctrine of pagans
Hillelism, doctrine of Hillel (Jew 112 B.C.) viz: "What is hated to thee do not unto thy fellow-men"
Hinduism, modified Brahmanism
idolatry, doctrine which attributes divine power to natural agencies
Islam, Mohammedanism
Jesuitism, the principles of Jesuits
Judaism, doctrine of Jews
latitudinarianism, doctrine which is active over a wide religious range
lexotheism, doctrine that the universe is governed by nature
materialism, doctrine that matter is the cause of spiritual phenomena
Methodism, the religion of Methodists
Mohammedanism, doctrine founded by Mohammed
Mormonism, doctrine of Mormons
neologism, any new religious doctrine
neology, a new doctrine at variance with orthodox belief

DOGMA (Continued)
Nihilism, doctrine which denies that anything can be known
oantheism, lexotheism
ophiolatry, doctrine based on snake-worship
orthodoxy, adherence to accepted doctrine
paganism, idolatrous doctrine
pantheism, cantheism
Papacy, Catholicism
polytheism, doctrine of the plurality of gods each taking a part in the conduct of nature
Presbyterianism, doctrine of Presbyterians
Protestantism, doctrine of Protestants
Puritanism, doctrine of Puritans
ritualism, doctrine based on excessive forms of worship
Sabianism, doctrine based on the heavenly hosts as symbols of the deity
Shintoism, Japanese doctrine based on ancestor worship
theocracy, doctrine based on mixed rule
theocrasy, mixed worship of polytheism
theism, doctrine based on the existence of a personal God
theodicy, doctrine based on the vindication of the dealings of God
theology, doctrine of divine government
theosophism, theosophy
theosophy, doctrine of God-wisdom extraordinarily imparted to man
theurgy, doctrine based on the divine effect on human affairs
Tractarianism, doctrine based on the religious principles of certain High Church interests
zoolatry, doctrine based on animal worship

82C

RELIGIOUS INSTITU-TIONS, Etc.

Ecclesiastical Dominion

church, jurisdiction of Christianity

clergy, jurisdiction of a clergyman

ecclesiasticism, jurisdiction of ecclesiastics

hierarchism, church government by a hierarchy

hierarchy, priesthood

Institutional Church, a governing church

institutionalism, spirit that exalts religious institutions

(Continued)

ministry, jurisdiction of ministers

priestcraft, the conduct or institution of priests

priesthood, office of a priest

Vaticanism, Papal Supremacy

Ecclesiastical Office

abbacy, office of an abbot

archbishopric, jurisdiction of an archbishop

bishopric, jurisdiction of a bishop

caliphate, caliph's office

chaplaincy, office of a chaplain

(Continued)

deaconship, office of a deacon

diocese, bishopric

episcopate, bishopric

episcopacy, prelacy

Papacy, office of the Roman Catholic Church

Popedom, jurisdiction of the Pope

prelacy, office of a prelate

rectorate, office of a rector

Vatican, office of the Pope

vicarage, office of a vicar

82D

RELIGIOUS SUPPORT-ERS, Etc.

Unorthodox

agnostic, adherent of agnosticism

atheist, adherent of atheism

fanatic, adherent of an extravagant faith

heretic, atheist

idolator, supporter of idolatry

idolatress, as above (fem.)

jumper, adherent of a dancing sect

latitudinarian, supporter of liberal range in matters religious

materialist, adherent of materialism

shaker, jumper

Orthodox

Arian, adherent of Arianism

Baptist, member of the Baptist Church

Buddhist, member of Buddhism

Calvinist, member of Calvinism

Catholic, member of the Catholic Church

cenobite, member of a cenobite convent

(Continued)

Christian, adherent of Christ

conformist, member of the Church of England

deist, believer in a personal God

dervish, monk

Episcopalian, adherent of the Episcopal Church

fatalist, adherent of fatalism

Fohist, Chinese adherent of Buddha

hadji, Mohammedan holyman

halleluiah-lass, female member of the Salvation Army

Hebrew, Jew

Jesuit, member of the Society of Jesus

Jew, adherent of Judaism

Kafir, non-Mohammedan

Methodist, adherent of Methodism

Mohammedan, adherent of Mohammedanism

monk, member of a monastic order

Mormon, member of Mormonism

Nihilist, supporter of Nihilism

(Continued)

Pagan, adherent of Paganism

Presbyterian, adherent of Presbyterianism

Protestant, supporter of Protestantism

Shintoist, adherent of Shinto

Sabian, worshiper of the heavenly hosts

stone-worshiper, adherent of a stone-worshiping sect

theist, adherent of the faith in the existence of God

Wycliffite, a follower of John Wycliffe, who first translated the entire Bible into English

Indefinite Churchman

churchman, adherent of a church

convert, neophite

gentile, one who is not a Jew

neophite, convert to a faith

parishioner, churchman

pilgrim, one who is drawn to a sacred place

professor, adherent of a religious sect

sectarian, adherent of a sect

82E

GOD—SPIRITUAL BEINGS

Allah, Mohammedan god
Almighty, God Omnipotent
angel, God's messenger
archangel, chief angel
Brahma, Creator (Hindu)
Buddha, incarnation of a divine intelligence
Christ, Messiah
Creator, God
Deity, God
demigod, inferior deity
Divinity, God
Father, God
God, Supreme Being
Godhead, Supreme Deity
Great Spirit, Indian term for God
Hanuman, monkey god of Hindu
Hecate, deity
Jehovah, God of the Jews
Joss, Chinese god
Juggernaut, god of Orissa
Lord, Jehovah
Madonna, The Virgin Mary
Maker, God
Manitou, Indian Great Spirit

(Continued)

Messiah, the Anointed One
Moloch, Fire-god
Omnipotence, God
oracle, prophetic deity
Redeemer, Jesus Christ
Savior, Redeemer
(B). Saviour
Supreme Being, God

NAME OF GOD
In Forty-Eight Languages

Aeolian, Doric, Ilos
Armorian, Teuti
Assyrian, Eleah
Arabic, Allah
Celtic, Gallic, Diu
Chaldaic, Eilah
Chinese, Prussa
Coromandel, Brahma
Cretan, Thios
Danish, Swedish, Gut
Dutch, Godt
English, Old Saxon, God
Finch, Jumala
Flemish, Goed
French, Dieu
German, Swiss, Gott
Greek, Theos
Hebrew, Elohim, Eloha

(Continued

Hindostanee, Rain
Irish, Dia
Italian, Dio
Japanese, Goezur
Lapp, Jubinal
Latin, Deus
Low Breton, Doue
Low Latin, Diex
Madagascar, Zannar
Malay, Alla
Modern Egyptian, Teun
Norwegian, Gud
Olalu Tongue, Deu
Old Egyptian, Teut
Old German, Diet
Pannonian, Istu
Persian, Sire
Peruvian, Puchecammae
Polish, Bog
Pollacca, Bung
Portuguese, Deos
Provencal, Diou
Runic, As
Slav, Buch
Spanish, Dios
Syriac, Turkish, Allah
Tartar, Magatal
Teutonic, Goth
Zemblain, Fetiza

82F

RELIGIOUS DOGMA—DOCTRINES—PERSONAGES   see—

vs. Disbelief—Heresy 30
vs. Dishonesty—Crime 130A
vs. Hell—Infernal Abodes 130N

See—(ASSOCIATIVE 82A)

82F

RELIGIOUS TEACHERS

apostle, Christian teacher
archpriest, chief priest
augur, religious interpreter
Brahman, one of the priestly cast (Hindu)
caliph, title of a successor of Mohammed
canonist, expounder of ecclesiastical law
chaplain, clergyman
clergyman, minister
curate, clergyman
divine, clergyman
Dominican, friar preacher

(Continued)

dominie, clergyman
Druid, ancient priest
ecclesiastic, clergyman
evangelist, itinerant preacher
fakir, Mohammedan mendicant, priest
flamen, Roman priest
hedge priest, one who has not received clerical orders
hiero, initiating priest
homilist, preacher

(Continued)

imam, Mohammedan priest
Jesuit, supporter of the Roman Catholic Society of Jesus
mufti, expounder of Mohammedan law
minister, clergyman
muezzin, Mohammedan priest
mullah, Turkish holyman who calls the faithful to prayer
(Continued on page 159)

82F
RELIGIOUS TEACHERS
(Continued)

neologist, one who teaches views opposed to the orthodox
parson, clergyman
pastor, minister
preacher, clergyman
presbyter, minister
priest, minister

(Continued)

prophet, augur
Rabbi, interpreter of Jewish law
rector, clergyman
reverend, divine
ritualist, one skilled in divine service

(Continued)

theist, expounder of the doctrine based on the existence of God
theologian, one who is versed in theology
theosophist, one who professes to explain the divine laws of nature

82G
See—(ASSOCIATIVE 82A)

82G
RELIGIOUS EXECUTIVES

abbess, lady superior of a convent
abbot, head of an abbey
acolyte, one who ranks below a Catholic subdeacon
archbishop, chief bishop
archdeacon, dignitary next below a bishop
beadle, parish officer
bishop, dignitary below an archbishop
canon, cathedral dignitary
cardinal, dignitary ranking below the Pope
churchwarden, church officer
deacon, minister's assistant

(Continued)

deaconess, as above (fem.)
dean, presiding ecclesiast
dean-and-chapter, governing body
diocesan, bishop
dignitary, ecclesiastic above a priest
elder, minister's assistant
hierarch, head of an ecclesiastical body
patriarch, Greek dignitary of the highest rank
Pontiff, Pope
Pope, supreme head of the Catholics
prelate, ecclesiastical dignitary

(Continued)

primate, highest dignitary of a national church
prior, head of a monastery
sacrist, sacristan
sacristan, sexton, etc.
sexton, one who officiates at certain church functions
suffragan, bishop
vicar, deputy ecclesiast
vicar-apostolic, missionary bishop with power from the Pope
vicar-general, assistant to a bishop

81 (Continued)
PERSONS (Continued)

scribe, teacher
teacher, instructor
trainer, disciplinarian
tutor, teacher

INSTITUTIONS

academy, educational institution
atheneum, educational institution
chair, professorship
college, institution of higher instruction
conservatory, musical academy
falconry, place for training falcons

INSTITUTIONS
(Continued)

gymnasium, school for the development of mind and body
hall, small college
hostel, unendowed college
kindergarten, school for children
library, institution for the dissemination of literature
lyceum, literary seminary
polytechnic, school of arts and sciences
preceptory, college, etc.
professorship, chair of learning
school, place of instruction
seminary, educational institution

INSTITUTIONS
(Continued)

university, colleges combined

MEDIUMS

catechism, book of instructions by questions and answers
horn-book, book containing the numerals, alphabet, and Lord's prayer
manual, compact volume
primer, a manual of instruction
text-book, book of instructions
theogony, treatise on the origin of deities

SCIENTIFIC DOCTRINES, ISMS AND OLOGIES		ASSOCIATIVE	

vs. Stupidity—Ignorance 110B
vs. Disbelief—Doubt 30

see—

Religious Doctrines 82A
Teaching—Education 81
Truth 61A
Truisms 61B
Intelligence—Wisdom 117

83

VERBS
(See TRUTH No. 61A)

ADJECTIVES
(See NOUNS for definitions)

anthropological
archeological
astronomic, —ical
biologic, —ical
botanical
dualistic
entomological
etymological
genealogical
geological
linguistic
ontological
philological
philosophic, —ical
scientific
seismographic
theurgic
etc., etc.

NOUNS

abiology, treatise on non-living things
acology, science of remedies
acoustics, science of sound
actinology, science of light
aerodynamics, science of atmosphere
aerology, description of the air
aerostatics, science of air travel
algebra, science of calculations
amphibiology, treatise on amphibious animals
anatomy, science of vital phenomena
angiology, science of lymphatics
animism, the doctrine of inherent life in matter
anthropography, treatise on race distribution
anthropology, science of the status of man
archeology, science of antiquities
archegony, doctrine of the origin of life

NOUNS (Continued)

aretology, philosophy treating on virtue
arithmetic, science of numbers
arteriology, science of arteries
astrology, science of stars
astronomy, science of cosmic conduct
atmology, science of aqueous vapor
atomology, treatise on atoms
automatism, doctrine which assigns all animal functions to the action of physical laws
bacteriology, science of bacteria
ballistics, science of projectile motion
barology, science of gravity
bibliography, scientific description of books
biodynamics, science of vital forces and energies
biogenesis, science of life development
biology, science which deals with the origin and life of plants and animals
botany, science of plants
carcinology, a department of zoology
casuistry, science which deals with the conscience
catacoustics, science of sound reflection
cerebralism, theory of brain functioning
chemistry, science of change in matter
climatology, science of atmospheric phenomena
cosmism, Spencer's evolutionary philosophy
cosmography, treatise on the world's origin
cosmology, science of the universe
criminology, treatise on crime
demography, science on vital and social condition of the people

NOUNS (Continued)

dualism, treatise on the good and evil in man
embryology, science of embryonic development
entomology, science of insects
ethnography, scientific description of the races
ethnology, science of racial characteristics
ethology, science of ethics
etiology, science of first cause
etymology, origin and source of words
eugenics, science of securing the birth of healthy children
evolution, theory of development from matter to transcending forms, life, etc.
genealogy, treatise on family succession
geology, treatise on the structure and conduct of the earth
glossology, treatise on language
gnomonics, science of dialing
gnosiology, science of cognition
grammar, art of expression
hedonism, doctrine that pleasure is the chief end of life
hexicology, science of habit and environment
hierology, science of hieroglyphics
hymnology, study and use of hymns
ichthyology, branch of fish knowledge
idealism, doctrine that all knowledge of objects is a knowledge of ideas
identism, the doctrine that subject and object are one
ideology, science of ideas
ichnology, science which treats of fossil footprints
(Continued on page 161)

NOUNS (Continued)

Lamarckism, Lamarck's teaching that species may be altered by adaptation to conditions

lexicology, science of words, meaning and application

linguistics, comparative philology

magnetics, science of magnetism

metaphysics, science of mental philosophy

meteorology, science of atmospheric phenomena

metrology, science of weights and measures

monism, doctrine of the identity of mind and matter

mutualism, ethical doctrine of mutual dependence in social development

nominalism, philosophy which holds that only names exist

onomatology, treatise on the derivation of words

ontogeny, history of the evolution of individual organisms

ontology, metaphysics

organography, science of man's status

organology, science of organic functions

ornithology, science of birds

orismology, treatise of terms in natural history

orthology, the right description of things

pantology, science of universal knowledge

penology, science of punishment, etc.

paleontology, subject of art in antiquity

phenomenalism, metaphysical doctrine that visible things are really phenomena

philology, science of languages

phonetics, science of sound in speech

phonics, science of sound

philosophy, treatise on the cause of phenomena

NOUNS (Continued)

physiognomy, science of facial analysis

physics, physical science

physiology, science of vital functions

pneumatology, science of the mind or spiritual existence and its operation

pragmatism, doctrine that practical results are the sole test of truth

psychics, psychology

psychoanalysis, science of mental analysis

psychology, mental science

psychophysics, science of the correlation of mind and matter

realism, doctrine of existence in immediate knowledge

science, conduct in natural law and truth

scientism, theories and practices of scientists

seismology, science of earthquakes

sinology, Chinese systematized knowledge of science, history, etc.

supernaturalism, doctrine of revelation

theurgy, science of divine relations to man

toxicology, science of poisons

vitalism, theory of vital phenomena

PERSONS

anthropologist, one versed in the science of man

antiquary, one versed in antiquities

archeologist, one versed in ancient things

astronomer, one versed in astronomy

biologist, one versed in the science of living forms

botanist, one versed in the science of plants

dualist, a supporter of dualism

embryologist, one versed in embryology

entomologist, one versed in the knowledge of insects

etymologist, one versed in words

PERSONS (Continued)

evolutionist, one versed in the science of evolution

genealogist, one versed in the art of tracing lineage

geologist, one versed in the structure of the earth

grammarian, one skilled in grammar

hedonist, one who maintains the doctrine that pleasure is the chief end of life

ideologist, one devoted to ideology

logician, one skilled in logic

mineralogist, one versed in minerals

naturalist, one versed in natural history

ontologist, metaphysician

Orientalist, one versed in Oriental languages, subjects, etc.

ornithologist, one versed in ornithology

paleontologist, one versed in fossil remains

penologist, one versed in penology

phenomenalist, one who maintains the doctrine of phenomenalism

philologist, one versed in language

philosopher, one versed in the phenomena of mind and matter

phrenologist, one versed in the science of the brain

pundit, one versed in Sanskrit language, laws, Hindu religion, etc.

physicist, one versed in natural science

physiognomist, one versed in characteristics of the countenance

physiologist, one versed in the vital functions of animals and plants

scientist, one versed in natural law

seismologist, one versed in seismology

sensationalist, one who holds that ideas are sensations transformed

toxicologist, one versed in poisons

EXPLANATION—
TRANSLATION
see—
vs. Ambiguity 57
vs. Nonsense 60
vs. Secrecy 103A

ASSOCIATIVE

Pithiness 58
Preciseness 134A
Verbosity 56
Narration 85A
Disclosure 78
Announcement 79
Assertion 80
Enumeration 86

Show—Indicate 95A
Proof—Citation 93
Truth 61A
Truisms 61B
Teaching 81
Accuracy 134A
Prophecy 77
Wisdom—Wit 59

VERBS

Explain
characterize, particularize
(B). characterise
define, describe
describe, delineate
detail, depict
explain, expound
expound, make clear
formulate, state definitely
orient, define bearings
premise, explain previously

Illustrate
allegorize, analogize
(B). allegorise
analogize, allegorize
(B). analogise
compare, analogize
demonstrate, point out
exemplify, illustrate
illustrate, exemplify
represent, describe

Exploit
account, give reason
develop, unfold
exploit, explain at length
recount, give particulars
state, detail
tell, explain
unfold, detail

Portray, Etc.
delineate, depict minutely
depict, describe vividly
paint, depict
portray, paint

Elucidate
blazon, explain technically
elucidate, illustrate
illuminate, elucidate

Signify
actualize, make clear
(B). actualise
convince, make clear
establish, define
evince, make evident
inscribe, state in writing
prove, establish
purport, make known
show, convince
signify, make known

Imply
allude, mention
imply, state indirectly
mention, imply

VERBS (Continued)

Interpret
construe, interpret
interpret, explain
mean, make known, signify
rationalize, be logical
(B). rationalise

Criticize
comment, explain
criticize, comment, define
moralize, explain morally
(B). moralise
review, write critically

Annotate
amplify, broaden
annotate, mark by note
broaden, make clear
descant, comment freely
paraphrase, explain freely

Provide
condition, stipulate
particularize, characterize
(B). particularise
provide, stipulate
specify, particularize
stipulate, provide
term, particularize

Transcribe, Etc.
copy, transcribe
render, translate
transcribe, translate
translate, interpret
turn, translate

ADJECTIVES

Explanatory
adjectival, definitive
characteristic, defining in
  particular
definitive, explanatory
descriptive, explanatory
explanatory, definitive
explicable, explanatory
explicative, explicable
interpretative, explanatory

Illustrative
allegoric, analogical
allusive, figurative
analogical, figurative
apposite, definitive
demonstrative, illustrative
exegetic, interpretative
exemplary, illustrative
figurative, metaphoric

ADJECTIVES (Continued)
illustrative, definitive
metaphoric, metaphorical
metaphorical, expressing
  likeness
parabolic, allegoric
pertinent, apposite

Exploitative
circumstantial, detailed
declarative, explanatory
exploitative, serving to
  exploit
exponential, expository
expository, manifest

Lucid
articulate, said distinctly
clear, definite
distinct, definite
graphic, depicting vividly
intelligible, clear
legible, clear
lucid, intelligible
luminous, lucid
manifest, clear
overt, open, plain
perspicuous, clear
plain, definite
simple, intelligible
understandable, clear
vivid, graphic

Significant
broad, comprehensive
comprehensive, clear
conclusive, decisive
convincing, indisputable
decisive, convincing
denotive, significant
determinable, defining
determinant, definitive
determinate, definitive
expressive, significant
inscriptive, descriptive
pregnant, significant
significant, made known by
  sign, token, etc.

Critical
commentative, explanatory
critical, analytical

Annotative
annotative, marked by
  notes
apropos, having bearing on
  the subject
(Continued on page 163)

ADJECTIVES (Continued)

interlinear, explaining between lines
paraphrastic, explaining additionally
parenthetic, explaining parenthetically
tautological, giving definition in different words

Provisional

conditional, provisional
explicit, definite
express, explicit
imprescriptible, having inherent significance
provisional, specific
stipulated, provisional

Definite

analytic, detailed
categorical, absolute
critical, exact
definite, absolute
detailed, specific
exact, explicit
finite, definite
minute, precise
particular, specific
precise, definite
puristic, precise
specific, definite

Direct

blunt, plain-spoken
downright, to the point
direct, pointed
emphatic, clear, direct
flat, downright, pointed
peremptory, positive
pointed, explicit
positive, declarative
pronounced, strongly defined

Absolute

absolute, definite
apodictic, indisputable
authentic, authoritative
authoritative, absolute
implicit, absolute
indisputable, unequivocal
logical, reasonable
rationalistic, through pure reasoning
unequivocal, clear
unmistakable, unequivocal

Transcriptive, Etc.

identical, literal
literal, as worded
metaphrastic, noting close or literal translation
transcriptive, translatable
verbatim, word for word

NOUNS

Explanation

adjective, descriptive term
characterization, description

NOUNS (Continued)

(B). characterisation
definition, description
demarcation, definition
description, depiction
explanation, elucidation

Illustration

allegory, analogy
allusion, account by comparison
analogy, similarity without identity
application, practical demonstration
apposition, addition of a characterization, as John, the fisherman
comparison, illustration
demonstration, illustration
example, illustration
exegesis, interpretation of a Bible text, etc.
exemplification, illustration
hermeneutics, science of interpreting scripture, etc.
illustration, exemplification
imagery, representation by images
instance, example
key, that by which anything is explained
metaphor, figure of speech intended to depict more vividly
metonymy, the use of one word for another
precedent, example
representation, description
rule, precedent
simile, illustration
trope, figurative word or representation

Exploitation

account, treatise
disquisition, dissertation
dissertation, explanatory treatise
development, detailed characterization
exploitation, lengthy explanation
exposition, explanation
homiletics, treatise on sermons
ritual, book of rites
terminology, explanation of technical words
treatise, written explanation
word-building, description

Portrayal

delineation, minute description
depiction, characterization
painting, portrayal
picture, vivid description

NOUNS (Continued)

portraiture, vivid delineation
portrayal, description
word-painting, vivid description

Elucidation

elucidation, a rendering intelligible
illumination, elucidation
lucidity, clearness of representation

Significance

blazonment, technical explanation
blazonry, art of describing coats of arms
import, significance
postulate, self-evident problem
purport, significance
significance, import
signification, significance

Interpretation

construction, interpretation
exponent, that which interprets
implication, inference
impressionism, description
inference, interpretation
interpretation, explanation
meaning, sense
rationale, reasoned exposition
reason, explanation
sense, meaning
solution, explanation
version, account

Criticism

comment, explanation
commentary, comment
criticism, critical explanation
critique, careful analysis of a production
eclaircissement, full explanation

Annotation

annotation, notation
excursus, added explanation
gloss, elucidation
interlinear, translation
marginalia, marginal notes
paraphrase, additional explanation
parenthesis, parenthetic explanation
scholium, explanatory note
tautology, different representation of the same idea

Provision

condition, provision
prerequisite, condition
(Continued on page 164)

NOUNS (Continued)

provision, stipulation
stipulation, condition
term, particular limitation

Particulars

circumstantiality, fullness
of detail
definiteness, definition
detail, minute account
emphasis, particular sig-
nificance
explicitness, definiteness
finiteness, definiteness
minuteness, exactness
minutiæ, particulars
particularity, circumstantiality
prolixity, minute detail
prospectus, sketch, plan or
outline
specification, detailed
statement
statement, explanation

Inscription

cartouch, inscription
chronogram, inscription
entry, inscription
epigraph, inscription
epitaph, inscription
etiquette, instruction in
decorum
hicjacet, "here lies," inscription on a tomb

NOUNS (Continued)

inscription, significant
writing

Model, Formula

exemplar, example, pattern
formula, recipe
model, example
pattern, example
plank, representation of a
political policy
prescription, written specification
recipe, formula

Transcription, Etc.

copy, transcript
crib, literal translation
pony, explanation or key in
translation
rendering, translation
rendition, translation
transcript, translation
transcription, transcript
translation, a rendering
from one language to
another

PERSONS

annotator, one who makes
annotations
augur, interpreter
cicerone, guide who ex-
plains the features of
a place

PERSONS (Continued)

commentator, one who
makes comments
critic, one who analyzes or
defines
criticaster, petty critic
delineator, one who de-
scribes or delineates
demonstrator, illustrator
dragoman, interpreter
elucidator, interpreter
examinee, one who ex-
plains under examination
exponent, one who inter-
prets principles, etc.
expositor, expounder
expounder, elucidator
gnomon, interpreter
illustrator, expounder
interpreter, translator
logician, an elucidator
orthographer, one who de-
fines by letters
purist, one who is precise
in style of representation
scholiast, commentator
speller, one who defines by
letters
stylist, a master of literary
representation
translator, interpreter

85A

RECITATION—

PUBLICATION see—

vs. Secrecy 103A
vs. Reservation ..132C

ASSOCIATIVE

Explanation	84	Teaching	81
Disclosure	78	Truth	61A
Speech	55A	Truisms	61B
Conversation	90	Enumeration	86
Announcement	79	Verbosity	56
Poems, etc.	85C	History, etc.	85D

85A

VERBS

Declaim

accost, address
address, speak or write
declaim, recite
harangue, deliver an ora-
tion or harangue
lecture, deliver a dis-
course
preach, sermonize
rant, declaim noisily
recite, narrate
rhapsodize, write or utter
rhapsodies
(B). rhapsodise
sermonize, preach
(B). sermonise

Narrate

account, relate
narrate, recite

VERBS (Continued)

recount, repeat
relate, narrate
romance, tell stories
speak, recite
tell, narrate

Write

collaborate, write jointly
compose, write
construct, compose
indite, compose
improvise, compose
pen, write
scribble, write
write, issue

Edit

edit, publish
issue, publish
promulgate, publish

VERBS (Continued)

publish, print and circu-
late
report, recount
republish, publish anew
sound, publish

ADJECTIVES

Declamatory

declamatory, recitative
oratorical, recitative
recitative, oratorical
rhapsodic, containing
rhapsody

Narrative

anecdotal, recitative
anecdotic, anecdotal
epic, narrative
narrative, recitative
(Continued on page 165)

ADJECTIVES (Continued)
telling, narrative

Literate

epistolary, pertaining to letters
literary, pertaining to literature
literate, pertaining to writing
stenographic, in shorthand

Miscellaneous

autobiographical, writing one's life
dramatic, represented theatrically
epigrammatic, pertaining to epigrams
episodic, pertaining to an episode
historic, recounting the past
histrionic, dramatic

Bardic

bardic, poetic
iambic, bardic
idyllic, pertaining to pastoral poetry
lyric, poetic

ADJECTIVES (Continued)
Parnassian, pertaining to poetry
poetic, expressing poetry

Fictional

fabulous, fictional
fictional, romantic
legendary, fabulous
mythic, legendary
mythological, mythic
romantic, storied
storied, told in story
traditional, recounted through generations

Editorial

editorial, by an editor
journalistic, editorial

NOUNS
Declamation

address, speech
allocution, formal address
declamation, recitation
dedication, address
dissertation, formal discourse
discourse, sermon, etc.
harangue, extemporary address

NOUNS (Continued)
homily, sermon
lecture, formal address
oration, speech
prelecture, lecture
recital, narrative
recitation, memorized speech
sermon, discourse
speech, oration
topic, discourse

Narration

account, narrative
anecdote, account
narration, narrative
narrative, account
relation, narration
statement, account
telling, narrative

Fiction

fable, fictitious narrative
fiction, story
mythology, tradition
romance, fanciful story
story, romance
tale, narrative
tradition, transmission of ancient practices

85B
See—(ASSOCIATIVE 85A)

85B
BOOKS—COMPOSITION

Book, Etc.

book, printed volume
brochure, pamphlet
opus, brochure
opuscule, unimportant work
pamphlet, brochure
volume, book

Periodical, Etc.

gazette, newspaper
journal, news publication
magazine, literary periodical
newspaper, news edition
periodical, publication
rag, low-class newspaper
serial, tale issued in parts

Composition, Etc.

act, thesis
article, composition
composition, a writing
construction, composition
contribution, a writing contributed with others
disquisition, elaborate essay
document, a writing
editorial, leading article
episode, incidental story

(Continued)
essay, short treatise
lucubration, studied composition
page, episode
piece, literary composition
thesis, essay
tract, short treatise
treatise, elaborate composition

Narrative, Etc.

drama, story of life
dramaturgy, dramatic composition
fiction, literary production
journalism, newspaper and magazine literature and its influence
literature, written or printed compositions
narrative, story
press, general literature
publicity, news
romance, fiction
scribble, careless writing
story, fictitious narrative

Miscellaneous

autobiography, written account of one's self

(Continued)
cento, patchwork composition
epic, heroic narrative
erotic, amatory composition
libretto, words of an opera or oratorio
novel, tale or romance
novelette, small novel
pornography, treatise on prostitutes
psalter, book of psalms
remain, work published after an author's death
rhapsody, composition
shocker, sensational novel
symposium, various views written on the same subject

Publication

edition, publication
extra, irregular edition
issue, publication
publication, a book or other press matter

Subject

burden, oft repeated subject
(Continued on page 166)

BOOKS—COMPOSITION
(Continued)
subject, theme
text, original words of an author
theme, essay
topic, subject

Communication
billet, note or letter
billet-doux, love letter
communication, letter, etc.
dispatch, official document
epistle, letter
letter, missive
missive, letter, message

(Continued)
message, missive
note, communication
valentine, love missive

Original Writing
autography, an original manuscript
holograph, M. S. in the author's handwriting
manuscript, a writing
original, first work
palimpsest, M. S. written on partially erased parchment

(Continued)
Transcript
copy, transcript
rifacimento, rewriting or recast of book or play
transcript, copy
transcription, transcript

News
intelligence, tidings
news, tidings
tidings, news

RECITATION—PUBLICATION see—
vs. Secrecy 103A
vs. Reservation ..132C

85C, 85D
ASSOCIATIVE
Explanation 84
Disclosure 78
Speech 55A
Conversation 90
Announcement 79
Narration 85A
Teaching 81
Truth 61A
Truisms 61B
Enumeration 86
Verbosity 56
Books, etc. 85B

85C
POEMS, ETC.
Alexandrine, a verse of six iambic feet
anthology, collection of poems, epigrams, etc.
bucolic, pastoral poem
canto, part of a poem
couplet, two lines which rhyme
distich, couplet
doggerel, verse devoid of sense of rhyme
eclog, pastoral poem
epic, heroic narrative poem
epigram, verse ending in a witty term
epode, last part of an ode
erotic, love poem
georgic, poem on agriculture
iambic, verse
idyl, pastoral poem

(Continued)
limerick, stanza of five lines
lyric, song or poem
lyric-poetry, poetry adapted for singing
macaronic, a burlesque or incongruous poem
madrigal, pastoral poem
monody, plaintive poem or song
ode, lyric poem
parody, burlesque poem
pastoral, poem of rural life
pentameter, a verse of five meters
philter, love poem
poem, poetic conception
poetry, metrical composition
posy, poetical inscription
prose, unmetrical composition
rhyme, verse

(Continued)
rondeau, poem of thirteen lines
rondel, poem of fourteen lines
sextain, six-lined stanza
sonnet, poem of fourteen lines
spondee, poetic foot of two long syllables
stanza, group of rhymed lines
tetrameter, verse of four measures
theogony, poem on the origin of deities
tribrach, poetic foot of three syllables
verse, line of poetry
versicle, a little verse
versification, composition or verse

85D
HISTORY—LEGEND
annals, history or chronicle
biography, recorded life of a person
fable, tradition, fiction

(Continued)
history, chronological narrative of facts
legend, incredulous story
memoir, account from personal knowledge

(Continued)
myth, legend
tradition, oral handing down of events

85E
PERSONS
abbe, literary ecclesiastic
amanuensis, stenographer
author, composer, etc.
bard, poet
bas-bleu, blue-stocking
bibliographer, authority on books
biographer, chronicler of lives
blue-stocking, literary woman
chronicler, one who chronicles
collaborator, co-worker in a literary work
composer, author
compositor, typesetter
editor, journalist
essayist, writer of essays
fictionist, writer of fiction
hack, petty author
historian, expert in history
historiographer, writer of history
idylist, pastoral poet
improviser, one who composes extemporaneously
improvvisatrice, as above (female)
journalist, editor, etc.

PERSONS (Continued)
laureate, poet-laureate
lecturer, one who lectures
librettist, writer of a libretto
literator, literary man
literati, those engaged in literature
lyrist, poet
minstrel, poet, etc.
mythologist, one skilled in mythology
narrator, relater
novelist, writer of novels
orator, skilled speaker
parodist, writer of parodies
poet, composer of poetry
poetaster, inferior poet
poet-laureate, poet to a sovereign, etc.
preacher, one who discourses on religion
prelector, lecturer
publicist, writer on public interests
publisher, producer of books, papers, etc.
ranter, noisy speaker
reader, university lecturer
relater, narrator

PERSONS (Continued)
rhapsodist, one who recites or writes rhapsodies
scald, Scandinavian poet
scribe, writer
scribbler, literary hack
secretary, amanuensis
sensationalist, a sensational writer or speaker
sonneteer, minor poet
spellbinder, intense orator
stenographer, amanuensis
stump-speaker, speaker on public questions
teller, narrator
troubadour, lyric poet
versifier, poet
writer, composer, etc.

BEINGS
Clio, muse of history
Apollo, god of poetry, etc.
Calliope, muse of eloquence and epic poetry
Muse, a goddess of poetry, art, etc.

SOURCE
Pierian Springs, fabled springs—source of poetic inspiration

86

| LIST—CLASSIFICATION | see— | ASSOCIATIVE |

86
VERBS
List, Record
book, record
docket, record
enter, list
impanel, list
list, catalogue
mark, record
note, record
record, register
register, enter
slate, register
take, record
write, record

Enlist, Etc.
conscript, enrol
enlist, enrol
enrol, enlist
matriculate, register in college
recruit, enlist

Enumerate
account, enumerate

VERBS (Continued)
enumerate, list
numerate, enumerate
score, keep account
tally, score
tell, enumerate, count

Itemize, Etc.
catalogue, list
detail, enumerate
inventory, list
invoice, list valuables
itemize, list details
table, index

Classify
arrange, classify
assort, arrange
classify, catalogue
compile, classify
co-ordinate, arrange
distribute, classify
group, classify
resolve, assort
subsume, classify

VERBS (Continued)
Chronologize
calendar, list
chronicle, record
chronologize, chronicle
(B). chronologise
genealogize, detail lineage
(B). genealogise
schedule, list

Index
alphabetize, arrange letters
(B). alphabetise
index, list names, etc.
tabulate, list

Summarize
recapitulate, summarize
recite, recapitulate
summarize, list concisely
(B). summarise

Blacklist
blacklist, except
except, blackball
proscribe, list the excepted
(Continued on page 168)

ADJECTIVES
Miscellaneous

analectic, noting recorded extractions
anthological, noting a digest of literary extracts
archival, noting records of state
categorical, systematized
chronological, in historical sequence
classificatory, categorical
conscript, enrolled in service
coördinate, classed together
demographic, treating on races
demological, treating on vital or social conditions
encyclopædic, in summarized knowledge
enlisted, recorded
enrolled, enlisted
genealogical, noting lineage
necrological, noting death registration
obituary, necrological
paragraphic, in paragraphs
registered, recorded
statistical, noting collective facts
tabular, listed by tables

NOUNS
Enlistment, Etc.

conscription, enrolment
enlistment, enrolment
enrolment, enlistment
matriculation, registration in college
muster, register for troops
registration, record
roster, list of names

Enumeration

account, statement
enumeration, account
numeration, enumeration
score, tally
tabulation, tabular forms
tally, account

Statement, Etc.

account, statement
bill, account of values
detail, enumeration
inventory, list of goods
invoice, bill of goods
manifest, invoice of a cargo
reckoning, statement
statement, account
specification, enumeration
table, list of particulars

NOUNS (Continued)
Classification

arrangement, classification
assortment, arrangement
classification, enumeration
compilation, arrangement
coördination, arrangement
distribution, classification

Chronology

annals, chronicle
chronicle, historical record
chronology, order of events
docket, digest
genealogy, pedigree
history, recorded events
itinerary, record of travel
pedigree, genealogy
program, schedule
schedule, tabular record
synchronism, tabular grouping of historical events

Chronological Record

almanac, yearbook
atlas, a tabulated work
calendar, record of yearly periods
daybook, journal
diary, register of daily interests
diurnal, daybook
ephemeris, astronomical almanac
gazette, journal of official announcements
journal, daybook
ledger, account book
log, log-book
log-book, ship's journal

Entry, Note, Etc.

article, entry
entry, record
inscription, entry
marker, score
memorandum, note
minute, memorandum
note, memorandum
notation, short note
record, entry
score, record
tally, score
index, list of entries

Summation

balance-sheet, proof-sheet
compend, abridgment
compendium, summary
recapitulation, summary
summary, compendium
summation, aggregate sum

Abridgment, Etc.

abbreviature, compendium
abridgment, epitome
abstract, summary
brief, epitome
conspectus, synopsis
digest, summary

NOUNS (Continued)

epitome, abridgment
sketch, outline
syllabus, epitome
synopsis, summary

Collected Facts

ana, collection of savings
analects, collected extracts
anthology, collection of epigrams, poems, etc.
catalogue, arrangement of represented articles
library, collection of books
memorabilia, account of worthy things
psalter, book of psalms
repertoire, list of dramas and songs
statistics, collected facts

Register, Etc.

list, catalogue
record, register
register, record
roll, register
scrip, written list

Name Lists

blacklist, list of undesirables
calendar, list of persons to be tried
canon, catalogue of saints
necrology, death register
obituary, record of death
panel, schedule of prospective jurors
roundrobin, a circle of signatures with the first signature unknown
slate, list of candidates

Prospectus

budget, financial outline
outline, synopsis
prospectus, outline

Census, Etc.

census, enumeration of a population
demography, statistical data of a people
directory, book of names and addresses
ethos, statement of characteristics of a people, nation, etc.

Inscription, Etc.

epigraph, epitaph
epitaph, memorial inscription
hicjacet, epigraph
inscription, a writing
memoir, account of worth

Bill of Fare

carte, menu
menu, bill of fare
(Continued on page 169)

NOUNS (Continued)
Laws, Code, Etc.

code, classified laws
codex, volume of statutes
pandect, digest of Roman or civil laws

Word Book, Etc.

alphabet, arrangement of letters
category, highest arrangement of knowledge
concordance, dictionary of words or passages
cyclopedia, encyclopedia
dictionary, arrangement of defined words
encyclopedia, cyclopedia
formulary, book of forms, rituals, etc.
gazetteer, dictionary of geographical names
glossary, dictionary of obsolete, obscure, or technical words
gradus, dictionary of Greek and Latin prosody

NOUNS (Continued)

lexicography, the compilation of dictionaries
lexicon, dictionary
nomenclature, words of an art, science, profession, etc.
pantology, an arrangement of all knowledge
sinology, systematized record of the Chinese language, knowledge, etc.
thesaurus, lexicon or dictionary
vocabulary, alphabetical list of words
word-book, vocabulary

PERSONS

accountant, bookkeeper
actuary, registrar
annalist, compiler of annals
anthologist, compiler of epigrams, poems, etc.
bibliographer, describer of books

PERSONS (Continued)

biographer, a chronicler of lives
bookkeeper, accountant
chronologist, one who orders accounts in sequence
compiler, one who places material in fresh form
composer, writer
diarist, one who records daily events
encyclopedist, compiler of an encyclopedia
genealogist, recorder of pedigrees
journalist, one who keeps a journal, editor
recorder, registrar
registrar, recorder
remembrancer, recorder
statist, classifier of facts
statistician, compiler of statistics
writer, composer

87

ADVICE—SUGGESTION

vs. Discouragement 13
vs. Scare—Menace 33

see—

ASSOCIATIVE

87
VERBS

advise, counsel
counsel, give advice
dissuade, advise against
preach, give advice

Suggest

allude, state indirectly
breathe, insinuate
buzz, whisper
hint, suggest
imply, allude
insinuate, hint
intimate, hint
mention, hint
prompt, suggest
remind, suggest
suggest, hint
whisper, suggest

Propose

commend, recommend
offer, commend
opine, propose
propose, offer for consideration

VERBS (Continued)

propound, propose
recommend, commend
refer, recommend

ADJECTIVES
Miscellaneous

advisable, noting advice
advisory, giving advice
allusive, hinting
analogical, bearing reference
associative, mnemonic
commendatory, serving to commend
dissuasive, implying advice against
ideographic, noting suggestion by a symbolic figure
mnemonic, assisting the memory
propositional, containing proposal
recommendatory, containing recommendation

ADJECTIVES (Continued)

referential, offered for consideration
snaky, insinuating
suggestive, insinuating

NOUNS
Advice

advice, counsel
counsel, advice
dissuasion, advice against

Suggestion

allusion, hint
clue, hint
cue, hint
hint, suggestion
imputation, insinuation
inkling, intimation
innuendo, oblique hint
insinuation, direct hint
intimation, suggestion
suggestion, hint
whisper, suggestion

Proposal

commendation, recom-
(Continued on page 170)

ANSWER—REPLY see—

88

VERBS

Miscellaneous

answer, respond
correspond, answer
rebut, answer
rejoin, answer
reply, respond
respond, answer
retort, reply
return, retort
rationalize, reply
(B). rationalise

ADJECTIVES

Miscellaneous

accountable, answerable
answerable, liable to answer
antiphonal, in responsive singing
antiphonary, antiphonal
correspondent, answering in accord with another
oracular, containing an inspired answer
respondent, responsive
responsible, implying response
responsive, answering
responsory, responsive
snappish, retorting sharply

NOUNS

Answer

answer, response
oracle, inspired response
reply, answer
response, reply

Rejoinder

facer, retort
quip, sarcastic retort
rejoinder, reply
repartee, witty reply
retort, sharp answer
roarback, a lie in answer
sockdolager, decisive reply

Rebuttal, Etc.

countercharge, answering charge
rebuttal, answer
replication, plaintiff's reply
rescript, answer having the force of law
rescription, an answering letter
surrebutter, reply to a rebutter
surrejoinder, reply to a rejoinder

Responsibility

accountability, containing account or reply

NOUNS (Continued)

accountancy, answer
responsibility, ability to respond satisfactorily

Password

password, prearranged answer
watchword, password

Gradual

antiphon, musical reply
antiphonary, book of responses
antiphony, responsive chanting
counterblast, answer with a challenging bugle
gradual, musical response

PERSONS

co-respondent, joint respondent in a divorce suit
oracle, the deity who answered inquiries
rebutter, one who rebuts
respondent, one who answers

---

87 (Continued)

NOUNS (Continued)

mendation
datum, situation offered as a basis for inference
motion, proposition
offer, overture
opinion, belief offered for consideration
overture, proposal
proposal, overture
proposition, proposal
recommendation, commendation
reference, recommendation

NOUNS (Continued)

referendum, reference to the people for final decision
theorem, proposition offered for proof

Mnemonics

auto-suggestion, self-suggestion
ideograph, suggestion by symbol
mnemonics, art of assisting the memory

NOUNS (Continued)

remembrancer, reminder
reminder, suggestion

PERSONS

adviser, counselor
attorney, counselor
barrister, attorney
councilor, member of a common council
counselor, adviser
council, advisory assembly
councilman, councilor

89

VERBS

Promise

accept, promise or agree to pay
agree, promise
negotiate, come to agreement
promise, pledge
treat, agree

Pledge

assure, give confidence by promise
guarantee, assure
indorse, guarantee
pledge, promise
subscribe, promise
swear, vow
vouch, guarantee
vow, pledge
warrant, guarantee

Plight

betroth, pledge one's troth
espouse, betroth
plight, promise

ADJECTIVES

Miscellaneous

assuring, guaranteeing
auspicious, promising
conditional, promising provisionally
contributive, liable to an impost, condition, etc.
devout, sincerely pledged
espousal, noting promise of marriage
leal, pledged to a cause

ADJECTIVES (Continued)

negotiatory, in agreement
promising, auspicious
promissory, giving promise
prospective, promising
sacramental, solemnly pledged
sponsorial, having promise
votive, consecrated by vow

NOUNS

Promise

agreement, promise
assumpsit, contract
negotiation, agreement
promise, agreement
word, promise

Pledge

assurance, agreement
guarantee, assurance
guaranty, legal guarantee
oath, vow
obligation, pledge
parole, promise, especially by a prisoner
pledge, promise
sacrament, solemn pledge
security, assurance
surety, guarantee
truce, promise of truthful performance
voucher, guarantee
vow, solemn promise
warranty, guarantee

Plight

affiance, betrothal
betrothal, mutual promise of marriage

NOUNS (Continued)

espousal, promise of a wife
plight, pledge
troth, promise of fidelity

Terms

condition, proviso
provision, stipulation
proviso, provision
purview, stipulation
stipulation, provision
terms, agreement

Indorsement, Etc.

acceptance, subscription or promise
indorsement, guarantee
sponsion, solemn promise for another
sponsorship, sponsion

PERSONS

contributor, subscriber
godfather, sponsor at baptism
godmother, as above (fem.)
guarantor, one who guarantees
indorser, guarantor
promiser, one who promises
promisor, promiser
sponsor, guarantor
trusty, one who is trusted on promise of good conduct
subscriber, promiser by subscription

CONVERSATION—
    CORRESPONDENCE   see—   ASSOCIATIVE

	Speech 55A
	Disputation 66
vs. Quiescence—Rest 11B	Answer 88
vs. Reserve 132C	Verbosity 56

90

VERBS

Converse
chat, converse easily
confab, talk familiarly
converse, discuss
gossip, talk idly
hobnob, talk familiarly
soliloquize, talk with
  one's self
(B). soliloquise
talk, converse

Commune
commune, converse
communicate, converse
correspond, commune by
  letter

Confer, Etc.
confer, consult
consult, confer
interview, question on
  opinions, etc.
negotiate, hold intercourse
palaver, confer
parley, hold a conference
temporize, parley
(B). temporise
treat, discourse

Discuss
agitate, discuss openly
canvass, discuss
debate, discuss
discuss, converse
exhaust, discuss fully

ADJECTIVES
Miscellaneous
colloquial, noting ordinary
  conversation
communal, implying con-
  versation
conversant, proficient in
  conversation
conversational, pertaining
  to conversation

ADJECTIVES (Continued)
conversable, inclined to
  social conversation
interlocutory, intermedi-
  ately conversational
negotiatory, noting trade
  conversation
sociable, conversing
  sociably
social, sociable
synodical, pertaining to
  religious consultation

NOUNS
Conversation
chat, easy conversation
colloquialism, common
  conversation
colloquy, conversation
confab, conversation
confabulation, confab
conversation, familiar talk
gossip, idle conversation
monologue, soliloquy
sociability, friendly
  conversation
soiree, social confab
soliloquy, discourse with
  one's self
talk, conversation
talking, conversation

Communion
communication, intercourse
communion, communica-
  tion
correspondence, communi-
  cation by letters
dialogue, talk of two
discourse, talk, sermon,
  etc.
intercourse, communion
interlocution, dialogue
tete a tete, confidential
  conversation

NOUNS (Continued)
Conference, Etc.
conference, discussion
congress, conference
consultation, conference
interview, conversation on
  opinions, etc.
negotiation, conversation
palaver, public conference
parlance, conversation
parley, conference between
  opponents
pourparler, diplomatic
  consultation
synod, consultation at a
  religious meeting
treaty, parley

Discussion
agitation, open discussion
burden, conversation on
  which one dwells
canvass, discussion
collocution, mutual discussion
conversazione, conversa-
  tion
debate, agitation
discussion, conversation
dissertation, formal dis-
  cussion
noise, public or frequent
  conversation
powwow, political discus-
  sion
ventilation, free discus-
  sion

PERSONS
agitator, one who inces-
  santly discusses
conversationalist, one who
  is skilled in conversation
correspondent, one who
  corresponds

INTERJECTION—EXCLAMATION
        vs. Quiescence 11B
        vs. Reserve 132C

ASSOCIATIVE

91

VERBS

Interject, Etc.

ejaculate, interject a sharp utterance
exclaim, interject a vociferation
gush, intervene extravagant sentiment
interject, introduce a word or exclamation

Interpose

apostrophize, interject a digressive address
(B). apostrophise
insinuate, introduce
intercede, interpose
interrupt, break in upon
interpose, intervene
intervene, interfere
introduce, intervene
mediate, interpose

Insert

insert, intervene
intercalate, intercalate, introduce as Feb. 29th in leap year, etc.
interline, insert between lines
interpolate, insert new or spurious matter

ADJECTIVES

Miscellaneous

apostrophic, noting an interposition in an address
ejaculatory, exclamatory
exclamatory, uttering exclamation
expletive, noting interjection
interlinear, noting insertion
interlocutory, interposing
parenthetical, noting insertion by parenthesis

NOUNS

Interjection, Etc.

ejaculation, exclamation
exclamation, interjection
expletive, an inserted word
gush, outburst
interjection, exclamation
slant, an interposed or added remark

NOUNS (Continued)

Interposition

apostrophe, digressive address
insinuation, indirect introduction
interlocution, interposed conversation
interposition, a breaking in between
interruption, interposition
intervention, interposition

Insertion

embolism, intercalation
insert, insertion
insertion, matter inserted
inset, insertion
intercalation, insertion, as Feb. 29th in leap year, etc.
parenthesis, the insertion of further exemplification

EXCLAMATIONS

Notice

ahem, exclamatory notice
behold, exclamatory notice
lo, behold

Joy

aha, exclamatory satisfaction
all-hail, exclamation of good wishes
amen, exclamation of approval
bravo, approving exclamation
bully, bravo
gramercy, exclamatory thanks
ha, exclamation of joy
hurrah, exclamation of joy
vive, exclamation of good wishes

Surprise

ah, interjectional surprise
fact, indeed
indeed, exclamation of surprise
quotha, indeed

Derision

fiddledeedee, nonsense
fiddlesticks, fudge
fudge, exclamation charging nonsense

EXCLAMATIONS
(Continued)

hoity-toity, exclamation of rebuke
nonsense, fudge

Impatience

faugh, exclamation of disgust
fie, a shaming exclamation
fugh, faugh
hem, exclamation of disgust
lush, exclamation of contempt
pish, lush
pshaw, pish
pugh, lush

Quiet

cease, exclamation ordering a stop
hark, hist
hist, hush
ho, stop
hush, exclamatory "be still"
oye, silence
stay, stop
stop, ho
tut, hush

Dismissal

abas, down with
begone, leave
go, begone
leave, go
off, begone

Regret

alack, exclamatory regret
alas, alack
peccavi, confessional exclamation
prithee, solicitous exclamation

Farewell

adieu, good-by
farewell, adieu
good-by, farewell
heigh-ho, exclamation of languor

PERSONS

interpolator, one who inserts news or spurious matter

NAME—TITLE—TERM
(Symbolic Expressions)   see— {Define 84
vs. Ambiguity 57   {Appointment 139A
vs. Generality ....132D   {Decree 94
        ASSOCIATIVE

92

VERBS

Name
assign, appoint
call, name
denominate, name
entitle, style
name, give a name
nickname, add a name
nominate, name
predicate, term
style, name
surname, give a family name
term, name
title, entitle

Represent
allegorize, represent
(B). allegorise
represent, characterize in likeness
symbolize, represent
(B). symbolise

Establish
appoint, ordain
confirm, establish
establish, ordain
induct, introduce
ratify, establish definitely

Introduce
acquaint, name
introduce, acquaint
mention, name casually

Dedicate, Etc.
baptize, christen
christen, name, dedicate
consecrate, dedicate
dedicate, christen, name
devote, dedicate
dub, confer name or rank
hallow, consecrate
inscribe, dedicate
ordain, appoint
pronounce, utter, state

Classify
characterize, style
(B). characterise
classify, characterize
rank, classify

Specify
designate, particularize
formulate, term concisely
individualize, characterize
(B). individualise
phrase, style peculiarly
specify, name particularly
stipulate, specify

Estimate
appraise, name a price

VERBS (Continued)
assay, appraise
estimate, appraise
reckon, estimate

Numerate
enumerate, name singly
number, denominate
numerate, enumerate

Sign
autograph, sign
countersign, sign additionally
indorse, sign as evidence
initial, write one's initials
sign, write one's name

ADJECTIVES

Nominative
appellative, serving to name
classificatory, giving class or rank
denominate, specifying
denominative, nominal
nominal, having name
nominative, giving name
specific, special
special, named particularly
substantive, denoting name
titular, nominal
yclept, called by name

Representative
allegoric, figurative
analogous, represented in likeness
characteristic, a marking or naming
equivalent, expressed in likeness
figurative, representative
homologous, identical but varying in term
homophonous, alike in name but different in meaning
imitative, representing in likeness
onomatopœic, sound-resembling
parabolic, allegoric
paronymous, having the same pronunciation of something different in significance
pronominal, representing by pronoun
representative, denotive of similitude or type

ADJECTIVES (Continued)
synonymous, named in likeness

Named After
eponymous, named after some person
matronymic, named after one's mother
patronymic, named after an ancestor

Dedicatory
baptismal, dedicative
dedicatory, christening, naming, etc.
inscriptive, dedicative

Symbolic
cuneiform, represented by wedge-shaped characters
hieroglyphic, representing likeness by picture writing
phonetic, naming elementary sounds
phonographic, phonetic
runic, noting representation by the earliest alphabet
typographical, represented by type

Anonymous
anonymous, nameless
inconnu, unnamed
nameless, anonymous

Pseudonymous
incognito, having an assumed name
pseudonymous, incognito
sol-disant, self-styled

Signatory
autograph, self-signed
autographic, as above
signatory, autographic

ADVERBS

Namely
namely, giving name
viz, namely

NOUNS

Nomination
announcement, introduction
appointment, stipulation
assignment, appointment
characterization, denotation
(B). characterisation
(Continued on page 175)

NOUNS (Continued)

classification, specification

denomination, a naming

designation, nomination

denotation, designation

enumeration, a naming singly

introduction, a naming

nomenclature, names belonging to an art, science, profession

nominalism, a philosophy which holds that only names exist

nomination, a naming

numeration, a naming

specification, enumeration

stipulation, special mention

terminology, designation of technical terms

Representation

allegory, figurative representation

analogue, object which bears analogy to something else

representation, name, etc.

simile, a likening or representation

Name

agnomen, an additional name, as Milton the poet

appellation, name

appellative, common name

cognomen, surname

eponym, surname

name, title or term

namesake, the same name as another

patronymic, name derived from an ancestor

prænomen, name prefixed to the family name, as John

surname, family name

Dedication, Etc.

baptism, christening

consecration, dedication

dedication, the naming of something devoted to some person or thing

ordination, consecration

inscription, dedication

Class, Rank

class, order

denomination, class

family, class

kind, species

office, particular post

order, rank, class

position, office

rank, station

sect, denomination, etc.

station, class

NOUNS (Continued)

species, name for a common group

Heading, Title

caption, title

heading, title

headline, title of an article

style, title

title, name, heading

Estimation

appraisal, the naming of a price

assay, the naming of a valuation

assizement, statement of weight, etc.

character, reputation

estimation, repute

opinion, estimation

reputation, repute

repute, estimate of character

Number

denominator, numerative name

nominal, in algebra a single term

number, denomination

numeral, number

numerator, name or number

Grammatical Names

adjective, appellation

antonym, a name of opposite meaning

binomial, two terms, quantities, or names

consonant, a letter naming a sound other than a vowel

diphthong, two letters representing two vowel sounds in one syllable

gerund, verbal noun

homomorph, a similar character or mark

homonym, word alike in sound but different in meaning

homophone, letter representing the same sound as another

nominative, nominative case

noun, name

onomatopœia, name given to represent sound

paronym, divergent name

phonogram, character representing a particular sound

phonograph, character noting a spoken sound

NOUNS (Continued)

pronoun, word used for a name

rebus, phrase or picture, as a bolt and ton—bolton

substantive, noun

synecdoche, rhetorical figure in which the whole is put for a part or a part for the whole

synonym, name or word nearly like another

term, name

verbal, noun derived from a verb

vocable, word, term

vowel, open sound

word, name

Anonymity

anonym, a nameless something

anonymity, namelessness

misnomer, incorrect term

nondescript, that which is difficult to name

Pseudonym

alias, assumed name

bookname, names in textbooks of plants, animals, etc.

cryptonym, secret name

epithet, appellation

inconnu, unfamiliar representation

nickname, epithet

pseudonym, fictitious name

sobriquet, nickname

Signature

allograph, signature made for another

autograph, signature

indorsement, documentary signature

monogram, symbolized name

signature, autograph

Topic, Etc.

subject, name

talk, subject

theme, subject

topic, subject

Password

parole, password of a camp

password, watchword

shibboleth, password

watchword, password

Escutcheon, Etc.

escutcheon, representative inscription

hicjacet, a representative inscription on a tomb

scutcheon, nameplate

(Continued on page 179)

PROOF—QUOTATION— WITNESS see—	ASSOCIATIVE	
vs. Falsehood 62	Disclosure ....78 Show ....95A Conspicuity ....95E Assertion 80	Explanation ....84 Answer ....88 Truth ....61A Truisms 61B

93

VERBS

Prove

assure, certify
convince, cause to believe
evidence, prove
manifest, place beyond doubt
probate, register proof of a will
prove, establish as genuine
show, prove
warrant, authenticate

Confirm

aver, verify
confirm, ratify
establish, confirm
ratify, confirm
validate, ratify
verify, prove true

Corroborate

adduce, bring forward as proof
circumstantiate, verify in every particular
corroborate, confirm
strengthen, ratify
substantiate, establish as true
support, vouch
uphold, maintain
vouch, attest
witness, give evidence

Cite

cite, quote in substantiation
demonstrate, prove beyond doubt
excerpt, quote
extract, quote
instance, give example
quote, adduce in proof
refer, instance a circumstance

Refute

convict, prove guilty
explode, prove false
refute, prove false

Affirm

affirm, confirm
allege, affirm
assert, declare
asseverate, affirm
certify, testify
declare, affirm
maintain, affirm

Attest, Vow

attest, certify as true
avouch, affirm

VERBS (Continued)

avow, declare openly
depose, testify on oath
swear, testify on oath
testify, attest
vow, swear

Authenticate

authenticate, establish as genuine
autograph, attest by one's signature
certificate, certify in writing
indorse, evidence by signature
seal, ratify by seal
sign, attest by signature
subscribe, attest by signature

ADJECTIVES

Proven

absolute, decisive
cogent, convincing
conclusive, apodictic
convincing, conclusive
decisive, conclusive
evincive, in absolute proof
final, decisive
incontestable, conclusive
incontrovertible, authentic
indisputable, testamentary
indubitable, irrefutable
irrefragable, irrefutable
irrefutable, conclusive
predominant, absolute
proven, apodictic
positive, testamentary
undeniable, convincing
unmistakable, valid
unquestionable, indisputable
valid, absolute

Confirmatory

apodictic, proving with evidence
confirmatory, ratifying

Corroboratory

adducent, giving evidence
adductive, adducent
circumstantial, corroborative
corroborative, verifying
corroboratory, verifying
presumptive, proven circumstantially
substantial, real, authentic
substantive, substantial

ADJECTIVES (Continued)

vindicatory, serving to vindicate

Citatory

citatory, adducent
demonstrative, conclusive
documentary, evidenced by record
quotative, citing
referential, quotative
testamentary, documentary or according to a will
testate, testamentary

Evident

bare, evident
clear, obvious
conspicuous, clear
evident, manifest
manifest, plain
naked, bare
obvious, evident
open, plain
plain, clear
undisguised, bare

Affirmative

affirmative, substantiating
declaratory, affirmative

Authentic

approved, sanctioned
authentic, implying truth or fact
autograph, attesting by signature
autographic, as above
indented, evidenced by notches on documents
notarial, attested by a notary
sealed, authenticated
signatory, attested by signature

NOUNS

Proof

assurance, testimony intended to inspire confidence
authority, authenticity
evidence, proof
postulate, a problem having the significance of self-evidence
proof, evidence
witness, evidence

Confirmation

confirmation, ratification
establishment, ratification

(Continued on page 177)

NOUNS (Continued)
ratification, confirmation
verification, proof

Corroboration

adduction, the bringing forward of proof or substantiation
apologetics, the vindication of the principles of Christian belief
compurgation, the verification of one person's testimony or veracity by the testimony of another
corroboration, verification
defense, plea in justification
substantiation, proof
testimony, substantiation
vindication, support by proof

Citation

analect, extract in evidence
citation, quotation cited in proof
demonstration, proof
excerpt, quotation
extract, quotation
instance, something offered in substantiation
quotation, the adduction (of a passage) from an author, as authority or proof
reference, evidence

Evidence

clew, circumstance
circumstance, evidence
finger-print, a finger mark
mark, evidence
record, written evidence
sign, evidence
trace, mark
vestige, evidence of something preceding

Refutation

alibi, proof of presence elsewhere
confutation, refutation
disproof, refutation
refutation, proof of invalidity

Affirmation

affirmation, averment
allegation, statement of proof

NOUNS (Continued)
assertion, defense
averment, verification
maintenance, affirmation

Attestation

attestation, certification or testimony
avowal, averment
certification, testimony
deposition, deponent's statement
oath, vow
testification, attestation
vow, sworn statement

Authentication

authentication, evidence of authorship
authenticity, as above
autograph, attestation by one's signature
check, confirmation
indentation, authentication by notches on documents
indenture, seal
indorsement, evidence by signature
paraph, flourish to a signature to attest genuineness and prevent forgery
seal, ratification
signature, signed name
subscription, attestation by signature

DOCUMENTS, ETC.

affidavit, testimony in writing
archive, preserved proof
bond, security evidenced in writing
certificate, written voucher
check, ticket
codicil, appendix to a writing
covenant, agreement in writing
credential, written authority
debenture, written acknowledgment of debt
deed, written attestation of property transference
deposition, affidavit
diploma, certificate conferring honor

DOCUMENTS, ETC.
(Continued)

document, written attestation
frank, free passage certificate
guarantee, warrant
indenture, covenant
instrument, attestation in writing
manifest, authentic invoice of a cargo
marque, certificate authorizing reprisals on enemy ships
mortgage, security in writing
pass, certificate of authorized passage
passport, certificate authorizing travel in foreign countries
probate, copy of a will that has been officially proven
receipt, certificate of acknowledgment
rider, codicil
scrip, credential
signature, one's name written in testimony
testament, sworn statement in writing
testimonial, testament
ticket, certificate of privilege
voucher, certificate
warranty, certificate
warrant, voucher

PERSONS

adductor, one who produces proof
affirmant, attester
attester, one who testifies
deponent, one who testifies
indorser, surety
notary, attester
signatory, one who attests by signature, especially for a state
surety, one who is jointly an indorser with another
testator, one who attests a will
witness, attester

COMMAND—DECREE—LAW   see—   **ASSOCIATIVE**

vs. Timidity 32

vs. Appeal 40B

Rule—Domination	.....................133A
Appointment	.................................139A
Demand	..................................41B
Announce	79

VERBS

Decide

abjudicate, adjudge
adjudge, decide
arbitrate, judge
decide, judge
judge, decree
rule, decree
umpire, decree

Adjure, Etc.

adjure, command on oath
bid, command
charge, command
cite, summon
command, order
dictate, direct
direct, command
enjoin, decree
instruct, command
order, command
summon, cite

Legalize

decree, direct
enact, decree
legalize, decree
(B). legalise
legislate, legalize
prescribe, direct
ratify, legalize
result, decree

Sentence

condemn, pronounce sentence
convict, pronounce judgment
damn, condemn
doom, condemn
pronounce, state authoritatively
sentence, condemn

ADJECTIVES

Decisive

arbitrary, decisive
decisive, final
decretory, decisive
dictatorial, absolute in decree
imperious, dictatorial
judicial, decretory
judiciary, judicial
magisterial, authoritative

Authoritative

authoritative, positive
constitutional, legal
lawful, legal
legal, constitutional
legitimate, lawful

ADJECTIVES (Continued)

Commanding

commanding, imperative
mandatory, imperious
preceptory, containing precept
prescript, directed
prescriptible, decretory
statutory, preceptory

Peremptory

absolute, imperious
final, decisive
flat, final
imperative, peremptory
peremptory, final
positive, peremptory

NOUNS

Decision

adjudgment, adjudication
adjudication, judicial decision
arbitration, arbitrament
arbitrament, decision
award, judgment
decision, decree
dictum, dogmatic decree
judgment, judicial decision
judicature, adjudication
result, decree
ruling, judgment
verdict, judgment

Authority

authority, rule
equity, law developed by the courts
government, rule
jurisdiction, legal authority
jurisprudence, legal science
polity, form of legal government
regime, rule, governmental system
regimen, rule

Authorization

authorization, award
(B). authorisation
legislation, the making of laws
legitimation, act of making lawful
ratification, corroborative decree
sanction, ratification

Law, Decree

act, decree
appointment, decree
bull, Papal decree

NOUNS (Continued)

canon, law, rule, decree
commandment, precept
criterion, law, rule, etc.
law, edict
decretal, Papal decree
edict, decree having the force of law
enactment, decree
law, edict
ordinance, rule, law
plebiscite, decree by vote
plebiscitum, plebiscite
precept, rule
prescription, prescribed rule
proclamation, edict
regulation, rule for government
rescript, the answering edict of an emperor or Pope
rule, precept or law
statute, legislative law

Kind of Law

blue-sky law, law to prevent bogus sale
civil law, Roman law
common law, unwritten law based on usage
International Law, laws governing nations
municipal law, common law of a city or country
statute law, statute

Code, Etc.

code, classified law
constitution, law
decalogue, ten commandments
institute, established law
pandect, digest of Roman or civil law

Adjuration

adjuration, solemn charge
behest, command
bidding, command
charge, command
command, order
dictation, direction
direction, charge
hest, behest
imperative, command
instruction, direction
mandate, command
order, command

Summons

citation, summons
(Continued on page 179)

NOUNS (Continued)

summons, command
subpœna, appearance command
warrant, command to arrest
writ, court order

Injunction, Etc.

caveat, injunction
injunction, authoritative order
mandamus, superior court command to an inferior court
mittimus, a writing of commitment to prison

Sentence, Etc.

condemnation, damnation
conviction, verdict
damnation, judgment of doom

NOUNS (Continued)

doom, condemnation
sentence, judgment

Court, Etc.

assize, judicial session
court, tribunal
judiciary, assize
tribunal, court

PERSONS

adjudicator, one who pronounces judgment in court
assizer, juror
arbiter, judge
arbitrator, arbiter
critic, judge
deemster, judge or umpire
director, one who directs
directorate, directors collectively

PERSONS (Continued)

judge, one who passes judgment
juror, one with the power to judge cases
jury, jurors collectively
justice, judge or magistrate
judiciary, judges collectively
legislator, lawmaker
legislature, a legislative body
magistrate, officer vested with certain judicial power
referee, umpire
senator, legislator
surrogate, substitute for a probate judge
umpire, arbiter

PRONOUNS

Singular	Plural
First Person	
I	we
me	us
myself	ourselves
Second Person	
you	you
thou	ye
thee	yourselves
yourself	
Third Person	
he	they
him	them
himself	themselves
	those
	who
she	whom
her	whoever
herself	whomever

PRONOUNS

Singular	Plural
Third Person	
who	whosoever
whom	whomsoever
whoever	
whomsoever	
whosoever	
whomever	
Indefinite	
it	they
that	them
this	those
which	which
what	what
whatever	that
whatsoever	

PRONOUNS (POSSESSIVE)

Singular	Plural
First Person	
my	our
mine	ours
Second Person	
your	your
yours	yours
thy	
thine	
Third Person	
his	their
her	theirs
hers	whose
its	whosesoever
whose	
whosesoever	
Indefinite	
its	whose
whose	their
	theirs

SHOW—SHOWING MEDIUMS

SHOW—DISCLOSURE

see—

vs. Secrecy 103A
vs. Reservation ..132C

ASSOCIATIVE

95A

VERBS

Show

demonstrate, evidence
display, exhibit
exhibit, display
illustrate, demonstrate
present, exhibit
represent, exemplify
show, display
visualize, show

Designate

denote, signify
designate, indicate
direct, indicate
guide, direct
indicate, show
point, indicate

Signify

betoken, signify
evince, demonstrate
express, show
import, signify
manifest, evince
purport, signify
signify, show

Adumbrate

adumbrate, shadow forth
bode, portend
forebode, presage
foreshadow, adumbrate
portend, foreshadow
presage, forebode
prognosticate, foreshadow

Uncover

bare, expose
denude, make bare
uncover, disclose
unearth, uncover
unmask, expose
unveil, reveal

Reveal

disclose, reveal
discover, make known
expose, uncover
nail, expose
reveal, disclose
unfold, disclose

ADJECTIVES

Showing

demonstrative, expository
expository, noting ex-
position

ADJECTIVES (Continued)

graphic, vivid
presentative, denotive
significant, indicatory
significatory, significant
telltale, significant

Designative

barometric, indicating
change of weather
denotative, indicative
designative, indicative
indicant, indicating
indicative, indicant
indicatory, serving to
indicate
periscopic, showing by
periscope

Adumbrative

adumbrant, shadowing
forth
adumbrative, adumbrant
boding, foreboding
phenomenal, indicating
by phenomena
precursory, premonitory
premonitory, giving
notice beforehand

Auspicious

auspicious, favorable
ostensible, holding to
view
propitious, auspicious
seeming, ostensible
specious, plausible

Ominous

admonitory, monitory
ill-omened, indicating ill
inauspicious, ominous
monitory, ominous
ominous, foreboding evil
portentous, ominous

Symptomatic

diagnostic, having
symptomatic indication
prognostic, foreshowing
symptomatic, diagnostic

NOUNS

Showing

circumstantiality, a showing of details
demonstration, exhibition
display, exhibition
example, demonstration
exhibition, a showing
illustration, example

NOUNS (Continued)

manifestation, that which
shows clearly
precedence, exemplary
significance
precedent, significant
example
presentation, exhibit
representation, example
show, indication
showing, indication
view, manifestation
vista, view

Designation

attribution, designation
designation, indication
indicant, that which
indicates
indication, a pointing
pointer, indicator

Significance

expression, manifestation
import, significance
purport, significance
significance, import
signification, act of
signifying

Adumbration

adumbration, a fore-
shadowing
augury, omen
boding, portent
foreboding, omen
omen, a sign of good or
evil
phenomenon, unusual
significance
precursor, omen
premonition, precursor
presage, portent
portent, omen
shadow, adumbration

Auspice

auspice, boding of promise
avatar, incarnate mani-
festation

Ominousness

death's head, an emblem-
atic warning of death
monition, warning notice
ominousness, a foreboding
of evil
warning, foreboding
(Continued on page 183)

INDICATING DEVICES

vs. Hiding—Secrecy 103A

DFI — Device for indicating

This classification contains only a partial list of indicating devices but it shows clearly how all indicating devices must necessarily come under this heading

95B

DEVICE—INSTRUMENT

Index (Indefinite)

annunciator, indicator
detector, DFI a thing
dial, indicator
gage, measure
guide, indicator
index, pointer
indicator, index
measure, DFI quantity
meter, DFI amount
pointer, indicator

Index (Graph, Etc.)

chart, graph
drawing, design
design, pattern
graph, outline
map, graph
model, plan
outline, drawing
pattern, model
plan, design
sketch, outline

Index (Rule, Etc.)

formula, rule
rule, guiding method

Index (Miscellaneous)

abacus, DFI quantities
absorptiometer, DFI gas absorbed by a unit vol. of fluid
acidimeter, DFI the quality of certain acids
acoumeter, DFI sensibility to sound
actinograph, DFI variations of light
actinometer, DFI intensity of heat
aeolian, instrument whose strings respond to the influences of the air
aethrioscope, DFI change of temperature
altimeter, DFI altitudes

DEVICE—INSTRUMENT
(Continued)

altiscope, mirrored instrument for showing beyond intervening objects
ambulator, DFI steps and distance walked
ampere-meter, DFI power of an electrode
anemograph, DFI force or direction of the wind
anemometer, DFI pressure of the wind
anemoscope, DFI direction of the wind
aneroid, barometer
annunciator, indicator
arithmometer, DFI a mechanical computation
astrolabe, DFI altitude of the sun
astrometer, DFI magnitude and luster of the stars
astrophotometer, DFI the intensity of the light of stars
ataxiagraph, DFI irregularities in ataxia
atmidometer, DFI evaporation from ice and snow
audiometer, DFI power of hearing
auriscope, DFI condition of the ear
balance, DFI weight
balloon d'essair, balloon for indicating the direction of air currents
barograph, DFI atmospheric pressure
barometer, DFI weight and pressure
baroscope, DFI variations of atmospheric pressure
bathometer, DFI depths
binocular, DFI more clearly
brontograph, DFI sound waves
calipers, compasses
camera, kodak
chromoscope, DFI optical effects of colors
chromometer, color-indicating scale
chronograph, DFI minute intervals of time

DEVICE—INSTRUMENT
(Continued)

chronometer, DFI accurate measurements of time
chronoscope, DFI velocity of projectiles
compass, DFI direction
coherer, DFI electromagnetic waves
cyclometer, DFI revolutions of wheels
cyclonoscope, DFI atmospheric currents
colorimeter, DFI degree of heat
declinagraph, DFI astronomical declinations
declinator, DFI declination and inclination of a plane
declinometer, DFI declination of the magnetic needle
dendrometer, DFI height of trees, etc.
detector, DFI a thing
diagometer, DFI relative conductivity
dial, indicator
divining-rod, DFI location of minerals
durometer, DFI hardness of steel
dynactinometer, DFI intensity of light and its quickness of action in photography
dynamograph, DFI grip or muscular power
dynamometer, DFI force in a moving load
electro-dynamometer, DFI strength of an electric current
electrometer, DFI quantity of electrical force
electroscope, electrometer
embryoscope, DFI development of an embryo
ergmeter, electrodynamometer
extensometer, DFI expansion of the body
galvanometer, DFI extent and direction of a current

(Continued on page 183)

DEVICE—INSTRUMENT
(Continued)

galvanoscope, DFI delicate currents of electricity
gasometer, DFI gases
glossograph, DFI vibrations of the tongue in speaking
gnomon, a style which indicates time by its shadow
goniometer, DFI angles
graphometer, DFI degrees in angles
gravimeter, DFI specific gravity
gyrostat, DFI dynamics of rotating bodies
haemadromometer, DFI velocity of the flow of blood
heliometer, DFI small angles in the heavens
helioscope, DFI phases of the sun by refraction
hoppet, dish for indicating measurements of ore
hydrometer, DFI specific gravity, etc., of fluids
hygroscope, DFI atmospheric moisture
hypsometer, DFI altitudes
index, alphabetic indicator
index-finger, indicating finger
indicator, instrument for indicating certain effects
inductometer, DFI rate of induction
iriscope, DFI prismatic color
kaleidoscope, DFI variations of symmetrical forms
kodak, camera
koniscope, DFI quantity of dust contained in the air
lactometer, DFI specific gravity of milk .

DEVICE—INSTRUMENT
(Continued)

level, DFI the horizontal line of a plane
log, DFI speed of a ship
macrometer, DFI degree or size of inaccessible objects
magnetograph, DFI terrestrial magnetism
magnetometer, DFI intensity of magnetic force
manometer, DFI density of air or gases
meter, DFI the amount measured
metrograph, DFI mileage and stops of a locomotive
metronome, DFI measure of beaten time
micrometer, DFI diameters noted by a telescope
odometer, DFI the revolutions of a carriage wheel
oleometer, DFI relative density of air
ophthalmoscope, DFI interior of the eye
opsiometer, DFI limitation of distinct vision
optigraph, a landscape camera
optometer, DFI range of vision
pantometer, DFI angles, elevations, distances, etc.
pedometer, ambulator
periscope, a device for revealing objects through angles
perambulator, pedometer
pulsimeter, device for indicating pulse
pyrometer, DFI expansion from heat
pyroscope, DFI intensity of heat
quantometer, DFI induced currents

DEVICE—INSTRUMENT
(Continued)

radio-beacon, DFI variation from directness
regulator, DFI regularity
rheometer, DFI intensity of a current
rheoscope, DFI presence of a current
rule, DFI measurement
saccharometer, DFI quantity of sugar in liquids
scale, DFI measurements of weights
searchlight, device for signaling a position
seismograph, DFI action of an earthquake
semaphore, device for signaling by means of arms, lanterns, flags, etc.
sirene, DFI the relation of vibration to pitch
spectacle, instrument for aiding vision
speedometer, DFI speed
spirometer, DFI capacity of lungs
spherograph, DFI certain positions
spherometer, DFI curvature, thickness, etc.
style, gnomon
tachometer, DFI velocity
tapeline, DFI distance
taximeter, DFI mileage or fare
telltale, DFI quantity, amount, etc.
thermometer, DFI temperature
thermopile, DFI variations in temperature
thermoscope, DFI quantity, amount, etc.
voltameter, DFI a voltaic current
zymometer, DFI degree of fermentation
zymoscope, zymometer

NOUNS (Continued)
Symptom

diagnostic, a symptom
prognostic, omen
prognostication, presage
symptom, the indication from which a cause may be determined

NOUNS (Continued)
Revelation

disclosure, revelation
discovery, disclosure
exposure, disclosure
revelation, disclosure
television, electrical showing

PERSONS

cantor, precentor
exhibitor, showman
fugleman, one who shows soldiers how to drill
precentor, singing leader
significator, one who shows

95C

VERBS

Miscellaneous

appear, become apparent
arise, rise
crop, appear suddenly
emerge, arise
face, appear
look, face
loom, show
peep, begin to appear
rise, emerge
seem, appear
show, appear
spring, appear suddenly
start, rise suddenly

ADJECTIVES

Miscellaneous

apparent, capable of being
  perceived
apprehensible, discernible
conceivable, apparent
discernible, conceivable
extern, visible
perspective, noting a vista
  or view
perceptible, discernible
present, apparent
scenic, having the aspect of
  scenery
seeming, apparent
unforeseen, now apparent
visible, perceptible

NOUNS

Appearance

apparition, looming object
appearance, visibleness
emergence, appearance
emersion, appearance

NOUNS (Continued)

peep, a beginning to
  appear
presentiment, apparition
rise, emergence

Visibility

light, visibility
perceptibility, visibility
visibility, perceptibility

Aspect, Phase

air, aspect
aspect, appearance
circumstance, evidence
circumstantiality, appearance in detail
complexion, aspect
expression, phase of
  countenance
front, appearance
look, aspect
phase, appearance as
  viewed from different
  angles
phenomenon, unusual
  appearance
semblance, appearance
spectacle, unusual
  appearance
surface, scope

Bearing, Poise

address, bearing
attitude, bearing
bearing, manner of
  appearance
carriage, bearing
demeanor, manner of
  appearance or deport-
  ment
guise, external appearance
manner, demeanor

NOUNS (Continued)

mien, air, look
poise, bearing
pose, demeanor
posture, attitude
presence, bearing

Figure

contour, profile
feature, lineament
figure, appearance
lineament, feature
profile, figure

Face

countenance, face
face, countenance
physiognomy, face
visage, countenance

Scene, Outlook

landscape, aspect of a
  country
outlook, appearance
perspectiveness, vista, view
prospect, scene
scene, spectacle
scenery, aspect
scope, outlook
sight, view
view, outlook
vision, outlook
vista, view

Impression

effect, impression
ichnolite, fossil footprint
impression, visible sign
path, trail
scintilla, trace
sign, trace
trace, a sign
track, path
trail, track
vestige, trace

95E (Continued)

NOUNS (Continued)

bareness, nakedness
nakedness, nudity
nudeness, nakedness
nudity, nakedness

Distinction

aspect, significance
attribute, characteristic
blazonment, a distinguishing mark
brand, mark
character, distinctive
  quality

NOUNS (Continued)

characteristic, distinctive
  trait
clew, evidence
delineation, demarkation
demarkation, distinctive
  marking
distinction, significance
earmark, distinctive mark
mark, demarkation
marking, mark
phase, aspect

AMPLIFYING INSTRU-
MENTS

binocular, telescope, etc.
lens, magnifying glass
lorgnette, opera-glass
microscope, lens
opera-glass, binocular
periscope, submarine outlook
polyscope, a lens
spy-glass, small telescope
telescope, binocular, etc.

OSTENTATION—
POMP see—

vs. Hiding	103A	Conspicuity	95E
vs. Darkness	97	Show—Indication	95A
vs. Reserve	132C	Artistry	100A
		Entertainment	99A
		Signals—Gestures	98A

Blazing—Meteoric	101D
Crimson—Scarlet	102A
Disclosure	78
Explanation	84
Brag—Bombast	76

95D

VERBS

Flaunt
air, display
display, be ostentatious
exhibit, display
flaunt, show ostentatiously
show, exhibit

Blazon
array, dress showily
blaze, make or be con-
spicuous
blazon, display
dangle, display
deck, array showily
emblazon, blazon
flare, be offensively showy
flash, flare
flourish, display
gush, display extravagantly
splurge, display

Pretend
affect, assume an
appearance
pretend, make a show
simulate, affect

Parade
mince, step primly and
showily
parade, march with pomp
prance, strut
promenade, walk for show,
etc.
sport, wear ostentatiously
stalk, walk pompously
strut, walk ostentatiously
swagger, strut with
affected superiority
swank (slang), swagger

Solemnize, Etc.
celebrate, distinguish by
solemn ceremony
chair, carry triumphantly
in a chair
dedicate, solemnize
dramatize, display with
stage effect
solemnize, impress with
ceremony

ADJECTIVES

Ostentatious
ostentatious, showy
ostensive, exhibiting
showy, ostentatious

Spectacular
bravure, striking

ADJECTIVES (Continued)
dangling, showy
extravagant, striking
fine, showy
flamboyant, gorgeous
flourishing, ostentatious
glaring, gaudy
gorgeous, showy
loud, ostentatious
spectacular, flamboyant
spreadeagle, ostentatiously
and defiantly bombastic
striking, spectacular

Stately
august, majestic
dignified, august
grand, imposing
imposing, impressive
impressive, striking
lofty, stately
magnificent, pompous
majestic, stately
stately, dignified

Flashy
flashy, showy
foppish, ostentatious in
dress
garish, gaudy
gaudy, in showy finery
gimcrack, showy
rococo, noting vulgar and
showy ornamentation
tawdry, gaudily showy
tinsel, excessively showy

Pretentious
affected, arrogant
brash, pretentious
ostensible, held up for
show
pedantic, displaying
learning
pretending, ostensible
pretentious, ostensible
specious, ostensible

Pompous
big, pompous
grandiloquent, pompous
grandiose, showy
highfalutin, affectedly
pompous
pompous, stately
proud, ostentatious
snobbish, vulgar
stiff, stilted
stilted, pompous

ADJECTIVES (Continued)
stuck-up, affecting the
bearing of one's superior
swank (slang), swagger-
ing
tumid, pompous
turgid, pompous
vain, proud

Airy
airy, showy
jaunty, airy
mincing, affecting
elegance
perky, jaunty
priggish, having osten-
tatious airs
smart, showy

Presumptuous
arrogant, presumptuous
audacious, cheeky
cheeky, impudent
forward, presumptuous
impudent, audacious
presumptuous, forward
unabashed, cheeky

Indelicate
bawdy, obscene
flashy, bawdy
immodest, indecent
indecent, indelicate
indelicate, immodest
meretricious, offensively
showy
obscene, indecently showy
ribald, obscene
unchaste, immodest

CEREMONIOUS
Miscellaneous
bacchic, noting Bacchus-
like ceremonies
ceremonial, pertaining to
impressive ceremonies
ceremonious, noting ostentatious ceremony
commemorative, noting
ceremonious commem-
oration
demonstrative, ceremonious
dramatic, displaying with
grand effect
formal, ceremonious
functional, formal
imposing, impressive
impressive, ceremonious
(Continued on page 186)

CEREMONIOUS
(Continued)
liturgic, ritualistic
Pharisaic, religiously ceremonious
ritual, ritualistic
ritualistic, noting forms or excessive forms of ceremony
solemn, ceremonious
striking, impressive
triumphal, triumphant
triumphant, victoriously demonstrative

NOUNS
Ostentation
demonstration, display
display, ostentatious show
exhibition, display
flaunt, ostentatious flare
ostentation, purposeful showiness
show, display
showiness, ostentation

Gaudiness
blazonment, blazonry
blazonry, display
bravura, display
dash, display
emblazonry, display
finery, outward show
gaud, ostentation
gaudiness, showiness
gush, extravagant display
splash, display
splurge, great display

Flashiness
flashiness, gaudiness
foppery, ostentatious attire
tinsel, anything showy
tawdriness, ostentation without elegance

Pretension
affectation, presumption
ostensibility, showy pretense
pretense, affectation
pretension, pretense
speciousness, pretense

Strutting
flourish, showy parade
priggism, assumed airs
promenade, a walk for ostentatious show
stalk, pompous walk
strut, ostentatious walk
swagger, affected walk

Pomp
dandyism, foppery
grandiloquence, pomp

95D (Continued)
NOUNS (Continued)
knight-errantry, ostentatious chivalry
pomp, proud display
pomposity, showy splendor
pedantry, display of learning
pride, self-esteemed air
turgessence, pompousness
vanity, empty display
vaunt, vain display

Presumption
arrogance, presumption
forwardness, presumption
presumption, arrogance

Indelicacy
bawdiness, showy obscenity
bawdry, bawdiness
indecency, indelicacy
indelicacy, obscene display
obsceneness, obscenity
obscenity, showy indecency
ribaldry, obscenity

CEREMONY, ETC.
Ceremony
celebration, ceremony
ceremonial, ceremony
ceremonialism, prescribed ceremonial display
ceremony, religious display, royal pomp
commemoration, celebration
dedication, a ceremonious setting aside
liturgics, ritualistic ceremonies
obsequies, funeral ceremony
rite, solemn ceremony
ritual, rite
ritualism, prescribed ceremony
solemnity, religious ceremony
solemnization, solemnity

Festivity
Bacchanalia, Roman ceremonious festival in honor of Bacchus
carnival, ceremonious festival
festival, joyful commemoration
festivity, ceremonious commemoration
fete, celebration
gala, festival, pomp

CEREMONY, ETC.
(Continued)
jubilee, triumphant celebration by the Jews
ovation, public demonstration

Impressiveness
array, ceremonious display
demonstration, pomp, display
drama, dramatic display
extravaganza, display
fanfare, ostentatious parade
grandeur, splendid display
impressiveness, ceremony
magnificence, pomp
notabilia, spectacle
pageant, showy spectacle
pageantry, demonstrative display
parade, ceremonious procession
pomp, parade
pomposity, show of splendor
spectacle, pageant
splendor, pomp
(B). splendour
tableau, statuesque display by persons

INTERJECTIONS
behold, see
lo, behold
see, behold

PERSONS
attitudinarian, one who affects or studies attitudes
cynosure, a conspicuous object or person of general interest
dandy, a neat parader
dude, ostentatious dresser
fop, pretentious dandy
jackanapes, conceited upstart
knight-errant, one who is ostentatiously chivalrous
pedant, one who displays his learning
pretender, one who is presumptuous
prig, one who puts on airs
puppy, fop
snob, one who is vulgarly ostentatious
wiseacre, a pretender to learning

CONSPICUOUS—

see—
vs. Obscure 97
vs. Ambiguous 57

Puzzling Show, etc. 96A
Ostentation 95D
Show—Indication 95A
Indicating Devices 95B
Brilliancy 101A

ASSOCIATIVE

Crimson, Scarlet 102A
Disclosure 78
Explicitness 84
Truth 61A

95E
VERBS

Miscellaneous

bedazzle, make dazzlingly
  conspicuous
blaze, mark conspicuously
blazon, blaze
brand, mark with a brand
characterize, make dis-
  tinctive
delineate, mark clearly
distinguish, make distinct
earmark, mark, brand, etc.
evidence, make plain
evince, make evident
feature, make prominent
label, mark with a label
loom, appear conspicuously
mark, render distinct
pose, simulate a posture
rubricate, mark with red
shine, render brilliant
signalize, make con-
  spicuous
signify, show clearly
stamp, mark with a stamp
ticket, label
underscore, make
  conspicuous

ADJECTIVES

Conspicuous

conspicuous, strikingly
  obvious
marked, prominent
outstanding, conspicuous
prominent, conspicuous
pronounced, notable
salient, conspicuous
striking, outstanding
vivid, intensely apparent

Brilliant

blazing, radiant
bright, resplendent
brilliant, blazing
dazzling, resplendent
flashing, bright
glaring, dazzling
radiant, flashing
resplendent, radiant
shining, brilliant
splendid, conspicuous

Impressive

bold, striking to the eye
commanding, imposing
grand, magnificent
great, grand
imposing, conspicuously
  impressive

ADJECTIVES (Continued)

impressive, striking
magnificent, impressive

Extraordinary

amazing, astonishing
astonishing, remarkable
astounding, sensational
extraordinary, remarkable
miraculous, phenomenal
phenomenal, remarkably
  significant
portentous, wondrous
remarkable, outstanding
sensational, amazing
spectacular, phenomenal
wonderful, remarkable
wondrous, wonderful

Obvious

aboveboard, manifest
apparent, manifest
evident, obvious
manifest, apparent
obvious, apparent
ostensible, apparent
overt, manifest
palpable, obvious
perspicuous, evident
pregnant, significant
significant, evident
significatory, evident

Plain

definite, definitive
direct, plain
plain, evident
point-blank, plain
pointed, plainly significant
undisguised, plain

Bare

bald, uncovered
bare, unconcealed
denuded, naked
naked, bare
nude, naked
stark, bare
stripped, undressed
undressed, naked

Distinctive

characteristic, apparent
  from circumstances
circumstantial, apparent
  from circumstances
complexioned, distinct
definitive, distinctive
diacritical, having dis-
  tinctive significance
distinct, marked, obvious
distinctive, outstanding

ADJECTIVES (Continued)

graphic, vivid
legible, distinct
readable, legible

Clear

clear, distinct
crystal, clear
crystalline, clear
lucid, clear
pellucid, clear
transparent, clear
unclouded, distinct
undimmed, unclouded

Public

exoteric, public
open, public
patent, open to all
public, open

Shameless

barefaced, unashamed
brazen, shameless
shameless, boldly open
unblushing, shameless

Notorious

arrant, notorious
exposed, open
flagrant, conspicuously
  bad
notorious, manifest

Notable

celebrated, renowned
distinguished, distinctive
famous, conspicuous
illustrious, renowned
eminent, conspicuous
notable, conspicuous
renowned, famous

NOUNS

Conspicuity

conspicuity, obviousness
cynosure, object or person
  of general interest
evidence, obvious
  significance
import, significance
manifestation, immediate
  significance
purport, significance
prominence, conspicuous-
  ness
significance, evidence

Bareness

baldness, bareness
(Continued on page 184)

AMAZING—	ASSOCIATIVE	
PUZZLING see—	Frightfulness 33	Darkness 97
	Disguise 103B	Ambiguity 57
vs. Conspicuity 95E	Falsehood 62	Disorder 125A
	Difficulty 13	Conspicuity 95E

96A

VERBS

Amaze
amaze, astonish
astonish, surprise
astound, astonish
dismay, astonish
electrify, surprise
excite, agitate
fascinate, overpower
glamour, fascinate
startle, surprise
surprise, astonish

Confuse
bamboozle, mystify
bewilder, perplex
confound, astonish
confuse, disconcert
discompose, disconcert
disconcert, disorder
dumbfound, bewilder
flabbergast, (col.) amaze
flurry, bewilder
fluster, agitate
nonplus, bewilder
obfuscate, bewilder
perturb, bewilder
petrify, dumbfound
pother, confuse
rattle, disconcert
shock, stagger
stagger, bewilder

Stupefy
besot, stupefy
benumb, stupefy
dope, stupefy
dull, stupefy
fuddle, stupefy
inebriate, intoxicate
intoxicate, excite
muddle, confuse
stultify, stupefy
stun, astonish
stupefy, nonplus

Mystify
maze, bewilder
mystify, perplex
overwhelm, dumbfound
perplex, embarrass
puzzle, perplex
razzle-dazzle, confound
stump, dumbfound
swamp, confound

Embarrass
abash, confound
affright, confuse
agitate, excite
bedevil, worry
boggle, embarrass

VERBS (Continued)
distract, confuse
distress, perplex
embarrass, disconcert
tantalize, fluster

ADJECTIVES

Amazing
amazing, astonishing
astonishing, astounding
astounding, confounding
dismaying, astonishing
exciting, discomposing
rousing, exciting
sensational, exciting
startling, surprising
striking, surprising
surprising, astonishing

Confusing
bewildering, confounding
confounding, disconcerting
confusing, bewildering
discomposing, confusing
disconcerting, confusing
obfuscating, bewildering

Stupefying
benumbing, stunning
dumbfounding, bewildering
staggering, astounding
stunning, benumbing
stupefying, dumbfounding

Mysterious
cryptic, puzzling
enigmatic, mysterious
enigmatical, enigmatic
magic, mystifying
mazy, bewildering
mysterious, enigmatic
mystifying, puzzling
perplexing, puzzling
puzzling, mystifying
strange, puzzling
theurgic, magic
uncanny, mysterious

Embarrassing
bedeviling, embarrassing
distracting, embarrassing
distractive, perplexing
distressing, embarrassing
embarrassing, confusing
shocking, bewildering

Phantasmal
chimerical, phantasmal
eery, exciting fear
ghostly, spirit-like
phantasmal, spectral
spectral, eerie
spiritual, ghostly

ADJECTIVES (Continued)

Prodigious
colossal, prodigious
monstrous, amazing
prodigious, astonishing
stupendous, amazing
tremendous, dismaying

Wonderful
extraordinary, surprising
marvelous, astonishing
(B). marvellous
miraculous, astonishing
remarkable, surprising
wonderful, astonishing
wondrous, amazing

Incredible
fabulous, incredible
incomprehensible, mysterious
incredible, amazing
indefinable, mysterious
indescribable, indefinable
inexpressible, indefinable
nondescript, enigmatic
unbelievable, incredible
unfathomable, confounding
unimaginable, confounding

NOUNS

Amazement
amazement, astonishment
astonishment, something amazing
excitation, astonishment
excitement, excitation
fascination, overpowering charm
jolt, unpleasant surprise
marvel, something amazing
surprise, act of surprising
wonder, something astonishing

Confusion
bewilderment, maze
confusion, distraction
difficulty, embarrassment
distraction, confusion
embarrassment, entanglement
mystification, perplexity
perplexity, entanglement
prodigy, anything astonishing

Mystery
charade, enigma
conundrum, riddle
enigma, puzzle

(Continued on page 189)

NOUNS (Continued)

magic, mystification
miracle, an amazing wonder
mystery, puzzle
nondescript, something puzzling
nonplus, enigma
poser, puzzling proposition
puzzle, enigma
rebus, enigmatic symbol
riddle, enigma
tickler, enigma

Complicacy

complicacy, intricacy
complication, complicacy
entanglement, difficulty
intricacy, maze
knot, intricacy
labyrinth, maze
maze, perplexing labyrinth
wilderness, perplexing maze

NOUNS (Continued)

Phantasm

chimera, phantasm
ignisfatuus, eery delusion
mirage, an illusion
phantom, puzzling apparition
phantasm, phantom
specter, puzzling vision
vision, perplexing specter

GHOST—SPECTER, ETC.

apparition, phantom
brownie, goblin
elf, hobgoblin
elfin, fairy
fairy, elf
fantom, phantom
fay, fairy
ghost, apparition
gnome, spirit
gnomide, spirit (fem.)
goblin, fairy

GHOST—SPECTER, ETC. (Continued)

hallucination, vision
hobgoblin, elf
ignisfatuus, will-o'-the-wisp
illusion, false appearance
imp, hobgoblin
monster, something astonishing
nymph, semi-divine being
oread, nymph
phantom, apparition
pigwiggen, fairy
specter, phantom
sphinx, mysterious person, etc.
spirit, fairy, elf, etc.
spook, ghost
vision, hallucination
will-o'-the-wisp, ignisfatuus
wraith, specter

97

DARKNESS—NEBULOSITY

vs. Conspicuity 95E

see—
ASSOCIATIVE

97

VERBS

Make Obscure

adumbrate, shadow forth
blur, dim
cloud, obscure
darken, obscure
dim, darken
eclipse, obscure temporarily
extinguish, eclipse
lower, darken
obscure, darken
overshadow, eclipse
shade, darken
shadow, shade
vanish, fade

Become Obscure

evanesce, fade gradually
fade, evanesce
gloom, grow dark
lower, appear gloomy
wane, become dark

ADJECTIVES

Black

black, in darkness
cimmerian, intensely dark
ebony, pitchy
fuliginous, soot-like
inky, black
pitchy, inky
sable, black

ADJECTIVES (Continued)

sooty, soot-like

Dark

dark, gloomy
darkish, twilight
darkling, dimly nebulous
darksome, gloomy
dusky, darksome
gloaming, in twilight
gloomy, dismal, obscure
glum, gloomy
lowering, gloomy
moody, gloomy
somber, murky, gloomy
saturnine, gloomy
twilight, shaded

Cloudy

blurred, obscured
clouded, obscured
cloudy, clouded
dingy, gloomy
dismal, gloomy
drab, dark-colored
foggy, misty
hazy, dim with haze
misty, obscure
murky, hazy, obscure
nebular, cloud-like
nebulous, nebular

Dim

dim, faint
evanescent, disappearing

ADJECTIVES (Continued)

faint, dim
obscure, dark
vague, obscured

Shadowy

shadowy, having shadows
shady, out of the sun
umbrageous, shady

Opaque

inscrutable, impenetrable
impenetrable, intensely dark
opaque, not transparent

NOUNS

Blackness

blackness, ebony
pitchiness, cimmerian darkness

Darkness

dark, darkness
darkness, night
dusk, darkness
gloam, partial darkness
gloaming, twilight
gloominess, gloam
moodiness, gloominess
twilight, light before sunrise or night

(Continued on page 192)

98A

VERBS

Signal

beck, nod or gesture
beckon, signal
gesticulate, signal
gesture, signal
motion, gesture
nod, signal with the head
point, signify a direction
signal, communicate by signals

Flag

flag, signal
signalize, signal
wag, gesticulate
wave, beckon
wigwag, signal

Flaunt

cock, tilt the head jauntily
flaunt, wave
fling, flounce
flirt, shoot rapid motions
flounce, fling the body petulantly
shrug, signify with the shoulders
toss, jerk the head

Posture

attitudinize, pose
pose, attitudinize
posture, pose

Menace

brandish, wave threateningly
bridle, hold the head in scorn
flourish, brandish
menace, poise threateningly
snub, meet contemptuously

ADJECTIVES

Miscellaneous

attitudinal, signifying with posture
beckoning, waving
brandishing, waving threateningly

ADJECTIVES (Continued)

flaunting, waving
flirting, motioning
flouncing, moving petulantly
gesticulating, signaling
motioning, gesticulating
menacing, brandishing
nodding, motioning with the head
shrugging, motioning with the shoulders
waving, signaling
wigwagging, waving
signal, signaling

NOUNS

Signal

beck, gesture
gesticulation, significant motion
gesture, gesticulation
motion, gesture
signal, significant motion

Flaunt

cast, significant motion
flaunt, a flutter
fleer, gesture of contempt
fling, flounce
flirt, a toss
fillip, sudden jerk
flounce, impatient jerk
jerk, significant motion

Posture

air, bearing
attitude, significant posture
bearing, attitude
carriage, mien
manner, mien
mannerism, affected bearing
mien, air, carriage
poise, bearing
pose, attitude
posture, pose
presence, mien

Menace

brandish, threatening waving

NOUNS (Continued)

flourish, a brandish
menace, threatening attitude

Innuendo

grip, significant handclasp
handsel, grip of sincerity
innuendo, nod
nod, motion of the head
shrug, motion with the shoulders

Code

code, signals
dactylology, communication by fingers

SIGNAL DEVICES

Miscellaneous

beacon, signal or guide
buoy, floating signal
buoyage, buoys collectively
cock, vane
crescent, beacon, etc.
cynosure, North Star
flag, see Flags No. 104E
flambeau, torch
heliostat, signaling mirror
lighthouse, mariner's beacon
pharos, lighthouse
pointer, directional signal
pylon, one of a series of towers for guiding aviators
rocket, signal light sent up
torch, signal, hand-light
vane, weathercock
weathercock, vane

PERSONS

cantor, precentor
fugleman, a soldier who shows drill movements
mannerist, one who affects characteristics to excess
precentor, the leader of a choir

98B (Continued)

NOUNS (Continued)

simper, an affected smile
smile, amused expression
smirk, simper
sneer, sardonic look

NOUNS (Continued)

snicker, snigger
snigger, sniggle
sniggle, snicker
squint, oblique look

NOUNS (Continued)

twinkle, a winking of the eyes
wink, a signal with the eyelids

FACIAL EMOTIONS see—

ASSOCIATIVE

98B

VERBS

Miscellaneous

blanch, become pale
blush, become red
brighten, become bright
crimson, blush
face, turn the face to
fleer, sneer contemptuously
flush, blush
frown, scowl
gape, open the mouth in wonder
gasp, gape
glare, stare fiercely
glower, stare threateningly
grimace, smirk
grin, show the teeth significantly
leer, give a significant sidelook
lighten, brighten
look, glare
pale, turn pale
pant, gasp
scowl, wrinkle the brow
simper, smile affectedly
smirk, simper
sneer, look with contempt
snicker, smile with a sniggle
smile, wear an amused or cheerful aspect
snigger, snicker
snub, meet with contemptuous mien
squint, look obliquely
sulk, have a sullen look
twinkle, open and shut the eyes rapidly
wink, motion with the eyelids

ADJECTIVES

Smiling

agrin, grinning displeasure
grinning, in suppressed laughter
laughing, joyous
smiling, in suppressed laughter
smirking, smiling affectedly
simpering, smirking
snickering, sniggering
sniggering, snickering

Bright

beaming, radiant
bright, radiant
glowing, beaming
radiant, bright

ADJECTIVES (Continued)

shining, radiant
sparkling, radiant
sunny, shining
twinkling, with sparkling eyes

Joyous

delighted, joyous
exuberant, joyous
gay, genial
genial, exuberant
gleeful, joyous
joyous, gay
merry, gay

Flushed

blushing, flushed
crimson, flushed
flushed, crimson
shamefaced, blushing

Gaping

gaping, open-mouthed
gasping, gaping
open-mouthed, gaping
staring, wide-eyed
yawning, gaping

Calm

calm, tranquil
composed, calm
peaceful, calm
placid, peaceful
quiet, calm
serene, tranquil
tranquil, serene
unclouded, tranquil
undisturbed, calm
unperturbed, calm
unruffled, composed

Dignified

dignified, stately
grand, dignified
majestic, dignified
stately, majestic
sublime, stately

Solemn

grave, solemn
sage, grave
sedate, serious
serious, grave
severe, austere
solemn, serious

Harsh

austere, harsh
fleering, sneering
frowning, scowling
glaring, staring fiercely
glowering, glaring

ADJECTIVES (Continued)

grimacing, smirking
harsh, austere
leering, looking slyly
mean, harsh
sardonic, scornful
scowling, frowning harshly
sneering, sardonic
sour, austere
sullen, mean

Gloomy

black, dismal
dark, dismal
dismal, gloomy
gloomy, melancholy
moody, gloomy
somber, melancholy

Pale

blanching, pale
colorless, pale
emaciated, bloodless
gaunt, emaciated
ghastly, haggard
haggard, gaunt
pale, colorless
pallid, wan
wan, pale

Cheerless

cheerless, dismal
dejected, dispirited
dispirited, dejected
disconsolate, sad
downcast, sad
hapless, sad
melancholic, dejected
melancholy, melancholic
morose, sullen
pathetic, hapless
pensive, sad
sad, sorrowful
sorrowful, pathetic

NOUNS

Miscellaneous

blush, having a crimson aspect
cast, significant look
flush, a blush
frown, a scowl
glare, fierce look
grimace, a smirk
grin, suppressed smile
leer, sly look
look, stare
mouth, grimace
pout, a sullen look
scowl, mean frown
shame, a blushing

(Continued on page 190)

SALUTATION   see—   **ASSOCIATIVE**

vs. Menace 33

Signal—Gesture 98A	Foreword—Opening 73
Facial Emotions 98B	Musical Openings 68C
Laughter 71B	Start 4
Esteem—Regard 38	

98C

Verbs

Salute
curtsy, salute
greet, salute
salute, greet in any manner
welcome, salute with kindness

Bow
bow, bend in salutation
courtesy, bend the knees in salutation
curtesy, as above
kneel, make obeisance
kowtow, touch the forehead in low salutation
salaam, salute
scrape, bow by awkwardly drawing back the foot

Grovel
cringe, bow servilely
grovel, be basely prostrated in salutation
prostrate, bow in humble reverence

Clasp
clasp, embrace
embrace, hug
grip, clasp hands
hug, embrace

Caress
caress, fondle
chuck, pat gently
cuddle, pet
cuddle, embrace

VERBS (Continued)
dally, exchange caresses
dandle, fondle, caress
fondle, caress
pat, pet
pet, fondle

Kiss
beslobber, kiss effusively
kiss, salute with the lips
osculate, kiss
smack, kiss

ADJECTIVES
Miscellaneous
complaisant, courteous
courteous, in graceful salutation
courtly, courteous
debonair, having gentle manners
groveling, in debased salutation
osculatory, kissing
polite, courteous
salutatory, containing greetings
urbane, polite

NOUNS
Miscellaneous
blandishment, token of affection
bow, salutation
buss, kiss

NOUNS (Continued)
caress, a fondling
complaisance, courtesy
courtesy, salutation
courtliness, elegance of manner
curtesy, courtesy
cringe, a servile bow
debut, salutatory appearance
embrace, hug
genuflection, worshipful bending of the knee
greeting, salutation
hello, greeting
hug, embrace
kiss, caress with the lips
kowtow, Chinese salutation
obeisance, bow
osculation, kiss
prostration, humble salutation
reverence, obeisance
salaam, oriental salutation
salutation, salute
salute, a greeting gesture
salvo, artillery salute
scrape, awkwardly backward bow
smack, loud kiss

PERSONS
debutant, one who makes a first or introductory appearance in public
saluter, one who salutes

---

97 (Continued)

NOUNS (Continued)
Cloudiness
blur, dim appearance
cloudiness, nebula
haze, dimness
haziness, haze
murk, darkness
murkiness, murk
nebula, cloudiness
nebulium, the greenish lines in a spectrum caused from a substance in nebula
nebulosity, haziness
phosphorescence, uncertain light from phosphorus
dimness, obscureness

NOUNS (Continued)
Dimness
evanescence, a fading from sight
invisibility, inscrutability
obscureness, darkness
obscurity, dimness
vagueness, uncertainty of appearance

Shadow
adumbration, vague shadow
eclipse, obscuration
night, darkness
penumbra, partial shadow on the exterior of the perfect shadow of an eclipse

NOUNS (Continued)
shade, shadow
shadow, obscuration
umbra, the dark cone of a shadow on a planet's side opposite from the sun

Opaqueness
inscrutability, opaqueness
occultation, temporary obscuration
opacity, imperviousness
opaqueness, not transparent

BEING
Hodur, Norse god of night

ENTERTAINMENT see—

vs. Boredom 130B

99A

VERBS

Entertain

amuse, entertain
disport, amuse
divert, entertain
entertain, amuse

Gratify

convulse, delight
delight, please
felicitate, make happy
gladden, felicitate
gratify, delight
please, gratify
tickle, gratify

Interest

absorb, engross
engage, interest
engross, engage
interest, divert

Be Humorous

burlesque, ridicule enter-
   tainingly
jest, joke
joke, jest
jolly, inspirit mirth
travesty, burlesque

Feast

banquet, entertain richly
feast, entertain sumptu-
   ously
fete, entertain festively
junket, feast

Fascinate

beguile, entertain
bewitch, charm
captivate, bewitch
charm, delight exquisitely
enchant, charm
enthrall, fascinate
fascinate, charm
glamour, fascinate

Transport

elate, cause exultation
enliven, exhilarate
enrapture, please greatly
entrance, enchant
exhilarate, make joyous
inflate, elate
inspirit, exhilarate
ravish, transport
regale, entertain richly
thrill, give an exquisite
   sensation
transport, ravish

Perform

act, perform histrionically

VERBS (Continued)

perform, play
play, entertain
show, perform
star, entertain as a star

ADJECTIVES

Entertaining

amusing, entertaining
diverting, entertaining
entertaining, amusing
playful, amusing

Gratifying

admirable, enjoyable
agreeable, pleasing
cheery, gladdening
delectable, delightful
delightful, pleasing
enjoyable, pleasurable
gladdening, gratifying
gladsome, joyous
gratifying, pleasing
pleasing, engaging
pleasurable, pleasing

Interesting

absorbing, engrossing
engaging, pleasing
engrossing, engaging
interesting, diverting

Gay

blithe, gay
blithesome, blithe
convivial, jovial
frolicsome, sportive
gay, jovial
jolly, inspiring mirth
jovial, convivial
joyful, jovial
joyous, merry
merry, delightful
mirthful, merry
vivacious, gay

Laughable

bizarre, grotesque
droll, ridiculous
fantastic, bizarre
gelogenic, producing
  laughter
gleeful, having the interest
  of minstrelsy
hilarious, gelogenic
laughable, humorous
ludicrous, laughable
queer, amusing
ridiculous, ludicrous

Humorous

antic, comic

ADJECTIVES (Continued)

buffo, comic
burlesque, with entertaining ridicule
clownish, comic
comic, ludicrous
comical, comic
facetious, humorous
farcical, having the interest
  of farce
funny, humorous
grotesque, ridiculous
harlequin, humorous
humorous, amusing
humorsome, diverting
(B). humoursome
jesting, jocose
jocose, sportive
jocular, waggish
jocund, jocose
sportive, humorous
waggish, sportive

Fascinating

beguiling, fascinating
bewitching, delightful
captivating, bewitching
charming, delightful
enchanting, bewitching
enthralling, captivating
fascinating, delightful
glamorous, fascinating

Transporting

ecstatic, entrancing
enlivening, exhilarating
entrancing, delightful
exhilarating, enlivening
exquisite, ecstatic
ravishing, transporting
transporting, ravishing

Remarkable

amazing, astounding
astounding, exciting
colossal, grand
dazzling, resplendent
extraordinary, remarkable
glorious, resplendent
gorgeous, resplendent
grand, wonderful
inspiring, sensational
magnificent, inspiring
marvelous, exciting
  interest
(B). marvellous
miraculous, wonderful
remarkable, sensational
resplendent, gorgeous
sensational, astounding

(Continued on page 194)

ADJECTIVES (Continued)

spectacular, grand
stupendous, colossal
thrilling, sensational
unsurpassed, remarkable
wonderful, remarkable

Histrionic

dramatic, having the interest of drama
histrionic, having the interest of the stage

ADJECTIVES (Continued)

magical, having the interest of magic
melodramatic, histrionic
operatic, having the interest of opera

Histrionic

primrose, histrionic
scenic, dramatic
stage, histrionic
talismanic, magically diverting

ADJECTIVES (Continued)

thaumaturgic, miraculously diverting
theatrical, histrionic
Thespian, dramatic

TOYS

top, a spinning toy
toy, a plaything, etc., etc.

NOUNS on 99B, 99C

99B, 99C
See—(ASSOCIATIVE 99A)

99B
NOUNS

Entertainment

amusement, entertainment
diversion, entertainment
divertissement, amusement
entertainment, amusement

Comedy

buffoonery, entertainment by buffoons
burlesque, ludicrous entertainment
comedy, farce
drollery, buffoonery
extravaganza, burlesque
farce, comedy
harlequinade, buffoonery
mimicry, ludicrous acting
pantomime, mimicry
tomfoolery, comedy
travesty, burlesque

Legerdemain

hocus, jugglery
hocus-pocus, jugglery

NOUNS (Continued)

jugglery, sleight-of-hand
legerdemain, jugglery
magic, legerdemain
prestidigitation, legerdemain
thaumaturgy, legerdemain

Stunt, Etc.

act, stage entertainment
feat, extraordinary performance
stunt, performance
trick, legerdemain

Kind of Show

acrobatism, acrobacy
acrobacy, acrobatic performance
bouffe, comic opera
burletta, comic opera
charade, acted enigma
drama, theatrical entertainment

NOUNS (Continued)

dramaturgy, stage effect
mime, mimic play
melodrama, histrionic entertainment
opera, musical drama, etc.
parody, burlesque
pyrotechnics, fireworks
tragedy, drama
trilogy, historical drama in a series of three
vaudeville, histrionic entertainment

Exhibition

exhibition, public divertissement
exposition, exhibition
histrionicism, stage
performance, entertainment
play, amusement
representation, performance
show, spectacle
spectacle, exhibition

99C
NOUNS

Beguilement

amusement, beguilement
beguilement, charm
bewitchery, charm
charm, enchantment
cheer, beguilement
delicacy, delight
delight, pleasure
delectability, delightfulness
enchantment, fascination
enthrallment, beguilement
fascination, charm
fun, frolic
merriment, mirth
pleasure, merriment
playfulness, sportiveness
thrill, charm
transport, enchantment

Jollification

comicality, humor
high-jinks, jollification
humor, jocularity

NOUNS (Continued)

(B). humour

jest, jesting
jesting, fun
jocosity, humor
jocularity, merriment
jocundity, humor
jollification, merrymaking
jollity, mirth
sport, sportiveness
sportiveness, jollification
waggery, jocularity

Merrymaking

banquet, rich entertainment
conviviality, joviality
festival, fete
festivity, festive celebration
fete, festive entertainment
revelry, festivity
saturnalia, riotous revelry
shindy, spree

NOUNS (Continued)

spree, frolic
symposium, merrymaking
wassail, merrymaking

Enlivenment

enlivenment, beguilement
entertainment, amusement
frolic, amusement
gaiety, joviality
glee, exhilaration
joviality, conviviality
lark, merriment
mirth, gaiety
pastime, beguilement
vivacity, sportiveness

Party, Etc.

holiday, day of diversion
infare, merrymaking
kettledrum, tea party
party, social entertainment
picnic, pleasure excursion
week-end, week-end merrymaking

99D

PERSONS

Actor
actor, histrionic performer
actress, as above (fem.)
artiste, actor
performer, actor
player, actor
soubrette, actress
stager, player
Thespian, an actor
troupe, company of
  performers

Actors (Miscellaneous)
dramatis persona, charac-
  ter in a play
ingenue, actress in the part
  of an artless girl
tragedian, actor in tragedy
tragedienne, as above
  (fem.)

Humorist
antic, clown
buffo, buffoon
buffoon, clown
clown, comic actor
comique, comedian
comedian, humorous actor

PERSONS (Continued)
comedienne, as above
  (fem.)
cut-up, buffoon
doll, puppet
droll, buffoon
harlequin, pantomime
humorist, fun-maker
merry-andrew, buffoon
mimic, buffoon
mummer, actor, masker
pantaloon, buffoon in
  pantomime
punch, buffoon
punchinello, hump-backed
  figure in a puppet show
puppet, doll or person in a
  mock drama
zany, merrymaker

Conjurer
conjurer, juggler
famulus, assistant
  magician
funambulist, rope
  performer
illusionist, conjurer
juggler, prestidigitator
magician, expert in magic

PERSONS (Continued)
prestidigitator, juggler
sorcerer, magician

Impersonator
impersonator, character
  actor
pantomime, one who acts
  (imitates) in a play
pantomimist, pantomime
personator, impersonator

Acrobat
acrobat, athletic performer
athlete, one skilled in
  strength
contortionist, an actor who
  contorts the body
tumbler, acrobat

Star
diva, prima donna
prima donna, principal
  female actress
star, principal actor

BEING
Euphrosyne, one of the
  Graces; she conferred
  joy

99E

AMUSEMENT PLACES, ETC.
aquarium, place for exhibiting fish, etc.
amphitheater, circus
(B). amphitheatre
arena, amphitheater
biograph, kinetograph
boards, stage
cabaret, restaurant which
  gives entertainment
carnival, a gathering for
  feasting and merry-
  making
casino, place for dancing
  entertainment

(Continued)
cinema, motion-picture
  show
cinematograph, cinema
circus, amusement arena
cockpit, arena for cock-
  fighting
colosseum, amphitheater
field, arena
footlights, stage
gridiron, football field
gymnasium, athletic hall
hippodrome, circus
kermess, carnival
kinetograph, motion-
  picture exhibition

(Continued)
Mardigras, last great day
  of a carnival
merry-go-round, revolving
  amusement device
nickelodeon, 5c amusement
  place
opera house, theater
opera, opera house
resort, place of diversion
show, amusement place
stage, theater
theater, playhouse
(B). theatre
Zoo, place for exhibiting
  animals

99F

DANCING—DANCES—DANCERS   see—   ASSOCIATIVE

99F

VERBS
dance, move the feet grace-
  fully, rhythmically, en-
  tertainingly, and artis-
  tically
flit, move lightly

VERBS (Continued)
jig, dance a jig
skip, flit
waltz, dance a waltz

ADJECTIVES
saltant, dancing
saltatory, saltant
Terpsichorean, pertaining
  to dancing
(Continued on page 196)

NOUNS

ballet, artistic dance
bayadere, spectacular dance
bolero, airy Spanish dance
breakdown, stamping dance
cachucha, bolero-like dance
cakewalk, grotesque negro dance
cancan, indelicate French dance
carmagnole, a wild dance
chacone, Spanish dance
cotillion, dance by eight
cushion, former wedding dance
czardas, Hungarian dance
dance, rhythmic foot movement
fandango, Spanish dance
farandole, French dance
fling, Scotch dance
fox-trot, modern dance
gallop, a kind of dance
gallopade, a brisk dance
gavot, a round dance
(B). gavotte

NOUNS (Continued)

highland fling, Scotch dance
jig, lively dance
lancers, dance by sets
masquerade, mask dance
maxixe, elaborate dance
mazurka, Polish dance
minuet, graceful dance
nautch, dance in India
pavan, stately dance
polka, three-step dance
polonaise, Polish dance
quadrille, dance by sets
reel, Scotch dance
redowa, Bohemian dance
ridotto, dance and song
rigadoon, lively dance
roundelay, dance in a circle
saltation, a leaping and dancing
saltarello, Spanish dance
saraband, stately Spanish dance
schottische, polka-like dance
seguidilla, Spanish dance

NOUNS (Continued)

siciliana, a dance of the Sicilian peasantry
strathspey, Scottish dance
strophe, dance by the chorus
tambourine, French stage dance
tango, a modern dance
tarantella, savage dance
turkey-trot, a dance
Virginia reel, a dance
waltz, dance by a couple

PERSONS

bayadere, Hindu dancing girl
dancer, one who dances
danseuse, female dancer
figurant, opera dancer
funambulist, rope dancer
geisha, Japanese dancing girl
minuet, graceful dancer
nautch girl, dancing girl of India
Terpsichore, muse of dancing, a ballet-dancer

Also: Fire dance, flower dance, kermess, May dance, medicine dance, passepied, Salmon dance, sun dance, snake dance, skirt dance, etc., and modern dances of transient and possibly enduring significance.

100A

ARTISTRY   see—

vs. Unskilfulness 126D
vs. Ugliness 109A

ASSOCIATIVE

Skill 134B	Monuments 104H
Operatives, etc. 144D	Paints—Pigments 102D
Entertainment 99D	Colors—Hues 102A
Dancers—Dances 99F	Jewels, etc. 107C
Melody—Music 68A	Beauty 108

100A

VERBS

Paint, Etc.

crayon, depict with crayon
dash, paint rapidly
daub, paint unskilfully
limn, paint or draw
paint, depict with pigments
pencil, sketch in pencil

Produce Variously

caricature, represent in exaggerated form
daguerreotype, to photograph by Daguerre's process
emboss, form in relief
fresco, paint in fresco
lithograph, produce lithographically

VERBS (Continued)

pink, form by punching holes
produce, form a work of art
profile, depict in profile
silhouette, form in profile

Delineate

chart, outline graphically
delineate, sketch
depict, portray
design, draw
draw, delineate
illustrate, delineate
map, sketch
mark, depict
outline, sketch
portray, depict in likeness
sketch, outline
trace, delineate
trick, delineate with color

VERBS (Continued)

Engrave, Etc.

engrave, cut or carve
etch, form by an acid process
grave, engrave
intaglio, engrave with a sunken design

Chisel, Etc.

carve, form by cutting
chisel, carve
sculpture, make statuary

Form

cast, form by mold
form, mold, shape, draw
model, form in likeness
mold, form with a cast
shape, form
(Continued on page 197)

ADJECTIVES
Delineatory
cartographic, pertaining to map-making
delineatory, graphic
diagrammatic, delineatory
sketchy, delineatory

Statuesque
parian, pertaining to the famed marble or porcelain used in statuettes
sculptural, produced in sculpture
statuesque, statue-like

Vivid
graphic, vividly formed
lithographic, formed in lithograph
photographic, produced by photography
pictorial, pertaining to pictures
picturesque, produced realistically
vivid, graphic

Miscellaneous
accolated, having profiles overlapped
anaglyphic, pertaining to art in relief, not sunken as an intaglio
arabesque, pertaining to artistic inlaying
artistic, characteristic of art

ADJECTIVES (Continued)
decorative, artistic
encaustic, pertaining to the art of painting in burnt wax
glyptic, pertaining to engraving in relief, anaglyphic
panoramic, having a wide scenic view
scenic, pertaining to scenery

NOUNS
Miscellaneous
ambrotype, a photographic process
amphitype, the process of producing positive and negative photography simultaneously
anaglyptography, the art of reproducing relief work on paper, glyphography
art, skill in the portrayal of imagery
artistry, the pursuits, interests, or products of art
cartography, the art of drawing maps
calcography, the art of drawing with colored chalk
dactylioglyphy, the art of engraving on gems

NOUNS (Continued)
daguerreotype, photography on a silvered surface
embossing, tracery in relief
glyphography, the production of engraving in relief, anaglyptography
hyalography, the art of engraving on glass
lithography, the art of reproducing impressions from stone
photography, the art of making photographs
photogravure, the art of making photographic plates
photochromy, the art of photographing colors
pornography, obscene painting
portraiture, images portrayed in portraits
portrayal, portraiture
realism, the representation of nature and life as it is
sciagraphy, the art of producing shadows as they appear in nature
sculpture, the art of fashioning figures
sketchiness, representation by sketching

PICTURES, ETC. 100B
ARTISTS, ETC. 100C

PICTURES—STATUARY, ETC.   See—(ASSOCIATIVE 100A)

Photo, Etc.
cabinet, photograph
cabinet-picture, a picture of small dimension
half-tone, a half-tone picture
heliochrome, heliochromotype
heliochromotype, a photograph in colors
kitcat, a 28 x 36 portrait showing half the length
kodak, snapshot
negative, photographic lights and shades represented opposite to those in nature
photograph, a likeness
photo, photograph
portrait, photograph, etc.
snapshot, instantaneous photographic likeness

(Continued)
vignette, a portrait of the head and bust

Painting, Etc.
canvas, a painting
depictment, portraiture in realistic imagery
drop, a painted theater curtain
flourish, fancy design
lithograph, reproduction
lithotint, lithograph from a drawing executed with a camel's hair pencil
mezzotint, a variety of copper engraving
miniature, a very small painting, especially a portrait on ivory
opuscule, a petty work
painting, painted picture
picture, painting, photograph

(Continued)
piece, an artistic production
tattoo, a design made by tattooing

Polychrome, Etc.
aquatint, etching in India ink resembling water-colors, etc.
chromo, picture produced by chromo-lithography
crayon, a crayon drawing
duograph, a picture in two colors
grisaille, a solid body represented in bas-relief by the employment of grey tints
monochrome, a painting in tints, of one color, relieved by light and shades
(Continued on page 198)

(Continued)

monotone, a picture in a single tint
oleograph, a lithograph in oil colors
polychrome, a work executed in many colors

Subjects (Miscellaneous)

battle, war painting
caricature, an exaggerated portraiture
cartoon, caricature
elaboration, an elaborate painting, etc.
frontispiece, a production on the front page
genre, a painting representing some scene of common life
landscape, picture of a country
marine, a sea-piece
nocturne, a night scene
pastoral, a production of rural life on canvas, etc.
pictograph, a picture of an idea
pornograph, obscene painting
seascape, a scene at sea

Holy Paintings

eikon, a holy image or picture
Madonna, a picture of the Virgin Mary
sudarium, Christ's face imaged on a napkin

Plate, Types

daguerreotype, a picture produced on a silver plate
ferrotype, a photograph upon an iron plate
ivorytype, an ivory-like photograph
pictoglyph, a picture carved on a hard surface
plaque, a figured metal or terra cotta plate

Profile

contour, profile
figure, drawing, painting, statue, etc.
form, figure
lineament, outline
outline, a first sketch
profile, side view
silhouette, outline filled in with black or shade

Sketch, Etc.

alignment, ground-plan
delineation, sketch
design, a drawing

(Continued)

device, a fanciful design or pattern
diagram, a drawing
draft, outline
elevation, representation of the principal side of a building
illustration, picture
plan, drawing, as of a building
projection, plan represented on a plane
protraction, a drawing of dimensions
sciagraph, the vertical section of a building showing its interior
sketch, outline
study, sketched ideas of a painter for future reference

Chart, Etc.

chart, map
hydrograph, map of the earth's waters
hyetograph, rain-chart
map, a chart of surface locations, etc.

Panorama, Etc.

cosmorama, various views of the world
cyclorama, connected scenes
diorama, pictures exhibited on a movable screen
panorama, extended scene

Relief, Etc.

alto-relievo, relief figure
anaglyph, a work carved in relief, distinguished from an intaglio
arabesque, production in low relief
bas-relief, a production in low relief
relief, a design above a plain surface
rilievo, relief

Intaglio, Etc.

engraving, an engraved production
etching, an etched production
glyptograph, an engraving in relief on gems, etc.
hatching, a drawing or engraving by crossed lines
intaglio, design cut on a gem or stone, distinguished from an anaglyph
niello, ornamental engraving on door brasses, escutcheons, etc.

(Continued)

Original

archetype, prototype
ecorche, manikin
example, type
manikin, model of the human body for anatomical study
model, a standard copy
original, a first production by an author
prototype, original model for copying
standard, model
type, original design

Copy

copy, duplicate of an original
counterfeit, imitation
duplicate, reproduction
imitation, likeness
likeness, photograph, etc.
print, a reproduction
replica, a copy
reproduction, copy
tracing, a copy made over thin paper

Fresco, Etc.

fresco, wall painting
graffito, a rude sketch on walls as in ancient Rome
secco, painting on dry plaster
tablature, painting on walls or ceilings, etc.

Statuary

acrolith, sculptured figure
Atlantes, columnar statuary
bust, statue of the head, shoulders and breast
Persian, a sculptured male figure used in column
sculptuary, statuary
sculpture, a carved work
statuary, statues collectively
statuette, little statue
statue, sculptured image

Daub, Etc.

cacotype, a defective production
daub, a rudely executed painting
scratch, a badly executed piece

Masterpiece

chef-d'oeuvre, masterpiece
masterpiece, virtue
opus magnum, great work
paragon, masterpiece
vertu, works of art
virtue, vertu

100C

PERSONS

artisan, one skilled in any art or trade
artist, one skilled in art
caricaturist, a producer of caricature
chartographer, map maker
copyist, a producer of transcripts
crayonist, crayon artist
cubist, erratic painter
decorator, decorative artisan
designer, drawer

PERSONS (Continued)

draughtsman, a delineator of plans, etc.
drawer, draughtsman
enameler, one who decorates with enamel
engraver, one who engraves
idylist, pastoral painter
illustrator, sketcher
impressionist, one who depicts forms without elaboration of details
lapidary, an artificer who cuts precious stones

PERSONS (Continued)

limner, painter, illuminator
painter, an artist who is skilled in painting
pornographer, painter of obscene art
profilist, profile artist
sculptor, an artist skilled in sculpture
sculptuary, sculptor
sketcher, outliner

BEING

Apollo, god of the fine arts, etc.

101A

LIGHT, ETC.   see—

vs. Darkness 97
vs. Hiding 103A

ASSOCIATIVE

Burning 131B
Colors—Hues 102A
Paints—Pigments 102D
Jewels, Etc. 107C

Beauty 108
Show 95A
Conspicuity 95E
Ostentation 95D

101A

VERBS

Miscellaneous

achromatize, lighten without color
beam, shine
bedazzle, overcome with brilliance
blaze, to flame
bloom, glow
brighten, lighten
coruscate, glitter
daze, dazzle
dazzle, bedazzle
enlighten, illuminate
flame, blaze
flare, burn unsteadily
flash, blaze suddenly
flicker, shine unsteadily
fire, illuminate
finish, polish
gild, illuminate
glare, dazzle
gleam, shine
glimmer, flicker
glisten, glitter
glitter, sparkle
glow, shine intensely
ignite, incandesce
illuminate, light up
illumine, illuminate
incandesce, glow
irradiate, illuminate
light, illuminate
lighten, illumine
opalesce, to shine like the opal
phosphoresce, to shine with a phosphorous-like light

VERBS (Continued)

polish, to shine
radiate, irradiate
scintillate, sparkle
sheen, glisten
shimmer, glimmer
shine, glow
smooth, polish
sparkle, glitter
twinkle, glimmer

ADJECTIVES

Brilliant

bright, luminous
brilliant, dazzling
dazzling, blazing
garish, dazzling, showy
glaring, dazzling
sunny, bright
vivid, forming brilliant images

Iridescent

glamorous, splendid
golden, lustrous
gorgeous, resplendent
iridescent, rainbow-like
lustrous, brilliant
nacreous, having iridescence
pyrotechnic, like fireworks
resplendent, brilliant
refulgent, resplendent
splendent, brilliant
splendid, brilliant

Sparkling

blazing, brilliant
flaring, flaming

ADJECTIVES (Continued)

flashing, blazing
flashy, brilliant
glistening, glittering
glittering, sparkling
meteoric, transitorily bright
radiant, emitting rays
scintillant, flashing
sparkling, glittering

Ablaze

ablaze, brilliant
aflame, ablaze
alight, lighted
flaming, blazing

Candent

aglow, glowing
ardent, glowing
candent, glowing
gleaming, bright
glowing, incandescent
incalescent, heating
incandescent, candent

Flickering

beamy, having rays
flickering, glimmering
lambent, flickering
tinsel, glittering
twinkling, glimmering

Shining

glossy, lustrous
sericeous, silky
silky, glossy
sleek, glossy
sheen, shiny
(Continued on page 200)

ADJECTIVES (Continued)

shining, radiant
shiny, shining
smooth, lustrous

Luminous

achromatic, lighting without coloration
achromatous, achromatic
illuminant, giving light
light, bright
lucernal, lighted by lamp
luminiferous, luminous
luminous, giving light
omnilucent, giving light in all directions
phosphorescent, having greyish luminescence
photo, prefix meaning light

Transparent

clear, bright
crystal, clear
crystalline, crystal
diaphanous, transparent
glassy, transparent
hyaline, transparent
lucid, bright
pellucid, clear
translucent, semi-transparent
transparent, transmitting light

Starry

astral, starry
dim, nebular
nebular, faint
nebulous, nebular
solar, of the sun
starry, stellar
stellar, star-like
stellate, stellar

NOUNS

Iridescence

brilliance, splendor

NOUNS (Continued)

effulgence, refulgence
glory, splendor
iridescence, rainbow-like radiance
irradiance, luster, light
luster, brilliance
opalescence, iridescence of opals
refulgence, splendor
resplendence, splendor
resplendency, refulgence
splendor, brilliancy
(B.) splendour

Sparkle

dazzle, splendor
glare, a dazzle
glitter, brilliancy
radiance, darting rays
scintillation, flashing sparkle
sparkle, scintillation

Spark, Flash

flash, sudden light
lightning, flashing light
scintilla, a spark
spark, a small flash

Blaze

blaze, a bright flame
flame, a transient fire

Fire

combustion, act of burning
conflagration, fire
coruscation, flashing light
fire, conflagration
ignition, incandescence

Candence

candescence, incandescence
fulgency, brightness
gleam, stream of light
glow, intense light
incandescence, glowing light or heat

NOUNS (Continued)

Flicker

flare, unsteady glare
flicker, unsteady light
glim, a light
glimmer, faint light
starriness, glimmer

Shine

burnish, a gloss
glint, gleam of light
gloss, a luster
glossiness, luster
luster, gloss
(B.) lustre
sheen, glitter
shine, luster
shimmer, unsteady gleam

Luminescence

illumination, brilliant lighting
light, irradiance
luminescence, light
phosphorescence, light from phosphorus
radiation, the diffusion of light
sunlight, sunshine
sunniness, sunshine
sunshine, sunlight

Transparency

lucidity, brightness
transparency, light transmission

Beam

beam, parallel light rays
pencil, light rays converging to a point
ray, pencil of light

X-ray

Roentgen rays, rays which permit vision through impervious objects
X-rays, Roentgen rays

101B

HALO—LUMINOUS REFRACTIONS

alpenglow, a purple gleam on the snow of the Alps before sunrise and sunset
anthelion, halo round a sun-shadowed object, etc.
aura, a subtle emanation of light from the body
aureola, halo
aurora, the rising light of the morning
aurora australis, the southern light

(Continued)

aurora borealis, the ascending streams of light from the north horizon
chromosphere, rose-colored envelope of the sun
coma, nebulous hair-like envelope surrounding the nucleus of a comet
halation, halo on a photographic plate
halo, a circle of light around certain objects

(Continued)

limelight, the light in which one shines
nimbus, halo employed for divinities
parhelion, a mock sun
spectrum, graduated light formed by a spectroscope
zodiacal light, luminous triangular tract with its base on the horizon, seen in twilight

101C
ARTIFICIAL ILLUMINA-TORS

achromatic lens, light transmitter, without coloration
arc-lamp, arc-light
arc-light, electric light
argand lamp, oil-lamp
astral lamp, oil-lamp
bale-fire, signal fire
beacon, lighthouse
bluelight, signal light
bonfire, fire in the open
bougie, candle
burner, the burning part of a lamp
candle, tallow light, etc.
candlestick, candle holder
candelabrum, lamp-stand
chandelier, girandole
clerge, ceremonial candle
cresset, torch
davy, miner's safety lamp

(Continued)

fizgig, a firework made of damp powder
flambeau, torch
flashlight, electric flash
gaselier, a gas-burning chandelier
girandole, a branching chandelier
glim, candle
illuminant, that which illuminates
illuminator, illuminant
incandescent lamp, electric lamp
jesse, a branching candle-stick
lantern, portable lamp
lamp, lighting device
light, illuminator
lighthouse, pharos

(Continued)

link, torch made of pitch and tar
louver, roof lantern
lucifer, match
match, lucifer
phantasmagoria, magic lantern
pharos, lighthouse
radiant, a luminous point
reflector, signal device
rocket, a firework
sconce, a hanging or projecting candlestick
spangle, a glittering ornament
spectroscope, instrument for forming a spectrum
taper, wax candle
tinsel, a glittering object
torch, flambeau
wick, burner

101D
CELESTIAL FORMS

aerolite, meteorite
bolide, a meteor
comet, a celestial body
constellation, "fixed" stars designated by name
Galaxy, the Milky Way
Lucifer, Venus as the morning star

(Continued)

luminary, a body which emits light
meteor, a transient luminous body in the sky
meteorite, meteor
moon, celestial body
parhelion, a mock sun
Phoebus, the sun

(Continued)

rainbow, celestial arch
sun, the luminous center of our worlds
star, celestial body
Venus, etc., etc.

BEING
Janus, god of light

102A

COLOR (COLOUR) see—

vs. Dirty 129A

{ Light 101A
{ Conspicuity 95E

ASSOCIATIVE
Jewels, etc. 107C
Beauty 108
Clothing 106B

Colors cannot be arranged logically except according to spectrumatic divisions. The arrangement herewith is a practical exposition of colors which commence with BLACK, blending into intermediate colors and progressing to WHITE.

102A
VERBS
Distinctive Coloration
black, blacken
blacken, make black
ebonize, stain with ebony
ink, blacken
smut, blacken with smut
brown, make brown
bronze, make bronze
tan, make brownish
empurple, make purple
redden, make red
crimson, make deep red
vermilion, make a brilliant red

VERBS (Continued)
ensanguine, cover with blood or blood-red
rouge, make red
rubricate, mark with red
ruddy, make ruddy
ruddle, make red with ochre
blush, crimson
flush, become crimson
gild, make gold-colored
whiten, render white
whitewash, whiten with whitewash

VERBS (Continued)
etiolate, blanch by excluding from sunlight
blanch, whiten
bleach, blanch
silver, color like silver

ADJECTIVES
Distinctive Hues
BLACK, darkest in hue
jet, deep-black
blackish, black-like
sable, black
pitchy, black
(Continued on page 202)

ADJECTIVES (Continued)
ebony, black-colored
inky, black
sooty, soot-colored
raven, raven-colored
fuliginous, soot-like
murky, dark
dingy, dark
dusky, incipiently dark
dull, dark
sad, dark-colored
BROWN, chestnut-colored
dun, dull-brown
brunette, brown-complexioned
buff, buff-colored
bronze, bronze-colored
chestnut, reddish-brown
chocolate, brownish
cinnamon, light-brown
dark, swarthy
drab, dull-brown
dusky, dark
foxy, reddish-brown
roan, chestnut, sorrel
sorrel, reddish-brown
swart, swarthy
swarthy, tawny-hued
tan, brownish
tawny, yellowish-brown
BLUE, sky-colored
azure, sky-blue
bluish, blue-like
cerulean, sky-colored
cyaneous, azure
PURPLE, red-blue
amaranthine, purplish
amethystine, violet purple
heliotrope, bluish-pink
lavender, pale-lilac
lilac, pale-purple
mauve, lavender-colored
puce, brownish-purple
tyrian, richly purple
violet, violet-colored
RED, scarlet to pink
auburn, brownish-red
blowzed, high-colored
bay, reddish
carbuncular, red
carnationed, flesh-colored
cherry, ruddy
claret, dark-red
coralline, pinkish-red
crimson, deep-red
flamy, flame-colored
florid, flushed with red
maroon, brownish-crimson
murrey, dark-red
reddish, red-like
roseate, rose-colored
rouge, red
rubicund, inclined to red
ruby, crimson-colored

ADJECTIVES (Continued)
rubescent, becoming red
ruddy, florid
russet, brownish-red
rutilant, red
sanguineous, blood-colored
sarcoline, flesh-colored
vinaceous, wine-colored
GREEN, verdant
emerald, deep-green
glaucous, sea-green
greenish, green-like
olive, olive-green
umber, olive-brown
verdant, fresh-green
YELLOW, golden-colored
amber, yellowish
aureate, golden-yellow
aureous, golden-colored
buff, light-yellow
canary, bright-yellow
ceraceous, having the color
of new wax
fallow, reddish-yellow
flav, prefix for yellow
flaxen, golden
fulvous, saffron
golden, gold-colored
jaundiced, yellowish
lurid, greyish-orange
orange, orange-colored
primrose, pale-yellow
rufous, reddish-yellow
saffron, deep-yellow
tawny, brownish-yellow
xanthic, tending to yellow
xantho, prefix for yellow
WHITE, snow-hued
achromatic, not colored
argent, silvery-white
ashen, pale
bleak, pale
blond, light-colored
cadaverous, pale
calcareous, lime-colored
chalky, chalk-colored
colorless, pale
(B). colourless
creamy, cream-colored
cretaceous, lime-colored
etiolate, blanched
fair, spotless
ghastly, pale
gray, hoar
grey, gray
hoar, greyish-white
leaden, lead-colored
niveous, snow-colored
pale, wan
pallid, pale
sallow, pale
silvery, silver-colored
snowy, snow-colored
uncolored, colorless

ADJECTIVES (Continued)
wan, pale
whitish, white-like

NOUNS
Definite Hues
BLACK, the darkest color
blackness, pitchiness
inkiness, blackness
pitchiness, dense blackness
sootiness, soot-like blackness
BROWN, dark color inclined to yellow
bronze, the color of bronze
chestnut, reddish-brown
drab, dull-brown
russet, reddish-brown
swarthiness, tawny hue
tan, light-brown
tawniness, yellowish-brown
BLUE, azure
alpen-glow, purple glow on the snow of the Alps
azure, sky-blue
azurine, grayish-blue
bloom, a blue
berylline, greenish blue
celestine, sky-blue
gridelin, greyish-violet
heliotrope, bluish-pink
lapis lazuli, rich blue
mauve, lilac or purple
purple, blended color of blue and red
ultramarine, beautiful blue
violet, violet color
RED, color from scarlet to pink
auburn, brownish red
bay, a red
blush, red color
carnation, rose-pink
carnification, making flesh-colored
color, redness
(B). colour
crimson, deep red
carmine, rich crimson
damask, deep pink
efflorescence, redness of the skin
maroon, brownish crimson
pink, light red
roan, dark color with shade of red
rose, rose color
ruddiness, redness of complexion
rutile, shining red
sanguine, blood-red
(Continued on page 203)

NOUNS (Continued)
scarlet, bright-red
GREEN, the color of verdant grass
aquamarine, pale bluish-green
olive, olive color
patina, green rust-color on ancient bronze, coins, etc.
verdancy, greenness
verdigris, blue-green which forms on copper, brass, etc.

NOUNS (Continued)
verdure, greenness of vegetation
YELLOW, a gold-like color
amber, yellow color
buff, light-yellow
orange, golden-yellow
orpiment, king's yellow
orpin, yellow of various intensity
saffron, deep-yellow
xanthosis, yellow

NOUNS (Continued)
WHITE, color of snow
argent, silvery white in designs signifying purity, spotlessness
blond, fair or light color
etiolation, whitish color due to the exclusion of sunlight
pallor, paleness
ghastliness, pale color

102B
VERBS
Neutral Hues
achromatize, deprive of the power of giving color
bloom, become fresh in flower or color
color, render a color
(B). colour
dye, color
grain, paint in imitation of wood
ingrain, give lasting color
paint, give a paint color
shade, color
stain, color with stain

VERBS (Continued)
tinge, stain or color
tint, color slightly
tone, harmonize colors
varnish, give gloss with varnish

ADJECTIVES
Neutral in Hue
beige, in natural color
colored, having a color
chromatic, in colors
ecru, unbleached
isochromatic, in identical color

ADJECTIVES (Continued)
tinctorial, in tints
unbleached, natural

NOUNS
Miscellaneous
color, hue
(B). colour
hue, shade
nuance, shade
shade, hue
stain, tint
tinge, color slightly
tint, tinge
tone, color

102C
VERBS
Render Variegated
bespeckle, mark with spots
blend, variegate or mingle colors
blot, discolor, blur
blur, discolor
checker, variegate with checkers
dapple, variegate with spots
dot, speckle
discolor, change from natural color
(B). discolour
fleck, variegate
fluoresce, make complexional
freckle, variegate with freckles
gradate, blend
mackle, blot or blur
shade, mark with gradations of light or color
speckle, variegate with spots
streak, variegate with streaks
stipple, color with short touches
stripe, variegate with lines

VERBS (Continued)
tattoo, pierce the skin with dotted designs
variegate, cover with various colors
vex, variegate

ADJECTIVES
Variegated
checkered, in checks
chiaroscuro, pertaining to shades in painting
colorful, complexioned
(B). colourful
complexional, fluorescent
complexioned, as above
dapple, spotted
discolored, mottled
(B). discoloured
drab, mixed or grey
florid, brilliantly varied
fluorescent, complexioned
freckled, with freckles
gray, white and black
grayish, gray-like
grey, gray
grizzly, grayish
harlequin, parti-colored
heterogeneous, mottled
high-colored, florid

ADJECTIVES (Continued)
inky, discolored with ink
iridescent, rainbow-like
kaleidoscopic, symmetrically colored
livid, black and blue
macled, spotted
motley, heterogeneous
mottled, marked variously
nacreous, iridescent
naevus, spotted
naif, natural colored
opalescent, opal-like
opaline, opalescent
parti-colored, variegated
pavonine, iridescent
peacock, pavonine
pearly, pearl-colored
pied, spotted
piebald, colored in patches
polychromatic, polychrome
polychrome, polychromatic
prismatic, spectrumatic
punctate, spotted
rubican, grey-black
spectrumatic, prismatic
spotted, marked with spots
spotty, having spots
streaky, having streaks
(Continued on page 204)

ADJECTIVES (Continued)

striped, having stripes

tabby, variegated

tinctorial, having tincture

variegated, having various colors

vivid, intensely colored

NOUNS

Variegations, Etc.

beige, natural color

bloom, flesh-colored

cast, tinge

chiaroscuro, treatment or effect of light and shades in painting

complexion, complex color of the skin, etc.

cyanosis, blueness of the complexion due to lack of aeration

discoloration, disordered colors

distemper, opaque coloration

NOUNS (Continued)

fluorescence, a color different from an inherent color

freckle, brownish variegation

gradation, gradual blending of colors

graining, texture in imitation

grey, white mixed with black

gray, grey

grissette, treatment or effect of a solid body represented in grey tints

heliosis, variegated sunspots on leaves due to the inequality of exposure, etc.

hue, tint, shade, etc.

iridescence, coloring like that of the rainbow

primary colors, various pure colors

NOUNS (Continued)

prismatic colors, various colors formed by a prism

shade, gradation of light or color

spectrum, various colors separated by refraction through a prism

spottiness, spotted color

stain, tinged color

stripes, narrow markings

streak, line of color different from the ground color

stripe, streak

tincture, shade or tinge of color

tinge, slight degree of gradation of some color

tint, slight coloring distinct from a principal color

tone, colors in harmony

variegation, diversity of colors

PAINTS—STAINS

102D, 102E

See—(ASSOCIATIVE 102A)

102D

PAINTS—PIGMENTS—STAINS

BLACK, black pigment or dye

blacking, black polish

blacklead, plumbago

jet, deep-black variety of lignite

plumbago, lead-pencil material

BROWN, brown pigment

bister, dark-brown pigment

sepia, brown pigment

sienna, brown pigment

umber, brown pigment

BLUE, blue pigment

azure, sky-blue pigment

azure-stone, ultramarine pigment

azurite, lazulite

amethyst, violet purple or variety of quartz

bice (bise), two pigments: blue bice and green bice

blue-spar, lazulite

bluing, indigo

indigo, blue dye

induline, blue dye

lapis-lazuli, rich blue stone originally yielding ultramarine

(Continued)

lazulite, azure-blue mineral

mauve, lilac or purple aniline

purple, bluish pigment

smalt, deep-blue pigment

ultramarine, lapis-lazuli pigment

zaffer, substance of intensely blue color

RED, red pigment

azarine, bright-red dye

brazilin, red coloring

carmine, rich crimson pigment

cochineal, scarlet dye

coralline, orange-red dye

knotting, red lead for protecting metal

lake, transparent red pigment

madder, red dye and pigment of the plant rubia

magenta, red animal dye

rouge, red cosmetic

ruddle, red ochre

turacine, red pigment

vermilion, brilliant red pigment

GREEN, green pigment

(Continued)

aquamarine, pale bluish-green variety of beryl

beryl, vari-colored mineral commonly green or greenish-blue

bice, or **bise,** two pigments: green bice and blue bice

cerulean, olive-green dye

emeraldine, dark-green colored dye

patina, age-green rust or coloring on ancient coins or bronze

verdigris, blue-green which forms on copper or brass

verditer, green or blue pigment

YELLOW, yellow pigment

crocus, saffron pigment

gamboge, yellow coloring or pigment

gilding, gold-like material

ocher, or **ochre,** yellow or brown-colored coloring

saffron, deep-yellow dye or coloring

xanthein, yellow coloring matter of plants, etc.

(Continued on page 207)

HIDING—SECRECY see—

vs. Disclosure 95A

ASSOCIATIVE

Reserve	............132C	Falsehood	62
Disguise	............103B	Ambiguity	57
Mystification	........96A	Darkness	97
Dishonesty	..........130A	Dogmatism	............82A

103A

VERBS

Hide

burrow, hide
bury, hide
cache, hide provisions
conceal, hide
hide, conceal
secrete, hide

Cloak, Etc.

blind, screen
cloak, cover
cover, hide
curtain, cloak
enshroud, shroud, hide
mask, hide
screen, curtain
shelter, conceal
shroud, hide
veil, cover

Obscure

blear, obscure
darken, obscure
dim, darken
obscure, conceal
shadow, shelter, shroud

Steal

creep, steal
lurk, be concealed
stalk, steal along
steal, creep

Miscellaneous

blindfold, hoodwink
camouflage, conceal
closet, seclude
collude, do secretly
couch, conceal
dissemble, disguise, mask
eclipse, obscure
ensconce, shelter
hoodwink, blindfold
lay, place secretly
mum, hide, mask
mystify, bewilder
seclude, ensconce
smother, conceal
suppress, conceal

ADJECTIVES

Hidden

covert, concealed
concealed, hidden
cryptic, secret
disguised, hidden
hid, hidden
hidden, concealed
latent, hidden
secluded, hidden

ADJECTIVES (Continued)

Cloaked

cloaked, concealed
draped, screened
screened, hidden
sheltered, cloaked
shrouded, concealed

Inscrutable

inconspicuous, not evident
indefinite, vague
indistinct, inconspicuous
indistinguishable, hidden
imperceptible, hidden
inscrutable, hidden
invisible, hidden
obscure, covered
undefined, indistinct
vague, abstruse

Puzzling

abstruse, hidden
abstrusive, abstruse
enigmatic, evasive
enigmatical, as above
incomprehensible, hidden
indefinable, enigmatic
impenetrable, obscured
mysterious, enigmatic
mystic, occult
occult, secret
occulted, hidden
puzzling, hidden
recondite, hidden

Delusive

deceptive, illusory
delusive, deceptive
illusive, delusive
illusory, deceptive
strategic, deceptive
unreal, deceptive

Collusive

clandestine, secret
collusive, confidential
collusory, confidential
confidential, secret
esoteric, secret
intimate, confidential
privy, clandestine
secretarial, confidential
surreptitious, secret

Cautious

cautious, secret
chary, circumspect
circumspect, cautious
discreet, circumspect
prudent, circumspect
reserved, cautious
reticent, reserved

ADJECTIVES (Continued)

Evasive

creeping, sneaking
elusive, evasive
elusory, evasive
evasive, secretive
feline, furtive
furtive, secretive
insidious, secret
lurking, creeping
skulking, circumspect
sly, furtive
slow, creeping
snaky, sly
sneaking, furtive
stealthy, furtive

Quiet

mum, secretive
quiet, secluded
silent, mum
still, silent
taciturn, reserved

Private

perdu, hidden
private, secret
postern, private
retired, private
seclusive, secluded
secret, hidden
secretive, reserved
sequestered, secluded

NOUNS

Cloak

blind, a cover
cloak, cover
cover, a hiding
curtain, screen
drapery, covering
eclipse, obscuration
occultation, eclipse
obscuration, eclipse
portiere, door-curtain
screen, curtain
shade, shadowy conceal-
ment
shroud, cover
veil, concealing fabric

Inscrutability

imperceptibility, inscrutability
inscrutability, deepest
secrecy
invisibility, inscrutability
suppression, concealment

(Continued on page 207)

DISGUISE—
    PRETENTION see—

      vs. Disclosure 95A

ASSOCIATIVE

Hiding 103A	Dishonesty 130A
Mystification 96A	Darkness 97
Falsehood 62	Reserve 132C
Ambiguity 57	Dogmatism 82A

103B

VERBS

Disguise
camouflage, simulate
disguise, mask
mask, disguise
masquerade, mask
mum, mask

Falsify
copy, imitate
counterfeit, simulate
doctor, make deceptive
falsify, counterfeit
forge, simulate
misrepresent, falsify

Deceive
deceive, disguise
delude, deceive
fool, deceive
humbug, deceive

Simulate
affect, simulate
assume, simulate
attitudinize, pose
dissemble, disguise
dissimulate, disguise
enact, imitate
feign, pretend
imitate, simulate
impersonate, imitate
malinger, feign illness
personate, imitate
personify, imitate
pose, simulate
pretend, simulate
sham, pretend
simulate, imitate
soldier, simulate

Mimic
ape, imitate
mimic, imitate
mime, mimic
mock, mimic

ADJECTIVES

Disguised
disguised, masked
incog, disguised
incognita, disguised (fem.)
incognito, disguised in
  name or character
masked, disguised

False
brummagem, false
counterfeit, simulated
false, counterfeit
pseudo, false
sham, false
unreal, affected

ADJECTIVES (Continued)

Deceptive
artificial, feigned
deceitful, pretentious
deceptive, deceitful
guileful, deceitful
insincere, pretentious
ostensible, pretentious
pretentious, specious
specious, ostensible

Illusive
delusive, illusory
fantastic, unreal
illusive, delusive
illusory, deceptive
puzzling, deceptive
whimsical, fantastic

Simulating
affected, assumed
assumed, artificial
feigned, pretended
hypocritical, pretentious
imitative, simulative
sanctimonious, hypocritical
simulated, counterfeit
simulating, imitative
would-be, pretentious

Mimic
mimetic, imitative
mimic, mimetic
mock, false
pantomimic, imitative

Arrogant
arrogant, affecting
  importance
ostentatious, pretentious
pragmatic, assuming
  business airs
snobbish, pretentious
uppish, pretentious

NOUNS

Disguise
camouflage, deception
cryptography, a writing in
  disguised symbols
disguise, a masquerading
incognita, disguise
masquerade, disguise

Mask
domino, masquerade hood
loup, half mask
mask, disguise
masque, a masquerade

Falseness
copy, imitation
counterfeit, simulation
fakement, pretense

NOUNS (Continued)
falsification, fakement
forgery, simulation
sham, pretense

Deception
artifice, deception
chicane, pretense
deceit, chicane
deception, deceit
humbuggery, pretense
misrepresentation, decep-
  tion
pretense, pretension
pretension, pretext
pretext, specious excuse
quackery, pretension
speciousness, pretentious
  fairness
stratagem, deception
strategy, artifice

Illusion
delusion, deception
illusion, deception
illusiveness, deception

Simulation
affectation, simulation
dissimulation, disguise
feint, pretension
hypocrisy, pretension
impersonation, assumption
  of another person's
  form
malingering, a feigning
  illness
personification, impersonation
pose, simulation
simulation, imitation
solemnity, feigned
  seriousness

Mimicry
buffoonery, masquerading
mimicry, imitation
mockery, mimicry
mummery, masked per-
  formance
pantomime, imitation

Arrogation
arrogance, pretention to
  importance
arrogation, as above
coxcombry, pretense
ostentation, pretense
presumption, arrogance
priggism, assumed airs
snobbishness, vulgar pre-
  tention

(Continued on page 207)

NOUNS (Continued)
vanity, vain display
vaunt, vanity

Enactment
enactment, imitation
imitation, simulation
show, sham

PERSONS
camoufleur, a disguiser
chameleon, simulator
coxcomb, vain pretender
dandy, coxcomb

PERSONS (Continued)
enactor, imitator
fop, coxcomb
forger, falsifier
faker, pretender
humbug, quack
hypocrite, humbug
imitator, simulator, etc.
incognita, a woman with an assumed name
incognito, one with an assumed name

PERSONS (Continued)
jackanapes, a pretentious upstart
mimic, imitator
mummer, one who makes sport while masked
pantomimist, mimic
pretender, hypocrite
prig, coxcomb
puppy, coxcomb
quack, pretender
snob, pretentious upstart
would-be, pretender

103A (Continued)
NOUNS (Continued)

Hiding Place
cache, concealment for food
crypt, secret vault
hiding, concealment

Disguise
camouflage, concealment
disguise, mask
domino, masquerade hood
loup, half mask
mask, concealment

Puzzle
arcanum, secret
mystification, nonplus
mystery, nonplus
nonplus, puzzle
puzzle, mystery

Collusiveness
clandestinity, secrecy
collusion, secret fraud
collusiveness, secrecy
conclave, secret assembly
confidence, secret
intimacy, confidence

NOUNS (Continued)
intrigue, secret activity
privity, joint secrecy
secretaryship, privity

Caution
caution, prudence
discretion, reserve
prudence, taciturnity
reserve, secretiveness

Evasion
artifice, evasion
evasion, subterfuge
furtiveness, secrecy
slyness, stealth
stealth, secretiveness
stealthiness, stealth
subterfuge, artifice

Quiet
quiet, silence
silence, secrecy
taciturnity, reserve

Privacy
concealment, a hiding
latency, a hiding
privacy, secrecy

NOUNS (Continued)
retirement, retreat
retreat, sanctum
sanctuary, sacred privacy
sanctum, private place
sanctum-sanctorum, place of utmost privacy
seclusion, privacy
secrecy, secretiveness
secret, secret silence
secretiveness, secrecy
sequestration, seclusion
solitude, privacy

PERSONS
confidant, a confident
confident, one who holds a secret
confidante, as above (fem.)
camoufleur, one skilled in camouflage
suppressor, concealer

BEING
Cybele, goddess of the mystery in nature
sphynx, a mystery monster

PAINTS—PIGMENTS—STAINS
(Continued)
xanthophyl, yellow coloring of withering leaves
WHITING, white coloring

(Continued)
bleaching-powder, material for bleaching
ceruse, white-lead pigment

(Continued)
whitewash, coloring liquid of white

102E
PAINTS (Indefinite)
alterant, substance used in dyeing to change or modify a color
alumnia, material used in dyeing
amaranth, color-mixture
aniline, dye or coloring mixture
bezetta, a dye

(Continued)
brilliantine, material for imparting gloss
calcimine, tinting wash
chalk, crayon
color, paint or hue
(B.) colour
crayon, chalk pencil
distemper, colors for mural work

(Continued)
dye, coloring matter
enamel, coloring substance
ink, writing fluid
paint, coloring pigment
pigment, paint
stain, a dye
varnish, material for imparting a gloss

SYMBOLIZATION see—

vs. Difference 126A

104A

VERBS

Miscellaneous

emblazon, symbolize with emblematic or heraldic figures, etc.

symbolize, represent by symbols

ADJECTIVES

Miscellaneous

armorial, pertaining to the emblematic arms or escutcheons of a family

caducean, pertaining to the winged staff or insignia of Mercury

emblematic, symbolic

emblematical, as above

figurative, symbolic

figured, emblazoned

hieroglyphic, in the picturesque symbols of the ancient Egyptians

iconic, represented in symbol or image

ideographic, pertaining to symbols representative of ideas

ADJECTIVES (Continued)

imaged, figured

mystic, emblematic

mnemonic, pertaining to relative or symbolic aids

representative, symbolic

symbolic, emblematic

zoomorphic, representing animals as in carving

NOUNS

Miscellaneous

grip, symbolic sign

blazonry, heraldic emblem

death's-head, death symbol of skull and crossed bones

effigy, image

emblem, symbol

figurehead, figure symbolic of a ship's nationality, ownership, etc.

horoscope, sign or representation at the time of birth

image, symbolic figure

imagery, images collectively

NOUNS (Continued)

ideography, symbolism

keepsake, symbol, souvenir

label, ticket

memento, keepsake

mnemonics, relative symbolical aids

presentation, representation

presentment, representation

representation, symbolization

significant, symbol

simulacrum, effigy, etc.

sign, symbol

symbol, emblem

souvenir, memento

symbolism, representation by symbols

ticket, an identifying inscription, label

token, sign

zoomorphism, representation of the deity with the attributes of an animal

---

104B
SYMBOLS OF VICTORY, DISTINCTION, HONOR

Miscellaneous

achievement, symbolic escutcheon

augmentation, additional charge on a coat of arms bestowed as a mark of honor

badge, token of achievement or distinction

blazon, coat of arms, etc.

blue ribbon, symbol of honor or success

chaplet, wreath or garland symbolic of honor, victory, etc.

chevron, V-shaped symbol of rank

coronal, crown or garland

decoration, badge or insignia of honor

device, heraldic emblem

ensign, badge or symbol

epaulet, shoulder badge

escutcheon, emblazoned heraldic arms of a family

favor, token

garland, wreath of laurel or oak leaves and acorns, emblem of glory, etc.

garter, badge of the Order of the Garter

hatchment, symbolic escutcheon, or armorial bearing of a deceased person

cross, decoration for war service

insignia, badges of honor or office

iron-cross, symbol of bravery in battle

medal, symbolic coin or emblem of glory, achievement, etc.

palm, palm branch symbolic of victory, etc.

trophy, symbol of victory, success, etc.

Victoria Cross, symbol of honor or great achievement in battle

wreath, garland, chaplet, etc., symbolic of some event

croix de guerre, French decoration for bravery

104C

RELIGIOUS IMAGERY

cross, emblem of the Christian faith
crucifix, image of Christ crucified
fetish, idol
flammule, a flame symbolizing the deity
icon, sacred image or picture

(Continued)

idol, sacred image
image, idol
osculatory, image of Christ or the Virgin Mary for worshipers to kiss
pax, small crucifix
rood, cross or crucifix
sudarium, imaged napkin of Christ's face

(Continued)

totem, symbol of a tribe for worship
zoomorphism, symbolization of the deity with the attributes of an animal
thummim, breast-plate symbol of perfection worn by Jewish priests

104D

SYMBOLS OF SOVEREIGNTY RANK—OFFICE

Scepter, Etc.

baton, staff used as a badge of office, etc.
bauble, court jester's staff
fasces, ancient symbol of authority
mace, crowned staff formerly borne before judges, magistrates, etc.
scepter, staff, emblem of authority, etc.
staff, wand or badge of office, etc.
trident, scepter
truncheon, staff of authority
verge, mace
wand, staff of authority

Crown, Etc.

coronet, head-dress or insignia of an inferior crown
crown, insignia of sovereignty or regal power

(Continued)

diadem, insignia of supreme sovereignty
tiara, triple crown or insignia of the Pope, etc.

Investiture

ermine, emblem, dignity, or office of a judge, etc.
investiture, robes or symbols of office
pall, the symbolic scarf of an archbishop worn when consecrated
purple, symbolic robe of royalty
regalia, ensigns of sovereignty, etc.
toga, garb or insignia of the Roman citizen as opposed to that of the foreigner, slave, etc.

Heraldry

arms, armorial bearings
bearing, heraldic device
emblazonment, heraldry
heraldry, arms

(Continued)

spread-eagle, the heraldic emblem of the U. S. A.

Seal, Etc.

cachet, mark of distinction
seal, stamping symbol, or seal of authority or ratification
signet, seal or insignia of sovereign ratification
stamp, seal

Miscellaneous

caduceus, winged staff or insignia of Mercury
chevron, symbol on the sleeve of a noncommissioned officer
epaulet, shoulder-piece variously marked to indicate rank
throne, chair or insignia of dignity, power, etc.
thummim, breast-plate, symbol of perfection, worn by Jewish priests

104E

FLAGS, STANDARD, ETC.

banderole, mast-flag, or lancehead flag
banner, emblematic flag or cloth
black-flag, black-jack
black-jack, pirate's ensign
blue-peter, a sailing signal
color, a military or naval flag
eagle, military standard of ancient Rome
ensign, flag, badge, symbol
fanion, small banner

(Continued)

flag, cloth or bunting symbol or standard
gonfalon, standard, usually with streamers
guidon, flag of a guild or fraternity
oriflamme, ancient flame-shaped standard of France
pendant, pennant
pennant, the symbol or bunting at the masthead of a man-of-war

(Continued)

pennon, swallow-tailed flag of a war ship
standard, national ensign
streamer, narrow flag or pennon, etc.
union-jack, a national flag

BEACON—GUIDE—REMINDER

(See 98A)

104F
STEEPLE—DOME, ETC.

cupola, a spherical roof
dome, a roof symbolic of
a cathedral, etc.

(Continued)

spire, steeple above the
tower, symbolic of a
church

(Continued)

steeple, spire

104G
SYMBOLS OF PEACE, PROSPERITY, ETC.

calumet, N. American
Indian pipe, symbol of
peace.

(Continued)

cornucopia, a horn, symbol
of prosperity, plenty
key, symbol of open hospitality, etc.

(Continued)

olive-branch, symbol of
peace

104H
MONUMENTS— MEMORIALS

Miscellaneous

altar, structure for worship,
memorial
barrow, mound of earth or
stone forming the mark
of a prehistoric grave
bier, tomb
cromleich, ancient monument of rough stones
cairn, a conical heap of
stones erected as a mon-
ument
cenotaph, empty tomb or
monument of a person
buried elsewhere
column, monument,
memorial
dolmen, sepulchral monument
grave, earthen mound over
buried body
gravestone, stone placed at
a grave

(Continued)

hatchment, armorial bearings of a deceased person
placed on a tomb, in a
church, etc.
mausoleum, the sepulchral
monument of King Mau-
solus, which was regarded
as the seventh wonder,
hence a stately monu-
ment
memorial, something designed to keep in re-
membrance a person,
event, etc.
monolith, pillar or column
formed of a single stone
monument, anything designed to perpetuate the
memory of a person or
event
mound, prehistoric earth-
pile marking a burial
place, fortification, etc.

(Continued)

obelisk, lofty tapering four-
sided pillar with a pyra-
midal top
pedestal, statue
pillar, monument, etc.
pyramid, sepulchral tomb
shaped like a pyramid
sepulcher, grave or tomb
statue, memorial of a person, made of solid ma-
terial
tablet, ancestral monument
tomb, vault or monument in
memory of its dead
tope, mound-shaped Buddhist monument contain-
ing relics
totem, totempole
tower, memorial structure
tumulus, artificial hillock
raised over a grave
vault, arched tomb, etc.

106A (Continued)
NOUNS (Continued)

love-lock, extra hair-lock
ringlet, curl
tress, lock of hair

Coiffure, Etc.

coiffure, headdress
periwig, small wig
queue, tail of a wig
scalp, skin and hair of the
head
scalp-lock, the lock grown
on or scalped from the
head
toupee, wig or curl
wig, false hair

Beard, Etc.

barb, beard
beard, face-hair
goatee, goat-like tuft

NOUNS (Continued)

imperial, tuft of chin-hair
moustache, hair on the
upper lip
whiskers, hair on cheeks

Eyebrow, Etc.

brow, eye-brow
cilia, hair of the eyelids
eyebrow, hairy arch above
the eyes
eyelash, ridge of hair that
lines the eyelids

Tail

brush, hairy tuft or tail
scut, deer's tail, etc.
tail, brush, etc.

Feathers

crest, tuft of feathers on
the head

NOUNS (Continued)

estrich, ostrich down
feather, fluffy or hair-like
growth
plumage, feathers
plume, a feather

Miscellaneous

cowlick, irregular tuft of
hair on the forehead
fetlock, hair-tuft behind a
horse's pastern joint
gare, leg-wool of sheep
mane, neck-hair of animals
pelage, hair or covering of
an animal

Awn, Etc.

awn, beard on grains, etc.
floss, down on husks
villi, soft hair on plants

105

VERBS

Exemplify

bespeak, betoken
betoken, exemplify
characterize, represent by
similarities
exemplify, make a copy,
transcript, etc.
idealize, represent in likeness of a preconceived
and ideal conception
instance, exemplify
represent, render a counterpart

Compare

agree, compare
compare, resemble
correspond, be similar
identify, make, prove, or
consider as the same
liken, compare
parallel, render similar
sample, take a likeness or
equivalence

Equal

copy, make similar
duplicate, copy
equal, be similar
image, make in likeness
match, make similar
render, form into a specific
character or likeness
reprint, reproduce in type
reproduce, produce in likeness
stereotype, reproduce in
metal type

Resemble

approach, approximate
approximate, resemble
favor, appear in likeness
(B). **favour**
resemble, bear likeness
seem, resemble
simulate, approximate

Typify

model, pattern in likeness
pattern, model
paragon, pattern
excellently
standardize, conform
typify, be of a type, etc.

Identify

brand, place identity upon
label, identify
print, stamp in likeness
stamp, reproduce

VERBS (Continued)
ticket, label

Foreshadow

adumbrate, reflect
foreshadow, adumbrate
mirror, reflect in likeness
portray, depict in likeness
reflect, mirror

Equalize

balance, even
conform, correspond
equalize, render uniform
even, conform
level, even
proportion, conform

ADJECTIVES

Equivalent

alike, similar
correspondent, tantamount
duplicate, corresponding
with another
equal, equivalent
equivalent, alike, equal
homologous, identical
idealistic, having likeness
or character of a precon-
ceived ideal
identical, alike
lifelike, similar to life
like, similar
replicate, copied in likeness
same, identical
similar, like
tantamount, equal

Resembling

analogical, resembling
analogous, having similarity
approximative, resembling
comparable, conformable
conformable, in likeness
corresponding, conformable
homogeneous, composed
similarly
parallel, corresponding
resembling, similar
seeming, appearing like
seemly, alike in character

Representative

archetypic, pattern-like
characteristic, typical
exemplary, representative
figurative, illustrative
illustrative, representative
representative, characteristic

ADJECTIVES (Continued)

Compensative

affinitive, having conative
likeness
balanced, even
commensurate, equivalent
compensative, equable
equable, equal
even, level
level, even
proportional, equable

Uniformity

common, uniform
customary, usual
regular, customary
typical, in common likeness
uniform, in like form
usual, common

Adumbrative

adumbrative, casting a
faint resemblance
reflective, showing likeness

NOUNS

Example

comparison, simile
example, pattern, sample
instance, example
parallel, resemblance
precedent, example
sample, specimen
specimen, example

Equivalence

agreement, correspondence
bisymmetry, likeness of
right or left part
coincidence, agreement
correspondence, likeness
equality, likeness
equivalence, equality
identity, practical
sameness
likeness, resemblance
parity, likeness
reflection, likeness
sameness, identity
similarity, likeness
symmetry, similarity
twin, that which bears a
close resemblance
uniformity, conformity to
criterion

Resemblance

analogue, anything analogous to something else
analogy, similitude of
relations
approximation, similarity
(Continued on page 212)

NOUNS (Continued)

homogeneity, similarity
resemblance, similarity
seeming, seemliness
seemliness, likeness
similitude, similarity
vraisemblance, resemblance
  to truth

Conformity

adaptation, conformation
affinity, inherent likeness
conformation, likeness of
  adaptation
conformability, uniformity
conformity, resemblance
correlation, similarity,
  relationship

Copy

autotype, facsimile
configuration, an equivalent
  shape or form
copy, duplicate
counterpart, facsimile
double, duplicate
duplicate, counterpart
duplication, production in
  duplicate
facsimile, exact likeness

NOUNS (Continued)

homologue, similarity of
  form and analogous
  functioning
homotype, that part of an
  animal which corresponds
  with another part
image, counterpart
impression, copy
prototype, original copy
replica, copy
reproduction, counterpart
simile, likeness employed to
  illustrate
symbol, simile
type, image

Pattern

archetype, pattern
copy, pattern
criterion, standard
ecorche, manikin
example, pattern
ideal, pattern, model
manikin, model
model, pattern
original, prototype
paradigm, pattern
paragon, pattern of
  excellence

NOUNS (Continued)

pattern, model
prototype, original from
  which others are copied
rule, standard
sampler, pattern
standard, criterion
touchstone, criterion

Chart, Plan

atlas, maps
chart, diagram
design, plan
diagram, draft
draft, design
map, plan in detail
plan, draft

Reflector

glass, mirror, reflector
looking-glass, mirror
mirror, pattern
reflector, mirror
speculum, concaved mirror

BE LIKE

as   so
is   such
be   that
am   etc.
exist

HAIR AND FEATHER FORMATIONS

106A.

see— ASSOCIATIVE
  Personal Ornamentation 107B
  Beautification 107A
  Clothing 106B

vs. Conspicuous—Uncovered 95E
106A

VERBS

feather, to cover or become
  covered with feathers

ADJECTIVES

Downy, Etc.

downy, having down
feathery, having feathers
flaxen, flax-like
floccose, wooly
flocculent, wooly
flossy, downy
fluffy, feathery
furry, covered with fur
fuzzy, downy
lanate, wooly
nappy, covered with nap
pilose, hairy
pubescent, covered with
  down
velvety, downy
wooly, having fine hair

Bristly, Etc.

awny, bearded
barbate, bearded
bearded, having a beard
bristly, stiff-haired

ADJECTIVES (Continued)

bushy, shaggy
ciliated, having eyelashes
fibrillose, covered with
  small fiber
hairy, covered with hair
hirsute, shaggy, hairy
hispid, bristly
shaggy, rough with hair
tomentose, thick with hair
tufted, having a tuft
villous, tomentose

NOUNS

Down, Etc.

Angora wool, hair of the
  Angora goat
down, fine hair or feathers
finos, sheep's wool
fleece, wool
flix, soft fur
flocculence, wooly growth
flocculus, a tuft of down or
  wool-like hair
floccus, as above
flue, fluff
fluff, light down

NOUNS (Continued)

fur, soft hair
fuzz, fine down
hair, fibrous growth
nap, down
pile, the nap on cloth
tuft, bunch of hair
velvet, down
wool, fine hair

Bristle, Etc.

bristle, stiff hair
kemp, coarse hair or wool
shag, wooly mass
whisk, small bundle of hair

Curl, Etc.

bang, hair fringe across
  the forehead
buckle, curl of hair
curl, ringlet of hair
elf-lock, lock of hair intricately formed
forelock, a hair-lock
frizette, a small tuft worn
  as a bang
frizzle, crisp lock of hair
lock, tuft of hair
(Continued on page 210)

CLOTHING—CLOTH, ETC.   see ⎰

vs. Bareness, Conspicuousness 95E

106B
VERBS
Miscellaneous
apparel, clothe
array, deck or dress
accouter, dress
caparison, attire richly
clothe, put on raiment
costume, clothe fittingly
deck, array in finery
don, put on dress
drape, costume
dress, clothe
enrobe, array
garb, clothe
gear, dress, harness, etc.
habit, dress
incarnate, clothe with flesh
robe, array
shift, dress in fresh
  clothing
shoe, place shoes upon
wear, be habited

ADJECTIVES
Miscellaneous
ermined, vested in ermine
habited, wearing dress
sericeous, silky
silky, like silk

NOUNS
Act of Attiring
arrayal, act of clothing
dressing, arrayal
incarnation, act of clothing
  in flesh
wear, act of wearing
Indefinite Apparel
accouterment, dress
(B). accoutrement

NOUNS (Continued)
apparel, clothing
array, attire
arrayal, clothing
attire, vesture
caparison, rich clothing
clothes, dress
clothing, garments in
  general
costume, dress in general
covering, dress
dishabille, careless attire
drapery, costumes represented in sculpture,
  paintings, etc.
dress, clothing
duds, clothes
equipment, accouterment
finery, caparison
foppery, neat, trim, and
  ostentatious attire
frippery, old clothes, etc.
garb, dress, etc.
garment, any article of
  clothing
gear, accouterment
guise, dress, etc.
habiliment, clothing
habit, dress
harness, the accouterment
  and armor of a knight,
  etc.
livery, the particular costume worn by servants
mufti, civilian dress of naval or military officers off
  duty
outfit, clothing in general
paraphernalia, ornaments
  of dress generally

NOUNS (Continued)
rags, mean dress
raiment, clothing
regalia, ensigns of sovereignty, etc.
regimental, uniforms worn
  by troops of a regiment
rig, dress
slop, ready-made clothing
suit, corresponding attire
tailoring, tailored clothing
tatters, mean dress
toggery, clothing
togs, loose outer clothing
toilet, attire, etc.
trappings, paraphernalia
uniform, dress of distinction or place
vestment, attire
vesture, clothing
wardrobe, wearing apparel
wear, attire

PERSONS
coiffeur, hairdresser
draper, one who drapes, as
  with garments, etc.
dresser, draper
haberdasher, dealer in
  small wares
hairdresser, coiffeur
milliner, hat maker, etc.
modiste, fashionable dressmaker
seamstress, woman who
  sews
tailor, one who makes
  clothing

106C
GENERAL DEFINITE
  ATTIRE
bandoleer, ammunition belt
  worn over the shoulder
  and across the breast
bib, chin-cloth
choker, necktie
collar, neck-piece
collaret, fichu of lace
cravat, neck-piece

(Continued)
cuff, ornamental band for
  the wrist
dicky, shirt-front
fichu, collar-like neck-piece
four-in-hand, necktie
glove, covering for the
  hand
mitten, fingerless glove
mourning, dress for a
  mourner

(Continued)
necktie, cravat
ruff, frilled collar
scarf, tie
shawl, large scarf
sleeve, covering for the
  arm
stock, stiff cravat
tie, cravat
veil, face covering

106D

ATTIRE FOR BOTH SEXES

academicals, costumes worn by university students
blazer, bright-colored jacket
caftan, kaftan
cape, shoulder covering
cardigan, knitted jacket
cloak, sleeveless garment
coat, upper garment
comforter, long scarf
cutaway, a style of coat
dishabille, negligent attire
dressing-gown, gown worn while dressing
dolman, Turkish outer garment
fleshings, flesh-colored tights
fustanelle, shirt worn by modern Greeks
gabardine, mock-frock formerly prescribed for Jews

(Continued)

garibaldi, a blouse-shaped shirt
guernsey, woolen shirt
haik, Arab's garment
jacket, tailless coat
jerkin, coat or jacket
jersey, close-fitting shirt
kaftan, oriental vest
kilt, petticoat of the Scotch highlanders
kirtle, upper garment
mackintosh, rain-coat
muffler, wrapper
mantle, cloak or cape
masquerade, the dress of masqueraders
overcoat, outside coat
pall, cloak or mantle
pinafore, loose apron
plaid, checkered cloth of the Scotch highlanders
poncho, loose garment
raglan, loose cloak
redingote, long coat
reefer, short jacket

(Continued)

robe, outer garment
roundabout, coat or jacket
scarf, neckcloth
serape, blanket or shawl worn by Mexicans
shawl, shoulder cloth
shirt, under garment
shroud, attire for the dead
spencer, short jacket
surtout, long coat
surcoat, overcoat
sweater, knitted outer-garment
tights, close-fitting garb
tippet, narrow cape
toga, loose outer garment worn by Romans
ulster, overcoat
vest, short body-garment
victorine, fur cape
visite, light cape
waterproof, storm-coat
wrap, shawl
wrapper, upper garment

106E

MALE ATTIRE

banian, loose gown for men
bolero, short jacket worn by bullfighters, etc.
breeches, garment for men
coat, outer garment
doublet, close-fitting man's garment
duck, sailors' clothing worn in hot climates
frock-coat, a coat

(Continued)

fustanella, shirt worn by modern Greeks
jumper, workman's jacket
knickerbockers, wide breeches gathered in below the knees
overalls, outer garb
pantaloon, trousers
pants, trousers
peajacket, seaman's jacket

(Continued)

smock-frock, outer shirt worn in farm-work
tabard, mantle worn over armor, etc.
trousers, breeches
tuxedo, coat for light occasions
waist-coat, sleeveless coat

106F

FEMININE OUTER GARMENTS

apron, dress covering
basque, woman's jacket
bib, child's clothes-protector worn in front
bloomer, female costume
blouse, loose overgarment
bodice, close-fitting waist or body of a woman's dress
capote, long mantle for a woman
cardinal, woman's short cloak with a hood
crinoline, hoopskirt
Dolly Varden, a brightly figured dress
farthingale, hoopskirt
frock, dress
gown, outer garment

(Continued)

hobble-skirt, close-fitting skirt
jumper, frock
kimono, loose outer robe of the Japanese
mantilla, woman's light cloak
mourning, the dress of a mourner
negligee, loosely fitting gown or dress
obi, Japanese shawl
opera cloak, evening dress worn at the theater
pelerine, long cape with tapering ends
pelisse, woman's silk habit
placket, a petticoat
polonaise, a body and skirt made together

(Continued)

robe, loose outer garment
sash, scarf, etc., worn around the waist or over the shoulder
scarf, sash
shawl, shoulder-cloth
shirtwaist, woman's blouse
skirt, a lower garment
skirting, skirts collectively
slip, outer garment
smock, smock-frock, chemise
tablier, over-shirt
trousseau, bride's outfit
weeds, a widow's mourning garments
wrapper, loose outer garment

106G
WOMAN'S UNDERWEAR
Miscellaneous

brassiere, a woman's underwaist
bustle, pad worn beneath the skirt
chemise, a woman's undergarment
chemisette, short chemise worn over the breast
corsage, a bodice
corset, a bodice
drawers, underwear for both sexes

(Continued)

guimpe, chemisette
linen, underclothing
lingerie, underclothing
nightgown, a gown worn at night
nightshirt, a shirt worn at night
pajamas, a kind of sleeping costume
pantalettes, loose drawers for women and children

(Continued)

petticoat, loose underskirt
shirt, an undergarment
shift, a chemise
stomacher, ornamental breast covering
smock, chemise
tucker, a linen or other shading for the breasts of women
tunic, an undergarment worn in ancient Rome
underwear, underclothing

106H
HEADDRESS OR COVERING
Crown, Etc.

coronet, inferior crown
crown, royal headdress
diadem, tiara
tiara, Pope's crown

Ecclesiastical Cap

amice, a former headdress worn by the clergy
biretta, a square ecclesiastical cap
capouch, cowl
cowl, monk's hood
domino, ecclesiastical hood
miter, headdress of Jewish high priests
wimple, nun's head-covering

Cap

calotte, skull-cap
cap, a brimless hat
caul, a head covering
zuchetto, a skull-cap

Helmet, Etc.

chapeau, a hat (French)
helmet, head armor
kepi, a military cap
sallet, helmet

(Continued)

shako, a military cap

Hats (Miscellaneous)

bonnet, a woman's hat
calash, a woman's hood
cardinal, a woman's hood or cloak
crush-hat, collapsible hat
derby, stiff hat
fez, close-fitting felt hat
hat, head covering
headdress, head covering
hood, head covering
leghorn, a bonnet
maharmah, head and face covering worn in Turkey
millinery, woman's headdress
mobcap, woman's headdress
sombrero, broad-brimmed hat
sunbonnet, sun hat
tam o' shanter, cap with a large flat top
tarboosh, oriental's fez
tile, a hat
toque, bonnet
turban, oriental's headdress

(Continued)

vizor, forepiece of a cap

Wig, Etc.

chignon, a hair roll for the head or coiffure
frizette, rat or hair-pad
periwig, a small wig
peruke, a wig
toupee, small wig or curl
wig, false hair for the head

Plait, Queue, Etc.

coiffure, headdress
cue, queue
pigtail, long hair-twist
plait, braided hair
queue, the tail of a wig
tress, braid or lock of hair

Plume

aigret, a plume on a helmet or woman's hat
crest, plume of feathers
plume, a head-feather

Fillet, Etc.

bandeau, a head-ribbon
braid, a fillet
fillet, a hair-band
snood, a hair-ribbon

106I
ECCLESIASTICAL ATTIRE

alb, white priestly vestment worn by Catholic clergy
amice, neck-piece worn by priests
biretta, ecclesiastical square cap
canonicals, dress worn by the clergy when officiating
capouch, cowl

(Continued)

cassock, a close-fitting ecclesiastical garment
cloth, ecclesiastical attire
cope, semicircular vestment worn by certain ecclesiastics
cowl, monk's hood
dalmatic, tunic worn by deacon during ceremonials
domino, ecclesiastical hood

(Continued)

ephod, priestly vestment
gremial, ecclesiastical vestment
maniple, a priest's scarf
miter, headdress of Jewish priests
orphrey, gold or silver bands worn across the front by an ecclesiast
pall, ecclesiastical robe
(Continued on page 216)

106I (Continued)
ECCLESIASTICAL ATTIRE (Continued)

pontificals, the full dress worn by an officiating priest or bishop

rochet, vestment worn by a bishop

scapular, part of the habit of certain ecclesiastics

soutane, priest's cassock

(Continued)

surplice, white garment worn over other dress by the clergy

stole, long scarf worn by bishops, etc.

thummim, breastplate symbol of perfection, worn by Jewish priests, etc.

(Continued)

tiara, pope's crown

tunicle, close-fitting vestment worn by Catholic bishops, etc.

vestment, priestly attire

106J
FOOTWEAR AND LEG-WEAR

babboosh, oriental slippers
Balmoral, laced boots
blucher, strong half-boot
bootees, small boots
boots, heavy footwear
brogans, heavy shoes
brogues, brogans
buckskins, leather shoes
buskin, a high shoe
clog, wooden shoe
footwear, wear for the feet
gaiter, ankle covering
galosh, an overshoe
greaves, covering for protecting the legs from ankle to knee

(Continued)

highlows, laced shoes reaching to the ankles
hose, foot and leg covering
hosiery, stockings
hessian, top-boots
jackboots, boots reaching above the knees
leggings, low gaiters
moccasins, deerskin sandals of N. American Indians
patten, wooden shoe for wet weather
pump, a light shoe
puttee, leggings
rubbers, overshoes

(Continued)

sabot, wooden shoes of the French peasant
shoes, footwear
sandals, a kind of shoe
ski, snowshoes
slipper, a low shoe
snowshoes, shoes for walking on snow
socks, short stockings
spatterdashes, leggings
stockings, coverings for the lower limbs
top-boots, high boots with light-colored tops
wellingtons, long-legged boots of the 19th century

106K
CLOTH, LEATHER, ETC.

Leather, Skin

astrakhan, young lamb's skin
basil, tanned sheepskin
budge, dressed lambskin
chamois, soft leather
cordovan, Spanish goatskin leather
cowhide, tanned cow skin
kip, untanned young skin
lambskin, skin with wool on
leather, tanned skin
leatherette, imitation leather
nutria, the fur or skin of the otter, etc.
pelt, raw hide
parchment, skin
shagreen, tanned skins of various animals
shammy, chamois
skin, pelt

Cloth

alamode, thin, black silk
alpaca, fabric made from the silky wool of the alpaca

(Continued)

Angora, Angora-wool cloth
bagging, coarse cloth
baize, coarse woolen stuff
balayeuse, plaited muslin
batiste, cambric
Bengaline, a fabric made of silk and hair
Bengal-Stripes, a gingham with colored stripes
bergamot, tapestry
bezan, Bengal cotton cloth
blanketing, blanket-cloth
bombazet, thin woolen cloth
bombazine, twilled cloth
book-muslin, fine muslin
broadcloth, woolen cloth with smooth finish
brocade, silk variegated with gold, silver and flowers
brocatel, figured fabric of silky texture
buckram, coarse linen cloth
bunting, flag-cloth
cabeca, Indian silk
calico, cloth with printed designs on one side

(Continued)

cambric, fine linen
cambric-muslin, cotton cambric
camlet, finely woven fabric
canvas, coarse cloth
carpeting, carpet-cloth
cassimere, twilled cloth
cassinette, cloth of mixed materials
cashmere, dress fabric in imitation of that made of the downy hair of Cashmere goats
cerecloth, waxed cloth
cerement, shroud-cloth
challis, light fabric
cheviot, rough wool cloth
chiffon, gauze fabric
chintz, printed cloth
clout, cloth for patching or other uses
corduroy, stout cotton fabric
cloth, woven fabric
cotillion, woolen shirt material in black and white

(Continued on page 217)

CLOTH, LEATHER, ETC.
(Continued)

cotton, cotton cloth
crash, heavy linen
cravenette, waterproof cloth
crape, thin black gauze
crepon, crepe-like material of wool, silk, etc.
cretonne, printed fabric
crewel, twisted worsted
damask, silk fabric elaborately patterned
delaine, light fabric
dimity, cotton cloth
doeskin, fine woolen cloth
dowlas, coarse linen cloth
drilling, twilled cloth
drugget, woolen fabric
duck, strong linen untwilled fabric
everlasting, stout woolen material
fabric, woven, felted, or knitted material
faille, soft untwilled silk
felt, fabric of pressed materials
felting, felt
flannel, soft cloth
flannelette, soft cotton cloth
forel, parchment for book-covers
foulard, light silk or cotton fabric
frieze, shaggy cloth
fustian, twilled cotton
galatea, striped fabric
galloon, cotton, silk or worsted fabric
gauze, light silk or cotton fabric
genappe, worsted yarn
gimp, interlaced silk
gingham, cotton dress cloth dyed in the yarn before weaving
glace, thin shiny silk
gossamer, gauze fabric
grenadine, gauzy dress fabric
gros, silk fabric
grosgrain, stout silk

(Continued)

gunny, coarse sack-cloth
gurrah, coarse muslin
hammercloth, cloth for coach-box covers
holland, fine linen
homespun, heavy cloth
huckaback, toweling cloth
jaconet, cotton material
kalmuck, hairy cloth
kendal, coarse green cloth
kersey, smooth cloth
khaki, light-drab cloth
lasting, twilled fabric used for making shoes
lawn, fine cambric
leno, cotton gauze
linen, cloth made of flax
longcloth, superior cotton cloth
luster, lustrous dress-cloth (B). lustre
melton, broadcloth
miniver, squirrel fur
mohair, fabric made of Angora-goat hair
moleskin, twilled fustian cloth
moreen, figured woolen fabric
mousseline-de-laine, woolen dress material
mousseline-de-soie, silk-muslin
mull, muslin cloth
muslin, thin cotton fabric
muslinet, coarse muslin
nacarat, dyed linen or crape
nainsook, thick muslin
nankeen, buff cotton fabric
organdy, a muslin
organzine, silk fabric
osnaburg, coarse linen
percale, cotton fabric with a linen finish
pique, figured cotton fabric
plaid, checkered woolen cloth
plush, woolen velvet
pongee, inferior kind of silk
poplin, fabric of silk and worsted

(Continued)

rag, fragment of cloth
ratteen, twilled fabric
rattinet, inferior ratteen
ruche, frilled lace or silk
sackcloth, coarse cloth
sacking, coarse cloth for making sacks
sarcenet, fine woven silk used for ribbons, linen, etc.
sateen, closely woven cotton fabric in imitation of silk
satin, closely woven glossy silk
satinet, thin satin
serge, twilled woolen fabric
shalloon, twilled worsted
shirting, material for shirts
shot-silk, silk fabric
silesia, linen cloth
silk, cloth made of silk
skirting, cloth material for skirts
stuff, textile fabrics
taffeta, fine glossy silk
tammy, woolen or worsted cloth
tapestry, ornamented textile fabric
tarlatan, dress muslin
tarpaulin, canvas
tartan, woolen cloth
tat, coarse cloth
tiffany, thin gauze or silk
tinsel, cloth ornamented with gold and silver
tissue, fabric
toweling, cloth for towels
tobine, twilled silk fabric
tweed, wooly cloth
twill, fabric
Valentia, coat material
velvet, silk fabric
velveteen, imitation velvet
web, thread-like material
webbing, cotton fabric
wigan, cotton fabric
woolen, cloth made of wool
worsted, cloth fabric

ORNAMENTATION	See—	ASSOCIATIVE

107A

VERBS

Ornament

adorn, beautify
beautify, embellish
bedeck, adorn
bishop, trick a horse
decorate, adorn
elaborate, adorn
embellish, make beautiful
garnish, decorate
ornament, beautify
plume, deck with showy finery
prettify, make pretty
trick, decorate
trim, decorate

Grace

enrich, embellish
fashion, grace
glorify, beautify
grace, adorn

Damask

damask, work flowers upon
damaskeen, decorate with metallic designs
flower, ornament with flowers

Chase, Inlay

chase, beautify with embossing, etc.
emboss, raise a design upon a surface
inlay, ornament

Beglitter

bead, adorn with beads
bedizen, bedeck with vulgar finery
bejewel, ornament with jewelry
bespangle, adorn with spangles
spangle, adorn with spangles
tinsel, adorn with tinsel

Illumine

blazon, embellish
brighten, make gay
emblazon, make bright or brilliant
illuminate, adorn with lights
illumine, brighten

VERBS (Continued)

Gild, Etc.

braze, ornament with brass
bronze, ornament with bronze
gild, adorn with gold
nickel, plate with nickel
plate, adorn with metal
silver, plate with silver

Polish

burnish, polish
furbish, polish
planish, polish
polish, make glossy

Flute, Border

crimp, adorn with flutes
embroider, embellish with needlework
festoon, decorate with festoons
fillet, adorn with a fillet
flounce, adorn with a flounce
fluff, ornament with feathers
fret, ornament with interlaced work
hemstitch, adorn with an ornamental stitch
plait, braid or interweave
purl, fringe with a waved edge
scallop, ornament with a curved edge
scollop, scallop
tuft, adorn with tufts

Marcel, Etc.

curl, make ringlets
frizz, frizzle
frizzle, curl the hair
marcel, wave the hair
wave, curl

Smarten

perk, make trim or smart
prank, prink
preen, trim or primp
prim, deck with affected nicety
primp, dress one's self in a prim manner
prink, deck in ostentatious finery
smarten, decorate
tidy, make neat
titivate, make smart

VERBS (Continued)

Attire

accouter, array in dress
(B). accoutre
apparel, array
array, deck
attire, adorn
drape, dress
dress, embellish

Enrobe

caparison, array with rich dress
costume, array in costume
deck, array in finery
enrobe, attire
robe, array

ADJECTIVES

Miscellaneous

cosmetic, beautifying
decorative, embellishing
elaborate, highly ornamental
ornamental, decorative
tonsorial, pertaining to a barber

NOUNS

Miscellaneous

adornment, embellishment
applique, a method of ornamentation
appointment, adornment
beautification, adornment
bon-ton, adornment in the height of fashion
chic, Parisian elegance in dress
decoration, embellishment
elaboration, beautification
embellishment, ornamentation
emblazonment, embellishment
emblazonry, decoration as with heraldic devices
fagoting, a method of ornamenting fabrics
finish, careful elaboration
garnish, embellishment
garnishment, embellishment
garniture, embellishment
ornamentation, adornment
(Continued on page 219)

107B
ORNAMENTAL ARTICLES FOR PERSONS, ETC.

Adornment
adornment, an embellishment
beautyspot, spot for heightening beauty
embellishment, ornamentation
finery, personal adornment
fixing, ornamentation
garnish, an ornament
garniture, embellishment
improver, device for improving personal appearance, etc.
ornament, adornment
ornamentation, ornament
trappings, dress ornamentation
trimming, embellishment

Bauble, Etc.
bauble, a trifle finery
bead, an ornamentation
beading, beads for ornamentation
bijou, any small and elegant article
brooch, ornamental clasp
bugle, glass bead
button, ornament or convenience for clothing
chatelaine, bunched trinkets worn by ladies
gewgaw, bauble
spangle, glittering ornament
tassel, ornamental pendant
trinket, small ornament

Bouquet, Etc.
bouquet, nosegay
boutonniere, buttonhole bouquet
flower, figured ornament
nosegay, bouquet
posy, bunch of flowers

Bowknot
bow, ornamental knot
bowknot, bow
favor, bunch of ribbons worn on special occasions
(B). favour
rose, knot of ribbons

(Continued)
rosette, cluster of ribbons arranged like a rose
tuft, ornamental bunch or knot

Plume, Curl, Etc.
feather, plume, etc.
marcel, hair-wave effect
plumage, showy raiment
plume, feathery ornament
ringlet, curl

Lace, Etc.
Brussels-lace, lace made in Brussels
cordonnet, slightly raised border of point-lace
embroidery, ornamental work of gold, silver, silk, etc.
filigree, gold or silver lacery
fret, interlaced work
grille, lattice-like lace
guipure, heavy lace
Honiton-lace, a lace
insertion, embroidery, etc.
knotting, lace-work
lace, woven ornamentation
lisle, fine lace
orphrey, costly embroidery
orris, gold or silver lace
ruche, plaited lace, etc., for edging dresses
tatting, narrow lace for edging
tinsel, gold and silver lacery; anything showy

Edging, Frill, Etc.
border, edging
cartouch, ornament in the form of an open scroll
chenille, dress-trimming
chevron, fret ornament
edging, ornamental edge
festoon, garland hanging in a curve
flounce, decorative trimming
flouncing, material for a flounce
frill, ruffling, etc.

(Continued)
frilling, as above
fringe, ornamental border
furbelow, plaited flounce
galloon, cotton or silk dress trimming
pinking, figured or scalloped ornamentation
purl, puckered border
ruffle, plaited ornamentation

Band, Etc.
bandlet, a small band
band, belt
cockade, ribbon worn on the hat
ribbon, fillet or strip of silk

Belt
baldric, belt worn around the waist or over the shoulder and across the breast
belt, girdle
girdle, belt
Sam Brown, a baldric

Wreath
chaplet, wreath
garland, chaplet or wreath made of flowers
wreath, garland or chaplet

Cane
cane, stick
stick, walking-stick
walking-stick, cane affected in walking

Miscellaneous
afghan, a bright carriage robe
arras, tapestry
bishop, woman's dress improver
brocade, gold and silver flowered silk stuff
brocatelle, figured fabric of silky texture
bustle, underskirt pad
collar, neck-piece
tapestry, fabric with raised ornamentation
tidy, ornamental covering

107A (Continued)

PERSONS
barber
beautifier
decorator

PERSONS (Continued)
elaborator
jeweler
(B). jeweller

PERSONS (Continued)
trimmer
manicurist

107C
JEWELS, ETC.

anklet, ankle ornament
bangle, ankle or wrist ornament
bijou, a jewel
bijouterie, jewelry or small articles of virtue
bort, inferior diamond
bloodstone, dark-green stone
bracelet, wrist ornament
brait, rough diamond
brilliant, brilliant diamond
brooch, ornamental clasp
cabochon, unpolished gem
cacholong, pearl opal
cameo, stone with figures in relief
carbuncle, deep-red gem
chain, linked metal or jewelry

(Continued)

chrysolite, green gem
demantoid, emerald
diamond, brilliant gem
earring, ear pendant
emerald, deep-green gem
garnet, precious gem
gem, precious stone
girasol, fire-opal
gold, precious metal
hyacinth, variety of zircon used as a jewel
intaglio, gem with a design cut into its surface
jewel, precious stone
jewelry, jewels collectively
(B). **jewellry**
lapis lazuli, rich-blue stone
la valliere, neck-piece
locket, small case used as a pendant

(Continued)

moonstone, translucent stone with pearly reflections
necklace, jewelry worn around the neck
opal, milk-hued stone
pearl, iridescent gem from the pearl oyster
pendant, earring
ruby, carmine-red gem
sapphire, blue gem
sard, deep-red stone
silver, precious metal
sunburst, diamond ornament
topaz, gem in various colors
torque, twisted necklace worn in ancient times
turquoise, precious stone

107D
SEMI-PRECIOUS STONES

agate, variety of quartz
amethyst, violet-purple quartz
beryl, mineral of blue and green variations
bullion, uncoined gold
chalcedony, variety of quartz

(Continued)

coral, mineral polyps, etc.
heliotrope, green-colored chalcedony
jade, green, translucent stone
jasper, many-shaded variety of quartz
onyx, variety of agate

(Continued)

peridot, greenish, semi-precious stone
plasma, grass-green variety of chalcedony
spinel, mineral of various colors

107E
NON-PERSONAL ORNAMENTATION

accolade, molding
astragal, ornamental strip
bratticing, ornamental cresting
bric-a-brac, fancy ware
buhl, inlaying
carpet, patterned floor-cloth
cartouch, open scroll
corbel, figured projection
curio, bric-a-brac
engrailment, embellishing ring around the edge of coin or medal
epergne, ornamental stand for holding flowers, etc.
faience, decorated majolica ware

(Continued)

festoon, hanging decorations
foliage, architectural decoration
fretwork, open ornamental work
frieze, ornamented tablature
gaslog, imitation log in a fireplace
gaud, finery
gimcrack, useless pretty thing
glome, cluster of flowers
gobelin, French tapestry
guilloche, twisted ornamentation
kickshaw, knickknack

(Continued)

knickknack, ornamental trifle
lambrequin, festooned drapery
linoleum, floor-cloth
molding, ornamental strip
parterre, ornamental series of flower beds
patera, flat ornament on a frieze
pendant, hanging ornament
perianth, floral envelope
portiere, hanging curtain
rug, floor cover
tapestry, ornamented fabric
tracery, design on stone, etc.

BEAUTY—ELEGANCE, ETC.   see—

ASSOCIATIVE

108

VERBS

Miscellaneous

adorn, grace
beam, be radiant
bewitch, enchant
brighten, shine
captivate, charm
charm, enchant
dazzle, sparkle
delight, enrapture
enchant, entrance
enrapture, charm
entrance, ravish
fascinate, charm
felicitate, delight
glow, beam
grace, radiate charm
infatuate, captivate
ravish, transport
shine, glow
sparkle, dazzle
thrill, enrapture
transport, enchant
(See Ornamentation 107A)

ADJECTIVES

Beautiful

beautiful, charming
beauteous, beautiful
bonny, handsome
buxom, comely
comely, handsome
fair, handsome
handsome, attractive
lovely, adorable
pretty, comely

Charming

alluring, charming
attractive, alluring
bewitching, charming
captivating, alluring
charming, fascinating
engaging, attractive
enchanting, charming
entrancing, fascinating
fascinating, captivating
glamorous, enchanting
magnetic, attractive
rapturous, fascinating
winning, attractive
winsome, pretty

Elegant

dainty, elegant

ADJECTIVES (Continued)

delicate, delightful
elegant, exquisite, graceful
exquisite, delicate
fine, exquisite
graceful, elegant
nice, dainty, delicate
refined, exquisite
rich, beautiful
sweet, attractive

Admirable

admirable, attractive
adorable, admirable
delectable, delightful
delicious, highly pleasing
delightful, affording delight

Grand

august, grand
dignified, stately
grand, magnificent
majestic, magnificent
manly, dignified
noble, magnificent
princely, magnificent
proud, stately
queenly, adorable
regal, royal
royal, majestic
stately, majestic

Impressive

imposing, stately
impressive, imposing
lofty, stately
pompous, grand
portly, stately
prepossessing, attractive

Striking

amazing, marvelous
astounding, amazing
glorious, magnificent
gorgeous, resplendent
magnificent, grand in appearance
marvelous, wonderful
(B). marvellous
remarkable, marvelous
romantic, fascinating
splendid, magnificent
spectacular, wonderful
striking, remarkable
stunning, remarkably fine

ADJECTIVES (Continued)

sumptuous, magnificent
superb, elegant
surprising, striking
thrilling, wonderful
wonderful, amazing

Matchless

consummate, classic
excellent, consummate
exceptional, superior
faultless, perfect
incomparable, sublime
inimitable, matchless
matchless, incomparable
peerless, matchless
perfect, consummate
recherche, matchless
surpassing, superb
superior, surpassing
superlative, consummate
unrivaled, inimitable

Resplendent

brilliant, gorgeous
dazzling, gorgeous
glittering, brilliant
lustral, bright
refulgent, splendid
resplendent, brilliant
scintillant, sparkling
sparkling, resplendent

Immaculate

chaste, pure
immaculate, virgin
innocent, clean
pure, untainted
simple, fine
snowy, chaste
spotless, unsullied
stainless, innocent
undefiled, untarnished
virgin, pure

Esthetic

aesthetic, see esthetic
Attic, classic, elegant
celestial, sublime
classic, ideal
columbine, sublime
divine, sublime
esthetic, classic
(B). aesthetic
ideal, aesthetic
(Continued on page 222)

ADJECTIVES (Continued)
seraphic, sublime
sublime, celestial

Ornate
adorned, ornate
arabesque, ornate
beautified, finished
callisthentic, adorned with physical beauty
decorated, ornate
elaborate, finished
embellished, adorned
figured, adorned
floriated, beflowered
flowery, floriated
finished, highly elaborated
luxuriant, ornate, florid
ornate, beautified
picturesque, beautiful
prettified, embellished
rosy, charming
shapely, handsome
sightly, pleasing

Chic, Etc.
alamode, stylish
chic, elegantly dressed
dandified, nobby
dapper, trim
dressy, pleasingly attired
fashionable, alamode
gay, elegantly attired
genteel, fashionable
modish, stylish
natty, neat
neat, tidy, nice
nobby, modish
prim, formally neat
smirky, spruce
spruce, neat
sleek, dapper
smug, prim
smart, spruce
stylish, fashionable
tidy, trim
tricksy, pretty
trim, neat

Graceful
graceful, lithe
lissom, graceful
lithe, lissom
lithesome, graceful
supple, lithe

ADJECTIVES (Continued)
Debonair, Etc.
bland, suave
chivalrous, gallant
courtly, elegant
courteous, polite
debonair, elegant
felicitous, delightful
gallant, courteous
gentle, courteous
gracious, felicitous
polite, gentle
suave, urbane
urbane, elegant

Becoming
becoming, seemly
decorous, becoming
seemly, comely

NOUNS
Miscellaneous
beau-ideal, faultless beauty
beauty, the quality which gives the eye intense pleasure
bloom, fresh beauty
brilliancy, sparkling beauty
charm, fascinating beauty
chic, Parisian elegance and beauty in dress
comeliness, beauty
delicacy, luxuriousness of appearance
dignity, stateliness
eclat, splendor
elegance, beauty
fairness, comeliness
glamour, splendor
goodliness, grace
gorgeousness, resplendence
grace, elegance
grandeur, magnificence
handsomeness, beauty
loveliness, the quality of being lovely, admirable, etc.
magnificence, grandness of appearance
majesty, grandeur
pomposity, stateliness
portliness, stateliness
prettiness, comeliness
pride, elegance

NOUNS (Continued)
radiance, brilliant splendor
refinement, exquisiteness
resplendence, magnificence
shapeliness, comeliness
sightliness, pleasing appearance
splendor, magnificence
(B). splendour
stateliness, dignity
sublimity, grandeur
urbanity, refinement
pulchritude, beauty

MISCELLANEOUS BEAUTY
butterfly
peacock
flower
lily
rose
etc., etc.

PERSONS—BEAUTY GODS
Adonis, a youth of rare beauty
Antinous, a beautiful youth, favorite of the Emperor Adrian
Aphrodite, Greek goddess of beauty, love, etc.
Apollo, god of youth and manly beauty
belle, a reigning beauty
beau, a handsome man, a dandy
cherub, a beautiful child
Cupid, Roman god of love, etc.
goddess, a woman of superior charm
Hebe, goddess of youth, etc.
Houri, nymph of the Mohammedan Paradise
Hyperion, Helois, or the sun-god, incarnation of light and beauty
Narcissus, a handsome youth who fell in love with his reflected image
nymph, handsome young woman
Venus, goddess of beauty and love

UGLINESS—QUEERNESS

vs. Beauty—Comeliness 108

109A

VERBS
(See Dirtiness, 129A)
(See Disorder, 125A)

ADJECTIVES

Ugly

dowdy, inelegant
gross, unseemly
inelegant, unseemly
unbecoming, unseemly
ugly, offensive to the eye
unlovely, unseemly
unseemly, unbecoming
unsightly, ugly

Plain

homely, plain-featured
ordinary, plain
plain, devoid of beauty
simple, plain
unimposing, unimpressive
unimpressive, plain

Unadorned

bald, bare
bald-headed, without hair
bare, unadorned
naked, bare
nude, naked
stark, bare
unadorned, plain
unembellished, bare

Faded

faded, withered
haggard, hollow-eyed
passe, worn out
weazen, withered
withered, faded
wizen, weazen

Incongruous

antiquated, archaic
archaic, old-fashioned
baroque, grotesque
bizarre, grotesque
freakish, queer
incongruous, absurd
nondescript, queer
odd, queer
outlandish, incongruous
peculiar, odd
preposterous, absurd
quaint, singular
queer, peculiar
rococo, debased in style
of ornamentation
singular, peculiar
strange, queer

Whimsical

absurd, ridiculous

ADJECTIVES (Continued)

curious, queer
flamboyant, grotesque
funny, queer
grotesque, incongruous
ludicrous, incongruous
ridiculous, absurd
risible, ridiculous
whimsical, odd in appearance

Ungraceful

awkward, ungraceful
clumsy, unseemly
gawky, graceless
graceless, unseemly
impolite, indecorous
uncouth, ungainly
ungainly, unbecoming
ungraceful, ungainly

Indecorous

indecent, indecorous
indecorous, unseemly in
conduct
obscene, indecent
offensive, abominable
shameless, indecent
unblushing, shameless

Beastly

apish, ape-like
baboonish, baboon-like
barbaric, unshaved
beastly, beast-like
gorgonean, hideous
grisly, terrible
monstrous, horrible

Horrible

abhorrent, repulsive
abominable, odious
appalling, horrible
dreadful, horrible
fearful, frightful
forbidding, repulsive
frightful, grotesque
ghastly, horrible
gruesome, horrible
hideous, offensive
horrible, hideous
horrid, horrible
odious, offensive
repulsive, disgusting

Odious

disgusting, repulsive
loathsome, offensive
mawkish, loathsome
nasty, loathsome
odious, loathsome

NOUNS

Miscellaneous

abomination, monstrosity
absurdity, unseemliness
baboonery, baboon-like
conduct
curiosity, oddity
dreadfulness, frightfulness
eyesore, extreme ugliness
fright, ridiculous attire
frightfulness, abomination
frippery, ridiculous appearance in old clothes
gorgoneion, a gorgon-like
mask
homeliness, plainness
horribleness, frightfulness
impoliteness, indecorum
incivility, impoliteness
indecency, indecorum
indecorum, unseemliness
inelegance, unseemliness
monstrosity, hideousness
nastiness, repulsiveness
nondescript, something
strange
obscenity, vulgarity
oddity, curiosity
repulsiveness, abomination
ridiculousness, absurdity
slouchiness, ungainliness
staleness, triteness
triteness, unloveliness
ugliness, unloveliness
unloveliness, absence of
beauty
vulgarity, nastiness

PERSONS

beldam, an ugly old woman
bugaboo, bugbear
bugbear, object of terror
fright, a ridiculous person
goblin, a frightful creature
gorgon, a repulsively ugly
woman
gorgonia, a horrible
monster
guy, oddly dressed person
hag, an ugly old woman
monster, frightful being
nondescript, an odd person
ogre, a frightful monster
scarecrow, a cause of
fright
slouch, an ungainly fellow

109B

VERBS

(See Error—Defect....126C)
(See Disorder................125A)

ADJECTIVES

Deformed

abnormal, deformed
crippled, deformed
crooked, deformed
deformed, ill-formed
disfigured, injured in form
disproportioned, abnormal
distorted, unshapely
lumpy, having lumps
lame, crippled
malformed, deformed
shapeless, disfigured
unfeatured, deformed

Beefy

beefy, corpulent
bulky, gross
corpulent, gross
dumpy, abnormally short
dwarfish, stunted in shape
 or form
fat, corpulent
gross, thick
hulking, bulky
obese, corpulent
squat, short and fat
stout, corpulent

Flabby

bloated, swollen
flabby, puffy
protuberant, swollen
puffed, pursy
pursy, swollen
swollen, bloated
tumid, swollen

Shriveled

shriveled, wizen
shrunken, shriveled
wasted, withered
weazen, wizen
withered, shriveled
wizen, wasted

Thin

lank, slender
lanky, lank

ADJECTIVES (Continued)

lean, thin
peakish, having thin
 features
skinny, lank
slabsided, flat-sided
slim, lank
thin, slim

Bony

bony, lean
gaunt, bony
gnarled, knotty
rawboned, having protrud-
 ing bones
scraggy, rawboned

Humpbacked

bent, stooped
gibbous, hunchbacked
humpbacked, hunchbacked
hunchbacked, humped in
 the back
stooped, humpbacked

Bow-legged, Etc.

bow-legged, having bowed
 legs
club-footed, having a club-
 like foot
flat-footed, having flat
 feet
knock-kneed, having bent-
 in knees
pigeon-toed, toeing in
slue-footed, having feet
 that turn or twist when
 walking

Flat-nosed

flat-nosed, simous
platyrhine, broad-nosed
simous, flat-nosed

Miscellaneous

excrescent, abnormal in
 outgrowth
labrose, thick-lipped
lantern-jawed, having a
 long, thin face
nanocephalous, noting disproportionate smallness
 of the head

NOUNS

Miscellaneous

abnormity, deformity
blemish, deformity
cacotype, defective type
club-foot, club-like foot
corpulence, excessive
 fatness
deformity, malformation
disfiguration, an injured
 form or shape
enormity, something out of
 normal
excrescence, unnatural
 growth
flabbiness, puffiness
gnarl, a knot
harelip, a malformed lip
hump, protuberance
knot, gnarl
lankiness, thinness
lump, protuberance
malformation, an ill-
 formation
monstrosity, an unnatural
 production
nanocephaly, smallness of
 the head
obesity, corpulence
protuberance, a swelling
scragginess, condition of
 being bony
skinniness, lankiness
whale, a whipmark

PERSONS

cripple, a lame person
dwarf, an undergrown
 being
grampus, gross loud-
 breathing person
monster, an abnormal
 being
scrag, a raw-boned person
squab, a short, fat person
wizen, a withered person

SHABBINESS—UNTIDINESS   see—   **ASSOCIATIVE**

    vs. Beauty—Comeliness 108

109C

VERBS

dishevel, disorder the hair
muss, dishevel, etc.
(See Dirtiness, 129A)
(See Disorder, 125A)

ADJECTIVES

    Ragged

ragged, tattered
rough, coarse
seedy, shabby
shabby, worn
tattered, ragged
threadbare, tattered
worn, threadbare

    Dirty

bedraggled, befouled
befouled, defiled
blotchy, blotched
blotty, having blots
dirty, unclean
defiled, filthy
filthy, foul
foul, dirty

ADJECTIVES (Continued)

grimy, foul
sordid, vile
squalid, extremely foul
vile, foul

    Slovenly

disheveled, having disordered hair
dowdyish, slovenly
dowdy, ill-dressed
frowzy, untidy
matted, disheveled
mussy, disordered
slatternly, slovenly
slipshod, slovenly
slovenly, untidy
sluttish, slovenly
unkempt, disheveled, etc.
untidy, disordered

NOUNS

    Miscellaneous

blemish, derangement
blot, blemish

NOUNS (Continued)

blotch, clumsy daub
derangement, disarray
dirtiness, uncleanliness
disarray, negligent dress
dowdiness, slovenliness
filthiness, uncleanliness
raggedness, in rags
seamy-side, sordidness
seediness, shabbiness
shabbiness, threadbareness
slovenliness, untidiness
sordidness, squalor
squalor, filthiness
untidiness, disarray

PERSONS

slattern, slovenly woman
slob, a slovenly person
sloven, an untidy person

QUALITY OF SENSE REACTION

CONSTITUTIONAL REACTION

FIVE SENSES

FIVE BASIC STIMULI

Dichotomized Classifications

(Shown elsewhere) suggest the various psychological functions.

INSENSIBILITY—APATHY   see—   ASSOCIATIVE

vs. Perception—Conscience 111

110A

VERBS

Miscellaneous

doze, drowse
droop, lose spirit
drowse, nap
languish, droop
nap, doze
pine, languish
sleep, slumber
slumber, sleep
snooze, nap

ADJECTIVES

Dormant

dormant, torpid, inactive
inactive, inert
inert, inactive, sluggish
latent, phlegmatic

Sleeping

asleep, slumbering
drowsy, sleepy
sleeping, slumbering
sleepy, drowsy

Lethargic

apathetic, insensible
comatose, lethargic
dull, sluggish
lethargic, sluggish
numb, dull, insensible
phlegmatic, apathetic
sluggish, dull
stagnant, spiritless
stunned, rendered senseless
torpid, inactive

Hazy

foggy, hazy
hazy, stupefied
stupefied, fuddled
vague, foggy

Unsober

besotted, drunk
drunk, intoxicated
fuddled, groggy
groggy, tipsy
inebriated, drunk
intoxicated, inebriated

ADJECTIVES (Continued)

shot, intoxicated
sodden, drunk
tipsy, intoxicated
waterlogged, sodden

Analgesic

anaesthetic, noting insensibility to feeling
analgesic, insensible to
pain

Callous, Etc.

callous, insensible
cataleptic, in suspended
sensation
impassive, apathetic
insensate, apathetic
insensible, apathetic
spiritless, dead
unconscious, insensate

NOUNS

Dormancy

dormancy, inactivity
inertia, inertness
inertness, sluggishness

Sleep

narcolepsy, neurotic drowsiness
nap, short sleep
siesta, midday nap
sleep, slumber
sleepiness, approach to
sleep
slumber, sleep
snooze, a nap
somnolence, drowsiness

Lethargy

apathy, hebetude
benumbment, stupefaction
hebetude, sluggishness
languor, spiritlessness
lethargy, apathy
listlessness, languor
numbness, torpidity
sluggishness, apathy
stagnancy, sluggishness

NOUNS (Continued)

stagnation, apathy
stultification, torpor
torpidity, torpor
torpor, numbness

Haziness

amnesia, loss of memory
haziness, muddle
letheomania, forgetfulness
from drugs
stupefaction, insensibility
stupor, lethargy

Insobriety

besotment, stupefaction
drunkenness, stupor
inebriation, intoxication
inebriety, drunkenness
insobriety, drunkenness
intoxication, insobriety
narcosis, stupefaction
from drugs
razzle-dazzle, stupefaction
from alcohol

Analgesia

anaesthesia, insensibility
to pain
analgesia, insensibility
to pain

Callousness, Etc.

asphyxia, condition of
lifelessness
catalepsy, suspended sen-
sation
coma, insensibility
impassiveness, apathy
insensibility, apathy
oblivion, insensibility
paralysis, loss of power
paresis, softening of the
brain, motor paralysis
palsy, paralysis

PERSONS

drunk, drunkard
drunkard, sot
inebriate, drunkard
sot, inebriate

110B

STUPIDITY—IDIOCY   see—   **ASSOCIATIVE**

vs. Intelligence—Wisdom 117
{
Foolishness—Nonsense 60
Defective Vision 119B
Amazement—Perplexity 112
}

110B
VERBS

dote, be mentally or
  physically weak
drivel, be weak or foolish
forget, lose from memory

ADJECTIVES
Stupid

backward, slow to learn
doltish, stupid
dummy, dull
gross, dull
muzzy, stupid
pigheaded, stubbornly
  stupid
poky, stupid
sottish, stupid
stolid, dull
stupid, asinine

Brutish

apish, foolish
asinine, stupid, silly
bovine, dull
brutish, bovine

Crass

blunt, dull
crass, dense, stupid
dark, unenlightened
dense, grossly dull
dull, stupid
obtuse, silly
raw, inexperienced
unimaginative, dull

Rustic

arcadian, rurally simple
backwoods, uncivilized
Boeotian, stupid
boorish, rude
bucolic, in rustic
  ignorance
green, inexperienced
pastoral, sylvan
rural, simple
rustic, artless
sylvan, rustic
verdant, unsophisticated

Simple

artless, simple
ingenuous, artless
innocent, artless
naive, ingenuous
simple, naive

Childish

childish, foolish
infantile, childish
puerile, childish

Silly

daffy, foolish
daft, silly

ADJECTIVES (Continued)

dizzy, giddy
driveling, weak, foolish
fantastic, foolishly fanciful
fatuous, silly
featherbrained, foolish
foolish, reasonless
giddy, foolish
harebrained, giddy
infatuated, foolish
maudlin, sentimentally
  foolish
nonsensical, absurd
oafish, silly
scatterbrained, giddy
silly, foolish

Superficial

callous, dull, shallow
narrow, superficial
prosaic, narrow-minded
shallow, superficial
small, superficial
superficial, shallow

Provincial

barbarous, ignorant
heathenish, ignorant
insular, narrow
parochial, narrow-minded
Philistine, narrow-minded
provincial, narrow
tramontane, barbarous

Untaught

ignorant, destitute of
  knowledge
illiterate, ignorant of
  letters
incompetent, inexperienced
inexperienced, unlearned
uncultured, unlearned
uneducated, illiterate
unenlightened, ignorant
uninformed, ignorant
unintellectual, uneducated
unintelligent, ignorant
unlearned, untrained
unschooled, illiterate
unsophisticated, inexperienced
untaught, unschooled
untrained, inexperienced
untutored, untaught

Unwise

impolitic, unwise
indiscreet, unwise
injudicious, indiscreet
unwise, injudicious
witless, stupid

ADJECTIVES (Continued)
Unreasonable

absurd, foolish
bigoted, blindly unreasonable
preposterous, absurd
unreasonable, absurd
unsound, unreasonable

Senseless

blind, devoid of sight or
  understanding
brainless, silly
empty, senseless
forgetful, lapsing in
  memory
insensate, senseless
insensible, senseless
senseless, foolish
vacant, empty, vacuous
vacuous, empty

Aberrant

aberrant, mentally de-
  ranged
cracked, crazy
crazy, insane
delirious, insane
demented, insane
deranged, demented
idiotic, mentally weak
imbecile, mentally im-
  potent
irrational, without reason
insane, irrational
loony, crazy
lunatic, insane
mad, insane
maniacal, having mania
moonstruck, insane
rabid, mad

NOUNS
Stupidity

asininity, stupidity
hebetude, dullness
obtuseness, dullness
stupidity, hebetude

Crassness

crassness, dullness
darkness, ignorance
stolidity, intellectual
  dullness

Rusticity

rusticity, simplicity
verdancy, inexperience

Simplicity

artlessness, simplicity
naivete, ingenuousness
(Continued on page 229)

NOUNS (Continued)

puerility, childishness
simplicity, naivete

Silliness

foolery, absurdity
fooling, foolish conduct
foolishness, nonsense
giddiness, nonsense
nonsense, foolishness
silliness, nonsense

Ignorance

ignorance, want of sense
illiteracy, ignorance of
letters
incapacity, inexperience
incompetence, incapacity
inexperience, want of experience
insularity, ignorance
nescience, ignorance
nonage, inexperience
unfamiliarity, ignorance

Senselessness

blindness, ignorance
insensibility, dullness
senselessness, vacuity
vacancy, vacuity
vacuity, vapidity

Aberration

aberration, mental derangement
amentia, imbecility
crankiness, craziness
craziness, insanity
delirium, aberration
delirium-tremens, mental
derangement
dementia, insanity
derangement, insanity
dotage, foolish old age
fatuity, idiocy
frenzy, temporary madness
hysteria, morbid excitement
idiocy, imbecility
imbecility, mental or physical weakness
insanity, dementia
lunacy, dementia
mania, violent insanity
monomania, insane regard
for one subject
paranoia, kind of monomania

110B (Continued)

NOUNS (Continued)

paresis, insanity with
general motor paralysis

Absurdity

absurdity, nonsense
absurdness, foolishness

Imprudence

impolicy, lack of wisdom
imprudence, impolicy

PERSONS

Numskull

blockhead, stupid fellow
bonehead, blockhead
booby, dunce
bumpkin, blockhead
chump, blockhead
dolt, blockhead
duffer, dullard
dullard, dolt
dummy, dull fellow
dunce, ignoramus
dunderhead, dolt
fool, idiot
gawk, simpleton
ignoramus, dunce
log, dull fellow
loggerhead, blockhead
lourd, dullard
lummox, stupid fellow
milksop, effeminately
weak person
mollycoddle, milksop
nincompoop, fool
numskull, blockhead
oaf, blockhead
plug, dummy
saphead, blockhead
slob, stupid person
tomfool, great fool
yap, foolish person

Calf, Etc.

ape, fool
ass, stupid fellow
buzzard, dull fellow
calf, stupid person
colt, foolish youth
donkey, stupid fellow
goose, silly person
lamb, dupe

Rustic

backwoodsman, ruralist

PERSONS (Continued)

greenhorn, ignoramus
greeny, simpleton
heathen, uncultured person
jay, greenhorn
popinjay, rustic
ruralist, rustic
rustic, countryman with
simple manners

Simpleton

dotard, aged dullard
gump, simpleton
ninny, simpleton
noddy, simpleton
noodle, simpleton
silly, simple person
simpleton, foolish person

Philistine, Etc.

ingenue, artless girl
philistine, narrow-minded
person
sciolist, one with a superficial knowledge
tenderfoot, one who is inexperienced
wiseacre, sciolist

Dupe

April-fool, dupe
butt, dupe
child, one who is immature in judgment
dupe, gull
gudgeon, dupe
gull, gudgeon
laughing-stock, dupe

Imbecile

bedlamite, madman
crank, fanatic
degenerate, imbecile
demoniac, lunatic
idiot, mental weakling
imbecile, idiot
lunatic, insane person
moron, one stunted in mind
maniac, lunatic
monomaniac, one who is
insane on one subject
paranoiac, monomaniac
weakling, imbecile

SYMBOL

fool's cap, symbol of
stupidity

---

116 (Continued)

PERSONS (Continued)

student, disciple
understudy, one who
studies under another, as
a potential successor

Students Collectively

class, pupils

PERSONS (Continued)

school, pupils collectively

Bookman, Etc.

blue-stocking, bookwoman
bookman, studious man
bookwoman, studious
woman

PERSONS (Continued)

bookworm, one who is devoted to study
dig, one who plods at
learning
sap, an assiduous student

111

VERBS

Miscellaneous

advert, apprehend
animadvert, perceive
apprehend, perceive
awake, wake
catch, perceive
cerebrate, act mentally
conceive, form ideas
feel, be conscious
imagine, form ideas
occur, come to mind
perceive, apprehend
sense, apprehend
take, perceive
view, perceive
wake, become conscious
waken, awake

ADJECTIVES

Conscious

advertent, attentive
attentive, cognizant
awake, advertent
aware, conscious
cognitive, conceptive
cognizant, aware
conscious, aware

Sensitive

impressionable, inceptive
receptive, impressionable
sensational, sensitive
sensible, sensitive
sensitive, susceptible
sentimental, impressionable
susceptible, impressible

Perceptive

animadversive, perceptive
conceptive, having conception
perceptive, inceptive
percipient, perceiving

Imaginative

ideal, perceived in the
mind
imaginary, conceiving
images
imaginative, having imagination

Subjective

inceptive, presentient
intuitional, spontaneously
perceptive
intuitive, perceiving immediately
presentient, perceiving in-
tuitively

ADJECTIVES (Continued)

psychic, noting sentience,
intuition, etc.
subconscious, inherently
conscious
subjective, having thought
arising within

Conceivable

apprehensible, having perception
conceivable, imaginative
imaginable, conceiving
ideas

Cerebral

cerebral, having brain-
action
cerebric, as above
mental, having mind
sensorial, sensible

NOUNS

Conscience

advertence, attention
advertency, advertence
attention, awareness
awareness, consciousness
cognizance, perception
conscience, awareness
consciousness, awareness
view, perception
vision, view

Sensitiveness

impressibility, awareness
sensibility, sensation
sensitiveness, percipience
susceptibility, sensitiveness

Percipience

apprehension, mental perception
conception, conative apprehension
discernment, perception
impression, conception
inception, mental apprehension
percipience, perception
percept, perception derived through the senses
perception, percipience
perceptivity, perception of
external things through
the senses

Sensation, Etc.

allopathy, passive reception of impressions

NOUNS (Continued)

animadversion (capacity
for) perception
apperception, perception
which makes itself its
object; the relation of
new ideas to old ones
arousal, an awakening
awakening, incipient
consciousness
inspiration, apprehension
of an elevating in-
fluence
sensation, mental perception
sentience, perception

Conceivability

conceivability, faculty of
conception
perceptibility, act of perceiving, etc.

Cerebration

cerebration, conscious or
voluntary action of the
brain
faculty, power of the mind
to receive and retain per-
ceptions
imagination, formation of a
mental picture
intuition, spontaneous perception without the aid
of reasoning; it is anal-
ogous to radioactive re-
ceptivity
sense, faculty of perception
telepathy, apprehension of
an exterior mind without
visible communication; it
is analogous to radioac-
tive receptivity

BRAIN—MIND, ETC.

brain, cerebrum
cerebellum, little brain
cerebrum, seat of the
mental functions
intellect, mind
mind, sensorium
sensorium, seat of perception and mental or physi-
cal expression or activity
sensory, sensorium
soul, inherent faculty of
conative conception and
rhythmic preservation

AMAZEMENT—PERPLEXITY   see—   ASSOCIATIVE

vs. Calmness—Equanimity 132B

112
VERBS

Miscellaneous

blanch, pale
blush, flush
crimson, blush
doubt, be undetermined
faint, swoon
ferment, be excited
fluctuate, waver
flunk, break down, faint
flush, blush
flutter, hesitate
fuddle, be fuddled
gasp, gape in wonder
hesitate, vacillate
marvel, wonder
misapprehend, misconceive
misconceive, misjudge
misjudge, misapprehend
misunderstand, be confused
reel, stagger confusedly
stagger, be fuddled
swim, reel confusedly
swoon, vacillate, waver
vacillate, waver
waver, hesitate
wonder, marvel
pale, blanch
flounder, fuddle

ADJECTIVES

Perplexed

bewildered, flustered
nonplussed, puzzled
perplexed, confused
puzzled, mystified
quizzical, puzzled

Indecisive

doubtful, undetermined
dubious, doubtful
inconclusive, unsettled
indecisive, inconclusive
irresolute, wavering
pending, undecided
uncertain, doubtful
undecided, uncertain
wavering, perplexed

Uneasy

restive, uneasy
restless, restive
troubled, embarrassed
uneasy, embarrassed

Distressed

annoyed, discomposed
distracted, nonplussed
distrait, confused
distraught, bewildered
distressed, distracted

ADJECTIVES (Continued)

frenzied, delirious
frantic, distracted
nervous, excited

Discomposed

abashed, confused
confounded, confused
confused, disconcerted
discomposed, confused
disconcerted, bewildered
disturbed, distressed
embarrassed, perplexed
excited, nonplussed
flabbergasted (colloq.)
   amazed
flurried, bewildered
flustered, confused
obfuscated, perplexed
perturbed, ruffled
ruffled, embarrassed
uncomposed, ruffled

Muddled

befuddled, bewildered
foggy, bewildered
fuddled, perplexed
muddled, mystified
stupefied, dazed

Drunk

drunk, intoxicated
drunken, drunk
groggy, tipsy
inebriated, intoxicated
intoxicated, drunk
moony, intoxicated
sodden, fuddled
tipsy, groggy

Dazed, Etc.

aghast, amazed
dazed, stunned
dizzy, bewildered
dumb, awe-struck
stunned, dumfounded

Awe-struck

awe-struck, bewildered
breathless, spellbound
dumfounded, confused
speechless, spellbound
spellbound, awe-struck
thunderstruck, awe-struck

Amazed

aback (adv.), surprised
amazed, astonished
astonished, dumfounded
astounded, astonished
dazzled, flustered
fascinated, amazed
startled, surprised
surprised, amazed

ADJECTIVES (Continued)

Hazy

blank, dazed
hazy, obfuscated
nebulous, perplexed
vague, hazy

NOUNS

Perplexity

bewilderment, perplexity
dilemma, perplexity
perplexity, embarrassment
quandary, perplexity

Indecision

doubt, nonplus
doubtfulness, doubt
fluctuation, hesitation
hesitancy, hesitation
hesitation, incertitude
incertitude, doubt
indecision, doubt
suspense, uncertainty
uncertainty, doubt
vacillation, hesitation

Uneasiness

agitation, excitement
disquietude, perturbation
distress, trouble
inquietude, excitement
misapprehension, dilemma
perturbation, agitation
restiveness, uneasiness
restlessness, restiveness
trepidation, agitation
trouble, worry
uneasiness, trepidation
worry, perplexity

Distress

consternation, surprise
distraction, bewilderment
panic, trepidation
stampede, panic

Discomposure

commotion, agitation
confusion, perplexity
discomposure, agitation
embarrassment, discom-
   posure
stultification, confusion

Excitement

delirium, mental excite-
   ment
excitability, ready agitation
excitation, excitement
excitement, roused emotion
fermentation, excitement
flurry, excitement
(Continued on page 235)

vs. Disbelief—Doubt 30
vs. Knowledge 117

{ Wonder—Amazement 112
  Dogma—Faith 82A
  Phantom—Ghost 96A

113

VERBS

Suppose
conjecture, guess
deem, have opinion
esteem, consider
estimate, guess
guess, conjecture
opine, suppose
reckon, suppose
regard, consider
repute, regard
surmise, suppose
suppose, opine
suspect, suspicion
suspicion, guess
think, opine

Believe
accept, believe
accredit, believe as true
believe, be credulous
credit, trust
depend, trust
rely, trust
trow, believe
trust, have faith

Presume
arrogate, presume
assume, suppose
consider, believe
entertain, assume
hold, believe
preconceive, presuppose
presume, assume
presuppose, presume
take, assume
understand, suppose

Theorize
hypothesize, assume for inference
postulate, hold as true
theorize, form a theory

Divine, Etc.
augur, judge from signs
divine, conjecture
dogmatize, form beliefs
idealize, form ideals

Imagine
dream, fancy
fancy, suppose
fantasy, soar
imagine, conjecture
soar, rise in fancy
visualize, fancy
ween, fancy

Misconceive
misapprehend, misconceive
misbelieve, misjudge

VERBS (Continued)
misconceive, mistake
misjudge, misconceive
mistake, misbelieve
misunderstand, mistake
overestimate, misjudge

ADJECTIVES

Suppositional
conjectural, suppositional
notional, suppositional
suppositional, hypothetic
suspicious, conjectural

Believing
anticipative, expectant
assured, convinced
confident, reliant
convinced, confident
dependent, trustful
expectant, presumptive
faithful, orthodox
fiduciary, trustful
fiducial, as above
implicit, reliant
reliant, trustful
sanguine, confident
trustful, reliant

Gullible
credulous, gullible
deceivable, credulous
easy, deceivable
gullible, credulous
verdant, gullible

Presumptive
assumptive, presumptive
forward, presumptuous
presumptive, assumptive
presumptuous, expectant
presuppositious, conjectural

Theoretical
abstract, theoretical
hypothetic, suppositional
hypothetical, as above
speculative, theoretical
theoretical, speculative

Divining
deistic, believing in a personal God
doctrinal, dogmatic
dogmatic, religious
orthodox, having belief in an established faith
religious, orthodox
theistic, believing in God

ADJECTIVES (Continued)
Idealistic
ideal, idealistic
idealistic, Utopian
quixotic, romantic
romantic, ideal
Utopian, idealistic

Imaginative
chimerical, fanciful
dreamy, visionary
fanatic, visionary
fancied, imaginary
fanciful, visionary
fantastic, unreal
flighty, fantastic
imaginary, illogical
imaginative, fanciful
whimsical, fanciful

Glamorous
extravagant, flighty
fictitious, fanciful
glamorous, romantic
romantic, visionary

Visionary
hollow, vain
idle, unfounded
impalpable, unreal
maggoty, whimsical
unfounded, visionary
unreal, unfounded
vain, unreal
vaporous, fanciful
visional, chimerical
visionary, imaginary

Prejudicial
biased, prejudiced
bigoted, intolerant
hidebound, opinionated
obsessed, prejudiced
opinionated, biased
opinionative, prejudicial
partial, biased
partisan, prejudicial
prejudiced, biased
prejudicial, having bias
superstitious, illogical

Conceited
arrogant, conceited
conceited, self-important
egotistic, conceited
flatulent, overweening
overweening, conceited
priggish, conceited
proud, arrogant
stuck-up, conceited
(Continued on page 233)

NOUNS

Supposition
conjecture, guess
estimation, conjecture
guess, surmise
idea, supposition
judgment, opinion
notion, opinion
opinion, conjecture
reputation, belief that a circumstance exists
repute, belief as to the circumstance of a person or thing
surmise, conjecture
supposition, opinion
suspicion, notion

Belief
acceptation, common belief
anticipation, expectancy
belief, credulity
credence, belief
credit, trust
dependence, reliance
expectancy, trust
reliance, confidence
trust, reliance

Gullibility
credulity, ready belief
gullibility, credulity

Confidence
assurance, confidence
assuredness, assurance
confidence, trust
esteem, confidence
faith, trust
fealty, faith, trust
sanguineness, confidence

Presumption
arrogation, presumption
assumption, arrogation
presumption, supposition

Theory
concept, general notion
conception, view
datum, assumption used as a basis for argument, etc.
hypothesis, assumption used as a basis for inference
postulate, position claimed as self-evident
presupposition, presumption
prognosis, opinion of probable results of a disease
speculation, theory
theorem, assumption held for proof
theory, assumption
view, opinion

NOUNS (Continued)

Divination
casuistry, determination of dogma
deism, belief in God, etc.
divination, conjectural dogma, prophecy, etc.
dogma, belief
dogmatism, established belief
fetishism, superstition
orthodoxy, belief in established doctrine
tenet, belief in a dogma
theism, belief in God

Idealism
ideal, idea of perfection
idealism, ideas that strive for a perfect state
ideality, ideal
quixotism, fanciful ideal
romanticism, idealism
Utopianism, idealism

Imagination
chimera, incongruous fancy
crotchet, whim or fancy
daydream, idle fancy
dream, fancy in sleep
fancy, imagination
figment, imagination
imagery, fanciful forms
imagination, illusion
kink, whim
pipe-dream, fancy
vagary, wild notion
whim, capricious fancy
whimsy, whim

Vision
apparition, specter
bogle, bugbear
bogy, bugbear
bugaboo, hallucination
bugbear, imaginary specter
delusion, illusion
fantasm, imaginary appearance
fantasy, fantastic idea
fantom, apparition
ghost, hobgoblin
glamour, delusion
goblin, bugbear
hallucination, delusion
hobgoblin, imaginary terror
illusion, hallucination
mare's-nest, fancied find
misapprehension, vagary
misconception, hallucination

NOUNS (Continued)
nightmare, oppressive dream
phantasm, fantasm
shade, ghost
specter, ghost
(B). spectre
spirit, shade
spook, ghost
vision, fanciful creation
wraith, ghost

Prejudice
bent, bias
bias, presupposition
bigotry, unreasonableness
conviction, strong belief
favor, bias, partiality
(B). favour
inclination, bent
obsession, prejudice
partiality, prejudice
prejudice, bias
prepossession, bias
superstition, obsession

Conceit
arrogance, conceit
conceit, self-esteem
donnishness, academic arrogance
flatulence, conceit
prigism, prig's conceit
sufficiency, conceit
vanity, conceit

PERSONS

Miscellaneous
abstractionist, idealist
believer, one who believes
bigot, one who is hidebound to an opinion
casuist, one who makes theological dogma
doctrinaire, casuist, etc.
dreamer, visionary
dupe, credulous person
extremist, dreamer
faddist, one with a fad
fan, fanatic
fanatic, visionary
flat, dupe
gudgeon, dupe
gull, dupe
gullible, gull
idealist, visionary
ideologist, theorist
illusionist, fanatic
prig, one who assumes airs
theorist, one who theorizes
visionary, dreamer

114

VERBS

Deliberate

absorb, be engrossed
bethink, reflect
concentrate, deliberate
debate, deliberate
deliberate, ponder
premeditate, deliberate
  beforehand
reconsider, consider again
retrospect, reconsider
think, cogitate

Plan

dope, plan
hammer, work in the mind
plan, scheme
plot, plan deliberately
scheme, plot

Meditate

brood, ponder
chew, meditate
cudgel, think
meditate, ponder
muse, think leisurely
ponder, deliberate
reflect, think, ponder
revolve, ruminate
ruminate, meditate

Reason

cogitate, reflect, reason
philosophize, reason like a
  philosopher
ratiocinate, reason by
  deduction
reason, ratiocinate
reckon, reason

Scrutinize

con, peruse carefully
consult, regard
examine, contemplate
peruse, examine
regard, consider closely
scrutinize, regard
study, deliberate
view, survey mentally

Consider

attend, think
consider, contemplate
contemplate, study deeply
entertain, consider
heed, regard carefully
mind, heed
weigh, consider

Compare, Etc.

analogize, compare
collate, compare critically
compare, study relation

VERBS (Continued)

test, compare

Theorize

speculate, theorize
theorize, speculate

ADJECTIVES

Deliberative

careful, thoughtful
contemplative, meditative
deliberate, slow in
  deliberation
deliberative, weighing
  mentally
intense, bending the mind
intent, mindful
painstaking, deliberative
premeditated, deliberated
premeditative, preoccupied
prepense, premeditated

Meditative

absorbed, engrossed
engaged, absorbed
engrossed, deeply absorbed
immersed, engrossed
meditative, pondering
musing, leisurely thoughtful
pensive, thoughtful
preoccupied, engrossed in
  meditation
reflective, attentive to
  thoughts as they pass
  in the mind
speculative, contemplative
thoughtful, contemplative
wistful, sadly meditative

Reasoning

cogitative, contemplative
dialectic, reasoning logically
logical, reasoning correctly
philosophical, reasoning in
  the interest of truth and
  order
platonic, pertaining to Pla-
  to's philosophic method
  of reasoning
ratiocinative, noting rational deliberation
rational, reasonable
reasonable, consistent with
  reason
reasoning, rational
valid, logical

Scrutinous

circumspect, deliberative

ADJECTIVES (Continued)

regardant, considering with
  attention
regardful, as above
scrupulous, having deliberative regard for pro-
  priety, etc.
scrutinous, regardful
studied, premeditated
studious, deliberative

Considerate

conscientious, discrim
  inately considerate
considerate, contemplative
minded, intent
mindful, considerate

Comparative

a posteriori, reasoning
  from effect to cause;
  opposed to a priori
a priori, reasoning from
  cause to effect; opposed
  to a posteriori
comparable, comparative
comparative, considered
  comparison
introspective, self-
  examining
metaphysical, reasoning
  from abstract thought
retrospective, reflective
transcendent, noting speculations concerning matters outside the range of
  human intellect or experience
transcendental, speculative,
  metaphysical

Theoretical

abstract, theoretical
theoretical, reasoning
  through speculations,
  suppositions, etc.

Rationalistic

psychic, pertaining to the
  mental functions
psychical, psychic
psychological, reasoning as
  in metaphysics, or psy-
  chology
rationalistic, having the
  faculty of reasoning, etc.

NOUNS

Deliberation

advisement, deliberation
(Continued on page 235)

NOUNS (Continued)
cogitation, reasoning
concern, regard
deliberateness, circumspection
deliberation, consideration
premeditation, meditation beforehand
reconsideration, consideration for correction
speculation, intellectual examination

Meditation
daydream, reverie
engrossment, deep attention
meditation, abstract thinking
meditativeness, contemplation
pensiveness, thoughtfulness
reflection, meditation
reflectiveness, reflection
retrospection, reflection
reverie, a waking dream or brown study
rumination, meditation
thought, meditation, reflection
thoughtfulness, consideration
vein, train of thought

Reasoning
dialectics, art of reasoning
logic, correct reasoning
philosophy, examination into the principle of things
ratiocination, process of reasoning
reason, ratiocination

NOUNS (Continued)
reasoning, speculation

Scrutiny
circumspection, deliberation
consultation, co-deliberation
examination, contemplation
perusal, examination
regard, attentive consideration
scrupulosity, conscious regard for propriety
scrutiny, regard

Consideration
attention, consideration
consideration, deliberation
contemplation, reflection
conscientiousness, deliberation
heed, careful attention
interest, concern
intent, intensity of mind

Comparison
analogy, a reasoning from cause to effect
autology, science of self-study
collation, comparison
comparison, a comparing
introspection, the examination of one's thoughts
metaphysics, mental philosophy, a reasoning from abstract thoughts
rationale, reasons assigned for action, etc.
rationalism, reasoning by deduction
synthesis, deduction of complex ideas from simple ones

NOUNS (Continued)
Theorization
theorem, the contemplation of a subject for solution
theorization, speculation
theory, contemplation, speculation

Rationality
ideation, the shaping of ideas
psychology, examination and analysis of mental phenomena
rationality, power of reasoning

PERSONS
Miscellaneous
analogist, one who reasons from comparison
collator, one who compares differences
freethinker, one who speculates regardless of the opinions of others
latitudinarian, one who holds widely speculative views
metaphysician, one skilled in metaphysics
peripatetic, an Aristotelian philosopher
philosopher, one who is fond of examining into the principle of things
psychologist, one skilled in psychology
rationalist, one who interprets by reasoning
ruminator, one who meditates
theorist, one who reasons from theory

NOUNS (Continued)
tension, excitement
Muddle
fix, dilemma
fog, bewilderment
muddle, bewilderment
pickle, embarrassing condition
scrape, predicament

Drunkenness
dizziness, razzle-dazzle
drunkenness, intoxication
grogginess, tipsiness, shock

NOUNS (Continued)
inebriation, intoxication
inebriety, drunkenness
insobriety, drunkenness
intoxication, excitement
razzle-dazzle, intoxication
tipsiness, grogginess

Amazement
amaze, astonishment
amazement, dismay
astonishment, amazement
dismay, astonishment

NOUNS (Continued)
surprise, astonishment
wonder, amazement

Haziness
haziness, perplexity
mystification, perplexity
nebulosity, perplexity
nonplus, perplexity

PERSONS
(See Apathy, 110A)

CONCLUSION—SOLUTION   see—

vs. Perplexity—Amazement 112	
vs. Supposition 113	
vs. Disbelief—Doubt 30	

ASSOCIATIVE

115
VERBS

Conclude

collate, determine from comparison
conclude, determine by inference
decide, determine
deem, judge from premises
determine, conclude
excogitate, deliberate conclusively

Judge

adjudge, determine in controversy
adjudicate, adjudge
arbitrate, decide
decree, determine, adjudge
judge, adjudge
rule, decide
umpire, judge

Appraise

appraise, value
appreciate, estimate
assay, determine quality
estimate, compute a result
rate, reckon a value or rank
value, estimate

Calculate

account, compute
audit, determine a status
calculate, determine a consequence
compute, calculate
count, determine a quantity
figure, calculate
number, count
reckon, calculate

Measure

admeasure, quantify
gage, measure
measure, admeasure
plumb, measure depth
quantify, measure
sound, fathom

Analyze, Etc.

analyze, determine constituent elements
diagnose, determine from symptoms
resolve, determine from premises

Infer

deduce, infer
deduct, deduce

VERBS (Continued)

derive, deduce
educe, deduce
evolve, educe
gather, infer
generalize, infer inductively
glean, gather
infer, conclude from premises
induce, infer inductively
reason, infer conclusively

Discriminate

differentiate, discriminate
discriminate, determine difference
distinguish, discriminate
difference, distinguish

Anticipate

anticipate, infer or conclude beforehand
prejudge, predetermine
predetermine, judge beforehand

Discover

ascertain, determine
decipher, determine a secret significance
discern, judge
discover, find
fathom, ascertain
find, ascertain
solve, ascertain
unravel, determine

ADJECTIVES

Conclusive

cognizable, noting decision
conclusive, decisive
decided, determined
deciding, determinative
decidable, determinative
decisive, conclusive
definitive, determinate
determinate, decisive
determinative, deciding

Judicious

decretive, judicial
decretory, decretive
judicial, decisive
judiciary, judicial
judicious, discreet in conclusions

Appraising

appraising, determinative
appreciative, discriminative

ADJECTIVES (Continued)

assessorial, determining valuation

Calculative

accounting, determining
calculating, calculative
calculative, noting conclusion from reckoning

Analytic

analytic, determining constituents
diagnostic, determining from symptoms
logical, having correct inference
metaphysical, determined as in metaphysics
psychological, analytical
qualitative, determining the nature of constituents
ratiocinative, making conclusions as by argumentative deduction from premises
synthetic, building up of particulars to inclusive wholes

Inferential

adducent, drawing to a conclusion
adductive, adducent
consequential, inferential
deductive, inferential
derivable, noting conclusion from derivation
derivative, derivable
inductional, inductive
inductive, adductive
inferable, noting inference
inferential, concluding from premises

Discriminatory

dioristic, distinguishing
discreet, discriminative
discretionary, determining at one's will
discriminating, determinative
discriminative, noting determination, etc.

Anticipative

anticipative, concluding beforehand

Measured

measured, ascertained

(Continued on page 237)

NOUNS
Conclusion
agreement, conclusion
collation, determination by comparison
concept, conclusion
conception, conclusion
conclusion, decision
consequence, inference
decision, determination
excogitation, conclusive reasoning
impression, conclusion
reason, correct judgment

Judgment
adjudgment, adjudication
adjudication, judicial decision
arbitration, arbitrament
arbitrament, decision
conviction, judgment
finding, verdict
judgment, conclusion
judicature, power of prudent decision and concomitant dispensation of justice
verdict, decision

Appraisal
appraisal, calculative conclusion
appreciation, just valuation
assay, analytic determination
assessment, determination of values
estimation, appraisal
valuation, estimation

Calculation
account, determined valuation
accountancy, the determination of values
audit, accountancy
calculation, determination through reckoning
computation, calculation
count, a reckoning
enumeration, a counting
numeration, a reckoning
reckoning, computation
tale, a counting or reckoning

Mathematics, Etc.
autometry, self-measurement
automorphism, judgment of others by comparison with self
bathymetry, determination of sea depths
calculus, branch of mathematical calculation
calibration, determination of diameter

NOUNS (Continued)
calorimetry, measurement of heat
geometry, science of determining figures and angles
mathematics, science of determining quantity
sounding, determination of depth
spherics, spherical geometry

Measurement
admeasurement, determination by measuring
measure, determination of quantity, area, capacity, etc.
measurement, as above
mensuration, measurement

Analysis
analysis, resolution or determination of a compound
analytics, science of determining constituents
diagnosis, conclusion from symptoms
inductive, philosophy, induction from deliberation to conclusion
logic, science of reasoning to right conclusions
metaphysics, science of determining first principles
prognosis, conclusive knowledge of effects as determined from symptoms
psychology, mental analysis
ratiocination, conclusion from premises
resolution, analysis
synthesis, conclusion of complex ideas from simple ones

Inference
connotation, inference from object to quality
corollary, additional inference
deduction, inference
derivation, deduction
generalization, conclusion
idea, inference
illation, inference
induction, deduction
inference, conclusive deduction

Discrimination
acumen, discrimination
discernment, discrimination
discretion, discrimination

NOUNS (Continued)
discrimination, determination
distinction, discrimination
tact, nice discrimination

Anticipation
anticipation, preconclusion
preconclusion, anticipation

Discovery
answer, solution
ascertainment, resolution
determination, conclusion
discovery, discernment
solution, determination

PERSONS
Miscellaneous
accountant, one who determines values
actuary, one who determines and fixes insurance rates
adjudicator, one who judges
analyst, one who resolves a compound into its constituents
appraiser, one who determines valuation
arbiter, judge, umpire
arbitrator, arbiter
arithmetician, mathematician
assayer, one who determines by analysis
assessor, appraiser
assizer, one who determines justice
auditor, accountant
calculator, one who determines computations
collator, one who determines by comparison
critic, one who judges critically
deemster, umpire
elector, one who determines by choice
electorate, electors collectively
geometer, mathematician
judge, one who makes judicial decisions
logician, one skilled in logic
mathematician, one skilled in calculations
metaphysician, one skilled in metaphysics
prud'homme, in France an arbiter for trades
psychoanalyst, one who analyzes the mind
psychologist, psychoanalyst
referee, judge, umpire
umpire, arbiter

LEARNING—STUDY—LEARNERS

ASSOCIATIVE

		see—
vs. Idleness	126B	
vs. Stupidity	110B	

Search—Scrutiny—Probe 119E
Deliberation—Meditation 114
Acquirement—Absorption 49A
Intelligence—Wisdom 117

116

VERBS

Learn

commit, learn by heart
con, fix in the mind by
repetition
learn, acquire knowledge
memorize, commit to
memory

Experience

acquaint, become conversant with
apprehend, seize mentally
discover, find
elicit, draw out or learn
explore, examine
experience, learn
familiarize, acquaint
find, experience
receive, gain knowledge

Assimilate

ascertain, learn
assimilate, absorb mentally
digest, assimilate mentally
get, learn
imbibe, absorb learning

Cultivate

cultivate, improve by
study
dig, study hard
grind, dig, study hard
plod, study closely
pore, study patiently
study, examine and learn
trench, learn deeply

Read

browse, assimilate through
reading
peruse, read attentively
read, peruse

ADJECTIVES

Studious

accultural, acquiring improvement from foreign methods
apprehensive, learning
quickly
assiduous, constant in application
autodidactic, self-learned
bookish, fond of study
studious, devoted to learning

Academic, Etc.

abecedarian, learning rudiments
academic, noting academic
learning, etc.

ADJECTIVES (Continued)

scholarly, scholastic
scholastic, scholar-like

Apt, Etc.

apt, susceptible
capable, susceptible
disciplinable, readily receiving instruction
docile, disciplinable
educable, learning readily
impressible, impressionable
impressionable, susceptible
impressional, susceptible
receptive, susceptible
susceptible, learning
readily
teachable, tractable
tractable, easy to learn

NOUNS

Learning

commitment, a memorizing
learning, act of studying
memorization, commitment

Studiousness

application, devotion to
study
assiduousness, constant
application
grind, hard study
lucubration, study by lamplight or at night
perusal, act of reading or
studying
psychogenesis, mental self-development
studiousness, application
study, application to
learning

Acculture

acculture, adoption of foreign methods
assimilation, act of
learning

Aptitude

aptitude, readiness in
learning
capability, susceptibility
docility, tractability
receptivity, susceptibility
susceptibility, aptitude
tractability, docility

Culture, Etc.

culture, moral or intellectual acquisition
discipline, strict course of
learning

NOUNS (Continued)

elicitation, act of learning
from

PERSONS

Beginner

apprentice, novice in learning a craft, etc.
beginner, novice
catechumen, beginner in
receiving religious instruction
explorer, neophyte
neophyte, novice
novice, beginner in learning
pioneer, explorer
probationer, novice
recruit, green soldier
tyro, beginner, novice

Rank of Learner

abecedarian, one engaged
in rudimentary learning
freshman, college student
in his first year
junior, a student in his
third year at college
senior, a student in his
fourth year at college
sophomore, a student in his
second year at college

Graduates

alumna, woman graduate
alumnus, graduate of a
university, etc.
graduate, one who has attained an academic degree

Students, Etc.

academic, student
cadet, a potential officer
taking military or naval
training
classman, student who has
gained distinction; opposed to passman
collegian, college student
disciple, pupil
extern, day student
humanist, student of
human nature
medic, medical student
passman, student who advances without distinction
pupil, scholar
scholar, student
(Continued on page 229)

INTELLIGENCE see—	ASSOCIATIVE	
vs. Stupidity 110B	⎧ Sensibleness 59	Seeing—Vision 119A
vs. Nonsense 60	⎨ Skill—Mastery 134B	Conception 111
	⎩ Learning 116	Preciseness 134A

117
VERBS

Understand
appreciate, perceive clearly
comprehend, compass
understandingly
ken, know
know, understand
perceive, understand
realize, know fully
understand, know
wit, to know

Recollect
acknowledge, own
bethink, recall
commemorate, call to
memory
mind, recollect
own, recognize
recall, remember
recognize, recollect
recollect, know again
recur, recollect
reflect, bethink
remember, recollect

ADJECTIVES

Intelligent
intellectual, intelligent
intelligent, having knowledge
rational, wise, judicious
sane, mentally sound
sensible, intelligent

Understanding
cognitive, having the power
of knowing or ap-
prehending
knowing, intelligent
understanding, knowing

Capable
able, mentally strong
capable, qualified
competent, able
proficient, qualified
qualified, capable
responsible, having capacity for correct judgment
skilled, qualified

Accomplished
accomplished, qualified
endowed, having a gift or
quality
gifted, talented
precocious, prematurely
qualified
talented, having ability or
excellence

Clever
apt, keen

ADJECTIVES (Continued)
artful, cunning
clever, witty
cute, clever
skilful, discriminating
witty, having wit or
understanding

Fertile
conversant, familiar
fertile, rich in resourcefulness or invention
ingenious, clever
inventive, fertile
resourceful, versatile
versatile, variously en-
dowed
versed, well informed

Brainy
brainy, intellectual
bright, witty
brilliant, accomplished
smart, brilliant

Discerning
acute, crafty
astute, sagacious
discerning, astute
discriminating, acute
intuitive, immediately
perceptive
judicious, sagacious
keen, knowing
penetrating, discerning
perspicacious, mentally
acute
piercing, perspicacious
quick, shrewd, sharp
sagacious, acute
sapient, sagacious

Shrewd
canny, shrewd
crafty, artful
cunning, crafty
foxy, crafty
politic, shrewd
sharp, intellectually acute
shrewd, sharp-witted
subtile, cunning
subtle, crafty
vulpine, cunning
wily, cunning

Familiar
acquainted, familiar
familiar, knowing well
intimate, familiar

Experienced
empiric, experienced
experienced, having prac-
tical knowledge
hard-bitten, veteran

ADJECTIVES (Continued)
liberal, wise, free from
narrowness
metropolitan, sophisticated
sophisticated, worldly-wise
veteran, experienced

Urbane
bland, suave
smooth, suave
smug, bland
suave, urbane
unctious, suave
urbane, metropolitan

Literate
cultured, learned
educated, scholarly
erudite, learned
learned, educated
lettered, learned
literate, lettered
scholarly, endowed with
learning
scholastic, scholarly
studied, scholastic

Profound
abstruse, profound
deep, profound
esoteric, having knowledge
of an enlightened few
gnostic, esoteric
profound, intellectually
deep
recondite, deeply profound

Wise
oracular, wise
omniscient, infinitely wise
sage, wise
wise, having wisdom

Esthetic
æsthetic, see esthetic
Augustan, intellectual
esthetic
(B). aesthetic, appreciative
of practical beauty
Hellenistic, implying Greek
wisdom
humanistic, having comprehension of human nature
as distinguished from
brute nature
theosophic, having divine
wisdom

Aware
aware, having knowledge
cognizant, aware
conscious, aware
(Continued on page 240)

ADJECTIVES (Continued)

ocular, knowing from actual sight

Recollective

mindful, keeping in mind
remindful, calling to mind
reminiscent, recollecting

Sure

accurate, exact
certain, sure
definite, precise
distinct, definite
exact, precise
logical, accurate
precise, specific
specific, certain
sure, aware
unequivocal, definite
unerring, exact

Absolute

absolute, perfect
consummate, utter
faultless, perfect
genuine, incontrovertible
incontrovertible, positive
infallible, perfect
perfect, consummate
positive, absolute
thorough, consummate

Mental

mental, intellectual
psychical, having soul faculty

NOUNS

Intelligence

brain, intelligence
enlightenment, intelligence
intellect, superior knowledge
intellectualism, intellectual power
intellectuality, intellect
intelligence, understanding
intelligibility, perceptive intelligence
knowledge, intelligence
nous, common sense

Understanding

acceptation, understanding
appreciation, correct understanding
apprehension, cognition
cognition, mental apprehension
comprehension, knowledge
ken, knowledge
understanding, the faculty of comprehension

Compass

breadth, comprehension
compass, comprehension
liberality, mental breadth
range, scope
scope, outlook

NOUNS (Continued)

sphere, range of knowledge

Capability

ability, talent
aptitude, mental capacity
capability, qualification
capacity, capability
grasp, intellectual capacity
potency, mental power
proficiency, capability
qualification, needed ability

Accomplishment

accomplishment, qualification
attainment, accomplishment
endowment, natural talent
forte, one's special talent
gift, talent
point, one's special talent
talent, ability

Cleverness

cleverness, wit, skill
facetiae, cleverness of wit
humor, wit
wit, knowledge
wittiness, cleverness

Fertility

fertility, richness of resources or invention
genius, remarkable aptitude
ingenuity, inventive ability
inventiveness, genius
savoir-faire, intuitive knowledge of what is correct
skill, capability in any art or science
subtlety, acuteness of intellect
versatility, the state of being variously endowed
wizardry, sorcery

Discernment

acumen, sagacity
acuteness, acumen
discernment, insight
insight, penetration
intuition, instinctive knowledge
judgment, intelligence
keenness, penetration
penetration, acuteness
perspicacity, penetration
sagacity, acumen
sapience, sagacity
sharpness, insight

Shrewdness

craftiness, cunning
cunning, cleverness
cuteness, cunning
foxiness, shrewdness

NOUNS (Continued)

shrewdness, acumen

Familiarity

acquaintance, familiarity
familiarity, intimate knowledge

Experience

empiricism, knowledge from practical experience
experience, practical knowledge
experientialism, empiricism
quackery, empiricism

Literacy

culture, enlightenment
education, intellectual culture
erudition, learning
learning, intellect
literacy, erudition
lore, learning
scholasticism, scholarliness
scholarship, attainment in literature or science

Profundity

depth, profundity
gnosis, higher knowledge or insight
profundity, deep intellectuality

Wisdom

omniscience, infinite wisdom
sageness, wisdom
wisdom, practical knowledge

Estheticism

æstheticism, see estheticism
art, intellectuality in representing or adapting natural power
estheticism, knowledge of development of practical beauty
Hellenism, Greek culture or wisdom
humaniculture, æstheticism, understanding of human nature as distinguished from brute nature
humanism, culture in the arts

Occultism, Etc.

clairvoyance, power of unusual perception under mesmeric influence
divination, foreknowledge
magic, wizardry
necromancy, sorcery
occultism, divination
sciolism, superficial knowledge

(Continued on page 241)

NOUNS (Continued)

sorcery, supernatural divination
theosophism, pretension to theosophic knowledge
witchcraft, sorcery

Foresight

foresight, foreknowledge
outlook, foresight
precocity, premature intellect
precognition, foreknowledge
presentiment, previous apprehension
prescience, foreknowledge
prevision, foreknowledge
privity, mutually secret knowledge

Awareness

awareness, cognizance
cognizance, cognition
conscience, awareness
realization, understanding

Mind, Sense

mind, intellectual faculty
rationality, reasoning power
reason, mental faculty
saneness, mental soundness
sense, intellect
sensibleness, sense
sensibility, sensibleness
sensitiveness, acuteness of sense
synesthesia, realization of a sensation derived from a sensation caused by a different stimulus

Recollection

acknowledgment, recognition
memory, recollection
recollection, remembrance
recognition, a knowing again
recurrence, recollection
reflection, recollection
remembrance, recollection
reminiscence, recollection
retrospection, remembrance

Sureness

assurance, confidence
certainty, absolute knowledge
certitude, assurance

NOUNS (Continued)

confidence, certitude
conviction, assurance
sureness, absolute knowledge

Established Knowledge

eclecticism, system of philosophic knowledge
history, knowledge of facts
jurisprudence, knowledge of man's rights
philosophy, knowledge of phenomena
science, proven knowledge of natural phenomena

PERSONS

alumna, university graduate (fem.)
alumnus, as above (male)
authority, one who is recognized as having special knowledge
bachelor, one having the lowest university degree
bookman, scholar
bluestocking, learned woman
clairvoyant, one having the power of unusual perception
classic, one who is highly versed
classicist, classic
connoisseur, a wise judge, especially of art, music, etc.
dean, most distinguished representative of the literature of a country
doctor, one learned in any branch of knowledge, a university official
esoterist, one having the confidential knowledge of the enlightened few
fox, cunning person
genius, one having remarkable aptitude
gownsman, one who wears a gown professionally
graduate, alumnus
Hellenist, one learned in Greek art
highbrow, highly intellectual person

PERSONS (Continued)

humanist, one versed in human nature
intellectual, scholar
litterateur, a literary man
Magi, wise man of the East
magician, wizard
oracle, person of reputed wisdom
philosopher, one noted for correct judgment and practical wisdom
poilu, veteran
pundit, one versed in Hindu lore, etc.
quidnunc, pretender to knowledge of current events
recognizer, one who recognizes
recognizor, one who enters into a recognizance
sage, man of wisdom and venerable age
savant, man of learning
scientist, one who has a knowledge of science
sciolist, one who knows a little of many things
sophist, one versed in philosophy, politics, etc.
scholar, man of letters
sorcerer, wizard
sorceress, as above (fem.)
stoic, one of a school of Greek philosophers
theosophist, one who has pretension to theosophic knowledge
veteran, one long experienced
wiseacre, would-be wise person
wit, witty person
witch, woman supposed to have supernatural power
wizard, one having supernatural power

BEINGS

Athena, Greek goddess of wisdom
Ganesa, god of wisdom
Jinnee, wise spirit
Minerva, Roman goddess of wisdom
Psyche, soul spirit
Thoth, god of learning
Urania, muse of astronomy

HEARING see— **ASSOCIATIVE**

vs. Insensibility—Apathy 110A

118

VERBS

attend, listen
eavesdrop, listen surreptitiously
hark, harken
harken, listen
hear, apprehend aurally
listen, attend closely
overhear, hear what is private
scout, gain audible information, etc., for those that follow
shrive (write), now means to hear or receive a confession

ADJECTIVES

acoustic (to hear), pertaining to the ear, hearing, sound, etc.
audible, hearing or capable of being heard
audient, listening
auditory, pertaining to hearing
aural, pertaining to the ear or hearing
auricular, aural
ausculative, detecting by ausculation
deaf, hearing indistinctly, or not at all
earminded, apprehending or learning by the ear
stethoscopic, pertaining to instrumental detection by the ear

NOUNS

acoustics (to hear), science of hearing and sound
auricle, external ear
ausculation, audient detection by means of the stethoscope or by direct application of the ear
clairaudience, the hearing of sounds ordinarily inaudible
deafness, indistinctness or lack of hearing
ear, delicate perception of sound
hearing, aural apprehension
oyer, legal hearing, etc.
preaudience, right of being heard
stethoscopy, stethoscopic hearing

MEDIUMS FOR HEARING

audiometer, instrument for gauging the power of hearing
audiphone, instrument for aiding hearing through the teeth and auditory nerves
auricle, external ear
auditorium, auditory
auditory, place allotted to an audience

MEDIUMS FOR HEARING (Continued)

ausculator, instrument for detecting sound
confessional, place for hearing confessions
dentiphone, audiphone
ear, organ of hearing
listening-post, place for listening
lug, the ear
mute, stethoscope
stethoscope, instrument for audient detection of chest-diseases

PERSONS

acoustician, expert in acoustics
addressee, auditor
audience, assembly of hearers
auditory, hearer
client (to hear), one who aurally receives professional service
clientage, clients collectively
deaf-mute, a deaf person

INTERJECTIONS

hark, hist
hear, listen
hist, hear
listen, hist
oyez, "hear ye"

---

124 (Continued)

VERBS (Continued)

Influence

affect, cause a change
cause, influence
effect, influence
influence, produce a sensible effect

ADJECTIVES

Miscellaneous

affecting, exciting the emotions
contagious, affecting by contact or disease
influential, imparting influence
lambent, touching lightly, etc.

ADJECTIVES (Continued)

palpable, meaning originally AFFERENT and now EFFERENT and capable of being felt by touching, etc.
tactile, perceptive to feeling
touching, tactual
tactual, effecting by touch
tangent, touching
ticklish, touching lightly

NOUNS

Miscellaneous

contact, touch
contiguity, contact

NOUNS (Continued)

extension, contiguity
graze, a rubbing touch
palpability, perceptible influence
palpation, perceptible pulsation
pique, the term uttered when a fencer makes a touch
tactility, perceptible touch
tangibility, tactility
thriller, that which affects with a thrill
tickler, that which tickles
titillation, a tickling touch, act of touching

SEEING—VISION, ETC.　　see—

vs. Insensibility—Apathy 110A

ASSOCIATIVE

Conception—Conscience 111
Search—Scrutiny—Probe 119E
Discovery—Identification 119F
Watchfulness—Vigilance 119G

119A

VERBS

Perceive
behold, look upon
observe, take notice
perceive, observe
see, perceive
sight, see
view, behold
visualize, make visible
witness, see

Discern
discern, distinguish
distinguish, perceive
mark, take notice

Glimpse
blink, get a glimpse
glance, look hurriedly
glimpse, glance
notice, see

Look
gaze, look earnestly
leer, cast a side-look
look, see with the eye

VERBS (Continued)

peer, look narrowly
quiz, peer

ADJECTIVES

Miscellaneous
binocular, for both eyes
bird's-eye, seen from above
dioptric, aiding vision as
with a lens, etc.
ocular, seeing
optic, implying sight
orbital, relating to the eye
perceptive, having per-
ception
visional, visual
visionary, having vision
visual, pertaining to sight

NOUNS

Perception
discernment, perception
observance, observation

NOUNS (Continued)

notice, observation
perception, ocular appre-
hension
observation, visual notice
view, vision
vis, (vision) used in the
phrase "vis-a-vis"
vision, ocular apprehension

Eyesight
eyesight, ocular perception
perceptibility, perception
perspicuity, ocular or mental discernment
perspicacity, perspicuity
perceptivity, perception
sight, vision

Glimpse
glance, look
gliff, glimpse
glimpse, quick look
look, act of viewing

119B

ADJECTIVES

Defective Sight
blind, seeing indistinctly
cock-eyed, eyes crossed
cross-eyed, cock-eyed
color-blind, unable to distinguish colors
(B). colour-blind
presbyoptic, having far
sight while near objects
are indistinct
purblind, dim sighted
sightless, without sight
short-sighted, myopic

NOUNS

Defective Sight
ablepsia, blindness
amblyopia, dimness of
vision

NOUNS (Continued)

amaurosis, confused vision
followed by blindness
astigmatism, variation of
sight due to unequal
focus
blindness, lack of sight or
dim-sightedness
catopsis, morbidly keen
vision
daltonism, color-blindness
dichromatism, color-blindness
emblyopia, dimness of
sight
hæmalopia, vision which
perceives objects as ap-
pearing red
hemeralopia, day-blindness
or night-blindness

NOUNS (Continued)

hemiopia, vision by which
only half of an object is
seen
hypermetropia, far-sighted-
ness
illusion, unreal vision
lippitude, blearedness of
the eye
macropsis, vision which
exaggerates objects to
grotesqueness
misconception, wrong per-
ception
myopia, shortsightedness
nyctalopia, night-blindness
presbyopia, farsightedness
with indistinct near-
vision

119C

VISUAL ORGANS

eye, organ of sight
eyespot, a rudimentary
visual organ
cornea, medium of the eye

iris, medium of the eye
optic, eye
orb, eye

pupil, medium of sight in
the eye
retina, medium of sensation
of the eye

119D

PERSONS

beholder, observer
clairvoyant, one who pro-
fesses to see the ordi-
narily imperceptible

PERSONS (Continued)

daltonian, color-blind
person
observer, spectator
percipient, one who per-
ceives

PERSONS (Continued)

spectator, beholder
witness, one who bears
witness

SEARCH—SCRUTINY
see— {
vs. Negligence......126B

ASSOCIATIVE

Inquiry—Quest 41A
Deliberation 114
Watchfulness 119G

Study—Learning 116
Sight—Vision 119A
Desire—Hope 39

119E
VERBS

Search
ferret, search by cunning methods
hunt, search
look, hunt, search
nose, pry into
quest, search
ransack, rummage
rummage, ransack
search, seek, inspect
seek, search

Scrutinize
eye, scrutinize
pry, scrutinize
quiz, peer
scan, scrutinize
scrutinize, inspect closely
spy, explore secretly

Stare, Etc.
gaze, look intently
glance, view quickly
gloat, gaze earnestly, etc.
ogle, look upon fondly
peep, pry
peer, look narrowly
stare, gaze

Contemplate
behold, observe carefully
contemplate, view
mark, observe critically
observe, regard attentively
regard, observe closely
speculate, regard earnestly
view, regard

Inspect
analyze, examine
bolt, examine with care
compare, note difference
con, seek, test, examine
consider, examine
examine, inspect
inspect, examine narrowly
investigate, seek to learn
research, investigate
sift, scrutinize
study, examine
winnow, examine

Experiment
experiment, seek to discover some truth, etc.
test, seek through experiment, etc.
try, examine

Probe
delve, probe or seek for things hidden
fathom, sound
feel, probe
fumble, grope

VERBS (Continued)
grabble, feel for confusedly
grope, seek blindly
probe, feel for, search
sound, probe for depth

Pursue
chase, course
course, hunt
follow, course
pursue, search
pussy-foot, seek stealthily
stalk, seek stealthily

Adventure
adventure, search for advantage or pleasure
prospect, search
venture, seek adventure

Survey, Etc.
explore, search
pierce, explore
reconnoiter, examine, survey
scour, search thoroughly
survey, examine critically
traverse, survey carefully

Search, Etc.
botanize, explore botanically
canvass, examine
coyote, seek gold or adventure singlehanded or as by chance
dissect, examine visually or mentally
etymologize, investigate the original significance of words
forage, search for food
maraud, search for plunder
overhaul, overtake and scrutinize
trek, seek settlement by wagon travel

ADJECTIVES
Scrutinous
curious, scrutinous
discerning, percipient
hawk-eyed, keen-eyed
keen, hawk-eyed
keen-eyed, penetrating
lynx-eyed, keen-eyed
penetrating, discerning
percipient, perceiving keenly
perspicacious, keenly discerning
piercing, perspicacious

ADJECTIVES (Continued)
prying, curious
scrutinous, examining closely
spying, exploring secretly
searching, seeking

Contemplative
attentive, observant
askance, observing from the corner of the eye
considerate, attentive
contemplative, regardant
mindful, attentive
observant, mindful
observing, observant
regardant, looking backward or behind
regardful, regardant
speculative, contemplating uncertainly

Miscellaneous
experimental, with searching experiment
nomadic, wandering searchingly

NOUNS
Search
quest, search
search, a seeking after

Scrutiny
discernment, penetration
espionage, a spying
penetration, discernment
scrutiny, close inspection
surveillance, a spying supervision

Stare, Etc.
cast, glance
glance, quick look
ogle, side look
stare, fixed look

Contemplation
consideration, examination
contemplation, considerate observation
observance, observation
observation, regardful examination
perspicacity, ocular or mental discernment
regard, observation
view, survey

Inspection
disquisition, systematic investigation, etc.
examination, critical inspection
(Continued on page 245)

NOUNS (Continued)

exploitation, examination for development
inspection, examination
investigation, inquiry
perlustration, inspection all over
research, examination
study, careful examination

Experiment

balloon d'essair, test used in determining the direction of air currents; hence a feeler for public opinion
experiment, search by trial
test, examination

Probe

probation, a probing for character, moral trial
probe, examination

Pursuit

hunting, search for game
pursuit, search
venery, act of hunting

Adventure

adventure, hazardous venture
venture, search for advantage, pleasure, etc.

Survey

exploration, geographical investigation
perambulation, annual survey of a parish
reconnoiter, survey, especially during war
reconnaissance, preliminary examination for military purposes

NOUNS (Continued)

survey, close examination

Search, Etc.

autopsy, personal examination
dissection, minute examination
foraging, search for provisions
ophthalmoscopy, examination of the eye

PERSONS

adventurer, one who seeks fortune or pleasure in doubtful enterprises
detective, one engaged in espionage
digger, one who pursues or strives, as by digging or ardent effort
examiner, investigator
hunter, searcher
huntsman, one who hunts for game
inspector, scrutinizer
investigator, examiner
nomad, a searcher for food and pasture
observer, one who observes
pioneer, explorer
prospector, one who searches for minerals
pursuer, hunter
pussy-foot, a sneaking underhanded worker
prier, pussy-foot
sleuth, detective
spectator, one who sees or beholds

PERSONS (Continued)

spotter, sleuth
spy, one who covertly seeks enemy plans, etc.
surveyor, one who inspects with a view of determined action
visitant, visitor
visitor, inspector, etc.

OBSERVATION PLACES

belfry, watch tower
belvedere, edifice for viewing surrounding scenes
blimp, observation balloon
crow's-nest, lookout
gazebo, belvedere
lookout, outlook
observatory, building fitted for making observations
outlook, observation post
panopticon, an observation arrangement affording a view of prisoners, employees, etc., without their knowledge
searchlight, an observatory light for searching out objects
stand, a raised platform for observers
turret, a tower on a man-o'-war

BEING

Diana, goddess of woods and hunting, of moon and light, of childbirth and of departed souls

---

119F

DISCOVERY—RECOGNITION	see—	ASSOCIATIVE

vs. Failure—Misfortune 127B

119F

VERBS

Discover

detect, find out
discover, detect
espy, discover
foresee, see beforehand
find, discover
ken, recognize
spy, discover

Notice

glimpse, catch sight of
note, take notice

VERBS (Continued)

notice, observe
observe, discern
sight, spy
witness, see personally

Discern

discern, distinguish
discriminate, discern
distinguish, discriminate
identify, recognize
recognize, discover

ADJECTIVES

Miscellaneous

askance (adverb), seeing from the corner of the eye
astrological, by means of stars
auspicious, favorable
cognizant, noting discovery, perception, etc.

(Continued on page 246)

ADJECTIVES (Continued)

discernible, noting discernment, cognizance, etc.

discreet, recognizing and choosing the best course of action

discriminate, observing or recognizing difference

introspective, looking inward or discovering one's thoughts, etc.

intuitional, noting the faculty of recognition, as more subtle than conclusion from reasoning

intuitive, as above, analogous to radioactive perception

noticeable, implying recognition, etc.

prescient, recognizing beforehand

provident, discreet

providential, prescient

prospective, recognizing promising subjects or objects within reach of sight

ADJECTIVES (Continued)

provisional (before-see), providing necessity concomitant with recognition for future requirements

provisory, as above

retrospective, taking discriminate notice

retrospective, discovering or observing things past

NOUNS

Miscellaneous

animadversion, recognition, indentification

cognizance, judicial notice

detection, a finding

discernment, discrimination, identification

discovery, detection

discretion, power of recognizing difference

discrimination, discernment, recognition

finding, discovery

foresight, discovery beforehand

NOUNS (Continued)

identification, retrospective recognition

intuition, mental faculty of recognition

notice, detection

prescience, fore-knowledge or recognition

prevision, recognition beforehand

provision, means provided as necessary to meet the recognized requirements of the future

prudence, foresight

recognition, identification

recognizance, recognition

retrospection, a looking on the past

PERSONS

astrologer, one who discovers and forecasts events

discoverer, explorer

explorer, discoverer, etc.

spy, one who spies or discovers, as in espionage

119G

WATCHFULNESS—VIGILANCE		ASSOCIATIVE
vs. Negligence—Laziness 126B	see—	Seeing—Sight—Vision 119A
		Inspection—Examination 119E
		Discovery—Recognition 119F

119G

VERBS

advert, turn attention

attend, watch closely

await, look for

beware, heed

bivouac, watch in open-air encampment

guard, keep vigil

heed, regard with care

mind, heed

regard, mind

sentinel, watch over

vigil, watch, as during hours of sleep

wake, watch, etc.

watch, be attentive or vigilant

ADJECTIVES

advertent, attentive

agape, watching eagerly or with open mouth

alert, watchful

argus-eyed, watchful

attentive, alert

canny, cautious

ADJECTIVES (Continued)

circumspect, watchful on all sides

careful, watchful

cautious, circumspect

guarded, cautious

heedful, guarded

mindful, heedful

painstaking, careful

precautionary, alert

prospective, watchful beforehand

regardful, watchful

sleepless, wary

vigilant, alert

watchful, circumspect

wakeful, watchful

wary, circumspect

NOUNS

advertence, heedfulness

advertency, attention

alertness, watchfulness

attention, watchfulness

attentiveness, attention

bivouac, a watch in open-air encampment

NOUNS (Continued)

care, attention

caution, heedfulness

circumspection, watchfulness

heed, careful regard

mindfulness, watchfulness

precaution, care

regard, attention

surveillance, close watch

sleeplessness, watchfulness

vigil, watch

vigilance, watchfulness

wake, a vigil

watch, vigilance

watchfulness, circumspection

wariness, caution

PERSONS

guard, sentinel

sentinel, sentry

sentry, a watch

watcher, one who watches

watchman, watcher

SMELL—
OLFACTORY PERCEPTION   see—

vs. Insensibility—Apathy 110A

ASSOCIATIVE
Taste—Appetite 51A
Feeling—Sensation 121
Hearing—Aural Apprehension 118
Sight—Visual Apprehension 119A

120
VERBS
nose, smell, scent
savor, smell with delight
scent, smell
smell, inhale odor
smoke, inhale tobacco
 smoke
sniff, scent

VERBS (Continued)
snuff, sniff

ADJECTIVES
olfactory, pertaining to
 smelling

NOUNS
smell, act of smelling

NOUNS (Continued)
smelling, smell
scent, olfactory perception
sniff, a smelling
smoke, a smoking

ORGANS OF SMELL
nose, the organ of smell
olfactory, the nose

121

FEELING—SENSIBILITY*   see—

vs. Insensibility—Apathy....110A

ASSOCIATIVE
Taste ....51A   Mirth—Gladness 71A
Smell 120   Laughter 71B
Hearing 118   Sorrow—Pain 31
Sight 119A

121
VERBS
Feel
experience, feel emotion
feel, be conscious of touch
 or effect
handle, feel
perceive, become conscious
 of sensation, etc.
touch, perceive by feeling

Thrill, Etc.
fornicate, feel sexually
itch, feel a tingling with
 a desire to scratch
thrill, feel an exquisite
 sensation
tickle, feel titillation
tingle, thrill
titillate, having a tickling
 or gratifying sensation

Kiss
kiss, touch with lips
osculate, kiss
smack, kiss

Caress
caress, fondle
cuddle, hug
dally, cuddle
dandle, fondle
fondle, handle fondly
pet, caress

Embrace
clasp, embrace
embrace, hug
hug, clasp fondly
pat, touch fondly

ADJECTIVES
Sensate
sensate, perceiving by the
 senses
sensational, having sensation, etc.
sensible, having perception
 by the senses, etc.
sensorial, noting perception
 by the sensorium
sensual, having sensation
sentient, sensate

Sensitive
alive, sensitive
highstrung, highly sensitive
itching, feeling an un-
 easiness in the skin
quick, sensitive
sensitive, feeling quickly
tender, sensitive
ticklish, sensible to slight
 touches
touching, perceiving by the
 sense of feeling

Emotional
compassionate, sympathetic
emotional, having excited
 feeling
heartfelt, deeply felt
sentimental, having feeling
 provoked by a condition
 of excellence, object of
 affection, or other ex-
 traordinary state
soulful, sensate

ADJECTIVES (Continued)
spirituelle, characterized
 by a conscious bearing
 of exquisite grace, delicacy, and refinement
sympathetic, heartfelt

Perceptive
infelt, felt within
palpable, feeling easily
perceptive, having sensi-
 tiveness
tactile, perceiving by the
 sense of touch
tactual, pertaining to the
 organs of touch

Feeling Hot
burned, wounded by heat
heated, hot
hot, uncomfortably warm
scorched, burned
warm, heated

Feeling Cold
chilled, frigid
chilly, cold
cold, uncomfortably below
 warmth
frigid, icy
frozen, frigid
icy, frozen

NOUNS
Feeling
feeling, consciousness of
 touch
(Continued on page 248)

---

*Feeling is the issue of contact, environment, or other influence upon matter or life,
and the words listed herewith express the variations of this function, or the variations
of the significants used to express FEELING.

FRAGRANCE—(ODOR)   see—   **ASSOCIATIVE**
vs. Stink—Stench 123   Food—Drink—Condiments 48P
Smell—Olfactory Perception 120

122

VERBS

Miscellaneous
flavor, impart smell or taste
perfume, impart fragrance
reek, smell
savor, have a peculiar smell, etc.
(B). savour
scent, impart odor
smell, emit an odor

ADJECTIVES

Fragrant
ambrosial, exquisitely sweet-smelling
aromatic, fragrant
balmy, fragrant
fragrant, sweet-smelling
musky, fragrant
odoriferous, diffusing fragrance
odorous, fragrant
pungent, stimulating
redolent, fragrant
scented, sweet-smelling
savory, having aroma
spicy, aromatic
sweet, fragrant
thuriferous, producing or bearing frankincense

Exquisite
delicate, exquisite
delightful, pleasing
exotic, strangely sweet
exquisite, delightful

ADJECTIVES (Continued)
pleasing, delightful

NOUNS

Fragrance
aroma, fragrance
breath, fragrance
fragrance, sweet smell
perfume, fragrance
redolence, fragrance
savor, perfume
(B). savour

Odor
flavor, particular smell, etc.
(B). flavour
odor, smell
(B). odour
scent, smell
smell, odor
thurification, odor of frankincense

Perfumery, Etc.
cordial, aromatic spirit
eau, a water-perfume
elixir, perfume
essence, perfume
lavender, perfume
perfume, fragrant fluid
perfumery, various perfumes

Aromatics
aloes, fragrant resin or wood
ambergris, material used in perfumery
ambrosia, anything pleasing to the smell, etc.

NOUNS (Continued)
aromatic, fragrant drug
balm, fragrant exudation
balsam, aromatic
bandolin, perfumed substance
bergamot, lemon-rind oil used in perfumery
flavoring, fragrant essence
(B). flavouring
frankincense, fragrant resin
incense, diffused fragrance
mint, aromatic herb
musk, fragrant material
myrrh, aromatic resin
pastil, aromatic paste
pomade, perfumed ointment
savory, aromatic herb
spice, aromatic flavoring

Nosegay, Etc.
cachou, aromatic pill
nosegay, fragrant posy
posy, nosegay
sachet, perfumed bag

VESSELS
censer, incense-burning vessel
thurible, censer
vinaigrette, box for smelling-salts, etc.

PERSONS
thurifer, thurible bearer

---

121 (Continued)

NOUNS (Continued)
palpitation, throbbing of the heart
sensation, sensibility
sentience, sensation
touch, sense of feeling

Sensitiveness
sensitiveness, acute mental or physical perception
tenderness, sensitiveness
touchiness, sensitiveness

Emotion, Etc.
affection, the sensation of emotion
compassion, sympathy
emotion, excited feeling
passion, strong feeling
pathos, deep feeling
pity, sympathy
sentiment, sensibility

NOUNS (Continued)
sentimentalism, sentimentality
sentimentality, the state of being readily affected and reacting without reason
sympathy, mutual feeling of pleasure or pain

Perceptivity
palpability, the quality of easily perceiving mentally or physically
perceptivity, sensitiveness
sensibility, mental or physical perception
tactility, perceptibility by touch

Thrill, Etc.
formication, sexual intercourse

NOUNS (Continued)
fornication, unlawful sexual intercourse
itch, a teasing feeling
sensualism, sensuality
sensuality, gratification of the senses
thrill, exquisite feeling
titillation, a tickling or exquisite feeling

MEDIUMS
antenna, the feelers upon the heads of insects
feeler, that which feels
quick, sensitive parts
sensorium, the seat of sensation

PERSONS
sensualist, one who indulges the senses

STINK—STENCH

vs. Fragrance 122

see—

ASSOCIATIVE

Dirt—Grime—Filth 129A
Impurity—Adulteration 146C
Rottenness—Decay 128C

123

VERBS
reek, stink
stink, give bad odor

ADJECTIVES

Stinking
effluvial, having offensive
exhalations
empyreumatic, smelling
like burnt wood
fetid, stinking
frowzy, musty
foul, fusty
fulsome, offensive
fusty, ill-smelling
hircine, having a goat-
like smell
inodorous, devoid of smell
malodorous, foul
mephitic, reeking
miasmal, giving polluting
exhalations
nocent, noxious
noisome, ill-smelling
noxious, offensive
odious, offensive
reeking, foul
stinking, ill-smelling
suffocating, stifling with
noxious air
stifling, suffocating

Putrid, Etc.
moldy, fusty

ADJECTIVES (Continued)
musty, fusty
nasty, disgusting
putrescent, putrid
putrid, rotten, etc.
rancid, rank-smelling
rank, rancid, etc.
rotten, putrid
sour, foul
stale, impure

Disagreeable
abominable, offensive
bad, odious
beastly, abominable
disagreeable, unpleasant
disgustful, nasty
loathsome, disgustful
loud, strong-smelling
obnoxious, odious
offensive, foul
pernicious, noxious
revolting, loathsome
unpleasant, unwholesome
unwholesome, noxious

NOUNS

Stink, Etc.
breath, exhalation
effluvium, exhalations from
decaying matter
empyreuma, odor from
decay

NOUNS (Continued)
exhalation, an emitted
vapor
fetor, stench
fume, suffocating exhala-
tions
fustiness, ill smell
halitus, breath, etc.
miasma, polluting
exhalations
mustiness, fustiness
offensiveness, stench, etc.
ozostomia, bad breath
putridity, rottenness,
foulness
rancidity, rank odor, etc.
stench, stink
stink, disgusting smell

ANIMALS
fitch, polecat
goat, hircine-smelling
animal
polecat, skunk-like animal
skunk, animal which emits
a fetid secretion

MEDIUMS—PLANTS
asafetida, a fetid drug
(B). asafoetida
garlic, strong-smelling root
etc., etc.

TACTILITY—TOUCH*

vs. Feeling—Sensibility 121
vs. Insensibility—Apathy 110A

see—

ASSOCIATIVE

Excitation—Inspiration 8
Influence—Importance 135B
Adjacency—Nearness 149M
Feeling—Sensibility 121

---

*The classification TACTILITY, No. 124, and FEELING, No. 121, give definite dis-
tinction, through the respective forces of EFFERENCE and AFFERENCE, to a class
of words that are commonly confused with one another.

124

VERBS

Touch
abut, touch
extend, reach or touch
graze, touch or rub lightly
handle, feel or touch
reach, touch
tickle, touch lightly
titillate, tickle

VERBS (Continued)
touch, to perceive by the
sense of feeling (AFFER-
ENT); also to affect, im-
press, strike, etc. (EF-
FERENT)

Touch Hard
contact, touch
dent, indent

VERBS (Continued)
hit, strike
impress, stamp
indent, impress
nudge, touch gently
pound, strike
stamp, make impression
strike, contact forcibly
(Continued on page 242)

DISORDER

CRIME—INJURY—DESTRUCTION

DISORDER—	ASSOCIATIVE

125A

VERBS

Disorder
confuse, disorder
demoralize, disorganize
disorder, confuse
disorganize, disorder
disqualify, render unfit
upset, disorder

Agitate
agitate, unsettle
convulse, agitate violently
discompose, disarrange
disturb, disorder
jar, disturb
jolt, jar
perturb, disturb
stampede, start a panic
swell, increase in violence
trouble, agitate
unsettle, confuse

Jumble
derange, confuse
disarray, disorder
dishevel, disarray
jumble, confuse
muddle, confuse
scramble, mix confusedly

Mix, Etc.
disarrange, disarray
displace, misplace
misplace, disarrange
mix, jumble
shuffle, disarrange

Tangle
entangle, tangle
involve, entangle
mat, entangle
muss, disorder
snarl, entangle
tangle, entangle
tousle, disorder

Litter
clutter, litter
litter, scatter carelessly
scatter, confuse

Distort, Etc.
contort, twist
distort, disfigure
twist, distort
wrench, wrest
wrest, distort
yank, twist

Rumple, Etc.
crinkle, bend irregularly
crumple, rumple

VERBS (Continued)
roughen, make irregular
rumple, crumple
ruffle, disarrange
wrinkle, crinkle

Disfigure
deflower, despoil beauty, etc.
deform, mar
disfigure, deform
mar, disfigure

Debase
abuse, violate
debase, mar
pervert, debase
profane, debase
prostitute, debase
violate, abuse

ADJECTIVES
Chaotic
acephalous, without head or ruler; disorganized
anarchic, in confusion
chaotic, disordered
confused, disordered
desultory, unsystematic
disordered, without order
disorderly, orderless
disorganized, disordered
haphazard, desultory
inharmonious, disordered
lawless, without order
orderless, disordered
promiscuous, scattered, mingled
topsy-turvy, disordered
unorganized, chaotic
unsystematic, without order
wild, chaotic

Discrepant
ameliorable, imperfect
discrepant, inharmonious
imperfect, discrepant
inappropriate, unfit
ineligible, unsuited
infelicitous, inappropriate
negative, not conforming
unfit, discrepant
unsuitable, unfit

Agitated
agitated, turbid
convulsive, tumultuous

ADJECTIVES (Continued)
obstreperous, implying disturbance
pellmell, in confused violence
riotous, chaotic
tumultuous, turbulent
turbulent, in riotous tumult
turbid, agitated

Mixed
indiscriminate, discrepant
mixed, confused
shuffled, disorganized

Tangled
entangled, tangled
knotted, knotty
knotty, irregular with knots
matted, tangled
mussed, tangled
tangled, intricately confused

Littered
junky, disordered
jungly, densely tangled
littered, mussy
mussy, disordered
scattered, confused
trashy, junky
untidy, disordered

Distorted
crooked, distorted
distorted, twisted
twisted, crooked
wry, twisted

Irregular
askew (adverb), awry
awry (adverb), disorderly
irregular, uneven
lopsided, unbalanced
ramshackle, disordered and shaky
unbalanced, discrepant
uneven, irregular
zigzag, uneven

Rumpled
bent, crooked
crinkled, rumpled
jagged, rough
rugged, uneven
rumpled, wrinkled
rough, irregular
wrinkled, rumpled
(Continued on page 252)

STORMS—WINDS, ETC.   see—   **ASSOCIATIVE**

                     Disorder Index 125

vs. Calmness ....132A { Disorder—Confusion 125A

                     Anger—Wrath 29

125B

VERBS

Miscellaneous

blast, blow violently
blow, gale
breeze, blow gently
gale, blast
storm, blow violently

ADJECTIVES

Miscellaneous

airy, breezy
breezy, blowing gently
cyclonic, tempestuous
inclement, stormy
rough, inclement
stormy, tempestuous
tempestuous, turbulent
turbulent, tempestuous
violent, turbulent
windy, breezy

NOUNS

Storm, Etc.

blizzard, hurricane
bayamo, tempest
bora, fierce wind
cyclone, violent storm
gale, stormy wind

NOUNS (Continued)

hurricane, violent gale
simoon, sand-laden wind
sirocco, desert wind
solano, hot wind
squall, violent wind
storm, tempest
storminess, violent weather
storming, storminess
tempest, hurricane
tornado, whirlwind
tramontana, blighting wind
typhoon, tornado
whirlwind, spiral wind

Wind, Etc.

anti-trade, an opposite
  trade wind
foehn, warm wind
head-wind, contrary wind
monsoon, periodical wind
norther, north wind
pampero, pampas wind
wind, breeze

Puff, Etc.

afflatus, blast of air
blast, sudden wind

NOUNS (Continued)

draught, sudden wind
flurry, sudden gust
gust, sudden squall
puff, short blast
whiff, sudden wind, etc.

Breeze

breeze, gentle gale
breath, gentle wind
sigh, slight breath
zephyr, gentle breeze

Miscellaneous

hailstorm, violent hail
  fall
lightning, cloud flash
rain, cloud fall in drops
rainfall, shower
rainstorm, violent rain
shower, rain
snow, snowstorm
snowstorm, violent snow
thunder, lightning report

BEINGS

Aeolus, god of winds
Thor, god of thunder, etc.
Zeus, god of storms, etc.

125A (Continued)

ADJECTIVES (Continued)

Disfigured

deformed, malformed
disfigured, deformed
malformed, deformed
unfeatured, deformed

NOUNS

Chaos

anarchism, confusion
chaos, disorder
desultoriness, irregularity
disorder, chaos

Agitation

ado, confused bustle
agitation, disturbance
bedlam, uproar
bustle, commotion
commotion, agitation
confusion, commotion
convulsion, tumult
discomposure, agitation
disturbance, agitation
excitement, pother
ferment, commotion
flurry, confusion
fray, riot
furore, great confusion
fuss, disorderly stir

NOUNS (Continued)

hubbub, uproar
huddle, crowded commotion
hurly-burly, tumult
hurry, bustle
hurry-scurry, pother
imbroglio, confusion
pandemonium, uproar
panic, wild alarm
perturbation, disturbance
pother, confusion
riot, hubbub
rumpus (colloq.), riot
ruction, disturbance
stampede, panic
stir, confusion
tumult, hubbub
turbulence, tumult
turmoil, disturbance
unrest, confusion
uproar, turmoil

Tangle, Etc.

derangement, disorder
disarrangement, disorder
entanglement, wilderness
jungle, wilderness
tangle, entanglement
waste, wilds
wilderness, wilds

NOUNS (Continued)

wilds, wild country

Litter, Etc.

debris, rubbish
jumble, confused mass
junk, discarded refuse
litter, scattered waste
medley, jumble
mess, confused mass
mix, jumble
muss, litter
muddle, mess
raff, jumble
remains, ruined mass
riffraff, rubbish
rubbish, raff
trash, rubbish
waste, litter

Jetsam, Etc.

driftage, rubbish
flotsam, goods lost at sea
jetsam, cast-off goods
wreckage, ruined mass

Desolation

desolation, ruin
destruction, desolation
ruin, waste

EXCESS	125C	ASSOCIATIVE	
EXTRAVAGANCE	125C-1	Destruction	130-O
VIOLENCE	125C-2	Overplus	26
INCONTINENCE	125C-3 see—	Generosity	43A
		Passion	39B
vs. Reserve	132C	Desire	39
vs. Calmness	132B	Boldness	42
		Mightiness	137B
		Haste—Hurry	9
		Sin—Crime	130A

125C EXCESS—Also see 125C-1, 125C-2, 125C-3

VERBS

Exceed

exceed, go beyond
excel, surpass
surpass, exceed

Set Free

free, set loose
loose, free
unbind, unleash
unleash, free
untie, unleash

ADJECTIVES

Excessive

excessive, extreme
extreme, uttermost
intense, excessive
sheer, utter
ultra, extreme
utter, unqualified
uttermost, extreme

Forward

familiar, forward
forward, unconstrained
pert, forward
precocious, forward

Immoderate

immoderate, inordinate

ADJECTIVES (Continued)

imprudent, unrestrained
inordinate, excessive
intemperate, unrestrained
licentious, intemperate
undue, excessive
unreserved, withholding
nothing

Unrestrained

exempt, unrestricted
free, unrestricted
immune, exempt
independent, free
loose, unrestrained
unconstrained, loose
unbridled, unrestrained
unincumbered, free
unrestrained, free
unrestricted, unrestrained

Unconditional

absolute, unconditional
autocratic, absolute
unconditional, absolute
unlimited, unrestricted
unqualified, absolute

NOUNS

Excess

excess, excessiveness

NOUNS (Continued)

excessiveness, exorbitance
exorbitance, excess
exuberance, superabun-
dance
pass, state of extremity
profusion, excess
superabundance, excess

Freedom

abandon, unrestraint
abandonment, abandon
catholicity, liberalism
freedom, liberty
immunity, freedom
independence, freedom
latitude, unrestraint
liberalism, unconserva-
tiveness
liberty, license
license, freedom
privilege, immunity
savagery, wildness
unrestraint, freedom

PERSONS

extrane, one who is
extreme
liberal, a non-conservative

125C-1 EXTRAVAGANCE—Also see 125C, 125C-2, 125C-3

VERBS

Miscellaneous

dissipate, squander
fritter, waste slowly
lavish, squander
trifle, fritter
squander, dissipate
waste, squander

ADJECTIVES

Miscellaneous

exorbitant, extravagant
extravagant, unsparing
exuberant, lavish
generous, lavish
improvident, prodigal
lavish, extravagant

ADJECTIVES (Continued)

liberal, lavish
prodigal, wasteful
profuse, generous
spendthrift, prodigal
tall, extravagant
thriftless, prodigal
unsparing, lavish
wasteful, improvident

NOUNS

Miscellaneous

exorbitant, extravagant
extravagance, wastefulness
exuberance, lavishness
generosity, lavishness

NOUNS (Continued)

improvidence, thriftless-
ness
imprudence, improvidence
indiscretion, imprudence
lavishness, extravagance
liberality, generosity
prodigality, wastefulness
profusion, exuberance
thriftlessness, imprudence
waste, wastefulness
wastefulness, prodigality

PERSONS

spendthrift, wastrel
wastrel, profligate
profligate, spendthrift

| VIOLENCE | see— { | (ASSOCIATIVE 125C) |
| vs. Reserve ....132C | { | |

125C-2
VERBS
Miscellaneous
burst, explode
explode, burst
flare, act violently
plunge, act suddenly
sky-hoot, rush violently

ADJECTIVES
Violent
fierce, violent
irrepressible, ungovernable
mighty, vehement
mortal, violent
riotous, unrestrained
strong, violent
unchecked, unrestrained
ungoverned, unrestrained
unrestrained, wild
vehement, violent
violent, regardless
Devilish
devilish, diabolical
diabolical, fierce
hellish, diabolical
Wild
savage, wild
tameless, wild
untamed, wild
wild, violent
wildcat, rampant
Headlong
breakneck, precipitate
hasty, rash

ADJECTIVES (Continued)
headlong, precipitous
heady, precipitate
impetuous, heedless
precipitate, impetuous
precipitous, impetuous
scorching, precipitous
sky-hooting, breakneck
Reckless
desperate, rash
foolhardy, rash
harum-scarum, reckless
heedless, precipitous
impulsive, unreserved
incautious, heedless
indiscreet, indiscriminate
indiscriminate, impetuous
rampant, overleaping
rash, reckless
regardless, heedless
reckless, heedless
unbridled, unrestrained
unreserved, rash
Stormy
inclement, tempestuous
stormy, tempestuous
tempestuous, violent
Explosive
bursting, explosive
crashing, violent
explosive, bursting or
  acting violently
volcanic, precipitate

NOUNS
Miscellaneous
burst, explosion
explosion, a bursting
force, violence
heat, vehemence
heedlessness, rashness
hell, extreme violence
impetuosity, unrestraint
inclemency, tempestuous-
  ness
paroxysm, uncontrol
precipitation, impetuosity
rashness, recklessness
recklessness, heedlessness
spurt, precipitation
temerity, rashness
tempestuousness, violence
vehemence, rashness
violence, vehemence

PERSONS
blade, highflyer
devil, bold fellow
highflyer, a wild liver
hotspur, madcap
jehu, fast driver
madcap, a reckless driver
plunger, hotspur
scorcher, a fast driver
spark, a dashing fellow
speeder, jehu

| INCONTINENCE | see— { | (ASSOCIATIVE 125C) |
| vs. Temperance ....132C | { | |

125C-3
VERBS
Miscellaneous
carouse, revel
debauch, carouse
revel, riot
riot, sensualize
sensualize, be without
  carnal restraint

ADJECTIVES
Miscellaneous
abandoned, profligate
adulterous, dissolute
animalistic, sensual
Bacchanalian, dissipating
bawdy, unchaste
bestial, sensual
brash, shameless
brassy, brazen
brazen, shameless
carnal, dissolute
dissipating, dissolute

ADJECTIVES (Continued)
dissolute, licentious
erotic, having inordinate
  sexual interest
fast, dissipating
immodest, immoral
immoral, dissolute
impudent, immodest
impure, unchaste
incestuous, unchaste
incontinent, wanton
indelicate, immodest
lewd, licentious
libertine, licentious
licentious, dissolute
meretricious, unchaste
profligate, abandoned
Saturnalian, dissolute
sensual, dissolute
shameless, immodest
unchaste, shameless
wanton, unrestrained

NOUNS
Miscellaneous
adultery, incest
animalism, sensuality
bawdiness, licentiousness
bazoo, a carouse
bestiality, sensualism
blow-out, a carouse
Bohemianism, unconven-
  tional living
brass, impudence
carnalism, eroticism
carousal, debauch
debauch, revelry
debauchery, intemperance
dissipation, intemperance
eroticism, inordinate sex
  interest
erotomania, eroticism
fling, debauchery
forwardness, brass
(Continued on page 258)

DIFFERENCE—
    IRREGULARITY

ASSOCIATIVE

126A
VERBS
Miscellaneous

alienate, estrange
alter, make different
Americanize, make American
barbarize, uncivilized
bastardize, make bastard
characterize, distinguish
conjugate, vary
contrast, differentiate
deviate, vary
differ, make unlike
differentiate, distinguish
digress, deviate
distinguish, characterize
diversify, vary
estrange, alienate
individualize, particularize
individuate, individualize
innovate, invent
invent, innovate
modify, alter
naturalize, nationalize
nationalize, conform to nation
originate, innovate
particularize, distinguish
specialize, particularize
vary, modify

ADJECTIVES
Different

another, different
different, dissimilar
diverse, different
other, different
unlike, different

Irregular, Etc.

aberrant, abnormal
abnormal, irregular
amorphous, anomalous
anomalistic, irregular
anomalous, irregular
asymmetrical, unproportioned
atypic, irregular
baroque, oddly shaped
disproportionate, irregular
heterologous, abnormal
irregular, variable
nondescript, abnormal
subnormal, below normal
variable, irregular

Miscellaneous

assorted, miscellaneous
diverse, different
heterogeneous, dissimilar

ADJECTIVES (Continued)

miscellaneous, various
multifarious, varied
several, divers
sundry, several
various, miscellaneous

Opposite

antithetical, opposite
contradistinctive, opposite
contrasting, different
contrary, opposite
discrepant, opposite
dissimilar, unlike
heteronomous, differing
opposite, contrary

Irrelevant

ill, unfit
immaterial, unrelated
impertinent, irrelevant
improper, unsuitable
inapposite, inept
inappropriate, unsuitable
incompatible, incongruous
inconsistent, discrepant
incongruous, inept
inept, unsuitable
inharmonious, incongruous
irregular, improper
irrelevant, inapposite
malapropos, unseasonable
unbecoming, unsuited
undue, improper
unfit, unsuitable
unimportant, immaterial
unseemly, improper

Foreign

alien, foreign
barbarous, foreign
exotic, foreign
extraneous, foreign
foreign, alien
uncivilized, wild
wild, barbarous

Strange

incredible, unbelievable
indescribable, strange
inexplicable, strange
inexpressible, strange
nameless, unknown
outlandish, strange
strange, unusual
unaccountable, unknown
unearthly, unnatural
unnatural, monstrous

Unknown

outlandish, foreign
strange, unknown
trackless, uncharted

ADJECTIVES (Continued)

unaccustomed, unfamiliar
uncustomary, unusual
unexplored, strange
unfamiliar, uncommon
unfathomed, unknown depth
unfathomable, trackless
unknown, strange
uncharted, unexplored
untrodden, strange

Antiquated

ancient, antiquated
antiquated, old-fashioned
archaic, obsolete
obsolete, unused
old, ancient
old-fashioned, queer
primitive, old-fashioned

Uncommon

recherche, rare
rare, uncommon
uncommon, unusual
unusual, exceptional

Unsuitable

inadvisable, inauspicious
inauspicious, unfavorable
inexpedient, inadvisable
inopportune, untimely
unfavorable, unpropitious
unpropitious, inauspicious
unsuitable, unseemly
unseasonable, untimely
untimely, inopportune

Immature

aborted, immature
crude, immature
immature, unfit
premature, unfit

Monstrous

freakish, odd
Gargantuan, monstrous
heteronomous, monstrous
monstrous, freakish

Odd, Queer

bizarre, queer
crotchety, whimsical
curious, odd
eccentric, peculiar
erratic, eccentric
grotesque, incongruous
odd, peculiar
peculiar, singular
quaint, singular
queer, strange
rum, queer
singular, particular
(Continued on page 256)

ADJECTIVES (Continued)

unique, singular
whimsical, odd

Absurd

absurd, preposterous
funny, queer
preposterous, outlandish
ridiculous, preposterous

New, Novel

brand-new, quite new
fast, ahead of custom
fresh, new
new, novel
novel, unusual
new-fangled, queer

Extraordinary

exceptional, outstanding
extraordinary, unusual
miraculous, remarkable
outstanding, distinct
phenomenal, unusual
remarkable, unusual

Incomparable

incomparable, unequaled
unequaled, singular
unexampled, unequaled
unparalleled, incomparable
unprecedented, unequaled

Special

chief, distinguished
distinct, particular
distinctive, exceptional
especial, particular
express, special
foremost, chief
main, chief
particular, special
principal, chief
separate, distinct
special, distinctive
specific, particular

Informal

easy, informal
free, informal
informal, unceremonious
unceremonious, informal
unconventional, informal

Personal

idiosyncratic, individual
individual, idiosyncratic
individualistic, distinct
personal, idiosyncratic

NOUNS

Difference

difference, dissimilarity
disparity, inequality
discrepancy, variation
exception, imparity
imparity, inequality
inconsistency, disparity
inequality, difference
misfit, inequality
oddment, imparity

NOUNS (Continued)

odds, inequality

Irregularity, Etc.

aberration, abnormality
abnormality, irregularity
amorphism, formlessness
anomaly, irregularity
asymmetry, unsym-
metricalness
crudity, imperfection
disproportion, asymmetry
irregularity, variation
nonconformity, incongruity
unfitness, unsuitableness
variability, irregularity

Variation, Etc.

allotropism, variation
conjugation, variation
deviation, variation
digression, variation
heterogenesis, variation
heteromorphism, deviation
variableness, variation
variance, difference
variant, variation
variation, diversity

Miscellaneous

assortment, oddments
miscellanies, oddments
miscellany, miscellanies
oddments, miscellanies
sundries, oddments
variety, miscellany

Oppositeness

antithesis, contrast
contradistinction, difference
contrariness, oppositeness
contrast, difference
differentiation, difference
differential, difference
dissimilarity, unlikeness
dissimilitude, contrast
diversity, dissimilitude
heterogenity, dissimilarity
oppositeness, contrast

Irrelevancy, Etc.

impertinence, irrelevance
impropriety, unfitness
inappropriateness, un-
fitness
incompatibility, incon-
gruity
incongruity, unfitness
ineptitude, unsuitableness
irrelevancy, impertinence

Monstrosity

flam, freak
freak, oddity
monstrosity, prodigy
prodigy, monstrosity

Absurdity

absurdity, oddity
curio, curiosity
curiosity, oddity

NOUNS (Continued)

kickshaw, nameless trifle
oddity, peculiarity
peculiarity, singularity
quaintness, oddness
rareness, singularity
singularity, peculiarity
strangeness, oddity

Occupation

avocation, recreative work
business, pursuit
calling, profession
employment, occupation
forte, specialty
interest, pursuit
job, work
occupation, business
profession, higher calling
pursuit, occupation
specialty, special calling
specialism, particularity
specialization, specialty
trade, special handicraft
vocation, occupation
work, occupation

Class, Degree

class, order
condition, state
degree, order
order, class
rank, degree
situation, condition
state, condition
station, class
title, rank

Quality, Kind

character, distinction
fashion, style
kind, species
manner, sort
mode, fashion
quality, sort
sort, kind
style, manner

Characteristic

attribute, characteristic
characteristic, trait
distinction, kind
feature, point
mark, characteristic
peculiarity, characteristic
point, attribute
property, characteristic
specialty, peculiarity
species, kind
trait, characteristic

Personality

idiosyncrasy, personality
individualism, idiosyn-
crasy
individuality, distinctive-
ness
personality, individuality
(Continued on page 260)

NEGLIGENCE—SLOWNESS   see—

ASSOCIATIVE

126B
VERBS
Neglect, Etc.
dawdle, idle
dally, delay
dilly-dally, loiter
drone, idle
idle, loiter
fritter, waste by degrees
loll, dally
neglect, omit
trifle, fritter
Forget, Etc.
forget, overlook
overlook, miss
Omit
disregard, slight
ignore, disregard
miss, omit
omit, neglect
pass, omit
procrastinate, omit
renege, ignore
scamp, omit a duty
skimp, neglect
skip, miss
slight, neglect
Poke, Drag
crawl, lag
creep, lag
drag, creep
inch, move slowly
poke, move sluggishly
Delay, Defer
check, delay
defer, delay
delay, lag
retard, delay
scotch, retard
slacken, lag
slow, slacken
temporize, delay
Shirk, Lapse
default, fail
fail, lapse
forsake, neglect
lapse, fail in duty
relent, lapse
shirk, default
Lag, Linger
lag, linger
linger, loiter
pause, rest
relax, procrastinate
rest, pause

VERBS (Continued)
tarry, linger
Lounge
deliberate, be unhurried
loiter, idle
loaf, loiter
lounge, loll
saunter, stroll
stroll, saunter
ADJECTIVES
Neglectful
care-free, careless
careless, neglectful
happy-go-lucky, care-free
lax, loose, careless
loose, careless
neglectful, careless
negligent, neglectful
perfunctory, negligent
slack, inattentive
thriftless, neglectful
Forgetful
absent-minded, inattentive
apathetic, unconcerned
forgetful, thoughtless
heedless, careless
impassive, apathetic
inadvertent, heedless
inattentive, neglectful
inconsiderate, heedless
indifferent, unconcerned
oblivious, forgetful
regardless, indifferent
remiss, heedless
thoughtless, inattentive
unguarded, negligent
unthinking, thoughtless
Idle
idle, unemployed
improvident, neglectful
imprudent, improvident
inactive, sluggish
unemployed, inactive
unoccupied, unemployed
vagrant, shiftless
Poky
drowsy, dull
dull, slow
languid, inactive
lethargic, listless
listless, sluggish
lymphatic, sluggish
phlegmatic, sluggish

ADJECTIVES (Continued)
poky, sluggish
sleepy, drowsy
slothful, inactive
slow, dilatory
sluggish, lethargic
torpid, inactive
Lazy
indolent, supine
lazy, indolent
shiftless, lazy
supine, indolent
unenterprising, indolent
Dilatory
averse, reluctant
backward, loath
dilatory, slow
laggard, backward
loath, unwilling
reluctant, backward
restive, reluctant
tardy, dilatory
unwilling, sluggish
Leisurely
casual, nonchalant
deliberate, leisurely
gradual, leisurely
leisurely, unhurried
nonchalant, unconcerned
unconcerned, leisurely
unhurried, leisurely
Delinquent
culpable, blamable
delinquent, neglectful
derelict, remiss
regrettable, remiss
truant, neglectful
undutiful, neglectful
unfilial, undutiful
Ungrateful
thankless, neglectful, ungrateful
unappreciative, undutiful
ungrateful, unappreciative
NOUNS
Neglect
carelessness, negligence
laxity, carelessness
looseness, laxity
neglect, omission
negligence, want of due application
(Continued on page 258)

NOUNS (Continued)
perfunctoriness, carelessness
slackness, negligence
　Forgetfulness
apathy, indifference
forgetfulness, oblivion
inadvertence, heedlessness
inattention, inadvertence
indifference, unconcern
oblivion, forgetfulness
oversight, forgetfulness
　Omission
disregard, indifference
omission, neglect
skip, omission
slip, omission
　Idleness
idleness, unemployment
improvidence, negligence
imprudence, inattention
vagrancy, aimless wander-
ing
　Pokiness
ennui, listlessness
inactivity, sluggishness
languor, lassitude
lassitude, inactivity
lethargy, sluggishness
pokiness, sluggishness
sleepiness, dullness
slowness, tardiness
sluggishness, lethargy
torpidity, inactivity
torpor, sluggishness
　Laziness
indolence, laziness

NOUNS (Continued)
laziness, indolence
sloth, idleness
supineness, indolence
　Dilatoriness
dilatoriness, tardiness
disinclination, backward-
ness
reluctance, disinclination
tardiness, dilatoriness
　Leisure
deliberateness, slowness
leisure, deliberateness
nonchalance, unconcern
relaxation, leisure
unconcern, leisure
　Shortcoming
defection, default
failing, fault
fault, omission
foible, slight fault
relentment, remissness
remission, relentment
remissness, negligence
shortcoming, remissness
truancy, delinquency
　Delinquence
arrear, the state of being
in default
arrearage, default
default, omission
delinquency, neglect
dereliction, omission
failure, neglect
　Delay
dalliance, delay
delay, dilatoriness
procrastination, delay

NOUNS (Continued)
　Ingratitude
ingratitude, indifference
undutifulness, ingratitude

PERSONS
creeper, one who moves
lazily
dawdler, trifler
defaulter, delinquent
delinquent, neglectful
person
drone, sluggard
idler, lazy person
laggard, loiterer
lazzarone, idler
loafer, idler
poltroon, sluggard
quitter, welsher
roustabout, loafer
slacker, defaulter
sluggard, lazy person
snail, lazy person
straggler, idler
tramp, vagrant
trifler, idler
truant, delinquent
vagabond, vagrant
vagrant, idler
welsher, dishonest
delinquent

INTERJECTION
heigh-ho, expression of
languor

BEING
Somnus, god of sleep

125C-3 (Continued)
NOUNS (Continued)
free love, animalism
harlotry, prostitution
immoderateness, ribaldry
immodesty, sensuality
immorality, licentiousness
incest, carnalism
incontinence, debauchery
indecency, immodesty
infidelity, profligacy
intemperance, debauchery
jamboree, a carouse
lewdness, licentiousness
liaison, profligacy
libertinism, debauchery
licentiousness, immorality
lubricity, carnalism
profligacy, abandon
prostitution, harlotry
revelry, ribaldry
ribaldry, licentiousness
riot, revelry
sensualism, sensuality
sensuality, profligacy
spree, a carouse

NOUNS (Continued)
vice, immorality
voluptuousness, sensuality

PERSONS
adulterer, paramour
adultress, as above (Fem.)
Bacchus, god of revelry
bat, a loose woman
carnalist, libertine
courtesan, prostitute
debauchee, rake, drunkard
demi-mondaine, one of the
demi-monde
demi-monde, the circle of
prostitutes
Dionysos, god of wine, etc.
Don Juan, libertine
cocotte, courtezan
fornicator, sensualist
fornicatress, as above
(Fem.)
gill, wanton girl
gipsy, hoydenish girl
harlot, prostitute

PERSONS (Continued)
harridan, dissolute woman
hoyden, bold girl
holden, as above
hussy, strumpet
jade, vicious girl
libertine, debauchee
Lothario, libertine
minx, pert girl
paramour, adulterer
profligate, libertine
prostitute, adultress
quean, dissolute woman
rake, loose liver
reprobate, profligate
ribald, libertine
romp, hoyden
roué, sensualist
seducer, libertine
sensualist, voluptuary
strumpet, prostitute
voluptuary, sensualist
wench, jade
whore, prostitute

ERROR—FAULT see—	ASSOCIATIVE	
vs. Accuracy 134A	Sin—Crime 130A	Awkwardness 126D
	Negligence 126B	Misfortune 127B
	Stagger—Shamble 18A	Falsehood 62
	Stray—Ramble 18B	Supposition 113
	Excess—Unrestraint ..125C	Irregularity 126A
	Stupidity 110B	Ambiguity 57

126C

VERBS

Err
blunder, make a mistake
err, make an error
slip, miss
stumble, err
trip, stumble

Miscarry
deviate, depart from
digress, deviate
lapse, fail
miscarry, go wrong

Misjudge
misapprehend, misunderstand
misconceive, misapprehend
misjudge, judge erroneously
mistake, err
underestimate, underrate
underrate, rate too low
undervalue, underrate

Miscellaneous
blemish, leave a flaw
boggle, bungle
botch, leave or make flaws
bungle, botch
cobble, patch coarsely
flaw, make a blemish
misplay, play incorrectly
misspell, spell incorrectly
miss, err
misunderstand, misapprehend
overestimate, estimate as too much
misplace, place wrongly

ADJECTIVES

Erroneous
errant, erring, etc.
erratic, aberrant
erroneous, incorrect
fallacious, false
false, erroneous
inaccurate, erroneous
inexact, not precise
incorrect, erroneous
mistaken, incorrect
undervalued, misvalued
wrong, incorrect

Fallible
culpable, having fault
fallible, erring
peccable, prone to err

ADJECTIVES (Continued)

Imperfect
ameliorable, imperfect
bad, defective
crude, culpable
defective, having defect
faulty, erroneous
imperfect, defective
inaccurate, inexact
incomplete, inperfect
jerry, badly built

Incongruous
anachronistic, in error as to time
discrepant, inconsistent
impertinent, incongruous
inapposite, inharmonious
incompatible, incongruous
incompetent, unqualified
incongruous, incorrect
inconsistent, discrepant
inharmonious, incompatible
irrelevant, impertinent
unqualified, unfit

Amiss
aberrant, straying
amiss, wrong
astray, aberrant
awry, erroneous
desultory, erratic
fitful, unreliable
misguided, stray
stray, erring in duty
unintentional, mistaken
unreliable, untrustworthy
untrustworthy, aberrant
unwitting, unintentional
wild, amiss

Imprudent
imprudent, injudicious
impolitic, injudicious
indiscreet, imprudent
indiscriminate, indiscreet
injudicious, indiscreet

Blundering
blundering, erring
bungling, blundering
stumbling, blundering

Illogical
absurd, inconsistent
eccentric, erratic
foolish, absurd
illogical, irrational
incoherent, irrational
irrational, wrong

ADJECTIVES (Continued)
nonsensical, absurd
preposterous, absurd
Ptolemaic, inconsistent
unreasonable, illogical
unsound, inconsistent

Inordinate
excessive, immoderate
exorbitant, inordinate
immoderate, inordinate
inordinate, excessive

Indecorous
impolite, wanting manners
improper, erroneous
indecorous, improper
inelegant, indecorous
rude, culpable
ungentlemanly, indecorous

NOUNS

Error
erratum, error in printing
errata, plural of erratum
error, mistake
fallacy, mistake
fault, error
faux pas, error or slip, especially in manners or morality
lapsus, slip or mistake
mistake, error
peccadillo, a trifling fault
slip, fault in effort

Fallibility
culpability, blamable fault
failing, minor fault
fallibility, mistake, liability to err
foible, imperfection in character
peccability, proneness to sin or err

Imperfection
blemish, defect
botch, poor work
crudeness, imperfection
crudity, crudeness
defect, fault, error
flaw, blemish
imperfection, faultiness

Incongruity
absurdity, inconsistency
defection, culpability
discrepancy, error
(Continued on page 262)

AWKWARDNESS—CARELESSNESS

vs. Skilfulness—Mastery 134B

ASSOCIATIVE

see— { Error—Fault—Slip 126C
Staggering—Shambling 18A
Stupidity 110B

126D

VERBS

Miscellaneous

boggle, bungle
botch, perform carelessly
blunder, be grossly careless
bungle, botch
flounder, attempt awkwardly
fudge, do in a bungling manner
fumble, handle awkwardly
miss, muff
muff, blunder
skimp, botch
stumble, trip or fall
trip, stumble

ADJECTIVES

Awkward

awkward, wanting in dexterity
blundering, clumsy
bungling, awkward
clumsy, awkward
floundering, awkward
fumbling, bungling
gangling, graceless
gawky, ungainly
graceless, awkward
inelegant, unpolished
left-handed, awkward
stodgy, clumsy
stumbling, blundering
uncouth, clumsy
undignified, inelegant
ungainly, awkward
ungraceful, inelegant

Boorish

boorish, awkward
brutish, irresponsible
gauche, awkward
green, lubberly, raw
lubberly, clumsy
raw, lubberly

ADJECTIVES (Continued)

rural, rustic
rustic, awkward

Unskilled

artless, unskilled
crude, unskilful
ill, unskilful
inartistic, crude
inexperienced, inexpert
inexpert, unskilful
maladroit, unskilful
tactless, without tact
unexercised, unskilled
unskilled, incompetent
unskilful, awkward

Inefficient

inadequate, incapable
incapable, incompetent
incompetent, wanting ability
inefficient, incompetent

Careless

careless, artless
harum-scarum, careless
inattentive, indifferent
inconsiderate, indifferent
indifferent, heedless
negligent, careless
offhand, perfunctory
perfunctory, careless

Incautious

incautious, inconsiderate
indelicate, indiscreet
indiscreet, indifferent
rash, reckless
reckless, heedless
thoughtless, indiscreet
unguarded, careless
unwary, heedless

Precipitate

hasty, heady
headlong, heedless
heady, precipitate

ADJECTIVES (Continued)

heedless, harum-scarum
precipitate, heedless
snap, without care
wild, heedless

NOUNS

Miscellaneous

awkwardness, clumsiness
carelessness, incompetence
clumsiness, gawkiness
crudeness, incompetence
crudity, crudeness
gawkiness, awkwardness
inability, incompetence
incompetence, want of ability
inefficiency, incompetence
inexperience, unskilfulness
mediocrity, inexpertness
recklessness, heedlessness
rudeness, unskilfulness
supineness, indolence
thoughtlessness, indifference

PERSONS

blunder, bungler
bungler, clumsy fellow
Goth, one who is destitute of artistic taste
gawk, awkward person
hobble-de-hoy, gawky fellow approaching manhood
looby, awkward fellow
lout, looby
lubber, raw sailor
mountebank, quack
quack, pretender to skill
ruralist, rustic
rustic, ruralist
slouch, awkward fellow
swab, lubber

126A (Continued)

PERSONS

barbarian, foreigner
bastard, illegitimate child
Bohemian, unconventional person
fogy, old-fashioned person
foreigner, outlander
gipsy, Bohemian

PERSONS (Continued)

guy, oddly dressed person
individual, person, thing, etc.
innovator, introducer
madcap, eccentric person
monster, prodigy
original, eccentric person

PERSONS (Continued)

outlander, stranger
prodigy, unusual person
specialist, one with a specialty
sport, monstrosity
stranger, foreigner
Etc., etc.

UNCERTAINTY—ACCIDENT

vs. Certainty—Destiny 134C

127A
see—

ASSOCIATIVE

Bad Luck 127B
Good Luck 134D
Changeability 3A

127A

VERBS

Befall
befall, happen
betide, befall
fall, happen
light, fall by chance
supervene, occur

Happen
chance, betide
eventuate, happen
hap, happen
happen, befall
occur, happen

Risk
hazard, risk
jeopard, jeopardize
jeopardize, hazard
risk, hazard

Bet, Wager
bet, risk a wager
flip, determine by the
chance turn of a coin
hedge, bet both ways
stake, wager
wager, bet

Venture
adventure, risk
brave, venture
dare, hazard
plunge, risk heavily
speculate, hazard an
investment
undertake, venture
venture, risk

ADJECTIVES

Accidental
accidental, unexpected
fluky, done by a fluke
sudden, unexpected
unexpected, accidental
unforeseen, unexpected
unsuspected, accidental

Chance
adventitious, casual
casual, chance
chance, accidental
circumstantial, incidental
coincident, happening
together
episodic, incidental
eventful, episodic
fortuitous, casual
incident, happening
incidental, casual
occasional, incidental

Uncertain
doubtful, uncertain

ADJECTIVES (Continued)

dubious, doubtful
indefinite, uncertain
indeterminate, uncertain
uncertain, untrustworthy

Tentative
conjectural, debatable
controvertible, unsettled
debatable, uncertain
disputable, debatable
inconclusive, indefinite
indecisive, inconclusive
provisional, tentative
tentative, conjectural

Aimless
aimless, at random
cursory, uncertain
haphazard, chance
indiscriminate, left to confused chance
promiscuous, implying
chance in confusion
random, haphazard

Unintentional
unintentional, unexpected
unpremeditated, capricious
unwitting, unintentional

Untrustworthy
fugitive, unreliable
irresponsible, unreliable
punic, untrustworthy
transitory, unreliable
unreliable, untrustworthy
untrustworthy, unreliable

Capricious
capricious, casuistic
fickle, capricious
flip, frivolous
flippant, frivolous
frivolous, trifling
giddy, fickle
impulsive, capricious
petulant, capricious
trifling, fickle

Arbitrary
arbitrary, capricious
casuistic, implying the
chance conduct of
conscience
critical, uncertain

Unsteady
fitful, spasmodic
fluctuating, uncertain
inconstant, uncertain
mercurial, fickle
slippery, doubtful
spasmodic, capricious
unstable, unsteady

ADJECTIVES (Continued)

unsteady, volant
volant, fluctuating
vacillating, wavering
wavering, uncertain

Risky
critical, perilous
dangerous, perilous
hazardous, risky
perilous, hazardous
precarious, uncertain
risky, hazardous
ticklish, precarious
treacherous, untrustworthy

Lucky
lucky, fortuitous

Probable
apt, likely
contingent, liable
eventual, contingent
liable, likely
likable, having likelihood
likely, liable
possible, uncertain
probable, likely
providential, implying
chance occurrence of
providence

Improbable
improbable, inconclusive
questionable, improbable
unlikely, improbable

Venturesome
excursive, venturesome
speculative, risky
venturesome, speculative

NOUNS

Accident
accident, chance event
casualty, accident
contretemps, unhappy
incident
mishap, casualty

Happening
event, incident
incident, chance occurrence
hap, casual event
happening, incident
occurrence, happening

Incidence
case, incident
circumstance, incident
incidence, chance fall
occasion, occurrence

Chance
accidental, incidental
(Continued on page 262)

NOUNS (Continued)
circumstantiality, inci-
  dentalness
coincidence, corresponding
  incident
coincident, as above
chance, happening
incidental, fortuity, etc.

    Uncertainty
doubtfulness, uncertainty
indefiniteness, uncertainty
uncertainty, possibility

    Aimlessness
aimlessness, random
haphazard, accident
random, chance action

    Caprice
caprice, uncertain whim
fickleness, inconsistency
frivolity, fickleness
giddiness, fickleness
levity, frivolity

    Unsteadiness
changeableness, instability
inconsistency, levity
instability, inconstancy
slipperiness, uncertainty
unstableness, instability
unsteadiness, instability

    Risk
crisis, peril
danger, peril
hazard, risk

NOUNS (Continued)
jeopardy, hazard
peril, hazard
risk, hazard

    Luck
fluke, lucky stroke, etc.
fortuity, lucky occurrence
fortune, fortuity
hit, lucky event, fluke
luck, fortuity

    Probability
contingence, probable
  occurrence
contingency, as above
eventuality, contingency
liability, possibility
likelihood, probability
probability, possibility
possibility, contingency
providence, contingency
  from God

    Improbability
improbability, unlikeliness
unlikelihood, improbability

    Bet, Wager
bet, a stake
gamble, chance or interest
  involving risk
stake, wager
sweepstake, sweeping bet
toss-up, equal chance
wager, money, etc., risked
  on a chance outcome

NOUNS (Continued)
    Venture
adventure, hazard
speculation, risky investment
venture, hazard
venturesomeness, hazard

PERSONS
adventurer
adventuress
gambler
plunger
speculator

BEING
Fortuna, goddess of chance,
  etc.

ADVERBS
may, possibly
might, may
peradventure, by chance
perchance, perhaps
perhaps, possibly
possibly, perchance

CONJUNCTIONS
either, one or the other
if, noting contingency
lest, implying possibility
or, implying either
unless, implying con-
  tingency

NOUNS (Continued)
impolicy, unsuitableness
impracticability, incon-
  gruity
incoherence, incongruity
incompatibleness, defect
incongruity, exorbitance
inconsequence, want of
  logical sequence
inconsistency, discrepancy
inexactness, want of
  precision

    Miscarriage
deviation, digression
digression, error
exorbitance, digression
  from course, rule, or
  propriety
lapse, slight fault
miscarriage, miss
miss, failure to accomplish

    Imprudence
imprudence, indiscretion
indiscretion, imprudence

NOUNS (Continued)
    Misconception
inadvertence, mistake
misapprehension, error in
  understanding
misunderstanding, miscon-
  ception
misconception, wrong con-
  ception
sophistry, fallacious
  reasoning
sophism, mistaken argu-
  ment

    Blunder
blunder, clumsy error
boggle, bungle
bungle, boggle
stumble, error
trip, stumbling error

    Indecorum
impoliteness, culpability
impropriety, fault
incivility, indecorum
indecency, faux pas

NOUNS (Continued)
indecorum, impropriety
indelicacy, indecency
inelegance, culpable choice
  without propriety

    Incongruity (Miscel.)
anachronism, misrepresen-
  tation in point of time
caco-economy, bad govern-
  ment
cacography, incorrect spell-
  ing
maladministration, caco-
  economy
salad days, days of youthful error
solecism, breach of rules
  of syntax, etc.

PERSONS
cobbler, botch workman
sophist, fallacious reasoner
vulgarian, indecorous
  person

127B

VERBS

Bankrupt, Etc.
bankrupt, fail in business
break, bankrupt
collapse, fail suddenly
fall, drop from grace
flop, fail (slang)
slump, fall, sink, or fail
smash, bankrupt
tumble, suffer a sudden
   setback

Fail
fail, fall short
fizzle, fail soon after
   starting
flunk, fail
miss, fail

Miscellaneous
bleed, lose freely, as
   money, etc.
forfeit, lose (possession or
   advantage) by a breach
   of conditions
lose, suffer dispossession
miscarry, fail
slip, miss footing
snap, miss fire
spill, suffer loss from a
   vessel, etc.
stumble, trip or fall
trip, stumble

ADJECTIVES

Ruined
bankrupt, suffering failure
defeated, ruined
destroyed, ruined
disabled, disqualified
disappointed, balked
gone, lost, ruined
helpless, disabled
irreclaimable, lost
irrecoverable, irreparable
irredeemable, lost
irreparable, ruined
lost, gone, ruined
prostrate, crushed
ruined, bankrupt, defeated
sunk, ruined

Unfortunate
infelicitous, unfortunate
regrettable, unfortunate
unfortunate, unlucky
unlucky, unfortunate
untoward, unfortunate

Futile
fruitless, unsuccessful

ADJECTIVES (Continued)

futile, unavailing
ineffective, inefficient
ineffectual, ineffective
inefficient, incapable
inoperative, ineffectual
Sisyphean, unavailing
unavailing, futile
unsuccessful, disappointed
useless, futile

Sinister
adverse, unfortunate
bad, adverse, unfortunate
evil, unfortunate
ill, unfortunate
sinister, unlucky

Inauspicious
inauspicious, unlucky
unfavorable, inauspicious
unpropitious, inauspicious
unseasonable, unpropitious
untimely, unseasonable

Hapless
bereft, deprived, despoiled
hapless, unfortunate
hopeless, futile
unhappy, bereft

Deserted, Etc.
abandoned, forsaken
deserted, abandoned
destitute, bereaved
forgotten, hapless
forlorn, abandoned
forsaken, forlorn
lorn, forsaken
marooned, abandoned
neglected, forsaken
orphan, orphaned, bereft
perdu, forlorn
stranded, helpless

Baffled
baffled
balked
foiled
frustrated
rebuffed
thwarted

Subdued
beaten
bowed
conquered
crushed
curbed
dominated
muzzled
overcome
overpowered

ADJECTIVES (Continued)

quelled
silenced
squelched
subdued
subjugated
suppressed
tamed
vanquished

Excelled
distanced
eclipsed
exceeded
excelled
outstripped
outwitted
passed
surpassed

Apprehended
apprehended
captured
collared
ensnared
entrapped
hooked
intercepted
shanghaied
snared
trapped

Confined
besieged
bottled
boxed
caged
confined
cooped
cornered
corralled
entombed
immured
impounded
imprisoned
incarcerated
jailed
penned
surrounded

NOUNS

Ruin
bankruptcy, failure
collapse, utter failure
defeat, failure
disappointment, failure
downfall, defeat
dud, flop (slang)
fall, failure
(Continued on page 266)

WEAKNESS—   ASSOCIATIVE
   EXHAUSTION see— ⎧ Sickness ....128B   Cowardice 32
                         ⎪ Misfortune ....127B   Decay 128C
     vs. Strength ....137B ⎩ Apathy—Stupor ....110A   Stupidity 110B

128A
VERBS

Weaken
decline, become weak
droop, lose vigor
languish, droop
weaken, tire

Tire
fag, grow weary
fatigue, tire
flag, fag
irk, tire
jade, fatigue
tire, lose strength

Die, Expire
decease, die
depart, die
die, succumb
drop, fall dead
drown, perish by water
expire, perish
perish, die
succumb, die

Miscellaneous
bare, disarm
collapse, be exhausted
disarm, remove arms
dote, be aged and weak
expose, make unsecure
fade, droop
faint, swoon
famish, starve
impoverish, render poor
lurch, roll helplessly
pauperize, impoverish
pine, waste away
shake, tremble wearily
stagger, move haltingly
starve, famish
swoon, lose power
tremble, shake wearily
wither, droop

ADJECTIVES
Weak
asthenic, feeble
enfeebled, weak
feeble, weak
invalid, enfeebled
low, feeble
meager, weak
puny, weak
tiny, puny
weak, feeble

Senile
anile, old-womanish
decrepit, weak with old age
infirm, decrepit
senile, feeble in age

ADJECTIVES (Continued)
shaky, unsteady
unsteady, feeble

Tired
blasé, wearied as by
  dissipation
droopy, fatigued
fagged, fatigued
fatigued, weary
languid, fatigued
listless, languid
tired, wearied
weary, tired

Frail
delicate, frail
effeminate, delicate
feminine, delicate
flimsy, thin and weak
fragile, weak
frail, fragile
limpsy, flimsy
slight, feeble
tender, weak

Spiritless
invertebrate, not firm
limp, weak
numb, benumbed
soulless, spiritless
spineless, spiritless
spiritless, languid

Bloodless
anaemic, bloodless
bloodless, anaemic

Emaciated
emaciated, thin
famished, starved
jejune, dull, lifeless
inanimate, inane
starved, low from hunger
underfed, undernourished

Exhausted
dispersed, dissipated
dissipated, wasted
done, exhausted
effete, worn out
exhausted, emptied
extinct, exhausted
gone, exhausted
spent, dissipated
wasted, spent

Unproductive
barren, sterile
castrated, emasculated
emasculated, castrated
fruitless, barren
impotent, barren
infertile, sterile
sterile, unproductive

ADJECTIVES (Continued)
sterilized, made infertile
unfertile, exhausted
unfruitful, unproductive
unproductive, barren
unsexed, sterilized

Arid
arid, barren
bare, barren
blank, empty

Immature
abortive, undeveloped
childish, weak
embryonic, undeveloped
immature, deficient
infantile, immature
meager, immature
puerile, immature
undeveloped, immature
unripe, immature

Futile
dormant, inactive
frustrate, vain
futile, useless
impotent, without power
ineffective, unavailing
ineffectual, unavailing
inefficient, ineffectual
inoperative, ineffectual
nugatory, useless
passe, faded
powerless, impotent
Sisyphean, futile
unavailing, nugatory
vain, futile

Useless
frothy, empty
idle, useless
useless, worthless
worthless, passe

Empty
devoid, destitute
empty, exhausted
inane, empty, void
vacuous, empty
void, vacuous

Unimportant
immaterial, unimportant
impalpable, immaterial
inappreciable, unimportant
inconsequent, of no avail
inconsiderable, trifling
insignificant, unimportant
intangible, inappreciable
little, insignificant
petty, unimportant
trifling, useless
(Continued on page 265)

ADJECTIVES (Continued)

unimportant, insignificant

Unsubstantial
impertinent, nugatory
invalid, without effect
irrelevant, impertinent
unsubstantial, immaterial

Innocuous
harmless, futile
innocuous, harmless
innocent, innocuous
innoxious, not hurtful
inoffensive, harmless

Deficient, Etc.
deficient, lacking
disqualified, deficient
incapable, inefficient
incapacitated, disqualified
incompetent, incapable
ineligible, disqualified
obsolescent, going obsolete
obsolete, useless
unfit, unqualified
unqualified, incompetent

Needy
beggarly, poor
beggared, reduced
bereft, made destitute
destitute, poor
impecunious, poor
indigent, poor
insolvent, without funds
necessitous, needy
needy, poor
penniless, poor
poor, necessitous
reduced, impoverished

Defenseless
defenseless, unprotected
disarmed, defenseless
endangered, exposed
exposed, unprotected
helpless, harmless
insecure, endangered
perishable, violable
pregnable, insecure
unfortified, exposed
unprepared, defenseless
unprotected, exposed
unsafe, insecure
vincible, conquerable
violable, unprotected
vulnerable, assailable

Endangered
disarmed, exposed
endangered, unprotected
exposed, unprotected
helpless, defenseless
imperiled, endangered
unarmed, disarmed
unprotected, defenseless

Disabled, Etc.
capsized, overturned
crippled, disabled

ADJECTIVES (Continued)

deluged, inundated
disabled, disqualified
dying, moribund
halt, lame
injured, hurt
lame, crippled
maimed, mutilated
moribund, dying
mutilated, wounded
paralyzed, unnerved
scuttled, disabled
stricken, hurt
wounded, injured

Subjugated
beat, overcome
beaten, subjugated
bowed, subdued
conquered, vanquished
crushed, suppressed
dominated, overpowered
muzzled, subjugated
overcome, overpowered
overpowered, bowed
quelled, subdued
silenced, quelled
squelched, subdued
subdued, subjugated
subjugated, subdued
suppressed, quelled
tamed, dominated
vanquished, subjugated

Destroyed
annihilated, destroyed
blasted, blighted
blighted, blasted
demolished, destroyed
desolate, devastated
destroyed, demolished
depopulated, devastated
devastated, annihilated
exterminated, annihilated
quashed, ruined
ruined, destroyed
smashed, quashed
subverted, overthrown

Killed
assassinated, murdered
beheaded, decapitated
butchered, slaughtered
crucified, martyred
decapitated, beheaded
decimated, killed by tens
defunct, dead
disemboweled, dispatched
dismembered, torn apart
dispatched, killed
electrocuted, executed
executed, killed formally
guillotined, decapitated
killed, murdered
massacred, murdered
murdered, killed

ADJECTIVES (Continued)

Dead
bleak, bare, barren
dead, deceased
deceased, gone
lifeless, dead

NOUNS

Weakness
adynamia, debility
anemia, bloodlessness
asthenia, debility
atony, weakness
cacotrophy, debility
debility, weakness
debilitation, enervation
enervation, enfeeblement
enfeeblement, debilitation
flaccidity, weakness
weakness, impotence

Senility
anility, dotage
decrepitude, infirmity
decline, infirmity
dotage, imbecility
foible, infirmity
imbecility, dotage
infirmity, weakness
senility, infirmity of age
shakiness, infirmity

Tiredness
ennui, listlessness
fag, fatigue
fatigue, weariness
languor, feebleness
lassitude, languor
oppression, lassitude
tiredness, fatigue
tiresomeness, weariness
weariness, fatigue

Frailty
delicacy, fragility
filmsiness, weakness
femininity, delicacy
fragileness, weakness
fragility, delicacy
frailty, delicacy

Emaciation
emaciation, inanition
inanition, exhaustion
starvation, cacotrophy

Futility
deficiency, incapacity
futility, incompetence
impotence, futility
incapacity, lack of power
incompetence, inability
inefficiency, inefficacy
inefficacy, incapacity
nugatoriness, insignificance

Nothingness
naught, nothing
nihility, nothingness
nil, nothing
(Continued on page 266)

NOUNS (Continued)
nonentity, nonexistence
nothing, naught
nullity, nonentity
void, nothingness
zero, nullity

Unimportance
inconsequence, invalidity
insignificance, inconse-
quence
pettiness, insignificance
unimportance, insignifi-
cance

Need, Poverty
beggarliness, poverty
beggary, poverty
deprivation, destitution
destitution, poverty
impecuniosity, indigence
indigence, poverty
pauperism, poverty
penury, poverty
poverty, indigence

NOUNS (Continued)
privation, destitution
strait, poverty

Danger
danger, exposure
exposure, jeopardy
jeopardy, risk
peril, exposure
risk, peril
vulnerability, exposure

Death
death, end of life
decease, death
demise, death
dissolution, death
end, death
quietus, death
rest, death

Miscellaneous
aridity, barrenness
barrenness, emptiness
collapse, exhaustion
dearth, famine

NOUNS (Continued)
decay, impaired state
desert, barrenness
depletion, exhaustion
disability, incapacity
emptiness, exhaustion
exhaustion, collapse
goneness, collapse
infecundity, barrenness
insolvency, depletion
lameness, incapacity
prostration, exhaustion
sterility, barrenness

PERSONS
beggar
crone
dotard
eunuch
imbecile
invalid
pauper
weakling
Etc., etc.

127B (Continued)
NOUNS (Continued)
flop, failure (slang)
frost, utter failure
frustration, failure
goneness, failure
hors de combat, a state of
being prostrate or out of
the fight
misadventure, fall, failure
prostration, defeat
smash, bankruptcy
tumble, fall, failure

Misfortune
adversity, misfortune
curse, mischief, evil
evil, misfortune
inclemency, adversity
ill, misfortune
mischance, misfortune
mischief, misfortune
misfortune, calamity
mishap, misfortune

Failure
failure, defeat
fiasco, ludicrous failure
flunk, complete failure
miss, failure
slip, miss

Disaster
bale, disaster
bane, scourge
calamity, disaster
cataclysm, disaster
catastrophe, calamity

NOUNS (Continued)
debacle, disaster
death, extinction
deluge, resistless calamity
demolition, destruction
desolation, ruin
destruction, ruin
devastation, desolation
disaster, catastrophe
epidemic, widespread bane
fatality, calamity
fate, death
havoc, devastation
hydra, baneful evil
pestilence, bane
plague, epidemic
ruin, devastation
scourge, death
stroke, calamity

Destitution
abandonment, desolation
desolation, abandonment
destitution, state of being
deprived
forlornness, destitution
loss, privation
privation, destitution

PERSONS, ETC.
bankrupt, one who fails
financially
bastard, one who is born
out of wedlock

PERSONS (Continued)
castaway, one who is
ship-wrecked
Davy Jones, sea devil
Davy Jones' Locker, bot-
tom of the ocean, grave
of the drowned
exile, one who is banished
foundling, a child whose
parents are unknown
goner, one who is lost
Lilith, (a beguiling woman)
hence an unlucky person
or harbinger
maroon, one who is
marooned
orphan, a child bereft of
parents
outcast, exile
scapegoat, one who bears
the blame of others
slink, the young of beasts
prematurely born
waif, homeless wanderer
wastrel, waif

BEINGS, ETC.
Fortuna, goddess of chance
Frankenstein, self-made
evil
hoodoo, cause of ill luck
jinx, hoodoo (slang)
Jonah, supposed bad luck
accompanying a person

SICKNESS	see—	ASSOCIATIVE	
vs. Health 137A		Weakness 128A	
		Apathy 110A	
		Decay 128C	
		Disease—Bane 130E	

128B
VERBS

relapse, become sick again
sicken, become sick

ADJECTIVES

Sick, Diseased
debilitated, indisposed
diseased, vitiated
ill, sick
indisposed, slightly ill
infected, diseased
infirm, debilitated
morbid, sickly
poor, somewhat sick
sick, indisposed
sickly, inclined to sickness
tainted, infected
unhealthy, indisposed
unsound, unhealthy
unwell, sick
valetudinarian, sickly
vitiated, infected

Miscellaneous
asphyxiated, suffocated
bilious, having disorder of
the liver
carbuncular, inflamed
choleric, having cholera
consumptive, suffering
homesick, sick for home

ADJECTIVES (Continued)

hysterical, morbidly
excited
inflamed, morbidly
affected
inflammatory, as above
leprous, having leprosy
mangy, having mange
nauseated, having nausea
nostalgic, homesick
poisoned, suffering poison
raw, sore
sea-sick, sick from waves
smothered, stived
sore, inflamed
suffocated, smothered
stifled, suffocated
ulcerous, ulcerate
ulcerate, diseased

NOUNS

Sickness
affliction, disease
ailment, sickness
disease, malady
disorder, sickness
illness, sickness
indisposition, illness
infirmity, sickness

NOUNS (Continued)

invalidism, sickness
malady, disease
sickness, illness
sickliness, chronic illness

Miscellaneous

ache, pain
biliousness, disorder of the
liver
gripe, pinching distress
nausea, feeling of sickness
nostalgia, homesickness
pain, pang
pang, pain
qualm, sudden sickness
relapse, return to sickness
smart, a quick pain
spasm, violent muscular
contraction
surfeit, sickness caused by
excess
twinge, a smart

PERSONS

consumptive, a person af-
fected with consumption
invalid, a sickly person
leper, a victim of leprosy
valetudinarian, invalid

129B (Continued)
PERSONS (Continued)

scut, frowsy, ill-behaved
person
spalpeen (Irish), scamp
tatterdemalion, ragged
person
whiffet, useless trifler
whipper-snapper, whiffet

Vagabond

hobo, tramp
loafer, tramp
rapscallion, vagabond
roustabout, loafer
straggler, vagabond
tramp, vagrant
vagabond, tramp
vagrant, idler

Ruffian, Etc.

anathema, person anathe-
matized or cursed
blackguard, scoundrel
caitiff, despicable wretch
cur, surly fellow
degenerate, degraded per-
son
knave, disreputable fellow

PERSONS (Continued)

miscreant, vile wretch
monster, vile person
recreant, despicable person
reprobate, one lost to all
sense of righteousness
rascal, knave
reptile, mean, groveling
person
rowdy, bounder
ruffian, base character
scamp, rascal
scapegrace, unprincipled
fellow
scoundrel, despicable rascal
thug, ruffian
tough, ruffian
varlet, villain
villain, scoundrel
vulgarian, rich person with
vulgar ideas
wretch, despicable person
yahoo, loathsome person

Outcast

derelict, one who is for-
saken

PERSONS (Continued)

exile, outcast
Ishmaelite, social outcast
outcast, pariah
pariah, despised outcast

PERSONS (Plural)

canaille, the lowest order
of the populace
commonality, common
people
dregs, canaille
mob, rabble
proletariat, the populace
whose capital is children
rabble, populace of the
lower order
raff, canaille
rag-tag, the rabble
ruck, mob
scum, canaille
trash, raff
vermin, low, despicable
folk
underworld, the lower class

128C

VERBS

Decay

addle, become putrid
blet, decay internally
canker, corrode
decay, rot, deteriorate
fester, rot
mortify, become gangrenous
putrefy, become corrupt
rot, decay
spoil, decay

Decompose

crumble, disintegrate
decompose, decay
disintegrate, crumble
fray, abrade
fret, wear, corrode
molder, crumble to mold

Corrode

abrade, corrode
corrode, rust
erode, corrode
rust, corrode

Emaciate

atrophy, degenerate
consume, waste away
emaciate, lose flesh
fade, wither, droop, decay
fail, waste away
shrivel, deteriorate
waste, disintegrate
wither, waste
wizen, waste and become dry

Degenerate

decline, deteriorate
degenerate, decline
deteriorate, degenerate

Retrograde

relapse, return to a lower state
retrograde, become less organized

ADJECTIVES

Decayed

cancerous, with cancer
carious, affected with decay
cankerous, corroding
decayed, rotten
dilapidated, in decaying ruin

ADJECTIVES (Continued)

gangrenous, suffering mortification
maggoty, full of maggots
purulent, containing pus
putrefactive, implying rottenness
putrescent, putrefactive
putrid, rotten
rotten, decayed
septic, promoting putrefaction
spoiled, decayed

Corrosive

abradant, wearing away
corrosive, rusting
caustic, corrosive
erosive, gradually eating away
rusty, corrosive

Degenerate

decadent, deteriorating
degenerate, declining

Retrogressive

atavistic, reverting to ancestry
retrogressive, deteriorating

Moldy

moldy, having mold
(B). mouldy

NOUNS

Decay

abscess, morbid pus
blet, decay in fruit
cancer, an eating disease
canker, a corroding
caries, decay in bones, etc.
corruption, putrescence
decay, rot
gangrene, mortification
purulence, generation of pus
pus, decomposed matter
putrefaction, rot
putrescence, rottenness
putridness, rottenness
rot, decay
rottenness, rot
sepsis, a putrefactive condition
staleness, decay

Carcass, Etc.

carcass, a decaying body

NOUNS (Continued)

carrion, putrefying flesh
corpse, decaying carcass

Decomposition

decomposition, disintegration
disintegration, gradual decay
disorganization, disintegration
mortification, decomposition

Corrosion

abrasion, a wearing away
causticity, corrosion
corrosion, rust, wear
erosion, corrosion
rust, corrosive degeneration
rustiness, rust

Emaciation

atrophy, wasting of tissue
consumption, a wasting
emaciation, a wasting away
marasmus, atrophy

Degeneration

degeneracy, deterioration
degeneration, morbid impairment
deterioration, decay, etc.
decadence, state of decay
declension, decline, deterioration
decline, deterioration
dilapidation, decaying ruin

Mold

mildew, mold
mold, decaying matter
moldiness, mold
(B). mouldiness
punk, fungus decay
rubigo, rust or mildew on plants

Retrogression

atavism, reversion to ancestry
regression, retrogression
relapse, a falling back to former low state
retrogression, degeneration
return, retrogression

DIRTINESS—GRIME—FILTH see— **ASSOCIATIVE**

129A
VERBS
Miscellaneous
addle, muddle
bedabble, spatter
bedraggle, soil by dragging
befoul, sully
begrime, make grimy
bemire, soil in the mire
beslaver, smear with spittle
beslobber, beslaver
besmear, mar by smearing
besmirch, dirty
besot, bespatter
bespatter, soil by spatter-
ing
blacken, make sooty
blemish, stain, mar
blot, spot
blotch, blot
blur, sully
botch, mar or soil
contaminate, corrupt
corrupt, vitiate
crock, blacken with soot
daub, smudge
defile, make foul
dirty, make unclean
discolor, daub
drabble, bemire
draggle, bedraggle
foul, befoul
grime, make dirty
mar, soil
mess, dirty
mire, bemire
muddle, muddy
muddy, dirty
pollute, defile
puddle, muddy
reek, foul with smoke or
steam
sanguine, stain with blood
smear, soil with a smear
smirch, smear
smudge, smear or stain
smut, crock
soil, dirty
spatter, foul
splash, bespatter
spoil, ruin
stain, mar
spot, discolor
sully, soil
taint, blemish
tarnish, sully
thumb, soil with the thumb
tinge, mar
wallow, roll in filth

VERBS (Continued)
welter, wallow

ADJECTIVES
Dirty
dirty, unclean
foul, filthy, dirty
grimy, dirty
soiled, dirty
squalid, extremely dirty
sullied, dirty
thumbed, fouled with the
thumb
trashy, fouled with trash
Befouled
bedraggled, soiled from
dragging
befouled, dirty
begrimed, dirty
bemired, fouled with mire
beslavered, fouled with
slaver
beslobbered, beslavered
besmeared, besmirched
besmirched, spattered
bespattered, befouled
bloody, stained with blood
blotchy, fouled with
blotches
blotted, blotchy
gory, fouled with blood
mired, bemired
smeared, fouled with
smears
smirched, soiled
smudged, fouled with dirt
spattered, bespattered
spotted, blotchy
stained, fouled
tarnished, fouled
weltered, dirtied from
wallowing
Slovenly
beastly, abominable
dowdy, slovenly
slovenly, unclean
sluttish, slovenly
Scurvy, Etc.
lousy, unclean with lice
scabby, scurfy
scaly, scurfy
scurfy, fouled with loose
matter
scurvy, scabby
Defiled, Etc.
contaminated, defiled
corrupt, befouled
defiled, befouled

ADJECTIVES (Continued)
filthy, unclean
leprous, unclean
marred, vitiated
miasmal, polluted
nasty, filthy
polluted, unclean
reeking, soiled by smoke,
etc.
sordid, filthy
tainted, vitiated
tinged, vitiated
unclean, filthy
vitiated, debased
Offensive
abominable, offensively
unclean
bad, vitiated
obscene, offensive
offensive, abominable
Discolored
blackened, sooty
blurred, soiled
dingy, dirty
discolored, dirty
smutty, fouled with smut
sooty, fouled with soot
Musty, Etc.
dusty, covered with dust
mildewed, fouled with
mildew
moldy, covered with
mold
(B). mouldy
musty, damp with mold
Clammy
clammy, offensively
fouled
slimy, clammy
stodgy, mucky
Excremental
excremental, pertaining to
excrement
fæcal, excremental
mucky, filthy
Dreggy
dreggy, like worthless
sediment
sedimentary, pertaining to
sediment
Turbid
feculent, muddy, turbid
muddy, turbid
turbid, muddy
(Continued on page 270)

NOUNS

Dirtiness

abomination, unclean-
liness
defilement, corruption
dirtiness, uncleanliness
dowdiness, slovenliness
griminess, dirtiness
slovenliness, uncleanliness
squalor, foulness
trashiness, dirtiness
uncleanliness, abomination

Dirt

dirt, any foul or filthy
matter
filth, foul matter
grime, ingrained dirt
mess, unclean disorder

Discoloration

blemish, foul effect
blot, spot or stain
blotch, daub or smudge
blur, smudge
discoloration, blotch
flaw, offensive blemish
smear, smudge
smudge, blur
spatter, foul spots
speck, blemish
spot, blot
splash, spatter
stain, blemish
taint, spot or stain
tarnish, taint

Filthiness, Etc.

blight, smuttiness, mildew
clamminess, offensive
stickiness
corruption, foul quality
filthiness, offensive dirtiness
miriness, muddiness
muddiness, wet earthiness
mustiness, damp mold-
iness
scabbiness, scurviness
scurviness, scabbiness
sootiness, foulness of soot
smut, spot or stain

Mire, Etc.

mire, wet clayey earth
mud, wet viscous earth
ooze, slime, mud
slime, viscous matter
slush, melted snow, etc.

Garbage, Etc.

carrion, filth, garbage
garbage, refuse
offal, refuse, waste meat
scavage, garbage, muck
sewage, sewer filth

NOUNS (Continued)

slop, dirty water, etc.

Excreta, Etc.

dung, anything filthy,
excrement
excrement, discharge from
animals, etc.
excreta, discharged matter
fæces, feces
feces, excrement
muck, moist dung
urine, liquid excretion

Spit

expectoration, spit
mucus, viscid fluid of the
mucous membrane
phlegm, mucus
saliva, spittle
spit, sputum
spittle, spit
sputum, spittle

Scurf, Etc.

crust, hard accretion
dander, dandruff
dandruff, loose scalp-
matter
exuviæ, cast-off skins
scab, wound crust
scurf, loose foul matter
tartar, the foul deposit on
teeth

Dregs

dottle, refuse of a pipe
draff, refuse from malt
dregs, worthless matter
feculence, dregs
grounds, dregs
lees, dregs
residuum, that which is
left after a chemical
process
residue, as above
sediment, dregs

Detritus, Etc.

alluvium, deposit from
floods, etc.
detritus, broken-off rocks,
debris, waste, talus
dust, accumulated particles
earth, soil
goaf, coal waste from a
mine
shale, argillaceous rock
silt, mud or sand deposit
soil, earthy material
talus, detritus

Debris

debris, rubbish
junk, discard

NOUNS (Continued)

litter, rubbish
mull, dust or rubbish
paltry, refuse, trash
raff, refuse, jumble
riff-raff, rubbish, refuse
rubbish, refuse
trash, rubbish

Waste, Refuse

discard, off-cast
off-cast, discard
offscouring, refuse, etc.
off-scum, offscouring
refuse, garbage, anything
worthless
scum, anything worthless
stuff, refuse
waste, refuse

Refuse (Miscell.)

chaff, grain husks
crumbs, fragments
husk, worthless outer
covering
kemp, refuse of fur
parings, worthless scraps
pealings, parings
rags, cloth scraps, etc.
sawdust, dust made by
saw-teeth
scraps, discarded fragments
shavings, parings
straw, anything worthless

Ashes, Dross

ashes, waste of something
burned
cinders, slag
clinkers, slag
dross, refuse, cinders
slag, dross
soot, finely divided carbon

Mold. (B). Mould

mildew, mold
mold, foul growth
(B). mould

PERSONS, ETC.

beast, filthy person
draggle-tail, slovenly
woman
mud-hole, wallow
slattern, draggle-tail
sloven, person who is
habitually untidy and
unclean
slut, dirty, untidy woman
wallow, mud-hole, etc.
welter, a wallow or foul
situation

LOWLINESS
   (Base, Humble) see—

   vs. Excellence 140B

129B

VERBS

Be Lowly

cringe, grovel
crouch, cringe meanly
fall, be in disgrace
grovel, crawl meanly
kneel, be on the knees in submission
prostitute, do basely

Make Debased

brutalize, make brutal
brutify, brutalize
debase, lower in character
derogate, detract from honor
disgrace, bring shame upon
dishonor, disgrace
humble, bring low
humiliate, humble
lower, humble
mortify, humble
pervert, debase
stigmatize, disgrace
vitiate, debase

ADJECTIVES

Common

common, low, inferior
commonplace, common
humdrum, commonplace
mediocre, ordinary
ordinary, commonplace
plebeian, common, vulgar
proletarian, plebeian
unrefined, vulgar
vulgar, common, coarse

Inferior

cheap, low, base, common
degenerate, inferior
inferior, low in state
measly, contemptible
paltry, contemptible
peddling, trifling
petty, contemptible
poor, insignificant
scrubby, mean and small
slight, insignificant
subnormal, inferior
unequal, inferior
unfit, base

Insignificant

insignificant, trivial
pitiful, insignificant
puny, petty

ADJECTIVES (Continued)

trifling, trivial
trivial, trite, commonplace

Worthless

counterfeit, worthless
precious, worthless (irony)
raca, worthless
sorry, mean, worthless
spurious, worthless, base
unworthy, without worth
useless, worthless
valueless, worthless
worthless, unfit

Despised

abhorred, despicable
abominated, abhorred
accursed, bad
cursed, accursed
damned, execrably bad
despised, abhorred
detested, despised
disdained, despised
hated, despised
loathed, despised
scorned, despised
spurned, scorned

Contemptible

abhorrent, repulsive
abominable, loathsome
contemptible, despicable
deplorable, lamentable
despicable, contemptible
detestable, contemptible
disagreeable, disgusting
disgusting, contemptible
distasteful, loathsome
hateful, meriting hate
insufferable, obnoxious
intolerable, insufferable
lamentable, despicable
loathsome, disgusting
mawkish, loathsome
obnoxious, offensive
odious, offensive

Disgraced

characterless, base, vile
degraded, disreputable
disgraced, derelict
disgraceful, infamous
disreputable, disgraceful
notorious, inglorious
scandalous, disgraceful
shameful, disgraceful
soulless, mean
vagrant, tramp-like

ADJECTIVES (Continued)

Humble, Etc.

groveling, base, crawling
hangdog, low, degraded
humble, low, meek, submissive
meek, humble
menial, mean, servile
miserable, wretched
modest, humble
obscure, humble
prostrate, lying humbly
retiring, modest
servile, abject
wretched, low, miserable

Low

abject, low, mean, despicable
base, low, worthless
dastard, pusillanimous
disingenuous, ignoble
ignoble, low, base
ignominious, inglorious
inglorious, ignoble
low, humble, base
lowly, abject
mean, inferior, low
pusillanimous, mean-spirited
recreant, pusillanimous
underbred, vulgar
unwholesome, repulsive

Sordid

beggarly, sordid
mercenary, sordid
prostitute, sordid
sordid, mercenary
venal, mercenary

Bestial

barbarous, brutal
bestial, brutish
beastly, brutish
brutal, savage
brutish, brute-like
illbred, vulgar
monstrous, hideous
reptilian, groveling
savage, barbarous
swinish, bestial, mean

Horrid

dreadful, unhallowed
forbidding, repulsive
foul, loathsome, frightful
frightful, unhallowed
(Continued on page 272)

ADJECTIVES (Continued)

gruesome, frightful
harrowing, offensive
hideous, horrible
horrible, abhorrent
horrid, gruesome
offensive, disgusting
repellent, repulsive
repulsive, disgusting
revolting, disgusting
ugly, morally repellent

Bad, Vile

atrocious, infamous
awful, heinous
bad, despicable, depraved
blackguard, vile, vicious
caitiff, mean, vile
corrupt, bad, dishonest
depraved, corrupt
evil, bad, worthless
heinous, abominable
infamous, unhallowed
shocking, vile
unearthly, unhallowed
unhallowed, depraved
unworthy, unfit
vicious, depraved, corrupt
vile, odiously base

Unwanted

abandoned, base, degraded
derelict, abandoned
forsaken, abandoned
outcast, pariah-like
reprobate, abandoned
undesirable, unfit
unenviable, poor
unenvied, as above
unpopular, insignificant
unsought, unworthy
unwanted, unworthy

Comp. Superl.

worse, (comp. of bad)
worst, (superl. of bad)

NOUNS

Commonness

commonness, vulgarity
commonplaceness, ordinariness
mediocrity, commonplaceness
plebeianism, vulgarity
vulgarity, plebeianism

Inferiority

cheapness, inferiority
inferiority, low state

Insignificance

insignificance, pettiness
littleness, pettiness
pettiness, contemptibleness
smallness, paltriness
triviality, insignificance

Worthlessness

baseness, unworthiness
unfitness, baseness

NOUNS (Continued)

unworthiness, unfitness
worthlessness, baseness

Antipathy

abhorrence, cause of repugnance
anathema, thing anathematized or cursed
antipathy, cause of aversion

Disgrace

disgrace, dishonor
dishonor, disgrace
fall, disgrace
ignominy, public dishonor
infamy, public disgrace
stigma, disgrace

Humility

abasement, base humility
humble-pie, humility
humiliation, abasement
humility, self-abasement
obscureness, lowliness
subordination, abasement

Lowliness

abjection, degradation
debasement, degradation
degradation, dishonor
depression, abasement
ignobleness, low birth
lowliness, depression

Sordidness

beggarliness, meanness
mercenariness, sordidness
prostitution, mercenariness
sordidness, prostitution
venality, prostitution of talents

Bestiality

bestiality, brutishness
heathenism, vulgarity
savagery, heathenism

Vileness

repulsiveness, despicableness
sorriness, despicableness
turpitude, inherent baseness
vileness, odious baseness

PERSONS

Plebeian

countryman, rustic
groveler, recreant
peasant, rustic
plebeian, common person
proletarian, plebeian
rustic, countryman
swain, rustic
yokel, rustic

Barbarian

barbarian, savage
boor, ill-mannered person
heathen, barbarian
savage, barbarian

PERSONS (Continued)

Beast

baboon, epithet of contempt
bear, uncouth person
beast, brute-like person
brute, beast
hound, brute-like person
monkey, term of contempt
skunk, contemptible fellow
worm, debased creature

Nobody

cipher, one of no value
insect, petty person
nobody, nonentity
nonentity, person of no account

Brat, Etc.

bastard, illegitimate child
brat, child (contemptuously)
chit, forward girl
imp, mischievous child
pickle, imp
street-arab, street urchin
tomboy, wild girl

Hussy, Etc.

crone, withered old woman
hag, ugly old woman
hecate, hag
holden, romp
(B). hoyden
hussy, worthless woman
quean, worthless woman
romp, rough girl
slattern, untidy woman
slut, term of contempt for a woman
wench, forward woman

Churl, Etc.

bloke, despised person
bounder, rough fellow
bumpkin, lout
cad, churl
churl, low-bred fellow
clown, rustic
coot, epithet of contempt
galoot, bloke
hoodlum, rowdy, hooligan
hooligan, tough
lout, uncouth fellow
menial, servile domestic
mumbo-jumbo, vulgar bugbear
pilgarlic, mean domestic
ragamuffin, disreputable fellow
rake, dissolute fellow
scalawag, scamp
sanculotte (French), one without breeches, term of contempt
scrub, sorry fellow
(Continued on page 267)

DISHONESTY—
SIN—CRIME   see—

vs. Goodness 140A
vs. Christianity 82D

ASSOCIATIVE

Impropriety	...............126C	Oppression	...............130B
Intemperance	...........125C	Attack	...........130F
Dishonor	...................129B	Chastizement	...........130N
Theft	...............49F	Brutality	...........130M
Robbery	...................49G	Torture	...........130N
Falsehood	62	Destruction	...........130-O

130A
VERBS

Fail, Lapse

decline, fall into sin
fall, trip into sin
lapse, sin slightly
misbehave, lapse
slip, lapse
trip, fall, slip, fail

Sin

blaspheme, profane
err, sin
profane, violate
sin, transgress or offend
propriety, order, or
religion

Outrage

out-Herod, exceed in evil
outrage, out-Herod
violate, outrage

Encroach

encroach, intrude
grasp, encroach
intrude, force into
invade, infringe
trench, encroach

Pervert

bishop, manipulate as in
horsetrading
counterfeit, manipulate
falsify, forge, etc.
forge, defraud by altera-
tion or deception
gerrymander, alter unfairly
manipulate, falsify
misapply, pervert
mutilate, pervert
pervert, misapply
tamper, pervert
vitiate, pervert

Deceive

bamboozle, deceive
beguile, impose upon
circumvent, impose de-
ception
deceive, impose upon
dupe, deceive
fake, deceive
foist, deceive
gull, deceive
hocus, impose
hocus-pocus, as above
hoodwink, deceive
illude, deceive
misrepresent, deceive
sham, deceive

VERBS (Continued)

Defraud

bam, cheat
cajole, cheat
cheat, defraud
defraud, swindle, cheat
jockey, cheat
juggle, cheat
mump, cheat
palm, defraud
swindle, defraud

Ensnare

betray, seduce
ensnare, entrap, seduce
entangle, ensnare
entrap, catch by imposition
seduce, draw into evil

Victimize

frame, foist an imposition
plant, frame
sell, betray
victimize, dupe

Betray

betray, victimize treach-
erously

Conspire

abet, aid criminally
apostatize, desert prin-
ciples
cabal, plot
connive, abet
conspire, concert in crime
intrigue, conspire
pack, unite for an unjust
purpose
plot, conspire
suborn, incite to crime

Perpetrate

batten, thrive at the ex-
pense of others
commit, perpetrate
contravene, transgress
force, violate
infringe, violate a law
misdemean, do a wrong
perpetrate, do wrong
transgress, violate law
trespass, transgress

Deprave

corrupt, make bad
debase, corrupt
demoralize, corrupt
deprave, corrupt

ADJECTIVES

Fallible

fallible, liable to sin
peccable, fallible

Failing

aberrant, wandering from
rectitude
failing, falling from
grace
lax, inclined to sin
loose, lax
remiss, lax
slack, peccable, lapsing

Mischievous

disobedient, reprehensible
impish, mischievous
injurious, bad, unjust
maleficent, mischievous
mischievous, bad
naughty, perverse, bad

Depraved

abandoned, dissolute
bad, wicked
corrupt, bad
criminal, wicked
debased, corrupt
depraved, debased
dishonest, discreditable
dissolute, wicked
felonious, criminal
ill, evil
immoral, corrupt
incorrigible, depraved
profligate, abandoned
unconscionable, un-
scrupulous
unprincipled, unscrupulous
unscrupulous, unprincipled

Sinful

blasphemous, profane
godless, impious
impious, profane
irreligious, ungodly
irreverent, impious
profane, blasphemous
sacrilegious, impious
sinful, impious
ungodly, wicked
ungracious, ungodly
unhallowed, wicked
unholy, evil
unrighteous, wicked
wayward, sinful
(Continued on page 274)

ADJECTIVES (Continued)

Outrageous
arrant, atrocious
atrocious, heinous
black, wicked
dreadful, wicked
enormous, diabolic
evil, wicked
flagitious, atrocious
flagrant, openly wicked
frightful, wicked
gross, flagrant
heinous, flagitious
infamous, notoriously bad
iniquitous, wicked
malevolent, evil
malignant, wicked
monstrous, atrocious
nefarious, very wicked
outrageous, over-wicked
perverse, bad
piacular, atrocious
scandalous, flagitious
sinister, evil
vicious, violent
villainous, wicked
violent, severely unjust
wicked, bad, sinful

Fiendish
demoniac, diabolical
devilish, diabolical
diabolic, fiendish
diabolical, fiendish
fiendish, devilish
hellish, diabolical
infernal, fiendish
satanic, diabolic
Stygian, infernal
unearthly, diabolic

Lawless
anarchic, lawless
disorderly, lawless
lawless, uncontrolled
uncontrolled, disorderly

Reprehensible
blamable, culpable
blameworthy, blamable
censurable, blamable
culpable, criminal
reprehensible, blamable
unprovoked, reprehensible

Abominable
abominable, loathsome
detestable, offensive
disgraceful, dishonorable
loathsome, detestable
odious, abominable
offensive, odious
regrettable, evil
shameful, disgraceful
shocking, wicked

Unspeakable
unmentionable, atrocious
unspeakable, atrocious
unutterable, shocking

ADJECTIVES (Continued)

Unjust
backhanded, unfair
dishonorable, unjust
foul, unfair
inequitable, unjust
invidious, unfair
tricky, dishonest
unfair, unjust
unjust, unfair
wrong, unjust
wrongful, wrong, blamable

Perverse
bogus, counterfeit
counterfeit, spurious
false, counterfeit
indirect, unfair
perverse, tampering with
sham, counterfeit
spurious, illegitimate
underhand, unjust

Deceitful
circumventive, deceptive
deceitful, delusive
deceivable, misleading
deceptive, deceitful
delusive, deceptive
disingenuous, deceitful
fallacious, deceitful
hollow, insincere
insincere, deceitful
meretricious, deceptive
pseudo, false

Crafty
crafty, insidious
cunning, treacherous
feline, treacherous
insidious, treacherous
surreptitious, fraudulent

Fraudulent
fraudulent, deceitful
knavish, dishonest
mendacious, dishonest
swindling, cheating
thievish, dishonest

Treacherous
apostate, treacherous
disloyal, faithless
faithless, untrue
intriguing, insidious
perfidious, treacherous
Punic, perfidious
recreant, false
treacherous, violating
allegiance
unfaithful, treacherous
untrue, disloyal
untrustworthy, faithless

Conspiring
accessorial, aiding criminally
clandestine, collusory
collusive, concerted in
fraud

ADJECTIVES (Continued)
conspiring, joined in evil

Guilty
damned, execrably bad
guilty, punishable
inexcusable, unpardonable
red-handed, fresh in crime
unforgivable, devilish
unpardonable, diabolical

NOUNS

Fallibility
fallibility, peccability
peccability, tendency to sin

Failing
aberration, dereliction
dereliction, laxity
failing, fault, sin
lapse, slight sin
laxity, remissness
laxness, remissness
remissness, slackness
slackness, failing

Mischief
delinquency, offense
disobedience, dereliction
escapade, misdeed
fault, slight crime
maleficence, evil deed
mendacity, dishonesty
misbehavior, offense
(B). misbehaviour
misconduct, misdemeanor
misdemeanor, misbehavior
(B). misdemeanour
mischief, badness
naughtiness, misbehavior
peccadillo, slight sin
prank, peccadillo

Depravity
badness, depravity
bane, vice or sin
corruption, depravity
depravity, wickedness
immorality, wickedness
rascality, crime, etc.
vice, depravity
villainy, wickedness

Sinfulness
blasphemy, profanity
desecration, profanation
impenitence, wickedness
impiety, irreverence
irreverence, impiety
original sin, first sin
profanation, violation
sacrilege, profanation
sin, transgression
sinfulness, ungodliness
ungodliness, wickedness

Outrage
atrocity, enormous evil
deviltry, wickedness
enormity, atrocity
(Continued on page 275)

NOUNS (Continued)

evil, wickedness
fiendishness, deviltry
hell, extreme evil
ill, evil
infamy, badness
iniquity, wickedness
outrage, extreme evil
perversity, peccancy
vileness, wickedness
wickedness, evil

Lawlessness

anarchy, lawlessness
disorder, lawlessness
lawlessness, disorder, crime
outlawry, lawlessness

Unjustness

dishonesty, knavery
hardship, injustice
improbity, dishonesty
inequity, injustice
injustice, unfairness
oppression, injustice
unfairness, injustice
unjustness, unfairness
unrighteousness, wrong
wrong, injustice

Encroachment

encroachment, intrusion
intrusion, illegal entry
invasion, encroachment

Perversion

manipulation, falsification
falsification, a tampering
 with
forgery, falsification
misapplication, manipula-
 tion
mutilation, perversion
perversion, misapplication
sham, counterfeit
spoliation, mutilation
vitiation, perversion

Deception

beguilement, imposition
circumvention, deception
cunning, trickery
deceit, knavery
deceitfulness, deception
deception, imposition
delusion, imposition
fake, deception
guile, deception
hocusing, trickery
imposition, imposture
imposture, deception
jugglery, imposture
obliqueness, guile
trickery, deception
trickiness, as above
wile, deception

Fraud

cheating, deception
chicane, unfair artifice

NOUNS (Continued)

fakement, fraud
flummery, fraud
fraud, swindle, deceit
fraudulence, fraud
knavery, fraud
malpractice, evil practice
sell, a swindle
swindle, a cheating

Treachery

apostasy, treachery
betrayal, treachery
perfidy, treachery
recreancy, treachery
treason, treachery
treachery, violation of
 allegiance

Conspiracy

abetment, connivance
barratry, unlawful incitement for the inciter's
 benefit
cabal, intrigue
collusion, complicity
complicity, connivance
connivance, complicity
conspiracy, collusion, plot
embracery, corruption
intrigue, secret plot
machination, plot
plot, conspiracy
subornation, act of
 inducing crime

Perpetration

breach, violation
contravention, violation
crime, iniquity
felony, crime
infraction, violation
infringement, violation
malfeasance, unlawfulness
malignancy, wickedness
malversation, corruption
offense, sin, crime
(B). offence
peccancy, sinfulness
perpetration, violation
transgression, violation
trespass, transgression
umbrage, offense
violation, breach of law,
 etc.
violence, outrage

Guilt

criminality, guilt
guilt, a liability to
 punishment
guiltiness, as above

Abomination

abomination, wickedness
culpability, wickedness
disgrace, infamy
scandal, culpability

PERSONS

Delinquent

delinquent, misdemeanant
misdemeanant, offender
pickle, mischievous child

Sinner

blasphemer, sacrilegist
desecrater, sacrilegist
impenitent, hardened
 sinner
offender, transgressor
profaner, desecrater
sacrilegist, profaner
sinner, offender
transgressor, sinner

Rascal

apache, Parisian criminal
blackguard, villain
miscreant, evil-doer
rascal, scoundrel
reprobate, miscreant
ruffian, outlaw
scamp, rascal
scapegrace, miscreant
scoundrel, rascal
thug, ruffian
varlet, scoundrel
villain, scoundrel
viper, crafty person

Fiend

demon, devilish person
devil, wicked person
fiend, demon
monster, demon

Outlaw

anarchist, opponent, and
 destroyer, of govern-
 ment
outlaw, a violator of
 established order

Interloper

interloper, impostor

Charlatan

charlatan, quack
humbug, impostor
knave, rogue
mountebank, charlatan
mumper, cheating beggar
quack, knave
rogue, trickster
trickster, knave

Swindler

bam, a cheat
beat, a dead-beat
cheat, swindler
dead-beat, cheat
defrauder, cheat
duffer, cheat
faker, swindler
fraud, swindler
gouger, swindler
huckster, knave
impostor, knave
shyster, trickster

(Continued on page 280)

OPPRESSION—
    ANNOYANCE see—
    vs. Consolation 136A

ASSOCIATIVE

Lashing	130G	Misfortune	127B
Punishment	130N	Difficulty	13
Cruelty	130M	Disease	130E
Death	130-O	Lowness	129B

130B

VERBS

Annoy

ail, cause worry
annoy, distress
badger, pester
bait, harass
bother, worry
disturb, trouble
harass, annoy, worry
harry, harass
molest, annoy, vex
pester, plague
pique, annoy
plague, annoy
pother, harass
tease, annoy
trouble, distress
worry, harass

Embarrass

abash, make ashamed
chagrin, mortify
disappoint, chagrin
discomfit, embarrass
embarrass, abash
faze, worry, annoy
humiliate, mortify
mortify, abash

Disgust

disgust, cause loathing
nauseate, sicken
sicken, disgust
turn, nauseate

Distress

abuse, ill-treat
afflict, distress
assail, abuse
beset, embarrass
crowd, press closely
discomfort, distress
distress, cause suffering
dragoon, harass
grieve, cause grief
maltreat, abuse
persecute, ill-treat
press, distress
scourge, harass greatly
stab, injure secretly
torment, harass
torture, vex

Depress

damp, discourage
dash, depress
deject, dishearten
depress, dispirit, deject
desolate, dispirit
discourage, dispirit
dishearten, discourage
dispirit, deject

VERBS (Continued)

sadden, deject

Smother

choke, suffocate
smother, stive
stifle, smother
stive, stifle
suffocate, smother

Aggravate

aggravate, add to distress
aggrieve, add to distress
bore, annoy
chafe, irritate
fret, irritate
gall, vex, fret
grind, harass
irritate, aggravate
ruffle, vex
tantalize, torment
vex, annoy

Inconvenience

discommode, inconvenience
incommode, inconvenience
inconvenience, discommode

Tire, Weary

fag, fatigue
fatigue, tire
jade, weary
tire, weary
weary, tire

Harm

harm, injure
hurt, harm
injure, harm
pain, distress
pinch, distress
twinge, cause pain
wound, hurt

Oppress, Etc.

burden, discomfort
encumber, burden
haze, impose distress
impose, burden
oppress, burden
saddle, burden
tyrannize, oppress

ADJECTIVES

Annoying

annoying, vexing
bothersome, troublesome
disturbing, annoying
harassing, annoying
offensive, annoying
pesky, annoying
plaguy, vexatious
provoking, annoying
troublesome, annoying

ADJECTIVES (Continued)

trying, troublesome
vexatious, worrisome
vexing, annoying
worrisome, troublesome

Embarrassing

discomfiting, embarrassing
embarrassing, distressing
humiliating, distressing
mortifying, vexatious

Disgusting

disgusting, nauseous
nauseous, loathsome
odious, disgusting

Distressing

abusive, offensive
disagreeable, unpleasant
discomforting, distressing
distressing, annoying
distressful, disagreeable
infelicitous, unpleasant
mischievous, harmful
piquant, offensive
uncomfortable, unpleasant
unpleasant, disagreeable

Depressing

cheerless, depressing
comfortless, cheerless
cumbrous, vexatious
depressing, distressing
discouraging, depressing
dismal, dreary
dispiriting, discouraging
drear, depressing
dreary, cheerless

Suffocating

close, oppressive
suffocating, smothering
sultry, suffocating

Aggravating

aggravating, morbidly distressing
galling, irritating
irritating, distressing
tantalizing, tormenting

Severe

afflictive, painful
austere, severe
cruel, pitiless
dolorous, causing grief
grievous, oppressive
hard, severe
harsh, severe
merciless, severe
pitiless, cruel
rigorous, severe
ruthless, pitiless

(Continued on page 277)

ADJECTIVES (Continued)
severe, ruthless
stringent, severe
unbearable, cruel

Pestilential
calamitous, distressing
pernicious, injurious
pestiferous, pestilential
pestilential, pernicious

Inconvenient
incommodious, inconvenient
inconvenient, troublesome

Wearisome
fatiguing, wearisome
irksome, wearisome
laborious, toilsome
onerous, burdensome
Sisyphean, ceaselessly toilsome
tiresome, irksome
tedious, wearisome
toilsome, laborious
wearisome, troublesome

Harmful
aching, causing pain
griping, distressing
harmful, hurtful
hurtful, afflictive
injurious, harmful
noxious, harmful
painful, causing pain
poignant, painful
pricking, painful
shocking, distressing
sore, distressing

Oppressive
burdensome, oppressive
oppressive, depressing
tyrannical, oppressive
tyrannous, as above

NOUNS
Annoyance
abomination, bother
annoyance, vexation
bother, annoyance
botheration, bother
discomfiture, discomfort
disturbance, annoyance
embarrassment, discomfiture
molestation, annoyance

NOUNS (Continued)
nuisance, annoyance
pest, annoyance
trouble, embarrassment
vexation, annoyance
worry, distressing trouble

Distress
abuse, ill treatment
distress, trouble
mischief, harm
piquancy, severity

Depression
damper, incubus
depression, damper
discouragement, incubus
grief, a cause of sorrow
incubus, depression
monotony, irksomeness
mortification, repression
nauseation, disturbance
nausea, nauseation
repression, mortification
skeleton, secret annoyance
tedium, wearisomeness

Aggravation
aggravation, morbid vexation
boredom, bother
disagreeableness, unpleasantness
discomfort, that which distresses
grievance, cause of complaint or suffering
irritant, pain
irritation, aggravation

Severity
austerity, severity
harshness, severity
inclemency, severity
pressure, severity
rigor, severity
(B). rigour
rigorism, severeness
severity, inclemency
strait, severe difficulty
stringency, severity
tenterhook, that which strains severely

Affliction
affliction, calamity
calamity, affliction

NOUNS (Continued)
plague, anything annoying

Harm
ache, pain
agony, extreme pain
harm, injury
hurt, injury
injury, harm
pain, pang
painfulness, pain
pang, sudden pain
pinch, distress
poignancy, pain
stab, secret injury
twinge, sharp pain

Oppression
burden, oppression
hazing, distressing burden
imposition, burden
onus, burden
oppression, burden
pill, onus
responsibility, burden
tyranny, oppression

Ordeal
cross, ordeal
fire, severe trial or affliction
ordeal, severe trial
persecution, oppression
sweat, ordeal
tantalization, annoyance
travail, severe toil
trial, ordeal
tribulation, severe affliction

Miscellaneous
inconvenience, annoyance
offense, annoyance
offensiveness, as above
toil, tedium
weight, something oppressive
worriment, worry
work, severe toil

PERSONS
bore
depressor
oppressor
persecutor
tyrant

130C (Continued)
NOUNS (Continued)
sauciness, impudence
Miscellaneous
abhorrence, abomination
abomination, cause of dislike, anger, etc.
disaffection, provocation
exasperation, that which enrages
indecency, shamelessness
indelicacy, indecency
intrusiveness, officiousness

NOUNS (Continued)
invidiousness, provocation to ill-will
irritant, cause of irritation
offense, invidiousness
(B). offence
officiousness, meddlesomeness
outrage, wanton mischief
rowdyism, riotous offense
rusticity, rudeness
vulgarity, rudeness

PERSONS
boor, ill-mannered person
chit, pert child
churl, ill-bred person
hamfatter, actor who displeases
hornet, disagreeable person
rowdy, indecorous person
vixen, turbulent woman
wasp, shrew
shrew, vixen
vulgarian, boor

ANGERING— ENRAGING (Cause of Anger) see— vs. Gladdening........99A	ASSOCIATIVE	
	Annoyance 130B	Punishment 130N
	Ugliness 109A	Cruelty 130M
	Derision 72	Death 130-O
	Reproof 64	Misfortune 127B
	Quarrel 66	Difficulty 13
	Wrath 29	Disease 130E
	Lashing 130G	Lowness 129B

130C

VERBS

Provoke
annoy, aggravate
bedevil, vex
bother, annoy
disaffect, provoke
meddle, be officious
provoke, exasperate
tease, vex
vex, nettle
worry, tease

Aggravate
aggravate, add indignity
badger, irritate
fret, nettle
irritate, exasperate
nettle, irritate
rankle, irritate
ruffle, irritate

Displease
displease, irritate
disturb, vex
intrude, disturb
offend, provoke
perturb, vex
pique, irritate

Embitter
chagrin, embitter
embitter, exasperate
envenom, exasperate

Inflame
excite, inflame
incense, provoke
inflame, provoke
kindle, inflame
rouse, provoke
stir, rouse

Exasperate
anger, madden
enrage, madden
exasperate, enrage
frenzy, enrage
infuriate, madden
madden, enrage
roil, infuriate

Insult
affront, insult
insult, be insolent
outrage, insult
trample, insult

ADJECTIVES

Provocative
aggravating, annoying
annoying, offensive

ADJECTIVES (Continued)
bothersome, annoying
irritating, aggravating
provocative, aggravating
provoking, as above
rankling, irritating

Discourteous
discourteous, uncivil
impolite, indecorous
uncivil, rude

Displeasing
displeasing, provoking
intrusive, offensive
invidious, displeasing
meddlesome, intrusive
objectionable, displeasing
obnoxious, offensive
offensive, invidious
officious, meddlesome
waspish, invidious

Indecent
immodest, indelicate
indecent, immodest
indecorous, provocative
indelicate, obscene
obscene, indecorous
shameless, impudent

Inflammatory
inflammatory, provocative

Exasperating
enraging, inflammatory
exasperating, vexatious
maddening, exasperating
vexing, vexatious
vexatious, aggravating

Insulting
brazen, impudent
brazen-faced, impudent
impertinent, impudent
impudent, insolent
insolent, impertinent
insulting, provocative
outrageous, exasperating
pert, insolent
saucy, insolent

Churlish
blunt, rude
churlish, rude
coarse, gross
gross, rude
harsh, rough
rough, rude, uncivil
rowdy, rough
rude, invidious

ADJECTIVES (Continued)
surly, churlish
vulgar, gross

Beastly
barbarous, boorish
bearish, beastly
beastly, boorish
boorish, rude
heathenish, boorish

Abominable
abominable, detestable
abhorrent, abominable
contemptible, detestable
despicable, despisable
despisable, contemptible
detestable, despicable
disgusting, abominable
hateful, abominable
heinous, outrageous
loathsome, invidious
odious, loathsome
repellent, repulsive
reprehensible, despicable
repugnant, repulsive
repulsive, repugnant
revolting, abhorrent

NOUNS

Provocation
aggravation, irritation
annoyance, vexation
bedevilment, offense
irritation, provocation
provocation, incitation to
  anger, etc.
provocative, that which
  provokes
vexation, provocation

Discourtesy
discourtesy, impoliteness
impoliteness, indecorum
incivility, discourtesy
indecorum, invidiousness
rudeness, incivility

Infuriation
infuriation, exasperation

Insult
effrontery, impudence
impertinence, impudence
impudence, sauciness
indignity, insult
insolence, impudence
insult, effrontery
pertness, sauciness

(Continued on page 277)

IMPAIRMENT—	ASSOCIATIVE	
DEPRIVATION see—	Attack 130F	Fatefulness 134C
	Beating 130G	Weakness 128A
vs. Nutriment 48A	Cruelty 130M	Disease 130E
vs. Generosity 43A	Punishment ....-............130N	Annulment 131A
vs. Teaching 81	Burning 131B	Oppression 130B

130D

VERBS

Impair

debase, degrade
decrease, diminish
degrade, lower
deteriorate, disqualify
diminish, impair
impair, diminish
lessen, decrease
lower, weaken
reduce, diminish

Invalidate

counteract, neutralize
countervail, neutralize
invalidate, make impotent
neutralize, render ineffective

Weaken, Etc.

debilitate, enfeeble
enervate, devitalize
enfeeble, weaken
fag, make tired
fatigue, fag
flag, fag
irk, make weary
tire, fag
weaken, impair strength
weary, cause weariness

Deprive

beggar, impoverish
bereave, deprive
deprive, impoverish
impoverish, deprive

Drain

deflate, empty
drain, empty
empty, drain
exhaust, empty
strip, empty, drain

Endanger

endanger, expose
expose, endanger
imperil, endanger
jeopard, jeopardize
jeopardize, endanger
risk, jeopardize

Injure

blemish, injure

VERBS (Continued)

damage, injure
harm, injure
hurt, impair
injure, hurt
mar, injure
scathe, injure
wear, injure

Lacerate

lacerate, rend, injure
rend, lacerate
rip, rend
tear, rend

Cripple

cripple, disable
hamstring, disqualify by cutting the tendons of the hams
lame, cripple
maim, cripple
mangle, mutilate
mutilate, maim

Devitalize

castrate, emasculate
devitalize, make effete
emasculate, deprive of seed
sterilize, devitalize

Dilute

dilute, weaken by mixture
thin, dilute
water, dilute
weaken, dilute

Disqualify

capsize, disqualify
disable, disqualify
disqualify, disable
founder, disable
incapacitate, disqualify
paralyze, unnerve
sap, devitalize
undermine, sap
unnerve, devitalize

ADJECTIVES

Miscellaneous

damaging, injurious
deleterious, harmful
detrimental, injurious

ADJECTIVES (Continued)

exhaustive, depriving of force
fatiguing, wearisome
harassing, fatiguing
harmful, injurious
hurtful, harmful
ill, harmful
irksome, wearisome
injurious, deleterious
mischievous, harmful
nocent, hurtful
noisome, harmful
scathing, injurious
tiresome, wearisome
wearisome, fatiguing

NOUNS

Miscellaneous

castration, emasculation
damage, impairment
debilitation, impairment
deprivation, impairment
deterioration, impairment
detriment, injury
emasculation, castration
enervation, devitalization
enfeeblement, impairment
harm, injury
hurt, harm
ill, harm
impairment, deterioration
injury, harm
laceration, impairment
mayhem, mutilation of defense
mischief, injury
mutilation, a laming
nocence, harm
sabotage, injury by workmen
sterilization, a making sterile
tiresomeness, wearisomeness
wear, impairment
wearisomeness, a wearing fatigue

DISEASE—BANE—POISON
(Cause of Sickness)

ASSOCIATIVE

see—
Decay	128C
Fatefulness	134C
Misfortune	127B
Defective Sight	119B

vs. Cure—Remedy 136B
vs. Health—Recovery 137A

130E

VERBS

Miscellaneous

attack, make sick
blight, corrupt
canker, poison
contaminate, canker
corrupt, contaminate
curarize, poison
derange, distemper
disease, derange
distemper, to disease
envenom, poison
indispose, make unfit
infect, to disease
poison, corrupt
sicken, make sick

ADJECTIVES

Miscellaneous

baneful, pernicious
cancerous, affected with
  cancer
gangrenous, having gan-
  grene
infectious, baneful
insalubrious, unwholesome
mawkish, sickening
morbid, unhealthy
morbific, producing disease
noxious, pernicious
pernicious, injurious
pestiferous, baneful
pestilential, baneful
poisonous, baneful
sickening, causing illness
unwholesome, baneful
toxic, poisonous
venomous, poisonous

NOUNS

Disease, Etc.

affection, disease
ailment, sickness
derangement, malady
disease, malady

NOUNS (Continued)

disorder, disease, etc.
humor, morbid condition
(B). humour
ill, disease, etc.
illness, ailment
infection, disease
leaven, pernicious influence
malady, disease
sickness, illness

Wound, Etc.

hurt, injury
injury, bane
sore, diseased part
wound, injury or hurt

Poison

atropine, a poisoning
atropism, poisoning by
  atropine
curare, poison
poison, venom
toxicant, any poison
virus, poisonous matter

Visitation

affliction, attack
attack, visitation
bane, disease, scourge
epidemic, plague
perniciousness, thorough
  bane
pestilence, perniciousness
plague, epidemic
scourge, pestilence
visitation, retributive affliction

Miscellaneous

abscess, morbid sore
alcoholism, alcoholic disease
allopathy, ailment sub-
  stituted to offset another
alopecia, disease which
  causes loss of hair
bacilli-pestis, species of
  deadly plague

NOUNS (Continued)

blight, plant disease
burn, injury by fire
cancer, a disease
canker, ulcerous disease
catarrh, disorder of the
  mucous membrane
cholera, violent disease
consumption, pulmonary
  disease
convulsion, violent muscular disorder
distemper, disease
gangrene, mortification
gripe, pinching distress
heartburn, an affection
hydrophobia, rabies
hysteria, morbid emotion-
  alism
inflammation, morbid
  state
itch, irritating disease
leprosy, skin disease
mange, disease
paroxysm, convulsion
rabies, hydrophobia
rash, cutaneous eruption
scald, injury by heat
scratches, a disease
singe, a burn
tumor, morbid swelling
ulcer, sore
ulceration, ulcer formation

BEINGS

Pandora, Greek woman who
  symbolized all the evils
  that afflicted mankind
Kali, Hindu goddess of epi-
  demics
  See a medical dictionary
for a more complete list of
diseases also classifiable.

130A (Continued)

PERSONS (Continued)

swindler, defrauder

Conspirator

abetter, partner in crime
accomplice, abetter
barrator, one guilty of
  barratry
cat's-paw, one who serves
  the deceptive ends of
  another
conniver, abetter
conspirator, accomplice
gangster, accomplice
intrigant, plotter (male)

PERSONS (Continued)

intrigante, plotter (fem.)
procurer, one who supplies
  women for prostitution
procuress, as above (fem.)
stool-pigeon, decoy for
  another

Traitor, Etc.

apostate, traitor
derelict, recreant
recreant, apostate
renegade, traitor
traitor, renegade

PERSONS (Continued)

Criminal

convict, convicted crim-
  inal
criminal, felon
culprit, criminal
felon, culprit
malefactor, criminal
perpetrator, offender
violator, transgressor

SYMBOL

Cloven Hoof, symbol of sin

<table>
<tr><td>

ATTACK—
    ENCOUNTER   see—

vs. Cowardice 32
vs. Retreat 15

</td></tr>
</table>

ATTACK—
ENCOUNTER see—

vs. Cowardice 32
vs. Retreat 15

ASSOCIATIVE

Contention 41D		Whipping 130G
Opposition 27		Punishment 130N
Anger—Fury 29		Brutality 130M
Hate—Enmity 28		Robbery 49G
Oppression 130B		Destructiveness 130-O

130F

VERBS

Attack

aggress, attack
assail, attack
assault, assail
attack, assault
attempt, attack
charge, attack
mob, attack with a crowd
onslaught, assail
storm, attack violently
tackle, attack

Waylay

ambush, waylay
waylay, ambush

Combat

battle, beset
combat, conflict
close, conflict
conflict, wage a conflict
contend, conflict
contest, contend
engage, conflict
fight, make war
skirmish, fight slightly

Militate

crusade, war for religion
militate, beset
war, militate

Siege

beset, attack on all sides
besiege, beset
compass, besiege
siege, besiege

Invade

infest, attack
invade, enter hostilely

Miscellaneous

bombard, attack with cannon
box, fight with fists
cannonade, bombard
duel, fight in a duel
enfilade, fire on a straight file of men

ADJECTIVES

Militant

bellicose, warlike
belligerent, militant
combative, pugnacious
fighting, combative
hostile, pugnacious
martial, militant

ADJECTIVES (Continued)

militant, warlike
offensive, aggressive
warlike, belligerent

Miscellaneous

aggressive, attacking
agonistic, noting athletic contest
amuck, in frenzied attack
assailant, hostile
besetting, aggressive
conflicting, assailant
fistic, pugilistic
gladiatorial, combative-like gladiators
guerrilla, in petty warfare
military, martial
paleomachic, noting obsolete warfare
pugilistic, fighting with fists
pugnacious, bellicose
snappish, pugnacious
tigerish, in ferocious attack

NOUNS

Attack

aggression, unprovoked attack
attack, onset
assault, onslaught
attempt, attack, assault
charge, attack
offense, assault
(B). offence
offensive, attack
onset, assault
onslaught, furious attack
storm, violent assault

Outbreak

ambush, attack from hiding
ambuscade, ambush
outbreak, hostile eruption
sally, sudden attack by the besieged
sortie, sally

Combat

affray, public fight
battle, combat
brush, slight encounter
clash, conflict
combat, struggle

NOUNS (Continued)

conflict, fight
collision, antagonism
encounter, conflict
engagement, encounter
fight, combat
fisticuffs, fistic fight
fracas, noisy fight
fray, fracas
melee, affray
pitched battle, encounter
rencounter, hostile collision
scrimmage, rough contest
scuffle, struggle
skirmish, slight conflict
struggle, fracas
tilt, conflict with lances
tussle, scuffle

Contest

bout, fistic combat
contest, any contention
duel, combat between two persons
joust, mock combat
prize-fight, fistic combat
set-to, boxing match

Militancy

antagonism, hostility
belligerency, warfare
fighting, a combat
hostility, warfare
militancy, warfare
militarism, warfare preparedness
war, military conflict
warfare, war

Siege

besetment, attack
besiegement, besetment
siege, belligerent surrounding

Invasion

crusade, religious invasion
foray, predatory incursion
incursion, raid
inroad, incursion
invasion, hostile incursion
irruption, hostile incursion
pogrom, attack (by Russian soldiers) on villages to obtain supplies, etc.
raid, predatory incursion
(Continued on page 282)

NOUNS (Continued)

Gun-fire

artillery preparation, bombardment before a charge
barrage, offensive firing
bombardment, cannonade
broadside, united firing from a vessel's side
cannonade, bombardment
fusillade, simultaneous firing
gun-fire, attack with guns
round, a volley
shot, single attack by a firearm
volley, simultaneous discharge of arms

Ordnance

artillery, ordnance
musketry, warfare with firearms
ordnance, artillery

PERSONS, ETC.

(See Officers 133A)

adversary, opponent
aggressor, one who begins an aggression
archer, one who uses the bow and arrow
artilleryman, cannoneer
assailant, assailer
assaulter, assailant
belligerent, combatant
besieger, assailer
bombardier, artilleryman
cannoneer, gunner
carbineer, soldier armed with a carbine
cavalier, armed horseman
cavalryman, trooper
charger, cavalry horse
chasseur, light-armed soldier
combatant, belligerent
cossack, one of the warlike tribe of S. Russia
cuirassier, cavalry soldier

PERSONS (Continued)

dragoon, cavalryman
doughboy, infantryman
enemy, foe
foe, foeman
foeman, enemy
free-lance, mercenary soldier
gladiator, contestant
grenadier, English soldier
guerrilla, irregular soldier
gunman, professional murderer
gunner, artilleryman
hoplite, heavily armed foot-soldier
hussar, cavalry soldier
lancer, cavalry soldier
marine, naval soldier
mercenary, soldier hired into foreign service
militant, fighter
musketeer, foot-soldier
myrmidon, one who is ruthless in the execution of orders
militiaman, member of the militia
onager, one who attacks wildly
opponent, adversary
picador, in bull-fighting, one who incites the bull with lances
piou-piou, French infantryman
poilu, French soldiers
private, common soldier
pugilist, prize-fighter
recruit, new soldier
regular, regular soldier
rifleman, rifle soldier
sapper, soldier employed in digging trenches
sepoy, soldier of India in the British service
sniper, sharpshooter
soldier, military subject
trooper, cavalryman

PERSONS (Continued)

warrior, soldier, fighter
zouave, infantry soldier of France

PERSONS (PLURAL)

armament, war forces
army, military body
battalion, body of infantry
battery, large arms and soldiers
brigade, division of an army
cavalry, horse soldiers
company, assemblage of troops
corps, body of troops
commando, military force
detachment, troops for special service
forces, army
fusileer, former British regiment
garrison, troops in a fortified place
host, army
infantry, foot soldiers
landsturm, last reserve of the German army
landwehr, the militia of the German army
military, body of soldiers
militia, drilled citizens
navy, ships and men of war
platoon, division of soldiers
regiment, companies of soldiers
rifle-corps, force armed with rifles
soldiery, soldiers collectively
squad, small party of soldiers
squadron, division of cavalry
troops, troop, army

BEINGS

Ares, Greek god of war
Mars, Roman god of war

BLOWS—INFLICTION

see—

vs. Remedy 136B

130G
VERBS

Strike

hit, strike
knock, strike
pelt, strike by throwing
rap, hit sharply
smite, strike
souse, strike violently
stone, strike with a stone
strike, hit
swat, smite
swipe, strike with a swing
whack, strike resound-
   ingly

Club, Cudgel

bang, thump with a club
cudgel, beat with a cudgel
club, cudgel
maul, beat, thump
pommel, club, cudgel
sandbag, strike with a
   footpad's sandbag

Slap, Etc.

box, strike with the palm
cuff, box
ferule, hit with ferule
paddle, spank
slap, strike with a flat
   instrument
spank, slap

Switch

bamboo, flog
swinge, whip
switch, swinge

Whip, Lash

chastize, whip
cowhide, flog
crop, whip
flagellate, whip
flog, lash
horsewhip, flog
lace, lash
larrup, thrash
lash, whip
leather, to strap
scourge, whip
strap, beat with a strap
stripe, lash
swash, flog
tan, beat
whip, beat, lash

Beat, Thrash

batter, give heavy blows
beat, thrash
belabor, beat soundly

VERBS (Continued)

drub, beat
lick, beat
manhandle, handle roughly
mistreat, treat badly
punch, hit with the fist
thrash, flog
trounce, beat soundly
wallop, beat soundly

Thump

bump, strike violently
butt, strike with the head
elbow, hunch
hunch, elbow
jostle, elbow, bump
nudge, hunch
thump, strike, beat

Kick, Stamp

boot, kick
kick, strike with the foot
stamp, strike upon with
   the foot
stomp, stamp
trample, tread under foot

Bruise, Etc.

bruise, injure without
   laceration
contuse, bruise
wound, bruise, stab

Abrade

abrade, chafe
chafe, make sore by
   rubbing
fret, abrade
gall, chafe

Gore, Etc.

goad, jab
gore, pierce with the horn
gouge, tear by gouging
hook, gore
jab, punch, puncture
prod, goad

Stab

bayonet, stab with a
   bayonet
harpoon, spear
lance, wound with a lance
lunge, thrust into
pierce, stab
prick, puncture, sting
puncture, pierce
spear, pierce
stab, stick with a weapon
stick, stab
sting, pierce

VERBS (Continued)

thrust, stab
tilt, thrust with a lance

Transfix

fix, transfix
impale, thrust upon a stake
impinge, strike upon
transfix, pierce through

Cut, Etc.

cut, wound by gashing
gash, cut
knife, wound by cutting
saber, cut or wound
slash, cut

Lacerate

claw, tear with the claws
lacerate, tear
mangle, lacerate
rend, lacerate
scratch, lacerate slightly
snag, wound roughly
tear, lacerate

Bite, Etc.

bite, wound with teeth
nip, pinch
pinch, squeeze sharply
snap, bite suddenly

Fell, Etc.

fell, knock down
flatten, prostrate
floor, fell
prostrate, floor

ADJECTIVES
(See VERBS)

abradant, abraiding
backhanded, striking with
   the back of the hand
flagellant, using a whip or
   scourge
galling, chafing
impinging, striking upon
pricking, piercing
rapping, striking upon
trenchant, unsparing

NOUNS
   (Also Employ VERBS)

Stroke, Blow, Etc.

bang, violent blow
blow, hostile stroke
bump, thump
butt, thrust of the head
cuff, blow

   (Continued on page 284)

NOUNS (Continued)

drive, strong blow
flick, whip-blow
hunch, elbow thrust
kick, blow of the foot
knock, blow
lash, blow with a whip
lick, blow
pass, thrust
pelt, a blow from something thrown
punch, blow
rap, sharp blow
slam, violent blow
slap, flat blow
smack, sharp blow
sockdolager, decisive blow
strike, blow
stroke, blow
swipe, strong blow
tap, slight stroke
thump, dull blow
wallop, blow
whack, smart blow

Thrashing

beating, whipping

NOUNS (Continued)

chastizement, whipping
dressing, beating
flogging, beating
hiding, beating
lacing, beating
lashing, whipping
pommeling, beating
scourging, severe whipping
spanking, a slapping
thrashing, flogging
trouncing, beating
whipping, a scourging

Stab

lunge, thrust, stab
pierce, stab
prick, sharp laceration
ripost, a lunge following a parry
stab, piercing thrust
stick, pierce
sting, sharp stab
thrust, lunge
tilt, thrust

Miscellaneous

abrasion, a chafing
attrition, abrasion

NOUNS (Continued)

bite, a wounding with the teeth
bruise, wound
collision, a violent striking together
contusion, bruise
cut, gash
empalement, act of empaling
friction, attrition
gash, cut
impact, collision
impalement, act of impaling
laceration, tear
nip, pinch
pinch, a sharp squeeze
scratch, slight laceration
snap, sudden bite
wound, cut, stab, bruise

PERSONS (See VERBS)

spanker, one who spanks
whipper, one who whips
Etc., etc.

130H

CUTTING WEAPONS, ETC.

Sword, Etc.

backsword, sword with one sharp edge
bilbo, sword
blade, sword
broadsword, sword with a broad blade
claymore, broadsword
cutlas, sword
falchion, sword
foil, fencing weapon
rapier, sword
saber, cavalry sword
scimiter, simitar
simitar, curved sword
steel, sword
sword, keen-edged weapon

(Continued)

Toledo, sword of the finest temper
yataghan, a saber

Dagger, Etc.

bolo, knife-like weapon
bowie knife, hunting knife
dagger, dirk
dirk, dagger
stiletto, small dagger

Ax, Etc.

ax, a war-like weapon, utilitarian instrument
celt, ancient ax or chisel
halberd, ax-like weapon
hatchet, small ax
tomahawk, hatchet-like weapon

(Continued)

Miscellaneous

antler, stag's horn
bayonet, sharp attachment for a gun
brier, thorn
glave, pointed weapon
goad, pointed instrument
horn, natural weapon on head of animals
splinter, sharp splint
spur, spiral goad
sting, sharp weapon of an insect
spine, thorn
tenter, tenter-hook
thorn, sharp formation on plants

130I

NOUNS

(Arms for Discharging Missiles)

air-gun, pneumatic rifle
armament, cannon, small arms, etc.
arm, weapon
arms, weapons of war
artillery, cannon, ordnance
battering-ram, besieging engine
battery, cannon and their complement

NOUNS (Continued)

blunderbuss, obsolete firearm
boomerang, missile used as a weapon
Bertha, a German cannon
blow-gun, pipe for blowing missiles
blow-pipe, blow-gun
bow, a weapon for discharging arrows
breech-loader, a firearm
cannon, large gun

NOUNS (Continued)

carbine, rifle
carronade, short cannon
cartridge, an explosive
catapult, engine for hurling missiles
crossbow, gun-shaped stock with a bow across the end
culverin, 16th century cannon
derringer, pistol
(Continued on page 285)

NOUNS (Continued)

fieldpiece, cannon
firearms, rifles, cannons, etc.
flintlock, a gun discharged with flint
fusil, flintlock
Gatling-gun, gun with numerous small barrels that are fired successively
gun, firearm
hackbut, harquebus

NOUNS (Continued)

harquebus, firearm
horse-pistol, firearm
howitzer, short cannon
mortar, short cannon
machine-gun, firearm
matchlock, obsolete firearm
musket, firearm
muzzle-loader, firearm loaded through the muzzle
ordnance, artillery

NOUNS (Continued)

pistol, hand-gun
repeater, revolver
revolver, hand-gun
rifle, musket
shooter, firearm
shotgun, firearm
sling, a flexible device for hurling missiles
weapon, destructive instrument
Winchester, repeating rifle

130J

NOUNS (Missiles)

ammunition, powder, balls, etc.
arrow, barbed missile
arrowhead, arrow-point
ball, bullet
bar-shot, linked balls
bolt, arrow
bomb, explosive missile
boomerang, missile

(Continued)

bullet, shot, ball
dart, lance, spear
dumdum, explosive bullet
fire-ball, grenade
grenade, bomb for throwing
harpoon, spear
javelin, spear
jereed, javelin

(Continued)

lance, spear-headed shaft
missile, projectile
pike, lance
projectile, missile
shaft, arrow
shot, bullet, missile
spear, weapon for thrusting or throwing
torpedo, destructive missile

130K

NOUNS (Explosives)

dunnite
dynamite
explosive
guncotton
gunpowder

(Continued)

lyddite
melinite
powder
pyrocollodion
rendrock

(Continued)

tonite
trinitrotoluol
T.N.T., trinitrotoluol
Etc., etc.

130L

NOUNS
(Striking Instruments)

billy, short bludgeon
blackjack, flexible bludgeon
blacksnake, pliant whip or rawhide
bludgeon, stick used as a weapon
bullwhack, bull-whip
cat, cat-o'-nine-tails (formerly)
cestus, loaded glove

(Continued)

club, heavy stick
cowhide, whip
cudgel, club
ferule, rod
fist, hand used as a club
flail, medieval weapon
horsewhip, heavy whip
knout, leather-thonged whip
lash, whip
mace, massive staff

(Continued)

rawhide, cowhide
rod, ferule
sandbag, flexible cudgel
scourge, whip
shillalah, cudgel
strap, lash
thong, whip
truncheon, cudgel
whip, scourge

130N (Continued)

PUNITIVE INSTITUTIONS
Hell

Acheron, Hades
Abaddon, (poetic) hell
abyss, hell
Erebus, region of the dead
Gehenna, hell
hell, place of punishment for souls of the wicked
Hades, hell
inferno, place of torment
pandemonium, place of evil spirits
Pit of Acheron, Greek hell
Sheol, (Jewish) hell
Tartarus, fabled hell

(Continued)

Topheth, hell

Hells (Descriptive)
bottomless pit, hell
Everlasting fire, hell
Everlasting torment, hell
Habitation of fallen angels
hell-fire, hell
Infernal regions, hell
Lake of fire and brimstone
Place of torment, hell
Realms of Pluto, hell

Purgatory, Etc.
Avernus, entrance to hell
Cocytus, river in Hades

(Continued)

limbo, place of misery
limbus, purgatory
purgatory, place of temporary punishment

Miscellaneous
court-martial, military court for justifying or punishing accused
dungeon, underground cell
penitentiary, an institution for the punishment and correction of criminals
star-chamber, ancient court of injustice and punishment

CRUELTY—
    BRUTALITY   see—

vs. Mercy 47

ASSOCIATIVE

Punishment 130N	Anger 29
Attack 130F	Hate 28
Blows 130G	Oppression 130B
Impairment 130D	Misfortune 127B
Death 130-O	Bane 130E

130M

VERBS

Miscellaneous

abuse, treat hurtfully
afflict, cause pain
aggravate, make worse
asphyxiate, suffocate
choke, strangle
cripple, disable
deface, disfigure
disable, injure seriously
disfigure, destroy beauty
excruciate, inflict pain
harm, injure
hurt, abuse
inflict, cause injury
injure, hurt
maltreat, treat badly
mar, injure
mutilate, disfigure
out-Herod, exceed in
  cruelty, etc.
outrage, injure violently
pain, cause suffering
scathe, injure severely
smother, suffocate
stive, suffocate
stifle, stive
strain, injure to excess
strangle, choke
stun, knock senseless
suffocate, smother
throttle, choke
tyrannize, oppress
violate, injure forcibly
vitiate, injure

ADJECTIVES

Cruel

atrocious, cruel
bloodthirsty, cruel
bloody, cruel
brutal, cruel
brute, brutal
coldblooded, brutal
cruel, merciless
heartless, cruel
merciless, cruel
pitiless, merciless
remorseless, merciless
ruthless, pitiless
sanguinary, cruel
tyrannical, cruel
unmerciful, pitiless

Excruciating

agonizing, painful
crucial, excruciating
excruciating, agonizing

ADJECTIVES (Continued)

grievous, causing suffering
painful, causing pain
tragic, causing suffering

Unfeeling

flinty, pitiless
inhuman, unfeeling
stony, cruel
unearthly, inhuman
unfeeling, cruel
unsympathetic, heartless

Insufferable

insufferable, intolerable
intolerable, extremely
  hurtful
unbearable, insufferable
unendurable, unbearable

Severe

acute, severe
bitter, poignant
grim, cruel
hard, unfeeling
harsh, severe
immovable, pitiless
inclement, severe
oppressive, severe
poignant, severe
relentless, remorseless
rigorous, severe
severe, relentless
trying, severe
tyrannous, oppressive
unrelenting, remorseless

Violent

barbarous, cruel
calamitous, extremely
  distressing
fell, cruel, fierce
ferocious, savage
fierce, violent
furious, rabid
rabid, rageful
rageful, furious
rough, violent
savage, brutal
tempestuous, calamitous
towering, violent, furious
unbridled, unrestrained
unconscionable, unbridled
unrestrained, violent
violent, severe
wrathful, rageful

Fiendish

demoniac, diabolical
devilish, diabolical
diabolic, diabolical
diabolical, atrocious

ADJECTIVES (Continued)

fiendish, diabolical
hellish, diabolical
infernal, diabolical
Stygian, infernal

Malignant

envenomed, vindictive
malicious, mischievous
malevolent, malicious
malignant, heinous
revengeful, vengeful
spiteful, vengeful
splenetic, spiteful
truculent, ferocious
vengeful, vindictive
venomous, malignant
vicious, malignant
villainous, cruel
vindictive, revengeful

Pernicious

abusive, inflictive
afflictive, hurtful
aggravating, more hurtful
baleful, pernicious
deleterious, pernicious
harmful, injurious
hurtful, painful
inflictive, injurious
injurious, hurtful
malign, hurtful
mischievous, hurtful
noxious, pernicious
pernicious, injurious

Wicked

evil, malicious
flagitious, atrocious
flagrant, heinous
heinous, atrocious
nefarious, atrocious
outrageous, violent
scathing, withering
ungodly, wicked
unmentionable, heinous
vile, evil
wicked, heinous

Dreadful

appalling, dreadful
awful, appalling
dreadful, horrifying
enormous, atrocious
fearful, frightful
frightful, horrible
gruesome, horrible
harrowing, dreadful
hideous, dreadful
horrible, terrible
(Continued on page 287)

ADJECTIVES (Continued)
horrid, dreadful
monstrous, hideous
shocking, frightful
terrible, dreadful

Murderous
deadly, fateful
fatal, deadly
fateful, fatal
lethal, deadly
murderous, deadly

NOUNS
Cruelty
abuse, flagrancy
astringency, severity
atrocity, shocking cruelty
barbarity, brutality
brutality, cruelty
cruelty, inhumanity
enormity, atrocity
excruciation, severe in-
   fliction
extremity, utmost violence
ferocity, brutality
flagrancy, atrocity
inhumanity, cruelty
mutilation, impairment
ordeal, severe trial
outrage, atrocity
poignancy, severity
ruthlessness, cruelty

NOUNS (Continued)
savagery, cruelty
scathe, injury
severity, cruelty
spoliation, defacement
trial, ordeal
truculence, savagery
tyranny, oppression

Violence
affliction, calamity
calamity, severe blow
inclemency, harsh cruelty
oppression, calamity
violence, severity
virulence, inhumanity

Perniciousness
bale, injury, pain
damage, injury
defacement, injury
harm, injury
hurt, injury
injury, cause of harm
ill, harm
impairment, injury
infliction, injury
mischief, injury
pain, that which injures
perniciousness, bale

PERSONS
adder, viper
barbarian, brute

PERSONS (Continued)
beast, brute
brute, a savage person
desperado, a vicious person
dragon, violent person
fiend, brute
gangster, desperate
   character
imp, mischievous child
marplot, one who injures
   maliciously
monster, fiend
mutilator, marplot
oppressor, one who causes
   suffering
reptile, malicious person
ruffian, brute
savage, barbarian
scorpion, virulent person
serpent, reptile
thug, ruffian
tyrant, oppressor
viper, malicious person
werwolf, one who has the
   characteristics of wolves

BEINGS
Furies, three sisters who
   tormented the wicked—
      Alecto,
      Tisiphone,
      Megaera

130N

PUNISHMENT— TORTURE see—		ASSOCIATIVE	
vs. Forgiveness 47	Retaliation 45	Hate 28
vs. Reward 45	Blows 130G	Anger 29
	Attack 130F	Misfortune 127B
	Cruelty 130M	Bane 130E
	Oppression 130B	Burning 131B
	Poison 130E	Death 130-O

130N
VERBS
Punish
impose, punish
penalize, punish
punish, chastize, correct

Chastize
bastinado, beat the soles
   of the feet
castigate, punish
chasten, chastize
chastize, punish
discipline, chastize
ferule, chastize

Revenge
avenge, punish in retaliation
requite, revenge
retaliate, requite
revenge, punish maliciously

VERBS (Continued)
Torture, Etc.
agonize, torture
distress, cause suffering
dragoon, persecute
excoriate, strip off the skin
excruciate, torture
flay, torture
grill, torture by grilling
grind, oppress exceedingly
harry, torment
inflict, punish
keelhaul, drag under the
   keel of a boat
martyr, torture
persecute, martyr
rack, torture on the rack
start, punish with a rope's
   end

VERBS (Continued)
torment, torture
torture, excruciate

Strangle, Etc.
asphyxiate, suffocate
choke, strangle
garrote, strangle with a
   garrote
smother, suffocate
stifle, smother
stive, stifle
strangle, choke
suffocate, stifle
throttle, strangle

ADJECTIVES
Miscellaneous
agonizing, giving pain, etc.
avenging, revengeful
(Continued on page 288)

ADJECTIVES (Continued)

castigatory, punitive
condign, implying merited punishment
devilish, infernal
diabolical, hellish
disciplinarian, pertaining to punitive methods to compel docility
disciplinary, pertaining to discipline
excruciating, agonizing
fiendish, diabolical
hellish, infernal
infernal, diabolical
penal, punitive
penitential, giving punishment
penological, penal
plaguy, tormenting
punitive, awarding or giving punishment
purgatorial, pertaining to cleansing or punishing after death (Catholic)
racking, torturing
retaliative, retributive
retributive, punitive
revengeful, punitive
ruthless, revengeful
satanic, devilish
Stygian, hellish
unbearable, diabolical
vengeful, inflicting or intending punishment

NOUNS

Punishment

boomerang, Nemesis, reprisal
infliction, punishment
Nemesis, retributive vengeance
penalty, legal punishment
punishment, pain, loss, or penalty inflicted for injury
retribution, punishment
visitation, retribution

Chastizement

bastinado, Oriental punishment by beating the soles of the feet
castigation, punishment
chastizement, punishment
correction, chastizement
discipline, chastizement
gruelling, chastizement
whipping, chastizement

Revenge

reprisal, retaliation for injury
requital, retaliation
retaliation, reprisal
revenge, return for injury

NOUNS (Continued)

vengeance, retaliative punishment

Torture, Etc.

anguish, torture
excoriation, act of galling or stripping off the skin
excruciation, torture
grilling, torture
martyrdom, persecution
ordeal, severe trial
persecution, torture or vengeance, especially for religious opinion
torment, torture
torture, infliction of punishment

Miscellaneous

damnation, punishment in a future state
doom, damnation
execution, capital punishment
feud, vendetta
fury, vengeance
gauntlet, punishment inflicted upon a culprit running between two lines
pain, penalty
penology, prison management or retributive punishment
vendetta, blood-feud or retaliation

PERSONS, ETC.

avenger, Nemesis
castigator, punisher
disciplinarian, one who employs punitive measures to enforce conduct
penologist, one versed in scientific punishment
persecutor, avenger

BEINGS

demon, devil
deuce, devil
devil, evil one who punishes after death
devilkin, little devil
Eblis, Mohammedan devil
Furies, three sisters who tortured the wicked—
    Alecto,
    Tisiphone,
    Megaera
Fury, one of the three goddesses of vengeance
imp, infernal devil
Lucifer, devil
nick, devil

BEINGS (Continued)

Nemesis, goddess of vengeance
Pluto, god of the underworld
Satan, devil

CASTIGATORY INSTRUMENTS (also see 130L)

blacksnake
bullwhack
cat-o'-nine-tails
cat
colt
ferule
knout
lash
rod
rawhide
scourge
strap
whip

PUNITIVE DEVICES

boot, an instrument formerly used in torturing
crank, an instrument of prison discipline (like a paddle-wheel)
cross, a gibbet used in crucifixion
cucking-stool, a chair for the exposure and punishment of scolds, disorderly females, etc.
ducking-stool, an instrument formerly used for ducking disorderly females
iron-heel, instrument of torture
pillory, punitive instrument
rack, device for torturing
stocks, punitive device
strait-jacket, disciplinary jacket used in prisons, etc.
thumbscrew, device used in punishment by compressing the thumbs
treadmill, punitive device
wheel, instrument of torture
whipping-post, post used when chastizing culprits, etc.
wooden-horse, instrument of torture
(See any book on ancient torture devices)
(Continued on page 285)

DESTRUCTION—DEATH
see—
vs. Guardianship ..34
vs. Construction ..144B
vs. Invention 144A
vs. Begetting 141A

130-O

VERBS

Destroy

annihilate, destroy
blast, destroy
consume, destroy
deface, destroy
destroy, demolish, kill
devour, annihilate
efface, destroy
end, destroy
eradicate, destroy utterly
evert, destroy
exterminate, annihilate
extirpate, eradicate

Demolish

confound, ruin, overthrow
crash, smash
crush, destroy
demolish, wreck
dismantle, demolish
explode, demolish
mash, smash
overthrow, demolish
raze, destroy, level
shatter, destroy
smash, crush
squash, beat into pulp
squelch, crush
wreck, destroy

Devastate

desolate, devastate
devastate, lay waste
harry, lay waste
infest, overwhelm
ravage, lay waste

Ruin

blight, ruin, destroy
nip, blast, destroy
outrage, commit violence
paralyze, destroy or render
  ineffective
pervert, ruin, corrupt
ruin, raze
spoil, destroy
subvert, ruin utterly
violate, ruin
waste, destroy wantonly

Flood, Etc.

capsize, overturn, ruin
deluge, flood
drown, kill by drowning
flood, deluge
inundate, overwhelm
overflow, flood
overwhelm, destroy utterly

VERBS (Continued)

scuttle, sink (a ship) by
  making holes in its
  bottom
sink, submerge
submerge, flood
swamp, plunge into inex-
  tricable ruin
whelm, overwhelm

Murder

butcher, slaughter
despatch, put to death
dispatch, put to death
execute, put to death
finish, kill
kill, slay, murder
lethalize, cause death
murder, kill
slay, kill
smite, kill, as in battle

Murder (How)

assassinate, murder foully
brain, dash out the brain
crucify, execute on a cross
dismember, sever limb
  from limb
electrocute, execute by
  electricity
empale, put to death by
  fixing upon a pale
fusillade, shoot down as by
  simultaneous firing
imbrue, drench, especially
  with blood or death
immolate, kill as a sacrificial victim
impale, empale
lapidate, kill by stoning
lynch, execute by mob-law
martyr, put to death for
  adherence to a faith,
  etc.
oslerize, kill when life has
  passed the period of usefulness
persecute, martyr
proscribe, punish with
  civil death
poison, kill with poison
sacrifice, immolate
shoot, kill with a shot
smother, destroy over-
  whelmingly
suicide, destroy self
torpedo, destroy with a
  torpedo

VERBS (Continued)

vivisect, dissect the living
  body

Slaughter, Etc.

decimate, execute every
  tenth man
depopulate, destroy or
  eliminate a population
massacre, slaughter indis-
  criminately
slaughter, slay in numbers

Behead

behead, decapitate
decapitate, behead
decolate, behead
guillotine, behead with a
  guillotine

Hang

gibbet, hang on a gibbet
hang, execute by hanging

Choke

choke, garrote
garrote, execute with a
  garrote
strangle, choke to death
throttle, choke

Disembowel

disembowel, eviscerate
draw, disembowel
eviscerate, disembowel
gut, disembowel

ADJECTIVES

Destructive

destructible, baneful
destructive, ruinous
exterminatory, destructive
extirpative, destructive

Crushing

crushing, destructive
smashing, crushing
swashing, crushing

Ruinous

outrageous, violent
pernicious, destructive
perverse, ruinous
perversive, as above
ruinous, destructive

Baneful

atrocious, violent, horrible
baleful, deadly
baneful, destructive
deleterious, deadly
dragoon, destructive
fated, implying death,
  destruction, evil, etc.

(Continued on page 290)

ADJECTIVES (Continued)

noxious, deadly
violent, baneful

Epidemic

epidemic, affecting many
pestiferous, noxious
pestilent, pestilential
pestilential, destructive

Subversive

calamitous, disastrous
cataclysmal, violently
  destructive
cyclonic, violent
disastrous, destructive
seismic, noting destruction
  by an earthquake
subversive, destroying
  utterly
subvertible, pertaining to
  or capable of subversion
volcanic, violently destructive

Poisonous

mephitic, poisonous
poisonous, noxious
toxic, poisonous, deadly
venomous, poisonous
viperous, venomous
virulent, poisonous

Murderous

amuck, noting indiscrimi-
  nate slaughter
bloodthirsty, murderous
bloody, murderous
deadly, fatal
fatal, causing death or
  destruction
fateful, baleful
homicidal, pertaining to
  the killing of a human
  being
killing, murderous
lethal, deadly
mortal, fatal
murderous, deadly
proscriptive, implying civil
  death
sanguinary, attended with
  bloodshed or death
slaughtering, murderous
telling, fatal
tragic, fatal

Miscellaneous

infanticidal, pertaining to
  murder of an infant
internecine, mutually de-
  structive
matricidal, pertaining to
  the murder of one's
  mother
parricidal, pertaining to
  parent murder
procrustean, violent in
  deadly conformity

ADJECTIVES (Continued)

regicidal, pertaining to the
  murder of a king
sacrificial, noting slaughter
  or destruction for gain
suicidal, pertaining to self-
  murder

NOUNS

Destruction

annihilation, destruction
defacement, ruin
demolition, destruction
destruction, extermination
destructiveness, demolition
effacement, destruction, etc.
excision, destruction
extermination, annihilation
extinction, extermination
extirpation, extermination
perdition, total destruction
wreck, complete destruction

Devastation

desolation, ruin
devastation, desolation
havoc, devastation
ruin, devastation
waste, ravage of time

Flood, Etc.

avalanche, baneful debacle
cataclysm, baneful deluge
cataract, downpour
cloudburst, destructive rain
debacle, baneful flood
deluge, baneful overflow
downpour, cloudburst
flood, baneful deluge
inundation, baneful deluge
maelstrom, resistless bane
Niagara, resistless bane
surge, rushing wave
tide, rushing surge
undertow, pernicious flow
  contrary to surface flow
washout, ruin by flood
wave, resistless surge
whirlpool, maelstrom

Banefulness

bale, calamity, disaster
bane, that which causes
  death or ruin
hell, extreme calamity
hydra, baneful evil
perniciousness, destruc-
  tiveness
vandalism, wanton de-
  struction

Epidemic

epidemic, widespread bane
pestilence, widespread bane
plague, malignant epidemic

Subversion

calamity, baneful disaster
catastrophe, calamity
disaster, destruction

NOUNS (Continued)

downfall, utter ruin
earthquake, baneful up-
  heaval
fall, destruction, ruin
fatality, calamity
fate, death, destruction
overthrow, ruin
smash, complete ruin
subversion, overthrow
sweep, general destruction
upheaval, destructive
  violence from within

Murder

chance-medley, justifiable
  homicide
euthanasia, painless killing
execution, proscription
hanging, execution by
  hanging
homicide, murder
manslaughter, unpre-
  meditated murder
murder, homicide
proscription, civil death

Murder (How)

assassination, foul murder
cannibalism, the practice
  of destroying and eating
  one's kind
crucifixion, death by
  crucifying
electrocution, death by the
  electrical chair
lapidation, a stoning to
  death
lynching, death by a mob
lynch-law, execution by a
  mob
martyrdom, death for a
  religious opinion
sacrifice, an offering, especially a victim
strangulation, murder or
  death by choking
thuggee, person murdered
  by thugs
thuggism, murder by thugs
vivisection, the dissection
  of a living body scientif-
  ically
voodoo, savage rites in
  cannibalism

Slaughter, Etc.

butchery, slaughter
carnage, great slaughter
decimation, death to every
  tenth man, destruction
  on a large scale
hecatomb, great sacrifice of
  victims
holocaust, general sacrifice
  or slaughter
(Continued on page 291)

NOUNS (Continued)

immolation, killing of sacrificial victims
killing, slaughter
massacre, slaughter
slaughter, great destruction of life
slaughtery, butchery

Killing of a Kin

feticide, destruction of an unborn child
fratricide, killing of one's brother or sister
infanticide, infant murder
matricide, murder of a mother by her child
parricide, the murder of one's parent
patricide, the murder of one's father
sororicide, the murder of one's sister

Decapitation

decapitation, a beheading
decolation, decapitation

Suicide

hara-kiri, suicidal disemboweling
suicide, self-destruction
sutteeism, Hindu woman's self-sacrifice on her husband's funeral pile

Death

casualty, incidental death
death, extinction of life, destruction of accustomed forces
mortality, fatality
quietus, death

PERSONS

Murderer, Etc.

apache, Parisian murderer or ruffian
assassin, treacherous murderer
butcher, one who slaughters cattle or cruelly murders
bravo, assassin, bandit
Cain, the murderer of one's brother or brother-man
cutthroat, murderer
desperado, murderous ruffian
garroter, one who garrotes his victims
gunman, desperado who kills for hire or revenge
homicide, murderer
killer, slaughterer
knacker, one who butchers horses

PERSONS (Continued)

matador, the bull-fighter who kills the bull
murderer, homicide
murderess, as above (fem.)
regicide, a king-murderer
Septembrist, murderer
slayer, one who kills
slaughterer, slayer
thug, one who murders in secret (India)
vulpicide, one who kills a fox unethically

Executioner, Etc.

ace, an aviator credited with destroying five or more enemy airplanes
crucifier, one who crucifies
electrocuter, one who electrocutes, executioner
executioner, one who puts to death
hangman, one who puts to death by hanging
headsman, one who beheads
Jack Ketch, hangman or executioner
lyncher, member of a lynching mob
vivisectionist, one who vivisects

Murderer of a Blood Relation

filicide, one who kills his child
fratricide, the slayer of one's brother
infanticide, infant murderer
matricide, one who murders one's mother
patricide, one who murders one's father

Cannibal

anthropophagi, cannibals
cannibal, one who practices the destruction and eating of one's kind

Suicide

felo de se, a suicide by one's own hand or as by running into another's sword
suicide, one who destroys self
suttee, Hindu widow who sacrifices herself on her husband's funeral pile

Destroyer

destroyer, one who destroys
devastator, destroyer

PERSONS (Continued)

dragon, destructive person
extirpator, one who exterminates
iconoclast, image breaker
vandal, ruthless destroyer
wrecker, destroyer

MEDIUMS OF DEATH

(Also see ARMS, Etc.)

abattoir, slaughter house
bale-fire, funeral pyre
cross, ancient instrument of torture or execution
destroyer, torpedo-boat destroyer
electric chair, an electrocution chair
exterminator, extirpator
extirpator, that which exterminates
gallows, structure for executing criminals by hanging
garrote, instrument for strangling criminals
gibbet, gallows
guillotine, structure for decapitation
infernal machine, maliciously designed machine of destruction
Juggernaut, Hindu god on wheels to crush self-sacrificing devotees
maiden, guillotine
pyre, funeral or sacrificial pile
ram, battering machine
scaffold, gibbet

BEINGS, Etc.

Briareus, giant buried by Jupiter under Mt. Etna, and who causes earthquake when he turns over
cockatrice, fabulous scorpion that killed with the glance of an eye
Melpomene, muse of tragedy
ogre, fabled man-eating monster or giant
Siva, Hindu (god) destroyer
vampire, fabled demon that sucked the blood of persons asleep

ANNULMENT—CANCELLATION—OBLITERATION see—	ASSOCIATIVE
vs. Authorship 144A	Banishment 35A
vs. Guardianship 34	Destruction—Disaster 130-O
vs. Construction 144B	Impairment—Deprivation 130D
vs. Invention 144A	Dissolution 145J
	Burning 131B
	Bane 130E

131A

VERBS

Annul

annihilate, reduce to nothing
annul, make void, abolish
nullify, void
void, obliterate, annul

Abolish

abolish, annul
abrogate, abolish, repeal
debar, preclude
eliminate, remove
preclude, make ineffective
supersede, render null and void
supplant, supersede
suspend, debar

Expurgate

dele, delete
delete, blot out, erase
expurgate, remove
expunge, blot out

Eradicate

eradicate, destroy
extirpate, eradicate
remove, eradicate
uproot, eradicate

Obliterate

efface, obliterate
erase, obliterate
obliterate, efface, void
scratch, erase, void
wipe, efface

Extinguish

destroy, void
douse, extinguish
extinguish, nullify
perish, cause to pass away
quash, annul
rid, clear out, destroy

Repudiate

disavow, recant
disclaim, disavow
disfranchise, invalidate
recant, retract
renounce, repudiate
repudiate, disclaim
retract, rescind

Repeal

recall, revoke
repeal, abrogate, revoke

VERBS (Continued)

rescind, annul, revoke
revoke, countermand

Invalidate

cancel, strike out
countermand, revoke
invalidate, void
reverse, declare void

Counteract

counteract, neutralize
counterbalance, countervail
countervail, neutralize
neutralize, render inactive

Dissolve, Etc.

disburse, clear from mistake
dissipate, scatter completely
dissolve, annul
explode, dissipate

ADJECTIVES

(See VERBS)

deleterious, (blot out) pertaining to injurious eradication
expurgatory, noting removal of objections
extirpative, noting eradication

MATERIAL ANNULMENT

aerophore, counteracting apparatus used to prevent explosions in spinning factories
eraser, that which effaces
extirpator, that which eradicates
extincteur, extinguisher
extinguisher, that which extinguishes

NOUNS

Annulment

annihilation, act of reducing to nothing
annulment, invalidation

NOUNS (Continued)

extinction, a putting out
nullification, act of nullifying
veto, act of voiding

Abolition

abolition, annulment
abrogation, authoritative repeal
cassation, abrogation
desuetude, discontinuance
discontinuance, disuse
dissolution, dissipation
repeal, abrogation
revocation, act of repealing

Expurgation

deletion, annulment, erasure
expurgation, removal
rescission, act of annulling
riddance, act of ridding

Obliteration

cancellation, annulment
effacement, obliteration
erasure, effacement
obliteration, effacement

Repudiation

recantation, retraction
renunciation, repudiation
repudiation, recantation
retraction, revocation

Invalidation

countermand, revocation
invalidation, annulment of validity
reversal, annulment

Counteraction

counteraction, counterbalance
counterbalance, neutralization
defeasance, counteractive condition

PERSONS

abolitionist, one in favor of abolition
expurgator, one who removes offensiveness
nullifier, one who nullifies

FIRE—BURNING
(Effect by Fire) see—

vs. Protection 34

ASSOCIATIVE

131B
VERBS
Miscellaneous

blaze, flame
brand, inflict, stigmatize, or distinguish by burning
burn, affect by fire
cauterize, sear with heat
char, burn partially
cremate, reduce to ashes
consume, reduce by fire
deflagrate, set fire to
fire, deflagrate
flame, burn
heat, make hot
ignite, fire
incinerate, burn to ashes
inflame, set on fire
kindle, fire
parch, heat to a crisp
scald, burn with steam, etc.
scorch, burn the outside
sear, burn partially
seethe, burn, singe
singe, burn slightly
smolder, burn slowly
warm, heat

ADJECTIVES
Miscellaneous

ablaze, aflame
aflame, burning
blazing, burning
brisk, burning freely
burning, ablaze
candent, white-hot
caustic, searing
combustible, inflammatory

ADJECTIVES (Continued)

crematory, implying cremation
fiery, hot
flaming, blazing
hot, burning
igneous, pertaining to fire
incalescent, growing hot
incandescent, candent
incendiary, pertaining to criminal burning
inflammable, combustible
inflammatory, implying combustion
live, burning
Plutonian, igneous
searing, scorching
solar, fiery
warm, heating

FIRE MEDIUMS

bale-fire, pyre
cremator, crematory
crematory, place for burning the dead
crucible, melting pot
furnace, heating place
igniter, match
ignition, that which ignites
incinerator, furnace for reducing matter to ashes
kiln, furnace, oven
lucifer, match
match, lucifer
oven, stove
pyre, funeral pile
stove, heating device

NOUNS
Miscellaneous

arson, criminal burning
causticity, intense heat
cauterization, burning with hot iron
combustion, consuming heat
conflagration, great fire
cremation, reduction to ashes
ember, live ash or coal
fire, combustion
flame, fire
flammule, little flame
heat, intense temperature
incendiarism, arson
incineration, reduction by fire
inflammability, combustibility
inflammation, heat, act of inflaming
ignition, act of igniting
pyromania, impulse to destroy by fire

PERSONS

firebug, an incendiary
firebrand, firebug
incendiary, one who employs arson
pyromaniac, one who insanely destroys by fire

BEINGS

Agni, Hindu fire god
Moloch, fire god

ORDER—STATE OF HARMONY

ORDER—HARMONY

vs. Disorder ....125A $\left\{\begin{array}{l}\end{array}\right.$

Calmness ....132B   Compliance 46A
Custom ....132D   Accuracy 134A
Government ....133A   Skill 134B

132A
VERBS

Arrange
address, arrange
arrange, order
array, order
form, arrange
marshal, arrange
order, arrange
range, arrange

Coordinate
coaptate, coordinate
collocate, conform
concordinate, order reciprocally
coordinate, harmonize
reconcile, harmonize

Harmonize
accord, reconcile
attemper, adapt
attune, accord
harmonize, concur
key, attune
moderate, adapt
modulate, adapt
temper, adjust

Concur
agree, correspond
coincide, concur
concur, agree
cooperate, help
correspond, coincide
synchronize, coincide
tally, correspond

Prepare
dispose, order
fettle, prepare
foreordain, predetermine
ordain, dispose
prearrange, prepare
predetermine, prearrange
predestinate, predestine
predestine, foreordain
predispose, prearrange
prepare, predispose
provide, prepare
qualify, prepare

Methodize
engineer, plan
methodize, systematize
regulate, coordinate
set, regulate
systematize, methodize

Organize
institute, organize
organize, methodize

VERBS (Continued)
plan, organize

Adapt
accommodate, conform
adapt, conform
adjust, fit
apply, adapt
befit, to fit
conform, adjust
convert, conform
fit, adapt
fix, adjust
match, conform
proportion, conform
shift, adapt
suit, match

Smooth, Etc.
brush, smooth
comb, brush
curry, brush
dress, curry
even, smooth
groom, curry
level, even
smooth, even
unravel, untangle
untangle, comb

Restore
rally, cooperate anew
readjust, adjust again
recover, rally
reduce, reclaim to order
reform, readapt
regain, recover
restore, readjust

Perfect, Etc.
consummate, perfect
finish, perfect
mature, perfect
perfect, consummate
ripen, perfect

ADJECTIVES
Arranged
arranged, ordered
arrayed, arranged
disposed, ordered
formed, ordered
ranged, ordered

Coordinate
accordant, consonant
agreeable, consistent
congruent, agreeable
congruous, harmonious
consentaneous, concordant

ADJECTIVES (Continued)
consentient, consonant
consistent, congruous
cooperative, concordant
coordinate, agreeable
correspondent, coordinate
corresponding, accordant
unanimous, concordant

Harmonious
concordant, consonant
consonant, harmonious
even, harmonious
harmonious, concordant

Concurrent
coincident, coordinate
concurrent, coordinate
simultaneous, synchronous
synchronous, coincident

Preparatory
predeterminate, provisional
preliminary, preparatory
preparatory, provisional
provisional, preparatory

Methodical
cosmic, harmonious
measured, uniform
methodical, orderly
monotonous, uniform
orderly, congruous
systematic, orderly
regular, uniform
uniform, accordant

Adaptable
accommodative, adaptive
adaptable, apposite
applicable, adaptable
applicatory, applicable
apt, suitable
coaptative, adaptive
conformable, adaptable

Suitable
apposite, appropriate
appropriate, suitable
becoming, fitting
fitting, fit
meet, fit
seemly, fitting
sizeable, suitable
suitable, appropriate

Opportune
advisable, expedient
apropos, opportune
convenient, suitable
expedient, suitable
(Continued on page 296)

ADJECTIVES (Continued)

felicitous, appropriate
likely, suitable
opportune, seasonable
seasonable, suitable
timely, seasonable

Pertinent

adequate, suitable
commensurate, adequate
compatible, suitable
competent, adequate
equal, adequate
germane, pertinent
pertinent, relevant
proper, suitable
relevant, germane

Perfect, Etc.

complete, finished
consummate, perfect
esthetic, consummate
(B). aesthetic
developed, ripe
done, fit
finished, consummate
fit, suitable, mature
grown, mature
mature, ripe
perfect, suited
ready, fit
ripe, fit

NOUNS

Arrangement

arrangement, conformation
collocation, arrangement
disposal, arrangement
disposition, arrangement
lay, arrangement
ordering, arrangement
permutation, arrangement

Coordination

accord, agreement
agreement, harmony
conformity, agreement
congruence, harmony
congruity, harmony
consentaneousness, accord
consentience, agreement
consistency, congruity
coordination, conformation
propriety, fitness

Harmony

accompaniment, adaptation
accordance, harmony
concert, accordance

NOUNS (Continued)

concord, harmony
concordance, agreement
consonance, concord
correspondence, congruity
harmony, perfect accord
rapport, harmony

Concurrence

coincidence, agreement
concurrence, agreement
synchronization, accord
teamwork, concord

Order

cosmos, harmony
order, harmony

Balance

balance, equilibrium
equality, balance
equilibrium, agreement
equipoise, equilibrium
equiponderance, equipoise

Unison

monotony, uniformity
uniformity, agreement
unison, harmony
unity, concord
virtue, harmony

Preparation

measure, provision
ordination, qualification
predisposition, organization
preparation, predisposition
provision, preparation
qualification, preparation

Method

gradation, regulation
method, orderly manner
regulation, coaptation
system, order

Organization

institution, organization
organization, collocation
plan, organization

Adaptation

accommodation, adjustment
adaptation, accommodation
adjustment, conformation
application, adaptation
apposition, adaptation
coaptation, adaptation
conformation, adaptation
conversion, coaptation

Suitability

adaptability, suitability
appositeness, suitability

NOUNS (Continued)

aptitude, aptness
aptness, suitableness
commensurability, suitability
cooperation, coordination
conformability, suitability
counterpoint, fitting point
fitness, adaptability
suitability, fitness

Opportuneness

advisability, suitability
convenience, suitability
expediency, convenience
expedient, convenience
felicity, suitability
opportuneness, felicity
seasonableness, fitness
seemliness, suitability

Pertinence

adequacy, suitability
compatibility, suitability
competence, suitableness
pertinence, suitability
relevancy, pertinence
sufficiency, competence

Restoration

rally, reorganization
rapprochement, reunion
reconciliation, adjustment
recovery, rally
reorganization, restoration
restoration, recovery
reunion, reconciliation

Perfection

consummation, perfection
culmination, perfection
maturity, suitability
perfection, consummateness
ripeness, suitableness

MATERIAL CONFORMERS

brush
comb
curry
last

PERSONS

adjuster
conciliator
regulator

BEING

Themis, goddess of law

CALMNESS—EQUANIMITY see—

		ASSOCIATIVE
vs. Disorder—Confusion 125A		Order—Harmony 132A
vs. Storm—Wind 125B		Custom—Habit 132D
vs. Unrestraint 125C		Stability 11B

132B

VERBS

Calm
becalm, compose
calm, compose
compose, calm, quiet
still, calm
subside, settle
tame, quiet
tranquillize, calm

Appease
allay, quiet, appease
ameliorate, mitigate
appease, assuage, allay
assuage, mitigate, soften
lull, calm, soothe
meliorate, propitiate
melt, soften, attemper
mitigate, assuage
mollify, soften, calm
soften, assuage
soothe, allay, assuage

Propitiate
abate, mollify, accord
accord, reconcile
conciliate, reconcile
harmonize, reconcile
pacify, calm, appease
propitiate, conciliate
reconcile, harmonize

Intercede
arbitrate, mediate
intercede, interpose for
  reconciliation
intervene, intercede
mediate, intercede

Moderate
adjust, harmonize
attemper, temper
moderate, attemper
modify, moderate
temper, mitigate, calm

Repose
lay, settle, calm
repose, compose
rest, repose
settle, grow calm

Sleep
doze, sleep lightly
nap, doze
sleep, slumber
slumber, sleep
snooze, nap

Quiet
hush, soothe
quell, quiet

VERBS (Continued)
quiesce, become reposed
quiet, calm

Behave
behave, be moderate
comport, behave
demean, behave

ADJECTIVES

Calm
calm, tranquil
halcyon, peaceful, calm
pacific, peaceful
peaceable, calm
peaceful, quiet, calm
placid, calm, peaceful
stormless, calm
tranquil, calm

Appeasive
appeasive, quieting
ameliorative, mitigative
assuaging, ameliorative
lulling, soothing
mollifying, calming
quieting, appeasive
soothing, pacifying
soporific, causing sleep

Propitiatory
conciliatory, conciliating
mediatorial, reconciling
pacifying, quieting
propitiatory, conciliatory
reconciliatory, harmonizing

Moderate
clement, mild
mild, calm, composed
moderate, mild, calm
propitious, clement
tempered, moderate
temperate, moderate
uneventful, tame, calm

Reposeful
fixed, still
impassive, imperturbable
imperturbable, cool, calm
motionless, quiet, calm
orderly, peaceable
reposeful, at rest
smooth, mild, calm
stable, steady
steady, smooth
still, quiet, calm
undisturbed, still, calm
unwavering, steady

Quiet
noiseless, quiet

ADJECTIVES (Continued)
quiescent, quiet, calm
quiet, calm, peaceable
reposed, quiet
silent, still

Gentle
dispassionate, calm, cool
docile, gentle
gentle, peaceful
passionless, calm
tame, docile

Indifferent
indifferent, unconcerned
nonchalant, unconcerned
unconcerned, nonchalant
unembarrassed, cool
unhurried, unperturbed
uninterested, indifferent

Composed
collected, cool
composed, calm
cool, calm, composed
demure, sober
poised, composed
sedate, calm, composed
serene, calm, placid
sober, even-tempered
staid, sober, sedate
stoical, undisturbed
stolid, staid, stoical
unemotional, unmoved
unmoved, calm
unperturbed, cool, calm
unruffled, calm, staid
untroubled, quiet, calm

NOUNS

Calm
calm, serenity
calmness, tranquillity
harmony, tranquillity
peace, tranquillity, freedom
  from war
peacefulness, peace
placidity, peacefulness
tranquillity, serenity

Lull
abatement, moderation
lull, abatement

Appeasement
amelioration, mitigation
appeasement, assuagement
assuagement, abatement
melioration, amelioration

(Continued on page 301)

HOLD—ABSTAIN—
FORBEAR see—

vs. Unrestrained ..125C
vs. Generosity 43A
vs. Brag 76

ASSOCIATIVE

Capacity 53A
Bind—Glue 52B
Hide—Conceal 103A

Silence 11B
Calmness 132B
Cowardice 32

132C

VERBS

Possess

contain, hold
hold, keep
keep, retain
possess, hold
retain, keep
withhold, retain

Depend

depend, hang on
hang, hold on
rely, depend

Preserve

conserve, preserve
maintain, preserve
preserve, save
reserve, retain
save, preserve
scrimp, be miserly
skimp, scrimp
stint, conserve

Economize

economize, preserve
husband, economize

Abstain

abstain, forbear
care, forbear
desist, forbear
fast, abstain
forbear, refrain
forego, forbear
inhibit, hold in
leave, desist
refrain, abstain
repress, refrain

Hesitate

falter, hesitate
hesitate, be in suspense
vacillate, hesitate
waver, hesitate

Avoid

avoid, refrain
decline, refuse
refuse, decline
reject, refuse

ADJECTIVES

Possessive

composite, inclusive
comprehensive, inclusive
inclusive, possessive
possessive, proprietary
possessory, possessive
proprietary, owned as property

ADJECTIVES (Continued)

retentive, holding

Deep-rooted

deep-rooted, inveterate
firm, unyielding
fixed, firm
inextricable, inveterate
inveterate, deep-rooted

Preservative

conservant, preserving
conservative, conserving
conservatory, preservative
preservative, conservant
saving, frugal

Economic

chary, sparing
economic, frugal
frugal, sparing
provident, economical
sparing, frugal
sumptuary, economical
thrifty, economic

Miserly

miserly, meanly close
niggardly, miserly
parsimonious, miserly
penurious, parsimonious

Stingy

close, closefisted
closefisted, stingy
illiberal, frugal
inhospitable, uncharitable
mean, stingy
stingy, niggardly
tight, parsimonious
tightfisted, stingy
uncharitable, inhospitable
ungenerous, illiberal

Abstinent

abstemious, temperate
abstentious, abstinent
abstinent, abstemious
constrained, restrained
continent, abstinent
restrained, constrained
teetotal, abstinent

Temperate

decent, decorous
decorous, circumspect
dispassionate, temperate
humble, modest
moderate, restrained
modest, duly restrained
temperate, abstemious

ADJECTIVES (Continued)

unassuming, modest
undemonstrative, modest
unemotional, impassive
unimpassioned, dispassionate
unobtrusive, unassuming

Prudent

careful, prudent
cautious, prudent
circumspect, cautious
considerate, circumspect
heedful, prudent
judicious, prudent
provident, prudent
prudent, circumspect
stealthy, cautious
wary, cautious
watchful, wary

Discreet

conscientious, scrupulous
discreet, prudent
discretionary, discreet
scrupulous, cautious
squeamish, scrupulous

Prudential

considered, prudential
providential, prudential
prudential, prudent
respectable, considerate

Gentle

easy, gentle
gentle, mild
mild, easy
soft, mild
tender, gentle

Quiet

mum, silent
mute, mum
quiet, still
quiescent, quiet
silent, taciturn

Hesitant

faltering, irresolute
hesitant, faltering
irresolute, undecided
undecided, faltering

Chaste

chaste, virtuous
maidenly, virtuous
modest, chaste
prudish, extremely modest
vestal, virginal
(Continued on page 299)

ADJECTIVES (Continued)

virginal, virtuous
virtuous, chaste

Demure

bashful, shy
coy, demure
coyish, coy
demure, modest
diffident, modest
sedate, demure
shy, bashful
staid, sedate

Unwilling

loath, unwilling
reluctant, unwilling
unwilling, reluctant

Disinclined

aclinic, disinclined
disinclined, unwilling
distant, reserved
stiff, aclinic

Reticent

evasive, noncommittal
impassive, noncommittal
neutral, impassive
noncommittal, reserved
reserved, taciturn
reticent, silent
retiring, reticent
taciturn, reticent

Unyielding

inexorable, unyielding
unrelenting, inexorable
unyielding, unrelenting

Unutterable

incommunicable, impassive
ineffable, unutterable
unutterable, ineffable

NOUNS

Possession

hold, retention
keep, maintenance
maintenance, possession
possession, hold
retention, maintenance
retentiveness, retention
seizin, possession
tenure, a holding, as land

Ownership

droit, ownership
equity, ownership
interest, ownership
ownership, equity

NOUNS (Continued)

right, ownership
title, ownership

Preservation

conservatism, conservation
conservation, preservation
preservation, economy
saving, conservation

Economy

economy, frugality
frugality, thrift
husbandry, thrift
thrift, economy
thriftiness, thrift

Miserliness

miserliness, mean hoarding
niggardliness, miserliness
parsimony, stinginess
stinginess, niggardliness

Abstinence

abstention, abstinence
abstemiousness, abstinence
abstinence, abstemiousness
continence, abstinence
forbearance, self-restraint
inhibition, a holding in
self-denial, continence
teetotalism, abstinence

Temperance

behavior, forbearance
decency, decorum
decorum, modesty
moderation, temperance
modesty, decency
reserve, modesty
temperance, moderation

Prudence

care, prudence
caution, circumspection
circumspection, prudence
heed, circumspection
prudence, discretion
sagacity, watchfulness
wariness, caution

Discretion

consideration, caution
discretion, prudence
qualms, scruples
scruple, caution
scrupulosity, caution

Hesitation

abeyance, suspense
hesitancy, hesitation
hesitation, indecision

NOUNS (Continued)

indecision, suspense
suspense, indecision
vacillation, indecision

Chastity

chastity, virtue
prudery, extreme virtue
virtue, virtuousness
virtuousness, chastity

Demureness

coyness, demureness
delicacy, scrupulosity
demureness, modesty
diffidence, modesty
sedateness, staidness
shyness, coyness

Avoidance

aversion, reluctance
avoidance, evasion
evasion, avoidance
refusal, an unyielding

Unwillingness

disinclination, inhibition
indisposition, reluctance
reluctance, unwillingness
unwillingness, disinclination

Reticence

neutrality, disinterest
reserve, reticence
reticence, taciturnity
silence, taciturnity
taciturnity, reticence

PERSONS

adherent, conservative
abstainer, abstentionist
abstentionist, teetotaler
conservative, adherent
economist, close manager
holder, possessor
incumbent, benefice holder
keeper, possessor
maiden, virgin
miser, niggard
niggard, miser
owner, proprietor
possessor, holder
proprietor, legal owner
prude, prudish woman
retainer, holder
scrimp, miser
teetotaler, an abstainer
virgin, chaste maiden

132D

VERBS

Regulate
adjust, regulate
attemper, regulate
govern, conventionalize
methodize, regulate
order, regulate
regulate, govern
standardize, regulate
steady, regulate
systematize, methodize
temper, regulate

Accustom
accustom, habituate
familiarize, accustom
habituate, accustom

Prescribe
civilize, conventionalize
conventionalize, train
domesticate, convention-
  alize
generalize, standardize
modernize, conventionalize
naturalize, conventionalize
popularize, conventionalize
prescribe, direct usage

Practice
drill, train
exercise, practice
practice, ply
rehearse, drill
train, drill

Proceed
carry, conduct
conduct, carry on
continue, ply
proceed, continue in
  progress

Ply, Work
drudge, toil
employ, use
labor, work
ply, work diligently
toil, labor
use, employ habitually
work, ply

Inure
acclimatize, acclimate
acclimate, inure
harden, inure
inure, accustom
season, inure
wean, accustom

ADJECTIVES

Regular
general, usual
methodical, regular
normal, regular
practicable, practical
practical, conforming to
  practice
regular, usual
standard, customary
systematic, methodical
typical, normal
usual, customary

Uniform
equal, equable
equable, uniform
even, equal
harmonious, rhythmic
rhythmic, regular
steady, regular
sustained, continuous
uniform, regular

Accustomed
accustomed, habitual
customary, habitual
habitual, commonplace
inveterate, habitual
routinary, customary
wont, accustomed
wonted, habitual

Commonplace
common, usual
commonplace, usual
dull, commonplace
hackneyed, commonplace
humdrum, monotonous
monotonous, dull
ordinary, customary
prosaic, commonplace
tolerable, ordinary
trite, hackneyed

Familiar
beaten, routinary
easy, beaten
familiar, common
free, easy
simple, unconventional

Unconventional
domestic, common
household, domestic
informal, unceremonious
Philistine, conventional
popular, common
public, common

ADJECTIVES (Continued)
unceremonious, simple
unconventional, informal

Average
average, medium
mean, average
mediocre, ordinary
medium, ordinary

Cosmic
astronomic, cosmic
astronomical, astronomic
cosmic, divinely prescriptive
natural, orderly
naturalistic, natural
universal, cosmic

Prescriptive
ceremonial, prescriptive
ceremonious, ceremonial
conventional, customary
ethical, prescriptive
formal, ethical
modal, usual
ordered, orderly
orderly, methodical
prescriptive, ethical
proper, orderly
stated, prescriptive

Inured
acclimatized, inured
hardened, inured
inured, accustomed
seasoned, acclimatized
used, accustomed

NOUNS

Regularity
equability, uniformity
equality, uniformity
regularity, uniformity
rhythm, measured recur-
  rence
uniformity, regularity
unity, uniformity

Habit
behavior, usual conduct
(B). behaviour
conduct, behavior
deportment, conduct
habit, usual conduct
habitude, habit
mannerism, usual habit
moral, life conduct

(Continued on page 301)

NOUNS (Continued)
wont, habit

Routine
domesticity, convention-
   ality
localism, local usage
routine, practice
use, practice

Prescription
ceremonial, ceremony
ceremony, formal usage
convention, practice
conventionalism, custom
conventionality, usage
custom, practice
ethics, habitual usage
etiquette, usual usage
fad, fashion
fashion, conventional use
form, observance
NOUNS (Continued)

formality, conventionality
go, custom
modality, conventionality
observance, ceremony
order, settled usage
prescription, custom
propriety, etiquette
regimen, standard living
regime, social custom
regulation, prescription
rule, prescription
style, custom
vogue, usage

Practice
exercise, practice
practice, usage
usage, custom

Procedure
course, procedure
manner, method

NOUNS (Continued)
means, method
method, order
mode, method
operation, procedure
policy, course
proceeding, formal usage
procedure, proceeding
process, procedure
system, method
way, manner

PERSONS, ETC.
addict
ascetic
devotee
genera
genus
habitué
user
votary

NOUNS (Continued)

Propitiation
adjustment, act of harmo-
   nizing
conciliation, mediation
pacification, peacemaking
propitiation, act of making
   favorable
reconciliation, adjustment

Intercession
intercession, mediation
intervention, mediation
mediation, intercession

Moderation
evenness, equanimity
mildness, moderation
moderation, mildness
temperateness, moderation

Repose
repose, rest, composure
rest, repose, tranquillity
subsidence, a settling

Sleep
nap, brief sleep
siesta, nap
sleep, slumber
slumber, sleep
snooze, nap

NOUNS (Continued)
somnolence, sleepiness
sopor, deep sleep

Quietude
quiescence, repose
quiet, calm
quietude, repose
silence, quiet
sleep, quiescence
stillness, calm

Behavior
behavior, moderate
   conduct
comportment, behavior
conduct, behavior
demeanor, conduct
deportment, comportment
virtue, behavior

Gentleness
docility, gentleness
gentleness, demureness
lenity, mildness

Poise
aplomb, self-possession
balance, poise
poise, equanimity

Indifference
coolness, equanimity
indifference, nonchalance

NOUNS (Continued)
nonchalance, cool in-
   difference
sang-froid, cool composure

Composure
composure, tranquillity
demureness, soberness
equanimity, composure
imperturbability, com-
   posure
serenity, calmness
sedateness, composure
sobriety, sedateness
staidness, sobriety
stolidity, staidness

PERSONS
go-between, intermediary
intercessor, mediator
intermediary, intercessor
mediator, reconciler
moderator, tranquilizer
mollifier, one who assuages
pacificator, assuager
pacifist, moderator, etc.

BEING
Somnus, god of sleep

RULE—GOVERNMENT	see—	ASSOCIATIVE	

133A

VERBS

Rule

govern, control
reign, rule
rule, govern

Dominate

dominate, govern
domineer, lord over
lord, domineer
monopolize, prevail
predominate, prevail
preponderate, predominate
prevail, have mastery
rein, govern with a rein
sway, prevail
will, control

Organize

methodize, regulate
organize, order
regulate, govern
systematize, organize

Legislate

federalize, organize
feudalize, make feudal
legalize, legislate
legislate, make laws

Guide

administer, minister
command, control
conduct, direct
control, govern
direct, conduct
guide, conduct
lead, preside
minister, preside
office, preside
preside, rule

Manage

boss, direct
manage, govern
order, command
superintend, supervise
supervise, manage

Function, Do

do, transact
employ, use
function, perform
handle, manage
manipulate, handle
operate, function
perform, do
transact, perform
use, utilize
utilize, employ
wield, handle

VERBS (Continued)

Compel

compel, force
enforce, compel
force, compel
impose, compel

ADJECTIVES

Ruling

controlling, ruling
governing, ruling
overruling, controlling
overwhelming, overruling
ruling, governing

Fundamental

basal, fundamental
basic, fundamental
fundamental, basal
primary, fundamental

Leading

chief, ruling
leading, ruling
main, leading
premier, chief
principal, chief

Dominant

absolute, supreme
dominant, ruling
monopolistic, prevailing
omnipotent, dominant
paramount, controlling
predominant, prevailing
preponderant, predominant
prevailing, ruling
supreme, paramount

Managerial

administerial, executive
administrative, administerial
authoritative, commanding
commanding, compelling
conductive, managerial
executive, administrative
managerial, administrative
ministerial, executive
ministrant, ministerial
proctorial, managerial
supervisory, ministerial

Sovereign

august, regal
dynastic, sovereign
imperial, sovereign
imperialistic, sovereign
kingly, regal
monarchical, sovereign
palatine, royal

ADJECTIVES (Continued)

regal, royal
regnal, sovereign
regnant, in royal authority
royal, kingly
sovereign, in supreme power

Popular

autonomic, self-governing
autonomous, self-governing
civic, civil
civil, civilian
civilian, civic
congressional, legislative
democratic, popular
governmental, administrative
legislative, congressional
municipal, self-governing
politic, political
political, governmental
popular, widely favored
republican, popular

Ruling Variously

aristocratic, oligarchic
autocratic, despotic
despotic, autocratic
dictatorial, imperious
federal, allied in rule
feudalistic, in feudalism
hierarchic, ruling ecclesiastically
Machiavellian, unscrupulous in government
oligarchic, aristocratic
prescriptive, governing through custom, etc.
regimental, governing by soldiers, officers, etc.
theocratic, hierarchic
tyrannous, despotic

Representative

embassadorial, officiating as an embassador
gubernatorial, noting the governing staff
magisterial, authoritative
official, in executive capacity
plenipotentiary, in full power
preconsular, in power as a preconsul
presidential, sitting in authority
(Continued on page 303)

ADJECTIVES (Continued)
vested, having authority
vicarious, in substitute authority
viceregal, in authority as a viceroy
Similarly other adjectives may be derived from personal nouns

NOUNS

Rule

authority, dominion
governance, government
government, regime
jurisdiction, authority
regime, system of rule
rule, government, dominion

Regulation

cardinal, ruling virtue
cardinal virtues, ruling principles
guide, directing virtue
institute, established law
keynote, ruling principle
law, rule or regulation
policy, plan or rule
regulation, rule
rule, law, guide

Fundamental

basis, ruling principle
fundamental, principle
hypostasis, fundamental
principia, first principle
principle, natural law
rudiment, first principle

Dominance

absolutism, predominancy
ascendency, control
dominance, supreme power
domination, dominance
dominion, rule
mastery, dominion, etc.
monopoly, prevalence
omnipotence, supremacy
predomination, prevalence
predominance, sway
preponderance, ascendency
prevalence, authority
primacy, supremacy
reign, supreme power
superiority, prevalence
supremacy, predominance
sway, rule, prevalence
virtue, rule, power

Management

administration, government
command, authority
control, command
conduct, management
direction, command
extraterritoriality, permit of an embassador to exercise his office as if in his own country
guidance, leadership

NOUNS (Continued)
leadership, authority
management, guidance
menage, management
ministration, management
regulation, rule, control
superintendence, direction
supervision, management

Sovereignty

dominion, supreme authority
empire, supreme dominion
imperialism, imperial government
kingdom, royal authority
monarchism, rule by a monarchy
monarchy, kingdom, empire
royalism, government by royalty
sovereignty, supreme

Popular Government

autonomy, self-government
Bolsheviki (the greater), popular government
Bolshevism, revolutionary government
commonweal, public influence or good
commonwealth, a republican government
democracy, government by the people
politics, civil government
republic, sovereignty by the people
republicanism, government by vote of the people

Various Government

aristocracy, rule by the nobility, etc.
bureaucracy, centralized government by bureaus, departments, etc.
cacoeconomy, bad government
communalism, government by communes
congregationalism, a democratic form of church government
despotism, absolute power
dictatorship, absolute rule
dynasty, reign by succession of a particular family
federalism, government by union
feudal system, feudality
feudality, a system of military control
feudalism, as above
gynarchy, female rule
gynecocracy, gynarchy
hegemony, leadership, ruling ascendency of a city

NOUNS (Continued)
hierarchism, rule by ecclesiastics
oligarchy, government in hands of a few
plutocracy, rule by the rich
regency, vicarious government
regimentation, enforced socialism
socialism, theocratic government through common ownership
sultanate, rule of a sultan
suzerainty, paramount authority
terrorism, government by terror
theocracy, government by ecclesiastics
trident, sovereignty of the seas
tyranny, government by a tyrant

Office, Etc.

capitol, place of government
chair, official seat
court, hall of justice
headquarters, place or seat of authority
office, headquarters
seat, place of action
throne, empire

Military Office

adjutancy, office of an adjutant
Admiralty, seat of the British Naval Government
captaincy, rank of a captain
colonelcy, rank of a colonel
generalship, office of a general
lieutenancy, office of a lieutenant
(Also derivatives from persons—see NOUNS)

Realm, Etc.

domain, empire
dominion, domain
district, territory
empire, domain
jurisdiction, extent of command
kingdom, empire
precinct, territorial district
realm, kingdom
territory, district

Miscellaneous Jurisdiction

bailiwick, jurisdiction of a bailiff
banate, office of a ban

(Continued on page 304)

NOUNS (Continued)

baronage, dignity of a baron

barony, domain of a baron

beylik, domain of a bey

curia, Papal Court

Duma, lower house of the Russian Parliament

duchy, jurisdiction of a duke

dukedom, seat of a duke

embassy, office of an ambassador

extraterritoriality, right of an embassador to conduct his office as if in his own country

khanate, jurisdiction of a khan

khediviate, jurisdiction of a khedive

lordship, jurisdiction of a lord

margraviate, domain of a margrave

marquisate, the dignity of a marquis

mayoralty, office of a mayor

ministry, office of a minister

municipality, governing center

palatinate, province of one having royal privilege

parish, ecclesiastical district

prefecture, office of a civil governor   (French)

presidency, office of the president

proconsulate, consular headquarters

proconsulship, office of a Roman official over a province

viceroyalty, domain of a viceroy

PERSONS

　　Sovereigns, Nobles, Etc.

absolutist, despot

alcalde, magistrate (Spain)

ameer, prince, governor

archduchess, wife of an archduke

archduke, a prince

aristocrat, a supporter of aristocracy

autocrat, an unrestricted ruler

baron, a person next below a viscount

baroness, a baron's wife

begum, princess (E. India)

bey, governor. (Turkey)

PERSONS (Continued)

boyar, one of the ancient Russian aristocracy

bureaucrat, member of a bureaucracy

Caliph, title of the successor of Mohammed

chevalier, knight

count, title of nobility

countess, wife of an earl or count

Czar, former Russian emperor

Czarevitch, Czar's eldest son

Czarevna, wife of the Czarevitch

Czarina, wife of the Czar

daimo, Japanese feudal lord possessing 10,000 measures of grain

decemvir, magistrate of ancient Rome

despot, autocrat, tyrant

dey, former Turkish governor

dictator, autocrat

doge, foreign chief magistrate

dowager, widow of a king, prince, or person of rank

duke, one of the highest order of the British peerage

duchess, wife or widow of a duke

earl, nobleman below a marquis

emir, Mohammedan prince

emperor, head of an empire

empress, as above (fem.)

fidalgo, Portuguese nobleman

Grand Vizier, Turkish chief magistrate

hidalgo, nobleman of the lowest rank   (Spain)

hierarch, chief church ruler

imperialist, subject of imperialism

Inca, Peruvian chief

Infanta, royal princess of the house of Spain

Kaiser, emperor

khan, Asiatic prince, chief, or ruler

khedive, title of the viceroy

king, male sovereign

knight, one who holds the dignity of Sir Knight

liege, lord or sovereign

lord, ruler or governor

lordling, little lord

magnifico, courtesy title of Venetian nobleman

PERSONS (Continued)

maharajah, title of many Hindu princes

mandarin, Chinese official

marchioness, wife or widow of a marquis

margrave, German title of nobility

marquis, nobleman ranking next below a duke

Mikado, Japanese emperor

Mogul, the emperor of Delhi was the Great Mogul

monarch, sovereign

nabob, a deputy. (India)

nobility, nobles collectively

noble, nobleman

nobleman, peer

oligarch, one of a government in which a few possess supreme authority

pasha, Turkish title of a high official

peer, a noble

peeress, wife of a peer

plutocrat, ruler through riches

potentate, sovereign

premier, prime minister

prince, ruler, sovereign

princess, daughter of a sovereign, consort of a prince

queen-consort, wife of a king

queen-dowager, widow of a king

queen, female sovereign, consort of a king

queen-regnant, queen in her own right

rajah, Hindu king, prince, or chief

rajput, Hindu of royal descent

regent, one who governs in the absence of a ruler

royalist, adherent of royalty

royalty, the person of a king or sovereign

ranee, Hindu queen or prince

ruler, sovereign

sahib, title for European gentlemen   (India and Persia)

shah, a sovereign

sheik, head of a tribe or plan

sovereign, king, queen, or emperor

sultan, Mohammedan sovereign

(Continued on page 305)

133A (Continued)

PERSONS (Continued)

suzerain, paramount ruler
tetrarch, Roman governor over the fourth part of a province
thane, title of honor for having large territorial possessions
tsar, another form of Czar
tycoon (great ruler), Japanese generalissimo
tyrant, despot
viceroy, governor ruling by authority of his sovereign
viscount, one below an earl

Naval and Military Officers

adjutant, officer who assists the commanding officer
adjutant-general, chief staff-officer of an army
admiral, chief commander of a fleet
aide-de-camp, officer who assists in general
boatswain, ship's petty officer
brigadier, brigade commander
cacique, aboriginal chief
captain, commanding officer
centurion, commander of 100 men
chief, ruler, leader, head
chieftain, chief
coastguard, guard in charge of the coast
colonel, chief officer of a regiment
commandant, officer in command
commander, naval officer next below a captain
commissariat, commandant of supplies
commissary, officer in charge of subsistence, etc.
commodore, commander of a squadron
cornet, formerly the lowest rank among cavalry officers
corporal, officer just above the rank and file
ensign, lowest rank in the navy
feudalist, member of a feudal system
field-marshal, highest rank in the British army
first-mate, naval officer next to a captain
fugleman, drill-soldier

PERSONS (Continued)

general, highest rank in the U. S. army
generalissimo, commander in chief
havildar, sergeant (Hindu)
lieutenant, officer below a captain
major, rank above a captain
major-general, rank below a lieutenant-general
marshal, chief military officer (French)
martinet, strict disciplinarian
officer, one commissioned to direct affairs
patrol, corporal's guard to preserve order
precisian, martinet
quartermaster, officer in charge of supplies
rear-admiral, naval officer next below an admiral
sachem, Indian chief
sagamore, Indian chief
serang, captain on the Malaysian waters
seraskier, Turkish commandant of land forces
sergeant, officer ranking next below a lieutenant
sergeant-major, warrant officer
skipper, sea-captain
subaltern, commissioned officer under the rank of captain
subordinate, one inferior in rank
supercargo, superintendent of a cargo on a voyaging ship
tycoon (great ruler), Japanese generalissimo

Politician, Etc.

congregationalist, adherent of congregationalism
congressman, member of congress
legislator, one of the legislative body
politician, statesman
quæstor, officer in charge of certain legislative assemblies
senator, member of the senate
statesman, one who is active in government

Political Adherents

autonomist, a subject of self-government

PERSONS (Continued)

civilian, subject of a civil government
democrat, a subject of democracy
federalist, a member of the federal party
republican, member of the republican party
theocrat, a subject of theocracy

Official

barnacle, tenacious official
commissioner, public officer
dignitary, one who holds a high position
functionary, an official
officer, person commissioned for an office
official, officer, etc.

Governor, Etc.

ban, foreign term for governor
governor, chief ruler
palatine, governor of a county (France)

Magistrate, Etc.

ædile, Roman magistrate
alderman, magistrate next in rank to a mayor
archon, one of the nine magistrates of Athens, etc.
Attorney-General, chief law officer of a state
burgomaster, chief magistrate (Holland, Belgium, Germany)
consul, chief magistrate
consul-general, chief consul
magistrate, civil officer
mayor, chief magistrate
prefect, magistrate, etc.
proconsul, magistrate
provost, chief magistrate of a town (Scotch)

Chairman, Etc.

chairman, president of an assembly, etc.
chamberlain, head of a city or corporation treasury
chancellor, a judge, etc.
croupier, vice-chairman
dean, head of a college
leader, one who leads
president, chief head of a nation, etc.
principal, leader
rector, head master of a school
ringleader, one in control of an organized band or body
syndic, government official
(Continued on page 306)

PERSONS (Continued)

vice-president, substitute president

Constable, Etc.

bailiff, subordinate civil officer
constable, official of state, etc.
cop, policeman
copper, policeman
gendarme, policeman
patrol, mounted police
patrolman, policeman
policeman, civil officer
sheriff, chief officer
warden, head official, etc.

Manager, Etc.

administrator, one who administers affairs
boss, overseer
director, manager
executive, director
factotum, director of affairs
foreman, overseer
ganger, boss of a gang
head, leader
intendant, superintendent
leader, boss, director, etc.
manager, superintendent
master, leader, manager
official, director
overseer, superintendent
principal, head, leader
steward, manager
superintendent, director
supervisor, overseer
taskmaster, boss

Envoy, Etc.

ambassador, see embassador
ambassadress, as above (fem.)
commissary, delegate
delegate, one sent to act for another

PERSONS (Continued)

deputy, one appointed to act for another
embassador, minister of high rank
emissary, one who is authorized to act on a private mission
envoy, a public officer sent from one country to another
plenipotentiary, minister of state with full power
vicegerent, one deputized to exercise the functions of another country

Agent, Etc.

agent, one who acts for another
controller, one who controls
curator, superintendent of a place of art, etc.
engineer, manager of an enterprise
executor, one appointed to carry out terms of a will
majordomo, steward
matron, female overseer
proctor, agent
procurator, proctor, agent
prudhomme, one of the board-of-trade masters who settles disputes
senior, one who is prior in rank or office
superior, principal

Plural Command

committee, an empowered body
commonwealth, the people and their influence as a whole
congress, U. S. Legislature
constabulary, policemen collectively

PERSONS (Continued)

corps diplomatique, the ministers accredited to a government
decemvirate, body of ten in authority
delegation, body of persons in authority
diplomatic corps, those organized for skillful negotiations
directorate, body of directors
hierarchy, body of ecclesiastical rulers
junta, legislative council
junto, secret council of state
knightage, knights collectively
legislature, legislative body
mote, assembly for considering the management of affairs
officials, officers collectively
parliament, legislative assembly
quorum, competent body for transacting business
senate, upper house of congress
soviet, Russian republic
tribunal, hall of justice
vigilance committee, protective organization in a new country

BEINGS, ETC.

Athena, goddess of wisdom in the arts of government, warfare, etc.
trident, three-pronged emblem-symbol of sovereignty over the sea
utræus, serpent emblem-symbol of sovereignty

134A (Continued)

NOUNS (Continued)

(B). rigour
severity, strictness
strictness, discipline
stringency, strictness
tenseness, strictness

Formality
ceremony, strict observance

NOUNS (Continued)

decorum, propriety
discipline, strictness
formalism, ceremony
formality, strict form
propriety, ethical conduct
punctilio, formal exactness
red-tape, formality

PERSONS

disciplinarian, martinet
formalist, precisian
martinet, disciplinarian
precisian, precise person

134A

VERBS

Correct

correct, rectify
edit, revise
rectify, make right
remedy, correct
revise, correct

Fit, Adapt

adapt, fit
adjust, adapt
finedraw, fit perfectly
fit, adapt perfectly

Perfect

consummate, perfect
finish, perfect
perfect, finish

ADJECTIVES

Accurate

accurate, correct
correct, accurate
infallible, unerring
mathematical, exact
right, correct
unerring, exact

Specific

particular, special
pointed, definite
special, specific
specific, precise

Perfect

consummate, perfect
faultless, perfect
flawless, faultless
impeccable, faultless
perfect, consummate
Utopian, ideally perfect

Absolute

absolute, perfect
incontrovertible, genuine
indisputable, faultless
thorough, consummate
unqualified, utter
unquestionable, absolute
utter, absolute

Punctual

appointed, regular
prompt, punctual
punctual, exact
regular, exact

Exact

certain, sure
even, exact
exact, precise

ADJECTIVES (Continued)

finedrawn, precise
hairsplitting, finedrawn
minute, precise
precise, exact
sure, unerring
unmistaken, sure
unmistakable, unerring

Tidy, Trim

neat, in strict order
prim, prudish
prudish, affectedly proper
smart, trim, neat
smug, trim, nice
spruce, smart, trim
tidy, neat
trim, precise

Fastidious

dainty, delicate
delicate, neatly accurate
exquisite, fastidious
fastidious, squeamish
finical, fastidious
meticulous, finical
nice, precise
pernickety, meticulous
scrupulous, precise
squeamish, scrupulous

Critical

careful, scrupulous
critical, precise
drastic, exceeding
exacting, harshly exact
exceeding, critical

Strict

grave, solemn
harsh, severe
puritanic, scrupulous
religious, strict
serious, solemn
severe, Lycurgan
spartan, severe
stern, severe
straitlaced, strict
strict, rigidly precise
stringent, severe
tense, strict

Inflexible

austere, strict
buckram, stiff
inflexible, Lycurgan
Lycurgan, severe
rigid, inflexible
rigorous, severe

ADJECTIVES (Continued)

stilted, formal

Formal

ceremonious, formal
disciplinary, strict
formal, ceremonious
punctilious, exact in
  etiquette
solemn, formal
starched, formal

Unequivocal

categorical, unequivocal
definite, precise
distinct, definite
explicit, definite
express, exact
identical, precise
literal, exact
positive, explicit
unequivocal, definite
unexaggerated, precise
verbatim, word for word

Authentic

authentic, genuine
genuine, true
true, perfect

NOUNS

Accuracy

accuracy, precision
correctness, accuracy
exactitude, accuracy
perfection, exactness
preciseness, accuracy
precision, preciseness

Exactness

certainty, accuracy
certitude, precision
definiteness, preciseness
exactness, preciseness
explicitness, exactness
identity, exactness
minuteness, exactness
positiveness, certainty
punctuality, exact time
sureness, accuracy

Fastidiousness

fastidiousness, finicality
finicality, squeamishness
nicety, minuteness
scrupulosity, exact regard

Strictness

austerity, strictness
rigor, strictness
(Continued on page 306)

SKILL—MASTERY—PROFICIENCY	see—	ASSOCIATIVE

134B

VERBS

Miscellaneous

conduct, manage
contrive, invent or devise
control, regulate
direct, control
excel, be superior
finesse, use artifice
guide, conduct skillfully
handle, manipulate
invent, contrive
juggle, perform with skill
    or artifice
manage, conduct skillfully
maneuver, move adroitly
manipulate, perform
    skillfully
master, excel
order, regulate, manage
regulate, make orderly
steer, guide
strategize, conduct skillfully
trick, perform artfully or
    deceptively

ADJECTIVES

Skillful

adept, skilled
adroit, dexterous
apt, expert
artistic, skillful
crack, dexterous
Dædalian, ingenious
deft, dexterous
dexterous, skillful, adroit
expert, skillful, adroit
facile, dexterous
handy, dexterous
manipulative, dexterous
masterly, skillful, clever
skillful, dexterous, adroit
sure, expert

Clever

acute, cunning
artful, cunning
clever, dexterous
cute, clever
ingenious, clever
sharp, subtle, clever
shrewd, smart
smart, clever

ADJECTIVES (Continued)

Cunning

canny, artful, shrewd
crafty, cunning, artful
cunning, crafty, deft
downy, cunning
foxy, crafty
slick, clever
sly, crafty
smooth, slick, clever
sophistical, fallaciously
    subtle, etc.
stealthy, cunning
subtile, artful, cunning
subtle, cunning, crafty
tricky, artful, cunning
vulpine, cunning
wily, crafty

Versatile

diplomatic, tactful
expedient, versatile
ready, expedient
resourceful, versatile
shifty, full of expedients
strategic, skillful in con-
    ducting forces
tactful, delicately skillful
versatile, full of expedients

Accustomed

accustomed, adept
acquainted, accustomed
conversant, proficient
empiric, experienced
experienced, accomplished
familiar, conversant
practiced, skilled
trained, thorough
versed, skilled

Talented

endowed, gifted
gifted, clever, skillful
inventive, skillful
talented, endowed with
    eminent ability

Competent

able, skillful
accomplished, proficient
capable, competent
fit, capable
competent, efficient
proficient, expert, skilled
qualified, fit, capable

ADJECTIVES (Continued)

reliable, good, thorough
responsible, reliable

Efficient

effective, efficacious
effectual, efficient
efficacious, efficient
efficient, qualified
telling, effective

Graceful

graceful, lithe
light, graceful
lithe, lithesome
lithesome, graceful
lissom, graceful, supple
supple, lithe

Excellent

excellent, consummate
incomparable, peerless
inimitable, matchless
matchless, incomparable
superlative, incomparable
surpassing, superlative
unparalleled, surpassing
unprecedented, incompar-
    able

Consummate

consummate, perfect
exquisite, consummate
Magian, magical
magical, consummate
perfect, consummate
sublime, supreme
superb, perfect
supreme, sublime
thorough, consummate

Miscellaneous

ambidextrous, using both
    hands equally well
architectonic, skilled in
    architecture
artificial, pertaining to
    production by artifice
factitious, artificial
pancratic, excellent in
    gymnastics
scientific, conforming to
    science
tactical, pertaining to
    scientific maneuvering
(Continued on page 309)

ADJECTIVES (Continued)

technical, (art) skilled in the art of an interest

thaumaturgic, noting legerdemain

NOUNS

Skillfulness

adroitness, dexterity

ambidexterity, skill with both hands

aptitude, expertness of operation or conduct

chic, manual dexterity

dexterity, manual skill

handicraft, manual skill

knack, adroitness

manipulation, skillful handling

skill, dexterity

slight, dexterity, cunning

technique, artistic execution

vertu, artistic skill

virtue, efficacy

Cleverness

cleverness, adroitness

genius, remarkable aptitude

magic, occult power in producing effects

mastery, eminent skill

shrewdness, cleverness

wizardry, magic

Cunning

artfulness, craftiness

artifice, cunning, craft

chicane, artifice

craftiness, skill, cunning

cunning, cleverness

subtileness, artfulness

subterfuge, artifice, trick

subtlety, cunning

trick, artifice, stratagem

wile, sly artifice

Versatility

address, tact, adroitness

diplomacy, special tact

expedience, readiness

finesse, artifice, stratagem

generalship, skillful tactics

ingenuity, cleverness in contriving

readiness, adroitness

resourcefulness, versatility

savoir-faire, intuitive conduct in propriety

statecraft, political skill

NOUNS (Continued)

statesmanship, skill as a statesman

stratagem, skillful handling of military forces

strategy, artifice

tact, delicate skill

versatility, adroitness

Talent

endowment, talent

gift, endowment

invention, skill in innovation

inventiveness, skillful artifice

talent, skill

Competence

ability, capability

capability, competence

competence, ability

faculty, skill, ability

proficiency, thorough skillfulness

qualification, fitness

Efficiency

efficacy, ability

efficiency, proficiency

Miscellaneous

esthetics, art, beauty, science, estheticism

archery, skill with the bow and arrow

art, skillful adaptation to an esthetic order

artificiality, craft

artistry, quality of an artist

craft, manual skill

horsemanship, skill in riding

jugglery, legerdemain

legerdemain, nimbleness in juggling

logistics, skill in moving and supplying armies

maneuver, adroitness in military affairs

sportmanship, skill in sports

tactics, skillful military maneuvers

PERSONS

abstractionist, one who is skilled in abstractions, ideals, etc.

adept, one who is highly skillful

PERSONS (Continued)

ambidexter, a man of unusual dexterity

archer, an adept with the bow and arrow

artificer, a skillful worker

artisan, one skilled in an art

artist, skilled worker

artiste, an expert cook, dancer, singer, etc.

conjurer, magician

corker, an adept

crackerjack, corker

craftsman, a skilled artisan

diplomat, one skilled in diplomacy

evolutionist, tactician

expert, master

famulus, assistant magician

genius, one having phenomenal ability

idealist, one active in developing an ideal state

illusionist, juggler

journeyman, an artisan who has served his apprenticeship

juggler, dexterous performer

maestro, master in any art

magician, wizard

manipulator, dexterous person

marksman, one skilled in shooting

master, expert

operative, artisan

proficient, an expert

strategist, one versed in strategy

tactician, expert in tactics

thoroughbred, one who is highly accomplished

virtuoso, one skilled in the fine arts

wizard, conjurer

BEINGS

elfin

fairy

fay

genie

gnome

nymph

oread

pigwiggen

spirit

CERTAINTY—DESTINY　　see—　　**ASSOCIATIVE**

vs. Chance—Incident ....127A　{ Preciseness—Accuracy 134A
　　　　　　　　　　　　　　　　　　　Skill—Mastery 134B
　　　　　　　　　　　　　　　　　　　Cause—Causation 1

134C

VERBS

Destine
cause, destine
decide, destine
destine, fix unalterably
determine, fix definitely
fix, place permanently
occasion, cause
predestinate, ordain beforehand
prepare, arrange for a definite course

Direct
conduct, guide
direct, ordain a definite course
guide, direct
lead, conduct

Qualify
appoint, ordain
institute, set up, ordain
ordain, appoint
qualify, prepare

Brew
brew, plot
concoct, brew
plan, decide a course of action
plot, plan or destine

Mold
cast, mold to form
crystallize, bring into definite form
form, shape
mold, cast
shape, mold

ADJECTIVES

Certain
certain, sure, inevitable
definite, certain
positive, certain
sure, infallible
unfailing, certain

Indubitable
assured, made certain
dependable, undoubted
indubitable, certain
infallible, certain
reliable, dependable
undoubted, certain

ADJECTIVES (Continued)
unquestionable, undoubted

Conclusive
conclusive, final
decisive, conclusive
final, decisive
ultimate, final

Destined
destined, fixed unalterably
determined, destined
fixed, settled
immutable, unchangeable
invariable, absolute
stated, definite, fixed
unalterable, invariable

Absolute
absolute, free as to condition, positive
predominant, prevailing
prevailing, absolute
primordial, absolute
sheer, absolute
utter, absolute

Inviolable
incontestable, absolute
insuperable, absolute
invincible, absolute
inviolable, invincible
invulnerable, inviolable
irrepressible, unfailing

Inescapable
inescapable, unavoidable
inevitable, destined
irresistible, irrepressible
overruling, inevitable
resistless, irrepressible
unavoidable, inevitable

Fated
doomed, fated
fatal, fraught with destiny
fatalistic, overruling
fated, destined
fateful, immutable

NOUNS

Cause
agent, active cause
agency, cause
cause, a determining agent
design, determining agency
force, agency

NOUNS (Continued)
virtue, force

Mold
cast, mold
die, mold or stamp
matrix, mold
mold, matrix, etc.
stamp, die

Miscellaneous
absolutism, certainty
assuredness, certainty
certainty, destiny
certitude, certainty
cinch, a sure thing
destination, destiny
destiny, inevitable lot
doom, evil destiny
fatalism, fate
fatality, destiny
fate, destiny
foredoom, doom beforehand
fortune, fate
inevitability, destiny
infallibility, certainty
kismet, fate
lot, destiny
positiveness, certainty
predestination, unalterable destiny
Rubicon, cause for irrevocable action
sureness, certainty
surety, certainty

PERSONS
fatalist, supporter of fatalism
predestinator, adherent to the doctrine of predestination

BEINGS
Atropos, goddess of destiny who cut the thread of life when man was to die
Clotho, goddess of destiny who held the distaff in spinning the thread of life
Lachesis, goddess of destiny who spun the thread of life

LUCK—GOOD FORTUNE   see—

vs. Misfortune 127B

ASSOCIATIVE
Gain 49A	Wealth 135B
Success 50	Health 137A
Discovery 119F	Aid—Help 5A

134D

VERBS

Miscellaneous
discover, find
draw, win
find, fall in with
fluke, score luckily
gain, win
hit, score luckily
profit, gain
prosper, succeed
score, win
scratch, gain by a fluke
strike, hit
succeed, win
win, gain

ADJECTIVES

Lucky
fluky, lucky
fortunate, lucky
lucky, fortunate
providential, God-given

Felicitous
felicitous, fortunate
halcyon, happy
happy, lucky
palmy, fortunate
rosy, happy
Saturnian, golden aged

Opportune
advantageous, favorable
apropos, pertinent
auspicious, favorable
convenient, advantageous
favorable, opportune

ADJECTIVES (Continued)

(B). favourable
opportune, seasonable
propitious, auspicious
seasonable, favorable
timely, fortunate

Prosperous
profitable, advantageous
prosperous, fortunate
successful, prosperous

NOUNS

Luck
boon, good fortune
fortune, chance good or ill
godsend, good fortune
luck, good fortune
potluck, luck in common
providence, godsend
windfall, good fortune

Fluke, Etc.
discovery, a find
find, fortunate discovery
fluke, lucky stroke
hit, lucky event
master-stroke, great success
scratch, fluked score

Felicity
blessing, boon
cheer, luck
felicity, prosperity
golden age, blissful age
happiness, good fortune

NOUNS (Continued)

Opportuneness
opportuneness, timeliness
seasonableness, opportuneness
timeliness, seasonableness

Advantage
advantage, seasonableness
behoof, advantage
occasion, opportunity
odds, advantage
opportunity, advantage
vantage, advantage

Prosperity
gain, advantage
profit, gain
prosperity, success
success, good fortune
vails, unexpected profit

PERSONS
mascot, a person, animal, or thing, used for luck
medalist, medal winner
winner, victor
victor, successful contestant

BEING
Fortuna, goddess of fortune

SYMBOL
swastika, symbol of good luck

135A

WEIGHT—LOAD   see—

vs. Impotence 128A
vs. Nullity 131A

ASSOCIATIVE
Quantitative Weight 147C
Importance 135B

135A

VERBS

Miscellaneous
burden, load
gravitate, weight toward
lade, load
load, weigh down
overweigh, outweigh
preponderate, overweigh
weigh, bear down

ADJECTIVES

Heavy
burdensome, heavy
cumbersome, burdensome
cumbrous, cumbersome

ADJECTIVES (Continued)
equiponderant, counterpoised
heavy, weighty
incumbent, weighing upon
laden, loaded
loaded, heavy
massive, ponderous
ponderable, having weight
ponderous, weighty
preponderant, outweighing
solid, weighty
weighty, heavy

Light Weight
buoyant, relatively light

ADJECTIVES (Continued)
imponderable, without weight
light, relatively ponderable

NOUNS

Weight
ballast, balancing weight
burden, load
cargo, freight
deadweight, oppressive weight
freight, cargo
gravity, weight
(Continued on page 314)

INFLUENCE—WEALTH
see—
vs. Impotence 128A

ASSOCIATIVE

135B
VERBS

Miscellaneous

bias, influence
circumstance, prevail
descend, weigh upon
environ, circumstance
exert, act upon
import, be of moment
influence, sway
permeate, pervade
pervade, permeate
prejudice, bias
preoccupy, prejudice
prevail, influence
sway, influence

ADJECTIVES

Influential

consequential, important
considerable, important
important, momentous
influential, causing effect
momentous, important
suant, (follow, seek after)
    suffusing in virtue; as
    water seeks its level, cul-
    ture spreads to man, etc.

Prominent

commanding, impressive
conspicuous, eminent
eminent, important
imposing, commanding
impressive, imposing
notable, prominent
notorious, conspicuous
outstanding, prominent
prominent, important
pronounced, outstanding
remarkable, memorable
significant, important
striking, impressive

Wealthy

affluent, wealthy
financial, monetary
heeled, wealthy
independent, wealthy
monetary, financial
moneyed, wealthy

ADJECTIVES (Continued)

opulent, wealthy
rich, affluent
wealthy, rich

Substantial

appreciable, material
material, important
solid, important
substantial, important

Prevalent

absolute, unrestricted
catholic, universal
ecumenical, universal
infinite, universal
national, prevailing widely
preponderant, predominant
predominant, prevailing
prevailing, influential
prevalent, predominant
rampant, prevalent
rife, prevalent
universal, prevailing
wide-spread, prevailing

Miscellaneous

big, important
Cæsarian, powerful
great, weighty
mighty, momentous
ponderous, weighty
powerful, mighty
weighty, important

NOUNS

Influence

bias, influence
circumstance, influence
environment, influence
influence, sway
power, influence
pull, influence
sway, influence
surroundings, environment
weight, importance

Importance

consequence, importance
import, significance
importance, significance
moment, importance

NOUNS (Continued)

prestige, importance
significance, importance

Prominence

greatness, importance
impressiveness, import
magnitude, importance
prevalence, predominance
prominence, importance

Wealth

affluence, wealth
bond, debt-certificate
chattels, goods
commodity, goods
estate, possessions
fortune, estate
funds, money
goods, merchandise
holdings, possessions
interest, holding
mammon, wealth
means, wealth
merchandise, commodity
money, worth
opulence, wealth
plenty, wealth
possession, property
property, holdings
real estate, property
resources, property
riches, affluence
securities, collateral
treasure, riches
valuables, goods
wealth, riches
worth, wealth

Character

attribute, trait
character, moral force
quality, character
trait, stroke
virtue, quality, power

BEINGS

Plutus, god of riches
Lakshmi, Hindu goddess of
    wealth, prosperity, etc.

COMFORT—BENEFIT
see—
vs. Annoyance 130B

Goodness—Justice ....140A Entertainment 99A
Aid—Assistance ....5A   Good Fortune—Luck....134D
Cure—Remedy ....136B   Friendliness 38

136A
VERBS

Comfort
comfort, console
disburden, relieve
relieve, allay

Sympathize
commiserate, condole
condole, sympathize with
pity, have compassion
sympathize, have compassion

Console
cheer, gladden
console, solace
enliven, exhilarate
exhilarate, cheer
hearten, comfort, cheer
inspirit, cheer
solace, comfort

Alleviate
allay, relieve
alleviate, allay
assuage, mitigate
ease, relieve
extenuate, mitigate
mitigate, palliate
mollify, ease, assuage
palliate, extenuate
soothe, mitigate

Help
befriend, succor
favor, befriend
(B). favour
foster, succor
help, succor
succor, help
(B). succour

Gratify
appease, allay, satisfy
content, satisfy
gratify, indulge
indulge, gratify
pacify, appease
pamper, indulge greatly
please, satisfy
satisfy, gratify

Delight
delight, please
enrapture, delight
entrance, enrapture
regale, delight
tickle, please
transport, enrapture

Beguile
beguile, charm

VERBS (Continued)
bewitch, fascinate
captivate, bewitch
charm, captivate
enchant, bewitch
fascinate, charm

Beatify
beatify, make supremely
happy
bless, give happiness
felicitate, beatify
gladden, felicitate

Miscellaneous
calm, soothe
bolster, ease with a pillow
fan, cool with a fan
quench, satisfy
slake, quench
warm, comfort

ADJECTIVES

Comforting
comfortable, imparting
comfort
comforting, heartening
Corinthian, luxuriously
pleasing
cozy, warm, comforting
luxurious, richly comfortable
restful, imparting rest
snug, warm, comforting
sumptuous, luxurious
warm, comforting

Kind
benign, kind
benignant, benign
boon, jovially kind
considerate, kind
friendly, well disposed
genial, kind, pleasant
good, kind
grateful, pleasurable
hearty, well disposed
kind, charitable
kindly, benevolent

Polite
affable, courteous
Chesterfieldian, suave
civil, complaisant
courteous, pleasing in
manner
courtly, courteous
debonair, pleasing in
manner

ADJECTIVES (Continued)
decorous, suitable
genteel, polite
gentle, courtly, kind
polite, pleasing in manner
suave, pleasant in manner
urbane, polite

Sympathetic
commiserate, condolatory
compassionate, deeply
sympathetic
condolatory, sympathetic
ruthful, compassionate
sympathetic, compassionate
tender, sympathetic

Consolatory
cheering, heartening
cheerful, imparting cheer
consolatory, comforting
cordial, cheering
heartening, friendly

Beneficent
altruistic, benevolent
beneficent, conferring
benefit
benevolent, kind
charitable, benevolent
humane, compassionate
humanitarian, humane

Alleviative
alleviative, mitigative
assuaging, alleviative
demulcent, softening
emollient, assuaging
lenitive, assuaging
mitigative, alleviative
mollifying, assuaging
palliative, mitigative
soothing, heartening
unctuous, soothing

Gratifying
agreeable, pleasing
complaisant, disposed to
please
congenial, agreeable
gratifying, satisfying
indulgent, kind, complaisant
pleasing, agreeable
satisfying, gratifying

Delightful
delectable, delightful
delightful, gratifying
(Continued on page 314)

ADJECTIVES (Continued)
ecstatic, transporting
gracious, pleasing
pleasant, agreeable

Beguiling

beguiling, charming
bewitching, fascinating
charming, captivating
enchanting, bewitching
engaging, engrossing
engrossing, captivating
entrancing, enchanting
fascinating, bewitching

Beatific

beatific, conferring happiness
celestial, heavenly
divine, God-like
Elysian, yielding heavenly joy
empyrean, heavenly
heavenly, good
Olympian, celestial
paradisiacal, heavenly
supernal, celestial

NOUNS

Comfort

comfort, that which contributes to ease
ease, relief
luxury, rich comfort
warmth, comfort

Kindness

amenity, geniality
benignity, kindness
bonhomie, goodheartedness
complaisance, desire to please
congeniality, agreeableness
cordiality, geniality

NOUNS (Continued)
favor, kindness
(B). favour
friendliness, altruism
geniality, pleasing disposition
goodness, kindness
kindness, goodness
lenity, humanity

Politeness

civility, courtesy
courtesy, politeness
courtliness, pleasing manner
decorum, pleasing manner
gentility, agreeable refinement
politeness, courtesy
politesse, affected politeness
suavity, urbanity
urbanity, politeness

Sympathy

commiseration, pity
compassion, condolence
condolence, sympathy
consideration, goodheartedness
pity, compassion
ruth, compassion
solace, comfort in sorrow
sympathy, compassion
tenderness, kindness

Consolation

balm, any solace
cheer, consolation
consolation, solace

Beneficence

altruism, benevolence
beneficence, active goodness
benefit, kindness

NOUNS (Continued)
benevolence, kindness
charity, benevolence

Alleviation

alleviation, mitigation
assuagement, alleviation
mitigation, palliation
palliation, assuagement
unction, something soothing

Help

help, succor
succor, relief
(B). succour

Deliverance

deliverance, rescue
relief, succor
rescue, relief

Gratification

appeasement, assuagement
gratification, indulgence
indulgence, gratification
satisfaction, indulgence

Beguilement

beguilement, captivation
bewitchment, enchantment
charm, bewitchment
enchantment, fascination
fascination, charm

MEDIUMS

fan, device for cooling
punka, swinging fan
snuggery, cozy place

PERSON

altruist, benevolent person

BEING

Parvati, Hindu goddess in her beneficent form

NOUNS (Continued)
heaviness, burden
heft, weight
incumbency, weight
load, burden
massiveness, ponderosity
onus, burden
ponderability, weight
ponderosity, heaviness
ponderousness, heaviness

NOUNS (Continued)
preponderance, superior weight
pressure, weight
weight, load
weightiness, heaviness

Lightness

buoyancy, relative weight
levitation, buoyancy
levity, lightness
lightness, buoyancy

NOUNS (Continued)
imponderableness, imperceptible weight

Equipoise

counterpoise, equipoise
equilibrium, equipoise
equipoise, equal weight
gravitation, reciprocal weight
poise, equipoise
equiponderance, equipoise

CURE—REMEDY—
RESTORATION
see—

vs. Bane 130E

ASSOCIATIVE

Comfort—Succor 136A
Aid—Assistance 5A
Goodness—Justice 140A

Strength 137B
Improvement 6
Purification 138B

136B

VERBS

Administer
administer, minister
doctor, treat medically
foster, nurse
minister, treat
nurse, care for, foster
treat, apply remedies

Medicate
foment, apply a medicated
lotion
medicate, treat medicinally
physic, administer medicine

Alleviate
allay, mitigate
alleviate, mitigate
assuage, allay
ease, assuage
help, ease
mitigate, palliate
mollify, assuage
palliate, meliorate
relieve, assuage
salve, soothe
soothe, assuage

Correct
adjust, correct
correct, remedy
readjust, correct
rectify, correct
reform, make better
remedy, repair

Improve
emend, improve
improve, assuage
meliorate, improve

Mend
clout, patch
cobble, mend
darn, mend
fettle, repair
mend, repair
patch, mend
repair, remedy
retouch, restore, work over

Rescue
reclaim, reform
rescue, restore
save, rescue, restore

Revive
freshen, revive
resuscitate, revivify
revive, restore

Restore
rebuild, restore
reconstruct, construct
anew
reestablish, rehabilitate
rehabilitate, restore to
former state

VERBS (Continued)

reinstate, restore
restore, repair, reinstate

Animate
animate, energize
energize, enliven
invigorate, animate
reanimate, revivify
recreate, reanimate
recruit, reinvigorate
refresh, freshen
regenerate, renew
rejuvenate, restore to
youthfulness
reinvigorate, restore vigor
renew, regenerate
renovate, restore
revivify, reanimate
stimulate, animate

Cure
cure, heal
heal, cure, make sound

ADJECTIVES

Alleviative
alleviative, assuaging
anodyne, assuaging
assuaging, alleviative
balmy, soothing
demulcent, lenitive
emollient, soothing
lenitive, emollient
mitigative, alleviative
mitigatory, mitigative
mollifying, assuaging
palliative, mitigative
paregoric, mitigating pain
sedative, alleviative
soothing, healing
unctuous, soothing

Corrective
amendatory, corrective
corrective, remedial

Preventive
hygeian, pertaining to
health
hygienic, promoting health
preventive, prophylactic
prophylactic, guarding
against disease
sanatory, hygienic

Reanimative
recreative, reanimative
refreshing, reinvigorating
regenerative, reformatory
regeneratory, as above
staminal, tonic
stimulative, conducive to
action

ADJECTIVES (Continued)

tonic, invigorating

Therapeutic
allopathic, healing by
counteraction
antidotal, corrective
antifebrile, alleviating
fever
antimonial, healing like
antimony
antiphlogistic, antifebrile
antipyretic, noting a
remedy for fever
antiscorbutic, noting a
remedy for scurvy
antispasmodic, implying
a remedy for spasms
antisplenetic, noting a
remedy for spleen
medical, medicinal
medicinal, healing
therapeutic, having healing
qualities

Curative
balmoral, healing
balsamic, having the effect
of balsam
curative, healing
detergent, cleansing and
healing
healing, curative

Restorative
remedial, corrective
restorative, remedial
resuscitative, restorative

Healthful
beneficent, wholesome
healthful, conductive to
health
salubrious, healthful
salutary, healthful
wholesome, salubrious

NOUNS

Alleviation
alleviation, relief
assuagement, alleviation
easement, relief
help, alleviation
mitigation, alleviation
palliation, mitigation

Correction
adjustment, correction
amends, reparation
correction, emendation
rectification, correction
remedy, correction
reparation, remedy
(Continued on page 316)

NOUNS (Continued)

repair, reparation

Improvement

improvement, melioration
melioration, improvement

Revivification

reanimation, restoration of vitality
resuscitation, reanimation
revival, resuscitation

Restoration

reconstruction, restoration
refreshment, restoration of liveliness
rehabilitation, reparation
rejuvenescence, restoration to youthfulness
renaissance, revival
renascence, renewal of birth or life
renewal, revival
renovation, restoration
restoration, rehabilitation

Healthfulness

balminess, salubrity
healthfulness, salubrity
salubrity, balminess
wholesomeness, salubrity

Kind of Practice

allopathy, method of treating disease
anaplasty, plastic surgery
dentistry, treatment of teeth
eugenics, promotion of offspring
euthenics, condition which improves the race
hygiene, science of the preservation of health
sanitation, promotion of health
surgery, remedial operations

Medicines, Drugs

aconite, drug
alleviative, medicine
alleviator, alleviative
alterative, medicine
anaesthetic, drug for preventing pain
analgesic, an anodyne
anodyne, an alleviative
antisepsis, preventive to bacteria
antifebrin, fever medicine
antidote, a counteractive for poison, etc.
antiphlogistic, remedy for inflammation
antipyretic, fever remedy

NOUNS (Continued)

antipyrine, as above
antiseptic, preventive to putrefaction
antiscorbutic, medicine for scurvy
antispasmodic, medicine for spasms
antisplenetic, medicine for spleen
antitoxin, counteractive remedy
balm, healing medium
balsam, as above
bracer, stimulator
carminative, remedy for flatulence
catholicon, panacea
cocoa, tonic
cordial, medicine
corrective, medicine
curative, remedy
demulcent, alleviative
detergent, cleansing medicine
drench, medicine
electuary, purgative
elixir, cordial
emetic, medicine for producing vomiting
emollient, lenitive
enema, injection
expectorant, medicine for promoting expectoration
febrifuge, fever medicine
fomentation, applied lotion
injection, enema
lenitive, emollient
medicament, healing agency
medicine, remedial compound
mollifier, lenitive
nostrum, quack medicine
ointment, a remedy, etc.
palliative, alleviative
panacea, cure-all remedy
paregoric, medicine to assuage pain
physic, medicine
pill, medicinal pellet
prophylactic, health preservative
pulmonic, lung medicine
purgative, emetic
remedy, a medicine
restorative, corrective
salve, ointment
sedative, alterative
stimulant, bracer
stimulator, stimulant
stimulus, stimulant

NOUNS (Continued)

supplement, something added to complete or correct
tablet, disk-like medicine
tincture, cordial
tonic, medicine
unction, anything soothing
vermifuge, medicine for expelling worms
For additional and related medicines see a medical index

INSTITUTIONS

hospital, place for the care of the sick
reformatory, place for reforming the wayward
sanatorium, institution for the treatment of ills

PERSONS

accoucheur, obstetrician
alienist, specialist in insanity
alopecist, one who treats baldness
aurist, ear specialist
chiropodist, hand and foot specialist
chiropractor, one who heals by manipulation
corrector, improver
dentist, dental surgeon
doctor, physician
emendator, corrector of a text, etc.
healer, physician, etc.
interne, physician or resident in a hospital
medic, doctor of medicine
medicine-man, Indian doctor
masseur, one who massages
nurse, one who cares for the wounded, sick, etc.
obstetrician, specialist in midwifery
oculist, eye specialist
optician, specialist in optics
optometrist, specialist in optometry
osteopath, one who practices osteopathy
physician, doctor of medicine
practitioner, physician
psychiatrist, specialist in mental diseases
(Continued on page 319)

HEALTH—RECOVERY—CONVALESCENCE

vs. Sickness 128B

ASSOCIATIVE

see—
{
Cure—Remedy 136B
Strength 137B
Happiness—Laughter 71A
}

137A

VERBS

Miscellaneous

convalesce, recover health
freshen, recover
heal, become whole or well
improve, mend
mend, recover
recover, recuperate
recuperate, rally
rally, revive
rest, repose, refresh
repose, rest
revive, recover strength

ADJECTIVES

Convalescent

convalescent, recuperative
improved, convalescent
juvenescent, becoming
  young again
recuperative, convalescent

ADJECTIVES (Continued)

Restored

cured, healed
healed, sound, cured
remedied, restored
restored, rehabilitated
resuscitated, revived
revived, recuperated

Regenerate

refreshed, restored
regenerate, reformed, etc.
rehabilitated, remedied
rejuvenated, made young

Fresh

blooming, fresh
fresh, unfaded
unfaded, blooming
unwithered, fresh
young, fresh
youthful, young

Healthy

hale, healthy, strong

ADJECTIVES (Continued)

healthy, sound, well
hearty, healthy
sound, healthy, strong
strong, healthy
well, healthy

NOUNS

Miscellaneous

convalescence, recovery
health, soundness of body
improvement, con-
  valescence
juvenescence, a growing
  young
rally, revival
recovery, recuperation
recuperation, rally
rest, recuperation
revival, recovery

BEING

Hygeia, goddess of health

137B

STRENGTH—ENERGY

vs. Weakness 128A

ASSOCIATIVE

see—
{
Soul—Inherence 137C
Rule—Domination 133A
Religious Sway 82B
Conquest 50
Weight 135A
Importance 135B
Stimulation 8
}
{
Restoration 136B
Skill—Proficiency 134B
Aid—Assistance 5A
Health 137A
Custom—Habit 132D
Destiny—Certainty 134C
Bravery 42
}

137B

VERBS

Endure

bear, support
endure, support steadily
stand, endure
support, sustain
sustain, bear

Prevail

overbear, bear against
predominate, prevail
prevail, be effectual
sway, be powerful

Harden

harden, toughen
inure, toughen
starch, stiffen
stiffen, make rigid
toughen, make strong

Qualify

accouter, equip
arm, equip with arms
empower, give power, arm
enable, empower
equip, qualify

VERBS (Continued)

harness, equip
qualify, make capable

Generate

engender, generate
generate, produce energy

Energize

animate, vivify
electrify, energize
energize, vitalize
innervate, give nervous
  energy
inspirit, animate
instil, engender
reanimate, revivify
revive, reanimate
revivify, revive
vitalize, animate
vivify, vitalize

Invigorate

augment, strengthen
enrich, give added power
fortify, strengthen
invigorate, energize

VERBS (Continued)

nerve, strengthen
reenforce, strengthen anew
reinforce, as above
stimulate, animate
strengthen, invigorate
sustain, strengthen

ADJECTIVES

Mighty

almighty, all-powerful
mighty, powerful
omnipotent, all-powerful
potent, strong, powerful
powerful, strong, mighty
strong, muscular, powerful

Invincible

absolute, all-powerful
indefeasible, invincible
infrangible, inviolable
insuperable, invincible
inviolable, invincible
invincible, almighty
(Continued on page 318)

ADJECTIVES (Continued)

irrepressible, mighty
irresistible, absolute
resistless, irresistible
utter, absolute

Brawny
able-bodied, strong
brawny, muscular
husky, muscular
leonine, powerful
lusty, robust, vigorous
manly, strong
masculine, manly
muscular, brawny, strong
robust, strong, powerful
sinewy, strong, brawny
stalwart, sturdy, strong
strapping, strong
sturdy, robust, stout
virile, strong, sturdy
wiry, lean and sinewy

Herculean
Cyclopean, powerful, huge
giant, titanic
gigantic, herculean
herculean, mighty
titanic, herculean

Doughty
doughty, redoubtable
formidable, redoubtable
redoubtable, mighty
Spartan, formidable

Hardy
flourishing, vigorous
hardy, hale, strong
hearty, strong, vigorous
staminal, having vigor
stanch, strong, vigorous
staunch, as above

Sound
consistent, solid
firm, solid, strong
hale, sound, strong
hard, firm, strong
solid, firm, strong
sound, solid, strong
substantial, solid, strong

Stout
inflexible, firm, rigid
rigid, strong
stark, rigid, strong
stiff, rigid, strong
stout, strong
tense, rigid
tough, strong
unyielding, inflexible

Capable
able, potent
capable, strong, able
competent, able
fit, competent
potential, able, powerful
puissant, powerful, strong
qualified, competent

Practical
applied, practicable

ADJECTIVES (Continued)

practicable, capable
practical, capable

Energetic
active, animate
alive, in vigor
animate, lively, live
athletic, muscular
dynamic, powerful, mighty
electric, dynamic
energetic, vigorous
lively, forcible
live, animate
spirited, animated
vigorous, strong

Forcible
drastic, vigorous
forceful, vigorous
forcible, vigorous
intense, strenuous
rigorous, forcibly severe
strenuous, vigorous, violent

Efficient
effective, efficient
efficacious, efficient
efficient, capable
pithy, strong, forcible
telling, effective

Animative
animative, imparting life
calisthenic, promoting
  strength
corroborative, intensive
intensive, serving to add
  force
stimulative, animative
stimulating, as above
tonic, strengthening
vivifying, animative

NOUNS

Might
almightiness, omnipotence
might, power, strength
mightiness, great power
omnipotence, almightiness
potency, powerfulness
potential, ready force
potentiality, as above
power, strength, ability
predominance, superior
  power
prevalence, superior
  strength
strength, power
weight, power

Brawn
bottom, stamina
brawn, strength
juvenility, youthful vigor
lustiness, strength
manhood, vigor
manliness, manhood
muscle, muscular strength
muscularity, brawn
sinew, strength

NOUNS (Continued)

stamen, strength, vigor
stamina, vigor, backbone
sturdiness, hardiness
thews, strength, brawn
virilescence, manhood,
  strength
virility, manliness
youth, virility

Doughtiness
doughtiness, redoubtableness
endurance, fortitude
forte, strength in which
  one excels
fortitude, power, firmness
  of character
hardihood, strength
prowess, valor, strength
redoubtableness, might
valor, strong bravery
(B). valour

Soundness
consistence, firmness
firmness, soundness
soundness, consistency

Stoutness
hardness, toughness
rigidity, strength
rigor, strong harshness
(B). rigour
rigorism, strong support
stiffness, rigidity
stoutness, toughness
toughness, strength

Capability
ability, capability
avail, powerful ability
capability, power
capacity, capability
competence, ability
faculty, capability
puissance, power, strength
qualification, capacity

Energy
activity, energy
brunt, stress
brute force, violent force
compulsion, force
dint, force, power
electricity, dynamic power
energy, inherent power
force, active power
heartiness, vigor
heft, active exertion
heyday, greatest vigor
intensity, relative strength
impulse, sudden force
leaven, silent working
  cause
life, spirit
main force, violent force
pressure, active power or
  weight
salutariness, vitality, vigor
(Continued on page 320)

SOUL—LIFE—ENTITY   see—   ASSOCIATIVE

vs. Death—Naught—Nullity..........131A

Strength—Force 137B
Weight 135A
Custom—Habit 132D
Tendency 2

137C

VERBS

Be, Exist
be, to exist
breathe, be alive
exist, have being
inhere, be innate
live, be alive
subsist, inhere

Pulse
beat, pulsate
palpitate, pulsate
pulsate, throb vitally
pulse, pulsate
throb, palpitate

ADJECTIVES

Innate
congenital, inbred
constitutional, inherent
hereditary, congenital
inborn, innate
inbred, inborn
incorporal, spiritual
indigenous, innate
ingrained, inherent
inherent, innate
innate, inbred, inherent
native, inborn
paternal, hereditary

Natural
cosmic, natural
natural, constitutional

Instinctive
alive, living
animate, live
impetuous, impulsive
impulsive, instinctive
instinctive, spontaneous
live, living
lively, intensely alive
living, vital
spontaneous, inherent
virtual, vital
vital, having the rhythm of
life
voluntary, instinctive

Substantial
existent, having entity

ADJECTIVES (Continued)
material, substantial
substantial, real
tangible, substantial

Real
actual, real
real, intrinsic
true, real

Essential
cardinal, constitutional
essential, constitutional
immanent, inherent
intrinsic, inherent
inveterate, deeprooted

Inseparable
imprescriptible, inalienable
inalienable, inherent
infrangible, inseparable
inseparable, inherent

Pulsing
breathing, living
habitual, constitutional
palpitating, pulsing
pulsing, habitual
rhythmic, habitual
throbbing, vital
vibrant, throbbing

NOUNS

Innateness
character, inherent trait
constitution, inherent
quality
essence, inherent nature
immanency, inherence
inbeing, life, inherence
inherence, state of being
inbred and inseparable
innateness, inbeing
inveteracy, constitution
nature, inherent conduct
noumenon, essence
quiddity, essence
quintessence, essential
constitution
temper, natural constitu-
tion

NOUNS (Continued)
temperament, constitution

Instinct
instinct, spontaneousness
spontaneity, instinctive
quality
voluntarism, instinct

Entity
being, entity
entity, life, inherent being
existence, being
individuality, entity
life, vital rhythm
soul, sustained inherence
spirit, inherent rhythm

Substance
gist, substance
pith, essence
substance essence

Vitality
blood, vital fluid
breath, life
juice, sap, blood
marrow, essence
rhythm, measured vitality
sap, vital fluid
virtue, inherent power
vitals, inherent essentials
vitality, vital rhythm

Momentum
impetus, momentum
kernel, essence
momentum, inherent action

Climate
climate, constitutional temperature
season, periodic climate
temperature, constitutional
climate

BEINGS
God, supreme being, es-
sence of all existence
Nymph, goddess of nature
Om, spiritual essence
Psyche, the maiden who
personifies the soul

136B (Continued)

PERSONS (Continued)
quack, pretender to medical
skill
reformer, one who reforms
renovator, one who
renovates

PERSONS (Continued)
resuscitator, reviver
revivalist, one who revives
an interest
surgeon, doctor of surgery

BEINGS
Apollo, god of medicine,
etc.
Vishnu, Hindu preserving
god
Æsculapius, god of healing

CLEANSING—ABSTERSIVES see— ASSOCIATIVE

vs. Dirt—Grime 129A
{ Purification—Purgation 138B
{ Cleanliness—Purity 138C

138A
VERBS
Cleanse
clean, free from dirt
cleanse, clean
renovate, restore freshness
scavenge, clean streets, etc.
Wash
bathe, wash
lave, bathe or wash
launder, wash and iron
rinse, cleanse with water
shampoo, cleanse (the head) with soap and water
sponge, clean with a sponge
tub, wash
wash, cleanse with water
Scrub
scour, clean by friction
scrub, rub with a wet brush
swab, clean with a swab
Flush
drench, wet thoroughly
flush, sluice
sluice, cleanse with water
Wipe
dust, brush
polish, wipe
rub, wipe
scrape, clean by rubbing
wipe, rub or dust
Brush
brush, rub, sweep, cleanse
curry, dress or clean
sweep, brush with a broom
whisk, brush off

ADJECTIVES
Miscellaneous
abluent, cleansing with liquid

ADJECTIVES (Continued)
abstergent, abstersive
abstersive, cleansing
cleansing, making clean
detergent, cleansing

NOUNS
Miscellaneous
ablution, bath
abstersion, cleansing
bath, ablution
cleaning, act of making clean
flushing, sluicing
lavation, bathing
renovation, restoration to cleanliness
shampoo, cleansing the head
sluicing, flushing
tub, sponge-bath
wash, act of washing

PERSONS
laundress, washerwoman
laundryman, washerman
scavenger, street cleaner

INSTITUTIONS, ETC.
bagnio, bath
bath, bathhouse
bathhouse, bagnio
bidet, a portable bath
laundry, place where clothes are washed and ironed
lavatory, place for washing, etc.

CLEANING MEDIUMS
Cleanser
abstergent, cleanser
abstersive, cleanser

(Continued)
abluent, that which cleanses
cleaner, that which cleans
cleanser, cleaner
lotion, liquid wash
wash, washing preparation
Brush, Etc.
besom, broom
broom, brush or besom
brush, instrument for cleaning by rubbing
duster, brush or cloth
hog, rough broom for scrubbing a ship's bottom under water
mop, swab
squeegee, pavement-cleaner
sponge, mop, etc.
swab, mop for cleaning deck floors
Towel, Etc.
bandana, highly colored handkerchief
diaper, towel-like cloth
handkerchief, nose cloth
sudarium, cloth for removing perspiration
sudary, towel
towel, cloth for drying
Napkin, Etc.
doily, napkin
napkin, cloth for use when eating
serviette, table napkin
Miscellaneous
mat, foot wiper
soap, cleansing agent
vacuum cleaner, device which cleans by suction

137B (Continued)
NOUNS (Continued)
sanguinariness, vitality
spirit, rhythmic force
stress, pressure, force
tension, straining
vigor, force
(B). vigour
vim, energy
vitality, vigor
Efficiency
effectiveness, efficacy
efficacy, effective energy
efficiency, effectual power

STRENGTHENING FACTORS
athletics, promotion of gymnastic ability
calisthenics, promotion of grace and strength

(Continued)
electrification, act of making dynamic
gymnastics, development of physical powers
mainstay, chief support
support, reenforcement

PERSONS
athlete, gymnast
giant, a Samson
gymnast, athlete
Hercules, one having Herculean strength
husky, strong person
Samson, strong person
Titan, man of great strength

BEINGS
Antæus, wrestler, invincible while in contact with the earth, crushed by Hercules who lifted him into the air
Apollo, god of youth, etc.
Atlas, Titan supporting the pillars of heaven on his shoulders
Cyclops, mythological one-eyed giant who forged the thunderbolts of Zeus
Goliath, a giant of Gath
Hebe, goddess of youth
Hercules, one of Herculean size and strength (a god)
Samson, one of abnormal strength
Titan, fabled giant

PURIFICATION—PURGATION   see—   ASSOCIATIVE

vs. Adulteration—Impurity ....146C { Cleansing—Abstersives 138A
vs. Dirtiness—Grime ....129A { Cleanliness—Purity 138C
                                         { Exoneration 138D

138B
VERBS

alcoholize, purify spirits
cauterize, burn away
  impurities
chasten, purify, refine
circumcise, purify
clarify, purify
defecate, refine, purify
deodorize, disinfect
deterge, cleanse wounds,
  etc.
disinfect, remove disease
  germs, etc.
expurge, clean out
filter, purify, as a liquid
filtrate, as above
fire, cauterize
flush, cleanse with water
fumigate, disinfect with
  smoke or vapor
purge, free from impurities
purify, render pure
rectify, refine
refine, clear of impurities
scour, purge
strain, filter
ventilate, purify by air

ADJECTIVES

abluent, purifying
ablutionary, abluent
abstergent, purging
abstersive, purging
antiseptic, eliminating negative germs, disease, or
  putrefaction
aperient, purgative
carminative, relieving flatulent gas from the
  stomach
cathartic, purgative
detergent, cleansing

ADJECTIVES (Continued)

emetic, causing vomiting
expurgatory, cleansing
  thoroughly
laxative, purgative
lustral, cleansing
purgative, purging
purgatorial, tending to
  purge from sin
purificative, purifying
purifying, making pure

NOUNS

ablution, a purifying
abstersion, a purifying
cauterization, removal of
  impurities by burning
circumcision, spiritual
  purification
clarification, act of making
  pure
cupellation, refinement in a
  cupel
defecation, clarification
disinfection, removal of
  disease germs
fining, clarification
lustration, purification
purgation, act of clearing
  away impurities
purification, act of making
  pure
rectification, purification
refinement, act of refining
ventilation, purification by
  free passage of air

PURIFIERS

abaiser, bone-black used in
  refining
abluent, a purifier

PURIFIERS (Continued)

abstergent, that which
  purges
abstersive, as above
antiseptic, that which pre-
  vents putrefaction
aperient, mild laxative
cathartic, purgative
clyster, enema
defecator, purifier
deodorizer, disinfectant for
  destroying odors
detergent, that which
  cleanses wounds
disinfectant, disease or
  germ remover, not applied
  to persons
electuary, purgative
emetic, that which induces
  vomiting
enema, that which flushes
  the rectum
expurgator, that which removes impurities
laxative, purgative
physic, cathartic
purgative, cathartic
purifier, that which
  purifies
vermifuge, medicine for
  expelling worms from the
  body

PURIFYING DEVICES

filter, device for purifying
  liquids
refinery, place for refining
  various substances
strainer, filter
ventilator, device or opening for affording the escape of noxious fumes

138D (Continued)
NOUNS (Continued)

maintenance, vindication
mitigation, palliation
palliation, extenuation
purgation, a clearing from
  imputed guilt

NOUNS (Continued)

purification, a cleansing
  from guilt
refutation, confutation
vindication, justification

PERSONS

whitewasher, one who
  falsely clears from
  imputation

CLEANLINESS—PURITY

vs. Dirtiness—Grime 129A
vs. Adulteration—Impurity 146C

see—

ASSOCIATIVE

Cleansing—Abstersives 138A
Purification—Purgation 138B
Modesty—Abstention 132C

138C

VERBS

Miscellaneous

clarify, make or become clear
purify, become pure
settle, clarify

ADJECTIVES

Clean

aseptic, not putrid
clean, not defiled
cleanly, clean, pure
immaculate, undefiled
kosher, pure, clean

Unsullied

neat, chaste
simple, pure
snowy, pure
spotless, immaculate
stainless, undefiled
unsullied, immaculate
untarnished, spotless

ADJECTIVES (Continued)

white, pure

Pure

clear, pure
fine, pure
genuine, unadulterated
intrinsic, genuine
pure, undefiled
sterling, pure

Incorrupt

incorrupt, without taint
unadulterated, pure
unalloyed, pure
undefiled, unpolluted
unpolluted, undefiled
untainted, undefiled

Thoroughbred

blooded, thoroughbred
thoroughbred, pure-blooded

Chaste

chaste, pure
innocent, pure

NOUNS

virgin, pure
virginal, chaste
virtuous, chaste

Miscellaneous

argent, symbol of purity
chastity, moral purity
cleanliness, purity
cleanness, pureness
fineness, degree of purity
health, purity
immaculateness, purity
innocence, purity
maidenhead, virginity
maidenhood, virginity
pureness, undefiled state
purity, pureness
simplicity, innocence
virginity, purity
virtue, purity

PERSONS

maid, virgin
maiden, virgin
virgin, a chaste woman

138D

EXONERATION
(Act of clearing from fault)
vs. Accusation—Condemnation 65

see—

ASSOCIATIVE

Goodness—Honesty 140A
Pardon—Forgiveness 47

138D

VERBS

Exonerate

absolve, clear of guilt
belie, remove falsity
confute, prove to be false
disprove, belie
exculpate, clear of fault
exonerate, free from imputation
justify, prove just
maintain, exonerate
purge, clear from accusation
vindicate, palliate
refute, confute

Extenuate

extenuate, absolve partly
gloss, palliate
gloze, palliate

Whitewash

mitigate, palliate
palliate, absolve partly
varnish, palliate
whitewash, render fair

VERBS (Continued)

Acquit

acquit, free from accusation
discharge, exonerate
excuse, justify, apologize

ADJECTIVES

Miscellaneous

absolvable, implying absolution
absolvatory, implying exculpation
apologetic, excusing
deprecatory, apologetic
exculpatory, implying a clearing of fault
excusable, justifiable
expiatory, exculpatory
extenuatory, palliative
justifiable, implying justification
mitigative, palliative
palliative, absolving party

ADJECTIVES (Continued)

pardonable, excusable
vindicatory, exculpatory

NOUNS

Miscellaneous

absolution, act of freeing from consequence of fault
apologia, vindication of one's principles
apologetics, vindication of Christian belief
apology, justification
confutation, removal of falsities
discharge, acquittal
excuse, extenuation
exculpation, a freeing from blame
exoneration, vindication
extenuation, palliation
justification, vindication
(Continued on page 321)

APPOINTMENT—INAUGURATION— ORDINATION   see—

ASSOCIATIVE

vs. Ban—Prohibition 35
vs. Banishment 35A

{ Exaltation 139B
Command—Decree 94
Name 92

139A
VERBS

Appoint

appoint, empower
assign, appoint
commission, delegate
delegate, authorize
depute, appoint
deputize, appoint

Introduce

create, invest
establish, constitute
found, establish
house, establish in a house
institute, establish
introduce, conduct or bring in
place, station
plant, establish
settle, establish
usher, introduce or escort

Confer

award, elect
confer, appoint
elect, invest
nominate, introduce

Invest

clothe, invest
constitute, appoint
dub, confer a rank, etc.
endue, invest
induce, bring on or into
induct, install into office
invest, clothe with office
ordain, institute
vest, invest

VERBS (Continued)

Empower

accredit, empower
authorize, empower
benefit, empower
empower, authorize

Inaugurate

chair, install
inaugurate, install
install, invest
instate, induct
lodge, install temporarily
quarter, lodge, station
seat, install
station, appoint

Enthrone

cap, crown
crown, invest with a kingdom
enthrone, crown
throne, enthrone

Consecrate

anoint, consecrate
canonize, enroll as a saint
consecrate, dedicate
dedicate, set apart as sacred, etc.

ADJECTIVES
Miscellaneous

beneficial, contributing to advantage, station, etc.
inaugural, pertaining to inauguration
inauguratory, inaugural
introductory, inaugural

ADJECTIVES (Continued)

nominative, pertaining to appointment

NOUNS
Miscellaneous

appointment, establishment by decree
assignment, appointment
benefit, advantage, appointment, etc.
commission, delegation
coronation, enthronement
delegation, commission containing representative authority
deputation, appointment
enthronement, coronation
establishment, act of stationing
inauguration, formal induction into office, etc.
induction, introduction into office
infare, installation of a minister
installation, induction
introduction, a placing, conducting, or bringing in
investiture, inducting of a bishop into office, etc.
lodgment, temporary installation
mission, delegation
nomination, appointment
ordination, investiture

EXALTATION	see—	ASSOCIATIVE

		Appointment—Inauguration 139A
vs. Defamation 65	{	Praise—Acclaim 63
		Rising—Transcending 17

139B

VERBS

Exalt
brevet, promote temporarily
elevate, exalt, ennoble
exalt, elevate in rank
lift, exalt
promote, elevate
rear, exalt

Glorify
aggrandize, make great
dignify, invest with rank, dignity, etc.
distinguish, confer a mark of distinction
ennoble, exalt
glorify, raise in honor or dignity
honor, glorify
(B). honour
immortalize, glorify by perpetuation
lionize, treat a person as a celebrity

Enthrone
enshrine, glorify
enthrone, invest with sovereignty
shrine, enshrine
throne, enthrone

Popularize
celebrate, extol, honor, distinguish
commemorate, celebrate with honor

VERBS (Continued)
popularize, distinguish
renown, make famous

Deify, Etc.
apotheosize, deify
beatify, declare blessed and worthy of homage; exalt above others
canonize, deify
consecrate, canonize, apotheosize
deify, exalt to the rank of a deity
idolatrize, make an idol of
idolize, as above
sanctify, consecrate

ADJECTIVES

Miscellaneous
commemorative, celebrating
crowning, glorifying
distinguishing, making popular, etc.
emeritus, honorary
ennobling, glorifying
glorifying, raising in honor or dignity
honorary, conferring honor
immortalizing, making immortal

NOUNS

Miscellaneous
advancement, promotion
aggrandizement, exaltation

NOUNS (Continued)
apotheosis, deification
brevet, temporary promotion
canonization, apotheosis
celebration, glorification
commemoration, celebration
consecration, canonization
deification, exaltation to the rank of a deity
distinction, exaltation
elevation, exaltation
exaltation, elevation in rank, dignity, etc.
glorification, aggrandizement
honor, glorification
(B). honour
lift, elevation
preferment, promotion, especially in the church
promotion, advancement
raise, exaltation
regeneration, sanctification
sanctification, consecration

PERSONS
commemorator, one who commemorates
immortalizer, one who immortalizes
glorifier, one who exalts

140A (Continued)

NOUNS (Continued)
fidelity, honesty, integrity
integrity, honesty
loyalty, fealty

Magnanimity
altruism, benevolence
beneficence, active goodness
benignity, goodness
benevolence, goodness, altruism
generosity, magnanimity
goodwill, benevolence

NOUNS (Continued)
graciousness, agreeableness
magnanimity, graciousness

TRIBUNALS
Areopagus, any high court
court, hall of justice
tribunal, court of justice

PERSONS
altruist, benevolent person
heritage, God's people

PERSONS (Continued)
loyalist, loyal person
Magdalen, Magdalene, reformed prostitute
Samaritan, benevolent person
trusty, trusted person

BEINGS
Astræa, goddess of justice
God, the essence of all goodness

GOODNESS—HONESTY—
JUSTICE

vs. Badness—Dishonesty 130A

ASSOCIATIVE

see—
- Truth—Frankness 61A
- Abstention—Decorum 132C
- Justification 138D
- Superlativeness 140B

140A
VERBS

Miscellaneous

abstain, refrain
behave, be proper
contain, live in continence
desist, forbear
forbear, desist
forego, refrain
refrain, forbear

ADJECTIVES

Good

decent, respectable
desirable, wholesome
ethical, respectable
good, righteous
high, honorable
high-toned, high-principled
moral, ethical
reputable, honorable
respectable, upright
wholesome, righteous

Blameless

blameless, guiltless
faultless, sinless
guiltless, innocent
incorrupt, guiltless
innocent, sinless
sinless, good

Holy

godly, holy
holy, preeminently good
impeccable, holy
pious, holy
reverential, pious

Worthy

creditable, meritorious
desirable, worthy
enviable, praiseworthy
exemplary, worthy
meritorious, worthy
noteworthy, praiseworthy
praiseworthy, meritorious
reformed, made good
worthy, creditable

Just

equable, just
equitable, impartial, just
fair, just, honest
honest, righteous, just
honorable, upright
(B). honourable
just, upright, fair
reasonable, equitable

ADJECTIVES (Continued)

righteous, just, honest
upright, just, honest
valid, just

Impartial

impartial, fair, just
Lycurgan, sternly just
Rhadamanthin, sternly just
rigid, severely just
square, just, righteous
unbiased, unprejudiced
unprejudiced, just

Lawful

justifiable, righteous
lawful, legal
legal, legitimate
legitimate, justifiable
rightful, justifiable
unimpeachable, upright

Sincere

bona fide, in good faith
frank, fair
ingenuous, frank
sincere, honest
single, straightforward
straightforward, honest

Plausible

ostensible, plausible
passable, tolerable
plausible, fair
specious, fair
tolerable, passably good

Reliable

dependable, reliable
incorruptible, firm
reliable, trustworthy
responsible, trustworthy
trustworthy, true
trusty, true

Loyal

constant, faithful
faithful, loyal
firm, steadfast, loyal
leal, loyal
loyal, true, steadfast
steadfast, constant
staunch, trustworthy
true, faithful
true-blue, loyal

Magnanimous

altruistic, benevolent, just
beneficent, altruistic
benevolent, good
benign, benignant
benignant, good, kind

ADJECTIVES (Continued)

generous, honorable
gracious, benignant
magnanimous, great-souled
unselfish, equable, just

NOUNS

Goodness

decency, respectability
goodness, righteousness
honor, magnanimity
(B). honour
innocence, sinlessness
propriety, approved con-
duct
rectitude, honesty
repute, honor
respectability, uprightness
uprightness, honesty
virtue, rectitude
wholesomeness, beneficence
worthy, worthiness
worthiness, goodness

Holiness

holiness, sacredness
piety, holiness

Justice

equability, fairness
equity, justice
fairness, equitableness
honesty, righteousness
impartiality, equability
justice, uprightness
reasonableness, equitableness
righteousness, justice
validity, justice

Lawfulness

justification, fairness
legitimacy, lawfulness
rightfulness, justice

Plausibility

plausibility, fairness
sincerity, honesty
speciousness, fairness

Reliability

probity, uprightness
reliability, probity
trustiness, faithfulness
trustworthiness, loyalty

Loyalty

allegiance, fealty
constancy, fidelity
fealty, constancy
(Continued on page 324)

EXCELLENCE—	**ASSOCIATIVE**	
SUPERLATIVENESS	Exaltation 139B	Bravery 42
see—	Goodness 140A	Nobility 133A
vs. Lowliness 129B	Beauty 108	Conquest 50
	Skill 134B	Transcendency 17
	Honesty 140A	Might 137B

VERBS

Excel
cap, top
crown, surmount
eclipse, excel
exceed, excel
excel, be superior
outstrip, surpass
predominate, eclipse
preponderate, predominate
prevail, predominate
rise, surmount
surmount, predominate
surpass, excel
top, surmount
transcend, excel

ADJECTIVES

Excellent
ascendant, predominant
excellent, matchless
extreme, exceeding
incomparable, peerless
inimitable, matchless
matchless, incomparable
peerless, unequaled
predominant, superior
superior, excellent
surpassing, unrivaled
transcendent, surpassing
unapproachable, matchless
unchallenged, unrivaled
uneclipsed, unprecedented
unequaled, unrivaled
unexcelled, unrivaled
unparalleled, unequaled
unprecedented, unparalleled
unrivaled, incomparable

Fine
capital, tiptop
choice, exquisite
dandy, fine
exquisite, excellent
fine, choice
first-class, first-rate
first-rate, tiptop
rare, valuable
select, choice
splendid, fine
tiptop, choicest

Costly
costly, expensive
dear, costly
expensive, valuable
inestimable, priceless
invaluable, inestimable
precious, very valuable
priceless, invaluable

ADJECTIVES (Continued)
sterling, valuable
valuable, precious

Grand
Babylonian, magnificent
exceptional, outstanding
glorious, illustrious
grand, magnificent
great, eminent
immense, great
imposing, grand
magnificent, splendid
sublime, grand, majestic

Remarkable
amazing, astonishing
astonishing, astounding
astounding, amazing
bewildering, astounding
electrifying, thrilling
exciting, stirring
extraordinary, wonderful
fabulous, incredible
incredible, hard to believe
indescribable, unthinkable
inexpressible, bewildering
magnificent, marvelous
marvelous, wonderful
(B). marvellous
memorable, unforgettable
miraculous, phenomenal
phenomenal, marvelous
remarkable, extraordinary
sensational, amazing
spectacular, extraordinary
staggering, astounding
startling, surprising
striking, notable
stunning, astounding
surprising, astonishing
thrilling, exciting
unbelievable, incredible
undreamed, unimaginable
unforgettable, memorable
unimaginable, unbelievable
unique, exceptional
unmentionable, unthinkable
unthinkable, unbelievable
wonderful, remarkable

Consummate
Augustan, classic
classic, excellent
consummate, perfect
faultless, flawless
flawless, perfect
ideal, perfect
perfect, ideal
unblemished, faultless

ADJECTIVES (Continued)

Superlative
excelsior, transcendent
ideal, most excellent
nonpareil, unequaled
paramount, supreme
perfect, supreme
preeminent, transcendent
sublime, supreme
superb, perfect
supernal, most excellent
superlative, supreme
supreme, most excellent
Utopian, superexcellent

Heroic
chivalrous, noble
epic, heroic
gallant, brave
heroic, chivalrous
leonine, heroic, kingly
lion-hearted, fearless
romantic, epic
valiant, heroic

Lovable
admirable, exciting praise
adorable, lovable
angelic, cherished
beloved, held dear
cherished, beloved
cherubic, angelic
darling, dearly beloved
dear, precious
honey, sweet, darling
lovable, beloved
lovely, sweet
precious, adorable
sweet, loved

Esteemed, Etc.
admired, appreciated
adored, worshiped
appreciated, esteemed
cherished, loved
elected, honored by ballot
ennobled, laureate
esteemed, valued
favored, honored
(B). favoured
favorite, preferred
(B). favourite
glorified, highly honored
honored, esteemed
(B). honoured
idolized, glorified
immortalized, glorified
laureate, laureled
laureled, crowned with a laurel

(Continued on page 327)

ADJECTIVES (Continued)

lionized, glorified
loved, adored
preferred, favored
prized, esteemed
respected, honored
revered, esteemed
toasted, honored by toasting
treasured, prized
valued, prized
venerable, honored
worshiped, adored

Noble, Etc.

aristocratic, imperial
Belgravian, aristocratic
illustrious, eminent
lordly, aristocratic
magnanimous, noble
noble, illustrious
patrician, noble

Imposing

commanding, impressive
dignified, stately
elegant, stately
important, imposing
imposing, dignified
impressive, important
portly, stately
prepossessing, dignified
stately, commanding

Distinguished

conspicuous, distinguished
distinguished, celebrated
distingue, distinguished
outstanding, prominent
prominent, conspicuous

Celebrated

acclaimed, famed
celebrated, renowned
famed, celebrated
famous, renowned
notable, distinguished
noted, distinguished
popular, celebrated
renowned, famed

Exalted

eminent, exalted
exalted, eminent
high, exalted
lofty, eminent
paramount, eminent
supereminent, preeminent

Royal

august, eminent
imperial, majestic
kingly, royal
majestic, august
princely, magnificent
queenly, majestic
regal, kingly
royal, princely

Foremost

chief, most eminent
dominant, prevailing

ADJECTIVES (Continued)

first, foremost
foremost, chief
head, leading
leading, chief
main, chief
outstanding, leading
predominant, leading
preeminent, outstanding
principal, chief
supreme, chief
transcendental, foremost

Divine

angelic, celestial
celestial, heavenly
cherubic, angelic
divine, celestial
ethereal, heavenly
Godly, divine
hieratic, sacred
holy, divine
heavenly, divine
sacred, holy
sacrosanct, sacred
saintly, holy
seraphic, angelic
supernal, celestial

ADVERBS

most
more
greater
better
farther
wider
higher
bigger
broader
beyond
above
over
utmost
utter
best

NOUNS

Excellence

beau ideal, ideal excellence
choice, the most excellent
cream, the choicest
excellence, superiority
exception, rarity
flower, the best or choicest
grace, excellence
ideal, perfection
incomparableness, matchless superiority
merit, excellence
nonpareil, superlativeness
perfection, excellence
primeness, supreme excellence
quality, excellence
rarity, exception
superexcellence, nonpareil

NOUNS (Continued)

superiority, excellence
superlativeness, highest quality
supremacy, excellence
virtue, excellence

Miscellaneous

chef-d'œuvre, masterpiece
dandy, something superior
marvel, a wonder
masterpiece, paragon
paragon, something of extraordinary excellence
wonder, remarkable thing

Costliness

costliness, dearness
credibility, merit
dearness, worth
desirability, goodness
goodness, virtue
merit, worth
value, merit
virtue, worth
worth, worthiness
worthiness, goodness

Lovability

lovability, that which attracts love
loveliness, lovability

Distinction

celebrity, renown
dignity, rank, elevation
distinction, prominence
elegance, queenliness
elevation, eminence
eminence, lofty rank
fame, renown
glory, sublimity
grandeur, greatness
greatness, eminence
loftiness, exaltedness
lordliness, loftiness
majesty, sublimity
magnanimity, nobleness
magnificence, sublimity
nobleness, greatness
prestige, prominence
prominence, distinction
queenliness, grandeur
rank, elevation
renown, distinction
splendor, magnificence
(B). splendour
sublimity, magnificence
supremacy, supereminence
transcendency, supremacy

Celebrity

bay, honor
celebrity, renown
cordon bleu, highest distinction in any profession
eclat, renown
fame, renown
(Continued on page 328)

NOUNS (Continued)
immortality, immortal
fame
laurel, honor
renown, fame

Divinity
divinity, sacredness
heavenliness, sacredness
holiness, heavenliness
sacredness, holiness
saintliness, holiness
sanctitude, holiness
sanctity, sacredness

PERSONS
Dignitary, Etc.
aristocrat, noble person
colossus, highly distin-
guished person
dignitary, one who holds a
position of distinction
magnate, person of distinction
notability, notable person
notable, personage
personage, distinguished
person
prince, highly esteemed
person
swell, person of the ultra
fashionable set (slang)
worthy, man of eminent
worth

Gentry, Etc.
aristocracy, nobility
elite, the most distin-
guished in society,
etc.
galaxy, an assemblage of
splendid persons
gentry, upper class
nobility, nobles collectively
notability, persons of note
peerage, the nobility

Idol, Etc.
appointee, an elect
celebrity, renowned person
champion, successful rival

PERSONS (Continued)
classman, student who has
gained distinction
demigod, deified hero
god, idolized person
hero, esteemed adventurer
idol, one revered to excess
immortal, person worthy of
immortality
laureate, one who is
crowned with laurel
lion, one who excites ad-
miration
medalist, one who receives
a reward
star, distinguished person

Darling, Etc.
baby, darling
beloved, one who is loved
cherub, beloved child
daddy, sweetheart (slang)
darling, dear
dear, one who is dear
dearie, darling
fairy, dear, pet, etc.
gem, jewel, pet, darling,
etc.
girlie, girl endeared
honey, darling
honey-boy, pet, sweetheart
jewel, precious, pet
love, sweetheart
mamma, sweetheart
(slang)
pal, intimate associate
papa, sweetheart (slang)
pearl, gem, pet, darling
pet, dear, darling
precious, dear, darling
queen, darling, honey, pet
rogue, term of endearment
sweetheart, object of love
sweety, sweetheart, dear
sweetness, sweetheart
sugar, sweetheart, dear

Respectability
dom, gentleman's title
(Portugal and Brazil)

PERSONS (Continued)
don, courteous title
(Spain)
donna, lady (Italian)
esquire, title of courtesy
madam, complimentary
title for a married
woman
mademoiselle, young wom-
an's complimentary title
miss, unmarried woman's
title
mister, man's title
senior, title of honor
senor, Spanish title of
courtesy
senorita, Spanish title for
a miss
signor, Mr. (Italian)
signora, Miss (Italian)
sir, term of respect

Miscellaneous
belle, reigning beauty
brick, first-class fellow
corker, admirable fellow
crackerjack, corker
gentleman, well-bred man
goddess, superior woman
hero, honored man
jewel, one held dear
lady, gentlewoman
meteor, one who dazzles for
the moment
mogul, superior person
nymph, graceful girl
pearl, beautiful woman
pippin, attractive woman
ripper, first-rate fellow
trump, good fellow
witch, fascinating woman

BEINGS
angel, God's messenger
celestial, angel, saint
God, heavenly ruler
saint, one blessed in
heaven
seraph, angel

The following auxiliary adjectives are immediately conductive to sparkling brilliance in the description of extraordinary qualities.

BEAUTIFUL
(See 108)
beautiful, attractive
charming, bewitching
chic, fashionable
esthetic, classic
graceful, lithe
immaculate, spotless

BRILLIANT
(See 101A)
brilliant, dazzling
dazzling, blazing

BRILLIANT (Continued)
glamorous, splendid
gorgeous, resplendent
iridescent, rainbow-like
meteoric, passing bright
resplendent, brilliant
sparkling, flashing
spectacular, meteoric
splendent, brilliant

BRAVE
(See 42)
aweless, brave

BRAVE (Continued)
bold, daring
brave, dauntless
courageous, aweless
daring, fearless
dauntless, aweless
fearless, dauntless
intrepid, courageous

IMMORTAL
(See 11A)
deathless, eternal
(Continued on page 329)

IMMORTAL (Continued)

eternal, perpetual
immortal, imperishable
imperishable, undying
interminable, eternal
perpetual, interminable
undying, deathless

SOPHISTICATED

(See 117)

bland, suave
smooth, bland
smug, smooth
sophisticated, urbane
suave, urbane
unctious, suave
urbane, metropolitan

GAY

(See 71A)

boon, gay
gay, gleeful
genial, boon
gleeful, joyous
joyful, gleeful
joyous, jubilant
jubilant, gleeful
merry, joyous
rollicking, jovial
vivacious, gay

GENEROUS

(See 43A)

generous, liberal
gracious, magnanimous
lavish, extravagant
liberal, generous
munificent, lavish
princely, munificent
rich, lavish

DELICIOUS

(See 48P)

ambrosial, delicious
delectable, delightful
delicious, exquisite
exquisite, delectable
luscious, delicious
palatable, savory
savory, delectable
sweet, sugary

COMICAL

(See 99A)

comical, funny
farcical, harlequin
funny, humorous
humorous, amusing
jocund, sportive
sportive, humorous
waggish, sportive

SPECTRAL

(See 96A)

chimerical, phantasmal
eery, exciting fear
ghostly, spectral
phantasmal, spectral
spectral, eery
spiritual, ghostly

RESOUNDING

(See 69B)

clangorous, clamorous
clarion, loud
crashing, clamorous
deafening, violently loud
loud, clarion
resounding, reverberatory
riotous, noisy
roaring, unroarious
smashing, crashing
sonorous, loud-sounding
stentorian, loud-voiced
thundering, thunder-like
tumultuous, riotous
turbulent, noisy
unroarious, tumultuous

MUSICAL

(See 68A)

dulcet, harmonious
harmonic, concordant
lyric, musical
mellifluent, sweet-sounding
melodious, dulcet
musical, melodious
Orphean, melodious
sweet, Orphean
symphonic, orchestral
tuneful, harmonic

SPEEDING

(See 9)

booming, rushing
bounding, springing
bustling, hurried
dashing, rushing
fleet, swift
flying, fleet
headlong, bounding
hurtling, bounding
leaping, bounding
racing, speeding
ripping, rushing
speeding, dashing

COUNTLESS

(See 147I)

countless, innumerable
extravagant, profuse
incalculable, countless
inexhaustible, infinite
innumerable, numberless
multitudinous, legionary
munificent, bountiful
myriad, innumerable
numberless, countless
overwhelming, profuse
profuse, copious
swarming, legionary
teeming, overflowing

BIG

(See 147J)

big, large, great
colossal, gigantic
Cyclopean, colossal
enormous, huge
great, huge, large
gigantic, colossal
Herculean, gigantic,
  mighty
huge, immense
mighty, huge
powerful, Herculean
prodigious, enormous
stupendous, prodigious
titanic, huge, enormous
tremendous, magnitudinous

GENESIS—

BEGETTING   see—

vs. Barrenness ..128A
vs. Death, Etc.....130-O

ASSOCIATIVE

Parturition, Delivery ..141B	Progenitors (plural) 141G
Sexual Intercourse........146D	Offspring (single) 142B
Wedlock 146H	Offspring (plural) 142C
Start, Origin 4	Animal Life 143A
Generative Organs........141C	Aquatic Life 143B
Birthplace 141D	Feathered Life 143C
Seeds, Eggs, Sperm.....:..142F	Bugs, Insects 143D
Shoots, Sprouts 142A	Plant Life 143E
Progenitor (Animal)....141F	Reptiles, etc. 143F

141A
VERBS
Engender
conceive, engender
create, cause to exist
engender, beget
gender, engender
inbreed, breed within
originate, create
start, engender

Impregnate
fecundate, impregnate
fertilize, fecundate
impregnate, fecundate

Plant
inhere, root into
plant, inhere
root, plant
transplant, replant

Vitalize
animate, impart life
inspirit, infuse spirit
quicken, impart life
vitalize, animate
vivify, endue with life

Beget
beget, procreate
generate, procreate
get, procreate
procreate, engender
produce, generate
propagate, produce or
  spread by generation
regenerate, cause to be
  born again, etc.
sire, procreate

ADJECTIVES
Miscellaneous
acinaceous, pregnated with
  kernels
asexual, noting generation
  without sex
autogenous, noting self-
  generation, or generation
  within self
conative, reciprocally generated or born
creative, causing to exist
embryonic, rudimentary in
  form

ADJECTIVES (Continued)
fissi, prefix denoting propagation by fission or sexual generation by the
  splitting of a parent body
  into two parts, which become separate individuals
formative, giving form,
  germinal
gamic, (marriage) noting
  sexual congress for the
  development of an ovum;
  opposed to parthenogen-
  esis
genetic, noting genesis
generative, implying the
  engendering and be-
  getting of young
genital, denoting genera-
  tion
genitival, genitive
genitive, noting origin, generation, relation, etc.
germinal, pertaining to
  germ or seed-bud
gono, prefix denoting generation
holoblastic, wholly
  germinal
male, noting the sex (op-
  posite the female) that
  begets young
masculine, male
nascent, beginning to grow
  or exist
original, genitive
parental, noting the function of parents in begetting young
pregnant, with young
protoplasmic, pertaining to
  generative organism
protoplasta, pertaining to
  original generative or-
  ganisms
puberal, noting the age at
  which persons beget, or
  may beget, young
pubescent, as above, having
  generative faculty
seminal, pertaining to
  seeds, germs, or primal
  elements; germinal

ADJECTIVES (Continued)
spermatic, pertaining to
  the seminal fluid of
  animals
staminal, noting the pollen-
  bearing organ of a flower
staminiferous, stamen-
  bearing
syngenetic, producing by
  the agency of both male
  and female
uterine, pertaining to the
  organ, of females, in
  which the young is
  generated

NOUNS
Miscellaneous
abiogenesis, spontaneous
  generation
advolution, process of nas-
  cently rolling toward or
  attending to a final end
anatomism, implying basic
  life in organization
arboriculture, growing rare
  trees
archebiosis, generation of
  living from non-living
asexuality, potential
  paternity
atavism, reversion to the
  ancestral type of a
  species
aviculture, the breeding of
  birds
biogenesis, generation from
  living parents or germs
  alone
conation, voluntary
  generation
conception, genesis
creation, the act of creat-
  ing, originating, bringing
  forth, etc.
cytogenesis, cell formation
ectogenesis, the production
  of structure from without
  instead of from within
embryogeny, development
  of the embryo in the
  ovule
(Continued on page 331)

141A (Continued)

NOUNS (Continued)

eugenics, the promotion of healthy child-birth

epigenesis, germ creation by the division of a fecundated cell

evolution, transcending development, natural growth

fecundation, impregnation

fertilization, impregnation

fission, the spontaneous segmentation or division of a simple organism into two parts each of which become a new individual

formation, genesis

germination, growing or occurring in pairs

generation, procreation

genesis, process of generating or producing

germination, first development of seed, etc.

heredity, transmission of qualities to offspring

heterogenesis, production by certain organisms of different offspring which revert to the production of original types in subsequent progeny

NOUNS (Continued)

homogenesis, evolutional genesis in which the offspring of a higher organism passes through the same cycle of existence as the parent or ancestry

homogamy, assortive mating and procreation by beings in the wildest state

implantation, impregnation, introduction for development

impregnation, infusion of genetic principle, etc.

indogenesis, spontaneous generation without determinable cause

metabolism, genesis through which, on the one hand, dead food is built up into living matter, and by which, on the other hand, the living matter is broken down into simpler products within the cell or organism

monogenesis, sexual production from a single cell.

origin, genesis, first production, existence, etc.

NOUNS (Continued)

parthenogenesis, reproduction by unimpregnated germs or ova, as in plant lice, some kinds of bees and hymenoptera

palingenesis, new birth or generation, inherited evolution

pregnancy, conception, a carrying young

primogeniture, seniority of birth

procreation, the generation and production of offspring

puberty, the age for begetting young

pubescence, puberty

regeneracy, regeneration

regeneration, causing to be born again

source, creation, origin

syngenesis, sexual reproduction

virility, power of procreation

Xenogenesis, production of forms which pass through different development from those of the parent and do not return to the cycle of the parent

---

141G (Continued)
PROGENITORS (Plural)

(Continued)

house, family or race
line, descent
lineage, ancestral line of descent
maternity, motherhood
motherhood, maternity
origin, parentage
parentage, extraction

(Continued)

paternity, authorship, origin, fatherhood
pedigree, genealogy
race, lineage
root, strain
sex, women in general, also man or woman
stem, branch of a family

(Continued)

stirps, family, lineage
stock, race, lineage
strain, lineage, race
succession, lineage
womanhood, womankind
womankind, women collectively

142A
PLANT OFFSPRING

bud, shoot, gemmule
gemmule, bud
imp, offshoot

(Continued)

shoot, young branch or sucker of a plant
spray, shoot

(Continued)

sprig, shoot
sprout, shoot
twig, shoot

PARTURITION—DELIVERY OF
YOUNG, Etc.   see— ⎰
                              (ASSOCIATIVE 141A)

vs. Barrenness—Impotence............128A ⎱

141B

VERBS

Bear
bear, deliver
deliver, bear young
produce, bring forth

Foal, Etc.
calve, bear calf
farrow, bear young, as pigs
foal, bear young, said of a mare
litter, bear in litters
pup, produce puppies
yean, bring forth, as sheep

Hatch
brood, sit on eggs
hatch, produce from eggs
incubate, hatch
set, hatch
sit, incubate

Bud
bud, sprout
emanate, issue
germinate, sprout or bud
issue, spring
shoot, sprout
spring, bud
sprout, germinate

Blossom
bloom, produce blooms
blossom, to flower
effloresce, blossom
flower, blossom, bloom

Fruit
breed, bear young, hatch
fructify, bear fruit
fruit, fructify
lay, produce eggs
multiply, fructify
reproduce, multiply
spawn, bear eggs or roe
teem, be full of young

Abort
abort, miscarry in birth
miscarry, abort
slink, miscarry

ADJECTIVES

Parturient
parturient, producing young
puerperal, implying childbirth

Pregnant
gestatory, implying pregnancy
gravid, pregnant
pregnant, with young, fruitful

ADJECTIVES (Continued)
teeming, full, as though ready to produce young

Maternal
female, in motherhood
feminine, as above
maternal, implying motherhood
matronly, maternal
mother, native, maternal
motherly, maternal
womanly, maternal

Natal
ancestral, pertaining to parentage
genealogical, implying lineal procreation
hereditable, passing or implying the passage of a quality to a progeny
hereditary, passing from ancestor to descendant
homogeneous, of the same origin of nature
indigenous, natal
lineal, ancestral
natal, (to be born) implying birth, indigenous
native, implying birth or production by nature

Viviparous
larviparous, producing young through larvæ
oviculture, implying the genital qualities of an egg
oviparous, producing young by eggs
ovoviviparous, implying the production of eggs containing young in a living form
viviparous, producing young by eggs

Fruitful
exuberant, copiously fruitful
fecund, prolific
fertile, productive
fruitful, fecund
procreant, implying the production of young
procreative, producing young
productive, generative
proliferous, producing offspring
prolific, productive

ADJECTIVES (Continued)
propagable, implying production and spreading by generation
regenerative, implying rebirth
regeneratory, reproductive
renascent, implying regeneration
reproductive, regenerative
rich, fruitful
virile, procreative

Multiparous, Etc.
biferous, bearing fruit twice a year
biparous, pertaining to birth in twos
geminate, growing or occurring in pairs
multiparous, bearing many
uniparous, producing one at birth

Bisexual, Etc.
androgynous, bisexual
bisexual, implying the combination of the productive organs of both sexes in one individual
hermaphrodite, bisexual
hermaphroditic, as above

Adnascent
adnascent, pertaining to generation or growth on something else
adnate, born together
congenital, born with one

Evolutional
atavistic, implying reversion to ancestry
evolutional, implying the function of evolution
evolutionary, as above
homogeneous, generating through the same cycle as the parent
metabolic, generating progressively or retrogressively

Miscellaneous
abortive, in premature birth
antenatal, before birth
autogenous, producing within by self-generation
ectogenous, producing structure from without; opposed to endogenous

(Continued on page 333)

ADJECTIVES (Continued)

efflorescent, blossoming

endogenous, autogenous; opposed to ectogenous

germinant, sprouting

heterogenetic, producing differences, etc.

neoplastic, forming newly

posthumous, born after the death of the father

pythogenic, implying generation or production by means of filth

thalassic, implying birth in the sea

NOUNS

Birth

accouchement, parturition

birth, bringing forth young

childbirth, confinement

confinement, parturition

delivery, parturition

labor, parturition

parturition, act of bringing forth young

travail, bringing forth of young

NOUNS (Continued)

Blossom

blossom, state of flowering

efflorescence, state of flowering

florescence, efflorescence

flowering, production of flowers

Fruitfulness

exuberance, fruitfulness

fatness, fertility, productiveness

fecundity, productiveness

fertility, fruitfulness

fructification, bearing of fruit, etc.

fruitfulness, fecundity

fruition, bearing of fruit

productiveness, fertility

propagation, successive production

reproduction, regeneration

Abortion

abortion, untimely birth

miscarriage, premature parturition

Miscellaneous

arboriculture, the production of trees

NOUNS (Continued)

aviculture, the breeding of birds

bastardy, birth out of wedlock

blastogenesis, reproduction by budding

gestation, pregnancy

incubation, act of hatching

metamorphosis, transformation in which insects and some animals develop from eggs, etc., to full maturity

pisciculture, artificial breeding of fish

pregnancy, state of being with young

primogeniture, seniority of birth

schizogamy, production in which a sexual form originates by fission or by building from a sexless one

sericulture, culture of silkworms

141C

GENERATIVE ORGANS

ovary, female organ in which the ovum, or first germ of life, is formed; male organ of a flower

penis, male organ of generation

(Continued)

ramus, male generative organ

testicle, seminal gland

stamen, male organ of a flower

uterus, womb

(Continued)

vulva, female generative organ

womb, organ in which young are developed

141D

BIRTHPLACE (See 53D, 53F)

aery, eagle's nest

arboretum, place for the growth of rare trees

birthplace, origin

cradle, birthplace

creation, source

earth, source, origin

eyrie, nest of a predatory bird

farm, place for crops

fatherland, nativity

(Continued)

foundation, origin, source

fountain, source

garden, small farm

hatchery, place for hatching eggs artificially

home, nativity

incubator, hatchery

nativity, place of birth

nature, cradle of all existence

nest, birthplace of birds

nidus, nest

(Continued)

nursery, place for cultivation of plants, etc.

orchard, place for growing fruit

origin, source

rookery, group of nests

root, origin

source, nature, origin

spring, source

universe, creation

**BREEDING—BEGETTING—
BEGETTERS—SEED** see—

vs. Destructiveness—Death 130-O
vs. Barrenness—Impotence 128A

(ASSOCIATIVE 141A)

141E
PERSONS (Progenitor)
abortionist, one who produces untimely birth
ancestor, forefather
ancestress, as above (fem.)
androgyne, hermaphrodite
author, creator
begetter, progenitor
beldam, grandmother
benedict, married man
bigamist, one who is wedded to more than one wife
concubine, inferior wife, a man's unmarried consort
consort, husband or wife
creator, one who creates or brings into being
dad, father
Eve (woman), first woman
father, male parent
female, sex as distinguished from the male
feme coverte, married woman
forbear, ancestor
forefather, forbear
generator, progenitor

PERSONS (Continued)
goodman, master of a house
goodwife, mistress of a house
grandfather, father of one's father or mother
grandmother, mother of one's father or mother
grandparent, parent of one's parent
grandsire, grandfather
hermaphrodite, one in whom are combined the organs of male and female
husband, head of a family
lady, mistress of a house
Lilith, wife of Adam before Eve
male, sex opposite the female
man, adult male
matron, married woman, especially one who has borne children
mother, female parent
mamma, mother

PERSONS (Continued)
mate, consort
mistress, concubine
pa, dad, father
papa, pa, father
parent, father or mother
patriarch, founder of a family
predecessor, ancestor
procreator, one who begets
progenitor, ancestor
propagator, procreator
queen consort, wife of a king
sire, progenitor
spouse, married person
squaw, N. American Indian woman or wife
wife, husband's consort
woman, female of the human species

BEINGS
Demeter, goddess of fertility
Diana, goddess of childbirth, of woods and hunting, etc.

141F
PROGENITORS (NON-HUMAN)
babouine, female baboon
bitch, female of the dog species
boar, male of swine, etc.
buck, male begetter of the fallow deer, goat, rabbit, hare, etc.
bull, male begetter of any bovine animal
cock, male bird
cow, female of the genus bos or ox, and of various other animals as elephant, whale, etc.

(Continued)
dam, mother or female parent (beast)
doe, female of fallow deer, antelope, rabbit, hare, etc.
drake, male duck
ewe, female sheep
gander, male goose
goose, female of the goose species
hen, female of birds
horse, male of horse species
jenny, female, as jenny wren, jenny ass, etc.

(Continued)
mare, female of horse
planarian, worm capable of reproducing lost parts, including the head
ram, male of sheep
roe, female of hart
sire, male of beasts
sow, female pig
stag, male of deer, etc.
stallion, breeding horse
vixen, she fox

141G
PROGENITORS (Plural)
(See 146I)
ancestry, line of one's descent
authorship, origin
birth, lineage
blood, extraction, lineage

(Continued)
branch, off-shoot, lineage
clan, tribe or lineage under one chief
descent, birth
extraction, lineage
family, descent

(Continued)
fatherhood, paternity
femininity, womankind
generation, single succession
genealogy, lineage, family
(Continued on page 331)

BREEDING—BEGETTING—
   BEGETTERS—SEED   see—
                                    (ASSOCIATIVE 141A)
   vs. Destructiveness—Death 130-O
   vs. Barrenness—Impotence 128A

142B

OFFSPRING (Single)

baby, infant
bastard, one born out of
  wedlock
changeling, ill-favored
  child supposed to have
  been substituted
child, offspring
creature, created being
daughter, female issue of
  parents
demoiselle, young lady

(Continued)

descendant, offspring
elfchild, changeling
foster child, child reared
  by one not its parent
girl, female child
grandchild, child of one's
  son or daughter
granddaughter, daughter of
  one's son or daughter
grandson, son of one's son
  or daughter

(Continued)

infant, baby, child
issue, offspring
lass, girl
lassie, girl
offshoot, offspring
offspring, descendant
scion, descendant
son, male issue of parents
unigeniture, the only
  begotten one

142C

OFFSPRING (Plural)

children, young of parents
fetus, (foetus) young in
  the womb or egg
generation, progeny

(Continued)

offspring, progeny
posterity, descendants,
  future generations

(Continued)

progeny, offspring
young, offspring

142D

OFFSPRING
  (Non-Human)
colt, young horse

(Continued)

cub, young of the fox, lion,
  etc.
whelp, cub

(Continued)

zooid, animal in one of its
  inferior stages of development

142E

OFFSPRING
  (Non-Human, Plural)
aery, brood of hawks or
  eagles
breed, progeny or stock
  from the same parents
brood, offspring, hatch of
  young birds

(Continued)

covey, hatch or brood
farrow, litter of pigs
fruit, young of man or
  animal
fruitage, as above
fry, swarm of young fish
hatch, brood

(Continued)

kit, brood
litter, young from one
  birth
nide, brood of pheasants
team, brood, litter

142F

SEED, EGGS, SEMEN,
  Etc.
acorn, seed of the oak
ameba, amoeba, cell having
  finger-like extensions
  with which it absorbs
  food; animalcula
animalcula, infusoria
animalculum, animalcule
anther, fertilizing medium
  of flowers
bacteria, pl. for bacterium
bacterium, organism, germ
bacillus, bacteria
bioplasm, protoplasm
bioplast, bioplasm having
  formative powers
blastema, embryonic
  protoplasm

(Continued)

blastoderm, the germinal
  spot in an ovum
cocoon, egg-like larvae
caviar, spawn
cell, unit of reproductive
  protoplasm
compost, fertilizing
  material
cytoblastema, the protoplasm of vegetable cells
ectoplasm, the exterior
  protoplasm of a cell
egg, ovule which repro-
  duces young
embryo, first germ or rudiment of an organism
fertilizer, impregnating
  material

(Continued)

flyblow, larvæ of a fly
gemmule, ovule
germ, plasm of an egg,
  ovum or ovule from
  which a new indivudual
  is formed
guano, fertilizing material
germule, incipient germ
idiochromosome, minute
  colorable body in the
  germ cell supposed to
  determine sex
infusoria, animalcula
kernel, grain or seed
(Continued on page 342)

BREEDING—BEGETTING—
   BEGETTERS—SEED   see— ⎰
                                       (ASSOCIATIVE 141A)
     vs. Destructiveness—Death 130-O
     vs. Barrenness—Impotence ....128A ⎱

143A

ANIMAL LIFE

agouti, rodent
ai, sloth
albino, person or animal with white skin and pink eyes
alpaca, llama
amphibian, form of life which lives on land and in water
ape, tailless monkey
Angora cat, species of cat
Angora goat, species of goat
animal, brute, beast
ant bear, species of bear
anteater, mammal that feeds on ants
anthropoid, man-like ape
Anthropoidea, sub-order of primate mammals
antelope, deer-like animal
apod, animal without feet
armadillo, mailed quadruped
ass, donkey
aswail, sloth-bear
aurochs, European bison
aye-aye, monkey-like animal
Ayrshire, breed of cattle
axis, hog-deer
baboon, monkey-like animal
babuina, female baboon
bandicoot, large rat
bandog, mastiff
badger, carnivorous mammal
beagle, hunting hound
bear, carnivorous mammal
beast, animal
beaver, rodent
behemoth, hippopotamus
Bengal tiger, tiger of India
bighorn, mountain sheep
biped, two-footed animal
bison, buffalo
black-cattle, cattle raised for food
bloodhound, species of dog
bluebuck, antelope
boa, serpent
boa constrictor, boa
boar, wild hog
brant-fox, species of fox
brock, badger
broncho, unbroken horse
bruin, brown bear

(Continued)

bucentaur, fabulous half man and half horse
buffalo, one of the ox family
bull, male of various animals
bulldog, species of dog
bullock, ox, grown steer
bull-terrier, a dog
burro, Mexican ass
calf, young bovine
camel, a large quadruped
camelopard, giraffe
caribou, reindeer
cat, domestic quadruped
catamount, wild-cat
cattle, live stock
cave-bear, fossil bear
cayuse, horse
cheetah, hunting leopard
chestnut, reddish horse
cheviot, sheep
chimpanzee, ape
chinchilla, a rodent
collie, sheep dog
colt, young horse
cow, female of ox family
coyote, prairie wolf
deer, one of genus cervus
dog, species of canine
donkey, ass
dromedary, camel
elephant, a large mammal
ermine, weasel-like animal
ewe, female sheep
eyra, wild cat
fauna, animals in an area
fawn, young deer
feline, cat
ferret, polecat
fice, a cur dog
filly, young mare
fitch, polecat
flying squirrel, squirrel that can volplane
fox, a canine mammal
fox-hound, hunting dog
fox-squirrel, tree-squirrel
galloway, horse
gaur, Bengal bison
gazelle, antelope
gelding, castrated horse
gemsbok, African antelope
genet, a Spanish horse
giraffe, camelopard
gnu, buffalo-like animal
goat, horned quadruped
gorilla, large ape

(Continued)

greyhound, a swift hound
grimalkin, old she-cat
grison, weasel-like animal
ground-hog, woodchuck
guanaco, llama
Guernsey, breed of cattle
guinea-pig, rodent
glutton, carnivorous animal
hamster, a great rat
Hanuman, old grey ape
hare, rabbit
harrier, hunting dog
hart, male of red deer
hartbeest, African antelope
hedgehog, spine-covered animal
heifer, young cow
hexapod, six-legged animal
hinny, offspring of horse and she-ass
hippopotamus, river horse
hog, swine
horse, solid-hoofed animal
hound, dog
howler, American monkey
human, human being
hyena, wolf-like animal
hyrax, horse-like animal
ibex, wild goat
ichneumon, weasel-like animal
Ichthyosaurus, huge fossil of fish-lizards
iguana, lizard
jackal, dog-like animal
jackass, donkey
jaguar, leopard-like animal
jerboa, leaping mouse
kangaroo, Australian animal
kinkajou, animal with prehensile tail
lamb, young sheep
lapdog, pet dog
lemur, monkey-like animal
leopard, cat-like beast
leveret, young hare
lion, carnivorous beast
lizard, saurian reptile
llama, camel-like animal
lynx, cat-like animal
macaco, lemur
mammal, animal
mammoth, extinct elephant
man, human being
mandrill, baboon
mare, female of the horse
(Continued on page 337)

ANIMAL LIFE
(Continued)

marmose, opossum-like animal
marmoset, small monkey
Marsupialia, pouch-bearing animals
marmot, prairie dog
marten, weasel-like animal
mastiff, large dog
mastodon, elephant-like animal
merino, a sheep
mice, pl. of mouse
miniver, squirrel
mink, weasel-like animal
moke, donkey
mole, a burrowing animal
mongoose, weasel-like animal
monitor, large lizard
monkey, human-like animal
moose, elk-like animal
mouflon, a wild sheep
mule, offspring of male ass and mare
mouse, rodent
musk-deer, hornless deer
muskrat, aquatic rodent
mustang, semi-wild horse
nylghau, antelope
ocelot, Mexican cat
octopod, eight-legged animal
okapi, giraffe-like animal
onager, wild ass
opossum, carnivorous mammal
orang-outang, ape-like animal
otter, weasel-like animal
ounce, leopard-like animal
ox, cow-like animal
pachydactyl, thick-toed animal

(Continued)

paco, llama-like animal
palfrey, small saddle horse
panther, cat-like animal
pard, any spotted beast
pig, a young swine
plantigrade, man-like walking animal
pointer, a dog
polar bear, bear of the arctic regions
polecat, skunk
pony, small horse
porcupine, spine-covered rodent
porker, pig
pug, species of dog
puma, mountain lion
puppy, whelp, young dog
prairie dog, small rodent
Quadrumana, order of mammalia including the monkey
quadruped, four-footed animal
quagga, zebra-like animal
rabbit, a rodent
ram, male sheep
ranger, variety of dog
rat, rodent
reindeer, domesticated deer
renard, fox
reynard, fox
rhesus, India's sacred monkey
rhinoceros, horn-snouted animal
rodent, rat-like animal
sable, weasel
saiga, Russian antelope
sajou, S. American monkey
saki, S. American monkey
sambur, elk (India)
sasin, Indian antelope
sea-bear, polar bear

(Continued)

setter, hunting dog
sheep, a ruminant animal
sheltie, Shetland pony
skunk, weasel-like animal
sloth, slow-moving mammal
sow, female pig
spaniel, dog
springbok, gazelle
squirrel, a rodent
stag, male deer
stallion, breeding horse
steer, bullock
steinbok, antelope
stoat, weasel
swine, a pig
tabby, cat
tahr, wild goat
talapoin, monkey
tamandua, anteater
tamarin, monkey
tapeti, hare
tapir, hog-like animal
teledu, badger
tiger, a fierce animal
tit, a small horse
unicorn, one-horned animal
vicuna, llama-like animal
wanderoo, bearded monkey
wapiti, elk
weasel, carnivorous animal
wether, castrated ram
wildcat, undomesticated cat
wolverene, wolf-like animal
wolf, dog-like animal
wow-wow, ape
woodchuck, ground hog
yak, ox-like animal
yapock, opossum
zamouse, buffalo
zebu, cow-like animal
zobo, ox-like animal
zoril, skunk
zebra, horse-like animal

143F
REPTILE—TURTLE, Etc.

aboma, large boa
adder, viper
alligator, lizard-like reptile
anaconda, boa
asp, viper
aspic, asp
batrachian, frog
blindworm, a species of lizard
boa, a large serpent
boa constrictor, boa
bull-frog, a species of frog
cobra-de-capello, the cobra of India
cobra, a venomous snake
cochlea, snail
constrictor, boa

(Continued)

crocodile, large lizard-like reptile
eft, salamander
frog, web-footed amphibian
garter-snake, yellow striped snake
gavial, crocodile
gopher, rat-like rodent
hawkbill, turtle
leatherback, turtle
naga, a snake
natterjack, rush-toad
newt, eft
Ophidia, order of reptiles
ophidian, reptile
python, boa-like serpent
rattler, snake with a rattler on his tail

(Continued)

rattlesnake, rattler
reptile, crawling animal
salamander, amphibious animal
serpent, reptile
snail, gastropod of the genus Helix
tapeworm, flat ribbon-like intestinal worm
terrapin, tortoise
toad, frog
tortoise, reptile of the family Testudinidae
turtle, tortoise
viper, serpent
worm, small creeping animal
yacare, crocodile

BREEDING—BEGETTING—
BEGETTERS—SEED   see—

vs. Destructiveness—Death 130-O
vs. Barrenness—Impotence 128A

(ASSOCIATIVE 141A)

143B

AQUATIC LIFE

alligator, crocodilian reptile
amphioxus, lancelet fish
anchovy, a fish
angle-fish, species of shark
archer fish, fish that preys upon insects by darting water on them
argonaut, octopus
bass, a fish
basking shark, Northern Sea shark
beluga, white whale
blackfish, black sea bass, etc.
bleak, a brilliant fish
blindfish, fish with rudimentary eyes
bream, carp-like fish
brill, flat fish
brit, young of herring
bullhead, catfish
cachalot, whale
caplin, smelt
carp, a fish
catfish, species of fish
cephalopod, octopus
cetacean, whale
chimera, a fish remarkable for its appearance
coral, marine polyps
cob, herring
cockle, shellfish
cod, a fish
codling, young cod
crawfish, crab-like fish
crab, division of crustacea
crustacea, crabs and lobsters
cuttle, cuttlefish
cuttlefish, octopus-like fish
crocodile, alligator-like reptile
dab, flounder
dog-fish, littoral shark
dory, a fish
dugong, aquatic animal
eel, elongated fish
finback, whale
fish, aquatic animal
flounder, flat sea fish
flying fish, fish that can fly
garfish, fish with a spear-like snout
garpike, garfish
garter-fish, species of fish
gilling, second-year salmon

(Continued)

globe-fish, inflating fish
goby, a fish
gold-carp, the gold-fish
grampus, sea dog
growler, perch
grunt, a fish
gudgeon, a fish
gwiniad, trout
gymnotus, electrical eel
haddock, codfish
hake, codfish
halibut, a flat fish
halicore, dugong
hornbeak, garpike
horseshoe, king crab
houndfish, shark-like fish
huck, German trout
jack, pike
jerkin, young salmon
king-crab, species of crab
kipper, salmon
leech, aquatic worm
loach, fish
loggerhead, sea turtle
lumpfish, horned fish
mackerel, fish
manatee, sea cow
mango-fish, a fish
menhaden, herring-like fish
minim, small fish
minnow, small fish
mullet, a fish
namaycush, trout
narwhal, whale-like mammal
nautilus, cephalopod
octopus, cephalopod
oyster, bivalve
parr, young salmon
penfish, kind of eelpout
perch, fresh-water fish
physeter, sperm whale
pike, fish
pilchard, herring-like fish
plaice, flat fish
pollard, cub fish
pollack, codfish
polyp, extensive group of radiated sea animals
porpoise, sea dog
pout, kind of codfish
prawn, shrimp-like fish
ray, cartilaginous fish
roach, a fish
rorqual, whale
ruff, a fish

(Continued)

salmon, a fish
salmon-peel, young salmon
salmon trout, trout-like fish
sardine, small fish
saury, pike-like fish
sawfish, fish with a saw-like snout
scad, shad
sculpin, a fish
sea-bat, flying fish
sea-calf, seal
sea-cow, walrus
sea-dog, seal
sea-elephant, seal
sea-fox, shark
sea-hog, porpoise
sea-horse, walrus
seal, marine animal
sea-leopard, kind of seal
sea-lion, species of seal
sepia, cuttlefish
shad, a fish
shark, a large fish
shrimp, a shellfish
skate, a fish
smelt, a fish
smolt, young salmon
sound, cuttlefish
sparling, smelt
sponge, species of spongida
sprag, young salmon
sprat, small fish
squid, cuttlefish
stingaree, the stingray
sturgeon, a fish
tadpole, aquatic larva
tautog, fish
tench, fish
toadfish, large-headed fish
trout, a fish
tunny, mackerel-like fish
turbot, flat fish
walrus, marine mammal, with tusks
weakfish, silvery fish
weaver, a fish
whale, a great fish
whitebait, a fish
wrymouth, eel-shaped fish
zingel, perch-like fish

ADJECTIVES

crustacean, pertaining to crabs, etc.
crustaceous, crustacean

BREEDING—BEGETTING—
BEGETTERS—SEED   see—

(ASSOCIATIVE 141A)

    vs. Destructiveness—Death 130-O
    vs. Barrenness—Impotence 128A

143C

FEATHERED LIFE

aigret, heron
albatross, sea bird
apteryx, wingless bird
auk, a diving bird
bantam, a fowl
barn owl, species of owl
barb, pigeon
bat, winged animal
bee-eater, a bird
bell-bird, American bird
bernicle, bernicle goose
bird, feathered creature belonging to the class Aves
bittern, wading bird
blackbird, species of bird
blackcap, black-crested bird
blackcock, heath cock
bobolink, American song-bird
booby, West Indian bird
brant-goose, species of wild goose
buffalo-bird, bird which eats parasites off buffaloes
bullfinch, song-bird
bunting, sparrow-like bird
butcher-bird, shrike
butter-bird, rice bunting
buzzard, vulture of the hawk species
canary, a singing bird
canvasback, duck
carrion-crow, common crow
chaffinch, a bird
chanticleer, cock
chick, small chicken
chicken, fowl
chickadee, titmouse
cheeper, young game bird
cob, sea gull
cock, male bird
cockerel, young cock
coot, waterfowl
cormorant, a diving bird
crossbill, a bird
crow, one of the species corvus
daw, jackdaw
demoiselle, Numidian crane
dodo, extinct bird
dorking, domestic fowl
dotterel, plover
dove, species of pigeon
drake, male duck

(Continued)

duck, waterfowl
eagle, a bird of prey
eider, duck
epiornis, fossil bird
falcon, predatory bird
fantail, pigeon
finch, canary-like bird
finikin, variety of pigeon
fish-hawk, osprey
flamingo, red-colored bird
flicker, woodpecker
fowl, domestic or wild bird
fox-bat, species of bat
francolin, partridge-like bird
frigate-bird, pelican-like bird
gadwall, a duck
gander, male goose
gannet, a sea bird
godwit, curlew-like bird
golden, pheasant
goldfinch, song bird
goose, web-footed bird
goshawk, hawk-like bird
gosling, young goose
grebe, diving bird
grosbeak, finch-like bird
grouse, partridge
guan, S. American bird
guillemot, auk
guinea-fowl, species of fowl
harrier, species of hawk
hawfinch, grosbeak
hawk, falcon-like bird
hen, domestic fowl
heron, wading bird
hobby, falcon
hooper, swan
hoopoe, a beautiful bird
hornbill, horn-crested bird
humming-bird, a small bird
ibis, wading bird
jackdaw, crow
jack-snipe, small snipe
jay, crow-like bird
kea, parrot
kestrel, hawk
kingfisher, a fishing bird
kite, a rapacious bird
kittiwake, gull
kiwi, a long-billed bird
knot, sandpiper
lanner, hawk
lapwing, plover-like bird
leghorn, a fowl
leipoa, pheasant of Australia

(Continued)

lorikeet, parrot
lory, parrot
love-bird, small parrot
lyre-bird, Australian bird
magpie, a chattering bird
mallard, duck
marabou, stork
martin, swallow-like bird
merganser, duck-like bird
merlin, falcon
mocking-bird, song bird
musk-duck, Australian duck
nightingale, song bird
noddy, sea fowl
notornis, fowl-like bird
oriole, golden thrush
ortolan, a small bird
osprey, fish hawk
ostrich, African bird
ousel, blackbird
owl, nocturnal bird
parrakeet, small parrot
parrot, tropical bird
partridge, game bird
peacock, bird with handsome plumage
pecker, woodpecker
pelican, large-billed bird
petrel, oceanic bird
pheasant, bird with brilliant plumage
philomel, nightingale
pigeon, bird of the genus Columbæ
plover, a bird
pochard, sea duck
poe-bird, parson-bird
poult, pullet
poultry, domestic fowls
pouter, pigeon
puffin, diving bird
pullet, young hen
puttock, hawk
Raptores, strong-clawed birds
Rasores, birds that scratch for food
raven, bird of the crow species
redbreast, robin
redshank, red-legged sandpiper
redstart, song bird
regent-bird, bird with handsome plumage
reremouse, bat
rhea, ostrich
(Continued on page 340)

FEATHERED LIFE

(Continued)

ricebird, bobolink
rifle-bird, Australian bird
ring-dove, wood-pigeon
ring ousel, thrush-like bird
robin, redbreasted bird
roc, a great bird
roller, species of crow
rook, bird of the crow species
rooster, cock
Royston-crow, hooded crow
ruff, snipe, pigeon
sanderling, wading-bird
sandpiper, species of snipe
scaup, duck
screamer, wading bird
sea-bar, sea-swallow
seagull, gull
sea-pheasant, pin-tailed duck
secretary-bird, a predatory bird
sheldrake, duck

(Continued)

shanghai, a fowl
shrike, butcher-bird
skimmer, marine bird
skylark, a singing bird
smew, duck
snipe, fen-fowl
sparrow, a bird
spoonbill, a wading bird
squab, nestling pigeon
starthroat, hummingbird
stonechat, bird
swallow, migratory bird
swan, web-footed bird
teal, duck
tercel, falcon
tern, gull-like bird
throstle, song-thrush
thrush, song-bird
tiercel, male hawk
tinamou, partridge-like bird
tit, small singing bird
titmouse, small bird
tomtit, titmouse
trumpeter, a pigeon

(Continued)

tumbler, a pigeon
turbit, pigeon
vampire, a bat
vulture, a bird of prey
wagtail, a bird
waxwing, a bird
whattlebird, honey-eating bird
wheather, a bird
whippoorwill, a bird
white-throat, a bird
willet, snipe-like bird
woodcock, snipe-like fowl
woodpecker, a bird
wren, a small bird
wrybill, plover
wryneck, woodpecker-like bird
yucker, flicker-bird
yunx, wryneck
yutu, a bird

ADJECTIVES

avian, pertaining to birds

143D

INSECT LIFE

ant, an insect
ant-lion, an insect
aphid, plant louse
army-worm, larva of a destructive moth
bedbug, a flat insect
bee, insect
bee-moth, moth whose larvæ feeds upon the wax of bees
beetle, insect
bluebottle, a fly
blowfly, fly which deposits its eggs upon flesh
bot, larva of the gadfly
butterfly, a species of insect
centipede, one of the class of Myriapoda
cockroach, an insect
cootie, trench louse
demoiselle, dragon fly
dragon-fly, large fly

(Continued)

ephemera, May-fly
firefly, insect which emits light
fly, insect
gadfly, insect
gallinipper, mosquito
glow-worm, beetle
gnat, insect
grasshopper, locust-like insect
greenfly, plant louse
grig, grasshopper
grub, larva of insect
honey-bee, common hive bee
hook-worm, a parasite
horse-fly, large fly
io, butterfly
insect, one of the articulate animals
larva, insect in the first stage of its metamorphosis after leaving the egg

(Continued)

locust, a winged insect
louse, a parasitic insect
maggot, larva of a fly
microbe, minute organism
milleped, insect with numerous feet
mite, insect
mosquito, an insect
moth, an insect
parasite, form of life that nourishes upon another
pismire, ant
scorpion, a poisonous insect
skipper, cheese bug
spider, insect
tarantula, spider
tick, a parasite
vermin, noxious animals or insects

BREEDING—BEGETTING—
BEGETTERS—SEED   see—

    vs. Destructiveness—Death 130-O
    vs. Barrenness—Impotence 128A

(ASSOCIATIVE 141A)

143E

PLANT LIFE

acacia, a plant
acanthus, a plant
aconite, a plant
acotyledon, a plant
ærophyte, air plant
agave, century plant
air-plant, plant that lives
   in the air
alder, birch-like shrub
alga, division of plants
alkanet, plant used in
   making dye
aloe, common succulent
   plant
amaranth, a plant
anil, indigo plant
anise, a plant
arbor-vitæ, evergreen tree
arnica, an herb
arrow-head, aquatic plant
artichoke, food-plant
ash, a tree
aspen, species of poplar
asphodel, plant of the
   genus Asphodelus
aspic, a plant
aster, genus of flowering
   plant
autumnal, plant that flowers in autumn
azalea, flowering plant
bamboo, tropical giant
   grass
banyan-tree, fig tree
baobab, huge African tree
bachelor's button, a flowering plant
bay, laurel tree
beaver-tree, sweet-bay
beech, a nut-tree
begonia, flowering plant
Bermuda grass, a grass
betony, flowering plant
Bignonia, species of oblong
   plant
birch, a shrub
black-currant, garden plant
bluebell, wild hyacinth
bluebottle, a field plant
blue grass, a grass
bluette, flowering plant
bloom, blossom
blossom, flower of a plant
bo-tree, pippul tree
box, evergreen shrub

(Continued)

bracken, brake fern
brake, fern
bramble, blackberry plant
brome-grass, a grass
broom, shrub bearing
   yellow flowers
buttercup, flowering plant
button, mushroom (young)
cacao, cocoa tree
cactus, a spiny plant
calamus, a palm
calla-lily, a flower
caltrop, a plant with
   prickly fruit
carnation, a flower
carob, evergreen
cassava, tropical plant
cassia, legume
cedar, an evergreen
century-plant, plant sup-
   posed to flower once in
   a hundred years
chickweed, a wild flowering
   plant
chicory, flowering plant
chrysanthemum, a showy
   flower
cleavers, goose grass
cocoa, cocoanut palm
columbine, flower
comfrey, a plant
cornflower, a wild plant
creeper, a plant
crocus, a flower
daisy, a flower
darnel, a grass
deodar, a cedar
dogwood, the cornel
elder, a shrub
evergreen, shrub or tree
everlasting, a flowering
   plant
exogen, plant which in-
   creases year by year by
   new outside layers
fern, a plant
fir, a tree
flag, a plant of the genus
   Iris
flaxglove, a plant
fleabane, a plant
flora, plants of a region
flower, bloom
forget-me-not, a flower
foxtail, a plant or grass

(Continued)

geranium, flowering plant
germander, flowering plant
gillyflower, flowering plant
gladiolus, sword lily
globe-flower, flowering
   plant
gloriosa, a lily-plant
gloxinia, flowering plant
goldenrod, flowering plant
goldilocks, flowering plant
gourd, dipper-shaped fruit
   vine
grass, pasture herbage
groundsel, flowering weed
guava, tropical fruit tree
hackberry, a tree
hackmatack, larch tree
hawkweed, flowering plant
hawthorn, shrub of the
   rose family
hazel, shrub or tree
heartsease, pansy
heartseed, climbing plant
heath, evergreen
heliotrope, flower
hemlock, evergreen
henbane, a poison plant
henna, tropical plant
herb, succulent plant
hickory, nut-bearing tree
holly, a shrub
hollyhock, flowering plant
holm, evergreen oak
honey-locust, bean tree
honeysuckle, flowering
   plant or vine
hyacinth, flower
hydrangea, flowering plant
hydrophyte, water plant
immortelle, everlasting
   flower
indigene, native plant
inflorescence, group of
   flowers rising upon a
   common main axis
ivy, clinging evergreen
jacinth, hyacinth
jasmine, flowering plant
jonquil, flowering plant
kava, a plant
knapweed, flowering plant
larch, coniferous tree
larkspur, flowering plant
laurel, evergreen shrub

(Continued on page 342)

PLANT LIFE

(Continued)

leek, onion-like plant
legume, a plant
lichen, fungus plant
lilac, flower
lily, flowering plant
lin, American linden
linden, flowering tree
lintel, a plant
litchi, fruit tree
lotus, a genus of tree or
  shrubs
love-apple, tomato
love-lies-bleeding, a flower
lupine, a plant
lustwort, the plant sun-
  dew
magnolia, flowering shrub
mahogany, hardwood tree
maidenhair, a fern
mangrove, a fruit tree
maple, sugar tree
martagon, lily plant
mignonette, flowering
  plant
milfoil, a plant
millet, grain plant
mistletoe, evergreen
  parasite
moonwort, fern
mullein, a plant
moss, lichen
myrtle, evergreen shrub
narcissus, flowering plant
nasturtium, flowering
  plant

(Continued)

nyssa, greenish flowering
  dog-wood
oak, species of tree
oleander, flowering shrub
orchid, flowering plant
palm, tropical tree
palmetto, palm tree
pansy, heartsease
passion-flower, flower representing the inflictions
  of Christ at the
  Crucifixion
petunia, flowering plant
phlox, flowering plant
pink, a flower
plant, shrub, etc.
pine, a tree
poinsettia, flowering plant
polyanthus, flowering plant
poplar, a tree
poppy, flowering plant
primrose, flowering plant
rhododendron, genus of
  flowering evergreen
rhubarb, vegetable plant
rose, a flower
rosemary, evergreen shrub
rush, wet-ground plant
sallow, willow tree
salsify, vegetable plant
sapling, young tree
sapodilla, tropical tree
scion, plant
sedge, coarse grass
Sequoia, genus of the
  cypress family

(Continued)

shea, a tropical tree
shrub, woody plant
shrubbery, collection of
  shrubs
snowdrop, a plant
spruce, fir tree
tamarind, tropical tree
tamarisk, flowering tree
tiger-flower, flowering
  plant
tiger-lily, flowering plant
tuberose, flowering plant
tulip, flowering plant
umbel, fan-like
  inflorescence
vegetation, plants
  collectively
violet, a flower
wallflower, flowering plant
walnut, nut tree
watercress, a creeping
  herb
willow, a tree
wintergreen, a berry plant
zamia, a tree

ADJECTIVES

arboraceous, relating to
  the nature of trees
arboreal, as above

BEING

Flora, goddess of flowers

143F

REPTILES

(See listed on 143A)

142F (Continued)

SEED, EGGS, SEMEN, Etc.

(Continued)

myxomycete, organisms
  commonly called slime
  mold; a life with very
  low animal-like charac-
  teristics
neoplasm, newly formed
  tissue
nucleus, generative organ
  as the center of development
ova, plural of ovum
ovoplasm, protoplasm of
  the yolk of an egg
ovule, germ of a plant

(Continued)

which develops the seed
ovum, egg-like form in the
  ovary
protoplasm, viscid sub-
  stance and the basis of
  physical life
protoplast, original germ
protoplasta, original germ
protozoa, lowest division of
  the animal kingdom rep-
  resented by single or
  group cells
roe, spawn of fishes

(Continued)

seed, ovule from which a
  plant may be reproduced
semen, sperm, seed of
  plants
spat, spawn of shellfish
spawn, eggs of fishes, am-
  phibians, mollusks, etc.
sperm, seminal fluid or
  spawn
spore, germinating form

BEING

Ceres, goddess of seedtime

INVENTION—CREATION—AUTHORSHIP

see—

ASSOCIATIVE	
Construction—Manufacture	144B
Breeding—Engendering	141A
Discovery	119F

vs. Destruction 130-O
vs. Stupidity 110B
vs. Barrenness 128A

144A

VERBS

Invent

concoct, devise
contrive, devise, invent
devise, contrive
improvise, devise without preparation
innovate, introduce
invent, contrive, devise

Develop

develop, contrive
evolve, develop
promote, develop

Cause

cause, create
create, originate
found, originate
institute, originate
neologize, originate and introduce new words, phrases, religions, etc.
originate, bring a new order into existence
produce, create
raise, institute

Constitute

constitute, compose, etc.
form, invent
model, form after a model
organize, found

ADJECTIVES

Miscellaneous

creative, inventive
extemporaneous, composing on the spur of the moment

ADJECTIVES (Continued)

extempore, noting unpremeditated action, etc.
formative, creative
imaginative, inventive
impromptu, extempore
ingenious, having inventive ability
inventive, creative
offhanded, impromptu
quixotic, like Quixote, aiming at the establishment of an extravagant ideal.
romantic, pertaining to fictitious compositions, etc.
Utopian, imaginative

NOUNS

Invention

coinage, invention
concoction, invention
creation, invention, origination
improvisation, extemporaneous composition
innovation, invention
invention, origination
inventiveness, originality
neology, invention in religion or language
originality, inventiveness
pregnancy, inventive power

Development

development, act of contriving
formation, development
modeling, creation in plastic materials
organization, development

NOUNS (Continued)

Cause

authorship, origination
causation, origination
cause, authorship
origin, creation
origination, invention

PERSONS

architect, one who develops structural plans
artificer, inventor
artist, creator in art
author, originator, creative writer
authoress, as above (fem.)
beginner, originator
composer, author
creator, originator
deviser, inventor
founder, originator
inventor, originator
modeler, one who models
neologist, inventor in language or religion
organizer, promoter, founder
pioneer, beginner
promoter, organizer
sculptor, carver of statuary
statuary, sculptor, etc.

BEINGS

Brahma, Hindu creator
Creator, God
God, Supreme Being
Hermes, god of invention

144E (Continued)

PRODUCT-ISSUE

(Continued)

consequent, result, effect
crop, produce
distillate, product of distillation
distillation, as above
effect, result
emblements, annual crops
end, outcome
fruit, product
goods, produce, etc.
growth, result

(Continued)

handiwork, product of the hand
invention, thing invented
issue, product
merchandise, wares
mold, cast, that which is molded
outcome, consequence
output, product
precipitate, resultant of precipitation

(Continued)

proceeds, result, product
produce, upshot, result
product, result
production, product
result, product
resultant, result
staple, product of a country, etc.
upshot, outcome
wares, merchandise
work, result of labor
yield, product

PRODUCTION see—	ASSOCIATIVE

vs. Neglect 126B
vs. Destruction ..130-O

Invention 144A
Aid—Assistance 5A
Skill 134B

Breeding—Begetting ..141A
Restoration 136B
Subordinates 46B

144B

VERBS

Produce

fabricate, manufacture
make, fabricate
manufacture, produce
produce, manufacture
yield, produce
weave, fabricate

Function

act, do
do, perform
function, operate
operate, perform
perform, effect
proceed, act

Work

bustle, work
fuss, bustle
hammer, work hard
labor, work
ply, hammer
speed, execute rapidly
toil, work
work, ply

Cultivate

accrete, grow
cultivate, farm
farm, grow agriculturally
grow, cultivate
nurse, cultivate
raise, grow
till, cultivate

Forge, Etc.

carve, form
chisel, carve
contrive, fashion
cast, mold
fashion, mold
forge, fashion
form, forge
mold, fashion
shape, mold

Erect

build, construct
construct, build
erect, construct
rear, build

Promote

cultivate, produce
develop, produce
elaborate, develop
exploit, elaborate
promote, exploit

VERBS (Continued)

Effect

discharge, perform
effect, execute
execute, perform

Miscellaneous

acetify, make into vinegar
braid, weave
carbonize, make carbon
cook, prepare food
decoct, cook
distill, make spirits
generate, produce force
monetize, make money

ADJECTIVES

Busy, Etc.

assiduous, diligent
bustling, busy
busy, active
constant, steadfast
determined, persistent
diligent, steadfast
earnest, sedulous
energetic, bustling
enterprising, busy
indefatigable, constant
industrious, enterprising
persevering, resolute
persistent, resolute
purposeful, steadfast
resolute, purposeful
sedulous, assiduous
steadfast, unflagging
steady, steadfast
unflagging, unwavering
unwavering, steady

Miscellaneous

accretive, growing
agricultural, farming
architectural, masonic, etc.
collaborative, coöperant
constructive, erective
coöperant, doing jointly
coöperative, coöperant
culinary, by cooking
efficacious, productive
efficient, efficacious
erective, constructional
functional, performing
horticultural, agricultural
industrial, productive
institutional, industrial
laborious, industrious
masonic, constructional
productive, constructive

NOUNS

Production

fabrication, manufacture
manufacture, production
production, manufacture

Function

action, operation
faculty, operative agency
function, action
operation, performance

Work

activity, employment
employment, work
exertion, labor
fuss, activity
industry, labor
labor, toil
toil, productive labor
work, toil

Cultivation

agriculture, tillage
cultivation, tillage
farming, agriculture
floriculture, flower growing
horticulture, gardening
husbandry, agriculture
tillage, cultivation

Erection

construction, erection
erection, construction

Promotion

constructiveness, development
development, promotion
elaboration, development
exploitation, development
formation, fabrication
promotion, exploitation

Efficacy

dispatch, performance
efficacy, efficiency
efficiency, effective work
execution, dispatch
performance, action

Miscellaneous

carbonization
carpentry
coinage
distillation
masonry
monetization
navalism
Etc., etc.

PRODUCTION—MANUFACTORIES see—

vs. Destruction 130-O
vs. Neglect—Laxity 126B

ASSOCIATIVE

Invention—Creation 144A
Breeding—Begetting 141A
Aid—Assistance 5A
Remedy—Restoration 136B
Skill—Proficiency 134B
Subordinates 46B

144C

PRODUCTIVE INSTITUTIONS

agency, productive power
apiary, beehives
bakery, place where bread, pastries, etc., are baked
beehive, place where bees make honey
cannery, canning place
creamery, place where butter, cheese, etc., are made
dock, place for constructing ships
establishment, institution
factory, manufactory

(Continued)

farm, agricultural institution
fishery, fishing industry
forge, smithy, workshop
garden, place where plants are cultivated
generator, mechanical producer of electricity
institution, productive establishment
kitchen, cookroom
laboratory, place where scientific products are developed

(Continued)

manufactory, place for the manufacture of goods
mill, manufactory, etc.
oven, cooking device
pharmacy, place where drugs are compounded
plantation, large farm
shop, workplace
smithy, blacksmith shop
still, distillery
stove, cooking device
workhouse, place where convicts work
Etc., etc.

144D

PERSONS

(Workers, Operatives)
Artificer

artificer, artisan
artisan, skilled workman
craftsman, skilled workman
journeyman, skilled workman
operative, artisan or skilled worker
operator, as above
workman, operative, artisan

Builder

architect, one who plans or builds edifices
builder, architect, etc.
constructor, builder
engineer, skilled constructor
erector, builder

Farmer, Etc.

agriculturalist, one who produces farm products
agriculturist, as above
crofter, small farmer
farmer, husbandman
floriculturist, one who cultivates flowers
florist, as above

PERSONS (Continued)

gardener, one who cultivates plants
horticulturist, gardener
husbandman, one who produces by agriculture
planter, farmer

Tailor, Etc.

dressmaker, mantua-maker
mantua-maker, dressmaker
modiste, fashionable dressmaker
seamstress, woman sewer
sempstress, needleworker
tailor, garment maker

Miscellaneous

agent, a producing cause or person
apothecary, one who prepares drugs
baker, bread maker, etc.
blacksmith, a smith
carpenter, artificer in wood
chef, professional cook
confectioner, sweetmeat manufacturer
cook, chef, food preparer
cordwainer, leather worker

PERSONS (Continued)

founder, one who casts metals
functionary, one who discharges some trust
jeweler, maker of jewelry
(B). **jeweller**
lapidary, cutter and setter of jewels
locksmith, lockmaker
mechanic, skilled workman with machinery
machinist, constructor of machines, etc.
manufacturer, one who produces various products
mason, builder in stone
mechanician, maker of machines, parts, etc.
navvy, railway construction laborer
pharmacist, apothecary
potter, pot maker
producer, manufacturer, etc.
pyrotechnist, fireworker
roustabout, ship's laborer
shoemaker, shoeworker
smith, blacksmith
weaver, one who weaves
wheelwright, wheelworker

144E

PRODUCT—ISSUE

aftermath, supplementary result
article, product

artifact, handiwork
cast, product cast
clip, season's shearing

concoction, the concocted
consequence, result
(Continued on page 343)

SEPARATION AND UNITY
SEPARATION—A PARTING FROM UNITY

UNITY, RELATION, ASSEMBLAGE

DIVISION—
SEPARATION   see—
vs. Unity 146A

ASSOCIATIVE

Break—Rupture 145E
Cut—Severance 145F
Crumble, Grind, etc.......145H
Spread—Expansion 145I
Liquefaction 145J
Alone—Single 145K

145A

VERBS
Divide
bisect, divide
deploy, unfold
diverge, divide
divide, separate
halve, divide
intersect, divide
partition, divide
segment, make segments

Separate
detach, disconnect
disconnect, disunite
disengage, disconnect
dissociate, separate
loose, disengage
loosen, disconnect
part, separate
separate, disconnect
sunder, disunite
unbind, unfasten
unclasp, disengage
uncouple, disconnect
unfasten, disengage

Subdivide
branch, be branch-like
ramify, divide branch-like
subdivide, divide a part

Unjoint
disjoin, disconnect
dislocate, disjoin
disunite, disjoin
joint, disjoint
unjoint, disjoint

Disunite
anatomize, dissect
disassemble, dismantle
dismantle, take apart
dissect, anatomize
disunite, disassemble
strip, dismantle

Untangle
disentangle, unravel
unfold, open
unravel, disentangle
untangle, unravel

Distribute
allocate, allot
allot, distribute
apportion, allot
assort, classify
circulate, distribute
dispense, deal out
dispose, distribute
distribute, apportion
parcel, divide
share, divide
sort, assort

VERBS (Continued)
Sift, Etc.
bolt, sift
gin, separate lint from seed
screen, size
sieve, sift
sift, screen
size, sieve
thrash, winnow
winnow, sift

Strain, Etc.
filter, filtrate
filtrate, filter
percolate, filter
strain, separate by straining

Remove
dislodge, displace
displace, dislodge
eliminate, remove
remove, displace

Isolate
isolate, place apart
neutralize, make neutral
quarantine, seclude
seclude, isolate
segregate, isolate
sequester, seclude
single, isolate

Sheath
case, incase
incase, sheath
insulate, isolate
sheath, scabbard
scabbard, sheath

Estrange
alienate, estrange
disaffect, alienate
divorce, separate
estrange, alienate
wean, estrange

Disband
demobilize, disband
disband, demobilize
disorganize, disband

Free
dehisce, open or divide
free, release
open, unfasten
unchain, unfetter
unfetter, free
unlock, open
untie, free

Liberate
discharge, free
emancipate, liberate
enfranchise, set free
liberate, release
manumit, emancipate
release, free

VERBS (Continued)
Reduce, Etc.
analyze, resolve
decompose, resolve
distill, resolve by distilling
eliquate, separate by melting
ferment, decompose
reduce, resolve
resolve, separate parts
secrete, separate (from blood or sap) and make into new matter
skim, separate

ADJECTIVES
Miscellaneous
ablative, noting separation
analytic, resolvent
critical, decisive
dehiscent, parting
disjunctive, disconnecting
distributive, divisional
divisible, noting division
divisional, separative
fermentative, decomposing
fissile, splitting
parting, dividing
resolvable, solvable
resolvent, separative
schismatic, causing schism
separable, divisible
separative, separating

NOUNS
Division
divergence, parting
division, separation
intersection, division
juncture, joint
parting, separation
schism, split in a church

Separation
detachment, disconnection
disconnection, disunion
dislocation, disunion
dissociation, separation
separation, detachment

Distribution
allocation, allotment
allotment, division
assortment, distribution
apportionment, allotment
circulation, distribution
distribution, apportionment
disposal, distribution
disposition, disposal

Isolation
insulation, isolation
isolation, insulation
removal, separation

(Continued on page 348)

NOUNS (Continued)

segregation, separation
separation, isolation

Estrangement
alienation, estrangement
disaffection, alienation
divorce, separation
estrangement, disaffection

Liberation
emancipation, liberation
liberation, release

NOUNS (Continued)

manumission, emancipation
release, liberation

Reduction, Etc.
ablactation, a weaning
analysis, resolution
decomposition, resolution
fermentation, decomposition
percolation, filtration
ramification, subdivision
reduction, analysis

NOUNS (Continued)

resolution, reduction
segmentation, division

ADVERBS, ETC.
apart, off
aside, apart
away, off
from, apart
of, apart from others
off, apart from
out, away

SEPARATIVE MEDIUMS   See—(ASSOCIATIVE 145A)

145B

NOUNS

Border, Etc.
border, boundary
boundary, dividing line
divide, watershed
divort, watershed
horizon, line of observation
intersection, dividing line
line, border
terminator, planetary line between darkness and light
watershed, divide

Partition, Etc.
asbestos, insulator
bar, dividing rail
diaphragm, organic partition
dura mater, organic insulation
fence, dividing structure

NOUNS (Continued)

hedge, fence of bushes
insulation, insulator
insulator, insulation
midriff, diaphragm
neurilemma, sheath
partition, dividing medium
rail, dividing bar
railing, rails
scabbard, sheath
sheath, scabbard
wall, dividing structure

Separators
colander, separating device
filter, strainer
percolator, filter
screen, coarse sieve
separator, separating device
sieve, separating device
strainer, filter
skimmer, separator

NOUNS (Continued)

Resolvents
alkahest, supposed universal solvent
flux, outflow
resolvent, divider
solvent, dissolvent

Miscellaneous
cremator, crematory
crematory, incinerator
crucible, melting pot
deflagrator, combustion device
furnace, closed apparatus for heating
gin, lint separator
incinerator, crematory
oven, baking device
pyre, funeral pile
retort, glass vessel for distilling
stove, heating device
thrasher, grain separator

145C

NOUNS

Separative Space
chap, longitudinal crack
chasm, gorge
chink, small fissure
clearance, dividing space
crack, rupture
cranny, chink
crevasse, fissure

NOUNS (Continued)

crevice, crack
cut, gash
fent, placket
fissure, crack
gap, chasm
gash, cut
gorge, deep ravine
hiatus, chasm

NOUNS (Continued)

laceration, rent
notch, shallow cut
placket, skirt slit
rent, tear
rupture, rent
space, dividing void
tear, rent

145D

NOUNS (See 145H)

Section, Portion, Etc.
annex, part added
atom, elemental particle
branch, subdivision
chapter, division of writing
chip, small section
chunk, lump
component, constituent part

NOUNS (Continued)

composite, component part
constituent, component part
course, portion
department, division
dividend, share
division, part
electron, part of an atom
element, component part

NOUNS (Continued)

fraction, part
fragment, broken part
hunk, large piece
installment, part
lay, share of profits
lamina, plate or scale
lump, small mass
molecule, elemental part
(Continued on page 349)

NOUNS (Continued)

paragraph, division of
  writing
parcel, small part
part, section
particle, small part
partition, section
piece, part

NOUNS (Continued)

portion, part
schist, rock forming part of
  a slab
scrap, fragment
seam, vein
section, portion
segment, section

NOUNS (Continued)

share, portion
slab, piece
slice, section
sliver, splinter
splint, splinter
splinter, sliver
vein, layer of mineral

145E

BREAK—RUPTURE   See—(ASSOCIATIVE 145A)

145E

VERBS

Break, Etc.

breach, break through
break, fracture
burst, rend violently
calve, become detached or
  broken from a glacier
crack, fracture
dash, break by collision
disrupt, part forcibly
dynamite, explode with
  dynamite
explode, burst violently
fly, part violently
fracture, crack

VERBS (Continued)

pick, break with a pick
rupture, burst
shatter, burst
snap, break with a snap

ADJECTIVES

Rupture, Etc.

abrupt, broken short
broken, ruptured
cracked, fractured
disruptive, parting
  violently
dissilient, bursting
explosive, disruptive

ADJECTIVES (Continued)

fractured, ruptured
ruptured, shattered, etc.
shattered, ruptured

NOUNS

Break, Etc.

abruption, disruption
breach, act of breaking
disruption, explosion, etc.
dissilience, a bursting
explosion, a bursting
fracture, a break
rupture, a bursting

ACCESSORIES

NOUNS (Explosives)

Atlas powder
bellite
dunnite
dynamite
guncotton

130K

(Continued)

gunpowder
lyddite
maximite
melinite
powder

(Continued)

pyrocollodion
rendrock
shimose
tonite
trinitrotoluol (T. N. T.)

145F

CUT—SEVERANCE   See—(ASSOCIATIVE 145A)

VERBS

Cut

bisect, cut in two
cut, sever
dissever, cut in two
incise, cut into
slice, cut thin
sunder, sever

Amputate

amputate, cut off
circumcise, cut off prepuce
dehorn, cut off horns
eradicate, root out
excise, amputate
lance, cut
operate, anatomize
remove, cut off
sever, cleave asunder
trepan, operate with a
  trepan

Dissect

anatomize, dissect
carve, cut, as meat

VERBS (Continued)

dismember, amputate, etc.
dissect, anatomize
vivisect, dissect a living
  body

Emasculate

castrate, emasculate
emasculate, castrate

Cleave

cleave, cut, split
rive, split, rend, tear
shiver, splinter, sliver
slit, split
sliver, whittle
splinter, shiver
split, cleave
whittle, sliver

Chop

chisel, cut, carve
chop, cut, hew
hack, chop
hew, hack, chop
slash, cut at random

VERBS (Continued)

Gash

bite, gash with teeth
gash, cut deeply
nick, notch
notch, cut slightly

Tear

lacerate, rend
rend, tear or split
rip, tear
tear, rend

Crop

bob, cut short
clip, cut off
crop, cut off short
hog, cut hair short
mow, cut or reap
reap, cut or crop
shave, cut or pare
shear, cut or clip
snip, cut or clip

(Continued on page 350)

VERBS (Continued)

Trim

manicure, trim fingernails
pare, trim
prune, trim
top, cut off at the top
trim, prune

Bore

bore, cut piercingly
drill, bore
penetrate, pierce
pierce, cut, puncture
perforate, pierce
puncture, pierce
tunnel, penetrate

Dig

dig, excavate
dredge, scoop deeply
excavate, scoop out
grub, dig
pick, dig with a pick
scoop, shovel or dig out
shovel, scoop

Scrape

file, cut with a file
rasp, cut with a rasp
scrape, rub or file

ADJECTIVES

Incisory, Etc.

anatomical, implying dissection
cutting, incisory
dental, biting, etc.
incisive, cutting into
incisory, having cutting qualities
keen, sharp
sectile, cutting, capable of piercing
sectorial, adapted for cutting
sharp, capable of cutting or piercing
trenchant, cutting deeply
penetrating, piercing
piercing, cutting

Rent, Parted

blasted, shivered
cleft, cloven
cloven, divided
cracked, fractured
parted, rendered apart
rent, torn
riven, split
severed, riven
shivered, shattered
split, severed
torn, ruptured

NOUNS

Cut

abscission, severance

NOUNS (Continued)

bisection, a cutting into two parts
chop, a cutting
clip, cut, split, etc.
cut, incision
disseverance, severance
incision, a cutting into
recision, a cutting off
severance, a cleaving asunder
slash, cut
snip, clip

Amputation

amputation, a cutting off
bronchotomy, bronchial incision
Cæsarian operation, operation on the abdomen for effecting childbirth
circumcision, operation on the prepuce
excision, a cutting out
operation, anatomical cutting
trepanning, skull operation

Dissection

anatomy, dissecting art
anatomism, anatomical analysis
dissection, operation, etc.
vivisection, dissection of a living body

Emasculation

castration, emasculation
emasculation, castration

Cleavage

cleavage, a splitting
fission, act of cleaving
rive, a splitting
slit, split
split, rupture

Tear

laceration, rent or tear
rent, a tear
rip, a tear
tear, rent

Miscellaneous

dentition, cutting through of teeth
excavation, a cutting or digging into earth
mowing, cutting of grass, etc.
perforation, a piercing through
puncture, perforation
shave, act of shaving
teething, dentition

CUTTING MEDIUMS

(See cutting weapons 130H)

CUTTING MEDIUMS
(Continued)

Knife, Etc.

fleam, lancet
knife, cutting instrument
lance, surgical instrument
lancet, surgeon's knife
machete, heavy knife
razor, shaving blade
scalpel, surgical knife
skiver, paring tool, as for leather
spud, stout knife

Ax, Etc.

adz, cutting tool
ax, cutting tool
blade, cutting instrument
cleaver, butcher's hatchet
flang, double-pointed pick
hatchet, chopping tool
mattock, cutting pickax
pickax, excavating tool

Auger, Etc.

auger, boring tool
drill, boring tool
gimlet, auger

Saw

bandsaw, endless saw
fret saw, fine-toothed saw
saw, toothed cutting tool
trap, surgical saw

Tooth

fang, long tooth
incisor, cutting tooth
teeth, incisors, etc.
tooth, an incisor, etc.
tusk, pointed tooth

Miscellaneous

awl, piercing tool
broach, awl
chisel, cutting tool
clipper, clipping device
crowbar, entrance lever
cutlery, cutting mediums
excavator, scooping device
file, a rasp
gouge, hollow chisel
graver, cutting tool
hackle, spiked hemp stripper
hoe, tool for cutting weeds, etc.
hook, sickle
jemmy, crowbar
jimmy, jemmy
lever, medium for forcing entrance, expansion, lift, etc.
rasp, a file
ripple, comb for cleaning flax
scissors, small shears
scythe, mowing blade
shear, large scissors
sickle, reaping hook

(Continued on page 351)

CUTTING MEDIUMS
(Continued)

spade, digging tool
trephine, surgical instrument
wedge, pointed medium for forcing a division

PERSONS

anatomist, one who practices anatomy
anatomizer, anatomist
dissector, anatomist

PERSONS (Continued)

surgeon, one who practices surgery
vivisectionist, one who dissects living forms

145G

SKIN—PEEL, ETC.   See—(ASSOCIATIVE 145A)

145G

VERBS

Skin, Peel, Etc.

bark, decorticate
decorticate, remove bark, husks, etc.
excoriate, strip off the skin, flay
flay, skin
hull, peel
husk, remove husk
pare, peel
peel, pare, remove rind
scale, remove scales
scalp, remove scalp
skin, strip off skin
strip, make naked

VERBS (Continued)

Shedding, Etc.

denude, undress
disrobe, undress
divest, make bare
doff, disrobe
exfoliate, shed or scale
mew, shed or molt
molt, shed feathers, hair, etc.
scale, come off in scales
shed, let fall or peel off
undress, divest

ADJECTIVES

(Skin, Peel, Etc.)
deciduous, shedding
(See Verbs)

NOUNS (See Verbs)

Skin, Peel, Etc.

decortication, act of husking or peeling
denudation, act of stripping
divestiture, act of stripping
excoriation, act of stripping off skin
excortication, the stripping off of bark
exfoliation, act of peeling off
molting, act of shedding feathers, hair, skin, etc.

145H

CRUMBLE—GRIND, ETC.   See—(ASSOCIATIVE 145A)

VERBS

Crumble

buck, break small
crush, reduce by crushing
crunch, grind
comminute, make smaller by grinding
crumble, reduce to bits
disintegrate, break up, crumble
granulate, form into grains
grind, reduce by grinding
reduce, break up, powder
scrunch, crunch
stamp, pulverize

Pulverize

atomize, pulverize, etc.
bray, pulverize
calcine, reduce to powder by heat
levigate, reduce to impalpable powder
mill, pulverize
pound, pulverize
powder, pulverize
pulverize, reduce to powder
triturate, pulverize

Harrow, Etc.

harrow, break by harrowing

VERBS (Continued)

hoe, break the soil by hoeing
plow, break by plowing

Fritter, Etc.

chip, cut small
fritter, cut small
hash, chop small
mince, fritter, hash

Chew, Etc.

bite, crush with teeth
champ, chew
chew, crush or grind
gnaw, bite away persistently
masticate, chew
munch, chew
nibble, bite into small bits
ruminate, reduce by chewing

ADJECTIVES

Miscellaneous

arenaceous, sandy
calculous, gritty
comminute, reducing to, or denoting, small particles
crumbled, broken small
dusty, powdered

ADJECTIVES (Continued)

farinaceous, crumbly like meal
flaky, flake-like
frangible, breaking easily
friable, crumbling easily
granular, grain-like
granulated, granular
gritty, grit-like
mealy, fine like meal
sandy, fine like sand

NOUNS (See Verbs)

Crumbling, Etc.

bite, a crushing with teeth
calcination, reduction to powder by heat
comminution, act of grinding smaller
crumbling, a breaking small
disintegration, a breaking into component parts
granulation, formation into fine particles
pulverization, reduction to powder
rumination, chewing
(Continued on page 352)

145I

VERBS

Scatter

bestrew, scatter
distribute, spread
intersperse, scatter among
lay, spread
permeate, spread or pervade
scatter, spread about
sow, scatter, as seed
spray, scatter in fine drops
spread, scatter, extend
sprinkle, scatter in drops
strew, scatter loosely

Suffuse

circumfuse, pour or spread around
dash, suffuse
diffuse, spread abroad
disseminate, diffuse
irrigate, suffuse
pervade, spread throughout
propagate, spread, diffuse
suffuse, overspread, as with vapor, fluid, or color, etc.

Disperse

dispel, dissipate
disperse, dissipate
dissipate, disperse utterly

Expand, Etc.

dilate, expand
distend, expand
expand, disseminate
extend, diffuse
stretch, spread, distend
swell, expand

VERBS (Continued)

Miscellaneous

electroplate, to diffuse and cover with a coat of metal by means of electricity

ADJECTIVES

Miscellaneous

broad, in wide diffusion
diffusible, implying diffusion
diffusive, dispersive
dispersive, diffusive
effusive, diffusive
elastic, stretchy
expansive, expanding far
patent, spreading widely
suant, (follow, seek after) spreading equally over the surface, as water over a level, as culture spreads to man, etc.
suffusive, spreading over as with fluid, etc.
swelling, expanding
swollen, turgid
tumid, distended
turgescent, growing inflated
turgid, distended beyond nature

MEDIUM, ETC.

dilator, one who or that which dilates
disseminator, diffuser
distributer, spreader
spreader, distributor
stretcher, distender
tumor, a swelling, etc.

NOUNS

Scattering

distribution, a spreading
scattering, diffusion
spread, dissemination
sprinkling, a scattering
sprinkle, a sprinkling

Suffusion

affusion, a pouring upon
circumfusion, a pouring or spreading around
diffusion, a pouring or spreading abroad
dissemination, a scattering abroad, as seed, etc.
effusion, diffusion
pervasion, prevalence
prevalence, general diffusion
propagation, diffusion
suffusion, an overspreading as with fluid, color, etc.

Dispersion

dispersion, diffusion
dissipation, a scattering completely

Expansion

dilation, expansion
distension, expansion
elasticity, expansiveness
expansion, a spreading
inflation, swelling
stretch, distension
swelling, turgescence
tumidity, inflation
turgidity, inflation
turgescence, a growing inflated

145H (Continued)

NOUNS (Continued)

trituration, pulverization

Reducing Mediums

atomizer, atomizing device
grinder, grinding device
gristmill, grain mill
harrow, soil-breaking device
mangler, meat chopper
mill, grinding device

NOUNS (Continued)

plow, soil-breaking device
pulverizer, atomizer, etc.
teeth, chewing mediums
tooth, as above (single)

Particles

brash, loose deposits underlying alluvial soil
crumb, small particle
dust, fine particles

NOUNS (Continued)

granule, a small grain
granulose, starch granules
grit, crumbly particles
gravel, coarse sand, etc.
powder, fine particles
pounce, powder
sand, particles of rock
talus, rocks, etc., at the foot of a cliff

LIQUEFACTION—
   VAPORIZATION
       see—
vs. Solidification 145K

ASSOCIATIVE

Spreading 145I
Separation 145A
Crumble—Grind 145H
Cut—Severance 145F

Break—Rupture 145E
Skin—Peel, etc. 145G
Alone—Single 145K
Fire—Burning 131B

145J

VERBS

Liquefy

deliquesce, melt and liquefy by absorbing moisture
dilute, make watery
dissolve, melt, liquefy
flow, run or liquefy
flux, melt, fuse
fuse, melt, liquefy
liquefy, melt, make liquid
melt, liquefy by heat
run, melt
thaw, dissolve, melt

Soften

anneal, make soft or malleable
digest, soften by heat or moisture
macerate, soften by soaking
saturate, soak
soften, render less hard
soak, soften

Vaporize

atomize, reduce to spray
effervesce, to give off bubbles of gas
evaporate, disperse in vapor
exhale, cause to evaporate
vaporize, convert into vapor
volatilize, evaporate

Rarefy

attenuate, rarefy, etc.
rarefy, attenuate
thin, attenuate

Heat

heat, intensify temperature
warm, heat

Boil, Etc.

bake, cook
boil, make bubble with heat
broil, cook
cook, boil, roast, bake
fry, cook
grill, broil
roast, cook
seethe, boil
simmer, boil gently
stew, boil slowly

Burn

burn, reduce to ashes
cremate, incinerate
deflagrate, burn
flame, burn
fire, burn
incinerate, burn to ashes

VERBS (Continued)

parch, scorch
scorch, burn

Moisten

dabble, soften by dipping or sprinkling
foment, apply lotions
imbrue, moisten, soak
moisten, wet, soften

Water

bedew, moisten with dew
water, moisten
wet, moisten

ADJECTIVES

Liquefacient, Etc.

alkalescent, having solvent qualities
attenuant, making thin, diluting
deliquescent, becoming liquid by absorption of moisture
dissoluble, causing, or capable of, solution
dissolvable, dissoluble
effervescent, implying a state of ebullition
fugacious, volatile
fugitive, volatile, effervescent
liquescent, melting or having a tendency to melt
liquefacient, serving to liquefy
resoluble, causing, or capable of, melting
resolutive, solvent
resolvent, causing solution
soluble, causing, or capable of, solution
solvent, resolvent
volatile, evaporating rapidly

Soft

mellow, soft
soft, not hard
soggy, wet, soaked

Rare

rare, thin, tenuous
sparse, tenuous
tenuous, thin, rare
thin, tenuous

Hot

hot, caustic
temperate, moderately warm
torrid, hot

ADJECTIVES (Continued)

warm, mildly hot

Burning

burning, caustic
caustic, burning
crematory, incinerative
fiery, hot
incinerative, reducing to ashes
parching, burning

Gaseous

æriform, gaseous
gaseous, gas-like

Vaporous

brumal, misty
cloudy, vaporous
foggy, vapory
misty, vapory
nebular, gaseous
steaming, vaporous
vaporous, like vapor

Moist

damp, moist
dank, damp
humid, damp, moist
moist, wet

Foamy

foamy, frothy
frothy, foamy
sudsy, like suds

Liquid

fluid, wet, liquid
liquid, fluid
rainy, watery
watery, like water
wet, watery

NOUNS

Liquefaction

deliquescence, liquefaction by the absorption of moisture
dilution, act of making thin or watery
dissolution, act of dissolving or liquefying
flux, fusion
fusion, a melting
liquation, a melting
liquefaction, act of liquefying
thaw, a melting

Vaporization

effervescence, state of ebullition
evaporation, a vaporizing
exhalation, evaporation
(Continued on page 354)

NOUNS (Continued)
vaporization, evaporation
volatilization, a vaporizing

Heat
climate, average temperature
heat, melting or unaccustomed temperature
temperature, degree of heat
warmth, moderate heat

Boil
boil, boiling state
ebullition, a boiling

Burning
burning, combustion
causticity, a burning
combustion, generation of heat by chemical combination
conflagration, great burning
cremation, incineration
fire, a consuming gas
flame, blaze of intense gas
incineration, a burning to ashes

Gas, Etc.
æther, ether
air, atmosphere
atmosphere, æriform fluid surrounding the earth

NOUNS (Continued)
ether, supposed medium filling all space, etc.
gas, æriform substance

Mist, Etc.
cloud, vaporous body
cumulus, wooly cloud
fog, vapor
fogginess, foggy state
haze, fog
mist, vapor
nebula, gaseous matter
nebulosity, nebula
scud, light cloud
smoke, vapor
spray, mist
steam, vapor, exhalation
vapor, mist, steam, gas
(B). vapour

Moisture
bree, moisture
dampness, moisture
humidity, dampness, moisture
humor, moisture
(B). humour
moisture, dampness

Foam
barm, malt foam
foam, spume
froth, foam
frothiness, frothy state

NOUNS (Continued)
lather, froth
spume, froth
suds, soapy water

Liquid
fluid, watery substance
fluidity, fluid-like state
liquid, water, etc.
water, fluid
wet, wetness, rain

Rain
dribble, drizzle
drizzle, light rain
mizzle, drizzle
rain, drops from clouds
serein, fine rain

Miscellaneous
alkahest, universal solvent
attenuation, a thinning by dilution, etc.
exhalation, vapor
fomentation, application of a lotion
rarefaction, a rendering rare or less dense
rarity, thinness
solubility, dissolvability
solution, liquid formed by a solvent
solvent, liquid that dissolves another substance
tenuity, thinness, rareness

NOUNS (Continued)
completeness, entirety
ensemble, whole
entirety, totality
fullness, completeness
gross, entire amount
integral, whole
integer, whole
integrity, completeness
macrocosm, universe
net, nondeductible sum
resume, summary
sum, total
summary, condensed sum
summation, aggregate
total, aggregate
totality, entirety
unit, whole
unity, wholeness
universe, infinite whole
whole, entireness

Unison
collaboration, concurrence
concurrence, unison
harmony, unison
monism, harmony of substance
rapprochement, harmony

NOUNS (Continued)
teamwork, unison
unison, harmony
unanimity, unison

Cluster
bunch, cluster
clump, cluster
cluster, bunch
group, cluster
sheaf, bundle

Bundle
bale, bulky bundle
bundle, group
fascicle, bundle

Package
lot, parcel
pack, bundle
package, bundle
parcel, package
truss, package

Set
batch, set
series, connected things
set, lot
setting, set

NOUNS (Continued)

Coil
coil, folded rope, etc.
roll, convoluted mass
skein, coiled thread

Pile
drift, accumulation
heap, mass
mass, accumulation
pile, mass

Miscellaneous
adherence, attachment
articulation, a joining
bias, uniting seam
concatenation, a linking
concomitance, inseparableness
conjugation, combination
correlation, reciprocal union
inherence, innate, relation
relation, inherent unity
splice, union
syncopation, slurring music
valency, combining power
vinculum, bond of union

DIVISION—	ASSOCIATIVE	
SEPARATION see—	Break—Rupture 145E	Spread—Expansion 145I
	Cut—Severance 145F	Liquefaction 145J
vs. Unity 146A	Crumble—Grind, etc.....145H	Alone—Single 145K

145K

ALONE—SINGLE

VERBS

(See Separation, 145A)

ADJECTIVES

Alone

alone, lone
lone, single
single, alone
sole, single
solitary, single

Heartwhole

divorced, legally parted
heartwhole, unengaged
unengaged, single
unmarried, single
wifeless, single
widowed, bereaved of husband

Free

free, unattached
independent, separate
loose, unattached
neutral, dissociated
partisan, interested apart

Seclusive

cloistral, secluded
exclusive, private
private, secluded
recluse, solitary
reclusive, seclusive
retired, seclusive
secluded, solitary
seclusive, withdrawn
sequestered, secluded
withdrawn, retired

Desolate

bereaved, destitute
desolate, lonely
destitute, alone
lonely, lonesome
lonesome, lonely
orphan, bereaved of parents

Forsaken

abandoned, deserted
deserted, forsaken
forgotten, neglected
forlorn, without help
forsaken, abandoned
lorn, forlorn
marooned, abandoned
neglected, forlorn

Isolated

insular, isolated

ADJECTIVES (Continued)

insulated, placed apart
isolated, insulated
segregated, isolated

Separate

detached, separate
disconnected, loose
disjoined, disconnected
dissociated, separate
separate, apart

Distinct

distinct, separate
individual, singular
particular, separate
peculiar, singular
respective, several
several, separate
singular, isolated
specific, particular

Divergent

bicuspid, double-pointed
bifid, divided into two
bifurcate, forked
bipartite, equally divided
cloven, divided
divergent, branching apart
open, apart
partite, almost divided
ramified, branching
stellate, divided star-like

Fractional

aliquant, fractional
aliquot, part
fractional, part
fragmentary, in parts
part, fractional
partial, in part
sectional, in sections
segmental, in segments

Foreign

extrinsic, foreign
extraneous, extrinsic
foreign, extraneous

Miscellaneous

abstract, considered apart
abstracted, apart
archipelagic, grouped
    separately
atomic, atom-like
dis, meaning separation
incoherent, segmental
molecular, like molecules
sporadic, occurring apart

ADVERBS

Lone, Single, Etc.

aloof, apart
apart, not connected
aside, apart
asunder, apart

ISLAND, ETC.

atoll, ring-like coral
    island
island, water-bordered land
isle, island (poetic)
oasis, fertile desert spot

NOUNS

Solitude, Etc.

bereavement, desolation
celibacy, sexual aloneness
desolation, destitution
destitution, solitude
isolation, insulation
loneliness, desolation
reclusion, solitude
seclusion, reclusion
solitude, loneliness

Miscellaneous

alienage, foreignness
incohesion, separateness
insulation, isolation
neutrality, dissociatedness
partisanship, party interest
recision, retired position
severalty, separateness

PERSONS (Alone, Single)

alien, foreigner
anchoret, hermit
anchorite, anchoret
ascetic, hermit
bachelor, unmarried man
celibate, unmarried person
cloisterer, cloister dweller
eremite, hermit
divorce, a divorced man
divorcee, divorced woman
foreigner, an alien
grass widow, deserted wife
hermit, anchoret
neutral, one dissociated
recluse, hermit
relict, widow
spinster, unmarried woman
widow, husband's survivor
widower, a wife's survivor

UNITY—		ASSOCIATIVE	
COMBINATION	Binding—Adhesion 52B	Accumulation 49E
see—	Solidification 146B	Mixture 146C
vs. Division 145A	Fellowship 146L	Compilation 86
	Sex and Family 146G	Army 147I
	Sex Relations 146H	Visit 19A

146A—UNION—CONNECTION

VERBS

Connect
articulate, join
center, focus
close, unite
combine, unite
conjoin, connect
conjugate, join in pairs
connect, unite
converge, run together
copulate, couple
couple, join
focus, bring (rays) to a
  point
join, connect
piece, join
unify, combine
unite, connect

Adjoin
add, unite with
adjoin, unite
affix, attach
annex, connect
append, attach
attach, connect with
complement, supplement
subjoin, unite with
supervene, add
supplement, add

Collide
clash, collide
collide, crash
coincide, fall together
crash, collide
dash, collide
meet, come together

Fold
contract, wrinkle
crease, fold
fold, crease
knit, contract
wrinkle, crease

Interlock
dovetail, scarf
interlock, dovetail, etc.
scarf, unite by jointing

Associate
adapt, suit
adjust, conform
ally, associate
associate, combine
circumstance, relate
conform, adapt
correlate, relate reciprocally
collocate, place together
fit, adapt

VERBS (Continued)

relate, connect mutually
suit, fit

Involve
implicate, connect with
imply, implicate
involve, implicate

Convolve
convolve, roll together
spin, twist into thread
twine, convolve
wind, encircle upon

Amass
accumulate, amass
aggregate, collect
amass, collect
bank, heap
collect, gather
gather, aggregate
lump, heap
heap, pile
mass, collect
pile, heap

Compound
agglomerate, mass together
commingle, mingle
compound, mix
conglomerate, mass
  coheringly
corporate, incorporate
embody, mingle
mingle, mass
mix, see 146C

Ingraft
bud, graft
graft, unite in growth
ingraft, graft
inoculate, ingraft a bud
inarch, graft together

Incorporate
amalgamate, mass closely
consolidate, embody closely
incorporate, unite closely
integrate, bring together

Cluster
bunch, cluster
bundle, bunch
cluster, bunch
group, cluster

ADJECTIVES

Connecting
articular, joining
connecting, junctional
copulative, uniting

Adjunctive
accessory, supplemental

ADJECTIVES (Continued)

additional, adding
adjunctive, uniting
afferent, forming unity
appurtenant, accessory
complemental, supple-
  mental
cumulative, adding
subordinate, subsidiary
subsidiary, auxiliary
supplemental, additional
supplementary, auxiliary

Associated
associated, allied
allied, related
correlated, related
correlative, relating
  mutually
related, correlated
relative, having relation
relevant, fitting
respective, relative
substantial, essentially
  conforming
together, in union

Involving
apropos, regarding
concerning, implicating
implying, involving
involving, concerning
regarding, concerning
respecting, regarding

Inclusive
comprehensive, inclusive
inclusive, comprehensive
synthetic, inclusive

Inherent
congenital, inherent
constitutional, inherent
fast, inveterate
inalienable, inseparable
indigenous, inherent
indissoluble, inalienable
indivisible, inseparable
inherent, vitally united
innate, inherent
inseparable, inherent
intrinsic, inherent
inveterate, inherent
native, innate

Coexistent
attendant, concomitant
coeval, contemporary
coexistent, contemporary
coincident, meeting
(Continued on page 357)

ADJECTIVES (Continued)

concomitant, belonging
together
contemporaneous, coeval
contemporary, coeval

Convergent
concurrent, meeting
confluent, concurrent
convergent, confluent

Massed
heaped, agglomerate
massed, conglomerate

Compound
agglomerate, heaped up
agglomerative, heaping up
aggregative, combining
composite, compound
compound, mixed
conglomerate, massed
glomerate, conglomerate

United
adnate, growing together
annexed, joined
articulate, united
attendant, connected with
coalescent, growing
together
coherent, connected
component, constituent
composite, combined
concatenated, linked
concentric, concurrent
concurrent, connecting
conjoint, united
conjugate, united in pairs
connate, joined at the base
connected, joined
consistent, held together
constituent, constituting
converged, united in a
point
convolute, rolled together
corporeal, incorporated
imbricated, overlapped
incorporated, united
involute, folded inwards
joined, united
joint, united
linked, concatenated
unanimous, united in
thought
united, connected

Entire
aggregate, whole
all, entire
catholic, entire
complete, entire
each, every
entire, all
every, aggregate
full, entire
gross, whole
holo, prefix (whole)
intact, whole
integral, forming a whole

ADJECTIVES (Continued)

monistic, in infinite unity
net, not subject to
deduction
plenary, entire
unbroken, entire
universal, infinitely whole
whole, entire

Tight
close, fast
fast, tight
firm, closely united
tight, close

Clustered
bunchy, clustered
clustered, bunched
concentrated, together

CONJUNCTION, PREP., ETC.

Combining
and, combining with
at, with
by, at
near, by
on, upon
to, with
toward, leading to
upon, connected with or on
with, combining with

ADVERBS, ETC.

In Addition
again, further
also, besides
besides, moreover
further, besides
furthermore, moreover
more, in addition
moreover, further
too, besides

NOUNS

Connection
commissure, junction
conjuncture, juncture
connection, union
conjunction, connectio
joinder, a joining
junction, union
juncture, junction
union, a joining

Adjunct
accessory, adjunct
accompaniment, accessory
addendum, addition
addition, annexation
adjunct, addition
annexation, addition
appendage, addition
appendix, appendage
attachment, adherence
complement, supplement
increase, addition

NOUNS (Continued)

supervention, following
upon
supplement, addition

Collision
collision, violent meeting
concussion, violent meeting
percussion, collision

Convolution
circumvolution, a rolling
upon
convolution, a rolling
together
involution, an infolding

Convergence
concurrence, confluence
confluence, convergence
convergence, a coming
together

Concentration
centralization, concentration
concentration, centralization
focus, centralized rays

Amassment
accumulation, amassment
aggregation, collection
amassment, accumulation
collection, mass
congeries, collection
cumulation, heap

Compound
agglomeration, accumula-
tion
composition, compound
compound, mixture
conglomeration, accumu-
lation
mixture, compound

Incorporation
coalescence, fusion
consolidation, incorpora-
tion
fusion, union by melting
incorporation, combination
integration, unification
syncretism, unification of
differences
synthesis, combination into
new forms

Union
collation, a bringing
together
collocation, a placing
together
combination, unification
embodiment, unification
inclusion, embodiment
unification, embodiment
union, embodiment

Entireness
aggregate, whole
aggregation, whole
(Continued on page 354)

SOLIDIFICATION—HARDNESS　see—

vs. Liquefaction 145J

146B

VERBS

Solidify

cement, concrete
concrete, coalesce, harden
crystallize, form solid
　crystals
fix, make solid or firm
fossilize, petrify
harden, compress, solidify
indurate, harden
ossify, convert into bone
petrify, form into a stone-
　like hardness
solidify, make solid, harden
vitrify, convert into glass

Embody

amalgamate, unite inti-
　mately
coalesce, grow together
consolidate, solidify
embody, coalesce

Compress

compress, condense
concentrate, condense
condense, compress,
　solidify
pack, press
press, compress

Congest

congest, crowd, surcharge
　with blood
crowd, congest
crush, squeeze
jam, squeeze
squeeze, press together
stuff, pack
wedge, press closely

Freeze

chill, harden by cooling
congeal, harden from cold
cool, condense with cold
freeze, congeal by cold
glaciate, harden by cold or
　make ice
ice, convert into ice
refrigerate, cool or freeze

Coagulate

cake, become solid
clot, coagulate
coagulate, congeal, clot
curdle, coagulate
inspissate, thicken by boil-
　ing and evaporation
set, congeal
thicken, clot

Contract

contract, condense, shrink

VERBS (Continued)

desiccate, dry or harden by
　removing moisture
dry, desiccate
parch, dry, desiccate
shrink, contract
shrivel, contract into a
　wrinkled mass

Constrict

constrict, compress
gripe, constrict painfully

ADJECTIVES

Making Solid

coagulative, congealing
coalescent, growing
　together
compressive, causing to
　compress
concretive, becoming
　concrete
condensable, implying
　condensation
congestive, causing to
　congest
constrictive, compressive
constringent, contracting
contractile, shrinking
freezing, causing
　glaciation
petrifactive, causing or
　tending to petrify
refrigeratory, freezing, as
　foodstuffs

Solid, Etc.

coalesced, solidified by
　growth
concrete, coalesced, hard
consistent, solid
crystallized, made crystal
solid, hard, firm
solidified, made solid
substantial, solid
vitrified, made glass

Coagulated

caked, coagulated
clotted, coagulated
coagulated, thickened
inspissated, condensed by
　evaporation or boiling
jellied, congealed, made
　jelly

Bony

bony, osseous
callous, hardened, etc.
cartilaginous, gristly
gristly, like cartilage

ADJECTIVES (Continued)

osseous, having bone for-
　mation
ossified, made bone

Contracted

contracted, shrunk
desiccated, dried or
　hardened
dry, desiccated
parched, desiccated
seared, hardened
shriveled, shrunken
shrunk, contracted
shrunken, contracted

Condensed

compressed, condensed
condensed, made close
serried, crowded

Congested

close, compact
compact, dense
congested, crowded, close
crowded, dense
dense, close, solid
thick, compact, dense

Hard

firm, solid
hard, solid
hardened, solidified
indurate, hardened
unyielding, solid

Impervious

athermanous, impervious to
　radiant heat
impenetrable, impermeable
imperforate, without holes,
　solid
impermeable, impervious
impervious, impenetrable,
　solid
imporous, without pores,
　solid
incompressible, solid be-
　yond compression

Insoluble

indissoluble, perpetually
　substantial
insoluble, indissoluble

Stony

adamantine, impenetrably
　hard
calculous, stony
flinty, adamantine
lithic, stone-like
stony, stone-like

Fossilized

fossil, petrified
(Continued on page 359)

ADJECTIVES (Continued)

fossiliferous, having fossil
petrified, made stony

Frozen

cold, frigid
congealed, frozen
frappe, chilled with ice
frigid, cold
frosty, frigid, ice-like
frozen, ice-like
glacial, implying a state of iciness
icy, glacial, cold
polar, frigid

Stable

absolute, invariable
fast, fixed
fixed, immovable
immovable, stable
invariable, stable
stable, fixed

NOUNS

Solidification

coalescence, act of growing together
coalition, union of body or mass
consolidation, close unification
crystallization, conversion into crystals
fixation, reduction of a fluid to a solid
fossilization, conversion of organisms into stone-like formation
induration, process of hardening
ossification, conversion of tissue into bone
petrification, fossilization
precipitation, chemical process of solidification
solidification, act of making solid

Compression

compressibility, compression
compression, condensation
condensability, condensation
condensation, a pressing together
concentration, condensation

NOUNS (Continued)

constriction, compression
pressure, compression

Congestion

congestion, crowding, etc.
crush, a squeeze
jam, a crushing
squeeze, compression

Freezing

congelation, freezing
freezing, congelation
refrigeration, a freezing
regelation, freezing together pieces of ice

Coagulation

coagulation, act of coagulating
gelatination, conversion into jelly
gelation, solidification, especially by cooling
inspissation, thickening by boiling and evaporating

Contraction

contractibility, the contracting quality in organic tissues
contractility, condensing or shrinking
contraction, shrinking
desiccation, hardening by the removal of moisture
shrinkage, contraction

Solidifying Mediums

coagulator, that which produces coagulation
coagulant, as above
coagulin, coagulant
cold, cooling or freezing temperature
coldness, as above
compressor, compressing device
condensor, condensing medium
constrictor, compressor
frigeratory, refrigerator
frigidity, freezing temperature
precipitant, precipitating chemical
press, machine for compressing
refrigerator, cooling device
refrigerant, substance that cools or freezes

NOUNS (Continued)

Solids, Etc.

adamant, real or imaginary hard substance
bone, osseous form
callus, hardened skin, etc.
cartilage, gristle
coagulation, congealed clot
coagulum, clot
clot, coagulated mass
concrete, hardened mass
crystal, solid mineral
flint, hard stone
fossil, petrified form
frost, frozen particles
glacier, solid ice floe
gristle, cartilage
hoarfrost, frozen moisture
ice, frozen liquid
icicle, pendent ice
iceberg, high mass of ice
iron, hard metal
knot, hard lump
marble, hard stone
material, substantial matter
matter, material
precipitate, solid substance precipitated
rock, hard mineral
snow, frozen vapor
solid, substantial form
stone, solid mineral
etc., etc.

Solidness

callosity, hardness of the skin, etc.
compactness, closeness
congestion, a crowding
consistence, firmness
consistency, as above
density, solidness
firmness, consistency
hardness, solidity
impenetrability, impermeability
impermeability, imperviousness
imperviousness, impenetrability
imporosity, solidness
iciness, icy state
indissolubility, substantial consistence
insolubility, as above
solidity, solidness
solidness, substantialness

MIXTURE—   **ASSOCIATIVE**
    IMPURITY—   Dirtiness ....129A   Unity 146A
    INFUSION   see—   Stench 123   Sexual Unity 146D
    vs. Purity....138B, 138C   Vileness ....129B   Species 146F

146C

VERBS

Mix

admix, mix
commingle, mix
dilute, admix
exosmose, commingle
intermingle, mix
intermix, mingle
mingle, mix
mix, compound
osmose, admix by osmose
stir, mix

Conglomerate

agglomerate, compound
confound, confuse
confuse, mingle
conglomerate, mingle
hash, chop and mix
jumble, mix
scramble, mix
tangle, interweave

Mass

heap, agglomerate
lump, heap
mass, heap

Combine

alloy, combine by fusion
amalgamate, compound
associate, combine
blend, mix intimately
coalesce, blend, fuse
combine, compound
compound, combine
fuse, blend by melting
gradate, blend gradually
incorporate, blend

Communicate

communicate, infect
impregnate, imbue
imbue, tinge
infect, communicate
infuse, imbue
inoculate, communicate
instil, infuse
leaven, imbue

Taint

stain, imbrue, tinge
taint, infect
tincture, imbue
tinge, stain

Adulterate

adulterate, corrupt
attaint, corrupt
contaminate, pollute
corrupt, contaminate
debase, pervert
debauch, corrupt
defile, contaminate
demoralize, corrupt

VERBS (Continued)

deprave, corrupt
pervert, corrupt
pollute, defile
slur, contaminate
subvert, corrupt
violate, pollute
vitiate, contaminate

Water

dampen, moisten
drench, soak
imbrue, wet
infiltrate, introduce
moisten, infiltrate
saturate, soak
soak, saturate
sprinkle, moisten
steep, imbue
water, wet
wet, imbrue

ADJECTIVES

Mixing

adulterant, corruptive
contaminative, pollutive
infectious, pollutive
miscible, noting mixture
osmotic, noting mixture
perversive, vitiative

Mixed

acetated, mixed with acid
agglomerate, admixed
admixed, mixed
alluvial, in mingled soils
complex, composite
composite, compound
compound, complex
decomposite, compounded
decompound, decomposite
heterogeneous, mixed
indiscriminate, confused
miscellaneous, various
mixed, composite
motley, heterogeneous
promiscuous, confused
sedimentary, residuary
various, mixed

Corrupt

addled, corrupt
adulterated, perverted
bad, not good
befouled, vitiated
contaminated, corrupt
corrupt, impure
debauched, corrupt
defiled, contaminated
foul, impure
impure, corrupt
infected, vitiated

ADJECTIVES (Continued)

muddy, impure
polluted, vitiated
sordid, vile
stagnant, foul
tainted, tinged
tinged, vitiated
turbid, muddy
vile, vitiated
vitiated, defiled

NOUNS

A Mixing

admixture, mixture
amalgamation, a compounding
association, incorporation
atomicity, combining power of atoms
diffusion, a mingling
diosmose, reciprocal mingling of fluids
endosmose, reciprocal mingling of fluids
exosmose, reciprocal mingling
gradation, a blending
incorporation, association
influx, a commingling
mixture, a compounding

Infusion, Etc.

dilution, a weakening by mixture
impregnation, saturation
infection, communication
infiltration, a passing into
infusion, a pouring into
inoculation, infection
saturation, impregnation
taint, corrupting cause
tinge, taint

Mixtures

alloy, mixed metals
alluvium, earthly deposits, mingled soils
amalgam, metallic mixture
blend, mixture
composition, compound
compound, mixture
conglomeration, hotchpotch
half-and-half, half mixture
hash, mixture
heterogeneity, intermixture
hotchpotch, mixture
jumble, confused mass
medley, mixture
miscellanea, mixed collection

(Continued on page 362)

MIXTURE— ASSOCIATIVE
HYBRIDIZATION
see— { Impurity ....146C   Unity—Unification 146A
vs. Purity....138B, 138C   Dirtiness—Dregs ....129A   Vileness—Lowness 129B
                              Stench—Bad Odor 123   Species—Progeny 146F

146D

VERBS

Sexual Mixture

adulterate, corrupt
corrupt, debase
debase, defile
debauch, corrupt
defile, corrupt
deflower, outrage
deprave, corrupt
dishonor, violate
hybridize, cause hybrids
impregnate, make pregnant
outrage, dishonor
pervert, seduce
pollute, corrupt
profane, pollute
prostitute, offer lewdly
ravish, violate
seduce, dishonor
violate, ravish
vitiate, violate

Cohabit

bed, fornicate
cohabit, bed
copulate, cohabit
fornicate, copulate
masturbate, pollute one's
  self sexually
tread, copulate (as birds)
whore, fornicate

ADJECTIVES

Sexual Mixture

adulterous, immoral

ADJECTIVES (Continued)

bawdy, dissolute
carnal, erotic
copulative, intimate
depraved, corrupt
dissolute, immoral
corrupt, depraved
erotic, wanton
immodest, lewd
immoral, wanton
incestuous, immoral
incontinent, wanton
intimate, copulative
lascivious, wanton
lewd, immoral
licentious, lewd
meretricious, wanton
profligate, dissolute
sexual, venereal
unchaste, immoral
venereal, sexual

NOUNS

Pertaining to Sex

adultery, infidelity
amour, illicit love
bawdiness, depravity
carnality, sensuality
concubinage, unmarried
  intimacy
copulation, intimacy
debauchery, immorality
depravity, debauchery
eroticism, sensuality

NOUNS (Continued)

erotomania, eroticism
fornication, copulation
free-love, license
harlotry, prostitution
hetærism, concubinage
immodesty, lewdness
immorality, licentiousness
incest, sex relations with
  blood kin
incontinence, incest
infidelity, adultery
intimacy, sexual inter-
  course
intercourse, copulation
lewdness, licentiousness
liaison, amour
licentiousness, depravity
lubricity, immorality
masturbation, onanism
obliqueness, depravity
onanism, masturbation
profligacy, infidelity
prostitution, whoredom
rape, ravishment
ravishment, rape
sensuality, lewdness
seduction, enticement to
  intimacy
venery, fornication
vice, immorality
whoredom, harlotry

146E

PERSONS

Copulators

adulterer, debauchee
adulteress, as above. (fem.)
carnalist, profligate
concubine, mistress
courtesan, prostitute
copulator, fornicator
debauchee, libertine
demi-mondaine, prostitute
demi-monde, the circle of
  prostitutes

PERSONS (Continued)

Don Juan, libertine
fornicator, carnalist
fornicatress, adulteress
harlot, prostitute
hussy, strumpet
jade, strumpet
libertine, debauchee
lothario, libertine
mistress, concubine
paramour, adulterer

PERSONS (Continued)

prostitute, harlot
quean, low woman
rake, debauchee
ribald, libertine
roué, demi-mondaine
seducer, libertine
strumpet, prostitute
whore, prostitute

146F

PERSONS

**Offspring from Sex-
ual Mixture**

bastard, illegitimate child
creole, native of Spanish
  America and of Euro-
  pean parentage

PERSONS (Continued)

crossbreed, offspring of
  different bloods
cur, mongrel dog
Eurasian, one partly European and partly Asiatic
greaser, Mexican creole
half-blood, cross-breed

PERSONS (Continued)

half-breed, half-blood
half-caste, one who is half
  E. Indian and half European
hybrid, mongrel
love-child, bastard
(Continued on page 367)

SEX AND FAMILY RELATIONS see—

vs. Divorce 145A

ASSOCIATIVE

Sexual Intercourse........146D
Begetting—Breeding ..141A
Alliance—Fellowship ..146K
Combination 146A

Inherence—Soul 137C
Offspring 146F
Ancestry—Line 141G
Mixture 146G

146G

VERBS

Engagement

affiance, betroth
betroth, affiance
engage, espouse
espouse, betroth
promise, betroth

ADJECTIVES

Engaged

affianced, engaged

ADJECTIVES (Continued)

antenuptial, before marriage
betrothed, affianced
engaged, betrothed

PERSONS

Betrothed

affianced, one betrothed
betrothed, affianced
espoused, affianced

PERSONS (Continued)

fiance, betrothed man
fiancee, betrothed woman

NOUNS

Engagement

betrothal, espousal
engagement, betrothal
espousal, betrothal
troth, betrothal

146H

VERBS

Wed, Unite

affiliate, consort
ally, unite
cohabit, live as man and wife
conjugate, unite
consort, mate
couple, unite
join, unite
marry, wed
match, mate
mate, pair
pair, couple
relate, ally
sort, consort
splice, unite
unite, splice
wed, marry
wive, consort

ADJECTIVES

Mated

bigamous, married to two women
bridal, nuptial
conjugal, connubial
connubial, matrimonial
hymeneal, nuptial
marital, matrimonial
marriageable, marital
married, wedded

ADJECTIVES (Continued)

mated, paired
matrimonial, connubial
monandrous, married to one husband
morganatic, denoting the married state of a person of rank with a woman of less degree
nuptial, matrimonial
paired, mated
polyandrous, married to more than one husband at the same time
polygamous, married to more than one wife at the same time
spliced, wedded
wedded, married

NOUNS

Wedlock, Etc.

affinity, mutual bond
alliance, union
bigamy, illegal second marriage
bridal, wedding
cohabitation, coverture
concubinage, a mating without formal marriage
conjugality, married state
coverture, wedlock

NOUNS (Continued)

free-love, promiscuous mating
hetærism, open concubinage
hymen, marriage
marriage, wedlock
matrimony, marriage
mesalliance, misalliance
misalliance, mesalliance
monogamy, marriage with one wife
Mormonism, (formerly) marriage with more than one wife
nuptial, marriage
polyandry, marriage with more than one husband
polygamy, marriage with more than one wife
spousal, marriage
union, wedlock
wedding, marriage
wedlock, wedding

BEING

Demeter, goddess of marriage
Hymen, god of marriage

BLOOD-RELATIONS

Next page

146C (Continued)

NOUNS (Continued)

miscellany, miscellanea
mixture, compound
oddments, miscellanea
variety, intermixture

Corruption

abomination, corruption

NOUNS (Continued)

adulteration, debasement
contamination, corruption
corruption, defilement
debasement, corruption
defilement, contamination
impurity, corruption

NOUNS (Continued)

vileness, impurity
infection, defilement
perversion, corruption
pollution, defilement
stagnation, impurity
stagnancy, impurity

SEX AND FAMILY RELATIONS see—	ASSOCIATIVE

Sexual Intercourse 146D
Begetting—Breeding ..141A
Alliance—Fellowship ..146K
Combine—Unite 146A

Inherence—Soul 137C
Offspring 146F
Ancestry—Line 141G
Mixture 146G

146I

VERBS—(Blood-relation)

affiliate, fix paternity
father, beget offspring
mother, bear offspring
relate, connect by blood
  (See Begetting 141A)

ADJECTIVES

Miscellaneous

akin, related
brotherly, like brothers
clannish, closely related
cognate, congenital
congenital, cognate
consanguineous, related by blood
fraternal, brotherly
filial, related to parents as son or daughter
german, of the same parents
germane, closely related
kindred, related
maternal, having motherly relation
matronly, maternal
paternal, having fatherly relation
patriarchal, implying relation to the founder of a family, etc.
related, allied by blood
relative, related
uterine, noting the relation to one born of the same mother but by a different father

NOUNS

  (See Lineage 141G)
affiliation, relationship
blood, consanguinity
brotherhood, relation of brothers
consanguinity, blood-relationship
correlation, kindred relation
family, relation of parents and children
fraternity, brotherhood
hearth, household
household, family circle
kin, consanguinity
kindred, consanguinity
maternity, relation of a mother
paternity, paternal relationship
relationship, consanguinity

PERSONS

Blood-relations

aunt, sister of a parent
brother, male born of the same parents
brother-german, brother
brother-uterine, brother born of the same mother but different father
cousin, child of one's uncle or aunt
cousin-german, first cousin

PERSONS (Continued)

dad, child's father
father, male parent
foster-brother, brother by nursing but not by birth
grandchild, child of one's son or daughter
granddaughter, daughter of one's son or daughter
grandfather, father of one's father or mother
grandmother, mother of one's father or mother
grandparent, parent of one's parent
grandsire, grandfather
grandson, son of one's son or daughter
kinsman, relative
mother, female parent
nephew, son of a brother or sister
niece, daughter of one's brother or sister
pa, father
papa, father
parent, father or mother
patriarch, founder of a family, etc.
relative, blood-relation
sire, father
sister, female relative born of one's parents
uncle, brother of one's father or mother

146J

PERSONS

Mate, Etc.

bigamist, one who is married to more than one wife
benedict, newly married man
bride, new wife
bridegroom, new husband
consort, husband or wife
couple, man and wife
feme, wife
feme covert, wife
goodman, husband

PERSONS (Continued)

goodwife, wife
groom, bridegroom
husband, married man
mate, consort (male or female)
matron, married woman
mistress, consort
polygamist, man married to more than one wife
queen, wife of a king
spouse, married person
squaw, N. American Indian woman or wife
wife, husband's consort

PERSONS (Continued)

Related by Law

brother-in-law, brother of one's wife or husband
daughter-in-law, wife of a son
father-in-law, father of one's husband or wife
mother-in-law, mother of one's husband or wife
sister-in-law, wife of one's brother
son-in-law, husband of one's daughter

ASSEMBLAGE—
FELLOWSHIP see—

vs. Isolation 145K

ASSOCIATIVE

146K

VERBS

Assemble
aggregate, come together
assemble, meet
centralize, congregate
collect, assemble
concentrate, congregate
congregate, gather
convene, meet, assemble
convoke, convene
foregather, assemble
gather, assemble

Congest
congest, crowd
crowd, mass
fill, crowd
huddle, scrouge
scrouge, crowd
throng, crowd

Flock
flock, assemble
herd, throng
hive, live crowded
horde, be in hordes
mass, horde
swarm, throng

Group
cluster, form in groups
clump, cluster
group, cluster

Mobilize
mobilize, form into active
   unity
muster, assemble
recruit, mobilize
troop, form as troops

Mingle
associate, unite
commingle, mingle
hobnob, associate
intermingle, mingle with
mingle, commingle
mix, mingle
neighbor, be associated

Reunite
reassemble, reunite
rally, reunite
rejoin, reunite
reunite, unite again

Incorporate
amalgamate, become
   mutually blended in
   blood or race
consolidate, unite
incorporate, associate

VERBS (Continued)

merge, consolidate
pool, unite in a pool

Affiliate
affiliate, join with
ally, unite
band, ally
federalize, form a federacy
fraternize, be as brothers
league, combine mutually

Populate
colonize, make a colony
inhabit, populate
people, populate
populate, people

Overtake
catch, overtake
overhaul, come up with
overtake, overhaul

Arrive, Reach
arrive, meet, reach
come, reach, assemble
enter, join with
join, combine
land, arrive, meet
meet, rendezvous
reach, arrive, meet
rendezvous, assemble

Cooperate
accompany, join with
attend, accompany
collaborate, work together
concert, concur
concur, unite, combine
consort, keep company
cooperate, collaborate
team, unite in effort

ADJECTIVES

Associative
associative, uniting in
   relation
companionable, sociable
communistic, associative
confederative, associative
congestive, crowding
congregational, con-
   gregating
convocational, assembling
federative, forming a
   league
sociable, companionable

Assembled
assembled, commingled
centralized, congregated

ADJECTIVES (Continued)

commingled, united
collocated, associated
congregated, assembled
foregathered, assembled
sessional, in session

Congested
congested, crowded
crowded, scrouged
herded, huddled
huddled, crowded
scrouged, thronged
thronged, crowded

Grouped
bunched, clustered
clustered, grouped
grouped, congregated

Banded
banded, allied
clannish, allied
gregarious, living in flocks
serried, joined in rows

Affiliated
affiliated, allied
allied, united
brotherly, fraternal
confederate, leagued
federalized, confederate
federal, united by treaty
federated, united
fraternal, associated
hanseatic, leagued as
   hansetowns
identified, associated
leagued, federated

Consolidated
amalgamated, incorporate
consolidated, incorporate
corporate, incorporated
incorporate, corporated
merged, corporate

Comprehensive
comprehensive, incorporate
ecumenic, universal
international, related
   nationally
universal, comprehensive

Concerted
accompanying, attendant
associated, allied
associate, united
attendant, accompanying
concerted, united
joint, united

(Continued on page 365)

ADJECTIVES (Continued)

Social
fellow, associated
intimate, associated
mutual, intimate
related, associate
social, mutual

NOUNS

Assemblage
aggregation, collection
association, assemblage
assemblage, gathering
attendance, congregation
caucus, political meeting
  for selecting candidates,
  concerting measures, etc.
collection, gathering
colonization, assemblage
  into a colony
confluence, a flocking
  together
convention, caucus
gathering, assemblage
session, assemblage

Congestion
congestion, a crowding
crowding, congestion
thronging, congestion

Reunion
mobilization, act of
  mobilizing
rally, a reuniting for
  fresh effort
reunion, a reassembling

Incorporation
amalgamation, consolidation
consolidation, amalgamation
incorporation, amalgamation
merger, consolidation
partnership, joint interest

Affiliation
affiliation, alliance
alliance, affiliation
communism, associative
  interest
coalition, alliance
confederation, alliance
entente, alliance
federation, a uniting into
  a federal government
union, confederation

Arrival
advent, arrival
arrival, a meeting
meet, meeting
meeting, assemblage

Cooperation
collaboration, team-work
complicity, concert in
  crime

NOUNS (Continued)
cooperation, collaboration
participation, a united
  sharing
team-work, concerted
  interest

Fellowship
bee, social gathering
camp-meeting, gathering
  for religious persons
communion, fellowship
conference, meeting
fellowship, association
intercourse, fellowship
sociableness, fellowship

Rendezvous
assignation, love-meeting
intimacy, close relation
rendezvous, a meeting
resort, rendezvous
tryst, rendezvous

Round-up
drive, annual gathering of
  cattle for branding
rodeo, a round-up
round-up, drive

PERSONS (In Plural Fellowship)

Assemblage
assemblage, gathering
assembly, gathering
concourse, assembly
confluence, a flocking
  together
congeries, gathering
congregation, assembly
convention, assembly
convocation, assembly
gathering, assemblage
gemot, assembly
mote, assembly
session, assemblage

Congestion
conflux, crowd
congestion, press
crowd, body, populace
huddle, crowd
press, dense throng

Multitude
army, host
drove, crowd
herd, crowd
hive, swarm
horde, multitude in common association
host, multitude
mob, riotous crowd
multitude, host
Sabaoth, hosts
swarm, throng
throng, crowd

Detachment
contingent, detachment
corps, division

PERSONS (Continued)
detachment, troops or ships
  detached for a special
  service
division, number of men,
  soldiers, etc.
quota, division

Group
aggregation, collection
bunch, group
cluster, bunch, group
collection, group
covey, flock
flock, congregation
fold, flock
group, assemblage

Body
body, corporation
corps, crew
crew, organized group
gang, clique
pack, gang
squad, small party
team, persons united in a
  purpose

Column
column, file formation
cue, waiting persons in
  file
file, column
line, row
queue, waiting line
row, line of persons

Complement
centumvirate, 100 men
complement, full number
majority, quorum
quorum, competent
  majority

Conclave
cabal, conclave
conclave, assembly within
  locked doors
conference, council
conventicle, religious
  assembly
faction, cabal
synod, religious council

Alliance
affiliation, alliance
alliance, allied group
entente, alliance

League
band, persons in league
combine, ring, cabal
confederacy, league
federation, league
hanse, confederated
  merchants
hanse-town, town confederated with another
league, federation
ring, pugilists, etc.
(Continued on page 366)

PERSONS (Continued)

syndicate, combination of capitalists

Chamber

chamber, political or commercial body
congress, assembly of ambassadors
constituency, the body of electors voting for a member of congress, etc.
council, assembly in consultation
diet, legislative assembly
soviet, council

Association

association, persons associated
company, association
concern, a firm
corporation, organized body
firm, company

Fraternity

brethren, brotherhood
brotherhood, fraternity
chapel, association of journeymen
fraternity, brotherhood
lodge, fraternity
order, lodge
union, persons united in a common interest

PERSONS (Continued)

Club, Guild

circle, coterie
clique, coterie
club, guild
coterie, circle
gild, association
guild, same as gild
sect, guild
set, circle
society, persons united in a common interest

Comradeship

companionship, company
comradeship, companionship
entourage, associates
party, company, etc.

Sorority

sisterhood, sorority
sorority, woman's club

Galaxy

bevy, group, usually women
constellation, assemblage of splendid persons
galaxy, brilliant group
ridotto, joyous assembly

Army

army, organized force
cohort, armed body
muster, troops assembled for inspection

PERSONS (Continued)

posse, improvised body of men (colloq.)
soldiery, army
troop, company, gathering

Populace

colony, body of immigrants or their descendants
community, body politic
neighborhood, associated neighbors
parish, congregation
populace, the masses
population, people of a place

Nation (See 53F)

clan, tribe, association
country, nation
nation, race
people, nation
race, tribe
tribe, race

Miscellaneous

committee, members assigned to some mission
cortege, train of attendants
retinue, cortege
seance, session of spiritualists
troupe, actors, etc.
vestry, parishioners in meeting

146L

PERSONS (In Single Fellowship)

Pal, Partner

buddy, pal
bunky, comrade
chap, fellow associate
chappie, companion
chum, pal
companion, associate
comrade, companion
crony, pal
fellow, companion
friend, adherent, ally
intimate, confidential friend
mate, companion
pal, mate, chum
partner, associate
playmate, pal

Associate

ally, confederate
associate, companion
collaborator, one who is in concerted purpose with another

(Continued)

colleague, fellow member
compeer, associate
confederate, associate
confrere, colleague

Miscellaneous

accomplice, associate in crime
acquaintance, a slight associate
adherent, one who adheres
assemblyman, member of an assembly
attache, member
attendant, companion
brother, member of an associated interest
charge, protege
communist, member of a community
compatriot, brother countryman
consort, mate

(Continued)

constituent, a represented person
contemporary, one living at the same time with another
convert, one who has joined others in opinion, faith, or interest
countryman, compatriot
escort, attendant
friar, brother or member in a monastery
groomsman, attendant to a bridegroom
member, associate
neighbor, member in a neighborhood
proselyte, convert
protege, one who is under the charge of another
visitant, visitor
visitor, one briefly associated with another

146M

PERSONS (Who Unite)

fusionist, one who has joined or fused political parties

(Continued)

incorporator, one who forms corporations

(Continued)

schatchen, matrimonial match-maker

146F (Continued)

PERSONS (Continued)

mestee, offspring of a white and a quadroon

mestizo, offspring of a Spaniard or creole and an Indian

mongrel, hybrid

PERSONS (Continued)

mulatto, offspring of a negro and a white

octoroon, offspring of a white person and a quadroon

PERSONS (Continued)

offspring, young of parents

progeny, offspring

quadroon, offspring of a mulatto and a white

sambo, offspring of a black and a mulatto

QUANTITY—TIME—PLACE—SHAPE
QUANTITY

TIME

PLACE—SPACE

SHAPES

147A NUMERICAL VERBS

Miscellaneous

quarter, divide into four parts
quadrate, divide into quarters
divide, halve
halve, divide into two equal parts
unite, make one
pair, join in couples
couple, unite two
double, duplicate
duplicate, make double
treble, make threefold
triple, treble
cube, raise to the third power
quadruple, increase fourfold
centuple, multiply one hundredfold
multiply, increase a number as many times as there are units in another

ADJECTIVES
(Arabic, Roman, Written)

1—I
a, one, an
an, one, a
alone, sole
another, one more
any, one
anything, aught
aught, one or any part
desolate, solitary
each, one of several
exclusive, sole
first, ordinal of one
isolate, alone
individual, single
lone, solitary
mono, prefix meaning one
none, not one
once, alone
one, single, alone
only, sole, single
respective, separate
separate, individual
single, one
singular, single
sole, single

ADJECTIVES (Continued)

solitary, single, sole
the, singling from others
unique, single, singular
2—II
bi, (prefix) double, two
bifold, double
bifoliate, having two leaves
binary, twofold
both, twofold
couple, two
double, two together
dual, two, twofold
duplex, double, two
second, after the first
twain, two
twice, double
twin, double
two, one and one
twofold, two, double
3—III
ternary, combining three
tertiary, third
third, next after second
three, two and one
threefold, three
treble, triple
triad, triadic
triadic, united in three
tri, (prefix) meaning three
triple, threefold
triplicate, threefold
triune, three in one
4—IV
four, three and one
fourfold, four
fourth, next after three
quad, fourfold
quadruple, fourfold
quarto, fourfold
tetra, (prefix) four
5—V
five, four and one
fivefold, five
fifth, next after four
quinary, containing five
quinque, (prefix) five
quintuple, fivefold
6—VI
hexa, (prefix) six
sex, (prefix) six
six, five and one
sixfold, six
sixth, next after five
senary, denoting six

ADJECTIVES (Continued)

sextuple, sixfold
7—VII
hept, (prefix) seven
seven, six and one
sevenfold, seven
seventh, next after six
septa, (prefix) seven
septuple, sevenfold
8—VIII
eight, seven and one
eightfold, eight
eighth, next after seven
octa, (prefix) eight
octuple, eightfold
9—IX
nine, eight and one
ninefold, nine
ninth, next after eight
10—X
deca, (prefix) ten
decimal, pertaining to ten
decuple, tenfold
ten, nine and one
tenfold, ten
tenth, next after nine
11—XI
hendeca, (prefix) eleven
eleven, ten and one
eleventh, next after ten
12—XII
twelve, eleven and one
duodecimal, reckoning by twelves
duodenary, pertaining to twelve
13—XIII
thirteen, twelve and one
14—XIV
fourteen, thirteen and one
15—XV
fifteen, fourteen and one
16—XVI
sixteen, fifteen and one
17—XVII
seventeen, sixteen and one
18—XVIII
eighteen, seventeen and one
19—XIX
nineteen, eighteen and one
20—XX
twenty, nineteen and one
score, twenty
(Continued on page 370)

ADJECTIVES (Continued)

30—XXX
thirty, twenty and ten
40—XL
forty, thirty and ten
50—L
fifty, forty and ten
quinquagesima, fiftieth
60—LX
sixty, fifty and ten
sexagenary, implying sixty
sexagesimal, as above
70—LXX
seventy, three score and
ten
80—LXXX
eighty, seventy and ten
fourscore, eighty
90—XC
ninety, eighty and ten
100—C
hundred, ten times ten
cental, pertaining to
hundred
centenary, implying a
hundred
centuple, hundredfold
centesimal, hundredth
hecto (prefix), meaning
100
500—D
900—CM
1,000—M
thousand, ten hundred
myriad, ten thousand
milli, (prefix) 1000th
demi, (prefix) half
hemi, (prefix) half
semi, (prefix) half
sesqui, whole and a half

NOUNS

(Arabic, Roman,
Written)
1—I
one, the number one
ace, a unit
digit, numeral denoting
one
integer, a whole, one
monad, a unit
unit, one
2—II
two, sum of two ones
brace, pair
couple, two of a kind
deuce, two, etc.
doublet, pair
duality, combination of
two
pair, couple
twain, two
twin, two
yoke, couple
3—III
three, two and one

NOUNS (Continued)

leash, three creatures of a
kind
tern, group of three
ternary, the number three
tierce, set of three
triangle, three angles
trio, triplet
triad, union of three
triplet, three united
triune, three in one
4—IV
four, three and one
quadruple, a fourfold
number
quartet, four
tetrad, the number four
5—V
five, four and one
cinque, five, as the five on
dice
quinary, five, group of five
quinque, five
quint, a set of five
6—VI
six, five and one
7—VII
seven, six and one
8—VIII
eight, seven and one
9—IX
nine, eight and one
ninefold, nine
ninth, next after eight
10—X
ten, nine and one
decade, group of ten
decimal, fraction based on
the number ten
11—XI
eleven, ten and one
12—XII
twelve, eleven and one
dozen, twelve
duodecimal, sum of twelve
units
13—XIII
thirteen, twelve and one
long-dozen, thirteen
14—XIV
fourteen, thirteen and one
15—XV
fifteen, fourteen and one
16—XVI
sixteen, fifteen and one
17—XVII
seventeen, sixteen and one
18—XVIII
eighteen, seventeen and
one
19—XIX
nineteen, eighteen and one
20—XX
twenty, nineteen and one
score, twenty

NOUNS (Continued)

30—XXX
thirty, twenty and ten
40—XL
forty, thirty and ten
50—L
fifty, forty and ten
60—LX
sixty, fifty and ten
70—LXX
seventy, sixty and ten
80—LXXX
eighty, seventy and ten
90—XC
ninety, eighty and ten
100—C
hundred, ninety and ten
century, hundred
centumvirate, 100 men
hecatomb, sacrifice of 100
bulls
1,000—M
thousand, ten hundred
chiliad, thousand
myriad, ten thousand
million, 1,000 thousand
billion, 1,000 million
trillion, 1,000 billion
quadrillion, 1,000 trillion
quintillion, 1,000 quadrillion
sextillion, 1,000 quintillion
septillion, 1,000 sextillion
octillion, 1,000 septillion
nonillion, 1,000 octillion
decillion, 1,000 nonillion

Fractions

centesimal, hundredth part
decimal, tenths or ten
eighth, half of a fourth
fifth, one of five equal
parts
fourth, quarter
half, one of two equal parts
of a whole
hemi, prefix meaning half
moiety, prefix meaning half
ninth, one of nine equal
parts
quarter, one of four equal
parts of anything
sixteenth, half of an eighth
sixth, one of six equal
parts
seventh, one of seven equal
parts
tenth, one of ten equal
parts
thousandth, one of a thousand equal parts
third, one of three equal
parts
tithe, tenth part

QUANTITY—NUMBERS—
MEASURES, ETC.   see— {   (ASSOCIATIVE 147A)

vs. Unity—Infinity 146A

147B—MONEY (Partial List)

Money Unit	Country	Value in U. S. Money (Variable)
balboa,	Panama	$1.0000
bolivar,	Venezuela	.1930
boliviano,	Bolivia	.3893
Canton,	China	.7985
colon,	Costa Rica	.4653
colon,	Salvador	.5000
cordoba,	Nicaragua	1.0000
crown,	Esthonia	.2680
crown,	Norway	.2680
dollar,	U. S. A.	1.
dollar,	British Honduras	1.
dollar,	Canada	1.
dollar,	Dominican Republic.	1.
dollar,	Liberia	1.
dollar,	Newfoundland	1.
dollar,	Straits Settlement	.5678
dinar,	Jugo-Slavia	.1930
drachma,	Greece	.1930
florin,	Netherlands	.4020
franc,	Belgium	.1930
franc,	France	.1930
franc,	Switzerland	.1930
escudo,	Portugal	1.0805
gourde,	Haiti	.2000
Haikwan,	China	.8149
kran,	Persia	.0899
krona,	Sweden	.2680
krone,	Denmark	.2680
lat,	Latvia	.1930
leu,	Roumania	.1930
lev,	Bulgaria	.1930
libra,	Peru	4.8665
lira,	Italy	.1930
litas,	Lithuania	.1000
mark,	Germany	.2385
markka,	Finland	.0252
milreis,	Brazil	.5462
Nankin,	China	.7925
Pekin,	China	.7804
pengo,	Hungary	.1749
peso,	Argentine Republic	.9608
peso,	Chile	.1217
peso,	Colombia	.9733
peso,	Cuba	1.
peso,	Honduras	.4885
peso,	Mexico	.4985
peso,	Paraguay	.9648
peso,	Philippine Islands	.5000
peso,	Uruguay	1.0342
peseta,	Spain	.1930
piaster,	Indo-China	.5276
piaster,	Turkey	.0440
pound,	Egypt	4.9431
pound sterling,	Great Britain	4.8665
quetzal,	Guatemala	1.
rupee,	India (British)	.33
ruble,	Russia	.5146
schilling,	Austria	.1407

(Continued)

sucre,	Ecuador	.4867
tical,	Siam	.3709
yen,	Japan	.4985
cent,	U. S. A.	.0100
nickel,	U. S. A.	.0500
dime,	U. S. A.	.1000

quarter, half dollar, dollar, eagle, etc.

147C—WEIGHTS

Apothecaries' Weight

grain, 1/20th scruple
scruple, 20 grains
dram, three scruples
ounce, eight drams
pound, 12 ounces

Avoirdupois Weight

dram, 27 11/32 grains
ounce, 16 drams
pound, 16 ounces
quarter, 25 pounds
hundredweight, four quarters
ton, twenty hundredweights
stone, 14 pounds (usually)
cental, 100 pounds
quintal, 100, or 112 pounds

Troy Weight

pennyweight, 24 grains
ounce, 20 pennyweights
pound, 12 ounces
carat, 3.168 Troy grains, 1/24 part pure gold

Metric Weights

milligram, .001 gram or .01 grain
centigram, .01 gram or .15 grain
decigram, .1 gram or 1.54 grain
gram, 15.43 grains troy
decagram, 10 grams or 5.64 drams avdp.
hectogram, 100 grams or 3.52 oz. avdp.
kilogram, 1,000 grams or 2.20 lbs. avdp.
quintal, 50 kilograms or 110.23 lbs. avdp.
millier, 500 kilograms or 1,102.31 lbs. avdp.
tonne, 1,000 kilograms or 2,204.62 lbs. avdp.

147D—PAPER MEASURE

sheet, 1/24 of a quire
quire, 24 sheets
ream, 20 quires
bundle, 2 reams
bale, 10 reams
medium, sheet 24 x 19
pot, sheet 12½ x 15 inches
duodecimo, sheet folded into twelve leaves
twelvemo, duodecimo
quarto, four leaves or sheets

QUANTITY—NUMBERS—
    MEASURES, ETC.   see—⎰

(ASSOCIATIVE 147A)

  vs. Unity—Infinity ....146A ⎱

147E—LINEAR AND SUR- FACE MEASURE

Linear Measure
inch, 1/12 foot
foot, 12 inches
yard, three feet
rod, 5½ yards
furlong, 40 rods
mile, 5,280 feet
league, three miles
pole, 5½ yards
line, 1/12 inch
nail, 2¼ inches
hand, 4 inches
palm, 3 or 4 inches
span, 9 inches
cubit, about 18 inches
ell, 45 inches

Surveyors' Measure
link, 7.92 inches
chain, 100 links
acre, 10 sq. chains

Square Measure
square foot, 144 sq. inches
square yard, 9 sq. feet
square rod, 30¼ sq. yards
acre, 160 sq. rods
sq. mile, 640 acres
section, 640 acres

Mariner's Measure
fathom, 6 feet
cable, 120 fathoms
mile, 7½ cables
statute mile, 5,280 feet
nautical mile, 6,085 feet
knot, nautical mile, 2,025
  yards
furlong, ⅛ mile

Circular Measure
minute, 60 seconds
degree, 60 minutes
right angle, 90 degrees
circle, 360 degrees

(Continued)
Linear Measure
(Metric)
millimeter, .03 inch
centimeter, .39 inch
decimeter, 3.93 inches
meter, 3.28 feet
hectometer, 328.08 feet
kilometer, 1,093.63 yards
myriameter, 6.21 mi.

Superficial Measure
(Metric)
centiare, 1.19 square yards
are, .09 rood
hectare, 2.47 acres

147F—LIQUID & DRY MEASURE

Apothecaries' Fluid Measure
minim, one drop, (roughly)
fluid dram, 60 minims
fluid ounce, 8 fluid drams
pint, 16 fluid ounces
gallon, 8 pints

Liquid Measure
gill, ¼ pint
pint, 4 gills
quart, 2 pints
gallon, 4 quarts
pottle, 4 pints
noggin, 1 gill

Dry Measure
pint, 4 gills
quart, 2 pints
peck, 8 quarts
bushel, 4 pecks

Casks, Barrels, Etc.
firkin, cask of 12 gals.
kilderkin, cask of 18 gals.
barrel, cask of 36 gals.
hogshead, cask of 54 gals.
puncheon, cask of 72 gals.

(Continued)
butt, cask of 110 gals.
leaguer, cask of 164 gals.
pipe, 2 hogsheads
tun, measure of 252 gals.
cade, cask of 500 herrings
chaldron, bu. of coke

Liquid Measure
(Metric)
centiliter, .01 pint
deciliter, .17 pint
liter, 1.76 pint
decaliter, 2.2 gals.
hectoliter, 22. gals.
kiloliter, 220. gals.

147G—SOLID MEASURE

Cubic Measure
cubic foot, 1,728 cu. inches
cu. yard, 27 cu. feet
perch, 24 cu. feet

Wood Measure
cord foot, 16 cu. feet
cord, 8 cord feet

Solid Measure
(Metric)
decistere, 3 cu. feet
stere, 1.31 cu. yards
decastere, 13 cu. yards

147H—TIME MEASURE
second, 1/60 minute
minute, 60 seconds
hour, 60 minutes
day, 24 hours
week, 7 days
month, (roughly) 1/12 year
year, 365 days
leap year, 366 days
century, 100 years
(see Duration of Time
  148H)

147I

VERBS

Miscellaneous

abound, surpass in quantity
flourish, abound
infest, swarm
outnumber, exceed
overflow, abound
swarm, be in great
    numbers
teem, abound

ADJECTIVES

(See Assemblage 146K)

Many

many, numerous
multiplex, manifold
multiple, many
numerous, many

Countless

countless, innumerable
incalculable, countless
innumerable, numberless
legionary, countless
multitudinous, legionary
myriad, innumerable
numberless, countless
swarming, legionary

Abundant

abounding, abundant
abundant, plentiful
affluent, abounding
bountiful, ample
bounteous, plentiful
copious, abundant
extravagant, profuse
exuberant, copious
flourishing, abundant
flowing, copious
full, abounding
galore, in abundance
generous, abundant
lavish, profuse
liberal, abundant
luxuriant, superabundant
manifold, abounding
munificent, bountiful
overflowing, profuse
plenteous, plentiful
plentiful, abundant
profuse, copious
prolific, flourishing
rich, abundant

Limitless

absolute, unlimited
exhaustless, unlimited
illimitable, innumerable
inexhaustible, infinite
infinite, limitless
limitless, inexhaustible

ADJECTIVES (Continued)

unlimited, infinite
utter, absolute

Excessive

beyond, surpassing
exceeding, surpassing
excessive, plethoric
exorbitant, excessive
plethoric, over-full
redundant, superfluous
superabundant, excessive
superfluous, excessive
surpassing, exceeding
teeming, overflowing
very, extreme

Utmost

all, utmost
every, all
extreme, utmost
replete, full
rife, replete
teetotal, utmost
ultra, extreme
utmost, utter

Much

appreciable, considerable
considerable, in large part
much, considerable

Majority

greatest, maximum
major, greater
majority, greater
maximum, most
most, utmost

Additional

additional, more
greater, more
more, greater in amount
other, additional

Ample

ample, abundant
enough, sufficient
plenty, sufficient
sufficient, ample

Entire

complete, entire
entire, whole
universal, whole
whole, universal, infinite

NOUNS

Abundance

abundance, great quantity
affluence, abundance
bounty, abundance
exuberance, profusion
generosity, bounty
incalculability, multiplicity
innumerability, myriad

NOUNS (Continued)

lavishness, exuberance
liberality, lavishness
luxuriance, superabundance
multiplicity, great number
munificence, bounty
plentitude, abundance
plenty, full supply
profusion, abundance

Multitude

army, great number
array, arrayed forces
cloud, multitude
crowd, multitude
drove, crowd
flock, crowd
herd, crowd
hive, swarm
horde, vast multitude
host, army
legion, host
mass, horde
multitude, host
myriad, a great number
Sabaoth, host, army
school, great number
shoal, large numbers (fish)
swarm, multitude
throng, multitude
troop, multitude

Lot, Heap

heap, great mass
lot, a great many
pile, heap
pot, large amount
sight, great number
store, great quantity
stack, large number
world, a great number or
    quantity

Excess

de trop, (too many) a
    person too many and not
    wanted
excess, overplus
exorbitance, excess
glut, superabundance
overabundance, super-
    abundance
plethora, overabundance
redundance, superfluity
repletion, plethora
superabundance, excess
superfluity, repletion
surplus, excess

Majority

majority, larger number
maximum, greater number
    or quantity

LARGE

see—

vs. Small ....147K }

(ASSOCIATIVE 147A)

147J
VERBS
Miscellaneous
enlarge, expand
exceed, surpass
excel, exceed
expand, enlarge
grow, wax, increase
increase, grow
surpass, exceed
wax, grow larger

ADJECTIVES
Huge
enormous, huge
great, huge, large
huge, immense
immense, vast, great
magnitudinous, immense
mammoth, immense
massive, weighty
mighty, huge
prodigious, enormous
stupendous, prodigious
thundering, very great
titanic, huge, enormous
tremendous, magnitudinous

Large
ample, large
big, large, great
capacious, large
large, big, great
sizeable, quite large
spacious, capacious
voluminous, great, large

Boundless
boundless, vast
exceeding, great
immeasurable, interminable
infinite, boundless
interminable, boundless

Extraordinary
extraordinary, remarkable
fabulous, incredible
incredible, miraculous
marvelous, extraordinary
(B). marvellous
miraculous, extraordinary
unparalleled, miraculous

Whopping (slang)
bouncing, strapping
spanking, strapping
strapping, large

ADJECTIVES (Continued)
whopping, unusually large
whacking, whopping

Gigantic
Brobdingnagian, gigantic
colossal, gigantic
cyclopean, colossal
elephantine, huge
Gargantuan, enormous
giant, gigantic
gigantic, colossal
herculean, gigantic, mighty
monstrous, huge, enormous

Corpulent
bloated, puffed, obese
corpulent, bulky, fat
fat, corpulent
gross, corpulent
obese, corpulent
portly, corpulent
squab, bulky
stout, corpulent

Bulky
bulky, large in bulk
burly, bulky, large
hulking, bulky

Wide
broad, wide
expansive, extending
extensive, far-reaching
long, far-reaching
vast, great in extent
wide, spacious

ADVERBS
Large
enormously, exceedingly
excessively, exorbitantly
extremely, immeasurably
indefinitely, infinitely
inordinately, intensely
intensely, monstrously
preeminently,
  preposterously
remarkably, strikingly
superlatively,
  tremendously
unusually, stupendously,
  Etc., etc.

NOUNS
Miscellaneous
amplitude, magnitude
bigness, largeness
breadth, vastness
bulk, mass
bulkiness, great bulk
burliness, largeness
corpulence, obesity
expanse, vast area
fatness, corpulence
grandeur, vastness
greatness, immensity
height, great stature
hugeness, vast size
illimitableness, boundless
  space
immeasurability,
  illimitableness
immenseness, vastness
immensity, magnitude
infinitude, illimitableness
largeness, hugeness
latitude, breadth
magnitude, great size
mass, magnitude
massiveness, hugeness
obesity, excessive
  corpulence
plumpness, fullness
vastness, great extent

BEINGS, ETC.
Miscellaneous
Brobdingnagian, giant
colossus, huge person
Cyclops, Titan
Gargantua, immense giant
giant, man of huge size
Goliath, Philistine giant
jumbo, huge person
leviathan, anything huge
monster, very large animal,
  person or thing
monstrosity, monster
mountain, huge mass, etc.
ogre, man-eating giant
sockdolager, whopper
thumper, something huge
Titan, giant
troll, giant or giantess
whopper, something
  unusually large

147K

VERBS

Miscellaneous
decrease, diminish
diminish, dwindle
dwindle, wane
drop, fall
evanesce, dwindle
fall, lapse
lapse, dwindle
subside, fall
wane, grow less

ADJECTIVES

Small
diminutive, very small
homeopathic, small in quantity
little, small
miniature, very small
petit, small
petty, inconsiderable
small, little, etc.
tiny, very small
wee, tiny

Microscopic
atomic, infinitesimal
infinitesimal, imperceptible
irreducible, infinitesimal
microscopic, infinitesimal
minute, very small
molecular, infinitesimal

Imperceptible
impalpable, inappreciable
imperceptible, too small for perception
inappreciable, inconsequent
intangible, inappreciable

Inconsequent
cheap, inexpensive
inconsequent, of little moment
inconsiderable, paltry
inexpensive, small in value
mere, trifle
negligible, trivial
nugatory, trifling
paltry, insignificant
pusillanimous, small in spirit or courage
puny, petty
slight, unimportant
trifling, inconsequent
trivial, unimportant
unimportant, trifling

Fragmentary
fine, powder-like
fragmentary, broken small
granular, grain-like

Least
least, smallest
minimum, least

ADJECTIVES (Continued)
minor, inconsiderable
smallest, least

Dwarf-like
bantam, diminutive
dumpy, short
dwarf, small
elfin, small like an elf
manikin, dwarf-like
pigmean, dwarf-like
pigmy, small
pony, small
pygmean, dwarf-like

Rare
few, not many
less, smaller
lesser, not greater
rare, scarce
scarce, scant, few

Meager
frugal, meager
insubstantial, inconsequent
meager, scant
mild, moderate
moderate, frugal
scant, wanting a trifle to complete
ungenerous, meager

Remaining
balance, remainder
remaining, residual
residual, remaining
residuary, residual
unexpended, remaining
unexpired, remaining

ADVERBS (not defined)
barely, comparatively, faintly, hardly, imperceptibly, merely, miserably, only, purely, rather, scarcely, simply, slightly, somewhat

NOUNS

Mite, Jot
bit, small quantity
iota, a jot
jot, a little bit
mite, jot
monad, ultimate atom
scintilla, a tiny spark, etc.
spark, speck, scintilla
speck, small particle
suspicion, smallest part
tit, a bit
tittle, iota
tract, mite

Mote, Whit
triviality, unimportance
bagatelle, trifle

NOUNS (Continued)
dab, small soft lump
driblet, trifle
drop, bit of moisture
minim, a drop
modicum, small portion
morsel, small piece
mote, small particle
particle, small part
picayune, trifle
tithe, a small part
tot, anything insignificant
trifle, bit
whit, smallest particle
wisp, a small bunch

Fragment
crumb, fragment
fragment, small piece
fritter, small piece, as of meat
screed, fragment
sliver, small splinter
snip, piece snipped by scissors

Pittance
dole, petty allowance
groat, trifling sum
pittance, small allowance
pocket, small quantity

Remainder
balance, remainder (coloq.)
leavings, remains
remainder, residue
remains, leavings
remnant, remainder
residuum, residue
residue, remainder

Miscellaneous
aught, something small or great
insignificance, small importance
minimum, less than the maximum
minority, less than the majority
minuteness, smallness
nil, nothingness
nonage, minority
nonentity, a mere nothing
nullity, nil
paltriness, insignificance
paucity, smallness of number or quantity
pettiness, smallness
rareness, scarceness
rarity, scarcity
scantiness, scarcity
scarceness, rareness
scarcity, rarity

(Continued on page 377)

147L

VERBS

Miscellaneous

account, give a reckoning
average, proportion
calculate, enumerate
compute, enumerate
count, sum up
enumerate, score
equalize, equate
equate, reduce to an average
figure, calculate
number, enumerate
numerate, reckon
proportion, relate divisionally
quantify, account
reckon, compute
score, keep account
sum, account

ADJECTIVES

Arithmetical

algebraic, implying quantity or number expressed in terms of algebra
arithmetical, pertaining to quantity or numbers
logarithmic, implying number or quantity in logarithm
mathematical, pertaining to the science of quantities
etc., etc.

Several

several, sundry
sundry, indefinite in number, etc.
various, several

Equal

commensurate, equal
concomitant, implying suitable relationship or value
equal, having the same value, etc.
equivalent, having equal value
proportional, same in quantity, numbers, etc.
proportionate, divisionally related
tantamount, equivalent

Miscellaneous

dimensional, noting size
finite, implying limit
marginal, implying amount reserved
numerary, pertaining to number
numerical, arithmetical

ADJECTIVES (Continued)

plural, more than one
quantitative, implying quantity
somewhat (adv.), more or less
such, implying type, quality or quantity
the, implying type, quality, or quantity

NOUNS

Quantity

bag, a certain quantity
batch, a quantity
deal, quantity, etc.
dose, a measured quantity of medicine
quantity, indefinite extent, measure, etc.
some, a quantity
wad, small mass or quantity

Sum

amount, sum
complement, full quantity
figure, number
number, numerical quantity
outcome, result
product, quantity resulting from multiplication
quantum, amount
result, value
slump, gross amount or mass
strength, number or value
sum, result
summation, sum or result
total, sum
whole, total

Portion

allotment, amount allotted
allowance, sum granted
component, constituent
constituent, component part
part, partial quantity
piece, part
portion, part
share, part
something, part or portion

Value

charge, price
cost, value
fare, passage-money
price, sum, amount
value, price, sum

Equality

equality, equalness of value, etc., equivalence

NOUNS (Continued)

equation, equality
equivalence, equality
equivalent, an equal value, etc.
proportion, relative magnitude, number, or degree
proportional, any quantity or number proportional to another
rate, ratio
ratio, proportion
tie, equality in score, etc.

Par, Etc.

average, medium
mean, middle quantity or value
medium, mean
par, nominal value
parity, par

Reserve

margin, amount reserved
reserve, margin
store, reserve

Size

dimension, size, measure
measure, size, amount
size, dimension

Catch

catch, fare
fare, quantity of fish taken by a smack
take, quantity received or caught, especially fish

Set, Series

series, number of things in succeeding order
set, a number of things
setting, set

Task

job, amount of work
task, job, amount of work
work, task

Mathematics

algebra, mathematical branch
arithmetic, science of computation
geometry, mathematical branch
mathematics, arithmetic
etc., etc.

Arithmetical Terms

aliquant, part of a number which does not divide it without a remainder
aliquot, part of a number which will divide it equally

(Continued on page 377)

NOUNS (Continued)

coefficient, known quantity used as a multiplier to an unknown quantity

decimal, quantity, representing a decimal fraction

denominator, the part of a fraction below the line which shows into how many equal parts the unit is divided

discount, amount allowed for prompt payment

dividend, number or quantity to be divided

divisor, the number by which another is divided

factor, one of two or more quantities used in multiplication

fraction, quantity representing the part of a whole

logarithm, exponent of a power to which a fixed number must be raised in order to produce a given number

multiple, a divisible quantity

multiplicand, number to be multiplied

multiplier, multiplying number

147L (Continued)

NOUNS (Continued)

numeral, symbol expressing a number

numerator, number which indicates how many parts of a unit are taken

percentage, portion by the hundred, etc.

quotient, quantity resulting from the division of one number by another

subtrahend, quantity to be subtracted from another

Etc., etc.

Distance, Length

caliber, cylindrical diameter

cast, distance thrown

circumference, boundary of a circle

diameter, distance through a circular middle

distance, reach

drop, fall

extent, distance

fall, distance of a fall

girth, circumference

latitude, scope or extent

magnitude, size

mileage, length in miles

pace, a step

pitch, distance between gear teeth

reach, extent

range, firing distance

NOUNS (Continued)

size, comparative magnitude or bulk

step, pace, small distance

sweep, range, extent

throw, distance cast

Degree, Rank

circumstance, situation

condition, circumstance

degree, relative rank, station, or importance

estate, position or quality

grade, degree

quality, rank

position, standing

rank, position

reputation, standing

situation, status

standing, rank

state, condition

status, rank

status quo, previous rank or position

Miscellaneous

content, quantity contained

cypher, the symbol 0

finiteness, size, quantity

purse, sum of money

quantivalence, worth of chemical affinity

quota, sum or money assigned

quotum, quota

stature, natural height or dimension

147K (Continued)

NOUNS (Continued)

shade, a hair's breadth

superficiality, slight knowledge, etc.

triviality, unimportance

BEINGS, ETC.

elf, dwarf

dwarf, being or plant below average size

BEINGS, ETC. (Continued)

dot, diminutive child

insect, something minute and contemptible

lilliputian, diminutive person

midget, tiny being

pigmy, person belonging to one of the small races

BEINGS, ETC. (Continued)

pigwiggen, diminutive person or thing

pygmy, pigmy

runt, dwarfed animal

shrimp, insignificant person or thing

titmouse, small bird

tomtit, titmouse

148A (Continued)

PERSONS (Single)
(Continued)

antediluvian, one who lived before the flood

preadamite, one who existed before Adam

PERSONS (Plural)

aborigines, first inhabitants

ancestors, forefathers

ancients, people of a past age

forefathers, people of a past age

BEINGS

Norna, one of the fates— Past, Present, Future

TIME PRECEDING see—

vs. Following 148B

148A

VERBS

Miscellaneous
antedate, date earlier
date, mark with a date
precede, occur or exist before
was, implying time past
were, as above (Plural)

ADJECTIVES

Preceding
antecedent, preceding
anterior, prior, earlier
before, preceding
bygone, former
early, near the beginning
former, preceding
olden, bygone
past, former
pluperfect, expressing past time prior to some other past time
preceding, time before
previous, former
preterit, belonging to the past
prior, former
quondam, former
remote, bygone (also future)

Old, Ancient
aged, ancient
ancient, having great age
antiquarian, ancient
antiquated, ancient, old
antique, ancient
archaic, antiquated
immemorial, ancient
mediæval, medieval
medieval, pertaining to the Middle Ages
old, aged
oldish, old
paleo, noting the earliest division of the stone age
pristine, pertaining to earliest time
quaint, antique

Original
aboriginal, primitive
beginning, original
first, beginning
fundamental, primary
original, first in order
primal, first

ADJECTIVES (Continued)
primary, original
primeval, primitive
primitive, original
prime, first in time, rank
primordial, original

Before What Follows
antemeridian, preceding noon, abbreviated A.M.
antenatal, before birth
antenuptial, before marriage
antepaschal, before Easter
anteprandial, before dinner
matin, pertaining to morning
matutinal, pertaining to the morning, early
untimely, happening before the usual time
yesterday, the day before to-day

Hoar, Etc.
fossil, ancient
hoar, ancient, grey with age
musty, ancient
stale, old

Prehistoric
antediluvian, noting time before the flood
antemundane, before the beginning of the world
preadamite, before Adam
prehistoric, preceding the recording of events

Historical
historical, relative to the past
legendary, traditional
traditional, referring to transmitted knowledge

ADVERBS
ago, in time gone by
before, previously
beforehand, before
earlier, more early
ere, before this time
since, before this
sooner, earlier
ultimo, in the preceding month
yore, long ago

PRETERIT VERBS
been
did
had
has
have
was
were

NOUNS

Precedence
antecedence, priority
anteriority, priority
precedence, anteriority
priority, precedence in time
seniority, priority in age

Origin
birth, origin
beginning, origin
origin, primary source

Dawn, Etc.
cockcrow, early morning
dawn, first period, morning
daybreak, dawn
dayspring, dawn
morning, early day
sunrise, beginning of the day or sunshine

Legend
history, past
legend, tradition
tradition, past knowledge

Miscellaneous
antedate, an earlier date
antiquity, great age
distance, remote past
eve, period before an event
past, former time
primitiveness, state of being original
primogeniture, seniority of birth
primary, that which is first in time

THINGS
antique, something of great age

PERSONS (Single)
aborigine, an original inhabitant
ancestor, forefather
ancient, one who lived in ancient times

(Continued on page 377)

148B

VERBS

Miscellaneous

abide, await
await, wait
belate, postpone
bide, wait
defer, postpone
delay, postpone
ensue, follow
eventuate, follow
follow, succeed in time
postdate, date later than the present
postpone, delay
procrastinate, defer
recur, follow again
retard, belate
succeed, take place after
wait, defer

ADJECTIVES

Future

after, following
coming, future
early, later
following, succeeding
future, in the hereafter
later, future
next, succeeding
posterior, subsequent
secondary, second in sequence
sequent, succeeding
subordinate, secondary
succeeding, subsequent
subsequent, following in order of time

Remote

dim, remote
distant, remote
far, distant
remote, implying distant future or past

Ultimate

eventual, ultimately
final, ultimate
last, following all
ultimate, last in sequence
utmost, last

Successive

consecutive, successive

ADJECTIVES (Continued)

recurrent, recurring
recurring, following again
subalternate, successive
successive, following in succession

Delayed

behindhand, late
belated, delayed
delayed, late
late, following usual time
tardy, late

Following

mesozoic, noting the secondary age of reptiles
postdiluvial, after the flood
postglacial, following the glacial epoch
posthumous, born after the death of the father
post-meridian, following noon, P.M.

ADVERBS

Afterward

afterward, subsequently
hereinafter, subsequently
since, after a past time
then, after
thence, from that time
thereafter, afterward

Soon

directly, presently
immediately, presently
presently, shortly
shortly, presently
soon, shortly

FUTURE AND PROGRESSIVE VERBS

am
are
does
shall
will
would

NOUNS

Future

beyond, the great future

NOUNS (Continued)

future, time following the present
futurity, future
hereafter, future
posterity, future issue

Remoteness

distance, remote future
infinity, infinite future
remoteness, distant future

Succession

advent, occurrence, or arrival after absence
consequence, sequence
course, regular sequence
eventuality, consequence
recurrence, repeated succession
sequence, succession
subsequence, succession
succession, a following in time or order

Delay

deferment, postponement
delay, postponement
postponement, a postponing
procrastination, deferment
prolongation, delay
protraction, delay

Eve, Morrow

afternoon, time following noon
dusk, twilight
eve, evening
evening, time following the close of day
eventide, evening
gloaming, twilight
morrow, to-morrow
night, time following day
sundown, sunset
sunset, time after sunshine
to-morrow, morrow
to-night, night following the present day
twilight, time after sunset

PERSONS

procrastinator, one who delays, etc.
protractor, procrastinator

LONG TIME

see—

vs. Short Time 148D

(ASSOCIATIVE 148A)

148C

VERBS

(See Continuation 11A)

ADJECTIVES

Eternal

ceaseless, continued
deathless, immortal
enduring, perpetual
eternal, without beginning
  or end
everlasting, perpetual
immortal, everlasting
infinite, interminable
interminable, perpetual
permanent, enduring
perpetual, everlasting
unceasing, perpetual

ADJECTIVES (Continued)

Secular, Etc.

aperiodic, continuing without period
chronic, enduring long
indefinite, aperiodic
indeterminate, indefinite
lasting, enduring
long, lasting
mundane, world-old
secular, in the course of
  ages
termless, indeterminable
temporal, secular

NOUNS

Miscellaneous

æon, an immense duration

NOUNS (Continued)

age, time of life or being
eternity, infinite time
immortality, life-everlast-
  ing
infinitude, infinity
infinity, limitless duration
life, age, time of being
longevity, great age
permanence, perpetuity
perpetuation, permanence
perpetuity, everlastingness

ADVERBS

ay, forever
(B). aye
forever, eternally

SHORT TIME

see—

vs. Long Time 148C

(ASSOCIATIVE 148A)

148D

VERBS

(See Haste 9)

ADJECTIVES

Brief

brief, short in time
momentary, in the smallest
  possible time
short, brief
temporary, brief

Swift

fast, rapid
fleeting, transient
flying, transitory
hasty, quick
quick, sudden
rapid, quick
swift, quick

Immediate

abrupt, instantaneous
immediate, without in-
  terval

ADJECTIVES (Continued)

instant, immediate
instantaneous, momentary
sudden, immediate

Punctual

exact, punctual
forward, prompt
prompt, immediate
punctual, prompt
ready, prompt

Transitory

ephemeral, transitory
fugacious, transient
fugitive, not permanent
temporal, transient
transient, transitory
transitory, existing for a
  short time

NOUNS

Moment, Etc.

flash, trice

NOUNS (Continued)

gliff, moment
jiffy, moment
instant, flash, twinkle
minute, short time
moment, smallest possible
  time
second, a short time
trice, an instant

Briefness

briefness, expedition
expedition, promptness
immediateness, promptness
instantaneousness, immediateness
promptitude, instantane-
  ousness
punctuality, promptness
temporariness, short duration
transitoriness, briefness

TIME PRESENT see—
vs. Time Future ....148B { **(ASSOCIATIVE 148A)**

148E

VERBS
dawn, appear new or present

ADJECTIVES

Immediate
immediate, present
instantaneous, immediate
prompt, immediate
punctual, prompt
present, current
exact, punctual

Simultaneous
coeval, contemporaneous
coincident, occurring at the same time
concurrent, current
contemporaneous, implying the same time of occurrence or presence
current, concurrent
incident, attending
incidental, as above
isochronous, happening in equal times
simultaneous, occurring or present at the same time

ADJECTIVES (Continued)
synchronal, happening at the same time, concurrent
synchronous, as above

Timely
opportune, timely
seasonable, timely
timely, opportune

Modern
current, modern
fresh, new, modern
green, new, fresh
late, recent
modern, new, present, recent
neo, prefix meaning new
neoteric, recent, late
new, modern
recent, modern, new
young, fresh

ADVERBS
during, (prep.) in the time of

ADVERBS (Continued)
forthwith, immediately
here, at present
immediately, now
now, at present
still, yet
this, now
to-day, on the present day
yet, as soon as now

NOUNS

Miscellaneous
blood, freshness
freshness, newness
modernism, present time or state
newness, recency
present, time now here
recency, comparative newness
to-day, present day

BEING
Norna, one of the fates—Past, Present, Future

148F—TIME INDICATORS
chronograph, instrument for recording minute intervals of time
chronometer, instrument for measuring time with extreme accuracy
chronoscope, instrument for measuring time of velocity in projectiles

(Continued)
clock, time-piece
dial, sundial
gnomon, the part of a dial which by its shadow, shows the time
horologue, instrument for indicating hours
horometer, clock-like instrument

(Continued)
hourglass, instrument for indicating the hour by running sand
sundial, indicator for showing time of the sun's shadow
time-piece, time indicator
watch, pocket time-piece

148G—NOUNS—CHRONICLES
annals, record of events in sequence of time
anachronism, chronological error
almanac, chronological record of seasons, tides, planting time, etc.
calendar, register of days, months, years, events, etc.
chronicle, annals
diary, register of daily or dated events, etc.
ephemeris, almanac showing daily positions of sun, moon, and planets
horology, art of determining time

DURATION (Definite)

see—

(ASSOCIATIVE 148A)

vs. Duration (Indefinite) 148I

148H

VERBS
(See Continuation 11A)

ADJECTIVES
Miscellaneous

centenarian, aged or lasting 100 years
centenary, lasting 100 years
centennial, aged 100 years
diurnal, lasting a day
decennial, lasting ten years
ephemeral, diurnal
hebdomadal, composed of seven days
hibernal, lasting through winter
horal, lasting an hour
millennial, lasting a thousand years
octogenarian, aged eighty years
perennial, lasting through the year
quadrennial, comprising four years
quinquagenarian, aged fifty years
quinquennial, lasting fifty years
septenary, composed of seven years

ADJECTIVES (Continued)

septennial, lasting seven years
septuagenary, aged 70 years
septuagesima, septuagenary
sexagenary, aged 60 years
tercentenary, lasting 300 years
triennial, lasting three years
undecennial, lasting 11 years

NOUNS
Miscellaneous

advent, period including the four Sundays before Christmas
bicentenary, 200 years
bissextile, leap-year
centennial, centennium
centennium, century
century, 100 years
day, 24 hours
decade, 10 years
fortnight, 14 days
hour, 60 minutes
leap-year, 366 days
lunar-month, 29½ days
lunation, time from one new moon to another

NOUNS (Continued)

lunar-year, 354 1/3 days
majority, legal age of 21 years
millennium, 1,000 years
minute, 60 seconds
month, loosely four weeks, one of the twelve divisions of the year
quinquagesima, 50 days
quinquennial, 5 years
quinquennium, 5 years
second, 1/60 minute
semester, six months
sennight, a week
septennate, seven years
week, seven days
year, 365 days

PERSONS, Etc.

sexagenarian, one 60 years old
septuagenarian, one 70 years old
octogenarian, one 80 years old
nonagenarian, one 90 years old
centenarian, one 100 years old
Methuselah, son of Enoch, who lived 969 years

DURATION (Indefinite)

see—

(ASSOCIATIVE 148A)

vs. Duration (Definite) 148H

148I

VERBS
(See 148B)

ADJECTIVES

autumnal, noting the season between summer and winter
finite, limited
limited, finite

ADVERBS, ETC.

awhile, for a period
during, (prep.) in the time of
till, (prep.) until
to, (prep.) till
until, (prep.) till

NOUNS
Duration

duration, continuance of time
lapse, period of passing time

NOUNS (Continued)

period, interval of time
space, period, duration
span, period of time
spell, space of time
term, period of time
time, period of duration
while, spell, duration
Era, Epoch
Christian era, time reckoned from the birth of Christ
Dark Age, period between 600 to 1300 A. D.
dynasty, period of reign
epoch, interval of time or series of years, memorable for extraordinary events
era, period of years dating from an event or fixed point
ice age, glacial epoch
reign, period of rule

NOUNS (Continued)
Periodicity

bout, a round
cycle, period of revolution recurring in like order
periodicity, interval
revolution, cycle
rotation, complete period, or regular recurrence
round, time of a recurrence, or one of a series of activities
Rhythm
rhythm, timed regularity
tempo, rate of rhythm
Continuance
continuance, time of stay
prolongation, period continued
protraction, prolongation
stay, time of continuance
Suspension
abeyance, suspension
(Continued on page 383)

LIFE (Indefinite)   see—   (ASSOCIATIVE 148A)

vs. Duration (Definite) 148H

148J

VERBS
age, grow old

ADJECTIVES
Infantile
babyish, infantile
childish, infantile
infantile, in the period of
infancy
Juvenile
adolescent, implying the
period between puberty
and maturity
callow, unfledged
juvenile, young
unfeathered, young
unfledged, callow
young, recently born
youthful, juvenile
Mature
adult, grown
grown, mature
mature, ripe in age
pubescent, mature
Senior
aged, very old
elder, older
elderly, somewhat old
old, aged
older, having more age
oldest, older than all
oldish, not young
senior, elder

NOUNS
Infancy
babyhood, infancy
childhood, infancy
infancy, period of child-
hood
Juvenility
adolescence, period be-
tween puberty and ma-
turity
boyhood, period of mascu-
line youth
girlhood, period of
feminine youth
juniority, period of
younger state

NOUNS (Continued)
juvenility, youth
teens, years of one's age
ending in teen
youth, early life
Maturity
maturity, period of full
growth
prime, period of vigor
pubescence, age at
maturity
seniority, period greater
than juniority
Seniority
age, period of life, etc.
generation, the period of a
single succession or na-
tural descent
life, period between birth
and death
longevity, length of life
secularity, period of
present life

PERSONS
Infant
babe, infant
baby, infant
bambino, baby
infant, young child
papoose, infant (N. American Indian)
pickaninny, negro child
Child
bairn, child (Scotch)
bantling, young child
brat, child
chick, child
chit, child
child, infant
kid, child
Youth
boy, male child
bub, boy
gossoon, lad
junior, younger person
juvenile, youth
lad, youth

PERSONS (Continued)
stripling, youth
shaver, lad
urchin, small boy
yonker, stripling
youngster, lad
youth, boy
Lass
damsel, maiden
girl, female child
lass, girl
maid, girl
maiden, lass, girl
Adult
adult, mature person
elder, a senior
gaffer, old man
greybeard, old man
Methuselah, very old man
patriarch, old man
senior, one who is older
than another

ANIMALS
Indefinite Age
calf, young of a cow,
whale, and other animals
chick, young chicken
chicken, young fowl
colt, young of the horse
cub, whelp, etc.
ephemera, that which
exists but for a day
fledgling, bird just fledged
foal, young of an ass, or
camel
hinny, offspring of she-ass
by stallion
kitten, young cat
lamb, young of a sheep
pullet, young hen
puppy, whelp, etc.
whelp, young of lion, dog,
fox, etc.
yearling, colt or calf less
than two years old
Etc., etc.

148I (Continued)

NOUNS (Continued)
delay, time of suspension
detention, delay
postponement, period of
delay
procrastination, period of
delay
suspension, period of delay
Interval
interim, intervening time

NOUNS (Continued)
intermission, interval
interregnum, period be-
tween reigns
interval, time between
Pause
entracte, interval between
acts
moratorium, time allowed
for payment after ma-
turity

NOUNS (Continued)
pause, period of cessation
reprieve, interval of
respite
respite, interval of temporary cessation, etc.
season, a division of the
year
truce, period of cessation

148K

WHEN (Definite)   see— ⎰

vs. When (Indefinite) ....148L ⎱   **(ASSOCIATIVE 148A)**

148K

VERBS

chronicle, record in order of time
date, mark with a date
time, determine a time

ADJECTIVES (See Nouns)

Graduating to More Remote Time

direct, immediate
immediate, at once
instant, direct
instantaneous, immediate
present, immediate
prompt, immediate
horal, hourly
hourly, every hour
matutinal, morning
morning, at dawn
noon, at midday
noonday, at noon
nightly, every night
daily, every day
diurnal, daily
quotidian, daily
tertian, every 3 days
quartan, every 4th day
quintan, every 5th day
hebdomadal, weekly
weekly, every week
biweekly, every two weeks
fortnightly, biweekly
menstrual, monthly
monthly, every month
bimonthly, every 2 months
biannual, twice a year
semi-annual, half-yearly
anniversary, occurring yearly
annual, yearly
hibernal, each winter
yearly, every year
biennial, once every two years
triennial, every three years
bissextile, every leap-year
quadrennial, every 4 years
quinquennial, every 5 years
septenary, every 7 years
septennial, every 7 years
decennial, every 10 years
undecennary, every 11 years
centuple, every 100 years
bicentenary, every 200 years

ADJECTIVES (Continued)

millennial, every 1,000 years
tercentenary, every 1,000 years
medieval, in the 8th to 15th century
mesozoic, in the reptile age
neolithic, in the polished-stone age
Saturnian, in the golden age

ADVERBS

forthwith, immediately
now, at once
straightway, now

NOUNS

Miscellaneous

afternoon, time after midday
autumn, time before winter
bedtime, retiring time
curfew, retiring time (archaic)
dawn, beginning of day
dawning, dawn
daybreak, dawn
dayspring, daybreak
dusk, twilight
eve, evening (poetic)
evening, beginning of night
fall, autumn
forenoon, time before midday
gloaming, twilight
meridian, midday
midday, middle of the day
midnight, 12 P. M.
midsummer, middle of summer
morn, early day
morning, early day
night, time of darkness
noon, midday
noonday, noon
noontime, midday
spring, season of growing
springtide, springtime
summer, time after spring
sundown, sunset
sunset, time of sunset
sunrise, time after dawn
twilight, dawn
winter, the cold season

DAYS OF THE WEEK

Sunday
Sabbath
Monday
Tuesday
Wednesday
Thursday
Friday
Saturday

MONTHS OF THE YEAR

January
February
March
April
May
June
July
August
September
October
November
December

NOUNS (Events, Etc.)

advent, time of Christ's coming, etc.
All-Hallows, Nov. 1st.
Arbor Day, tree-planting day
Ascension Day, 40th day after Easter
Annunciation, March 25th
anniversary, annual commemoration
bicentenary, 200th anniversary
birthday, the anniversary of a birth
Candlemas, Feb. 2nd
Christmas, Dec. 25th
Christmastide, Yuletide
doomsday, judgment day
Easter, a Sunday falling between Mar. 22nd and Apr. 25th
Epiphany, Jan. 6th
Halloween, Oct. 31st
Jubilee, Jewish festival celebrated every 50th year
New Year, Jan. 1st
Yule, Christmas
Yuletide, Dec. 24th

BEING

Vertumnus, god of seasons

WHEN (Indefinite)	see—	(ASSOCIATIVE 148A)
vs. When (Definite) 148K		

148L

VERBS
(See Adjectives, Etc.)

ADJECTIVES

Frequent
accustomed, frequent
frequent, recurring often
often, frequently (adv.)
periodic, occurring at
    regular intervals
periodical, as above
recurrent, recurring
    repeatedly
regular, periodic

Infrequent
infrequent, seldom
occasional, recurring at
    rare periods
rare, seldom
seldom, occurring rarely
sometime, at an indefinite
    time

Forthcoming
anon, soon (adv.)
betimes, soon
early, soon (adv.)
forthcoming, soon

ADJECTIVES (Continued)
soon, early

Simultaneous
coeval, contemporaneous
coexistent, coeval
coincident, occurring at
    the same time
concurrent, current
contemporaneous, living or
    being at the same time
    with another
contemporary, at the same
    time
current, existing or active
    at the same time
incident, concurrent
incidental, as above
isochronous, happening in
    equal times
opportune, timely
seasonable, opportune
simultaneous, occurring at
    the same time
synchronal, happening at
    the same time
synchronous, as above
timely, concurrent

NOUNS

Frequency
frequency, frequent
    recurrence
oftenness, frequency
periodicity, recurrence at
    regular intervals

Infrequency
infrequency, recurrence at
    long intervals
rareness, seldomness

Simultaneousness
accord, unison
coexistence, existing at
    the same time
coincidence, concurrence
    of two or more incidents
concurrence, meeting in
    time and circumstances
seasonableness, timeliness
simultaneousness, concur-
    rence in time
synchronism, concurrence
    in time
timeliness, opportuneness
unison, accord

149A (Continued)
NOUNS (Continued)

Omnipresence
omnipresence, presence
    everywhere
ubiquity, omnipresence

Direction
bearings, position
direction, position
drift, general direction
presentation, position of a
    child at parturition
trend, drift, direction

Collocation
arrangement, distribution

NOUNS (Continued)
collocation, a placing
distribution, a specific
    placing
installation, a placing
localization, a local placing
removal, replacement

Arrangement
arrangement, order
disposition, arrangement
order, situation

Miscellaneous
latitude, geographical point
    horizontal

NOUNS (Continued)
longitude, geographical
    point perpendicular
status, relative position
status quo, relation or po-
    sition in which a person
    or matter, has been, is,
    or may be
topography, featured
    regions

BEING

Terminus, god of boundary
    lines

PLACE (Indefinite) see—

vs. Direction 149B

149A

VERBS

Place
deposit, place
lay, place
place, situate
put, place

Move
change, move
move, change place
remove, replace
replace, change

Throw
cast, pitch
fling, hurl
hurl, throw
pitch, place by a toss
throw, place by a toss
toss, place by a throw

Lodge
beach, land
land, place ashore
lodge, rest temporarily
moor, tie to a moor
park, place a car

Set
seat, place
set, place
stand, place upright

Station
establish, locate
install, place
quarter, lodge
station, situate

Arrange
arrange, place, situate
collocate, station
dispose, arrange
distribute, locate
specifically
localize, limit to a place
locate, situate
order, range
orientate, place eastward
range, arrange
situate, locate

Mislay
lose, mislay
mislay, misplace
misplace, place wrongly

ADJECTIVES

Local
insular, on an island
local, referring to place

ADJECTIVES (Continued)
territorial, on earth or
  territory
topical, local
topographical, referring to
  places in particular

Geographical
anthropological, pertaining
  to the divisions or
  localities of the races
continental, situated in, or
  pertaining to, a conti-
  nent
geographical, implying
  situation on earth
mundane, on earth
terrene, mundane
terrestrial, on earth

Terraqueous
amphibious, living on land
  and in water
terraqueous, referring to
  earth and water

Omnipresent
omnipresent, present
  everywhere
throughout, in every part
ubiquitous, omnipresent

Missing
absent, missing
lost, astray
misplaced, lost
missing, lost

Miscellaneous
eccentric, away from the
  center
latitudinal, noting position
  of latitude
locative, noting place
longitudinal, noting position of longitude
oriental, relating to the
  orient
situate, placed
spacial, in space

ADVERBS, ETC.
absent, away
afield, in a field
anywhere, any place
ashore, on shore
astray, lost
at, prep. denoting place
away, absent

ADVERBS (Continued)
there, at that place
whence, from what place
where, at which place
whereabouts, what place

NOUNS

Space
room, space
space, unoccupied place
vacancy, room
void, space

Place
locale, locality
location, place
place, position
position, situation
post, position
seat, site
site, situation
situation, locality
station, place
venue, place where an
  action in law is laid

Locality
area, location
locality, place
premises, particular position or section in real
  estate
quarter, region
region, locality
section, location or portion
  of country
whereabouts, place
zone, section

Point
mark, spot
point, exact spot
spot, place

Rest
footing, position
landing, footing
moor, mooring place
parking, parking place
rest, stopping place

Habitat
habitat, natural location
  of animals and plants
nativity, place of birth
vivarium, natural location
  for animals
(Continued on page 385)

DIRECTION N., E., S., W., Etc. see—

vs. Place (Indefinite) 149A

(ASSOCIATIVE 149A)

149B

VERBS

(See Adjectives, etc.)

ADJECTIVES

antarctic, noting the south-polar regions
arctic, northern
austral, southern
boreal, northern
easterly, eastern
eastern, noting the locality in the direction of sunrise
eastward, easterly
north, northern
northern, located on the left of a person facing the rising sun

ADJECTIVES (Continued)

occidental, pertaining to countries west of Asia and the Turkish dominions
polar, arctic
south, southern
southern, opposite the north
west, western
western, opposite the east
westerly, nearly west
westward, westerly

PERSONS

easterner
northerner
Oriental
southerner
westerner, etc., etc.

NOUNS

cardinal points, north, east, south, west
north, locality on the left of a person facing the rising sun
Occident, countries west of Asia and the Turkish dominions
Orient, the East, especially those countries in Asia east of the Mediterranean
south, locality opposite the north
east, locality towards the rising sun
west, locality opposite the east

POSITION—STRAIGHT, LEVEL see—

vs. Oblique, Sloping 149D

(ASSOCIATIVE 149A)

149C

VERBS

aline, form a line
even, smooth
flatten, level
grade, level
lengthen, aline
level, make horizontal
smooth, flatten
sprawl, lie spread
straighten, grade

NOUNS (Related)

elongation, a lengthening
extensor, muscle that straightens a limb

ADJECTIVES

awash, level with waves
direct, not circuitous
even, smooth
flat, level
flush, level
horizontal, level
lengthwise, longitudinal
level, even
longitudinal, lengthwise
parallel, side by side and equidistant
plane, flat
rectilineal, in straight-lined position
smooth, level
straight, direct

NOUNS

alinement, formation of a line, etc.
flat, a level
evenness, levelness
length, state of being short or long
level, flat surface
levelness, smoothness
parallelism, parallel position
plane, flat surface
smoothness, evenness
straightness, evenness

SLOPE—OBLIQUENESS

see—

(ASSOCIATIVE 149A)

vs. Level, Flat 149C

149D

VERBS

bend, incline
cant, tilt
careen, incline sidewise
incline, lean, slope
lean, incline
list, lean over
slant, incline
sheer, slope away
slope, incline, slant
taper, slope to an apex
tilt, incline

ADJECTIVES

abrupt, precipitous
acclivous, sloping up
arduous, hard to climb
bluffy, abrupt
bold, steep

ADJECTIVES (Continued)

gradient, ascending or
  descending
lopsided, inclined un-
  naturally
oblique, slanting
precipitous, steep
sheer, steep
slanting, oblique
sloping, inclined
steep, precipitous

ADVERBS

acock, in a cocked position
apeak, nearly vertical
askance, obliquely
askew, obliquely
aslope, slopingly
aslant, obliquely

ADVERBS (Continued)

atilt, tilted
awry, obliquely

NOUNS

acclivity, upward slope
bend, curved incline
cant, inclination
declivity, downward slope
diagonal, oblique line
grade, slope
inclination, slope
incline, slope
list, inclination
obliqueness, slant
pitch, degree of slope
slant, incline
slope, slant

149E

UPRIGHTS—
PERPENDICULARITY

see—

(ASSOCIATIVE 149A)

vs. Flatness 149C

149E

VERBS

Miscellaneous

elevate, rise or raise
heighten, elevate
hill, make into a hill
rise, tower aloft
spire, shoot upward
tower, rise high

ADJECTIVES

Miscellaneous

alpine, mountainous
broken, hilly
erect, vertical
hilly, hill-like
lofty, very high
mountainous, lofty
peaky, peak-like
perpendicular, upright
ridgy, rising in ridges
rugate, ridgy
sheer, perpendicular
tall, towering
towering, lofty
transcendent, rising above
upright, erect
vertical, perpendicular

NOUNS

Elevation

acclivity, ascent

NOUNS (Continued)

ascension, rise
ascent, ascension
bank, acclivity
elevation, rise
perpendicularity, upright
  position
rise, elevation
rising, rise

Tower

spire, steeple
steeple, spire above the
  roof of a church
tower, lofty structure
turret, small tower

Hill, Etc.

glacier, mountainous ice
highland, mountainous
  region
hill, high elevation
iceberg, floating ice-hill
mount, mountain
mountain, lofty formation
  of earth, rock, etc.
peak, hill
sierra, ridged mountain
tor, high hill

Hillock

barrow, mound
dune, sand-hill
hillock, small hill

NOUNS (Continued)

hummock, rising ground
knob, knoll
knoll, hillock
kopje, hillock (S. Africa)
mound, hillock

Bump, Etc.

bump, protuberance
hump, a rise
prominence, protuberance
protuberance, knob

Craig, Cliff

bluff, steep bank
brae, hillside
butte, abrupt hill
cliff, steep bank
craig, steep rock
precipice, nearly perpendicular elevation
reef, chain of rocks
ridge, long elevation
shoal, sand-bank

Stalagmite

stalactite, cone-like formation on the ceiling of
  caverns
stalagmite, cone-like formation on the floor of a
  cavern

149F

HEIGHT—ALTITUDE

see— $\left\{\begin{array}{l}\end{array}\right.$ (ASSOCIATIVE 149A)

vs. Lowness 149G

149F
VERBS

Miscellaneous
bestride, straddle
cap, superimpose
hover, flutter over
perch, sit upon
roost, perch
sit, rest upon
straddle, bestride
stride, straddle
superimpose, place upon
surmount, rise above
top, superimpose
tower, overtop
transcend, surmount
uplift, raise aloft

ADJECTIVES

Miscellaneous
aerial, soaring
altitudinal, noting height
ascendant, above the
  horizon
astraddle, astride
elevated, high, above
eminent, lofty
exalted, raised on high

ADJECTIVES (Continued)

high, lofty
highest, above all
lofty, high
meridian, highest
mounted, perched upon
overhead, upper, above
perching, sitting elevated
soaring, high
tip-top, top
top, uppermost
topmost, at the very top
towering, lofty
upper, highest
uppermost, highest

ADVS. & PREPS.

above, overhead
aloft, on high
astride (adv.), perching
  with legs apart
beyond (prep.), above
on (prep.), resting on
over, above
up, on high
upon (prep.), on

NOUNS

Height
altitude, elevation
elevation, height
eminence, high place
height, altitude
loftiness, eminence

Pinnacle
acme, highest point
apex, tip or summit
climax, acme
culmination, highest point
meridian, highest point
peak, summit
pinnacle, topmost point
sky, apparent vault
summit, apex
tip-top, apex
top, summit
vertex, summit
zenith, point overhead

Cap, Brow
brow, hilltop
crest, summit
cap, top
hilltop, summit
nap, hilltop

149J (Continued)
NOUNS

Miscellaneous
adjacency, juxtaposition
broadside, entire side of a
  ship above the water line
contiguity, adjacency
flank, side of an army,
  regiment, or building
juxtaposition, contiguity

NOUNS (Continued)

laterality, state of proceeding from, or acting upon,
  the side
larboard, left side of a
  vessel, port
lee, sheltered side
left, side opposite the right
offside, side to the right of
  the driver
port, larboard

NOUNS (Continued)

right, side opposite the
  heart
side, lateral part as distinguished from front, back,
  top, or bottom
siding, side-track
starboard, the right side of
  a vessel looking towards
  the bow

LOW—BELOW

vs. Height 149F

(ASSOCIATIVE 149A)

149G
VERBS

Lower
deepen, increase depth
dip, lower (a flag) for a
   moment
drop, lower
lower, let down

Suspend
dangle, hang loosely
depend, suspend
hang, droop or hang down
suspend, hang
swing, hang

Settle
droop, lean or hang down
hog, droop at both ends,
   said of a ship
settle, sink
sink, droop

Lie, Lay
flatten, become prostrate
lay, cause to lie
lie, be prone
prostrate, lie flat
recline, lean, lie down
repose, lie at rest
sprawl, lie
underlie, lie under

Stoop
bow, bend or incline
crouch, stoop low
squat, crouch
stoop, bend low

Decline
bend, incline
decline, bend down
descend, slope
incline, lean
lean, incline, bend over
slant, incline
slope, slant
tilt, incline
tip, tilt

ADJECTIVES

Low
abysmal, bottomless
bottom, lowest
bottomless, abysmal
deep, subjacent
deepest, lowest
low, below something else
lower, below

ADJECTIVES (Continued)
lowermost, lowest
lowest, undermost

Descending
declinate, curved down
declivitous, declining
   steeply
decurrent, extending down,
   said of a plant
decursive, running down
defluent, running down
descending, decursive
down, downward
downward, sloping down
netherward, descending
precipitous, headlong and
   downward
proclivous, slanting forward
   and downward

Inclining
dipped, tilted
gradient, descending or
   ascending in a certain
   proportion
inclined, leaning
inclining, inclined
leaning, inclining
reclinate, reclined
reclining, leaning
tilted, inclined

Hanging
drooped, bent down
drooping, bending down
hanging, suspended
pendent, hanging
suspended, pendent

Lying
decumbent, prostrate
depressed, flattened
flat, prostrate
horizontal, level
level, without elevations
lying, recumbent
procumbent, lying down
prone, prostrate
prostrate, lying flat
recumbent, lying down

Stooping
bent, stooped
bowed, drooped
crouched, squat
squat, crouching
stooped, bowed

ADJECTIVES (Continued)
stooping, stooped

Under
nether, beneath
subjacent, lying below
subterranean, below the
   surface of the earth, etc.
under, lowermost
underground, under earth
undermost, lowest

Submerged
immersed, submerged
submerged, under water
sunken, under water

ADVERBS
below, under
beneath, below
under, beneath
underneath, beneath

NOUNS
Decline
declination, a bending or
   moving downward
decline, a leaning down-
   ward
declivity, gradual descent
descent, decline
drop, decline
fall, drop
incline, slant
reclination, a bending
   downward
slant, slope
slope, downward inclina-
   tion

Prostration
proneness, prostration
prostration, a lying flat
recumbency, state of
   reclining

Miscellaneous
base, bottom
bottom, lowest part
depth, penetration down-
   ward
depression, a sink below
   the surface
horizon, level
level, smooth, erect
nadir, heavens directly
   under observer
squat, a crouch

BEFORE—IN FRONT   see—   **(ASSOCIATIVE 149A)**
(Time Preceding 148A)

  vs. Behind—In Back ....149I   (Beginning ....4)

149H
VERBS

Miscellaneous
accost, confront
antecede, precede
confront, stand face to face
face, front
forerun, precede
front, confront, be in front
jut, project
precede, go in front
project, shoot forth or be in front
protrude, project

ADJECTIVES

Foremost
advance, forward
first, preceding
foremost, first
forward, in front
front, at the front
leading, first
preceding, foremost
principal, first
primary, first

Before
anterior, more to the front, especially as in time
before, in front
fore, before
former, preceding

Chief
chief, first
head, front
main, leading
paramount, first

Antecedent
antecedent, preceding
precedent, anterior
precursory, preceding
preliminary, preceding

Protrusive
excurrent, pressing forth or through
frontal, pertaining to the forehead
gibbous, protuberant
projecting, jutting in front
prominent, protruding
protruding, projecting
protrusive, projecting
protuberant, prominent
salient, prominent

Opposite
opposite, in front
vis-a-vis, face to face

ADVERBS
ahead, in front
forth, forward
fore, forward
forward, ahead

NOUNS

First
anteriority, priority
beginning, the first
first, forward object, etc.
preliminary, the first
primary, that which is first in place

Front
forepart, the first
front, forepart
head, forepart
lead, head

Foreground
facade, front elevation
face, front
foreground, front
frontage, front

Vanguard
advance, vanguard
salient, advance wedge of attacking troops
van, front of an army or fleet
vanguard, advance guard of an army

Antecedence
antecedence, precedence
precedence, lead
principal, that which leads
priority, place in front

Protrusion
projection, protrusion
projecture, projection
prominence, projection
protuberance, prominence
protrusion, projection
spur, projection

Opposition
opposite, front to front, or back to back
opposition, position confronting another

OBJECTIVE

These groups contain words that are variations of the term OBJECTIVE— the object or incentive that beckons us to struggle for achievement.

Objective
goal, destination, mark

OBJECTIVE (Continued)
ideal, ultimate objective
mecca, destination
Mekka, goal of Mohammedan pilgrimage
object, aim, end, goal
objective, aim, goal

Destination
bourne, destination
destination, point or goal ahead
end, goal
issue, end
terminus, destination

Aim
aim, object, goal
design, purpose
motive, aim
purpose, aim, end
sake, end, purpose

Mark
mark, target
point, aim
record, mark, score
target, mark, goal

Incentive
ambition, object of interest
incentive, inducement
inducement, motive
interest, influence
opportunity, promise

Influence
impulse, instigation
incitement, instigation
influence, incitement
instigation, goading influence

Challenge
challenge, a call to conquest
dare, challenge
ultimatum, final offer

Game
game, object of pursuit
quarry, game
prey, quarry

PERSONS
antecessor, one who goes before
leader, one who leads
pioneer, one who precedes in a work
predecessor, one who precedes
vis-a-vis, one who is face to face with another

BEHIND—IN BACK   see—   {   (ASSOCIATIVE 149A)

vs. Before—In Front ....149H   (Time Following 148B)

149I
VERBS
Miscellaneous
follow, go or come after
pursue, follow
succeed, follow
tag, follow closely

ADJECTIVES
Behind
after, next, following
behind, back of
following, succeeding
hind, hinder
hinder, at the back
next, following nearest
subsequent, following
succeeding, following in
   order

Backward
back, at the rear
backward, toward the back
behindhand, backward
dorsal, located at the back
rear, back

Successive
ordinal, denoting sequence,
   as 1st, 2nd, etc.
posterior, subsequent in
   place, etc.
sequent, following
successive, sequent

ADJECTIVES (Continued)
Final
conclusive, final
dernier, last, final, as
   dernier resort (French)
final, last
hindmost, at the extreme
   rear
last, behind all
ultimate, final

Miscellaneous
antepenultimate, noting the
   last but two
mizzen, noting the hindmost
   of fore and aft sails
penult, last but one
post-nasal, lying behind
   the nasal tract
secondary, after the first

ADVERBS
aback, backward
abaft, astern
aft, at or towards the
   stern
after, behind
astern, at the hinder part
   of a ship
back, behind
behind, aft

NOUNS
Back
back, hind part
background, rear
backside, hind part
end, rear
rear, hind part
stern, after part of a vessel

Miscellaneous
antepenult, the last syllable
   but two of a word
antepenultimate, that
   which is last but two
breech, hinder part
buttock, hinder part
extreme, end
nape, back of the neck
omega, end
penult, last syllable of a
   word but one
poop, raised stern of a
   vessel
posteriority, state of being
   behind
scruff, nape
tow, that which is drawn
   behind
train, something drawn
   behind
wake, track in water at the
   rear of a vessel

149J
VERBS
flank, move to, or be at,
   the side
juxtapose, put side by side
parallel, to move or be
   parallel with
sidle, move side foremost

ADJECTIVES
Flanking
bordering, flanking
collateral, side by side
flanking, at the side
lateral, pertaining to the
   side
leeward, pertaining to the
   lee or sheltered side
littoral, pertaining to the
   shore; between high and
   low-water marks
parallel, side by side

ADJECTIVES (Continued)
parietal, pertaining to a
   side or wall
riparian, on the side or
   bank of a water-course
sidelong, lateral

Adjacent
adjacent, adjoining
adjoining, contiguous
contiguous, adjacent
immediate, adjacent

Right
dexter, right-hand
off, on the right-hand side
right, noting the side
   opposite the heart
right-handed, noting the
   right side
starboard, the right-hand
   side facing the bow of a
   vessel

ADJECTIVES (Continued)
Left
gauche, left-handed
larboard, on the left side of
   a ship
left, opposite the right
left-hand, left
left-handed, on the left
   side
sinister, on the left side,
   etc.

ADVERBS
abreast, side by side
alongside, close beside
at, by
aweather, toward the wind
   side
beside, at the side
by, on the side

(Continued on page 389)

OUTSIDE—SURROUNDING see—$\left\{\begin{array}{l}\end{array}\right.$ **(ASSOCIATIVE 149A)**

vs. Inside 149L

149K
VERBS

Miscellaneous
border, encompass
bound, circumscribe
circumscribe, border
compass, encircle
encircle, encompass
enclose, encompass
encompass, surround
envelope, inclose
environ, surround
inclose, encompass
surround, border

ADJECTIVES

Outside
centrifugal, outward
exo, prefix meaning outside
exterior, external
external, outside
outer, external
outside, exterior
outlying, outside
outward, external

Surrounding
bordering, surrounding

ADJECTIVES (Continued)
circumjacent, surrounding
circumambient, encompass-
 ing
encircling, encompassing
encompassing, circumambi-
 ent
surrounding, outside

Extrinsic
extrinsic, outside the nature
 of an object or case
superficial, pertaining to
 the surface

Extraneous
exotic, outside
extramundane, beyond the
 limits of the world
extramural, outside the
 walls of a city or university
extraneous, foreign
foreign, outside

ADVERBS
about, around the outside
around, encircling
without, externally

NOUNS

Miscellaneous
border, outer edge
boundary, border
brim, margin, as of a river
brink, edge
edge, extreme border
environment, exterior
exterior, the outside.
extraneity, externality
extroversion, the turning of
 an inner part outward
 and vice versa
frontier, boundary
ledge, shelf-like edge
margin, border
outport, outside port
outpost, outside station
outside, exterior
outskirts, outer precinct
precinct, outer boundary
rim, border
superficiality, surface
superficies, external area
surface, upper exterior
surroundings, environment
verge, border

149L

INSIDE—WITHIN see—$\left\{\begin{array}{l}\end{array}\right.$ **(ASSOCIATIVE 149A)**
(Entrance ....20)
(Submersion ....21)

vs. Outside 149K

149L
VERBS

Miscellaneous
center, place in the center
(B). centre
centralize, bring into the
 center
ensheathe, sheathe
enter, place or go within
inject, introduce
inlay, lay within
inlet, insert
inset, set between
insert, place within
intern, shut within
interpose, place between
introduce, insert
introvert, turn in
sack, place in a sack
sheathe, place in a
 scabbard

ADJECTIVES

Inside
endo, (prefix) within
inmost, central

ADJECTIVES (Continued)
inner, interior
inside, within
interior, internal
within, interior

Central
center, in the middle
(B). centre
central, middle
centric, central
concentric, having a com-
 mon center
eccentric, near the center
focal, central
median, pertaining to the
 middle
mesial, middle
middle, central
middlesome, nearest the
 middle

Between
between, intermediate
betwixt, between
intermediate, middle
intervening, intermediate

ADJECTIVES (Continued)
Endemic.
endemic, within a country,
 district, locality, or
 people
geocentric, noting the center of the earth
indoor, within doors
inland, in the interior
inshore, inland
internal, endemic
intramural, within the walls
 of a city or institution
littoral, situated between
 high and low-water
 marks

Inward
centripetal, inward
inward, toward the center

Medium
average, mean
mean, middle
medium, intermediate
mezzo, mean
(Continued on page 394)

NEAR—ADJACENT   see—

vs. Distant—Remote 149N

(ASSOCIATIVE 149A)
(Tactility ....124)

149M

VERBS

Miscellaneous

abut, border upon
adjoin, lie next to
approach, draw near
approximate, draw near
border, adjoin
localize, neighbor
near, approach
neighbor, adjoin
nestle, lie close
nuzzle, nestle close
snuggle, nestle close
verge, come near

ADJECTIVES

Near

approximate, close together
approximative,
   approximate
close, near
imminent, impending
impending, close upon
near, close by
proximate, nearest

Adjacent

adjacent, contiguous
adjoining, adjacent
bordering, adjoining
conterminous, contiguous
contiguous, adjoining

Present

hard-by, near, immediate
immediate, close

ADJECTIVES (Continued)

next, nearest
present, at or near

Handy

convenient, handy
handy, close at hand
intimate, mutually close

Neighboring

frontier, bordering
local, neighboring
neighboring, adjacent
suburban, adjacent

ADVERBS, ETC.

about, on every side
against, hard-upon
around, about
at (prep.), near
beside, near
by, near
here, at this place
hither, to this place

NOUNS

Nearness

approximation, nearness
attendance, presence
juxtaposition, nearness
nearness, closeness
nighness, proximity
propinquity, nearness

Adjacency

abutment, a bordering upon
adjacency, contiguity

NOUNS (Continued)

contiguity, adjacency
immediateness, adjacency
presence, adjacency, state
   of being present
proximity, adjacency

Vicinity

entourage, environment
environment, immediate
   surroundings
environs, suburbs
neighborhood, vicinity
purlieu, adjacent district
suburbs, environs of a
   community
vicinage, vicinity
vicinity, proximity,
   neighborhood

Precinct

border, frontier
borderland, frontier
confines, border
fringe, border
frontier, bordering region
precinct, outward limit

PERSONS

borderer, one who lives on
   the border
bystander, one who stands
   near
neighbor, one who resides
   in the vicinity
suburbanite, resident of a
   suburb

149L (Continued)

ADVERBS, PREP., ETC.

abed, in bed
aboard, on or within
amid, prep. amidst
amidship, in the middle of
   the ship
amidst, prep. among
among, mingled with
amongst, prep. among
herein, within
in, prep. among, amidst
into, prep. to the inside
intro, prefix meaning
   within
on, aboard
within, inside

NOUNS

Miscellaneous

axis, lineal center of a
   form
center, middle
(B). centre
centralism, centrality
centrality, central position
centricity, centrality
concentricity, common
   center
core, center
focus, central point
inset, insert
insert, that which is
   inserted

NOUNS (Continued)

inside, that which is within
intrados, interior and inner
   lining of an arch
mean, middle point
middle, center
midst, middle, etc.
nucleus, central form
   Introduction, Etc.
centralization, conversion
   centrally
injection, insertion
insertion, introduction
introduction, a placing
   within
introversion, a turning in

149N

VERBS

extend, continue farther
lengthen, extend
stretch, extend or draw
    out

ADJECTIVES

Distant

distant, far away
extensive, far-reaching
far, distant
far-flung, extensive
far-reaching, reaching far
remote, far removed

Further

farther, more distant
further, more remote
longer, farther
ulterior, farther

Farthest

extreme, farthest
farthest, furthest
futhermost, most remote
furthest, most distant
outermost, farthest
ultimate, utmost
utmost, farthest

Absent

absent, away, missing
gone, lost
lost, missing
missing, absent
off, away

ADJECTIVES (Continued)

stray, lost, gone

Nonresident

antipodal, on the opposite
    side of the earth
antipodean, residing or per-
    taining to the opposite
    side of the earth
exotic, foreign
foreign, distant
nonresident, foreign
occidental, pertaining to
    the west or countries
    constituting the occident
oriental, noting the East
tramontane, beyond the
    mountain, foreign
ultramontane, tramontane

ADVERBS

abroad, beyond one's home
    or country
afar, at a distance
ahead, farther on
along, farther
aloof, at a distance
astray, lost
away, absent
beyond, farther on
gone, afar
lost, gone
onward, ahead
yonder, beyond

NOUNS

Miscellaneous

absence, presence
    elsewhere
absenteeism, absence, as
    from an estate or one's
    country
alibi, proof of absence
antipodes, position or re-
    gion on the opposite side
    of the earth
beyond, farther away
extension, extent
extent, reach
distance, remoteness
farness, distance
occident, the West
offing, off from the shore
reach, distance
remoteness, distance off
truancy, absence

PERSONS

absentee, one not present
antipodean, a resident on
    the other side of the
    earth
antipodes, residents on the
    other side of the earth
barbarian, foreigner
foreigner, antipodean, etc.
nonresident, foreigner
truant, absentee

150C (Continued)

NOUNS (Continued)

arch, curvature
arching, arch
crescent, figure like a new
    moon
hemisphere, half sphere

Concave

concave, hollowed surface

NOUNS (Continued)

concavity, hollow curve
convex, protruding curve
convexity, as above

Cylinder

cylinder, figure of uniform
    diameter whose ends are
    equal parallel circles

NOUNS (Continued)

cylindroid, cylindric form
    with elliptical ends
tube, cylinder

MEDIUMS

curler, device which curls
flexor, bending muscles
Etc., etc.

SHAPES—FORMS—
OUTLINES   see—

vs. Space 25A
vs. Land, etc. 25G

ASSOCIATIVE

Shapes (Indefinite) 150A
Circular Shapes 150C
Angular Shapes 150D
Pointed Shapes 150E
Straight—Flat, Etc. 149C

Radial Shapes 150F
Irregular Shapes 150B
Corporeal Shapes 150G
Vegetative Shapes 150H
Land Bodies....................25G

150A
VERBS

carve, form by chiseling
cast, shape in a mold
chisel, carve
fashion, mold
figure, form or shape
forge, fashion
form, fashion
make, construct
mold, form
outline, shape
pattern, shape after
proportion, form harmoni-
ously
sculpture, carve
shape, form
symmetrize, proportion

ADJECTIVES

figured, having shape
pantamorphic, taking all
shapes
proportional, proportion-
ately formed
shapely, symmetrical
symmetrical, well propor-
tioned

NOUNS

area, plane surface
aspect, side, surface, or
form
cast, form or shape
configuration, form

NOUNS (Continued)

contour, outline, profile
figure, outline, shape
form, shape
guise, appearance, form
mold, figure from a cast
outline, figure
pattern, shape for copying
plane, even surface
profile, contour
proportion, symmetry
shape, outward form
shapeliness, good shape
surface, undefined area
symmetry, harmony of
form

150B
IRREGULAR SHAPES   see—

vs. Beauty 108	(ASSOCIATIVE 150A)
vs. Uniformity 132D	(Disfiguration ......109B)

150B
VERBS

Twist
contort, twist
twist, distort
warp, twist

Bend
bend, crook
crook, make crooked
dent, bend or puncture
turn, bend

Deform
deform, distort
disfigure, deform
distort, twist

Crinkle
corrugate, wrinkle
crease, corrugate
crinkle, corrugate
crumple, rumple
ridge, dent, rumple
ruffle, rumple
ruck, crease
rumple, wrinkle
wrinkle, crinkle

Miscellaneous
fold, crease, etc.
pucker, wrinkle
purse, pucker

ADJECTIVES
Twisted
contorted, twisted

ADJECTIVES (Continued)

skew, twisted
tortile, twisted, bent
tortuous, crooked
twisted, tortile
warped, twisted

Bent
bent, crooked
crooked, irregular

Deformed
amorphous, shaped irregu-
larly
deformed, disfigured
disfigured, shapeless
distorted, irregular
irregular, uneven
shapeless, illformed
uneven, irregular

Rough
broken, rough, rugged
craggy, rugged
deckle-edged, rough-edged
erose, deckle-edged, etc.
jagged, craggy
ridged, rugged
rugate, ridged
rugged, uneven
rough, broken, rugged
zigzag, irregular

Crinkled
corrugated, crinkled
crinkled, wrinkled

ADJECTIVES (Continued)

crumpled, crinkled
rumpled, wrinkled
wrinkled, crinkled

NOUNS

Miscellaneous

asperity, roughness
bend, a curve or crook
contortion, a twist
corrugation, a crinkle
crease, wrinkle
crinkle, wrinkle
crook, a bend
crumple, a rumple
deformity, irregularity
dent, punctured bend
distortion, a warp
fold, a crease
irregularity, tortuousness
plait, crease
pucker, small fold
ruck, crease
ruffle, plait
rumple, wrinkle
unevenness, irregularity
warp, twisted shape
wrinkle, crinkle

ADVERBS

awry, crooked

CIRCULAR AND CURVED SHAPES

see— (ASSOCIATIVE 150A)

vs. Angular Shapes 150D

150C

VERBS

Miscellaneous

arch, form an arch
bend, curve
circumscribe, mark around
circumflect, bend around
coil, wind
crescent, form a crescent
curl, coil spirally
curve, bend
querl, coil
sinuate, turn, wind
turn, sinuate
wind, bend, curve

ADJECTIVES

Circular

annular, ring-shaped
annulose, ringed
circular, round
circumferential, circular
circumflex, winding
circumscriptive, periphery
clock-wise, circling right
globular, globe-shaped
orbed, spherical
orbicular, orb-shaped
orbital, orb-like
peripheral, circumferential
periphery, as above
rotund, spherical
round, cylindrical
spherical, globular

Circuitous

circuitous, roundabout
roundabout, circuitous
sinuate, in alternate curves
sinuous, bending in and out
winding, curving
zigzag, having short turns

Curly

crispate, curled
curly, wavy
wavy, curling

Spiral

cochleate, screw-like
helical, spiral-shaped
helicoid, coiled like the
  shell of a snail
spiral, screw-like
volute, spiral-like

Curvate

bent, curved
curvate, curved
curved, waved, coiled, etc.
curvilineal, curved
deflective, bending
recurvate, curved back

ADJECTIVES (Continued)

Elliptic, Etc.

elliptic, like an ellipse
oblate, flat at the poles
oblong, egg-shaped
oval, egg-shaped
ovate, as above
ovoid, as above
prolate, elongated at the
  poles
spheroidal, not quite round

Conic

campanulate, bell-shaped
conic, cone-shaped
conical, as above
coniferous, cone-shaped
conoid, cone-like
conoidal, conical
mitriform, conical
parabolic, shaped like a
  parabola
pineal, like a pine cone

Arching

arching, arch-like
arched, arch-like
curved, arched
horseshoe, U-shaped

Concave, Etc.

concave, hollowed
concavo-convex, recipro-
  cally hollowed
convex, having a protrud-
  ing curve
convexo-concave, convexed
  on one side and con-
  caved on the other
convexo-convex, convexed
  one one side as well as
  on the other
lenticular, double-convex

Cylindric

cylindric, cylinder-like
tubal, cylindric
tubate, tubal

NOUNS

Circle

ambit, circumference
annulation, ring-like formation
annulet, little ring
circle, a round
circlet, small circle
circuit, circumference
circumference, circle
circumscription, act of
  drawing a line around
compass, circular course

NOUNS (Continued)

gibbosity, roundness
orbit, circular path
perimeter, ambit, etc.
ring, circle
round, circle, sphere, etc.
sphere, globular figure
sphericity, roundness
spherule, little sphere

Globe

ball, globe
disk, circular form
globe, a round form
globule, small globe
orb, circular body
pellet, little ball

Spiral

coil, series of circles
helicoid, spiral
helix, spiral shape
screw, a spiral form
spiral, a screw-shape
volute, spiral-like form

Curve

bight, river-bend, etc.
circumflexion, curve
curvation, a curving
curve, bending line, etc.
curvilineal, curve
curvature, a bending
deflection, a bending form
deflexure, a bending down
flexion, curve
flexure, curve or fold
involute, inward curve
involution, an incurving
sinuosity, wave-like lines

Ellipse, Etc.

ecliptic, path of the sun
ellipse, oval-like figure
ellipsoid, spheroid
ellipticity, oval-like form
loop, curve-like course
oval, egg-like form
spheroid, roundish figure

Cone

cone, solid whose base is a
  circle which rises taper-
  ingly to a point
hyperbola, the figure made
  when a cone is cut
  parallel to its axis
parabola, the figure made
  when a cone is cut
  parallel with one side

Arch, Etc.

apse, semicircular recess
arc, segment of a circle
(Continued on page 395)

150D
VERBS
Miscellaneous
angle, make angular
bend, turn sharply
basil, to form a chisel-edged angle
deflect, bend from a straight line
facet, cut a facet upon
inflect, bend
reflex, bend or turn back
refract, bend from a direct course
square, make square
triangulate, make triangular

ADJECTIVES
Scaled to show increasing angularity
Angular
angular, having angles
geometric, having dimensional shapes
reflex, bent or turned back
refracted, bent back at an acute angle
refrangible, implying refraction
Acute
acuminate, ending in an acute point
acute, sharp-pointed
cuneate, wedge-shaped
cuneiform, wedge-shaped
pointed, point-like
tangent, meeting a line or surface at a point but not intersecting it
tapering, diminishing to a point
Rectangular
abeam, at right angles to the keel of a ship
orthogonal, rectangular
rectangular, right-angled
Obtuse
blunt, obtuse
obtuse, more than a right-angle
retuse, blunt
salient, having an angle less than two right-angles

    bi-, (prefix) two
    di-, (prefix) two
    duo-, (prefix) two
biangular, having two angles
diagonal, oblique
dihedral, having two plane faces or sides

ADJECTIVES (Continued)
oblique, diagonal
    tri-, (prefix) three
triangular, three-sided
trigonal, three-cornered
trihedral, three-sided
trilateral, three-sided
    tetra-, (prefix) four
deltoid, diamond-shaped
diamond, rhomboid-shaped
quadral, four-cornered
quadrangular, having four angles and four sides
quadrate, having four equal sides and right-angles
quadratic, pertaining to a square
quadrifrontal, having four fronts or faces
rhombic, rhomb-shaped
square, having four right-angles and equal sides
tetrahedral, four-sided
    quinque-, (prefix) five
pentagonal, pentahedral
pentahedral, having five sides
quinquangular, having five angles
quinquelatteral, five-sided
quinqueangled, quinquangular
    sex-, (prefix) six
    hexa-, (prefix) six
cube, having six equal square faces
cubic, cube
hexagonal, six-sided
hexahedral, having six planes
rhombohedral, having six rhombic planes
sexangular, having six angles
    hepta-, (prefix) seven
    septa-, (prefix) seven
heptagonal, having seven angles
heptahexahedral, having seven six-faced planes
septi, seven-sided
    octa-, (prefix) eight
octangular, having eight angles and eight sides
octahedral, having eight equal sides
octangular, having eight equal sides
    non-, (prefix) nine
    enne-, (prefix) nine

ADJECTIVES (Continued)
nonagon, noting a figure with nine planes and nine angles
enneagon, nonagon
    deca-, (prefix) ten
decagonal, noting a figure with ten planes and ten angles
didecahedral, having form of a ten-sided prism with a five-sided base
    hendeca-, (prefix) eleven
hendecagonal, having eleven angles
    dodeca-, (prefix) twelve
didodecahedral, noting a prism with twelve sides and a six-sided base
dihexahedral, hexahedral in form with trihedral summits
duodenary, denoting twelve
Polyagonal
polyagonal, many-sided
prismatic, prism-shaped
Conic, Etc.
conic, shaped like a cone
coniferous, cone-shaped
pyramidal, pyramid-like
Retiform
retiform, net-shaped
reticular, having network shape
reticulate, as above

NOUNS
Scaled to show increasing angularity
Angle
axil, angle formed by the upper side of a branch with the stem to which it is attached
angle, space between two lines or planes meeting at a point
corner, angle
refraction, refracted angle
Acute Angles
basil, angle of a cutting edge
bezel, basil, as above
tangent, meeting of a straight line and a curve without intersection
(Continued on page 399)

NOUNS (Continued)
Obtuseness, Etc.

obtuseness, angularity greater than a right-angle
right-angle, angle made by lines meeting perpendicularly
salient angle, an angle less than two right-angles
  bi-, (prefix) two
  di-, (prefix) two
  duo-, (prefix) two
dihedron, figure with two sides or surfaces
  tri-, (prefix) three
delta, triangular surface
hypotenuse, side of a right-angled triangle
isosceles, triangle having two equal sides
scalene, triangle having all sides unequal
spandrel, triangular form
triangle, figure having three sides
trihedron, form having three sides
  tetra-, (prefix) four
diamond, oblique-angled parallelogram
lozenge, rhombus
quad, quadrate
quadrangle, plane with four sides and four angles
quadrate, square area
quadrilateral, plane with four sides and four right-angles
rectangle, figure with four right-angles
rhomb, rhombus
rhomboid, four-sided figure having its opposites equal but not right-angled
rhombus, four-sided figure whose sides are equal and parallel and whose opposite angles are obtuse and acute
square, parallelogram having four equal sides and four right angles
tetragon, plane with four sides and angles
tetrahedron, solid having four triangles

NOUNS (Continued)
trapezium, quadrilateral without parallel sides
trapezoid, quadrilateral with two parallel sides
  quinque-, (prefix) five
pentagon, form of five sides and five angles
pentahedron, form having five sides
  sex-, (prefix) six
  hexa-, (prefix) six
cube, figure with six equal square sides
hexagon, plane having six angles and sides
hexahedron, form bounded by six plane faces
parallelopiped, prism with six faces, all parallelograms
rhombohedron, figure bounded by six rhombic planes
  hepta-, (prefix) seven
  septa-, (prefix) seven
heptagon, plane having seven angles and seven sides
heptahedron, form with seven sides
  octa-, (prefix) eight
octagon, plain figure with eight angles and sides
octahedron, figure contained by eight equal equilateral triangles
  non-, (prefix) nine
  enne-, (prefix) nine
nonagon, plane with nine sides and angles
enneagon, nonagon
  deca-, (prefix) ten
decagon, plane with ten sides and angles
decahedron, solid bounded by ten plane faces
  hendeca-, (prefix) eleven
hendeca, form with eleven plane faces
hendecagon, form with eleven sides and eleven angles

NOUNS (Continued)
undecagon, form with eleven sides and eleven angles
  dodeca-, (prefix) twelve
dodecagon, a polygon of twelve angles and sides
dodecahedron, solid with twelve faces

Polygon, Etc.

cone, figure with a circle base that tapers up to a vertex
equilateral, figure with equal sides.
facet, minute plane on a diamond, etc.
frustum, figure represented by the lower part of a pyramid cut off parallel to its base; the same applies to the cone
icosahedron, form having twenty planes
isogen, figure with equal angles
parallelogram, plane whose four-sided opposite sides are parallel and equal
parallax, angular difference due to view from different positions
polygon, figure having many angles
polyhedron, form having many sides or faces
prism, figure whose ends are equal and parallel polygons and whose sides are parallelograms
prismoid, figure with two faces that are parallel polygons and the remaining faces triangles or quadrilaterals
pyramid, figure with a square base and triangular sides terminating in a point at the apex
solid, figure having length, breadth, and thickness

Angularity

angularity, the quality of having angles
refrangibility, refraction

SHARP OR POINTED SHAPES   see—

vs. Obtuse Shapes 150D

(ASSOCIATIVE 150A)
(Pin, Nail ....52D)

150E

VERBS

Miscellaneous
hone, sharpen
sharpen, give a keen edge
taper, come or bring to a
    point

ADJECTIVES

Sharp
fine, keen
keen, sharp
sharp, having a fine edge

Pointed
acuminate, sharp-pointed
acute, pointed
cuneate, wedge-shaped
cuneiform, wedge-shaped
pointed, having a point
punctate, pointed
punctiform, point-shaped
tapering, diminished to a
    point

ADJECTIVES (Continued)

Lanciform, Etc.
ancipital, two-edged
arrow-headed, arrow-
    pointed
cusped, cusp-like
cuspidate, having a spear-
    like point
lanciform, lance-shaped

Spiky
aculeate, having a sting or
    prickles
aciform, needle-shaped
clavate, nail-like
pectinate, pectinated
pectinated, shaped like the
    teeth of a comb
spicate, spike-like
spicular, dart-like
spiky, spike-like

Tooth-like
dentate, toothed

ADJECTIVES (Continued)
dentiform, tooth-shaped
dentoid, tooth-shaped
odontoid, tooth-like

Furcated
bicuspid, having two
    points
bifurcated, forked
forked, fork-like
furcated, forked
serrated, notched like a
    saw

Sword-like
ensiform, sword-shaped
gladiate, sword-shaped
sword-like, gladiate

NOUNS
cusp, a point
point, sharp end
spicule, pointed body
spike, nail, wedge
wedge, pointed form

150F

RADIAL OR BRANCHING FORMS see—

vs. Straight 149C

(ASSOCIATIVE 150A)

150F

VERBS

Miscellaneous
cross, place crosswise
intersect, cross each other
radiate, branch out from a
    center

ADJECTIVES

Radial
asterial, radiating, as star-
    rays
radial, branching from a
    center like rays
radiative, radial

Stelliform
actinoid, starfish-shaped
asteroid, star-shaped
astral, star-like

ADJECTIVES (Continued)
stellate, star-like
stelliform, having radiat-
    ing points

Cruciform
antiparallel, running in
    parallel opposite direc-
    tions
cross, not parallel
cruciform, cross-shaped
decussate, intersected
transverse, crosswise

Branched
bifurcate, divided into
    branches
branched, divided branch-
    like
ramose, branched

ADJECTIVES (Continued)
tridentate, having three
    prongs

ADVERBS
across, transverse
athwart, crosswise
crosswise, cross-shaped
thwart, crosswise

NOUNS

Miscellaneous
cross, crucifix, etc.
crossing, intersection
crucifix, the Christcross
fork, diverting branch
intersection, crossing place
radius, radial form

CORPOREAL SHAPES

vs. Vegetative Shapes....................150H

(ASSOCIATIVE 150A)

150G

VERBS

Miscellaneous
dimple, form a dimple
pucker, purse, wrinkle
purse, pucker
wrinkle, crease the brow

ADJECTIVES

Well-shaped
clean-cut, well-shaped
clear-cut, clean-cut
delicate, clean-cut
symmetrical, clean-cut

Slim
gaunt, lean
lank, slim
lanky, lank
lean, thin
long, not short
peakish, thin-featured
skinny, lank
slabsided, flat-sided
slender, slim
slim, thin
thin, slim

Chunky
chubby, plump
chunky, dumpy
dumpy, stocky
dwarfish, abnormally short
podgy, short and round
short, not long
stumpy, stubby
stubby, chubby

Fleshy
beefy, corpulent
bulky, corpulent
corpulent, fleshy
fat, corpulent
fleshy, plump
gross, thick
hulking, bulky
obese, corpulent
plump, rotund
portly, corpulent
rotund, corpulent
squat, short and stout
stocky, short and stout
stout, corpulent
thick, chunky

Stooped
bent, stooped
gibbous, hunchbacked
hucklebacked, round-
shouldered
humpbacked, hunchbacked
hunchbacked, humpbacked
stooped, humpbacked

Flat-footed, Etc.
bandy, bowlegged

ADJECTIVES (Continued)
bowlegged, bandy
club-footed, club-shaped
flat-footed, having flat feet
knock-kneed, having bent-
in knees
pigeon-toed, toeing in
slue-footed, turning or
twisting the feet when
walking

Flat-nosed
flat-nosed, simous
platyrhine, broad-nosed
simous, platyrhine

Aquiline
aduncous, hooked
aquiline, beak-nosed
hooked, aquiline
hook-nosed, aquiline
rostral, beak-like

Bald
bald, hairless
dipilos, bald
glabrous, bald
hairless, bald

Horned
cornuted, having horns
horned, having horns
horny, as above

Tailless, Etc.
bobtailed, short-tailed
caudate, tail-like
escaudate, tailless
tailless, without tail

Winged, Etc.
alar, wing-shaped
aliform, wing-shaped
aliped, wing-footed
apteral, without wings
apterous, as above
bipennate, two-winged
dipterous, double-winged
wing-like, aliform

Miscellaneous
actinoid, starfish-shaped
auriform, ear-shaped
bilabiate, having two lips
bimanous, two-handed
biped, two-footed
bipedal, as above
crural, leg-shaped
decapod, having ten feet
or ten arms
digitate, finger-shaped
dimply, having dimples
equine, horse-like

NOUNS
lingulate, tongue-shaped
ophidian, snake-like
pinnate, feather-shaped
polypod, having many feet
quadrumanous, four-
handed
simian, monkey-like
Etc., etc.

Head, Etc.
brow, forehead
cranium, skull
crown, top of the head
forehead, head above the
eyes
head, upper part of body
pate, head
skull, brain case

Tail
fox-brush, fox's tail
scut, a short tail
tail, hind pendant

Abdomen
abdomen, belly
belly, stomach
stomach, abdomen

Hip, Etc.
buttock, hip
haunch, buttock
hip, haunch
huckle, hip
rump, the body behind

Corpulence, Etc.
chubbiness, plumpness
corpulence, rotundity
embonpoint, plumpness
plumpness, chubbiness
portliness, corpulence
rotundity, plumpness
stockiness, stoutness

Miscellaneous
aduncity, shape of a
parrot's bill
ankle, joint above foot
armpit, shoulder cavity
axilla, armpit
body, animal form
bosom, breast
chin, point below the
mouth
dimple, cheek or chin
indentation
elbow, joint above wrist
finger, digit
heart, center of the
vascular system
knee, joint below thigh
knuckle, finger joint, etc.
leg, supporting limb
palm, inner hand
(Continued on page 402)

150H

VERBS (See Adjectives)

ADJECTIVES

Miscellaneous

arborescent, tree-shaped
arboreous, as above
bifoliate, two-leaved
branchy, having branches
bushy, growing thick
coniferous, bearing cones
dendroid, arborescent
emarginate, notched on
edges
foliaceous, leaf-shaped

NOUNS

Miscellaneous

arborescence, tree-like formation, as in certain
crystals
bough, tree-branch
branch, minor limb
branchlet, small limb
bush, thick shrub
frond, palm-leaf
evergreen, shrub or tree
herbage, herbs collectively
grass, herbage

NOUNS (Continued)

leaf, flat and thin appendage of a plant
limb, tree-branch
shoot, young branch
shrub, woody plant
shrubbery, shrubs collectively
sprout, shoot
tree, plant with trunk,
branches, and leaves
trunk, stem of a tree
Etc., etc.

150G (Continued)

NOUNS (Continued)

physique, the body
shank, leg below knee
tarsus, ankle, heel

NOUNS (Continued)

toe, digit of the foot
wrist, joint above hand
Etc., etc.

PERSONS

butter-ball, short, stout
woman
grampus, corpulent person

INDEX

absolve 47, 138D
absorb take in 49A
 drink 51B, 8, 99A,
 114
absorbent 49A, 51B
absorptiometer 95B
absorption 49A
absorptive 49A, 51B
abstain refrain 132C
 behave 140A
abstemious 132C
abstentious 132C
abstergent
 cleansing 138A
 purification 138B
abstersive 138A,
 138B
abstinence
 forbearance 132C
abstinent 132C
abstract
 take from 49A,
 145A, 145K,
 58, 86, 113, 114
abstraction 145A,
 49A
abstractional 145A
abstractionist, 113,
 134B
abstruse
 obscure 57, 13, 117
 hidden 103A
absurd
 foolish 60, 110B
 ridiculous 109A
 fantastic 57
 inconsistent 126C
 preposterous 126A
absurdity*
abundance
 much 147I, 26,
 43A
abundant*
abuse 65, 125A,
 130M, 130B
abusive 130M, 130B
abut 149J, 124, 149M
abutment 149J, 53R,
 53G
abuzz buzz-like 69A
abysm gulf 25H
abysmal 149G, 25
abyss 25H, 149G,
 96A, 139N
acacia plant 143E
academic
 educational 81,
 116
academicals 106D
academician 81, 116
academy 81
acanthus plant
 143E
accede comply 46A
accelerando 9
accelerate 9
acceleration 9
accelerator 9

accent 10
 stress 69B, 55B,
 69C
accentual 69B, 10,
 69C
accentuate 69B, 10,
 69C
accept receive 49B
 acquiesce 46A
 promise to pay 89
 yield in belief 113
 understand 117
acceptability 49B
acceptable 49B
acceptance 49B, 89
acceptation 49B,
 113, 117
access opening 25,
 25B
accessibility 25
accessible 25
accession
 attainment 49B
 agreement 46A
 increase 10
 commencement 4
accessional 49B, 10,
 46A, 4
accessory 130A
 increasing 10
 aid 5A, 146A
accidence
 inflection 3A
accident
 contingency 127A
 mishap 127B
accidental 127A
acclaim praise 63
acclamation 63
acclamatory 63
acclimate 132D
acclimatize 132D
acclivity slope 149D,
 149E
accolade 107E
accolated 146A,
 100A
accommodate aid 5A
 adapt 132A
 supply 43B
 lend 46A, 45
accommodation*
accommodative*
accompaniment
 68B, 146A, 68A,
 132A
accompanist 68H
accompany 68A,
 24A, 146K
 join 146A
accomplice aid 5A
 associate 146L
 abettor 130L,
 130A
accomplish
 achieve 50, 12
 know 117

accomplished
 learned 117
 perfect 132A,
 134B
accomplishment 50,
 117, 134B
accord
 reconcile 132A,
 46A, 68A, 132B,
 148L
accordant 132A, 46A
accordion
 instrument 68G
accost speak to 55A
 to front 149H,
 85A
accouchement
 parturition 141B
accoucher 136B
account explain 84
 reckon 115
 statement 86, 85A,
 147L
accountability 88
accountable
 answerable 88
accountancy 88, 115
accountant 86, 88,
 115
accouter
(B). accoutre
 equip 132A
 dress 106B, 107A,
 137B
accredit believe 113
 authorize 94, 139A
accrescent
 growing 144B
 increasing 10
accrete adhere 52E
 unite 146A
 gain 49A
 increase 10, 144B
accretion 146A, 10,
 49A
accroachment
 usurpation 49G
accrue attain 49A,
 10
accrument 49A, 10
acultural 6, 116
accumbent 149C
accumulation
 amassment 49E
 mass 147I, 146A
accumulative 49E,
 10
accuracy
 preciseness 134A
 truth 61A
accurate 134A, 61A,
 117
accursed 129B
accusation blame 65
accusative 65
accusatory 65
accuse blame 65
accustom 132D

accustomed 132D,
 148L
 practiced 134B
ace unit 147A, 42,
 130-O
acentric not in
 center 149A
acephala
 bivalve 143B
acephalous 112,
 125A
acerbity
 acrimony 64
 harshness 29
 sourness 48Q
acetanilide 5C
acetate 5C
acetic acid 5C
acetification 3A
acetify 3A, 144B,
 48Q
acetimeter 95B
acetin 5C
acetone 5C
acetylene 5C
ache pain 31, 128B
acheron 130N
achievable
 subject 46B
achieve gain 49A,
 50
achievement 49A,
 escutcheon 104B,
 50, 149H
aching suffering 31,
 130B
achromatic 101A,
 102A
achromatize 101A,
 102B
achromatous 101A
acid sour 48Q
acidic 48Q
acidific 48Q
acidification 48Q
acidify 48Q
 embitter 130C
aciform
 pointed 150E
acinaceous 142F,
 141A
acknowledge
 admit 61A
 confess 78, 38, 117
acknowledgment
 appreciation 38
aclinic 132C
acme highest
 point 149F
acne eruption 16
acock 149D
acology
 remedy 136B, 83
acolyte 82G
aconite plant 142A,
 143E, 136B
aconitina drug 136B

acorn seed 142F
acotyledon 142A,
   143E
acoumeter 95B
acoustic 118, 83
acquaint
   announce 79, 81,
    92
   familiarize 116,
    117
acquaintance 117,
   146L
acquiesce agree 46A
   submit 46B
acquire attain 49A
acquirement 49A
acquisition 49A
acquisitive 49A .
   greedy 39
acquit free 47
   exonerate 138D
acquittal 47, 138D
acquittance 47,
   138D
acre 147E
acreage 25G
acrid sharp 48Q, 64
acridity 48Q, 29, 64
acrimony 48Q
   anger 29, 64, 28
acrobacy 99B
acrobat 99D
acrobatism 99B
acrolith 100B
acrophobia 32
acropolis
   citadel 36B
across 150F
acrostic 61B
act start 4, 3A
   decree 94
   an acting
    part 99B, 99A
   thesis 85A, 85B
   make 144B
   play 99A, 99B
   move 19A
acting ruling 133A
actinic 3A
actinism 3A
actinium 5D
actinograph 95B
actinoid 150F
actinology 83
actinometer 95B
action change 3C
   start 4, 19A
   production 144B
actionable 3A
active moving 19A,
   3A, 1, 3C, 144B
   aiding 5A
   constant 11A
   lively 9, 137B
activity*

actor 99D
actress 99D
actual true 61A, 1,
   137C
actuality 61A
actualize 61A, 84
actuary
   registrar 86, 115
actuate start 4, 7, 8
actuation 4, 19A, 8
aculeate sharp 150E
acumen
   discrimination 115
   insight 117
acuminate
   sharp 150E, 150D
acute pointed 150E
   discriminating
    115, 117, 134B
   59, 130M, 150D
   130B
ad 79
adage proverb 61B
Adam's ale
   water 48J
adamant
   hardness 146B,
    137B
adamantine 146B,
   137B
adapt
   to fit 132A, 134A,
    146A
adaptation 132A, 105
add unite 146A
   sum up 115
   affix 74
   increase 10
addendum 74, 10,
   146A
adder 143F, 130M
addict devotee 39,
   38, 71A, 132D
addition
   appendix 74
   unity 146A
   increase 10
additional 74, 146A,
   10, 147I
addle 146C, 128C,
   129A
address
   straighten 132A
   redress 45
   speak, write 55A,
    55B
   consign 43B
   bearing 95E, 95C,
    145B, 40, 85A,
    134B
addressee 118
adduce prove 93
   conclude 115
adducent 93, 115
adductive 93, 115

adenoid 25E
adept skilled 134B
adequacy
   fitness 132A
   repletion 26, 147I
adequate 132A, 26,
   147I
adhere stick 52E,
   52A
adherence 52E
   affection 39A
   attachment 146A
adherent 52E
   follower 146K, 38,
    39, 132C, 146L
adhesion 52E
adhesive 52F, 52E
adieu 15, 63, 91
adit passage 25
adjacency 149M,
   149J
adjacent 149M, 149J
adjectival 84, 55A
adjective 84, 92,
   55A
adjoin unite 146A,
   149J, 149M
adjourn postpone 12
adjournment 12
adjudge decree 94
   determine 115
adjudicate 94, 115
adjudication 94, 115
adjunct 146A, 5A
adjunctive 146A
adjuration 94
adjure 94, 40B
adjust fit 132A,
   134A, 136B,
   132B, 132D,
   146A
adjustment*
adjutancy 133A
adjutant 133A
adjutant-general
   133A
admeasure
   measure 115, 147L
admeasurement*
administer
   manage 133A
   dispense 43B
administration*
administrator*
administratrix*
admirable attrac-
   tive, 108, 140B,
   48P, 99A
admiral 133A
admiralty 133A
admiration
   fondness 38, 63
   wonder 112
admire esteem 38

admission
   frankness 61A, 78
   permission 46A
   acceptance 49B
admit*
admittance*
admix mix 146C
admixture 146C
admonish reprove 64
   warn 79
   threaten 33
   prophesy 77
admonition*
admonitory*
adnascent 141A,
   141B
adnate 141A, 146,
   141B
ado confusion 125A
adobe 5B
adolescence 148J, 10
adolescent 148J, 10
Adonis 108
adopt choose 49A
adoption 49A
adoptive 49A
adorable
   attractive 108
   lovable 140B
adoration esteem 38
   love 39A
adore 38, 39A
adorn
   beautify 107A,
    108
adornment 107A,
   107B
adown down 149G
adrift aimless 18B
adroit
   dexterous 134B
adulation praise 63,
   40
adulator 63
adulatory 63
adult 148J
adulterant 146C
adulterate 146C
adulterer 146E, 39C,
   125C-3
adulteress*
adulterous 146C,
   39C, 125C-3,
   146D
adultery 146C, 146D,
   39C, 125C-3
adumbrant shadow-
   ing 95A
adumbrate
   to shadow 95A,
    97, 76
   show 95E
   resemble 105
adumbration*
aduncous
   hook-like 150G

advance
  proceed 19A
  aid 5A, 6
  pay beforehand 45
  increase 10
  offer 40A
  front 149H
advancement 139A, 139B
advantage
  benefit 5A
  luck 134D, 40A, 50
advantageous 5A, 134D
advent 148H
  arrival 146A
advent 148K, 148B 148H
adventitious
  by chance 127A
adventual 148K
adventure
  boldness 42, 127A, 119E
adventurer 42, 127A, 39, 119E
adventurous 42, 39
adventuress 42, 127A
adverb defining word 55A
adverbial 55A, 55B
adversary 41D, 130F
adversative
  adverse 27
adverse opposed 27
  unfortunate 127B
  dispute 66, 67A
  resentful 28
adversity 127B
  misery 31
advert apprehend 111, 119G
advertence*
advertent*
advertise publish 79
advertisement 79
advice
  information 78
  suggestion 87
advisability 132A
advisable 132A
advise
  inform 78, 87, 79
advised cautious 32
advisement 114
advisory 78, 87
advocacy
  appeal 40B
advocate 40B, 5A, 63
advolution 141A
advowee 43A, 49B
advowson 43A
adynamia 128A
adz 145F

aedile edile 82G, 133A
Æolian harp 68D
Æolus 125B
æon eon 148C
aerate 146C
aeration 7
aerial 23, 149F
aerie 53D
aeriform 145J
aero 149F
aerocyst 53Q
aerodrome 53B
aerogram 55A, 55B
aerolite 101D
aerology 83
aerometer 95B
aeronaut 23
aeronautic 23
aerophone 55C
aerophore 131A
aerophyte 143E
aeroplane 24I
aerostat balloon 24I
aerostatic 24I
aerostatics 83
aery eagle's nest 53D, 142E, 141D
Æsculapius 136B
æsthetic 117, 132A, 119F, 108, 134B
æstheticism*
æther 145J
æthrioscope 95B
afar distant 149N
affability 46A, 38
affable 46A, 38
  inviting 40A, 40B, 136A
affect actuate 8, 19A
  have liking 39, 103B, 95D, 124
affectation*
affecting 8, 124, 130B
affection
  fondness 38, 39, 121
  love 39A
  disease 130E
affectionate 38, 39A
afferent 146A
affiance
  betroth 89, 146G
affidavit proof 93
affiliate 146I, 146K, 49A, 146H, 146A
affiliation*
affinity likeness 105
  consanguinity 146I, 146H
  sexual attraction 39B, 39
affirm assert 80
  confirm 61A, 93

affirmance*
affirmant*
affirmation*
affirmative 80, 61A, 93
affix append 74
  attach 52B
  unite 146A
afflatus wind 125B
  exaltation 71A
afflict distress 130B
  cause pain 130M
affliction 130B, 130M
  suffering 31, 128B, 130E
afflictive 130M
affluence
  riches 135B, 49E
affluent 135B, 49E
  abundant 147I
afflux increase 10
afford
  supply 43A, 43B
affranchise
  permit 46A
  free 47
affray
  fight 41D, 130F
affright
  frighten 33, 96A
affront 42, 130C, 28, 64
affusion
  pouring 16, 145I
afghan robe 107B
afield 149N, 149A
aflame alight 101A
  afire 131B
afloat 23
afoot 19B
aforementioned 73
aforesaid 73
afraid 32
afresh 148E, 75
African 54C
Africander 54C
aft, 149I
after 149I, 148B
after-clap 127B
aftergrass 49A
aftermath 49A
  result 144E
afternoon 148B, 148K
afterward 148B, 149I
again 75, 146A
against 27, 149M
agape
  watchful 119C, 119G
agate 107D
agave plant 143E
age 148I, 148C, 148J
aged 148A
agency aid 5A, 144C, 134C

agent 5A, 144C, 46B, 133A, 134C, 144D
agglomerate 146A, 146C
agglomeration*
agglomerant 52E
agglutinant uniting 52E, 52F
agglutinate 52E
aggrandize 139B, 10
aggravate
  trouble 130B, 13, 130C, 10, 130M
aggregate
  amass 49E
  unify 146A, 146K
aggregation 146A, 146K
aggress
  attack 130F
  oppose 27
aggression*
aggrieve
  oppress 130B
aghast
  frightened 32
  perplexed 112
agile 3C, 9, 19B
agility 3C, 9
agio premium 45
agiotage
  exchange 49D
agitate excite 8, 96A
  discuss 66
  deliberate 114, 90
  disorder 125A
agitation 8, 66, 125A, 112
agitator 8, 66, 67A, 90
aglow glowing 101A
aglutition 128B
agnail whitlow 128B
agni 131B
agnomen name 92
agnostic 30, 110B, 67A, 82D, 130F
agnosticism 30, 110B, 82B
ago past 148A
agog eager 39, 71A
agnostics 41D
agonize suffer 31
  torture 130N, 130M
agony anguish 31, 130B
agouti rodent 143A
agrarian 43B
agree consent 46A
  harmonize 132A, 105
  promise 89

agreeable 46A, 132A, 38, 89, 99A, 136A
agreement 46A, 132A, 89, 105
mutual understanding 115
agricultural 144B
agriculture 144B
agriculturist 144D
agrin, grinning 98B
aground
impotent 128A
ague fever 128B
ah 91
aha 91
ahead 149H, 149N
ahem 91
ahoy a hail 41B
ai sloth 143A
aid help 5A, 136A
aide-de-camp 133A
aigret plume 106H
bird 143C
ail suffer 31
cause pain 130B
ailment 128B, 130E
aim endeavor 41C, 39
tend 2, 12, 149H
aimless 127A
air space 25A, 95D, 95A, 95C, 145J, 78, 98A, 68B
air brake 12
air craft 24I
air gun 130H, 130I
airily joyously 71A
airiness gaiety 71A
airing exposure 78
airman 23
airplane 24I
air plant 143E
airship 24I
airy breezy 125B, 95D
gay 71A
aisle passage 25, 25B
ajar open 25
discordant 70
ajax 42
akimbo 149J
akin related 146I
alabaster 5C
alack 91
alacrity
briskness 19B, 9
readiness 2, 3C, 71A
alalus
ape-man 143A
alamode
in style 108
a silk 106K
alar 23, 150G

alarm fear 32
warning 79, 76
menace 33
alarming 33
alary 150G, 23
alas 91
alate 23
alb 106I
albata 5C
albatross bird 143C
airship 24I
albeit 27
albino 142B, 143A
album 100A
albumen 5C
albumin 5C
alcalde 133A
alchemist 3A
alchemy 3A
alcohol 48L
alcoholic 48L
alcoholism 130E
alcoran 82A, 82B
alcove 53E
alder 143E
alderman 133A
ale 48L
alecto 130M, 130N
alee 149J
alert watchful 119G, 2, 39
alevolate 25
alexandrine 85C
alfalfa 48N
algae plant 143E
algebra 147L, 83
algebraic 147L
alias name 92
alibi 149N, 93
alien foreign 126A, 145K, 54C
alienable 145K
alienage 145K
alienate 145K, 126A, 3A, 43B, 145A
alienation 145K, 43B, 3A
alienism 145K, 126A
alienist 136B
aliform 150G
alight descend 22
lighted 101A
align 149C
alignment 149C, 100B
alike 105
aliment food 48A
allowance 43B, 45
alimental 48A, 43B
alimentary 48A
alimentary canal 25E
alimentation 48A, 25E
alimentiveness 51A
instinct for food 39

alimony 45
aline 149C
aliped 150G
aliquant 147A, 145K, 147L
aliquot 147A, 145D, 145K, 147L
alive 9, 121, 137B, 137C
alkahest 145B, 145J
alkali 5C
alkaline 5C
alkaloid 5C
alkanet plant 143E
all 147I, 146A
all along 146A
all-hail 91
Allhallowe'en 148K
Allhallows 148K
allopathy 130E
all-round 117
all-sorts 146C
Allah 82E
allay calm 132A
abate 12
relieve 136A, 136B
allegation
declaration 80, 61A
proof 93
allege affirm 61A, 80, 93
allegiance 146K, 140A
allegoric
figurative 92, 81, 57, 84
allegorize 92, 81, 84
allegory 92, 81, 84
alleviate lessen 14
aid 5A
succor 136A, 136B
alleviation*
alleviative 14, 136B
alley lane 25B
alliaceous 48P
alliance union 146A, 146H, 146K
alligation 115
alligator 143F, 143B
alliteration 75
alliterative 75
allocate 43B, 43A, 145A
allocation 43B, 43A
allocution 85A
allodial 54A
allodium 54A, 53D
allograph 92
allomorphism 3A
allopath 136B, 31
allopathic 136B, 111
allopathy 136B, 111
alloquialism 55A
allotment 43B, 145A, 147L
allotropic 3A

allotropism 126A, 3A
allotropy 3A
allow yield 46A
provide 43B
allowance
concession 46A
grant 43A, 45, 43B
sum 147L
alloy 146C
allspice 48P
allude 57, 84, 87
allure
persuade 40A, 39, 108
allurement 40A, 12, 40
allusion 57, 84, 87
allusive 57, 84, 87
uncertain 127A
alluvial 146C
alluvion 146C
alluvium 146C, 129A
ally 5A, 146K
unite 146A, 146H
almagra 102D
almanac 86, 148G
almightiness 137B, 1
almighty 137B
God 82E
almond 48G
almoner 43A
almonry 43A
almost 127B
alms 43A
almshouse 43A
aloe 143E
aloes 122
aloft 149F
alone 145K, 145A, 147A
along 149H, 149N
alongside 149J
aloof 149M, 145A, 145K, 149N
haughty 28
alopecia 130E
aloud 69B
alpaca fabric 106K
llama 143A
alpen-glow 101B, 102A
alpen-horn 68G
alpenstock 53R
alpha 4, 73
alphabet 55B, 86
already 2
also 146A, 10
altar 53G, 104H
altazimuth 95B
alter 3A, 126A
alterant 3A, 102E
alteration 3A, 3B
alterative 3A, 136B
altercate 66, 41D
altercation 41D, 66
alternate 3A, 149G

alternant 149J, 102E
alternation 3A,
  149G, 68B, 3B
alternative 46A,
  49A, 136B
alternator 3A
alt-horn 68G
although 27
altimeter 95B
altimetry 115
altisonant 68A
altitude 149F
alto 68A
altogether 146A
alto-relievo 100B
altruism 43A, 136A,
  140A
altruist 43A, 136A,
  140A
altruistic*
alum 5C
alumina 102E
aluminite 5C
aluminum 5D
alumna 116, 117
alumnus 116, 117
alveolated 25H
always 11A
am 11A, 134C, 105,
  148B
amain 137B, 148D
amalgam 146C
amalgamate 146C,
  146A, 146B,
  146K
amalgamation*
amanuensis 85E,
  55B
amaranth 143E,
  102E
amaranthine 102A
amass 49E, 146A
amassment 49E,
  146A
amateur 38, 39, 71A
amative 39A
amativeness 39A,
  39B
amatory 39A
amaurosis 119B
amaurotic 119B
amaze
  wonder 112, 140B
  bewildering 96A
amazement 112
amazing 96A, 95E,
  99A, 108, 140B
Amazon 42
ambassador 133A
ambassadress 133A
amber 5C, 102A
ambergris 122
ambidexter 134B
ambidexterous 134B,
  62
ambient 149K

ambiguity 57, 103B,
  127A
ambiguous*
ambit 150C
ambition 39, 149H
ambitious 39
amble 19B
amblyopia 119B
ambrosia 48F, 122
ambrosial 48F, 122,
  48P
ambrotype 100A,
  100B
ambulance 24H
ambulant 19B
ambulation 19B
ambulator 19B, 95B
ambulatory
  walking 19B
  temporary 148D
  passage 25B
ambuscade 130F
ambush 130F, 49F
ameba 142F
ameer 133A
ameliorate 5A, 6
  improve 132B
amen verily 61A, 91
amenable 46B
amend 136B
amendment 136B
amends
  reparation 136B
  compensation 45
amenity 38, 136A
amenorrhea 12
amentia 110B
amerce exaction
  41B
  payment, fine 45
amercement 41B, 45
American 54C
Americanism 126A
amethyst 102D,
  107D
amethystine 102A
amiability 38, 46B
amiable 38, 46B
amicable 38
amice 106I, 106H
amid 149L
amidship 149L
amiss 126C
amity 38
ammonia 5C
ammonite 146B
ammunition 130I,
  43B
amnesia 110A
amnesty 47
amoeba 142F
among 149L
amorous 39A
amorphism 126A
amorphous
  formless 150B
  anomalous 126A
  deformity 109B

amortize 43A, 44
amount 147L
amour 39C, 39B,
  146D
ampere 147M
Amphibia 143F
amphibian 143F,
  143A
amphibious 143F,
  149A
amphibolic 57
amphibrach 55B
amphioxus 143B
amphitheatre
(B). amphitheatre
  99E, 25A
amphitype 100A
amphora 53N
ample 147I, 147J,
  25
ampliative 10
amplification 10
amplify 10, 147J,
  56, 84
amplitude 147L,
  147J
ampulla 53N
amputate 145F
amt 133A
amt-man 133A
amuck 130F, 130-O
amulet 34
amusement 99A,
  71A, 99C
amuse 99A
amygdalin 5C
amyl 5C
amylene 5C
an 147A, 92
ana 86
anachronism 126C,
  148G
anachronistic 126C
anaconda boa 143F
anadromous 149D
anaesthesia 110A
Ananias 62
analytic 84
anarchic 125A
anaemic 128A
anemia 128A
anesthetic 136B,
  121, 110A
anaglyph 100B
anaglyptograph
  100B, 100A
anagram 55A
anal 25E
analect 86, 93
analectic 86, 93, 37
analgesia 110A
analgesic 136B,
  110A
analgetic 110A
analogical 105, 87,
  132A
analogism 114
analogist 114

analogize 114
  explain 84
  liken 105, 92
analogous 105, 92
analogue 105, 92
analogy 105, 84, 114
analysis 115, 145A
analyst 115
analyze 115, 145A
  119E
anapest 55A
anaphrodisiac 136B
anaplasty 136B
anarchic 125A, 130A
anarchism 125A
anarchist 130A
anarthrous 146A
anastrophe 3A
anathema 64, 65,
  129B
anathematize 64, 65,
  35A
anatomism 145A, 84
anatomist 145A,
  145F
anatomize 145A,
  145F
anatomy 145F,
  145A, 83
ancestor 141E, 148A
ancestral 141A,
  141B
ancestress 141E
ancestry 141G
anchor 52A, 49C
anchorage 149M
anchoret 145K, 15,
  54B
anchovy 143B
ancient 148A, 126A
ancillary 5A, 46B
ancipital 145F, 150E
ancon 53R
and 146A
andesite 5C
andirons 53P
androcephalous
  150G
androgynous 141B
androsphinx 150G
anecdote 85A
anemia 128A
anemograph 95B
anemometer 95B
anemoscope 95B
aneroid 95B
aneurism 128B
anew 75
angel 24F, 79, 82E
  140B
angel-fish 143B
angelic 24F, 82E,
  24A, 79, 140B
angelus 40B
anger wrath 29
  provoke 130C
angina pectoris
  128B

angiology 83, 82B
angle to fish 41D
   shape 150D
   slope 149D
angler 41D
anglican 82D
anglicanism 82B
anglicism 55A
anglicize 55A
Anglophobia 28
Angora 106K, 106A
Angora-cat 143A
Angora-goat 143A
angriness 29
angry 29
anguish 31, 130N
angular 150D
angularity 150D
angustate 150D
anhydride 5C
anil 143E
anile 128A
aniline 102E
anility 128A
animadversion 111
   censure 64, 119F
animadversive 111
animadvert 111, 64
animal 143A
animalcular 142F
animalcule 142F
animalculum 142F
animalia 143A
animalism 125C
animalistic 125C
animate enliven 8, 9
   live 137B, 141A,
     136B, 137C
animation 8, 9, 3A
animative 8, 9
animism 83, 82C,
   82B
animosity 28
animus 28, 2
anise 143E
ankle 150G
anklet 52A, 107C
ankylosis 130E,
   146A
ankylostomiasis
   130E
ankylotic 130E
annalist 86
annals 86, 85B,
   148G, 85D
anneal 146B, 145J
annex 146A, 145D,
   74
annexation 146A, 74
annihilate 130-O
   wipe out 131A
annihilation 130C
anniversary 148L,
   148K
annotation 84
announce 77, 79
announcement 79,
   92
announcer 55C

annoy trouble 13
   abuse 130B
   offend 130C
annoyance 130B, 13,
   130C
annual 148K
annuitant 49B
annuity 45
annul 131A
annular 150C
annulate 150C
annulation 150C
annulet 150C
annulment 131A
annulosa 143D
annulose 150C
annunciate 77, 79
annunciation 77, 79,
   148K
annunciator 95B
anode 150C
anodyne 136B
anoint 94, 139A
anomalistic 126A
anomalous 126A, 57
anomaly 126A, 57
anon 75, 148L
anonym 92
anonymity 92
anonymous 92
Anopheles 143D
another 147A,
   126A
answer reply 88
   solution 115
ant 143D
ant-bear 143A
ant-eater 143A
ant-lion 143D
antacid 136B
Antæus 137B
antagonism
   hostility 28
   dispute 66, 67A
   attack 130F, 41D
antagonist 41D, 66
antagonistic 28, 66,
   67A, 130F
antagonize 41D, 27
antarctic 149B
antecede 148A,
   149H
antecedence 148A,
   149H, 73
antecedent 149H, 73
antecessor 149H
antechamber 53E
antedate 148A
antediluvian 148A
antelope 143A
antemeridian 148A
antemetic 136B
antemundane 148A
antenatal 148A,
   141B
antenna 121
antenuptial 148A,
   146H, 146G

antepaschal 148A
antepenult 149I
antepenultimate
   149I
anteprandial 148A
anterior 149H, 148A
anteriority 149H,
   148A
anteroom 149H, 53E
anthelion 101B
anthem 68B
anther 142F
antheroid 142F
anthological 86
anthologist 86
anthology 86, 85C
anthracene 5C
anthracite 5C
anthrax 128B
anthropography 83
anthropoid 143A
Anthropoidea 143A
anthropological 83,
   149A
anthropologist 83
anthropology 83
anthropometric
   150G
anthropometry
   150G
anthropomorphism
   82E, 82B
anthropophagi 51A,
   130-O
anthropophagous
   51A
anti-aircraft 36
antic 99A, 99D
Antichrist 30
antichristian 30
anticipant 49A,
   149H
anticipate 49A, 39,
   115
anticipation 49A,
   113, 39, 115
anticlimax 12, 74,
   72
anticyclone 125B
antidotal 136B
antidote 136B
antifebrile 136B
antifebrine 136B
antimoniate 5C
antimony 136B, 27,
   5D
antimonianism 27,
   82B
antinomy 27, 28
Antinous 108
antiparallel 150D,
   150F
antipathetic 28, 27
antipathic 27, 28
antipathy 28, 129B
antiperiodic 136B
antiphlogistic 136B
antiphon 68B, 88
antiphonal 68B, 88

antiphonary 88, 68B
antiphonetic 88, 68B
antiphony 88, 68B
antiphrasis 72
antipodal 149N
antipode 149N
antipodean 149N
antipodes 149N
antipyretic 136B
antipyrin 136B
antiquarian 148A,
   83
antiquarianism
   148A
antiquary 148A, 83
antiquated 148A,
   109A
antique 148A, 148J
antiquity 148A
antiscorbutic 136B
anti-Semitic 27
antisepsis 136B,
   138B
antiseptic 136B,
   138B
antislavery 27
antispasmodic 136B
antisplenetic 136B
antistrophe 68B
antithesis 27, 126A
antithetic 27, 126A
antitoxin 136B
antitrade 125B
antler 130H
antonym 92, 55A
anurous 150G
anus 25E
anvil 5B
anxiety 31, 32 39,
   37
anxious 31, 32, 39
any 147A, 57
anyhow 27
anything 57, 147A
anyway 27
anywhere 149A
anywise 27
aortitis 128B
apace 19B
Apache Indian 54C
   murderer 130-O
   outlaw 130A
apart 145A, 145K
apartment 53E, 53D
apathetic 110A,
   126B
apathy 110A, 126B
apatite 5C
ape monkey 143A
   fool 110B
   imitate 105
apeak 149D
aperient 138B
aperiodic 148L, 148C
aperture 25H, 150D,
   25
apex 149F
aphid 143D

aphorism 61B
aphorize 59, 61B
aphrodisiac 8
Aphrodite 108
aphthong 55A
apiary 53D, 144C
apiece 147A
apish, foolish 110B
  ugly 109A
aplomb 132B
Apocalypse 82A
apocope 58, 35A
apocrypha 82A, 57
apod 143A
apodictic 84, 93
apodosis 55A, 55B
apogean 149A
Apollo 68H, 77, 85E,
  100C, 108, 136B,
  137B
apologetic 40B,
  138D
apologetics 40B, 93
apologist 40B, 36G
apologize 40B, 138D
apologue 61B
apology 40B, 138D
apoplectic 128B
apoplexy 128B
aport 149J
apostasy treason
  130A
  abandonment 15
  opposition 27
  dispute 66
apostate 15, 27, 66,
  62, 67A
apostatical 15, 66, 65
apostatize 15, 66,
  67A, 130A
aposteriori 114
apostle 82F
apostles' creed 82A
apostolate 82C, 82A
apostolic 82A
apostrophe 91
apostrophic 91
apothecary 144D
apothegm 61B
apotheosis 139A,
  139B
apotheosize 139A
appal 33
appalling 33, 109A,
  130M
apparatus 5A
apparel 106B, 107A
apparent 95E
apparition 95E, 95C,
  113
  ghost 96A, 57
appeal 40B
appear 95C, 95E
appearance 95C,
  95E
appease 132B, 136A
appeasement 132B
appellant 40B

appellate 40B, 114
appellation 40B
  name 92
appellative 92
appellatory 40B
appellee 27
append 52B, 146A,
  22, 74
appendage 145D, 10,
  74
appendicitis 128B
apperception 111
appertain 52G, 53A
appetence 51A
appetite 39
appetizer 48P
applaud 63
applause 63
apple 48G
appliance 5A
applicable 132A, 5A
applicant 40B
application request
  40B
  assiduity 39
  explanation 84
  study 116
  fitness 132A
applied 137B
applique 107A
apply 40B, 132A
appoint name 92,
  139A, 94, 134C
appointee 49B
appointment 92,
  107A, 139A, 94
apportion 43B, 145A
apportionment 43B
apposite 132A, 84,
apposition 132A, 84
appositional 84
appraisal 92, 115
appraise 92, 115, 79
appraisement 92,
  115
appraiser 92, 115
appreciable 135B,
  147I
appreciate 10
  esteem 38
  estimate 115, 117
  be glad 71A
appreciation 38,
  71A, 45, 115,
  117
apprehend fear 32
  seize 49C
  perceive 111
  learn 116
  expect 39
  hold 52A
apprehension 32
  49C, 111, 116,
  39, 52A, 117
apprehensive 32, 39
apprentice 116
apprize 79

approach 149M
  19A, 105, 25B
approbate 63, 46A
approbation 63, 46A
appropriate fit 132A
  take 49A
  deprive 49G, 43A
appropriation 49A,
  49G, 43A, 49C
approval 63, 46A
approximate
  approach 19A
  near 149M
  resemble 105
approximation*
appurtenance 5A,
  53A, 146A,
  132C, 52A
apricot 48G
April 148K
apriori 114
apron 106D, 34,
  106F
apropos 84, 132A,
  134D, 146A
apse 150C
apt 132A, 116, 2,
  117, 134B, 127A
apteral 150G
apteryx 143C
aptitude fitness
  132A, 2, 116,
  117, 134B
aqua 145J
aquafortis 5C
aquamarine 102D,
  102A
aquarium 53C, 99E
aquatic 23
aquatint 100B
aqueduct 25F
aquiform 145J
aquiline 150G
Arab 54C
arabesque 107E,
  100B, 100A, 108
arable 141B
arbiter 94, 115
arbitrament 94, 115
arbitrary despotic
  27
  discretionary 115,
  94, 127A, 132B
arbitration*
arbor 25B
arboreal 54A
arboreous 143E
arborescence 150H
arboriculture 144B,
  141B
arborous 150H
arbor-vitæ 143E
arc 150C
arc-lamp 101C
arc-light 101C
arcade 25D
Arcadia 53H

arcadian 110B
arcanum 103A
arch 150C
archaic 109A, 126A,
  148A
archeologist 83
archeology 83
archaism 148A, 55A
archangel 24F, 82E
archbishop 82G
archdeacon 82G
archduchess 133A
archduke 133A
archebiosis 141A
archegony 84, 83
archenemy 28
archeology 83
archer 36G, 134B,
  130F
archer fish 143B
archery 134B
archetype 100B, 105
archetypic 105
Archibald 130I
archiepiscopacy 82C
arching 150C
archipelagic 145K
archipelago 25I
architect 144A, 144D
architecture 144A,
  144B
architrave 53R
archival 86
archive 53B, 93
archly 72, 32
archness 32
archon 133A
archpriest 82F
archway 25
arcograph 150C
arctic 149B, 146B
arctic circle 150C
ardent 39, 2, 101A
ardor
(B). ardour
  desire 39
  passion 39B
  bent 2
arduous 13, 149D
are 11A, 147E, 148B
area 25G, 25A,
  149A, 150A
arena 25A, 99E
arenaceous 145H
Areopagus 133A,
  140A
Ares 130F
argent 102A, 138C
argentite 5C
argil 5C
argillite 5C
argon 5D
argonaut 143B
argosy 24J
argot 55A
argue 66
argument 66

argus-eyed 119G
aria 68B
Arian 82A, 82D
Arianism 82A, 82B
arid 128A
arietta 68B
aright 140A
ariolation 77
arise start 4
  mount 17
  appear 95A, 95C
  ascend 149F
aristocracy 133A
  nobility 140B
aristocrat 133A
  140B
aristocratic 140B
aristocratism 133A
arithmetic 83, 147L
arithmetician 115
arithometer 95B
ark 24J, 53D, 34
arm 150G
  weapon 130I,
  137B, 36
armada 24J
armadillo 143A
armament 130I,
  130F
armature 36, 36C
armchair 53-O
armful 147L
armistice 12, 132B
armlet 25I
armoire 53E
armor 36C
(B). armour
armorial 105, 104A
armory 53B, 53C
armpit 150G
arms 130I, 104D
army 130F, 147I,
  146K
army-worm 143D
arnica 143E
aroma 122
aromatic 122
aromatous 122
arose 17, 8
around 149K, 149M
arousal 111
arouse 8
arow 149C
arraign 65, 41B
arraignment 41B,
  65
arrange 132A, 86,
  149A
arrangement 132A,
  86, 149A
arrant 130A, 95E
arras 107B
arrasene 52C
array 132A, 95,
  106B, 95D,
  107A, 147I
arrayal 106B, 95D

arrear 149I, 148B,
  126B
arrearage 126B
arrest stop 12
  seize 49C, 50, 52A
arris 150D
arris-wise 150D
arrival 146K
arrive 146K
  76, 38, 41B,
arrogance 28, 95D,
  103B, 113
arrogant 28, 95D,
  76, 38, 103B, 113
arrogate assume
  103B
  fancy 113, 41B,
  49A
arrogation*
arrow 130J
arrowroot 5C
arroyo 25I
arsenal 53B
arsenic 5D
arsenite 5C
arsis 55A
arson 131B, 130A
art 100A, 134B, 117
arterial 25E, 25
arterialization 3A
arterialize 3A
arteriology 83
arteriosclerosis
  128B
arteriotomy 145F
artery 25E
artesian well 16
artful witty 59
  cunning 117, 57
  skillful 134B
arthritis 128B
artichoke 48K, 143E
article 86, 55A, 85B,
  144E
articular 145D
articulate 55A, 84
  unite 146A
articulation 55A
artifact 144E
artifice 57, 134B, 62,
  103A, 103B
artificer 134B, 144D,
  144A
artificial 134B, 103B
artillery 130I, 130F
artisan 134B, 144D,
  100C
artist 100C, 144A
artiste 134B, 68I,
  99D
artistic 100A, 134B
artistry 100A, 134B
  144A, 68A, 144B
artless 126D, 110B,
  61A
as 105
asafetida 123

(B). asafoetida
asbestos 5C, 145B
ascend 17, 149F
ascendancy 50, 133A
ascendant 17, 149F,
  140B
ascension 17, 149F,
  149E
ascent 17, 149F,
  149E
ascertain 115, 116
ascertainment 115
ascetic 145K, 132D
asceticism 132C
ascribe 65, 80, 84
aseptic 138C
ascetic 15
asexual 141A
ash 143E
ashamed 112, 32
ashen 102A
ashes 129A
ashore 149A
Ashur 50
aside 149J, 145A,
  145K
asinine 110B
asininity 110B
ask request 40B
  question 41A
  invite 40A
askance 119G, 119E,
  119F, 149D
askew 149D, 125A
aslant 149D
asleep 11B, 110A
aslope 149D
asp 143F
asparagus 48K, 143E
aspect 95C, 95E,
  150A
aspen 143E, 3B
asper 28, 150B
asperity 28, 64, 150B
asperse 65
aspersion 65, 145I
asphalt 5C
asphodel 143E
asphyxia 110A
asphyxiate 130M,
  130N
aspic 143F, 143E,
  48D
aspirant 39
aspirate 69A, 55A
aspiration 69A, 39
aspiratory 51A
aspire 39, 51A, 17
aspirin 136B
asquint 119A
ass 110B, 143A, 24G
assail 130F, 130B
assailant 130F
assassin 130-O
assassinate 130-O
assassination 130-O

assault 130F
assay 115, 92
assemblage 146K
assemble 146K, 49E
assembly 146K
assent 46A
assentation 46A
assentient 46A
assert 61A, 80, 93
assertion 61A, 80, 93
assess 115
assessment 115
assessor 115
assets 49E, 45
asseveration 80
assibilate 55A, 69A
assibilation 55A,
  69A
assiduity 39, 11A,
  41C, 116
assiduous 39, 41C,
  116, 11A, 38,
  39A, 144B
assign 43B, 44, 94,
  80, 92, 139A
assignation 146D,
  44, 146K
assignee 49B
assignment 43B, 44,
  94, 92, 139A
assignor 44
assimilable 132A
assimilate 51A, 116
assimilation 51A,
  116, 49A
assist 5A
assistance 5A
assistant 5A, 46B
assize 115, 92, 94
assizement 115, 92
associate 146L,
  146K, 146C
associative 146L, 87,
  146A
assonance 68A
assonant 68A
assort 145A, 86, 43B
assortment 145A, 86,
  126A
assuage 132B, 136A,
  14
assuagement*
assume 113, 49A,
  49C, 41B, 103B
assumpsit 89
assumption 113, 49A
assurance proof 93
  encouragement 7
  confidence 42, 113,
  117
  promise 89
assure 89, 7, 93
assuredness 42,
  134C, 113
Assyrian 54C
Assyriology 83
aster 143E

asteriated 150F
asterisk 150F, 55B
asterism 150D
astern 149I
asteroid 150F
asthenia 128A
asthenic 128A
asthma 128B
astigmatic 136B, 119B, 70
astigmatism 119B
astir 19A, 19B
astomatous 150G
astonish 96A, 62, 140B
astonishment 112
astound 96A, 140B
astraddle 149F
Astræa 140A
astragal 107E
astragalus 150G
astrakhan 106K
astral 101B, 150F, 101A
astral lamp 101C
astray 18B, 149N, 126C, 149A
astrict 52B
astriction 52B
astride 149F
astringency 130M
astringent 52B
astrolabe 95B
astrologer 77, 119F
astrological 77, 119F
astrology 83, 77
astrometer 95B
astronomer 83
astronomic 83, 132D
astronomy 83
astrophotometer 95B
astrotheology 82B
astute 117, 59
asunder 145K
aswail 143A
asylum 53C
asymmetrical 126A
asymmetry 126A
asyndeton 55A
at 146A, 149A, 149J, 149M
atavic 3A
atavism 128C, 141A, 3A
atavistic 128C, 141B
ataxia 126A
ataxiagraph 95B
ataxic 126A
ate 51A
atelier 144C
atheism 82B, 30
atheist 30, 82D
atheistic 30, 82A
Athena 117, 133A
atheneum 81
athermanous 146B

athirst 39
athlete 41D, 137B, 99D
athletic 137B
athwart 150F
atilt 149D
atlantes 100B
atlas 86, 100B, 105, 137B
atmidometer 95B
atmology 83
atmometer 95B
atmosphere 145J, 25A
atmospheric 145J
atoll 145K
atom 145D
atomic 145D, 147K
atomicity 145D, 147K, 146B
atomize 145J, 145H
atomizer 145J, 145H
atone 31, 45
atonement 31, 45
atonic 128A
atony 128A
atrip 145A
atrium 53E
atrocious 80, 130M, 28, 129B, 130A, 130-O
atrocity 80, 130M
atrophy 128C
atropin 130E
atropism 130E
Atropos 134C
attach fasten 52B, 74, 49C, 146A
attache 146L
attachment 52B, 38, 39A, 49C, 146A
attack 130F, 130E
attain 49A, 50, 117
attainder 49A
attainment 49A, 117, 50
attaint 65, 146C
attemper 132D, 132B, 132A
attempt 2, 41C, 130F
attend aid 5A, 24A
  regard 119G
  wait upon 46B
  regard 114
  listen 118
  accompany 146K
attendance 146K, 149J, 149M
attendant 146L, 46B, 146A, 146K
attention 111, 114, 119G, 38, 119E
attentive*
attenuant 145J
attenuate lessen 14, 146J

attest 61A, 93
attestation 93, 61A
attic 53E, 108
Attica 108
Atticism 68A
Atticize 68A
attire 106B, 107A
attitude 98A, 132A, 95C
attitudinal 98A, 132A
attitudinarian 95D
attitudinize 98A, 103B
attorney 36G, 40B, 87
attract 49A, 40A, 39
attractile 49A
attraction 49A, 40A, 12, 39
attractive 108, 49A
attribute ascribe 80
  assign 43B
  trait 135B, 126A
  characteristic 95A, 95E
  defamation 65
attribution 65, 43B, 80, 95A
attrite 32, 31
attrition 32, 31, 130G
attune 68A, 132A
attunement 68A
atypic 126A
auburn 102A
auction 44
auctioneer 44
audacious 42, 64, 95D
audacity 42, 64, 28, 95D
audible 69A, 118
audience 118
audient 118
audiometer 95B, 118
audiphone 118
audit 115
auditor 118, 115
auditorium 118
auditory 118
auger 145F
aught 148K, 57, 147A
augment 10, 73, 137B
augmentation 10, 49A, 104B
augmentative 10, 74
augur 77, 84, 95A, 82F, 145F, 113
augury 77, 95A
august 107A, 140B, 95D, 108, 133A, 148K
Augustan 140B, 117
auk 143C
aula 53E

aulic 53E
aunt 146I
aura 101B
aural 118
aureate 102A
aureola 101B
aureous 102A
auricle 118
auricular 118
auriferous 144B
auriform 150G
auriscope 95B
aurist 136B
aurochs 143A
aurora 101B
aurora australis 101B
aurora borealis 101B
auscultate 118
auscultation 118
auscultator 118
auspice 77, 95A, 34
auspicious 89, 95A
  fortunate 134D
  helpful 5A
austere sour 48Q
  crabbed 29
  precise 134A
  harsh 130B, 67A, 98B
austerity*
austral 149B
authentic true 61A, 93, 134A, 84
authenticate 93
authenticity 61A, 93
author 144A, 141E, 85E
authoress*
authoritative
  permissive 46A
  assertive 80
  absolute 84, 61A
  positive 94
  ruling 133A
authority 46A, 117, 93, 94
  dominion 133A
authorize 46A, 94, 139A
auto 24H
autobiographic 85A
autobiography 85A, 85B
autochthon 54B
autocracy 133A
autocrat 133A
autocratic 133A, 125C
autocycle 24H
autodidactic 116
autodynamic 2, 137B, 4
autogenous 141B, 141A
autograph 92, 93

autographic 92, 93
autography 85B
autohypnotic 90
autolatry 38
autology 114
automat 48B
automatic 2, 4
automatism 2, 83
automaton 2
automatous 2, 4
autometry 115
automobile 24H
automorphism 115
automotor 2
autonomist 133A
autonomous 133A
autonomy 133A
autonym 92
autophon 68G
autoplasty 136B
autopsy 119E
autosuggestion 87
auto-truck 24H
autotype 105
autumn 148K, 14
autumnal 148K,
    49E, 143E, 10,
    148I
auxiliary 5A, 46B
avail 49A, 50, 137B
availability 46B
avalanche 130-O
avarice 39
avaricious 39
avatar 95A, 3A
avaunt 35A
ave 91
avenge 130N, 45
avenue 25B
aver 61A, 80, 93
average 132D, 147L,
    149L
averment 61A, 80, 93
Avernus 130N
averse 27, 28, 126B
aversion 27, 28, 132C
avert 15, 36
avian 143C
aviary 52H
aviation 23
aviator 23, 19A
aviculture 141A,
    141B
avidity 39, 51A
avocation 49A, 71A,
    126A
avoid 15, 18C, 28,
    132C, 32
avoidance 15, 18, 28
avoirdupois 135A
avouch 61A, 80, 93,
    78
avow 61A, 80, 78, 93
avowal*
await 39, 11A, 119G,
    148B
awake 8, 111

awaken 111, 8
award 45, 43B,
    94, 139A
aware 111, 117
awash 149C
away 149N, 145A,
    149A
awe 32, 33
aweather 149J
awesome 32
awe-struck 112
awful 33, 129B,
    130M
awhile 148I
awkward 18A, 126D,
    109A, 45
awl 145F
awn 106A
awning 34
awny 106A
awry 125A, 126C,
    149D, 150B
ax 145F, 130H
axial 149L, 150D
axiferous 53R, 150D
axiform 149L, 150D
axil 150D
axile 150D
axilla 150D, 150G
axiom 61B
axiomatic 61B
axis 150D, 143A,
    149L
ay 11A, 148C
(B). aye
ayah 46B
aye 46A
(B). ay
aye-aye 143A
Ayrshire 143A
azalea 143E
azimuth 150C
azote 5C
Aztec 54C
azure 102A, 102D
azurine 102A, 102D
azurite 102D

B

B 55B
baa 69B
Baalism 82B
babble verbosity 56
    tell secrets 78
    talk foolishly 60
babbler*
babe 148J
babiroussa 143A
bablah 36F
baboo 140B
baboon 143A, 129B
baboonery 109A
baboosh 106J
babuina 143A, 141F
baby 148J, 140B,
    142B
babyhood 148J

Babylonian 140B
bacca 48G
baccalaureate 81
bacchanal 51B, 71A
bacchanalia 51B,
    125C-3, 71A
bacchante 51B, 71A
bacchic 51B, 71A,
    95D
Bacchus 48L, 125C-3
bachelor 145K, 117
bacillus 142F
back boat 24J
    hinder part 149I
backbite 64, 65
backbone 53R, 27,
    42
backer 5A
backgammon 41D
background 149I
backhand 55B, 57
backhanded
    unfair 130A
    ambiguous 57
    hitting 130G
backsheesh 43A
backside 149I
backslide 15
backstays 52C
backsword 130H
backward 149I,
    148A, 126B, 27,
    110B, 32
backwater 15
backwoods 110B
backwoodsman 110B
bacon 48, 48D
bacteria 142F
bacteriologist 83
bacteriology 83
bacterium 142F
bad evil 130A
    depraved 129B
    corrupt, 146C,
    126C, 127B,
    123, 129A
badderlocks 143E
badge 104B
badger 143A, 130B,
    130A, 130C
badger-game 49G
badiaga 143E
badinage 72
badness 130A
baffle elude 15, 13
    defeat 50
bag 53J
    quantity 147L
    steal 49F
    capture 49C
bagasse 129B
bagatelle 147K
baggage 5A
baggala 24J
bagging 106K
baggy 3C
bagnio 53C, 138A

bagpipe 68G
bah 64
bail 45
bailee 49B
bailiff 133A
bailiwick 133A
bailment 45
bailor 45
bairn 148J
bait 40A, 130B
baize 106K
bake 145J
baker 144D
bakery 144C
bakshish 43A
balance 95B, 132A,
    135A, 147L, 105,
    132B, 147K
balance-reef 52C
balance-sheet 86
balancer 132A
balata 5C
balayeuse 106K
balboa 147B
balconet 36I
balcony 36I
bald 109A, 95E,
    150G
bald-head 109A
balderdash 60
baldric 107B
bale 24A, 146A, 31,
    127B, 130M,
    147D
bale-fire
    beacon 101C
    pyre 131B
    direful 130M
    woe 31
baleful 28, 130M,
    130-O
balk 27, 36A, 18C,
    50
ball 24D, 130J, 150C
ballad 68B
ballast 135A
ballastage 45
ballet 68B, 99F
ballistics 83
balloon d'essai 24I,
    119E, 95B
balloon 24I
balloonist 23
ballot 49A
ball up 125A
ballyhoo 69B
balm 122, 136A,
    136B
balmoral 106J, 136B
balmy 122, 136B, 8
balsam 136B, 122
balsamic 136B, 122
baluster 36I
balustrade 36I
bam 49F, 130A
bambino 148J
bamboo 143E, 130G

beamy 101A
bean 48M
bear carry 24A
 suffer 31
 support 53R
 contain 53A
 cherish 39A
 be fruitful 141B
 mammal 143A, 14,
 129B, 39A, 137B
beard 106A
bearing 95C, 53A,
 98A, 104D, 149A
bearish 130C
beast animal 143A
 rude person 129B
 filthy person 129A,
 130M, 109A, 123,
 130C
beastly*
beat, strike 130G
 excel 50
 throb 3B, 137C
 stroke of time
 148D
 course 25A, 25B
 bad debtor 130A
 exhausted 128A
beaten 128A, 127B,
 132D
beatific 136A, 71A
beatify 136A, 139B
beating 130G, 3B
beatitude 71A
beau 39A, 108
beau-ideal 108, 140B
beau monde 108,
 140B
beauteous 108
beautiful 108
beautify 107A
beauty 108, 140B,
 68A
beauty-spot 107B
beaver 143A, 106H
beaver-rat 143A
beaver-tree 143E
becalm 132B
because 1
beche-de-mer 48D
beck 98A
becket 52A
beckon 98A
become 4, 49A
becoming fit 132A
 proper 134A
 seemly 108
bed 53-O, 146D
bedbug 143D
bedstraw 53-O
bedtick 53-O
bedazzle 96A, 95E,
 101A
bedding 53-O
bedeck 107A
bedevil 130C, 96A
bedevilment 130C

bedew 145J
bedizen 107A
bedlam 125A, 69B
bedlamite 110B
Bedouin 54C
bedraggle 129A
bedroom 53E
bee, insect 143D
 gathering 146K
 busy person 144D
bee-bread 48E
beech 143E
bee-eater 143C
beef 48D
beefeater 46B
beefy 109B, 150G
beehive 53D, 144C
bee-line 149C, 25A,
 25B
bee-moth 143D
been 148A
beer 48L
beery 48L
beestings 48J
beet 48K, 143E
beetle 143D
befall 127A
befena 43A
befit 132A
before 148A, 149H
beforehand 149H,
 148A
befoul 129A, 146C
befriend 38, 136A
befuddled 112
beg 40B
began 4
beget 141A, 141B
begetter 141E
beggable 40B
beggar 40B, 14,
 128A, 130D
beggarliness 40B,
 128A, 129B
begin 4, 73
beginner 4, 116,
 144A
beginning 149H, 4,
 148A, 73
begone 35A, 91
begonia 143E
begot 141B
begotten 141B
begrease 129A
begrime 129A
begrudge 39, 28
beguile
 persuade 40A
 cheat 130A
 divert 99A, 8
 deceive 62, 49F,
 136A
beguilement 12, 99C
begum 133A
begun 4
behalf 5A

behave accord 132B,
 140A, 132C,
 132D
behavior*
behead 130-O
beheld 119F
behemoth 143A
behest 94
behind 149I
behindhand 149I,
 148B
behold 119A, 119E,
 95D, 91
beholden 46B
behoof 49A, 134D
behoove 46B
beige 102B
being 11A, 137C
bejewel 107A
belabor 130G
(B). belabour
belate 148B
belated 148B
belay 52B
belaying-pin 52D
belch 16, 70
beldam 109A, 148J,
 141E
beleaguer 41D
belfry 53E, 119E
Belgravian 140B
belie 65, 62, 138C
belief 113, 82B
believe 113
belike 127A
belittle 65
bell 68E
bell-bird 143C
bellman 79
bell-wether 24A
belladonna 136B
belle 108, 140B
belles-lettres 85B, 64
bellicose 66, 130F,
 67A
bellied 150G
belligerence 41D,
 27, 130F
belligerent 41D, 27,
 67A, 130F
bellow 69B, 66, 67A
bellows 8
belly 53Q, 150G
belly band 52C
belong 53A, 146A
belonging 146A, 49E
beloved 140B
below 149G
belt 107B
beluga 143B
belvedere 119E
bemire 129A
bemoan 31, 67A
bench 53-O

bend 150C, 3A, 46B,
 18C, 149D,
 149G, 150B,
 150D
bends 128B
beneath 149G
benedict 146J, 141E
benediction 63, 40B
benefaction 43A
benefactor 43A, 6
benefice aid 5A, 6,
 43A, 43B, 48A,
 49B, 136A,
 136B, 134D,
 45, 140A
beneficent*
beneficial*
beneficiary 49B, 43A
benefit
 see benefice
benevolence 140A,
 136A, 38, 43A
benevolent*
bengal 106K
Bengal tiger 143A
benign 140A, 136A,
 43A
benignity*
benison 63
bent propensity 2
 determined 27,
 150C, 113, 38,
 109B, 125A,
 149G, 150B,
 150G
benumb 96A, 130E
benumbment 96A,
 126B, 110A
benzene 5C
benzine 5C
benzoin 5C
bequeath 43A
bequeathment 43A
bequest 43A
berate 64
berceuse 68B
bereave 145A, 145K,
 130D
bereavement 145K,
 31
bereft 128A, 127B
bergamot 48G,
 106K, 122
beriberi 128B
Bermuda grass
 143E
Bermudian 54C
berry 48G
berth 53E, 53-O,
 53A
Bertha 130I
Bertillon 86
beryl 102D, 107D
berylline 102B, 102A
berryllium 5D
beseech 40B
beset 130F, 130B
besetment 130F

beshrew 64, 40B, 65
beside 149J, 149M
besides 10, 147L, 146A
besiege 130F, 52H
besiegement 130F
beslaver 63, 129A
beslobber 63, 129A, 98C
besmear 129A
besmirch 129A, 65
besom 138A
besot 96A, 129A
besotment 110B, 110A
besought 40B
bespangle 107A
bespatter 65, 129A
bespeak 40B, 104A, 105
best 140B, 108
best man 46B
bestial animal 129B
  intemperate 125C-3
  sensual 39B
  brutal 130M
bestir 4, 8, 9
bestow 43A, 43B
bestraddle 149F
bestrew 145I
bestride 17, 149F
bet 41D, 127A
betake 49A
betel 48P
betel-nut 48C
bete-noire 129B, 33
bethel 53D
bethink 114, 117
betide 127A
betimes 132A, 148A, 148L
betoken 95A, 104A, 105
beton 5C
betony 143E
betray 78, 130A
betroth 89, 146G
betrothal 89, 146G
better 140B, 6
betterment 10, 136B
betting 41D
between 149L
betweenwhile 148L
betwixt 149L
bevel 150D
bevel-gear 5B
beverage 48J
bevy 146K
bewail mourn 31
  weep 67B
  appeal 40B
bewailment*
beware 32, 119G
bewilder 96A

bewilderment 96A, 13, 112, 8
bewitch charm 50, 99A, 8, 40A, 108
bewitching 50, 99A, 108, 136A
bewitchment 50, 40, 99A, 40A, 68A, 99C
bewray 78
bey 133A
beylik 133A
beyond 17, 149K, 149B, 147I, 149F, 149N
bezan 106K
bezel 150D
bezetta 102E
bezique 41D
bezoar 5C
bhang 48L
bi 147A, 150D
biangular 150D
biannual 148K
bias prejudice 113
  seam 146A
  propensity 2
  misrepresent 62
  weight 135B, 38
biauriculate 150H
biaxial 150D
bib 34, 106C, 106F
bibber 51B
Bible 82A
Biblical 82A
Biblicist 82F
bibliographer 86, 85E
bibliography 83
biblioklept 49F
bibliolater 38
bibliolatry 38
bibliology 82A
bibliomania 39
bibliomaniac 39, 38
bibliophile 38
bibliopole 44
bibliotheca 86, 81
bibulous 51B
bice 102D
bicentenary 148K, 148H
bicentennial 148K
bicephalous 150G
biceps 150G
bichloride 5C
bichromate 5C
bicipital 105G
bicker 66
biconcave 150C
biconvex 150C
bicorn 150G
bicorporal 150G
bicuspid 150G, 145F, 145K, 150E
bicycle 24H
bicyclist 24E

bid 40A, 94
biddable 46B
bidder 40A
bidding 40A, 94
biddy 148J
bide 148B, 11A, 31, 54A
bident 49C, 150F
bidental 145F, 150G
bidet 24G, 143A, 138A
biennial 148K
bier 24H, 104H
bifacial 105, 150G
biferous 141B, 43A
biff 130G
bifid 145K
bifilar 150F
bifold 147A
bifoliate 147A, 150H
bifurcate 150F, 147A, 145K, 150E
big large 147J
  important 135B
  pompous 95D
bigamist 146J, 141E
bigamous 146H
bigamy 146H
bighorn 143A
bight 25I, 150C
bignonia 143E
bigot 27, 113, 110B
bigoted 27, 113, 110B
bigotry 27, 113
bigwig 140B
bijou 107C, 107B
bijouterie 107C
bike 24H
bilabiate 150G
bilander 24J
bilateral 149J
bilberry 48G
bilbo 52A, 130H
bile 29
bilge 150C
bilge-ways 53R
bilin 5C
bilingual 55A
bilious 29, 128B
biliousness 128B
bilk 49F, 130A
bill 86
bill of lading 86
bill of sale 44
billet 85B
billet-doux 85B
bill-book 145F
billiards 41D
Billiken 71A
billingsgate 64, 65
billion 147A
billow 17, 16
billy 130L
billy-goat 143A

bilobate 150F
bimanous 150G
bimonthly 148K
bin 531
binary 147A
bind 52B, 146A
binding 52B
bing 146A
binocle 95B, 119A
binocular 119A
binomial 92
biodynamics 83
biogenesis 83, 141A
biograph 99E
biographer 85E, 86
biography 85B, 85D
biologist 83
biology 83
bioplasm 142F
bioplast 142F
biotaxy 86
biparous 141B
bipartite 145K
bipartition 145D
biped 143A, 150G
bipedal 150G
bipennate 150G
biplane 24I
biplicate 147A, 146A
birch 143E
bird 143C
birdlime 52F
birdman 23
biretta 106I, 106H
birth 4, 141B, 141G, 148A
birthday 148K
birthplace 1, 141D
birthright 43A, 49B
biscuit 48E
bisect 145F, 145A
bisection 145F
bisector 145F
bisexual 141A, 141B
bishop beverage 48J
  church dignitary 82G
  dress improver 107B, 107A
  deceive 130A, 49F
  disguise 103B
bishopric 82C
bisk 48D
bismuth 5D
bison 143A
bisque 5C
bissextile 148K, 148H
bister 102D
bisulfate 5C
bisulphite 5C
bisymmetry 105
bit 52A, 145F, 147K
bitch 143A, 141F
bite 130H, 145F, 130G, 145H

bitter 48Q, 28, 29, 64, 130M
bittern 143C
bitters 48P, 48L
bitumen 5C
bituminous 5C
bivalve 147A, 143B
bivouac 53D, 119G, 53C
biweekly 148K
bizarre odd 126A
  jocular 72
  ugly 109A
  fanciful 99A
blab 78
black darkest
  hue 102A, 102D
  darkness 97
  forbidding 33
  evil 130A
  wrathful 29, 98B
blackamoor 54C
blackball 35, 86
blackberry 48G
blackbird 143C
blackbirding 49G
blackboard 46B
black-canker 128B
black-cap 143C, 48G
black-cattle 143A
black-cock 143C
black-current 143E
blacken defame 65
  make black 102A
  dirty 129A
black-fish 143B
black-flag 104E
black-fly 143D
black-friar 82F
blackguard revile 65
  a vile person 130A
  a low person 129B
blackguardism 65
black-hole 52H
blacking 102D
black-jack
  bludgeon 130L
  drinking cup 53M, 53N
  pirate's ensign 104E
blacklead 102D
blackleg 49F, 49G
black-letter 55B
black-list 35, 86
blackmail 49G
Black Mass 65
Black Pope 82B
blacksmith 144D
bladder 53Q
blade cutter 145F
  weapon 130H
  reckless fellow 125C, 2
blamable 130A
blame 64, 65

blameless 140A
blameworthy 130A
blanch uncolor 102B, 102A
  become pale 98A, 98B, 112
bland affable 38
  soft 69A, 108, 117
  persuasive 40A
blandishment 40A, 63, 98C
Blank
  confounded 112
  empty 128A, 46A
blanket 34
blanketing 106K
blare 69B
blarney flattery 63
  persuasion 40A, 40B
blarney-stone 63
blasé 26, 128A
blaspheme 64, 130A, 65
blasphemous 64, 130A, 65
blasphemy 64, 130A, 65
blast 125B, 69B, 130-O
blastema 142F
blastoderm 142F
blastogenesis 141A
blatant 69B, 76
blather 60
blatherskite 110B, 60
blaze flame 131B, 101A
  mark 148
  blazon 95D, 95E
blazer 106D
blazon display 95D, 95E
  show 95A
  symbolize 104A, 104B
  explain 84
  embellish 107A
  proclaim 79, 76
blazonment*
blazonry*
bleach 102A
bleachery 102D
bleak 128A, 143B, 102A
blear 103B, 103A
bleat 40B, 69C, 69B
  lose steadily 127B
bleed lose blood 16, 49G, 127B

blemish
  tarnish 129A
  injure 130D
  defame 65
  deformity 109B, 109C
  defect 126C
blench 32, 15
blend 146C, 102B
blende 5C
blennorrhea 16
bless praise 63
  invoke 40B
  make happy 136A
blessedness 71A, 136A
blessing
  benediction 63
  comfort 136A
  supplication 40B
  good fortune 134D
blet 128C
blewits 48K
blight disease 130E
  mildew 129A
  destroy 130-O
blimp 24I, 119E
blind sightless 119B
  undiscriminating 110B
  secret 130A, 37
blind-fish 143B
blindfold 96A, 103A
blindness 119B
blindworm 143F
blink 119A
blinker 96A
bliss 71A
blister 53Q
blithe 71A, 99A
blizzard 125B
bloat 11H, 14
bloater 48D
blob 53Q
block 36, 53R, 36B
block-head 110B
block-house 36B
blockade 36B, 52H
blockage 36B
bloke 129B
blond 102A
blonde-lace 107B
blood lineage 141G
  vitality 137B, 2, 42, 137C, 146I, 148E
blooded 138C
bloodhound 143A
bloodiness 130-O
bloodless 128A
blood-money 49G, 45
bloodstone 107C
blood-thirsty 28, 130M, 130-O
bloody cruel 130M
  murderous 130-O
  blood-stained 129A

bloody-flux 16
bloom glow 101A
  blue of freshness 102A, 102B
  growth 10
  health 137A, 141B
  blossom 143E
  beauty 108
bloomer 106F
bloomery 144C
blooming 129B, 137A
blossom 143E, 10, 141B
blot 129A, 102B, 109C
blotch 129A, 109C
blotted 129A
blouse 106F
blow a knock 130G
  blossom 143E
  boast 76, 78
  expel breath 16
  blast of air 125B
blow-fly 143D
blow-out 125C-3
blow-pipe 130I
blowzed 102A
blubber weep 31
  deplore 67B
blucher 106J
bludgeon 130L
blue azure 102A, 102D
  unhappy 31
blue-bell 143E
blue-blood 140B
blue-book 86
bluebottle 143E, 143D
bluebuck 143A
blue-devils 31
bluegrass 143E
blue-gum 143E
blueing 102D
bluejacket 24E, 23
bluelight 101A, 101C
blue-peter 104E
blue-ribbon 104B
blue-spar 102D
blue-stocking 85E, 116, 117
blue-stone 5C
bluette 143E
bluff 33, 149D
bluffer 33
bluffy 149D, 58
bluish 102A
blunder 126C, 126D
blunderbuss 130I
blunt out-spoken 84
  stupid 110B, 150C, 130C, 150D
blur 129A, 97, 102B
blurb 76
blurt 78

blush reddish 102A
red from shame
32, 98A, 98B
112, 71A
bluster 76, 33
boa 143F, 143A
boa-constrictor
143F, 143A
boar 143A, 141F
board timber 53R
entertainment
99A, 99E
food 48A
provision 43B
obtain food 51A
go on board 20
boarish 130M
boast 76
boastful 76
boat 24J, 24A, 23
boatman 23
boatswain 133A
bob 145F
bobbin 24A
bobolink 143C
bob-stay 52C
bob-tail 150G, 129B
bobtailed 150G
bock-beer 48L
bode 95A, 77
bodice 106F
boding 95A
body 150G, 146K
body-blow 130G
body-color 102E
body-snatcher 49F
Boeotian 110B
Boer 54C
bog 25G, 21, 13
bogle 113
boggle bungle 126C
be clumsy 126D
embarrass 96A
boggy 33, 113, 13
bogie 24H
bogus 130A
bogy 113
bohea 48J
Bohemian 126A, 18B
Bohemianism 126A,
125C, 3
boil seethe 145J, 29,
14, 128B
boisterous 69B, 70
bolas 49C
bold 42, 95E, 149D
bole 150G, 5C
bolero dance 99F
tune 68B
jacket 106E
bolide 101D
bolivar 147B
boliviano 147B
boll 53I
bollard 53R
bolo 130H
bolometer 95B

Bolshevik 133A
bolster 53R, 136A,
5A, 53-O
bolt arrow 130J
depart 15
pin, rod 52D
roll of cloth 106K
shoot forth 19B
spring 9
fasten 52B, 78,
51A, 145A,
119E, 49C
bolus 150C
bomb 130J
bomb-ketch 24J
bombard 130F, 41A
bombardier 130F
bombardment 130F
bombardon 68G
bombast 76
bombazet 106K
bombazine 106K
bombshell 130J
bona-fide 140A
bona-fides 140A
bonanza 49E
bonbon 48F
bond fastening 52B,
52A, 52C
imprisonment
52H
obligation 45, 93,
146A, 135B
bondage 50
bone 53R, 49F
bone-black 5C
boneless 128A
bonfire 101A, 101C
bonhomie 136A
boniface 43B, 48A
bon-marche 147K
bonnet 106H
bonny 108, 71A
bonspiel 41D
bon-ton 108, 136A,
107A
bonus 45
bony 109B, 146B
boo 64
booby 110B, 143C
boobyish 110B
boodle 49G, 45
boodler 45
boo-hoo 69B
book 85B, 86
book-case 53P
bookman 116, 117
book-muslin 106K
book-name 92
book-talk 118
book-worm 116
booking-office 44
bookish 116
booklet 86
book-stall 44
boom 9, 23, 24C,
36A, 69B, 63,
24A

boomerang 130J,
130I, 130N
boon gay 71A
kind 136A
gift 43A
privilege 46A
prayer 40B
good luck 134D,
36B
boor 130C, 129B
boorish 130C
awkward 126D
illiterate 110B
brutal 130M
boost 24A, 24B, 17,
7
boot 45
kick 130G, 53J
torture device
130N
foot covering 106J
booth 53E
boots 46B, 106J
booty 45, 49G
booze 48L, 51B
bora 125B
boracic 5C
borax 5C
Bordeaux 48L
border 36H, 107B,
149J, 149K
boundary 145B
adjoin 149M
bore drill 145F, 20,
25
weary 130B
boreal 149B
boredom 28, 130B
boride 5C
born 137C
bornite 5C
boroglyceride 136B
boron 5D
borough 53F
borrow 49D, 49A
bort 107D, 107C
boscage 34
bosh nonsense 60
humbug 62
bosket 34
bosky 34
bosom passion 39B
breast 150G
boss 133A
bot 143D
botanic 83, 143E
botanist 83
botanize 119E
botany 83
botch 128B, 126C,
129A, 126D
both 147A
bother trouble 13
annoy 130B
offend 130C
bothersome 13,

130B, 130C
bo-tree 143E
bots 142F
bottle 53N, 52H
bottom base 149G
ship 24J
river 25I, 16
stamina 137B
bottomry 49A
bouche 145F
boudoir 53E
bouffe 99A, 99B
bough 150H
bought 49D
bougie 101C
bouilli 48D
bouillon 48D
boulangerite 5C
boule 133A
boulevard 25B
bounce rebound 3C
leap 9
dismiss 35A
bound 52H, 150C,
3C, 9, 149K
boundary 145B, 52H
bounder 129B, 33
boundless 147J, 11A
bounteous 11A, 43A,
147I
bountiful 43A, 147J,
147I
bounty 43A, 147J,
45, 147I
bouquet 107B
bourbon 68G
bourgeois 44
bourgeoisie 44
bourn stream 25I
goal 12
place 149H
bourse 44
bout 41D, 148L,
130F, 148I
boutonniere 107B
bovine 110B
bow salute 98A, 98C
bend 150C
subdue 50
weapon 130I,
107B, 149G
bow-net 49C
bow-saw 145F
Bowdlerize 35A
bowel 25E
bower 53E, 25B
bowery 25B
bowie-knife 130H
bowl 53N, 25, 24D,
24C, 25H
bowlder 150C
bowline 62C
bowsprit 53R
bowspring 52C,
130-O

box receptacle 53J, 53-O, 53I
compartment 53B
shrub 143E
house 53D, 53E
fight with fists 130F, 41D, 52H, 130G
boxhaul 18C
boxiana 85B
boy 148J
boyar 133A
boycott 35
boyer 24J
boyhood 148J
boyish 148J
brace 53R, 147A, 150C, 52C, 48D
bracelet 107C
bracket 53R, 55B
brackish 48Q
brad 52D
brae 149E
brag 76
braggadocio 76
braggart 76
bragger 76
brahma 143C
Brahma 82B, 82E, 144A
Brahman 82F
Brahmin 82F
Brahminee 82D
braid weave 144B
intertwine 150B
fillet 106H
brail 52C
braille 55B
brain 111, 117, 130-O
brainless 110B
brain-storm 110B
brainy 59, 117
braise 48D
brait 107C
brake 52A, 34, 143E
bramble 143E
brambly 13, 34
bran 48M
brancard 24H
branch limb 53R
stream 16, 25I
off-shoot 141A
subdivision 145D
ancestry 141G, 150F, 145A, 150H
branchiae 25E
branchiate 25E
branchlet 53R
branchy 150F, 150H
brand mark 95A, 95E
infamy 65
stigma 129B
burn into 131B, 105

brandish 98A, 33
brand-new 126A
brandy 48L
brant-fox 143A
brant-goose 143C
brash 128A, 95D, 16, 145H, 42, 125C, 3
brass 5C, 64, 125C, 28
brassard 36C
brassiere 106G
brassy 64, 125C-3
brat 129B, 148J
brattice 145D
bratticing 107E
bravado 42, 66
brave 42, 127A
bravery 42
bravo praise 63
assassin 130-O
interjection 91
daring 42, 67A
bravura 68A, 95D
brawl 66
brawn 137B
brawny 137B
braxy 128B
bray cry 69B
beat fine 145H
harsh cry 70
braze 52E, 107A, 52B
brazen
shameless 42, 95E
impudent 64, 130C, 125C-3
brazier 53M
brazilin 102E, 102D
Brazil-nut 48C
breach gap 25, 25H
violation 130A
break 145E
bread 48E
bread-fruit 48E
breadth 25A, 117, 147J
break 145E, 127B, 50, 126C
breakdown 127B, 99F
breaker 16, 149E
breakfast 48A, 51A
breakneck 125C-2
breakwater 36H
bream 143B
breast to brave 42
milk organs 25E
stem 27
contend 41D
breastfast 52C
breastplate 36C
breastwork 36B

breath life 137B, 1
respiration 51A, 48A
exhalation 16, 122, 123, 125B, 137C
breathe inhale 51A
live 137B, 137C
disclose 78, 55A
exhale 16
insinuate 87
inspire 7
whisper 69A
breathing 51A, 137C
breathless 112, 128A, 71A
bree 48D, 145J
breech 149I
breeches 106E
breeching 52C, 52A
breech-loader 130I
breed
procreate 141B, 141G, 142E
breeze 125B
brethren 146K
breve 148H
brevet 46A, 139B
breviary 82A
brevier 55B
brevity 58
brew plot 134C
produce 144B
brewery 144C
Briareus 130-O
bribe tempt 41A, 40A
pay 45
gain 49D
bribery 41A, 45, 40A
bric-a-brac 107E
brick 5C, 140B
bricole 52C, 52A
bridal 146H
bride 146J
bridegroom 146J
bridesmaid 5A
bridewell 52H
bridge 25B, 41D
bridle curb 52A
control 50
scorn 28, 98A
brief 58, 148D, 79, 86
brier 130H
brig 24J
brigade 130F
brigadier 133A
brigand 49G
brigantine 24J

bright radiant 101A, 98B
witty 59, 117
glorious 140B, 95E
brighten 101A, 98A, 98B, 107A, 108
brill 143B
brilliance 68A
brilliancy 101A, 108
brilliant bright 101A, 95E, 108
distinguished 140B
diamond 107C
accomplished 117, 59
brilliantine 102E
brim 149K, 36H
brimful 26
brimstone 5C
brine 5C
bring 24A
brink 149K, 36H
briny 48Q
briquette 5C
brisk 9, 19B, 101A, 3C, 131A
bristle 106A
brit 143B
Briton 54C
brittle 128A, 3C
britzska 24H
broach awl 145F
spike 52D
spire 104F
begin 4, 73, 55A
broad wide 25
comprehensive 84
diffused 145I
unrestrained 125C
evident 95E
bold 42
river 25I, 117, 147J
broadcast 79
broad-cloth 106K
broadside 130F, 64, 149J
broadsword 130H
broaden 10, 84, 25
Brobdingnagian 147J
brocade 106K, 107B
brocatelle 106K, 107B
broccoli 48K
brochure 85B
brock 143A, 52D
brogan 106J
brogue 106J, 55A
broil 145J, 66, 29
brokage 45
broke 145E
broken 145E, 149E, 150B

broker 44, 49D
brokerage 45
broma 51A
brome-grass 143E
bromide 5C
bromine 5D
bronchia 25E
bronchitis 128B
broncho 143A, 24G
bronchopneumonia 128B
bronchotomy 145F
bronchus 25E
brontograph 95B
bronze 102A, 102D, 107A
brooch 107B, 107C
brood hatch 142E
  ponder 114, 31, 141B
brook 25I, 31, 16
brooklet 25I, 16
broom 138A, 143E
brose 48D
broth 48D
brothel 53D
brother 146I, 146L
brother-german 146I
brother-in-law 146J
brother-uterine 146I
brotherhood 146I, 146K
brougham 24H
brow 106A, 149E, 149F, 150G
browbeat 33
brown 102A, 102D
brownie 96A
browse 51A, 48N, 116
bruin 143A
bruise 130G
bruit 78, 79
brumal 145J
brummagem 103B
brunette 102A
brunt 130F, 137B
brush cleanse 138A, 130F, 132A, 106A
brusque 58, 70
Brussels-lace 107B
Brussels-sprouts 48K
brutal 130M, 129B
brutality 130M
brutalize 130A, 129B, 65
brute 130M, 129B, 110B
brutify 130A, 129B, 65
brutish 130M, 126D, 110B, 129B
bub 148J

bubble 128A
bubo 128B
bubonocele 128B, 145E
buccal 150G
buccaneer 49G
bucentaur 24J, 143A
buchu 136B
buck 143A, 41D, 145H, 27, 141F
buckboard 24H
bucko 146L
buck-shot 130J
buck-wheat 48M
bucket 53N
buckle fasten 52B
  twist 146A
  bend 150C
  confine 52H, 2, 1, 4, 49C, 106A
buckra 54C
buckler 36C
buckram 106K, 134A
bucolic 85C, 110B, bud 141B, 146A, 142A
Buddha 82E
Buddhism 82B
Buddhist 82D
budge 3A, 106K
budget 86, 53B, 53J
buff 102A
buffalo 143A
buffalo-bird 143C
buffer 46A
buffet 41D, 53E, 53P
buffo 72, 99A, 99D
buffoon 72, 99A, 99D
buffoonery 72, 99A, 99B, 103B
buffy 102A
bug 143D
bugaboo 33, 109A, 113
bugbear 96A, 33, 109A, 113
buggy 24H
bugle 68G, 107B
buhl 107E
build 144B
building 53B, 53D
bukshish 43A
bulbous 150H
bulk 147L, 147J
bulk-head 145D
bulky 147J, 150G, 109B
bulkiness 147J, 150G
bull 143A, 141F, 94, 62, 79
bulldog 143A, 42
bulldoze 33
bullet 130J

bulletin 79
bull-finch 143C
bull-fight 41D
bull-frog 143F
bullhead 143B
bullion 107C
bullock 143A
bull-terrier 143A
bully 33, 63, 91
bully-rag 33
bulwark 36B
bullwhack 130L, 130N
bumboat 24J
bummer 129B
bump 130G, 149E
bumper 48J, 48L
bumpkin 110B, 129B
bumptious 76
bun 48E, 106A
bunch 146A, 146K
bunchy 146A
bunco 49F
buncombe 40A, 76
bund 36A
bundle 146A, 35A, 15, 147D
bung 36A
bungalow 53D
bungle 126C, 126D
bunk 53-O
bunker 53I
bunky 146L
bunting 106K, 143C
buntline 52C
buoy 98A, 7, 11A
buoyage 98A
buoyancy 135A, 71A
buoyant light 135A
  sustaining 11A
  gay 71A
  floating 23, 5A
  inspiring 7
burden load 135A
  oppression 130B
  difficulty 13
  capacity 53A
  chorus 68B
  topic 90, 85B
burdock 143E
bureau 53P, 5A
bureaucracy 133A
bureaucrat 133A
burgess 54B
burgh 54B
burgher 54B
burglary 49F
burgomaster 133A
Burgundy 48L
burial 52H
burlap 106K
burlesque 72, 99A, 99B
burletta 99B
burly 137B, 147J

burn consume 131B
  reduce 145J
  have anger 29, 39B, 39, 130E, 25I, 16
burner 141C, 101C
burnish 107A, 101A
burro 143A, 24G
burrow 103A, 53D, 25
bursar 49B, 53B, 45
burst 145E, 125C-2
bury 52H, 103A
bus 24H
bush 34, 150H
bushel 147F, 147I
Bushman 54C
bushranger 49G
bush-whacker 145F
bushy 34, 106A, 130H, 150H
business 44, 126A
buskin 106J
buss 24H, 98C, 24J
bust 100B
bustle tumult 125A
  quickness 9, 19B
  be busy 144B
  pad 107B, 106G
busy 144B, 39, 11A
busybody 36G, 13
but 27
butcher 130-O
butcher-bird 143C
butchery 130-O
butler 46B
butt thrust 130G
  end 12
  target 149H, 95A
  dolt 110B
  cask 53N, 147F
  hill 149E
butte 149E
butter 48I, 63, 48P
butter-ball 150G
butter-bird 143C
buttercup 143E
butterfly 143D
buttermilk 48J
butternut 48C
buttery 53B
buttock 149I, 150G
button fastening 49C, 52B
  ornament 107B
  mushroom 143E
  page boy 24F
buttress 53R, 53G
butyrate 5C
buxom 108, 71A
buy 49D
buzz 69A, 87
buzz-saw 145F
buzzard 143C, 110B
buzzer 79

by 146A, 149J, 149M
bygone 148A
by-law 46A, 133A

C

cab 24H, 24A
cabal 130A, 146K
cabala 103A
cabaret 48B, 99E
cabbage 48K
cabeca 106K
cabin 53D, 53E
cabin-boy 46B
cabinet 53E, 53P, 100B
cable 52C, 55C, 55B, 147E
cablegram 79
cabochon 107C
caboose 53E
cabriolet 24H
cacao 143E
cache 103A, 13, 53B
cachalot 143B
cachet 104B, 104D
cachinnate 71B
cachinnation 71B, 71A
cacholong 107C
cachou 122, 48P
cacique 133A
cackle 60, 69B, 70
cacography 126C
cacophonous 70, 133A
cacotype 100B, 109B
cactus 143D
cad 129B
cadaver 128C
cadaverous 102A
caddie 46B
caddy 53J
cade 53N, 147F
cadence 68A, 69C
cadenza 68A
cadet 116
cadge 49F
cadmium 5D
caducean 104A
caduceus 104D
Caesarean 135B, 145F
Caesarism 133A
caesium 5D
cafe 48B
cafeteria 48B
caffeine 5C
cage 52H
cahoots 130A
Cain 130-O
caique 24J
cairn 104H
cairngorm 5C
caisson 53J
caitiff 32, 129B
cajole 40A, 130A

cake 48E, 146B
cake-walk 99F
calabash 48G, 53I 53N
calaboose 52H
calamitous 127B, 31, 130M, 130B, 130-O
calamity*
calamus 143E
calash 24H, 106H
calcareous 5C, 102A
calcify 3A
calcimine 102E
calcination 145H
calcine 145H
calcite 5C
calcium 5D
calcography 100A
calculable 115
calculate 115, 147L
calculation 115, 113
calculator 115
calculous 145H, 146B
calculus 115, 147L
caldera 25H
caldron 53M
calendar 86, 148G
calender 132A
calenture 128B
calf 143A, 110B, 148J
caliber 147L
calibrate 115
calibration 115
calico 106K
calligraphy 55B
calipers 95B
caliph 133A, 82F
caliphate 82C
calisthenic 137B, 108
call 41B, 92, 40B, 40A, 119E, 12, 41B
calligraph 55B
calligraphy 55B
calling 126A
calliope 68G, 85C, 85E
callous 146B, 110B, 110A
callow 128A, 148J
callus 146B
calm 132B, 98A, 98B, 136A, 11B
calomel 136B
calorimeter 95B
calorimetry 115
calotte 106H
caltrop 143E
calumet 104G
calumniate 65
calumnious 65

calumny 65
calve 141B, 145E
Calvinism 82B
Calvinist 82D
Calvinistic 82B, 82A
camatose 37
camber 150C
cambist 44
cambric 106K
camel 143A, 24G
cameo 100B, 107C
camera 95B
camion 24H
camlet 106K
camouflage 103B, 57, 103A
camoufleur 103B, 103A
camp 53C, 54A
campaign 40B, 25G, 41D
campanile 104F
campanulate 150C
can 53N, 137B, 11A
Canadian 54C
canaille 129B
canal 25F, 25E, 25I
canaliculate 25
canard 62
canary, bird 143C
    color 102A
    wine 48L
cancan 99F
cancel 131A
cancer 130E, 128C
cancerate 128C
cancerous 130E, 128C
candelabrum 101C
candent 101A, 131A
candescence 101A
candid 61A
candidate 41D, 39, 40B
candle 141C, 101C
Candlemas 148K
candor 61A
candy 48F
cane 143E, 130G, 107B
canine 143A
canister 53M
canker 130E, 128C
cankerous 128C
cannabis 52C
cannibal 130-O, 51A
cannibalism*
cannon 130I
cannonade 130F
cannula 25F
cannular 25F
canny shrewd 117
    cautious 119G
    artful 134B, 57
canoe 24J, 24A

canoeist 24E, 23
canon Godly law 82A
    law 133A
    catalogued saints 86, 82G
    decree 94
canon law 82A, 94
canon 25H
canonical 82A
canonicals 106I
canonicity 82A
canonist 82F
canonization 139B, 94
canonize 139B, 94, 139A
canopy 34
canorous 68A
cant 31, 55A, 62, 149D, 18C, 40B
cantaloupe 48K
cantankerous 66, 27, 29, 67A
cantata 68B
cantatrice 68B, 68I
canteen 53N, 44, 48B
canter 19B, 9, 43B
canterbury 53P
canticle 68B
cantilever 53R
cantillation 68B, 68A
canto 68A, 85C
canto-fermo 68B
canton 147B
cantonment 53C
cantoon 106K
cantor 68I, 95A, 98A
Canuk 54C
canvas 106K, 100B, 5B
canvas-back 143C
canvass
    examine 119E
    discuss 90
    solicit 40B
canyon 25H
canzona 68B
canzonet 68B
caoutchouc 5C
cap top 149F, 106H, 140B, 50, 139A
capability 117, 137B, 134B, 116
capable*
capacious 25, 53A, 147J
capacity 117, 137B, 53A, 6
caparison 107A, 106B
cape 106D, 25G
caper 9, 71A, 18B

capillary 49A, 25E
capilliform 150G
capital 53F, 140B, 53R
capitalist 49E
capitally 140B
capitation 45, 49A
capitol 133A
capitulate 46B
capitulator 46B
caplin 143B
caponiere 36B
capote 106F
capouch 106H, 106I
caprice 127A, 3C
capricious 127A, 3C
capriole 19B, 9
Capsicum 48P, 143E
capsize 130D, 130-O
capsular 53I
capsule 53I, 53Q
captain 133A
caption 73, 92
captious carping 64
  resentful 27, 67B, 49C, 57
captivate 50, 40, 99A, 8, 40A, 108, 136A
captivation 50, 40A
captive 46B
captivity 52H, 49C
captor 49A, 49C
capture 49C, 49A
caput 150G
car 24H
carack 24J
caracole 18C, 25C
caramel 48F
carapace 36F
carat 147C
caravan 24H, 24E, 19A
caravaneer 24E
caravansary 53D, 48B
caravel 24J
carbine 130I
carbineer 130F
carbon 5D
carbonize 3A, 144B
carboy 53N
carbuncle 107C
carbuncular 102A, 128B
carburetor 145J
carcase 128C, 53R
carcinology 83
card 79
card-sharp 49F, 41D
cardia 137B, 25E
cardialgia 128B
cardigan 106D

cardinal 133A, 4
  cloak 106H, 106F, 82G, 137C, 149B
care 39, 13, 119G, 132C
careen 149D
career 9, 19B
care-free 126B
careful 39, 119G, 114, 32, 61A, 132C, 134A
careless 126D, 126B
carelessness 126B, 126D
caress 98C, 121
caret 55B
cargo 135A
caribou 143A
caricature 100B, 100A, 72
caricaturist 100C
caries 128C
carillon 68E, 68B
cariole 24H
carious 128C
cark 39, 31
carl 137B, 129B
carline 53R
carminative 136B, 138B, 16
carmine 102A, 102D
carnage 130-O
carnal 39B, 125C-3, 146D, 39C
carnalist 146E
carnation 143E, 102A
carnification 102A
carnival
  revelry 99A, 99E
  feasting 51A, 71A
  ceremony 95D
carnivorous 51A
carob 143E
carol 68B, 68A
carouse 51A, 125C-3, 71A
carp 64, 66
  fish 143B
carpenter 144D
carpentry 144B
carpet 107E
carpet-bag 53J
carpeting 106K
carriage
  vehicle 24H
  transportation 24A
  deportment 98B, 95C, 98A
carrier 24E
carrier-pigeon 143C
carrion 128C, 129A

carrion-crow 143C, 51A
carronade 130I
carrot 48K, 143E
carry 24A, 50, 132D
cart 24H, 24A
cartage 24A, 45
carte 86
carte blanche 46A
cartel 42
cartilage 146B
cartographer 100C
cartography 100A
cartoon 100B
cartouch 100B, 84, 92, 107B, 107E
cartridge 53I, 130I
carve cut 145F
  sculpture 100A, 150A, 144B
caryatid 100B
cascade 16
casco 24J
case 53J, 127A
casemate 36B
casement 25
cash 45
cashbook 86
cashier 49E
cashmere 106K
cash-register 95B
casino 53D, 99E, 41D, 53C
cask 53N
casket 53L
casque 36C
Cassandra 77
cassation 131A
cassava 143E
cassia 143E
cassimere 106K
cassinette 106K
cassock 106I
casson 53J
cast throw 24C
  defeat 50
  condemn 65
  form 150A, 98A, 98B, 100A, 119E, 134C, 144B, 144E, 147L, 149A, 114, 102B
castanets 68E
castaway 127B, 129B
caste 54C, 145D, 145K
castellated 36B
caster 53I, 150C, 24D, 53N
castigate 130N, 64
castigation*
Castilian 54C
castle 53D, 36B

castrate 35A, 130D, 145F
casual 127A, 60, 126B
casualty
  injury 130-O
  misfortune 127B
  accident 127A
casuist 113
casuistic 113, 57, 127A
casuistry
  doctrine 83
  equivocation 57, 62
  theory 113
cat 143A, 24J, 130L, 130N
cat-o'-nine-tails 130L, 130N
catabolism 3A, 14
cataclysm 130-O, 127B, 16
catacomb 53L
catacoustics 83
catafalque 53R
catalepsy 11B, 110A
cataleptic 11B, 110A
catalogue 86
catalysis 3A
catamaran 24J, 29, 67A
catamount 143A
cataphoric 137B
catapult 130I
cataract 16, 25I, 130-O
catarrh 16, 128B, 130E
catastrophe 130-O, 74, 127B
catawba 48G
catboat 24J
catcall 64, 72
catch seize 49C
  accept 49B, 111, 146K, 147L
catchpenny 49A
catchup 48P
catechetical 81
catechism 81
catechize 81
catechumen 116
categorical 84, 134A, 86
category 86
cater 43B, 48A
caterpillar 24G
caterwaul 70
catfish 143B
catgut 52C
cathartic 138B
cathead 53R
cathedral 82C, 53C

catholic 135B, 146A, 82A, 82D
Catholicism 82B
catholicity 82B, 125C
catholicon 136B
catopsis 119B
catoptrics 83
cattle 143A
Caucasian 54C
caucus 146K
caudal 150G
caudle 48L
caul 106H
cauliflower 48K
causal 1, 144A
causality 1
causation 1
causative 1, 134C
cause principle 1
 excitation 8
 authorship 144A, 137B, 134C, 124
causeway 25B
caustic
 burning 131B
 sarcastic 64
 hateful 28, 48Q, 128C, 145J
causticity 131B, 128C
cauterization 131B
cauterize 131B, 138B
caution warn 79
 fear 32, 103A
 watchfulness 119G
 reserve 132C
 threaten 33
cautious fearful 32
 circumspect 119G
 reserved 132C
 secret 103A
cavalcade 24E, 19A
cavalier gallant 39A
 armed horseman 130F
 gay 71A
 supercilious 28, 38
cavalry 130F
cavatina 68B
cave den 53D
 hollow 25H
cave bear 143A
caveat 94
cavern 25H
cavernous 25H, 25
caviar 142F
cavil 66
cavity 25H, 25
cavo-rilievo 100B
cavort 19B, 9
caw 69B
cayenne 48P
cayuse 143A
cease 12, 91

ceaseless 11A, 148C
cedar 143E
cede 46B
ceil 34
ceiling 34
celandine 143E
celebrant 140B
celebrate 95D, 63, 139B
celebration 95D, 63
celebrity 140B
celerity 9
celery 48K
celeste 102A
celestial 140B, 108, 54C, 136A
celibacy 132C, 145K
celibate 145K
cell 53D, 53E, 52H, 142F
cellar 53E
cello 68D
cellular 142F
cellulose 142F
celt 130H
Celt 54C
Celtic 54C
cement 52F, 146A, 146B, 52E
cementation*
cemetery 53L
cenobite 82D
cenotaph 104H
censer 53I, 122
censor 133A, 35A
censorious 64
censorship 35A
censurable 64, 130A
censure 64
census 86
cent 147B
cental 147C, 147A
centare 147C
centaur 143A
centenarian 148H
centenary 148H, 147A
centennial 148H
center 149L, 146A
(B). centre
centesimal 147A
centiare 147C
centigrade 147A
centigram 147C
centiliter 147F
centime 147B
centimeter 147E
centipede 143D
cento 85C, 68B, 85B
central 149L
centrality 149L
centralize, 149L, 146A, 146K
centric 149L
centricity 149L

centrifugal 149L, 15, 149K
centrifugence 15, 149L
centripetal 19A, 20
centumvirate 133A, 146K, 147A
centuple 147A, 148K
centurion 133A
century 148H, 147A
century-plant 143E
cephalalgia 128B
cephalic 149H
cephalitis 128B
cephalopod 143B
Cephalopoda 143B
ceraceous 102A
ceramic 144A
cerate 136B
ceratin 146B, 36F
cereal 48M
cerebellum 111
cerberean 34
cerberus 34
cerebralism 83
cerebrate 111
cerebration 111
cerebric 111
cerebrum 111
cerecloth 106K
cerement 106K
ceremonial 95D, 132D
ceremonialism 132D
ceremonious 95D, 134A, 132D
ceremony 95D, 134A
Ceres 48G, 48M, 142F
cerium 5D
cerography 55B
certain 134A, 117, 134C
certainty 134A, 117
certes 134A, 117
certificate 93
certify 93, 61A
certitude 117, 134A, 134C
cerulean 102A, 102D
cerumen 129A
ceruse 102D
cervical 150G
cessation 12, 46B
cession 46B
cessionary 46B
cesspool 53B, 130A
cestus 130L
cetacean 143B
chafe 130G, 31, 39B, 130B
chaff 72, 129B, 129A
chaffweed 143E
chagrin, 29, 130C, 130B

chain 52B, 50, 147E. 52C, 107C
chain-mail 36C
chair seat 53-O
 official seat 133A
 professorship 81
 install 139A, 94, 95D
chairman 133A
chaise 24H
chalcedony 107D, 5C
chaldron 147F
chalet 53D
chalice 53I
chalk 102E
chalky 102E, 102A
challenge invite 40A
 dispute 66
 summons 41B
 dare 33, 12, 42, 149H
challis 106K
chamber 53E, 146K
chamberlain, 133A, 46B
chameleon 103B, 3A
chamfer 25F
chamois 106K
champ 145F, 39, 145H
champagne 48L
champaign 25G
champerty 43B, 41D, 36
champion 50, 140B
chance 127A, 148L
chancel 53E
chancellor 133A
chance-medley 130-O
chandelier 101C
change alter 3A
 exchange 45
 taint 146C
 convey 24A
 deteriorate 128C, 14, 149A
 small coin 147L
changeability 3A, 3C
changeable 3A, 46B
changeling 142B
channel 25F, 25I
chant 68B, 68A
chanter 68I
chantey 68B
chanticleer 143C
chantry 53C
chaos 125A
chaotic 125A
chap 146L, 148C, 25H
chaparral 34
chap-book 85B
chapeau 106H
chapel 53C, 146K
chaperon 34

chapfallen 31
chaplain 82F
chaplaincy 82C
chaplet 104B, 107B
chapman 44
chapple 146L
chapter 145D, 82F
char 46B, 131B
character 55B
  distinction 126A,
    68A, 95E, 135B,
    137C
characteristic 126A,
    84, 95E
characterization
    126A, 92, 84,
    95A, 95E, 105
characterize 126A,
    95E, 105, 92, 84
characterless 129B
charade 57, 96A, 13,
    99B
charcoal 5C
charge 41B, 13, 64,
    65, 130F, 94, 45,
    147L
charge d'affaires
    133A
charger 24G, 130F,
    143A
chariot 24H
charioteer 24E
charitable 43A, 38,
    136A
charity 43A, 136A,
    38
charivari 68B, 70
charlatan 130A, 62
charm subdue 50, 8
  delight 99A, 68A,
    71A, 99C, 108,
    136A
  allure 40A, 40
  protection 34
charnel 128C
chart 100B, 95B,
    100A, 105
charter 46A
chartographer 100C
chary 32, 132C, 103A
chase 41D, 41C, 35A,
    107A, 24H, 119E
chasm 25H, 37, 145C
chassepot 130I
chasseur 130F
chassis 53R
chaste pure 138C,
    108
  modest 132C
chasten 138B, 130N
chastize 130N, 130G
chastity 138C, 132C
chat 55A, 90
chateau 53D
chatelaine 107B

chattels 135B
chatter 56, 60
chatterbox 56
chauffeur 24E
Chauvinism 38
cheap 147K, 129B
cheapen 14, 147K
cheat 49F, 130A
check restrain 52A,
    50
  reproof 64, 126B,
    93, 12, 36A
checker 102C, 102B
checkmate 50
cheek 42, 28, 64, 95D
cheep 69C
cheeper 143C
cheer applaud 63,
    71A, 134D, 7,
    99C, 136A
cheerful 71A, 136A
cheeriness 71A
cheerless 31, 98B,
    130B
cheery 71A, 99A
cheese 48I
cheese cake 48I
cheetah 143A
chef 144D
chemical 3A
chemise 106G
chemisette 106G
chemist 3A
chemistry 3A, 83
chenille 107B
cherish 38, 39A, 7,
    34
cheroot 48-O
cherry 48G, 102A,
    48L
cherub, 108, 140B
cherubic 140B
chess 41D
chest 53J
Chesterfieldian 38,
    136A
chestnut 48C, 102A,
    143A
chesty 28, 76
chevalier 133A
Cheviot 106K, 143A
chevron 104B, 104D,
    107B
chew 145F, 114,
    145H
chiaroscuro 100A,
    102B
chic 108, 134B, 107A,
    134B
chicane 103A, 62, 57,
    103B, 130A,
    134B
chick 143C, 148J
chickadee 143C
chicken 143C, 148J

chickweed 143E
chicory 143E
chide 64
chief leader 133A
  eminent 140B,
    149H, 126A
chieftain 133A
chiffon 106K
chiffonier 53P
chignon 106A, 107B,
    106H
chikara 143A
chilblain 128B
child 148J, 110B,
    142B
childbirth 141B
childe 148J
childhood 148J
childish 148J, 128A,
    110B
childless 145K, 128A
childlike 110B
children 148J, 142C
chiliad 148H, 147A
chill 146B, 28
chilli 48P
chilly 121
chime 68E, 68A
chimera fancy 113,
    96A
  ambiguity 57
  fish 143B
chimerical 57, 113,
    96A
chimney 25F
chimpanzee 143A
chin 150G
china 53M
chinchilla 143A
Chinese 54C
chink 25H, 145C
chinkapin 48C
chintz 106K
chip 145F, 145D,
    145H
chipper 9, 3C
chirography 55B
chiromancy 77
chiropodist 136B
chiropractic 136B
chiropractor 136B
chirp 68B, 68A, 69C,
    69B
chisel 145F, 144B,
    150A, 100A
chit 148J, 129B,
    130C
chitchat 60
chivalresque 42
chivalrous 42, 38,
    108, 140B
chivalry 42, 38
chloral 136B, 48L
chloralism 136B,
    128B

chlorin 5D
chlorodyne 136B
chlorophyll 102D
chlorosis 128B
chocolate 48F, 102A,
    48J
choice 49A, 140B
choir 68I
choke 130N, 130-O,
    130B
choker 107B, 106C
choler 29
cholera 128B, 130E
choleric 128B, 29
choose 49A, 39
chop 145F
chop-suey 48D
choral 68A, 68B
chorale 68B
chord 68A
chores 144B
chorister 68I
chortle 71B, 71A
chorus 68B, 68I
chosen 49A
chouse 49F
chowder 48D
Christ 82E
christen 92
Christendom 82C,
    82B
Christian 82D, 82A
Christianity 82C,
    82B
Christmas 148K
Christmastide 148K
chromascope 95B
chromatic 102B,
    68A
chromatometer 95B
chromium 5D
chromo 100B
chromogen 102E
chromosphere 101B
chronic 11A, 148C
chronicle 148G
chronicler 85E
chronogram 84
chronograph 86,
    95B, 148C
chronological 86,
    148A, 148B
chronology 86
chronometer 95B,
    148F
chronopher 98A
chronoscope 95B,
    148F
chrysanthemum
    143E
chrysolite 107C
chubby 150G
chuck 24A, 24C, 98C

club-foot 109B, 150G
club-haul 18C
clue 87, 95E
clump 34, 146A, 146K
clumsy 126D, 18A, 109A
cluster 146A, 146K
clutch 49C
clutter 125A
clyster 138A, 138B
coach 24H, 81
coagulate 146B
coagulin 146B
coagulum 146B
coal 5C
coalesce 52E, 146A, 52G, 146B, 146C, 52F
coalition 146A, 146K, 146B
coal-scuttle 53N
coamings 53R
coaptation 132A
coarse 70, 126A, 130C
coarseness 126A, 70
coast sail 23, 25G
   shore 36H
   descend 22
   proceed 19A
coaster 24J
coastguard 34, 133A
coastwise 149J
coat 106D, 106E
coax 40A
cob 143B, 143C
cobalt 5D
cobble 136B, 126C, 24J
cobra 143F
cobweb 48J, 49F, 53D
coca 136B
cocaine 136B
cochineal 102A, 143D, 102D
cochlea 143F
cochleate 150C
cock, 143C, 141F, 98A
cockade 107B
cockatrice 130-O
cockboat 24J
cockcrow 148A
cockerel 143C
cock-eyed 119B
cock-fight 41D
cockle 150B, 143B
cockney 54C
cockpit 25A, 53E, 99E
cockroach 143D
cocktail 48L

cocoa 48J, 143E, 136B
cocoanut 48C
cocoon 142F
cocotte 39B, 125C-3
cocytus 130N
cod 143B
coddle 38, 98C
code 98A, 86, 94
codeine 136B
codex 86
codger 39, 29
codicil 93
codify 86
codling 143B
coefficient 147L, 5A
coerce 52A, 50
coercion 52A, 50
coeval 148L, 146A, 148E
coextensive 149A
coffee 48J
coffer 53J
coffin 53L
cog 5C, 130A, 24J
cogent 93
cogitate 114
cogitation 114
cognac 48L
cognate 146I
cognition 117
cognitive 117, 111
cognizance 117, 111, 119F
cognizant*
cognomen 92
cohabit 145D, 146H
cohere 52E
coherence 52E, 52G, 115, 146A
coherer 95B
cohesion 52E
cohesive 52E
cohort 146K
coiffeur 107A, 106B
coiffure 106H, 106A
coign 150D
coil 150C, 146A
coin 147L
coinage 144B, 144A
coincide 132A, 146A, 105
coincident 127A, 148L, 105, 148E
coition 146D, 146A
coke 5C
colander 145B
cold 146B, 28, 121
cold-blooded 28, 130M
cole 48K
cole-slaw 48D
colewort 48K
colic 128B

collaborate 5A, 144B, 85A, 146K
collaboration*
collaborator 5A, 144D, 146L, 46B, 85E
collapse 127B, 128A, 22
collar seize 49C
   restraint 52A, 52C
   neck-piece 107B, 106C
collarette 106C
collate 114, 115, 146A
collateral 46B, 149J
colleague 146L
collect 146K, 49E, 40B, 146A
collected 132B
collection 49E, 146A
college 81
collegian 116
collegiate 81
collide 130G, 146A
collie 143A
collier 24J
collision 130G, 146A, 130F
collocation 132A, 149A, 146A
collocution 90
colloquial 55A, 90
colloquy 90
collude 103A
collusion 103A, 130A, 5A
collusive 103A, 130A, 5A, 62
colon 55B, 147B
colonel 133A
colonial 146K
colonist 54B
colonization 146K
colonize 146K
colonnade 53R
colony 146K, 53E
color 102B, 102E, 104E, 102D
color-blind 119B
colorimeter 95B
coloring 102B, 102E
colorist 100C
colossal 147J, 96A, 99A
colosseum 99E, 25A
colossus 147J, 140B
colportage 43B
colporteur 43B
colt 143A, 148J, 110B, 130N, 142D
columbine 143E, 108
column 53R, 55B, 146K, 104H

columnar 150C
coma 110A, 101B
comatose 110A
comb 132A
combat 41D, 130F
combatant 41D, 130F
combine 146A, 146K, 146C
combustible 131B
combustion 131B, 101A, 145J
come 19A, 146A, 146K
comedian 99D, 72
comedy 99D, 72, 99B
comely 108
comet 101D
comfit 48H
comfort
   console 136A
   inspirit 7, 71A
comfortable 71A, 136A
comforter 136A, 106D
comfortless 130B, 31
comfrey 143E
comic 99A
comicality 99A, 99C
coming 146A, 148B
comique 99D
comity 38
comma 55B
command 41B, 94, 95E, 133A
commandant 133A, 82A
commandeer 49C
commander 133A
commandment 94
commando 146K, 130F
commemorate 11A, 139B, 63, 95D, 117
commemoration*
commence 4, 73
commencement 4, 73
commend 63, 87
commendation 63, 87
commensurability 132A, 45
commensurable*
commensurate 26, 105, 147L, 45, 132A
comment 84, 55A
commentary 84
commentator 84
commerce 44, 49D
commercial 44, 49D
commingle 146K, 146C, 146A
comminute 145H

condescend 46A, 46B
condescension*
condign 132A, 45, 130N
condiment 48P
condition 126A, 89, 84, 147L
condole 31, 136A, 7
condolence 7, 136A
condonation 47
condone 47
conduce 10, 43B, 1, 2, 5A
conducive 10, 43B, 1, 24A
conduct 24A, 132C, 134B, 132D, 133A, 134C
conductance*
conduction 24A
conductive 24A, 1, 6
conductor 24E, 25F
conduit 25F
cone 150C, 150D
confab 90
confection 48F
confectioner 144D
confectionery 48F
confederacy 146K
confederate 146L, 5A, 146K
confederation 146K
confer, consult 41A
converse 90, 43A, 43B, 139A
conference 90, 41A, 146K
confess 46A, 61A, 78
confession*
confessional 78, 118
confessor 78, 46A
confidant 38, 42, 103A
confide 78
confidence 113, 42, 38, 39, 78, 103A, 117
confident 42, 113, 61A, 103A, 117
confidential 78, 103A
configuration 149A, 150A, 105
confine 52H
confinement 52H, 141B
confines 149M
confirm 93, 61A, 92
confirmation*
confiscate 49C
conflagration 131B, 101A, 145J
conflict 41D, 130F
conflicting 130F, 27
confluence 16, 146A, 25I, 146K
conflux 16, 146A, 146K

conform 132A, 105, 146A
conformation 132A, 105
conformist 82D
conformity 132, 105
confound 57, 13, 96A, 146C, 130-O
confrere 146L
confront 149H, 42, 27
confuse 57, 13
  jumble 125A
  mingle 146C
  bewilder 96A
confusion 125A, 112
confutation 138D, 67A, 93, 61A
confute*
con-game 130A
congeal 146B, 52E
congelation*
congenial 136A, 146I
congeniality 136A
congenital 141B, 137C, 146A, 146I
congeries 49E, 146A, 146K
congest 146B, 146K
congestion 146K, 26, 146A
conglomeration 146C, 146A
conglutinate 52E
conglutination 52E
congratulate 63
congratulatory 63
congratulation 63
congregate 146K
congregation 146K
congregational*
Congregationalism 133A
Congress 146K, 90, 133A
Congressional 133A
Congressman 133A
congruent 132A
congruity 132A
congruous 132A
conic 150C
coniferous 141B, 150C, 150H
coniform 150C
conine 5C
conjectural 113, 57, 127A
conjecture 113, 57
conjoin 146A
conjoint 146A
conjugal 146H
conjugality 146H
conjugate 3A, 146I, 126A, 146A, 146H

conjugation 3A, 146H, 126A
conjunction 146A, 55A
conjunctive 146A
conjuncture 146A, 3A
conjuration 40B, 50
conjure 40B
conjurer 99D, 134B
conjuror 146L, 40B
connate 146A
connaught 106K
connect 52B, 146A
connection 52B, 146H, 146A
connective*
conning 94
connivance 130A, 46A
connive 130A, 103A
connoisseur 117, 49E
connotation 115
connotative 80
connote 80
connubial 146H
conoid 150C
conoidal 150C
conquer 50
conqueror 50
conquest 50
consanguineous 146I
conscience 111, 117
conscientious 114, 117, 132C
conscious 111, 112, 117
conscript 49C, 86
conscription*
consecrate 92, 94, 63, 139A, 139B
consecration*
consecutive 75, 148B
consensus 46A
consent 46A, 46B
consentient 46A, 46B, 132A
consequence 28
  result 144E, 74
  significance 95A, 115, 148B
consequent 144E
consequential 135B, 115
conservable 132C
conservation 11A, 132C
conservative 132C
conservator 34, 11A
conservatory 132C, 11A, 81
conserve 132C, 11A
consider 113, 114, 119E
considerable 147I, 135B

considerate 114, 132C, 136A, 113, 119E
consideration 114, 136A, 113, 132C
consign 24A, 43B
consignee 49B
consignment 43B, 24A
consignor 43B
consist 53A
consistence 137B, 146A, 132A, 146B
consolation 136A, 71A
console 136A, 53P
consolidate 146B, 146K, 146A
consomme 48D
consonant 68A, 132A, 92, 55C
consort
  partner 146L, 146J, 141B, 146H, 146K
conspectus 58, 86
conspicuous 95E, 140B, 93, 135B
conspiracy 130A
conspirator 130A
conspire 130A
constable 133A
constancy 11A, 39A, 140A, 38, 39, 144B
constant*
constellation 101D, 146K
consternation 112, 32
constipate 146B
constipation 146B
constituency 146K
constituent 145D, 37, 146A, 146L, 147L
constitute 53A, 144B, 94, 139A, 144A
constitution 137B, 2, 35, 46A, 94
constitutional 35, 46A, 4, 137B, 19B, 52G, 53A, 94, 137C, 146A, 2
constrain 52A, 50
constraint*
constrict 52B, 146B
constriction 52B
constrictor 143F
constringent 52B, 146B
construct 144B, 85A, 144A

construction 144B, 144A, 53D, 84, 53B, 85B
constructive 144B
constructiveness*
constructor 144D
construe 84
consubstantial 137B
consubstantiation 82C
consul 133A
consul-general 133A
consulate 133A
consult 41A, 90, 114
consultation*
consume 51A, 131B, 128C, 130-O
consummate 12, 50, 132A, 140B, 134B, 134A, 108, 117
consummation 12, 50
consumption 128B, 130E, 128C
consumptive*
contact 124
contagion 124
contagious 124
contain 53A, 140A, 132C
container 53B, 53N
contaminate 130E, 146C, 129A
contamination 146C
contemplate 114, 119E
contemplation*
contemplative*
contemporaneous 148L, 146A, 148E
contemporary*
contempt 28
contemptible 129B, 130C
contemptuous 28
contend assert 80
dispute 66, 27, 41D, 130F
content gratify 136A
contentment 71A
contention 27, 66, 41D, 67A, 147L
contentious*
contentment 71A
conterminous 149M
contest oppose 27
dispute 66
contend 41D
struggle 130F
contestant 41D, 27, 130F
context 74
contiguity 149M, 124, 149J

contiguous*
continence 132C
continent 132C, 25G
continental 149A
contingence 127A
contingent 127A, 146K
continual 11A, 148I
continuance*
continuation*
continue 11A, 148I, 132D
continuity*
continuous*
contort 150C, 125A, 150B
contortion*
contortionist 99D
contour 150A, 100B, 95C
contraband 35
contrabandist 49F
contrabasso 68D, 68A
contract shorten 58
condense 146B
incur 49D, 14
agreement 89, 146A
contraction 58, 146B
contractor 44
contra-dance 99F
contradict 66, 67A
contradiction*
contradictory 66, 67A
contradistinction 126A
contradistinguish 119F
contralto 68A, 68I
contrariety 27, 60
contrary 27, 60, 67A, 126A
contrast 126A
contravallation 36B
contravene 27, 66, 67A, 130A
contravention*
contretemps 127B, 127A
contribute 43B, 5A, 43A, 10, 85B, 89
contribution*
contributor 43A
contributory*
contrite 31
contrition 31
contrivance 5B, 5A
contrive 144A, 144B, 134B
control 50, 132D, 133A, 134B
controller 93, 133A
controversial 66, 57, 67A
controversialist 66

controversy 66
controvert 66, 27, 67A
contumacious 27
contumelious 27, 28, 65
contumely 27, 28, 64, 65
contuse 130G
contusion 130G
conundrum 57, 96A, 103B, 13
convalesce 137A
convalescence 137A
convalescent 137A
convene 146K
convenience 5A, 132A, 46B
convenient 5A, 132A, 46B, 149M, 134D
convent 53C, 52H
conventicle 146K
convention 146K, 132D
conventional 132D
conventionality 132D
converge 146A
convergence 146A
convergent 146A
conversant 90, 117, 134B
conversation 90
conversational 90
conversationalist 90
conversazione 90
converse 90, 3A
conversely 3A
conversion 3A, 132A
convert 3A, 132A, 82D, 146L
covetous 49A
convex 150C
convexity 150C
convexo-concave 150C
convexo-convex 150C
convey 24A, 55A, 43A, 43B, 44
conveyance 24H, 24A, 5A, 24J
conveyancer 86, 24E
conveyancing 86
convict 93, 94, 130A
conviction 93, 94, 113, 115, 117
convince 93, 50, 84
convivial 71A, 38, 99A
conviviality 71A, 99C
convocation 40B, 41B, 146K
convocational 40B, 41B, 146K

convoke, 40B, 41B, 146K
convolution 150C, 146A
convolve 150C, 146A
convoy 24A, 34
convulse 71B, 71A, 125A, 72, 99A
convulsion 125A, 130E
convulsive 72, 125A
coo 55A, 69A, 40
cook 144B, 145J, 144D
cookery 144B
cooky 48F
cool 146B, 132B, 28
cooler 146B
coolie 24E
coon 117
coop 52H
cooper 144D
cooperant 144B, 5A
cooperate 144B, 5A, 132A, 146K
cooperation*
cooperative*
coordinate 132A, 86
coordination 132A, 86, 144B
coot 143C, 129B
cop 49C, 133A
copaiba 136B
copal 5C
coparcener 146L, 130A
cope 106I, 41D
copeck 147B
copious 147I, 43A, 26, 56
copper 5D, 133A
copperhead 143F
copse 34
copulate 146D, 146A
copulative 146A
copy likeness 105
imitate 103B
original work 100B
transcript 84, 85B
reproduce 75
copyist 100C, 105
copyright 46A
coquet 40
coquetry 40
coquette 40
coracle 24J
coral 143B, 107D
coralline 142D, 102A, 102D
corbeil 36E
corbel 107E
cord 52C, 147G
cordage 52C
cordate 150G

cordial hearty 38
  medicine 136B
  cheering 136A
  aromatic 122
cordiality 38, 136A
cordiform 150G
cordilla 52C
cordillera 149E
cordite 130K, 145B
cordoba 147B
cordon 36B, 52C
cordon bleu 117,
  140B, 50
cordonnet 107B
cordovan 106K
corduroy 106K
corduroy road 25B
cordwainer 144D
core 137B, 2
co-respondent 88
Corinthian 108,
  136A
cork 36A
corker 134B, 117,
  140B
cormorant 143C, 51A
corn 48M
cornea 119C
corner 150D, 53I,
  49C
cornerstone 53R
cornet 68G, 133A,
  106H
cornflower 143E
cornstarch 48M
cornucopia 104G,
  147I
cornuted 150G
corollary 115
corona 101B, 149F
coronal 104B, 101B
coronation 94, 139B
coroner 133A
coronet 104D, 106H
corporal 133A, 150G
corporate 146K
corporation 146K,
  146A
corporeal 150G,
  146A
corps 130A, 146K
corpse 128C
corpulence 150G,
  109B, 147J
corpulent 150G,
  109B, 147J
corpus 86
corral 52H, 49C
correct 136B, 134A,
  61A, 130N
correction*
correctional 136B
correlate 146A
correlation 146A,
  105, 146I
correspond 90, 88,
  132A, 105

correspondence 90,
  88, 105
correspondent*
corridor 25D
corrigible 46B
corroborate 93, 137B
corroboration 93
corrode 128C
corrosion 128C
corrosive 128C
corrugate 150B
corrugation 150B
corrupt 128C, 146C,
  129B, 125A, 65,
  129A, 130A,
  130E, 146D
corruption*
corsage 106G
corsair 49G
corset 106G
corselet 36C
cortege 46B, 146K
Cortes 133A
corundum 5C
coruscate 101A
coruscation 101A
corvette 24J
cosmetic 102E, 107A
cosmic 132A, 132D
cosmism 83
cosmogony 132A, 83
cosmography*
cosmology*
cosmopolitan 54B,
  132B
cosmorama 100B
cosmic 137C
cosmos 132A
Cossack 130F
cost 45, 147L
costermonger 44
costive 146B, 128B
costly 140B
costume 106B, 107A
cosy 136A
cot 53-O, 53D
cote 53D, 147I
contemporary 148L
coterie 146K
cotillion 99F, 68B,
  106K
cottage 53D
cotton 106K, 52C
couch 53-O, 103A,
  5A, 55A
couchant 32
cough 16
council 87, 41A,
  146K
councilman 133A, 87
counsel advise 87
  consultation 41A
  reveal 78
counselor 87
count 133A, 115,
  147L

countenance
  allow 46A
  appearance 95E,
  95C, 95A
counter 53P, 27
counteract 3C, 27,
  131A, 130D
counterbalance 3C,
  131A
counterblast 88
countercharge 88,
  64, 65
counterfeit 105, 62,
  100B, 103B,
  129B, 130A
counterfoil 86
counterfort 36B
counter-light 101A
countermand 131A
counterpane 34
counterpart 105
counterpoint 132A
counterpoise 3C,
  135A
counterscarp 149D
countersign 92
countervail 45,
  131A, 27, 130D
countess 133A
countless 147I
country 53F, 25G,
  146K
countryman 129B,
  146L
county 53F
coup 50, 49A
coupe 53E
couple fasten 52B
  unite 146A
  pair 147A
  copulate 146D,
  146H, 146J
couplet 85C
coupon 49D, 93
courage 42
courageous 42
courier 24F
course 25A, 16, 19A,
  25B, 25I, 41D,
  132D, 145D, 9,
  19B, 148B,
  119E, 23
courser 24G, 143A
court 25D, 40, 94,
  53E, 133A, 140A
courteous 38, 136A,
  98C, 108
courtesan 125C-3,
  146E, 39C
courtesy 38, 98C,
  136A
courtier 40
courtly 136A, 98C,
  108
courtship 40
courtyard 25D

cousin 146I
cousin-german 146I
cove 25I, 16
covenant 93, 46A
cover 103A, 34
covering 34, 106B
coverlet 34
covert 103A, 104A,
  34, 53D
coverture 34, 146H
covet 39, 39B, 49A
covetous 39, 39B
covetousness*
covey 142E, 147I,
  146K
cow 143A, 141F, 33
cowcatcher 36A
coward 32
cowardice 32
cower 32, 46B
cowhide 130L, 106K,
  130G
cowl 106H, 106I
cowlick 106A
coxcomb 28, 113,
  103B
coxswain 133A
coy bashful 32
  modest 132C
coyness 32, 132C
coyote 143A, 119E,
  130A
cozen cheat 130A,
  49F
  entice 40A
cozy 71A, 136A
crab 145B, 48G, 15
crack 145E, 25H,
  140B, 76, 134B,
  145C
cracked 110B, 70
cracker 48E
crackerjack 140B,
  134B
crackle 69C, 69A
crackling 69C
cracknel 48E
cracksman 49F
cradle 53P, 141D,
  1, 4, 53-O
craft skill 134B
  fraud 49F
  vessel 24J
craftsman 134B,
  144D
crafty cunning 117,
  59, 62, 130A
  skillful 134B
crag 149E
craggy 149E, 150B
cram 146B, 51A
cramp 31, 49C, 52B
cranberry 48G
craniology 83
cranium 53Q, 150G
crank 110B, 130N

cranky 110B, 29, 126A
cranny 25H, 145C
crape 106K
crapulent 51A, 51B
crash clash 146A, 69B, 106K, 130-O
crass 110B
crate 53K
crater 25H
cravat 106C
crave 39, 40B
craven 32, 40B
cravenette 106K
craving 39
craw 53Q
crawfish 143B, 15
crawl 19B, 18A, 52H, 126B
crayon 102E, 100B, 100A
crayonist 100C
craze 39, 39A
crazily 110B
craziness 110B
crazy 110B
crazy-work 126A
creaky 69C
cream 48I, 140B
creamy 102A
creamery 144C
crease fold 146A, 150B
create 141A, 144A, 94, 139A
creation 141A, 144A, 1, 141D
creative 141A, 144A
creator 141A, 144A 82E, 1, 141E
creature 143A, 54B, 142B
creche 5A
credence 113
credenda 82A, 113
credential 93, 113
credible 140A, 127A, 61A
credit trust 46A
  sell on trust 44
  believe 113
creditor 44, 113
credulity 113
credulous 113
creed 82A
creek 25I
creel 53K, 49C
creep 19B, 103A, 18A, 126B
creeper 19A, 143E, 143C
creepy 32
cremate 131B, 145J
cremation*
crematory 131B, 145B

crenate 150H
crenelle 36B
creole 146F
creosote 102E
crepitate 69C, 69A
crepon 106K
crescent 150C, 10, 98A
cresol 5C
cresset 101C
crest summit 149F, 106A, 36C, 28, 38, 42, 71A, 106H
crestfallen 31
cretinism 128B, 130E
cretonne 106K
crevasse 25H, 145C
crevice 25H, 145C
crew 146K
crewel 106K
crib bed 53-O
  manger 53E, 53D, 49F, 84
cribbage 41D
cribriform 25
crick 128B
cricket 41D
crier 79
crime 130A
criminal 130A
criminate 65
crimination 65
criminology 83
crimp decoy 40A
  entrap 49F
  make fluted 107A
crimson 102A, 98B, 112
cringe 32, 98C, 129B
crinkle 150B, 125A
crinoline 106F
cripple disable 130D, 109B, 130M
crippling 53R
crisis 3A, 37, 127A
crisp 58, 150C
crispin 144D
criterion law 94
  standard 105
crith 147C
critic 64, 84, 94, 115
critical 84, 127A, 3A, 13, 134A, 145A
criticaster 64, 84
criticize 64, 84
criticism 64, 84
critique 84
croak 64, 69B, 70, 72
crochet 107A, 144B
crock 53N, 129A
crockery 53N
crocket 107E
crocodile 143F, 143B
crocus 102D, 143E

crofter 144D
croix de guerre 104B
cromlech 104H
crone 128A, 129B, 148J
crony 146L
crook 49F, 150C, 150B
crooked 125A, 150B
croon 68A, 69A
crop produce 144E
  bird's craw 53Q
  whip 130L, 130G
  cut, clip 145F
  appear 95C
croquet 41D
croquette 48D
cross cross piece 150F
  crucifixion 130-O
  decoration 104B, 104C
  suffering 31
  oppression 130B, 131A, 36, 29, 130N
cross-bill 143C
crossbow 130I
cross-breed 146F
cross-examination 41A
cross-eyed 119B
cross-grained 29
crossing 25B, 150F
cross-tie 53R
cross-wind 125B
crosswise 150F
crotch 49C
crotchet 68K, 113, 55B
crotchety 126A, 113
croton-bug 143D
crouch 32, 149G, 129B
croup 128B
croupier 44, 133A
crow 143C, 76, 69B
crowbar 5B, 145F
crowd host 146K
  to press 146B, 40B, 130B, 147I
crown
  head-dress 104D, 106H
  complete 50
  top 149F, 150G, 139B, 94, 45, 139A, 140B, 147B
crow's-nest 119E
crucial 119E, 115, 130M
crucible 131B, 53M, 145B
crucifix 104C, 150F
crucifixion 130-O
cruciform 150F

crucify 130-O
crude raw 126A
  awkward 126D, 126C
crudeness*
cruel 130M, 130B
cruelty 130M
cruet 53N
cruise 23, 19A
cruiser 24J
crumb 145H, 147K, 129A
crumble 145H, 128C. 125A
crumple 150B, 125A
crunch 145H
crupper 52C, 150G
crural 150G
crusade 41D, 130F, 36, 49C
cruse 53N
crush crumble 145H
  ruin 130-O, 13, 50, 146B
crush-hat 106H
crust 146B, 129A
Crustacea 143B
crustaceous 150G
crusty 146B, 29
crutch 53R
cry have grief 31
  call aloud 69B
  proclaim 79
  implore 40B
  protest 66, 67B
  demand 41B
crypt 53E, 13, 103A
cryptic secret 103A
  bewildering 96A
  hidden 57, 13
cryptogram 55B
cryptography 55B, 103B
cryptonym 92
chrysolite 107C
crystal 101A, 5C, 95E, 146B
crystalline 101A, 5C, 95E
crystallize 11B, 14, 134C, 3A, 146B
cub 143A, 148J, 142D
curbature 114, 147L
cubby 53D
cube 150D, 147A
cubeb 48P
cubic 150D
cubit 147E
cucking-stool 130N
cuckold 129B
cuckoo 143C
cucumber 48K
cud 48A
cuddle 98C, 121
cuddy 24G

cudgel 130L, 114, 130G
cue end 12, 74
  hint 87
  queue 106H, 106A, 146K, 5B
cuff blow 130G
  sleeve-fold 106C
cuirass 36C
cuirassier 130F
cuisine 53E, 48B, 48P
cul-de-sac 52H
culinary 144B
cull 49A
culminate end 12, 74, 17, 50, 132A, 149F
culmination*
culpable 126C, 130A, 126B
culprit 130A
cult 82B, 38
cultch 142F
cultivate 5A, 39, 6, 10, 81, 144B, 116
cultivator 6
cultural 6, 81
culture 6, 116, 81, 117
culverin 130I
culvert 25F
cumber hinder 52A
  embarrass 13
  oppress 130B
  perplex 96A
cumbersome 135A, 13, 130B
cumin 143E
cumulative 10, 49E, 146A
cumulus 145J
cuneate 150E, 150D
cuneiform 150E, 55B, 92, 150D
cunning designing 130A
  crafty 134B, 117
  witty 59
  deceit 103B
cup vessel 53M
  prize 104B, 45
  potation 48L
cupboard 53P
cupel 53N
cupellation 138B
Cupid 39A, 108
cupidity 39, 39B
cupola 104F
cupule 53M
cur 143A, 129B, 32, 146F
curacy 45
curare 136B, 130E
curarize 130E
curate 82F

curative 136B
curator 133A
curb restrain 52A
  subdue 50
  curbstone 36H
curd 48I
curdle 146B
cure 136B
curfew 148K
curia 133A
curio 107E, 126A
curiosity 39, 41A, 126A, 109A
curioso 49E
curious 39, 41A, 119E, 109A, 126A
curl 106A, 150C, 107A
curly 150C
curmudgeon 39
currant 48G
currency 3A, 132D
current 79, 16, 113, 2, 148E
curricle 24H
curriculum 81
currier 107A
currish snappish 29
  cowardly 32
  quarrelsome 66
curry 40B, 138A, 132A, 48D, 48P
curse 65, 64, 127B
cursed 129B
cursorial 9, 19B
cursory hasty 9
  superficial 60, 113, 127A
curt 58
curtail 58, 14
curtailment 14
curtain 103A
curtesy 98C
curtsy 98C
curvate 150C
curvature 150C
curve 150C, 18C
curvet 18B
curvelinear 150C
cushion 53-O, 99F
cusp 150E
cuspidate 150E
cuspidor 53M
custard 48E
custodian 34, 52H
custody 52H
custom 132D, 45, 38, 49A
customary 132D, 75, 105
customer 49D
cut sever 145F
  stab 130G, 25I, 25F, 145C
cutaneous 36F
cutaway 106D

cutch 142F
cute 117, 134B, 108, 59
cuticle 36F
cutlas 130H
cutler 144D
cutlery 145F
cutter 24J, 24H
cut-throat 130-O
cuttle 143B
cutwater 149H
cutworm 143F
cyanate 5C
cyaneous 102A
cyanosis 102A, 102C
cybele 103A
cycle 150C, 24H, 148I
cyclic 150C
cyclist 19A, 24E
cycloid 150C
cyclometer 95B
cyclone 125B
cyclonic 125B, 130-O
cyclonoscope 95B
Cyclopean 137B, 147, 33
cyclopedia 86
Cyclops 137B, 147J
cyclorama 100B
cyclostyle 55B
cylinder 25F, 150C
cylindric 150C
cylindroid 150C
cymbal 68E
cynic 64, 28
cynical 64, 28
cynosure 95E, 95D, 98A
cypher 147L
cyprian 39B, 146D, 125C
cyst 53Q
cystoplast 53Q
cystoscopy 119E
cystotaenia 143F
cystotome 145F
cytoblastema 142F
cytode 142F
cytogenesis 141A
Czar 133A
czardas 99F
Czarevitch 133A
Czarevna 133A
Czarina 133A
Czech 54C
Czecho-Slovak 54C

D

dab small bit 147K
  clever 134B
  fish 143B
dabble 129A, 145J
dabster 134B, 117
dacoit 49G
dacoity 49G

dactyl 55B
dactylography 100A
dactylology 83, 98A, 55B
dad 141E, 146I
daddle 18A
daedalian 134B
daffodil 143E
daffy 110B
daft 110B
dagger 130H, 55B
Dagon 82E
daguerreotype 100B, 100A
dahabiyeh 24J
daily 148K, 98C
daimio 133A
dainty 108, 48F, 134A
dairy 44
dais 53R
daisy 143E
dal 48D
dale 25G
dalliance 126B
dally 126B, 121
dalmatic 106H, 106I
Daltonism 119B
dam 36A, 36, 52H, 64, 36H
  parent 141E
damage impair 130D
  wound 130M, 45
damask fabric 106K
  deep pink 102A, 107A
damaskeen 107A
dame 148J
damn sentence 94
  curse 64, 65
damnation 94, 64, 65, 130N
damnatory 65,64
damned 130A, 129B
damnify 65, 130D
damosel 148J
damp moist 145J
  depress 130B, 31
damper 132D, 13, 130B
damsel 148J
dance 99F
dandelion 143E
dander 29, 129A
dandruff 129A
dandle 98C, 121
dandy 140B, 95D, 103B
danger 127A, 33, 13, 128A
dangerous*
dangle 95D, 149G
dank 145J
danseuse 99F
dapper 108
dapple 102C
darbies 52A

dare challenge 67A, 42, 33, 127A, 149H
dare-devil 42
daring 42
dark obscure 97
  ambiguous 57, 110B, 98B
  brunette 102A
darken 97, 13, 103A
darkness 97, 110B
darling 140B
darn 136B
darnel 143E
dart 9, 24A, 130H, 24C, 130J
dash throw 24C
  break 145E
  suffuse 145I, 130B, 125A, 100A, 23, 9, 18A, 55B, 146A, 95D
dastard 32, 129B
date fruit 48G, 148L, 148A, 148K
datum 113, 87
daub paint 100A, 100B, 129A, 63, 52F
daughter 142B
daunt 33
dauntless 42
davenport 53-O
davy 101C
Davy Jones 127B
daw 143C
dawdle 126B
dawn 4, 148A, 148E, 148K
day 148K, 101A, 147H, 148H
daybook 86
daybreak 148A, 148K
daydream 116, 113, 114
dayspring 148A, 148K
daze 101A, 96A, 112
dazzle 101A, 96A, 108, 95E
deacon 82G
dead 110A, 128A, 11B
deadbeat 49F, 130A
deaden 14, 128A
deadhead 49C
dead-lift 135A, 41C
deadlock 13
deadly, 130-O, 130M
dead-weight, 135A
deaf 118, 37
deafen 69B, 130D
deafening 69B, 130D
deaf-mute 118
deafness 118
deal 43B, 147L
dealer, 43B, 44, 49D

dean 82G, 117, 140B, 133A
deanship 82C
dear 140B, 38
dearborn 24H
dearth 37, 128A
death 128A, 128C, 12, 130-O, 127B
death's-head 33, 95A, 104A
deathless 11A, 148C
deathly 130-O
debacle 16, 130-O, 50, 127B
debar 35, 35A, 131A
debark 15
debarkation 15
debase 65, 129B, 146C, 125A, 130A, 130D, 146D
debasement*
debatable 57, 127A
debate dispute 66
  deliberate 114
  discuss 90
debauch lewdness 125C-3
  pollute 146D, 39C, 146C, 51B
debauchee 146E
debauchery 125C-3, 146D, 39C, 51B
debenture 93
debilitate 130D
debilitation 128A, 130D
debility 128A
debit 49D
debonair 38, 136A, 98C, 108
debouch 15, 25
debouche 44
debris 129A, 125A
debt 49D
debtor 49D
debut 95C, 98C
debutant 98C, 95C
deca 147A, 150D
decade 148H, 147A
decadence 128C
decagon 150D
decagonal 150D
decagram 147C
decahedron 147C
decaliter 147F
decalog 82A, 94
decalogue 82
decamenter 147E
decamp 15
decant 16, 24C
decanter 24C, 53N
decapitate 130-O, 145F
decapod 150G
decare 147E

decastere 147G
decay 128C, 128A
decease 128A
deceit 103B, 130A, 62, 49F
deceitful feigned 103B
  false 62
  ambiguous 57
  dishonest 130A
deceitfulness*
deceive mislead 103B
  lie 62, 57, 49F, 130A, 134C
December 148K
decemvir 133A
decemvirate 133A
decency 134A, 140A
decennial 148H, 148K
decent 134A, 132C, 140A
deception 103B, 62, 49F
deceptive 103B, 62, 57, 103A, 130A
declare 147E
decide conclude 115
  resolve 39, 2, 94, 134C
deciduous 22, 145G
decigram 147C
deciliter 147F
decillion 147A
decilux 147D
decimal 147A, 147L
decimate 130-O
decimation 130-O
decimeter 147E
decipher 115
decision 115, 94
decisive 12, 115, 27, 50, 58, 84, 93, 94
decistere 147G
deck array 106B, 107A
  display 95D
  flooring 25A, 25D
decker 24J
declaim, 85A, 68A, 69A
declamation*
declamatory*
declaration 79, 93, 61A, 80
declarative 79, 61A, 80, 84, 93
declare proclaim 79, 80
  witness 93
  affirm 61A
  say 55A
declension 14, 128C, 149D, 3A
declinate 150C, 149G

decline 35
  incline 149D
  diminish 14
  refuse 27, 67A
  lean 22
  become weak 128A, 128C, 130A, 132C, 149G
declinograph 95B
declinometer 95B
declivitous 149D, 149G
declivity 149D
decoct 144B
decoction 48A, 144B
decoit 49G
decoity 49G
decollate 145F, 130-O
decollete 149G, 95E
decompose 128C, 145A
decomposite 146C
decomposition 128C
decompound 146C
decorate 107A, 104B
decoration*
decorative 107A, 100A
decorous
  proper 134A
  decent 132C
  pleasing 136A, 108
decorticate 145G
decorum, see decorous
decoy 40A 49F
decrease 14, 130D, 147K
decree 94, 115, 50
decrement 14
decrepit 128A
decrepitude 128A
decrescent 14, 12
decretal 85B, 94, 82A
decretive 94, 115
decrial 65, 64
decry 64, 65
decumbent 149C, 149G
decuple 147A
decurrent 149D, 16, 149G
decursive 149D, 149G
decussate 150F
dedicate
  inscribe 85A, 63
  decree 94
  name 92, 43A, 95D, 139A
dedication*
dedicatory, 92, 94, 63
deduce 115
deduct infer 115
  take from 49A
  decrease 14

deduction*
deed document 93
 sale 44
 achievement 50
deem 115, 113
deemster 115, 94
deep 25H, 149G, 96A,
 69B, 70, 25I, 13,
 25, 117
deepen 149G, 10
deepness 115, 96A,
 149G
deer 143A
deerhound 143A
deface 130-O, 130D,
 130M
defacement 130-O,
 130D, 130M
defalcation
 theft 49F
 diminution 14
defalcator 49F
defamatory 65, 129B
defame 65, 129B
default 49F, 126B
defaulter 49F, 126B
defeasance 131A
defeat 50, 127B
defecate 16, 138B
defecation 16, 138B
defect 126C, 126B
defection 15, 126B
defective 125C,
 126B, 126C
defend 34, 36
defendant 27, 36G
defense 34, 36, 93
(B). defence
defenseless 128A
defensive 36, 36B
defer 12
 delay 126B, 148B
 comply 46A
deference 46A, 38
deferent 24A
deferential 46A, 38
deferment 46A, 38,
 12, 148B
defiance 67A, 42, 33
defiant*
deficiency 37, 128A
deficient*
deficit 37
defilade 36
defile
 corrupt 146C,
 146D
 tarnish 129A, 25B,
 109C
defilement*
define 84
definite defined 84
 exact 134A, 68A,
 117
 destined 134C,
 95E, 95A, 75
definition*

definitive*
deflagrate 131B,
 145B, 145J
deflate 130D
deflect 150B, 150C,
 18C, 150D
deflection
 150B, 150C
deflective*
deflector 150C, 18C
deflexure 150C
deflower 146D, 125A
deforest 125A
deform 150B, 109B,
 125A
deformity
 109B, 150B
defraud 49F, 130A
defray 45
deft 134B
defunct 128A
defy 67A, 42, 33
degenerate 128C,
 129B, 14, 110B
degeneration*
deglutition 51A, 51B
degradation 129B,
 14, 65
degrade 65, 129B,
 14, 130D
degree 147L, 126A,
 147E 147L
dehiscence 16, 145A
dehiscent 16, 145A
dehorn 145F
deification 139B
deify 139B
deign 46A
deism 82A, 82B
deist 82D, 113
deistic 82A, 113
Deity 82E
deject 130B, 33
dejection 31
dejeuner 48A
delaine 106K
delay 12, 148B, 148I,
 126B
dele 131A
delectable 48P, 71A,
 99A, 99C, 108,
 136A
delectation 71A, 51A
delegate commit 94
 send 24A, 133A,
 139A
 messenger 24F,
 133A
delegation 133A, 94
delete 131A
deleterious 130D,
 130M, 130-O,
 131A
deliberate 114, 126B
deliberation 114

delicacy
 agreeableness
 48P, 48F, 99C,
 108
 frailness 128A, 3C,
 32
 reserve 132C
delicate 57, 108, 122,
 128A, 134A,
 150G
delicatessen 48B
 48F
delicious 48P, 108
delight 71A, 99A, 63,
 99C, 108, 136A
delightful 99A, 108,
 48P, 122, 136A
delineate
 sketch 100A
 show 95A, 95E
 describe 84
delineation*
delineator*
delinquency 126B,
 130A
delinquent*
deliquesce 145J
deliquescent 145J
delirious 128B, 112,
 110B, 71A
delirium*
deliver convey 43B
 free 47
 submit 46B
 send forth 24A, 90,
 55A, 141B, 136A
deliverance*
delivery*
dell 25G
delta 25G, 150D
deltoid 150D
delude 49F, 62
deluge 16, 127B,
 130-O, 21
delusion deceit 103B,
 57
 imposition 130A
 illusion 113, 49F
delusive*
delve 119E
demagogic 64, 41B,
 65
demagogism 64, 65
demagogue 64, 41B,
 27, 65
demand 41B
demantoid 107C
demarcation
 84, 95A, 95E
demean 132C, 132A,
 132B
demeanor 132C, 95C
dement 96A
dementia 110B, 128B
Demeter 141E, 146H
demi 147A
demigod 82E, 140B
demijohn 53N

demimonde 125C-3,
 146-E
demise death 128A
 grant 43A
demobilize
 145I, 145A
democracy 133A
democrat 133A
democratic 133A
demography 86
demoiselle 140B,
 142B, 143D
demolish 130-O
demolition 130-O,
 127B
demon 130N, 130A
demoniac 130M,
 110B, 130A
demonolatry 82B
demonology 82B
demonstrate 84, 95A,
 93, 95D
demonstration*
demonstrative*
demoralize 125A,
 96A, 130A, 146C
demountable 46B
demulcent 14, 136B,
 136A
demur 66, 27, 67A
demure 132C, 132B
demureness*
demurrage 45
demurrer 66, 67A
demy 147D
den 53D
denaturalize 35A
denatured 146C
dendroid 150H
dendrology 83
dendrometer 95B
denial 27, 67A
denizen 54B
denominate 92
denomination 92
denominative 92
denominator 92,
 147L
denotable 95A
denotative 95A, 84
denote 95A, 92
denouement 74
denounce 64, 65
denunciatory 64
dense 146B, 110B
density 146B
dent 150B, 124
dental 145F, 55A
dentate 145F, 150E
denticulate 145F
 150E
dentiform 150E,
 150G
dentifrice 138A
dentiphone 118
dentist 136B
dentistry 136B

dentition 145F
dentoid 150E, 150G
denude 95A, 145G
denunciation 64, 65
deny 66, 67A, 27
deodar 143E
deodorize 138B
depart leave 15, 18C
  die 128A
  begone 35A
department 145D
departure leave 15
  deviation 18C
  death 128A, 131A
depend
  hang down 22,
    113, 46B, 132C,
    149G
dependence trust
  113
  connection 146A
  reliance 46B
depict describe 84
  portray 100A, 68A
depilatory 35A
deplane 15
depletion 128A
deplorable 31, 129B,
  127B
deplore 31, 67A, 67B
deploy 145A
deponent 93
depopulate 131A,
  130-O
deport 35A
deportment 132C,
  132B, 132D
depose 35A, 93
deposit place in 43B
  place 149A
  thing deposited
    49E, 45
depositary 34, 49B
deposition 93
depositor 43B
depository 53B
depot 53C
depravation 128C
deprave 65, 146C,
  130A, 146D
depraved 130A, 129B
depravity 130A,
  125C
deprecable 66, 64
deprecate 64, 67A,
  65
deprecation 65, 40B,
  64, 67B
deprecatory 66, 138D
depreciate 14, 64, 65
depredation 49G
depredator 49G
depress 33, 13, 14
  humble 129B
  lower 65
  oppress 130B
depressed 31

depression 31, 129B,
  14
  lowness 149G
deprivation 130D
  destitution 128A
  seizure 49C, 37
deprive take 49C
  debar 35, 35A
  impair 130D
  rob 49G
depth 149G, 117
deputation 94, 146K
depute 94, 139A
deputize 94, 139A
deputy 133A
derail 145A, 15
derange
  confuse 125A
  sicken 130E
  bewilder 96A
derangement 125A,
  110B, 109C
derby 106H
derelict 129B, 130A,
  126B
dereliction 15, 126B,
  129B, 130A
deride scorn 28
  ridicule 72
  gibe 64
derigible 24I
derision*
derisive 28, 72, 64
derivation 115, 49A
derivative 115, 55B
derive 49A, 49B, 115
derm 36F
derma 36F
dermatoid 36F
dermatology 83
dermic 36F
dernier 12, 74, 149I
derogate annul 131A
  detract 65, 64
  lessen 14, 129B,
    41A
derogation*
derogatory*
derrick 24B
derringer 130H, 130I
dervish 82D, 40B
descant song 68B
  comment 84
  teach 81
descend fall 22, 20,
  130F, 135B,
  149G
descendant 142B
descendent 22, 149G
descension 22, 14
descent fall 22
  ancestry 141G
describe 84
description 84
descriptive 84
desecrate 64, 65,
  129B

desecration*
desert 15, 128A,
  149D, 25G, 45,
  49A
desert reward 45,
  48F
deserve 140B, 49A
desiccate 146B, 11A
desiderate 37, 38, 39
desideratum 37, 38,
  39
design 2, 100B, 115,
  95B, 100A, 105,
  149H
designate 95A, 92
designation 95A, 92
designing 115, 114,
  130A, 130C, 1
desirable 140A, 140B
desire 39, 39B
desirous 39
desist, stop 12
  refrain 132C
  forbear 47
  yield 46B
  be just 140A
desk 53P
desolate destroy
  130-O
  lonely 145K, 147A
  sad 31
  overwhelm 130B,
    125A, 127B
desolation*
despair 31
despatch see
  dispatch
desperado, 130A,
  130-O, 42, 130M
desperate 125C-2, 42
despicable 129B,
  130C
despisable 130C
despise 28
despite 28, 27
despoil 49G
despond 31
despondency 31
despondent 31
despot 133A, 130B
despotic 133A, 130B
despotism 133A
dessert 48F
destination 149H,
  12, 74
  tendency 2
  destiny 134C
destine 134C, 1
destiny 134C, 50,
  37, 2
destitute 128A, 127B
  desolate 145K, 37
destroy 130-O, 131A
destroyer 130-O, 24J
destruction 130-O,
  125A, 127B
destructive 130-O

desudation 16
desuetude 131A
desultory cursory
  110B
  rambling 18B
  ambiguous 57
  erratic 126C,
    125A, 56, 60
detach part 145A
  send away 35A
detachment body of
  troops 146K, 130F,
  28
detail 86, 84
detain hold 52A
  stop 12
  delay 148B
detainment*
detect 119F
detection 119F
detective 119E
detector 95B
detent 12, 36A
detention 12, 36A,
  52A, 148I
detentive*
deter 12, 52A, 33
deterge 138B
detergent 138B,
  136B, 138A
deteriorate 128C,
  128A, 14, 130D
deterioration 128C
determinable 115, 84
determinant 84, 5A,
  1
determinate 84
determination 115,
  39, 42, 27, 134C
determine decide 115
  tend 2
  brave 42
  destine 134C, 1
determined 42, 27,
  11A, 39, 144B
determinism 83
deterrent 52A, 33
detest 28
detestable 129B,
  130A, 130C
detestation 28
dethrone 35A
detonate 69B
detour 18C, 25B
detract 14, 65
detraction 14, 65
detrain 15
detriment 130D, 13
detrimental 130D, 13
detrital 129A
detritus 129A, 145H
de trop 26, 147I
deuce 147A, 130N
deuteragonist 99D
deutoplasm 48A
devaporation 146B
devastate 130-O

devastation 130-O, 127B
develop 145A, 6, 10
  explain 84
  produce 144B, 95C, 144A
development*
devest 131A
deviate turn 18C
  vary 126A
  part from 145A
  err 126C
deviation*
device 5A, 104A, 100B, 104B
devil Satan 130N
  wicked person 130A
  bold fellow, 42, 125C
  malicious person 28
  to season 48P
devilish wicked 130A
  hateful 28, 125C-2, 130N, 130M
devilkin 130N
devilment 130A
deviltry 130A
devious 18B, 18C
devise 144A, 43A
devisee 49B
deviser 144A
devisor 43A
devitalize 130D
devoid 128A
devolution 3A
devolve 24A
devote 43A, 92
devotee 38, 39, 71A, 132A
devotion 38, 39A
devour swallow 51A
  annihilate 130-O
  enjoy 71A
devout 38, 89
dew, 145J
dewlap 36F
dewy 145J
dexter 149J
dexterity 134B
dexterous 134B
dextrin 52F
dextrose 48P
dey 133A
dhow 24J
di 150D
diabetes 128B
diablerie 130A
diabolic impious 130A
  hateful 28
  brutal 130M, 125C-2, 130N
diabolo 41D
diacaustic 150C

diaconal 82G
diaconate 82C
diacoustics 83
diacritical 55B, 95A, 95E
diadem 104D, 106H
diaeresis 55B
diagnose 115
diagnosis 115, 95A
diagnostic 115, 92, 95A
diagometer 95B
diagonal 149D, 150D
diagram 150D, 100B, 105
diagrammatic 100B, 100A
diagraph 100C
dial 95B, 148F
dialect 55A
dialectic 55A, 113, 114
dialectician 114
dialectology 83
dialogue 90
dialysis 145A
diameter 149L, 147L
diametrical*
diamond gem 107C
  angled figure 150D
Diana 119E, 141E
diapason 68A
diaper 138A
diaphane 100A
diaphanous 101A
diaphantograph 100C
diaphoretic 16
diaphragm 145B
diaphylactic 136B
diarist 86
diarrhea 16, 128A
diary 86, 148G
diastole 3B
diatonic 68A
diatribe 66, 64, 65
dibble 145F
dice 41D
dicer 41D
dichroism 101A, 101B
dichromatism 119B
dicker 49D, 44
dicky 106C
dicotyledon 143E
dictaphone 55B
dictate 55A, 94
dictation 55A, 94
dictator 55A, 94
dictatorial 94, 133A
diction 55A, 68A
dictionary 86
dictum 94, 133A, 61B, 80
did 148A
didactic 81
didactics 81

didactyl 150G
didecahedral 150D
die perish 131A, 12
  wither 128A, 100B, 55B, 134C
dieresis 55B
diesis 55B
diet 48A, 146K
dietary 48A
dietetic 48A
dieting 51A
differ contend 41D
  contrast 126A
  oppose 27
  dispute 66, 67A
difference*
different 126A
differentia 126A, 115
differential*
differentiate*
differentiation*
difficult 13, 96A, 57
difficulty knot 13
  scruple 30
  objection 27
  perplexity 112
  amazingness 96A
diffidence doubt 30
  modesty 32
  reserve 132C
diffident*
diffraction 150D
diffractive 150D
diffuse 145I, 56
diffusibility 145I
diffusion 145I 146C, 20
diffusive 145I, 56
dig 145F, 116, 25
digest classify 86
  abridgment 58
  assimilate 51A
  learn 116
  dissolve 145J
digestible 48A, 145J
digestion 51A
digestive 51A
digger 54C, 119E
digging 145F, 49A
digit 147A, 150G
digital 150G
Digitigrada 19B
dignified 98B, 108
dignify 139B
dignitary 82G, 140B, 133A
dignity 98B, 108, 68A, 140B
digress deviate 126A, 126C, 18C, 56
digression 18C, 57, 56, 126A, 126C
digressive*
dihedral 150D
dihexahedral 150D
dike 36H, 25F

dilapidation 128C
dilatation 10, 145I
dilate enlarge 10
  distend 145I
  expatiate 56
dilatory 126B
dilemma 13, 112
dilect 55A
dilectic 55A
dilettante 38, 116, 39, 71A
dilettanteism 38, 116
diligence 11A, 39, 41C, 49A
diligent 144B
dill pickle 48K
dilly-dally 126B
dilute 145J, 146C, 128A, 130D
dilution*
dim 97, 14, 101A, 103A, 148B
dime 147B
dimension 147L
diminish 14, 128A, 130D, 147K
diminuendo 68A
diminution 14
diminutive 147K
dimissory 46A
dimity 106K
dimorphism 3A
dimple 150G
din 69B, 75, 81, dinar 147B
dine 51A, 43B, 48A
ding 68A, 81, 75
ding-dong 68A
dingey 24J
dingle 25H
dingle-dangle 3B
dingy dirty 129A
  dark 97, 102B, 102A
dinner 48A
dint 137B, 150B, 1
diocesan 82C, 82A, 82G
diocese 82C, 53F
Dionysus 48G, 125C-3
dioptase 5C
dioptric 119A
diorama 100B, 95D
dioristic 115
diosmose 146C
dip 21, 149G, 22
diphtheria 128B
diphthong 55A, 92
diplos 150G
diploma 93
diplomacy 57, 62, 59, 134B
diplomat*
diplomatic*
diplomatics 116

diplomatist 134B, 57
dipper 53M
dipsomania 39, 128B
dipsomaniac 39,
   128B, 38
dipterous 150G
dire 33, 31
direct straight 149C
   command 94
   straightforward
     58, 84
   send 24C, 24A
   destine 134C, 95A,
     95E, 133A, 134A,
     148K, 149A
direction*
directness 58
director 94, 133A
directorate 94, 133A
directory 86
dirge 68B
dirigible 24I
dirk 130H
dirt 129A, 146C, 5C
dirtiness 129A, 109C
dirty 129A, 146C,
   70, 109C
dis 145K
disability 128A
disable impair 130D
   maltreat 130M
disabuse 78, 136B,
   131A
disaffect 145A, 33,
   130C
disaffection 145A,
   28, 130C
disagree 27, 66, 67A
disagreeable 130B,
   129B, 70, 123
disappear 15
disappearance 15
disappoint
   thwart 50
   incommode 13,
     130C, 130B
disappointment
   127B, 31
disapprove 64, 67A
disarm subdue 50
   unarm 128A
   deprive 130D
disarmament 128A
disarrange 125A
disarray 125A, 109C
disassemble 145A
disaster 127B, 130-O
disastrous*
disavow 66, 67A,
   131A
disband 145A
disbar 35
disbelief 30
disbelieve 30
disburden 35, 136A,
   35A, 5A

disburse 45, 44, 43B,
   131A, 49D
disbursement*
discard 35A, 129A
discern see 119A
   recognize 119F
   judge 115
discernible 95C
discernment 119F,
   111, 112, 115,
   119E
discharge gush 16
   send forth 24C
   dismiss 35A
   exonerate 138D
   free 47
   explode 145E,
     69B, 144B, 145A
disciple 116
disciplinarian 81,
   130N, 134A
disciplinary 81,
   130N, 134A
discipline teach 81
   chastizement
     130N
   mastery 134B, 116
   preciseness 134A
disclaim 66, 67A,
   131A
disclose 95A, 78, 61A
disclosure*
discolor 102C, 129A
discomfit 50, 130B
discomfiture 50,
   127B, 31
discomfort 30, 130B
discommode 130B,
   13
discompose
   abash 96A
   disarrange 125A
   anger 130C
discomposure 112,
   125A
disconcert 96A, 50
disconnect 145A
disconsolate 31, 98B
discontent 27, 37
discord dispute 66,
   67A
   dissonance 70
   noise 69B
discordant*
discount 14, 147L
discontinue 12
discourage 33, 13,
   130B
discouragement 32
discourse sermon 81
   recitation 85A
   conversation 90
discourteous 28,
   130C

discover find 115,
   116
   reveal 95A, 119F,
     134D
discovery*
discredit 30
discreet
   prudent 132C,
     103A, 119F
   discriminative 115
discrepancy 126A,
   126C, 125A
discrepant*
discrete apart 145A
   distinct 126A, 32
discretion 115, 132C,
   119F
discretionary*
discriminate
   115, 119F, 49A
discrimination*
discursion 57
discursive 18B, 60,
   57, 56
discursiveness*
discuss 90, 66
discussion*
disdain 28
disdainful 28
disease 130E, 128B
disembark 15
disembogue 15, 16
disembowel 130-O
disfiguration 109B
disfigure 109B,
   125A, 130M,
   150B
disfranchise 131A,
   35
disgorge vomit 16
   surrender 46B
   repay 45
disgrace shame
   130A
   dishonor 129B, 65
disgraceful*
disguise 103B, 103A
disgust dislike 28
   unsavoriness 48Q
   offend 130C, 130B
disgustful 123
disgusting 48Q,
   130C, 109A, 123,
   129B
dish 48A, 53M, 43B
dishabille 106B,
   109C, 106D
dishearten 33, 130B,
   13
dishevel 125A, 109C
dishonor
(B). dishonour
   disgrace 129B
   defamation 65
   violate 146D
   refuse 27
dishonorable 130A,
   129B

disinclination
   dislike 28
   opposition 27
   reserve 132C, 11B
     126B
disinfect 138B
disingenuous 130A,
   62, 65, 129B
disintegrate 128C,
   145H
disintegration*
disjunctive 145A
disk 150C
dislike 28
dislocate 145A
dislocation 145A
dislodge 35A, 145A
disloyal 130A, 27,
   62
dismal dark 97
   sorrowful 31, 98B,
     130B
   horrid 33
dismantle strip 145A
   demolish 130-O
dismay terrify 33, 13
   dispirit 128A
   perplexity 112,
     96A
   fear 32
dismember 145F,
   130-O
dismiss 35A
dismissal 35A
dismount 22, 15
disobedient 27, 130A
disobey 27, 130A
disorder derange
   125A
   irregularity 126A
   disease 130E,
     128B, 96A, 69B,
     130A
disordered 125A, 27
disorderly 125A,
   130A
disorganize 125A,
   145A
disown 66, 67A, 35A,
   27, 35
disparage 65
disparagement 65
disparity 126A
dispassionate 132B,
   132C
dispatch send off
   24A
   celerity 9
   kill 130-O
   finish 12, 85B, 79,
     144B
dispel dissipate 145I
   banish 35A
dispensable 43B, 45
dispensary 43B, 48B
dispensation 43B,
   46A, 47

dispense 43A, 43B, 47, 145A
disperse 145I, 35A
dispersion 145I, 35A
dispirit 33, 130B, 13
displace 3A, 35A, 125A, 145A
displacement 3A
display show 95A
 exhibit 95D
 bluster 76
 disclose 78
displease 130C
displeasure 28, 31
disport play 71A
 amuse 99A
disposal bestow 43B
 give 43A
 arrangement 132A, 145A, 149A
dispose*
 incline 149D, 2, 1, 35A, 43B, 132A, 145A
disposition*
disproof 93
disprove 67A, 138C
disputation 66, 67A
dispute 66, 67A
disqualify 65, 125A, 130D
disquisition, investigation 119E
 essay 85A, 84, 85B
 inquiry 41A
disrate 65, 14
disreputable 129B
disrobe 145G
disruption 145E
dissatisfaction 27, 31, 37, 39
dissect 145F, 119E, 145A
dissection*
disseize 49C
disseizin 49C
dissemble 103B, 103A
dissembler 62
disseminate 145I, 81
dissension 27, 66, 67A
dissent 27, 66, 67A
dissentient*
dissertation
 discourse 66, 85A
 explanation 84
 discussion 90
dissever 145F
dessicate 14
dissidence 66, 27, 67A
dissident 66, 27
dissilient 145E

dissimulate 103B, 57
dissimulation*
dissipate 145I
 squander 125C-1
 annul 131A
dissipation 125C-3 145I
dissociate 145A
dissoluble 145J
dissolute carnal 146D
 licentious 125C-3, 39C
 wicked 130A
dissolution 145J
 death 128A, 131A
dissolve 145J
 annul 131A
dissonance discord 70, 67A, 66
dissonant 70, 66
dissuade 87, 27, 40A
dissuasion*
dissyllable 55B
distaff 53R
distance length 147L, 149M, 149N, 148A, 148B
 space 25A
 aloofness 28, 132C
 leave behind 15, 50
distant 28, 132C, 149M, 148B, 149N
distaste 28
distasteful 129B
distemper disease 130C
 colors 102C, 102E, 130E
distend 145I, 10
distich 85C
distil trickle 16
 separate 145J, 145A, 144B
distillation 144E
distinct plain 95E
 different 126A
 separate 145K, 68A, 84, 117, 126A, 134A, 140B
distinction*
distinctive*
distingue 140B
distinguish show 95A, 95E
 honor 139B
 discriminate 115, 119F, 126A
 see 119A
distinguished 140B
 conspicuous 95E

distort, twist 150C, 150B
 misrepresent 62
 disfigure 109B, 150B
distortion 18C, 62, 125A
distract 96A, 13
distraction 112, 31
distractive 96A
distrain 49C
distrait 112, 126B
distraught 112
distress harass 130B
 pain 31
 perplex 96A, 112
 torture 130N
distribute allot 43B
 separate 145A, 149A, 145I, 86
distribution*
district 53F, 133A
distrust 30
distrustful 30
disturb trouble 13, 130C, 125A, 130B, 69B
disturbance*
disuse 131A
ditch 25F, 25H, 25, 145F
ditto 75
ditty 68B
diurnal daily 148K, 84, 86, 148H
diva 99D
divan 53-O, 53E
dive 21, 53D, 16
diverge 18C, 145A, 145K
divergence*
divergent*
divers 126A, 147L
diverse 126A
diversification 3A, 126A
diversify*
diversion fun 71A
 amusement 99A
 variation 3A, 18C
divert*
divertimento 68B
divertissement 68B, 71A, 99A, 99B
divest strip 35A, 49G, 145G
divestiture 46A, 46B, 35A
divide 145A, 145F, 145B, 147A
dividend 45, 145A, 145D, 147L
divi-divi 102E
divination 113, 117

divine guess 113
 God-like 136A
 good 140A, 108
 heavenly 140B
 clergyman 82F
 foretell 77
divining-rod 95B
divinity 82E, 82B, 140B
divisible 145A
division 145A, 145D, 146K
divisor 145A, 147L
divorce 145A, 145K
divort 145B
divulge 78, 61A
dizzy 112, 110B
do, work, 144B
 achieve 50, 105, 133A, 49F
docile 46B, 116, 132B
docility 46B, 116
dock 49A, 14, 144C, 143E, 25B
dockage 45
docket digest 58
 summary 86
dockyard 144C
doctor physician 136B
 savant 117
doctorate 117
doctrinaire 113
doctrinal 81, 82A, 113
doctrine 82A, 81, 82B
document 93, 85B
documentary 93
dodder 143E
dodeca 150D
dodecagon 150D
dodecahedron 150D
dodge 15, 28, 18C, 32, 35A
dodo 143C
doe 143A, 142D, 141E
does 148B
doeskin 106K
doff 35A, 145G
dog 143A
dogcart 24H
doge 133A
dogfish 143B
dogged 27
dogger 24J
doggerel verse 85C
 nonsense 60
doggish 29
dogma doctrine 82B, 82A
 exaggeration 62
 ambiguity 57
 belief 113, 80

dogmatic 80, 62, 113, 57, 82A
dogmatize 62, 57, 113, 82A
dog-trot 19B, 9
dogwood 143E
doily 138A
doings 3A, 144B
doldrums 125B, 31
depression 31, 130B
dole alms 43A, 43B, 147K
doleful mournful 31, 67B
doll 99D, 140B
dollar 147B
dolly 99D
dolman 106D
dolmen 104H
dolomite 5C
dolor 31
(B). dolour
doloroso 69A
dolorous 31, 130B
dolphin 143A
dolt 110B
dom 140B
domain 133A
dome 104F
domestic 132D, 46B
domesticity 132D
domicil 53D
domiciliary 54A
dominant 133A, 50, 140B
dominate 133A, 50, 1
domination 133A, 50
domineer rule 133A
compel 50
bluster 76
demonical 82B
dominical 82A
dominican 82F
dominie 81, 82F
dominion 133A, 50, 53F
domino hood 106H, 103B, 103A, 106I, 41D
don 106B, 140B
donate 43A
donation 43A
done 50, 128A, 12, 132A
donee 49B
doni 24J
donjon prison 52H
tower fort 36B
Don Juan 39C, 125C-3, 146E
donkey ass 143A, 24G, 27, 110B
donna 140B
donnishness 113
donor 43A

doom sentence 94
destiny 134C
punishment 130N, 45, 50
doomsday 148K
door entrance 25, 36A, 4, 36I
dope 96A
plan 114
magazine fillers 85A
Doric 55A
dorking 143C
dormant 11B, 110A, 128A
dormitory 53C, 53E
dormouse 143A
dorsal 149I
dory 24J, 143B
dosage 48P
dose 147L, 43B, 136B, 48A, 48J
dot 102C, 147K, 148J
dotage affection 39A
imbecility 110B
feebleness 128A
dotard 128A
dote 39A, 110B, 128A, 38
dotterel 143C
dottle 129A
double 147A, 105
double dagger 55B
doubleness 147A, 105
doublet 147A, 106E
doubloon 147B
doubt 30, 112
doubtful perplexed 112
uncertain 127A
ambiguity 57
doubtless 134C
douche 16
dough 48E
doughboy 130F
doughty 42, 137B
douse 21, 131A
dove 143C
dove-cote 53D
dovetail 145F, 132A, 52B, 146A
dowager 133A
dowdy 129A, 109C, 109A
dowel 52D
dower 43A
dowlas 106K
down 106A, 149G
downcast 31, 98B
downfall 127B, 22, 130-O
downgrade 127B
downpour 16, 130-O
downright 84
downward 22, 149G

downy in down 106A
soft 3C
artful 134B
not loud 69A, 57
dowry 45
doxology hymn 68B
praise 63
doze 11B, 110A, 132B
dozen 147A
drab 102C, 97, 102A
drabble 129A
drachma 147B
draff 129A
draft sketch 100B
outline 58, 105
a drinking 51B
a drink 48J
select 49C
drag 24A, 24H, 18A, 24G, 126B
draggle 129A
draggle-tail 129A
dragoman 84
dragon 143A
fierce person 130M, 130F, 130-O
dragon fly 143D
dragoon 130F, 50, 130B, 130N
drain empty 16
exhaust 128A, 130D, 25F, 49A,
drainage 16, 25F
drake 143C, 141F
dram 107C, 48L, 147C
drama 85A, 85C, 85B, 95D
entertainment 99B
dramatic 99A
dramatize 99B, 95D
drank 51B
drape 106B, 107A
drapery 106B, 106K, 103A, 107A
drastic 137B, 134A
draught 41D, 125B
Dravidian 54C
draw pull 24A
sketch 100A
raise 17, 149F
disembowel 130-O, 145A
take 49A
be in depth 21
entice 40A
receive 49B
win 134D
drawback 13, 127B
drawbridge 25B
drawee 45
drawer draftsman 100C
container 53I
garment 106G

drawing 100B, 95B
drawing-room 53E
drawl 55A, 70
drawn 146B, 57
dray 24H
dread 32, 33
dreadful 33, 129B, 109A, 130M, 130A
dreadnaught
brave 42
battleship 36B, 24J
dream 113
dreamer 113
dreamy 113
dreary 31, 97, 130B
dredge 145F, 49C
dreggy 129A
dregs lees 129A
canaille 129B
drench make wet 146C, 136B, 138A
Dresden 107E
dress 106B, 107A, 132A
dresser 53P
dressing attire 106B
beating 130G
sauce 48P
reprimand 64
dribble 16, 147K, 145J
drift flow 16
tendency 2, 146A, 149A, 25, 18B, 22, 25B
driftage 129A, 125A
drill, 145F, 20, 25, 75
train 81, 132D
drilling 106K
drink 48J, 48L, 51B
drip 16
drive impel 24C
urge 8
convey 24A
travel 19A
aim 39
hard blow 130G
road 24A, 25B, 35A
gathering 146K
drivel 16, 60, 110B
drizzle 16, 145J
droger 24J
droit 53A, 132C
droll 72, 99C, 99D, 99A, 99B
dromedary 143A, 24G
drone 69A, 70
lazy fellow 126B
drool 16, 60
droop sink 22, 104G, 128A, 110A, 149G
droopy 128A

ecthyma 16, 128B
ectoderm 36F
ectogenesis 141A
ectoplasm 142F
ectype 100B, 75
ectypography 100A
ecu 36C
ecumenic 146K, 146A, 132D, 135B
eczema 128B
edacious 51A
edacity 51A
eddy 16, 18C, 150C
Eden 53H
edge border 149K
  brink 36H
edging 107B
edible 48A, 48P
edict 94, 79
edification 81
edifice 53B
edify 81
edit 85A, 134A, 136B
edition 85B, 147L
editor 85E
editorial 85A, 85B
educate 81
education 81, 117
educationist 81
educator 81
educe 115
eduction 49A
eel 143B
eelbuck 49C
eelfare 19A, 142E
eerie gloomy 31, 96A, 33
efface 131A, 130-O, 35A
effacement 131A
effect touch 124
  get result 144B
  result 144E, 1, 8, accomplish 50, 95A, 95C, 134B
effective 137B, 134B, 1
effectual 137B, 134B
effeminancy 128A,
effeminate*
efferent 145A, 16, 15
effervescence 16, 145J, 14
effervescent*
effete 128A, 129B
efficacious 137B, 144B, 134B, 50
efficacy*
efficiency*
efficient*
effigy 105, 104A
efflorescence 141B, 102A
effluence 16

effluent 16
effluvial 123
effluvium 123
efflux 16
effort 41C, 2, 13
effrontery 130C, 28, 42, 64
effulgence 101A
effusion 16, 145I, 56, 71B
effusive*
eft 143F
egg 142F, 8
egging 8
egis 36C
eglantine 143E
ego 38, 39
egoism 38, 39, 76
egoist*
ego-maniac 38, 39, 76
egotism 38, 39, 76, 71A
egotist*
egotistic*
egregious 126A, 125C
egress 15
Egyptology 83
eider 143C
eidograph 100C
eight 147A
eighteen 147A
eighteenmo 147D
eighteenth 147A
eightieth 147A
eightscore 147A
eighty 147A
eikon 100B
either 147A, 127A, 25A
ejaculate 91
ejaculation 91
eject 35A
ejection 35A
ejectment 35A
ejoo-fiber 52C
eke 10
elaborate
  improve 136B
  refine 138B, 6
  beautify 107A
  produce 144B
  unsparing 125C
  innovate 126A
  beautiful 108
  complicated 13
elan zeal 39, 71A
  bent 2
elapse 131A, 15
elasticity 3C, 145I
elate excite 8
  exult 99A, 7
  jubilant 71A
elation 71A
elbow 150G, 130G
elder 143E, 148A, 82G, 148J

eldest 148J, 148A
El Dorado 135B, 49E
elect choose 49A, 115
  appoint 139A
  divine 140B
election 49A
electioneer 40B
electoral 49A, 115
electorate 49A, 115
electric 137B
electrician 144E
electricity 137B
electrify 8, 137B, 96A
electrocute 130-O
electrocution 130-O
electro-dynamom- eter 95B
electrography 100A
electrokinetics 83
electrolier 107E
electromassage 136B
electrometer 95B
electromotor 137B
electron 145D, 147K
electrophone 55C
electroplate 55B, 145I
electroscope 95B
electrotinting 55B
electrotype 55B
electuary 138B, 136B
eleemosynary 43A, 49B, 51A
elegance 108, 68A, 140B
elegant fine 108, 68A, 140B
elegiac 68A, 31, 68B
elegit 52A
elegy 68B
element 4
  principle 133A, 137B, 145D, 5D
elemental 4, 148A
elephant 24G, 143A
elephantiasis 128B
elephantine 147J
elephantoid 150G
elevate
  raise 149F, 17, 24B
  inspire 7, 8
  educate 81, 139B, 149E
elevation 24B, 100B, 149F, 149E
  high 17, 140B
elevator 24B, 53B, 24G
eleven 147A
eleventh 147A
elf 147K, 96A, 33
elf-child 142B
elfin 96A, 134B, 147K

elfkin 96A
elf-lock 106A
elicit 116, 40A
eligibility 46B
eligible 46B
eliminate 35A, 35, 131A, 145A
eliquate 145J, 145A
elision 58, 145A
elite 140B
elixir 122, 136B, 11A, 48J
elk 143A
ell 147E
ellipse 150C
ellipsoid 150C
elliptic 150C
ellipticity 150C
elocution 68A
elocutionist 55A
Eloes 38
eloge 63
Elohim 82E
elongate 10, 145I
elongation 10, 145I, 149C
elope 15
eloquence 68A
eloquent 68A
else 27
elsewhere 149N
elucidate 84
elude 15
elusive 15, 57, 103A
Elysian 136A, 71A
Elysium 53H, 71A
em 147E
emaciate 128C
emanate 16, 141B
emancipate 47, 145A
emancipation*
emarginate 150B, 150H
emasculate 35A, 130D, 145F
embalm 11A, 122
embank 36H, 36
embankment 36H, 36B
embargo 35
embark 149L, 42, 20
embarrass
  hinder 52A
  perplex 96A
  trouble 13
  annoy 130B
embarrassment* 112, 31
embassy 133A
embattled 36
embed 149L
embellish 107A, 107B
ember 131B, 101D
embezzle 49F
embitter 130C
emblazon 95D, 107A, 104A, 104D

emblazonry*
emblem 104A
emblemata 100B, 107E
emblematic 104A
emblements 144E
emblyopia 119B
embody 146A, 146B, 53A, 145A, 146K
embolden 7
embolism 91, 149L
embonpoint 150G
embosom 38, 34
emboss 100A, 107A
embouchure 25
embowel 130-O
embower 34
embrace 98C, 49C, 49B, 53A, 33, 49C, 121
embracery 130A, 52A, 33
embrasure 25
embrocation 136B
embroider 107A
embroidery 107B
embroil 66, 67A
embryo 142F, 4
embryogeny 141A
embryologist 83
embryology 83
embryonic 10, 141A, 141B, 4, 128A
embryoplastic 141B
embryoscope 95B
embryotomy 145F
emend 136B
emendation 136B, 6
emerald 102A, 107C
emeraldine 102D
emerge 17, 19A, 15, 95A, 95C
emergency
 necessity 37
 strait 13
 crisis 3A
emeritus 15, 140B
emersion 15, 95C
emetic 136B, 138B
emigrant 15
emigrate 15
eminence 149F
 height 149E
 exalted rank 140B
eminent
 exalted 140B
 conspicuous 95E, 17, 135B, 149F
emir 133A
emissary 133A
emission 16
emit issue 16
 circulate 145I
emollient 136A, 136B, 14

emolliotype 100B
emolument 49A, 45
emotion tendency 2
 passion 39B
 feeling 121, 3C
emotional*
emotive 8
empale 130-O
emperor 133A
emphasis 10, 69C, 69B, 115, 69A, 58
emphatic 10
 earnest 61A
 decisive 115, 58, 69C
 significant 84
empire 133A, 53F
empiric 117, 41C, 134B
empiricism 117
employ 49D, 133A, 38, 132D
employee 46B, 144D
employment 144B, 44, 49A, 38, 126A
emporium 44
empower 94, 46A, 137B, 139A
empresario 68J
empress 133A
empressement 38
emptiness 128A, 110B
empty vague 57, 60
 need 37
 destitute 128A
 stupid 110B
 void 131A, 24C, 16, 130D
empyreal 53H
empyrean 53H, 140B, 136A
empyreumatic 123
emu 143C
emulate 41D, 41C
emulgent 16
emulus 41D, 41C
enable 137B, 43B
enact 94, 105, 103B
enamel 102D
enamor 40, 50
encamp 54A, 53C
encampment*
encaustic 100A
enceinte 36B, 141B
enchain 52B, 52A
enchant charm 99A
 subdue 50
 excite 8, 40A, 99A, 108, 136A
enchantment 50, 99A, 8, 68A, 99C, 71A

encircle 52H, 150C, 149K
enclose 52H, 149K
enclosure 52H
encomiastic 63
encomium 63
encompass 52H, 149K
encore 63, 41B, 75
encounter 130F, 41D
encourage 7
encouragement 7
encroach 49F, 130A, 20
encroachment*
encumber 13, 36A, 36, 52A, 130B
encumbrance*
encumenical 135B
encyclical 79
encyclopedia 86
encyclopedic 86
end finish 12
 goal 149H
 outcome 144E
 annihilate 131A, 130-O, 74, 128A, 149I
endanger 128A, 130D
endear 38
endearment 38
endeavor 41C, 2
endemic 126A, 149L
endless 11A, 148C
endo 149L
endogen 143E
endogenous 141A, 141B
endosmose 16, 20, 146C
endosmosis 146C
endow 43A
endowment 43A, 117, 134B
endue invest 94, 11A
 furnish 43A, 43B, 8, 139A
endurance 137B, 11A, 31, 148C
endure 31, 137B, 11A
endways 149H
enema 136B, 138B
enemy 28, 130F
energetic 137B, 39, 41C, 58, 144B
energico 58, 69B, 115
energize 8, 137B, 136B
energy 137B, 2, 1, 58
enervate 130D
enfeeble 130D

enfeoff 44
enfilade 25, 130F
enforce 50, 133A, 8
enfranchise 46A, 47, 145A
enfranchisement*
engage 52B, 49D, 49C, 41D, 53A, 130F, 146G, 8, 99A
engagement 146G, 130F, 41D, 54A, 52B, 53A, 144B
engaging 99A, 50, 40A, 108, 136A
engender 141A, 8, 137B
engine 137B
engineer 24E, 132A, 133A, 144D
English 54C
engorge 51A
engraft 81
engrailment 107E
engrave 100A, 81
engraving 100B, 81
engross 55B, 49D, 53A, 8, 99A, 136A
engrossment 114, 49D, 55B, 53A
engulf 21, 130-O, 13
enhance 10, 5A, 6
enharmonic 68A
enigma 57, 96A, 103A, 13
enigmatic*
enjoin 94, 35, 50
enjoy 71A, 51A
enjoyable 48P, 99A
enjoyment 71A, 51A, 51B
enkindle 8
enlarge 10, 56, 147J
enlighten 81, 101A, 78
enlightenment 117
enlist 49A, 86, 146K
enliven 8, 99A, 136A
en masse 146K
enmity 28
ennoble 139B
ennui languor 128A
 dislike 28, 26, 126B
enormity 130A, 109B, 130M
enormous 147J, 130A, 130N
enough 26, 147L, 147I
enplane 20
enrage 130C
enrapt 71A

enrapture 99A, 50, 40, 108, 136A
enrich 43A, 107A, 137B, 6
enrobe 106B, 107A, 94
enrol 86
en route 19A
ensanguine 102A
ensconce 103A, 34
ensemble 145A, 146K, 146A
ensheathe 149L
enshrine 139A, 139B
enshroud 103A
ensiform 150E
ensign 104B, 104E, 133A
ensilage 48N
enslave 50, 46B
ensnare 49C, 130A, 49F
ensue 148B
entablature 53R
entail 10
estate in fee 43A
involve 126A, 57, 13, 37
entangle 13, 57, 125A, 130A, 36B, 96A
entente 46A, 117, 146K
enter 20, 25, 149L, 4, 86, 55B, 146K
enterprise 39, 42, 144B
entertain 99A, 48A, 114, 113
entertainment 99A, 48A, 99B, 99C
enthrall 50, 71A, 99A, 99C
enthrone 139B, 139A
enthuse 7, 8, 39, 71A
enthusiasm 39, 71A
enthusiast 39, 38, 71A
enthusiastic 39, 71A
enticement 40A, 12
entire whole 146A, 147L, 147I
entirety 146A, 147L
entitle 92
entity 2, 137C
entombment 52H
etomology 83
etomologist 83
entourage 146K, 149L, 149M
entracte 148I
entrails 25E
entrain 20, 24A, 149L

entrance 25, 25B, 50, 99A, 4, 20, 108, 136A
entrap 49C, 49F, 130A
entreat 40B
entreaty 40B
entree 20, 46A, 48F
entre nous 103A
entrust 45
entry entrance 25
passage 25B, 20
a listing 86
inscription 84
entwine 145A, 52B
enumerate 86, 115, 92, 147L
enunciate 55A, 79, 80
enunciation*
envelop 52H, 103A, 52B
envelope 53I, 149K
envelopment 52H
envenom 130D, 130C, 130E
enviable 140B
envious 39, 28
environ 135B, 149K
environment 135B, 149K, 149M
envoy 133A, 24F
envy 28, 39
enrap 52B
epact 147A, 148H
epaulet 104B, 107B, 104D
epergne 107E, 53N, 53M
ephemera 148H, 143D, 148J
ephemeris 86, 148G
ephod 106I
ephor 133A
epic 42, 85A, 85C, 85B, 140B
epicardium 36F
epicarp 36F
epicure 51A, 71A
Epicurean 51A, 71A
epicycle 150C
epidemic 130E, 130-O, 127B
epidermis 36F
epigamic 40
epigenesis 141A
epigram 61B, 85C
epigrammatic 61B, 59, 85C, 85A
epigraph 86, 84
epigraphy 83
epilogue 74, 85C
epiornis 143C
Epiphany 148K

Episcopalian 82D, 82A
episcopate 82C
episode 85B, 127A
episodic 85B, 127A, 85A
episperm 36F
epistemology 83
epistle 85B, 79, 85A
epitaph 86, 84
epithet 92
epitome 58, 86
epitomize 58, 14, 86
epoch 148L, 148I
epode 74, 68C, 85C
eponym 141E, 92
eponymous 92
equable 140A, 132D, 105
equal 147L, 105, 132D, 132A
equality 105, 132D, 132A, 147L
equalize*
equanimity 132B
equate 105, 147A, 147L
equation*
equator 149L, 145B
equatorial 145B
equerry 46B
equestrian 24E, 24A
equestrienne 24E
equilateral 150D
equilibrium 132A, 135A, 105
equine 150G
equinox 148K
equip 137B, 132A
equipage 24H, 5A
equipment 5A, 106B
equipoise 135A, 132A
equiponderant*
equitable 140A
equity 140A, 132C, 94
equivalence 26, 92, 105, 147L
equivalent*
equivocal 57, 105, 103B, 127A
equivocate 57, 62
equivoque 57
era 148I
eradicate 130-O, 138B, 131A, 145F
erase 131A, 35A
erasure 131A
erato 39A
erbium 5D
ere 148A
erebus 130N
erect 144B, 149E

erection 144B
eremite 145K
erethism 8
erg 147M
ergmeter 95B
erinite 5C
ermine 143A, 104D, 107B
ermined 106B, 140B
erode 128C
eros 39A
erose 150H, 150B
erosion 128C
erotic amorous 39A, 39B
poem 85C, 85B, 125C-3, 146D
eroticism 39A, 39B, 39C, 125C-3, 146D
erotomania 146D
err 126C, 130A
errand 19A, 79
errant 126C, 18B, 126A
erratic*
erratum 126C
erroneous 126C
error 126C
eructation 16
erudite 117
erudition 117
eruption 16
escadrille 24I, 130F
escalade 17, 25C
escalator 24B, 24H
escapade 126C, 130A
escape 15
escarpment 149D
eschew 15, 32
escort 34, 146L, 24A
escritoire 53P
escudo 147B
esculent 48P, 48A
escutcheon 92, 104B
Eskimo 54C
esophagus 25E
esoteric secret 103A
taught privately 81
profound 117
esoterist 117, 81
especial 126A
espionage 119E
esplanade 25B
espouse 89, 146G
esprit de corps 146K
espy 119F
Esquiman 54C
esquire 140B
essay 41C, 85B
essence spirit 137C
perfume 122, 2

essential 37, 137C, 138C
establish fix 11B
   prove 93, 84, 92, 94, 11A, 139A, 149A
establishment 144C, 94, 53D, 93
estate 147L, 146K, 135B
esteem 38, 113
esthete 38, 71A, 117
esthetic 108
estimable 140B
estimate 113, 115, 92
estimation*
estop 12, 35, 36
estoppel 35, 36, 36A
estrange 145A, 126A
estrich 106A
estuarial 25
estuary 25, 25I
et cetera 147L
etch 100A
etching 100B
eternal 11A, 148C
eternity 11A, 148C
etesian 125B
ether 25A, 145J
ethereal 145J, 140B
ethical 132D, 140B
ethics 132D
Ethiopian 54C
ethnic 132D
ethnography 83
ethnology 83
ethology 83
ethos 132D, 86
etiolate 102A
etiology 83
etiquette 132D, 84
etymologist 83
etymologize 116, 119E
etymology 83
etymon 55A
euchre 41D
eugenics 83, 141A, 136B
eulogistic 63
eulogize 63
eulogy 63
eunuch 46B, 128A
euphemism 68A
euphonic 68A
euphonious 68A
euphonium 68G
euphony 68A
Euphrosyne 71A, 99D
euphuism 68A
Eurasian 146F
eureka 79
euroclydon 125B
europium 5D

eustachian 25E
eutectic 145J
Euterpe 68H
euthanasia 130-O
euthenics 83, 136B
evacuate abandon 15
   discharge 35A, 16
evade 15, 28, 32
evanesce 97, 147K
evanescent 15, 14, 145J, 97
evangel 79
evangelical 82F
evangelism 82A
evangelist 82F
evangelize 81
evaporate 145J, 14, 16
evasion 15, 57, 62, 103A, 132C
evasive*
Eve 141E
eve 148A, 148B, 148K
even 149C, 132D, 105, 132A, 134A
evening 148B, 148K
event 127A
eventful 127A
eventide 148K, 148B
eventual 148B, 127A
eventuality*
eventuate*
ever 11A, 148L
everglade 25G
evergreen 143E, 150H
everlasting 11A, 148C, 143E, 106K
evermore 11A, 148C
evert 130-O
every 147I, 146A
evict 35A
eviction 35A
evidence 93, 95A, 95E
evident*
evil wicked 130A, 28, 65
   unfortunate 127B, 130-O, 129B, 130M
evil-eye 28
evince manifest 95A
   demonstrate 95E
   explain 84
evincive 93
eviscerate 130-O
evoke 40B
evolution 3A, 6, 19A, 141A, 83
evolutional 141A, 141B, 83

evolutionist 134B
evolve gender 141A
   work out 144A
   solve 115
   change 3A
ewe 142A, 141F, 143A
ewer 53N
exact correct 134A
   demand 41B, 84, 49G, 117, 148D, 148E
exaction 41B, 49G
exactly 134A
exaggerate 62, 10, 57, 113
exaggeration*
exalt 139B, 17
exaltation 71A
examination 114, 116, 41A, 119E
examine*
examinee 84
examiner 116, 119E
example 95A, 105, 84, 100B
exasperate 130C
ex cathedra 132A
excavate 25
excavation 145F, 25
exceed excel 125C
   cloy 26
   defeat 50, 140B, 134B, 147J
exceeding 147J, 134A, 134B, 147I
excel see exceed
excellence 140B, 134B
Excellency 140B
excellent 140B, 108, 134B
excelsior 140B, 5C
except 35, 27, 86
exception 35, 29, 126A, 140B
exceptionable 126A, 27
exceptional 126A, 140B, 108
excerpt 49A, 93
excess superfluity 26
   overplus 147I, 125C, 126C
excessive*
exchange change 3A
   barter 49D, 44
   repay 45
exchequer 52H, 53B
excise 49C, 145F, 49A
excision 145F, 130-O

excitability 2, 3A, 112
excitant 8, 96A
excitation 8, 112
excite 8, 96A, 4, 130C
excitement 112, 125A, 8, 96A, 71A
exciting 96A, 8, 140B
exclaim 91, 69B, 55A
exclamation 91, 55A, 55B
exclude 35
exclusion 35
exclusive 35, 145K, 147A
excogitate 115
excommunicate 35A
excoriate 145G, 64, 130N
excoriation*
excrement 16, 129A
excremental*
excrescence 109B
excrescent 16, 109B
excreta 16, 129A
excretion 16
excretory 16, 25E
excruciate 130M, 130N
excruciation 130M, 130N, 31
exculpate 138D
excurrent 150H, 149H
excursion 19A, 57, 56
excursive 18B, 57, 127A
excursus 57, 84
excuse pardon 47
   justify 138D
   plea 40B
   pretext 62, 103B
exeat 46A
execrate 65, 28, 64
execute 130-O, 50, 144B, 130N
execution*
executive 133A
executor 133A
exegesis 81, 84
exegetic 81, 84, 57
exemplar 84, 95A
exemplary 105, 140B
exemplify 105, 84
exempt 46A, 125C
exequatur 93, 133A
exercise 81, 132D, 38
exercitor 49B
exergue 128A, 46A

exert 41C, 2, 137B, 1, 13, 135B
exertion 1, 13, 41C
exfoliation 145G
exhalation 16, 123
exhale 16, 145J
exhaust empty 16
  drain 49A, 130D
  discuss 92, 90
exhaustion 37, 128A
exhaustless 147I
exhaustive 130D, 146A, 49A
exhibit 95A, 95D, 95E, 99A, 99B, 71A
exhibition*
exhilarate 71A, 8, 99A, 136A
exhort 8, 87, 40B, 79
exhortative 8
exhume 145F
exigency 37, 41B
exigent 37, 41B
exile 35A, 127B, 129B
exist 11A, 137C, 15, 51A, 105
existence 11A, 137C
exit 15
exo 149K
exode 68C
exodus 15
exogen 143E
exogenous 141A
exonerate 138D
exophthalmia 128B
exorbitance 125C, 126C, 147J, 147I
exorbitant*
exorcise 35A
exorcism 35A
exordium 73, 4
exosmose 16, 20, 146C
exoteric 81, 95E
exotic 126A, 149N, 122, 149K
expand 10, 145I, 147J
expanse 25A
expansion 10, 145I
expansive 25, 147K, 147J
expatiate 56, 84
expatriate 35A
expect 39, 127A, 113
expectant 113, 39
expectation 113, 39
expectorant 136B
expectorate 16
expectoration 129A

expediency 5A, 46B, 132A, 132D
expedient 132A, 132D, 5A, 46B, 134B
expedite 5A, 9
expedition haste 9
  march 19A
  promptness 148D
expeditionary 19A
expeditious 9, 19A
expel 35A
expend 43B, 45, 49D
expenditure*
expense 45, 49D
expensive 140B
experience 116, 117, 134B, 121
experimental 41C, 119E
experimentalism 117, 41C, 116, 119E
expert 134B, 117
expiate 45, 31, 138D
expiration 12
expire die 131A, 128A
  exhale 16
  finish 12
explain 84
explanation 84
expletive 91, 65
explicable 84
explicit 84, 134A
explode
  demolish 130-O
  refute 93, 131A
  dissipate 145E
  flare 125C-2, 69B
exploit 144B, 84, 42, 6
exploitation 136B, 119E, 84
exploration 119E
explore 119E, 116
explorer 119F
explosion 145E, 69B, 125C-2
explosive 130K, 145E, 69B, 125C-2
exponent 84
export 24A
expose 95A, 78, 128A, 130D
exposition 95A, 84, 99A, 78, 99B
expository 84, 95A
expostulate 41B, 66, 67A
exposure 95A, 128A, 78
expound 84

express utter 55A
  show 95A
  dispatch 24A
  definite 84, 126A
  precise 134A
  fast train 24H
expression 55A, 95C, 95A
expressive 55A, 84
expressman 24E
expropriation 35
expulsion 35A
expunge 131A, 130-O
expurgate 131A, 35A, 138B
expurgatory*
exquisite 108, 140B, 48P, 68A, 71A, 99A, 122, 134A, 134B
extant 137C, 11A
extemporaneous 55A, 144A
extempore*
extemporize 55A
extend 10, 145I, 124, 11A, 78, 149N
extensible 145I, 3A
extension 10, 11A, 25B, 145I, 124
extensive 147J, 25, 149N
extensometer 95B
extensor 25E, 145I, 149C
extent 25A, 147L, 149N
extenuate 14, 136A, 138C
extenuatory*
exterior 149K
exterminate 130-O
extern 116, 95C, 149N
external 149K
exterritoriality 46A, 133A
extinct 128A, 131A, 130-O
extinguish 131A, 97, 130D
extirpate 130-O, 131A, 138B
extirpative*
extol 63
extort 49G
extortion 49G
extortionate 49G
extra 10, 126A, 85B, 26
extract 49A, 93
extraction 49A, 141G

extradite 46B, 24A, 43B
extradition 24A, 46B
extramundane 149K
extramural 149K
extrane 149K, 125C
extraneous 149K, 126A, 145K
extraordinary
  rare 126A
  immense 147J
  eminent 140B, 96A, 95E, 99A
extravagant 43A, 125C, 60, 113, 57, 62, 95D, 147I
extravaganza 68B, 99B, 60, 95D
extravasate 16
extreme last 149I
  furthest 149N, 26, 125C, 140B
extremist 113
extremity 12, 125C, 149N, 130M
extricate 49A, 136A
extrinsic 149K, 145K
extroversion 149K
extrude 24C, 35A
exuberant 26, 147I, 56, 71A, 98B, 125C, 141B
exude 16
exult 71A, 71B
exuviæ 129A
eye 119C, 119E
eyeball 119C
eyebrow 106A
eyelash 106A
eyelet 25
eyelid 36F
eye-opener 96A, 57, 48L
eyesight 119A
eyesore 109A
eye-spit 119C
eye-tooth 145F
eyot 25G
eyra 143A
eyre 25B
eyrie 53D, 141D
eyry 53D

F

fable moral 61B
  falsehood 62
  fiction 85B, 85A, 85D
fabric cloth 106K
  building 53B

fabricate lie 62
  invent 144A
  make 144B
fabulist 62, 85E
fabulize 55A, 62
fabulous 62, 96A,
  85A, 140B
facade 149H
face front 149H
  oppose boldly 42
  countenance 95C,
  98B
  aspect 95C
facer 88
facet 95C, 150D
facetiae 59, 72, 117
facetious 72, 59,
  99A
facial 95C
facies 95C
facile helpful 5A
  yielding 46B
  dexterous 134B
facilitate 5A
facility 5A, 46B
facing 107E
facsimile 105
fact 61A, 91
faction 27, 146K
factious 27
factitious 103B,
  134B, 132D
factitive 1
factor agent 133A
  quantity 147L
  cause 1, 5A, 46B
factorage 49A
factory 144C
factotum 133A, 46B
factual 61A
facula 101B
facultative 46A, 46B
faculty ability 137B
  conscience 111, 1,
  2
  mental capacity
  117, 81, 144B,
  134B
fad 113, 132D, 15
faddist 113, 132D
fade 128C, 128A,
  14, 97
fæcal 129A
fæces 129A
fag
  grow weary 128A,
  130D, 130B,
  48-O
fag-end 149I, 128A
faggot 129B
fagot 146A, 48D
fagoting 107E, 107A
falence 107E

fail miscarry 127B
  omission 126B
  wane 14, 130A
  deteriorate 128C
  forsake 15
falling*
faille 106K
failure 127B, 126B
fain 46B, 71A, 39,
  46A
faint feeble 128A
  not loud 69A
  timid 32, 112,
  101A, 97
fair, beautiful 108
  just 140A, 61A
  not dark 102A
  spotless 138C
  reasonable 59
  market 44
fairy 96A, 134B,
  140B
faith 113, 82A, 82B
faithful loyal 38
  having faith 113
  honest 140A
  truthful 61A
faithless 30, 62,
  130A
fake 49F, 130A
faker 49F, 130A,
  103B
fakir 82F
falchion 130H
falcon 143C
falconry 81
faldstool 53-O, 53P
fallal 107E, 68B
fall, drop 22, 18A
  perish 128A
  be disgraced 129B
  sin 130A
  autumn 148K
  ruin 130-O
  water-fall 25I, 16
  decrease 14, 127B,
  127A, 147K,
  147L, 149G
fallacious 62, 130A,
  126C
fallacy 62, 60, 126C,
  130A
fallibility 126C
fallible 126C, 128A,
  130A
fallopian 25E
fallow 126B, 102A
fallow deer 143A
false 62, 103B, 130A
falsehood 62
falsetto 68A, 68I
falsify 62, 130A,
  103B
falsity*

Falstaffian jovial 72
  boastful 76
falter be timid 32
  utter weakly 69A,
  70, 132C
falty 126C
fame rumor 57
  report 79
  renown 140B
famed 140B
familiar affable 38
  intimate 117, 92,
  125C, 132D,
  134B
familiarity 117, 38,
  125C
familiarize
  habituate 132D
  teach 81
  know 117, 116
family lineage 141G
  household 146I
  class 92
famine 37, 128A
famish 37, 128A
famous 140B, 95E
famulus
  assistant 46B
  performer 99D
  magician 99D,
  134B
fan 113, 39, 136A,
  38
fanatic 113, 39, 82D,
  38
fanaticism 113, 39
fancier 38, 39
fanciful 113, 57
fancy 39, 71A, 113,
  38
fandango 99F
fanfare 76, 95D,
  69B
fanfaronade*
fang 145F
fanion 104E
fantail 143C
fantan 41D
fantasia 68B
fantasm 113
fantastic odd 126A
  unreal 103B, 99A,
  110B, 113
  ambiguous 57, 62
  fancy 107A
fantasy 113
fantom 96A, 113
far 149N, 147I, 148B
farad 147M
farce 99B, 95D
farcical 99B, 99A
farcy 128B

fare mood 121
  enjoy food, etc.,
  51A
  succeed 50, 45,
  147L
farewell 15, 91, 63,
  74
far-fetched 60
farina 48M, 145H
farinaceous*
farm 53D, 144B,
  144C, 144D,
  49D, 141D
farmer 144D
faro 41D
farrage 146C
farrow 141B, 142E
farther 149N, 140B
farthing 147B
farthingale 106F
fasces 104D
fascicle 146A, 86,
  49E
fasciculate 150H
fascinate excite 8
  captivate 50, 40A,
  40, 99A, 108,
  136A, 96A
fascination 8, 50,
  96A, 112, 40,
  40A, 71A
fascine 36E
fashion shape 150A,
  107A, 126A,
  144B, 132D
fashionable 107A,
  108
fast 132C, 126A
fast speedy 9
  at rest 11B
  aberrant 126A
  tight 52B, 52G,
  38, 137B, 125C-3,
  132C, 146A,
  146B, 148D
fasten 49C, 52B
fastening 52A
fastidious 134A, 28,
  49A
fastness 36B, 34
fat corpulent 150G
  stupid 110B, 45,
  147I, 109B,
  147J
fatal 130-O, 50, 130M
fatalism
  destiny 134C, 50,
  82B
fatalist 82D, 134C
fatalistic 134C, 50
fatality 130-O, 134C,
  50, 127B
fate 134C, 130-O,
  13, 127B
fated 134C

figured 107E, 108
  symbolized 104A
  shaped 150A
filament 52C
filbert 48C
filch 49F
file 145F, 86, 146K
filicide 130-O
filial 146I
filiation 146I
filibuster 148B, 49G, 36
filiform 52C, 107C
filigree 107B
Filipino 54C
fill make full 146A
  satisfy 46A
  finish 12
  crowd 146K, 146B
  satiety 26
fillet band 52C
  hair band 106H
  meat etc. 148D
  ornament 107B, 107A
fillip 24C, 98A
filly 143A, 125C, 24G
film 36F, 97
filose 52C
filter 138B, 16, 145B
filth 129A, 109C
filthy 129A, 70, 109C
filtrate 138B, 145A, 148B
final decisive 94, 27, 74, 93, 148B, 149I
finale end 12, 74
finality 12, 74, 50
finance 45, 43B
financial 135B
financier 49A
finback 143B
finch 143C
find attain 49A
  ascertain 115, 116
  discover 119F
  declare 80
  have luck 134D
finding 119F
  verdict 94, 115
fine money paid 45
  exact 41B, 13
  slender 150G
  fanciful 113, 57
  musical 68A
  beautiful 108
  noble 140B
  pure 138C
  showy 95D, 134B, 147K, 150E
finedrawn 134A, 13, 57
finery 106B, 107B, 95D
finesse 134B, 49F, 57
finger 150G, 49F, 49C

finial 107E, 134C
finical 134A, 49A
finikin 134A, 143C
finis 12, 74
finish end 12, 74
  complete 50
  perfect 134A, 132A
  polish 101A
  kill 130-O
  elaboration 107A
finite definite 84
  time 148L, 147L, 148I
finiteness 84, 148L, **finos** 106A
fiord 25I
fir 143E
fire 131B, 24C, 68A, 91
  discharge 35A
  ardor 39
  radiance 101A, 130C, 8, 138B, 130B, 145J
firearms 130I
fire-ball 130J
firebrand 130-O, 101C, 131B
firebug 130-O, 130A, 131B
firecracker 101C
fire-dog 53P
firefly 143D
fireside 53D
fire-water 48L
fireworks 101C
firkin 147F, 53N
firm, hard 146B
  steadfast 11B
  staunch 38, 2, 11A
  rigorous 137B, 52B, 146K, 132C, 140A, 146A
firmament 25A
firman 133A
first one 147A, 4
  in front 149H
  important 135B, 140B, 148A
first-aid 136B
first-class 108, 140B
first-fruits 49A
firstling 148A, 142B
first-mate 133A
first-rate 140B
firth 25I
fiscal 3A
fish
  attempt 41C, 41D
  fish 143B
  hoist 24B
  search 119E
fisherman 49C, 24J
fishery 144C
fishgig 49C

fishhook 49C
fishmonger 44
fishwife 44
fishy 62, 57
fissile 145A
fission 145A, 141A
fissiped 150G, 143A
fissure 145C, 25H
fist 130L
fistic 130F
fisticuffs 130F
fistula 25E, 25
fistulose 25E
fit adapt 134A, 6
  edible 48A, 48P, 134B, 137B, 146A
  orderly 132A
fitch 143A, 123
fitful 3C, 29, 127A, 126C
fitting 132A
five 147A
fivefold 147A
fix fasten 52B, 52G
  stable 11B, 11A
  adjust 132A
  transfix 130G
  make regular 132D, 1, 146B, 112, 134C
fixation 11B, 52B, 146B, 52G
fixative 11B, 146B
fixed
  lasting 11A, 11B
  destined 134C
  fastened 52B, 52G, 39, 27, 146B
fixedness 11B
fixing 107B
fixity 11B
fixture 53P
fizgig 101C, 40
fizz 48L, 69A
fizzle 127B
fjeld 25G
flabby 3C, 128A, 109B
flabellate 150F, 150C
flabellum 35A
flaccid 3C, 128A
flag 104E, 130D
  signal 98A
  plant 143E
  flagstone 25B
  tire 128A
flagellant 130G, 130M
flagellate 130G
flageolet 68G
flagging 25B
flagitious 130A, 28, 130M
flagofficer 133A
flagon 53N

flagrant
  wicked 130A, 95E
  heinous 130M
flagstone 25A, 25B
flail 130L
flake 145D, 145H
flaky 145H
flam freak 126A
  falsehood 62
flambeau 101C, 98A
flamboyant 69B, 76, 95D, 109A
flame fire 131B
  ardor 39
  passion 39B
  blaze 101A, 39A, 145J
flamen 82F
flamingo 143C
flammule 131B, 101A, 104C
flamy 101A, 102A
flang 145F
flange 132D
flank 149J, 150G
flanker 130F, 36G
flannel 106K
flannelette 106K
flap 34
flapjack 48E
flapper 40
flare light 101A
  unrestraint 125C-2
  be showy 95D, 39, 57, 62
flash blaze 101A, 95D, 148D
flashiness 95D
flashing 101A, 95E
flash-light 101C
flashy 95D, 101C
flask 53N
flat 149C, 149G
  positive 94
  downright 84, 80, 113
  dissonant 70, 68A
  plain 25G
  story or floor 53E, 53D
  nonsense 60
  insipid 48Q
flatfish 143B
flatten 148C, 130G, 149C, 149G
flatter 63, 40, 40A
flattery 63, 40, 40A
flatulence 60, 113, 76
flatwise 149C
flaunt
  display 95D, 76, 72, 98A
flav 102A
flavor 48P, 51A, 122
  (B). flavour
flavoring 48P
flaw 126C, 129A

fomentation 5A, 8
fond 38, 39A
fondle 38, 39B, 98C, 121
fondling 140B
font 55B
food 48A
fool idiot 110B
  disguise 103B
foolhardiness 42, 110B
foolhardy 42, 110B, 125C-2
fooling 60, 53G
foolish 60, 110B, 126C
foolishness 60, 110B
foolscap 147D, 110B
foot 147E, 150G, 53R, 55B
football 99A, 41D
footing 53R, 36B, 149A
footman 46B
footpad 49G
footwear 106J
fop 113, 103B, 95D
foppery 95D, 106B
for 1, 27
forage 48N, 51A, 48A, 119E, 43B
foraging 119E
foray 49G, 130F
forbear 46A, 47, 140A, 141G, 141E, 132C
forbearance 46A, 47, 140A
forbid ban 35
  oppose 27, 34
forbidding 35, 129B, 27, 109A
force power 137B
  overpower 50
  violence 125C-2, 130A, 2, 8, 1, 13, 68A, 134C
forceps 49C
forceful 58, 137B
forcible 137B, 125C
ford 19B, 25I, 24H
fore 149H
forebode 95A, 77
forecast 77, 119A
forecastle 149H
foreclose 146A, 49A
foredoom 134C
foregather 146K
forego refrain 132C, 46B, 46A
foregoing 73
forehead 149H, 150G
foreign
  remote 149N, 126A, 145K, 149K

foreigner 54C, 126A, 145K, 149N
forel 106K
forelock 106A
foreman 133A
foremost first 149H, 140B, 126A
forensic 66
forepart 149H
forerun 149H, 79
forerunner 77, 79
foreshadow 105
foresight 117
forespeech 73
forest 34, 25G
forestall 49D, 115
forestay 52C
forester 133A, 54B
forestry 144B
foretell 77
foretopmast 53R
forever 11A, 148C
forewarn
  inform 79
  caution 33
forfeit fine 45
  lose 127B
forfeiture 45, 127B
forever 148C, 11A
forefend 36
foreword 73
forge shape 150A, 144B, 144C
  counterfeit 103B
  defraud 130A
  invent 144A
forger 130A, 49E, 62, 103B
forgery 130A, 49F, 103B
forget 126B, 110B
forgetful 126B, 110B
forgive 47
forgiveness 47
forgotten 127B, 145K
fork 49C, 150F, 53M
forked 150F
forlorn bereft 145K
  miserable 31
  unfortunate 127B
form shape 150A, 141A, 144B, 100A, 132A, 132D, 134C, 144A
formal precise 134A
  conventional 132D
  ceremonious 95D
formalist 134A
formality 134A, 132D
formation 49E, 141A
formative 141A, 3B
former 148A, 149H
formication 121

formidable 42, 33, 137B
formula 84, 86, 95B
formulary 82A, 86
formulate 84, 92
fornicate 146D, 125C-3, 39C, 121
fornication 146D, 125C-3, 39C, 121
forsake 15, 126B
forsaken 127B, 129B, 145K
forsooth 61A
forswear 62, 66, 67A
fort 36B
forte 137B, 117, 126A
forth 149H, 149N
forthcoming 19A, 95C, 148B, 148L
forthwith 148D, 148B, 148E, 148K
fortification 36B, 137B
fortify 36, 137B, 7
fortitude courage 42
  strength 137B, 31, 46A
fortnight 148H
fortress 36B
fortuitous 127A
fortuity 127A
fortuna 127A, 127B, 134D
fortunate 134D
fortune
  (good) 134D
  (bad) 127B
  chance 127A
  wealth 135B
  fate 134C, 49E
forty 147A
forum 53C
forward aid 5A, 6
  front 149G, 148A, 148D
  presumptuous 113, 125, 125C, 39
  impertinent 64, 9, 136B, 24E, 24A, 42, 95D, 149H
fossil 146B, 148J, 148A
fossiliferous 146B
fossilize 146B, 14
foster nourish 48A
  help 5A, 6, 10
  nurse 136B
  succor 136A
  sustain 11A
  cherish 39A
foster-brother 146I

foster-child 146I, 142B
foul offensive 123
  impure 146C, 129A
  unfair 130A
  infamous 65, 70
  loathsome 129B, 109C
foulard 106K
found 94, 144A, 11B, 139A
foundation 1, 11B
  support 53R, 53G, 61A, 141D
  origin 4, 149A
  cause 1
founder
  author 144A, 21, 22, 128A, 130D, 144D
foundling 127B, 148J
foundry 144C
fount 16
fountain 16, 4, 141D
fountain-pen 55B
four 147A, 24J
fourfold 147A
fourgon 24H
four-in-hand 24H, 106C
fourscore 147A
foursome 147A
fourteen 147A
fourteenth 147A
fourth 147A
fowl 143C
fowling-piece 130I
fox 143A, 117
fox-bat 143A, 143C
fox-brush 106A, 150G
foxglove 143E
foxhound 143A
fox-squirrel 143A
foxtail 143E, 150G, 106A
foxy 49F, 117, 134B, 102A
foyer 25D
fracas 66, 130F
fraction 145D, 147L
fractional 145D, 147L, 145K
fractious 27, 29
fracture 145E
fragile 3C, 128A
fragility 3C, 128A
fragment 145D, 147K
fragmental*
fragrance 122
fragrant 122
frail 128A
frame 53R, 130A, 132A

framework 53R
franc 147B
franchise 46A
francolin 143C
frangibility 3C, 128A, 145H
frank candid 61A, 93, 92, 140A
Frankenstein 33, 127B
frankincense 122
frantic 31, 29, 32, 39, 112
frap 52B
frappe 146B
fraternal 146K, 146I
fraternity 146K
fraternize 146K
fratricide 130-O
fraud 49F, 130A
fraudulence 49F, 130A
fraudulent*
fraught 147C, 135A
fray riot 125A, 130F
  quarrel 66
  rub 145H, 128C
freak whim 113, 126A, 109A
freakish*
freckle 102C
free release 47, 145A
  unrestrained 125C, 126A, 43A, 132D
freebooter 49G
freedman 54B
freedom 125C, 46A
free-handed 43A
freehold 135B
free-lance 130F
freeman 54B
freethinker 114
freeze 146B
freight 135A, 24H, 24J, 24A, 24B, 149L
freightage 45
freight car 24H
freighter 24J, 24H
French 54C
French leave 15
frenzied 29, 112
frenzy 29, 112, 130C, 110B
frequent 3B, 38, 132D, 75, 54A, 148L
fresco 100B, 100A
fresh 126A, 148E, 137A
freshet 25I, 16

freshman 116
fret wear away 145H, 128C
  injure 130D
  vex 130C
  irritate 130B
  ornament 107A, 107B
  be irritated 31, 66, 67A, 130G
fretful 29
fret saw 145F
frette 108
fretwork 107E
friable 145H
friar 82F, 82G, 146L
fricassee 48D
fricative 55B
friction, riot 27
  attrition 130M
  stimulation 8
  irritation 29, 66, 13, 130G
Friday 148K
friend 38, 146L
friendless 145K
friendly 38, 136A
friendship 38, 136A
frieze 107E, 106K
frigate 24J
frigate-bird 143C
frigeratory 146B
fright 32, 33, 109A
frighten 33
frightful 33, 32, 109A, 129B, 130A, 130M
frigid 146B, 28, 121
frill 107B
frilling 107B
fringe 107B, 149K, 149M
frippery 106B, 129B, 109A
frisk 18B, 99F
frisket 53R
friskiness 3C, 9
frisky 3C, 9, 71A
frit 146C
frit fly 143D
frith 251
fritter cut up 145F
  waste 125C-1
  food 48, 48E, 126B
frivolous 3C, 60, 127A
frizette 106H, 106A
frizzle 107A, 106A
frock 106F
frock-coat 106E
frog 143F
frolic 71A, 99A, 99C
frolicsome 71A, 99A
from 145A
frond 150H

front foremost 149H
  aspect 95C
  boldness 42
frontage 149H
frontal 149H, 150G
frontier 25G, 149K, 149M
frontispiece 100B, 149H
frost 146B, 127B
frosty 146B, 28
frothy 76, 60, 128A, 145J
froward 27, 132C
frown 98B
frowzy 123, 109C
frozen 146B, 121
fructify 141B
frugal 132C, 147K
frugivorous 51A
fruit 48G, 144E, 141B, 142E
fruitage 48G, 144E, 142E
fruiterer 43B
fruitful 43A, 141B
fruition 141B, 50
fruitless 127B, 128A
frustrate 50, 36, 127B, 128A
frustum 149G, 150D
fry cook 145J
  swarm 146K, 147I 148J, 143B, 142E
fuddle 96A, 112
fudge story 62
  nonsense 60, 91, 126D
fuel 5C
fugacious 15, 3C, 9, 22, 145J, 148D
fugh 64, 91
fugitive 3C, 127A, 148D, 15
fugleman 95A, 98A, 133A
fugue 68B
fuguist 68J, 68H
fulfil 50, 45, 12
fulfillment 50, 45
fulgency 101A
fuliginous 97, 102A
full complete 146A
  much 147I, 69B
  clear, sonorous 68A
  replete 26
fulminate reprove 64, 65
  thunder 69B, 33
fulsome 123, 129B, 63
fulvous 102A
fumble 126D, 119E

fume 123, 29, 16
fumigate 138B
fun mirth 71A
  drollery 72
  entertainment 99A, 99C
funambulist 99D, 99F
function 144B, 95D, 5A
functionary 5A, 144D, 133A
fund 135B, 45
fundament 4, 149G
fundamental primary 148A, 149H
  foundation 4, 1, 61A, 133A
funeral 95D
funereal 31
funicle 52C, 25E
funicular 52C, 25E
funk 32
funnel 25F
funny 99A, 126A, 24J, 72, 109A
fur 106A
furbelow 107B
furbish 107A, 101A
furcate 150F
furies 130M, 130N
furious 29, 130M
furl 52B
furlong 147E
furlough 46A, 47
furnace 131B, 145J, 145B
furnish 43B, 132A
furniture 53P
furore 125A, 63, 69B, 71A
furrier 144D, 44
furrow 25F
furry 106A
further 149N, 5A, 6, 10, 146A
furthermore 10, 146A
furthermost 149N
furthest 149N
furtive 103A, 49F
fury, rage 29
  retribution 130N, 45
fuse 146C, 145J, 52E
fusee 141C
fusil 130I
fusileer 130F
fusillade 130F, 130-O
fusinist 100C
fusion 146C, 145J, 146A
fusionist 146M

geocentric 149L
geographer 95A, 100C
geographical 149A
geography 86, 149A
geologist 83
geology 83
geometer 115
geometric 150D
geometrician 115
geometry 83, 115, 147L
geophagism 51A
georgic 85C
geranium 143E
germ 142F, 137C, 4
German 54C, 146I
germander 143E
germane akin 146I
  appropriate 132A
germanium 5D
germicide 138B, 130-O
germinal 141B, 141A
germinate 141B
germination 141A
germule 142F
gerrymander 130A, 45
gerund 92, 55B
gestation 141A, 141B
gestatory*
gesticulate 98A
gesture 98A
get 49A
  realize 117
  learn 116
  procreate 141A
  depart 15, 35A
gewgaw 95D, 107B
geyser 16, 25I
ghastly 102A, 109A, 33, 98B
ghaut 25B
gherkin 48K
Ghetto 53F
ghi 48I
ghost 96A, 113
ghostly 96A, 31
ghoul 49F, 51A
giant 147J, 137B
giaour 30
gibber 60
gibberish 60
gibbet 130-O, 95A, 72, 78
gibbous 150G, 109A, 109B, 149H, 150C
gibe 72, 64
gid 130E
giddy 110B, 112, 127A

gift generosity 43A
  talent 117, 45, 134B
gifted 117, 134B
gig 24J, 24H, 18C
gigantic 147J, 137B
giggle 71B
gild 102A, 107A, 101A, 146K
gilding 100A, 107A, 102D
gill 25E, 25I, 147F, 16, 125C-3
gilling 143B
gillyflower 143E
gilt 102A
gimbal 132D
gimcrack 107B, 95D, 107E
gimlet 145F
gimp 106K
gin a drink 48L
  trap or snare 49C, 145B, 145A
ginger 48J
gingerale 48J
gingerade 48J
ginger-beer 48J
gingerbread 48E
gingerly 32
gingham 106K, 36J
ginkgo 143E
gin-mill 48B
gin-palace 48B
ginseng 143E
gippo 48I, 48D
Gipsy race 54C, 18B
  hoiden 39B, 125C-3, 126A
giraffe 143A
girandole 101C
girasol 107C
girba 53N
gird 52B, 64
girder 53R
girdle 52C, 106C, 52B, 107B
girl 142B, 148J
girt 52B
girth 52C, 147L, 150C
gist 137C, 58, 2
gittern 68D
give 43A, 46B, 3C
gizzard 53Q
glabrous 150G
glace 146B, 106K
glacial 146B
glacier 146B, 149E
glacis 36B
glad 71A
gladden 99A, 71A, 136A
glade 25G, 25A
gladiate 150E, 145F

gladiator 41D, 130F
gladiolus 143E
gladsome 71A, 99A
Gladstone 24H
glamour 40A, 96A, 12, 99A, 101A, 108, 113
gland 25E
glance 119E, 119A
glandule 25E
glare
  brilliance 101A
  scrutiny 119E, 98B
  dazzle 96A
  slippery 127A
  smooth 5A
glaring 101A, 95D
glass vessel 53M, 5C
  mirror 105, 95A
glaucous 102A
glave 130H
glaze 146B, 101A
gleam 101A, 98B
glean gain 49A, 49E
  collect 49E
  infer 115
glebe 135B, 53F
glee mirth 71A
  music 68B, 68A, 99C, 99A, 98B
gleet 16
glen 25G
glib voluble 56
  flippant 60
glide 22, 16, 23
gliff glimpse 119A
  fear 32
  interval 148D
glim 101C, 101A
glimmer 101A
glimpse 101A, 119A, 119F
glin 97
glint 101A
glissando 68D
glisten 101A
glitter 101A, 108
gloam 97, 101A
gloaming 97, 148K, 148B
gloat gaze 119E
  have lust 39B
global 150C
globate 150C
globe 150C
globe-fish 143B
globeflower 143E
globe-trotter 19A
globular 150C
glome 107B, 107E
glomerate 146C, 146A
gloom 97, 31

gloomy 97, 31, 98B
gloria 68B, 63
glorify praise 63
  exalt 139B
  worship 38
  beautify 107A
gloriole 101B
gloriosa 143E
glorious
  exalted 140B
  magnificent 108, 101A, 99A, 63, 71A, 101B
glory*
gloss luster 101A
  explanation 84
  excuse 138D
glossarial 84, 57
glossary 84, 86
glossograph 95B
glossographer 84
glossography 84
glossology 83
glossonomy 83
glossy 101A
glove 106C
glow 101A, 39A, 108
glower 98B, 33
glowworm 143F
gloxinia 143E
gloze 138D, 84
glucose 52F, 48P
glue 52F, 52E
glum 97, 31, 29
glut repletion 26
  oversupply 43B, 51A, 147I
gluten 52F, 5C
glutinous 52E
glutton 51A, 143A
gluttonous 51A
gluttony 51A
glyph 150B, 107B
glyphic 55B, 100A
glyphography 100A
glyptic 100A
glyptograph 100B
gnarl 109B
gnarled 109B
gnash 29, 67A, 27
gnat 143D
gnaw 145H
gnome
  goblin 96A, 113, 28
  a saying 61B, 34, 134B
gnomic 61B
gnomide 96A, 113, 34
gnomiometrical 115
gnomon 95B, 148F, 84
gnomics 83, 58
gnosiology 83

gnosis 117
gnostic 82A, 117
gnu 143A
go 19A, 15, 35A, 91, 132D
goad 8, 130H, 130G
goaf 129A
goal 149H, 12
goat 143A, 123
goatee 106A
gobble 51B, 69B, 70
gobelin 107E
go-between 132B
goblet 53M
goblin 96A, 113, 33, 109A
goby 143B
go-cart 24H
God 82E, 1, 137C, 140A, 144A
god 140B
goddess 140B, 108
godfather 89, 34
Godhead 82E
godless 130A
godly 140B, 140A
God-man 82E
godmother 89, 34
godroon 107B
God's-acre 53L
godsend 134D
Godspeed 63
godwit 143C
goer 19A, 24G
goffer 150B, 107A
goggle 119E, 36C
goglet 53N
going 19A, 15
Golconda 49E, 135B
gold 135B, 107D, 5D, 107C
gold-carp 143B
golden 102A, 101A, 43A
golden age 71A, 148K, 134D
golden pheasant 143C
golden rod 143E
golden rule 94, 82A
goldfish 143B
goldilocks 143E
goldsmith 144D
golf 41D
golgotha 53L
Goliath 137B, 147J
gommer 48M
gomuti 52C
gondola 24J, 24H
gondolier 24E
gondoline 24J
gone
    annihilated 131A
    exhausted 128A
    lost 127B, 149N
goner 127B
gonfalon 104E

gong 68E
goniometer 95B
gono 141A
gonophore 141C
gonorrhoea 130E
good fitness 140A
    kind 136A
    adept 134B, 38, 48P, 49G, 63
good-by 15, 63, 91
goodly 108, 136A, 140B
goodman 146I, 141E
goodness 140A, 136A
goods 5C, 144E
goodwife 146I, 141E
goodwill 140A, 38
goose 143C, 110B, 141F
gooseberry 48G
gopher 143A
gordian difficult 13
    tight 52B
Gordius 13
gore 130H, 146B, 130G
gorge 25H, 51A, 145C
gorgeous 108, 101A, 95D, 99A
gorget 36C
Gorgon 109A, 33
gorgoneia 109A, 33
gorilla 143A
gormand 51A
gormandize 51A
gory 129A
goshawk 143C
gosling 143C, 148J
gospel 82A, 61A
gossamer 106K, 106A
gossip 90
gossoon 148J
Goth 54C, 126A, 126D
Gothic 100A
gouge 130G, 145F, 130A
goulash 48D
gourami 143B
gourd 143E, 53N
gourde 147B
gourmand 51A
govern 133A, 132D
governance 133A
governante 81
governess 81
governing 133A, 134B
government 94, 133A
governor 133A, 132D, 81
gown 106F
gownsman 117
gowt 25F, 25

grab 49C, 24J
grabble 119E
grace beauty 108, 68A
    excellence 140B
    deference 46A, 63
    embellishment 107B, 107A
graceful 108, 134B
graceless 109A, 126D
gracious lovely 108
    deferential 46A, 38
    good 140A, 43A, 63, 136A
gradate 146C, 132D, 102C
gradation 19A, 132D, 146C, 10, 102C, 132A
gradatory 19A, 10
grade level 149C, 149D
    degree 147L
gradient 14, 19B, 149D, 22, 149G, 17, 149F
gradine 145F
gradual 126B, 88, 68B
graduate 132D, 116, 50, 117
graduation 50, 19A
graduator 100C
gradus 86
graffito 100B
graft join 146A
    incorporate 146C
    perquisite 45
    take a bribe 49B
grafter 49B, 49F
grail 53I
grain 48M, 147C, 102B
gram 147C
grama grass 143E
gramercy 45, 91
graminivorous 51A
grammalogue 55B
grammar 83
grammarian 83
grammatical 68A, 134A
grammatist 83
gramophone 55C
grampus 143A, 150G, 109B
granadilla 48G
granary 53B
grand great 147J
    illustrious 140B
    eloquent 68A
    magnificent 108, 95D, 95E, 98B, 99A
    piano 68D

grandam 146I
grandchild 146I, 142B
granddaughter*
grandee 133A
grandeur 147J, 140B, 95D, 108
grandfather 146I, 141E
grandiloquent 68A, 76, 95D
grandiose 68A, 95D
grandmother 141E, 146I
grandparent 146I, 141E
grandsire*
grandson 146I
Grand Vizier 133A
grange 53B, 53D
granivorous 51A
grant give 43A
    concede 46A
grantee 49B
grantor 43A, 43B
granular 145H, 147K
granulate 145H
granule 145H
granulose 145H
grape 48G
grape-shot 130J
graph 95B
graphic vivid 95E, 95A, 84, 100A
graphology 83
graphometer 95B
graphophone 68F
grapnel 49C
grapple 49C, 41C, 41D
grasp seize 49C
    encroach 130A
    hold 132C, 52A
    intelligence 117
grasping 49C, 39
grass 48N, 143E, 150H
grasshopper 143D
grass-widow 145K
grate 53I, 70
grateful 38, 136A, 63, 71A
graticulation 145A
gratification
    reward 45, 43B
    pleasure 71A
    pleasingness 136A
    compliance 46A
gratify humor 46A, 136A, 99A, 43B, 63
grating 70, 36A
gratis 43A
gratitude 71A, 38, 45, 63
gratuitous 43A

gratuity 43A, 45
gravamen 130C
grave serious 61A
  important 135B
  threatening 33,
    13, 27, 67A,
    98B, 134A
  engrave 100A
  burial place 53L,
    104H
gravel 145H
graver 145F
gravestone 104H
graveyard 53L
gravid 141B
gravimeter 95B
gravitate tend 2,
  135A
  fall flow 22
gravitation 2, 39,
  49A, 135A
gravity 2
  attraction 39
  weight 135A
  importance 135B
  solemnity 27, 33
gravy 48I
gray 102C, 102A
graze touch 124
  freed upon 51A
grease 48I, 5A
greaser 54C, 146F
greasy 5A, 13, 127A
great large 147J
  eminent 140B
  important 135B,
    95E, 117, 147I
greaves 36C, 106J
grebe 143C
greed 39
greediness 39
greedy 39, 51A
Greek 54C, 60
green 102A, 25G
  fresh 148E
  unripe 48Q, 110B,
    126D
greenfly 143D
greenhorn 110B
greenroom 53E
greensward 25G
greeny 110B
greet 98C, 63
greeting 98C, 63
gregale 125B
gregarian 146K,
  132D
gregarious 146K
Gregorian chant
  68B
gremial 106I
grenade 130J
grenadier 130F
grenadine 106K
grey 102C, 102A
greybeard 148J
greyhound 143A
griddle 53M

griddle-cake 48E
gridelin 102C, 102A
gridiron 53R, 25A,
  53M, 99E
grief 31, 130B
grievance
  sufferance 31,
    67A, 67B, 130B
grieve suffer 31
  complain 67A,
    67B
  cause grief 130B
grevious painful 31
  causing pain 130B
  atrocious 130M,
    130A, 67A
griffin 34
grig 143D
grill broil 145J
  torment 130N
grillade 130N, 48D
grillage 53R
grille 107B, 145J
grim hideous 109A
  forbidding 27, 33
  cruel 130M, 28
  unyielding 11B
grimace 98B
grimalkin 143A,
  148J
grime 129A, 109C
grimy*
grin 98B, 71B
grind
  pulverize 145H
    130B, 130N, 116
grindstone 150A
grip grasp 49C, 8
  bag 53J, 98A, 98C,
    104A, 25F
gripe seize 49C,
  130B, 130D,
  128B, 130E,
  146B
grisaille 100A, 100B
grisette 40
grisly 33, 109A
grison 143A
grist 48M
gristle 146B
grit sand, etc., 145H
  meal 48M, 42,
    67A, 137B
gritty*
grizzle 33
grizzly bear 143A
  greyish 102C
groan utter pain 31
  ridicule 72
  deplore 67A, 67B,
    71B
groat 147B, 147K
grocer 44, 43B
grocery*
grog 48L
groggery 48B
groggy 110A, 112
grogshop 48B

groom 146J, 132A,
  46B
groomsman 46B,
  146L
groove 25F, 25
grope 119E
gros 106K
grosbeak 143C
grosgrain 106K
gross bulky 150G
  rude 130C, 109A,
    109B, 130A,
    110B, 147A,
    146A
grotesque
  odd 126A, 113, 60,
    99A, 72, 109A
grotto 25H
grouch 29
grouchy 29
ground earth 25G
  cause 1, 5C, 11B,
    52G
  foundation 53R,
    53G
  place 149A
  instruct 81
ground hog 143A
groundless 110B, 60
grounds 129A
groundsel 143E
ground-swell 16, 25I
group 146K, 86, 146A
grouse 143C
grout 52F, 48M
grouty 29, 129A
grove 34
grovel be prone 98C,
  32, 129B
grow 10, 6
  cultivate 144B
  thrive 49A, 52B,
    52G, 147J
growl 67A, 69B, 64
growler*
  perch 143B
  cab 24H
grown 148J, 12, 132A
growth 10, 6, 49A,
  advancement 19A
  result 144E
grub food 48A
  dig 145F
  larvae 142F, 143D
grub-stake 43B,
  127A
grudge 28, 39
gruel 48D
gruelling 130N
gruesome 109A, 33,
  129B, 130M
gruff 70, 28
grumble 70, 67A
grumpy 29, 67A
grunt 70, 143B
gruyere 48I
grysbock 143A
guan 143C

guanaco 143A
guano 142F
guarantee 89, 134C,
  93, 34
guarantor 89, 34
guard 34, 119G, 36,
  52H, 36A
guarded 34, 119G
guardian 34, 52H
guardsman 34, 130F
guava 143E
gubernatorial 133A
gudgeon fish 143B
  dupe 113, 110B
guerdon 45
Guernsey 143A
guernsey 106D
guerrilla 130F, 49G
guess 113
guess-work 113
guest 49B
guff 60
guffaw 71B
guidable 46A, 46B
guidance 24A, 132A
guide lead 24A, 95A,
  95B, 132D, 133A,
  134B, 134C
guidon 104E
guild 146K
guilder 147B
guile 103B, 130A, 62
guileless 140A, 61A
guillemot 143C
guilloche 107B, 107E
guillotine 130-O
guilt 130A
guiltless 140A, 138D
guilty 130A
guimpe 106G
guinea 147B
guinea-fowl 143C
guinea-pig 143A
guipure 107C, 107B
guise 95C, 106B,
  150A
guitar 68D
gula 25E
gulch 25H
gulf 25I, 25H, 37, 16
gull sea-fowl 143C
  dupe 113, 110B,
    130A, 49F
gullet 25E
gullible 113
gully 25H
gulp 51B
gum 52F
gumbo 48D
gummy 52E
gump 110B
gumption 117
gun 130I
gunboat 24J
guncotton 130K,
  145E
gunfire 130F

gunman 130F, 130A, 130-O
gunner 130F
gunny 106K
gunpowder 130K, 145E
gun-shy 32
Gunter's chain 147E
gunwale 36A
gurgitation 18C, 16
gurgle 16, 69A
gurglet 53N
gurnet 143B
gurrah 106K
guru 81
gush flow 16
  outburst 91, 63, 95D
gusher 16
gusset 106K
gust 125B, 67A
gustful 48P, 71A, 51A
gusto*
gut
  organic canal 25E
  channel 25I, 130-O, 49G
gutter 25F, 16
guttural 70, 55A
guy rope, etc. 52C
  freak 126A, 109A, 72, 130A
guzzle 48L, 51B
guzzy 106K
gwiniad 143B
gymnasium 81, 99E
gymnast 137B, 134B
gymnastic*
gymnastics 134B
gymnotus 143B
gynarchy 133A
gynecocracy 133A
gynecology 83
gyneolatry 40, 39A
Gypsy 54C
gyrate 18C
gyratory 18C
gyre 52A
gyro 18C
gyroplane 24I
gyropter 24I
gyroscope 18C, 24H
gyrostat 95B
gyve 52A

H

ha 71B, 91
haberdasher 44, 106B
habergeon 36C
habiliment 106B
habilitate 132D
habit custom 132D, 106B, 38, 53A
habitable 54A
habitant 54B

habitat 53D, 149A
habitation 53D, 54A
habitual usual 132D
  repeated 75
  inveterate 137C, 54A
habituate 132D, 81
habitude 132D, 81
habitue 54B, 38, 39
hacienda 53D
hack cut 145F
  horse 24G, 24H, 85E
hackberry 143E
hackbut 68G, 130I
hackle 145F
hackman 24E
hackmatack 143C
hackmore 52A
hackney coach 24H, 24G, 130D
hackneyed 128A, 132D, 56
had 148A
haddock 143D
Hadean 97
Hades 130N
hadji 82D
haemadromograph 95B
haemalopia 119B
hafnium 5D
hag 109A, 129B
haggard 109A, 128A, 98B
haggle 41B, 66, 44
haik 106D
haikwan 147B
hail 73, 98C, 41B, 146B, 16, 63
hair 106A
hairdresser 107A, 106B
hairsplitting 134A
hairy 106A
hake 143B
halation 101B
halberd 130H
halcyon
  peaceful 132B
  happy 71A
  fortunate 134D
hale 137B
half 147A
half-blood 146F
half-breed 146F
half-caste 146F
half-tone 100B
halibut 143B
halicore 143B
halitus 123
hall 53E, 81, 25B
hallelujah 63, 68B
hallo 69B
halloo 73, 98C, 40B
hallow 38, 92
Halloween 148K

hallucination
  imagination 113, 126C, 57, 96A
halo 101B
halt limp 18A
  stop 12
  lame 128A
halter 52A, 52B, 50
halve 145A, 147A
halyard 52C
ham 48D, 53F
Hamburg 48G, 143A
hammerkop 143C
hamiform 150C
hamlet 53F
hammer 5B, 6, 75, 81
  deliberate 114
  forge 150A, 144B
hammer-beam 53R
hammer-cloth 106K
hammock 53-O
hamper 53K, 13, 130B, 52A
hamshackle 52A, 52B
hamster 143A
hamstring 130D
hand give 43A, 43B
  human clasp 49C, 150G
  four inches 147E
  dexterity 134B, 46B, 24A
hand-grenade 130J
handcuff 52A, 52B
handicap 13, 11
handicraft 134B
handiness 46B
handiwork 144E
handkerchief 138A
handle 5B, 124, 133A, 121, 134B
handmaid 46B
handscrew 24B
handsel 43A, 98A
handsome 108, 43A
handy skillful 134B
  46B, 149M, 5A
handyman 46B
hang 52B, 130-O, 149D, 22, 132C, 149G
hangar 53B
hangdog 32, 129B
hanging 130-O, 149G
hangman 130-O
hank 52C
hanker 39
hanky-panky 130A
Hanse 146K
hanseatic 146K
hansom 24H
Hanuman 82E, 143A
hap 127A
haphazard 127A, 125A
hapless 31, 127B, 98B

happen 31, 127A
happiness 71A, 134D
happy*
happy-go-lucky 71A, 126B
harakiri 130-O
harangue 85A
harass 128A, 130B
harassing 128A, 13, 130B, 130D
harbinger 77, 79
harbor haven 34
  water port 25I, 53G, 53C, 38
harborage 34, 53D
hard solid 146B
  difficult 13
  unyielding 27, 130B, 130M, 137B
hard-by 149M
harden 146B, 14, 132D, 137B
hardihood 42, 137B
hardness 146B, 137B
hardship 31, 130A
hard-tack 48E
hardware 5B
hare 143A
harebrained 110B
harefoot 150G
harehound 143A
harelip 150G, 109B
harem 53D
hare's-foot 143E
hare's-tail 143E
haricot 48D
hark 118, 39, 91
harken 118
harlequin 99D, 72, 99A, 102C
harlequinade 99B, 72
harlot 125C-3, 146E, 39C
harlotry 125C-3, 146E, 39C, 44, 146D
harm 130D, 130M, 130B
harmful*
harmless 128A
harmonic 68A
harmonica 68G
harmonious 68G, 68A, 132D, 132A
harmoniphon 68G
harmonist 68J, 68H
harmonium 68G
harmonize
  melodize 68A
  make orderly 132A
  reconcile 132B
harmony 68A, 132A

harness 52B, 106B, 52A
harp repeat 75
    dwell upon 56
    instrument 68D
harpoon 49C, 130H, 130G, 130I
harpsichord 68D
harpy 49G
harquebus 130I
harridan 29, 125C-3
harrier 143A, 143C
harrow 145H
harrowing 130M
harry plunder 49G
    lay waste 130-O
    harass 130B
    torture 130N
    anger 130C
harsh austere 28
    discordant 70
    unsavory 48Q
    hurtful 130D, 64, 67A, 98B, 130B, 130C, 130M, 134A
hart 143A
hartbeest 143A
harum-scarum 125C-2, 126D, 125A
harvest 49E
has 148A
hash 48D, 146C, 145F, 145H
hashish 48L
haslet 48D, 25E
hasp 49C
hassock 53-O
haste 9
hasten 9, 10
hasty 9, 125C-2, 39, 42, 126D, 148D
hat 106H
hatband 107B
hatch 141B, 142E, 36I, 25
hatch-boat 24J
hatchery 141D
hatchet 130H, 145F
hatching 100B
hatchment 104B, 104H
hatchway 25
hate 28
hateful 28, 130C, 129B
hatrack 53P
hatred 28
haubergeon 36C
hauberk 36C
haughty 28
haul 24A
haulage 45, 24A
haulm 53R
haunch 150G

haunt 53D, 119A, 146K, 19A
hautboy 68G, 68D
hauteur 28
Havana 48-O
have 53A, 132C, 148A
havelock 36C
haven 53D, 34
haversack 53J
havildar 133A
havoc 130-O, 127B
haw 48G
Hawaiian 54C
hawfinch 143C
hawk bird 143C, 16, 44, 49F
hawkbill 143F
hawker 44, 49A, 81
hawkeye 54B
hawkeyed 119A, 119E
hawkmouth 143D
hawkweed 143E
hawok 147B
hawser 52C
hawthorn 143E
hay 48N
haycock 146A, 48N
haymow 48N
hazard chance 127A
    to risk 42
    accident 127B
    danger 13, 41D, 128A, 33, 41C
hazardous*
haze fog 145J, 97
    dim light 102A, 130B, 112
hazel 143E
haziness 97, 145J
    nonplus 112, 110A
hazing 130B
hazy 97, 145J, 56, 57, 110A, 112
he 92
head
    top of body 150G
    chief 133A
    leader 133A
    top 149F
    forepart 149H
    intellect 117, 141D, 2, 27, 19A, 140B
header 21
heading 92
headland 25G
headline 92, 79, 73
headlong 125C-2, 42, 126D, 9
headsman 130-O
headstrong 27, 42
headwind 125B
heady 42, 125C-2, 126D
heal 136B, 137A
healer 136B

health 137A, 138C, 140A, 89, 136B
healthful*
healthy 137A, 137B
heap 146A, 147I, 49E, 146C
hear 118
hearken 118
hearsay 57
hearse 24H
heart an organ 25E, 150G
    spirit 137C
    courage 42
heartache 31
heart-broken 31
heartburn 31, 128B, 130E
hearten 7, 136A
heartfelt 121
hearth 146I, 53D
heartiness 38, 137B
heartless 130M
heartsease 143E
heartseed 143E
heart-whole 145K
hearty cordial 38
    strong 137B, 136A, 137A
heat 145J
    ardor 39, 39A, 131B
    passion 39B
    vehemence 125C, 41D, 8, 29
heater 136A, 145J
heath 25G, 143E
heathen 30, 110B, 129B
heathendom*
heathenish 30, 110B, 130C, 82B
heathenism*
heather 25G
heave 24C, 24B
    vomit 16
heaven 53H, 25A
Heaven 82E
heavenliness 140B
heavenly 140B, 136A
heavy 135A, 31, 13
hebdomadal 148H, 148K
Hebe 108, 137B
hebetude 110B, 110A
Hebraist 117
Hebrew 54C, 82D
Hecate 82E, 129B
hecato 147A
hecatomb 130-O, 147A
heckle 130B, 41A, 66
hectic 137C, 11A, 14
hectogram 147C
hector 33, 76, 42
hedge 36D, 127A, 145B

hedgehog 143A
hedge-priest 82F
hedonism 83
heed 132C, 46B, 119G, 114
heedful 132C, 119G
heedless 126B, 125C, 125C-2, 126D
heel 150G, 149D
heeled 135B, 36
heft handle 5B
    effort 41C
    weight 135A
    strength 137B
heifer 143A, 148J
heigh-ho 91, 128A, 126B
height 149F, 147J, 149E
heighten 10, 149F, 6, 149E
heinous 130A, 130C, 130M, 129B
heir 49B
heir-apparent 49B
heiress 49B
heirloom 43A, 104A
heir-presumptive 49B
helicoid 150C
helicopter 24I
heliochromotype 100B
heliolatry 82B
heliometer 95B
helioscope 95B
heliosis 102C
heliostat 98A
heliotrope 143E, 107C, 102A
heliotropic 18C
heliotropis 18C
helium 5D
helix 150C
hell 130N, 130A, 125C-2, 130-O
Hellenism 117, 38
Hellenist 117
Hellenistic 117
Hellenize 81
hellish 28, 125C-2, 130A, 130M, 130N
hellbound 33, 109A
hello 98C, 73
helm 24C, 36C
helmet 36C, 106H
helot 46B
helotry 46B
help aid 5A
    succor 136A, 43B, 43A, 136B, 46B, 40B
helper 46B
helpful 5A
helpless 128A, 127B
helter-skelter 125A

helve 5B
hem 91, 149K, 107B
hemeralopia 119B
hemi 147A, 150C
hemiopia 119B
hemisphere 147A, 150C
hemlock 143E, 130E
hemorrhage 16, 128B
hemorrhoids*
hemp 52C, 143E
hemstitch 107A, 107B
hen 143C, 143D, 141F
henbane 143E, 130E
hence 148B
henchman 46B, 5A
hendeca 147A, 150D
hendecagon 150D
hendecasyllable 85C, 55B
henna 143E
henpecked 32, 46B
hept 147A, 68D, 150D
heptaglot 55B
heptagon 150D
heptagonal 150D
heptahedron 150D
heptahexahedral 150D
heptarchy 133A
her 92
herald 79, 24F, 77
heraldic 79, 77
heraldry 79, 83, 104D
herb 143E
herbage 48N, 150H
herbivora 51A, 143A
herbivorous 51A
Herculean
strong 137B
huge 147J
difficult 13
Hercules 137B
herd 146K, 147I
here 149J, 148E, 149M
hereafter 148B
hereby 149J
hereditable 43B, 43A, 141B
hereditament 43A
hereditarily 137C
hereditary 137C, 141B
heredity 141A, 137C
herein 149L
hereinafter 149I
heresay 57
heresy 30, 82B
heretic 30, 82B, 82A, 82D
heretical*
heretofore 148A
heritable 49B

heritage 49B, 43A, 140A
hermaphrodite 141E, 141B
hermeneutics 84
Hermes 49A, 144A
hermetic 52H
hermit 145K, 15
hermitage 53D, 48L
hermit-crab 143B
hernia 145E, 128B
hero 42, 140B, 50
heroic 42, 140B
heroic verse 85C
heroine 42
heroism 42
heron 143C
hero-worship 38, 63
herpetology 83
herself 92
hesitate
vacillate 127A
be timid 32, 132C, 112, 30
hesitancy*
Hessian 106J
Hessian-fly 143D
hest 94
hetaerism 146H, 146D
heterodox 30, 82A
heterodoxy 30, 82B
heterogeneous 126A, 102C, 146C, 141A
heterogenesis*
heterogenetic 141B
heterologous 126A
heteromorphism*
heteronomous 126A
hew 145F
hexa 147A, 68D, 150D
hexagon 150D
hexahedron 150D
hexameter 85C
hexapod 143A
hexicology 83
heyday 71A, 137B
hiatus break 145E
gap 25H, 37, 145C
hibernal 148K, 148H
hibernate 54A
hiccough 16, 128B
hicjacet 84, 86, 92
hickory 143E
hid 103A
hidalgo 133A
hide 103A, 13, 36F
hidebound 52B, 113, 52G
hideous ugly 109A
frightful 33, 129B, 130M
hiding 103A, 130G
hie excite 8
hasten 9

hierarch 82G, 133A
hierarchic 82A, 133A
hierarchism 82B, 82C, 133A
hierarchy 82F, 82G, 82C
hieratic 82F, 82G, 140B
hiero 82F
hieroglyphic 55B, 92, 104C, 104A
hierology 83
higgle 44, 41B, 66
high lofty 149F
exalted 140B
honorable 140A, 137B, 69B
highbrow 117
high-colored 102B, 102C, 62, 57
highest 149F
highfalutin 76, 95D
high-flown 149F, 76, 28, 62
high-flyer 125C-1, 125C-2
high-handed 130A
high-jinks 99A, 72, 99C
highland 149E
highlows 106J
highness 149F, 140B
high-priest 82F
highroad 25B
highstrung 69B, 121
high-toned 69B, 134A, 140A
highwater 149F, 25I
highway 25B
highwayman 49G
hike 19B
hiker 19B
hilarious 71A, 71B, 99A
hilarity 71A, 71B
hill 149E
Hillelism 82B
hilly 149E
hilt 5B
him 92
himself 92
hind servant 46B, 143A, 141F, 149I
hinder 149I
hinder obstruct 36
restrain 52A
hamper 13
prevent, stop 12
hindermost 149I
hindmost 149I
hindrance 12, 36A, 52A, 13
Hindu 54C, 82D
Hinduism 82B
hinge 146A, 52A, 52B, 18C

hinny 146F, 142D, 143A, 148J
hint 87, 57
hip 53R, 150G
hipp 51A
hippodrome 99E, 49F
hippology 83
hippophagy 51A
hippopotamus 143A
hircine 123
hire lease 49D, 45, 46B
hireling 46B
hirsute 106A
his 92
hispid 106A
hiss 69A, 64, 55A
hist 91, 11B, 33, 118
histology 83
historian 85E
historic 85A, 148A
historiographer 85E
historiography 85D
history 85D, 117, 86, 148A
histrionic 99B, 85A, 99A
histrionicism 99B
hit strike 130G
lucky event 134D, 59, 124, 127A
hitch 52A, 36A, 52B
hither 149J, 149M
hive bee-house 53D
a swarm 146K, 54B, 147I, 54A
ho 91, 12
hoar white 102A
ancient 148A
hoard 49E
hoar-frost 146B
hoarhound 48P
hoarse 70
hoarseness 70
hoax 62
hob 53P
hobble 18A, 13, 52A
hobbledehoy 18A, 126D
hobble-skirt 106F
hobby 63, 71A, 143C
hobby-horse 24H
hobgoblin 96A, 113, 33
hobnob drink 51B, 90, 146K
hobo 18B, 129B
hock wine 48L, 45, 150G
hockey 41D
hocus
deceive 62, 49F
cheat 130A, 49F
juggle 99A, 99B
hocus-pocus 41B, 99B

hod 53I
hodge-podge 48D
hodman 46B
Hodur 97
hoe 145F, 145H
hog, 143A, 51A, 138A, 145F, 149G
hogshead 147F, 53N
holden (B. hoyden) 8, 39C, 129B
hoist 24C, 149F, 24B, 24H
hoity-toity 91, 64, 71B
hoki, 143B
hokey-poky 48F
hold retain 52A
  reserve 132C
  judge 113
  contain 53A, 52E, 11A, 53B, 53E
hold-up 49G
hole, hollow 25, 25H
  burrow 53D, 53E
  difficulty 13
holiday 99C, 148L
holiness 140A, 140B
holland 106K
hollo 69B, 98C
hollow 25H, 25
  superficial 60
  unreal 113, 62, 69A, 69B, 70 62, 130A
holly 143E
hollyhock 143E
Holm 143E, 25G
holmium 5D
holo 146A
holoblastic 141A
holocaust 130-O
holograph 85B
holster 53I
holt 34, 149E, 53D
holy 140A, 140B
homage 38, 63, 139B
homalo 149C
home 53D, 141D, 34
homeliness 109A
homeopathic 147K, 136B
home rule 133A
homesick 39, 128B
homespun 106K
homestead 53D, 141D
homicide 130-O
homiletics 84
homilist 82F
homily 85A
homing 19A
hominy 48M
homo 105
homogeneous 105, 141B
homogenous 141A, 141B

homograph 57, 55B
homologous 141A, 92, 105
homology 141A
homomorph 141A, 92
homonym 57, 141A, 92, 55B
homophone*
homophonous*
homotype 141A, 105
hone 150E
honest 140A, 61A
honesty 140A, 61A
honey 48H, 48P
  flatter 63
  darling 140B
honey-bee 143D
honey-boy 140B
honeycomb 53B
honeydew 48P
honey-locust 143E
honeymoon 39B, 71A
honeysuckle 143E
honiton 107B
honor (B. honour) 38, 140A, 140B, 139B, 63
honorable (B. honourable) 140A
honorarium 45
honorary 140A, 38, 139B
hood 106H
hoodlum bully 33, 129B
hoodoo 127B, 129B, 34
hoodwink 130A, 96A, 103A
hoof 150G
hook 49C, 52B, 145F, 130G
hooka 25F
hooked 150C, 150G
hooker 24J
hook-worm 143D
hooligan 129B
hoop 52A, 24D, 150C, 69B
hooper 143C
hoopoe 143C
hoot 64, 72
hop 9, 17, 99F
hope 38, 39
hopeless 31, 127B, 112
hoplite 130F
hopper 53K
hoppet 53K, 95B
hopscotch 41D
horal 148H, 148K
horde 146K, 147I
horizon 150C, 145B, 111, 149G
horizontal 149C, 149G
horn 130H, 68G, 53I

hornbeak 143B
hornbeam 143E
hornbill 143C
horn-book 81
horned 150G, 36
hornet 143D, 129B, 130C
hornpipe 99F, 68G
horny 150G
horologue 148F
horology 83, 115, 148G
horometer 148F
horoscope 95B, 100B, 104A
horrent 28, 33, 109A, 42
horrible 109A, 33, 129B, 130M
horrid 33, 29, 109A, 129B, 130M
horrify 33
horripilation 32
horror 32, 31
hors de combat 127B, 128A
hors-d'oeuvre 48D
horse 143A, 24G, 141F
horse-fly 143D
horse-laugh 71B, 72, 64
horsemanship 134B
horse-pistol 130I
horse-play 72
horse-power 137B
horseradish 48P, 143E
horseshoe 106J, 150C, 143B
hortative 7
horticultural 144B
horticulture 144B
hosanna 63, 40B
hose 106J, 25F
hosiery 106J
hospice 48B, 43A
hospitable 43A
hospital 53C, 136B
hospitality 43A
host crowd 146K
  multitude 147I, 130F, 48B, 48A
hostage 45
hostel 48B, 53C, 81
hostelry 48B, 53C
hosteau 53C, 136B
hostess 48A
hostile 28, 67A, 130F
hostility*
hostler 46B
hot fiery 131B, 121
  melting 145J
  passionate 39B, 39, 29, 48P
hotchpotch 48D, 146C

hotel 48B, 53C
hothead 27, 29
hothouse 144C, 53B
hotspur 42, 29, 125C-2
hound chase 41C
  dog 143A, 129B
houndfish 143B
hour 148H, 147H
hour-glass 148F
Houri 108
house 53D, 141G, 94, 53B, 54B, 139A
house-boat 53D, 24J
household 53D, 146I, 54B, 132D
housing 106B, 106K, 34
hovel 53D
hover
  move about 17
  be expectant 39, 149M, 149F
how 41A
howdah 53I
however 27
howitzer 130I
howl 69B
howler coward 32, 143A, 69B
however 27
hoy 24J
hub 52B
hubbub 69B, 125A
huccatoon 106K
huck 143B
huckaback 106K
huckle 150G
hucklebacked 150G, 109B
huckleberry 48G
huckster 44, 49F, 130A
huddle 146K, 125A
hue color 102B, 102C, 41B, 69B
huff blow 16
  bully 33
  anger 29, 64
hug 98C, 121
huge 147J
hugeness 147J
Huguenot 82D
hulk 24J
hulking 147J, 13, 109B, 150G
hull covering 36F
  to peal 145G
hullabaloo 69B, 66
hum 68B, 69A, 68A
human 143A
humane 38, 136A
humaniculture 117, 81
humanist 116, 117
humanitarian 136A
humanity 143A, 38

Page 459

humanize 132D
humankind 143A
humble
  debased 129B
  modest 132C
  submissive 46B,
    50, 65, 103A
humble-pie 46B,129B
humbug
  fraud 49F, 130A,
    62, 103B
humbuggery 130A,
    49F, 62, 103B
humdrum 132D,
    129B, 56
humid 145J
humidor 145J
humiliate 65, 129B
humiliation 65, 129B,
    32, 46B, 130B
humility*
hummer 9, 144D
humming-bird 143C
hummock 149E,146B
humor (B. humour)
  yield 46A
  wit 59, 117
  merriment 71A,
    71B, 99C
  petulance 29
  moisture 145J, 2,
    72, 128C, 130E
humorist 59, 72,
    99D
humorous 99A, 72,
    59, 71B
hump 150G, 9, 130B,
    109B, 149E
humus 146D, 142F
Hun 54C
hunch 150G, 109B,
    130G
hunchback*
hundred 147A
hundredth 147A
hundredweight 147C
Hungarian 54C
hunger 39, 37, 51A
hungry, 37, 39, 128A
hunk 145D
hunt 119E, 41D
hunter 119E, 41D
hurdle 13, 24H
hurdy-gurdy 68D
hurl 24C, 55A, 64,
    149A
hurly-burly 125A,
    69B
hurrah 91, 71A, 63,
    71B
hurricane 125B
hurry speed 9
  accelerate 10
  confusion 125A

hurry-scurry 125A, 9
hurt
  injure 130G, 130D,
    130-O, 130B,
    130E, 130M
hurtful*
hurtle 9, 24C
hurtleberry 48G
husband 146J, 141E,
    132C
husbandman 144D
husbandry 144B,
    132C
hush 69A, 11B, 132B,
    91
husk 36F, 129A, 145G
husky 70, 137B
hussar 130F
hussy 125C-3, 146E,
    39C, 129B
hustle 9, 24C
hustler 9, 144D, 46B
hut 53D
hutch 53J
hyacinth 143E,
    107D, 107C
hyal 101A
hyaline 101A
hyalography 100A
hybrid 146F
hybridize 146D
hydatoid 145J
Hydra 13, 33, 142F,
    127B, 130-O
hydrangea 143E
hydrant 25F
hydraulic 137B
hydro-aeroplane 24I
hydrodynamics 83,
    137B
hydrogen 5D
hydrokinetics 83,
    137B
hydrology 83
hydrometer 83, 95B
hydrophobia 128B,
    130E, 32
hydrophyte 143E
hydroplane 24I
hydrostat 95B
hyena 143A
hyetograph 100B
hyetology 100B
hygeian 136B
Hygeia 137A
hygiene 136B, 83
hygienic 136B
hygiology 136B
hygrometer 95B
hygroscope 95B
hymen 146H, 141C
hymeneal 146H
hymn 68B
hymnal 85B
hymnology 83

hypocephalus
    27, 110B
hyper 125C
hyperbola 150C
hyperbole 57, 62
hyperbolic 57, 62
hyperborean 149B,
    146B
hyperdulia 38
Hyperion 108
hypermetropia 119B
hyphen 55B
hypnotic 50
hypnotism 50
hypnotize 50
hypochondria 128B,
    32, 39, 31
hypochondriac 128A
hypocrisy 62, 103B
hypocrite*
hyporcheme 68B
hyporchesis 99F
hypostasis 133A
hypostrophe 18C
hypostyle 34
hypotenuse 150D
hypothesis 113
hypothetic 113, 57
hypsi 149F, 150G
hypsometer 95B
hyrax 143A
hyssop 143E
hysteria 31, 128B,
    110B, 130E
hysterical 31, 128B

I

I first person 92
iambic 85C, 85A
iambus 55B
ibex 143A
ice 146B
iceberg 146B, 28,
    149E
ice-boat 24J
ice cream 48F
ice field 25G
ichneumon 143A
ichnolite 100B, 95A,
    95C
ichnology 83
ichthyic 150G
ichthyography 85B
ichthyology 83
Ichthyosaurus 143F,
    143A
icicle 146B, 150E
icing 48P
icon 104C
iconoclast 130-O,
    67A, 64
icosahedron 150D
icy 146B, 28, 121
idea 111, 113, 115

ideal conceptive 111
  visionary 113, 105,
    108, 149H, 140B
idealize 105, 113
idealism 113, 140B,
    105, 134B, 38, 83
idealist*
idealistic*
ideality*
ideation 113, 114
identical 105, 84,
    134A
identify 119F, 105
identism 83, 105
identity 105, 134A
ideograph 55B, 105,
    87, 104A
ideographic*
ideography 100A,105
ideologist 113, 83
ideology 83
ideomotion 4, 19A
ideomotor 4, 1
idio 55B, 105
idiocy 110B
idiom 55A
idiomatic 55A
idiosyncrasy 126A
idiot 110B
idiotic 110B
idiotrophic 51A
idle empty 60, 128A
  fanciful 113
  neglect 126B
idler 126B
Ido 55A
idol 104C, 140B
idolater 38, 82D
idolatrous 38, 82A,
    39A
idolatry love 39,
    39A, 39C
  reverence 38
  a religion 82B
idolize 38, 139B
idyl 85C
idylist 85E, 100C
idyllic 85C, 85A
if 127A
igloo 53D
igneous 131B
ignis fatuus 96A, 57,
    40A
ignite 131B, 101A
ignition 131B, 101A
ignoble 129B
ignominious
    129B, 65, 130A
ignominy*
ignoramus 110B
ignorance 110B
ignorant 110B
ignore 28, 126B
Igorote 54C
iguana 143A

implant 10, 52G
  place in 149L
  instruct 81
  ingraft 146A
implement 5B, 5A
implicate 146A, 13,
  87, 93
implication 146A, 13,
  84, 115
implicit 84
  believing 113
  inferring 115
  submissive 46B
implore 40B
imploring 40B
imply embody 53A
  signify 84, 95A, 87,
  146A
impolicy 126C
impolite 126C, 130B,
  130C, 28, 109A
impoliteness*
impolitic 126C, 110B
imponderable 135A
imporosity 146B
imporous 146B
import bring in 49A
  signify 95A, 84,
  135B, 5C, 95E,
  135B
importance 135B,
  68A
  pride 28, 113
important 135B
  pompous 95D, 113,
  28, 140B
importation 49A
importunate
  appealing 40B
  troublesome 13
  urgent 7, 8, 40A
  exacting 41B
importune*
importunity*
impose cheat 130A
  burden 130B
  punish 130N, 50,
  133A
imposing 108
  impressive 135B
  conspicuous 95E,
  95D, 140B
imposition
  fraud 130A, 49F,
  50
  oppression 130B
impossibility 13
impossible 13, 126A,
  36
impost 49C, 45, 49A
impostor 130A, 62
imposture 130A, 62
impotence 128A
impotent 128A
impound 52H

impoverish 130D, 14,
  128C
impoverishment*
impracticable 126C
imprecate 65, 40B,
  64, 65
imprecatory*
impregnable 36
impregnate 141A,
  146D, 26, 10,
  146C
impresario 99D, 68J
imprescriptible 137C
  self-evidencing 84
impress mark 95A
  teach 81, 49C, 50,
  124
impressible 111, 116
impression
  mark 95A, 95C
  image 105
  conception 111
  notion 113, 115
impressionable 111,
  116, 3C
impressional 116
impressionism 84
impressionist 100C
impressionistic 135B
impressive 135B,
  95D, 33, 95E,
  108, 140B
impressiveness*
impressment 49C
imprimatur 46A
imprimis 73
imprint 55B, 81
imprison 52H
imprisonment 52H
improbability 127A
improbable 127A
improbity 130A
impromptu 144A,
  55A
improper 126C, 126A
impropriety*
improvable 125A,
  128A
improve 136B, 6,
  137A
improvement*
improver 107B
improvidence 126B,
  125C-1
improvident*
improvisation 144A,
  68B, 85B, 85A
improvisator 85E,
  68H, 68J
improvise 144A, 85A,
  68B
imprudent 126B,
  125C, 28, 42,
  95D, 110B, 126C,
  130C

impudence
  rudeness 130C
  shamelessness
  125C-3, 64, 95D,
  110B, 42
impudent*
impugn 67A, 66
impulse 4, 24C, 8, 1,
  2, 137B
impulsion 24B, 149H
  instigation 8
  force 137B
impulsive 9
  actuating 8, 2, 3C
  forcible 137B,
  125C-2, 137C,
  39B, 126A, 127A
impunity 34, 46A
impure 146C, 129A,
  125C-3
impurity*
imputation 65, 87
impute 65, 80
in 149L, 27
inability 128A, 126D
inaccessible 36
inaccurate 126C
inaction quiet 11B
  sluggishness 110A
  slowness 126B
inactive*
inadequate
  unfit 126B, 126D
  insufficient 37
  incapable 128A
inadmissible 35
inadvertence 126B,
  126C, 28
inadvertent 126B
inalienable 137C,
  11B, 146A
inamorata 39A, 146E
inamorato*
inane 25A
  empty 37, 128A
  senseless 110B
  silly 60
inanimate 128A, 37
inanition 128A, 37
inanity 128A, 110B,
  60
inapposite 126C
inappreciable 147K,
  128A, 28
inarch 146A, 146D
inarticulate 60,
  145A, 70
inartistic 126D
inasmuch 105
inattentive 126B, 27,
  126D, 28
inaugural 139A, 94
inaugurate*
inauguration*
inauspicious 127B,
  95A, 126A
inbeing 137C, 2

inborn 137C
inbred 137C
inbreed 141A, 146D
Inca 133A, 54C
incalculable 147I
incalescence 145J
incalescent 145J,
  101A, 131B
incandescence 101A,
  131B
incantation 68B, 40B
incantatory 68B,
  68A, 40B
incapable 126D,
  128A
incapacitate 130D,
  129B
incapacity 128A
incarcerate 52H,
  130D
incarceration*
incarnation 106B
incase 106B, 52H,
  145A
incast 45
incastellate 106B
incautious
  careless 126B,
  126D
  heedless 125C-2
  daring 42
incavo 100B
incendiary 130A,
  131B, 8, 27
incense 8, 130C, 122
incentive 8, 12, 40A,
  149H
inception 111, 4
inceptive*
incertitude 127A
  doubt 112
incessant 11A, 75
incest 146D, 125C-3,
  39B
incestuous 146D,
  125C-3, 39B
inch 147E, 14, 126B
inchoate 4, 10
inchoative*
incident
  happening 127A
  appertaining 53A,
  46B, 148E, 148L
incinerate 131B,
  145J, 145B
incineration*
incinerator*
incipient 4
incise 145F
incision 145F
incisor 145F
incitation 8
incite 8
incitement 8, 7, 149H
incivility
  offense 130C, 126C,
  109A

indistinct 97, 57, 69A, 103A
indistinguishable 97, 103A, 57
indite 55B, 85A
indium 5D
individual
  inborn 137C
  single 147A, 145K
  distinct 126A
individualism 126A
individualist 82D
individualistic 126A
individuality 126A
individualize 126A, 92
indivisible 146A, 137C
indocile 27
indoctrinate 81, 82A
indogenesis 141A
indolence 126B
indolent 126B
indomitable
  courageous 42
  conquering 50, 36
indoor 149L
indorse 93, 63, 89, 92
indorsement*
indubitable 61A, 93, 134C
induce
  persuade 40A, 7, 8, 40B, 92, 139A, 115
inducement 40A, 40B, 12, 149H
induct 92, 94, 139A
induction 94, 115, 139A
inductive 115
inductometer 95B
indue 43B, 81, 43B
indulge 46A, 136A, 71A
indulgence*
indulgent*
indulin 102D
indurate 146B, 27, 14
industrial 144B
industrialism 144B
industrious 11A, 144B, 39, 49A, 8
industry*
inebriate 110A, 112, 96A
inebriation*
ineffable 132C, 140B
ineffaceable 11B
ineffective 128A, 127B
ineffectual*
inefficacy 128A, 127B
inefficiency 128A, 127B, 126D
inefficient*

inelegance 126D, 109A, 18A, 126C, 70
inelegant*
ineligible 126A, 125A, 128A
inept 60, 126A
inequality 126A
inequitable 130A
inequity 130A, 126A
inert 11B, 110A
inertia*
inescapable 50, 134C
inestimable 147I, 140B
inevitable 134C, 50
inexact 126C
inexcusable 130A
inexhaustible 11B, 147I, 137B
inexorability 11B, 27, 39, 50, 130M, 132C
inexorable*
inexpedient 126A, 13
inexpensive 147K
inexperience 110B, 126D
inexperienced*
inexpert 126D, 126C
inexplicable 57, 96A
inexpressible 126A, 13, 96A, 140B
inextricable 52A, 132C
infallible 134A, 134C, 61A, 117, 126A
infamous 65, 130A, 129B
infamy*
infancy 148J, 148A
infant 148J, 142B
Infanta 133A
Infante 49B
infanticide 130-O
infantile 148J, 110B, 128A
infantry 130F
infare 99C, 139A
infatuate 7, 39B, 50, 40, 108
infatuation 8, 38, 39B, 146D
infection 130E, 146C
infect*
infectious 130E
infecundity 128A
infelicitous
  unfortunate 127B
  unhappy 31, 126A, 125A, 130B
infelicity*
infelt 121
infer 115
inference 115, 84
inferior low 129B
  subordinate 46B

inferiority*
infernal bad 130A
  hellish 130N
  brutal 130M
  fiendish 28
inferno 130N
infest 130F, 130-O, 147I
infidel 30, 82D
infidelity 30, 130A, 146D, 125C-3, 62
infiltration 146C
infinite vast 147J, 146A, 147K, 57, 11A, 148C, 135B, 147I
infinitesimal 147K
infinitive 57
infinitude 11A, 147J
infinity 147J, 146A, 11A, 148B, 148C
infirm 128A, 128B
infirmary 53C, 136B
infirmity 128B, 128A
inflame 131B, 8, 130C
inflammability 131B
inflammable 131B
inflammation 130E, 128B, 131B
inflammatory 130C, 131B, 8, 128B
inflate swell 10, 99A, 145I
inflect 3A, 150D
inflection 150C, 3A, 3C, 69C, 130N
inflectional 3A
inflexible 11B, 137B, 27, 134A
inflict 130G, 130M, 130N
inflorescence 141B, 143E
influence potency 135B, 124
  tendency 2
  excitation 8, 1, 50, 149H
influential*
influenza 128B
influx 146C, 146A, 20, 16
inform teach 81
  reveal 78
  announce 79
informal 126A, 132D
informant 78
information 78, 81
informer 78
infraction 130A
infrangible 11B, 137B, 52G, 137C
infrequence 148L
infrequent 148L
infringe 130A
infringement 130A

infuriate 130C
infuse teach 81
  pour into 146C, 24C, 10
infusion*
infusoria 142F
ingate 25
ingenious canny 117
  skillful 134B
  inventive 144A
ingenue 99D, 110B
ingenuity 117, 134B, 144A
ingenuous
  frank 61A, 140A
  artless 110B
Ingleside 53D
inglorious 129B, 65
ingraft 146A, 146C, 81, 10
ingrain 100A, 102B
ingratiate 38
ingratitude 126B
ingredient 145D
ingress 20, 25
inhabit 54A, 146K
inhabitant 54B
inhabitation 54A
inhalation 51A
inhale 51A
inharmonious 70, 126A, 125A, 126C
inhere 137C, 52E, 52G, 141A
inherence*
inherent 137C, 52E, 2, 146A
inherit 49B, 49A
inheritance 49B, 43A
inhibit 52A, 35, 132C
inhibitive 52A, 35
inhospitable 28, 27, 132C
inhuman 130M
inhume 52H
inimical 28, 67A, 27
inimitable 134B, 140B, 108
iniquitous 130A
iniquity 130A
initial 4, 92, 58
initiate begin 4
  instruct 81
initiation 4, 81
initiative 4
initiatory 4, 81, 73
inject 24C, 149L
injecta 81
injection 24C, 126B
injudicious 110B, 126C
injunction ban 35
  command 94
injure 130G, 130D, 130B

injurious hurtful
130G, 130D,
130B, 130M
unjust 130A
injury*
injustice 130A
ink 102E, 102A
Inka 133A
inkiness 102E, 102A
inkling 87
inky 102E, 97, 102A,
102C
inland 149L
inlay 107A, 149L
inlet 25I, 25, 149L
inly 103A
inmate 54B, 146A
inmost 149L
inn 48B, 53C
innate 137C
inner 149L
innervate 137B
innocence
goodness 140A
purity 138C, 61A
imbecility 110B
innocent*
innocuous 128A
innovate 144A, 126A
innoxious 128A
innuendo 87, 57, 98B,
98A
innumerable 147I
innutritious 128A
inoculate 146C, 10,
136B, 146A
imbue 81
inodorous 122, 123
inoffensive 140A,
128A
inoperative 128A,
127B
inopportune 127B,
126A
inordinate 125C,
126C
inquest 41A
inquietude 96A, 112
inquire 41A
inquiry 41A, 119E
inquisition 41A
inquisitive 41A
inroad 130F, 20, 49G
insalubrious 130E
insane 110B
insanity 110B
insatiable 39, 37
inscribe 55B, 84, 92
inscription 55B, 84,
92, 86
inscriptive*
inscrutable 97, 57,
103A
insect 143D, 147K,
129B
insectivorous 51A

insecure 128A
insensate 110B,
110A
insensibility 110A
insensible 110A,
110B
inseparable 52G,
137C, 146A
insert 149L, 91
insertion 149L, 91,
107B
inset 149L, 85B, 91
inshore 149M, 149L
inside 149L
insidious false 62
treacherous 130A
secret 103A, 28
insight 117
insignia 104B
insignificance 128A,
129B, 147K
insignificant*
insincere false 62
unfair 130A
dissembling 103A,
103B
insinuate 20
ingratiate 38
suggest 87, 57, 91
insinuation*
insipid 48Q
insist 41B, 27, 8
insistence 41B, 27
insistent 41B, 27,
95E, 8
insobriety 110A, 112
insolence 130C, 64
insolent 130C, 64, 28
insoluble 146B, 11B
insolvency 128A, 64
insolvent 128A, 64
insomnia 128B, 111
inspect 119E
inspection*
inspector*
inspiration
a breathing 51A
excitation 8, 71A
conception 111
inspire inhale 51A
exhilarate 8, 99A
imbue 81, 7
inspirit imbue 81, 7,
99A, 137B, 8,
141A, 136A, 99A
inspissate 146B
instability 3C, 127A
install 94, 39A,
139A, 149A
installation*
installment 145D,
139A, 45
instance proof 93,
84
likeness 105

instant 9
immediate 148D
urgent 8, 148I,
148K
instantaneous 148D,
148I, 148E,
148K
instanter 148D
instate 139A
instep 150G
instigate 8
instil teach 81
infuse 146C
engender 137C,
141A, 8, 137B
instinct 2
instinctive 2, 4, 137C
institute fix 11B
originate 144A
ordain 139A, 82A,
132A
legalize 133A
maxim 61B
command 94
destine 134C
institution 144C, 5A
institutional 144B,
61A, 4, 5A
institutionalism
82A, 82C
instruct teach 81
command 94
instruction 81, 94
instructive 81
instructor 81
instrument 5A
document 93
musical instru-
ment 68F, 68A
instrumental*
insubordination 27
insufferable 130M,
130N, 129B
insular
separated 145K
narrow 110B
insularity 110B,
145K, 149A
insulate 145A
insulation 145A,
145B
insulator*
insult 130C, 64, 28
insuperable 36, 134C,
137B, 13, 50
insurance 34, 45
insure 34
insurgent 27
insurrection 27
intact 146A
intaglio 100B, 107C,
100A
intake 49A
intangible 128A,
147K
integer 147A, 146A
integral 146A

integrant 145D
integrate 146A
integrity
goodness 140A
soundness 146B,
61A, 146A
integument 36F
intellect 117, 111
intellectual 117
intellectualism 117
intellectuality 117
intelligence
understanding 117,
79, 78, 85B, 59
intelligent*
intelligible 59, 84
intemperance
125C-3, 51B, 51A
intemperate*
intend 2
intendant 133A
intense replete 26
excessive 125C
strained 41C, 114,
39, 137B
intensify 10, 6
intensity force 137B
vehemence 39, 2,
68A
intensive 10, 137B,
2, 6
intent 2, 41C, 37, 39,
114
intention 2
inter 52H
intercalate 91
intercede plead 40B,
132B, 91
intercept 36, 49C
intercession 40B,
132B
interchange 3A, 45
intercourse 146D
connection 146A
conversation 90
exchange 3A
fellowship 146K
interdict 35
interest excite 8, 12,
99A, 39, 114,
49A, 45, 126A,
132C, 149H
interesting 8, 99A,
40A
interfere 13, 36, 35,
12, 36A
interim 148I
interior 149L
interjection 91, 55A
interline 91
interlinear 91, 84
interlocutory 90, 91,
149L
interloper 49G, 130A
interlude 68B, 68C
intermediary 132B,
5A

intermediate 149L
interment 52H
intermezzo 68C
interminable 8, 147J, 148C, 11A
intermingle 146C, 146K
intermission stop 12
  duration 148I
intermit 12
intermittent 3B
intermix 146C
intern 52H, 149L, 136B
internal 149L
international 146K
internecine 130-O
interpellate 41A
interpolate 91
interpose 12, 36A
  thrust in 91
  place between 149L
  interfere 36
interpret 84
interpretation 84
interregnum 148I, 12
interrogate 41A
interrogation 41A, 55B
interrogative 41A
interrupt delay 126B
  stop 12
  hinder 52A
  interfere 36, 36A, 91
interruption*
intersect 145F, 150F, 145A
intersection*
intersperse 145I
interstellar 149L
interstice 25H, 25
interstitial 25
intertidal 149L
interurban 146A
interval 148I, 25A
intervale 25G
intervene 36, 91, 35, 149L, 132B
intervention*
interview 90, 41A
intestinal 25E, 25
intestine 25E, 149L
intimacy 146K, 146D, 38, 103A
intimate declare 80
  hint 87, 57, 146D
intimate
  associated 146K
  confidential 103A, 79, 87, 52E, 117, 38, 149M, 146D, 146L
intimation 79, 87
intimidate 33
into 149L

intolerable 130M, 130N, 129B
intolerance 27
intolerant 27, 130M
intonation 68A, 69B
intone 68A, 69B, 69C
intoxicant 48L
intoxicate 96A
intoxication 110A, 112, 96A, 71A
intra 149L
intracellular 149L
intractable 27
intrados 150C, 149L
intramural 149L
intransigeant 27
intrench 36
intrepid 42
intrepidity 42
intricacy 13, 57, 96A
intricate 13, 57
intrigant 130A, 103A
intrigue 130A, 103A
intrinsic
  inherent 137C, 2, 146A
  genuine 138C, 61A
intro 149L
introduce 79, 73, 92, 10, 81, 91, 139A, 149L
introduction 4, *
introit 68B
intromission 73, 149L
intromit 149L
introspection 114, 119E
introspective*
introvert 149L
intrude 130C, 20, 130A, 13, 36
intrusion*
intrust 113
intuition 117, 111, 119F
intuitive*
inundate 21, 130-O, 147I, 16
inundation*
inure 132D, 137B
invade 130F, 20, 49G, 130A
invalid 128A, 131A
invalidate 131A, 130D
invaluable 140B
invariable 11A, 11B, 134C
invasion 130F, 20, 49G, 130A
invective 64, 65
inveigh 64, 65
inveigle 40A
invent 144A, 134B, 126A

invention 144A, 5A, 12, 62, 144E
inventive 144A, 117, 134B
inventory 86
inveracity 62
inverisimilitude 62, 126C, 60
inverse 3A, 27, 3C
inversion 3A
invert 3A, 18C
invertebrate 128A, 32
invest 49D, 139A
investigate 119E
investigation 119E
investor 49D
investiture 43A, 139A, 104D
investment 45, 49D
investor 45, 49D
inveterate 137C, 52G, 132C, 132D, 146A
invidious 130C, 130A, 28
invigorate 8, 137B, 136B
invincibility 134C, 36
invincible 134C, 1, 50, 61A
  impregnable 36
  indomitable 42
  mighty 137B
inviolable 134C, 1, 11B, 61A, 137B, 36
invisible 103A, 97
invitation 40A, 40B
invite*
invocation 40B, 40A
invoice 86
invoke 40B
involuntary 46B
involute 150C, 146A
involution*
involve
  complicate 126A
  confound 57, 144E, 53A, 13, 125A, 146A
invulnerable 36, 134C
inward 149L
inwardly 149L
inwrought 108
io 143D
iodine 5D
iota 147K
irascibility 29
irascible 29, 66
irate 29
ire 29
iridescence 102C, 101A

iridescent*
iridium 5D
iris 119C
iriscope 95B
irk 130D, 128A, 31, 13
irksome 13, 130D, 130B
iron fetter 52A, 146B, 137B, 5C, 5D
ironclad 36, 24J
ironical 57, 64, 28, 7?
irony 57, 64, 28, 72
irradiance 101A
irradiate 101A
irradicate 137C
irrational 60, 110B, 126C
irreclaimable 127B
irredeemable 127B
irredentist 49C
irregular 126A, 125A, 150B
irrelevant 126A, 128A
irreparable 127B
irrepressible 134C, 36, 125C-2, 137B, 50
irreproachable 140A
irresistible 134C, 50, 137B, 36
irresolute 112, 32, 132C
irrespective 126A
irresponsible 128A, 127A
irreverent 130A
irrevocable 11B
irrigate 141A, 146C, 145I
irritability 29
irritable 29
irritant 130B, 130C
irritate 130C, 130B
irritation 130C, 29
irruption 145E, 49G, 130F, 20
is 11A, 11B, 105
isagon 150D
Ishmaelite 129B
Islam 82E, 82B
island 25G, 145K
isle 145K, 25G
islet 145K, 25G
ism 83
isochromatic 102B
isochronous 148L, 148E
isogon 150D
isolate 145K, 145A, 147A
isolation 145K
isosceles 150D
Israelite 54C, 82D

jut 149H
jute 52C, 106K
juvenescence 148J,
137A
juvenescent*
juvenile 148J
juvenilia 145B
juvenility 148J,
137B, 137A
juxtapose, 149M,
149J
juxtaposition*

K

Kafir 54C, 82D, 30
kaftan 106D
kago 24H
kaiser 133A
kale 48K, 143E
kaleidoscope 95B
kali 130E
Kalmuck 54C, 106K
kama 39A
kamis 106D
kangaroo 143A
kava 143E, 48J, 48L
kavass 133A, 24F
kayak 24J, 53D
kazoo 68G
kea 143C
kedge 49C, 18C
keel 53R, 46B
keel-boat 24J
keelhaul 130N, 64
keelson 53R
keen sharp 150E,
145F, 59, 117,
119E
keening 31
keep hold 52A
maintain 132C
guard 34, 11A,
48A, 36B
keeping 132A, 132C
keepsake 104A
keeve 53N
keg 53N
kemp 106A, 129A
ken 117, 119F
kendal 106K
kennel lair 53D
gutter 25F
keno 41D
kepi 106H
kerite 145B
kermes 102D
kermess 71A, 99A,
51A, 99E
kernel 142F, 137C, 2
kersey 106K
kestrel 143C
ketch 24J
ketchup 48P
kettle 53M

kettledrum 68E,
71A, 99C
key 5A, 115, 84, 43A,
104G, 25G, 133A,
132A
keynote 133A, 55B
keyword 55B
khaki 106K
khan 133A, 48B
khanate 133A
khediviate 133A
khedive 133A
kick 130G, 27, 67A
kickshaw
delicacy 48D
fancy 113, 126A,
107E
kid 148J, 143A,
130A
kidnap 49G, 49F
kidney 25E
kilderkin 147F
kill 130-O
kiln 131B
kilogram 147C
kiloliter 147F
kilometer 147E
kilt 106D
kimono 106F
kiltie 130F
kin 146I, 68G, 68D
kind
benevolent 136A
affectionate 38
species 92, 126A,
46A
kindergarten 81
kindle 8, 131B, 130C
kindly 136A, 46A
kindness 136A, 5A,
38
kindred 146I
kinemacolor 99E
kinetoscope 99E
king 133A
kingdom 133A, 53F
kingfisher 143C
kink 13, 125A, 113,
71B
kinkajou 143A
kinsfolk 146I
kiosk 53D
kip 106K
kipper 143B
kirk 53C
kirtle 106D
kismet 134C, 50
kiss 98C, 121
kit 53N, 142C, 142E
kitcat 100B
kitchen 144C, 53E
kitchenette 53E
kite 24I, 143C
kith 146L
kitten 143A, 148J
kittiwake 143C
kiwi 143C

kleidoscopic 102C
kleptomania 49F
kleptomaniac 49F
knack 134B
knacker 130-O
knapsack 53J
knapweed 143E
knave 130A, 49F,
129B
knavish*
knead 146B
knee 25E
kneel 98C, 46B, 32,
129B
knell omen 77
bell-sound 69B
knickerbockers
106E
knick-knack 107E
knife 145F, 130H,
130G
knight 133A
knightage 133A
knight-bachelor
133A
knight-errant 42,
76, 95D
knit 146A, 98B
knob 5B, 149E
knock 130G
knock-out 35A, 50
knoll 149E
knot difficulty 13
entanglement
125A, 96A
a hardness 146B,
147E, 143C,
146A, 52B, 52C
knotting paint 102D
lace 107B
knotty 13, 125A, 57
knout 130L, 130N
know 117
knowledge 117
knuckle 150G, 46B
kodak 95B, 119C,
100B
koff 24J
kohlrabi 48K
koniscope 95B
kopi 54C
kopje 149E
Koran 82A
kosher 138C
koto 68D
koumiss 48L
kowtow 98C
kraal hut 53D
village 53F
kraken 143B
kran 147B
kriegspiel 41D
krona 147B
krypton 5D
kultur 81
kumquat 48G
kymograph 95B

L

laager 36B
label name 92
mark 95A, 86,
95E, 104A, 105
labial 55A, 55B
labiate 150G
labor make 144B
difficulty 13
pain 31
parturition 141B
serve 46B, 132D
laboratory 144C
laborious 13, 130B,
144B
labradorite 107E
labrose 109B
labrus 150G
labyrinth 13, 57,
96A
lace fabric 107B
a binding 52C, 52B
beat 130G
lacerate wound
130G
rend apart 145F
impair 130D
laceration 145C
Lachesis 134C
lachrymal 16, 31
lachrymose 31
lack 37
lackadaisical 121, 39
lackey 46B
laconic 58
lacquer 102E
lacrosse 41D
lactation 51B
lactometer 95B
lacuna 25H
lad 148J
ladder 25C
lade 135A, 24C, 24B
lading 135A
ladle 53M
ladrone 49G
lady 140B, 141E
lag 126B, 18A
laggard 126B
lagnappe 45
lagoon 25I
lair 53D
lake 25I, 102E
Lakshmi 135B
lama 82F
Lamarckism 83
lamb 143A, 148J,
110B
lambent 101A, 97,
124
lambrequin 107E
lambskin 106K
lambswool 106A

lame disabled 128A
staggering 18A
deformed 109B
unsound 110B
to cripple 130D
lament 31, 67A, 40B,
67B
lamentable 31, 129B
lamentation 31, 67A,
40B, 67B
lamina 145D
laminate 145A
lamp 101C
lampblack 102D
lampoon 72, 64
lanate 106A
lance cut 145F,
130H, 130G,
130I
lanceolate 150E
lancer dance 99F
soldier 130F
lancet 145F
lanciform 150E
land earth 25G, 5C
gain 49A
win 134D, 50
district 53F
place upon 149A,
49C, 146A, 146K
landau 24H
landaulet 24H
landgrabber 49G
landlord 133A
landrail 48E
landscape 100B, 95C
landsturm 130F
landwehr 130F
lane 25B
language 55A
languid 128A, 126B
languish
weaken 128A,
110A
pine away 31,
128B
long for 39
languor 128A, 126B,
110A
lank 109B, 150G
lanky 109B, 150G
lanner 143C
lantern 101C
lanthanum 5D
lanyard 52C
lap 25A, 150G, 51B,
25B
lapdog 143A
lapidary 100C, 144D
lapidate 130-O
lapis lazuli 102D
102A, 107C,
107D
lappitude 119B
lapse glide away 15
fall 22, 14

slip, error 126C
neglect 126B
sin 130A, 148L,
147K, 148I
lapsus 126C
lapwing 143C
larboard 149J
larcenous 49F
larceny 49F
lard 48I, 48P
lardaceous 48I
larder 48B, 53E
large 147J, 25
largeness 147J
largess 43A
lariat 49C, 52C
lark 71A, 99A, 99C
larkspur 143E
larrup 130G
larva 142F, 143D
larviparous 141B
lascivious 39B, 146D
lash
strike 130G, 130L
punish 130N
bind 52B, 64
lasher 36H
lashing 130G
lass 148J, 142B
lassie 148J, 142B
lassitude 128A, 126B
lasso 49C, 52C
last rear 149I
continue 11A, 12
lowest 129B, 149G
farthest 149N,
127A, 150A,
132A, 148B
lasting 106K, 11A,
148C
lat 147B
latch 49C, 52B
latchet 52C
late recent 148A,
126B, 148B,
148E
lateen 5B
latency 2, 11B, 103A,
110A
latent*
lateral 149J
lath 53R
lather 145J
latitude 149B
breadth 25A
freedom 125C,
25G, 147J, 147L,
149A
latitudinarian 25A,
82D, 114
latter 148E, 149I
lattice 36A
laud 63
laudable 63, 140B
laudanum 136B
laudatory 63

laugh 71B, 72
laughingstock 129B,
110B
laughter 71B
launch plunge 21
expatiate 56
boat 24J, 4, 41C,
20
laundress 138A
laundry 138A
laureate poet 85E,
63, 140B
laurel shrub 143E
distinction 140B
reward 45
lava 16, 146B
la valliere 107C,
107B
lavatory 138A, 53E
lave 138A
lavender 102A, 122
laver 53M
lavish profuse 147I
liberal 43A
waste 131A,
125C-1
law edict 94
license 46A
custom 132D
ban 35
rule 133A
lawful just 140A
allowable 46A
decretory 94
lawless 130A, 125A
lawn 25G, 106K
lawyer 40B
lax 126B, 128A,
130A
laxative 138B
laxity 126B, 130A
lay place 149A
spread 145I
flatten 149C
settle 11B
calm 132B
wager 41D
hide 103A
impute 65
lay eggs 141B
arrange 132A
share 145D
song 68B, 132D,
149G
layman 132D, 46B
lazaretto 136B, 53B
laziness 126B
lazulite 102D, 107D
lazy 126B
lazzaroni 126B
lea 25G
leachery 39B
leacherous 39B
lead conduct 24A, 4,
149H, 40A, 5D,
133A, 134C
leaden 102A, 126B

leader 133A, 4, 6,
149H, 52C
leaf 150H
league 147E, 146K
leak 16, 25I, 25
leakage 16
leal 38, 140A, 89
lean incline 149D
thin 109B
tend 2
sterile 128A, 137A,
149G, 150G
lean-to 53D
leap 9, 17
leap-year 148K,
148H
learn 116
learned 117
lease 46A, 49D
leash 52B, 147A,
52A, 52C
least 147K
leather 106K, 130G
leatherback 143F
leatherette 106K
leathern 106K
leave depart 15
permit 46A
except 35
desist 47, 132C
bequeath 43A
begone 35A, 91
leaven taint 146C, 1,
130E, 137B, 3A
lecher 125C, 146E,
39C
lechery 125C, 146E
lection 82A
lectionary 81
lector 81
lecture 85A, 81, 64
ledge 149K
ledger 86
lee 149J
leech 143F, 143B
leek 143E
leer 98B, 119A
lees 129A
leeward 149J
leeway 149J
left 149J, 15
left-handed 149J,
126A, 126D
leg 53R, 150G
legacy 43A
legal 46A, 94, 140A
legalism 133A
legality 46A, 94
legalize 94, 133A
legal tender 3A
legatee 49B
legation 133A, 53D
legend 85D, 148A
legendary 85D, 85A,
148A
legerdemain 99B,
134B

leggings 106J
leghorn bonnet 106H
  fowl 143C
legibility 95E
legible 95E, 84
legion 147I, 146K
legionary 147I
legislate 94, 133A
legislation 94, 133A
legislative 94, 133A
legislator 94, 133A
legislature 133A, 94
legitimacy 46A, 140A, 94
legitimate*
legitimation 94, 133A
legume 143E
leipoa 143C
leisure 71A, 46A, 126B
leisurely 126B
lemon 48G
lemonade 48J
lemur 143A
lend 46A, 43A, 45
length 147L, 148I
lengthen 10, 149C, 149N
lengthwise 149C
lengthy 56
leniency 47
lenient 47
lenitive 132B, 136B, 14, 136A
lenity 132B, 136A
leno 106K
lens 95E
lenticular 150C
lentil 143E, 48M
leonine 137B, 140B
leopard 143A
leper 128B
leprosy 130E, 128B
leprous 128B, 129A
lesion 128B
less 147K
lessee 54B
lessen 14, 147K, 130D
lesson 81
lest 127A
let 46A, 44
lessor 46A, 44
lethal 130-O, 130M
lethargy 110A, 126B
letheomania 110A
letter 55B, 85B, 79
leu 147B
lev 147B
levant 15, 35A
levee 36H
level 149C, 95B, 132A, 105, 149G
lever 24B, 145F
leverage 24B

leveret 143A
leviathan 147J, 143B
levigate 145H
levitation 135A, 71A
levity
  lightness 135A
  gaiety 71A, 71B
  inconsistency 60
  fickleness 3C
levy 49C, 49A
lewd 125C-3, 146D, 39B, 39C
lexicographer 86
lexicology 83
lexicon 86
liability 46B, 127A
liable 46B, 127A
liaison 39C, 146D, 125C-3
liar 62
libel 65
libelous 65
liberal
  generous 43A
  plentiful 147I
  intellectual 117
liberalism 125C
liberality 43A, 117, 125C-1
liberate 47, 145A
liberator 47
libertine 39C, 146E, 125C-3
libertinism 125C-3, 146D, 39C
liberty 46A, 125C
libidinous 39B
libra 147B
librarian 133A
library 86, 81
libratory 3B
librettist 85E
libretto 85B
lice 143D
license 46A, 125C-3
licentiate 46A
licentious 39B, 125C-3, 146D, 39C
lichen 143E
licit 46A
lick 51B, 130G
lickerish 48P
lickspittle 63
licorice 48P, 48F
lid 36I
lie rest 11B, 12, 62, 149G
liege 46B, 133A
lien 52A
lieu 149A
lieutenancy 133A
lieutenant 133A
life 137C, 148J, 1, 137B, 148C
lifeguard 34
lifeless 128A

lift 24B, 49F, 24H, 139B
ligament 52C
ligature 52C
light
  illuminate 101A 101C
  not heavy 135A
  gay 71A
  graceful 134B
  to kindle 8
  fall upon 22, 146A
  happen 127A, 5A
  lighten 95E, 101A, 95C
lighter 24J
lighthouse 101C, 98A
lightning 101A, 125B
like 38, 105, 51A
likely 2, 127A, 132A
liken 105
likeness 100B, 105
likewise 10
liking 38
lilac 102A, 143E
Lilith 141E, 127B
Lilliputian 147K
lilt 68B, 68A
lily 143E
limb 53R, 150G, 129B
limber 3C, 24H, 46B
limbo 130N
limbus 130N
lime 48G, 145B
limelight 101A, 101B
limerick 85C
limp 18A
limit 52A, 52H
limitation 52A, 13
limitless 11A
limn 100A
limousine 24H
limp 3C, 18A, 128A
limpsy 128A
lin 143E
linchpin 52D
linden 143E
line cord, etc., 52C
  1/12th inch 147E, 85B, 141G, 25B, 146K
lineage 141G
lineal 141G, 141B
lineament 100B, 95C
linear 149C
linen 106K, 106G
liner 24J
ling 143B
linger 126B
lingerie 106G
lingo 55A
linguist 55A
linguistic 55A, 83, 56
linguistics 83
lingulate 150G

liniment 136B
lining 106K
link connect 146A, 52B
  torch 101C
  a measure 147E
  golfing grounds 25G
linoleum 107E
linotype 55B
linseed 142F
lint 52C
lintel 53R, 143E
lion animal 143A
  courageous 42
lionize 63, 139B
lip 55A, 150G, 67A
lipped 150G
lippy 64
liquation 145J
liquefacient 145J
liquefy 145J
liquer 48L
liquid 145J, 16, 55A, 68A
liquidate 45, 43B
liquidation 45
liquor 48L
lira 147B
lisle 107B
lisp 69A, 70
lissom 3C, 9, 108, 134B
list catalogue 86
  incline 149D
listen 118
listerine 136B
listing 86
listless 126B, 128A, 110A
litany 88, 40B
litas 147B
litchi 143E
liter 147F
literacy 117
literal 84, 134A
literary 85B, 85A
literate 85B, 117, 84, 85A
literati 85E
literature 85B, 85E
lithe 3C, 9, 108, 134B
lithesome 3C, 9, 108, 134B
lithic 146B
lithium 5D
lithograph 100B, 100A
lithography 100A
lithotint 100B
litigant 27, 41D, 66, 41B
litigate 27, 41D, 41B, 66
litigation 27, 41D, 41B, 66

litigious 27, 41D, 66, 41B, 66
litter bedding 53-O
  carrier 24H
  rubbish 129A, 125A, 142E, 141B
litterateur 117
little 147K, 128A
littoral 149J, 149L, 25G
liturgic 40B, 95D
liturgy 40B, 95D
live have soul 137C
  subsist 51A
  reside 54A
  endure 11A
  quick 9, 137B, 131B, 2
livelihood 49A, 51A, 45
liveliness 9, 137B, 3C
lively 9, 137B, 3C, 71A, 137C
live-oak 143E
liver 25E, 150G
livery 106B
liveryman 46B
livid 102A, 102C
living 49A, 51A, 45, 137C
lixiviate 145J
lizard 143A
llama 143A, 24G
llano 25G
lo 91, 95D
loach 143B, 110B, 251
load 135A, 24B, 13, 149A
loaf 48E, 126B, 18A
loafer 126B, 129B
loan 45, 46A
loath 27, 132C, 129B, 126B
loathe 28
loathing 28, 31
loathsome 129B, 130C, 109A, 123, 130A
lobby 53E, 40B, 25B
lobbyist 40B
lobe 150G
lobster 143B
local 149M, 24H
localism 55A, 132D
locality 149A
localize 149A, 149M
locate 149A
location 149A
loach 25I
loch 25I
lock 49C, 106A, 52B
locker 53I
locket 107C
lockjaw 138B

lockout 35, 35A
lockup 52H
locomotion 19A
locomotive 24H, 19A
locust 143D
locution 55A
lodge 54A, 11B, 53D, 149A, 139A, 146K
lodger 54B
lodging 53D
lodgment 149A, 49E, 139A
loft 53E
loftiness 149F
lofty 149F, 28, 140B, 95D, 108, 149E
log a timber 53R, 86, 95B, 110B
logarithm 147L
logarithmic 147L
log-book 86
loggerhead 143F, 143B, 110B
logic 114, 115
logical 114, 115, 84, 59, 117
logician*
logistics 114, 134B, 24A, 43B
logograph 55B
logomachy 66
logrolling 146A, 63
loiter 126B, 18A
loll 126B
lone 145K, 147A
lonely 37, 31, 145K
lonesome*
long not short 147J, 56, 11A, 39, 148C, 149N, 150G
longboat 24J
longbow 130I
longcloth 106K
long-dozen 147A
longevity 148J, 148C
longhand 55B
longing 39
longitude 149J, 149A
longitudinal 149C
longshoreman 24E, 46B
loo 41D
looby 18A, 126D, 110B
look see 119A, 119E, 95C, 98B
lookout 119E
loom appear 95C, 5B, 95E
loop 150C
loophole 25
loony 110B
loord 110B

loose
  unfasten 145A
  lax 126B
  bad 130A, 125C, 145K
loosen 145A
loot 49G, 45
lop 145F
lopsided 149D, 125A
loquacious 56
loquacity 56
lorcha 24J
lord 82E, 133A
lordliness 140B, 28
lordship 133A
lore 117, 81
lorette 39C, 125C, 146E
lorgnette 95E
lorikeet 143C
loris 143A
lorn 127B, 145K
lorry 24H
lory 143C
lose 127B, 14, 149A
loss 127B, 14
lost 127B, 112, 149N, 149A
lot 147I, 134C, 146A, 13
Lothario 39C, 125C-3, 146E, 40
lotion 136B, 138A
lottery 127A
lotto 41D
Lotus 143E
louchettes 95E
loud noisy 69B
  showy 95D
  ill-smelling 123
lough 25I
lounge 126B, 53-O
loup 103A, 103B
louse 143D
lousy 129A
lout 126D, 129B, 18A
louver 101C
lovability 140B
lovable 140B, 38
love
  affection 39A, 39, 38, 40, 140B
love-apple 48K, 143E
love-bird 143C
love-child 146D
love-feast 51A, 95D
love-gift 45
loveliness 108, 140B
lovely 108, 140B, 40A
lover 39A, 38, 40
loving 39A, 39
low not high 149G
  depressed 31, 128A
  not much 147K, 69A, 68A, 69B, 70, 129B

lower lessen 14
  weaken 130D
  humble 65
  place low 22, 149G, 21, 97, 33
lowering 33, 97
lowermost 149G
lowland 25G
lowly 129B
loyal 38, 140A
loyalist 140A, 38
loyalty 38, 140A
lozenge 48P, 150D, 48F
lubber 126D, 110B, 18A
lubricate 5A
lubricator 5A
lubricity 39C, 125C-3, 57, 146D
lucerne 48N, 143E
lucernal 101A, 101C
Lucianism 82B
lucid 101A, 84, 95E
lucidity 101A, 84
Lucifer 130N, 101C, 101D, 131B
luck 134D, 127B, 127A
lucky*
lucrative 49A, 45
lucubration 85B, 116
ludicrous 99A, 72, 109A
luff 18C, 23
lug ear 118, 150G
  pull 24A
luggage 13
lugger 24J
lugsail 5A
lugubrious 31
lugworm 143F
lukewarm 128A, 145J
lull 132B
lullaby 68B
lumber 53R
lumberman 144D
luminary 81, 117, 101D
luminiferous 101A
luminous 101A, 84
lummox 110B
lump 146A, 146C, 109B, 145D
lumper 130F
lumpfish 143B
lumpy 146B, 109B
lunacy 110B
lunar 148K
lunate 150C
lunatic 110B
lunation 148H
lunch 51A, 48A
luncheon 48A, 51A
lung 25F
lunge 130G

lupine 49G, 143E
lurch 18C, 13, 128A
lure 40A, 12
lurid 102C, 97, 102A
lurk 103A
luscious 48P
lush 48P, 48L, 64, 91
list 39B
lust 39B
luster (B. lustre)
101A, 106K
lustful 39B, 137B
lustiness 137B
lustral 138C, 108,
138B
lustration*
lustrous 101A
lustwort 143E
lusty 137B
lute 68D
lutecium 5D
lutheran 82A, 82D
luxuriance
exuberant 26
lavish 43A, 147I,
108
luxuriant*
luxuriate 43A, 71A
luxurious 136A, 71A
luxury 136A, 71A
Lyceum 81
Lycurgan 134A, 140A
lyddite 145E, 130K
Lydian 128A, 39B
lying 62, 149C, 149G
lymphad 24J
lymphatic
110A, 126B
lynch 130-O
lynx 143A
lynx-eyed 119E
lyre 68D
lyre-bird 143C
lyric 68A, 85C, 68B,
85A
lyrist 68H, 85E

M

ma 146I, 141E
macaco 143A
macaroni 48E
macaronic 57, 85C
macaroon 48E
macaw 143C
mace 104D, 130L
macerate 145J, 130B
machete 145F
Machiavellian 5A
deceitful 62, 130A,
132D, 133A, 57
Machiavellianism*
machination 130A
machine 5B
machine gun 130K,
130I
machinery 5B

machinist 144D
mackerel 143B
mackintosh 106D
mackle 102C
macled 102C
macro 147J
macrocosm 146A
macrometer 95B
macropsis 119B
mad 29, 110B
madam 140B
madcap 125C-2,
126A, 129B, 42
madden 130C
madder 143E, 102E
made 144E
Madeira 48L
mademoiselle 140B
madonna 100B, 82E
madras 106K
madrigal 68B, 85C
Magdalen 140A
magenta 102D
maggot 143D
maggoty 129A, 113,
128C
Magi 117
Magian 134B, 95A
magic 99B, 96A, 99A,
117, 134B
magician 99D, 117,
134B
magisterial 133A, 94
magistracy 94
magistrate 133A, 94
magnanimity 140A,
43A
magnanimous 38, 42,
43A, 140A, 140B
magnate 140B
magnesium 5D
magnet 39, 137B,
140B
magnetic 39, 108
magnetics 83
magnetism 49A, 39
magnetize 8, 50
magnetograph 95B
magnetometer 95B
Magnificat 68B
magnificent 108,
95D, 140B, 68A,
95E, 99A
magnifico 140B, 133A
magnifier 10, 95E
magnify 10, 62, 63
magniloquent 68A,
76
magnitude 147L,
147J, 135B
magnolia 143E
magnum 53N
magpie 143C

maguey 143E
Maharajah 140A,
133A
maharmah 106H
mahatma 82F
Mahdi 82F
Mahdism 82B
Mahdist 82F
mahogany 143E
mahout 24E
maid 148J, 46B, 138C
maiden 148J, 138C,
130-O, 140A
maidenhair 143E
maidenhead 138C
maidenhood 138C
maidenly 138C
mail 36C, 79, 24A,
36
maim 130D
main 25I, 126A,
133A, 137B,
140B, 149H
mainmast 53R
mainsail 5B
mainsheet 5B
mainstay 53R, 137B
maintain
support 43B, 48A
hold 132C, 36, 11A,
138D, 80, 93
maintenance*
maize 48M
majestic 108, 140A,
95D, 98B
majesty 108, 140B
major 133A, 147L,
147I, 148H
major-domo 133A
major-general 133A
majority 147I, 148H,
146K
make 144B, 86, 50, 8,
150A
Maker 82E
makeshift 46B
maladroit 126D
malady 128B, 130E
Malaga 48L
malaise 31, 32
malapert 130C, 64
malapropism 60
malapropos 126A
malcontent 27, 37
male 148J, 141A
malediction 65, 64
malefactor 130A
malevolent 28, 130A,
130M
malfeasance 130A
malformation 109B
malice 28
malicious 28, 130M
malign hateful 28
slander 65, 130E,
130M
malignancy 28, 130A

malignant 28, 130A,
130M
maligner 28, 65,
130A, 62
malignity 28, 65
malinger 62, 103B
malison 65, 64
mall 5B, 25B
mallard 143C
malleable 3C
mallet 5B
mallow 143E
malmsey 48G
malodorous 123
Malpomene 130-O
malpractice 130A
malt 48M
Malthusian 132C,
52A
maltose 48P
maltreat 130B, 130M
malversation 130A,
49F
mamma 141E, 146I,
48A
mammae 48A, 43B
mammal 48A, 43B,
143A
Mammalia 143A, 48A
mammalian*
mammary 150G, 25E
mammillary 150G
mammodis 106K
mammon 135B, 39,
49E
mammoth 147J,
143A
man adult 148J
male progenitor
141E
male servant 46B
husband 146J, 34,
143A
manacle 52A
manage 133A, 132D,
134B
manageable 46A, 46B
management 133A,
134B
manager 133A, 48A
manatee 143B
manbote 45
mandamus 94
mandarin 133A, 48G,
102A
mandatary 46B
mandate 94
mandible 150G
mandolin 68D
mandrake 143E
mandrill 143A
mane 106A
manege 81, 134B
maneuver 134B,
24A
manful 42
manganese 5D

mange 130E
manger 53I, 53E
mangle 130G, 130D
mangler 145H, 130G
mango 48G
mango fish 143B
mangosteen 48G
mangrove 143E
mangy 128B
manhandle 130G
manhood 42, 137B
mania 38, 110B, 39
maniac 110B
manicure 107A, 145F
manifest show 95A
　　make plain 95E,
　　84, 86, 93
manifesto 80, 93, 79
manifold many 147I,
　　126A, 13, 57
manikin 100B, 105,
　　147K
manila 52C, 48-O
manioc 143E
maniple 106I
manipulate 134B, 62,
　　130A
manipulation*
manipulative*
Manito 82E
manis 143A
manliness 42, 137B
manly 42, 137B, 108
mannish 42, 137B
man-of-war 24J
manometer 95B
manor 133A, 53D
manse 53D
mansion 53D
manslaughter 130-O
mantel 53P
mantelet 36I, 53P,
　　130F, 36B
mantilla 106F
mantle 106D
mantuamaker 144D
manual 86, 81
manufactory 144C
manufacture 144B
manumit 47, 145A
manure 142F
manuscript 85B
many 147I
map 100B, 95B,
　　100A, 105
maple 143E
mar injure 130D,
　　109A, 125A,
　　129A, 130M
marabou 143C
marasmus 128C
Marathon 41D

maraud 49G, 119E
marble 5C, 24D, 146B
marcel 107A, 150C,
　　107B
March 148K
march 19B, 19A, 68B
marchioness 133A
marconigram 55C
Mardi Gras 99A,
　　99E, 148K
mare 143A, 142D,
　　141F
mare's-nest 113
margarine 48I
margin 149K, 147L,
　　36H
marginal*
marginalia 84
marginate 149K
margosa 143E
margot 143B
margravate 133A
margrave 133A
marigold 143E
marine 130F, 23,
　　100B, 24A, 24J
mariner 24E, 23
marionette 99D
marital 146H
maritime 23
marjoram 143E
mark signify 95A,
　　86, 95E, 100A,
　　126A
　　evidence 93
　　target 149H, 12
　　money 147B, 119A,
　　119E, 149A
marker 95A, 86
market 44, 49D
markka 147B
marksman 134B
marline 52C
marmalade 48F
marmite 53M
marmoset 143A
marmot 143A
maroon banish 35A,
　　127B, 102C,
　　102A, 145A
marplot 27, 36G,
　　130M
marque 46A, 93
marquetry 107E
marquis 133A
marquisate 133A
marriage 146H
marriageable 146H
married 146H
marrow 137C, 2
marry 146H
Mars 130F, 41D
Marseilles 106K
marsh 25G, 13
marshal 133A, 132A
marshy 13, 145J
marsupialia 143A

mart 44, 49D
martagon 143E
marten 143A
martial 130F
martial law 133A
Martian 54C
martin 143C
martinet 133A, 81,
　　134A
martingale 52A
martyr sufferer 31,
　　130N, 130-O
martyrdom 130N,
　　130-O, 31
martyrologist 83
martyrology 83
marvel wonder 112,
　　96A, 108, 71A,
　　140B
marvelous (B. mar-
　　vellous) 96A, 108,
　　99A, 140B, 95D,
　　147J
mascot 134D
masculine 42, 137B,
　　141A
mash 48D, 40, 130-O
masher 39A
mask 103B, 103A
mason 144D, 146L
Masonic 146K
masonry 144B
masque 103B, 103A
masquerade 103B,
　　99F, 106D, 103A
mass lump 146A
　　large body 146K,
　　49E, 146C, 147I,
　　147J
massacre 130-O
massage 136B
masseur 136B
massive 147J, 135A
massiveness*
mast 53R
masthead 53R
master 133A, 50,
　　134B
masterpiece 100B,
　　140B
mastery 134B, 50,
　　133A
masticable 48A
masticate 145J,
　　145F, 145H
mastication*
mastiff 143A
mastodon 143A, 147J
masturbation 146D
masurium 5D
mat 138A, 125A
matador 99D, 130-O
match a lucifer 101C
　　pair 147A, 146K,
　　105, 146H, 41D,
　　132A, 131B
matchboard 53R

matchless 108, 134B,
　　140B
matchlock 130K,
　　130I
mate
　　companion 146L
　　sexual mate 146J
　　to associate 146K,
　　133A, 146H,
　　141E
materfamilias 146I
material 5C, 135B,
　　1, 137C, 146B
materialism 82B
materialist 82D
materialistic 82A
materiality 146B, 5C
materialize 146B
materiel 13, 5C, 135B
maternal 146I, 141B
maternity 146I, 141B
mathematical 134A,
　　147L
mathematician 115
mathematics 115
matico 143E
matin 148A, 148K
matinee 99B
matriarch 146I, 141E
matriarchate 133A
matricide 130-O
matriculate 86
matriculation 86
matrimony 146H
matrix 141C, 150A,
　　134C
matron 146I, 141E,
　　133A, 148J
matronly*
matronymic 92
matted 125A, 109C
matter 5C, 146B
matting 107E
mattock 145F
mattress 53-O
maturation 2, 6
mature ready 2, 12,
　　48P, 148J, 132A
maturity 132A, 148J
matutional 148A,
　　148K
maudlin tearful 31,
　　121, 110B
maul 130G
maulstick 53R
mausoleum 104H,
　　52H
mauve 102A, 102D
maw 53Q
mawkish
　　sickening 130E,
　　129B, 109A, 48Q,
　　39
maxilliform 150G
maxim 61B
Maxim gun 130K
maximum 147I

maxixe 99F
May 148K
may 127A
mayhem 130D
mayonnaise 48D
mayor 133A
mayoralty 133A
maze difficulty 13,
  96A, 57
mazurka 99F
me 92
mead 25G, 45
meadow 25G, 48N
meager 147K, 128A
meal 48A, 48M
mealy 145H
mean intend 2
  vulgar 129B
  stingy 132C
  middle 149L, 130C,
    95A, 84, 98B,
    132D, 147L
meander 23, 18B, 13,
  16, 18C
meaning 2, 84
means 5A, 49E, 135B
measly 129B
measurable 115
measure
  determine 115
  instrument 95B
  law 133A
  allot 43B, 147L,
    145D
measurement*
meat 48D
mecca 12, 149H
mechanic 144D
mechanical 144B
mechanician 144D
medal 104A
medallion 104B
medalist 49A, 140B,
  49B, 50, 134D
meddle 13, 130C, 36
meddler 130C, 129B,
  13, 36G
meddlesome 13, 130C
mediæval 148A
mediævalism 148A
median 149L
mediate 91, 132B
mediation 132B
mediator 132B
mediatorial 132B
medic 136B, 116
medical 136B
medicate 136B
medicament 136B
medicine 136B
medicine-man 136B
medieval 148K
mediocre 132D, 129B
mediocrity*
meditate 114
meditation 114

medium 5A, 147D,
  132D, 147L, 149L
medley 146C, 125A
medulla 137C
Medusa 109A, 33
meed 45
meek 46B, 129B
meet unite 146A
  encounter 130F,
    146K, 132A
meeting 146K
Megaera 130M, 130N
megaphone 69B, 55B
melancholia 31
melancholic 31, 98B
melancholy*
melange 146C, 125A
melee 130F
melinite 145E, 130K
meliorate 6, 136B,
  132B
melioration*
mellifluent 68A
mellow 68A, 48P,
  145J
melodeon 68G
melodious 68A
melodist 68J, 68H
melodize 68A
melodrama 99B
melodramatic 99B,
  99A
melody 68B
melon 48G, 48K
melt 145J, 3A, 47,
  132B
melton 106K
member 146L
membrane 52C, 25E
membranous*
memento 104A
memoir 85B, 86, 85D
memorabilia 86
memorable 126A,
  140B
memorandum 58, 86
memorial 104A,
  104B, 104H, 63,
  93
memorize 116
memory 117
menace 33, 98A
menage 133A, 54B
menagerie 53D, 52H,
  99E
mend repair 136B,
  137A, 134A
mendacious 63, 130A,
  62
mendacity 63, 130A,
  62
mendicancy 40B
mendicant 40B
menhaden 143B
menial 46B, 129B
menses 16
menstrual 16, 148K

menstruum 145J,
  145B
mensuration 115
mental 111, 117
mentality*
mention say 55A
  say briefly 58, 87,
    84, 79, 92
Mentor 81
menu 86
Mephistophelian 64,
  28
mephitic 123, 130-O
mercantile 44
mercenary 44, 49E,
  46B, 130F, 129B
mercery 5A
merchandise 5A,
  135B, 144E
merchant 44, 49D,
  49A
merchantman 24J
merciful 47
merciless 130M, 130B
mercurial active 9,
  127A, 3C
mercury 5D, 5C
Mercury 44
mercy 47
mere 147K, 134A
merely 134A, 61A, 27
meretricious 39B,
  39C, 146D,
  125C-3, 44, 130A,
  40A, 49F, 95D
merganser 143C
merge 146K
merger 146M, 146K
meridian 148K, 149F,
  12
meringue 48F
merino 143A
merit earn 49A, 45,
  140B
meritorious 44, 40A,
  140A
merle 143C
merlin 143C
merlion 143C
mermaid 143B
merriment 71A, 99A,
  99C
merry 71A, 99A, 98B
merry-andrew 99D,
  72
mesa 25G
mesalliance 146H
mesh 25H, 25, 25I
mesial 149L
mesmerism 50, 96A
mesmerize 96A, 50
mesne 149L
Mesozoic 148A, 148K
mess diners 146K,
  51A
  confusion 125A,
    43B, 129A, 48A

message 79, 85B
messenger 24F, 79
Messiah 82E
messieurs 140B
messmate 146L
messuage 53D
mestee 146F
mestizo 146F
metabasis 3A, 19A
metabolian 143D, 3A
metabolic 3A, 141B
metabolism*
metagenesis 3A,
  141A
metal 5C
metallic 5C
metamorphic 3A, 3C
metamorphose 3A,
  141B
metamorphosis*
metaphor 84
metaphoric 84
metaphrastic 57, 84,
  115
metaphysics 114, 115,
  83
metaphor 84
metastasis 3A
metathesis 3A
mete 43B
metempsychosis 3A
meteor 101D, 140B
meteoric 101A
meteorite 101D
meteorography 86
meteorologist 83
meteorology 83
meter 95B, 55B,
  147E
methinks 113
method 132D
methodical 132D,
  132A
Methodism 82B
Methodist 82D
methodize 132D,
  132A, 133A
Methuselah 148H,
  148J
meticulous 134A, 32,
  49A
metonymy 84
metric 147L
metrical 147L
metriform 150C
metrograph 95B
metrology 83
metronome 95B
metronymic 49A
metropolis 53F
metropolitan 117
mettle 42
mettlesome 42
mew 145G, 69B
Mexican 54C, 146F
mezzanine 53E
mezzotint 100B

miasma 123
miasmal 123, 129A
mice 142E, 143A
mico 143A
micro 147K
microbe 143D
microcephalous 150G
micrococcus 142F
micrography 83
micrometer 95B
micromillimeter 147A
microphone 10, 55C
microscope 95E
miscroscopic 147K, 95E
microvolt 147M
microzyme 142F
midday 148K
middle 149L, 132C
middling*
midget 147K
midriff 145B
midshipmen 133A
midst 149L
mien 95C, 98B, 98A
might 137B, 127A, 1
mightiness 137B
mighty 137B, 147J, 125C-2, 135B
mignon 108
mignonette 143E
migrant 15, 19A
migrate 15
migratory 15, 19A, 18B
Mikado 133A
mild 132B, 132C, 48P, 147K
mildew 129A, 146C, 128C
mile 147E
mileage 45, 147L
milfoil 143E
militancy 130F, 41D, 27, 67A
militant*
military 130F
militate 130F, 41D, 66
militia 130F
milk 48J, 49A
milksop 110B
mill 144C, 41D, 147A, 145H, 18C
millennial 148H, 148K
millennium 148H
milleped 143D
miller 145H, 144D
millet 143E, 142F
millard 147A
millier 147A, 147C
milligram 147C
milliliter 147E
milliner 106B
millinery 106H

million 147A
millionaire 135B, 49E
millionth 147A
millrace 25I
milreis 147B
milt 141A, 142F
mime 99B, 103B
mimetic 105, 103B
mimic 103B, 99D
mimicker 99D
mimicry 103B, 99B
minatory 33
mince chop 145F, 145H, 132B, 98B, 95D, 68A
mince-meat 48E
mince-pie 48E
mind intellect 117, 111, 114, 119G, 46B
minded 2, 114, 119G
mindful 114, 119E, 119G, 117
mine tunnel 25B
store 53B, 135B, 49A, 49E, 92
mineralogist 83
mineralogy 83
Minerva 117
mingle 146C, 146K, 146A
miniature 147K, 100B
minim drop 147K, 147F, 143B
minimize 14, 147K
minimum 147K
minion 46B, 63
minister
servant 46B
agent 133A
clergyman 82F, 43B, 136A, 136B
ministrant 43B, 133A
ministration*
ministry 133A, 82A, 82C
miniver 143A, 106K
mink 143A
minnow 143B
minor 148J, 147K
minority 148J, 147K
minster 53C
minstrel 85E, 68H
minstrelsy 68A, 68B
mint 122, 43B, 143E
mintage 45
mint julep 48L
minuend 147L
minuet 99F, 68B
minus 14
minute small 147K
precise 134A, 84
1/60th hour 148H, 147E, 147H, 58, 86, 148D

minutely 134A
minuteness 147K, 134A, 84
minutiae 147K, 84
minx 125C-3
miracle 96A, 126A, 144A
miraculous 96A, 95E, 99A, 140B, 147J, 126A
mirage 96A, 113, 57
mire filth 129A, 13, 5C, 21
mirror 105
mirth 71A, 99A, 99C
mirthful*
mirthless 31
misadventure 127B
misalliance 146H
misanthrope 28
misanthropy 28
misapprehend 112, 113, 126C
misappropriate 49F
misbehave 130A
miscarriage 126C, 127B, 141B
miscarry*
miscellanea 126A, 146C
miscellaneous*
miscellany*
mischance 127B
mischief harm 130D, 127B, 130B, 130A, 130M, mischievous*
miscible 146C
misconceive 112, 113, 126C, 119B
misconception*
misconduct 130A
miscreant 130A, 129B
misdemean 130A
misdemeanor 130A
miser 99E, 39, 132C, 49E
miserable 31, 129B
misericorde 130H
miserly 99E, 39, 132C, 49A, 49E
misery 31
misfit 126A
misfortune 127B
mishap 127A
mislead 57
misnomer 92
misogynist 28
misogyny 28
misplace 126C, 149A, 125A
misrepresent lie 62, 103B, 130A
miss fail 127B
err 126C, 126B, 126D, 140B, 37

missal 86
missile 130J
missing 127B, 37, 149N, 149A
mission 46B, 45, 133A
missionary 82F
missioner 82F
missive 85B, 79
misspell 126C
mist 145J
mistake 126C, 110B
mister 140B
mistletoe 143E
mistral 125B
mistreat 130G
mistress 133A, 146I, 39A, 125C, 146E, 141E
mistrust 30
misty in mist 145J, 97, 101A, 57
misunderstanding 113, 126C, 27, 66
mite 143D, 147K
miter 106I, 106H
mitigate 14, 136B, 136A, 138D, 132B
mitigation*
mitrailleuse 130I
mitriform 150C
mitten 106C
mittimus 94
mix blend 146C, 146K, 125A, 146A
mixture 146C, 146A
mizzen 149I
mizzle 16, 145J
mnemonic 87, 104A
mnemonics*
moan 31, 67A
moat ditch 25F
fortress 36B, 36
mob rabble 129B, 146K, 130F
mobcap 106H
mobile 3C, 19A
mobility 3C
mobilize 146K
mobocracy 133A
moccasin 106J
mocha 48J
mock ridicule 72
mimic 103B
false 62
mockery*
mocking bird 143C
modal 132D
modality 132D
mode 132D, 126A
model pattern 105, 95B, 100B
example 84, 144A, 100A, 150A
modeler 100C, 144A, 105

modeling 144A, 100A
moderate lessen 14
  qualify 132A, 132C, 132B, 147K
moderation 132C, 132B
modern 148E
modernize 132D, 148E
modest 132C, 147K, 138C, 32, 129B
modesty*
modicum 147K
modification 3A, 126A
modify*
modish 108, 14, 132B
modiste 106B, 144D
modulate change 3A, 126A, 68A, • 132A
modulation 3A, 68A
Mogul 133A, 140B
mohair 106K
Mohammedan 82D, 82A
Mohammedanism 82B
moiety 147A
moist 145J
moisten 145J, 146C
moisture 145J
moke 143A
molar 145F
molasses 48H
mold rich soil 142F
  matrix 150A, 128C, 129A, 144B, 100A, 134C, 144E
molder decay 128C
molding 107E
moldy 128C, 129A
mole 143A, 36H
molecular 147K, 145D, 145K
molecularity*
molecule 145D
moleskin 106K
molest 130B
mollify 136B, 136A
mollusk 143B
mollycoddle 110B
Moloch 82E, 131B
molt 145G
molten 145J
molybdenum 5D
moment 148D, 135B
momentary 148D
momentous 135B, 2
momentum 137B, 2, 24C, 137C
monad 147A, 142F, 147K
monandrous 146H
monarch 133A

monarchism 133A
monarchist 133A
monarchy 133A
monasterial 53D, 53C
monastery 53C
monastic 53C, 54A
monasticism 133A
Monday 148K
monetary 137B, 135B
monetization 147B
monetize 147B, 144B
money wealth 135B, 147B, 45
moneyed 135B
moneyless 128A
monger 49D
mongoos 143A
mongrel 146F
monism 82B, 83, 146A
monist 83, 82D
monistic 82A, 146A
monition notice 95A, 77, 87, 33
monitive 79, 77, 33
monitor alarmer 79, 33, 77
  instructor 81, 24J, 36B, 143A
monitorial*
monitory*
monk 82D
monkey 143A, 129B
monkey-boat 24J
monkey-wrench 49C
mono 147A
monody 68B, 85C
monogamy 146H
monogenesis 141B, 141A
monogram 104A, 92
monograph 85B
monolith 104H, 53R
monologue 90
monomania 110B
monomaniac 110B
monoplane 24I
monopoly 49D, 53A
monopolize*
monosyllable 55B
monotone 100B, 70
monotonous 56, 70, 132D, 1, 69C
monotony 132D, 130B, 70
monsieur 140B
monsoon 125B
monster
  prodigy 126A, 96A
  cruel person 130M
  ugly person 109A, 109B, 130A, 33, 129B, 147J
monstrosity 109B, 109A, 126A, 130A, 129B, 96A, 130M, 147J

monstrous*
montebank 126D, 130A
month 148H, 147H
monthly 148K
monument 104H
monumental
  large 147J, 11A, 139B, 104A
moo 69B, 70
mood 2, 121
moody 31, 98B, 97, 29
moon 101D, 148H, 110A
moonsail 5B
moonshine 101A, 48I, 35
moonshiner 49F, 130A
moonstone 107C
moonstruck 110B
moonwort 143E
moony 110B, 121, 112, 113, 39A
moor secure 52B, 25G, 149A
moorage 49C, 52B
moorland 25G
mooring 49C, 52C
moose 143A
moot 40A, 46B
mop 138A
mope 31, 11B
moquette 107E
mora 143E
moral good 140A, 138C, 132C, 132D, 61B
morale 42
moralist 84, 81
morality 132D
moralize 84, 81, 61B
morass 25G, 13
moratorium 148B, 148L, 148I
morbid 128B, 130E
morbific 130E
mordant 11B, 64
more 10, 147I, 140B, 146A
moreen 106K
morello 48G
moreover 10, 84, 146A
morganatic 146H
morgue 53C, 53B, 95A
moribund 128A, 128B
morion 36C
Mormon 82A, 82D
Mormonism 82B, 146H
morning 148A, 148K
morocco 106K
moron 110B

morose sad 31, 27, 29, 98B
morphology 83
morrow 148B, 148K
morse 143B, 49C
morsel 147K, 48A
mort 143B
mortal fatal 130-O
  wicked 130A, 125C-2, 143A
mortality 130-O
mortar vessel 53M, 52F, 130I
mortgage 93, 45, 44
mortgagee 49B, 93
mortgagor 45
mortification 128C, 129B, 32, 130C, 31
mortify rot 128C
  repress 132C, 65, 129B, 130B
mortise 53I, 145F, 49B
mortuary 52H
Moslem 82A, 82D
mosque 53C
mosquito 143D
moss 25G, 143E
most 147I, 140B
mot 61B, 59
mote assembly 146K, 147K, 133A
motet 68B
moth 143D
mother 146I, 141E, 141D, 1, 48A, 141B
motherless 127B, 145K
mother-in-law 146J
motion change 3A
  progress 19A, 137C, 8, 39A, 39, 87, 16, 98B, 98A
motionless 132B
motivate 116
motive 1, 8, 12, 39, 149H, 4, 111
motley 146D, 102C, 146C
motmot 143C
motor 137B, 24J
motor-boat 24J
motor-car 24H
motorcycle 24H
motordrome 25A
motorist 24E
motorman 24E
motto 61B
mouflon 143A
moujik 54B, 54C
mouldy 123
moulin 25H, 145C
mound 149E, 104H
mount 149E, 17
mountain 149E, 147J

natatorium 53C, 23
nation 54B, 141D, 146K
national 54A, 135B
nationality 54C
native 54B, 54A, 141B, 137C, 2
nativity 141D, 149A, 1, 53F
natterjack 143F
natty 108
natural 132D, 137C, 61A, 2
naturalism 132D
naturalist 83
naturalistic 137C
naturalize 132D, 126A
naturalization 132D
nature 132D, 137C, 2, 1, 141D
nature faker 62
naught 131A, 128A
naughty 130A
nausea 128B, 28, 48Q, 130B
nauseate 128B, 130E, 48Q
nauseous 128B, 48Q, 130B
nautical mile 147E
nautch 99F
nautilus 143B
naval 23
navalism 23, 26
nave 52A
navigability 25A
navigate 23
navigation 23
navigator 24E, 23, 19A
navvy 46B, 144D
navy ships 24J, 36B, 130F
nay 27
neaped 127B
near close 149M, 146L, 117, 19A, 38, 146A
neat 108, 138C, 134A
nebula 97, 101A, 145J, 57
nebular*
nebulous 112
necessary 37
necessitate 37, 50, 8
necessitous 37, 128A
necessity 37
neck 150G
necklace 107C
necktie 106C
necrological 86
necrology 86
necromancy 77, 62, 117
necromantic*
necropolis 53L

nectar 48J, 48L, 48Q
nectareous 48P
nectarine 48G
nee 137C
need 37, 128A
needful*
needle 145F
needle gun 130K
needs 37
needy 37, 128A
nefarious 130A, 130M, 28
negation 66, 67A, 27
negative 27, 66, 67A, 100B, 125A
neglect 126B
negligee 106F
negligent 126B, 126D
negligible 147K
negotiability 3A, 46B, 45
negotiable*
negotiate 89, 44, 49D, 45, 90
negotiation*
negrillo 148J
negrito 54C
negro 54C
negroid 54C, 146F
negus 48L
Negus 133A
neigh 69B
neighbor 146M, 149J, 146L, 149M
neighborhood 53F, 149M, 146K
neighboring 149M
neighborliness 38
neith 34
neither 27
Nemesis 130N, 45
neo 148E
neodymium 5D
neolithic 148A, 148K
neologism 82B, 55B
neologist 82F, 82D, 144A
neologize 144A, 55A, 79
neology 82B
neon 5D
neontology 83
neophyte 116, 82D, 4
neoplasm 142F
neoplastic 141B
neoteric 148E
nephew 146I
Nephthys 34
nepotism 43A
Neptune 25I
nerve 25E, 42, 7, 52C, 137B
nervous 3C, 32, 112
nervy 42
nescience 110B
nest 53D, 54A, 141D

nestle 149J, 54A, 149M
nestling 142D, 148J
net 49C, 147L, 49A, 146A
nether 149G
nettle anger 130C
    plant 143E
neurilemma 145B
neurology 83
neuter 145K
neutral apart 145K
    reserved 132C
    indifferent 27
neutrality*
neutralize 145A, 130D, 131A
never 148C
nevertheless 27
new 148E, 126A
newel 25C
new-fangled 126A
news 79, 85B
newspaper 85B
newt 143F
next 149J, 148B, 149I, 149M
nexus 146A, 52C
Niagara 16, 130-O
nibble 145F, 145H
niblick 5B
nice good 140A, 134A, 108
nicety 134A, 134B
niche 25, 145C
Nick 130N
nick hack 145F, 95A, 49F
nickel 147B, 5D, 107A
nickelodeon 99E
nickname 92
nidana 52C
nidification 144B
nide 142E
nidus nest 53D
    birth-place 141D
niece 146I
niello 100B
niggard 132C, 39, 49E
niggardliness*
nigh 149M
nighness 149M
night 148K, 148B
    darkness 97
nightingale 143C, 68I
nightmare 113, 33
nightshade 143E
nihilism 82B, 30
nihilist 30
Nike 50
nil 147K, 131A, 128A
nimble 9, 3C
nimbus 101B
nincompoop 110B

nine 147A
ninefold 147A
ninepins 41D
nineteen 147A
nineteenth 147A
ninetieth 147A
ninety 147A
ninny 110B
ninth 147A
niobium 5D
nip pinch 130G, 130-O, 48L, 51B, 130G
nipper 148J, 49C
nipple 25E, 150G
Nirvana 53H
nit 142F
niton 5D
nitrogen 145J, 5D
niveous 102A
no 27, 131A
nob 103B
nobby 108
nobility 133A, 140B
noble excellent 140B, 108, 43A, 42, 133A, 140A
nobleman 133A
nobody 129B
nocent 123, 130D
nocturnal 148K, 97
nocturne 100B, 68B
nod 98A, 22
noddy 110B, 143C
noggin 53M, 147F
noise 69B, 79, 87, 70, 78, 90
noiseless 132B
noisiness 69B, 70, 69A
noisome fussy 123, 130D, 130B
noisy 69B, 70
nomad 19A, 18B, 119E
nomadic 19A, 119E
nomenclature 92, 86
nomial 92, 147L
nominal 92
nominalism 92, 83
nominate 92, 94, 139A
nomination*
nominator 92
nominee 92
nonage 147K, 110B
nonagenarian 148H
nonagesimal 147A
nonagon 150D
nonchalance 28, 132B, 126B
nonchalant 28, 132B, 126B
nondescript 126A, 96A, 13, 92, 109A

none 147K, 131A, 27, 147A
nonentity 131A, 129B, 128A, 147K
nonillion 147A
nonpareil 140B, 108
nonplus doubt 112
  to perplex 96A
  ambiguity 57, 103A
  difficulty 13, 36
nonresident 149N
nonsense 60, 110B, 91
nonsensical 60, 110B
noodle 110B, 48D
nook 53E
noon 148K
noonday 148K
noose 49C
nor 27
normal 132D
Norna 148A, 148E
north 149B
norther 125B
northern 149B
nose 120, 150G, 119E
nosegay 107B, 122
nostalgia 39, 128B
nostril 25E
nostrum 136B
not 27
notabilia 140B, 95D
notability 140B
notable 95E, 140B, 125C, 135B
notary 93
notation 58, 86
notch 145F, 25H, 145C
note brief 58
  explanation 84, 79
  sound 69C, 68A, 86, 55A, 85B, 119F
noted 140B
noteworthy 140A
nothing 131A, 147K, 128A, 129B
notice 79, 119F, 77, 119A
noticeable 95E, 140B, 119F
notification 79, 77
notify 79, 77
notion 113
notoriety 95E, 78
notorious 95E, 125C, 129B, 135B
notornis 143C
Notus 125B
notwithstanding 27
nougat 48F
noumenon 137C, 2
noun 92, 55A
nourish 48A, 81

nourishment 48A
nous 117, 59
novel 85B, 126A
novelette 85B
novelist 85E
novelty 126A
November 148K
novice 116, 4
novitiate 116
now 148E, 148K
noxious
  harmful 130B, 130C, 130-O, 123, 130E, 130M
nozzle 25F
nuance 102B
nubbin 142F, 48M
nucleus 149L, 49A, 142F
nude 95E, 109A
nudeness 95E
nudge 124, 98A, 130G
nudity 95E
nugatory 147K, 128A
nugget 150B, 146A
nuisance 130B, 130C, 13
null 131A, 128A
nullify 131A
nullity 131A, 147K, 128A
numb 110A, 11B, 128A
number unit 147A
  multitude 147I, 115, 147L, 92
numberless 147I
numeral 147L, 92
numerary*
numerate 147L, 92, 86
numeration 86, 92, 115
numerator 86, 92, 147L
numerous 147I
numskull 110B
nun 82F
nuncio 82G
nuncupative 92
nuptial 146H
nurse promote 144B, 136B, 48A, 132C
nursery 141D
nursling 148J, 142B
nutrition 48A
nurture 48A, 81, 6, 10
nut 48C
nutant 150C
nutmeg 48P
nutria 106K
nutrient 48A
nutriment 48A
nutrition 48A

nutritious 48A
nutritive 48A
nuzzle 149J, 149M
nyctalopia 119B
nye 142E
nymph 140B, 108, 96A, 134B, 137C
Nyssa 143E
nyxis 145F

O

oaf 110B
oafish 110B
oak 143E
oakum 52C
oantheism 82B
oar 5B, 24A, 23, 24C
oasis 141D, 145K
oat 48M, 143E, 142F
oath 89, 64, 93
obbligato 68B
obdurate 27
obdurateness 27
obedience 46B
obedient 46B
obeisance 98C
obelisk 104H, 150D, 55B
obese 150G, 109B, 147J
obesity*
obey 46B
obfuscate 96A, 57, 13
obi 34, 106F
obituary 79, 86
object 27, 67A, 149H, 12
objection 27, 67A
objectionable 130C, 13
objective 149H
objurgate 64, 65
objurgation*
oblate 150C
oblation 43A
obligation 46B, 13, 45, 50, 89
obligatory 46B, 8
oblige 8, 50, 46A, 44, 46B
obligee 44
obliging 46A
obligor 49D, 46B
oblique 149D, 57, 18C, 150D,
obliqueness 149D, 146D
obliterate 131A, 35A
obliteration 131A
oblivion 131A, 126B, 110A
oblivious*
oblong 150D, 150C
obloquy 64, 65

obnoxious 130C, 123, 129B
oboe 68G
obscene
  unchaste 146C
  offensive 130C, 129B, 95D, 129A, 70, 109A, 65
obscenity*
obscure dark 97
  ambiguous 57, 13, 103A, 127A, 129B, 65
obscureness*
obsecrate 40B
obsecration 40B
obsequies 95D
obsequious 46B, 38, 32
observance 95D, 119E, 119A, 132D
observant*
observation*
observatory 119E
observe 119A, 119E, 55A, 119F
obsession 113, 2, 38
obsolescence 131A, 129B, 128A, 14, 126A
obsolescent*
obsolete*
obstacle 36A
obstinacy 27
obstinate 27, 113
obstreperous 27, 69B, 41B, 70, 125A
obstruct 36
obstruction 36A
obstructionist 36G
obtain 49A, 11B
obtainment 49A
obtrude enter 20, 41B, 8, 13, 40A, 130C
obtrusion 130C, 130B, 8, 27
obtuse 150D, 110B
obverse 150D
obvert 18C
obviate 35A, 5A, 36, 35
obvious 95E, 93
oca 143E
occasion 127A, 1, 134D, 134C
occasional 127A, 148L
Occident 149B
Occidental 149B, 149N
occipital 149I
occiput 149I
occult 103A, 57
occultation 103A, 97
occulted 103A

occultism 103A, 117
occupancy 54A
occupant 54B
occupation 54A,
    49A, 49D, 44,
    126A
occupy 54A, 84,
    49D, 53A
occur 127A, 111
occurrence 127A
ocean 25I, 147J
oceanography 83
ocelot 143A
ocher 102D
octa 147A, 150D
octagon 150D
octagonal 150D
octahedral 150D
octahedron 150D
octangular 150D
octant 150C
octave 148H
octavo 147D
octennial 148K
octillion 147A
October 148K
octodecimo 147D
octogenarian 148H
octopod 143A
octopus 143B
octoroon 146F
octuple 147A
ocular 119A, 117
oculiform 119A,
    150G
oculist 136B
odd 126A, 126C, 57,
    109A
oddity*
oddments 126A, 146C
odds 126A, 134D
ode 68B, 85C
odeum 99E
odious 123, 129A,
    129B, 130B,
    130A, 130C,
    109A
odium 28
odometer 95B
odontoid 150G,
    150E
odontoscope 105
odor (B. odour) 122
odoriferous 122
odorous 122
of 145D, 145A
off 149N, 149J, 35A,
    91, 145A
offal 129A
off-cast 129A
offend 130C, 130A
offense (B. offence)
    130C, 129B,
    29, 130A, 130F
offensive 130C
    annoying 130B
    attacking 130F,
    129B, 109A, 123,
    129A, 130A

offer present 43A,
    40A, 87
offering 43A, 40A
office 53E, 133A, 92
officer 133A
official 133A
officiate 133A
officious 130C, 13
office 5A
offing 25I, 149M
offscouring 129A
offscum 129A
offset 142A, 45
offshoot 142B
offside 149J
offspring 142C,
    142B, 146F
often 148L, 3B
ogle 119A, 119E,
    39B
ogre 147J, 33, 51A,
    109A, 130-O
ogreish 147J, 33,
    51A
oh 91
oil 5A, 48P
oilcloth 106K
oil-color 102E,
    100B
oily easy 5A
    flattering 63
ointment 136B
okapi 143A
okeh 134A
old 148A, 126A,
    148J
olden 148A
oldish 148A, 148J
oleander 143E
oleograph 100B
oleometer 95B
olfactory 120
oligarch 133A
oligarchy 133A
olive 48G, 102A
olive-branch 104G
olivet 107C
olla 53M
olla podrida 48D
Olympian 82E,
    136A
Olympus 53H
Om 82E, 137C
ombrometer 95B
omega end 12, 74,
    149I
omelet 48D
omen 95A, 79, 77
ominous 95A, 33, 77
omission 126B, 35
omit 126B, 35
omni 148C
omnibus 24H
omnipotence 133A,
    137B, 1
omnipotent*
Omnipotent 82E
omnipresence 149J,
    82E, 149A

omniscient 117
omnivorous 51A
on 149F, 149H,
    146A, 149L
onager 143A, 130F
onanism 146D
once 147A
one 147A
onerous 13, 130B
onion 48K
only 147A, 147K, 27
onomatopoeia 92
onomatopoetic 92
onset 130F
onslaught 130F
ontogenesis 83
ontologist 83
ontology 83
onus 13, 130B, 46B,
    45, 135A
onward 19A, 149H,
    149N
onyx 107D
oology 83
oolong 48J
oomiak 24J
oosperm 142F
ootheca 142F
ooze 16, 129A
opacity 97
opal 107C
opalesce 101A, 102C
opalescent*
opaline 102C
opaque 97
opaqueness 97
open
    unobstructed 25,
    61A, 95E, 93,
    43A, 4, 73, 145A,
    145K
opening 25, 73
opera 99B, 68B, 99E
opera-cloak 106F
opera-glass 95E
operameter 95B
operate work 144B,
    145F, 136B,
    133A
operatic 99B, 68B,
    68A, 99A
operation 144B,
    145F, 132D
operative 144D,
    134B
operator 144D, 55C
operetta 99B, 68B
ophicleide 68G
Ophidia 143F
ophidian 143F, 150G
ophiology 83
ophthalmia 119B
ophthalmic 119C
ophthalmoscope 95B
ophthalmoscopy
    119E
opiate 136B
opine 113, 87

opinion 113, 87, 39,
    92
opinionated 113
opium 136B
opobalsam 136B
opossum 143A
opponent 27, 41D,
    66, 67A, 130F
opportune 134D,
    132A, 40A, 148L,
    132A, 134D,
    148E
opportuneness*
opportunism 49C,
    49A
opportunity 134D,
    40A, 46A, 149H
oppose 27, 41D, 66,
    67A
opposite 27, 149H,
    126A
opposition 27, 66,
    67A, 149H
oppress 50, 130B,
    130D
oppression 130B,
    128A, 31, 130A
oppressive 130B,
    130M, 50
oppressor 130B,
    130M
opprobrious 28, 64,
    65, 130A
opprobrium*
opsiometer 95B
optative 39
optic 119A, 119C
optician 136B
optigraph 95B
optimism 39, 82B
optimist 82D, 39
optimistic 39, 113
option 39, 49A, 46A
optional*
optometer 95B
optometrist 136B
opulence 135B, 49E
opulent 135B
opus 68B, 85B,
    100B
opuscule 85B, 100B
or 127A
oracle 88, 82E, 77,
    57, 117
oracular*
oral 55A
orange 48G, 102A
orangeade 48J
orang-outang 143A
oration 85A
orator 85E, 68A
oratorical 85E, 68A,
    85A
oratorio 68B
oratory 85E, 68A,
    68B
orb 119C, 150C,
orbed 150C

orbicular 150C
orbit path 25B, 150G, 150C
orbital 150C, 119C, 119A
orchard 144C, 143E
orchestra 68H
orchestral 68A
orchestration 68B
orchid 143E
orchis 143E
ordain 139A, 92, 134C
ordeal 31, 130M, 130N, 130B
order method 132A
  regularity 132D
  command 94
  class 92, 126A
  rule 133A, 146K, 134B, 149A
orderly
  methodical 132A
  regular 132D, 132B, 46B
ordinal 132A, 149A, 149I
ordinance 94
ordinary 132D, 129B, 115, 94, 109A
ordinate 149C, 149A
ordination 94, 92, 132A, 139A
ordnance 130K, 130F, 130I
ore 5C
oread 96A, 113, 134B
organ 68G, 25E
organist 68H
organization 132A, 144A, 146K
organize 132A, 144A, 146K, 133A
organography 83
organology 83
organon 133A, 84, 81
organzine 106K
orgasm 146D
orgy 125C, 71A, 99A, 51B
oriel 25
Orient 149B
orient 84
Oriental 149B, 54C, 149A, 149N
orientate 149A
Orientalism 126A
Orientalist 83, 117
orifice 25, 25E
oriflamme 104E
origin cause 1
  beginning 4, 149H, 148A, 141D, 141G
original first 149H

preceding 148A, 105
  beginning 4, 100B, 85B, 126A, 144A
originality 4, 144A
original sin 130A
originate start 4, ·144A, 126A, 141A
orillon 36B
oriole 143C
ornament 107A, 107B, 107E
ornamentation*
ornate 108
ornith 143C
ornithologist 83
ornithology 83
ornithopter 24I
orography 83
orotund 68A
orphan 127B, 145K
orphanage 53C
orphaned 127B
Orphean 68A
Orpheus 68H
orphrey 106I, 107B
orpiment 102A, 102D
orpin 102A
orpine 143E
orrery 95B
orris 107B, 119C
ortho 148C, 134, 61A
ortho 148C, 134A, 61A
orthodoxy*
orthoepy 92, 134A
orthogonal 150D
orthographer 55B, 84
orthography 55B
ortolan 143C
Oscan 54B, 54C
oscillate 3B
oscillator 3B
osculate 98C, 124, 18C, 121
osculation*
osculatory 98C, 104C
osier 143E
Osiris 82E
oslerize 130-O
osmium 5D
osmosis 146C, 3A
osmund 143E
osprey 143C
ossify 146B
ostensible 95D, 95E, 140A, 95A, 103B
ostensive 95D
ostentation 95D, 76, 103B
ostentatious*
osteologist 83
ostelogy 83

ostiary 25
ostracism 35A
ostracize 35A
ostrich 143C
Ostrogoth 54C
other 126A, 10, 147I
otherwise 27
otoscope 95E
otter 143A
Ottoman 54C
ottoman 53-O
ought 46B, 147L
ounce 147C, 143A
our 53A, 92
ourselves 92
ousel 143C
oust 35A
out 149K, 149N, 35A, 145A
outbreak 130F, 16
outcast 127B, 129B
outcome 74, 144E, 147L
outcrop 95C
outcry 41B, 40B, 70, 69B, 31
outer 149K, 149N
outfit 106B, 5A
outgo 45, 50
out-Herod 130A, 130M
outlander 54C, 126A
outlandish 126A, 109A, 65
outlaw 130A, 35
outlay 45
outlet 25
outline 100A, 95C, 86, 150A, 100B, 84
outlook 25, 95C, 117, 119E
outnumber 147I
outport 34, 149K
output 144E
outrage abuse 130A, 130C, 130M, 146D
outrageous*
outre 62
outrider 46B
outrigger 24J, 53R
outright 148D, 146A
outside 149K
outskirt 149K
outspoken 61A
outstanding 95E, 140B, 126A, 135B
outstrip 140B
outward 149K, 95C
outward-bound 149N
outwards 149K
outwit 50
outwork 36B
ova 142F
oval 150C

ovary 141C
ovate 150C
ovation 63, 95D
oven 131B, 145J, 144C, 145B
over 140B, 133A, 17, 149F
overalls 106E
overbear 1, 137B
overcoat 106D
overflow 16, 21, 147I
overhaul 146K, 119E
overhead 149F, 45
overhear 118
overplus 26
overpower 50
oversee 133A
oversight 126B
overt 95E, 84
overtake 146K
overthrow 50, 130-O
overture 73, 68B, 68C, 87, 40A
overweening
  conceited 113, 28, 71A, 62, 76, 38
overwhelm
  crush 130-O, 96A
  conquer 50
overwrought 62
ovicular 142F, 150C, 150G
oviculture 141B
oviparous 141B
ovoid 150C
ovolo 150C
ovoplasm 142F
ovoviviparous 141B
ovule 142F
ovum 142F
owe 46B
owing 46B
owl 143C, 49F
owlet 143C, 142D, 148J
own embody 53A
  possess 52A
  peculiar to 126A
  hold 132C, 78, 61A, 117
ownership*
ox 143A, 24G
oxygen 5B
oye 91
oyer 118
oyez "hear ye" 118
  silence 11B, 91
oyster 143B
ozone 5C
ozonometer 95B
ozostomia 123

P

pa 146I, 141E
pabulum 48A
paca 143A

pace step 19B, 147E, 147L
pachycarpous 53I
pachydactyl 143A
pachydermatous 36F, 150G, 36
pacific 132B
pacification 132B
pacifier 132B
pacify 132B, 136A
pack bundle 146A
great number 147I
press 146B, 146K, 35A, 15, 130A
package 146A
packet 24J
paco 143A
pad 53-O
padding 85B
paddle 24C, 23, 24A, 24J, 130G
paddock 52H
padlock 49C, 52B
paean 68B
pagan 82D, 30
paganism 82B
page 24F, 46B, 119E, 85B
pageant 99B, 95D
pageantry 95D
pagination 86
pagoda 53C
pail 53N
pain suffering 31, 128B
penalty 130N, 41C, 130B, 141B, 130M, 130N, 130B
painful 130B, 31, 130M
painstaking 114, 119G
paint 100A, 84, 68A, 102B, 102E, 102D
painter 100C, 52C
painting 100B, 84
pair 147A, 146H
pajamas 104G
pal 146L, 140B
palace 53D, 139A
palaeo 148A
palaeontologist 83
palaeontology 83
palaestra 25A, 99E
palanquin 24H
palatable 48P
palate 51A
palatial 108, 136A
palatinate 133A
palatine 133A
palaver 90, 56, 40B
pale wane 128A, 102A, 98B, 112
paleo 148A
paleomachic 130F

palette 53M
palfrey 143A
palimpsest 85B, 55B
palindrome 57
paling 36D
palingenesis 141A
palisade 36A, 36, 36B
pall cloak 106D, 106I, 104C, 104D, 128A
palladium 34, 5D, 36B
pallet 53-O
palliate
remedy 136B, 140A, 103A, 14, 138D
palliative*
pallid 128A, 102A, 98B
pallor 128A, 102A
palm 150G, 147E, 143E, 104B, 103A, 130A, 49F
palmate 150G
palmetto 143E
palmistry 77
palmy 134D, 135B
palpability 121, 95E, 124
palpable 121, 95E
palpitate 3B, 121, 69A, 124, 137C
palsy 110A, 128B
palter 62, 130A, 41B
paltry 129B, 129A, 147K
pampas 25G
pamper 48A, 136A
pampero 125B
pamphlet 85B
pan 53M
panacea 136B
panada 48E
pancake 48E
pancratic 137B, 134B
pandect 94, 58, 86
pandemonium
hell 130N, 53C, 69B, 125A
pander 43B
Pandora 130E
panegyrize 63
panel 53R, 86
pang 31, 128B, 130B
panhandle 25G
panic 32, 112, 125A
pannier 53K
panoplied 36C, 36
panoply 36C
panopticon 119E, 100B
panorama 100B
panoramic 100A, 119A

pansy 143E
pant breathe 16
desire 39
pantaloon 99D, 106E
pantamorphic 3A, 150A
pantheism 82B
pantheist 82D
pantheistic 82A
Pantheon 53C
panther 143A
pantochronometer 95B
pantology 86
pantometer 95B
pantomime 99D, 103A
pantomimic 99B, 103B
pantomimist 99D
pantophagous 51A
pantry 53E
pants 106E
pap 48D, 25E
papa 146I, 141E, 140B
papacy 82C, 82B
papaw 143E
paper 52C, 85B
papoose 148J, 142B
pappy 48P
paprika 48P
par 105, 147L
parable 61B
parabola 150C
parabolic 150C, 92, 84
paraboloid 150C
parachute 24I
parade 95D, 25A, 19A, 25G, 95D
paradigm 105, 55A
paradise 53H, 136A
paradox 61A, 57
paradoxical 61A, 57
paraffin 52F, 145B
paragon 105, 100B, 140B
paragraph 55B, 145D
paragrapher 85E
paragraphic 86
parallax 149C, 150D
parallel 149J, 105, 149C
parallelism 149J, 105
parallelogram 150D
parallelopipedon 150D
paralysis 128B, 110A
paralyze 130D, 130-O
paramount
eminent 140B, 149H, 133A,

paramour 39C, 40, 125C-3, 146E
paranoia 110B
paranoiac 110B
parapet 36B
paraph 93
paraphernalia 106B
paraphrase 84, 68B, 56
paraphrastic 84, 56
parasite 143D, 51A
parasitic 51A
parasitism 51A
parasol 36J
parathesis 84
parboil 145J
parbuckle 52C, 52B
parcel 146A, 145D
parcenary 49B
parcener 49B
parch 145J, 14, 131A, 146B
parchment 106K
pard 143A
pardon 47
pardonable 138D
pardoner 47
pare 14, 145F
paregoric 136B
parent 146I, 141E
parentage 141G
parental 146I, 141A
parenthesis 84, 55B, 91
parenthetical 84, 91
paresis 110B, 110A
parhelion 101B, 101D
pariah 129B
Parian 100A
parietal within 149L
wall 145B, 149J
parings 129A
parish district 53F, 146K, 133A
parishioner 54B, 82D
Parisian 54B, 54C
parity 105, 147L
park 25G, 53F, 149A
parlance 55A, 90
parley 90
Parliament 133A
parliamentary 133A
parlingenesis 141A
parlor 53E
Parnassian 85C, 85A
parochial 133A, 110B
parodist 68J, 85C, 68I, 85E
parody 68B, 85C, 72, 99B
parole 89, 92, 61A, 46A
paronym 92, 57
paronymous 92, 57

paroxysm 128B, 130E, 125C-2
parquet 25D
parquetry 107E
parr 143B
parrakeet 143C
parricidal 130-O
parricide 130-O
parrot bird 143C
repeat 75
parrot-fish 143B
parry 36
parse 84
parsimonious 132C, 39
parsimony 132C, 39
parsley 48K, 143E
parsnip 48K, 143E
parson 82F
parsonage 53D, 45
part 145D, 145A, 25G, 15, 145K, 147L
partake 49A
parterre 107E
parthenogenesis 141A
partial biased 113, 38, 39, 145A, 145K
partiality*
participant 49A
participate 49A
participation 49A, 145A, 146K
participial 55A
participle 55A
particle 145D, 147K, 55A
parti-colored 102C
particular 126A, 134A, 145K, 84, 49A
particularity 84, 134A, 126A
particularize 84, 126A
parting 145A, 15
partisan 146I, 113, 145K
partner 146L
partnership 146K, 145K
partite 145K
partition 145B, 145A, 145D
partner 146L
partridge 143C
parturition 141B
party 146K, 99A, 99C
Parvati 136A
parvenu 49B, 135B
pasha 133A
pasquinade 64, 72

pass proceed 19A
a passage 25B
transfer 24A, 18C
outstrip 50
omit 126B, 125C, 93, 46A, 43B, 130G
passable 25A, 140A
passage path 25B, 19A, 19B, 55B
passe 128A, 109C, 109A
passementerie 107B
passenger 19A
passing 19A
passion desire 39
love 39A, 39B, 29, 31, 121
passionate 29, 39B, 39
passion flower 143E
passionless 132B
passive still 11B, 31, 46B
passman 116
passport 93
password 92, 88, 61A
past 146A, 148A
paste 52E, 52F
pastel 100C
pastil 52F, 122
pastime 71A, 99A 99C
pastor 82F
pastoral 85C, 68B, 82A, 110B, 100B
pastorate 82C, 53D
pastry 48E
pasturage 48N
pasture 48N, 48A
pasty 52E
pat 130G, 134B, 134A, 98C, 121
patch 136B
patchouli 143E
pate 150G
patent apparent 95E
spreading 145I
a privilege 46A
disclosure 78, 79
patentee 49A
patera 53M, 107E
paterfamilias 146I, 141E
paternal 146I, 137C
paternity 141G, 146I
paternoster 40B
path 25B, 95C
pathetic 31, 121, 8, 98B
pathos 31, 121
patience 121, 31, 46A, 132C, 46B
patient*
patina 102D, 102A
patness 132A, 134A
patois 55A

patriarch 146I, 148J, 82F, 82G, 141E
patriarchate 82C, 82A
patrician 133A, 140B
patricide 130-O
patrimonial 43A, 49B
patrimony 43A, 49B
patriot 38, 54B, 54C
patriotic 38
patriotism 38
patrol 34, 133A
patron 43A, 34, 6
patronage 43B, 43A, 34, 6
patronize*
patronymic 92
patten 106J
patter 55A, 56, 69C, 69A
pattern 105, 84, 95B, 150A
paucity 147K
paunch 53Q
pauper 128A
pauperize 128A
pause 12, 148D, 32, 126B, 148I
pave 149C, 5A
pavement 25B
pavilion 53C
paving 25B
pavonine 102C, 101A
paw 52A, 150G, 49C
pawl 36A
pawn 45
pawnbroker 45, 49D
pawpaw 143E
pax 104C
pay 45
payee 49B
paymaster 45
payment 45
pea 142F, 48M
peace 132B, 74
peaceable 132B
peaceful 132B, 98B
peach 48G, 130A, 78, 62
peacock 143C, 102C
peahen 143C, 141F
pea-jacket 106F, 106E
peak 149F, 150E, 17, 149E
peakish 128A, 102A, 109B, 150G
peaky 150G, 149E
peal 69B
peanut 48C
pear 48G
pearl 107C, 140B
pearly 102C
peasant 46B, 54B, 129B
peasantry*

pecan 48C
peccability 126C, 130A
peccable*
peccadillo 126C, 130A
peccancy 128C, 130A
peccavi 40B, 91
peck 51A, 130G, 147F
pecker 143C
pectinate 150E
peculate 49F
peculation 49F
peculiar odd 126A, 57, 145K, 134A, 109A
peculiarity 126A
pecuniary 135B
pedagogic 81
pedagogics 81, 83
pedagogist 83
pedagogue 81
pedagogy 81, 83
pedal 19B, 150G, 24C
pedant 81, 76, 95D
pedantic 81, 76, 95D
pedantry*
peddle 43B, 44
peddler 43B, 44
pedestal 53G, 100B, 104H
pedestrian 19A, 19B
pediform 150G
pedigree 141B, 86, 141E
pedometer 95B
peel 36F, 145G
peeler 145G, 49G
peelings 129A
peep 119A, 119E, 69C, 69B, 95C
peephole 25
peer 119E, 119A, 146L, 105, 133A
peerage 133A
peerless 140B, 108
peevish 29
ped 52D
peg 52D
peignoir 106D
Pekin 147B
pelage 106A
pelerine 106F
pelf 135B, 49G
pelican 143C
pelisse 106F
pellet 150C
pellitory 143E
pellmell 125A, 125C
pellucid 95E, 101A
pelt 130G, 106K
peltry 106K
pemmican 48D
pen 52H, 85A, 55B
penal 130N
penalize 130N, 13

penalty 45, 130N, 13
penance 31
penchant 2, 39, 38
pencil 100A, 55B, 101A
pendant 107B, 107E, 104E, 107C, 107E
pendency 112, 132C
pendent 132C, 3B, 149G
pending 2, 112
pendulous 3B
pendulum 3B
penetrability 20, 145F
penetrable 20, 145F
penetralia 149L, 103A
penetrant 20
penetrate 20, 81, 25, 145F
penetrating 20, 117
penetration 20, 117, 119E
penetrativeness 117
pen-fish 143B
pengo 147B
peninsula 25G
peninsular 150B
penis 141C, 150G
penitence 31
penitent 31
penitential 31, 130N
penitentiary 130N, 52H
penknife 145F
penman 55B
penmanship 55B
pennant 104E
penniless 128A
pennon 104E
penny 147B
pennyweight 147C
penologist 130N, 83
penology 130N, 83
pension 45
pensionary 45, 49B
pensioner 49B
pensive 31, 114, 38, 39, 98B
pensiveness*
penta 147A, 68D
pentagon 150D
pentahedral 150D
pentahedron 150D
pentahexahedral 150D
pentameter 85C
Pentateuch 82A
penthouse 53D
penult 149I, 149L
penultimate 149I
penumbra 97, 101B
penurious 32, 132C 49E, 39
penury 39, 37, 128A

peon 46B
peony 143E
people 54B, 141G, 146K
pepper 48P
peppermint 48P
peppery 48P, 29, 67A
pepsin 48P
peptic 48P
peptones 48P
peradventure 127A
perambulation 19A, 19B, 119E
perambulator 19A, 19B, 24H, 95B
percale 106K
perceivable 95E, 111
perceive 111, 119A, 121, 117
percentage 147L
percept 111, 117
perceptibility 95E
perceptible 95E, 95C
perception 111, 119A
perceptive 121, 111, 119A
perceptivity*
perch 143B, 147G, 147E, 53D, 11B, 54A, 149F
perchance 127A
percipience 111, 119A
percipient 111, 119A, 119D, 119E
percolate 16, 145A
percolator 145B
percussion 146A
perdition 130-O
perdu 127B, 103A
peregrination 19A
peregrinator 19A
peremptorily 94
peremptory 94, 80, 58, 84
perennial 11A, 148H
perfect
    complete 146A
    consummate 132A
    pure 138C
    skilled 134B
    precise 134A, 140B, 108, 117
perfection*
perfidious 130A, 62, 30
perfidy 130A
perforate 145F, 20, 25
perforation 145F
perforce 137B, 125C
perform 50, 99A, 133A, 144B
performance 50, 99B
perfume 122
perfumery 122

perfunctory 126B, 126D
pergola 25B
perhaps 127A
perianth 107E
pericarp 53I, 53Q
peridot 107D
perihelion 149M
peril 128A, 33, 127A
perilous 33, 127B, 127A, 13
perimeter 149K, 150C
period 148I, 12, 55B
periodical 132D, 75, 85B, 3B, 148L
periodicity 132D, 75, 3B, 148I, 148L
peripatetic 115, 81, 19B, 114
peripheral 150C
periphrasis 57, 56
periphery 150C
periphrastic 57
periscope 95E, 95B
periscopic 119E, 95A
perish 128A, 131A, 12
perishable 128A
peristaltic 24A
peristyle 25D, 53E
periwig 106A, 106H
perjure 62
perjury 62
perk 107A, 119E
perky 98A, 98B, 9, 71A, 95D
perlustration 119E
permanence 11A, 11B, 148C
permanent*
permeability 25
permeable 25
permeate 20, 145F, 135B, 145I
permeation 20
permissible 46A
permission 46A
permit 46A
permutation 3A, 3C, 132A
pernicious
    hurtful 130B, 130D, 130-O, 130E, 123, 130M
pernickety 134A, 58
peroration 74
perpend 114
perpendicular 149E
perpetrate 130A, 50
perpetration 130A, 50
perpetual 11A, 148C
perpetuate*
perpetuation 11A
perpetuity 11A, 148C
perplex 96A, 57, 13

perplexity 112, 30, 13, 57
perquisite 43A, 45, 49A
perron 25C
persecute 130B, 130N, 130-O
persecution*
persecutor*
perseverance 11A, 39, 11B, 27
persevere*
Persian 100B
persiflage 72
persimmon 48G
persist 11A, 11B, 27
persistence 11A, 11B, 27, 39
persistent*
person 143A
personage 140B
personal 126A
personality 126A, 140B
personate 105, 103B
personator 103B, 99D
personification 103B
personify 103B
personnel 146K
perspective 95C
perspicacious 117, 119A, 119E
perspicacity*
perspicuity*
perspicuous 95E, 84
perspiration 16, 129A
perspire 16
persuade 40A, 40B
persuasion 40A, 40B
persuasive 40A, 40B
persuasiveness 40A
pert 130C, 28, 42, 64, 125C
pertain 53A, 132C
pertinacious 52E, 27, 39, 11A, 11B
pertinacity*
pertinence 132A, 134A, 5A, 53A, 84
pertinent*
perturb 130C, 96A, 125A
perturbation*
peruke 106A, 106H
perusal 116, 114, 119E
peruse*
pervade 20, 145I, 135B, 1, 145I
pervasion*
perverse 27, 29, 130A, 67A
perverseness*
perversion 27, 130A, 62

pervert 130A, 129B, 62, 125A, 130-O, 146C, 146D
pervious 25
peseta 147B
pesky 130B
peso 147B
pessimism 27, 82B, 113
pessimist*
pessimistic*
pest 130E, 130-O, 130B
pester 130B
pestiferous 130B, 130-O, 130E
pestilence 130E, 130-O, 127B, 130B
pestilent*
pestilential*
pestle 145B
pet 140B, 98C, 38, 121
peter 128A
petit 147K
petition 40B
petitionary 40B
petit-maitre 103B
petrel 143C
petrifaction 146B
petrify 146B, 96A, 33, 14
petroleum 5C
petticoat 106G
pettifogger 40B
pettish 29, 66, 67A
petty small 147K
  trifling 60
  insignificant 128A
  contemptible 129B
petulance 29, 66, 3C, 28, 67A
petulant*
petunia 143E
pew 53-O
phaeton 24H
phalanx 146K
phantasm 96A, 113, 57
phantasmagoria 99E, 101C
phantom 96A, 113, 57
pharisaic 82A, 95D, 134A, 62
pharisaism 82B, 62
pharisee 82D, 134A, 62
pharmaceutist 144D
pharmacology 83
pharmacopoeia 86
pharmacy 144B
pharos 101C, 98A
phase 95C, 95E
pheasant 143C
phenix 143C

phenomenal 96A, 95E, 95A, 95C, 126A, 140B
phenomenalism 96A, 82A, 83
phenomenalist 82D
phenomenon 95C, 96A, 95A
phial 53N
philander 40
philanthropic 38, 43A
philanthropist*
philanthropy*
philatelist 49E, 38
philately 49E, 38
philharmonic 38
Philippic 64, 65
Philistine 110B, 132D
philological 83, 38
philologist 83
philology 83
philomel 143C
philoprogenitive-
  ness, 39, 39A, 38
philosopher 83, 116, 114, 117
philosophic 83, 61A, 114
philosophize 114, 81
philosophy 83, 117, 114
philter 8, 39A, 68B, 85C
phiz 95C
phlegm 129A, 110A, 28, 132B
phlegmatic*
phlox 143E
Phoebus 101D
phone 55A
phonetic 55B, 92
phonogram 55B, 92
phonograph 55C, 55B, 92, 68F
phonographic 55B, 92
phonography 55B
phonology 83, 55B
phonoscope 55B
phonotype 55B
phosphoresce 101A
phosphorescence 97, 101A
phosphorescent*
phosphoric 101A
phosphorus 101A, 5D
photo 100B, 101A
photograph 100B
photography 100A
photogravure 100A
phrase 55A, 92, 55B
phraseology 55A
phrenologist 83
phylactery 82A

physeter 143B
physic 136B, 138B
physical 136B, 124
physician 136B
physicist 83, 116
physics 83
physiognomist 83
physiognomy 83, 95C
physiologist 83
physiology 83
physique 150G
phytophagous 51A
piacular 45, 130A
pianist 68H
piano 68E, 68D
pianoforte 68D, 68E
piaster 147B
piazza 25D
pibcorn 68G
pibroch 68B
picador 130F
picaroon 49G
picayune 147B, 147K
piccaninny 148J, 142B
piccolo 68G
pick select 49A
  pointed tool 145F, 49E, 145E, 51A, 49F, 49G
pickax 145F
pickelhaube 36C
picket 36D, 36, 34, 36B, 52A, 52D
pickle 48K, 11A, 13, 112, 129B, 130A
picklock 49F
picnic 99A, 51A, 99C
pictoglyph 100B
pictograph 100B
pictorial 100A
picture 100B, 84
picturesque 100A, 108
pie 48E, 146C
piebald 102C
piece 145D, 85B, 100B, 146A, 147L, 20, 145F, 119E
piecemeal 145A, 145K, 102C
pier 25B
pierce 25, 119E, 130G, 145F
piercing 69B, 70, 117, 119A, 119E
piety 140A, 38
pig 143A
pigeon 143C, 110B
pigeonhole 53E, 53I
pigeon-toed 150G, 109B
pigheaded 27, 110B
pigmean 147K, 150G
pigment 102E, 102D

pigmy 147K, 54C
pigsty 52H
pigtail 106A, 106H
pigwiggen 96A, 113, 134B, 147K
pike road 25B
  weapon 130H, 130J
  fish 143B
piker 49D, 130A
pilaster 53R, 36I
pilchard 143B
pile 143A, 106A, 49E, 146A, 147I
pilfer 49F
pilgarlic 129B, 127B
pilgrim 19A, 82D
pilgrimage 19A
pill 136B, 130B, 35, 35A
pillage 49G, 45
pillar 53R, 104H
pillion 53-O
pillory 52H, 130N
pillow 53-O
pilose 106A
pilot 24E, 24A
pilotage 24A, 45
pilot-cloth 106K
pilot-engine 24H
pimiento 48P
pimp 43B
pin 52D, 52B
pin-cloth 106K
pinafore 106D
pinaster 143E
pincers 49C
pinch inflict 130G, 130B, 49A, 49E, 13
pinchers 49C
pine 143E, 128A, 31, 110A, 39
pineal 150H, 150C
pineapple 48G
pinion 23, 150G, 52A
pink 102A, 143E, 24J, 140B, 100A
pinking 107B
pin-money 135B, 45
pinnace 24J
pinnacle 149F
pinnate 150G
pinochle 41D
pint 147F
pintle 49C
pioneer 25, 4, 116, 119E, 144A, 149H
pious 140A, 38
pipe 25F, 147F, 68A
pipe dream 113
piping shrill 69B, 70
pipkin 53M
pippin 48G, 140B
piquancy 27, 130B, 29

piquant*
pique 29, 130C, 130B, 106K, 124
piracy 49G, 49F
pirate*
piroque 24J
pirouette 99F, 18C
piscary 46A, 49C
piscatorial*
pisciculture 141B
pish 64, 91
pismire 143D
pistol 130I
pistole 147B
piston 24C
pit 49C, 25, 41D, 53E, 130N
pita 52C
pitch 5C, 24C, 18A, 21, 149D, 68A, 147L, 149A
pitcher 53N
pitchfork 49C
piteous 31, 121
pitfall 49C, 13
pith 137C, 2, 58, 137B
pithiness 58, 137C
pitiable 31
pitiful 31, 121, 129B
pitiless 130M, 130B
pitsaw 145F
pittance 147K, 43B
pity 121, 31, 136A
pivot 18C, 52D
placability 47
placable 47
placard 79
place 149A, 25A, 53F
placeman 133A
placid 132B, 98B
placidity 132B
placket 145C, 106G, 106F
plagiarism 49F
plagiarist 49F
plagiarize 49F
plague 130E, 130B, 127B, 130-O
plaguy 130B, 130C, 130N
plaice 143B
plaid 106K, 106D
plain flat 149C, 25G, 84, 58, 93, 95B, 109A, 95E
plaint 68B, 31, 67B, 40B
plaintiff 40B
plaintive 31, 40B
plaintiveness 31, 67B, 40B
plait 107B, 106A, 106H, 107A

plan drawing 100B, 105
invent 144A, 2, 114, 132A, 134C
plane flat 149C
level area 25G, 25A, 24I, 150A
planet 101D
plane-tree 143E
planisphere 150C
plank 53R, 84
plant 146A, 144C, 141A, 130A, 94, 52G, 139A, 143E
plantation 144C, 146K, 53F
planter 144D
plantigrade 143A, 19B
plantule 142A
plaque 100B
plash 25I
plasm 105
plasma 107D, 143D
plasticity 3C
plaster 52F, 136B
plastic 3C, 46B
plastrum 107B
plat 25G
plate a vessel 53M
prize 45, 107A, 150B
plateau 25G, 53M
platform 53R, 53G
platinum 5D
platitude 60, 56
platonic 114, 117
platoon 130F
platter 53M
platyrhine 150G, 109B
plaudit 63
plauditory 63
plausibility 140A, 63
plausible 140A, 63
play 99B, 99A, 71A, 68A
playful 71A, 99A
playfulness 71A, 99A, 99C
playmate 146L
plaza 25D
plea 40B
plead 40B
pleadings 40B
pleasant
agreeable 136A, 71A, 99A, 48P, 122
pleasantry 72, 71A
please 46A, 136A, 99A
pleased 71A
pleasing 136B, 99A, 122
pleasurable 99A, 136A

pleasure 71A, 99A, 99C
plebeian 129B
plebiscite 94
pledge 89, 45
plenary 146A
plenipotentiary 133A
plenitude 146A, 26
plenteous 147I
plentiful 147I
plenty 147I, 26, 135B
pleonasm 56, 75
pleonastic 56, 75
plethora 26, 147I
plethoric 26, 147I
plevin 94
pliability 3C, 46B
pliable 3C, 46B
pliancy*
pliant 3C, 46B
plicate 146A
pliers 49C
plight 89, 13
plinth 53R, 53G
plod 116, 13, 18A, 19B
plot 2, 114, 130A, 25G, 134C
plover 143C
plow 145F, 145H
pluck 49E, 49C, 42
plucky 42
plug stopper 52A, 110B
plum 48G, 135B, 49E
plumage 106A, 107B
plumb 95B, 115
plumbago 102E, 102D
plumcot 48G
plume 106A, 107B, 76, 106H, 107A, 147J
plump 150G, 41D
plumy 106A
plunder 49G, 45
plunge 21, 125C-2, 16, 18A, 22, 127A
plunger 125C-2
pluperfect 148A
plural 147L
plus 10
plush 106K
Pluto 130N
plutocracy 133A
plutocrat 133A
Plutonian 130N, 131A
Plutus 135B
pluvial 16
ply 40B, 8, 6, 39, 144B, 132D
pneumatic 3C
pneumatics 83
poach 49F
poacher 49F

pochard 143C
pocket 49C, 53B, 53J, 147K
pocketbook 53J
pod 53I, 53Q
podgy 150G
poe 48D
poe bird 143C
poem 85C, 55B
poesy 85C
poet 85E
poetaster 85E
poetic 85A, 140B
poet laureate 85E
poetry 85C, 68B, 55B, 68A
pogrom 130-O, 130F
poignancy 130G, 38, 64, 28, 130B, 130M
poignant*
poilu 130F, 117
poinsettia 143E
point 150E, 12, 55B, 58, 95A, 117, 126A, 149A, 149H
indicate 98A
pointblank 58, 95E
pointed direct 58, 59, 95E, 150D, 150E, 134A, 84, 61B
pointer 143A, 95B, 98A, 95A
pointless 60
poise 98B, 135A, 95C, 98A, 132B
poison 130E, 130-O
poisonous 130E, 130-O
poke 130G, 119E, 126B
poker 145F, 41D
poky 126B, 18A, 110B
polar 149B
polariscope 95B
pole 147E
polecat 143A, 123
polemic 66, 67A
polemical 66
police 34, 133A
policeman 34, 133A
policy 133A, 132D, 34
polish 107A, 138A, 101A
polite courteous 98C, 46A, 108, 38, 136A
politesse 38, 136A
politic 117, 133A, 113
political 133A
politician 133A
politics 133A
polity 94, 133A

prawn 143B
pray 40B
prayer 40B
prayer-book 40B
prayerful 40B
pre 148A
preach 81, 85A, 87
preacher 82F, 85E
preadamite 147A,
141G, 148A
preamble 73
preaudience 118
prebend 45
precarious 40B,
127A
precaution 119G
precautionary 119G
precede 148A, 149H,
73
precedence 148H,
149H, 84, 105,
73, 95A, 148A
precedent*
priceless 140B
precentor 95A, 98A,
68J
precept 61B, 82B, 94
preceptor 81
preceptory 81, 94
precession 19A
precinct 53F, 133A,
149K, 149M
precious 140B, 129B
precipice 149K, 149E
precipitance 9, 39
precipitant 9, 127B,
146B
precipitate
throw 24C
urge 8, 9
be rash 42
violent 125C-2,
146B, 126D,
144E
precipitation*
precipitous
steep 149D
hasty 9
rashly brave 42,
125C, 149G
precise 134A, 84, 17
preciseness*
precisian 134A, 133A
preclude 35, 36,
131A, 12, 36A
preclusion*
precocious
smart 117
unusual 126A,
125C, 130C
precocity*
precognition 117
preconceive 113
precursor 79, 77,
95A

precursory 149I,
149H
predatory 49G
predecessor 141E,
149H
preceder 149H
predestinarian 82D,
132A
predestinate 2, 134C,
132A
predestination 2,
134C
predestine 1
predetermine 1
predicability 80
predicable 80
predicament 13, 92
predicate 80, 92
predication 80
predict 77
prediction 77
predilection 2, 38,
49A
predispose 2, 1, 38,
132A
predisposition*
predominance 133A
137B, 50, 1
predominant
ruling 133A
conquering 50
strong 137B
weighty 135B,
135A, 143C, 93,
134C, 140B
predominate*
predomination*
preeminence 140B
preeminent*
preempt 49D, 46A
preemption*
preen 107A
preface 73, 149H
prefatory*
prefect 133A
prefecture 133A,
53D
prefer esteem 38,
78, 79, 149H,
49A
preference*
preferential*
prefix 73, 149H
pregnable 46B, 128A
pregnancy
begetting 141A,
144A, 141B,
95A, 84, 95E
pregnant*
prehensile 49C
prehension 49C
prehistoric 148A
prejudge 115, 113
prejudice bias 113,
62, 2, 13, 38,
135B

prejudicial 113
prelacy 82C
prelate 82G
prelatic 82G, 82A
prelection 85A
prelector 85E, 68J
preliminary 4, 73,
149H, 132A
prelude 68B, 73, 68C
prelusory 73
premature 126A,
148A
premeditate 114
premeditation 114
premier 148A, 149H,
133A
premiership 133A
premise 84, 73
premises 149A
premium 45
premonitory 77, 95A,
33
preoccupy 49C, 54A,
135B
preparation 2, 134C,
6
preparative 2, 5A, 1
preparatory 2, 5A,
73, 1, 4
prepare 5A, 2, 4, 6,
132A, 150A,
134C, 1
preparedness 2
prepay 45
prepense 114
preponderance 133A,
137B, 135A,
135B, 50
preponderant*
preposition 55A
prepositional 55A
prepossess 54A
prepossessing 140B,
108
prepossession 54A,
132C, 113, 53A
preposterous 60, 57,
110B, 109A,
126A, 126C
prerequisite 84
prerogative 46A,
49A
presage 77, 95A
presbyopia 119B
presbyter 82F, 82G
Presbyterian 82D,
82A
Presbyterianism
82B
presbytery 82G, 82C
prescience 117, 119F
prescient 117, 119F
prescribe 94, 132D
prescript 94

prescription 94, 84,
132D, 133A
presence 149J, 95C,
98A, 148E,
148D
present 43A, 148E,
148K, 149M
gift 43A, 79, 95A
presentation*
representation
105, 104A, 149A
presentative*
presentee 49B
presentient 111
presentiment 117,
32, 95C, 111
presentment 95A,
43B, 105, 104A
preservation 11A
preservative 11A,
132C
preserve 36, 11A,
48H
preserver 47
preside 133A
presidency 133A
president 133A
presidential 133A
press 8, 130B, 9, 24A,
50, 146B, 85B,
146K, 53N, 53E,
49C, 41B
pressing 8, 40B
pressure
force 137B
compression 146B
grievousness 130B
hurry 9
weight 135A, 41B
prestidigitation 99A,
99B
prestige influence
135B, 133A,
140B
pristine 148A
presume 113, 42
presumption 113, 42,
28, 71A, 95D,
103B
presumptive 113, 93,
95D
presumptuous*
presuppose 113
presupposition 113
pretend 62, 103B,
95D
pretended 103B, 62
pretender 62, 102B,
103B
pretense 103B, 95D
pretension*
pretentious 95D,
103B, 76
preterit 148A
pretext 62, 103B

prettify 107A
pretty 108, 132C
pretzel 48E
prevail 50, 133A, 1,
11B, 137B, 140B,
135B
prevalence 135B,
137B, 50, 133A,
145I, 1, 134C
prevalent *
prevaricate 62
prevaricator 62
prevent 12, 36A, 36,
136B, 35
prevention*
preventive*
preventorium 136B
previous 148A
prevision 117, 119F
prey 45, 49G, 51A,
48A, 149H
price 45, 147L
priceless 140B
prick 130G
pricking 130G, 130B
prickle 130H
prickliness 130G
pride 71A, 28, 38,
95D, 108
prier 41B, 119E
priest 82F
priestcraft 82A, 82C
priesthood 82C
priestliness 82F
priestly 82A
prig 95D, 113, 103B
priggish*
prim 108, 134A,
107A
primacy 133A
prima donna 68I,
99D
primage 45
primal 148A
primary 148A, 149H,
133A, 4
primary colors
102A
primate 82G
prime first 1, 148A,
149H, 148J,
135B, 134A, 34
primeness 140B
primer 81
primeval 148A
priming 34
primitive 148A,
126A
primitiveness*
primogeniture 49B,
148A, 149H,
141B, 141A
primordial
first 148A, 134C,
133A
primp 107A

primrose 143E,
102A, 71A, 99A
prince 133A, 140B
princely 140B, 108,
43A
princess 133A
principal 133A,
140B, 149H
principia 133A
principle 61A, 82B,
126A, 133A
prink 107A
print 55B, 100A,
100B, 105
prior former 148A
priory head 82F,
82G
priorate 82C
priority 148A, 149I,
149H
priory 82C, 53C
prism 150D
prismatic 150D,
102C
prismoid 150D
prison 52H
pristine 148A
prithee 40B, 91
privacy 103A
private secret 103A,
130F, 145K
privateer 49G, 24J
privation 128A, 127B
privative 27, 126A,
14
privilege 46A, 125C,
49A
privity 102A, 117
privy secret 103A
prize 45, 38
prize fight 41D, 130F
proa 24J
probability 2, 127A,
57, 61A
probate 93, 119E
probation 93, 41C
probationary 119E,
41C
probationer 116
probe 119E, 41A
probity 61A, 140A
problem 41A, 57
problematical 57,
127A
proboscis 49C
procedure 16, 19A,
132D
proceed*
proceeding 132D
proceeds 144E
process 132D
procession 19A,
146K
processional 19A
proclaim 79
proclamation 79

proclivity 2, 149D
proconsul 133A
proconsular 133A
proconsulate 133A
procrastinate 148B,
126B
procrastination 148I
procreate 141A,
141B
procreation*
procreative*
procreator 141E
procrustean 132A,
130-O
proctor 133A
proctorial 133A
procumbent 149C,
149G
procuration 43B,
49A, 130A
procurator 133A
procure 49A
procurer 43B, 130A
prod 130G
prodigal 43A,
125C-1, 147I
prodigality*
prodigious 147J, 96A
prodigy 96A, 126A
produce 144E, 144B,
100A, 141A,
141B, 144A
product 144E, 147L
production 144E,
144B
productive 144B,
141A, 141B
productiveness*
proem 73
profanation 65,
130A, 125A
profane 65, 130A,
146D
profanity 65, 130A
profess 78, 80
profession 80, 146K,
38, 44, 126A
professional 100A,
44
professionalism*
professor 82D, 81
professorate 81
professorial 81
professorship 81
proffer 40A
proficiency 134B,
117
proficient*
profile 100B, 95C,
100A, 150A
profilist 100C
profit 49A, 45, 50,
134D
profitable 134D, 45,
49A

profitableness*
profiteer 49A, 49C
profligacy 125C-3,
39C, 146D,
125C-1, 130A
profligate 146E
profound 117, 13
profundity 117, 68A
profuse 43A, 147I,
56, 26, 125C-1
profusion*
progenitor 141E
progeniture 141B
progeny 142B, 146F,
142C
prognosis 113, 57,
115, 77
prognostic 77, 95A,
57, 79
prognosticate*
prognostication*
prognosticator 77
program 86
progress 19A, 134B,
6, 10
progression 19A
progressive 19A, 6
prohibit 35, 52A, 12
prohibition*
prohibitionist 35
prohibitive 35
project 114, 24C,
149H, 2, 41C
projectile 130J, *
projecting 149H
projection
delineation 100B
a throwing 24C,
149H
projecture 149H
prolate 150C
proletarian 46B,
129B
proletariat*
proliferous 142A,
141B
prolific 141B, 147I
prolix 56, 57
prolixity 56, 84
prolocutor 73
prologue 73
prolong 10, 11A,
148B
prolongation 148I
promenade 19B,
25B, 95D
Promethean 8, 7
prominence 140B,
95E, 149H, 135B,
149E
prominent*
promiscuous 125A,
146C, 127A
promise 89, 40A, 7,
146G
promissory 89

promissory note 93
promontory 25G
promote 6, 139B, 144A
promoter 144A, 6
promotion 139A, 6
prompt 2, 148D, 8, 87, 9, 134A, 148E
promptitude*
promulgate 79, 85A
promulgation*
promulgator 79, 85A
prone 2, 149C, 149G
proneness 2, 149C
prong 49C
pronominal 92, 55A, 58
prononce*
pronoun 92, 55A
pronounce 92, 55A, 94, 79
pronounced 95E, 84, 135B
pronouncement 80, 94
pronunciamento 79
pronunciation 55A, 92
proof 93, 61A, 105, 100B
prop 53R, 5A
propaganda 81, 6
propagandist 81, 6
propagate 141B, 141A, 6, 10, 141E, 145I, 24C, 81
propagation*
propel 24C
propellent 24C
propeller 24C, 18C
propend 2
propensity 113, 2
proper 132A, 134A, 132D
property 135B, 49E, 126A
prophecy 77
prophesy 77
prophet 77, 82F
prophetic 77
prophylactic 136B
propinquity 148D, 149M
propitiate 142D, 45, 132B
propitiation 132D, 45, 132B
propitious 134D, 47, 5A, 95A
proponent 39
proportion 150A, 105, 147L
proportional 147L
proportionate 147L

proposal 40A, 87
propose offer 40A
    solicit 40B
    nominate 92
    suggest 87
proposition 55B
propositional 40A, 87
propound 41A, 87, 73
proprietary 132C
proprietor 132C
propriety 132D, 140A, 134A, 132A
propulsion 24C
propulsive 24C
prorogation 148B, 12
prorogue 148B, 40B
prosaic 132D, 110B, 56
proscenium 25D
proscribe 130N, 130-O, 35, 86
proscriptive*
prose 55A, 56, 85B, 55B, 85C
prosecute 41C, 41D, 50
prosecution*
prosecutor*
proselyte 146K, 146L
proselytism 146K, 3A
proselytize*
prosiness 56
prosody 81
prospect 119E, 95C, 39
prospective 39, 119F, 119G, 89
prospector 39, 119G, 119E
prospectus 100B, 84, 86
prosper 49A, 134D, 50
prosperity*
prosperous*
prostitute 39C, 146E, 125C-3, 44, 129B, 125A, 146D
prostitution*
prostrate 149C, 46B, 128A, 40B, 98C, 129B, 65, 127B, 130G, 149G
prostration*
protean 3A
protein 3C
protect 34, 36
protection*
protective*
protector 34

protectorate 36
protege 146L
proteids 142F
protest 67A, 27
Protestant 82D, 67A
Protestantism 82B
protestation 67A, 80
protocol 86
protoplasm 142F
protoplasmic 142F, 141A
protoplast*
protoplasta*
protoplastic 142F
prototype 100B, 105
protozoa 142F
protozoan 142F
protract 126B, 10, 11A
protracter*
protraction 10, 11A, 100B, 100A, 148B, 148I
protractionism 35
protractor 100C, 49A
protrude 149H, 24C
protrusion*
protrusive*
protuberance 149H, 109B, 149E
protuberant*
proud 28, 38, 95D, 71A, 76, 140B, 108, 113
provable 93
prove 93, 61A, 84
proven 93
provender 48N
proverb 61B
proverbial 61B, 117
provide 43B, 132A, 84
providence 132C, 127A, 134D, 119F
provident*
providential 132C, 119F, 134D, 127A
province 25G, 53F
provincial 54B, 110B
provincialism 55A
provision food 48A, 43B, 84, 89, 119F
provisional 43B, 84, 148D, 119F, 127A, 132A
proviso 89, 84
provisory 89, 84, 119F
provocation 8, 130C
provocative*
provoke 8, 130C, 130B
provost 133A

prowess 42, 137B
prowl 103A
proximate 149M
proximity 149M
proximo 148B
proxy 93
prude 132C
prudence 132C, 32, 117, 103A, 119F
prudent 132C, 117, 32, 103A
prudential 132C, 117
prudery 132C
prudhomme 132B, 133A, 115
prudish 132C, 134A
prune 48G, 145F, 14
prunella 48G
prurience 39B
prurient 39B
pry 41A, 119E
psalm 68B
psalmist 68I
psalmody 68B, 68A
Psalter 85B, 86
psaltery 68D
pseudo 62, 130A, 103B
pseudonym 92
pshaw 91, 28, 64
psyche 117, 137C
psychiatrist 136B
psychic 114
psychical 111, 114, 117
psychics 83
psychoanalysis 115, 83
psychogenesis 116
psychological 115, 114, 117, 83
psychologist*
psychology*
psychometry 83
psychophysics 83
Ptolemaic 126C, 57
puberal 141A
puberty 141A
pubescence 141A, 148J, 106A
pubescent*
public 132D, 95E, 146K
publication 85B, 79
publicist 85E
publicity 95E, 78, 79, 85B
publish*
puce 102A
puck 72
pucker 150G, 150B
pudding 48D
puddle 25I, 129A, 146C
pueblo 53D

puerile juvenile 148J, 128A, 110B, 129B
puerility*
puerperal 141B
puff 16, 125B, 63, 76, 9, 10
puffer 63
puffin 143C
puffiness 63, 150G
puffy 76, 63
pug 143A
pugh 64, 91
pugilism 41D, 130F
pugilist*
pugnacious 130F, 66, 27, 41D, 67A
pugnacity*
puissance 137B
puissant 137B
puke 16
pulchritude 108
pule 40B, 67A, 31, 67B
puling 31, 40B
pull draw 24A
    pluck 49C, 49A
    rend 145F, 41C, 41D, 135B
pullet 143C, 148J
pulley 24D, 18C
pulmonary 51A, 25E
pulmonic*, 136B
pulmotor 8
pulp 145J
pulpit 53G
pulque 48J
pulsate 3B, 137C
pulsation 3B
pulse 3B, 137C
pulsimeter 95B
pulverization 145H
pulverize 145H
puma 143A
pump 106J, 41A, 24B
pumpkin 48K
pun 72, 57
punch 130G, 48L, 99D, 25, 72
puncheon 147F, 53N
punchinello 99D
punctate 102C, 150E
punctiform 150E
punctilio 134A
punctilious 134A
punctual 134A, 148D, 148E
punctuality 134A, 148D
punctuate 145A, 150E, 102C
punctuation*
puncture 145F, 130G, 20
pundit 117, 83
pung 24H

pungent 48P, 122, 72, 64, 48Q
Punic 130A, 127A
punish retaliate 45, 130N, 136B
punishment*
punitive 130N
punk 60, 128C
punka 136A
punster 72, 57
punt 24J
puny weak 128A
    petty 147K, 129B
pup 141B
pupil 116, 119C
puppet 99D
puppy 148J, 142D, 95D, 113, 103B, 143A
purblind 119B
purchase 49D, 24A, 24B
pure 138C, 108
pureness 138C
purgation 138B, 138D
purgative 138B, 136B
purgatorial 130N, 138D, 138B
purgatory*
purge 138B, 138D
purging 16, 138B
purification 138B, 138D
purificative 138B
purifier 138B
purify 138B, 138C
purism 68A
purist 134A, 68A, 84
puristic 134A, 68A, 84
Puritan 82D, 82A, 134A
Puritanism 82B
purity 138C
purl 48L, 107B, 107A, 69A, 16
purlieu 149M
purlin 53R
purloin 49F
purple color 102A, 102D
    royal robe 104D
purport meaning 84, 95A, 95E, 2
purpose design 2, 149H, 12, 27, 39
purposeful 2, 39, 27, 144B
purse 53J, 150G, 98B, 147L, 150B
purser 43B, 45
pursuant 41C, 149I
pursue 41C, 119E, 38, 41D, 149I

pursuer 41C, 119E
pursuit 41C, 119E, 38, 41D, 126A
pursuivant 46B, 24F
pursy 150G, 109B
purulence 128C
purulent 128C
purvey 43B, 49D
purveyance*
purveyor 43B, 48A, 49D
purview 89, 84
pus 128C
push 24A, 130F, 13, 19A, 24C
push-cart 24H
pusillanimity 32
pusillanimous 32, 128A, 147K, 129B
puss 143A, 128C
pussy-foot 119E
put 149A
putative 113
putlog 53R
putrefaction 128C, 123
putrefactive*
putrefy*
putrescence*
putrescent*
putridity*
puttee 106J
putter 5B
puttock 143C
putty 52F
puzzle 96A, 103A, 57, 13, 112
pygmean 147K, 150G
pygmy 54C, 147K
pyjamas 106G
pylon 98A
pyramid 150D, 104H
pyramoid 150D
pyre 130-O, 131B, 145B
pyrocollodion 145E, 130K
pyromania 131B
pyrometer 95B
pyrotechnic 101A
pyrotechnics 101C, 99B
pyroxyline 145E, 130K
pyrrhonism 30
pyrrhonist 30
pythogenic 141A, 141B
Python 143F
pythoness 77
pythonism 77
pyx 104C, 53J

Q

quack 69C, 62, 103B, 130A, 126D, 136B
quackery 62, 130A, 117, 103B
quad 150D, 147A
quadra 150D
quadral 150D
quadrangular 150D
quadrant 150C
quadrat 145B
quadrate 150D, 147A
quadrature 150D
quadrennial 148H, 148K
quadrifrontal 150D
quadrilateral 150D
quadrille 99F
quadrillion 147A
quadrireme 24J
quadrivium 146A, 150F
quadroon 146F
Quadrumana 143A
quadrumanous 150G
quadruped 143A, 150G
quadruple 147A
quaestor 53B, 133A
quaff 51B
quagga 143A
quagmire 25G, 13
quail 32, 31, 15
quaint odd 126A, 57, 109A, 148A
quake 32
Quaker 82D
Quaker-gun 130K, 33
quaking 32, 3C
qualification 117, 134B, 6, 132A, 137B
qualificative 81, 136B
qualify 132A, 14, 6, 134C, 137B, 147L
qualitative 115, 132A
quality 126A, 2, 117, 134B, 135B, 140B
qualm 132C, 128B, 32
quandary anxiety 39, 112, 30, 13
quantify 147L, 115
quantity 147L
quantivalence 147L
quantometer 95B
quantum 147L
quarantine 35, 145A
quarrel 66
quarrelsome 66
quarry 53B, 49A, 149H

rash 9, 42, 125C-2, 126D, 16, 130E
Rasores 143C
rasp 145F
raspberry 48G
rat 143A, 15, 106A
rate 147L, 115, 64
rather 27
rathskeller 48B
ratification 11B, 61A
ratify 93, 94, 92, 61A, 46A
ratio 147L
ratiocinate 66, 114
ratiocination 114, 66
ratiocinative 114, 66, 115
ration 43B, 48A
rational wise 117
  reasonable 114
  sensible 59
rationale 114, 84
rationalism 114
rationalistic 114, 84
rationality 114, 117, 59
rationalize 84, 88
ratteen 106K
rattinet 106K
ratting 15
rattle 56, 60, 69B, 69C
  bewilder 96A
rattler 143F
rattlesnake 143F
raucity 69B
raucous 70
ravage 49G, 128C, 130-O
rave 29, 60, 67A
ravel 145A
raveln 36B
raven bird 143C, 102A, 49G, 51A, 130A
ravenous 51A, 49G, 39
ravine 25H
ravish 49G, 39C, 146D, 99A, 108
ravishment 146D, 39C, 71A
raw 48Q, 128B, 110B, 126D
rawboned 150G, 109B
rawhide 130L, 130N
ray 101A, 143B
raze 130-O
razor 145F
razzle-dazzle 112, 96A, 110A
reach 124, 146K, 49A, 50, 25I, 16, 25A, 147L, 149N
reaction 3C
read 116, 119E

reader 116, 85E
readiness 71A, 148D, 2
readjust 132A, 136B
ready 2, 132A, 134B
real 61A, 137C, 1
realism 83, 100A
realist 83
realistic 137C, 1
reality 137C, 61A
realization 117, 50
realize 117, 50
really 61A
realm 133A, 53F
realty 135B
ream 147D, 145F, 49E, 49B
reap 49B, 49D
reaper 49D
rear behind 149I, 17, 24B, 10, 139B, 139A, 81, 144B, 132A
rear-admiral 133A
reason 115, 117, 114, 1, 8, 40A, 84
reasonable 114, 61A, 140A
reasonableness*
reasonless 60
reassure 7, 134C
rebate 45
rebel 27
rebellion 27
rebellious 27
rebound 3C, 15
rebuff 36, 130F, 50, 27
rebuke 64, 130N
rebus enigma 96A, 105, 103B, 57, 13, 92
rebut 36, 88
rebuttal 36, 88
rebutter*
recalcitrant 27
recall 117, 40B, 41B, 131A
recant 27, 30, 131A, 67A
recantation*
recapitulate 75, 58, 86
recapitulation*
recaption 45, 130N
recede 15, 22
receipt 49B, 93
receivable 49B
receive 49B, 116
receiver 49B
recency 148A, 148E
recension 119E, 86, 136B
recent 148E, 148A
receptacle 53N, 53B

reception 49B, 38, 99A
receptive 49B, 111, 116
recess 15, 145K, 25H, 53E
recession 15
recessional 68B, 68C
recherche 126A, 140B, 108
recipe 84
recipient 49B
reciprocal 3C, 45, 46A
reciprocate 45, 3A, 3C, 43A, 49B
reciprocating 3B, 3C
reciprocation 3B, 3C, 45
reciprocity 3A, 43A, 49B, 45
recision 145F, 15, 14, 145K
recital 85A, 68B, 132D
recitation 85A, 75
recitative 85A, 68A
recite 85A, 68A, 35, 75, 132D, 86
reck 132C, 114
reckless 125C-2, 60, 62, 126D, 42
recklessness*
reckon 115, 113, 92, 114, 147L
reckoning 115, 114
reclaim 49A, 41B, 136B
reclinate 149D, 149G
reclination 149D, 11B
recline 149D, 11B, 149G
recluse 145K, 15
reclusive 145K
recognition 117, 119F
recognizance 80, 61A, 78, 93, 38, 119F
recognize 117, 119F, 46B
recoil 15, 32, 3C
recollect 117
recollection 117
recommend 87, 63
recommendation*
recommendatory*
recommit 43B
recompense 45
reconcilable 132A
reconcile 132A, 132B
reconciliation*
recondite 103A, 13, 117, 57
reconnoiter 119E
reconsider 114

reconstruct 144B
reconstruction 136B
record 86, 93, 149H
recorder 86
recount 85A, 84
recoup 49A, 45
recourse 49A, 40B
recover 49A, 137A, 3C, 132A
recovery 49A, 137A
recreant 32, 40B, 129B, 130A
recreate 136B, 71A
recreation*
recreative*
recriminate 65
recrimination 65
recriminatory 65
recruit 43B, 86, 136B, 130F, 137A, 146K, 49A, 116
recruiting 86
rectangle 150D
rectangular 150D
rectifiable 136B
rectification 136B, 138B
rectify 136B, 138B, 134A
rectilineal 150D, 149C
rectitude 140A
rector 82G, 133A, 82F
rectorate 82C
rectorial 82A
rectory 53D, 45
rectum 25E
recumbent 149C, 149D, 149G
recuperate 137A
recuperation 137A
recur 117, 95C, 75, 3B, 148B, 148L
recurrence*
recurrent*
recurvate 150C
recusancy 126A, 27
recusant 27
red 102A, 102D
redan 36B
redbreast 143C
red-coat 130F
redden 102A
reddish 102A
redeem 49D, 45, 49A, 34
redeemer 34, 49D
Redeemer 82E, 49A, 49D
redemption 49D, 34, 49A
redemptioner 49D
redemptive 49D
redemptory 49D
redgum 143E

red-handed 130A, 95E
red-hot 39
redingote 106D
redivivus 137A
redolence 122
redolent 122
redouble 10, 75, 9, 137B
redoubt 36B
redoubtable 42, 127B, 36, 33
redound 26, 43A
redowa 99F, 68B
redress 45
redshank 143C
redstart 143C
red-tape 134A
reduce 14, 58, 129B, 50, 132A, 145H, 130D, 145A
reduction*
redundance 26, 56, 75
redundant 26, 56, 75, 147I
reduplicate 75
reduplication 75
reecho 75, 69B
reed 143E, 68G, 25F
reef 149E
reefer 106D, 49G
reek 129A, 123, 16
reel 99F, 18A, 112
reenforce 137B
reenforcement 137B
refection 48A
refectory 48B
refer 87, 79, 80, 93, 41A
referee 94, 115
reference 87, 79, 93
referendum 87
referential 87, 79, 93
refine 138B, 81, 6, 134A
refinement 108, 138B
refinery 138B
refit 132A
reflect 114, 117, 64, 65, 105
reflection 105, 114, 117
reflective 114, 105
reflectiveness 105
reflector 105, 101C
reflex 150C, 150D
    reciprocal 3C, 2
refluent 15
reflux 16, 15
reform 136B, 3A, 132A
reformation 136B, 6
reformative 136B
reformatory 52H, 136B, 6
refract 150D, 150C

refraction 150D
refractory 27
refrain 132C, 68B
refrangibility 150D
refrangible 150D
refresh 136B, 8
refreshing 8, 48A, 48P, 136B
refreshment 48A
refrigerant 48A, 48F, 48P, 146B, 136B
refrigerate 146B
refrigeration 146B
refrigerator 146B
refuge 34, 36B, 53D, 53E, 15
refugee 15
refulgence 101A
refulgent 101A, 108
refund 45
refusal 35, 27, 49A, 39, 67A
refuse 67A, 27, 35, 132C, 129A, 129B
refutation 93, 27, 50, 67A, 138D
refute*
regain 43A, 49A, 132A
regal 133A, 140B, 108
regale 48A, 99A, 136A
regalia 106B, 104D
regard 119E, 114, 113, 119G, 38
regardant 119E, 114
regardful 119E, 119G, 114
regarding 119E, 53A
regardless 27, 125C-2, 126B
regatta 41D
regelation 146B, 52E
regency 133A
regeneracy 141A
regenerate 141A, 136B, 3A, 137A, 139B, 141B, 136B
regeneration*
regenerative*
regeneratory*
regent 133A, 81
regent bird 143C
regicidal 130-O
regicide 130-O
regime 132D, 133A, 94
regimen*
regiment 130A
regimental 130A, 106B, 133A
regimentation 133A

region 25G, 53F, 149A
register 86
registrar 86
registration 86
registry 86
regnal 133A
regnant 133A, 135B
regression 15, 128A, 128C
regret 31
regretful 31
regrettable
    bad 130A, 126B, 126C, 127B, 31
regular 132D, 134A, 130F, 132A, 75, 105, 148L
regularity*
regulate 132D, 134B, 133A, 94
regulation*
regulator 132D, 95B, 132A, 148F
regurgitate 26, 16
rehabilitate 139A, 136B
rehash 60, 56, 145F
rehearsal 6, 132D, 75
rehearse 6, 132D, 85A, 75
reign 133A, 148I
reimburse 45
reimbursement 45
rein 52A, 133A
reindeer 143A, 24G
reinforce 137B
reinforcement 137B
reinstate 136B, 139A
reiteration 75
reiterative 75
reject 27, 35, 66, 67A, 132C, 35A
rejective*
rejection*
rejoice 71A
rejoicing 71A
rejoin 88, 146A, 146K
rejoinder*
rejuvenate 136B, 8, 137B, 137A
relapse 128B, 128C
relate 85A, 80, 146A, 146H, 146I
related 146I, 146A
relation 85A, 146A, 146I
relationship*
relative 146I, 53A
relator 85E
relax 46B, 14, 71A, 126B, 47, 3A
relaxation*
    71A, 126B
relay 3A

release 47, 145A
relegate 35A
relegation 35A
relent 47, 126B
relenting 47
relentless 11A, 50, 130M
relevancy 5A, 132A, 146A
relevant 5A, 132A, 146A
reliability 140A, 134B
reliable true 61A
    worthy 140A, 5A, 134C
reliance 113, 42
reliant 113
relic 104A
relict 145K
relief 136A, 47, 136B, 5A, 100B
relieve 136A, 5A, 47, 145A, 136B
religion 82A, 82B, 140A, 38
religious 82A, 140A, 134A, 38, 113
relinquish 15, 46B, 47
relinquishment
    abandonment 15, 46B
reliquary 53B, 53J
relique 104A
relish 51A, 71A, 48A, 48P
reluctance 32, 27, 28, 132C, 126B
rely 46B, 113
remain 11A, 11B, 54A, 125A, 85A
remand 43B
remark 55A, 119A
remarkable 126A, 140B, 96A, 95E, 99A, 108, 135B
remedial 136B
remedy 136B, 134A
remember 117, 38
remembrance 117
remembrancer 87, 86
remind 87
remindful 117
reminiscence 117, 114
reminiscent 117, 114
remise 15
remiss 126B, 46B, 130A
remission 47, 45, 126B
remit 45, 43B, 47, 35A, 14
remittal 46B, 24A
remittance 45

remittant 3B
remnant 147K
remonstrance 67A, 41B
remonstrant*
remonstrate*
remorse 31
remorseful 31
remorseless 130M
remote 149N, 148A, 148B
remoteness*
removal 24A, 35A, 131A, 145A
remove 24A, 3A, 145F, 130-O, 145A, 35A, 149A
remunerate 45
remuneration 45
remunerative 45, 49D
Renaissance 136B, 141B
renard 143A
renascent 141B, 136B
rencounter 41D, 130F
rend 145F, 130D, 130G
render change 3A, 45, 43B, 24A, 46B, 95A, 105, 84
rendezvous 146K
rendition 84, 46B
rendrock 145E, 130K
renegade 15, 27, 130A
renege 126B
renew 136B
renewal 136B
renounce reject 27, 64, 67A, 126B, 15, 131A
renouncement*
renovate 136B, 138A
renovation*
renown 140B, 139B
renowned 140B
rent 145F, 25H, 45, 46A, 49D, 145C
rental 45, 86
renunciation 27, 15, 64
rep 106K
repair 136B, 45, 49A
reparation 136B, 45
reparative*
repartee 88
repast 48A
repay 45
repeal 131A
repeat 75, 3B
repeater* 130I
repel 27, 36

repellent 36, 27, 130C, 129B
repent 31
repentance 31
repentant 31
repertoire 86, 53B
repertory 53B
repetition 75
repine 31, 67B, 40B
replace 149A, 3A
replenish 43B
replenishment 43B
replete 26, 147I
repletion 26, 147I
replevin 49A, 45, 49D
replevy*
replica 105, 100B
replication 88, 75, 105, 40B
reply 88
report 85A, 79, 57, 69B, 78
reportorial 79
reposal 132D
repose 12, 132D, 11B, 137A, 149A, 53D, 132B, 149G, 149D
repository 53B, 49B
repousse 107E
reprehend 64, 65, 52A
reprehensible 130A, 130C
reprehension 64, 65
reprehensive 64, 65, 52A
represent 95A, 84, 105, 104A, 92
representation*
representative*
repress 52A, 132C, 50, 36, 130B
repression*
repressive*
reprieve 12, 148B, 148I
reprimand 64
reprint 105
reprisal 45, 130N
reproach 64, 65, 129B
reproachful 64
reprobate 64, 27, 130A, 129B, 35A, 35, 125C-3
reprobation 64, 130-O
reproduce 75, 141B
reproduction 105, 100B, 141B
reproof 64
reprove 64
reptile 143F, 129B, 130M
reptilian 129B
republic 133A
republican 133A

republication 85B
republish 85B, 85A
repudiate 27, 66, 67A, 131A
repudiation*
repudiator 27, 66
repugnance 28
repugnant 28, 130C, 129B
repulse 36, 27
repulsion 36, 27
repulsive 33, 36, 109A, 129B, 130C, 27
repulsiveness*
reputable 140A, 61A
reputation 116, 92, 113
repute 116, 140A, 92, 113
request 40B
requiem 68B
require 37, 41B
requirement*
requisite 37, 41B
requisiteness 37, 41B
requisition 37, 41B
requital 45, 130N
requite 45, 130N
reredos 36I, 145B
reremouse 143A, 143C
rescind 131A
rescission 131A
rescript 94, 88
rescue 11A, 136A, 47, 49A, 136B
research 119E
resemblance 105
resemble 105
resent 27, 28, 29, 67A
resentful*
resentment*
reservation 132C
reserve 132C, 103A, 147L
reservoir 53B
reside 54A
residence 54A, 53D
resident 54B, 54A
residential 54A
residual 147K, 147L
residuary 147L
residue 147K, 147L, 129A
residuum 129A, 147L, 146K
resign 46B, 15
resignation*
resilient 3C
resin 5C
resist 27, 36
resistance 27, 36
resistant 27, 36
resistless 50, 137B, 134C

resoluble 145J
resolute 2; 27, 11A, 39, 42, 144B
resoluteness*
resolution 115, 39, 27, 42, 11A, 145J
resolutive 145J, 145A
resolve 145A, 115, 2, 27, 39, 42, 86
resolvent 145J, 145B
resonance 68A, 69B
resonant 68A, 69B
resort 53C, 53D, 99E, 146K, 49A, 19A
resound 69B, 79
resourse 5A, 43B, 135B
resourceful 117
resources 49E, 135B
respect 38
respectability 140A
respectable 140A, 132C, 38
respective 145K, 126A, 146A, 147A
respiration 51A, 16
respiratory 51A, 16
respire 51A, 16
respite 148B, 12, 47, 148I
resplendence 101A, 108, 68A
resplendent 101A, 105, 95E, 99A, 108
respond 88
respondent 88
respondentia 45
response 88
responsibility 13, 88, 130B, 140A
responsible 47, 140A, 46B, 61A, 117, 134B
responsive 88
responsiveness 88
rest stability 11B, 74, 132B, 71A, 137A, 148I, 12, 149A, 53D, 54A, 126B, 128A, 147L, 132B
restaurant 48B
restaurateur 48A
restful 136A, 132B
restitution 45
restive 32, 112, 126B, 27
restiveness*
restless 32, 112, 3C, 39
restoration 136B
restorative 136B
restore 136B, 45, 132A

restrain 52A, 50, 12
restraint 52A, 50
restrict 52H, 52A
restriction*
result 144E, 115, 94, 147L
resultant 144E
resume 146A, 147L, 4, 11A
resumption 4, 11A
resurrection 137A
resuscitate 136B, 8
resuscitation*
resuscitative 136B
resuscitator 136B
retail 44
retain 132C, 52H, 45, 52A
retainer*
retaliate 45, 130N
retaliation 45, 130N
retaliative 130N, 45, 28
retard 148B, 52A, 36, 12, 36A, 126B, 14
retardation*
retardative*
retch 16, 41C
retention 132C
retentive 132C
reticence 132C
reticent 132C, 103A
reticular 25, 150D
reticulate 25, 150D
reticule 53J
retiform 150D
retina 119C
retinue 46B, 146K
retire 15
retired 145K, 103A
retirement 15, 103A, 74
retiring 132C, 129B
retort 88, 145H, 145H
retouch 136B
retrace 19A
retract 131A, 27
retraction 131A, 27
retreat 15, 34, 53D, 103A
retrench 14
retrenchment 14, 36B
retribution 45, 130N
retributive 45, 130N
retrieve 49A
retriever 49A
retroactive 3A
retrocede 43A, 15, 43B
retrocession 15, 128C
retrograde 15, 128C
retrogression 15, 128C
retrogressive*

retrospect 119F
retrospection 119F, 119E, 114, 117
retrospective*
return reunite 146A, 88, 45, 79, 15, 49A, 18C, 19A, 20, 128C
retuse 150D, 36
reunion 146K, 132A
reunite 146A, 146K
reveal 95A, 61A, 78, 149E
reveille 68C
revel 71A, 51A, 125C-3
revelation 95A, 78, 61A
reveler 125C-3, 51A, 71A
revelry 71A, 125C, 51A, 99C
revenge 28, 130N, 45, 130N, 130M
revengeful*
revenue 49A, 49F, 45
reverberate 69B, 3B
reverberation*
reverberatory*
revere 38, 63
reverence 38, 98C, 63
reverend 140A, 140B, 38, 82F
reverent 38, 129B, 46B
reverential 38, 140A
reverie 114
reversal 50, 131A, 3A
reverse change 3A, 50, 131A, 127B, 18C
reversion 3A, 18C
reversionary 3A
revert 18C, 3A
revest 45
revetment 36B
review 119E, 84
revile 65
revise correct 136B, 119E, 134A
revision*
revival 8, 136B, 137A
revive 137A, 136B, 137B, 8
revivify 136B, 137B, 8
revocation 131A, 3A, 41B
revoke 131A, 41B
revolt 27, 28
revolting 130C, 129B, 123
revolution 18C, 75, 27, 148I

revolutionary*
revolutionist 27
revolutionize 3A
revolve 18C, 114, 3B
revolver 130I
revolving 18C
revulsion 3A
revulsive 3A
reward 45
reynard 143A
Rhadamanthine 140A, 134A
rhapsodic 60, 57, 71A, 85A, 85E
rhapsodist*
rhapsodize 56, 71A, 85A, 85B
rhapsody*
rhea 143C
rhenium 5D
rheometer 95B
rheoscope 95B
rheostat 3A, 132D
rheotrope 95B
rhesus 143A
rhetoric 68A
rhetorical 68A
rhetorician 85E
rheum 16
rhinoceros 143A
rhodium 5D
rhododendron 143E
rhomb 150D
rhombic 150D
rhombohedral 150D
rhombohedron 150D
rhomboid 150D
rhombus 150D
rhubarb 143E, 48K
rhumb 150D
rhumb line 150D
rhyme 105, 68A
  poetry 85C
rhythm 3B, 75, 148I
rhythmic 3B, 75, 68A, 132D, 137C
rib 53R
ribald 129B, 70, 72, 39C, 125C-3, 146D, 95D, 146E
ribaldry*
ribbon 107B, 52C
rice 48M
rice-bird 143C
rich plenty 147I
  wealthy 135B
  splendid 140B, 141B, 48P, 108, 68A, 43A
riches 49E, 135B
rick 48N
rickety 128A
ricochet 3C, 9
rid 131A, 35A
riddance 131A, 35A
riddle 96A, 57, 13
ride 24A

rideau 36B
rider 93
ridge 149E, 150B
ridicule 72, 64
ridiculous 72, 60, 64, 109A, 126A, 99A
ridotto 146K, 99F
rifacimento 85B
rife 132D, 1, 135B, 147I
riff-raff 129A, 129B, 125A
rifle 49G, 130I
rifle-bird 143C
rifle-corps 130F
rifler 49G
rift 25
rig 24H, 106B, 72
rigadoon 99F
rigging 52C
right 61A, 134A, 140A, 149J, 149E, 49A, 53A, 132C
right-angle 150D, 147E
righteous 140A
righteousness 140A
rightful 140A
rightfulness 140A
rigid strict 134A, 140A, 11B, 137B
rigidity 11B
rigmarole 60, 56
rigol 150C
rigor 134A, 130B, 58, 130M
(B). rigour
rigorism 134A, 130B
rigorist*
rigorous 134A, 130B, 11B, 137B
rilievo 100B
rill 25I, 16
rim 149K, 36H
rime 146B
rimose 25H, 150B, 25
rimple 150B
rind 36F
ring 150C, 25A, 99E, 146K, 68A, 69B, 69C
ringdove 143C
ringing 68A
ringleader 133A
ringlet 106A, 150C, 107C, 107B
ring-ouzel 143C
ringworm 143F
rink 25A
rinse 138A
riot 69B, 27, 71A, 125A, 125C-2, 125C-3
riotous*
rip 145F, 78, 64, 130D

riparian 36H, 149J
ripe 132A, 134A, 48P, 12
ripen 132A
ripeness 132A
riposte 130F, 130G, 88
ripper 140B
ripple 145B, 69A, 16, 145F
rippling 69A
rise ascend 17, 4, 10, 9, 149E, 95C, 28, 141D, 140B
risibility 71B
risible 71B, 72, 109A
rising 149E, 27
risk 127A, 128A, 130F, 42, 39, 41C
risky 33, 127A, 13
risorial 71B
risotto 48D
rissole 48D
rite 95D
ritornello 68B, 68C
ritual 95D, 84, 82A
ritualism*
ritualist 95D, 82F
ritualistic 95D
rival 27, 41D
rivalry 27, 41D
rive 145F
river 25I, 16
river-horse 143A
rivet 52D
rivose 150B
rivulet 25I, 16
roach 143D, 143B
road 25B
roadster 24H, 24G
roam 18B
roan 24G, 143A, 102A
roar 69B, 67A, 71B
roarback 88
roaring 69B
roast 145J, 72, 64
rob 49G, 49F
robber 49G, 49F
robbery 49G, 49F
robe 106D, 34, 106F, 107A
robin 143C
robot 2
roburite 130K, 145E
robust 137B
roc 143C
rochet 106I
rock 146B, 3B
rockaway 24H
rocket 101C, 98A, 17
rococo 109A, 95D
rod 130L, 130N, 147E
rodent 143A
rodeo 146K

rodomontade 76
roe 142F, 143A, 141F
rogation 40B
rogue 49F, 140B, 130A
roguery 49F
roguish 49F
roil 130C
roll 18C, 24A, 24C, 69B, 68A, 48E, 86, 146A, 48-O
roller 24D, 16, 52C
rollick 18B, 71A
rollicking 71A, 98B
rolling 18C, 3B
roly-poly 41D, 48H
romance 62, 85B, 85A
romantic 113, 85A, 62, 108, 144A, 140B
Romany 19A
romp 9, 18B, 129B, 71A, 125C-3
rondeau 85C, 68B
rondel 85C
rood 104C, 147E
roof 34
rook 49F, 143C
rookery 53D, 141D
rookie 130F
room 25A, 53E, 102D, 149A
roorback 62
roost 53D, 54A, 11B, 149F
rooster 143C, 141F
root 141D, 1, 55A, 141G, 137C, 141A
rope 52C, 52B
ropy 52E
rorqual 143B
rosary 86, 40B
rose 143E, 102A, 107B, 108
roseate 102A, 10
rosebud 142A, 140B
rosemary 143E
rosette 107B
roster 86
rostral 150G
rostrum 53R, 53G
rosy 102A, 108, 134D
rot 128C, 60
rotary 18C, 3B
rotate 18C, 3B
rotation 18C, 3B, 148B, 148I
rotative 18C
rote 75
rotograph 100B
rotten 128C, 123
rotund 150G, 150C
rotunda 53D, 53B
rotundity 150C, 150G
rouble 147B

roue 39C, 125C-3, 146E
rouge 102D, 102A
rouge-et-noir 41D
rough
   unordered 125A, 13, 70, 130C, 130M, 125C, 109A, 109C, 150B
roughen 150B, 125A
roulade 68A
roulette 41D
rounce 5B
round turning 18C, 150C, 150G, 146A, 147J, 68B, 130F, 148I
roundabout
   devious 18C, 57, 150C, 106D
roundelay 99F, 68B
roundhouse 53D
round-robin 86
rouse 8, 35A, 130C
rouser 125C
rousing 8, 125C
roustabout 126B, 129B, 46B, 144D
rout 15, 35A, 145I, 125A, 96A
route 25B
routinary 132D
routine 132D, 75, 53A
rove 18B
rover 18B, 49G
row 146K, 19A, 24A
row 66
rowan 143E
rowdy 33, 125C, 130C, 129B
rowdyism*
rowel 8
rowen 48N
royal 133A, 140B, 108
royalist 133A
royalty 133A, 45
Royston-crow 143C
rub 138A, 107A, 13, 5B, 35A
rubber 3C, 119E, 106J
rubber-neck 119E
rubbish 129A, 125A, 129B, 60
rubescent 102A
Rubicon 134C
rubicund 102A
rubidium 5D
rubied 102A
rubigo 128C
ruble 147B
rubric red 102A
rubricate 102A, 95E
ruby 102A, 107C

ruche 107B, 106K
ruck 150B, 129B, 34
ruction 66, 125A
rudder 24C
ruddiness 102A
ruddle 102D, 102A
ruddock 143C
ruddy 102A
rude 110B, 130C, 126C, 28, 70
rudeness*
rudiment 133A, 61A, 81, 4
rudimentary
   beginning 4
   undeveloped 128A
rue 31
rueful 31
ruff 107B, 106C, 143B, 143C
ruffian 130M, 129B, 49G, 130A, 33
ruffle 150B, 130B, 130C, 125A, 107B
rufous 102A
rug 107E
rugate 150B, 149E
rugged 150B, 125A
ruin 130-O, 127B, 31, 125A, 50
ruined 128A, 128C
ruinous 130-O
rukh 34
rule govern 133A, 81
   principle 84, 133A
   maxim 61B
   decree 94, 95B
   standard 105
   method 132D
   decide 115
ruler 133A
ruling 133A, 50, 94
rum 48L, 126A
rumble 69B
ruminate 145H, 114
rumination*
rummage 119E
rumor 79, 78, 57
rump 150G
rumple 150B, 125A
rumpus 69B, 125A
run speed 9
   flee 15
   race 41D
   flow 16
   melt 145J
   demand 41B
   smuggle 49F
   proceed 19A, 35A
runagate 15
runaway 15
runcinate 150C
rundle 53R
rung 53R
runic 55B, 92
runlet 25I

runnel 25I, 16
runner 24F
runt 147K, 150G
rupee 147B
rupture 145E, 145C
rural 110B, 149I, 126D
ruralist 110B, 149I, 126D
ruse 130A, 62
rush 9, 20, 143E, 129B
rusk 48E
russet 102A, 106K
rust 128C, 128A
rustic 110B, 46B, 54B, 126D, 129B
rusticate 54A, 35A
rustication 54A, 35A, 53D
rusticity 110B, 130C
rustle 9, 69A
rustler 38, 144D
rustling 69A
rusty 128C, 128B
rut 39B, 25B
rutabaga 48K, 143E
ruth 31, 136A
ruthenium 5D
ruthless 130M, 130N, 130B, 33
rutilant 101A, 102A
rutilous 102A
ruttish 39B
rye 48M
ryot 54B

S

Sabaoth 130F, 146K, 147I
  hosts 147I, 146N
Sabbatarian 134A
Sabbath 148K
saber 130H, 130G
Sabian 82D
Sabianism 82B
sable 143A, 102A, 97
sabot shoe 106J
sabotage 130D, 49A, 52A
sac 53Q
saccade 52A
saccharine 48P
saccharize 48P
saccharoid 150D
saccharometer 95E
saccule 53Q
sacerdotal 82F
sachem 133A
sachet 122
sack 53Q, 53I, 106F, 49G, 35A, 49C, 149L
sackbut 68D
sackcloth 106K
sacking 106K

sacrament 89
sacred 140A, 140B
sacrifice 43A, 130-O
sacrificial*
sacrilege 130A, 49F
sacrilegious*
sacrilegist 130A, 49F
sacrist 82G
sacristan 82G, 34
sacristy 53E
sacrosanct 140B
sad 31, 102A, 98B
sadden 31, 130B
saddle 53-O, 13, 130B
safari 19A
safe 34, 53B, 53J, 36B, 36, 134C
safeguard 34, 36B, 36
safety 34
saffron 102A, 102D
sag 22, 149G
sagacious 117, 59
sagacity 117, 59, 132C
sagamore 133A
sage 117, 59, 135B, 98B, 48P
saguaro 143E
saguin 143A
sahib 140C, 133A
saiga 143A
sail 5B, 24J, 23
sailer 24J
sailor 24E, 23
saint 140B
saintly 140B
sajou 143A
sake 1, 5A, 12, 149H
saki 48L, 143A
salaam 98C
salable 44
salacious 39B
salacity 39B
salad 48D
salad days 126A
salamander 143F
salaried 45
salary 45
sale 44
salience 9, 3C, 132C
salient 9, 3C, 95E, 150D, 130F, 149H
saliva spit 129A
salival 16
salivate 16
salivant 16
salivation 16
sallet 36C, 106H
sallow 128B, 102A, 143E
sally attack 130F
  rush forth 15, 59, 19A, 71A, 71B, 72
sallyport 25

salmagundy 48D
salmi 48D
salmon 143B
salmon-peel 143B
salmon-trout 143B
salon 53E
saloon 53E, 100B, 48B
salsify 143E
salt 48P, 23
saltant 9, 3C, 99F
saltarello 99F, 68B
saltatory 99F, 18C, 63
saltish 48Q
salubrious 136B, 137A
salubrity 136B, 137A
salutariness 136B
salutary 136B, 38, 48A, 137B
salutation 98C, 73, 63
salutatory 73, 98C, 38
salutatorian 73
salute 98C, 63
salvage 45
salvation 34, 11A
salve 136B
salver 53M
salvo 98A, 98C, 63, 69B
Samaritan 43A, 140A, 136A
samarium 5D
sambo 146F
sambur 143A
Sam Brown 107B
sambur 143A
same 105
sameness 105
samovar 53N
sampan 24J
samphire 143E
sample 105
sampler 105
Samson 137B
sanatorium 136B
sanatory 136B
sanctification 139B
sanctimonious 103B, 62
sanction 94, 63, 46A
sanctitude 140A, 140B
sanctity 140A, 140B, 139B
sanctuary 53, 103A, 53D, 53E
sanctum 103A, 53E
sand 145H, 5C, 42
sandal 106J
sandbag 130L
sanderling 143C
sanders 5C
sandpiper 143C
sandwich 48D

sandy 145H
sane 117
saneness 117
sangaree 48L
sang-froid 132B, 28
sanguinary 28, 130-O, 130M
sanguine 39, 113, 42, 102A, 129A
sanguineness 113, 39, 26
sanguineous 39, 137B, 102A
sanitarium 53C, 136B
sanitary 136B
sanitation 136B
sanity 117
sansculotterie 133A
sansculottes 129B
Sanskrit 55
sap 137C, 25F, 2, 116, 128A, 130D
sap-head 110B
sapid 48P
sapience 59, 117
sapient 59, 117
sapless 128A, 32
sapling 143E
sapodilla 143E
saporous 48P
sapper 130F
sapphire 107C
sappiness 137C
saraband 99F, 68B
sarcasm 72, 64
sarcastic 72, 64
sarcenet 106K
sarcoline 102A
sarcophagus 53L, 51A
sard 107C
sardine 143B
sardonic 28, 98B, 64
sarsaparilla 143E
sartorial 106B
sash 107B, 53R, 106F
sasin 143A
sassafras 143E
Satan 130N
satanic 130N, 28, 130A
satchel 53J
sate 51A
sateen 106K
satellite 101D, 46B
satiate surfeit 51A
satiety 51A, 26
satin 106K
satinet 106K
satire 64, 72
satirist 64, 72
satirize 64, 72
satisfaction 71A, 136A, 45
satisfactory 136A, 45
satisfy 136A, 45, 46A

saturate 146C, 145J, 26
saturation*
Saturday 148K
Saturnalia 71A, 99C
Saturnalian 71A, 125C-3
Saturnian 134D, 148K
saturnine morose 31, 97
sauce condiment 48P, 64
saucer 53M
sauciness 130C
saucy 130C, 28, 42, 64
sauerkraut 48K
saul 143E
saunter 18B, 126B
saury 143E
sausage 48D
savage 130M, 125C-2, 29, 129B
savagery 130M, 125C
savanna 25G
savant 117
save 11A, 34, 49E, 49A, 132C, 136B, 35, 36
saveloy 48D
savin 143E
saving 132C
Savior 11A, 34, 47, 49A, 82E
(B). Saviour
savoir-faire 117, 134A, 134B
savor 48P, 122, 51A, 120
(B). savour
savory 48P, 122
savoy 48K
saw 145F, 61B
sawfish 143B
sawfly 143D
sawyer 145F, 144D
saxhorn 68G
saxophone 68G
say 55A
saying 61B
scab 36F, 129A
scabbard 53I, 145A, 145B
scabby 129A
scabrous 150B
scad 143E
scaffold 53R, 130-O
scaffolding 53R
scalawag 129B
scald burn 130D, 85E, 130E, 131A
scale 36F, 95B, 68A, 68K, 145G, 17
scalene 150D

scallop 143B, 107A, 107B
scalp 36F, 145G, 106A
scalpel 145F
scaly 129A
scamp 129B, 130A, 126B
scamper 9
scan 119E
scandal 130C, 65, 130A
scandalize 65, 130C
scandalous 65, 130A, 129B
scandium 5D
scant 147K, 37
scantling 53R
scanty 147K, 37
scape 15
scapegoat 127B, 31
scapegrace 129B, 130A
scapular 104C, 106I
scar fish 143B, 149E, 109A
scarab 11A
scarce 147K, 37
scarceness 147K, 37
scare 33, 32
scarecrow 33, 113, 109
scared 32
scarf 106C, 106D, 106F, 146A
scarlet red 102A
scarlet runner 143E
scarp 149D
scary 33
scathe 130D, 130M
scathing 130D, 130M, 64, 65
scatter 145I, 125A
scatterbrained 110B
scaup 143C
scavage 129A
scavenge 128A, 138A
scavenger 143, 51A, 138A
scenario 58
scene 95C
scenery 95C
scenic 95C, 101A, 99B, 99A, 100A
scent 120, 122
scepter 104D
schatchen 146L
schedule 86
scheme 114, 113
schilling 147B
schism 145A, 27
schismatic 145A, 27
schist 145D
schizogamy 141B
Schizomycetes 142F

scholar 116, 117
scholarly 117, 116
scholarship 117
scholastic 117, 116, 134A, 81
scholasticism 117
schollast 84
scholium 84
school 81, 116, 147I
schooling 81
schooner 24J, 53M
Schottische 99F
sciagraph 100B
sciagraphy 100A
science 61A, 117, 83
scientific 61A, 134A, 132A, 117, 134B
scientism 83
scientist 83, 117
scimitar 130H
scintilla 101A, 147K, 95C
scintillant 108
scintillate 101A
scintillation 101A
sciolism 117, 60, 62
sciolist 110B, 117
scion 142A, 142B, 49B, 143E
sciopticon 99E
scissors 145F
scoff 72, 64
scoffer*
scold 64
scollop 107A
sconce 36B, 101C, 48E
scoop 53N, 145F, 53M
scoot 9
scope 25A, 25G, 2, 95C, 117
scorch 131B, 9, 145J
scorcher speeder 9, 125C-2
scorching 9, 125C-2
score 147A, 86, 134D, 50, 147L
scorn 28, 65
scornful 28, 27, 65
scorpion 143D, 130M
scotch 126B, 12
scoundrel 130A, 129B
scour 138A, 138B, 119E
scourge 130G, 130L, 130N, 130B, 127B, 130E
scout 34, 28, 72, 64, 118
scovel 138A
scow 24J
scowl 98B, 28, 33
scrag 150G, 109A
scragginess*

scramble 17, 49C, 146C, 41C, 125A
scranch 145H, 145F
scrap 145D, 130F, 129A
scrapbook 86
scrape 70, 138A, 49E, 50, 98C, 13, 112, 130F, 145F
scrapple 48D
scratch 130G, 131A, 134D, 106A, 41D, 100B
scratches 128B, 130E
scratch race 41D
scrawl 126B, 55B
scrawny 109A, 150G
scream 69B, 67A, 31, 67B
screamer 143C, 62, joke 72
screech 69B, 70
screed 145D, 69B, 70, 147K
screen 145B, 103A, 34, 36, 36I, 145A
screw 52D, 49C, 18C, 52B, 150C
scribble 60, 85B, 55B, 85A
scribbler 85E
scribe 85E, 46B, 81
scrim 106K
scrimmage 130F
scrimp 132C
scrimpiness 147K, 37
scrip 53J, 86, 93
script 55B
scriptural 82A
scripturalism 82A
scripture 82A
scrouge 130B, 146K, 146B
scrub 138A, 129B, 46B
scrubby 129B
scruff 150G, 106A, 149I
scrunch 145H
scruple 147C, 132C, 30, 32
scrupulosity*
exactness 134A
scrupulous 132C, 114, 134A, 32, 114, 49A
scrutinize 119E, 114
scrutiny 119E, 114
scud 23, 9, 15, 145J
scuffle 130F, 41D
scull 5B, 24C
scullery 53E
scullion 46B

sculpin 143B
sculptor 100C, 144A
sculptural 100A
sculpture 100A,
  100B, 150A
sculpturesque 100A
scum 129A, 129B
scupper 25, 35A
scurf 129A
scurfiness 129A
scurfy 129A
scurrile jocose 72
scurrility 72, 65
scurrilous 64, 72, 65
scurry 9
scurvy 129A, 129B
scut 106A, 150G,
  129B
scutcheon 92
scuttle 53N, 130-O,
  25, 9
scutum 36C
scylla 33
scythe 145F
sea 25I, 16, 147I
sea-bar 143C
sea-bat 143B
sea-bear 143A
sea-calf 143B
sea-cow 143B
sea-devil 143B
sea-dog 143B
sea-elephant 143B
sea-fox 143B
sea-gull 143C
sea-hog 143B
sea-horse 143B
seal 143B, 104D, 93,
  52E
sea-leopard 143B
sea-lion 143B
seam 146A, 145E,
  145D
seaman 23
sea-mew 143C
seamless 146A
seamstress 106B
seance 146K
sea-pheasant 143C
seaplane 24I
sear 131B
search 119E
searchlight 95E,
  119E, 95B, 101C
seared 130M, 146B,
  28
seasaw 3C
seascape 100B
season 148L, 148I,
  48P, 132D, 137C
seasonable 134D,
  132A, 148E,
  148L
seasonableness 134D,
  148L

seasoning 48P
seat 53-O, 133A,
  149A, 53D, 52B,
  52G, 139A
secant 145F
secco 100B
secede 15
secession 15
seclude 145A, 103A,
  35
seclusion 145K, 103A
second 147A, 46B,
  148H, 147H,
  148D
secondary after 149I,
  46B, 148B
secrecy 103A
secret 103A, 13
secretarial 103A
secretary 103A, 85E
secretary bird 143C
secretaryship 103A
secrete 103A, 145A
secretion 145A
secretive 103A
secretiveness 103A
secretory 145A
sect 82D, 146K, 92,
  82B
sectarian 146L, 27,
  38, 82D
sectarianism 146A,
  38
section 145F, 145D,
  149A, 147E
sectionalism 38
sector 150C
sectorial 145F
secular 39, 82F, 46B,
  148C
secularity 39, 148E,
  148J
secure 34, 42, 113,
  49A, 52B, 89,
  34, 36, 45
security 135B,*
sedan 24H
sedate 132B, 98B,
  132C, 27
sedateness 132B
sedative 136B, 14
sedentariness 11B
sedentary 11B
sedge 143E
sedilia 53-O
sediment 129A
sedimentary 129A,
  146C
sedition 15, 27
seditious 27, 41B,
  15
seduce 40A, 39C,
  146D, 130A
seducement*

seducer 40A, 39C,
  146D, 40, 125C-3
seduction 40A, 39C
seductive 40A, 39C
seductiveness 40A
sedulity 39, 11A
sedulous 39, 11A,
  41C, 144B
see 82C, 119A, 111,
  95D
seed 142F, 141A
seediness 109C, 31
seedy 109C, 31
seek 119E, 41C
seem 95C, 105
seeming 95C, 62, 95A
seemliness 134A, 108
seemly 134A, 108,
  132A
seer 77
seesaw 3B
seethe 145J, 131B
segment 145D, 145A
segmentation 145A,
  145K
segregate 145A
segregation 145A
seignior 140C
seigniorage 49C, 45,
  49A
seine 49C
seismic 3B, 130-O
seismograph 95B
seismography 83
seismologist 83
seismology 83
seize 49C, 117
seizen 49C, 132C
seizor 49C
seizure 49C
seldom 148L, 147K
select 49A, 140B
selection 49A
selector 49A
selenium 5D
selfish 39
sell 44, 130A
semaphore 95B
semblance 105, 95C
semen 142F
semester 148H
semi 147A
semiannual 148K
semicolon 55B
seminal 141A, 148A
seminary 81
sempstress 106B
senary 147A
senate 146N
Senate 133A
senator 133A, 94
senatorial 94
send 24C, 35A
Senegalese 54C
senile 128A

senility 128A
senior older 148A,
  116, 133A, 140B,
  148J
seniority 148A, 148J
sennight 148H
senor 140B
senorita 140B
sensate 121
sensation 121, 111
sensational 121, 111,
  8, 95E, 96A,
  99A, 140B
sensationalist 85E
sense 117, 111, 84
senseless 110B, 60
sensibility 117, 111,
  121
sensible 117, 121,
  111, 3C, 59
sensitive 121, 117,
  111
sensorial 111, 121
sensorium 111, 121
sensual 39B, 125C-3,
  121, 39C
sensualism 121,
  125C-3
sensualist 39C,
  125C-3, 146E,
  121
sensuality 39B,
  125C-3, 146D
sensualize 146D,
  39C, 8, 125C-3
sensuous 39B, 111,
  117
sentence 94, 115, 45,
  55B
sententious 58, 61B
sentience 121, 111
sentient 121, 111
sentiment feeling 121
  noble feeling 71A
  love 39A, 39, 111
  opinion 113
sentimental*
sentimentalism*
sentimentalize*
sentinel 34, 119G
sentry*
separability 145A
separable 145A
separate part 145A,
  126A, 145K,
  147A
separation 145A
separator 145B
sepia 143B, 102D
sepoy 130F
sepsis 128C
septa 147A, 150D
September 148K
Septembrist 130-O

septenary 148H, 148K
septenate 148H
septennial 148H, 148K
septet 68B
septi 150D
septic 128C
septillion 147A
septuagenarian 148H
septuagenary 147A, 148H
septuagesima 148K, 148H
septuple 147A
sepulcher 53L, 104H
sepulchral 69A, 69C, 70
sepulture 52H
sequel 74, 144E
sequence 148B, 149I, 74, 149A
sequent 148B, 149I
sequester 145K, 145A, 15, 49C
sequestered 145K, 103A
sequestration 49C, 15, 145K, 103A
sequestrator 49C
sequoia 143E
seraglio 53D
serang 133A
serape 106D
seraph 140B
seraphic 140B, 108
seraskier 133A
Serbonian 13
serein 16, 145J
serenade 68B, 68A
serene 132B, 98B
serenity 132B, 98B
serf 46B
serfage 46B, 50
serge 106K
sergeancy 133A
sergeant 133A
sergeant major 133A
serial 85B
sericeous 101A, 106A
sericulture 141B
series 146A, 147L
serious 98B, 13, 33, 67A, 61A, 39, 27, 114, 135B, 134A
sermon 81, 85E, 85A
sermonize 81, 85E, 85A
serpent 143F, 130A, 28, 130M
serpentine 103A, 150C
serrate 150B
serried 146B

servant 46B
serve 46B, 5A, 45, 132A, 43B
service 46B, 5A, 48A, 68B, 38
serviette 138A
servile 46B, 32, 129B
servility 129B, 32, 46B
servitude 46B, 52H
sesqui 147A
session 146K
sessional 146K
set to place 149A
  fix 52B, 52G
  plant 137C
  stabilize 11B, 12, 132A
  regulate 132D, 38, 149G, 22, 146B, 27, 146K, 146A, 147L, 141B
settee 53-O, 24J
setter 143A
setting 146A, 147L
settle 22, 149G, 45, 94, 132B, 132A, 11B, 54A, 138C 139A
settlement 53F, 45, 53D
settler 54B
setto 41D, 130F
seven 147A
sevenfold 147A
seventeen 147A
seventeenth 147A
seventh 147A
seventieth 147A
seventy 147A
seven-up 41D
sever 145F, 145A
several 126A, 145K, 147L
severalty 145K
severance 145F, 145B
severe 13, 130M, 134A, 28, 29, 64, 67A, 98B, 130B
severity*
service 5A
sew 146A, 52B
sewage 129A
sewer 25F
sewerage 25F
sex six 147A, 150D, 148H, 141G
sexagenarian 148H
sexagenary 147A, 148H
sexagesima 148K
sexagesimal 147A
sextain 45C, 85C

sextant 150C, 95C
sextet 68L, 68I
sextillion 147A
sexto 147D
sexton 82G
sextuple 147A
sexual 141B, 146D
sexuality 141B
shabby 109C, 129B
shack 53D, 48N, 129B
shackle 52A
shad 143B
shade 103A, 97, 102B, 102C, 147K, 113
shadow 97, 103A, 95A
shady 97, 57
shaft 25, 25B, 25F, 130H, 130J, 53R
shag 106A
shagginess 106A
shaggy 106A
shagreen 106K, 106A
shah 133A
shake 3B, 128A
shakedown 53-O
Shaker 82D
shako 106H
shaky 128A, 32
shale 129A
shall 46B, 148B
shalloon 106K
shallop 24J
shallow 60, 110B, 25, 25A, 147K
sham 130A, 62, 103B, 105
shamble 18A
shambling 18A
shame 96A, 129B, 65, 32, 31, 98B
shamefaced 32, 98B
shameful 132B, 130A, 129B
shameless 42, 95E, 129B, 130C, 109A, 125C-3
shammy 106K
shampoo 138A
shanghai 143C, 49C
shank 53R, 150G
shanty 53D
shape 150A, 105, 100A, 132D, 3A, 134C, 144B
shapeless 109B, 150B
shapely 150A, 108
share 49A, 43A, 145A, 145D, 147L
shark 143B

sharp 145F, 117, 59, 58, 68A, 150E, 48P, 48Q, 134B
sharpen 150E
sharper 49F
shatter 145E, 145H, 50, 130-O
shave 145F, 49G
shaver 148J, 142B
shaving 129A
shawl 106B, 106C, 106D, 106F
shawn 68G
shay 24H
she 92
shea 143E
sheaf 146A
shear 145F
sheath 53I, 145B
sheathe 149L, 145A
shebang 53D
shed 145G, 16, 145I, 53D, 53B
sheen 101A
sheep 143A
sheepish 32
sheer 138C, 149E, 125C, 134C, 149D
sheet 5B, 85B, 147D
sheik 141E, 133A
sheldrake 143C
shelf 53P
shell 36F, 145G, 53D, 53I
shelter 53D, 34, 36B, 36, 103A
sheltie 143A, 24G
shelve 149D, 149F
sheol 130N
shepherd 34
sherbet 48F
sheriff 133A
sherry 48L
shibboleth 55A, 92, 61A
shield 34, 36, 36C, 36I
shift 18C, 3A, 106B, 106G, 132A
shiftless 126B, 129B
shifty 3C, 134B
shillalah 130L
shilling 147B
shilly-shally 32
Shiloh 82E
shimmer 101A
shin 150G, 17
shindy 69B, 99A, 71A, 99C, 113
shine 101A, 95E, 108, 38
shingle 34, 53R
shining 102A, 140B
Shintoism 82B

Shintoist 82D
shiny 101A
ship 24J, 24A, 23
shipshape 132A
shirk 15, 126B, 32
shirt 106G, 106D
shirting 106K
shirtwaist 106F
shivaree 72
shiver 3B, 32, 145F
shoal 147I, 149E
shock 33
shocker 85B
shocking 96A, 33,
    109A, 130C,
    130A, 130B,
    130M, 129B
shoddy 106A, 106K,
    129B
shoe 106J, 106B
shoo 33
shoot 130-O, 130F,
    24C, 9, 22, 142A,
    141B, 150H, 25F
shooter 130I
shop 44, 144C
shoplifting 49F
shore 25G, 36H
short 37, 149M,
    148D, 58, 150G
shortage 37
shortcake 48E
shortcoming 126B,
    37
shorten 14, 58
shorthand 55B
shortly 148B
shortness 148D,
    150G
short-sighted 119B
shot 130J, 134B,
    110A, 24C, 130F
shot-gun 130I
shot-silk 106K
shout 69B
shove 24C, 13
shovel 145F, 53M
show 95A, 93, 99B,
    99A, 99D, 95D,
    81, 84, 95C, 62,
    103B
shower 16, 43A, 125B
showiness 95D
showy 95D
shred 145F, 145D
shrew 143A, 64, 29,
    130C
shrewd 117, 59, 134B
shrewish 64, 29
shriek 69B, 70
shrift 78, 47
shrike 143C
shrill 69B, 70
shrimp 143B, 147K
shrine 104H, 53R,
    139B

shrink 146B, 15, 14
    fear 32
shrinkage 14, 146B
shrive 78, 118
shrivel 146B, 14,
    128C
shroud 103A, 106D
shrub 143E, 150H
shrubbery 143E,
    150H
shrug 98A
shrunk 146B, 109B
shrunken 146B,
    109B
shuck 36F
shudder 3B, 32
shuffle 146C, 125A,
    18A, 24C
shuffling 18A
shun 15, 27, 28, 32
shunt 18C
shut 35, 36, 52H
shutter 103A, 36I
shy 32, 132C, 24C,
    18C
shyness 32
shyster 130A
sibilance 69A
sibilant 69A
sibilate 55A, 69A
sibilation 69A, 64
sibyl 77
Sibylline 77
sick 128B, 28
sicken 128B, 130E,
    130B
sickening 48Q, 130E
sickish 128B
sickle 145F
sickliness 128B
sickly 128B
sickness 128B, 130E
side 149J
sideboard 53P
sidelong 149J
sidewalk 25B
side-wheeler 24J
siding 149J, 25B
sidle 18C, 149J
siege 52H, 130F
sienna 102D
sierra 149E
siesta 11B, 132B,
    110A
sieve 145B, 145A
siffleur 68K, 72
sift 145A, 119E
sigh 69A, 16, 31,
    67B, 125B
sight 119A, 119F,
    95C, 147I
sightless 119B
sightliness 108
sightly 108

sigmoid 150C
sign 104A, 95A, 95C,
    92, 55B, 93
signal 98A, 55B,
    140B
signalize 95E, 98A
signatory 93, 92
signature 93, 92
signboard 95A
signet 104D
significance 95A, 58,
    95E
significant 95A, 95E,
    55A, 84, 135B,
    58, 104A
signification 95A, 84
significatory 95A,
    95E
signify 95A, 84, 95E
signiory 133A
signor 140B
signorina 140B
silence 132B, 69A,
    132C, 11B, 50, 12
silent*
silesia 106K
silhouette 100B,
    100A
silicon 5D
silk 106K, 52C
silken 106K
sill 53R
sillibub 48I
silliness 110B, 60
silly 110B, 60
silo 53B
silt 129A
silvan 34
Silvanus 34
silver 102A, 107C,
    5D, 107A
silvery 102A, 68A
simian 150G
similar 105
similarity 105
simile 105, 84, 92
simmer 145J, 14
simoniacal 49D
simony 49D
simoon 125B
simous 109B, 150G
simper 71B, 98B
simple 5A, 145K,
    138C, 108, 84,
    110B, 109A,
    132D
simpleton 110B
simplicity 61A, 110B,
    138C
simplification 5A
simplify 5A
simulacrum 105,
    104A
simulate 105, 103B,
    57, 62, 95D

simulation 105,
    103B, 57
simultaneous 105,
    148L, 132A,
    148E
sin 130A
since 148A, 148C,
    1, 148B
sincere true 61A,
    140A, 138C, 38,
    39
sincerity*
sinecure 45
sinew 137B, 52C,
    25E
sinewy 137B
sinful 130A
sing 68B, 68A
singe 131B, 130E
single 147A, 145K,
    140A, 145A
singleness 145K
singsong 70
singular 145K,
    126A, 140B,
    109A, 147A
singularity 126A
sinister evil 130A,
    33, 127B, 28,
    149J
sink 22, 21, 25F,
    130-O, 149G
sinless 140A
sinner 130A
sinology 83, 85D, 86
sinuate 150C, 18C
sinuosity 150C
sinuous 150C, 18C
siphon 25F, 24A
sip 51B
Sir 140B
sire 140B, 141E,
    141A, 146I, 141F
siren 40, 40A
sirene 95B
sirloin 49D
sirocco 125B
sirrah 64
sisal-grass 143E
sister 146I
sisterhood 146K
sister-in-law 146J
sisyphean 13, 127B,
    130B, 11A,
    128A
sit 149A, 141B,
    11B, 12, 149F
site 149A, 53D
sitting 146N
situate 149A
situation 149A,
    126A, 147L
siva 130-O
six 147A
sixfold 147A

sixscore 147A
sixteen 147A
sixteenmo 147A
sixteenth 147A
sixth 147A
sixtieth 147A
sixty 147A
sizable 147I, 132A, 147J
size 52F, 147L, 145A
sizzle 69A, 69C
skat 35A
skate 143B, 24H, 9, 23
skedaddle 15, 32, 35A
skein 146A
skeleton 53R, 103A, 130B
skeptic 30
skeptical 30
skepticism 30
sketch 100A, 100B, 86, 95B
sketchiness 100A
sketchy 100A
skew 32, 149D, 150B
skewer 52D, 52B
ski 106J, 24H, 23
skid 18C, 23
skiff 24J
skill 134B, 117
skillet 53M
skillful 134B, 117
skilly 48D
skim 145A, 9, 23, 116
skimmer 143C, 145B
skimp 126B, 132C, 126D
skin 36F, 106K, 145G, 49F
skinflint 49C, 49E, 39
skinny 109A, 150G, 109B
skip 9, 17, 126B, 53K, 99F
skipper 133A, 143D, 23
skirmish 130F, 41D
skirr 9
skirt 106F
skirting 106K, 106F
skit 64, 72
skittish 32
skiver 145F
skulk 15, 103A, 32
skull 150G
skunk 143A, 129B, 123
sky 53H, 150C, 149F
sky-hoot 9, 125C-2
skylark 143C

skylarking 71A
skyscraper 53D, 53B
slab 145D, 53G, 53R
slab-sided 109B, 150G
slack 126B, 130A
slacken 126B, 14, 46B
slacker 126B
slag 129A
slake 132A, 131A, 136A, 48A
slam 130G, 72
slander 65
slanderous 65
slang 55A
slant 149D, 91, 64, 149G
slanting 149D
slap 130G
slash 145F, 130G
slashing 64
slat 53R
slatch 125B
slate 86, 64, 55B
slattern 129B, 129A, 109C
slatternly 109C
slaughter 130-O
slave 46B
slaver 24J, 16
slavery 46B, 50
slavey 46B
slavish 46B
slaw 48D
slay 130-O
sleazy 128A, 3C
sled 24H, 24A
sledding 24A
sledge 24A, 5B
sleek 101A, 108
sleeky 108
sleep 132B, 11B, 110A
sleeper 53R, 24H
sleepiness 126B, 110A
sleepless 119G, 3B
sleepy 126B, 110A
sleet 16
sleety 16
sleeve 106C
sleigh 24H
sleight 134B
slender 150G, 128A
sleuth 119E
slice 145F, 145D, 145A
slick 5A, 134B
slide 23, 9, 24C
slight 128A, 147K, 129B, 126B, 134B
slim 150G, 109B

slime 129A
slimy 129A
sling 24C, 130I
slink 15, 127B, 141B, 32
slinky 150G
slip glide 23
  skid 18C
  miss footing 127B, 103A, 126C, 126B, 106F, 149D
slipper 106J
slipperiness 3C, 127A, 5A
slippery*
slipshod 109C
slit 145F, 25H
slither 23
sliver 145F, 145D, 147K
slob 119C, 109C, 110B
sloe 48G
slogan 41B, 61B, 146K
sloop 24J
slop 129A, 106B
slope 149D, 149G
slosh 129A
slot 145C
sloth 126A, 143A
slothful 126B
slouch 18A, 126D, 109A
slough 25G, 129A
sloven 119C, 129A, 109C
slovenliness 119C, 129A, 109C
slow 126B, 103A
slue 18C
slug bullet 130J
sluggard 126B
slugger 41D, 130F
sluggish 126B, 110A, 18A
sluice 25, 16, 138A
slum 53F
slumber 132B, 126B, 110A
slump 22, 13, 25G, 14, 146A, 147L
slur 65, 146C
slush 129A
slut 109C, 129B, 129A
sluttish 109C, 129A
sly 103A, 134B, 117
slyness*
smack 130G, 98C, 121, 48P, 24J, 51A
small 147K, 110B, 129B

smalt 102D
smart 130B, 59, 111, 31, 128B, 95D, 134B, 108, 134A
smarten 107A
smart-money 45
smash 130-O, 127B
smatter 60
smattering 117
smear 146D, 129A
smectite 5C
smell 122, 123, 120
smelling 120
smelt 143B, 146A, 145J
smerky 108
smew 143C
smile 71B, 71A, 98B
smirch 129A
smirk 71B, 98B
smite 130G, 130-O
smith 144D
smithereen 145D, 147K
smithing 144B
smithy 144C
smock 106F, 106G
smock-frock 106E
smoke 51A, 145J, 120
smoke-stack 25F
smokiness 145J
smolder 131B
smolt 143B
smooth
  not rough 5A, 16, 149C, 101A, 63, 40A, 132B, 132D, 132A, 134B, 48N
smother
  destroy 130-O, 31, 130A, 37, 50, 130B, 130M, 130N
smudge 129A
smudginess 129A
smug 134A, 108
smuggle 49F, 103A, 149M
smut 129A, 70, 102A
smuttiness 129A
smutty 129A, 70
smack 48A
snaffle 52A
snag 130G, 13
snail 143F, 126B
snake 143F
snakish 150G
snaky 150G, 103A, 62, 87
snap 145E, 64, 67A, 69C, 126D, 127B, 130G, 49C, 5A, 48E, 9, 130A
snappish 88, 130F, 29, 67A

sprinkle 145I, 146C
sprinkling 145I
sprint 9
sprout 142A, 141A, 141B
spruce 143E, 48L, 48J, 134A, 150H, 108
spry 9, 117
spud 48K, 145F
spume 145J
spunk 42
spunky 42
spur 8, 130H, 149H, 9, 19A
spurious 146C, 130A, 129B, 62
spurn 35, 28
spurt 16, 9, 125C-2, 41C
sputter 70, 69B, 69C
sputum 16, 129A
spy 119F, 119E
spyglass 95E
squab 53-O, 142B, 150G, 109B, 143C, 147J
squabble 66
squad 130F, 146K
squadron 130F, 146N
squalid 129A, 128A, 109C
squall 125B, 69B, 70
squally 125B
squalor 129A, 109C
squander 45, 125C
square 150D, 61A, 140A
squash 145H, 145E, 130-O, 48K
squat 54A, 149G, 109B, 150G
squatter 54B
squaw 146J, 141E
squawk 69B, 70
squeak 69B, 69C
squeal 69B, 69C
squeamish 128B, 134A, 28, 132C
squeegee 138A
squeeze 146B, 13
squelch 130G, 130-O, 145H, 50
squib 72, 64
squid 143B
squint 119A, 98B
squirm 31, 18C
squirrel 143A
squirt 16, 24C
stab 130G, 130D, 130-O, 130B
stability 11B, 11A
stable 11B, 11A, 132B, 146B, 53D, 53B
stack 147I, 146A, 147J, 25F
stadium 25A
staff 104D

stag 143A, 141F
stage 53R, 53G, 24H, 99B, 99A, 99E
stager 99D
stagger 18A, 30, 112, 128A, 96A
stagnancy 11B, 146C, 110A
stagnant 11B, 146C, 110A
stagnate 11B, 146C
stagnation 11B, 146C, 110A
staid 132B, 11B, 132C
stain 102C, 102E, 146C, 102, 129A
stainless 138C, 108
stair 25C
staircase 25C
stairway 25C
stake 53R, 41D, 127A, 52D
stalactite 150E, 149E
stalagmite 150E, 149E
stale 123, 128C, 128A, 129B, 148A, 48Q, 132D, 16
stalemate 12
stalk 41C, 28, 95D, 19B, 103A, 119E, 53R
stall 53B, 53D, 53E
stallion 143A, 141F
stalwart 42, 137B
stamen 137B, 141C
stamina 137B
staminal 137B, 2, 141A
staminiferous 141B, 141A
stammer 70
stammering 70
stamp 145H, 55B, 81, 95E, 104D, 105, 124, 130G, 134C
stampede 15, 112, 125A, 32
stanch 39, 27, 140A, 12, 38, 42, 137B
stanchion 53R
stand be erect 149E, 12, 11B, 137B, 146C, 11A, 31, 53C, 53B, 53G, 53P, 119E, 149A, 27
standard 104E, 105, 100B, 132D
standardize 132D, 105
standing 132D, 147L
standpatter 11B
stanhope 24H
stanza 85C

staple 144E, 52D, 5C
star 101A, 101D, 140B, 99D, 99A
starboard 149J
starch 52F, 11B, 137B
Star Chamber 49C, 130N
starched 11B, 134A
starchy 52E, 134A
stare 119E, 95E
stark 137B, 95E, 109A
starriness 101A
starry 101A
start 32, 4, 95C, 145A, 8, 130N, 141A
starthroat 143A
startle 8, 33, 32, 96A
startling 140B
starvation 37, 128A
starve 37, 128A
starveling 37, 128A
state 149A, 53F, 79, 80, 126A, 147L, 84
statecraft 134B
stated 132D, 11B
stateliness 108, 98B, 68A
stately 108, 98B, 95D, 140B
statement 86, 85A, 84
stateroom 53E
statesman 133A
statesmanship 133A, 134B
static 11B
station 149A, 53C, 94, 139A, 92, 126A, 139A
stationary 11B
statist 86
statistic 86
statistician 86
statistics 86
statuary 100C, 100B
statue 100B, 104H
statuesque 100A, 11B
statuette 100B
stature 147L, 149E
status 147L, 149A
status quo 147L, 149A
statute 94, 133A
statutory 94
staunch 137B, 140A
stay 52C, 53R, 11B, 11A, 91, 54A, 53D, 12, 52A, 5A, 18C, 148I
steadfast 11B, 11A, 140A, 132D, 27, 38, 39, 144B

steady 11B, 132D, 11A, 132B, 39, 144B
steak 48D
steal 49F, 103A
stealth 103A
stealthy 103A, 132C, 134B
steam 145J, 16
steamer 24J
steamy 145J
steed 24G, 143A
steel 5C, 137B, 130G
steelyard 95B
steep 21, 146C, 149D
steeple 104F, 149E
steer 143A, 24C, 24A, 134A
steerage 53E
steinbok 143A
stellar 101A
stellate 101A, 150F, 145K
stem 53R, 146I, 27, 36, 41D, 141G
stench 123
stencil 55B
stenograph 55B
stenographer 85E, 55B
stenographic 55B, 85A
stenography 55B
Stentor 69B
stentorian 69B
step 4, 19B, 147L, 25C, 25G
steppe 25G
stere 147G
stereometer 95B
stereoscope 95E
stereotype 55B, 105
sterile 128A
sterility 128A
sterilization 130D
sterilize 130D
sterling 138C, 140A, 140B
stern 149I, 11B, 98B, 27, 67A, 134A
stertorous 70, 69B
stethometer 95B
stethoscope 95B, 118
stethoscopy 118
stethoscopic 118
steve 24A, 124A
stevedore 24E
stew 48D, 13, 53D, 145J
steward 133A
stewardess 133A
stewardship 133A
sticcado 68E
stick 52E, 52A, 107B, 130G, 60, 11A, 5C
stickle 41D

stutter 70, 60
sty 52H
Stygian 28, 130A, 130M, 130N
style 92, 55A, 95B, 148F, 126A, 132D
stylish 132D, 108
stylist 85E, 84
stylistic 126A
suant 39, 81, 135B, 145I
suasion 40A
suasive 40A
suave 38, 136A, 63, 108, 117
suavity 38, 136A
subaltern 46B, 133A
subalternate 46B, 148B
subconscious 111
subdivide 145A
subdue 50, 14
subjacent 149G
subjacency 149G
subject 46B, 49C, 92, 85B, 80, 50
subjection 46B, 50
subjective 111
subjectiveness 111, 46B
subjectivism 83
subjoin 146A
subjugate 50
subjugation 50
subjugator 50
sublimate 145J, 138B
sublime 140B, 108, 139B, 98B, 134B
sublimity 140B, 108
submarine 24J, 21, 149G
submerge 21, 149G, 130-O
submersion 21, 16
submission 46B
submissive 46B
submit 46B, 87
subnormal 126A, 129B
subordinate 46B, 50, 133A, 146A, 148B
subordination 50, 46B, 129B
suborn 43B, 130A
subornation 43B, 130A
subpœna 94
subscribe 92, 93, 43A, 43B, 46A, 89
subscription*
subsequence 148B, 149I
subsequent 148B, 149I

subserve 46B, 144B, 136B, 137B
subside 14, 21, 22, 132B, 147K
subsidence*
subsidiary 146A, 46B, 5A, 43B
subsidize 43B, 43A, 5A
subsidy 43A, 5A
subsist 10, 11A, 132C, 53A, 51A, 137C
subsistence*
substance 5C, 2
substantial 146B, 137C, 135B, 137B, 146A, 93
substantiate 93
substantival 93
substantive noun 92, 55A, 137C
substitute 3A, 46B
substitution 3A
subsume 86
subterfuge 62, 103A, 134B
subterranean 149G
subtile 3C, 134B, 57, 59, 117
subtileness*
subtle*
subtlety 57, 117
subtract 14, 49A
subtraction 14, 49A
subtrahend 147L
subtreasury 53B
subulate 150E
suburb 25G, 149M
suburban 149M
subvention 43A
subversion 50, 130-O, 46B, 146C
subvert 50, 130-O
subway 25B
succeed 134D, 50, 148B, 149I
success 50, 134D, 49A
successful 50, 134D, 49A
succession 141G, 148B, 149I, 75
successional 75, 148B
successive 75, 148B, 3B, 149I
successor 50, 148B, 43A
succinct 58
succor 136A, 5A, 43A
(B). succour
succotash 48D
succulence 48P
succulent 48P
succumb 46B, 128A
such similar 105, 147L

suck 51B
sucker 51B
suckle 51B, 48A
suckling 51B, 142B
sucre 147B
suction 51B, 49A
suctorial 51B
sudarium 100B, 104C, 138A
sudary 138A
sudation 16
sudatorium 138A, 138B
sudden 148D, 9, 127A
sudoriferous 16
suds 145J
sudsy 145J
sue 41B, 40B, 40
suffer 31, 46A
sufferable 46A
sufferance 31, 46A
suffering 31
suffice 26
sufficiency 26, 113, 132A
sufficient 26, 113, 147I
suffix 74
suffocate 31, 130-O, 123, 130B, 130N
suffocation*
suffrage 46A
suffragette 41B, 41D
suffuse 145I, 16
sugar 48P, 40A, 63
sugary 48P
suggest 87
suggestion 87
suggestive 87
suicidal 130-O
suicide 130-O
suit 40B, 40, 106B, 132A, 146A
suitability 132A, 134A
suitable 132A, 134A
suite 146N, 53D
suitor 40, 39A
sulcate 150D
sulk 98B, 29
sulkiness 28, 29
sulky 29, 28, 24H
sullen morose 98B, 27, 29, 31
sully 129A
sulphur 5D
sultan 133A
sultanate 133A
sultry 130B, 145J
sum 147L, 146A
sumac 143E
summarily 58, 148D
summarize 58, 86, 75
summary 58, 86, 146A, 147L
summation*
summer 148K, 53R

summit 149F
summon 41B, 94, 40A
sumpit 130H
sumpitan 130I
sumptuary 49D, 132C
sumptuous 108, 136A
sun 101D
sunbonnet 106H
sunburst 107C
sundae 48F
Sunday 148K
sunder 145A, 145F
sundial 148F, 95B
sundries 126A, 147I
sundry 126A, 147I, 147L
sunk 149G, 127B
sunken 149G, 127B
sunniness 101A
sunny 101A, 98B
sunrise 148K, 148A
sunset 148K, 148B
sunshine 101A
sup 51A, 145D, 147K, 48J, 51B
super 125C, 46B
superabundance 26, 147I, 125C
superannuate 45
superannuation 45
superb 108, 140B, 136A, 134B
supercargo 133A
superciliary 149F
supercilious 28
superdreadnaught 24J
supererogation 43A
supererogatory 43A
superficial 149F, 60, 110B, 149K
superficiality 60, 110B, 149F
superficies 149F, 149K
superfine 140G
superfluity 26, 147I
superfluous 26, 56, 147I
superimpose 149F
superintend 133A
superintendence 133A
superintendent 133A
superior 140B, 133A, 50, 108
superiority 140B, 133A, 50
superlative 140B, 108, 134B
supernal 149F, 140B, 1, 136A
supernatural 126A, 1
supernaturalism 83
supernumerary 26, 10

superpose 149F
superscribe 92, 55B
superscription 92
supersede 131A, 149I, 3A
superstition 113
superstitious 113
superstructure 149F
supervene 127A, 10, 43B, 146A
supervise 133A
supervision 133A
supervisor 133A
supervisory 133A
supine 126B, 126D, 149D, 149C
supper 48A
supplant 131A, 3A
supple 3C, 108, 46B, 134B
supplement 43B, 10, 74, 146A
supplemental*
suppliant 40B
supplicate 40B
supplication 40B
supplicatory 40B
supplier 43B
supply 43B, 3A
support 48A, 11A, 93, 53R, 53G, 5A, 6, 7, 137B, 63, 43B
suppose 113
supposition 113
supposititious 113
suppress 50, 103A, 12, 35
suppression*
suppressor*
supreme 133A, 140B, 134B
sur 149F
surah 106K
surcease 12
surcharge 49D, 26
surcoat 106D
sure 11B, 61A, 134C, 134A, 134B, 34, 117
sure-footed 134A
surety 134C, 93, 89
suretyship 89
surf 16, 25I
surface 25A, 149K, 95C, 150A
surf-boat 24J
surfeit 26, 125C, 51A, 128B
surge 17, 16, 130-O
surgeon 136B, 145F
surgery 145F, 136B
surgical 145F, 136B
surliness 29
surly 64, 29, 130C
surmise 113

surmount 17, 149F, 140B, 26, 50
surname 92
surpass 140B, 26, 50, 108, 125C, 134B, 147I, 147J
surplice 106I
surplus 26, 147I
surprise 112, 96A
surprising 96A, 108, 140B
surrender 46B
surreptitious 103A, 49F, 130A
surrey 24H
surrogate 94
surround 52H, 149K
surtax 49C, 49A
surtout 106D
surveillance 119E, 119G
survey 119E
surveying 119E
surveyor 119E
survival 11A
survive 11A, 50
survivor 11A, 50
survivorship 11A
susceptibility 46B, 111, 116
susceptible 46B, 111, 116
suspect 30, 116, 127A, 113
suspend 22, 35, 52B, 12, 11A, 131A, 149G
suspender 52A
suspense 112, 127A, 132C, 38, 30, 39
suspension 12, 22, 30, 127A, 112, 148I
suspicion 113, 30, 147K
suspicious 113, 30
sustain 11A, 53R, 48A, 31, 43B, 137B
sustained 11A, 132D
sustenance 48A, 11A
sustentation 48A, 11A
susurration 69A
sutler 43B, 44
suttee 130-O
sutteeism 130-O
suzerain 133A
suzerainty 133A
swab 138A, 126D, 18A
swaddle 52B
swag 22, 49B
swagger 33, 76, 19B, 95D, 39A, 46B
swain 39A

swallow 51A, 143C, 25E, 51B, 129B
swamp 25G, 96A, 13, 130-O, 21
swan 143C
swap 3A, 44, 45, 49D
sward 25G
swarm 147I, 146K
swarthy 102A
swash 16, 130G
swashing 147I, 16, 76, 145E
swastika 134D
swat 130G
swathe 52B, 52C
sway 3B, 8, 135B, 133A, 50, 1, 137B
swear 93, 61A, 89, 64
sweat 16, 129A, 130B
sweater 106D
sweep 138A, 24A, 9, 130-O, 147L, 119E, 25A
sweepstakes 41D, 127A
sweet 108, 48P, 68A, 122, 48L, 140B
sweet-corn 48K
sweeten 48P, 63
sweet-flag 143E
sweetheart 39A, 140B
sweetmeat 48F
sweet-potato 48K
sweet-william 143E
swell 10, 16, 125C, 125A, 69B, 140B, 145I
swelter 16, 31
swerve 18C
swerving 18C
swift 9, 148D
swig 51B
swill 51B
swim 23, 112
swimmer 23
swimming 23
swimmingly 134D
swindle 49F, 130A
swine pig 143A
swing 3B, 23, 98A, 33, 18C, 149G
swinge 130G
swinish 129B, 51A
swipe 49F, 130G
swirl 18C, 16
swish 130G, 69C
switch 130G
swollen 109B, 145I
swoon 128A, 112
swooming 128A
swoop 22, 49C, 49G
sword 130H
sycamine 143E

sycamore 143E
sycophancy 63, 46B
sycophant 63, 46B
syllable 55B
syllabus 58, 86
sylph 96A, 113
sylvan 110B
symbiosis 146A, 146K, 51A
symbiotic*
symbol 104A, 55B, 105
symbolic 104A
symbolism 104A
symbolize 104A, 92
symmetrical 105, 132D, 132A, 150A, 150G
symmetrize 105, 132D, 150A
symmetry 105, 132D, 150A
sympathetic 7, 121, 136A, 3A, 47, 31, 38, 136A
sympathize 68A
sympathy*
symphonic 68A
symphony 68A, 68B, 68C, 74
symposium 51A, 51B, 71A, 85B, 99C
symptom 95A
symptomatic 95A
synagogue 53C
synchronism 86, 85D, 105, 148L, 148E
synchronize 105, 148L, 132A
syncopate 58, 146A
syncopation 68A, 69B, 58, 146A
syncretic 132A, 146A
syndic 133A
syndicate 146K
synecdoche 92
synesthesia 117
syngenetic 141A
synod 146K, 90
synodal 146J, 90
synodic 146J, 90
synonym 105, 92, 55A
synopsis 58, 86
synoptic 58, 86
synthesis 146A, 114, 115
synthetic 146A, 115
syringe 24C
syrup 48H
system 132A, 132D, 133A
systematic*
systematize*
systole 58

T

tab 52C, 95A
tabard 106E
tabasco 48P
tabby 102C, 143A
tabernacle 53C, 53I, 54A
tabes 128A, 128B, 14
tablature 100B
table 86, 48A, 53R
tableau 100B, 95D
tableau vivant 100B
table d'hote 48A
tableland 25G
tablet 104H, 136B
tabloid 104H, 58
taboo 35
tabor 68E
taboret 53-O
taborine 68E
tabular 86
tabulate 86
tachometer 95B
tacit 46A
taciturn 132C, 11B, 103A
taciturnity 132C, 11B, 103A
tack 52D, 10, 74, 52B, 18C
tacky 109C
tackle 49C, 130F, 52C
tackling 5A, 52C
tact 134B, 115, 134A, 121, 117, 59
tactical 134B
tactician 134B
tactics 134B
tactile 124, 121
tactility 124, 121
tactless 126D
tactual 121, 124
tadpole 143F, 143B
taffeta 106K
taffy 48F, 63
tafia 48L
tag 95A, 41D, 129B, 149I
tahr 143A
tail 150G, 15, 106A, 125C-1
tailor 106B
taint 129A, 146C, 65
take seize 49C, 49A
    receive 49B, 51B, 86, 111, 113, 24A, 147L, 46A, 51A, 51B, 115
taking 40A, 49B, 108
talapoin 143A
tale 85A, 62, 115, 147L
talent 117, 2, 134B, 147B

talented 117, 134B
talisman 45, 34
talismanic 34, 96A, 45, 99A
talk 55A, 90, 57, 92
talkative 56
talkativeness 56
talking 90
tall 149E, 125C
tallow 48P
tally 86, 50, 105
tally-ho 24H
talon 49C
talus 145H, 129A
tamale 48D
tamandua 143A
tamarin 143A
tamarind 143E
tamarisk 143E
tambour 68E, 36B
tambourine 68E, 99F
tame 50, 132A, 132B
tameless 125C-2, 125A
tammy 106K
tam o'shanter 106H
tamp 146B
tamper 13, 119D, 3A, 130D, 130A
tan 102A, 130G
tandem 24H
tang 48P, 69C, 69B
tangency 124
tangent 124, 150C, 150D
tangential 150C
tangerine 48G
tangible 124, 95E, 137C
tangle 125A, 13, 57, 146C
tango 99F
tank 53B, 24H
tankard 53M
tantalization 40A, 130N, 130B, 130C, 96A
tantalum 5D
Tantalus 40A
tantamount 105, 147L
tantrum 29, 67A
tap 130G, 25F, 25
tape 52C
tapeline 95B
taper 101C, 150E, 149D, 150D
tapering 150E
tapestry 106K, 107E, 107B
tapeti 143A
tapioca 48K
tapir 143A
taps 68B, 74, 94, 68C
tar 5C, 23

tarantass 24H
tarantella 99F
tarantula 143D
tarboosh 106H
tardiness 126B, 27
tardy 126B, 148B, 27, 132C, 18A
tare 135A
target 149H, 36C, 12
tariff 86
tarlatan 106K
tarn 25G, 25I
tarnish 129A
tarpaulin 106K
tarry 126B, 148B
tarsus 150G
tart 48P, 48E, 48Q, 64
tartan 106K, 24J
tartar 129A, 29
Tartarus 130N
task duty 45, 13, 147L
taskmaster 133A
tassel 107E, 107B
taste 117, 71A, 51A, 48P, 105, 49A
tasteful 48P, 108
tasteless 48Q
tasty 48P
tat 106K
tatter 106B
tatterdemalion 129B, 109C
tatting 107B
tattle 78, 60
tattoo 68B, 68C, 74, 100A, 100B, 102C
tattooing 100A
taunt 64, 72
tautog 143B
tautological 75, 61B, 84
tautology 75, 61B, 84
tavern 48B, 53C
tawdriness 95D
tawdry 95D
tawniness 102A
tawny 102A
taws 130L
tax 13, 45, 49A, 49C
taxation 49A, 49C
taxicab 24H
taxidermist 100C
taxidermy 100A
taximeter 95B
tea 48J
teach 81
teachable 116
teacher 81
teaching 81

teal 143C
team 24G, 24H, 142E, 146K
teamster 24E
team-work 132A, 146A, 146K
tear 145F, 9, 145A, 66, 76, 67A, 130D, 130G, 145C
tearful 16, 31
tease 130B, 130C
teaspoon 53M
teat 25E
techiness 29
technic 134B
technique*
technological*
technologist*
technology 83
techy 29
tedious 13, 130B, 56, 75
tedium 130B, 128A
teem 141B, 26, 147I
teeming 141B, 26, 147I
teen 148J
teepee 53D
teeth 145F, 145H
teething 145F
teetotal 132C, 146A, 147I
teetotaler 132C
teetotalism 132C
tegument 36F
tehee 71B
teledu 143A
telegram 55C
telegraph 55C, 55B
telegrapher 55C
telegraphic 55C
telegraphone 55C
telegraphy 55C
telepathy 55C, 111
telephone 55C, 55A
telephotography 100A
telescope 95E
telescriptor 55C, 55B
television 95A
tell 55A, 85A, 86, 78, 84
teller 49B, 45, 85E, *
telling 130-O, 134B, 137B
telltale 95A, 78, 95B
tellurium 5D
temerity 42, 125C-2
temper modify 3A, 132D, 146C, 2, 39, 39B, 28, 29, 137C, 132A, 132B
temperament*

temperamental*
temperance 132C, 14
temperate 132B, 132C, 145J
temperature 135B, 145J, 137C
tempered 137C, 146B
tempest 125B
tempestuous 125B, 29, 125C-2, 130M
temple 53C
tempo 69C, 148I
temporal 148D, 148C
temporality 148E
temporariness 148E
temporary 148E, 148D
temporize 46A, 90, 148B, 126B
tempt 40A
temptation 40A
tempter 40A
tempting 40A
ten 147A
tenable 46B, 53A
tenacious 52E, 27
tenacity 52E
tenament 53D
tenancy 54A
tenant 54B
tenantry 54B
tenary 147A
tench 143B
tend 34, 146K, 2, 18C, 43A
tendency 2
tender 3C, 121, 24J, 128A, 38, 39A, 68A, 136A, 40A, 132C
tenderfoot 110B
tenderling 121
tenderness 121, 39
tendon 52C, 25E
tendril 49C
tenement 53D
tenet 82A, 82B, 113
tenfold 147A
tennis 41D
tenor 68A, 68I, 137C, 105, 2
tense eager 39, 134A, 137B
tenseness 39, 134A
tension 13, 112, 11B, 39, 137B
tent 53D, 48L
tentacle 49C
tentacular 49C
tentative 41C, 127A
tenterhook 130B, 130G
tenth 147A
tenuity 145J, 150E
tenuous 145J, 150E

tenure 54A, 132C
tepefy 145J
tepidity 145J
terbium 5D
tercel 143C, 141F
tercentenary 148H, 148K
tergiversation 3C, 15, 27, 28, 62
term 148L, 148I, 92, 84, 89
termagant 69B, 125C, 29, 64, 67A, 70
terminal 12
terminate 12, 74
termination 12, 74
terminator 145B
terminology 83, 92, 84
Terminus 149A
terminus 12, 53C, 149H
termite 143D
termless 148C, 147J
tern 143C, 147A
ternary 147A
Terpsichorean 18C, 99F, 71A
terra 141D
terrace 25A, 25B, 25G
terra cotta 107E
terrapin 143F
terraqueous 25G, 25I, 149A
terrene 148E, 149A
terrestrial 149A
terret 52B
terrible 33, 130M
terribleness 33
terrier 143A
terrify 33
territorial 53F, 25G, 149A
territory 25G, 53F, 133A
terror 32, 33
terrorism 133A, 33
terrorist 33
terrorize 33
terse 58
terseness 58
tertian 148K
tertiary 147A, 148H
tessellate 107A, 150D
test 41C, 119E, 114
testa 36F
testaceous 36F
testacy 43A, 93
testament 93, 43A
Testament 82A
testamentary 93, 43A
testate 93, 43A

testator 93, 43A
testicle 53Q, 141C
testify 61A, 93
testimonial 93, 63
testimony 93
testiness 29
testudo 36B
testy 29
tete-a-tete 90
tete-de-pont 36B
tether 52A
tetra 147A, 150D
tetrad 147A
tetragon 150D
tetrahedral 150D
tetrahedron 150D
tetrameter 85C
text 85B, 81
text-book 81
Thalia 72
thallium 5D
thane 140C, 133A
thank 63, 38, 45
thankful 38, 45, 71A
thankless 126B
thanksgiving 63, 38
that 92, 84
thatch 53D
thaumatrope 95E, 99E
thaumaturgy 134D, 99A, 99B, 134B
thaw 145A, 47, 145J
the 126A, 92, 147A, 147L
theater 99E
(B). theatre
theatrical 99A
thee 92
theft 49F
their 92
theism 82A, 113, 82B
theist 82D, 113, 82F
theistic 82A, 113
them 84, 92
theme 92, 85A, 85B
themis 132A
then 149I, 148B, 148D
thence 148B, 149I
theocracy 82B, 133C
theocrasy 82B
theocrat 54B, 133A
theocratic 133A
theodicy 82B
theogony 83, 85C, 81
theologian 82F
theological 82A
theology 82A, 82B
theorem 61A, 87, 113
theoretical 113
theoretics 113
theorist 114, 113
theorize 114, 113
theory 113
theosophic 82A, 117

theosophism 82A, 117, 82B
theosophist 82D, 117, 82F
theosophy 82B
therapeutic 136B
there 149A
thereafter 148B
therefore 149I, 27
thereupon 149I
thermometer 95B
thermopile 95B
thermoscope 95B
thermostat 95B
thesaurus 53B, 86
these 92
thesis 93, 85A, 85B
Thespian 99A, 99D
theurgic 96A
theurgy 82B, 83
thews 137B
they 92
thick 150B, 146B, 136K, 110B, 137B, 150G
thicken 156B
thicket 34
thickset 150G
thief 49F
thieve 49F
thievish 49F, 130A
thigh 150G
thill 53R, 53G
thimble 36C
thin 150B, 109B, 145J, 14, 130D, 150G
thine 92
thing 145D, 126A, 57
think 113, 114, 117
third 147A
thirst 37, 39
thirstiness 37, 39
thirsty 37, 39
thirteen 147A
thirteenth 147A
thirtieth 147A
thirty 147A
this 148E, 92
thistle 143E
thither 149A
thong 52C, 130L
Thor 125B
thorium 5D
thorn 130H, 13
thorny 150E
thorough 134A, 134B, 117
thorough-bred 138C, 134B
thoroughfare 25B
those 149A, 92
Thoth 117
thou 92

though 27
thought 114
thoughtful 114, 39
thoughtless 126B, 60, 126D
thousand 147A
thousandth 147A
thraldom 46B, 50, 52H
thrall 46B, 50
thrash 130G, 145A
thrasher 143B, 145B
thrashing 130G, 145A
Thrason 76
thread 52C, 24A, 18B, 19A, 20
threadbare 109C, 128A
threat 33
threaten 33
threatening 33
three 147A
threefold 147A
threshold 25, 4
thrice 147A
thrift 132C, 49A, 143E
thriftiness*
thriftless 125C, 126B
thrifty 49A, 132C
thrill 8, 99A, 99C, 108, 121, 71A, 3B
thriller 8, 85C, 124
thrive 49A, 51A, 10
thriving 49A, 50
throat 25E, 25
throaty 70
throb 3B, 137C
throe 31
throne 133A, 104D, 139B
throng 146K, 146N, 147I
throstle 143C
throttle 130-O, 130M, 130N
through 50
throughout 149A
throw 24C, 147L, 149A
thrum 68A
thrush 143C
thrust 130G, 130F, 24C
thud 69C
thug 49G, 130A, 129B, 130M, 130N
thuggee 130-O
thulium 5D
thumb 150G, 129A
thumbscrew 130N
thummim 104C, 104D, 106I

thump strike 130G, 69C
thumper 62, 147J
thunder 69B, 64, 33, 125B
thunderbolt 33, 64, 69B, 42
thundering 69B, 147J
thunderstruck 112, 71A
thunderous 69B, 33
thurible 122
thurifer 122
thuriferous 122
Thursday 148K
thus 84
thwack 130G
thwart 27, 150F, 50, 36
thy 92
tiara 104C, 106H, 104D, 106I
tical 147B
tick 143D, 69A
ticket 93, 95A, 95E, 104A, 105
ticking 106K
tickle 124, 99A, 121, 136A
tickler 124, 13, 96A, 57
ticklish 124, 121, 127A, 13, 127A
tidal 16
tide 16, 148I, 3A, 2, 130-O
tidings 79, 85B
tidy 107A, 108, 107B, 134A
tie 52B, 52C, 106C, 105, 146A, 52A, 147L
tierce 147F, 147A
tiercel 143C, 141F
tiff 29, 66
tiffany 106K
tiger 143A
tiger-flower 143E
tight 11B, 52E, 52A, 52H, 146A, 132C
tighten 52B
tigress 143A, 141F, 29
tigrin 29
tigrish 29
tile 106H, 36D
till 53I, 49E, 148I, 10, 144B
tillage 144B
tiller 144D, 5A, 24C
tilt 53D, 41D, 130F, 149D, 130G, 34, 149G
timber 53R
timbrel 68E

time 148I, 132D, 148K
timeliness 134D
timely 134D, 132A, 148E, 148L
time-piece 95B, 148F
timid 32, 132C
timidity 32, 132C
timorous 32
tin 5D
tinamou 143C
tinctorial 102B, 102C
tincture 102B, 136B, 102C, 146C
tinder 5C
tinge 102B, 102C, 129A, 146C
tingle 121, 68A
tinker 136B
tinkle 68A, 69C, 69A
tinsel 106K, 107E, 95D, 101A, 101C, 107B, 107A
tint 102B, 102C
tintinnabulation 69C, 69A
tiny 147K, 128A
tip 149H, 43A, 45, 149D, 149G
tippet 106D
tipple 51B, 48L
tipsiness 112
tipster 78
tipsy 112, 110A
tiptop 149F, 140B
tirade 64, 65
tire 52C, 128A, 130D, 130B
tireless 11A, 137B
tiresome 130B, 130D
tiresomeness 130B
Tisiphone 130M, 130N
tissue 106K
tit 147K, 143A, 143C
Titan 137B, 147J
Titanic 147J, 137B, 48F
titanium 5D
tit-for-tat 45
tithe 147K, 147A
titillate 124, 121
titillation 124, 121
titivate 107A
title 92, 132C, 126A
titmouse 143C, 147K
titter 71B
tittle 147K
titubation 18A
titular 92
to 146A, 148I
toad 143F
toadeater 46B
toadfish 143B
toady 46B, 63

toadyism 46B, 63
toast 48E, 63, 89
tobacco 48-O
tobine 106K
toboggan 24H, 22
toby 53M
today 148E, 148K
toddle 18A, 19B
toddy 48L
to-do 9, 125A
toe 150G
toffy 48F
toga 104D, 106D
together 146A
toggery 106D
toil 130B, 130D, 31, 144B, 13, 46B, 41C, 132D
toilet 106B
toilsome 130B, 130D, 13
token 104A, 55B, 104A
Toledo 130H
tolerable 140A, 132D
tolerance 31, 46A
tolerant 46A, 31
tolerate 46A, 31
toleration 46A
toll 68A, 69B, 45
tomahawk 130H
tomato 48K
tomb 104H, 52H
tomboy 125C, 129B
tom-cat 143A, 141F
tomentose 106A
tomfool 110B
tomfoolery 60, 99A, 99B
tomorrow 148B, 148K
tomtit 143C, 147K
tom-tom 68E
ton 147C, 135A
tonality 68A
tone 68A, 102B, 14, 69C, 102C
tong 146N, 49C, 69C
tongue 150G, 59, 56, 55A, 64
tonic 136B, 137B
tonight 148K, 148L
tonite 145E, 130K
tonnage 135A, 147C
tonneau 24H
tonsorial 107A, 128A
tonsure 145F
too 26, 10, 146A
tool 5A, 5B
tooth 145F, 51A
toothsome 48P
toothsomeness 48P
toothwort 143E
top 149F, 50, 140B, 17, 99A, 18C, 145F

topaz 107C
top-boots 106J
tope 104H, grove 34, 51B
Tophet 130N
topic 92, 90, 85A, 85B
topical 92, 149M, 149A
toplofty 28
topographer 149A
topographic 149A
topography 149A, 150A
topple 22
topsy-turvy 125A
toque 106H
tor 149E
torch 101C, 98A
toreador 41D, 130-O
toreutic 100A
torment 130N, 31, 130B
torn 145F
tornado 125B
torose 150B
torpedo 130J, 130-O
torpedo-boat 24J
torpescent 110A
torpid 110A, 126B, 11B
torpidity*
torpor*
torque 107C, 106H
torrent 16, 25I
torrid 145J, 131B
torsion 18C
torso 150G
tortile 150B
tortoise 143F
tortuous 150B, 18C, 62
torture 31, 130N, 130B, 62
toss throw 24C, 98A, 149A
tossing 24C
toss-up 127A
tot 147K, 140F
total 146A, 147L
totality 146A
totem 104C, 104H
totter 18A
tottery 128A
touch 124, 121
touchiness 29, 121
touching 121, 8, 124
touchstone 105
touchy 29
tough 137B, 129B, 13, 33
toughen 137B
toughish 13, 137B
toupee 106A, 106H
tour 19A

tourist 19A
tournament 98C, 41D
tousle 125A
tout 40B, 78
tout ensemble 95A
touter 40B, 78
tow 24A, 149I
towage 24A, 45
toward 2, 116, 146A
towel 138A
tower 149F, 149E, 104H, 36B, 17
towering 149F, 149E, 29, 125C, 130M
town 53F
township 53F
toxic 130E, 130-O
toxicant 130E, 130-O
toxicologist 83
toxicology 83
toy 99A
trace 95A, 95C, 93, 100A, 147K, 52A
tracery 107A, 107E
tracing 100A, 95A, 100B
track 95A, 95C, 25B, 41C, 41D, 119E
trackless 13, 126A
tract 25A, 85B, 25G, 147K
tractable 46B, 116
Tractarianism 82B
tractate 81
tractor 24H
trade 44, 49D, 126A
trade-mark 104A
trader 44, 49D
trade-sale 44
tradesman 44, 49D
trading 44, 49D
tradition 85A, 81, 85D, 148A
traditional 85A, 81, 11B, 148A
traduce 65, 62
traffic 44, 49D
tragedian 99D
tragedy 99B, 130-O
tragic 130-O, 31, 130M
tragi-comedy 99B
tragi-comic 99B
trail 95C, 122, 41C, 119E
train 24H, 24A, 81, 132D, 149I, 46B
trainer 81
training 81, 116
traipse 18A
trait 95A, 126A, 135B
traitor 27, 62, 130A, 78

traitorous 62, 130A
trajectory 150C
tram 24H, 25B
trammel 52A, 49C
tramontana 125B
tramontane 149N, 126A, 110B
tramp 18B, 19B, 129B, 126B
trample 130G, 130C
trampoose 18B
tramway 25B
trance 71A, 128B
tranquil 132B, 98B
tranquilize 132B
tranquillity 132B
transact 50, 144B, 133A
transaction 50, 144B
transcend 17, 50, 140B, 149F
transcendency 17, 50
transcendent 140B, 50, 114, 149E
transcendental 114, 113, 140B
transcribe 84
transcript 85B, 84
transcription 85B, 84
transfer 24A, 43B, 44
transferee 49B
transference 24A
transfiguration 3A
transfigure 3A
transfix 130G
transfixion 130G
transform 3A
transformation 3A
transformer 3A
transfuse 24C, 16
transfusion 24C, 16
transgress 130A
transgression 130A
transgressor 130A
transient 148D, 19A, 9
transit 19A, 17
transition 3A, 19A
transitional 3A, 19A
transitive 3A, 3C
transitiveness 3A
transitoriness 148D
transitory 148D, 3C, 127A, 60, 131A, 149K
translate 24A, 84
translation 84
translator 84
translucent 101A
transmigration 3A, 19A
transmission 24A
transmit 24A
transmutation 3A
transmute 3A

transom 53R
transparency 101A
transparent 101A, 95E
transpiration 16
transpire 16, 78
transplant 141A, 3A, 52G
transplantation 3A, 24A
transport 24A, 24H, 99A, 99C, 108, 136A, 35A, 24J, 71A, 29
transportation*
transpose 3A
transposition 3A
transubstantiation 3A
transude 16
transverse 150F, 18C
trap snare 49C, 24H, 145F
trapezium 150D
trapezoid 150D
trapper 49C
trappings 106B, 107B
trash 129A, 129B, 125A
trashiness*
trashy*
travado 125B
travail 31, 13, 130B, 141B
travel 19A
traveler 19A
traverse 150F, 25D, 67A, 88, 36, 19B, 119E, 18C, 19A
travesty 72, 99B, 99A
trawl 49C
trawler 24J
tray 53M
treacherous 62, 130A, 49F, 127A
treachery 62, 130A
treacle 48H
tread 19B, 146D, 130-O, 50
treadmill 130N
treason 27, 130A, 62
treasure 135B, 147I, 49E, 38
treasurer 49E, 45, 53B, 49B
treasurership*
treasury 53B, 49B
treat 133A, 136B, 44, 89, 90
treatise 84, 85B
treatment 132D, 84, 133A
treaty 90, 146A, 46A
treble 147A, 68A

tree 143E, 150H
treenail 52D
trek 19A, 119E
trellis 53R
tremble 32, 3B, 128A
tremendous 147J, 33, 95E, 96A
tremolo 68A, 69C
tremor 3B
tremulous 32, 3B, 69C
trench 25F, 36B, 130A, 116
trenchant 145F, 64, 130G
trencher 53M
trend 2, 149A, 18C
trepan 145F
trephine 145F
trepidation fear 32, 112
  vibration 3B
trespass 130A, 130C
tress 106A, 106H
trestle 53R, 25B
trevis 53R
tri 147A, 150D
triad 147A
trial 41C, 13, 93, 130B, 130M, 41A, 119E
triangle 150D, 147A
triangulate 150D
triangulation 150D
tribal 54B
tribe 54B, 146K
tribrach 85C
tribulation 31, 130B
tribunal 140A, 94, 133A
tribune 140A
tributary 43A, 45, 43B, 46A, 46B, 25I, 16
tribute 43A, 45, 63, 49A
trice 148D
trichology 83
trichord 68D
trick 49F, 134B, 130A, 62, 96A, 13, 99A, 99B, 107A, 100A
trickery*
trickiness*
trickle 16, 25I
trickster 130A, 49F
tricksy 108
tricky 130A, 49F, 134B
tricycle 24H
trident 104D, 133A
tridentate 150F
tried 140A
triennial 148H, 148K

trifle 147K, 129B, 60, 127A, 125C, 126B
trifling 3C, 129B, 127A, 128A
trigamy 146H
trigger 8, 5B
trigonal 150D
trihedral 150D
trihedron 150D
trilateral 150D
trill 68A, 3B
trillion 147A
trilogy 99B
trim 107A, 108, 14, 134A, 145F
trimmer 107A
trinket 107B
trinitrotoluol 145E, 130K
trinomial 147A
trio 147A
trip journey 19A
  stumble 18A
  err 126C, 126B, 130A, 126D, 127B
triple 147A
triplet 147A
triplicate 147A
trireme 24J
trisect 145A
trisection 145A
trite 128A, 129B, 132D
triturate 145H
trituration 145H
triumph 71A, 50, 95D
triumphal*
triumphant 50, 71A
triumvirate 146N
triune 147A
trivial 147K, 129B
triviality 129B, 147K
trocha 25B
trochlear 18C
troll 147J
trolley 24H
trollop 39C
trombone 68G
troop 147I, 130F, 146K
trooper 130F
trope 57, 84
trophy 104B
tropic 131B, 149L
tropical 131B, 149L
trot 19B, 9
troth 146G, 89
troubadour 85E, 68I
trouble 112, 31, 13, 125A, 130B
troublesome 13, 130B
trough 25F, 53I
trounce 130G
trouncing 130G

troupe 146K, 99D
trousers 106E
trousseau 106F
trout 143B
trove 49A
trover 49A, 49D
trow 113
trowel 53M
troyweight 147C
truancy 126B, 149N
truant 126B, 149N
truce 12, 148D, 89, 148I
truck 24H, 44, 24A
truckle 46B
trundle-bed 53-O
truculence 29, 130-O, 130M
truculent 29, 130-O
trudge 18A, 13
true 61A, 134A, 140A, 38, 137C
true-blue 140A
truism 61B
truly 61A
trump 49A, 134D, 140B, 50
trumpery 95D, 129B
trumpet 63, 68G, 78, 69B, 76
trumpeter 143C, 63
truncheon 104D, 130L, 130G
trundle 24H, 24A
trundle-bed 53-O
trunk 53R, 53J, 150H
truss 53R, 146A, 52B
trust 113, 146N, 44, 38
trustee 49B
trustful 113
trustiness 140A, 113
trustworthy 61A, 140A, 5A
trusty 113, 89, 140A
truth 61A, 134A, 137C
truthful 61A, 137C
try 41C, 2, 119E
trying 13, 130B, 130M
tryst 146K, 89
Tsar 133A
Tsarina 133A
tsetse 143D
tub 53N, 138A
tubal 150C
tube 25F
tuberose 143E
tuck 130H, 146A
tucker 106G
Tuesday 148K
tuft 146A, 106A, 107A, 107B
tufthunter 51A, 63
tug 24J, 24A, 41C
tuition 81, 45, 34

tulip 143E
tumble 134D, 18A, 22, 127B
tumbler 53N, 53M, 143C, 143D, 99D
tumbrel 24H
tumid 95D, 76, 10, 109B, 145I
tumidity 10
tumor 130E, 145I
tumult 69B, 125A
tumultuous 69B, 125A
tumulus 104H
tun 147F, 53N
tundra 25G
tune 68B, 68A, 134A, 132B
tuneful 68A
tuneless 70
tuner 68J, 68H
tungsten 5D
tunic 106G
tunicle 106G, 106I
tunnel 25B, 20, 25, 145F
tunny 143B
turacine 102D
turban 106H
turbid 125A, 146C, 129A
turbine 24C
turbit 143C
turbot 143B
turbulence 69B, 125A, 27
turbulent*
tureen 53M
turf 25G, 25B
turfman 41D
turgescence 7, 76, 95D, 145I
turgid 7, 76, 95D, 145I
Turk 54C
turkeytrot 99F
turmoil 69B, 125A
turn 3A, 18C, 84, 130E, 128B, 150C, 130B, 150B
turnip 48K
turnkey 52H
turnpike 25B, 25
turpitude 129B, 130A
turquoise 107C
turret 119E, 149E
turtle 143F
turtle-dove 143C
tusk 145F
tussle 41C, 41D, 130F
tut 91, 11B
tutelage 34, 81
tutelary 34, 67A
tutor 81, 34
tutorial 81, 34

uneventful 132D,
132B
unexaggerated 134A,
61A
unexampled 126A
unexecuted 126B
unexercised 110B,
126D
unexpected 127A
unexpended 147K
unexpired 147K
unexplored 126A
unfading 11B
unfailing 134C, 11A
unfair 130A
unfairness 130A
unfaithful 130A
unfaithfulness 130A
unfaltering 11A,
140A
unfamiliar 126A,
110B
unfashionable 126A
unfasten 145A
unfatherly 28, 130B
unfathomable 96A,
126A, 13
unfathomed 126A
unfavorable 13,
127B
unfearing 42
unfeatured 109A,
109B
unfed 128A
unfeeling 110A,
130M
unfeigned 61A
unfertile 128A
unfetter 145A
unfettered 125C
unfilial 126B
unfilled 128A, 37
unfinished 37
unfit 126A, 129B,
48Q, 125A,
128A
unfitness*
unfitted 126A
unflagging 11A, 39,
144B
unflattering 64, 65
unflinching 42
unfold open 145A
disclose 95A, 78,
84
unforbidden 46A
unforeseen 126A,
95C, 127A
unforgivable 130A
unforgettable 140B
unforgotten 117
unforsaken 127A
unfortified 128A
unfortunate 127B
unfounded 113
unfrequented 126A
unfriendliness 28

unfriendly 28
unfrock 35A
unfruitful 128A
unfurl 145A
unfurnished 37
ungainly 126D, 109A,
18A
ungenerous 132C,
147K
ungentlemanly 126C,
28
ungifted 110B
ungird 145A
ungodliness 130A
ungodly 130A, 130M
ungovernable 27
ungoverned 125C-2
ungraceful 126D,
109A, 18A
ungracious 130A,
129B, 28, 130C
ungrammatical 70,
126C
ungrateful 126B
ungratefulness 126B
ungrounded 62
ungrudging 43A
unguarded 128A,
126B, 126D
unhallowed 130A,
129B
unhappiness 31, 127B
unhappy 31, 127B
unhealthy 128B
unhesitating 148D,
42
unholy 130A
unhurried 126B,
132B
unicorn 143A
unicycle 24H
uniform
regular 132D, 105,
106B, 102A
uniformity 132D,
105, 132A
unify 146A
unigeniture 141B,
142B
unimaginable 96A,
13, 140B
unimaginative 110B
unimagined 96A,
126A
unimpassioned 132C
unimpeachable 140A
unimpeded 11A
unimportance 128A
unimportant 128A,
6, 147K
unimpressive 128A,
109A
unincumbered 125C
uninfluential 128A
uninformed 110B
unintellectual 110B
unintelligent 110B

unintelligible 60
unintended 127A
unintentional 127A,
126C
uninterested 126C,
27
uninteresting 60,
128A
uninterrupted 11A
uninvited 35
uninviting 28, 27
union 146A, 146K,
146H
unionism 146K
Union-Jack 104E
uniparious 141B
unique 126A, 140B,
147L
unison 132A, 68A,
146A, 148L
unit 147A, 146A
Unitarian 82D
Unitarianism 82B
unite 146A, 146H,
146K, 52B, 52G
unity 146A, 132A,
132D
universal 146A,
132D, 135B,
146K, 147I
universe 146A, 141D
university 81
unjust 130A
unkempt 109C
unkind 28
unlawful 35
unlearned 110B
unless 127A
unlike 126A
unlikelihood 127A
unlikely 127A
unlimited 125C, 147I
unload 35A
unlock 145A
unloose 145A
unlucky 127B
unman 128A
unmanageable 27
unmannerly 129B
unmarried 145K
unmeaning 60
unmentionable
130A, 130M
unmistakable 84, 93,
134A
unmitigated
bad 130A, 11A
unmoved 132B, 27
unnatural 126A
unnecessary 26
unnerve 130D
unobtrusive 132C
unoccupied 126B
unparalleled 126A,
140B, 134B,
147J
unpardonable 130A

unpleasant 130B,
130C, 123
unpolluted 138C
unpopular 129B
unprecedented 126A,
140B, 134B
unprejudiced 140A
unpremeditated
127A
unprepared 126B,
148D, 128A
unpretentious 132C
unprincipled 130A
unproductive 128A
unprofessional 126C,
126A
unprofitable 127B
unpropitious 127B,
13, 126A
unprovoked 130A
unqualified 128A,
126C, 134A,
125C
unquenchable 37, 39
unquestionable 61A,
134A, 93, 134C
unraveled 145A, 84,
132A
unreal 113, 62, 103A,
103B
unreasonable 60,
110B, 126C
unregenerate 130A
unrelenting 130M,
11B, 132C
unreliable 127A, 57,
62, 126C
unremitting 11A
unreserved 125C-2
frank 61A, 39C
unrest 125A, 112
unrestrained 125C-2,
39C, 146D, 130M
unrighteousness
130A
unrivaled 140B, 108
unroll 145A
unruffled 132B
unruliness 27
unruly 27
unsafe weak 128A
unsatisfactory 37
unsavory 48Q
unscathed 146A
unschooled 110B
unscrupulous 130A
unseasonable 127B,
126A
unseemly 109A,
126A, 129B
unseen 103A
unsettle 125A
unsex 130D, 128A
unshaken 132B, 11B
unsightly 109A
unskillful 126C,
126D

Page 517

vaulted 150C
vaunt 76, 95D, 103B
vaunting 76
veal 48D
veer 18C
vegetables 48K
vegetarian 51A
vegetarianism 51A
vegetate 126B
vegetation 143E
vehemence 39, 29, 125C-2
vehement 39, 39B, 29, 125C-2, 9
vehicle 24H
vehicular 24H
veil 103A, 106C, 45
vein 25E, 53B, 2, 114
veinous 25E
veld 25G
velocipede 24H
velocity 9
velvet 106K, 106A
velveteen 106K
venal 45, 129B, 44, 25
venality 129B, 44
vend 44
vendee 49D
vendetta 28, 130-O, 130N
vendor 44
vendue 44
veneer 62, 95D
venerable 140B
venerate 38, 63
veneration 38, 63
venereal 39C, 146D
venery 39C, 146D, 119E
venesection 145F
vengeance 28, 130N
vengeful 28, 130N, 130M
venial 140A, 47, 49E
venison 48D
venom 28, 130E
venomous 130E, 130M, 130-O
spiteful 28, 65
venous 25
vent 25F, 25, 64, 55A
ventilate 78, 16, 138B, 90
ventilation*
ventilator 25F, 138B
ventricle 25E, 53Q
ventriloquism 55A
ventriloquist 55A
venture dare 42, 127A, 41C, 119E, 127A
venturesome 42, 41C, 127A
venue 149A

Venus 39A, 108, 71A, 71B, 101D
veracious 61A
veracity 61A
veranda 25D
verb 55A, 4
verbal 134A, 92, 55A
verbatim 134A, 84
verbiage 56
verbose 56
verbosity 56
verdancy 102A, 110B
verdant 102A, 110B, 113
verdict 94, 115, 80
verdigris 102D
verditer 102D
verdure 102A
verge 104D, 149K, 149M
verifiable 93, 61A
verification 93, 61A
verify 93, 61A
verily 61A
verisimilitude 61A, 105, 57
veritable 61A
verity 61A, 134A
vermifuge 136B, 138B
vermilion 102A, 102D
vermin 143D, 129B
vernacular 55A
versatile 3A, 117, 3C, 134B, 56, 59
versatility*
verse 85C
versed 117, 134B
versicle 85C
versification 85C
versifier 85E
version 84
versus 27
vertebra 53R
vertex 149F
vertical 149E
vertu 134B, 100B
vertumnus 148K
verve 39, 71A, 2
very 61A, 137C, 125C, 147I
vesicle 53Q
vespers 68B
vessel 24J, 53M, 53N, 25E
vest 106D, 139A
vesta 34
vestal 138C, 132C
vested 133A
vestibule 25D
vestige 95A, 93
vestment 106B, 106I
vestry 53E, 146K
vesture 106B
vetch 143E

veteran 117
veto 131A, 3b
vex 130B, 130C, 102C
vexation 31, 130B, 130C, 13
vexatious 130B, 13, 130C
vexed 29
vexing 130B
viaduct 25B
vial 53N
viands 48D, 48A
vibrant 3B, 137C
vibrate 3B
vibration 3B, 69C
vibratory 3B, 69C
vicar 82G
vicarage 82C, 45
vicar-general 82G
vicarious 46B, 133A
vice 130A, 146D, 125C-3, 38
vicegerent 46B, 133A
vice-president 133A
viceroy 133A
viceroyalty 133A
vice versa 3A
vicinage 149M
vicinity 149M
vicious 130A, 129B, 28, 130M
vicissitude 3A
victim 31, 127B
victimize 49F, 130A, 130B, 130-O
victor 50, 134D
victoria 24H
victorine 106D
victorious 50, 134D
victory 50, 134D
victual 48A, 43B
victualer 43B, 48A
vicuna 143A
videlicet 92, 84
vie 27, 41D
view 119A, 111, 119E, 114, 100B, 95A, 95C, 113
vigil 119G
vigilance 119G
vigilant 119G
vignette 100B
vigor 137B
(B). vigour
vigorous 137B, 58
viking 49G
vile 129B, 130A, 146C, 129A, 109C, 130M
vileness*
vilifier 65
vilify 65
villa 53F, 53L
village 53F
villager 54B

villain 129B, 130A
villainous 65, 130A, 129B, 130M
villainy 130A, 129B
villenage 46B, 50
villi 106A
villous 106A
vim 137B
vinaceous 102A
vinaigrette 53J, 122
vincible 46B, 128A
vinculum 146A
vindicate 93, 138D, 140A
vindication*
vindicator 138D
vindicatory 93, 138D
vindictive 28, 130M
vine 143E, 53R
vinegar 48P
vineyard 144C
vinic 48L
vin-ordinaire 48L
vinous 48L
vintage 48L, 144E
vintner 44, 49D
viol 68D
violable 128A
violate 130A, 130D, 65, 125C, 39C, 146D, 125A, 130M, 130-O, 146C
violation*
violator*
violence 125C-2, 39C, 146D, 130M, 29, 130F, 130A, 39, 125B
violent*
violet 143E, 102A
violin 68D
violinist 68H
violoncellist 68H
violoncello 68D
violone 68D
viper 143F, 28, 130A, 130E, 130M, 130-O
virago 29, 42, 137B
virgin 138C, 132C, 108
virginal 138C, 132C
virginity 138C, 132C
virile 137B, 141A, 42
virility*
virtue 137C, 138C, 132C, 137B, 1, 2, 42, 58, 100B, 132A, 132B, 133A, 134B, 135B, 140A, 140B, 61A
virtual*
virtuoso 68H, 134B, 68I

virtuous 138C, 132C
virulence 28, 130M, 130G, 130-O, 65
virulent*
virus 136B, 130E
vis 137B, 119A, 2
visage 95C
vis-a-vis 149H
viscid 52E
viscidity 52E
viscount 133A
viscous 52E
vise 49C
vishnu 136B
visibility 95A, 95C
visible 95A, 95C
vision 119A, 95A, 95C, 96A, 111, 113
visional*
visionary 119A, 113, 126C
visit 119A, 146K 119E, 19A
visitant 119A, 146L, 119E
visitation 119A, 119E, 130N, 130E
visite 106D
visitor 146L, 119E
vista 95A, 95C, 25B, 25
visual 119A
visualize 119A, 113, 8, 95A
vital 137C, 37, 130-O,
vitalism 83
vitality 137B, 1, 137C
vitalize 8, 141A, 137B
vitals 137C
vitamine 48A
vitascope 99E
vitiate 146C, 130A, 129B, 62, 130M, 146D
vitreous 101A
vitrescent 101A
vitric 101A
vitrify 146B
vitriform 101A
vituperate 64
vituperation 64
vituperative 64
viva 63, 91
vivacious 71A, 9, 3C, 40A, 99A, 99C
vivacity*
vivarium 52H, 53D, 149A
vive 91, 63
vivid 101A, 100A, 102C, 95E, 84
vivify 9, 8, 141A, 137B

viviparous 141B
vivisect 145F, 130-O
vivisection*
vivisectionist*
vixen 29, 66, 141F, 64, 67A, 130C
viz 92
vizor 106H
vocable 92, 55A
vocabulary 86
vocal 55A, 68A
vocalist 68I
vocalize 55A, 68A
vocation 44, 49A, 144B, 126A
vociferate 41B, 69B
vociferation*
vociferous*
vodka 48L
vogue 132D
voice 55A
voiceless 37
void 128A, 25A, 37, 131A, 16, 149A
volant 9, 3C, 127A, 23
Volapuk 55A
volatile 127A, 23, 145J, 9, 3C
volatility*
volatilize 145J
volcanic 145J, 16, 33, 125C-2, 130-O
volcanize 145J, 146A
volcano 145J, 149E
volition 39
volitive 39
volley 130F, 69B
volplane 22, 23
volt 147L
voltameter 95B
volubility 56
voluble 56
volume 85B, 68A, 69B
volumetric 147L
voluminous 147J, 147I
voluntary 125C, 39, 2, 40A, 43A, 137C
volunteer*
voluptuary 39B, 71A, 39C
voluptuous 39B, 108, 125C-3
voluted 150C
vomit 16
voodoo 82B, 50, 130-O
voracious 51A, 39
voracity 51A
vortex 16, 18C
votary 38, 71A
vote 49A
voter 49A
votive 89

vouch 93, 89
voucher 93, 89
vouchsafe 46A
vow 89, 80, 93
vowel 55A, 92
voyage 19A
voyager 19A
voyageur 19A
vraisemblance 105
vulcanize 52B, 52E
vulgar 129B, 132D, 130C, 70
vulgarian 130C, 129B, 126C
vulgarism 70, 129B
vulgarity 70, 129B, 109A, 130C
vulgus 129B
vulnerability 46B
vulnerable 46B, 128A
vulpicide 130-O
vulpine 134B, 117
vulture 49G, 143C, 51A
vulturine 49G, 51A
vulva 141C
vying 41D

W

wabble 18A
wad 146A, 147L
waddie 130L
wadding 106K
waddle 18A
waddler 18A
wade 19B, 21
wadi 25G
wady 25H, 25G
wafer 52F
waffle 48E
waft 23
wag 3B, 98A, 72
wage 130F, 41D, 45, 11A, 42
wageearner 49D
wager 41D, 127A
waggery 72, 99C
waggish 72, 99C, 99A
waggle 18A
wagon 24H
wagoner 24E
wagonette 24H
wagtail 143C
waif 127B
wail 31, 67A, 67B, 69B, 40B
wain 24H
wainscot 53R
wainscoting 53R
waist 149L
waistcoat 106E
wait 39, 11A, 119G, 148B
waiter 46B
waiting 46B
waits 68H

waive 46B, 46A
wake 8, 111, 119G, 149I, 95A
wakeful 119G
waken 8, 111
wale 119B
Walhalla 53H
walk 19B, 25B
walkingstick 107B
walkout 15
wall 36B, 36, 145B
wallet 53J
wallflower 143E
wallop 130F, 130G, 145J
wallow 129A
walnut 48C, 143E
walrus 143B
waltz 99F
wampee 48G
wampum 147B
wan 102A, 128B, 98B
wand 104D
wander 18B, 19A
wanderer 18B, 19A
wanderoo 143A
wane 14, 97, 147K
wanness 128B, 37
want 37, 39
wanting 37
wanton 39B, 39C, 125C-3, 146D
wapiti 143A
war 130F, 41D
warble 68A
warbler 68I
warbling 68I, 68A
war-cry 41B, 79, 61B
ward 34, 36
warden 34, 52H, 133A
warder*
wardrobe 106B, **53P**
wardroom 53C
warehouse 53B
wares 144E, 5C
warfare 130F, 41D
wariness 32, 119G, 132C
warm 71A, 39B, 121, 39, 8, 136A, 131A, 145J
warmth*
warn 79, 33, 64
warning 79, 33, 64, 77, 95A
warp 52C, 150B, 129B, 24A, 18C, 24C
warrant 89, 46A, 94, 34, 93
warranty*
warren 52H
warrior 130F
wary 32, 119G, **31**, 132C
was 148A

wash 138A
washer 138A
washerwoman 138A
wash-out 25H, 130-O
washing 138A
wasp 143D, 29, 67A, 130C
waspish 130C, 29, 67A
wassail 125C, 99C, 48L, 51B, 71A
waste 130-O, 14, 125C-1, 131A, 128A, 128C, 129A, 129B, 125A
wasteful 125C, 43A
wastrel 127B, 39C, 146D, 43A, 125C-1
watch 34, 148F, 95B, 119G
watchful 119G, 132C
watchmaker 144D
watchword 88, 61A, 92
water 145J, 25I, 48J, 130D, 146C
watercourse 25F
watercress 143E
waterfall 16, 25I
water-gauge 95B
water-logged 110A
watermain 25F
waterproof 34, 106D
water-shed 145B
waterspout 16
watery 145J
wattlebird 143C
wave 3B, 16, 98A, 107A, 130-O
waver 32, 132C, 112, 127A
wavering*
wavy 3B, 18C, 150C
wax 29, 10, 147J, 52E, 52F
waxiness 52F
waxwing 143C
waxy 52F
way 25B, 132D
wayfarer 19A
waylay 130F
wayward 27, 3C, 130A, 127A
we 92
weak 128A, 69A, 110B, 3C, 32
weaken 128A, 130D
weakfish 143B
weakling 110B, 128A
weal 134D, 50, 71A
weald 34
wealth 135B, 49E
wealthiness 135B
wealthy 135B
wean 145A, 14, 132D

weapon 130I
wear 130D, 95A, 18C, 11A, 14, 106B
weariness 128A
wearisome 130D, 130B
weary 128A, 130D, 13, 32, 130B
weasand 25E
weasel 143A
weasen 109A
weather 50, 135B
weather-cock 98A
weave 144A, 144B
weaver 144D, 143B
weazen 150G, 109B
web 106K
webbing 106K
wed 146H
wedding 146H
wedge 52B, 150E, 145F, 146B
wedlock 146H
Wednesday 148K
wee 147K
weed 143E, 48-O, 35A
weediness 129B
weedy 129B
week 148H
weekday 148L
weekly 148K
ween 113
weep 31, 67B
weeping 31
weaver 143B
weevil 143D
weft 52C
weigh 115, 13, 114, 135A, 130B
weight 135A, 13, 137B, 1, 135B, 50, 130B
weighty 135A, 135B, 2
weir 36H
weird 96A, 33, 126A
welcher 126B
welcome 38, 98C, 63
weld 52E, 52B
welfare 134D, 71A, 50
well 16, 25F, 25, 134D, 137A
well-bred 117, 140A
Wellingtons 106J
Welsh-rabbit 48D
welter 129A
wench 46B, girl 148J, 129B, 125C-3
wend 18B
went 15, 19A
were 148A
werewolf 130-O, 130M
Wesleyanism 82B

west 149B
western 149B
westward 149B
wet 145J, 146C
wether 143A
wet-nurse 43B
whack 130G
whacker 130G, 62, 147J
whale 147J, 143B, 109B
whaler 24J
wharf 25B
what 92, 80
whatever 92
whatnot 53P
whatsoever 92
wheat 143E, 48M
wheatear 143C
wheedle 40A, 63
wheel 24D, 18C, 130N, 5A, 24C
wheelbarrow 24H
wheeler 24E
wheelman 24E
wheelwright 144D
wheeze 70, 69C
wheezing 70
wheezy 70
whelm 130-O
whelp 148J, 142D
when 148B, 148L
whence 149A
where 149A
whereabouts 149A
whereas 61A
wherefore 1
wherry 24J
whet 150E, 8
whether 92
whey 48I
which 92
whiff 125B, 24J, 16
whiffet 129B
whiffle 18C, 62
whiffling 62
while 148I
whim 113
whimper 31, 67B, 40B
whimsical 113, 72, 103B, 109A, 126A
whimsy 113
whine 31, 40B, 67B
whining 67B
whip 130G, 130N, 8, 130L
whipper 130N
whipper-snapper 129B
whipping 130N, 130-G
whippoorwill 143C
whir 18C
whirl 18C, 16
whirligig 18C

whirlpool 16, 25I, 130-O
whirlwind 125B
whirr 69A
whisk 106K, 9, 138A
whiskers 106A
whisky 48L
whisper 55A, 69A, 87, 78
whist 41D
whistle 68B, 68A, 68G
whistler 68J
whit 147K
white 102A, 138C
whitebait 143B
white-feather 32
white-lie 62
white-livered 32
whiten 102A
white-squall 125B
white-throat 143C
whitewash 102A, 102D, 138D, 62
white-wine 48L
whither 149A, 128B
whittle 145F, 145H
whiz 69C
who 92
whoa 12
whoever 92
whole 146A, 137A, 147I, 147L
wholesale 147I, 44
wholesome 48A, 140A, 136B
wholesomeness 140A
whom 92
whomever 92
whomsoever 92
whoop 69B
whooper 62, 147J
whore 39C, 125C-3, 146E, 44, 146D
whoredom*
whortleberry 48G
whose 92
whosoever 92
why 1, 40B
wick 101C
wicked 130A, 130M
wickedness 130A
wicker 25
wicket 25
wicki-up 53D
wide 25, 147J
widen 10, 147J, 25
wideness 25A, 147J
widespread 135B
widgeon 143C
widow 145K
widower 145K
width 150A, 25A
wield 133A
wife 146J, 141E
wifeless 145K
wig 106A, 106H

wigan 106K
wigging 64
wigwag 98A
wigwam 53D
wild 125C-2, 125A, 29, 126C, 25G, 33, 126A, 126D
wildcat 143A, 125C-2
wilderness 13, 96A, 34, 25G, 125A
wile 134B, 40A, 130A, 71A
will 49A, 39, 2, 43A, 148B
willful 27, 125C, 11B
willet 143C
willing 2, 46A
will-o'-the-wisp 113, 96A
willow 143E
wilt 128C, 128A
wily 117, 134B, 57
wimple 106H
win 50, 134D, 49A
wince 15, 32, 31
Winchester 130I
wind 125B, 150C, 60, 18C, 146A
windfall 134D, 43A
windiness 125B, 60, 56, 76
winding 18C, 150C
windlass 24B, 18C
windmill 144C
window 25, 36I
windward 149A
windy 125B, 69B, 60
wine 48L
wing 23, 150G
wink 98B
winking 98B
winner 49A, 134D, 50
winning 108
winnow 145A, 35A, 119E
winsome 108
winter 148K, 54A
wintergreen 143E
wipe 131A, 138A, 35A
wire 52C, 25F, 55C, 55B
wireless 55C
wiry 3C, 137B
wisdom 117, 59
wise 117, 59
wiseacre 117, 110B, 62, 95D
wish 39
wishy-washy 128A, 60
wisp 146A, 147K
wistful 31, 39, 114
wit 117, 59, 72
witch 117, 50, 140B
witchcraft 117, 50

witchery 117, 50
with 146A
withdraw 15, 49A
white 52B, 52C
wither 128A, 128C, 14
withhold 132C, 52A
within 149L
without 149K
withstand 27, 36
witless 60, 110B
witness 93, 119A, 119F, 119D
witted 117
witticism 72, 117, 59
wittiness 117, 59
witty 117, 59, 72
wive 146H
wizard 117, 134B
wizen 128C, 109B, 109A
wobble 18A
wobbly 18A
woe 31
woebegone 31
woeful 31
wold 34
wolf 143A, 49G, 130M
wolfish 39
wolverine 143A, 51A
woman 146J, 46B, 141E
womanhood 141E
womankind 141E
womanly 141E, 141B
womb 141C
wonder 96A, 112, 39, 71A, 140B
wonderful 126A, 96A, 95E, 99A, 108, 140B
wonderland 96A
wont 132D
wonted 132D
woo 40
wood 34, 53R, 5C, 25G
woodchuck 143A
woodcock 143C
woodpecker 143C
wooer 40
wooing 40
wool 106A, 106K, 5C
woolen 106K
woolgathering 113
wooliness 106A
wooly 106A
woolsack 53J, 53-O
word 55A, 55B, 82A, 79, 89, 92
word-book 86
worded 84
wording 84
word-painting 84
wordy 56

work 144B, 45, 46B, 31, 13, 126A, 130B, 132D, 144E, 147L, 8
workhouse 52H, 53B, 144C
workman 144D, 46B
workmanship 144B, 134B, 144E
world 147I, 141D
worldliness 39
worldly 39
worm 143F, 129B
worn 109C
worried 31
worriment 31, 130B
worrisome 130B
worry 130B, 39, 32, 31, 13, 130C, 112
worse 129B
worship 63, 40B, 38
worshipful*
worshiper*
worst 129B, 50
worsted 106K
worth 140B, 140A, 135B
worthiness*
worthless 129B, 128A
worthy 140B, 140A
would 148B
would-be 62, 103B
wound 130G, 130B, 130E
wow-wow 143A
wrack 125A, 129A
wraith 113, 96A
wrangle 41B, 66
wrangler*
wrap 52B, 106D
wrapper 52B, 106F, 52C, 106D
wrath 29
wrathful 29, 130M
wreath 104B, 107B
wreathe 150C
wreck 130-O
wreckage 125A
wrecker 130-O, 49G
wren 143C
wrench 49C, 130D, 125A
wrest 49C, 130D, 125A
wrestle 41D, 41C, 27
wrestler 41D
wretch 31, 129B
wretched 31, 129B
wriggle 18C
wright 144D
wring 49G, 35A
wringer 35A
wrinkle 150B, 14, 125A, 146A, 150G
wrist 150G

writ 94
write 55B, 85B, 18C, 85A, 86
writer 85E, 86
writhe 31, 18C
wrong 130A, 126C
wrongful 130A
wroth 29
wry 150B, 62, 28, 125A
wrybill 143C
wrymouth 143B
wryneck 143C
wurbagool 143A
wurraluh 143C
wynkernel 143C

X

xanthein 102D
xanthic 102A
Xanthippe 29, 64
xantho 102A
xanthophyl 102D
xanthous 102A
xebec 24J
xenogenesis 141A
xenomania 39
xenon 5D
xylophagous 51A
xylophone 68E

Y

yacht 24J
yachting 23
yachtsman 24E, 23
yahoo 129B
yak 143A
yam 48K
yank 49C, 134B, 125A
yap 110B
yapock 143A
yard 3 feet 147E, 25A, 25G, 25D, 52H
yarn 106A, 52C, 62
yataghan 130H
yaw 18C, 126C
yawl 24J
yawn 145A, 51A
yawning 25, 98B
yawp 70
ycleped 92
ye 92
yean 141B
year 148H
yearling 148H, 148J
yearly 148H, 148K
yearn 39
yeast 145B
yeggman 49F
yell 69B, 70
yellow 102A, 102D
yellowish 102A
yelp 31, 69B, 67A, 67B

yen 147B
yes 46A
yesterday 148A, 148K
yet 10, 27, 148E
yield 46B, 43A, 46A, 144E
yielding 46B, 3C
yodel 68A, 68B
yoke 52A, 147A, 46B, 50, 52H, 5B
yokel 129B
yonder 149N
yore 148A
you 92
young 148J, 142C, 137A, 148E
youngish 148J
youngster 148J, 142B
younker 148J, 142B
your 92
yourself 92

youth 148J, 142B, 137B
youthful 148J, 137A
yttrium 5D
ytterbium 5D
yucker 143C
yule 148K
yuletide 148K
yunx 143C
yurga 143A
yutu 143C

Z

zaffer 102D
zamang 143E
zamouse 143A
zanella 106K
zany 72, 99D
zariba 36B
zeal 39
zealot 39, 38

zealous 39
zebra 143A
zebu 143A
zenana 53D
zendik 30
zenith 149F
zephyr 125B
Zeppelin 24I
zero 128A
zest 71A, 51A, 48P
Zeus 125B
zigzag 18C, 150B, 125A, 150C
zinc 5D
zingel 143B
Zion 82A, 82B, 53C, 53H
zirconium 5D
zither 68D
zobo 143A
zodiac 101D
zodiacal 101D

zone 149A, 145D
zoo 99E
zophile 38
zooid 143A, 142D
zoolatry 82B
zoological 83
zoologist 83
zoology 83
zoomorphism 82B, 104A, 104C
zoophilist 39
zoophyte 143A, 143E
zoosperm 142F
zoospore 142F
zorilla 143A
zouave 130F
zucchetto 106H
zymologist 83
zymometer 95B
zymoscope 95B
zythum 48L
zyxomma 143D